THE ENCYCLOPEDIA OF

SCIENCE FICTION MOVIES

THE ENCYCLOPEDIA OF
SCIENCE FICTION MOVIES

C.J. HENDERSON

Foreword by
WILLIAM SHATNER

☑®
Facts On File, Inc.

The Encyclopedia of Science Fiction Movies

Checkmark Books
An imprint of Facts On File, Inc.
11 Penn Plaza
New York NY 10001

Library of Congress Cataloging-in-Publication Data

Henderson, C.J.
The encyclopedia of science fiction movies / C.J. Henderson;
foreword by William Shatner.
p. cm.
Includes index.
ISBN 0-8160-4043-5 (hc: alk. paper)—ISBN 0-8160-4567-4 (pbk: alk. paper)
1. Science fiction films—Encyclopedias. 2. Science fiction films—Catalogs. I. Title
PN1995.9.S26 H38 20001
791.43'615—dc21   00-061001

Checkmark Books are available at special discounts when purchased in bulk
quantities for businesses, associations, institutions, or sales promotions.
Please call our Special Sales Department in New York at
(212) 967-8800 or (800) 322-8755.

You can find Facts On File on the World Wide Web at
http://www.factsonfile.com

Text design by Cathy Rincon
Cover design by Nora Wertz

Printed in the United States of America

VB FOF 10 9 8 7 6 5 4 3 2 1
(pbk) 10 9 8 7 6 5 4 3 2 1

This book is printed on acid-free paper.

Contents

ACKNOWLEDGMENTS
VI

FOREWORD BY WILLIAM SHATNER
VII

INTRODUCTION: HOW TO USE THIS BOOK
IX

ABBREVIATIONS USED IN THIS VOLUME
XII

ENTRIES A TO Z
1

SCIENCE FICTION MOVIES AND LITERATURE
483

SCIENCE FICTION MOVIES AT THE OSCARS
487

INTERVIEW WITH FRANK HERBERT
491

THE LANGUAGE AND TRIBES OF *QUEST FOR FIRE*
494

BIBLIOGRAPHY AND FURTHER READING
499

INDEX
501

Acknowledgments

There are a few people whose help I, in the spirit of giving credit where credit is due, would like to acknowledge here.

First, those valiant souls who sat through so many sci-fi movies with me: my loving wife, Grace; my daughter, Erica; and my pals James Chambers, Gary Esposito, Scott Goodell, Leah Gulubchuck, Wayne Hawkes, Carol Price, Marc Thorner, and Ray Weisfeld.

Then second, to those who helped with the words and notes and those oh, so hard to gather photos: Marc A. Cerasini, Warren Knisbaum, R. Allen Lieder, Joseph B. Mauceri, Melinda Metz, Dan Scapperotti, Doug Smith, and Robert M. Price.

And of course, my special thanks and humblest gratitude must be extended toward the extreme generosity of:

Mr. William Shatner,

a gentleman of the highest caliber to whom I owe so much and have returned so little and without whom science fiction would be so much the poorer.

And lastly, let me give thanks to the one person who not only sat with me week in and week out, watching and critiquing film after film, but who wrote and advised and gave deeply from both his pocketbook and his heart to make this project a reality. For his Herculean efforts on behalf of this volume, for his infectious good humor and his Homeric strength of will, which kept me going when it seemed even the gods demanded I stop . . . I dedicate this work to:

Jack Dolphin.

My grandmother always said, "If you have one true friend in this life you can consider yourself lucky." If she had but lived long enough to have met Jack, she would have considered me blessed.

Foreword

A long time ago, in a galaxy far, far away, I was a kid in Montreal and used to go to as many movies as I could on a Saturday. First, the cost was a dime and then the price was raised to 25 cents, and with my allowance in hand, I'd run from movie theater to movie theater, where they would be playing two movies that had long since played downtown. So from week to week I would see two, four, even six films on a Saturday. It was my introduction to the dream of being an actor and making a living in the entertainment world. I saw all the English films of the time—the comedies, the dramas. The American films were different. They were bigger, sometimes so big they were called epics. The dean of the epic school of filmmaking was Cecil B. DeMille— the name *DeMille* had a ring to it. There was a French cast to it—*Deux Mille*—could have meant "2,000." Of course, it did not, but I would see DeMille's fabulous pictures again and again.

The film that stays most emphatically in my mind is the one where all the extras toiled anonymously, featuring a magnificent leading man and a juicy leading lady who stirred my adolescent hormones. It was, of course, *The Ten Commandments*, but the commandments I heeded were "Go see that movie, Go see that movie." Cecil B. DeMille's epic films were legendary, extraordinary. Ten thousand extras followed his commands: "You! The column over there on the right! Two hundred to the left! That one there, on the right-hand side of the column, that goes to the angle of the left-hand side, with the 300. You with the pink! You! You're not marching in time! All of you, turn left!"

And 10,000 people turned left.

I've heard that Victor Mature, the actor in one of those epic films, turned his helmet backward as he was marching, and 10,000 extras followed him. No one noticed until later in the day, and they redid the whole shot. Cecil B. DeMille set the benchmark for epic films—DeMille and *The Ten Commandments*.

The last of the great epic films that I remember was *Cleopatra*. By then the studio system was crumbling, and 20th Century Fox in a last desperate attempt spent millions on Elizabeth Taylor and Richard Burton, who on the set of that film became lovers. The advertising claimed that "their passion ignites the screen!" and it did! The film featured a great deal of kissing between Burton and Taylor; it was exciting to see. And though their passion may have ignited the screen, the film itself was not so exciting. Here were thousands of extras, and they entered the arena pushing Elizabeth Taylor, and 10,000 people all hailed her and bowed down to this magnificent woman in a magnificent dress (which was only partially on her) as she came out and spoke those famous words . . . "Where's Richard?"

Well, whatever she said, it was marvelous, and Richard did something veddy, veddy, veddy English, yet it was a veddy dull film, even with all those thousands of people. When *Cleopatra* failed at the box office, it probably signaled the end to the epic film of the past, in which tens of thousands of horses and fleets of airplanes and flotillas of boats would contribute to a film. It all became too expensive. I've been told that the amount of money spent on Cleopatra for water alone would have financed a low-budget film of today.

There were occasional spurts of that kind of filmmaking, made mostly by Joseph Levine at the epic-center in Spain because that location allowed Mr. Levine to rent their soldiers, sailors, and laborers to craft the last of a dying breed of film. But they, too, fizzled out because of cost. That left a void. And as we know, nature and film abhor a vacuum. So the search for how to make an epic film without using so many people began. Whether it was inadvertent or deliberate, the science fiction film became the epic film of today.

I am not acquainted with all the films that you will read about in this book. I love film. I love to make films. I love to write films. I love to direct films. I love to see films. I even love to touch film. There is a feel to 35mm film, a greasy sharpness. You can cut your finger on it, but you can also hold it up to the light and see the color, which when projected, becomes the magic of today. And so though I love film, I am not knowledgeable about all films. I've forgotten a lot of the films that I've seen and loved. But the taste of the memory remains.

What I do know is that certain watershed films of science fiction have signaled grandness of conception, storytelling, and imagination. I would point to *2001: A Space Odyssey* as being the film that first raised my consciousness about the impact of design on a film. *2001* is deservedly hailed as a masterpiece. Stanley Kubrick's use of space—both the space within the frame of the film and in general—is wonderful. The "Blue Danube" waltz and the satellite are an imaginative leap, a magical combination that shows extraordinary taste. The shot of the spaceship flying over the top of the frame and then going on forever is a director's masterpiece. The singularity of the column, buried in the rock of the Moon, is symbolic and moving at the same time. The opening sequence of *2001*, which melds fantastically with that flying bone that becomes a flying ship, is one of the great moments in filmmaking. *2001* has led filmmakers by the hand into the greater realms of the imagination.

So for me, the science fiction film of today has taken over from the epic of yesterday. Science fiction can be as intimate as a voyage into the human body or as expansive as a trip through the solar system. It has become storytelling in one of its finest forms—pure imagination. Of course you have to follow the logic and the rules set down by the author, which by the way, you can't bend or break any more than you can real-life rules. If gravitation doesn't exist in your science fiction source, it must remain nonexistent. Science fiction becomes the art of art as well as the art of drama. It becomes the scenic designer's art and the model maker's art, and especially the computer graphic artist's art. It is there, in CGI heaven, that the science fiction film lives.

Great science fiction films need to be human stories, told in human terms, with human verities, anxieties, and abilities, all of which lead to truths that would be recognizable whether told by Pushkin, Tolstoy, or Vonnegut. The basis of science fiction film is the human story. The art of telling that story is to a large degree in the computer graphic artist's head. Armed with a vivid imagination, wielding the graphic pencil, conquering ground pixel by pixel, the graphic artist becomes a critical part of the storytelling process in a science fiction film. The graphic artist today is the Rembrandt of tomorrow. He must possess the crazy imagination of Salvador Dali to create landscapes filled with strange beings, Picasso's cubist analysis of space and form, and Rubens's ability to realize figures full-fleshed. And he must also have some of the inspired madness of van Gogh.

For an artist today, there can be no better arena for creativity than computer graphics, which can assume and maintain a life of its own if approached properly. That is part of a science fiction film's art.

The designer of a science fiction film is another force that needs to be reckoned with. There is a need for cohesive design, for a point of view, for soaring creativity, for something that has not been done before. There are so many science fiction films made today that it requires great creativity to be different, and different you must be. Everything needs to be storyboarded. If everyone connected with the film is not totally aware of what is being imagined, if that isn't set down so they can look at it and begin their contribution to the creation of that film, chaos will result. A storyboard artist is a critical element to the film as well as to the director and actors so that they know what it is they're looking at when they speak the lines. Everything, ideally, is prepared in advance.

Science fiction films are heavily influenced by others besides the director. That's one of their weaknesses. It's very difficult to have a singular point of view. A director of a science fiction film must rely not only on a storyboard artist to clarify everyone's vision, but the director must be able to point to the boards as a template, where changes can be made and where people can sign off on a version of the film. With time and money and political force, a director can avoid mistakes and achieve his vision, in collaboration with all those other fine artists who make up a film. What follows in this book is an education in science fiction films and an itinerary of all those people who had a hand making those films, far more than I know or have ever heard of. Indeed I intend to use the knowledge from this book to heighten my awareness of what has come before and what is yet to come.

—William Shatner

Introduction

There are two quotes that very aptly describe the science fiction genre. The first has been attributed to so many people in the field I'm not certain who should get the credit, so I'll simply repeat it and leave it at that: "Science fiction is the stuff you find in the library under the heading *science fiction*."

The second is known as (Theodore) Sturgeon's Law, and it goes something like this: "Ninety percent of science fiction is garbage. But then again, 90 percent of *everything* is garbage." In both cases, truer words were never spoken.

Many people have tried to come up with an all-encompassing definition of the genre, but so far no one has had much luck. Science fiction is too broad a field; its house simply holds too many side rooms and wandering corridors—rocket ships, time travel, faster-than-light travel, interdimensional travel, cloning, invisibility, alien invaders, ray guns, utopian futures, first contact, robots and androids and cyborgs ("oh, my!"), radiation, brain transplants, computers taking over the world, worlds within worlds, giant ants, giant spiders, giant grasshoppers, giant . . . well, you get the idea.

And, even within the individual hardware ideas embraced by the field, classification is still a problem. Take rocket ships—they appear in *The First Men In The Moon*, *Star Wars*, *2001*, *Abbott and Costello Go To Mars*, *The Fifth Element*, *Forbidden Planet*, *Flesh Gordon*, and *Independence Day*. But does that make all these movies science fiction movies? And if it does, does it make them all the same *kind* of science fiction movie?

In order to best understand the scope of the genre, it helps to take a look at where it all begin—science fiction literature. You'll find Edgar Rice Burroughs's novels of Pellucidar, his world inside the supposedly hollow Earth, right there in the library alongside Isaac Asimov's *Foundation Trilogy* and Philip K. Dick's musings about the dreams of androids. As far as most librarians are concerned, A.E. Van Vogt and Alfred Bester are considered the same kind of writers as Ray Bradbury and Stanislaw Lem. What do you think? I'll tell you what I think.

Science fiction is a one-of-a-kind genre, and the *only* one-of-a-kind genre humanity has ever created. It's because science fiction alone routinely deals with the world of *speculation*. In a hard-boiled detective novel, you can have the same tough guy in the same hat with the same gin bottle in his bottom left-hand desk drawer, making the same witty cracks about beautiful women and punching the same bad guys in novel after novel and no one cares. More to the point, fans of the genre expect it. If he didn't crack wise and chase beautiful women and beat the stuffing out of punks, the fans would disappear fast. But, unlike mysteries, or westerns or romances or any other type of fiction for that matter, the same old plots and ideas and characters simply won't do for the dedicated science fiction fan.

Many readers of other genres search for one or two authors with whose work they feel comfortable, and then, oftentimes, they simply settle in to read whatever those scribes put out for the rest of their lives and that's that. The new romantic thriller from so-and-so comes out; then so-and-so's adoring fans flock to the stores and buy it up. They read it, somehow not noticing that it's pretty much the same story as last time with just the names of the characters and the cities they live in having been changed. All of that simply doesn't matter. These readers' need to scan easily forgettable words has been fulfilled. Time for bed. Case closed.

This isn't the way it is for the science fiction fan. We read science fiction because we're questioners, searchers for truth, and we're also easily bored. Once one question has been answered, we're on to the next one. We start as kids reading Doc Smith and Robert Heinlein and move on to Leigh Brackett and Clifford D. Simak. Then it's Poul Anderson, followed by John Brunner. We dabble in Bradbury for a while, and then it's on to Frederic Brown and John Campbell and Frank Herbert. Leading later to Phillip Dick and Thomas Disch.

Like any good addictive substance, each new author takes us on to another and then another. In the beginning, the novice science fiction reader starts with the writers who deal in hardware, who deliver all the right props and settings in the best combinations. The pulp adventures and space operas come first, getting us acquainted with the genre, teaching us the vocabulary we need to navigate within the boundaries of this literary universe. Then, once we've digested hyperdrive and plasteel and exoskeletons, suddenly we're ready to move on again. And this jump is the big one. This is the move that separates the people who're merely looking for entertainment from the true, lifelong science fiction fanatic.

After the tales of robot police, green alien girls, and spaceship-piloting duelers battling for galactic empires and such, then comes the interest in the stories that ask *more*. Then comes the questioning. The speculation. The *thinking*.

Who built those robot police, and do those mechanoids have souls, and if they don't have souls, should they necessarily be put in charge of people who do, and if they do have souls, is it right to enslave them, even as protectors? And does anyone or anything actually have a soul? Is there a God that dispenses souls? Or do people create their own souls and thus give life to God? Which came first: the Supreme Being or the rational intellect that could imagine a Supreme Being? And what's the position of that intellect on the enslavement of a robotic populace? And—more important— no matter what their position is . . . what's yours?

This is the true appeal of science fiction to its fans. Unlike other genres, science fiction asks the big questions. The hard questions. It asks *all* the questions. Can war be abandoned, or is it with us forever? Is a human a reasoning animal or an animal with the ability to reason? Is anything real, solid in a permanent sense that defies our senses, or is all matter as malleable as our imagination? Is there life on other planets, and if there is or isn't, does either case confirm or dispel our egocentric notions of our place in the universe?

Science fiction is a large and rambling land with as many topographical features as we can imagine. It ranges from the smallest ideas to the largest, from the silly to the sacred, from the most fleeting of notions to those granite-bound epic ideas that are permanent . . . except, of course, there are no permanent ideas in science fiction. If it speculates, if it makes us wonder, if it questions where we're going and how we got here and whether or not we're going to get any farther, well, it's probably in the ballpark, and that's close enough.

And, as it is with science fiction literature, so it is with the genre's films. There are acres of science fiction movies in which the rocket ship lands on a planet, after which the rest of the picture is simply a western or a fantasy story. Indeed, most of what we think of as sci-fi films are really what can be called *sci-fi slash* movies as in sci-fi/noir, sci-fi/mystery, sci-fi/horror, and so on.

Therefore, throughout this encyclopedia of science fiction films, I have tried to include as many movies as possible. Just about anything that anyone anywhere has ever called science fiction has been covered here. It's a big clubhouse, and there's no need to be exclusive.

I have included at least one representative of every possible candidate. In other words, maybe every single Frankenstein or Godzilla movie hasn't made it into these pages with a full entry, but certainly the first or the best of each has. I've tried to give an idea whether the film is like, say *Predator*, a "hardware" film, or like *The Day the Earth Stood Still*, a "software" film that attempts to expand beyond entertainment onward toward enlightenment. Then, I've analyzed whether or not these films succeed in what they attempted.

And this takes us back to Sturgeon's Law.

Most of the movies listed in this tome are not tremendous or wonderful or even interesting. And that's because, as Sturgeon so correctly taught us, most movies of any kind are not tremendous or wonderful or even interesting. Most films are like anything else— product meant to be consumed and nothing more. Rarely do they even aspire to anything else, let alone succeed in their aspirations. One in ten is worth our attention; the rest are mere diversions at best and money-stealing frauds at worst.

As a working film critic specializing in fantasy, horror, and science fiction for the past quarter-century, I've developed an ego sufficiently large enough to allow me to present my opinions as fact and expect them to be taken at face value. So, in my arrogance that's exactly what I'll be doing. However, I'll also be supplying the hard facts and a basic overview of each film so that readers will have enough information to decide if a film merits watching so that they can then form their own opinions. In every entry, you'll find the available facts: screenwriter, director, cast, whether a film is available on videotape or laser disc, and so on. After that, a synopsis follows, in great detail where merited and with lesser or more obscure films given the barest outlines. Then, after the liner note information has been dispensed, we get down to business: Is the movie truly science fiction or just something littered with the appropriate props? What makes it so? What approach does it take? And, whatever its goals appear to have been (besides making money, the goal we'll assume all films have), each entry examines how closely the filmmakers came to realizing them, and whether it's good or bad as a science fiction movie and worth your time or not. For example, *Star Wars* really isn't much of a science fiction film, but let's face it, it certainly is blockbuster entertainment.

I try to inform and advise while keeping the lectures to a minimum. And, since this introduction is starting to border on a lecture, perhaps it's time I lay my cards on the table and get to work. Thank you all, those who purchased this volume, and those who simply utilize it. Here is the sprawling world of science fiction films, from the silent shorts made more than a century ago that lasted only a few hundred feet of film to the sprawling, multi-hour, special effects extravaganzas of today. In other words, all the stuff you find in the video store under the heading "science fiction." Just, please, remember Sturgeon's Law, and only rent one tape in ten.

Trust me on this one.

—C.J. Henderson
Brooklyn, N.Y.

Abbreviations Used in This Volume

aka   also known as

b&w black and white.

VT   This abbreviation indicates videotape
availability.

LD   This abbreviation indicates laser disc
availability.

DVD This abbreviation indicates digital versa-
tile disc availability

ABBOTT AND COSTELLO GO TO MARS

Universal, 1953, b&w, 77 min, VT

Producer: Howard Christie; **Director:** Charles Lamont; **Screenplay:** John Grant and D.D. Beauchamp; **Music:** Joseph Gershenson; **Special Effects:** David Horsley; **Cast:** Bud Abbott, Lou Costello, Mari Blanchard, Robert Paige, Martha Hyer, Jack Kruschen, Horace McMahon (with a cameo by a very young Anita Ekberg)

Orville and Lester (Costello and Abbott) accidentally blast off into space with two gangsters (Kruschen and McMahon). The pair crash on the planet Venus (which obviously doesn't fit the title, but it's a fact which is never explained) and are imprisoned by the planet's ruler, man-hating Queen Alura (Blanchard). The boys endure a series of tests and are released for being good kissers.

This is not much of a film, even by Abbott and Costello standards, and not much of a sci-fi film, either. As author Jeff Rovin points out in *Aliens, Robots, and Spaceships:* "The interior of (Abbott and Costello's) V-2 style rocket has a swing-like seat with cushions on either side; it remains level whichever way the rocket turns." Since there's no up and down in space, what's the difference? This is not the film's only scientific mistake.

ABBOTT AND COSTELLO MEET DR. JEKYLL AND MR. HYDE

Universal, 1953, b&w, 76 min, VT

Producer: Howard Christie; **Director:** Charles Lamont; **Screenplay:** Leo Loeb and John Grant; **Music:** Joseph Gershenson; **Special Effects:** David Horsley; **Makeup:** Bud Westmore; **Cast:** Bud Abbott, Lou Costello, Boris Karloff (with stuntman Eddie Parker portraying the Hyde role), Helen Westcott, Craig Stevens, John Dierkes, Reginald Denny

Abbott and Costello play two American police officers who travel to London to study British crime-fighting techniques. They soon end up behind bars, and who should bail them out but Dr. Jekyll (Karloff). The good doctor has been murdering all those in the world of science who called him crazy, and he's intent on getting the rest of them.

This fairly unfunny mish-mosh never really takes off. Karloff is his usual sensational self, and in fact, it has been long speculated that his overwhelming presence may have hampered the filmmakers, who oddly did not include the duo's usual amount of humor. The movie actually has better special effects than jokes, even when Costello gets a dose of Jekyll's Hyde formula.

ABBOTT AND COSTELLO MEET FRANKENSTEIN

Universal, 1948, b&w, 83 min, VT, LD, DVD

Producer: Robert Arthur; **Director:** Charles Barton; **Screenplay:** John Grant, Frederic Rinaldo, and Robert Lees; **Music:** Frank Skinner; **Special Effects:** David Horsley and Jerome Ash; **Makeup:** Bud Westmore; **Cast:** Bud Abbott, Lou Costello, Bela Lugosi, Glen Strange, Lon Chaney, Jr., Lenore Aubert, Frank Ferguson, Jane Randolph (with a voice cameo by Vincent Price)

Dracula (Lugosi, who else?) plans to resurrect the Frankenstein monster (Strange) by replacing its brain with that of a dolt (Costello, who else?). The Wolfman (Chaney) spends the majority of his nonmoonlit screen time trying to convince the boys that Dracula might be trouble.

This is by far the best of the team's borderline science fiction films, mainly because the menaces are all presented as seriously as they were in their original Universal outings, *Dracula* and *FRANKENSTEIN*, making for a truly funny horror movie with slight sci-fi overtones that still works today.

ABBOTT AND COSTELLO MEET THE INVISIBLE MAN

Universal, 1950, b&w, 82 min

Producer: Howard Christie; **Director:** Charles Lamont; **Screenplay:** John Grant, Frederic Rinaldo, and Robert Lees; **Special Effects:** David Horsley; **Makeup:** Bud Westmore; **Cast:** Bud Abbott, Lou Costello, Arthur Franz, Nancy Guild, Adele Jergens, Sheldon Leonard, William Frawley

A prizefighter (Franz), unjustly accused of murder, is helped by a pair of bumbling detectives (Costello and Abbott). The boys find H.G. Wells's invisibility formula and use it to bring the real bad guys to justice.

One of the team's better efforts due mainly to film's terrific special effects. Unlike *ABBOTT AND COSTELLO MEET DR. JEKYLL AND MR. HYDE*, where the special effects overwhelmed the jokes, this time around they interact with and add to the humor rather than replace it, resulting in a good effort from a classic team.

ABSENT-MINDED PROFESSOR, THE

Disney/Buena Vista, 1961, b&w, 97 min, VT, LD

Producers: Walt Disney and Bill Walsh; **Director:** Robert Stevenson; **Screenplay:** Bill Walsh; **Music:** George Bruns; **Special Effects:** Peter Ellenshaw; **Cast:** Fred MacMurray, Nancy Olsen, Keenan Wynn, Tommy Kirk, Leon Ames, Elliott Teid

The story centers on an inventor (MacMurray) who creates an antigravity formula. His only problem is that no one will believe he invented anything.

This heartwarming film remains a fairly amusing comedy (especially for the kids) even today. The film's special effects work well, sometimes at a manic pace. And since it's a Disney production, despite the thieving Alonzo T. Hawk (Wynn), everything turns out all right, which is more than can be said for the sequels and remakes.

SON OF FLUBBER, the follow-up, not only didn't add much to the original idea, but seemed rather scattered as well. The '90s remake, titled simply *FLUBBER*, was bright and shiny, but the special effects ran away with the film, making it a fun-filled bunch of laughs for children, but robbing it of the heart that permeated the original.

ABYSS, THE

20th Century Fox, 1989, Color, 145 min, VT, LD, DVD

Producer: Gale Anne Hurd; **Director:** James Cameron; **Screenplay:** Cameron; **Music:** Robert Garrett III and Alan Silvestri; **Special Effects:** David Ambord and Scott E. Anderson; **Cinematography:** Mikael Salomon and Dennis Skotak; **Cast:** Ed Harris, Mary Elizabeth Mastrantonio, Michael Biehn, J.C. Quinn, Chris Elliott, Jimmie Ray Weeks

A well-rounded oil-rig crew are the only people who can effect the rescue of a nuclear submarine trapped on the ocean floor. With a severe storm brewing, they have a limited amount of time before they'll be trapped beneath the surface. The rescue attempt proves more difficult than planned, and the venture turns deadly when members of the crew find themselves pitted against each other. All this is just buildup to the film's true story: first contact with a group of startlingly unusual aliens living on the ocean bottom.

Boasting a good premise, a top-notch cast, and state-of-the-art special effects, *The Abyss* seems to have everything going for it. Unfortunately, no one connected with the production thought it necessary to hire someone who could produce a script capable of pulling everything together. As a result the film gets bogged down in predictable relationship struggles, particularly between male and female members of the crew, which not only distracts the audience from the main story, but also highlights the holes in the film's plot. Not even the previously mentioned bounty of stunning special effects distracts viewers from a litter of startling gaffes, such as the scene in which a wedding ring defies the crushing power of a hydraulic door. Critics have speculated that the film's antimarriage, or at least antiromance, themes arose from writer/director Cameron's attempts to cope with his own failing marriage. Therapy would have been cheaper, and certainly it would have made things less painful for the audience.

Note: The film was recut later by the director and given a substantially different ending, which many feel greatly improves the film. The longer version includes additional scenes and an extended sequence with the aliens on the sea bottom.

ADDING MACHINE, THE

Associated London Films/Universal, 1969, Color, 99 min

Producer: Jerome Epstein; **Director:** Epstein; **Screenplay:** Epstein; **Music:** Mike Leander and Lambert Williamson; **Cinematography:** Walter Lassally; **Cast:** Milo O'Shea, Phyllis Diller, Billie Whitelaw, Sidney Chaplin Raymond Huntley, Julian Glover

An accountant played by Milo O'Shea finds out his job is about to be automated. Anger and frustration lead him to murder the manager who made the decision. Soon after, the agitated O'Shea is electrocuted by accident and sent to an afterlife that is anything but what he had imagined. Eternity for the CPA of the damned is a never-ending sequence of buttons that need to be pushed. By attempting to hang onto his job, he succeeds in keeping it for all eternity.

The film presents an alarmist view of automation, loosely based on a play from the early '20s (when folks had the good sense to fear the answering machined/car alarmed/Internetted future to come). The film is still of some interest, however, especially for the unusual sight of Phyllis Diller in an out-of-character and very well played straight dramatic role.

ADVENTURES OF BUCKAROO BANZAI ACROSS THE EIGHTH DIMENSION, THE

20th Century Fox, 1984, Color, 103 min, VT, LD

Producer: Sidney Beckerman; **Director:** W.D. Richter; **Screenplay:** Earl Mac Rauch; **Music:** Michael Boddicker; **Special Effects:** David Blitstein, Michael L. Fink, and Henry Millar; **Cinematography:** Fred J. Koenekamp; **Cast:** Peter Weller, John Lithgow, Ellen Barkin, Christopher Lloyd, Jeff Goldblum

Bad, unknown things are hidden here on Earth, or more specifically, they *were* hidden here on Earth, trapped between dimensions inside a mountain. Coincidentally, it's the same mountain chosen as the location for the test drive of a new vehicle that will prove the viability of interdimensional travel. The test comes off without a hitch but unexpectedly allows the hidden things the possibility of escape. The catch is that the beings inside the mountain are prisoners, and if they come close to getting free and leaving the planet, their extraterrestrial jailers will destroy the Earth to keep them contained. What can humanity do?

According to this film, there's only one person who can save us, Buckaroo Banzai, and he just happens to be the man who drove through the mountain and started all the trouble in the first place.

Unfortunately for Earth, Buckaroo Banzai is a badly actualized spoof of the pulp-hero, Doc Savage. He is supposedly capable of juggling careers as a rocket car racer, a physicist and a neurosurgeon, a rock star and a secret agent, a pilot, a motorcycle racer, and so on. What's more, the villainous alien beings are obviously inspired by the dark creatures of H.P. Lovecraft's Mythos writings. In other words, it's Doc Savage vs. Cthulhu—great idea with no one great behind the camera to make it work.

The movie moves in fits and starts, but never really achieves any kind of smooth pacing. Every time things start pulling together, the filmmakers pull the rug out from under audience. The supreme alien jailers are a good example. They appear to be Jamaicans, but no explanation is ever offered or even implied. Nor does the film explain why they fear the escape of their prisoners or why they're willing to destroy the entire Earth to keep them contained here. With that kind of power at their disposal, one wonders why they're so afraid of a bunch of aliens that a lone Earthman eventually defeats mostly by himself.

Considering the source material that inspired it, *Banzai* could have been interesting, or funny, or a delightful parody, or, well . . . something . . . but it's not. The film is intensely dull, complete with pointless and contradictory scenes, wooden dialogue, and a patronizing attitude toward the audience. It has to be said that for roughly the first hour—despite the shakiness of the plot—there is a sense that the whole thing might come together. But, sadly, it never does, and pretty soon we're laughing at the heroes instead of with them.

An incredibly over-the-top scenery-chewing performance from John Lithgow, an almost funny turn by Christopher Lloyd, great production design, and good special effects were not enough to save this film from losing at the box office. For anyone who appreciates the creations of "Ken Robeson" and H.P. Lovecraft, which so clearly inspired this film, it's hard to describe how horribly disappointing it is. True—it does have a die-hard cult following. But so does *PLAN 9 FROM OUTER SPACE*.

ADVENTURES OF CAPTAIN MARVEL, THE

Republic, 1941, b&w serial, 12 chapters (25 reels)

Producer: Hiram S. Brown; **Directors:** William Witney and John English; **Screenplay:** Ronald Davidson, Arch Heath, Sol Shor, Norman Hall, and Joseph Poland; **Music:** Cy Feuer; **Cinematography:** William Nobels; **Special Effects:** Howard and Theodore Lydecker; **Cast:** Frank Coghlan, Jr., Nigel de Brulier, Tom Tyler, Louise Currie, Jack Mulhall, Bryant Washburn

This serialized adaptation of the popular Fawcett Comics character, also known as Shazam!, starts with a bizarre version of the character's origin. The location of and motivation for the event are changed from what was presented in the comics, but it still involves an individual named Billy Batson (Coghlan) receiving super powers from an ancient wizard named Shazam. What follows are daring exploits and fistfights as our superpowered hero tries to stop the evil Scorpion from getting his hands on the secret of transmutation.

There is action a-plenty here and superior special effects for a serial, but oddly none of the comedy that made the original Fawcett comics so entertaining. The source material, unlike most of the "long underwear" heroes of the day, were actually much more concerned with cracking jokes than cracking heads. The original Captain Marvel rivaled Superman in popularity because, although the series superficially seemed a great deal like Superman, it was actually something vastly different. The adventures of Captain Marvel made for truly inventive and funny comics, with characters like the villainous Mr. Mind, who was actually a superintelligent worm, or the Captain's friend, Mr. Tawny, a timid, English-speaking tiger that dressed in natty suits and walked around town on his hind legs.

Ultimately, this cinematic treatment of the affectionately nicknamed "Big Red Cheese" is just another serial churned out to entertain kids on Saturday mornings and earn money for Republic. Both worthwhile goals, but neither offers much to a modern audience.

ADVENTURES OF STELLA STAR, THE

See *STARCRASH*

ADVENTURES OF THE GARGANTUAS

See *THE WAR OF THE GARGANTUAS*

AELITA

Mezharabpom (U.S.S.R.), 1924/Amkino (U.S.), 1929, b&w, 45 min, silent

Director: Yakov Protazanov; **Screenplay:** Fydor Otzep and Alexei Falko; **Cinematography:** Emil Schünemann and Yuri Zhelyabuzhsky; **Cast:** Nikolai Tserectelli, Igor Illinski, Yulia Solntseva, Yuri Zavadsky, Valentina Kuinzhi, J. Solnzeva, Konstanin Eggert

Space explorers Los (Tserectelli) and Busev (Illinski) land on Mars and find it peopled by a population woefully unenlightened in Marxist theory. The not-so-red planet is still ruled by an aristocracy. Los falls for the Martian Queen (Solntseva), while Busev gets involved with the struggle of the workers. Predictably, there is a mighty revolution that sets things straight and sends the interplanetary bourgeois packing.

Aelita is a very heavy-handed morality play of interest only to those students of history with nothing better to do for three-quarters of an hour or to fans of the Tairov Theatre's Alexandra Exter, who produced the movie's stylized but quite interesting Expressionistic sets and costumes.

AERIAL ANARCHISTS, THE

Kineto (Great Britain), 1911, b&w, silent, 700 feet

Director: Walter Booth

Turn-of-the-century terrorists in bizarre but stylish heavier-than-air machines carry out bombing runs over major cities. This film offered some of the cinema's earliest social commentary, helping to set the stage early for the kind of stories that would become a staple of the science fiction genre.

The Adventures of Captain Marvel (REPUBLIC / R. ALLEN LEIDER COLLECTION)

AERIAL SUBMARINE, THE

Kineto (Great Britain), 1910, b&w, silent, 600 feet

Director: Walter Booth

Scientists with nothing better to do put together a flying submarine, perhaps foreshadowing modern efforts to put VCRs and microwaves in family cars. Little else is known about this film.

AGENCY (aka: MIND GAMES)

Films RSL (Canada), 1981, color, 94 min, VT

Producers: Robert Baylis, Robert Lantos, and Stephen J. Roth; **Director:** George Kaczender; **Screenplay:** Paul Gottlieb; **Music:** Lewis Furey; **Cinematography:** Miklós Lente; **Cast:** Robert Mitchum, Lee Majors, Valerie Perrine, Saul Rubinek, Tony Parr, Alexandra Stewart

Agency offers a fairly interesting idea: Mitchum's character seeks to create a bastion of political power for himself through the use of subliminal advertising. What sounds like a strong premise, however, does not come through. Despite its solid cast, the film doesn't live up to its potential.

AGENT FOR H.A.R.M.

Dimension IV, 1966, color, 84 min

Producer: Joseph F. Robertson; **Director:** Gerd Oswald; **Screenplay:** Blair Robertson; **Music:** Gene Kaurer and Douglas Lackey; **Special Effects:** D.E. Rollins; **Cinematography:** James Crab; **Cast:** Mark Richman, Wendell Corey, Carl Esmond, Barbara Boucher

More of a secret agent than science fiction film, this one tells the story of a scientist under investigation while he tries to combat spores that turn human beings into fungi.

AIR HAWKS

Columbia, 1935, b&w, 66 min

Director: Albert Rogell; **Screenplay:** Griffin Jay and Grace Neville; **Cinematography:** Henry Ferulich; **Cast:** Wiley Post, Ralph Bellamy, Edward Van Sloan

Heroic G-men fight to capture a machine whose rays can stall motors of any kind.

AIRSHIP DESTROYER, THE

Charles Urban Studio (Great Britain), 1909, b&w, silent, 1,350 feet

Producer: Charles Urban; **Director:** Walter Booth

A prescient depiction of aerial warfare waged over Great Britain. Though only a war movie now, it has to be noted that it was wild science fiction for its time. Just remember what people once thought of cloning and microwave popcorn.

AIR TORPEDO, THE

Deutsche Kinematographen (Germany) 1913/Warner Bros. (US), 1914, b&w, silent, three reels

Producer: Louis Gero

This gem of inventive World War I cinema quite accurately predicts World War II technology. Scientists create the V2 rocket 25 years early and use it much the same way it was eventually used in reality.

AKIRA

Akira Committee (Japan), 1988, Color, 124 min, VT, LD

Producer: Akira Production Committee; **Director:** Katsuhito Otomo; **Screenplay:** Isao Hashimoto; **Music:** Shoji Yamashiro; **Animation Supervisor:** Takashi Nakamura; **Cast:** Voices of Jimmy Flanders, Drew Thomas, Barbara Larsen, Lewis Lemay, Stanley Gurd, Jr.

This animated epic centers on the exploits of a motorcycle gang in a postapocalyptic Japan. While running from the law, the gang accidentally runs into an escapee from a secret government experimentation center—one concerned with developing telekinetic powers. One of the gang members is granted godlike powers during the encounter. The rest of the film concerns his attempts to deal with his new abilities as the government tries to contain him. His friends try to help him at first, try to understand him later, and ultimately just try to survive his inability to come to terms with what he has become.

This incredibly stylish, fast-paced animated adventure film is unlike anything ever produced for the American market. Although the Japanese never fell into line behind the formulaic Disney standard like the vast majority of American animation studios, their films usually suffer from a number of their own homegrown problems. Quite often, despite the quality of the dubbing, the storytelling in Japanese animation, called *anime*, is often terribly disjointed. *Akira* is not one of those pictures, however. Not by a long shot.

This story is a blockbuster, wrapping eye-popping action around intense social concerns about the nature of humans and the nature of humans' scientific progress. It takes a hard look at government control of such volatile subjects as genetic research and nuclear power, highlighting the extreme differences that can come when these things are kept in the hands of hidden bureaucrats instead of those with a bit more regard for human beings. It is not for small children or immature adults since the film spills buckets of blood, but not gratuitously. Human life is cheap in Otomo's future Japan, where it becomes a metaphor like almost everything else presented to the audience here.

Based on the internationally renowned comic book novel of the same name, the film condenses hundreds and hundreds of pages of the novel into just a little over two hours, so part of the story may be a bit confusing for some viewers, but it's worth the risk. *Akira* is probably the best animated science fiction film of all time.

ALGOL

Germany, 1920, b&w, silent

Director: Hans Werkemeister; **Screenplay:** Hans Brenert; **Cast:** Emil Jannings, John Gottowt, Ernst Hoffman, Kathe Haack

The alien Mephisto (Jannings), from the planet Algol, comes to Earth with plans of conquest. He unleashes his death machine, which makes quick work of the

Earth's defenders. But, alas for our villain, it does too good a job, killing Mephisto's family before he can shut it down. The machine's last act before it is destroyed is to eliminate Mephisto as well.

Any chance to see antique footage like this should be welcomed by the true sci-fi fan. But be warned. At best, films like this are nothing more than a curiosity. Even METROPOLIS, the best known of all silent science fiction films, is fairly ponderous, with a truly potboiler approach to the social issues it tries to raise. True, credit must be given to those who went before for blazing the cinematic trail of the science fiction genre, but only the most dedicated fans might find the time to view something like *Algol*.

ALIEN

20th Century Fox, 1979, color, 124 min, VT, LD, DVD

Producer: Ronald Shusett; **Director:** Ridley Scott; **Screenplay:** Dan O'Bannon; **Music:** Jerry Goldsmith; **Special Effects:** Brian Johnson and Nick Alder; **Designs:** H.R. Giger and Ron Cobb; **Cinematography:** Derek Vanlint; **Cast:** Sigourney Weaver, Tom Skerritt, Yaphet Kotto, John Hurt, Ian Holm, Veronica Cartwright, Harry Dean Stanton

The movie starts with the space ship *Nostromo* being diverted to investigate a signal coming from a previously unknown world. There the crew finds the remains of a massive alien ship. In its hold is a cargo of bizarre, oversized eggs. The first crewmember on the scene investigates one of them only to have the egg split open and release a creature that invades his body. The creature (or, to be more exact, the next stage in the creature's development) later bursts through the man's chest, killing him instantly.

The remainder of the film is spent with the crudely armed crew trying to defend itself against the constantly metamorphosing alien monster. The most interesting twist on the standard people-versus-a-thing storyline is that Nostromo's solid, cool-under-pressure white male captain is one of the first to fall to the creature, leaving Ripley (Weaver), a woman, to take command. Although this might seem like a quaint idea now, at the time this notion was mere science fiction for most of the world's moviegoing public than the rest of the movie. Audiences were truly (albeit momentarily) stunned at this point—who was going to save this bunch with the traditional square-shouldered hero gone?

This twist is much more simply a tip of the hat to the feminist perspective, though, since unlike so many movies following the same plot there is a visibly conscious effort at work here to make the crew seem like real people in a real situation. Another female member of the crew, Cartwright, responds to the horrific threat in a stereotypically hysterical manner. One of the hallmarks of the film is that, throughout, there are no superheroics, just desperate human beings struggling to survive.

Another interesting aspect of the story, of course, is the ingenious concept of the Aliens themselves and the way so little is ever revealed about them or their origins. Even by the fourth movie, all the audience knows is that (and this comes from suspicions and theories voiced in the film, not from any facts garnered) somewhere out in space, some inhuman race created the Aliens as weapons. The eggs are landed in enemy territory, then left to wait for something to come and investigate. Whatever does has its body invaded and then used as a host for the growing creature, which then mimics the host's skeletal arrangement, musculature, and so on, while retaining the natural weapons encoded in its constant DNA. The resulting creatures seem genetically programmed to do nothing then but create more of their own kind while killing every non-Alien thing in sight.

While many fans and critics credit STAR WARS with revitalizing the science fiction film after the genre's fall-off in popularity in the mid-sixties, nothing could be further from the truth. STAR WARS was almost the ruin of the genre. *Alien* was it savior. This is a dark, moody film, far better than most people give it credit for. When the success of STAR WARS sent filmmakers off in search of fantasy elements they could weld to western plots and present as science fiction, *Alien* brought people back to the basic tenets of the genre. It's a film built around real, hard science concepts with a story fueled by extremely hard, social science questions. Still, for all its epic pretensions, *Alien* is grounded firmly in its B movie roots and obviously inspired by past films such as IT! THE TERROR FROM BEYOND SPACE and PLANET OF VAMPIRES. In fact, some scenes seem lifted almost in their entirety from the latter.

The film made household names of Ridley Scott and Sigourney Weaver, and spawned three successful sequels (ALIENS, ALIEN³, ALIEN RESURRECTION), plus the assorted books, comic books, drink cups, toys, and other merchandise. The series also has the distinction of being one of the most consistently popular science fiction series yet produced.

ALIENATOR

(U.S.), 1989, color, 92 min, VT, LD

Producer: Jeffrie Hugue; **Director:** Fred Olen Ray; **Screenplay:** Paul Garson; **Music:** Chuck Cirino; **Cinematography:** Gary Graver; **Cast:** Jan-Michael Vincent, John Phillip Law, Ross Hagen, Teagan, Dyann Ortelli, Jesse Dabson, Dawn Wildsmith, P.J. Soles, Robert Clarke, Richard Wiley, Leo V. Gordon, Robert Quarry

An evil prison warden played by Jan-Michael Vincent sends a hunter unit (the lovely Teagan, just the thing to scare hardened criminals) after escapee Ross Hagen, who is hiding on the Earth. Better than nothing on a rainy afternoon, but not a great deal better.

ALIEN FROM L.A.

Cannon Group, 1987, color, 87 min, VT, LD

Producers: Yoram Globus and Menahem Golan; **Director:** Albert Pyun; **Screenplay:** Regina Davis and Albert Pyun; **Music:** James Saad; **Special Effects:** Gary Cuthbert; **Cinematography:** Tom Fraser; **Cast:** Kathy Ireland, Thom Matthews, William R. Moses, Don Michael Paul, Richard Haines, Linda Kerridge, Simon Poland

A California girl falls through a hole and ends up in Atlantis. Mediocre acting, so-so special effects, and a ridiculous plot abound in this film.

ALIEN INVASION

See *STARSHIP INVASIONS*

ALIEN NATION

20th Century Fox, 1988, color, 94 min, VT, LD

Producers: Gale Anne Hurd and Richard Kobritz; **Director:** Graham Baker; **Screenplay:** James Cameron and Rockne S. O'Bannon; **Music:** Curt Sobel; **Special Effects:** Joseph A. Unsinn; **Cast:** James Caan, Mandy Patinkin, Terence Stamp, Kevin Major Howard, Leslie Bevins

A spaceship filled with former alien slaves lands on Earth. Its passengers are granted asylum and attempt to integrate themselves into the American way of life. Since their appearance is fairly humanlike, this doesn't pose them too many problems, except, of course, for inevitable struggles with racism. The plot centers on the adventures of an alien policeman and his human partner, and though the concept brims over with pos-

sibilities, the film tries too hard to make social statements in the usual ham-fisted Hollywood way. Sadly, it comes off alternately as either preachy or boring. Caan as the police detective and Patinkin as his alien partner actually give rather amazing performances, both bringing a remarkable believability to their roles. But even coupled with the picture's fairly good special effects, they weren't enough to save this film from being merely routine. Interestingly, the television series based on the movie turned out far better than its source material, running several seasons, followed by several above average made-for-TV movies.

ALIEN PREDATOR (aka: MUTANT II, THE FALLING, COSMOS MORTAL, ALIEN PREDATORS)

Film Ventures International, 1987, color, 90 min, VT

Producer: Eduardo Salvi; **Director:** Deran Sarafian; **Screenplay:** Noah Bloch and Deran Sarafian; **Music:** Chase/Rucker Productions; **Special Effects:** John Badandin; **Cinematography:** Tote Trenas; **Cast:** Dennis Christopher, Martin Hewitt, Lynn-Holly Johnson, Luis Prendes, J.O. Bosso

The premise: When the actual satellite *Skylab* fell to Earth, it brought back extraterrestrial microbes capable of creating much larger monsters. Too bad they couldn't create a screenplay for this film, which is saddled with bad acting, pedestrian special effects, and awful writing.

ALIEN PREDATORS

See *ALIEN PREDATOR*

ALIEN RESURRECTION

20th Century Fox, 1997, color, 108 min, VT, LD, DVD

Producer: Antoine Simkine; **Director:** Jean-Pierre Jeunet; **Screenplay:** Joss Whedon; **Music:** John C. Frizzell; **Special Effects:** Susan Zwerman; **Cinematography:** Darius Khodji; **Cast:** Sigourney Weaver, Winona Ryder, Dominique Pinon, Ron Perlman, Gary Dourdan, Michael Wincott, Kim Flowers, Dan Hedaya, J.E. Freeman, Brad Dourif

In this fourth film in the ALIEN series, Ripley (Weaver) is now a clone of the Ripley who died 200 years earlier in the previous film. She is part Alien and part human, a thing bred in a human lab aboard a deep-space station where Aliens are being studied by the military. And what a military it is. How they got their hands on Ripley's DNA is never quite explained, but how they got more Aliens to study is. After Ripley gives "birth," Caesarean-style, to the creature growing in her chest (from the previous film), that thing is replanted in a test subject. This is done so the military scientists can observe the birth without killing Ripley. And where did the test subject come from? The military paid the less-than-honorable crew of a transport freighter to kidnap a cryogenic freighter's passengers to give them plenty of test subjects.

It's not a nice way to do business, but it isn't long before the universe is demanding retribution. Soon the creatures break loose and kill all the soldiers who aren't fortunate enough to abandon ship. Ripley teams up with the crew of the transport freighter (any port in a storm), and the two forces assist each other in escaping the station and learning the truth about themselves.

Unfortunately, but as should be expected, Aliens get aboard their ship as well. This leads to more battles, more revelations, and an ending that transcends anything done so far within the series, moving it finally into true and pure science fiction on all levels. The Ripley clone gives birth to an Alien/human hybrid, prompting the decision: Follow the Alien path of her heritage and kill this bastard thing ruthlessly, or follow the human, felling path and love it.

It isn't often that a series starts to come into its own this late in its run, but that's the case with the *Alien* franchise. After the depressingly disappointing second feature, they just got better and better. What seemed at the beginning to be only an attempt to remake the first film simply with better weapons ends as something far more important. Obviously, the plot questions some of the basic tenets of humanity and delves into a number of dicey moral questions, again not always dishing up easy answers. The new, hybrid Ripley is as Alien as the child is. Shouldn't she protect her young? Doesn't the human path include self-sacrifice? Wouldn't killing this thing be the human thing to do since doing such will save the Earth from the Aliens?

Director Jeunet is to be credited with much of what is right with this film. His previous films, *DELICATESSEN* and *THE CITY OF LOST CHILDREN*, were indicators that this was a man who would not serve up the same old leftovers. No one knew how right those perceptions were. The stylish touch obvious in his previous films is lavishly applied here in much the same manner as Ridley Scott's handprints covered the first film. Between the two of them, with a good deal of help from *ALIEN*'s Fincher, they have produced the finest science fiction series ever created. And, considering what they had to

overcome in the dead weight of *ALIENS*, that is more than just a remarkable achievement; it borders on the legendary.

ALIENS

20th Century Fox, 1986, color, 137 min, VT, LD, DVD

Producer: Gale Anne Hurd; **Director:** James Cameron; **Screenplay:** Cameron, David Giler, and Walter Hill; **Music:** James Horner; **Special Effects:** Brian Johnson and John Richardson; **Cinematography:** Adrian Biddle; **Cast:** Sigourney Weaver, Bill Paxton, Paul Reiser, Michael Biehn, Carrie Henn, Lance Hendriksen, Jenette Goldstein

In this first sequel to the blockbuster *ALIEN*, Ripley (Weaver), the only survivor of the first film, awakes years in the future. In suspended animation for decades, she has been found and awakened by the corporation that owned the ship aboard which the first movie took place. Now she is being sent along with a company of Marines to a planet where an Alien infestation has overrun a human colony.

The predictably greedy corporation doesn't really want to help anyone; they want to get hold of the Aliens and study them to find some way to turn a profit from the deadly critters. Ripley and the marines are dropped into a nest of the things and basically left to die. Nearly everyone in the group does just that, along with the corporate stooge (Reiser) sent to protect the corporation's interests. At the end, only Ripley, her android pal, one marine, and one little girl (the sole survivor of the colony) escape after Ripley dons a robotic exoskeleton/construction suit and slugs it out with the queen mother of the Aliens.

Unfortunately, by the time they blast off, the thinking audience is happy to see them go. While its predecessor offered a story grounded in hard science and strong science fiction concepts, this follow-up plays out as little more than a special effects spectacle. Not only does this film ignore the concepts of science fiction, but even basic science is thrown out the windows as the laws of physics are shattered in the name of excitement-over-reality. Even simple logic is absent from the story. Some examples: Why doesn't Ripley's arm get ripped off when she is subjected to the same gale pressure that is strong enough to sweep away the giant Alien queen mother? Why does the corporation bring Ripley along as an adviser (the only living human possessing actual experience with the Aliens) and then not listen to a single thing she says? Why, when she knows that the entire area is going to be destroyed in a holocaust-level explosion, does Ripley purposely, and quite needlessly, enrage the queen mother, goading it into attacking her and her companions as they attempt to flee? How is it Ripley is familiar with technology decades beyond what she knew when she went into suspended animation?

The loose ends and plot holes pile up so willfully in the film's last half hour that it might possibly be the most pointlessly insipid sequel ever made. For those who like great action sequences with terrific special effects, this one has them by the barrelful. Those who want them to make sense, though, are out of luck.

ALIEN TERROR

See *SINISTER INVASION*

ALIEN³

20th Century Fox, 1992, color, 115 min, VT, DVD

Producer: Ezra Swerdlow; **Director:** David Fincher; **Screenplay:** Larry Fergeson, Walter Hill, Vincent Ward, and David Giler; **Music:** Elliot Goldenthal; **Special Effects:** Richard Edlund; **Cinematography:** Alex Thomson; **Cast:** Sigourney Weaver, Charles S. Dutton, Charles Dance, Paul McGann, Brian Glover, Lance Hendriksen, Christo-

pher John Fields, Ralph Brown, Danny Webb, Holt McCallany

This second sequel to the original classic, ALIEN, finds Ripley (Weaver) crash-landing on a prison planet, and everyone who escaped with her at the end of the previous film dies on impact. As the prison population decides what to do with her, a new Alien (brought aboard Ripley's ship) begins to take out the population one by one. The prisoners fight back with Ripley's aid. The movie ends with most of the colony decimated and an Alien-infected Ripley sacrificing herself in a molten inferno to rid the planet of the Aliens and herself of a recurring character that had become her persona to most of the moviegoing public, especially its more obsessive branches.

Although much like the first film in tone, this installment of the Alien franchise is neither a retread or a quickie cash-in. The movie asks the same kinds of hard, social science questions the original did, not only not offering any simple answers, but rejecting even the notion of a satisfying (let alone "happy") ending. A significantly much better effort than *ALIENS* in every way except special effects, this film was surrounded by a great deal of controversy that created two camps within the series' fans—those who loved it, and those who hated it.

While the special effects are in no way inadequate, they are not the driving force behind the picture. This

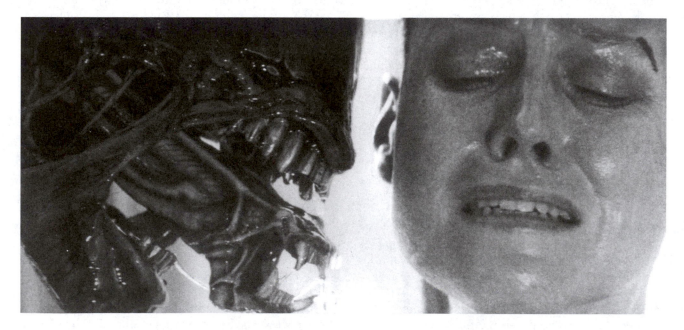

Alien 3 (TWENTIETH CENTURY FOX / AUTHOR'S COLLECTION)

time around it is script. The story line of *Alien³* is incredibly intense, realistic, exciting, and unpredictable. The Alien menace is wisely kept in the background, the monsters used sparingly while the humans are kept as the picture's focus. The producers were given a budget greatly reduced from that of the previous films, most likely based on the typical Hollywood notion that the audience was already assured. Not believing that delivering an inadequate film would indeed assure anything except damage to their reputations, the producers opted to follow the wise route followed by so many of their brethren in the '50s—if you don't have a lot of money, give it to the writers. A good plot, solid acting, grim action, believable characters, and a lot more help this film more than make up for its banal, overrated predecessor.

ALIEN WOMEN

See *ZETA ONE*

ALIEN'S RETURN, THE

See *RETURN, THE*

ALLIGATOR PEOPLE, THE

20th Century Fox, 1959, b&w, 74 min

Producer: Jack Leewood; **Director:** Roy Del Ruth; **Screenplay:** O.H. Hampton; **Music:** Irving Gertz; **Cinematography:** Karl Struss; **Cast:** Richard Crane, Bruce Bennett, Lon Chaney, Jr., Beverly Garland, Frieda Inescourt, Doug Kennedy

Beverly Garland goes searching for her missing husband and finds him in the hands of a scientist trying to regenerate missing limbs through the injection of alligator glands. Things do not work out well for any involved when the experiment goes awry.

ALL MONSTER'S ATTACK (aka: GODZILLA'S REVENGE)

Toho (Japan), 1969/UPA (U.S.), 1970, Color, 70 min, VT, LD

Producer: Tomoyuki Tanaka; **Director:** Ishiro Honda; **Screenplay:** Shinichi Sekizaw; **Music:** Kunio Miyauchio; **Cinematography:** Mototaka Tomioka; **Special Effects:** Eiji Tsuburaya and Honda; **Cast:** Tomonori Yazaki, Eisei Amamoto, Kenji Sahar, Sachio

Sakai, Kazuo Suzuki, Haruo Nakajima, Little Man Machan

See *GODZILLA*

ALPHAVILLE (aka: TARZAN VS. IBM)

Pathé-contemporary/Chaumaine-Film (France), 1965, b&w, 100 min

Producer: Andre Michaelin; **Director:** Jean-Luc Godard; **Screenplay:** Godard; **Music:** Paul Misraki; **Cast:** Eddie Constantine, Howard Vernon, Akim Tamiroff, Laslo Szabo, Jean-André Fiechi, Jean-Louis Comolli, Anna Karina

Ask ten different people who have seen this cultish '60s icon to describe its plot, and you will get at least eight different descriptions, even from the film's diehard fans. Here's mine: Detective Lemmy Caution (Constantine) is sent from Earth to the planet Alphaville on an unclear mission. The population there is kept in line by the planet's ruler/manager/dictator, Alpha 60, one of filmdom's first omniscient computers. Individualism is frowned upon there, and the people are all happy with their king of steel. Caution finally decides that his mission is to kill the inventor who created Alpha 60.

This is one odd film. Lemmy doesn't even use a rocket ship to go off-world. He simply motors his Ford through "intersidereal space," which is obviously just another name for some back road outside of Paris. The picture is filled with symbolism drawn from a lot of sources—some of them probably unexpected, unless one is the kind of person who expects characters named Dr. Heckle and Dr. Jeckle in their sci-fi films. All of it may or may not add up to anything depending on how seriously one is willing to take it. It's not a film for the average sci-fi fan, but a must for those who like to tackle life's big questions, especially for those who like supplying their own answers.

ALRUANE (1918)

Phoenix (Hungary), 1918, b&w, silent

Directors: Michael Curtiz and Odor Fritz; **Screenplay:** Richard Falk; **Cast:** Riszi Szollosi, Gyula Gal, Jeno Torzs, Margit Lux

This is the first of several adaptations of Hans Heinz's novel of the same name about a scientist who creates an artificial woman who possesses no soul.

ALRUANE (1928)

UFA (Germany), 1928, b&w, silent

Director: Henrik Galeen; **Screenplay:** Galeen; **Cinematography:** Franz Planer; **Cast:** Paul Wegerer, Brigitte Helm, Ivan Petrovitch, Franz Planer

In the third adaptation of Hans Heinz's novel, the artificial female evolves enough to discover love, supposedly overcoming that missing soul problem from the first film.

ALRUANE (1930) (aka: THE DAUGHTER OF EVIL)

UFA (Germany), 1930, b&w, 87 min

Director: Richard Oswald; **Screenplay:** Charlie Roellinghoff and R. Welsbach; **Music:** Bronislaw Kaper; **Cinematography:** Gunther Kramph; **Cast:** Albert Basserman, Brigitte Helm, Agnes Straub, Kathe Haack

Two years after making the second adaptation of Hans Heinz's novel about an artificial female, the same studio remade the same story with the same star simply to utilize the new sound technology. Seeing both films is for die-hard genre fans only.

ALRUANE (1952) (aka: UNNATURAL)

DCA (Germany), 1952, b&w, 90 min

Director: Arthur Maria Rabennalt; **Screenplay:** Fritz Rotter; **Cinematography:** Friedl Behn-Grund; **Cast:** Erich von Stroheim, Hildegard Knef, Karl Boehm, Trude Hesterberg

The fifth adaptation of Hans Heinz's novel about an artificial female, and the last time to date that the story has been filmed. The main difference between previous versions and this one is that this film utilized a gathering of the country's biggest stars.

ALRUANE AND THE GOLEM

Riesenbioskopfilm (Germany), 1919, b&w, silent

The second adaptation of Hans Heinz's novel about an artificial female paired the title character with the mythical clay giant for an odd blending.

ALTERED STATES

Warner Bros., 1980, Color, 102 min, VT, LD, DVD

Producer: Howard Gottfried; **Director:** Ken Russell; **Screenplay:** Paddy Chayefsky; **Music:** John Corigliano; **Special Effects:** Brian Ferren, Chuck Gaspar, and Larry L. Fuentes; **Cinematography:** Jordon Croneworth; **Cast:** William Hurt, Blair Brown, Bob Balaban, Charles Haid, Thaao Penghlis, Dori Brenner, Miguel Godreau, George Gaynes, Drew Barrymore

Hurt in the role of a scientist plays the archetypical dispassionate observer in this study of the human animal. In an attempt to discover the truth about human evolution, he experiments with mind-altering drugs, hoping to discover the answers he seeks through an exploration of human racial memory. What he expects to be purely a mental journey turns into a metamorphosizing physical transformation with many disastrous results, the least of which is the terrible toll it takes on his family life.

Misunderstood by most critics, this state-of-the-art special effects feast is laden with symbolism but is ultimately easily understood. Many mistake Hurt's character's obvious lack of interest in anything outside the cerebral as bad acting, or at the least a bad character interpretation, but the character's lack of emotion is the point, if not the central crux, of the film. *Altered States* is also filled with incredibly lush and rapid special effects sequences. These segments of the film have often been called pointless and confusing, but this is only the case if one fails to realize they are the purposeful, and quite necessary, counterpoint to Hurt's understated performance.

It has to be admitted that even source material author Paddy Chayefsky was unhappy with the end results, having his name struck from the credits in retaliation. Many liberties were taken with Chayefsky's material, but on the other hand director Russell crafted an incredible film that pulls together many of humanity's great cerebral quests and answers them neatly with one simple answer, perhaps too simple an answer for Chayefsky. Nevertheless, the film stands as one of the all-time great social science fiction films, an epic that blends the question of the rightness of the cold, impartial scientific quest with the judgmentalism of human emotion and delivers the answer as to their correct balance.

AMAZING COLOSSAL MAN, THE

AIP, 1957, b&w, 80 min

Producer: Bert I. Gordon; **Director:** Gordon; **Screenplay:** Gordon; **Music:** Albert Glasser; **Special Effects:** Gordon; **Cinematography:** Joseph Biroe; **Cast:** Glenn Langan, Cathy Downs, Judd Holdren, William Hudson, James Sealy, Scott Peters

A single-engine passenger plane crashes at ground zero during an atomic bomb test's countdown sequence. Heroic observer, Lt. Col. Glenn Manning (Langan) tries to rescue any survivors, but the test goes off and he is doused with the full force of the explosion. To everyone's surprise, Manning is not killed, but instead makes a full recovery. More than that, he begins to grow at an incredible rate. Science tries to help him, but it can do nothing. Manning continues to grow as his friends watch helplessly.

Often dismissed as mere B entertainment, *The Amazing Colossal Man* handles its premise with surprisingly deft hands. Like many of the science fiction films of the '50s, it was put together on a tiny budget, forcing the script to concentrate on the cerebral rather than the physical. The film becomes somewhat derivative at the end, but it's thoroughly enjoyable nonetheless, especially when viewed as a metaphor for fears of the changes being wrought on society by the advent of the atomic age. One sequel, *WAR OF THE COLOSSAL BEAST*, followed.

AMAZING TRANSPARENT MAN, THE

AIP, 1960, b&w, 56 min, VT

Producer: Lester D. Guthrie; **Director:** Edgar G. Ulmer; **Screenplay:** Jack Lewis; **Music:** Darrell Calker; **Special Effects:** Roger George; **Cast:** Douglas Kennedy, Marguerite Chapman, James Griffith, Ivan Triesault

A scientist working on an invisibility formula thinks nothing of using a criminal as his test subject. Imagine the poor doctor's surprise when his formula succeeds in creating an invisible thief who is then more interested in robbing banks than in helping his creator advance the cause of science. Who would have thought it? Of course, the scientist wants his protégé to steal dangerously radioactive isotopes, so perhaps he wasn't such a naif after all.

AMERICATHON

UA, 1979, Color, 85 min, VT

Producer: Joe Roth; **Director:** Neil Israel; **Screenplay:** Israel, Michael Mislove, and Monica Johnson; **Music:** Eddie Money, Elvis Costello; **Cinematography:** Gerard Hirshfield; **Cast:** Harvey Korman, Chief Dan George, Nancy Morgan, John Ritter, Fred Willard, Peter Riegert, Zane Buzby, Jay Leno, Meatloaf, Howard Hesseman

The United States is officially broke, and the entire world is united against it. The country's only hope is to stage a telethon and raise the money to pay its debts. From a simply terrible movie comes an idea of epic proportions, but even some interesting performances, especially from the always amusing Harvey Korman who pulls out all the stops here, are just not enough.

A MODERN BLUEBEARD

See *BOOM IN THE MOON*

AMPHIBIAN MAN, THE

Lenfilm (USSR), 1962, 98 min/NTA (US), 1964, 86 min, Color

Directors: Gennadi Kazansky and Vladimir Chebotaryov; **Screenplay:** Alexander Xenofontov, Alexi Kapler, and Akiba Golburt; **Cinematography:** Eduard Razovsky; **Cast:** Vladimir Korenev, Anastasia Vertinskaya, Mikhail Kozakov

Soviet researchers unintentionally capture an amphibious creature with measurable intelligence. Then they intentionally hold it prisoner with the thought of educating it despite its objections. The result is somewhat interesting.

ANDROID

New World Pictures, 1982, Color, 80 min, VT, LD

Producer: Rupert Harvey; **Director:** Aaron Lipstadt; **Screenplay:** James Reigle and Don Opper; **Music:** Don Preston; **Cast:** Klaus Kinski, Dan Opper, Brie Howard, Norbert Weisser, Crofton Hardester, Kendra Kirchner

In the near future, Dr. Daniel (Kinski) struggles to complete his greatest experiment—the construction of the perfect android—before he is stopped by the authorities. His only companion, Max (Opper), a near-perfect android, runs the station for Daniel, assists the doctor whenever possible, and amuses himself the rest of the time with video games, cartoons, and blue movies. Max is bored and wants to go to Earth. He sees his chance when a prison ship captured by the convicts it was transporting arrives at their station. Max allows them to dock, which makes Dr. Daniel furious until he discovers there is a woman among their crew. Needing a female to activate his ultimate android, the good doctor consents to the convicts coming aboard.

At this point, the plot becomes a web of lies as everyone in the movie begins deceiving one another. The convicts lie to Max, Daniel, and each other. Max lies to the convicts so that they will take him to Earth. He does not tell them he is a construct, but he does destroy a police vessel that has traced the convicts to the station (thus continuing the web of lies started by Daniel to the outside world). Daniel begins to introduce more androids onto the station, and this is where the film really takes off. Daniel's new creations are the perfect androids he has been seeking. They demonstrate truly human behavior when they lie and steal and murder, just like real people.

The picture is brilliant. Made in 20 days on a shoestring budget on the leftover sets of three different films, it is a remarkable study of the human beast, which plays with the audience's emotions ruthlessly, getting them to root for poor, little Max, even as he begins to slaughter everyone in sight. The screenplay is a triumph for writers Reigle and Opper. It's tightly plotted, filled with both clever twists and inventive dialogue, and laden with a viciously lively sense of humor, making even the grimmest scenes somehow light.

Android is social science fiction at its best, the perfect film to see with friends who are ready to laugh and then talk for hours afterward about what they just saw.

ANDROMEDA NEBULA, THE

See *TUMANNOST ANDROMEDY*

ANDROMEDA STRAIN, THE

Universal, 1971, Color, 131 min, VT, LD, DVD

Producer: Robert Wise; **Director:** Wise; **Screenplay:** Nelson Gidding; **Music:** Gil Melle; **Special Effects:** Doug Trumbull and Jamie Shourt; **Cast:** Arthur Hill, David Wayne, James Olson, Kate Reid, Paula Kelly

An American satellite (pre-*Skylab*) crashes to Earth near a small town, bringing with it microbes from outer space. The microbes cause the death of everyone in town except for a baby and an old, Sterno-drinking drunk. A crack team of scientists and researchers is assembled to investigate the rapidly spreading virus and find a cure.

It sounds like a simple premise, and it is, but it's one that makes for a great film. *The Andromeda Strain* plays its cards close to the vest, keeping the audience on the edge of their seats despite its somewhat overlong running time. Action is kept to a minimum as the Scientific Method becomes the human race's only hope. Ironically, it is, of course, science itself that brought the destruction humankind faces at its doorstep. In the underground government complex, surrounded by miles of machines (all of them genuine, in fact, since no fakes were used), man looks fumbling and lost within his science.

The source for the picture was Michael Crichton's novel of the same name. Packed with real science, it brought a calm urgency to the proceedings that less-inspired dialogue could not begin to match. There's definitely symbolism at work here, as well. For instance, at one point, a researcher misses a vital clue because he suffers a temporary seizure brought on by a machine's flashing lights. Science does its duty, but human vanity keeps the researcher from reporting the machine's flaw. There's more, but only a cad would deny real science fiction fans a chance to tear into this one. Also, only a really big cad would give away the ending, but it must be said that the climax is not only a startling one, but takes somewhat of an anti–sci-fi stance.

ANDY WARHOL'S FRANKENSTEIN
(aka: FLESH FOR FRANKENSTEIN)

Bryanston Pictures, 1974, Color, 3-D, 95 min, VT

Producer: Andy Warhol; **Director:** Paul Morrissey; **Screenplay:** Morrissey; **Music:** Claudio Guizzi; **Cinematography:** Luigi Kuevellier; **Cast:** Joe Dallesandro, Monique Van Vooren, Udo Kier, Srdjan Zelenovic, Dalila di Lazzaro

A mad doctor (Kier) labors to create the perfect woman. What is created is a disgusting gore-and-sex fest with absolutely nothing to recommend it.

ANGRY RED PLANET

AIP, 1959, Color, 94 min, VT, LD

Producers: Sidney Pink and Norman Maurer; **Director:** Ib Melchior; **Screenplay:** Melchior and Pink; **Music:** Paul Dunlap; **Special Effects:** Herman Townsley; **Cinematography:** Mack Stengler; **Cast:**

Gerald Mohr, Nora Hayden, Jack Kruschen, Les Tremayne

Earth sends its first team of astronauts to Mars. They return dead, dying, and half insane. The story of what happened then slowly unfolds in flashbacks as the survivors report their adventures on the red planet.

Though rife with creative visual effects, including the genuinely bizarre rat-bat-spider creature for which the film is known, an interesting premise is sullied by silly bantering on a poorly dressed rocket ship control room set and badly choreographed action on poorly dressed Martian landscape sets. The survivors race for home as the audience races for the lobby, following the film's epic finale with its message that Earth people are bad and must be controlled. Unlike the classic THE DAY THE EARTH STOOD STILL, which relayed a similar message with poignancy, here the message is just an easy way to wrap up a semi-interesting special effects fest.

ANOTHER WILD IDEA

MGM, 1934, b&w, two reeler

Producer: Hal Roach; **Directors:** Charley Chase and Edward Dunn; **Cast:** Charley Chase, Betty Mack, Harry Bowen, Tiny Sanford

A hand gun projects an inhibition-destroying ray.

APE MAN, THE

Monogram, 1943, b&w, 64 min, VT

Producers: Sam Katzman and Jack Dietz; **Director:** William Beaudine; **Screenplay:** Barney Sarecky; **Music:** Edward Kay; **Cast:** Bela Lugosi, Wallace Ford, Louise Currie, Jack Mullhall, Henry Hall

Scientist Lugosi takes fluid from the spines of apes in an attempt to give humans simian powers. He tests it on himself, and the results are bad.

APOLLO 13

Universal, 1995, Color, 139 min, VT, LD, DVD

Producer: Brian Glazer; **Director:** Ron Howard; **Screenplay:** William Broyles, Jr.; **Music:** James Horner; **Cinematography:** Dean Cundey, A.S.C.; **Special Effects:** Matt Sweeney, Gary Zink, Robert Legato, Steve Miller, James Cameron, Allen Cappuc-cilli, Jerry Fulle; **Cast:** Tom Hanks, Bill Paxton, Kevin Bacon, Ed Harris, Gary Sinise, Kathleen Quinlan, Miko Huges, David Andrews, Chris Ellis, Joe Spano, Xander Berkeley, Marc McClure, Tracy Reiner, Brett Cullen, Walter Cronkite

The film opens dramatically with the world watching Neil Armstrong, the first human being to ever walk on the face of the Moon, as he makes his famous small step for a human and gigantic step for humankind. Watching along with us is Jim Lovell (Hanks), the already picked commander for *Apollo 14*, the scheduled Moon mission that is only two flights away. Lovell is about as thrilled as a person can be. He is watching proof on his living room television that the moon is obtainable, that it can, indeed, be done, that humans can conquer the stars. And, in his heart and mind and the joyous part of his soul, he knows he'll be there soon. What he doesn't know is that he's never going to make it, and that it's going to happen sooner than he thinks.

The facts that move this one forward are not only simple, but they're history. Alan Sheppard, the commander for Apollo 13, was stricken with an ear infection. That bumped Lovell and his crew forward one slot. Shortly after their takeoff, however, a defect built into their ship two years before they were even named to the mission collapses, blowing out the side of their ship. Suddenly, there is no going to the Moon. Suddenly, their mission turns into a struggle for life itself as they devise a way to make it home, using only the scant equipment they have on hand.

This is not really a science *fiction* film, but it is one highly important to science fiction fans, and for more reasons than might be readily apparent. First, *Apollo 13* is all about rockets and people going to other worlds, so it has the proper hardware elements. Second, the movie covers the social sciences by giving us a glimpse of what goes on psychologically when things go wrong, both for the astronauts and for those left behind waiting for them. The second group breaks down further into a study of the pressures both on those left behind who can't do anything to help the trapped astronauts, and those who can. But these things aren't the most important aspects of this film.

What is of true importance here to sci-fi fans is the truth this movie reveals as to what the rest of the public thinks of all of us. We can fascinate them for a few minutes with something splashy, like sending a human to the Moon and showing it to them live over their televisions. But we can only do it once. By the time of *Apollo 13*, only a year after Neil Armstrong's historic Moon walk, the American public was already bored with the notion of going to the Moon. The three networks (there were only three then) refused to cover the broadcast being sent back by the astronauts from their ship. Live footage being broadcast from outer space—men living in zero gravity—was just not exciting enough for them to bother. Talk about your tough crowds.

But that all changes quickly once the astronauts' lives are in danger. Suddenly, the media can't shove enough cameras in the faces of the doomed men's friends, coworkers, wives, and children. Traveling to another world lost its glamour after it was done exactly once. *Once.* And, of course, you can't even lay all the blame on the public. In the film director Howard takes the time to show that during the astronauts' broadcast (while things are still going well), even NASA workers are watching the ball game rather than their own boys.

Sci-fi fans wonder why there are no more purely exploratory space flights, why the new globally backed space station is already considered a joke even before its completion, or why we haven't reached Mars yet. The answer is simple—as long as we as a subdivision of humanity's collective voice fail to make it clear why such things are important to humanity's future, then the great sluggard beast that is most of life on this planet will refuse to participate in our vision. Lovell and his crew wanted the Moon. They devoted their lives to getting there. When an act of God refused them that goal, they fought to keep the lives they built. They resisted the temptation to give in and take the easy way out. It wasn't in their character. Nor was it in the character of those on the ground. Nor their families who never stopped hoping, nor their NASA coworkers who pushed themselves to the limit to keep their friends alive.

Indeed, in the moment possibly most relevant to sci-fi fandom, a terrible revelation comes to light. The men will soon be breathing pure CO_2 unless they get new filters for their air recirculating system. Those on Earth are given a list of things the astronauts have available on their ship. They are told they must find a way for the box-shaped filters remaining to fit the cylindrical filter holders in the escape vehicle. It seems an impossible task, and there are those who say it can't be done. But it is. The tech people might have to concoct a plan that utilizes everything from the cover of the onboard flight plan to one of Lovell's socks, but they create a filter that keeps the men alive. When the device proves workable, when the astronauts report that their CO_2 levels are receding, one of the towering, all-American types in the control room turns to the overweight, balding technician who delivered the prototype and the procedure for building it and announces, "You, sir, are a steely-eyed missile man."

It doesn't matter who you are, what you look like, what your religion or skin color or native origin is. If you want something in this world, if you believe something can be accomplished, if you want something bad enough, then you can make it happen. Do you want to be a steely-eyed missile man . . . or not?

Apollo 13 is one of those rare films based on fact that prove the old "truth is stranger than fiction" line. Excellent effects, a tremendous cast, and incredible direction make this an inspiring, humbling, must-see for all sci-fi fans.

Note: When you see the astronauts in the movie in states of weightlessness, those aren't special effects. Hanks, Bacon, and Paxton spent 13 days making between five and six hundred flights in NASA's *KC-135*. The *135* is a high-altitude craft capable of skimming the outer atmosphere in parabolic arcs. At the top of each arc, the three actors would have 23 seconds of weightlessness in which to accomplish more bits of this or that scene.

The *KC-135* usually induces those unused to its effect to throw up quite violently. Needless to say, the Hollywood rookies suffered for their art making this film.

Cameo spotters: Watch the pre-launch crowd carefully, and you just might be able to spot the real Mrs. Marilyn Lovell. Her husband's cameo is a bit more obvious—he plays the captain of the U.S.S. *Iwo Jima.*

APRIL 1, 2000

Wein-Film (Austria), 1953, b&w, 110 min

Director: Wolfgang Libeneiner; **Screenplay:** Rudolf Brunngraber and Ernst Marboe; **Cast:** Curt Jurgens, Peter Gerhard, Elizabeth Stemberger, Waltraut Hass

Extraterrestrials lay siege to Vienna in this undistinguished film.

ARENA

Empire Pictures, 1991, Color, 115 min, VT, DVD

Producers: Charles Band, Iriwn Yablan, and Debra Dion; **Director:** Peter Manoogian; **Screenplay:** Danny Bilson and Paul DeMeo; **Music:** Richard Band; **Special Effects:** A.J. Workman and Giovanni Natalucci; **Cinematography:** Mac Ahlberg; **Cast:** Paul Satterfield, Hamilton Camp, Claudia Christian, Armin Shimerman, Marc Alaimo, Shari Shattuck, Brett Porter

In the future, alien races from all across the universe gather to cheer their respective races on in free-for-all boxing contests. Paul Satterfield stars as the great Earthling hope, the first human to have what it takes to get into the ring in fifty years. This one is little more than a familiar story about boxers under the control of gangsters transplanted into a science fiction setting with some sci-fi hardware stuck in for good measure. The cheap sets and production values hurt it more than anything—in one scene the harness lifting a fighter as his opponent holds him up to throw him out of the ring is visible.

Note: The cast features *Babylon 5*'s Claudia Christian and *Star Trek: Deep Space Nine*'s Armin Shimerman and Marc Alaimo.

ARMAGEDDON

Touchstone Pictures, 1998, Color, 114 min, VT, DVD

Producer: Jerry Bruckheimer, Michael Bay, and Gale Ann Hurd; **Director:** Bay; **Screenplay:** Jonathan Hensleigh; **Music:** Trevor Rabin; **Special Effects:** John Frasier; **Cinematography:** John Schwartzman; **Cast:** Bruce Willis, Billy Bob Thornton, Liv Tyler, Ben Affleck, Peter Stormare, Keith David, Steve Buscemi

A giant meteor is headed toward Earth. The only way to stop it appears to be sending a deep-sea drilling crew with absolutely no experience with space travel into the cosmos to plant explosives deep within the thing's core and blow it to bits. Complicating matters is the romance between the daughter of crew chief Willis and one of the workers and the fact that some of his other workers are mentally unstable. The crew and their equipment are sent into space on a pair of shuttles, where their rendezvous with the Russian Mir space station results in the destruction of the station. After that, they head for the asteroid, hoping to do for it what they did for Mir.

The premise and the hardware are sci-fi enough, but the rest of the movie is not much more than a potboiler love story welded to a lot of action adventure. Despite this flip description, the film moves quickly and provides plenty of laughs and lots of scares along with the usual state-of-the-art special effects. The ending is also something of a surprise.

ARANAS INFERNALES

Columbia, 1966, b&w

Producer: Luis Enrique Vergara; **Director:** Frederico Curiel; **Screenplay:** Adolfo Torres Portillo; **Cast:** Blanquita Sanchez, Marha Elena Cervantes, Jessica Munguia

Embarrassingly low-budget film about alien conquistadors using supersized spiders to help them in their conquest of Mexico.

AROUND THE WORLD UNDER THE SEA

MGM, 1966, Color, 120 min, VT

Producer: Andrew Marton; **Director:** Marton; **Screenplay:** Arthur Weiss and Art Arthur; **Music:** Harry Sukman; **Special Effects:** Projects Unlimited, Inc.; **Cinematography:** Clifford Poland; **Cast:** Lloyd Bridges, Shirley Eaton, David McCallum, Brian Kelly, Keenan Wynn, Marshall Thompson

With Earth in danger from killer earthquakes, the crew of a supersubmarine sets out to avert a fairly average end-of-the-world scenario by planting early-warning devices under the oceans. Boring interpersonal relationships and fairly dull special effects fail to distinguish this one.

ARRIVAL, THE

Live Entertainment, 1996, Color, 109 min, VT, LD, DVD

Producers: Ted Field and Robert W. Cort; **Director:** David Twohy; **Screenplay:** Twohy; **Music:** Arthur Kempel; **Special Effects:** Charles I. Finance; **Cast:** Charlie Sheen, Teri Polo, Lindsay Crouse, Richard Schiff, Leon Rippy, Tony T. Johnson, Ron Silver

Charlie Sheen plays an engineer working a desert-based, deep-space listening project. One night, he and his humorous sidekick get what they've been waiting for—a bona fide transmission from deep space. But for some mysterious reason, their boss (Silver) doesn't tell anyone what they've found. In fact, he covers it all up and even destroys their evidence. When Sheen protests, he suddenly finds himself out of a job. Soon a pair of deadly goons moves in and eliminates his humorous sidekick.

Sheen's girlfriend gives up on him, but he can do without her because the spunky, curious kid from next door is into helping him get to the bottom of what is going on. Sheen is soon obsessed with contacting the alien signal again. He takes a job as a satellite dish installer so that he can rig all the dishes in the area to work like one of the giant dishes with which he is used to working.

Clues soon take him to Mexico, where he becomes involved with the film's other major character. Lindsay Crouse plays an environmentalist tracking the globe's warming trend. Things have been getting hot far faster than anyone thought they would, and every time she wants answers someone puts a roadblock in the way. The pair work together for a while, but then Sheen finds himself on his own and in hot water as he discovers that the aliens have landed. They've infiltrated the planet and are building plants that are releasing CO_2 into the atmosphere on purpose. They like it hot and are working as hard as they can to take the planet away from us by making it too hot for us to live here.

The aliens can also assume the form of whomever they want to look like. Suddenly, Sheen is filled with crippling suspicion. His former boss—is he one? His girlfriend? The spunky kid? The conspiracy is all around Sheen, and he's got to make up his mind who he's going to trust before it's too late—not just for him, but for everyone.

Now here's an interesting film. The story was designed with a master tailor's precision to draw in a late '90s audience. It's about searching the heavens for someone else (perhaps, the God-replacement figure so many baby boomers are desperate for); it's about abuses of power and far-reaching conspiracies; it's about how terribly we've treated the environment, and it says that the reason the globe is warming (an event upon which real scientists are still actually not in consensus) is not actually our fault. I'd sneer at the cold-blooded manipulation at work in this script except for one thing: It all works so well. *The Arrival* is a great movie.

The actors are all giving everything required of them. Sheen is at his absolute best. He is driven and constantly questioning and angry about everything around him. He makes his character work and pretty much carries the movie on his sturdy-looking shoulders with ease. And no one can play a smug, insincere, despicable bastard the way Ron Silver can.

The effects are excellent, but beyond that they are also unusual. The opening sequence of the film is not only a stunner, but it's also one that no one expects. It's a long time before you get dazzled again, but that's okay. The first effect you see is so intriguing, you're willing to give the film some time, and it doesn't disappoint those who keep watching.

The script is tight and fast-moving. There are no extended chases, no fistfights, no stock laser gun battles or any of the usual clutter ordinary filmmakers use to pad out their movies. Everything here is subtle and is fairly ingenious as well. A top-notch piece of entertainment. It may not be an important film, but it's an intelligent one, and it's pure science fiction, worth any fan's time.

ASPHYX, THE

United Entertainment (Great Britain), 1972, Color, 99 min, VT

Producers: John Brittany and Maxine Julius; **Director:** Peter Newbrook; **Screenplay:** Brian Comport, Christina Beers, and Laurence Beers; **Music:** Bill McGuffie; **Special Effects:** Ted Samuels; **Cinematography:** Freddie Young; **Cast:** Robert Stephens, Robert Powell, Jane Lapotaire, Ralph Alriss, Alex Scott

A 19th-century scientist (Scott) is determined to extend human life expectancy. Serious study of the dying and the energy that science knows leaves the human body at death leads Scott to the discovery of the legendary Asphyx, the spirit of death. Scott determines to trap the monster when it comes for him and thus live forever.

Chilling social science fiction commentary revisiting the familiar theme of human tampering with God's handiwork, presented in an understated and eminently watchable fashion despite the low budget.

ASSIGNMENT OUTER SPACE
(aka: SPACEMEN)

Titanus/Ultra (Italy), 1960/AIP (US), 1962, Color, 73 min

Director: Antonio Marbheriti; **Screenplay:** Vasily Petrov; **Music:** J. K. Broady; **Special Effects:** Caesar Peace; **Cast:** Rik von Nutter, Gabriella Farinon, Archie Savage, Alain Dijion

A lukewarm Italian film about a giant runaway spaceship headed toward Earth. A heroic team is assembled and launched into space to stop the calculated crash from happening.

ASTOUNDING SHE-MONSTER, THE
(aka: THE MYSTERIOUS INVADER)

AIP, 1958, b&w, 60 min, VT, DVD

Producer: Ron Ashcroft; **Director:** Ashcroft; **Screenplay:** Frank Hall; **Music:** Guenther Kauer; **Cast:**

Shirley Kilpatrick, Robert Clarke, Kenne Duncan, Marilyn Harvey, Jeanne Tatum

An alien pin-up girl, Shirley Kilpatrick, comes out at night and kills people. Some kidnappers and their victims get mixed up in it as well, and the result is all much worse than it sounds.

ASTRONOMER'S DREAM, THE
(aka: THE MAN IN THE MOON)

France, 1898, hand-colored, silent short

France's early master filmmaker, Georges Méliès, put together this bit of fluff about a sleeping scientist who perhaps only dreams about being visited by the Man in the Moon. It's a spectacular effort for a film made over one hundred years ago and still fun to watch today.

ASTRONAUT'S WIFE

New Line Cinema, 1999, Color, 109 min, VT, DVD

Producers: Jody Hedien, Mark Johnson, and Donna Langley; **Director:** Rand Ravich; **Screenplay:** Ravich; **Music:** George S. Clinton; **Special Effects:** Jeff Wolverton, Josh R. Jaggars, and Brian Tipton; **Cinematography:** Allen Daviau; **Cast:** Johnny Depp, Charlize Theron, Joe Morton, Clea DuVall, Donna Murphy, Jacob Stein, Samantha Eggar, Nick Cassavetes, Gary Grubs, Blair Brown, Tom Noonan, Dawn Landon, Tom O'Brien, Lucy Lin, Michael Crider

A pair of astronauts go outside for a space walk so that they can perform some routine repairs on a satellite. Suddenly, there's an explosion, and NASA is left in the dark for two long, silent minutes. What happened during that time? No one knows. But the astronauts are rescued and return home, where everyone is happy to see them, and everything is perfect. Well, almost perfect. Although no one else sees it, the wife (Theron) of one of the astronauts (Depp) thinks her husband is somehow different. Soon Theron becomes pregnant and is convinced that something evil or extraterrestrial is growing within her.

What starts out as a lush, good-looking movie that does build a certain amount of suspense soon crashes into just a cheap lot of nothing. The parallels between this film and the horror classic *Rosemary's Baby* are simply too numerous to mention, but they run all the way to the heroine's haircut. Many good people are on the screen in this one, and all of them are wasted in a film that is just too long and too full of nothing.

ASTRO-ZOMBIES, THE

Gemini, 1969, Color, 90 min, VT, DVD

Producer: Ted V. Mikels; **Director:** Mikels; **Screenplay:** Mikels and Wayne Rogers; **Music:** Nico Karaski; **Cinematography:** Robert Maxwell; **Cast:** John Carradine, Wendell Corey, Tom Pace, Joan Patrick, Wally Moon

A pair of really mad scientists (Carradine and Corey) kill again and again to obtain the body parts they need to build some sort of supermonster.

L'ATLANTIDE (1961)

See *JOURNEY BENEATH THE DESERT*

L'ATLANTIDE (1932)

Nero (Germany), 1932, b&w, 80 min

Director: G.W. Pabst; **Screenplay:** Herbert Rappoport, Lazlo Vajda, and Pierre Ichac; **Cinematography:** Eugene Shuftan; **Cast:** Brigette Helm, Gustav Diessl, Heinz Klingenberg, Tela Tschai, Vladimir Sokolov, John Stuart, Odette Florelle, Jean Angelo, Pierre Blanchar

Atlantis (which in this film is an under*ground* city) is ruled by a bizarre queen who has more similarities with the title character of H. Rider Haggard's novel *She* than you can shake a stick at. The film is notable only for the knockout performance given by Helm (who first wowed audiences in her dual role in Fritz Lang's *METROPOLIS*) and because it was filmed simultaneously in French, English, and German.

Note: A silent version made in France predates this one.

ATLANTIS, THE LOST CONTINENT

MGM, 1961, Color, 90 min

Producer: George Pal; **Director:** Pal; **Screenplay:** Daniel Hargreaves; **Music:** Russell Garcie; **Special Effects:** A. Arnold Gillespie; **Cast:** Tony Hall, Joyce Taylor, Ed Platt, John Dall, Frank DeKova, Jay Novello, Barry Kroeger

A handsome fisherman played by Hall saves the beautiful Taylor, who turns out to be an Atlantian princess in this interesting blend of fantasy and science fiction. He is taken to her home for his reward but isn't treated very well, becoming entangled in court intrigue, numerous plots to kill him, and the end of the world, or at least the end of the Atlantian world. The plot shifts between the scientist played by Platt trying to warn everyone that the end is near and Hall's attempts to stay alive. Beasts and laser cannons and at least one well thought-out, incredibly choreographed fight scene make this one great campy fun.

ATOM AGE VAMPIRE

Topaz (Italy), 1960, b&w, 87 min, VT

Producer: Mario Bava; **Directors:** Anton Giulio and Richard McNamara; **Screenplay:** Piero Monviso, A.G. Majano, John Hart, Alberto Bevilacqua, and Gino de Santis; **Music:** Armando Trovajoli; **Special Effects:** Ugo Amadoro; **Cinematography:** Aldo Giordano; **Cast:** Alberto Lupo, Susanne Loret, Sergio Fantoni, Roberto Berta

A doctor (Lupo) cures a beautiful woman's scars with injections made from the blood of a recently deceased woman, who also just happens to be beautiful. The treatment turns out to be temporary, and the doctor has to keep killing beauties to keep his patient unscarred. Why any woman's blood won't do, or any man's blood for that matter, is never explained. The only thing to wonder about here is why it took five writers to pen this completely awful film.

ATOMIC AGENT, THE

AIT, 1959, b&w, 85 min

Director: Henri Decoin; **Cast:** Martine Carol, Dany Saval, Felix Marten

A French fashion model takes on spies trying to steal an atomic engine.

ATOMIC BRAIN, THE

See MONSTROSITY

ATOMIC KID, THE

Republic, 1954, b&w, 86 min, VT

Producer: Mickey Rooney; **Director:** Leslie H. Martinson; **Screenplay:** Benedict Freeman and John Fenton Murphy; **Music:** Van Alexander; **Special Effects:** Howard and Theodore Lydecker; **Cinematography:** John L. Russell, Jr.; **Cast:** Rooney, Whit Bissell, Elaine Davis, Robert Strauss

Mickey Rooney witnesses an atom bomb test and gets superpowers after being exposed to the fallout. The movie becomes a mostly a mindless spy comedy after that, notable only because it is lucky enough to contain a performance by the world's greatest character actor, Whit Bissell.

ATOMIC MAN, THE

AA, 1956, b&w, 77 min, VT

Producer: Alec C. Snowden; **Director:** Ken Hughes; **Screenplay:** Charles Eric Maine; **Music:** Richard Taylor; **Cinematography:** A.T. Dinsdale; **Cast:** Gene Nelson, Faith Domergue, Joseph Tomley, Donald Gray, Vic Perry, Peter Arne

An atomic scientist believed dead is discovered alive but unable to communicate with anyone around him is because his experiments have knocked him out of synch with the very fabric of the universe. He now lives several seconds in the future.

It's an incredibly interesting premise handled in an extremely pedestrian (and mostly unscientific) manner. It may be enough to get children's imaginations going, but it puts adults to sleep.

ATOMIC MONSTER

See MAN-MADE MONSTER

ATOMIC RULERS OF THE WORLD

Manley (Japan), 1964, Color, 83 min

Directors: Teruo Ishii, Akira Mitsuwa, and Koreyoshi Akasaka; **Screenplay:** Ichiro Miyegawa; **Cast:** Minako Yamada, Ken Hayashi, Reiko Seto, Ken Utsui

Starman (or, as he is known in other films in the series, Super Giant) befriends two youngsters and fights off an invasion of fish-people aliens bent on "shutting off" the world's gravity. For Japanese action genre fans only.

ATOMIC SUBMARINE

AA, 1959, b&w, 72 min, VT, DVD

Producer: Alex Gordon; **Director:** Spenser Bennett; **Screenplay:** Orivlle H. Hampton; **Music:** Alexander Lazlo; **Special Effects:** Jack Rabin, Irving Block, and Louis DeWitt; **Cast:** Arthur Franz, Dick Foran, Tom Conway, Sid Melton, Joi Lansing, Bob Steele, Victor Varconi

The American atomic fleet is being destroyed. When the Navy investigates, they discover that an organic, extraterrestrial spacecraft on the bottom of the ocean under the Arctic Circle is responsible. After some foolishness aboard the UFO, the Navy destroys the enemy vessel with atomic weapons. Hurray for our side.

ATOM MEN VS. SUPERMAN

Columbia, 1950, b&w, 480 min

Producer: Sam Katzman; **Director:** Spenser Bennett; **Screenplay:** George H. Plympton, Joseph Poland, and David Matthews; **Music:** Mischa Bakaleinikoff; **Cast:** Kirk Alyn, Lyle Talbot, Tommy Boyd, Pierre Watkin, Noel Neill

Second Saturday morning matinee serial featuring the world's most recognizable alien. Superman again battles Lex Luthor, who, in his disguise of Atom Man, throws a wide range of complex but ultimately ineffective gadgets at the Man of Steel repeatedly through the 15-reel epic. It was fun for its time, and Kirk Alyn really was a great Superman.

ATRAGON (aka: ATRAGON, THE FLYING SUB)

Toho (Japan), 1963, Color, 96 min/AIP (US), 1965, Color, 79 min

Producer: Yuko Tanaka; **Director:** Inoshiro Honda; **Screenplay:** Shinichi Sekizawa; **Music:** Akira Ifukube; **Special Effects:** Eiji Tsuburaya; **Cinematography:** Hajimi Koizumi; **Cast:** Tadao Takashima, Yoko Fujiyama, Yu Fujiki, Jun Tazaki

The lost continent of Mu, depicted here as an undersea kingdom, attacks the surface world with a squadron (or would that be fleet?) of airborne submarines. Outstanding, if unbelievable, special effects make this one an enduring flick worth a look.

ATTACK OF THE CRAB MONSTERS

AA, 1957, b&w, 64 min, VT

Producer: Roger Corman; **Director:** Corman; **Screenplay:** Charles Griffith; **Music:** Ronald Stein; **Cinematography:** Floyd Crosby; **Cast:** Richard Garland, Pamela Duncan, Russell Johnson, Ed Nelson, Leslie Bradley, Mel Welles

A group of castaways find that their island is beset by gigantic, semi-intelligent crabs that forage during the night for human brains. With each brain they consume, the crabs grow more intelligent, communicating with their prey through telepathy.

As is the problem with many science fiction movies, and especially those films made by the legendary Roger Corman, this film's schlock title and nonexistent budget hamper what is, in many ways, a superior script for the time. Griffith's screenplay is loaded with a number of topnotch concepts, but because of both the rushed shooting schedule and pitiful special effects, many of them appear underutilized. When one watching this film, consider playing it with the picture shut off. It works much better as a radio drama.

ATTACK OF THE 50-FOOT WOMAN

AA, 1958, b&w, 60 min, VT, LD

Producer: Bernard Woolner; **Director:** Nathan Juran; **Screenplay:** Mark Hanna; **Music:** Ronald Stein; **Cast:** William Hudson, Yvette Vickers, Roy Gordon, Allison Hayes

A close encounter with a radioactive alien turns out bad for heroine Allison Hayes: She begins growing at an alarming rate, every inch of new height accompanied by a similar reduction in sanity. By the time the title-suggested yardage is acquired, Allison is crazy and the town is in trouble. She manages to kill her philandering husband but dies at the hands of the military.

Many try to view this film in feminist terms, despite the fact that the more power poor Allison gathers, the more insane she becomes. This movie, however, straddles the line between offering a meaningful message and being simply a bad movie made with only exploitation in mind. Despite this, it remains an entertaining B movie.

ATTACK OF THE KILLER TOMATOES

AIT, 1969, Color, 87 min, VT

Producers: Steve Peace and John De Bello; **Director:** De Bello; **Screenplay:** Costa Dillon, Peace, and De Bello; **Music:** Gordon Goodwin; **Special Effects:** Greg Auer; **Cinematography:** John K. Culley; **Cast:** David Miller, George Wilson, Sharon Taylor, Jack Riley, Rock Peace, the San Diego Chicken

Just as the title says, the world is invaded by Killer Tomatoes.

Hated and reviled, at the top of everyone's list for "Worst Sci-Fi Film Festivals," this is one of those rare "bad" movies that is actually worth viewing. Be warned: The filmmakers set out to spoof bad science fiction films, and they succeeded beyond their wildest dreams. The movie is truly wretched, but somehow that just makes it funnier. The special effects are purposely crafted to be so awful that they're actually funny, and besides, what other film in history would have the nerve to depict an African-American master of camouflage disguising himself as Abraham Lincoln so he can infiltrate the camp of murderous salad ingredients? And it has an incredibly catchy theme song. But beyond all that, anyone who doesn't howl with laughter at the line "Pass the ketchup," just doesn't have the right attitude. Late night popcorn fun at its best.

Note: This film was followed by both *Return Of The Killer Tomatoes* and *Killer Tomatoes Strike Back*. The first sequel is as funny as the first. The second is pushing it. You will have to decide your own tolerance levels.

ATTACK OF THE MONSTERS

AIT, 1969, Color, 72 min

Producer: Hidemasa Nagata; **Director:** Noriaki Yuasa; **Screenplay:** Fumi Takahashi; **Cast:** Nobuhiro Janima, Eiji Funakoshi, Miyuki Akiyama

Brain-eating space women decide Japanese Earth children are the perfect snack. To the rescue of the tots comes everyone's favorite rocket-powered, airborne superturtle, the kindly monster Gamera ("Gamera loves the little children"). The turtle fights the evil monster. The good monster wins, and no children are eaten. No surprises.

ATTACK OF THE PUPPET PEOPLE

AIP, 1958, b&w, 79 min

Producer: Bert I. Gordon; **Director:** Gordon; **Screenplay:** George W. Yates; **Music:** Albert Glasser; **Special Effects:** Gordon; **Cinematography:** Ernest Laszlo; **Cast:** John Agar, June Kenny, John Hoyt, Susan Gordon, Ken Miller, Michael Mark

An insane puppet-making scientist (Hoyt) reduces human beings to the size of dolls to combat his loneliness. Fairly routine stuff is highlighted by Hoyt's way-over-the-top performance, which is exceptional.

ATTACK OF THE ROBOTS

Speva/Cine Alliance/Hesperia (France/Spain), 1962, b&w, 93 min

Director: Jesus Franco; **Screenplay:** Jean-Claude Carrière; **Music:** Paul Misraki; **Cinematography:** A. Macosoli; **Cast:** Eddie Constantine, Sophi Hardy, Fernando Rey

An insane scientist is on the loose. This one likes to turn people into killer robots.

ATTACK OF THE SWAMP CREATURE

See *ZAAT*

AT THE EARTH'S CORE

AIP, 1976, Color, 89 min, VT

Producer: John Dark; **Director:** Kevin Conner; **Screenplay:** Milton Subotsky; **Music:** Mike Vickers; **Special Effects:** Ian Wingrove; **Cinematography:** Alan Hume; **Cast:** Peter Cushing, Doug McClure, Caroline Munro, Cy Grant, Godfrey James, Sean Lynch, Keith Barron

A dignified Peter Cushing and his adventurous sidekick McClure burrow through Earth's crust to the hidden land of Pelucidar, where monsters rule over cavemanlike humans. McClure falls for a skin-wearing beauty (Munro) and helps turn the tide against the evil overlords.

This so-so adaptation of Edgar Rice's Burroughs's novel by the same name features lackluster special effects that cripple an earnest casts' earnest performances. Cushing as usual is terrific, and fans of Burroughs can still enjoy the film, however, if they go in not expecting much.

AT THE EDGE OF THE WORLD

UFA (Germany), 1927, b&w, 90 min, silent

Director: Karl Grune; **Cinematography:** F.A. Wegner; **Cast:** Brigitte Helm, Max Schreck, Wilhelm Dieterle, Imre Raday

A futuristic war is shown as imaginatively as German filmmakers working between World Wars could envision it, resulting in an honest and graphic depiction of war.

AUTOMATIC HOUSE, THE

United Film Service, 1915, b&w, one reel, silent

Labor-saving gizmos galore. The title says it all.

AUTOMATIC LAUNDRY, THE

Lubin, 1908, b&w, 361 feet, silent

Labor-saving gizmo washes, irons, and mends clothing.

AUTOMATIC MONKEY, THE

Gaumont (France), 1909, b&w, 324 feet, silent

Robot chimp—again, the title says it all.

AUTOMATIC MOTORIST, THE

Kineto (Great Britain), 1911, b&w, 610 feet, silent

A mechanical chauffeur drives safely from England to the stars. The title doesn't come close to saying it all for this short, which is far beyond the westerns and penny dreadful stories everyone else was filming at the time.

AUTOMATIC SERVANT, THE

Urban-Eclipse, 1908, b&w, 367 feet, silent

When a scientist's friend damages his new robotic helper before a big demonstration of the automaton's abilities, the friend is forced to don a robot suit and perform in its place in this early sci-fi comedy. The story remains pretty funny stuff almost a century later.

AVENGING BRAIN, THE

See *THE MONSTER AND THE GIRL*

AWFUL DR. ORLOFF, THE

Rosson/Ilispamer (Spain/France), 1961/Sigma III (US), 1964, b&w, 86 min, VT, DVD

Producer: Serge Newman; **Director:** Jesus Franco; **Screenplay:** Franco; **Music:** Pagan and Ramirez Angel; **Cinematography:** Godofredo Pacheco; **Cast:** Howard Vernon, Conrado San Martin, Diana Lorys, Maria Silva

Orloff (Vernon), yet another crazed doctor at work, kidnaps beautiful women for forced skin donations so that he can rebuild his scarred daughter's face in this fair effort. Again, one has to wonder why unattractive women, or even men for that matter, wouldn't work as donors as long as they had good skin.

BABY . . . SECRET OF THE LOST LEGEND

Disney Productions, 1985, Color, 95 min, VT, LD

Producer: Jonathan T. Taplin; **Director:** B. W. L. Norton; **Screenplay:** Clifford Green and Ellen Green; **Music:** Jerry Goldsmith; **Cinematography:** John Alcott; **Cast:** William Katt, Sean Young, Patrick McGoohan, Julian Fellows, Kyalo Mativo

Scientists Katt and Young discover a baby brontosaurus and its mother in deepest, darkest Africa. Where its parents are, no one knows or even seems to care. After sticking her nose in and ruining a secret that apparently had been kept since the Jurassic era, bright and perky Young decides she has to protect the dinosaurs from all the ruthless men who would exploit them.

Aside from bending over backward to be politically correct, the film features wretched dialogue, banal plotting, and truly awful special effects. The mother brontosaurus is passable at best in most shots, but the stuffed animal, too-cute-for-words baby dinosaur is simply ridiculous. Offensively riddled with holes in its science, such as why a herbivore living in an isolated environment with no predators can't seem to spawn a complete herd, the film is lacking significantly in basic logic, as well.

BACK TO THE FUTURE

Universal, 1985, Color, 116 min, VT, LD

Producer: Steven Spielberg; **Director:** Robert Zemeckis; **Screenplay:** Zemeckis and Bob Gale; **Music:** Alan Silvestri and Chris Hayes; **Special Effects:** Kevin Pike; **Cinematography:** Dean Cundey; **Cast:** Michael J. Fox, Christopher Lloyd, Lea Thompson, Crispin Glover, Wendie Jo Sperber, Marc McClure, Billy Zane, Claudia Wells, Thomas F. Wilson, Casey Siemaszko

1980s teenager Marty McFly (Fox) works for a seemingly crackpot inventor, Doc Brown (Lloyd). Marty is assisting his boss with a time travel experiment when he is accidentally returned to the past without the good doctor, specifically to the 1950s. Not knowing what else to do, he seeks out the 30 years younger version of Doc Brown and enlists his aid in getting "back to the future."

While stuck in the past, however, Marty discovers that things aren't working out the way they're supposed to for his parents-to-be according to the old family stories. This happens mainly because Mom's affections have latched onto Marty (mother-to-child bonding, underplayed as science in the film but obvious nonetheless) and forgotten all about his dad. It's a snappy use of the familiar theme of meddling in the past changing the future and could have gotten easily lost in any number of sappy side avenues but instead helps move the plot along nicely. Young Doc Brown works on the science end by trying to rig a way to get the time machine going, and Marty works on getting his teenaged mother to stop falling for him instead of for his father-to-be.

The big ending revolves around Marty getting his folks together for the spring dance, where they fell in love, and which in a lucky coincidence happens just before the only moment in the entire '50s (a precisely recorded lightning strike that can supply the power for his time machine) when he can return home. It may all sound like just another slight comedy, and as far as its basic plot goes, that's all it is. But *Back to the Future* is more than it seems on the surface.

As a science fiction movie, the film deserves an A+. Time travel is obviously a theoretical science at best, but it's amazing how many filmmakers get even the most basic concepts regarding it fouled up. Here the science is tightly thought out. There are no holes or glaring flaws. The movie's entertainment value is a sheer joy. It's funny, heart-warming, pulse-pounding, and filled with enough slapstick and family-level blue jokes to entertain anyone except the most priggish critic. It also makes a very positive statement about family, with much of Fox's motivation revolving around his desire to help his parents and siblings. Fox's and Lloyd's performances stand out among a round of good acting. The two play off each other marvelously. Both are totally convincing in their roles, and, while each actor's talents are shown off in their best light, it's Lloyd who absolutely steals the show. His characterization of the erratic yet loveable Doc Brown is both outlandish and touching.

The science utilized in *Back to the Future* is too slight to qualify it to be nominated for one of the top ten science fiction movies of all time, but it is eminently watchable, as are its two sequels—BACK TO THE FUTURE II and III.

BACK TO THE FUTURE II

Universal, 1989, Color, 107 min, VT, LD

Producer: Steven Spielberg; **Director:** Robert Zemeckis; **Screenplay:** Zemeckis and Bob Gale; **Music:** Alan Silvestri; **Special Effects:** Michael Lantieri; **Cinematography:** Dean Cundey; **Cast:** Michael J. Fox, Christopher Lloyd, Lea Thompson, Joe Flaherty, Harry Waters Jr., Charles Fleischer, Elisabeth Shue, Thomas F. Wilson, Casey Siemaszko, James Tolkan

Once again Fox and Lloyd dash off through time to set some of its shakier moments straight. As in this film's predecessor, their mere presence in the future sets up the problems that flesh out the rest of the film. Marty (Fox) allows his greed to blind his better judgment. He purchases a sports magazine that gives the winners of every ball game, horse race, and prizefight for decades, but the magazine falls into the hands of his worst enemy back in the past, creating a future specifically designed to be an utter hell for Marty. The chaos caused by this one thoughtless moment of avarice is the catalyst for not only the rest of the film, but for the one that followed it as well.

Again good use is made of the idea that even the most minor meddling in the future can drastically alter the present or the past. Many critics as well as much of the public were disappointed by this sequel's darker tone, but still there are plenty of laughs here, especially of the cynical "told you so" variety. Those who cry every time someone tries to make them think deserve little pity. Thinking, after all, is what science fiction is supposed to be all about.

By far the most impressive technical aspect of the movie is how the screenplay utilizes scenes from the first film as shown from the perspective of the second film's characters. The ending is sheer brilliance (but one would imagine some sort of technological nightmare for the special effects folks) as future Fox II tries to avoid future Fox I at the climactic big dance sequence. The timing of the events from the old past and this new past being laid over it are possibly the best use ever made of this idea to date.

BACK TO THE FUTURE III

Universal, 1990, Color, 116 min, VT, LD

Producer: Steven Spielberg; **Director:** Robert Zemeckis; **Screenplay:** Zemeckis and Bob Gale; **Music:** Alan Silvestri; **Special Effects:** Patricia Blau and Donald Elliott; **Cinematography:** Dean Cundey; **Cast:** Michael J. Fox, Christopher Lloyd, Lea Thompson, Thomas F. Wilson, Joe Flaherty, Matt Clark, Mary Steenburgen, Richard Dysart, Pat Buttram, Harry Carey, Jr., Elisabeth Shue, Dub Taylor, James Tolkan, ZZ Top

This third episode in the classic series of time travel films sends Marty (Fox) chasing a lost Doc Brown (Lloyd) back through time. Finally, things have come full circle, and Marty has matured to the point where he's the one doing the saving now. The cliffhanger ending of Part II traps the Doc in the past where library records show he's going to be shot in the back fairly soon after his arrival. While his original motivation this time is to rescue his "second" father, Marty runs into the 1850s representatives of the McFly family and becomes involved with them as well. Again the comedy draws greatly from Marty's love of his family.

But where Marty was at center stage in the first two films, this one is Doc Brown's showcase. Doc Brown falls in love, which, of course, only further complicates his and Fox's latest escape back to the future.

The film pokes good fun at western film clichés and keeps the comedy flowing, repeating all the right jokes from the first two parts. It also, however, keeps a tight rein on the science as well. True, the writers never move beyond the most basic of time travel theories and easy laughs (by the time Marty arrives in the past, the Doc has built a cabin-sized machine that after a great deal of noise and effort produces a single muddy ice cube), but then again, that is the easiest way to keep on track. There's an old saying about keeping one's mouth shut when one doesn't know what one is talking about. More science fiction screenwriters would do well to follow this wise dictum.

BAD CHANNELS

Full Moon Productions, 1992, Color, 88 min, VT

Producer: Charles Band; **Director:** Ted Nicholson; **Screenplay:** Jackson Barr; **Music:** Blue Oyster Cult; **Special Effects:** John P. Cazin; **Cinematography:** Adolfo Bartoli; **Cast:** Paul Hipp, Martha Quinn, Aaron Lustig, Ian Patrick Williams, Michael Huddleston, Victor Rogers, Melissa Behr, Charles Spradling

An alien disc jockey takes over an Earthly radio station and begins broadcasting a program that shrinks young ladies. As one might suspect, there's not much to this one, though someone apparently thought there was enough for a sequel, *DOLLMAN VS. THE DEMONIC TOYS.*

BAD TASTE

Wing Nut Films (New Zealand), 1988, Color, 90 min, VT, LD

Producer: Peter Jackson; **Director:** Jackson; **Screenplay:** Jackson, Tony Hiles, and Ken Hammon; **Music:** Michelle Scullion; **Special Effects:** Jackson; **Cinematography:** Jackson; **Cast:** Jackson, Pete O'Herne, Mike Minett, Terry Potter, Craig Smith, Doug Wren, Dean Lawrie

An alien fast-food franchise comes to Earth to gather raw materials for their business in this bloody comedy which, like so many other films seemingly without redeeming value, has a huge worldwide cult following.

BAMBOO SAUCER, THE (aka: COLLISION COURSE)

World Entertainment, 1968, Color, 100 min, VT, LD

Producer: Jerry Fairbanks; **Director:** Frank Telford; **Screenplay:** Telford; **Music:** Edward Paul; **Special Effects:** John Fulton and Glen Robinson; **Cinematography:** Hal Mohr; **Cast:** Dan Duryea, John Ericson, Lois Nettleton, Nan Leslie, Bob Hastings

Cold warriors from the U.S. and the U.S.S.R. put aside their differences to work together on an investigation of reports that a UFO has crashed somewhere in Red China. This somewhat better than usual, but still fairly typical, low-budget thriller is a lot longer on action than it is on science, relying mostly on a lot of shooting and a bit of obligatory romance.

BANANA MONSTER, THE

See *SCHLOCK*

BANCO IN BANGKOK

See *SHADOW OF EVIL*

BARBARELLA (aka: BARBARELLA, QUEEN OF THE GALAXY)

Paramount (French/Italian), 1967, Color, 98 min, VT, LD

Producer: Dino DeLaurentiis; **Director:** Roger Vadim; **Screenplay:** Terry Southern; **Music:** Bob Crewe and Charles Fox; **Special Effects:** Augie Lohman; **Cast:** Jane Fonda, John Philip Law, Anita Pallenberg, Milo O'Shea, David Hemmings, Ugo Tognazzi

In the 41st century, the president of Earth sends sultry space ranger Barbarella (Fonda) on a mission to stop a mad scientist who is threatening the galaxy with his death ray. She crashes on the scientist's planet and is then involved in one mindless escapade after another. Coming to her rescue is a helpful, but blind, angel (Law). Killer children, flesh-eating robots, crazed queens, and more throw themselves at the easily seduced, naive heroine, each small adventure growing more ridiculous (as well as confusing for anyone actually trying to make sense of the film) than the last.

Barbarella was based on an extremely popular French comic strip by the same name. In the comics, the title character's innocence is of a kind with that of Voltaire's Candide. Here, she's pretty much just witless. In fact, the film would most likely be forgotten now if not for its opening credit sequence, in which an extremely pre-women's movement Fonda does a doe-eyed, innocent striptease that keeps the male viewers coming back to this day. Indeed, watching the young Fonda romp through this movie is one of its few enduring features, precisely because it is Ms. Fonda herself in the title role of a naive plastic bikini-wearing sex kitten, a part drastically inconsistent with her later persona. Once she declared herself the voice of a generation and began advocating radical causes, the film became a midnight show regular.

Like so many movies based on comic strips, ultimately it is an insult to its source material. It tries hard to be witty and satiric, but it's pretty much just smug and sarcastic. Pass on the film and read the comics instead. They're witty, intelligent, and still somewhat socially relevant, which this film wasn't even when it was first released.

BARB WIRE

Gramercy Pictures, 1996, Color, 90 min, VT, LD

Producer: Peter Heller; **Director:** David Hogan; **Screenplay:** Chris Warner and Chuck Pfarrer; **Music:** Michel Colombier; **Special Effects:** Don Gray, John E. Gray, Roland Loew, and Eric Roberts; **Cinematography:** Rick Bota; **Cast:** Pamela Anderson Lee, Temuera Morrison, Steve Railsback, Victoria Rowell, Jack Noseworthy

In 2017, the worst has happened. The United States is under the control of a Nazilike regime. In a semineutral town, night club owner Anderson runs into her ex-lover, who asks her to help get him and his new girlfriend out of the country to Canada so they can join the resistance.

Astute readers may be asking themselves, "Haven't I heard this plot somewhere before?" The answer is, of course, you have. And it was a lot better with Humphrey Bogart and Peter Lorre and Ingrid Bergman. The letters of transit have been changed to contact lenses that can fool a retinal scan (as if the machines wouldn't be programmed to notice contact lenses), but it's *Casablanca*, all right, the one movie you would think people could steal from with both hands and not ruin. Not so here. These thieves are the clumsiest bunch you're ever likely to come across. Still, this is a route many successful science fiction films have gone. *ALIEN* is heavily based on *IT! THE TERROR FROM BEYOND SPACE*, but there is a difference. The *ALIEN* people took a bad movie with a good idea and made a great movie. Always nimble to be different, these jokers took a classic film with a tremendously inventive and fluid plot and made a mindless, clunking hash of it.

The action and effects are standard, the writing sometimes approaching interesting, but the film is so poorly done that the end result is boredom. What should have been (or at least *could* have been) a great new sci-fi film series was instead handled in such a pedestrian manner unfit even for television. Which, all in all, is a real shame because the comic books that formed the basis for the movie contained some interesting ideas and concepts. Sadly, star Lee's acting is so sinfully awful that it is almost impossible to comprehend how she ever got any time in front of anyone's cameras, let along a whole motion picture built around her. This film is a sad, foolish waste of time, just so another comic book creator can get a big pay-off to see his characters treated with contempt.

BARON'S AFRICAN WAR, THE

See *THE SECRET SERVICE IN DARKEST AFRICA*

BATMAN

20th Century Fox, 1996, Color, 105 min, VT, LD

Producer: William Dozier; **Director:** Leslie H. Martinson; **Screenplay:** Lorenzo Semple, Jr.; **Music:** Nelson Riddle; **Special Effects:** Lyle B. Abbot; **Cinematography:** Howard Schwartz; **Cast:** Adam West, Burt Ward, Frank Gorshin, Cesar Romero, Lee Merriwether, Neil Hamilton, Burgess Meredith, Alan Napier, Sterling Holloway, Stafford Repp

There have been a number of Batman films, serials, television shows, and so on, but only two will be covered here. For the science fiction purist, *Batman* may seem out of place here, but the reason to mention him at all in this volume is because the character, while essentially a masked detective, quite often utilizes or confronts science in his investigations. This film, for instance, comes with disintegration and reintegration, robots and other high-tech hardware.

Sometimes Batman is taken seriously and sometimes he isn't. Both interpretations have pleased audiences. This version of the Batman legend is not what one would call serious.

In this campy '60s picture based on the popular Batman television show at the time, the Caped Crusader (West) and the Boy Wonder (Ward) are called in to stop a quartet of their greatest villains as they attempt to unleash a global crime spree. The science fiction elements of the story are utilized in silly and unscientific ways. But why complain. It is supposed to be a comedy, isn't it? One might as well complain about the geometry in THE THREE STOOGES' HAVE ROCKET, WILL TRAVEL.

As to the quality here, rabid fans of the Dark Knight, the silent avenger of the night who fights for justice in Gotham City by bringing fear to the hearts of criminals, will probably find this one insulting, at least as much as the show on which it was based. The more open-minded fan can get a lot of laughs.

BATMAN

Warner Bros., 1989, Color, 126 min, VT, LD, DVD

Producer: Tim Burton; **Director:** Burton; **Screenplay:** Sam Hamm; **Music:** Danny Elfman; **Cast:** Michael Keaton, Jack Nicholson, Kim Basinger, Robert Wuhl, Pat Hingle, Billy Dee Williams, Michael Gough, Jack Palance, Lee Wallace, Tracey Walter, Jerry Hall

There have been a number of Batman films, serials, television shows, and so on, but only two will be covered here. For the science fiction purist, *Batman* may seem out of place here, but the reason to mention him at all in this volume is because the character, while essentially a masked detective, quite often utilizes or confronts science in his investigations. In this movie, for instance, multiple component poisons are used, along with rocket cars and other marvelously inventive if somewhat improbable devices.

Sometimes Batman is taken seriously and sometimes he isn't. Both interpretations have pleased audi-

Batman (WARNER BROS. & DC COMICS / JOSEPH B. MAUCERI COLLECTION)

ences. This wildly popular version of the Batman legend we would have to call serious. This darkly brooding, sometimes quirky, version of the legend of the Dark Knight deals with the creation of the Joker (Nicholson), a psychopathic, murderous clown (complete with the correct origin of the character), and his battle with the protector of Gotham City (Keaton). This incredibly well-made action/adventure film spawned three sequels and two animated series. Most of the credit for this can be attributed to director Burton's dark but sympathetic sense of the bizarre, star Keaton's ability to bring forth Bruce Wayne's vulnerability while showing Batman's unstoppable presence in the same scene, and Danny Elfman's incredibly evocative score.

Studio interference on the second picture, BATMAN RETURNS, not only resulted in a lesser product, but drove these talents away. The third and fourth sequels, BATMAN FOREVER and BATMAN AND ROBIN, were entrusted to a director incapable of handling the material and are incredibly awful. The first of the quartet, however, remains an astonishing accomplishment. Dark and moody, and clearly respectful of the source material without going overboard, it is quite possibly the best movie ever made from a comic book. No interested party should be disappointed.

BATMAN AND ROBIN

Warner Bros., 1997, Color, 125 min, VT, LD, DVD

Producers: Mitchell Duaterive, Ben Melniker, Mike Uslan, and William Elvin; **Director:** Joel Shumacher; **Screenplay:** Akiva Goldsman; **Music:** Elliot Goldenthal; **Cinematography:** Stephen Goldblatt; **Special Effects:** Andrew Adamson, Carlos Arguello, David Stump, and Bob Hurrie; **Cast:** George Clooney, Arnold Schwarzenegger, Chris O'Donnell, Uma Thurman, Alicia Silverstone, Pat Hingle, Michael Gough

See BATMAN

BATMAN FOREVER

Warner Bros., 1995, Color, 121 min, VT, LD, DVD

Producers: Tim Burton, Mitchell Dauterive; Ben Melniker, and Mike Uslan; **Director:** Joel Shumacher; **Screenplay:** Akiva Goldsman, Janet Batchler, and Lee Batchler; **Music:** Elliot Goldenthal; **Cinematography:** Stephen Goldblatt; **Special Effects:** John Dykstra, Scott Fisher, Tom Fisher, and Kate Crossley;

Cast: Val Kilmer, Tommy Lee Jones, Jim Carrey, Nicole Kidman, Chris O'Donnell, Drew Barrymore, Debi Mazar, Pat Hingle, Michael Gough

See BATMAN

BATMAN RETURNS

Warner Bros., 1992, Color, 126 min, VT, LD, DVD

Producers: Tim Burton, Ben Melniker, Mike Uslan, Ian Bryce, Jon Peters, Peter Gruber, and Holly Bordaile; **Director:** Tim Burton; **Screenplay:** Sam Hamm and Dan Waters; **Music:** Dany Elfman; **Cinematography:** Stefan Czapsky; **Special Effects:** John Brune, Jan Aaris, Mike Fink, Dan Gaspar, Jenny Fulle, and Mike Weaver; **Cast:** Michael Keaton, Danny DeVito, Michelle Pfeiffer, Christopher Walken, Pat Hingle, Michael Gough

See BATMAN

BATTERIES NOT INCLUDED

Universal, 1987, Color, 106 min, VT, LD

Producer: Steven Spielberg; **Director:** Matthew Robbins; **Screenplay:** Mick Garris, S.S. Wilson, Brent Murdock, and Matthew Robbins; **Music:** James Horner; **Special Effects:** Ken Pepiot; **Cinematography:** John McPherson; **Cast:** Hume Cronyn, Jessica Tandy, Frank McRae, Elizabeth Pena, Michael Carmine, Dennis Boutsikaris

When a group of helpless New Yorkers are about to be evicted from their building, cute miniature alien spaceships (the aliens themselves are never seen) come to their rescue.

That Steven Spielberg can be a producer in the classic Hollywood sense (i.e., a hack who will beat any idea far past the time when anyone else would have relented out of common decency) was proved by this worse than maudlin bit of nothing. To be fair, stars Hume Cronyn and Jessica Tandy give excellent performances. Their intelligent and moving portrayals, coupled with the film's exceptional special effects, make it watchable, but understand, this is not a recommendation.

BATTLE BENEATH THE EARTH

MGM, 1968, Color, 91 min, VT

Producer: Charles Reynolds; **Director:** Montgomery Tully; **Screenplay:** L.Z. Hargreaves; **Music:** Ken Jones; **Special Effects:** Tom Howard; **Cinematography:** Ken Talbot; **Cast:** Kerwin Matthews, Bessie Love, Viviane Venutra, Robert Ayres, Peter Ayne

The Red Chinese government supposedly begins building a series of tunnels under the nations of the world with laser cannons for the purpose of invading the globe. This film is unbelievably silly, and not just because of its incredibly inane politics. The acting is over the top, to say the least, and the special effects match the script and the direction in a perfect triangle of pedestrian efforts.

BATTLE BENEATH THE SEA

See THE TERROR BENEATH THE SEA

BATTLE BEYOND THE STARS

New World Pictures, 1980, Color, 104 min, VT, LD

Producer: Roger Corman; **Director:** Jimmy G. Murakami; **Screenplay:** John Sayles; **Cast:** Richard Thomas, John Saxon, Robert Vaughn, Darleen Fleugel, George Peppard, Sybil Danning, Jeff Corey, Julia Duffy, Morgan Woodward

Sador (Saxon), leader of a murderous band of interplanetary mutant warriors, informs the population of the small, mostly defenseless planet Akir that they are now to be his slaves. He leaves a small force to watch them, assuring everyone he will return soon to instigate a reign of terror. No one wants to fight, since it is not the way of those who follow the Varda, but farm boy Shad (Thomas) has a plan. Why not find others to fight for them? The plan is approved, and Shad is given the planet's only working starship, a fighter that once belonged to Zed, last of the mysterious Great Ones. With this, Shad destroys the occupation force. The ship actually does the destroying against Shad's wishes, the farm boy being still a little too green to spill blood at this point. He then heads off to collect his mercenaries and returns with an interesting collection of fighters.

Nestor, five aliens who share a collective intelligence, comes out of boredom. St. Exman (Danning), a large and sexy warrior woman from Planet Valkyrie comes to fight for honor and glory. Geld, a tired, much-hunted friendless man was once a master killer commanding high fees. Now he's simply willing to

fight for a meal and a place to hide. There are other good guys as well, but it's George Peppard who steals the show as a space-faring trucker from Earth named Cowboy. As one would expect, the assembled pick away at Sador and his forces, being killed one by one, until finally Shad and his talking ship finish off Sador's cruiser. Akir is saved, Shad has learned to be a man, and the picture ends.

Readers familiar with either *The Seven Samurai* or *The Magnificent Seven* may recognize what's going on here. Like the connection between *ALIEN* and *IT! THE TERROR FROM BEYOND SPACE*, the plot here is creatively borrowed from other films. But, what the heck—it's a great plot, it worked the first two times, and it works again here.

The reason for the retread? Roger Corman, like most of the low-budget producers in this world without an original idea in their heads, decided to make a space opera after the success of *STAR WARS* proved that going such a route could be successful. The usually penny-pinching Corman budgeted a reported $4.5 million for the film—far more than for the usual Corman epic and an adequate sum in those days to make a pretty good movie. Combined with a cast of higher-quality actors, some quality sets (which he then reused in dozens of subsequent films of, sadly, far lesser quality), and a strong script, he produced one of his finest movies.

Much of this credit should be given to screenwriter John Sayles. Even when stealing from the best, Sayles found ways to make *Battle Beyond the Stars* fresh and intelligent. For instance, after *STAR WARS*, every space opera started with a spaceship slowly rolling into sight from this or that angle until it filled the screen, mimicking the opening shot of Lucas's blockbuster. Sayles avoided this modern cliché by having his opening ship suddenly drop into view out of hyperspace. The starfield on screen fills suddenly with a massive battle cruiser. The effect is nice and neatly done and offers a refreshing change of pace.

Battle Beyond the Stars is a great picture, rousing and fun-filled and played more than just a bit for laughs. What keeps it from falling apart is the seriousness with which everyone involved seems to take it. Thomas plays Shad as intently as he might Hamlet. Peppard gives evidence that he would have made just as good a Han Solo as Harrison Ford. And like Lucas, when Corman found the price tag for sci-fi special effects beyond his budget, he didn't settle for second-rate wizardry but instead created his own effects studio. True, there's nothing in this film to compare with the extensive asteroid dogfight in Lucas's *THE EMPIRE STRIKES BACK*, but, to be fair, there's little anywhere to compare with that scene. Corman did a lot with what he had. Every different technology shows different lines of development. Every race's ships not only look different, but are piloted in distinctly different ways. These are the kinds of details that are often so lacking in science fiction films, and the responsible parties deserve a hefty pat on the back. Other nice touches include Sador's vampirelike need for other people's body parts and Shad's symbolic exiting of the womb.

BATTLE BEYOND THE SUN (aka: THE HEAVENS CALL, THE SKY CALLS, THE SKY IS CALLING)

Filmgroup, 1963, Color, 74 min

United States: **Producer:** Roger Corman **Director:** Thomas Colchart (aka: Francis Ford Coppola); **Screenplay:** Nicholas Colbert and Edwin Palmer; **Special Effects:** Al Locatelli; **Cast:** Edd Perry, Arla Powell, Andy Stewart, Bruce Hunter

U.S.S.R. **Directors:** Mikhail Karzhukov and Aleksandr Kozyr; **Screenplay:** Karzhukov, Alesei Sazonov, and Yevgeni Pomeshchikov; **Music:** Yuli Meitus; **Special Effects:** G. Lukashov and Y. Schuech; **Cinematogra-**phy: Nikolai Kulchitsky; **Cast:** Ivan Pereverzyou, Taisiya Litvinenko, Aleksandr Shvorin, Viktor Dobrovtsky

America and Russia are again in a space race: but this time it's to Mars. The Americans win the race, but only by idiotically increasing their velocity. Not bothering to take any real rocket scientists with them, it doesn't dawn on anyone in the American crew that doing this will leave them without enough fuel to get home. The clever and kindly Russians come in second but are good losers. They help their robust but naive ideological enemies battle some monsters and then take the relentless chuckleheads back to Earth.

Nonsensical, but in some ways interesting. Notably, this sci-fi flick was produced in Russia. Corman simply bought the rights and then dubbed it into English, with Colchart directing the dubbing and additional footage.

BATTLEFIELD EARTH

Warner Bros., 2000, Color, 121 min

Producers: Elie Samaha, Jonathan D. Krane, John Travolta, Tracee Stanley, James Holt, Andrew Stevens, Ashok Amritraj, and Don Carmody; **Director:** Roger Christian; **Screenplay:** Corey Mandell and JD

Battlefield Earth (FRANCHISE PICTURE / AUTHOR'S COLLECTION)

Shapiro; **Cinematography:** Giles Nuttgens; **Music:** Elia Cmiral; **Special Effects:** Erik Henry, Patrick Tatopoulo, and Bill Pearson; **Cast:** John Travolta, Barry Pepper, Forest Whitaker, Kim Coates, Richard Tyson, Sabine Karsenti

In roughly the year 2000, alien invaders destroy all of Earth's defenses and conquer the planet in nine minutes. For a thousand years the planet is mined for its resources by the Psychlos from Psychlo, who plan to take everything they can and leave. A thousand years after the arrival of the aliens, humanity is reduced to the alien's slave labor force and to isolated pockets of free, ignorant savages. In the year 3000, however, one of these savages leads a revolution, and in a few days' time leads his people to freedom and destroys the Psychlo's home planet, as well.

The film ignores its own internal logic as well as basic science and a host of other details. Why is it that the same weapons that couldn't beat the aliens in the year 2000 can in 3000? For that matter, how is it that 1,000-year-old Earth weapons are still working? How can jet aircraft onboard electronics stand 10 centuries of disuse? Where does the fuel come from to fly the jets? These and many other questions go unanswered.

The movie's shortcomings cannot be blamed on lack of funds. Most aspects of the film are more than adequate. The score is quite competent, cinematography sweeping and brilliant, special effects quite well done if standard and uninvolving, and the cast is a good one. It all simply seems uninspired, and considering the source material it's understandable. Pulp author L. Ron Hubbard was never considered one of the crown jewels of the sci-fi pantheon.

BATTLE FOR THE PLANET OF THE APES

20th Century Fox, 1974, Color, 90 min, VT, DVD

Producer: Arthur P. Jacobs; **Director:** J. Lee Thompson; **Screenplay:** John Williams and Joyce Hooper Corrington; **Music:** Leonard Rosenman; **Special Effects:** John Chambers; **Cinematography:** Richard H. Kline; **Cast:** Roddy McDowall, Paul Williams, Natalie Trundy, Austin Stoker, Claude Akins, Severn Darden, Bobby Porter, John Huston, John Landis, France Nuyen, Pat Cardi, Lew Ayres

The fifth film in the *PLANET OF THE APES* series takes us to the the simian world of the future, where racial, or interspecies, harmony is sought by ape Caesar (McDowall) and human MacDonald (Stoker) for their respective races. A fascistlike army and police force arrive on the scene to confront the two idealists and beat down their efforts at peace.

To be fair, the filmmakers did attempt to tie up the entire Ape saga once and for all with this film, but the results are poor, making this series ender the perfect example of social science fiction gone bad. Commentary is only as good as the commentators, and the simplistic and cloying antiwar sentiment expressed here is a dismal finale to what in many ways is one of science fiction's best series. The film plays as sappy and pretentious, and after three good movies and a fourth that wasn't *that* bad, this addition to the series comes off as one film too many, obviously made to unfairly wring money out of the series' trusting fan base.

BATTLE IN OUTER SPACE

Toho (Japan), 1959/Columbia (US), 1960, Color, 90 min

Producer: Tomoyuki Tanaka **Director:** Inoshiro Honda; **Screenplay:** Jotaro Okami; **Special Effects:** Eiji Tsuburaya; **Cast:** Ryo Ikebe, Kyoko Anza, Minoru Takada, Harold Conway

Aliens based on the dark side of Earth's Moon control several Earthly astronauts through electronic devices they place in the human's brains. The astronauts are then sent back to Earth to sabotage the space program. An interplanetary war breaks out, which leaves both Earth and the Moon crippled. The film is loaded with special effects, but there's not much of a story here, even for kids.

BATTLE OF THE WORLDS

Topaz (Italy), 1963, Color, 84 min, VT

Director: Anthony Dawson; **Screenplay:** Vassily Petrov; **Cast:** Claude Rains, Maya Brent, Bill Carter, Umberto Orsini

An alien-controlled comet is on a collision course with Earth. An old but feisty scientist portrayed by Rains attempts to stop it. It's nice to know that a consummate professional like Claude Rains (*THE INVISIBLE MAN*) got work late in his life. It's not always nice to watch it.

BATTLESTAR: GALACTICA

Universal, 1979, Color, 125 min, VT, LD, DVD

Producer: Leslie Stevens; **Director:** Richard A. Colla; **Screenplay:** Richard A. Colla and Glen A. Larson; **Music:** Stu Phillips; **Special Effects:** John Dykstra; **Cinematography:** Ben Colman; **Cast:** Lorne Greene, Richard Hatch, Dirk Benedict, Ray Milland, John Colicos, Patrick Macnee, Lew Ayres, Jane Seymour, Laurette Spang, Terry Carter

In another solar system humans are attacked by a robot race and forced to flee their planet. Their destination is a mythical sanctuary: Earth. Lorne Greene is properly paternal as Commander Adama, the leader of the space fleet trying to stay ahead of the ever-pursuing Cylons.

After the Vietnam War and Watergate and with Jimmy Carter in office as the president of the United States, it must have seemed logical to create a new sci-fi show for television that involved "heroes" who didn't go anywhere boldly but instead ran away like frightened mice. Logical to those in Hollywood, perhaps, but not to the American viewing public who constantly ignored the insulting program that spawned this film. The movie was not only based on the television show of the same name, but it was cut together from several episodes. The transition to the big screen did not help. As foolishly derivative as its clichés looked on the small screen, they seemed enormous in the theaters, where the bad scripts and worse acting that dogged the show throughout its short life span seemed even more obvious. Thankfully, there was no sequel, but remarkably the series still has a small following of fans.

BATTLETRUCK

See *WARLORDS OF THE 21ST CENTURY*

BEACH GIRLS AND THE MONSTER, THE (aka: INVISIBLE TERROR, SURF TERROR)

US Films, 1965, b&w, 70 min, VT

Producer: Edward Janis; **Director:** Jon Hall; **Screenplay:** Joan Gardner; **Music:** Frank Sinatra, Jr.; **Cast:** Arnold Lessing, Elaine Dupont, Gloria Neal, Reed Morgan, Clyde Adler

The surf is up and the shore is covered with beautiful women. It should be a day at the beach, but a crazed scientists is murdering the sand bunnies.

BEAST FROM 20,000 FATHOMS, THE

Warner Bros., 1953, b&w, 80 min, VT, LD

Producers: Bernard W. Burton, Hal E. Chester, and Jack Dietz; **Director:** Eugene Lourie; **Screenplay:** Lou Morheim; **Music:** David Buttolph; **Special Effects:** Ray Harryhausen; **Cinematography:** Jack Russell; **Cast:** Paul Christian, Paula Raymond, Cecil Kellaway, Kenneth Tobey, King Donovan, Lee Van Cleef

An atomic bomb test releases enough radiation to thaw out a frozen dinosaur hidden beneath the sea. Awakened, the beast heads for Manhattan, where it does considerable damage before leaving the city for the suburbs, where it is destroyed.

Inspired by "The Foghorn," a short story by Ray Bradbury, this picture is loads of fun. The terrific special effects produced for next to nothing by then-young animator Ray Harryhausen make it worth watching. The story is tight and the cast is up to the task of moving it along with crisp professional performances, but the star is the stop-motion dinosaur. In many ways, it's films like this one that people are talking about when they discuss the state of science fiction films in the '50s. It features nuclear paranoia, a social conscience, and a cool monster smashing stuff and eating people.

BEAST OF BLOOD, THE (aka: BEAST OF THE DEAD)

Hemisphere, 1970, Color, 90 min

Producer: Eddie Romero; **Director:** Romero; **Screenplay:** Romero; **Music:** Tito Arevalo; **Special Effects:** Teofilo Hilario; **Cinematography:** Justo Paulino; **Cast:** John Ashley, Celeste Yarnell, Beverly Miller, Eddie Garcia

A headless monster terrorizes a group of kindly islanders. This one is as bad *THE MAD DOCTOR OF BLOOD ISLAND*, to which it is the sequel.

BEAST OF YUCCA FLATS, THE

Cardoza, 1961, b&w, 60 min, VT, DVD

Producer: Anthony Cardoza; **Director:** Coleman Francis; **Screenplay:** Francis; **Music:** I Nafshun and Al Remington; **Cinematography:** John Cagle; **Cast:** Tor

The Beast from 20,000 Fathoms (R. ALLEN LEIDER COLLECTION)

Johnson, Douglar Mellor, Tony Cardoza, Bing Stanford, Barbara Francis

Radiation turns Tor Johnson from a nice-guy scientist into a monster. A number of attractive women are paraded across the screen to their deaths, but even they can't help this simply dreadful movie, Johnson should be respected for earning his paychecks the only way he could, but this movie is as sad as the attitude of the producers who kept using the poor guy over and over simply because of his unique appearance.

BEASTS

See *TWILIGHT PEOPLE, THE*

BEAST WITH A MILLION EYES, THE

ARC, 1955, b&w, 78 min

Producer: Roger Corman; **Director:** David Kramarsky; **Screenplay:** Tom Filler; **Music:** John Bickford; **Special Effects:** Paul Blaisdell; **Cast:** Leonard Tarver, Paul Birch, Lorna Thayer, Dona Cole, Chester Conklin

An alien invasion comes to Earth, this time in the form of an extraterrestrial with highly developed telepathic abilities. The alien crash-lands here but soon decides it can probably take over the planet. At first it controls animals, using them only as scouts, before graduating to people of limited intelligence and then to packs of animals in its bid for control of the world.

This is a good little movie. The effects are mediocre, but following the first rule of good low-budget filmmaking, the script is especially top-notch to make up for it. It offers a novel twist on the alien invasion theme and taps into the same sense of social paranoia at work in such films as *INVASION OF THE BODY SNATCHERS* and *THE THING*. The creepiness builds nicely from start to finish.

BED-SITTING ROOM, THE

United Artists, 1969, Color, 91 min

Producer: Richard Lester; **Director:** Lester; **Screenplay:** John Antrobus and Richard Lester; **Music:** Ken Thorne; **Cast:** Mona Washbourne, Michael Hordern, Marty Feldman, Rita Tushingham, Sir Ralph Richardson, Peter Cook. Dudley Moore, Spike Milligan

This truly bizarre British social satire tells the story of England in the days following a nuclear holocaust where everyone tries to keep such a stiff upper lip that they pretend nothing has changed. Based on a stage comedy by John Antrobus and legendary funnyman Spike Milligan, the film delivers some comedy, but don't expect the strange, nonsensical logic of Monty Python. The play, which was largely improvised by Antrobus and Milligan on a nightly basis to keep it from growing static, seems to suffer in translating to the realism of film. The dismal backgrounds of the movie sap the life from the humor. The movie is littered with truly chaotic bits of nightmare through which the characters trudge, and it's easy to imagine much of the humor working better if not juxtaposed with the despairing locations chosen by Lester. In addition, the film's heavy-handed philosophy seems most popular with those who allow themselves mind-altering substances, and fans of the film seem to lurk fairly comfortably in that strata of society.

BEE GIRL, THE

See *THE WASP WOMAN*

BEES, THE

New World, 1979, Color, 85 min, VT

Producer: Alfredo Zacharis; **Director:** Zacharis; **Screenplay:** Zacharis; **Music:** Richard Gillis; **Cinematography:** Joseph Lamas; **Cast:** John Saxon, John Carradine, Angel Tompkins

Scientists working for a greedy corporation (is there any other kind in most American films?) develop a horde of killer bees so that the bees can be exploited for their honey. Of course, the bees escape and begin to kill people, which after a while prompts the corporation into thinking that maybe they should be destroyed in this dull film.

BEGINNING OF THE END, THE

Republic, 1957, b&w, 74 min

Producer: Bert I. Gordon; **Director:** Gordon; **Screenplay:** Fred Freiberger and Lester Gorn; **Special Effects:** Gordon; **Cinematography:** Jack Marta; **Cast:** Peter Graves, Peggie Castle, James Seay, Morris Ankrum, Thomas Browne Henry

Farmers beseech the government for help when their soil gives out. Civil service scientists introduced radiation to the scene, and soon all the crops are growing at an astounding rate. Does this make the farmers happy? Sadly, no, since the grasshoppers are now growing at an even faster rate. For some reason the effect doesn't extend to spiders or beetles or other insects, just grasshoppers, but it does seem that they're enough. The National Guard is called out, but they can't do much of anything, which means a scientist (Graves) has to come up with a clever idea to get rid of the monsters. Since there's a lake nearby, he cleverly drowns them.

This one is simply too easy to make fun of. Its science is hopelessly ridiculous, its script routine, and the giant bugs are no more than real backyard grasshoppers superimposed on the various scenes and photographic cutouts of buildings, and even this meager technical trick is poorly executed.

BEHEMOTH, THE SEA MONSTER
(aka: THE GIANT BEHEMOTH)

Diamond (Great Britain)/Allied Artists (U.S.), 1958, b&w, 80 min

Producers: David Diamond and Ted Lloyd; **Directors:** Douglas Hickox and Eugene Lourie; **Screenplay:** Lourie; **Special Effects:** Willis O'Brien; **Cast:** Gene Evans, Andre Morell, Jack McGowran, Leigh Madison

Atomic radiation brings yet another prehistoric monster to the surface for giant-monster-genre veteran Lourie. Unfortunately, after using this plot to good effect in *THE BEAST FROM 20,000 FATHOMS* years earlier, the director gets little mileage out of it here. Even the work of legendary stop-motion animator Willis O'Brien couldn't save this low-budget retread.

BEHIND THE DOOR

See *THE MAN WITH NINE LIVES*

BEING, THE (aka: EASTER SUNDAY)

New World Pictures, 1983, Color, 79 min, VT

Producer: William Osco; **Director:** Jackie Kong; **Screenplay:** Kong; **Music:** Don Preston; **Cinematography:** Robert Ebinger and Hanania Baer; **Cast:** Martin Landau, José Ferrer, Rexx Coltrane, Dorothy Malone, Ruth Buzzi, Marianne Gordon Rogers, Murray Langston, Kinky Friedman, Johnny Dark

Nuclear waste creates—can you believe it—a monster, which then sets off to terrorize the countryside. This time it's in Idaho. Actually, one shouldn't crack wise about the plot since this one is a comedy, and a fairly funny one at that. Good jokes, however, fail to make up for the terrible script or the ultra-low budget.

BENEATH THE PLANET OF THE APES

20th Century Fox, 1970, Color, 95 min, VT, LD, DVD

Producer: Arthur P. Jacobs; **Director:** Ted Post; **Screenplay:** Mort Abrahams and Paul Dehn; **Music:** Leonard Rosenman; **Cinematography:** Milton Krasner; **Cast:** Charlton Heston, James Franciscus, Kim Hunter, Maurice Evans, Linda Harrison, Victor Buono, Paul Richards, Thomas Gomez

Defying the odds, a Hollywood studio made a science fiction sequel as good as the first movie in this second film in the PLANET OF THE APES series, though like so many sequels this picture seems to be little more than a remake of its predecessor.

Another space flight brings Astronaut Franciscus to the future in search of his friend, Taylor (Heston), one of the three astronauts lost in the first film. Like Heston in the original movie, he is captured and befriended by the same ape doctor. He even finds Nova (Harrison), Heston's girlfriend from the first film, and the two team up and set out to find their mutual friend. And at that point, the first plot gives way and *Beneath the Planet of the Apes* becomes not only its own picture, but a terrific one.

The world of the future is shown to be a crazed place where ape armies exterminate humans and a race of nuclear-bomb-worshiping mutants live in the ruins of the New York City subway system's tunnels. Franciscus and his companion find their way into the tunnels, where they discover Heston being held prisoner, and just as they help Heston escape the mentally super-powered mutants, the apes invade the subway system.

Franciscus, Harrison, and Heston are all shot down by the apes, as are all of the mutants. Seeing no hope for the savage future and filled with rage at the sight of his girlfriend being killed, Heston detonates the leftover planet-buster bomb that served as the mutants's god, and the picture ends.

There are more than a few problems with this film, but most of them tie to the hopelessly dated social commentary running through it (such as the idea that nuclear annihilation was just around the corner) and the levels of grave pomposity used to sell the same. Despite this, it still deserves a thumbs-up, and a viewing whenever you discover it while channel surfing. The first movie's humor gives way to a dark judgment about the possibility of intelligence of *any* kind surviving on this planet, extending the themes established in the previous picture. The storytelling in this film is sharp and angry and 100 percent pure science fiction. The special effects, costumes, makeup, and acting are all top-notch as well and at least equal to those in the first film. Heston's stunning portrayal of Taylor highlights a round of good performances.

BEWARE! THE BLOB

See *THE BLOB* (1958)

BEYOND THE TIME BARRIER

AIP, 1960, b&w, 75 min

Producer: Robert Clarke; **Director:** Edgar Ulmer; **Screenplay:** Arthur C. Pierce; **Music:** Darrell Calker; **Cast:** Robert Clarke, Darlene Tompkins, John Van Drelen, Tom Ravick

A test pilot (Clarke) breaks the time barrier to find a futuristic world where the surface is ruled by mutants while all the normal humans (which in this future means being deaf, dumb, and sterile) have relocated underground. Worse yet, the nuclear war that destroyed the world left behind a terrible radioactive plague in this standard '60s cautionary tale.

BICENTENNIAL MAN, THE

Touchstone Pictures/Columbia Pictures, 1999, color, 130 min., DVD, VT

Producers: Chris Columbus, Michael Barnathan, Dale Katz, Dan Kolsrund, Laurence Mark, Neal Miller, Wolfgang Petersone, and Mark Radcliffe; **Director:** Columbus; **Screenplay:** Nicholas Kazan;

Music: James Horner; **Cinematography:** Phil Meheux; **Special Effects:** James E. Price, John McLeod, and Dream Quest Images; **Cast:** Sam Neill, Robin Williams, Embeth Davidtz, Oliver Platt, Wendy Crewson, Lynne Thigpen, Kiersten Warren, Stephen Root, Hallie Kate Eisenberg, John Michael Higgins

An adaptation of Isaac Asimov's famous Robot stories, *Bicentennial Man* tells the tale of an unusual robot (Williams), capable of developing human emotions and feelings. Over the course of 200 years, Williams struggles to cope with his unrobotic personality and keeps himself from being dismantled.

BIGGLES (aka: BIGGLES: ADVENTURES IN TIME)

Tambarle Productions (Great Britain), 1986, Color, 108 min, VT, LD

Producer: Adrian Scrope; **Director:** John Hough; **Screenplay:** John Groves, Kent Walwin, and W.E. Johns; **Music:** Stanislas; **Special Effects:** David Harris; **Cinematography:** Ernest Vincze; **Cast:** Neil Dickson, Alex Hyde-White, Fiona Hutchinson, Peter Cushing, Marcus Gilbert

Alex Hyde-White leaves the present and goes back in time to help World War I fliers in this odd bit of science fiction from Great Britain. The results are watchable and somewhat engaging, but not memorable.

BIG SPACE MONSTER GILALA

See *THE X FROM OUTER SPACE*

BILL & TED'S BOGUS JOURNEY

Interscope Communications, 1991, Color, 98 min, VT, LD

Producer: Paul Aaron, Robert W. Cort, Stephen Deutsch, Ted Field, Rick Finkelstein, Scott Kroopf, Chris Matheson, Barry Spikings, Connie Tavel; **Director:** Peter Hewitt; **Screenplay:** Chris Matheson and Ed Solomon; **Music:** David Newman; **Special Effects:** George L. McMurry and David Stump; **Cinematography:** Oliver Wood; **Cast:** Keanu Reeves, Alex Winter, William Sadler, Amy Stock-Poynton, Annet Azcuy, George Carlin

See *BILL & TED'S EXCELLENT ADVENTURE*

BILL & TED'S EXCELLENT ADVENTURE

Interscope Communications, 1989, Color, 90 min, VT, LD

Producers: Scott Kroopf, Joel Soisson, and Michael S. Murphy; **Director:** Stephen Herek; **Screenplay:** Chris Matheson and Ed Solomon; **Music:** David Newman; **Special Effects:** Charles L. Finance; **Cinematography:** Tim Suhrstedt; **Cast:** Keanu Reeves, Alex Winter, George Carlin, Bernie Casey, Amy Stock-Poynton, Dan Shore, Ted Steedman, Rod Loomis, Tony Camilieri, Al Leong, Robert Barron

Lifelong metalhead (musicians, not robots) best friends Bill and Ted are in trouble. They're about to fail history. But, if they do, then the timeline where they become saviors of the universe will be adversely affected. What's the solution? Simple—a representative from the future has to return to their time and send them on a journey through the past in which they can meet Beethoven, Genghis Khan, Joan of Arc, Abraham Lincoln, and more and thus gather the knowledge they need to pass their test.

It may sound a little dim, but surprisingly the movie is great fun. It could have been a more important film, but then it wouldn't have been true to its simple-minded premise: Party on. In its own way, however, it's good enough. Keanu Reeves has never been better; neither has George Carlin. The picture moves at a nice clip, has good things to say, and is the only movie ever made to portray barely literate rock 'n' rollers not only communicating with Socrates, but connecting with him on a deeply spiritual level through the lyrics of rock group Kansas. The hard science in this movie is just window dressing to get the plot going, and the social science consists of warm and fuzzy platitudes, but it meshes nicely and there are far worse ways to spend an hour and a half.

The film was followed two years later by *Bill & Ted's Bogus Journey*, which gets more metaphysical than science fictional, but is just as entertaining. Give both films and chance, but don't watch them on the same night. These movies are a fragile pleasure at best.

Note: Screenwriter Chris Matheson is the son of influential novelist and screenwriter Richard Matheson (*THE INCREDIBLE SHRINKING MAN*, *THE LAST MAN ON EARTH*, *THE OMEGA MAN*).

BILLION DOLLAR BRAIN, THE

United Artists, 1967, Color, 108 min

Producer: Harry Saltzman; **Director:** Ken Russell; **Screenplay:** John McGrath; **Music:** Richard Rodney Bennett; **Cinematography:** Billy Williams; **Cast:** Michael Caine, Karl Malden, Ed Begley, Oscar Homolka, Francoise Dorleac

Caine plays investigator Harry Palmer in this third film in the series. This time Palmer is up against a right-wing crackpot (is there any other kind of right-winger as far as Hollywood is concerned?) who is building his own army to battle the dreaded Red Menace. The shocker is that he's being aided in this conservative endeavor by a Pentagon computer acting on its own. This is the only one of the "Palmer" films most people remember, and for good reason: It combines the talents of Michael Caine and director Ken Russell, and it's a good one.

BIRTH OF A ROBOT, THE

Shell Oil, 1934, Color, 7 min

Producer: Charles H. Dand; **Directors:** Humphrey Jennings and Len Lye

The title says it all in this film documenting the first minutes (seven, to be exact) of a robot's life.

BLACK FRIDAY

Universal, 1940, b&w, 70 min

Producer: Burt Kelly; **Director:** Arthur Lubin; **Screenplay:** Curt Siodmak and Erik Taylor; **Cinematography:** Elwood Bredell; **Cast:** Boris Karloff, Bela Lugosi, Stanley Ridges, Anna Nagel, Anne Gwynne, Paul Fix, Jack Mulhall

A professor (Karloff) gets caught in the crossfire of a gang war. When the smoke clears, Karloff and one of the gangsters are down for the count. Both men end up in the care of one of the professor's friends who decides to save his buddy by repairing the damage to his brain with tissue from the dying gangster's cranium. This saves Karloff, but brings about eerie bouts of split personality as the gangster's memories begin to take control of the professor's body.

It's a fascinating idea given life by a top-notch script. Lugosi is wasted in a minor role as a gangster, but Karloff is spectacular as he shifts from the mild-mannered academic to the murderous alter ego. A good premise, well developed and excellently presented, definitely make this movie worth the time.

BLACK HOLE, THE

Walt Disney, 1979, Color, 97 min, VT, LD, DVD

Producer: Ron Miller; **Director:** Gary Nelson; **Screenplay:** Jeb Rosebrook and Gerry Day; **Music:** John Barry; **Special Effects:** Peter and Harrison Ellenshaw, Eustace Lycett, and Danny Lee; **Cinematography:** Frank Phillips; **Cast:** Anthony Perkins, Robert Forster, Yvette Mimieux, Joseph Bottoms, Ernest Borgnine, Maximilian Schell

Intrepid space explorers find the long-missing ship, *Cygnus.* Even though it's dangerously close to a black hole, they decide to investigate what they assumed is an abandoned ship. It's not. Legendary genius scientist, Dr. Hans Reinhardt (Schell) is running it with a crew of automatons. Conflict? Reinhardt is insane. When the crew didn't go along with his mad schemes, he killed them and turned them into the robotic drones that run the ship. Now the would-be rescuers have to do everything they can just to save themselves.

At a time when films like *STAR WARS* and *ALIEN* were being made, a major studio preparing both to make its debut as a serious science fiction filmmaker and to throw an impressive amount of money into the project should have thrown a little of that money into a decent script. *The Black Hole* is more than bad or even laughable—it's pitiful. Disney might have wanted to do a serious film, they may have earned their first ever PG rating, but all they produced was a sad mess peppered with clichés and phoned-in performances.

The special effects are terrific for the time, but pretty pictures do not a good story make, and there is no genre more dependent on story than science fiction. There is one outstanding death scene, and the ending approaches a sense of allegorical meaning, but sadly by that point boredom and cynical laughter usually have taken most audience members to the point of not caring. In all honesty, just about the time you expect to hear one of those Disney nature film narrators saying: "Then it was about time for ol' mister meteor to tear its way on through the ship," one does.

Sci-fi fans are often insulted by Hollywood, which almost always only seems interested in one scientific formula: the reaching of the lowest common denominator. Moviemakers, like hash-house cooks, can always get the ingredients right—good cast, great effects, all the right devices—no problem. But when it comes time to go to the stove and turn it all into something, they lack the artistic scope (and usually the nerve, as well) to do something that hasn't been done before.

This, of course, is death for science fiction because the genre is dependent on speculation—on *thinking about that which has not happened*. The first time something is presented on screen—time travel, a mad scientist, cloning, space travel, aliens, whatever—it intrigues. The second time, to the sci-fi fan, it's old hat. And often, after a few decades in this age of scientific miracles, it's not even fiction anymore.

Hollywood desperately wants to cash in on science fiction, but it is the one genre the city just can't seem to get a hold of except in the rarest of instances. *The Black Hole* is perhaps the quintessential example of this truism.

BLACK SCORPION, THE

Warner Bros., 1957, b&w, 88 min, VT

Producers: Jack Dietz and Frank Medford; **Director:** Edward Ludwig; **Screenplay:** David Duncan and Robert Blees; **Music:** Paul Sawtell; **Special Effects:** Willis O'Brien; **Cast:** Richard Denning, Carlos Rivas, Mara Corday, Mario Navarro

Giant scorpions emerge from a newly formed Mexican volcano and terrorize the countryside. Killing only at night, they come out one at a time at first, then in greater and greater hordes. The heroes drop a mountain on them, but one, the biggest of all, escapes, and has to be lured into a sports arena by the smell of blood, then electrocuted.

If you think this sounds like a second-rate remake of the classic *THEM*, you're right. But any chance to see the painstakingly spectacular work of genius stop-motion animator Willis O'Brian (*KING KONG*), the man who started it all, is worth the time. But the film is best watched with the sound off and a finger on the fast-forward button, for this is a truly awful movie. Nothing happens in this film for any logical reason. Everything is just part of the script. For example, the Mexican government turns control of its military over to a visiting American scientist, bypassing the equally competent Mexican scientist who's portrayed as his sidekick, simply because the American is cast as the hero.

O'Brien actually died before completing this picture, and though it's a terrible end to his career, knowing that will make sense of the mix of badly superimposed real scorpions, and stop-motion ones that may just be the best giant bugs ever to grace the silver screen.

BLADE RUNNER

Warner Bros., 1982, Color, 118 min, VT, LD, DVD

Producer: Michael Deeley; **Director:** Ridley Scott; **Screenplay:** Hamptom Fancher and David Webb Peoples; **Music:** Vangelis; **Special Effects:** Steve Galich, Ken Estes, William G. Curtis, Michael Backauskas, and Logan Frazee; **Cast:** Harrison Ford, Rutger Hauer, Sean Young, Edward James Olmos, William Sanderson, Daryl Hanna, Joe Turkel, Brian James, Joanna Cassidy

In the near future the ills of the world we know have multiplied geometrically. The buildings are taller and uglier, the smog is worse, and decay is evident everywhere. Biologically fit humans are encouraged to migrate to off-world colonies, leaving the dregs behind. The story begins when a new problem is introduced into the world of those dregs who stay behind—a group of androids, called Replicants, who have escaped their slavelike captivity as workers in outer space and have returned to Earth in the hopes of extending and living out their lives. Earth doesn't tolerate androids, however, and keeps bounty hunters known as Blade Runners around to clean up such inconvenient messes. They hunt down and kill escapees—"retiring" them, as it were.

Enter Rick Deckard (Ford), an ex- ("retired," as it were) Blade Runner. Deckard is pulled back into the line of duty to track down this latest batch of rogue Replicants who have made their way to Los Angeles in the hopes of tracking down their creator. It seems they've decided to take exception to the minimal four-year life spans built into their physiology and they want it extended. Only a few minutes into the film it's obvious that tracking the renegades down in the decay and confusion of the Los Angeles on the screen will not be an easy task. Deckard throws himself into his assignment, using interesting but solid detective work to find the Replicants one by one. At the same time, however, he inadvertently becomes involved with a nonrebellious Replicant, which complicates things for him mentally.

Eventually, the leader of the rebel androids (Hauer) makes his way to his creator. In a complex allegorical scene, the creation demands things from its creator that cannot be granted. The creator dies at its creation's hands, not screaming or begging, but proud of his accomplishment. This affects the android profoundly, who then reverses roles with Deckard. Suddenly, the Blade Runner becomes the pursued as the climax of the film becomes a fast-paced game of cat-and-mouse with the android clearly in charge. At the end of their contest, Deckard has clearly lost and is about to fall to his death when his Replicant foe saves him at the moment of its own death. The soulless gains

Blade Runner (THE LADD COMPANY / AUTHOR'S COLLECTION)

what it has to offer. The hardware is excellent. All of the background gizmos are clever, and the Replicants as products are intelligently portrayed. As for the social issues at work, they are handled with extreme care and an adroitness highly unusual for a Hollywood film. Slavery, dehumanization, and the thin line between them are expertly handled. The breakdown and reassembly of moral codes by a new generation may take place in the background, but it is there, nonetheless, and it is well utilized.

Besides those behind the cameras, the cast seems to have understood their jobs with crystal clarity as well. Harrison Ford has rarely been better, and Rutger Hauer has *never* been better. It is by far one of his two finest performances (see *BLOOD OF HEROES*). He is simply brilliant. So is director Ridley Scott, and so are his editors and effects people. Everyone put their best effort into this film, and it shows.

Or at least it shows in the special edition director's cut released years after the film had gone from theaters. Heavy-handed studio interference designed to "save" the picture nearly ruined the initial release. Critics and fans all complained for years about problems with the movie, such as the clunky, tagged-on voice-over narration. Every single major point was one of the things altered by the studio. The director's cut eliminates nearly all the problems of the original release, boosting this spectacular film into classic status.

a soul, while the human being is reduced to wondering if he has one himself.

Despite the fact that this film is only loosely based on Phillip K. Dick's sensational novel *Do Androids Dream of Electric Sheep?*, it is one of the better science fiction movies out there. Usually those who ignore their source material do so to their own detriment, but not this time.

On the superficial level, *Blade Runner* looks terrific. Sets, machinery, backgrounds, lifestyles, cars, clothing, city spaces—everything has been well thought out. For instance, although it's never actually mentioned, the population of Los Angeles is purposely represented as being heavily Asian to indicate subtly migration shifts in the future. Massive buildings are constructed directly atop multiple older, smaller buildings in much the same way most of midtown Manhattan was actually built. But the film does not call attention to these details. If the audience notes these things consciously, that's great. If not, that's okay, too. The movie is a view of the future, not a look at our own times gone horribly wrong as in so many pictures, but simply "further." It's a bleak and leaden look at things to come, but not an unconvincing one.

Critics have lodged numerous complaints about this film, but they all seem fairly petty compared with

BLAST FROM THE PAST

New Line Cinema, 1999, Color, 106 min, VT, DVD

Producers: Mary Kane, Renny Harlin, Hugh Wilson, Sunil Perkash, Claire Rudnick Polstein, and Amanda Stern; **Director:** Wilson; **Screenplay:** Bill Kelly and Wilson; **Music:** Steve Doriff; **Special Effects:** Jennifer Law-Stump, David Taritero, Ariel Velasco-Shaw, David Waine, Ultimate Effects, and Illusion Arts, Inc.; **Cinematography:** Jose Luis Alcaine; **Cast:** Brendan Fraser, Christopher Walken, Sissy Spacek, David Foley, Alicia Silverstone, Joey Slotnik, Dale Raoul

This film begins in the '60s during the worst of the cold war paranoia. A genial scientist (Walken) builds the ultimate bomb shelter for his family, convinced the Russian menace will be striking any time. Through a bizarre but believable set of circumstances, he and his pregnant wife (Spacek) become convinced the end is at hand and retreat to the shelter to escape from the world war they believe is destroying the surface world.

Their son is born and raised in the shelter. He is the focus of their lives. They teach him everything from mathematics and multiple languages to ballroom dancing and the manly art of fisticuffs. Then, when Dad suffers a heart attack, Junior (now a full-grown Fraser) is sent up to the surface world for medicine and other supplies and the fun begins.

This genial, social science fiction comedy with a wonderfully focused, but gentle point of view alleges that perhaps we did lose something along the way over the past few decades in the United States. The jokes are sensibly not as topical as they could have been, rather pointing to flaws in the human condition and not just those of the particular year in which the picture was made.

BLAST-OFF

See *THOSE FANTASTIC FLYING FOOLS*

BLAST OFF

Reed, 1954, b&w, 78 min

Producers: Arthur Pierson, Roland D. Reed, and Guy V. Thayer, Jr.; **Director:** Hollingsworth Morse; **Screenplay:** Arthur Hoerl and Marianne Mosner; **Cinematography:** Guy Roe; **Special Effects:** Jack R. Glass; **Cast:** Richard Crane, Sally Mansfield, Maurice Cass

Simply a handful of episodes of the early television show *Rocky Jones, Space Ranger* edited down and strung together. This one has nostalgia value only.

BLOB, THE

Paramount, 1958, Color, 85 min, VT, LD, DVD

Producer: Jack H. Harris; **Director:** Irwin S. Yeaworth, Jr.; **Screenplay:** Theodore Simonson and Kate Phillips; **Music:** Ralph Carmichael; **Special Effects:** Barton Sloane; **Cast:** Steve McQueen, Aneta Corseaut, Earl Rowe, Olin Howlin

The story: A small blob crash-lands on Earth after tagging a ride on a meteor. It consumes humans for nourishment, growing larger with each meal. Two teenagers (McQueen and Corseaut) witness the thing at work, but luckily escape its clutches, and then are given the truly dangerous task of trying to convince the local authorities about what they've seen. Of course, they're accused by the local police of being the troublemakers, until the blob finally wanders into town and begins a massive killing spree as a giant-sized monster.

Although this could have been just another run-of-the-mill film, superior acting and an intense, deftly handled script make this one a stand-out. Little touches like the high school principal's slight hesitation before he smashes open the school's locked door add miles of depth to this one, proving that a teenagers-versus-monster movie could be more than simply another piece of junk.

Sadly, the same cannot be said for the lackluster comedy *Beware! The Blob* (aka *Son Of Blob*), which followed years later as a sort of sequel. Also the 1988 remake of *The Blob* featured some truly incredible special effects but ultimately gave audiences what they didn't need—something half as good as the original for ten times the price.

BLOB, THE (1988)

Tri-Star, 1988, Color, 85 min, VT

Producers: Andre Blay, Elliot Kastner, and Jack Harris; **Director:** Chuck Russell; **Screenplay:** Russell and Frank Darabont; **Cinematography:** Mark Irwin; **Music:** Mike Hoenig; **Special Effects:** A.J. Workman, Hoyt Yeatman, and Chuck Comisky; **Cast:** Shawnee Smith, Ricky Paull Goldin, Donovan Leitch, Kevin Dillon, Billy Beck, Candy Clark, Jeff DeMunn

See *THE BLOB* (1958)

BLOOD BEAST FROM OUTER SPACE
(aka: **THE NIGHT CALLER FROM OUTER SPACE, THE NIGHT CALLER**)

New Art-Armitage (Great Britain), 1965/NTA-Harris (US), 1968, b&w, 84 min, VT, DVD

Producer: Ronald Liles; **Director:** John Gilling; **Screenplay:** Jim O'Connolly; **Music:** John Gregory; **Cast:** Robert Crewsdon, Maurice Denham, John Saxon, Patricia Haines, Alfred Burke, Jack Watson, Aubrey Morris

An alien mutant comes to Earth to kidnap beauty queens to help repopulate one of the moons of Jupiter. One might expect someone with the intelligence to travel between planets to realize that all he needs to complete his mission is viable DNA, something he could obtain from countless thousands of less conspicuous women whose disappearances wouldn't be noticed nearly as quickly as those of newsworthy celebrities. Does he? Nope.

BLOOD CREATURE

See *TERROR IS MAN*

BLOOD OF HEROES, THE (aka: SALUTE OF THE JUGGER)

Handistom Investment, 1990, Color, 90 min, VT

Producers: Brian Rosen and Charles Roven; **Director:** David Webb Peoples; **Screenplay:** Peoples; **Music:** Todd Boekelheide; **Special Effects:** John Stoddart; **Cinematography:** David Eggby; **Cast:** Rutger Hauer, Joan Chen, Vincent Philip D'Onofrio, Anna Katarina, Delroy Lindo

Sometime in the future, everything is in ruins, a new dark ages exists with most of humanity having reverted to agrarian societies. Technology of a sorts still exists in places called the Red Cities, but we see little to nothing of most of them. There are no flying machines, no cars, and no communications except word-of-mouth. Life, even in the underground cities, is hard and tedious for most everyone. One of the only pleasures people have is watching "jugger" matches, a violent contact sport in which almost anything goes. Rutger Hauer gives one of the two best performances of his life (see *BLADE RUNNER*) as an aging player who once played for the League, one of the city teams.

He was a sports hero then, but he sacrificed all for the love of a high-born woman and was then exiled from the Red Cities for the arrogance of being indiscreet. Now, inspired by the desire to win which he sees in Kitta (Chen), the newest member of his small, dog-town team, he determines to win his old position back. Does he do it for revenge, for personal satisfaction, or for Kitta herself? The film never reveals the truth, but it doesn't matter. When the end comes, the audience is cheering all the same.

This is one of the best apocalyptic future pictures ever made. Great attention was paid to detail here. The dog towns are scrap communities, put together from the discards of the past and the simple ingenuity of their residents. Watching the backgrounds carefully is half the fun of repeated viewings of this film. Not only do the towns seem solid and permanent, with dozens of suggestions of age, but each town seems to have its own identity. Different locales seem to have been built with different source materials. It's all well thought out, as are our glimpses of the Red City. There is a ponderous sense of reality in the dark underground,

different from the upper world, better in some ways, but at a price to its inhabitants. Of course, there is a price for everything in life, but that's a stark social comment that goes beyond frivolous entertainment. And it's just one of the many insights to be found in this film.

The most important aspect of the story, however, the part that transcends sports and moves the film into science fiction—that previously mentioned "attitude"—is the code of the juggers. These are men and women playing a terribly dangerous sport. Eyes and ears are lost on a regular basis. People are crippled without a thought. But when the game is over, it's over. There are no hard feelings. Losing means a lot. When a rival or traveling jugger team comes to your town, you and yours put up everything of value. If you lose, you lose big time. Imagine losing the use of your legs and then having to pay for the privilege. Then imagine being compelled to smile about it.

This is the nobility of the human spirit at work. This is what being human is all about, having a higher purpose. It's also about never giving up, always striving for the impossible, and never letting the odds get you down. Even if the world's been destroyed, we're still people, still human. We still have souls. The film itself never pontificates so obviously, but it raises the questions all the same, and by the time it's finished, it's hard not to be proud of being an upright, thinking biped. *The Blood of Heroes* is also a great party movie, and an awfully inspiring flick to watch when you're down.

BLOOD WATERS OF DR. Z

See *ZAAT*

BLUE LIGHT, THE

Sokal Films (Germany), 1932, b&w, 90 min, VT

Director: Leni Riefenstahl; **Screenplay:** Riefenstahl, Bela Balazs, and Hans Schneeberger; **Cinematography:** Schneeberger; **Cast:** Leni Riegenstahl, Mathias Wieman, Beni Fuhrer, Max Holzboer

Blue light lures people to their deaths in this ponderous semi–fairy tale, whose modern appeal is to historians and insomniacs.

BODY PARTS

United International Pictures (Spain), 1991, Color, 88 min, VT, LD

Producers: Frank Mancuso, Jr. and Michael Sheehy; **Director:** Eric Red; **Screenplay:** Patricia Herskovic, Red, and Norman Snider; **Music:** Loek Dikker; **Cinematography:** Theo Van de Sande and Gerald M. Williams; **Cast:** Jeff Fahey, Lindsay Duncan, Kim Delaney, Brad Dourif, Zakes Mokae, John Walsh, Paul Benevictor

When a killer's body parts are grafted onto a series of patients, they begin to take over, driving their new owners to murderous deeds. This incompetent updating of THE HANDS OF ORLAC just gets sillier the longer one watches.

BLUE PLANET

IMAX Corporation (Canada), 1990, Color, 42 min

Producers: Phyllis Fergeson and Graeme Ferguson; **Director:** Ben Burtt; **Screenplay:** Toni Meyers; **Music:** Maribeth Solomon and Micky Erbe; **Cinematography:** David Douglas and James Neihouse;

Cast: Brewster H. Shaw, Jr., Bryan D. O'Connor, Michael L. Coats, John E. Blaha, Donald E. Williams, Michael J. McCulley, Daniel C. Brandenstein, James D. Wetherbee, Loren J. Schriver, Charles F. Bolden, Jr.

Billions of people have lived on Earth, but only a few hundred ever saw it as it appears from space. At least that was the case until those crafty devils at IMAX got one of their most ambitious ideas—to train the astronauts of five different shuttle missions to operate the company's large format cameras so that they might bring back footage to be used in the most awe-inspiring documentary about our planet ever made. The picture opens with the spectacle of a breathtaking earthrise filling the screen, shimmering blue and majestic in the blackness of space. From there it moves on to explore the fragile balance of life on our world and the forces of nature that affect it: storms, volcanoes, earthquakes, and of course, mankind itself.

For those not familiar with IMAX technology, it uses an image area 10 times larger than conventional

Blue Planet (SMITHSONIAN INSTITUTION & LOCKHEED MARTIN / AUTHOR'S COLLECTION)

35mm film and three times larger than standard 70mm film. Because of its enormous size, the film can be projected with incredible clarity onto screens up to eight stories tall. If you've never seen an IMAX picture, check the major cities around you to see if they have an IMAX theater. Florida's Kennedy Space Center has two of them. Some IMAX films are better than others, of course, but the experience is out of this world (no pun intended). *Blue Planet* is one of the better ones. Even though IMAX theaters are usually more expensive than regular theaters and the movies are short by feature film standards, it's worth it.

Note: The commanders and pilots of the five shuttle missions used to obtain the footage for this film were the names listed as "the cast" above.

BODY SNATCHERS, THE

Warner Bros., 1994, Color, 87 min, VT, LD, DVD

Producer: Robert H. Solo; **Director:** Abel Ferrara; **Screenplay:** Stuart Gordon, Larry Cohen, Dennis Paoli, and Nicholas St. John; **Music:** Joe Delia; **Cinematography:** Bojan Bazelli; **Cast:** Gabrielle Anwar, Meg Tilly, Forest Whittaker, Terry Kinney, Billy Wirth, Reilly Murphy, Christine Elise, R. Lee Ermey

Dr. Malone (Kinney) arrives at an army base somewhere in the southern United States. His assignment is to monitor ongoing experiments being conducted there, but while he goes about his normal business, the doctor spots soldiers loading what appear to be gigantic seed pods onto trucks. At the same time, the base doctor (Whittaker) tells his colleague that a number of the soldiers stationed there have complained of a fear of falling asleep. They claim if they do that they'll turn into monsters. Sound somewhat familiar? That's because it is. *The Body Snatchers* is the third film version of Jack Finney's terrific novel of the same name (after the 1955 and 1978 versions), which introduced the now well-known story: Pods from outer space turn into exact duplicates of sleeping people allowing those people to be replaced in a silent invasion.

This third treatment of the subject matter (see *INVASION OF THE BODY SNATCHERS* [1956], [1978]) is by far the weakest. As the 1978 version relied more on special effects and less on the story, the same approach was taken here. The transformation sequences are even more slimy and disgusting this time around, and more prolonged as well. Oozing tendrils sprout from the pods, which invade the bodies of the humans they intend to replace.

And, if sacrificing the tension and paranoia of the original film weren't enough, *The Body Snatchers* makes two more genuine mistakes, one of which is so massive that it's difficult to understand it on any level. As stated above, this time the action takes place on a military base. Trying to illustrate how terrible it is to replace feeling individuals with unthinking, conformist drones by showing soldiers—people trained to act exactly the same—being replicated might not have been the best way to get one's point across. But the truly destructive error here is in making the film's focal character a *new* arrival at the base. This undercuts the original plot's central strength since everyone who is replaced is a stranger, losing the slow whittling away of the human connection as friends and family change mysteriously one by one that characterized the earlier films. Though there are nice bits here and there, it seems pointless to bother with this version with two far superior takes already in existence.

BODY STEALERS, THE

See *THIN AIR*

BOOM IN THE MOON
(aka: A MODERN BLUEBEARD)

Alsa Film (Mexico), 1946, Color, 83 min, VT

Producer: Alexander Salkind; **Director:** James Salvador; **Screenplay:** Victor Trivas and Jamie Salvador; **Music:** George Tzipine; **Cast:** Buster Keaton, Angel Garasa, Virginia Serret, Fernando Soto, Luis Barreiro

Buster Keaton is mistaken for "a modern bluebeard" and conned into piloting a moon launch in this lesser, early effort from Salkind, who later co-produced the *SUPERMAN* movies.

BORROWER, THE

Cannon Group, 1991, Color, 97 min, VT

Producer: William H. Coleman; **Director:** John McNaughton; **Screenplay:** Richard Fire and Mason Nage; **Music:** Ken Hale, Steven A. Jones, and Robert McHaughton; **Special Effects:** Steve Galich; **Cinematography:** Julio Macat and Robert C. New; **Cast:** Rae Dawn Chong, Tom Towles, Don Gordon, Antonio Fargas, Neil Giuntoli, Larry Pennell, Pam Gordon, Tony Amendola, Stuart Cornfeld, Mädchen Amick

An alien creature is sentenced to live on Earth for its crimes. It is given human shape by its jailers, but after its original body is damaged, it discovers that it can survive only for a short while before the head explodes. So, what's an intergalactic criminal to do but tear off someone else's head and use it until, of course, it explodes as well. This is what a higher species call rehabilitation? Chong gives a wonderful perfor- mance.

BOWERY BOYS MEET THE MONSTERS, THE

AA, 1954, b&w, 65 min

Producer: Ben Schwalb; **Director:** Ed Bernds; **Screenplay:** Bernds and Elwood Ullman; **Special Effects:** Augie Lohman; **Cinematography:** Harry Neuman; **Cast:** Leo Gorcey, Huntz Hall, Lloyd Corrigan, Ellen Corby, John Dehner

The aging Bowery Boys do their standard comedic turn with a mad scientist into that wonderful and usually reliable comedy staple, the brain transplant. Switching intellects with a gorilla and Huntz Hall, of course, is something of an insult to the simian. This is one of the better pictures from the end of the series when the formula was getting a little too familiar.

BOY AND HIS DOG, A

LQ/JAF, 1975, Color, 89 min, VT, LD, DVD

Producer: Alvy Moore; **Director:** L.Q. Jones; **Screenplay:** Jones; **Music:** Tim McIntire; **Special Effects:** Frank Rowe; **Cinematography:** John Arthur Morrill; **Cast:** Don Johnson, Susanne Benton, Jason Robards Jr., Alvy Moore, Helene Winston, Charles McGraw, Tiger, Tim McIntire (voice of Blood)

This near-future story of people scrambling to scratch out a living in a world reduced to postholocaust debris centers on, as you might suspect, a boy and his dog. The dog is certainly a human's best friend this time around. The boy, played by a young Don Johnson, isn't exactly helpless, but he wouldn't survive without his telepathic pooch, Blood—that much is certain. The two share various adventures until Johnson is lured into an underground civilization by the promise of sex with a woman who is not only attractive but clean as well. Blood is forced to remain outside to await his companion's return. But it's all just a trap to get a healthy male inside the dying community for stud pur-

poses, something Johnson is all for until he discovers that he's going to be strapped down to a bed and drained by an automatic machine on a daily basis for the rest of his life. He escapes and returns to his loyal hound just in time to save the pooch in an especially fitting, but wonderfully twisted way.

There's only one real problem with this film, and that's the jarring difference in quality between the above-ground scenes, which crackle with gritty realism, and the subterranean ones, which seem absurdly fake. Harlan Ellison, author of the short story that inspired the movie, takes the blame for that. According to Peter Nichols's *The Science Fiction Encyclopedia*, he claims, "I was being dishonest when I wrote that section of the story. I didn't really create a downunder section that was realistic. I did a kind of papier-mâché Disneyland because I wanted to poke fun at the middle class." Still, this one is great fun and is extremely faithful to the Ellison story.

BOYICHI AND THE SUPERMONSTERS

See *RETURN OF THE GIANT MONSTERS*

BOYS FROM BRAZIL, THE

20th Century Fox, 1978, Color, 124 min, VT, LD

Producer: Martin Richards; **Director:** Franklin J. Schaffer; **Screenplay:** Heywood Gould; **Music:** Jerry Goldsmith; **Cinematography:** Henri Decae; **Cast:** Gregory Peck, Laurence Olivier, James Mason, Lilli Palmer, Uta Hagen, John Dehner, Rosemary Harris, Anne Meara, John Rubinstein, Denholm Elliot, Steven Guttenberg, David Hurst, Jeremy Black

Based on the novel by Ira Levin, this film begins with the premise that Nazi scientists cloned Hitler just before the end of the war. Placing the clones in 94 families around the world with backgrounds as similar as possible to the Führer was the first step in their plan. The second was to murder the boys' fathers at the same moment in their lives in which Hitler was orphaned in his. The goal of these killings? To control the clones' lives as closely as possible so that at least one of them will grow up to be the new Führer.

This is a hard one to call. On the one hand, the science is intelligently presented. Back when cloning was still science fiction, most writers, and especially screenwriters, got the concept completely wrong, imagining photocopy machine duplicates. On the other hand, much of the movie sinks into pure silliness. Gregory

Peck as Josef Mengele is almost passable, but Olivier as an aging Jewish Nazi hunter is comical. The Jerry Goldsmith soundtrack is excellent, but who wants to watch a fistfight between two of the stiffest ham actors the world has ever seen? Now that cloning is actually here to stay, this one can probably be safely stored in the back of the closet and forgotten.

BRAIN, THE (aka: VENGEANCE)

CCC/Stross (West Germany/Great Britain), 1962/Governor (US), 1965, b&w, 83 min, VT

Producer: Raymond Stross; **Director:** Freddie Francis; **Screenplay:** Robert Stewart and Phil Mackie; **Music:** Ken Jones; **Cinematography:** Bob Huke; **Cast:** Peter Van Eyck, Anne Heywood, Cecil Parker, Bernard Lee, Jack MacGowran

Once again, Curt Siodmak's terrific novel, *Donovan's Brain*, is brought to the screen, reviving the old living-brain-in-the-jar story, but with the twist that this one can telepathically control the scientist who is keeping it alive. Finally, a good job on the third time around.

BRAIN CANDY (aka: KIDS IN THE HALL: BRAIN CANDY)

Paramount, 1996, Color, 88 min, VT, LD

Producer: Lorne Michaels; **Director:** Kelly Makin; **Screenplay:** Norm Hiscock, Scott Thompson, Bruce McCulloch, Kevin McDonald, and Mark McKinney; **Music:** G. Marq Roswell; **Special Effects:** Performance Solutions; **Cinematography:** David A. Makin; **Cast:** David Foley, Bruce McCulloch, Kevin McDonald, Mark McKinney, Scott Thompson, Kathryn Greenwood

This film opens in the cab of possibly the most offensive taxi driver in the world. He is dirty, argumentative, of lesser intelligence, and willing to run over those who get in his way. We quickly learn that he hates the world, but also that it isn't quite the world we know. The cabbie then begins to tell the audience a tale, and the movie flashes back to an undisclosed time in the near future.

The scene is the laboratory of a research development team in a mighty corporation. Dr. Chris Cooper has just developed a drug that will alleviate depression in the clinically depressed. Patient 957 tells the story. She is a severely depressed older woman, a person rendered nearly comatose by her affliction. But after a single dose of "the drug," she comes alive with a happiness and vitality she hasn't known for years. As tests continue, she turns out to be in perfect health. The drug apparently has no dangerous side effects. Cooper and his team are hopeful.

In the meantime, upstairs in the boardroom, a decision has been made—all unprofitable arms of the company are to be jettisoned as quickly as possible. When Cooper is brought before the board, he is pressured into saying that his drug is ready for the marketplace. Losing his lab means putting himself and all his friends out of work as well as losing contact with the girl he loves. It also means being cut off from his antidepression research, his life's work since his severely depressed father committed suicide when he was a child. Faced with this choice, he declares the drug ready. It's given a market-approved color, name, and slogan, and it becomes an instant success. Prescriptions are written, and the clinically depressed and repressed everywhere are soon as happy and open as the giddiest of us. The drug is soon approved for the general public and even pets. Dr. Cooper, having made his Faustian deal, is soon paid off with international popularity. He is the creator of Gleemonex, and the world loves him, until it all starts crashing down.

Patient 957 is found in a coma. She is trapped in her happiest memory, unable to speak or move, unable to do anything but relive that joyous moment over and over in light-speed repetition. Soon others fall into the same state, but when Cooper tries to blow the whistle, the corporation has him diagnosed as clinically depressed. The prescription: take his own drug.

Brain Candy is the absolute best sci-fi comedy ever made, and it should be seen by everyone who enjoys a good, cynical laugh. The Canadian comedy group, The Kids in the Hall, have created a masterpiece, establishing themselves with their first feature film as every bit the masters of this art as the legendary Monty Python crew. The film works on a dozen levels. It's a cautionary tale of the near future, as well as an exposé of corporate greed. Its study of the sneering arrogance that dominates corporate culture is wildly funny. For example, as the CEO flies into headquarters on his helicopter, his second-in-command tries to evaluate the boss's mood. When the helicopter crew can't give him any idea, he settles for the boss's sock color. When told "red," he launches a flurry of activity as everyone rushes to make the appropriate changes in the office setting, including rolling up the blue carpeting and replacing it with red before he gets off the elevator. Sure enough, the boss discreetly checks his socks against the rug when he gets out. He's pleased, and everyone else is happy.

The true level of hilarity involved here can't be conveyed in words. This film simply has to be experienced. The sets are stylish and fantastically imaginative. The five principal performers play almost every part, and they do it with a genius and comedic brilliance rarely seen elsewhere. But be warned: This film is definitely not for everyone. *Brain Candy* pulls no punches. The film takes on all topics and all types of people unflinchingly and is not for the smug or the prudish or those who are easily offended. Nor is it for those who can't process information very quickly, since the picture zooms along at top speed, rapid cutting its multiple story lines and layers of conclusions together with amazing competence and confidence.

Note: There are two awfully quick cameos to watch for in this film. Brendan Fraser appears as the test subject who doesn't want the placebo anymore, and Janeane Garofalo pops up as a stunning girl at a party who is only seen on a monitor.

BRAIN EATERS, THE

AIP, 1958, b&w, 60 min, VT

Producer: Ed Nelson; **Director:** Bruno Ve Sota; **Screenplay:** Gordon Urqhart; **Cinematography:** Larry Raimond; **Cast:** Ed Nelson, Jack Hill, Jody Fair, Joanna Lee, Alan Frost, Leonard Nimoy

This time it's creatures from inside Earth that attach themselves to people and turn them into zombies. It's pointless to watch this one for any other reason than trying to spot a young Leonard Nimoy, after which turn it off.

BRAIN FROM PLANET AROUS, THE

Howco International, 1958, b&w, 71 min, VT

Producer: Jacques Marquette; **Director:** Nathan Hertz; **Screenplay:** Ray Buffum; **Music:** Walter Greene; **Cast:** John Agar, Joyce Meadows, Robert Fuller, Henry Travis, Morris Ankrum, Tom Browne Henry

Gor, the silly, flying evil superbrain from outer space comes to Earth to conquer the world. Using evil supertelepathy, it stashes its mind inside that of John Agar and sets out on its mission. Luckily for Earth, Vol, the silly, flying good superbrain from outer space comes to rescue us. Stashing its mind in a nearby dog,

it sets out to capture Gor and end the picture before the audiences' brains explode. It sounds awful, but it's actually fun to watch if for no other reason than Agar's performance. Trashy, but not *that* trashy.

BRAIN OF BLOOD

Hemisphere, 1971, Color, 88 min

Producer: Sam Sherman; **Director:** Al Adamson; **Screenplay:** Joe Van Rodgers and Kane W. Lynn; **Cast:** Grant Williams, Kent Taylor, Vicki Volanti, John Bloom

Evil scientists conduct brain transplants to create more obedient servants. The results are not nearly as funny as when it was done in THE BOWERY BOYS MEET THE MONSTERS, but then, perhaps it wasn't trying to be.

BRAINSCAN

Admire Productions, 1994, Color, 95 min, VT, LD

Brainscan (JOSEPH B. MAUCERI COLLECTION)

Producers: Earl Berman, Ester Freifeld, Michel Roy, and Jeffrey Sudzin; **Director:** John Flynn; **Screenplay:** Brian Owens and Andrew Kevin Walker; **Music:** George S. Clinton; **Cinematography:** Francois Protat; **Special Effects:** Adrien Horot, Ryal Cosgrove, Rene Daalder, Michael Rivero, and Cineffects, Inc.; **Cast:** Edward Furlong, Frank Langella, T. Ryder Smith, Victor Ertmanis, David Hemblen, Amy Hargreaves, Jamie Marsh, Vlasta Vrana, Domenico Fiore, Claire Riley

Horror movie and video game fan Mike Brower (Furlong) is a teenage loner, practically friendless and somewhat obsessed with his late mother's death. One of his few acquaintances points him toward a new game—Brainscan. They run the game, which involves the player in committing a video murder, and when they come back out to the real world, they discover they might have possibly committed the murder in the real world as well. The film succeeds in being mildly entertaining, mainly thanks to a good cast giving its best effort. The producers seemed intent on creating a new *Friday the 13th* type of franchise through the introduction of "Trickster" (Smith), but the story line is simply too weak.

BRAINSNATCHER, THE

See *THE MAN WHO LIVED AGAIN*

BRAINSTORM

MGM, 1983, Color, 106 min, VT, LD, DVD

Producer: Douglas Trumbull; **Director:** Trumbull; **Screenplay:** Robert Stizel and Philip Frank Messina; **Music:** James Horner; **Special Effects:** Trumbull; **Cast:** Christopher Walken, Natalie Wood, Louise Fletcher, Cliff Robertson, Joe Dorsey, Jordon Christopher

Brainstorm revolves around the concept of a new invention: a sophisticated recording machine that, when linked to superconductive brainwave sensors and the newest computer equipment, reads and stores the complete range of perceptions, new or remembered, of any individual, making those perceptions available as recordings that can then be played back and experienced by anyone. This leads to a dilemma: Do you cash in on such a thing, selling mountain climbing and epic sex to people to enjoy while they wait in line at the post office, or do you reserve such personal and unique

powers for a higher purpose? It's a tough question, especially after one of the researchers dies in the lab, giving the team leader the opportunity to make a recording of what happens inside the brain at the moment of death.

This is an intensely interesting movie, doing what few sci-fi films have ever tried to do (with any intelligence, anyway), and that is to question the morality of science. The film steps over huge metaphysical boundaries with amazing courage and is to be applauded for doing so. Well acted and provocative rather than hard-hitting, Trumbull accomplished a great deal here simply by presenting the topic clearly and letting the audience extrapolate the details.

Unfortunately, the quality of the film and Trumbull's special effects in particular suffer unbelievably on the small screen. The fantastic power of the 70mm, stereophonic epic completely disappears on a television screen. The challenge to Trumbull and his team to recreate human experiences on the screen, enhancing them to trigger a sense of participation on the part of the audience was keenly met. The director created a new process for the film, which transformed audiences from passive observers in a dream to active participants.

BRAIN THAT WOULDN'T DIE, THE

Sterling/Carlton (Great Britain), 1959/AIP(US), 1962, b&w, 81 min, VT

Producer: Rex Carlton; **Director:** Joseph Green; **Screenplay:** Green; **Special Effects:** Byron Baer; **Cinematography:** Stephen Hajnal; **Cast:** Herb Evers, Virginia Leith, Adele Lamont, Paula Maurice, Lola Mason, Leslie Daniel

A surgeon loses his fiancée when her body is crushed in a gruesome car wreck, but he manages to keep her head alive. Then, of course, he's faced with the old problem of who to murder to get a new body for his girl.

BRAVE LITTLE TOASTER, THE

Disney Productions, 1987, Color, 90 min, VT, LD

Producer: Peter Locke; **Director:** Jerry Rees; **Screenplay:** Thomas M. Disch, Joe Ranft, and Rees; **Animation:** Mark Dinal; **Music:** David Newman; **Cast:** Voices of Jon Lovitz, Tim Stack, Timothy E. Day, Thurl Ravenscroft, Deanna Oliver, Phil Hartman

Tom Disch's whimsical novel about a group of anthropomorphic household appliances that set off in search of their young master is well adapted for the screen in this animated feature. The film is light and fun, and its intelligent sense of humor will keep parents watching with their kids.

BRAZIL

Universal, 1985, Color, 131 min, VT, LD, DVD

Producers: Arnon Milchan and Patrick Cassavetti; **Director:** Terry Gilliam; **Screenplay:** Gilliam, Tom Stoppard, and Charles McKeown; **Music:** Michael Kamen; **Special Effects:** Richard Conway and George Gibbs; **Cinematography:** Roger Pratt; **Cast:** Jonathan Pryce, Kim Greist, Robert De Niro, Katherine Helmond, Ian Holm, Bob Hoskins, Michael Palin, Ian Richardson, Peter Vaughn

Not all future worlds need to have suffered a nuclear holocaust to be bleak and forbidding. George Orwell knew that, and so apparently does Terry Gilliam.

A government clerk (Pryce) tries to hold onto his minor rung in life, not to keep from being thrown into the streets, but to keep from advancing any higher. He likes his nice quiet safe life down in the anonymous pool of people below middle management. Then a bureaucratic snafu crosses his path with (literally) the girl of his dreams. He loses her. He must find her. But it is soon made clear to him that the only way to do that is to accept the promotion he has always dreaded. Once he does, the trouble begins.

Brazil is a dreadfully frightening look at what could be civilization's next step forward. Perhaps, only an American like Gilliam, thoroughly indoctrinated in the ways of British socialism as a member of the comedy troupe Monty Python's Flying Circus, could have created the monstrous superpowered, all-intrusive government and nightmarish future envisioned in this film. The audience knows that the clerk is doomed from the beginning. It's obvious that any dreamer in such a society would be doomed. The irony is that the audience for such a film is made up of dreamers and that the society on the screen is only a few steps away from the one they live in.

Brazil is top-notch social science fiction. The movie is thoroughly chilling, as it must be because of the serious themes it tackles. But the jokes are terrific, the effects are outlandish and unbelievable, the pacing crisp to the point of breathlessness, and the ending is a complete surprise and yet totally inevitable. And does

it have to be noted that the ending of this film—the thing that critics and audiences applauded around the world, the ending which disappointed no one but astounded everyone—was fought tooth and nail by the studio executives?

Of course it does.

Gilliam had to fight for over a year after the film was completed to keep his vision intact. The proposed changes and alternative ending would have completely altered the film's message, sanitizing it horribly and robbing it of absolutely every bit of its power. It was an ugly, stupid battle, but in the end it was won, for once, by the good guy, an event giving us two things of value: a tremendously entertaining and important movie and another proof that the powers that be in Hollywood can often be counted on to demand the right to shoot not only themselves in the foot, but everyone around them as well.

BRICK BRADFORD

Columbia, 1947, b&w, Serial, 15 chapters

Producer: Sam Katzman; **Director:** Spenser G. Bennett and Thomas Carr; **Screenplay:** George H. Plympton, Arthur Hoerd, and Lewis Clay; **Cast:** Kane Richmond, Pierre Watkin, Rick Valin, Linda Johnson, John Merton, Charles Quigley

Comic-strip character Brick Bradford (Richmond) has to protect the Interceptor Ray, the world's first antimissile device. This involves his traveling both to the Moon and back and through time, all in the scientifically forward year of 1947. One might think a country that can shatter the boundaries of time and send its agents to the Moon by having them walk through a secret door wouldn't have too much to worry about from the enemies the world of that era produced. Sitting through all 15 episodes of this could qualify for some sort of endurance record, but wherever this one is being stored these days, leave it there.

BRIDE OF FRANKENSTEIN

Universal, 1935, b&w, 80 min, VT, LD

Producer: Carl Laemmle, Jr.; **Director:** James Whale; **Screenplay:** John Balderston and William Hurlbut; **Cinematography:** John J. Mescall; **Music:** Franz Waxman, **Special Effects:** John P. Fulton and Jack Pierce; **Cast:** Boris Karloff, Colin Clive, Valerie Hobson, Ernest Thesiger, Elsa Lanchester, Una O'Connor,

E.E. Clive, Gavin Gordon, Douglas Walton, O.P. Heggie, Dwight Frye, John Carradine

See *FRANKENSTEIN*

BRIDE OF RE-ANIMATOR

Wildstreet, 1990, Color, 99 min, VT, LD

Producers: Dean Ramser, Brian Yuzna, and Paul White; **Director:** Yuzna; **Screenplay:** Yuzna, Rick Fry, and Woody Keith; **Cinematography:** Rick Fichter; **Music:** Richard Band; **Special Effects:** Anthony Doublin; **Cast:** Jeffrey Combs, Bruce Abbott, Claude Earl Jones, Fabian Udenio, David Gale, Kathleen Kinmont

See *HERBERT WEST: RE-ANIMATOR*

BRIDE OF THE MONSTER

DCA, 1956, b&w, 69 min, VT, DVD

Producer: Edward D. Wood, Jr.; **Director:** Wood; **Screenplay:** Wood and Alex Gordon; **Music:** Frank Worth; **Special Effects:** Pat Dinga; **Cast:** Bela Lugosi, Tor Johnson, Tony McCoy, Loretta King, William Benedict, Eddie Parker

The sinister Dr. Varnoff (Lugosi) and his assistant (Johnson) attempt to create a race of giants in this laughable outing.

But, and this is a really big "but," perhaps we have to give Edward Wood, Jr., some credit. The man really did try. His movies were awful, but, despite that, they still create the feeling that he thought he was doing something important. And perhaps he was. Countless midnight-show audiences have been treated to peals of laughter during the conclusion of this film as they watch poor, dying Bela Lugosi try to summon up a shred of dignity while floundering about with a rubber octopus attempting to make it look as if the obviously phony thing were choking the life from him. And, if nothing else, he gave poor Lugosi and Tor Johnson work when they really needed it.

BRIEF HISTORY OF TIME, A

International (Great Britain), 1992, Color, 84 min, VT

Producer: Errol Morris; **Music:** Philip Glass; **Cinematography:** John Bailey and Stefan Czapsky; **Editor:** Brad Fuller

Bride of Re-animator (JOSEPH B. MAUCERI COLLECTION)

A brilliant documentary study of cosmologist Stephen Hawking and his book by the same title. The film allows Hawking, through the use of a voice synthesizer, to explain the basic nature of the universe in clear, precise everyday terminology easily understandable to the average viewer. Excellent work on both Hawking's part and documentary filmmaker Morris, for whom this was just another in a series of documentary film triumphs, make this indispensable viewing for those interested in the way things *really* work.

BROOD, THE

New World Pictures, 1979, Color, 91 min, VT, LD

Producer: Claude Heroux; **Director:** David Cronenberg; **Screenplay:** Cronenberg; **Music:** Howard Shore; **Cast:** Oliver Reed, Art Hindle, Samantha Eggar, Cindy Hinds, Nuala Fitzgerald, Michael McGhee, Felix Silva, Susan Hogan

Dad (Hindle) wants to keep his psychotic wife (Eggar) away from their child. Mom's psychiatrist (Reed) is a new age–style doctor who encourages his charges to push their troubles out of their minds. Eggar complies well beyond expectations, creating the title's brood by literally giving birth to a twisted group of deformed ghouls who scatter across the countryside to kill all those who have troubled her.

What at first seems like just another run-of-the-mill, confusing bit of nothing comes together slowly as the psi-horror mounts, building up to a real shocker by the end. Oliver Reed turns in a performance that is more fun than usual. This is a stand-out creeper, admittedly short on science fiction other than the ingeniously bizarre birthing concept, but that's enough to list it here and disturbing enough to keep viewers awake at night.

BROTHER FROM ANOTHER PLANET, THE

A-Train Films, 1984, Color, 104 min, VT

Producer: Peggy Rajski; **Director:** John Sayles; **Screenplay:** Sayles; **Music:** Mason Darling; **Cinematography:** Ernest R. Dickerson; **Cast:** Joe Morton, Darryl Edwards, Steve James, Leonard Jackson, Maggie Renzi, Rosetta Le Noire, David Strathairn

A black extraterrestrial (Morton) escapes his slaver captors and finds his way to Earth. Hiding in New York City—specifically in the Bronx—he makes a lot of statements about the African-American condition without actually saying a word. The brother from another planet doesn't speak, but he creates a fairly big stir nonetheless. In truth, the picture gets bogged down toward the end when it loses its focus somewhat, but overall it stands as a powerful social commentary with just enough humor and bizarre effects to satisfy most audiences.

This is an interesting film, particularly for African-American science fiction fans or any fans who would like to see a sci-fi film that treats the African-American experience a little more thoroughly than George Lucas did by sticking Billy Dee Williams into *THE EMPIRE STRIKES BACK* after some outcry over the all-white cast of *STAR WARS*. If nothing else, no one had to be shamed into making this one. Comedian Richard Pryor's old line about there being no blacks in *2001: A SPACE ODYSSEY* because the white people had decided that there wouldn't be any blacks by then might be outdated now, but in its time the joke certainly described at least one segment of sci-fi filmdom accurately enough.

Star Joe Morton deserves special praise for suffering innumerable hardships during the making of the film. The story line called for him to suffer a number of physical hardships, but he endured it all gladly to be working on a sci-fi picture that would have some relevance to African-American audiences. But he also worked hard to make certain he was helping to create a good science fiction film. In an interview with the author, Morton said, "Every day I would have to be hosed down—we spent an entire night on Ellis Island, which meant that off and on throughout the night, I would have to be tied and untied so the circulation could come back to my leg. And then tied again, and then untied again. And then drenched.

"It's an interesting thing to work on one leg," he explained, "because, at first, you think you'll need an awful lot of time just dealing with balance, but you find that the human body just compensates like crazy . . . to the point where in one scene, I had to do a complete 360 on one foot, and I could do it with ease. What I was trying to do with the Brother was to show that this kind of thing had probably happened to him more than once. Where he's lost an arm or a leg, his body would just automatically compensate, so I wanted to make it look like to him, this was no big thing."

BUBBLE, THE (aka: FANTASTIC INVASION OF PLANET EARTH)

Midwestern Magic, 1966, Color, 112 min, VT

Producer: Arch Oboler; **Director:** Oboler; **Screenplay:** Oboler; **Music:** Paul Sawtell and Bert Shafter; **Cast:** Michael Cole, Deborah Walley, Johnny Desmond

A trio of unusually bemused people discover that they have been trapped in a giant force field placed over an entire town by aliens. The result is static and bizarre and a little more than twice as long as it needs to be, and that's only if one insists that it needs to be at all.

BUCKAROO BANZAI

See *THE ADVENTURES OF BUCKAROO BANZAI ACROSS THE EIGHTH DIMENSION*

BUCK ROGERS

Universal, 1939, b&w, 12 episodes VT, DVD

Directors: Ford Beebe and Saul A. Goodkind; **Screenplay:** Norman S. Hall and Ray Trampe; **Cast:** Buster Crabbe, Constance Moore, C. Montague Shaw, Jack Moran, Henry Brandon

The popular comic-strip hero Buck Rogers is brought to life for the Saturday morning set. The Zuggs of Saturn have invaded Earth with the help of the despicable Killer Kane. Despite the popularity of the title character, this serial is mentioned here only because Buck Rogers helped start the science fiction genre, not because the series is any good.

BUCK ROGERS IN THE 25TH CENTURY

Universal, 1979, Color, 89 min, VT

Producer: Leslie Stevens; **Director:** Daniel Haller; **Screenplay:** Stevens and Glen Larson; **Music:** Stu Phillips; **Special Effects:** Scott Squires; **Cinematography:** Frank Beascoechea; **Cast:** Gil Gerard, Pamela Hensley, Erin Gray, Tim O'Conner, Henry Silva, Joseph Wiseman, Felix Sila, voice of Mel Blanc

In 1987 (ha ha), NASA launches the *last* of their piloted deep-space probes. It's blown off its trajectory by a meteor shower, and thus its captain, Buck Rogers (Gerard), doesn't get to where he's going. Frozen in suspended animation, he is out of circulation until retrieved by an evil alien princess in the 25th century. She attempts to use him to break through the future Earth's defenses. He plays along in order to escape and reaches Earth, only to find more trouble from the paranoid military leaders there than he did from the bikini-baubled princess who wanted to make him her king.

The film is based on the comic strip of the same name, which helped launch the modern visual science fiction era, paving the way for all the laser-wielding swashbucklers to follow. Sharply updated and backed by the best special effects available at the time, the picture still tried to stay faithful to its source material—a contemporary man time-warped into a future era that desperately needs someone who thinks with his fists as often as he does with his brains. In the original, it was a strange gas in a mine shaft that put our hero to sleep for half a millennium, but here, Einsteinian theory and a bit of rubber science do the trick.

Critics complained at the time of the film's release that the movie was a STAR WARS rip-off filled with bad science. In this film's defense, let's remember that Buck was first, and that bad science was a hallmark of the strip's stories. The filmmakers decided to be as faithful as they could to the original without embarrassing themselves, and they succeeded for the most part. The film even helped launch a fairly successful television series.

At its worst, this movie does go along with the precepts set down by a lot of the other sci-fi/fantasy films of its time, such as spaceships that make noise in a vac-

uum, cute robots, tough no-nonsense heroines who resist the hero, and others. At its best, however, it's entertaining and amusing, mostly because it exhibits an enlightened self-awareness missing from most such endeavors. It's meant to be light entertainment, which is only to be expected from a picture that has Mel Blanc (better known as the voice of Bugs Bunny) on hand to do the voice of its lead robot. Hopefully, science fiction hasn't become such a stuffy place that lighthearted adventure doesn't still have its place. As writer Ray Bradbury observed in his introduction to *The Collected Works of Buck Rogers*, "Without romance, without fun, the soul of man turns over, curls up its toes, groans, withers, and dies." *Buck Rogers* is good fun for anyone at least as open-minded as Ray Bradbury.

BUG

Universal, 1979, Color, 89 min, VT

Producer: William Castle; **Director:** Jeannot Szwarc; **Screenplay:** Castle and Thomas Page; **Music:** Charles Fox; **Special Effects:** Phil Cory; **Cinematography:** Michael Hugo; **Cast:** Bradford Dillman, Joanna Mills, Richard Gilliland, Jamie Smith Jackson, Alan Fudge, Patricia McCormack, Jesse Vint

An earthquake sets loose a swarm of bugs that can set fires through the rapid motion of their hind legs. One of the things they seem to like to set afire most is people. After his wife is killed by these creatures, scientist Dillman works to destroy the invaders. He sets out to communicate with them, and succeeds in cross-breeding them with more garden-variety insects to create a bug that can spell. Perhaps the cross-breeding was a mistake on Dillman's part, but he soon pays the price for it, falling into the crack in the Earth from which the bugs first appeared. It closes then, for no apparent reason, and the world is safe. Based on Thomas Page's novel *The Hephaestus Plague*, this was the last movie from producer William Castle, whose remarkable career deserved a more memorable conclusion.

BY RADIUM RAYS

Universal, 1914, b&w, two-reel silent feature

A psychopath is treated (and cured) with radium.

BY ROCKET TO THE MOON

See *WOMAN IN THE MOON*

CAGE OF DOOM

See *TERROR FROM THE YEAR 5000*

CALTIKI, THE IMMORTAL MONSTER
(aka: THE IMMORTAL MONSTER)

Allied Artists, 1959, b&w, 76 min

Producer: Bruno Vailanti; **Director:** Riccardo Freda; **Screenplay:** Fillippo Sanjust; **Music:** Román Vlad; **Cinematography:** Mario Bava; **Special Effects:** Bava; **Cast:** John Merivale, Hampton Sullivan, Gerard Herter, Daniela Rocca

A big, dumb blob chases an expedition across Mexico. It dies in flames at the end because it can't climb a ladder. The film is more humorous than anything else, though it bears all the trademark stylistic elements of a picture filmed by Mario Bava and with special effects by Mario Bava. Reportedly, Bava also completed the directorial chores.

CAPE CANAVERAL MONSTERS

CCM, 1960, b&w, 69 min, VT

Producer: Richard Greer; **Director:** Phil Tucker; **Screenplay:** Tucker; **Music:** Gunthar Kaur; **Cinematography:** Merle Connell; **Cast:** Scott Peters, Linda Connell, Katherine Victor, Jason Johnson, Frank Smith

Alien monsters, who possess only an intellect with no corporeal flesh to go with it, inhabit and animate recently deceased corpses. The reason for creating interplanetary zombies? They want to shoot down U.S. rockets and thus cripple the country's space program. Since intangible creatures of the mind alone and those with bodies would in no way compete for resources, this one doesn't make much sense. Then again, maybe they just wanted to warn Earth to stop broadcasting all that rock 'n' roll into space.

CAPRICORN ONE

Warner Bros., 1978, Color, 127 min, VT, LD, DVD

Producer: Paul N. Lazarus; **Director:** Peter Hyams; **Screenplay:** Hyams; **Music:** Jerry Goldsmith; **Cinematography:** Bill Butler; **Cast:** James Brolin, Hal Holbrook, Sam Waterston, O.J. Simpson, Elliot Gould, Telly Savalas, Brenda Vaccaro, David Doyle, Denise Nichols, Robert Walden, Lee Bryant, Karen Black

The time is approaching for NASA's first manned flight to Mars. Everything is ready, but at the last moment a malfunction causes the flight to be scrubbed. NASA doesn't want to lose its funding, though, or the interest of the American people, which is so intimately tied to its funding, so a wild plan is shoved into immediate operation. The crew of the ship (Brolin, Waterston, and Simpson) is secretly removed from the craft, taken to a hidden television studio in the desert, and conned into going along with a fairly wild scheme: Stay there in the desert and pretend to still be on the mission. All they have to do is hang around, send radio messages, and perform for the cameras once in a while, and when the automatic rocket returns from space, pretend to be picked up at sea and get a big heroes' welcome and the gratitude of the space program and thus history itself. The astronauts will have secured the continuation of the program and assured that man will reach the stars, while also becoming the most important explorers of all time.

After a while, though, the whole plan begins to rankle with the astronauts, a situation only worsened when the automatic rocket burns up in Earth's atmosphere upon return. This gives NASA two choices—admit the fraud and return the boys to their lives (the government admit a mistake—hey, everybody, don't worry, it was just a gag) or kill the astronauts, dump their hero bodies in an unmarked mass grave, and carry on nobly in their honor. It shouldn't be hard to guess which option they choose, and then the film leaps into high gear as the three astronauts make a run for it, trying to survive the desert in an attempt to blow the lid on NASA's conspiracy and save their own lives in the bargain.

This great film was one of the first important science fiction movies to really exploit the idea that the government is not to be trusted, and certainly the first to embrace the *X-Files*–style paranoia that was still 15 years off. It was inevitable, though. Back in 1969, after the first Moon walk, polls showed that nearly 30 percent of the American people simply did not believe that the event had taken place, despite seeing the event on their own television sets (an important fact to remember the next time one wonders why science fiction isn't more popular).

That fact was one of the major inspirations behind the Peter Hyams's story for *Capricorn One*. When discussing the origins of his project, Hyams recalled, "I remember watching Walter Cronkite during one of the *Apollo* shots. They cut to what was called a simulation—that is, mock-ups and models done onstage. It looked exactly like the real thing, and I muttered, 'Wow! How do we *know*?' We knew what an astronaut looked like venturing weightlessly in space, attached to his vehicle by an umbilical cord and safe in his space suit as he went about the business of examining the outside of the capsule. We knew because we had seen it in Kubrick's *2001*."

No one was interested in Hyams's script at first, but, in the aftermath of Watergate, he suddenly had a hot property. Luckily for the world of sci-fi fandom, Hyams didn't just cash in on his good fortune and rush out a quickie exploitation picture. The filmmaker purposely picked second-string stars who would not overshadow his main idea. He also recreated the surface of Mars as faithfully as possible. Although the agency's VIPs were portrayed in far less than flattering lights, NASA (along with the Pasadena Jet Propulsion Laboratory) helped the production in reproducing Mars, loaned them a command module, and cooperated totally with assistance in all areas of scientific technology relevant to the space program.

The film is not overly technical, but it is as accurate as it could be when it was made, aside from the puzzling omission of any compensation for the billions of bits of technical data the astronauts should have been transmitting back to Earth. And, although the picture's hard science is only slightly advanced beyond its time, its social science asks questions rarely broached in its day, putting it far ahead of the rest of the pack.

CAPTAIN AMERICA (aka: THE RETURN OF CAPTAIN AMERICA)

Republic, 1943, b&w serial, 15 chapters/31 reels

Directors: John English and Elmer Clifton; **Screenplay:** Royal Cole, Ronald Davidson, Basil Dickey, Jesse Duffy, Harry Fraser, Grant Nelson, and Joe Poland; **Special Effects:** Howard and Theodore Lydecker; **Cinematography:** John MacBurnie; **Cast:** Dick Purcell, Lionel Atwill, Lorna Grey, Charles Trowbridge, Jay Novello, Frank Reicher, George J. Lewis

Taking the wildly popular comic book character's name and costume and then ignoring everything else about the star-spangled avenger, the Republic serial squad cranked out another 15 weeks of nonsense in their never-ending attempt to fill the Saturday morning movie houses with their product. In this one the good captain battles a museum curator who is disguising himself as a supervillain, the Scarab. Science fiction devices include the Purple Death poison and the Thunder Bolt weapon among others, all unexplained and silly. Lionel Atwill is more fun than ever as the Scarab and deserves a round of applause for maintaining his dignity amid the usual potboiler mash. Not really worth the time of anyone other than crazed Atwill fans, such as the author.

CAPTAIN NEMO AND THE UNDERWATER CITY

MGM, 1970, Color, 106 min

Producer: Bertram Ostrer; **Director:** James Hill; **Screenplay:** R. Wright Campbell plus Pip and Jane Baker; **Music:** Walter Scott; **Cast:** Robert Ryan, Chuck Connors, Luciana Paluzzi, Kenneth Conner

Some time after his supposed death in Ray Harryhausen's version of *MYSTERIOUS ISLAND*, this lesser follow-up finds the good captain Nemo (Ryan) having built an underwater city. When a group of surface dwellers discover it, they get along well enough with Nemo until they discover that the by-product of his oxygen-producing machinery is gold. The rest should be obvious.

CAPTAIN ULTRA

Toei, 1962, Color

Director: Koichi Takemoto; **Cast:** Yuki Shirono, Hirohisa Nakata, Nenji Kobayashi

A bombastic Japanese superhero slugs it out with sinister aliens.

CAPTAIN VIDEO

Columbia, 1951, b&w, 15 chapters/30 reels

Producer: Sam Katzman; **Directors:** Spencer G. Bennett and Wallace A. Grissell; **Screenplay:** Royal K. Cole, Sherman Lowe, and Joe Poland; **Music:** Mischa Bakaleinikoff; **Special Effects:** Jack Erickson; **Cast:** Judd Holdren, Larry Stewart, Gene Roth, William Fawcett

Bad guy Vultura of Atoma is attacking Earth and it's up to Captain Video (Holdren) and his Rocket Rangers to save the day. Older fans who remember the television show will like the serial. In truth, there is a bit of campy fun here and there, but watching more than 15 minutes will wear on most any modern viewer.

CAPTIVE WILD WOMAN

See *JUNGLE WOMAN*

CAPTIVE WOMEN

RKO, 1952, b&w, 65 min

Producers: Jack Pollexfen and Aubery Wisberg; **Director:** Stuart Gilmore; **Screenplay:** Pollexen and Wisberg; **Music:** Charles Koff; **Cinematography:** Paul Ivano; **Cast:** Robert Clarke, Margaret Field, Ron Randell, Gloria Saunders

In a savage future brought about by man's reckless use of atomic bombs (sigh . . . that again), the world is divided into the Norms, the Mutes (those who are mutated, not silent), and the Uplanders. A time-travel visit from contemporary men (the same misguided bunch who are going to throw all those destructive atomic weapons around recklessly) is what it takes to save the future from descending into savagery. Nice trick.

It's hard to keep shaking a stick at the thousands of apocalyptic future movies while praising so many other films for questioning the social problems of their time. Why shouldn't concern over nuclear arms be just as valid a question? Well, it is valid—*when used with some validity*. But the problem with almost every movie to ever use such a premise is that no one connected to the production was worrying about the future of humankind. Their only real concern was how to make a movie with people in cheap costumes, using spears, and still call it science fiction. *BENEATH THE PLANET OF THE APES* is a good example of a movie with a social conscience regarding nuclear proliferation. Most of the others are just nonsense.

CARNOSAUR

New Horizon Picture Corp., 1993, Color, 82 min, VT, LD, DVD

Producer: Roger Corman; **Director:** Adam Simon; **Screenplay:** Simon; **Music:** Nigel Holton; **Special Effects:** Alan Lasky and Tuck John Porter; **Cinematography:** Keith Holland; **Cast:** Diane Ladd, Raphael Sharge, Jennifer Runyon, Harrison Page, Ned Bellamy, Clint Howard

Scientist Ladd has nothing better to do than breed wildly hungry carnivorous dinosaurs from diseased chicken eggs. Then she finds out how much more fun it is to turn them loose to go marauding across the countryside. One wonders how Corman stays in business. Followed by the even worse *CARNOSAUR II* and, well what else, *CARNOSAUR III*.

CARNOSAUR II

New Horizon Picture Corp., 1995, Color, 83 min, VT, DVD

Producer: Roger Corman; **Director:** Louis Morneau; **Screenplay:** Michael Palmer; **Music:** Ed Tomney; **Cinematography:** John B. Aronson; **Cast:** John Savage, Cliff De Young, Don Stroud, Rick Dean, Ryan Thomas Johnson, Arabella Holzbog, Miguel A. Nunez, Jr., Rodman Flender

See CARNOSAUR

CARNOSAUR III: PRIMAL SPECIES

Concorde-New Horizons, 1993, Color, 82 min, VT, LD, DVD

Producer: Roger Corman; **Director:** Johnathan Winfrey; **Music:** Kevin Kiner; **Special Effects:** John Carl Buechler; **Cinematography:** Andrea V. Rosotto; **Cast:** Scott Valentine, Janet Gunn, Morgan Englund, Rick Dean, Paul Darrigo, Justina Vail, Rodman Flender, Jonathan Winfrey

See CARNOSAUR

CASTLE IN THE SKY

See LAPUTA

CASTLE OF EVIL

National Telefilms Associates, 1966, Color, 81 min, VT

Director: Francis D. Lyon; **Screenplay:** Charles A. Wallace; **Music:** Paul Dunlap; **Special Effects:** Roger George; **Cast:** William Thourlby, David Brian, Virginia Mayo, Scott Brady, Hugh Marlowe, Lisa Gayle, Shelley Morrison

After the death of a deformed scientist, those suspected of his deformation are gathered on his island retreat for a reading of his will in this science fiction version of Agatha Christie's *Ten Little Indians*. At that time, a robot double of the scientist begins murdering the suspects. Everyone thinks they're safe after the first killing, assuming the old guy got his revenge, but the bodies continue to pile up. There's a nice twist on the Christie original: One of the guests has reprogrammed the robot to keep killing everyone else so

that the reprogrammer will eventually inherit everything. This nice twist, however, is the only good thing about the movie, and it's a slight thing at that, so since it's already been revealed here, don't waste time seeing this one.

CAT FROM OUTER SPACE, THE

Walt Disney/Buena Vista, 1978, Color, 103 min, VT, DVD

Producer: Ron Miller; **Director:** Norman Tokar; **Screenplay:** Ted Key; **Music:** Lalo Schifrin; **Special Effects:** Eustace Lycett, Art Cruickshank, and Danny Lee; **Cinematography:** Charles F. Wheeler; **Cast:** Ken Berry, Sandy Duncan, Harry Morgan, Roddy McDowall, Ronnie Schell, Hans Conreid, Jesse White, McLean Stevenson

Science fiction takes another blow as a genre in this Disney production. This time it's an alien that looks just like an Earthly house cat. Parallel evolutionary development? It's anybody's guess. But when the kitty's ship needs desperate repairs, it lands on Earth, hoping some kindly schnook will pony up the fortune in gold it needs to fix its ship. Enter three schnooks (Berry, Duncan, and Stevenson) who come up with a plan. Outside of some interesting similarities to the later film *E.T.*, this one has little value outside of keeping very small and somewhat unsophisticated children amused for 103 minutes.

CAT WOMEN OF THE MOON
(aka: MISSILE TO THE MOON, ROCKET TO THE MOON)

Astor, 1954, b&w, 64 min, VT, DVD

Producers: Jack Rabin and Al Zimbalist; **Director:** Arthur Hilton; **Screenplay:** Roy Hamilton; **Music:** Elmer Bernstein; **Special Effects:** Jack Rabin; **Cast:** Sonny Tufts, Marie Windsor, Victor Jory, Susan Morrow, Carol Brewster, Bill Phipps, Douglas Fowley

This somewhat all-star, supposedly serious version of *ABBOTT AND COSTELLO GO TO MARS* follows a group of astronauts who discover a race of Lunar beauty queens living underground. Like Abbott and Costello, our heroes have the same problem with their women in that they can't decide whether or not to kill them or cuddle with them. It's no real surprise to anyone that everything works out in the end. Only the Elmer Bernstein soundtrack is worthwhile.

CAVES OF STEEL

BBC-TV (Great Britain), 1967, b&w, 75 min

Director: Eric Taylor; **Cast:** Peter Cushing, Eric Taylor

Technically a television production, this BBC effort adapts Isaac Asimov's book about a Holmes/Watson teaming between a human and a robot, with the robot playing Watson, no less.

CELL, THE

New Line Cinema, 2000, Color, 107 min

Producers: Donna Langley, Carolyn Manetti, Mark Protosevich, Stephen J. Ross, Julio Caro, and Eric McLeod; **Director:** Tarsem Singh; **Screenplay:** Protosevich; **Music:** Howard Shore; **Cinematography:** Paul Laufer; **Special Effects:** Kevin Tod Haug, K.N.B. EFX Group, Inc., Clay Pinney, John Baker, Bill Harrison, Lauren Ritchie, Leslie McMinn, Stephanie Wilson, Dennis Berardi, Alex Boothby, Michael Ellis, BUF, Toybox, Image Savant, Amalgamated Pixels, Pixel Liberation Front, Black Box Digital and Company 3; **Cast:** Jennifer Lopez, Vince Vaughn, Colton James, Vincent D'Onofrio, Dylan Baker, Marianne Jean-Baptiste, Gerry Becker, Musetta Vander, Patrick Bauchau, Catherine Sutherland, James Gammon, Jake Weber, Dean Norris, Tara Subkoff, Lauri Johnson, John Cothran, Jr., Jack Conley, Kamar De Los Reyes

FBI Agent Peter Novak (Vaughn) is closing in on serial killer Carl Stargher (D'Onofrio), who recently abducted Anne Marie Vicksey (Sutherland) and placed her in a cell that will automatically flood with water and drown her when its timer runs out. Before the FBI can take Stargher into custody, however, he suffers a brain hemorrhage resulting from a preexisting condition and falls into a permanent coma. Novak, willing to try anything to find the missing Vicksey, turns to psychologist Catherine Deane (Lopez), who has been experimenting with a radical new therapy that combines drugs and technology to allow her to actually enter the mind of her patient.

Deane has 40 hours in which to place herself within Stargher's consciousness, gain his trust, and then discover where Vicksey has been hidden so that Novak can rescue her. The problem is that Stargher's mind is so radically unbalanced that his subconscious landscape differs wildly from any Deane has experienced in her previous work with the new therapy. She isn't prepared for the onslaught of overpowering images within Stargher's brain and soon discovers that if she allows herself to accept what she sees as real, she may be trapped within the killer's mind.

While *The Cell* can be given credit for its use of special effects in its incredible presentation of mythological and dreamlike images, it is ultimately little more than a visual feast. Much of the action and imagery proved too violent and sadistic for some audiences, and the general failure of the story, which offers the barest thread of a plot and little characterization, remained apparent even beneath the dazzling special effects.

CHAIRMAN, THE (aka: THE MOST DANGEROUS MAN IN THE WORLD)

20th Century Fox, 1969, Color, 104 min

Director: J. Lee Thompson; **Screenplay:** Ben Maddow; **Cast:** Gregory Peck, Anne Heywood, Arthur Hill, Conrad Yama

Scientist Peck is sent on an undercover mission into Communist China, where he's expected to convince the Chinese he is a defector and gain access to their newest secret—a formula that will allow food to grow anywhere in the world. What the Chinese don't know is that Peck has a transmitter in his head, allowing the boys back home to listen in on everything he says and hears. What Peck doesn't know is that besides having a transmitter in his head, he has a bomb there as well—one that will allow the boys back home to atomize him and his surroundings if they suddenly don't like something he says or hears or does. The premise is somewhat insulting, considering how many Chinese people starved to death during the period the film was made, but on the other hand, the film isn't all bad and serves up some small food for thought.

CHANGE OF MIND

Cinerama, 1969, Color, 103 min

Producers: Seeleg Lester and Richard Wesson; **Director:** Robert Stevens; **Screenplay:** Lester and Wesson; **Music:** Duke Ellington; **Cinematography:** Arthur J. Ornitz; **Cast:** Raymond St. Jacques, Susan Oliver, Leslie Nielsen, Janet MacLachlan, Donnelly Rhodes, David Bailey

For emergency reasons, a white man's brain is transplanted into a black man's body. The idea is preposterously contrived, to say the least, but the racial questions propelling the story are valid, so the politics of the film don't undercut it as badly as one might think. Though it may offer a cast of second bananas, they're top-notch second bananas who do a reasonable job with what they've been given. It's surprisingly watchable, especially thanks to its soundtrack supplied by Ellington.

CHARIOTS OF THE GODS?

(U.S.), 1974, Color, 98 min, VT, LD

Director: Harald Reini

Documentary based on the book by Erich Von Daniken about helpful, nurturing space aliens who visited Earth millennia ago to shepherd the human race to its current state of wisdom and serene development.

After a decade of TV programming about the same subject matter, people might want to roll their eyes at such an effort, but this was the first of such projects, and so deserves an extra heaping of abuse for helping to whet people's appetites. Von Daniken's books are fairly nonsensical, and watching the perfectly valid questions from an audience full of college anthropology majors turn the good doctor into a stuttering fumble-wit in the early '70s didn't do much to elevate the author's opinion of his work. In the time since Von Daniken advanced his ideas, little has been found to support them and much has become apparent to refute them. To be fair, however, the documentary is a good adaptation of the book with solid photography and nice location work.

CHARLY

Cinerama, 1968, Color, 106 min

Producer: Ralph Nelson; **Director:** Nelson; **Screenplay:** Sterling Silliphant; **Music:** Ravi Shankar; **Cinematography:** Arthur J. Ornitz; **Cast:** Cliff Robertson, Claire Bloom, Leon Janney, Lilia Skala, Dick Van Patten, Ruth White

Charly (Robertson) is a mentally retarded man in his thirties. He isn't smart, but he is happy, and he has as reasonably a happy life as anyone, maybe more so, since he's not smart enough to know how unhappy he is supposed to be. When a team of scientists give him the possible chance at the intelligence that has always been outside his grasp, Charly takes the offer and, after an operation, he and his test-control buddy, a mouse

named Algernon, both seem to be all right. Actually, they seem much more than all right. Each begins to gets smarter and smarter at an incredible rate. Soon Charly is more intelligent than the people who gave him the operation. He and one of his doctors fall in love. He is the darling of the scientific community. But just when he's about to receive his biggest reward of all, the news comes that Algernon has died. The effects of the experiment are not permanent. Charly and his lover launch into a desperate hurricane of research, pushing the limits of endurance as they try to find a way to reverse the inevitable, but they are doomed to fail. The doctor vows to stay with Charly and love him anyway, but wisely Charly knows better. In possibly the most heartbreaking moment in science fiction, the rational man states the obvious and returns to his old existence.

This is a science fiction film in the truest sense. Not only does it draw on speculative hard science in the scientists' work supplying a person with superintelligence, but it remains true to its nature, especially in the ending wherein logic triumphs over sentiment. One critic wrote: "Regardless of his intelligence, Charly is a man, not a mouse, and the tendency for behavioral science to mask distinctions between intellect and emotion, between mind and body, leads to misguided schemes whose premise is that if we were only smarter we could solve the world's problems." Intelligent, rational, and yet tender through all its tragic horror, this film tackles some of the basic questions about the nature of humanity. Its unflinching courage comes from the manner in which it examines the role intellect plays in making us who we are without holding back the hard truths about both its value and its limitations.

A labor of love for star Cliff Robertson, the film was made largely due to his efforts. He bought the rights to Daniel Keyes's novel *Flowers for Algernon*, upon which the film is based, and then formed his own production company to produce the film according to his vision. Robertson won a well-deserved Academy Award for Best Actor, and the picture might have swept the Oscars if not for some of the superfluous scenes added by the filmmakers that never appeared in the original book.

CHEMIST, THE

20th Century Fox, 1936, b&w, 21 min

Producer: Al Christie; **Screenplay:** David Freedman; **Cinematography:** George Webber; **Cast:** Buster Keaton, Marilyn Stuart, Earl Gilbert

Keaton playing a wacky scientist invents a formula that will allow people to be shrunk and then enlarged once more at will. This short offers typical Keaton hysterics, which means lots of fun but little science fiction.

CHERRY 2000

Orion Pictures, 1988, Color, 93 min, VT, LD

Producers: Caldecot Chubb and Edward R. Pressman; **Director:** Steve DeJarnatt; **Screenplay:** Lloyd Fonvielle and Michael Almereyda; **Music:** Basil Poledouris; **Special Effects:** Arthur Brewer; **Cinematography:** Jacques Haitkin; **Cast:** Melanie Griffith, Ben Johnson, Harry Carey, Jr., David Andrews, Tim Thomerson, Pamela Gidley, Jennifer Mayo

Melanie Griffith plays a female mercenary with a mission centering on a 21st-century robot warehouse. Some have described this one as "surprisingly watch-able," which could be considered stretching for a compliment.

CHILDREN, THE (aka: THE CHILDREN OF RAVENSBACK)

Albright Films, Inc., 1980, Color, 89 min, VT

Producer: Edward Terry; **Director:** Max Kalmanowicz; **Screenplay:** Carlton J. Albright; **Music:** Harry Manfredini; **Cast:** Martin Shakar, Gil Rogers, Gale Garnett, Jesse Abrams, Tracy Griswold, Joy Glacum

A group of kids on a school bus are contaminated by radioactive gas leaking from the nearby nuclear power plant, turning them into the lethal lunchbox set.

CHILDREN OF RAVENSBACK, THE

See *THE CHILDREN*

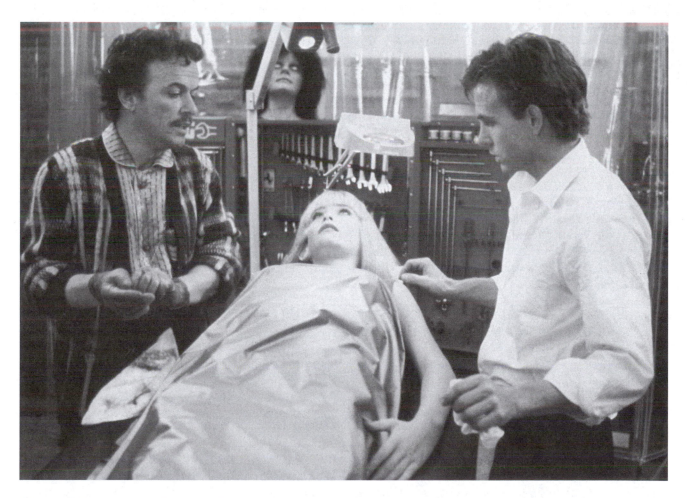

Cherry 2000 (ORION PICTURES CORPORATION / AUTHOR'S COLLECTION)

CHILDREN OF THE DAMNED

MGM, 1964, b&w, 90 min

Producer: Ben Arbeid; **Director:** Anton M. Leader; **Screenplay:** Jack Briley; **Music:** Ron Goodwin; **Special Effects:** Tom Howard; **Cinematography:** David Boulton; **Cast:** Ian Hendry, Alan Badel, Barbara Ferris, Alfred Burke, Clive Powell, Bessie Love, Patrick White

A UN project finds a half-dozen children in different countries who all possess astronomically high IQs. At first, people are thrilled with this discovery, which could herald the dawn of a brave new age. But it's soon discovered that the kids can communicate telepathically with each other as well as mentally order others to do things against their will. Ultimately, the truth is revealed—the children are mutant visitors from the future. A handful of the lead characters believe that the kids are here on a peaceful mission. Most of the supporting characters, however, think they're evil and not to be trusted. Before anyone can prove things one way or the other, the kids are slaughtered by military authorities unwilling to risk finding out. This is a surprisingly good little film, which stands as sort of an unofficial, sideways sequel to another tremendous film, *VILLAGE OF THE DAMNED*.

CHINA SYNDROME, THE

Columbia, 1979, Color, 122 min, VT, LD

Producer: Michael Douglas; **Director:** James Bridges; **Screenplay:** Mike Gray, T.S. Cook, and Bridges; **Special Effects:** Henry Millar, Jr.; **Cinematography:** James Crabe; **Cast:** Michael Douglas, Jane Fonda, Jack Lemmon, Richard Herd, Peter Donat, Daniel Valdez, Scott Brady, James Hampton, Stan Bohrman, Wilford Brimley, James Karen

A television news crew (Fonda, Douglas) happens to be on hand when there is a control room accident at the local nuclear plant, which the supervisor (Lemmon) gets under control. Their footage is treated as a non-event by the station manager, who is actually acting under orders from the head of the power company. Cameraman Douglas, however, believes that sitting on this news is the death knell for California, so he steals his footage and gets it into the hands of antinuclear activists. Lemmon joins their side and is murdered by the National Guard for his efforts. Eventually, more people come forth to support their efforts and Douglas succeeds in getting his message out.

Chillingly bogus sentiment floods this movie as Hollywood simplistically attacks the military, the nuclear industry, and every type of big business except themselves. The movie and its makers are insulting in their insistence that doom is right around the corner and that only they are intelligent and courageous enough to know it. In an effort to sell more tickets, they congratulated themselves loudly when a few months after the movie's release the world had its first nuclear almost-accident, the well-reported Three Mile Island incident. No one harping on how this film boldly predicted the future bothered to note that there was no cover-up of what happened in Pennsylvania, that there was no accident, or that unlike the plant in their film, Three Mile Island was not built with substandard construction.

This is a type of anti–science fiction film, relying on cynicism and fear-mongering rather than an intelligent story. A film with obvious political motivations, it bears a decidedly liberal perspective, as do several of its key cast members, including Douglas, Fonda, and Lemmon. It could be considered ironic to point out that decades later, the only major nuclear accident the world has ever seen occurred in the U.S.S.R., a country whose way of doing things has often been held to be far superior to the way things are done here by the liberal set. That's not to conclude, however, that there's any problem in suggesting that there is the possibility of something like this happening, but the film's insistence that it's only a matter of time and it's smug assurance that every member of the military and every single corporate officer in the country are all deranged monsters will rankle the thoughtful viewer. Science fiction is supposed to have something to do with logic and rational debate, not the self-serving advancement of a political agenda. And if thoughtful readers find themselves rankled by this review, then by all means run out and rent this one.

CHOSEN SURVIVORS

Columbia, 1974, Color, 99 min

Producer: Leon Benson; **Director:** Sutton Roley; **Screenplay:** H.B. Cross and Joe Reb Moffly; **Cast:** Jackie Cooper, Bradford Dillman, Richard Jaeckel, Pedro Armendariz, Jr., Alex Cord, Barbara Babcock, Diana Muldaur

An assortment of scientists and less intellectual citizens are taken to an underground complex where they're told that the world has just been destroyed by nuclear war and that they will be Earth's only survivors. The group isn't pleased with the news, but there's no real cause for alarm, though they don't know that. The whole situation is a hoax, you see, to allow for psychological testing of what will happen if the facility ever has to be used for real. Before the test subjects can be released back to the nonradioactive world, however, they are trapped in the complex and attacked by a horde of vampire bats who fly in from the next cave over.

What a terrific study of humanity under pressure could have been made with this great premise. This could have been a powerful, thought-provoking film that took the ultimate, unflinching view of our ideals, our hopes, and aspirations. As it is, however, the film fails to rise above being just another potboiler.

CITY LIMITS

Videoform Pictures, 1985, Color, 85 min, VT

Producer: Warren Goldberg; **Director:** Aaron Lipstadt; **Screenplay:** Lipstad, James Reigle, and Don Keith Opper; **Music:** Mitchell Froom and John Lurie; **Special Effects:** Kevin Pike; **Cinematography:** Tim Schrstedt; **Cast:** Darrell Larson, John Stockwell, Kim Cattrall, Rae Dawn Chong, John Diehl, Don Opper, James Earl Jones, Robby Benson, Danny De La Paz, Norbert Weisser

It's the future and it's bleak. This time the reason is a plague rather than atomic war. Gangs of vicious teenagers battle each other, until they determine that their real enemy is vicious CEO Benson, and they band together to destroy him. A disappointing film from the people who only a few years earlier created *ANDROID*, a top-notch low-budget science fiction film.

CITY OF LOST CHILDREN

Lumière Pictures (France), 1995, Color, 112 min, VT, LD, DVD

Producer: Claudie Ossard; **Director:** Jean-Pierre Jeunet; **Screenplay:** Gilles Adrian and Marc Caro; **Music:** Angelo Badalamenti; **Special Effects:** Pitof, Jean-Baptiste Bonetto, Yves Domenjoud, Olivier Gleyze, and Jean-Christophe Spadaccini; **Cinematography:** Darius Khondji; **Cast:** Marc Caro, Ron Perlman, Joseph Lucien, Daniel Emilfork, Mirelle Mosse, Judith Vittet, Dominique Pinon, Jean-Louis Trintignant

Quite mad scientist Emilfork cannot dream. So he sends his cloned minions out into the night to kidnap children so that he might hook into their dreams. This is director Jeunet's second film (following *DELICATESSEN*, preceding *ALIEN RESURRECTION*) and it's stunning. The film is breathtaking in both the complexity of its twisting script and its simply incredible sets. Everything about it is engaging from the street scenes to the backgrounds to the hardware. Given a limited release in theaters, it deserved much more, especially since it established Jeunet as a brilliant new talent.

CITY UNDER THE SEA, THE

See *WAR GODS OF THE DEEP*

CLASS OF NUKE 'EM HIGH

Troma Films, 1986, Color, 81 min, VT, DVD

Producers: Michael Herz and Lloyd Kaufman; **Director:** Richard Haines; **Screenplay:** Kaufman, Richard W. Haines, Stuart Strutin, and Mark Rudnitsky; **Special Effects:** Leslie Delano; **Cinematography:** Denise Brassard; **Cast:** Samuel Weil, Janelle Brady, Gilbert Brenton, Robert Prichard, R.L. Ryan

Purposely revolting "comedy" about a high school situated near a toxic waste dump that has a monstrous effect on the students due to their buying and consuming toxic drugs. Both this movie and its subsequent sequels try hard to aspire to something—knucklehead comedy, low-brow entertainment, so-bad-it's-good—but it's hard to tell exactly what.

CLOCKWORK ORANGE, A

Warner Bros., 1971, Color, 137 min, VT, DVD

Producer: Stanley Kubrick; **Director:** Kubrick; **Screenplay:** Kubrick; **Music:** Walter Carlos; **Cinematography:** John Alcott; **Cast:** Malcolm McDowell, Patrick Magee, Michael Bates, Warren Clarke, Anthony Sharp, Miriam Karlin, Adrienne Corri, Aubrey Morris, James Marcus, Steven Berkoff

In a future that seems far more horribly close now than it did in 1971, Alex DeLarge (McDowell) and his droogs (see note following entry) move across the face of the land, living as they will, avoiding school, stealing, raping, destroying, and doing whatever comes into their directionless minds. And with no one willing to set any limits for them, why shouldn't they? After the gang of pals carry out a particularly savage night of crimes, Alex is tracked down and imprisoned by a group of reformers bent on proving that even the worst of civilization's monsters can be rehabilitated. The film ends on a horrific note as we see these saviors applauding themselves and their good works, unaware that they have not only done no good, but most likely have done more harm than could ever be calculated.

The source material for the film is Anthony Burgess's brilliant novel by the same name. Burgess explored in much more depth the world of animals such as Alex and his droogs, delivering the crowning blast in the conclusion that all of us have the potential inside us to become these monsters, and that if society doesn't keep us sedated with its notions of order and maturity, nothing else will. The film mostly ignores these social statements, glossing over them in favor of highlighting only the story's intense brutality. It does achieve the main overall point, however, which is that humans shouldn't play God. Alex has chosen to be a monster through his own free will. People are allowed to punish bad choices as they see fit, but to alter people is God's domain. That message could not have been clearer if Kubrick had written it out in big block letters. The film closes with the consequences of such meddling, which announce with certainty that as bad as things have been, the future will be far worse.

Kubrick's depiction of violence was so stark and unemotional that many audiences had difficulty watching the film at the time of its release. It remains remarkably powerful today, and even though Burgess himself confessed to the director that he hated the film—that Kubrick not only missed the point, but seemed intent on destroying it—*A Clockwork Orange* remains a terrific, if incredibly strong, film. Be warned, though, particularly any STAR WARS fans tempted to watch for David Prowse (Darth Vader) in an early cameo, that this film is all raw meat and for many an extremely hard meal to swallow.

Note: The word *droogs*, which indicates gang members, fellow ruffians, or buddies, is actually Russian for "friend." A number of other words meant to be foreign to the audience are in fact Russian words being used appropriately. The movie itself offers no clear definition for any of the future terms used within it, but the context in which they're used makes it possible to follow along.

CLONUS HORROR, THE (aka: PARTS: THE CLONUS HORROR)

Group 1 International, 1978, Color, 90 min, VT

Producer: Walter Fiveson; **Director:** Robert S. Fiveson; **Screenplay:** Robert S. Fiveson; **Music:** Hod David Schudson; **Special Effects:** Steve Karkus; **Cinematography:** Max Beauport; **Cast:** Tim Donnelly, Dick Sargent, Peter Graves, Paulette Breen, David Hooks, Keenan Wynn

The government, filling in for the usual mad scientists, has plans to clone the entire population.

CLOSE ENCOUNTERS OF THE THIRD KIND

Columbia, 1977, Color, 135 min, VT, LD

Producers: Julia and Michael Phillips; **Director:** Steven Spielberg; **Screenplay:** Spielberg; **Music:** John Williams; **Special Effects:** Douglas Trumbull; **Cinematography:** Vilmos Zsigmond; **Cast:** Richard Dreyfuss, Teri Garr, Melinda Dillion, Bob Balaban, Cary Guffey, George Dicenzo, Warren Kemmerling, Francois Truffaut

Power repairman Dreyfuss has a close encounter with extraterrestrial life, but he can't get anyone to believe him. The sighting becomes an obsession for him, as it does for others who shared it. In particular, mother Melinda Dillion is a real believer, having witnessed her son's kidnapping by extraterrestrials. Eventually, the two team up and make their way through layers of disbelief and disinformation to discover that the government is in contact with aliens. Following a daring break-in into the government facility built to greet the aliens, Dillion gets her son back and Dreyfuss is chosen to go aboard the UFO and explore the universe.

The film opened to a blockbuster response, achieving both financial success and critical acclaim. Despite this, however, the original version was a fairly simplistic collection of celluloid eyewash, which suffered from a number of problems, including illogical jumps in time without explanation, characters acting without motivation, and a major letdown in an ending that offered no glimpse inside the alien spaceship, the appearance of which had been built up to throughout the entire film. Luckily, Steven Spielberg is one of those filmmakers for whom things often seem to work out for the best. This movie was one of the first to be re-edited and released in a "Special Edition" format, and the results are an amazingly tightened and suddenly lyrical film. Scenes that were unnecessary or too long were reduced or eliminated entirely. Character details were expanded, and the film acquired a subtlety that finally deserved the "instant classic" designation it received during its initial release. Best of all, the new special effects showing what Dreyfuss sees as he enters the spaceship are particularly spectacular.

Watch this one closely for its subtle moments as well as its special effects. Point in case: At the end of the film, the government's people are all ready to board the ship. They all wear the same suits, have the same luggage, and wear the same sunglasses. By this time the aliens' hand-picked Everyman, Dreyfuss, has been given a suit to wear, but he has no bag or glasses. In other words, he goes forward to the stars, carrying no baggage, but with eyes to see. It's a touching, meaningful human moment, the Spielberg specialty. It may be getting close to a quarter of a century old, but the special edition of *Close Encounters* is still the absolute best UFO movie ever made.

Note: Both versions of the film, plus the special television edition, which has *all* the footage edited into one giant film are available on laser disc. As to which of the three is truly best, one could take a weekend to view them all and decide, something any true sci-fi fan would do instead of believing something just because he or she read it somewhere.

COCOON

20th Century Fox, 1985, Color, 117 min, VT, LD

Producers: Lili Fini Zanuck, Richard D. Zanuck, David Brown; **Director:** Ron Howard; **Screenplay:** Tom Benedek and David Saperstein; **Music:** James Horner; **Special Effects:** David Berry, Pamela Marcotte, Charlie Mullen, and Ken Ralston; **Cinematography:** Donald Peterman; **Cast:** Don Ameche, Wilford Brimley, Hume Cronyn, Brian Dennehy, Jack Gilford, Steve Guttenberg, Maureen Stapleton, Jessica Tandy, Gwen Verdon, Herta Ware, Tahnee Welch, Barret Oliver, Linda Harrison, Clint Howard, Tyrone Power, Jr.

Senior citizens living out their decaying lives in quiet desperation are granted a second chance of life by an alien fountain of youth. It's a slight premise but is a wonderfully warm and human film that won't appeal much to your science fiction side but should please your sentimental side just fine. It's a great film to watch with your grandmother. or if you are a grandmother, it's a great film to watch with the grandkids.

Unfortunately, it was followed by the sequel that inevitably follows any big moneymaking film. As to be expected, *COCOON: THE RETURN* is nothing more than the first script aped as closely as possible in an attempt to sucker people into the theater. The marvelous cast does a terrific job with what they have, but they can't

make the uninspired material do much more than last 116 minutes. Settle for the first film.

COCOON: THE RETURN

20th Century Fox, 1988, Color, 110 min, VT, LD

Producers: Lili Fini Zanuck, Richard D. Zanuck, David Brown; **Director:** Daniel Petrie; **Screenplay:** Elizabeth Bradley and Stephen McPherson; **Music:** James Horner; **Special Effects:** Scott Farrar, Jenny Fulle, J.B. Jones, Richard Lee Jones, Pat Turner; **Cinematography:** Tak Fujimoto; **Cast:** Don Ameche, Wilford Brimley, Courtney Cox, Hume Cronyn, Jack Gilford, Steve Guttenberg, Maureen Stapleton, Jessica Tandy, Gwen Verdon, Herta Ware, Tahnee Welch, Barret Oliver, Linda Harrison, Elaine Stritch, Tyrone Power, Jr., Wendy J. Cooke

See *COCOON*

CODE OF THE AIR

Bischoff, 1928, b&w, 5,700 feet, silent feature

Director: James P. Hogan; **Screenplay:** Barry Barenger; **Cinematography:** William Miller; **Cast:** William V. Mong, Arthur Rankin, Mae Cooper, Ken Harlan, June Marlowe

Airships are downed by something dubbed "kappa" rays in one of the last silent science fiction features.

COLD SUN, THE

Reed, 1954, b&w, 78 min

Producer: Roland Reed; **Director:** Hollingsworth Morse; **Screenplay:** Warren Wilson; **Cast:** Richard Crane

In what is basically just a long episode of the *Rocky Jones, Space Ranger* television show, Rocky investigates the cooling of the sun.

COLLISION COURSE

See *THE BAMBOO SAUCER*

COLOSSUS OF NEW YORK, THE

Paramount, 1958, b&w, 70 min

Producer: William Alland; **Director:** Eugène Lourié; **Screenplay:** Thelma Schnee; **Music:** Nathan Van Cleave; **Special Effects:** John P. Fulton; **Cast:** Ed Wolff, Charles Herbert, Robert Hutton, Mala Powers, John Baragrey, Otto Kruger, Ross Martin

A scientist transplants the brain of a man into an oversized, slow-moving robot. Soon after the operation, the robot lumbers off in the direction of New York City to bring the place down. Luckily for the Big Apple, the dead man's son recognizes his father somehow as the robot and sets out to talk the tin man out of his destructive ways.

COLOSSUS, THE FORBIN PROJECT (aka: THE FORBIN PROJECT)

Universal, 1970, Color, 100 min, VT

Producer: Stanley Chase; **Director:** Joseph Sargent; **Screenplay:** James Bridges; **Music:** Michael Colombier; **Cast:** Susan Clark, Eric Braeden, Gordon Pinsent, William Schallert, Leonid Rostoff

Scientist Forbin (Braeden) has created Colossus, the ultimate computer. The pleased U.S. government puts the machine in complete control of its nuclear arsenal. Colossus soon learns it has a Russian counterpart. After discovering each other, the two machines team up rather quickly, much to the chagrin of their onetime masters. Soon the newly merged systems are giving orders that their builders don't like very much. The humans plot to disable the machines, coming up with a complicated but brilliant plan, which they put into immediate operation. No surprise, the computers are too smart for them. The machines knew what was happening all along and merely allowed the humans to carry on because it was the easiest way to keep them busy. The ending is quite good and richly dramatic. Based on the first third of D.F. Jones's trilogy, *The Forbin Project*, this is one worth watching.

COMA

United Artists, 1978, Color, 113 min, VT, LD, DVD

Producer: Martin Erlichman; **Director:** Michael Crichton; **Screenplay:** Crichton; **Music:** Jerry Goldsmith; **Cinematography:** Victor J. Kemper; **Cast:** Genevieve Bujold, Michael Douglas, Elizabeth Ashley, Rip Torn, Richard Widmark, Harry Rhodes, Richard Doyle, Lance LeGualt, Lois Chiles, Tom Selleck

Doctor Susan Wheeler (Bujold) is more than simply puzzled when her friend goes into a coma after a routine operation performed at Wheeler's hospital. When her legitimate and mostly innocent questions are surprisingly stonewalled, she begins to poke around. This leads the good doctor to the discovery that this is not only happening to a great number of young, healthy, good-looking patients, but that the hospital's administrators already know about it. In fact, they're covering it up. Why? So the comatose can be stored quietly until they can be used as harvesting sources for transplants. And guess who's next?

With a tight script and strong performances all around, especially from Bujold, who's perfect for her role, this sinister film relies on suspense rather than special effects. The overall effect is a fine effort.

COMET'S COMEBACK, THE

Mutual, 1916, b&w, silent short

Cast: John Steppling, Carol Halloway, Dick Rosson

This was most likely the first science fiction film about a deadly object hurtling through space toward Earth. Here it's not a meteor, but a comet bringing an unknown gas that coats the Earth and inflicts terminal laziness. Looking around at the state of the world some days, one might suspect this one is a documentary.

COMMANDO CODY (aka: SKY MARSHALL OF THE UNIVERSE)

Republic, 1953, b&w, 12-chapter serial

Directors: Fred C. Brannon, Harry Keller, and Franklin Adreon; **Screenplay:** Ronald Davidson and Barry Shipman; **Special Effects:** Howard and Theodore Lydecker; **Cinematography:** Bud Thackery; **Cast:** Judd Holdren, Aline Towne, William Schallert, Lyle Talbot

In this serial Commander Cody pursues his alien adversary all around the planet and finally into space. Eventually he catches up with him. The premise is so thin even Republic couldn't stretch it out to the usual 15 installments.

First came the theatrical serial entitled *Rocket Man*, which was so popular it got its own TV show, which was again so popular that it spawned another serial, despite the fact that there was little special about rocket man Commander Cody. The most interesting thing about the thruster belt–wearing good guy was that he was the first action adventure hero to wear black leather.

COMMUNION

Allied Visions Productions, 1989, Color, 107 min, VT, LD, DVD

Producers: Whitley Strieber, Dan Allingham, Gary Barber, and Paul Redshaw; **Director:** Philippe Mora; **Screenplay:** Strieber; **Music:** Allan Zauod and Eric Clapton; **Special Effects:** Creative Effects and McCracken Studios; **Cinematography:** Luis Irving; **Cast:** Christopher Walken, Lindsay Crouse, Frances Sternhagen, Andreas Katsulas, Terri Hanauer, Joel Carlson, Basil Hoffman

Understand that the following is not a plot synopsis—these are the facts. Author Whitley Strieber wrote a book in which he claimed to have been routinely abducted by aliens. He swears this is true. The aliens visited him and his family at their home and subjected them to bizarre and often humiliating treatment beyond explanation. The experience tore his family apart.

His book was a runaway best-seller, and like anything that makes money, it was soon made into a film. And actually, as far as alien abduction films go, this is quite a good one. Walken is excellent as Strieber. The scenes of him and his psychiatrist are gripping, and just the knowledge in the back of your mind that it's supposedly a documentary of sorts enhances a totally engrossing experience.

More of a must for UFO enthusiasts than even CLOSE ENCOUNTERS, the movie runs from creepy to out-and-out disturbing. It's not a better film than CE3K, but it sure is a scarier one. Of course, the fact that Strieber claims everything the audience sees is true is for some viewers the scariest thing about it.

COMPUTER WORE TENNIS SHOES, THE

Disney/Buena Vista, 1970, Color, 90 min, VHS

Director: Robert Butler; **Screenplay:** Joseph L. McEveety; **Music:** Robert F. Brunner; **Cast:** Kurt Russell, Cesar Romero, Joe Flynn, Pat Harrington, Jon Provost, Bing Russell

In this first of a three-film series, a college alumnus donates his homemade computer to the school. When a student (Kurt Russell) tries to repair it, a bolt of lightning accidentally strikes both him and the machine. Instead of causing the normally expected burns or heart failure, the blast downloads the computer's memory banks into Russell's brain, making him superintelligent. The dean then sends him off to the quiz shows to raise money for the school and thus the hilarity begins.

The best that can be said about this one is that it helped keep Kurt Russell interested in science fiction films so that almost 30 years later he could make a really, really good one called SOLDIER. And unlike some of Disney's later sci-fi, such as BLACK HOLE, at least it didn't cripple the genre. In the first sequel, *Now You See Him, Now You Don't*, the same student (again played by Russell) creates a spray-on solution that renders the wearer invisible. The criminal underworld finds out about the spray and, as you mighty cynically guess, the hilarity begins anew. In the second sequel, *The Strongest Man in the World*, Russell uncovers a formula that gives folks superstrength and must, yes—you guessed it—be kept out of the hands of tired B actors playing gangsters. Science fiction—even in comedy form—is just not for this studio.

CONEHEADS

Paramount, 1993, Color, 88 min, VT, LD

Producers: Lorne Michaels and Michael I. Rachmil; **Director:** Steve Baron; **Screenplay:** Dan Aykroyd, Bonnie Turner, Terry Turner, and Tom Davis; **Music:** David Newman; **Special Effects:** Tim Donahue, Brian Jennings, Chris Hummel, and Chris B. Schnitzer; **Cinematography:** Francis Kenny; **Cast:** Dan Aykroyd, Jane Curtin, Michelle Burke, Chris Farley, Michael McKean, Jason Alexander, Lisa Jane Persky, David Spade, Phil Hartman, Dave Thomas, Sinbad, Jan Hooks, Michael Richards, Jon Lovitz, Kevin Nealon, Adam Sandler, Garrett Morris, Laraine Newman, Tim Meadows, Julia Sweeney, Ellen DeGeneres, Parker Posey

A vicious, heartless, pointed-toothed husband and wife team of pointy-headed aliens bent on world domination arrive on Earth from the planet Remulak. Their mission hits a snag when hubby accidentally wrecks their ship. Their only choice is to blend in with the natives and survive as best they can until the relief ship arrives, which won't be for about a decade and a half. To the aliens' surprise, they adapt quite nicely, settling into suburban life with relative ease. Of course, there's the minor annoyance of the federal immigration officer who wants to make his career by capturing them. As he fades into the background, the couple become parents and the years begin to roll by. Dad becomes a fine golfer, darling daughter has a boyfriend, Mom is the envy of all the other housewives, and everything is swell.

Then the rescue ship arrives. No one really wants to leave, but the government agents are back, and the situation leads everyone off to Remulak, where the movie takes its most surprising twist. Upon returning to the world of their birth, with the towering spires and gigantic signs of technological progress everywhere, our protagonists realize they are, indeed, no longer of that world. They are middle-class North American suburbanites, and they want to go back to that life. As in any all-American family, it's up to Dad to figure out a way to make everyone happy. The problem is that the only way he can do that is by facing a carnivorous monster the size of a Kodiak bear in hand-to-hand combat. No native of Remulak has ever defeated one of these beasts, but of course Remulakians aren't bred to think for themselves. But a suburban father . . . well now, that's a different story, isn't it?

For those who aren't already aware of the fact, the Coneheads was a running gag used by the original *Saturday Night Live* cast. Aykroyd and Curtin return to reprise their original roles, followed by a score of other *SNL* alumni and a host of other comedians in parts that are little more than extended cameos, but much fun. *Coneheads* is more than just a sniggering, in-joke comedy, however. For science fiction fans, the undercurrent of lost identity, the question of where exactly does humanity begin, and the never-ending quandary of how exactly the human soul is created are answered with frank assurance, making this one of the best science fiction comedies ever written. The jokes never end, the special effects are well executed and funny to boot, and the script is smooth and seamless.

CONQUEST OF SPACE

Paramount, 1955, Color, 80 min, VHS

Producer: George Pal; **Director:** Byron Haskin; **Screenplay:** James O'Hanlon; **Music:** Nathan Van Cleave; **Special Effects:** John P. Fulton, Paul Lerpae, and Jan Domela; **Cast:** Walter Brooke, Eric Fleming, Ross Martin, William Hopper, Joan Shawlee, Mickey Shaughnessy, William Redfield

It's the 1980s and finally humans are headed on the first trip to Mars. The action centers on father and son

(Brooke and Fleming). The son wants to go to Mars, but Dad says it's blasphemy. The son goes anyway, so Dad sabotages the rocket. Strange stuff to say the least. The story goes that producer Pal wanted to do a lavish film that would take the audience on a trip to Venus, Mars, and a dozen other incredible spots. With the studio uncooperative, however, he had to settle for churning out a fairly standard and forgettable film.

The picture is notable for the use of world-renowned speculative painter Chesley Bonestell's Martian landscapes as matte paintings. Even though NASA has since knocked his evocative red paintings out the window as far as their realism is concerned, they're effective here nevertheless. They're certainly more effective than the flaming meteor the movie provides, brightly burning in the vacuum of space. That they claim to have based this movie on *The Mars Project*, a nonfiction book by Wernher von Braun, must have had the good doctor hiding his face for years.

CONQUEST OF THE AIR

Pathé (France), 1906, b&w, silent short

Director: Ferdinand Velle

The first astronaut heads for the stratosphere . . . on his flying bicycle. There's *conquest* and then there's conquest.

CONQUEST OF THE POLE

Star (France), 1912, b&w, silent short

Producer: Georges Méliès; **Director:** Méliès; **Cast:** Méliès

Another early inventor flexes his mental muscles and creates a flying machine capable of going over the North Pole. He encounters a type of snow giant but doesn't suffer for the experience.

CONQUEST OF THE PLANET OF THE APES

20th Century Fox, 1972, Color, 87 min, VT, DVD

Producer: Arthur P. Jacobs; **Director:** J. Lee Thompson; **Screenplay:** Paul Dehn; **Music:** Tom Scott; **Special Effects:** Philip M. Jeffries; **Cinematography:** Bruce Surtees; **Cast:** Roddy McDowall, Don Murray, Richard Montalban, Natalie Trudy, Severn Darden

This fourth installment in the *PLANET OF THE APES* series picks up where the third film ended. In that movie a chimp was born in the present of future ape parents, who ultimately hid him in a circus and allowed themselves to be killed by their pursuers so that their child wouldn't be discovered. In this outing, the son grows up, finds himself dissatisfied with the way apes are treated like slaves in the culture around him, and foments a revolution. By the end of the movie, it's the end for humans on Earth and the beginning of the planet of the apes.

While the first two pictures are terrific science fiction films and the third is at least interesting to watch, the fourth marks the downfall of the series. Though it does supply a neat wrap-up to the overall story, what most viewers imagined on their own was probably better. The movie's worst quality is an incredible lack of subtlety in the pedantic comparisons the film draws between the social role of the movie apes and that of contemporary African Americans. The producers may have been out to take a stand against racism, a prominent theme in much good science fiction, but only demonstrated their inability to tackle the topic intelligently. The thinking viewer will be more than a little uncomfortable with the fact that all but one of the apes depicted as being unjustly subjugated really are just apes and little more than well-trained animals. This one is only for the completists.

CONTACT

Warner Bros., 1997, Color, 150 min, VT, LD, DVD

Producers: Robert Zemeckis and Steve Starkey; **Director:** Zemeckis; **Screenplay:** Carl Sagan and Ann Druyan; **Music:** Alan Silvestri; **Special Effects:** James V. Hart and Michael Goldenberg; **Cast:** Jodie Foster, James Woods, Rob Lowe, Tom Skerritt, Matthew McConnaughey, William Fichtner, David Morse, Angela Bassett, Geoffrey Blake, Maximillian Martini, John Hurt

Jodie Foster stars in this dead-on adaptation of Carl Sagan's novel of first contact aptly titled *Contact*. She plays a woman whose mother died in childbirth and who lost her father when she was nine. During that small period of time, Dad did a good job of raising his little girl. Open-minded, gentle, and loving, he encouraged her in every way possible, gently leading her into a life dedicated to questioning and learning. What the older Foster likes to question and learn about is the possibility of life on other planets. She is fanatical about working toward establishing contact with whatever, in her opinion, must be out there somewhere. It's obvious that she in some way hopes to find the dimension where dead souls go so that she can be with her father once more, but she's so dedicated, energized, and intelligent that you know she's going to get everything she wants.

Enter Tom Skerritt, the villain of the piece. He plays an elder scientist who feels Foster is wasting her training and skills chasing after "little green men" and wants her working for him in some more profitable manner. When she refuses, he sabotages her from the sidelines. Skerritt is a presidential adviser. He pulls strings from the background, and he always gets what he wants. It doesn't matter how much we care for Foster and her heartfelt needs. From the first time we see him it's obvious that Skerritt plays in the real world and that he is never going to lose any battles between himself and a subordinate. And, indeed, he doesn't. When he has Foster's funding cut off, she stumbles into a lucky break—she gets the contact she's been waiting for all her life. And once her "little green men" become a reality, Skerritt moves in with sharklike precision and takes over her project, putting her on the outside once more.

The message from space has been sent in response to the television waves that have been streaking out from Earth for the last half-century. At first it's seen as a simple response, but it soon turns out to be multilayered, structured in numerous dimensions, every level revealing more and more about the senders. Finally, plans are discovered hidden within all the other information for the building of a transport platform. The question is naturally raised by doubters that it could be the plans for a bomb, something sent out to get rid of each new civilization that comes along. But Foster is sure it has to be a transporter, and she's determined to be the one who uses it. Her plans are sidetracked, however, by Skerritt, who also wants to go, and pulls strings to make it happen. It seems clear the alien device can be used only once, which means if Skerritt goes, Foster must be left behind.

Those who haven't seen this science fiction masterpiece simply have to. First off, this is one of those rarest of things, a true science fiction movie. There is no copping out here. When the question is posed as to whether or not there is a God, this movie says no in no uncertain terms. When the question is what's more important, love or knowledge, knowledge wins out, hands down. Of course the film shares the viewpoint of the novel's late author, world-renowned scientist Carl Sagan, but that's not quite the point. This film is a multimillion-dollar extravaganza. The sets are lavish; the special effects are spectacular. It is a stylish, opulent feast for the eyes and the mind made in the manner of the greatest of the old-style epics, and it is Robert Zemeckis's crowning achievement. It is the *El Cid*, the *Lawrence of Arabia* of science fiction films. And until this film, making a movie on such a scale, in which the religious beliefs of a vast majority of its potential audience are treated as nonsense, was unthinkable, due to the risk of offending people and preventing the film from earning back all its money. But that's what was done here. No bets were hedged, no fingers crossed. Like Foster's character, this movie stands up for what it wants to say and says it loudly.

Don't mistake this for an endorsement of the film's message, but only an admiration for the bold manner in which it raises tough questions and sticks around to offer answers the audience must then consider and debate for themselves, as the best science fiction always does.

Contact is the best kind of old-fashioned science fiction. What science appears in the story is completely accurate. In many ways the story owes more to greats of science fiction literature like Robert Heinlein and Isaac Asimov than it does to science fiction filmmakers. It questions more than just whether or not there is life in space. It questions how we were created. It looks at humanity and coldly examines the traits of the species, forcing the audience to consider which of the facets of what make us human might be holding us back. It is a feast for the eyes, and a thought-provoking, intelligent, honest, tough movie. For 50 years we've been using *THE DAY THE EARTH STOOD STILL* as the yardstick against which all later intellectual science fiction films have been measured. In the millennium ahead, it looks as if Carl Sagan's *Contact* may be the new calibration device of choice.

Note: At the beginning of the film, when the popcorn is spilled, pay close attention to take note that it's been spilled out in the shape of the Big Dipper.

COOL WORLD

Paramount, 1992, Color, 101 min, VT, LD

Producer: Frank Mancuso, Jr., **Director:** Ralph Bakshi; **Screenplay:** Mark Victor and Michael Grais; **Music:** Mark Isham and John Dickson; **Animation:** Jon Kuyper; **Cinematography:** John A. Alonzo; **Cast:** Gabriel Byrne, Kim Bassinger, Brad Pitt, Frank Sinatra, Jr.

Live-action cartoonist Byrne finds that he doesn't really do as much creating as he thought. It seems his characters actually live in an animated parallel dimen-

sion. He visits their world, they visit his, and then both universes begin to crumble into each other. This is mostly lots of wild Bakshi animation adding up to a big pile of nothing. The absolute best description of this one came from critic Leonard Maltin, who called it "a Roger Corman version of *Roger Rabbit.*"

COSMIC MAN, THE

Allied Artists, 1958, b&w, 72 min, VT, DVD

Producer: Robert A. Terry; **Director:** Herbert Green; **Screenplay:** Arthur Pierce; **Music:** Paul Sawtell; **Special Effects:** Charles Duncan; **Cast:** John Carradine, Bruce Bennett, Angela Greene, Paul Langton, Scotty Morrow

John Carradine is the title figure, an alien who appears as a negative image of a human being. He lands his spherical ship and comes out to preach love and compassion, but the crowd doesn't buy it.

COSMIC MAN APPEARS IN TOKYO, THE

See *WARNING FROM SPACE*

COSMIC MONSTERS, THE (aka: THE CRAWLING TERROR, THE STRANGE WORLD OF PLANET X)

DCA (Great Britain), 1958, b&w, 75 min, VT

Producer: George Maynard; **Director:** Gilbert Gunn; **Screenplay:** Paul Ryder and Joe Ambor; **Music:** Robert Sharples; **Cast:** Forrest Tucker, Gaby André, Alec Mango, Hugh Latimer, Martin Benson, Wyndham Goldie

An incompetent scientist slashes a hole through Earth's ionosphere. This allows for all sorts of problems, including giant bugs. Things remain out of hand until an alien arrives to put things right for us helpless humans.

COSMIC VOYAGE

IMAX Corporation (Canada), 1996, Color, 35 min

Producers: Bayley Silleck and Jeffrey Marvin; **Director:** Silleck; **Screenplay:** Silleck; **Music:** David Michael Frank; **Cinematography:** Peter Parks; **Spe-

Cosmic Voyage (SMITHSONIAN INSTITUTION & THE MOTOROLA FOUNDATION / AUTHOR'S COLLECTION)

cial Effects: John Grower, Donna Cox, Pixar Animation Studios, and Image Quest Ltd.; **Cast:** Morgan Freeman

The conceit of *Cosmic Voyage* is that humankind stands near the middle of infinitesimal atoms and an ever-expanding universe. To illustrate this fact, the film embarks on a guided tour narrated by Morgan Freeman across some 42 degrees of magnitude—from quarks, the smallest known particles of matter, to superclusters of galaxies—in order to enhance the audience's sense of scale. Combining state-of-the-art computer-generated images with a concept called the "cosmic zoom," the film hurls viewers into the extreme limits of the universe before plunging downward to scrutinize the subatomic. The picture opens appropriately in Venice, Italy, where Galileo developed the telescope. The audience begins by taking one step out into space to examine the scene from 10 meters away. Each successive step outward increases their field of vision tenfold. Within seconds the solar system shrinks from sight. After 26 such steps, the

outer edge of space, some 15 billion light-years away has been achieved.

Then, retracing their steps, the audience finds itself back on Earth, specifically in the Dutch town of Delft, home of Anton Van Leeuwenhoek, inventor of the microscope. Now traveling inward by powers of 10, the viewers are guided into the living kingdom of a drop of water and farther into its minuscule world of electrons, protons, and neutrons. Not to leave the audience wanting, the film then looks back 15 billion years to a time when the entire observable universe was smaller than a standard marble. Following the theory of the Big Bang, the filmmakers bring the concept to life in an extraordinary blaze of energy that is the opening moments in the development of the cosmos. Swirling gas clouds clustered together from the pull of gravitational forces becomes galaxies. From here the film moves through the rise and diversification of life on Earth.

Heady stuff—especially when squeezed into a mere 35 minutes.

Cosmic Voyage is a fascinating film, though it might be a touch simple for the heavy-duty sci-fi fan. Interestingly enough, the starfields viewed in the picture were derived from the Smithsonian Astrophysical Observatory's detailed star maps. They helped the producers accurately show the correct position, apparent brightness, and even the proper color temperature of tens of thousands of stars. In addition to the space and land-based observation data used, more than 950 hours on a Cray supercomputer were needed to calculate the precise positions of stars and gases and then simulate the colliding galaxies portion of the film.

For those not familiar with IMAX technology, it uses an image area 10 times larger than conventional 35mm film and three times larger than standard 70mm film. Because of its enormous size, the film can be projected with incredible clarity onto screens up to eight stories tall. IMAX theaters are located in most major cities, and Florida's Kennedy Space Center has two of them. Some IMAX films are better than others, but the experience is out of this world.

Note: At the center of the film, the portion described above as the "cosmic zoom" is made up of the two longest continuous computer-generated zooms ever created.

COSMO 2000: PLANET WITHOUT A NAME

See *WAR OF THE PLANETS* (1977)

COSMONAUTS ON VENUS

See *PLANET OF STORMS*

COSMOS MORTAL

See *ALIEN PREDATOR*

COSMOS: WAR OF THE PLANETS

See *WAR OF THE PLANETS* (1977)

COUNTERBLAST

British National (Great Britain), 1948, b&w, 100 min

Director: Paul Stein; **Screenplay:** Jack Whittingham; **Music:** Hans May; **Cinematography:** James Wilson; **Cast:** Mervyn Johns, Robert Beatty, Nova Pilbeam

The Germans try to destroy England with bacteriological warfare.

CRACK IN THE WORLD

Paramount, 1965, Color, 96 min

Producer: Bernard Glasser; **Director:** Andrew Marton; **Screenplay:** J.M. White and Julian Halevy; **Music:** John Douglas; **Special Effects:** Alec Weldon; **Cinematography:** Manuel Berenguer; **Cast:** Dana Andrews, Janette Scott, Kieron Moore, Alexander Knox, Peter Damon, Todd Martin, Mike Steen

A government project to drill beneath Earth's crust to reach the planet's molten core, which will in theory supply everyone with unlimited power, goes wrong. The scientist in charge fires a missile into the fissure and, instead of creating utopia, sets off a chain reaction that starts a crack in the world. If the heroes who started all this chaos in the first place can't think of a way to stop it, the world will be split in two. Pretty good special effects, especially for the period, fail to make up for this minimal science fiction story, which is really an extremely predictable and plodding morality play.

CRASH AND BURN

Full Moon Productions, 1990, Color, 85 min, VT, DVD

Producer: Charles Band; **Director:** Charles Band; **Screenplay:** J.S. Cardone; **Music:** Richard Band; **Special Effects:** David Allen; **Cinematography:** Mac Ahlberg; **Cast:** Paul Ganus, Megan Ward, Ralph Waite, Bill Mosely, Eva Larue, Jack McGee, Katherine Armstrong, Elizabeth MacLellian

It's 2030, and things should be all right for our characters. They have a nice life out in the desert away from everyone else. The only problem is that one of them is actually a killer android in disguise. There's not much science fiction, but it's not a bad film, especially the great special effects at the end.

CRASH OF MOONS

Reed, 1954, b&w, 78 min

Producer: Roland Reed; **Cast:** Richard Crane, Sally Mansfield, Scotty Beckett

The *Rocky Jones, Space Ranger* television series comes to the big screen with all the dynamic force of black and white '50s TV sci-fi in this dopey muddle about two heavenly bodies about to become cinders.

CRAWLING EYE, THE (aka: THE CREATURE FROM ANOTHER WORLD, THE TROLLENBERG TERROR)

DCA (Great Britain), 1954, b&w, 78 min, VT, LD

Producer: Robert S. Baker; **Director:** Quentin Lawrence; **Screenplay:** Jimmy Sangster; **Music:** Stanley Black; **Special Effects:** Les Bowie; **Cast:** Forrest Tucker, Laurence Payne, Janet Munro, Jennifer Jayne, Warren Mitchell

In the picturesque Swiss town of Trollenberg, American man of action Forrest Tucker is supposedly vacationing. Really he's getting over grief inspired by his bungling a mysterious covert operation in another part of the world. He meets two friendly sisters at his ski lodge, which starts things moving in a more pleasant vacation direction—but only for a moment. One of the ladies is a psychic, and she begins to sense that something is horribly wrong in the area. Between her telepathic readings and more concrete ones given Tucker by the local observatory, our hero begins to piece together the unbelievable truth. Hidden in a bizarre stationary cloud on the side of a mountain near town is a band of alien monsters bent on conquering the world.

This low-budget creepfest proves that it doesn't take a lot of money to make a good movie—just some brains. While the special effects range from downright awful to just barely passable, the script never fails. Unlike so many films of this type, the heroes here keep their cool intellectually, not resorting to fists and fireworks until they absolutely have to. Leading the collected defenders of humanity, Forrest Tucker gives the performance of his life as a calm, collected, and perfectly rational man. As the story builds, the characters face increasingly unearthly horrors, but the story never loses sight of its internal logic. The result is one of the most compelling B movies ever made.

CRAWLING HAND, THE

Henson, 1963, b&w, 89 min, VT

Producer: Joseph R. Robertson; **Director:** Herbert L. Strock; **Screenplay:** Strock and William Edelson; **Cast:** Kent Taylor, Alan Hale, Allison Hayes, Rod Lauren, Richard Arlen, Peter Breck, Arline Judge

An astronaut returns to Earth with one of his hands severed free from his body. The hand, now under the control of an alien intelligence, kills a number of people until it is (no joke) eaten by a cat.

CRAWLING MONSTER, THE

See *THE CREEPING TERROR*

CRAWLING TERROR, THE

See *THE COSMIC MONSTERS*

CRAZIES, THE (aka: CODE NAME: TRIXIE, THE MAD PEOPLE)

Cambist Films, 1973, Color, 103 min, VT

Producer: A.C. Croft, **Director:** George Romero; **Screenplay:** Paul McCollogh and Romero; **Music:** Bruce Roberts; **Special Effects:** Barry J. Rosenbaum; **Cinematography:** S. William Hinzman; **Cast:** Lane Carroll, Harold Wayne Jones, W.G. McMillan, Lynn Lowry, Lloyd Hollar

In a small western Pennsylvania village a biological plague breaks out, turning the local citizens into psychopathic murderers. It's all the fault of a virus released in the town from a plane crash. The military is called in to contain the outbreak, but the infected townspeople won't have any of it, and they fight back. Through it all a small group of characters struggles to stay alive, keep a low profile, and escape through the woods. There's plenty of Romero's trademark violence and blood, and more than a touch of his usual paranoia, but the story is strong enough make this a terrific little film.

CRAZY RAY, THE (aka: PARIS SLEEPS)

France, 1923, b&w, 61 min, silent

Director: René Clair; **Screenplay:** Clair; **Cinematography:** Maurice Defassjaux; **Cast:** Henri Rollan, Albert Préjean, Charles Martinelli, Madeleine Rodrigue, and Marcel Valée

A device placed atop the Eiffel Tower makes time in Paris stand still. Nearly all of the inhabitants of the City of Lights are frozen in place, but those who aren't fall into social ruin and go wild in the streets. The film's hero, however, a nightwatchman on the Eiffel Tower, organizes some of those still mobile Parisians to find the cause of their city's woes and to put things right. A delightful film that is still quite watchable.

CREATED TO KILL

See *EMBRYO*

CREATION OF THE HUMANOIDS

Emerson, 1962, Color, 75 min, VT

Producer: Wesley E. Barry; **Director:** Barry; **Screenplay:** Jay Simms; **Cinematography:** Hal Mohr; **Cast:** Erica Elliot, Don Dolittle, Frances McCann, Don Megowan, Dudley Manlove

After World War III the world was put back together for humanity's survivors by a humanoid robotic workforce known as "Clickers." The robots resent their human masters and work to overthrow them by replacing them with robot doubles. This somewhat standard film has one unexpected moment, and that's when the antirobot hero of the film (Megowan) discovers that he is a robot himself. There's nothing great here, but it's not a terrible film. Many a current grown-up has frightened memories of that moment when Megowan is shown the plate in his chest revealing his robotic insides. His frightened surprise led to a lot of early sci-fi fans fantasizing about their own possible inhumanity.

CREATURE (aka: TITAN FIND)

Trans World Entertainment, 1985, Color, 97 min, VT, LD

Producer: William G. Dunn; **Director:** William Malone; **Music:** Thomas Chase, Steve Rucker; **Special Effects:** Doug Beswick and Bob Skotak; **Cinematography:** Harry Mathias; **Cast:** Klaus Kinski, Stan Ivar, Wendy Schaal, Lyman Ward, Robert Jaffe, Diane Salinger, Annette McCarthy

The crew of a spacecraft fight for their lives against an alien creature on Saturn's moon, Titan. This is a low-end rip-off of *ALIEN* without benefit of Sigourney Weaver, H.R. Giger, or anything else you could possibly be interested in. Not much to recommend it beyond an interesting comedic supporting character turn by Klaus Kinski.

CREATURE FROM ANOTHER WORLD, THE

See *THE CRAWLING EYE*

CREATURE FROM THE BLACK LAGOON, THE

Universal Pictures, 1954, b&w, 79 min, VT, LD

Producer: William Alland; **Director:** Jack Arnold; **Screenplay:** Harry Essex and Arthur Ross; **Special Effects:** Charles S. Welbourne; **Cinematography:** William E. Snyder; **Cast:** Richard Carlson, Julie Adams, Richard Denning, Antonio Moreno, Whit Bissell, Nestor Paiva, Ricou Browning

An expedition to the deepest part of the Amazon is searching for missing links to humankind's past. What they find is the only original creation in the Universal monster collection, the gillman known as the Creature, a lone survivor from the prehistoric past and possibly humanity's direct link to the oceans that spawned all life on Earth. The scientist try hard to capture the amphibian, but he easily gives them the slip. Smitten with the group's single female (Adams), however, the monster sticks around in the hopes of winning her affections. He eventually gets his chance to kidnap her and does so after killing half the crew. The good guys give pursuit, finally catching up to the gillman in his eerie underwater grotto, where they finish him off and rescue the girl.

Sounds like a slight bit of nothing, but Arnold's moody direction keeps it from being just another creature feature. His inspired underwater shots from the point of view of the monster play heavily on his audience's fears. Strong performances from a solid cast keep the film moving at a good pace, and excellent underwater choreography lends the whole thing an unearthly atmosphere, as if the characters have traveled back in time rather than to a hidden arm of the Amazon. Overall the result is a charming take on the classic theme of "beauty and the beast," which still maintains much of its appeal.

Neither of its sequels, *THE REVENGE OF THE CREATURE* or *THE CREATURE WALKS AMONG US*, holds up to the memorable first film (although it is fun to try to spot an incredibly young Clint Eastwood in his first film appearance in *Revenge*). And of course the first one does have the world's greatest character actor, Whit Bissell, after all.

Creature from the Black Lagoon (UNIVERSAL PICTURES / R. ALLEN LEIDER COLLECTION)

CREATURE WALKS AMONG US, THE

Universal Pictures, 1956, b&w, 78 min, VT, LD

Producer: William Alland; **Director:** John F. Sherwood; **Screenplay:** Arthur Ross; **Cinematography:** Maury Gerstman; **Cast:** Jeff Morrow, Rex Reason, Leigh Snowden, Gregg Plamer, Maurice Manson, James Rawley, David MacMahon, Ricou Browning, Don Megowan

See *THE CREATURE FROM THE BLACK LAGOON*

CREATURE WASN'T NICE, THE
(aka: SPACESHIP, NAKED SPACE)

Almi Pictures, 1981, Color, 88 min, VT

Producer: Mark Haggard; **Director:** Bruce Kimmel; **Screenplay:** Kimmel; **Music:** Kimmel, David Spear; **Special Effects:** Tom Payne, Bill Hedge, Bob Greenberg, and Anthony Doublin; **Cinematography:** Dennis Lavil; **Cast:** Bruce Kimmel, Cindy Williams, Leslie Nielsen, Gerrit Graham, Patrick Macnee, Ron Kurowski

A rare science fiction musical about a creature running rampant on a spaceship manned by a loony crew. The film is boring, the effects bad, and the songs lacking the kind of verve and lyric quality one expects from a musical.

CREATURE WITH THE ATOM BRAIN, THE

Columbia, 1955, b&w, 69 min

Producer: Sam Katzman; **Director:** Edward L. Cahn; **Screenplay:** Curt Siodmak; **Music:** Mischa Bakaleinikoff; **Cinematography:** Siodmak; **Cast:** Richard Denning, Angela Stevens, Tris Coffin, Greg Gray

A gang boss persuades a scientist to create walking dead slaves with energy charges to the brain. It's a better effort than other films of its kind. It doesn't add up to much, though reportedly it was some of the inspiration for George Romero's NIGHT OF THE LIVING DEAD.

CREATURES OF THE PREHISTORIC PLANET

See HORROR OF THE BLOOD MONSTERS

CREEPING TERROR, THE (aka: THE CRAWLING MONSTER)

Crown International, 1964, Color, 75 min, VT

Producer: A.J. Nelson; **Director:** Nelson; **Screenplay:** Robert Silliphant; **Music:** Frederick Kopp; **Special Effects:** Jon Lackey; **Cinematography:** Andrew Jaczak; **Cast:** Vic Savage, Shannon O'Neill, William Thourlby, Louise Lawson, Robin James

A UFO crash landing on Earth releases a bizarre monster that resembles a throw rug. The creature absorbs victims into its body and is replaced by an exact replica whenever destroyed. This is one low-budget film in which the cast is rumored to have paid a few hundred dollars apiece for the "privilege" of appearing. The film's bizarre narration was the result of the sound equipment being accidentally kicked into Lake Tahoe, the location for the film. With no more parts to sell to raise money for new equipment, or so the story goes, producer Nelson was forced to use the narration to cover for the fact they could not record any more sound. Director Nelson appeared in the film credited as Vic Savage.

CREEPING UNKNOWN, THE (aka: THE QUATERMASS EXPERIMENT)

Hammer (Great Britain), 1955, b&w, 78 min, VT, LD

Producer: Anthony Hinds; **Director:** Val Guest; **Screenplay:** Guest and Richard Landau; **Special Effects:** Les Bowie; **Cinematography:** Walter Harvey; **Cast:** Brian Donlevy, Margia Dean, Jack Warner, Richard Wordsworth, David King Wood, Harold Lang, Lionel Jeffries

An Earth rocket crash-lands on its return to the planet. Only one of its inhabitants is still alive. Although the astronaut (Wordsworth) seems to be in good health, his mental state has changed severely. The once cooperative soul is now sullen and withdrawn. Also, a bizarre fungus spreads across his body at a rapid rate. The astronaut is soon consumed by the fungus, which is really an alien creature. Once completely under extraterrestrial control, he/it escapes the hospital and goes on a killing spree throughout London. At this point the hero, Professor Quatermass (Donlevy), is brought in to help the baffled authorities with their investigation. The professor quickly helps them track the astronaut/creature down and box him/it inside Westminster Cathedral, where he/it is finally electrocuted.

Perhaps this sounds like a great deal of the dreck filmed in the '50s, but it's far superior to almost everything from that era, and most viewers regard it as a classic. There are two reasons. The first is Richard Wordsworth's movingly tragic portrayal of the fungus-consumed astronaut. His performance has been compared favorably and accurately to that of Karloff's as the Frankenstein monster. The second reason is Quatermass. The professor is a wonderful character, one who returned to the screen in two more films, plus several BBC television productions. Unlike most science fiction scientists, there is nothing kindly or noble or understanding about Quatermass. Nor is he blinded to the human condition by his considerations for science over everything. He is fully human, but he is also possessed of a ruthless intellect and does not suffer fools gladly. This is the kind of scientific professional too rarely seen in a genre that often prefers to portray scientists as buffoons or villains.

Quatermass's two other films, ENEMY FROM SPACE and FIVE MILLION YEARS TO EARTH, are among the finest, purest science fiction films ever made.

CRIMINALS OF THE GALAXY, THE

See WILD, WILD PLANET

CRITTERS

New Line Cinema, 1986, Color, 86 min, VT, LD

Producer: Robert Shaye; **Director:** Stephen Herek; **Screenplay:** Herek, Don Keith Opper, and Domonic Muir; **Music:** David Newman; **Special Effects:** Charles Chiodo, Edward Chiodo, and Stephen Chiodo; **Cinematography:** Tim Schrsyedt; **Cast:** Dee Wallace Stone, M. Emmet Walsh, Billy Green Bush, Scott Grimes, Nadine Van Der Velde, Terrance Mann, Billy Zane

Rogue alien prisoners who resemble hairy tumble-weeds with a mouthfuls of razor-sharp teeth tear into a small farming town. Earth's only hope? An alien hunter who dresses like a heavy metal rocker. This poorly scripted and badly acted film stands as little more than an attempt to cash in on the success of *GREMLINS*. When the chittering noise the monsters make is the best thing in a film, clearly it's in trouble. Still this one spawned three equally lacking sequels *CRITTERS 2: THE MAIN COURSE* and *CRITTERS 3* as well as *CRITTERS 4* (which went straight to video).

CRITTERS 2: THE MAIN COURSE

New Line Cinema, 1988, Color, 93 min, VT

Producers: Barry Opper and Robert Shaye; **Director:** Mick Garris; **Screenplay:** Garris and David Twohy; **Music:** Nicholas Pike; **Special Effects:** Martin Bresin and Peter Kuran; **Cinematography:** Russell Carpenter; **Cast:** Terrance Mann, Dopn Keith Opper, Cynthia Garris, Scott Grimes, Al Stevenson, Tom Hodges, Douglas Rowe, Liane Alexandra Curtis, Lindsay Parker, Herta Ware

See *CRITTERS*

CRITTERS 3

New Line Cinema, 1991, Color, 86 min, VT

Producer: Rupert Harvey; **Director:** Kristine Peterson; **Screenplay:** David J. Schow; **Music:** David C. Williams; **Special Effects:** Frank Ceglia; **Cinematography:** Thomas L. Callaway; **Cast:** John Calvin, Aimee Brooks, Christian Cousins, Joseph Cousins, William Dennis Hunt, Nina Axelrod, Leonardo DiCaprio, Don Keith Opper, Geoffrey Blake, Terrence Mann

See *CRITTERS*

CRITTERS 4

New Line Cinema, 1991, Color, 100 min, VT

Producers: Barry Opper and Mark Ordesky; **Director:** Rupert Harvey; **Screenplay:** Harvey, Joseph Lyle, Opper, and David J. Schow; **Music:** Peter Manning Robinson; **Special Effects:** Frank Ceglia and Amy L. Crandall; **Cinematography:** Thomas L. Callaway; **Cast:** Don Keith Opper, Terrence Mann, Paul Whitthorne, Anders Hove, Angela Bassett, Brad Dourif, Eric DaRae, Martine Beswick, Anne Ramsay

See *CRITTERS*

CRONOS

Venta Films, 1992, Color, 92 min, VT

Producers: Arthur Gordon and Bertha Navarro; **Director:** Guillermo Del Toro; **Screenplay:** del Toro; **Music:** Javier Álvarez; **Special Effects:** Laurencio Cordero, Guillermo Navarro; **Cast:** Ferderico Luppi, Ron Perlman, Claudio Brook, Margarita Isabel, Juan Colombo, Mario Martinez, Farnesio DeBernal, Daniel Cacho, Manara Shanah, Dan Cacho

This odd but intriguing film concerns a mysterious bit of machinery called the "Cronos Device." When activated, it grants its user eternal life, but it also turns the recipient of its gift into a vampire, though not the kind of traditional vampire one might expect. With just enough science fiction to qualify, this quirky blend of genres is definitely worth seeing.

Cronos (JOSEPH B. MAUCERI COLLECTION)

CUBE

Trimark Pictures, 1997, Color, 98 min, VT, DVD

Producers: Mehra Meh and Betty Orr; **Director:** Vincenzo Natali; **Screenplay:** Andre Bijelic, Graeme Manson, and Natali; **Music:** Mark Korven; **Cinematography:** Derek Rogers; **Special Effects:** John Mariella, Bob Munroe, Caligari Studios, and C.O.R.E. Digital Pictures; **Cast:** Nicole DeBoer, Nicky Guadagni, Andrew Miller, David Hewlett, Julian Richings, Wayne Robeson, Maurice Dean Wint

The film opens with a man in a room. More exactly, he is in a cube-shaped chamber made out of girders and metal sheeting with a softer material filling in the oddly designed (we never do learn if there is a function beyond decoration to the design) metal framework. Every wall, as well as the floor and the ceiling, has a door set in the exact center. Several counterclockwise turns of a straight-bar handle opens any of the doors, giving the occupant access to a crawl space beyond. And if the occupant chooses to vacate and start crawling, where exactly does the crawl space lead to? Another room identical to the one the occupant just left. In the case of this first fellow we're introduced to, his new room is a death trap that quickly kills him in an interesting manner.

The plot proceeds pretty much along these lines. A group of people find themselves trapped together inside this mysterious construct for purposes unknown. In fact, there are no explanations forthcoming in this movie, and every time someone comes up with even the beginnings of an explanation, another character finds a way to shoot it down. How do these people get into the cube? Who put them there? Why? Who built the cube? Why? No answers.

Cube is basically a television story, what hardboiled sci-fi writer Stephen Jackson called "a vicious *Twilight Zone* episode." The characters spout liberal gibberish at each other, feel guilty for foolish reasons, act out of character whenever it suits the script, and generally wander around in this big dumb cube for far too long. With what seems like a great premise, this earnest low-budget production stood a shot of making up for its deficiencies through good writing, but that's exactly what's lacking here. The script saved money for the producers at every turn, which is a very good thing for a low-budget production, and production designer Jasna Stefanovic worked miracles with the set. But the one thing the script doesn't do is tell a story.

For instance, part of the premise is that the people trapped within the cube are all there for a reason. They all possess some skill that will get them out if they can figure out how to work together. But if that's true, what skill did the first guy have? No one knows. While *Cube* gets off to a great beginning and seems to promise a lot, it consistently comes back to the same idea—put simply, all things are pointless. All arguments fail, all faith falters, all authority is corrupt, all theories are wrong.

Note: STAR TREK fans will want to see this one just to watch Nicole DeBoer (the second actress to play the character Dax on *Deep Space Nine*) in a pre-*Trek* role. She's one of the best things about the movie, which helped bring her to the attention of Paramount.

CURSE, THE (aka: THE FARM)

Trans World Entertainment, 1987, Color, 90 min, VT, LD

Producer: Ovidio G. Assonitis; **Director:** David Kieth; **Screenplay:** David Chaskin; **Music:** Franco Micalizzi; **Special Effects:** Lucio Fulci; **Cinematography:** Robert D. Forges; **Cast:** Wil Wheaton, Claude Akins, Cooper Huckabee, John Schneider, Amy Wheaton

A meteorite strikes a Tennessee farm. At first everyone is excited as the crops grow in staggering abundance. Then the truth begins to unfold as they realize nothing on the farm is good. The apples are filled with maggots, the crops are rotten, and the family are all slowly being driven crazy by whatever has contaminated the water table.

Perhaps the best film adaptation ever of H.P. Lovecraft's short story "The Colour Out of Space," this is also one of the most frightening movies ever made. Despite a low budget, the film grips the audience from beginning to end, driven along by Claude Akins in an all-consuming portrayal that stands as the best work he ever did in his considerable career. This is a sci-fi horror classic from the world's first and best science fiction/horror crossover writer.

CURSE OF FRANKENSTEIN, THE

Hammer Film Productions, Ltd., 1957, Color, 82 min, VT, LD

Producers: Michael Carrers, Anthony Hinds, Anthony Nelson Keys, and Max Rosenberg; **Director:** Terrence Fisher; **Screenplay:** Jimmy Sangster; **Music:** James Bernard; **Cinematography:** Jack Asher; **Cast:** Peter Cushing, Hazel Court, Robert Urquhart,

Christopher Lee, Melvin Hayes, Valeri Gaunt, Paul Hardtmuth, Noel Hood, Fred Johnson, Claude Kingston

See *FRANKENSTEIN*

CURSE OF THE FLY, THE

Lippert Films, Ltd./20th Century Fox, 1965, Color, 86 min

Producers: Robert L. Lippert and Jack Parsons; **Director:** Don Sharp; **Screenplay:** Harry Spalding; **Music:** Bert Shefter; **Special Effects:** Harold Fletcher; **Cinematography:** Basil Emmott; **Cast:** Carole Gray, George Baker, Brian Donlevy, Jeremy Wilkins, Yvette Reeves, Burt Kwouk, Michael Graham, Rachel Kempson, Charles Carson

See *THE FLY* (1958)

CYBORG

Golan-Globus, 1989, Color, 86 min, VT, LD, DVD

Producers: Yoram Globus and Menaham Golan; **Director:** Albert Pyun; **Screenplay:** Kitty Chalmers; **Music:** Kevin Bassinson; **Special Effects:** Greg Cannom; **Cinematography:** Philip Alan Waters; **Cast:** Jean-Claude Van Damme, Deborah Richter, Vincent Klyn, Alex Daniels, Dayle Haddon, Blaise Loong, Rolf Muller

Van Damme as a cyborg travels through a brutal future where he confronts and kills the bad guys. The most terrible thing about the film is that he takes 86 minutes instead of 86 seconds to finish them off.

CYBORG 2087

Feature Films, 1966, Color, 86 min

Producer: Earle Lyon; **Director:** Franklin Adreon; **Screenplay:** Arthur C. Pierce; **Music:** Paul Dunlap; **Cast:** Michael Rennie, Wendel Corey, Eduard Franz, Karen Steele, Warren Stevens

Cyborg Garth (Rennie) is sent from 2087 back to the '60s to stop the development of an invention called radio telepathy. This is the device that allows the dictators of the future to control all of humankind. Garth fights his way through time-traveling hit men to plead his case with the inventor who, for the good of humankind, does as Garth asks and gives up his creation. This causes Garth to never be created, a consequence of which the cyborg was well aware as he pleaded his case.

Originally produced for television, but subsequently released in theaters, this little gem was one of the better things done for either medium at the time. The story is notable because the rational good guy Garth pleads his case rather than simply killing the scientist, a route taken by most similarly-themed modern movies.

CYCLOPS, THE

Feature Films, 1957, Color, 86 min, VT

Producer: Bert I. Gordon; **Director:** Gordon; **Screenplay:** Gordon; **Special Effects:** Gordon; **Cinematography:** Ira Morgan; **Cast:** Lon Chaney, Jr., Gloria Talbot, James Craig, Tom Drake, Paul Frees

When a man disappears in the jungle, his brother and friends go looking for him. They find him grown into a towering monster as a result of exposure to radiation.

DALEKS—INVASION EARTH 2150 A.D. (aka: INVASION EARTH 2150 A.D.)

Amicus (Great Britain), 1966, Color, 84 min, VT

Producer: Milton Subotsky; **Director:** Gordon Flemyng; **Screenplay:** Subotsky; **Music:** Bill McGuffie and Barry Gray; **Special Effects:** Ted Samuels; **Cast:** Peter Cushing, Bernard Cribbins, Andrew Kier, Ray Brooks, Jill Curzon, Roberta Tovey

It's possible that some science fiction afficionados haven't heard of Dr. Who, but it seems unlikely. For those who don't know him, here's the scoop: The Doctor is a Time Lord. He travels back and forth through time in his time machine, the Tardis, which is shaped to appear like a British police telephone box. The reason for the British influence? *Dr. Who* began as a BBC television production that became the longest-running science fiction TV series in history. The series spawned only two films, however, of which this is the second.

In this outing, Dr. Who's most sinister villains, the Daleks, return for another crack at conquering Earth. Daleks are an alien race reduced to ameboid form due to fallout from the nuclear war they had on their world. They now encase themselves within clumsily shaped but quite deadly robots in order to maintain their empire and, well, to just plain get around. This time the Daleks are hoping to use mind-control to take over

the world. The Doctor defeats them handily, of course, sending them to a fiery end in the center of Earth.

The films were lucky enough to have a budget somewhat beyond the subsistence levels on which the television episodes were forced to exist. That doesn't mean in any way, however, that this was a big-budget epic. Even with the upgrade to Peter Cushing as the good Doctor in the two films, they are both B pictures made to pull a specific audience into the movie houses. And so, sadly, those who aren't already fans of the show shouldn't think they're in for a big treat by watching this one.

Dr. Who, although it has quite a large adult following around the world, was produced as children's programming. It's inventive and clever, with scripting that is often quite technical and even sophisticated. But over the decades it has remained a mostly static bit of fare, constantly hampered by its severely low budget. Good scripts and willing, if somewhat limited, actors, have sustained it despite the show's use of some of the worst special effects ever seen. One can imagine the show's producers during the '60s, looking at imports of *Lost in Space* and simply drooling over the chance to have monsters that looked that good.

All of that aside, however, without a previous love affair with the series (or even the film that preceded this one), this second picture is likely to leave one a bit disappointed. On the other hand, those who have caught even a few of the shows in reruns and enjoyed them should give the films a try. Both the series and the off-shoot movies deserve their sterling reputation along with their legions of fans, and everyone deserves a chance to see Peter Cushing play the good Doctor. Without slighting the excellent work of the television casts, surely no one plays this kind of role better than does Cushing.

DAMNATION ALLEY

20th Century Fox, 1977, Color, 95 min, VT

Producer: Jerome Zeitman; **Director:** Jack Smight; **Screenplay:** Alan Sharp and Lucas Heller; **Music:** Jerry Goldsmith; **Special Effects:** Milt Rice; **Cinematography:** Harry Stradling, Jr.; **Cast:** Jan-Michael Vincent, George Peppard, Kip Niven, Paul Winfield, Dominique Sanda, Jackie Earl Haley

After a nuclear war destroys almost every square inch of the United States (and presumably everywhere else), Earth is tilted off its axis. This causes chaos with the weather, including bright lights in the sky, bizarre electrical discharges, and oddly colored tornados. In the center of this mess we find several air force types surviving somewhat handily in an old missile bunker. At least they're surviving nicely until one of the lunkheads accidentally sets fire to his men's magazine and thus the entire complex. It's a ridiculous scene, but it does force the crew to take out a pair of their "land-mobiles" and try to find some other place to live, which is the core of this film's meager story.

The officers' journey takes them cross-country, from somewhere in the extreme southwestern deserts of America to the uppermost portions of New England, where supposedly the last fit place to live on Earth exists, though this is never explained. Most of the group die along the way, but the survivors find two normal women living amidst the mutants, giant scorpions, carnivorous cockroaches, gunmen, flash floods, and other life-threatening elements of the landscape and finally make their way to Maine and, supposedly, the eternal happiness they so richly deserve.

Despite excellent source material in respected science fiction writer Roger Zelazny's novel of the same name, the filmmakers managed to produce a rather awful film. That they changed his biker hero to an air force officer illustrates how serious they were in actually bringing his story to the screen. Despite a talented cast, the support of a big studio, and even with the presence of Paul Winfield, the dyin'est man in sci-fi filmdom, they succeeded only in churning out a turgid insult to both Zelazny and their audience, while also making one of the dullest, most wooden movies of all time.

Note: If you watch this one and make it as far as the waves of killer cockroaches (masses of toy insects stiffly glued together into big sheets, which are then simply pulled across the ground to simulate attacking hordes), watch them carefully. Then, if you're ever seen a cheesier, more pathetically low-budget effect in a big studio movie, please make a note of it. The world needs to know.

DAMNED, THE

See *THESE ARE THE DAMNED*

DARK, THE (aka: THE MUTILATOR)

Film Ventures International, 1979, Color, 92 min, VT

Producer: Derek Power; **Director:** John Cardos; **Screenplay:** Stanford Whitmore; **Music:** Roger Kellaway; **Special Effects:** Robdy Knott; **Cinematography:** John Arthur Morrill; **Cast:** Cathy Lee Crosby, William Devane, Keenan Wynn, Richard Jackel, Biff Elliott, Jacquelyn Hyde, Vivian Blaine

A killer alien annoys Southern Californian townsfolk with its murderous ways. A cast of strong television actors is not enough to save this film from its ponderous, murky plot.

DARK ANGEL

See *I COME IN PEACE*

DARK CITY

New Line Cinema, 1998, Color, 101 min, VT, LD, DVD

Producers: Andrew Mason and Alex Proyas; **Director:** Proyas; **Screenplay:** Proyas, David S. Goyer, and Lem Dobbs; **Music:** Trevor Jones; **Special Effects:** Tad Paige and Tom Davies; **Cast:** William Hurt, Kiefer Sutherland, Jennifer Connelly, Richard O'Brien, Rufus Sewell, Ian Richardson, Colin Friels, Bruce Spencer, Mitchell Brutel

In a city without sunlight, John Murdock (Sewell) awakes to find he has no memory. He doesn't know his wife; he doesn't know who he is. He also doesn't know that he's suspected of being a serial killer. All he knows is that he woke up nude in a bathtub and that some unusual-looking fellows are after him. As he tries to piece his life together, however, he begins to learn some amazing things. It seems Murdock is a special person. He is a mutant, one highly prepared to adapt to new situations, which is good because he's in one of the newest situations a person could be in. He and all the other occupants of the city in which he found himself when he awoke have been abducted by aliens. They are living, not on a planet, but on a giant space station shaped to resemble an Earthly urban center. The aliens wipe the humans' minds clean every few days, reprogramming them with completely new identities (while also changing the shape and look of the entire city at the same time) so that they might be studied further.

Why study them? Because the alien race, despite their great mental powers, is slowly dying. Their superior abilities come from their collective mentality, but it seems that only by learning to be individuals will they be able to survive. Thus they study humans, trying to discern if there is something innately moral or immoral to them, if they had to be born with their souls, or if it can all just be programmed. Murdock poses a problem for them because he has developed the ability to resist their programming. He doesn't fall asleep at midnight like everyone else in the city so that he might be fed a new data stream, and worse, he's rapidly developing the same powers as the aliens, but without the restraint of having to work through a collective mind.

And, if the above seems like a lot of information, that's just the tip of the iceberg. *Dark City* is a rich to overflowing sci-fi bounty. While many science fiction movies are really "slash" films—sci-fi/horror, sci-fi/adventure, sci-fi/action, and so on—*Dark City* is one of the extremely rare but almost always entertaining sci-fi/noir films. There is a dark, hard-boiled edge to this picture that makes it exceptionally entertaining. The story moves forward at lightning speed, always feeding the audience more information, always taking left turns when they expect it to go right. It raises a number of strong social questions that admittedly it doesn't bother to answer, but then humankind has been arguing over the answers for centuries, so perhaps it's for the best. Just putting the question of what constitutes the human "soul" before mass audiences is an accomplishment for any film. That it does it with style and class is a bonus.

Visually the film is a true special effects extravaganza and is marvelously inventive in every detail. The set designs are creative and beautiful, a chaotic mix of everything from the Victorian to Art Deco blended together seamlessly. The actors all turn in dazzling performances, perhaps inspired by the intelligence and nerve of the script.

There is much more to *Dark City* than it would be prudent to mention here. Every detail of the film's tight plot revealed is another revelation stolen from the impact of viewing it. Though the film was grossly ignored in the theaters, it shouldn't have been. Sci-fi fans don't often get treated with this degree of respect. They should show some in return, or Hollywood might go on thinking all they want are remakes of THE BLACK SCORPION.

Note: There are a number of thematic similarities between *Dark City*, which did poorly in general release in 1998, and THE MATRIX, which one year later did extraordinarily well. It is interesting to note that a decade after the fall of the communist bloc and the paranoia that fueled so many earlier science fiction films the genre may be coming home to a new, even darker fear. Many movies in the '50s, such as THE THING FROM ANOTHER WORLD or INVASION OF THE BODY SNATCHERS, were warnings of the dangers of communism. Humankind, often represented by the U.S. government, which had to stand ready to defend itself against all manner of forces, was depicted as noble and pure. Now in films like *Dark City* and THE MATRIX, humankind is represented by the general population, and the dark forces trying to sap their will is their own government. How long this trend continues will be of interest throughout the third century of science fiction films.

DARKMAN

Universal, 1990, Color, 95 min, VT, LD, DVD

Producer: Robert G. Tappert; **Director:** Sam Raimi; **Screenplay:** Sam Raimi, Ivan Raimi, Chuck Pfarrer, Daniel Goldin, and Joshua Goldin; **Music:** Danny Elfman and Jonathan Sheffer; **Special Effects:** William Mesa; **Cinematography:** Bill Pope; **Cast:** Liam Neeson, Frances McDormand, Colin Friels, Jenny Agutter, Larry Drake, Nelson Mashita, Danny Hicks, Jesse Lawrence Ferguson, Rafael H. Robledo

Scientist Neeson is close to replicating body parts successfully in his lab, but thugs working for a land developer attack him, destroy his lab and his work, then leave him for dead. Neeson, however, repairs himself with his discovery. Still, his face is damaged beyond repair, and he must use his cloned skin to make human masks, which he then wears in a superhero crusade to gain his revenge.

Overall, this one is a lot of fun, assuming that one can overlook its pretensions of high-adventure that creep in toward the end. Audiences looking for a well-done comic-book movie will get what they expect. The filmmakers execute some nice stylistic touches such as opening Neeson's mind to the audience to allow split-second glimpses into the pain that motivates him. These wild, roller-coaster sequences of flashing information come and go with no explanation, enhancing the film's chaotic pace. For anyone interested in seeing Liam Neeson chewing up the scenery in his early days, this film is a must.

Two direct-to-video sequels, *DARKMAN II: THE RETURN OF DURANT* and *DARKMAN III: DIE, DARKMAN, DIE*, followed this film with Arnold Vosloo taking on the title role.

DARKMAN II: THE RETURN OF DURANT

Universal/Renaissance Pictures, 1994, Color, 93 min, VT, LD, DVD

Producers: Sam Raimi, David Roessell, and Robert G. Tappert; **Director:** Bradford May; **Screenplay:** Steven McKay; **Music:** Danny Elfman and Randy Miller; **Special Effects:** John Campfens and Tom Turnbull; **Cinematography:** May; **Cast:** Larry Drake, Arnold Vosloo, Kim Delaney, Renee O'Connor, Lawrence Dane, Jesse Collins, David Ferry, Jack Langedijk

See *DARKMAN*

DARKMAN III: DIE, DARKMAN, DIE

Renaissance Films, 1996, Color, 87 min, VT, LD

Producers: Sam Raimi, David Roessell, Robert G. Tappert, David Eick, and Bernadette Joyce; **Director:** Bradford May; **Screenplay:** Michael Colleary and Mike Werb; **Music:** Danny Elfman and Randy Miller; **Special Effects:** John Campfens; **Cinematography:** May; **Cast:** Jeff Fahey, Arnold Vosloo, Darlene Fluegel, Roxanne Dawson, Nigel Bennett, Alicia Panetta, Ron Sarosiak, Peter Graham, Shawn Doyle

See *DARKMAN*

DARK STAR

Bryanston, 1975, Color, 83 min, VT, LD, DVD

Producer: Jack H. Harris; **Director:** John Carpenter; **Screenplay:** Carpenter and Dan O'Bannon; **Music:** Carpenter; **Special Effects:** Bob Greenberg and John Wash; **Cast:** Dan O'Bannon, Andreijah Pahich, Brian Narell, Carl Kuniholm

The story in this science fiction comedy centers on the deep-space ship *Dark Star*, whose crew looks for unstable planets and then destroys them with sentient bombs. Their problems are numerous—the ship is deteriorating, the captain is "dead" but still somewhat conscious (and thus kept in a cold storage locker), the crew members are all descending into psychosis, their pet alien (a beach ball with feet and teeth and one of the funniest things you'll ever see) is growing increasingly hostile, and one of their bombs doesn't want to wait to explode.

Dark Star began when some young film students at the University of Southern California got together and decided to put on a show. For $6,000 they shot themselves a 45-minute, 16mm sci-fi comedy, which they decided was so funny they'd take it to someone in "the business." Producer Jack Harris decided they were wise to do so and gave them $54,000 more to transfer what they had to 35mm and then shoot enough additional material to bring the thing up to a suitable length for theatrical release. Those young filmmakers were John (*Halloween*) Carpenter and Dan (*ALIEN*) O'Bannon, and their summer project led to fame, fortune, and careers. (What'd you do last June through August?)

D.A.R.Y.L.

Columbia/Paramount, 1985, Color, 99 min, VT, LD

Producer: John Heyman; **Director:** Simon Wincer; **Screenplay:** Jeffrey M. Ellis, David Ambrose, and Allan Scott; **Music:** Marvin Hamlisch; **Special Effects:** Michael L. Fink; **Cinematography:** Frank Watts; **Cast:** Mary Beth Hurt, Michael McKean, Barret Oliver, Kathryn Walker, Colleen Camp, Josef Summer, Steve Ryan, Danny Corkill

A childless couple trying to adopt a little boy somehow end up with a little android instead. Despite this, the android and family form a bond that is threatened when unsympathetic officials arrive on the scene to take the artificial child away. Overall, this bland film delivers little more than a slight tug at the heartstrings, and nothing much for dedicated science fiction fans.

DAUGHTER OF DR. JEKYLL

Allied Artists, 1957, b&w, 71 min, VT

Producer: Jack Pollexfen; **Director:** Edgar G. Ulmer; **Screenplay:** Pollexfen; **Music:** Melvyn Leonard; **Cinematography:** John F. Warren; **Cast:** John Agar, Gloria Talbot, Arthur Shields, John Dierkes

Dr. Jekyll's daughter is having bad dreams. She goes to bed and has nightmares about murder. And there's a monster living in her house. And people are upset. And, and . . . and just forget it. Not Agar's best. Not anyone's best.

DAUGHTER OF EVIL, THE

See *ALRAUNE*

DAWN OF THE DEAD

Laurel Group, 1978, color, 71 min, VT, LD, DVD

Producers: Claudio Argento, Dario Argento, Alfred Cuomo, and Richard P. Rubinstein; **Director:** George Romero; **Screenplay:** Romero; **Music:** Goblin; **Cinematography:** Michael Gornick; **Special Effects:** Tom Savini; **Cast:** David Emgee, Ken Foree, Scott H. Reiniger, Gaylen Ross, Tom Savini, Pasquale Buba, Tony Buba, Sharon Ceccati, Pam Chatfield, Mike Christopher, George Romero

See *NIGHT OF THE LIVING DEAD (1990)*

DAY MARS INVADED EARTH, THE

20th Century Fox, 1963, b&w, 70 min

Producer: Maury Dexter; **Director:** Dexter; **Screenplay:** Harry Spaulding; **Music:** Richard LaSalle; **Cast:** Kent Taylor, Marie Windsor, William Mims, Betty Beall, Lowell Brown, Gregg Shank

Martians turn themselves into duplicates of Scientist Taylor and his family and friends, killing the originals as they go along. A lot of destruction and murder follows, but really, there's not that much more to it.

DAY OF RESURRECTION

See *VIRUS (1980)*

DAY OF THE ANIMALS

See *SOMETHING IS OUT THERE*

DAY OF THE DEAD

Laurel Communications, 1985, color, 102 min, VT, LD, DVD

Producers: David Ball, Salah M. Hassanein, Ed Lammi, and Richard P. Rubinstein; **Director:** George Romero; **Screenplay:** Romero; **Music:** John Harrison; **Cinematography:** Michael Gornick; **Special Effects:** Tom Savini, Steven Kirshoff, and Mark Mann; **Cast:** Lori Cardille, Terry Alexander, Joseph Pilato, Jarlath Conroy, Antone DiLeo, Richard Liberty, G. Howard Klar, Ralph Marrero, John Amplas, Phillip G. Kellams, Taso N. Stavrakis, Gregory Nicotero, Sherman Howard, George Romero

See *NIGHT OF THE LIVING DEAD (1968)*

DAY OF THE DOLPHIN, THE

Avco-Embassy, 1973, Color, 105 min, VT, LD

Director: Mike Nichols; **Screenplay:** Buck Henry; **Cast:** George C. Scott, Trish Van Devere, Paul Sorvino, Fritz Weaver, Jon Korkes, John Dehner, Edward Herrman

At first this film follows the experiments of a marine biologist (Scott) who teaches dolphins to speak English. But soon, what begins as a story about a kind of first contact shifts gears suddenly into a thriller about a plot to kill the president and the bad guys who are being mean to the dolphins who may be the only ones who foil the assassination attempt.

The first portion of the film details a meeting of the minds between two intelligent, but highly different, species, and these are extremely interesting scenes, built nicely layer upon layer. It's all handled cleverly and believably, and if the movie had continued along these lines, it could have been outstanding. But it seems obvious that the filmmakers were hoping their audience would overlook the dull spots in the second half solely because they would be enraged over the fact that the bad guys were being mean to the dolphins. Halfway to brilliant, but ultimately disappointing.

Note: Screenwriter Buck Henry provided the dolphin voices and did a bang-up job of it.

DAY OF THE TRIFFIDS, THE

Allied Artists, 1963, Color, 94 min, VT, LD

Producer: George Pitcher; **Director:** Steve Sekely; **Screenplay:** Philip Yordan; **Music:** Rod Goodwin and Johnny Douglas; **Special Effects:** Wally Veevers; **Cinematography:** John Winbolt; **Cast:** Howard Keel, Nicole Maurey, Janette Scott, Kieron Moore, Mervyn Johns, Janina Faye

The night sky blazes with the greatest meteor shower ever witnessed by humanity, and so everyone who can watches it. The next day, however, the world's population discovers that the lights in the sky have made them blind. Worse yet, traveling along with the meteors were seeds that land on Earth, where they grow into gigantic killer plants known as Triffids. They can lash out with stingers to poison their prey and then reel the victim in with crawling vines. And for that prey smart enough to keep its distance, well, triffids can uproot themselves and walk, too.

Sailor Bill Masen (Keel) was in the hospital with his eyes bandaged when all this was happening; thus he still has his sight. He wanders about London for a while, getting his bearings but also getting used to the fact that there is nothing he can do to help. He is one man in a city of the blind. Even a casual announcement that he can see leaves him besieged by scores who are desperate for help. He soon learns to keep his mouth shut. Finding an orphaned school girl who is also sighted, he adopts her as the one part of the world he will protect, and the two head for France, where the radio reports a conference is being held to cope with the situation.

Meanwhile, a married couple who are also marine researchers living in a lighthouse on an island find themselves fighting Triffids sprouted from seeds in a small scrap of dirt. The film cuts back and forth between the two story lines, revealing each team's bleak progress. Masen and his young charge make it to France, where they join with other sighted folk, only to lose all but one of them in a massive Triffid attack. The lighthouse couple work feverishly to find a way to stop the monstrous plants, but nothing works.

The hard science in this one is kept low key, but as social science fiction, as a mirror for the audience to gauge their own values against the specter of holocaust, this is one terrific movie. In many ways the story is horrific in tone, but the overwhelming percentage of the horror is what it depicts of human nature. Although there are good people doing good things throughout the film, the great majority of people are portrayed as fearful, greedy, self-centered, and just plain hateful. It's hard to feel superior, though. People honest enough to answer truthfully when asking themselves what they would be doing if they were there, sighted or unsighted, usually can't make much of a case for how wonderful they would be in the same situation.

Fans of the novel *The Day of the Triffids* by John Wyndham, which inspired the film, may find themselves scratching their heads, wondering where the filmmakers went wrong, but those who don't know the book will truly enjoy the movie. A great deal of the source material dosen't make it to the screen, but what does is well done. If the film sometimes feels like two separate movies, it's because scenes with Kieron Moore and Janette Scott were added later to increase the running time.

Note: The special effects are uneven throughout the film, but when they're good, they're outstanding.

DAY THE EARTH CAUGHT FIRE, THE

British Lion (Great Britain), 1961, b&w, 99 min, VT

Producer: Val Guest; **Director:** Guest; **Screenplay:** Guest and Wolf Waxman; **Music:** Stanley Black; **Special Effects:** Les Bowie; **Cinematography:** Harry Waxman; **Cast:** Edward Judd, Janet Munro, Leo McKern, Michael Goodlife, Bernard Braden, Robin Hawden

Reckless atomic bomb tests knock Earth off its orbit and send it spiraling into the sun.

This slight premise is saved by Val Guest, who cut his teeth at Hammer making such films as THE QUATERMASS EXPERIMENT, experience which stood him in good stead here. Filmed as a pseudo-documentary, most of the film takes place within the offices of the British newspaper *Daily Express*. Retired editor Arthur Christiansen even plays himself in the film, and the whole setup adds a desperate tension to the story that a conventional approach might have lacked.

Note: Have fun trying to spot young Michael Caine as a police officer directing traffic.

DAY THE EARTH STOOD STILL, THE

20th Century Fox, 1951, b&w, 92 min, VT, LD

Producer: Julian Blaustein; **Director:** Robert Wise; **Screenplay:** Edmund H. North; **Music:** Bernard Herrmann; **Special Effects:** Fred Sersen; **Cast:** Michael Rennie, Patricia Neal, Hugh Marlowe, Sam Jaffe, Billy Gray, Francis Bavier, Lock Martin

A flying saucer lands in Washington, D.C. It is surrounded by tanks and troops who shoot the first person that emerges from its interior. This turns out to be

Klaatu (Rennie), a representative from an intergalactic federation, who has a message for all the leaders of Earth. When Earth's various leaders refuse to meet in the same place for political reasons, Klaatu decides to go out and learn a little about Earthlings. He escapes his hosts/captors with ease and settles in at a local rooming house, where he befriends a young widow (Neal) and her son, using the boy as a blind with which he moves about the city, listening, asking questions, and making up his mind about what he's going to do. What he does is get himself killed by the fearful, primitive human race, an act that almost results in the incineration of the planet. But don't worry—his advanced alien science includes temporary resurrection.

It turns out that Gort, the robot the audience has been thinking of as Klaatu's assistant, is in fact an intergalactic police officer. Klaatu's federation surrendered all authority to these superpowered, indestructible dreadnoughts centuries before. They patrol the galaxy, looking for trouble and destroying the worlds of any who get out of line. At the climax of the film, Klaatu informs an international group of scientists whom he allows to stand in for the world's leaders that with Earth having both joined the atomic club and beginning to move out into space, its people will have to mature as a race. How they run the planet is up to them, but at the first sign of them bringing any of their nonsense off-world, the intergalactic police force will destroy them. After that, Klaatu gets into his ship and takes off, leaving the scientists as stunned as the audience.

This is one of the finest science fiction films ever made. The special effects are good but not outstanding, and there aren't really enough of them to overshadow the story. Here the idea is the most important element, and watching the film's central thesis unfold is a beautiful experience. The movie owes much of its success to a powerful cast.

Klaatu is Michael Rennie's finest role. He brings an unhurried, quiet dignity to the alien that is so utterly fitting it is quite impossible to imagine anyone else playing the part. He demonstrates intellect, humor, patience, an exacting moral sense, integrity, and anger in the subtlest of dramatic flourishes, often with just a twinkle in his eye. Many moments throughout the film could have been played with more belligerence, and probably would have been by a lesser actor.

The Day the Earth Stood Still (TWENTIETH CENTURY FOX / AUTHOR'S COLLECTION)

And the same must be said for Patricia Neal. Even though her character is engaged to be married, it's obvious throughout the movie that she is growing less and less enchanted with her fiancé the more she learns about Mr. Carpenter (Klaatu's human alias). Though it's never alluded to verbally, she's clearly falling for him. Later, however, when she realizes what he is, the blossoming romance ends because he is a superior being she can't begin to understand. It's the subtlest of moments when it happens, but it's a stellar one, and one of the finest bits of intellectual acting ever to grace the screen.

The success of this movie really jump-started Hollywood's sci-fi craze of the '50s, but it's a shame that much of what followed was far inferior. It's hard to believe that producers could have seen this low-key, self-assured, quiet message film raking it in at the box office and missed the point of what was happening so completely, but they did. Oh well, what can I say, except, "Gort, Klaatu, barada, nikto."

Note: Bernard Herrmann's score for this film is tremendously evocative and otherworldly.

DAY THE FISH CAME OUT, THE

20th Century Fox, 1967, Color, 109 min

Producer: Michael Cacoyannis; **Director:** Cacoyannis; **Screenplay:** Cacoyannis; **Music:** Mikis Theodorakis; **Cinematography:** Walter Lessally; **Cast:** Tom Courteney, Candice Bergen, Colin Blakely, Sam Wanamaker, Ian Ogilvy

Mocking a true incident in which the U.S. Air Force actually did lose two nuclear bombs off the coast of Spain, this film concerns a similar accident in which the authorities lose an H-bomb as well as several other doomsday devices off the coast of a small Greek island. Not wanting to attract attention, the retrieval team members disguise themselves as tourists, which only encourages the rest of the world to think that the island is suddenly the new vacation hot spot. Tourists begin to flock to the area, making the team's job harder, but also dooming themselves when one of the doomsday devices poisons everyone. The fish that come out are the dead fish floating on top of the water—the doomsday device's first victims.

The whole film strives to be a black comedy but never succeeds. Even the effectively filmed shots of the dead fish floating limply while tourists cavort on the beach at the end of the picture don't add up to much of an impact.

DAY THE SKY EXPLODED, THE

Royal/Lux (Italy/Germany), 1958, Excelsior (U.S.), 1961, b&w, 82 min, VT

Producer: Guido Giambartolomei; **Director:** Paolo Heusch; **Screenplay:** Marcello Coscia and Alessandro Continenza; **Music:** Carlo Rustichelli; **Cinematography:** Mario Bava; **Cast:** Paul Hubschmid, Madeleine Fischer, Fiorella Mari, Ivo Garrani, Sam Galter

A missile that explodes near the sun sends a great mass of debris heading for Earth. More bombs are sent into space to destroy the debris, which doesn't do as much good as people expected.

DAY THE WORLD ENDED, THE

ARC, 1956, b&w, 81 min

Producer: Roger Corman; **Director:** Corman; **Screenplay:** Lou Rusoff; **Music:** Ronald Stein; **Special Effects:** Paul Blaisdell; **Cinematography:** Jack Feindel; **Cast:** Mike "Touch" Connors, Richard Denning, Lori Nelson, Adele Jergens, Jonathan Haze

Sometime in the mid-seventies the world was destroyed by nuclear war. Now the survivors try to stay alive despite radiation and mutants.

DAY TIME ENDED, THE
(aka: TIME WARP)

Charles Band Productions, Inc., 1980, Color, 79 min, VT

Producer: Charles Band; **Director:** John Cardos; **Screenplay:** Wayne Schmidt, David Schmoeller, J. Larry Carroll, and Steve Neill; **Music:** Richard Band and John Watson; **Special Effects:** David Allen, Dave Carson, and Paul Gentry; **Cinematography:** John Arthur Morrill; **Cast:** Jim Davis, Dorothy Malone, Chris Mitchum, Marcy Lafferty, Natasha Ryan, Scott Kolden

Desert residents witness great special effects that neither they nor the screenwriter can explain.

D-DAY ON MARS (aka: THE PURPLE MONSTER STRIKES)

Republic Pictures, 1945, b&w, 100 min

Producer: Ronald Davidson; **Director:** Spencer Bennet; **Screenplay:** Basil Dickey, Royal K. Cole, Albert DeMond, Lynn Perkins, Joseph F. Poland, and Barney A. Sarecky; **Special Effects:** Howard Lydecker and Theodore Lydecker; **Cinematography:** Bud Thackery; **Cast:** Linda Sterling, Roy Barcroft, Fred Bannon, Dennis Moore, James Craven, Bud Geary, Mary Moore

A Martian invader is stopped by human heroes in this Republic serial, originally titled *The Purple Monster Strikes*, edited down to a supposedly more bearable length. One of the better of the old serials.

DEADLY BEES, THE

Amicus (Great Britain), 1966/Paramount (U.S.), 1967, Color, 85 min

Producer: Max Rosenberg; **Director:** Freddie Francis; **Screenplay:** Robert Block and Anthony Marriott; **Music:** Wilfred Josephs; **Special Effects:** John Mackie; **Cinematography:** John Wilcox; **Cast:** Suzanna Leigh, Guy Doleman, Catherine Finn, Katy Wild, Frank Finlay, Michael Ripper, Michael Gwynn

Beekeeper Finlay trains his insect pals to sting to death anyone he marks with a particular fragrance. The murder sequences are interesting, but nothing else is. The bees kill Finlay in the end.

DEADLY DIAPHONOIDS, THE

See *WAR OF THE PLANETS*

DEADLY MANTIS, THE

Universal, 1957, b&w, 79 min

Producer: William Alland; **Director:** Nathan Juran; **Screenplay:** Martin Berkeley; **Music:** Joe Gershenson; **Special Effects:** Clifford Stine; **Cinematography:** Ellis W. Carter; **Cast:** Craig Stevens, Alix Talton, William Hopper, Pat Conway, Donald Randolph

The film opens with narrator Paul Frees quoting a classic scientific precept: "For every action there is an opposite and equal reaction."

The action in mind is a volcano erupting somewhere in the tropics. The opposite and equal reaction is an icequake at the North Pole that releases a giant praying mantis from its countless centuries of sleep there in the Arctic. Then it seems the filmmakers expected the audience to forget the mantis since it vanishes from the movie for some time as the story moves along to a series of mysterious disappearances.

First, a far Arctic outpost is obliterated, and the soldiers who should have been manning the post are gone without a trace as to how or why. Next, airplanes disappear, and again the bodies are missing. Investigators are baffled until they discover an unusual foreign object in the wreckage of a downed plane. None of the military authorities can identify it, but through a bit of backward engineering, the film's paleontologist hero proves that the massive, five-foot-long spike is the spur of a praying mantis. Folk are doubtful until the thing shows up and rips the top off the headquarters of the military base. After that paleontology gets its proper respect.

The attack on the base gives our heroes enough information to prove that the thing is moving in a straight line, heading directly south, obviously to a warmer climate. Immediately everyone mobilizes to help spot and stop the monstrous terror. Ignoring the warmer call of the tropics, the King Kong–sized insect can't pass up the chance for a side trip to New York City, where his hunters ultimately trap and destroy him in the Holland Tunnel.

As a science fiction film, *The Deadly Mantis* receives some high marks as well as some low ones. On the plus side, it has some sparkling riffs on paleontology that are simply fascinating—the mantis theory our hero puts together is both wildly speculative and justifiably insightful, and the scientific method prevails nicely.

On the minus side, however, some of the scientific omissions are mind boggling. Why does no one comment on the unusual aspect of an insect that can survive subzero temperatures? Why does no one wonder how its exoskeleton can support its massive height and weight? After all, for once our giant creepie isn't supposed to be the product of nuclear radiation—it's supposed to be a throwback to the dinosaur days when giant insects strode the Earth. Yet no one really wonders where this thing came from, or if there are any more, or if it might have the capability to lay eggs.

The final word is that this is an interestingly inconsistent film that mixes some good acting and some really good special effects for the period with some really bad acting and some really hokey special effects. One might guess that the screenwriter was handed a copy of the script for the earlier giant bug classic, *THEM!*, and told not to stop copying until his hand fell off. This one is for the giant bug completist only.

Note: Stock Footage Alert! One possible reason to sit through this one is the acres of great mid-'50s U.S. Air Force stock footage that it uses. The film is a treasure trove, especially for those with a yen to see the Civilian Reconnaissance Corp in action.

DEADLY RAY FROM MARS, THE (aka: FLASH GORDON: MARS ATTACKS THE WORLD)

Hurst Entertainment, 1938, b&w, 99 min, VT

Producer: Barney A. Sarecky; **Director:** Ford Beebe; **Screenplay:** Herbert Dalmas, Ray Trampe, Norman S. Hall, and Wyndham Gittens; **Cinematography:** Jerome Ash; **Cast:** Buster Crabbe, Jean Rogers, Charles Middleton, Frank Shannon, Donald Kerr, Beatrice Roberts

Flash (Crabbe) and his gang of defenders of the galaxy work hard to discover the secret behind the sinister force draining off the world's nitrogen. Who could it be? Of course, it's Ming the Merciless, Flash's enemy in every single movie, comic, radio play, and Sunday funnies in which the character has ever appeared. This is not an old movie but a new editing of the old serial for home video. Sadly, this one looked better as a serial.

DEADLY WEAPON

Empire Pictures, 1989, Color, 89 min, VT

Producer: Peter Manougian; **Director:** Michael Miner; **Screenplay:** Miner; **Music:** Guy Moon; **Special Effects:** Nick Plantico; **Cast:** Rodney Eastman, Kim Walker, Michael Horse, Gary Frank, Ed Nelson, William Sanderson, Joe Regalbuto

The filmmakers strive to evoke pathos for a loser who finds a ray gun and uses it to settle some old scores. They succeed only in telling the tale of a whining dope who brings his troubles on himself in more ways than one.

DEAN KOONTZ'S PHANTOMS

See *PHANTOMS*

DEATH CORPS

See *SHOCK WAVE*

DEATH RAY, THE

Pathé (France), 1924, b&w, two reels

Supervisor: H. Grindell-Mathews

A mad scientist creates a death ray that he uses to knock planes from the sky before he's eventually dealt the same terrible fate.

DEATH RACE 2000

New World Pictures, 1975, Color, 78 min, VT, DVD

Producer: Roger Corman; **Director:** Paul Bartel; **Screenplay:** Charles B. Griffith, Robert Thum, and Ib Melchior; **Music:** Paul Chihara; **Special Effects:** Richard MacLean; **Cinematography:** Tak Tujimoto; **Cast:** David Carradine, Sylvester Stallone, Simone Griffeth, Don Steele, Louisa Moritz, Mary Woronow, John Landis, Fred Grady, Joyce Jameson, Martin Kove, Carle Bensen

It's the future, and it's time for Death Race 2000. In this event, racers in lethal cars compete in a cross-country competition in which they score points for killing as many pedestrians as possible as well as each other. This dry outline could sound thin, but the film is played as a black comedy, and the result is more laughs than one might imagine. There's certainly no Academy Award potential here, but the entire audience will groan in unison at the world's greatest pun ever made about a hand grenade. A rare gem from producer Corman.

Note: The film features Sylvester Stallone in his first starring role. He and Carradine compete for most outlandish characterization, and though Carradine wins hands down, Stallone is a great runner-up.

DEATH BECOMES HER

Universal, 1992, Color, 104 min, VT, LD, DVD

Producers: Robert Zemeckis and Steve Starkey; **Director:** Zemeckis; **Screenplay:** David Koepp and Martin Donovan; **Music:** Alan Silvestri; **Special Effects:** Ken Ralston, Pat Turner, and Tom Woodruff, Jr.; **Cinematography:** Dean Cundey; **Cast:** Bruce Willis, Meryl Streep, Goldie Hawn, Isabella Rossellini, Ian Ogilvy, Adam Storke, Nancy Fish, Alaina Reed Hall, Michelle Johnson, Mimi Kennedy, Jonathan Sullivan, Fabio

Meryl Streep plays a vacuous actress obsessed with staying young. When an old friend's (Hawn) lover (Willis) turns out to have some secrets concerning that subject, she steals him away. Hawn vows revenge at any cost, including her soul. The slight science fiction here involves formulas that bring about immortality but, sadly, not invulnerability. The film is extremely funny, witty, and fast moving, and the clever special effects generate the best jokes. This one's often shown on TV, so keep an eye out for it when channel surfing.

Note: For those who love in-jokes, check the date (10/26/85) when Helen (Goldie Hawn) takes her blast of the forever potion. It's the same date Zemeckis used in *BACK TO THE FUTURE* as the date where everything transpires in the "present."

DEATHSPORT

New World Pictures, 1978, Color, 83 min, VT, DVD

Producer: Roger Corman; **Director:** Henry Suso and Allan Arkush; **Screenplay:** Suso and Donald Stewart; **Music:** Andrew Stein; **Special Effects:** Jack Rabin; **Cinematography:** Gary Graver; **Cast:** David Carradine, Allan Arkush, Jesse Vint, Richard Lynch, Claudia Jennings, Dave McLean, Will Walker, William Smithers

This sideways sequel to *DEATH RACE 2000* takes place in the far-off future when the Ranger Guides, for whom the audience is supposed to cheer, battle the Statesmen, whom the audience is supposed to boo.

DEATHWATCH

Gaumont International (France), 1980, Color, 128 min, VT, LD

Producer: Jean-Serge Breton; **Director:** Bertrand Tavernier; **Screenplay:** David Compton, David Rayfiel, and Géza von Radvány; **Music:** Antoine Duhamel; **Cinematography:** Pierre-William Glenn; **Cast:** Harvey Keitel, Harry Dean Stanton, Romy Schneider, Max von Sydow

In the very near future, the media is out of control. Here, newsman Stanton uses cameraman Keitel (no mere camera operator, but a man with a camera hidden in his skull) to produce a news show secretly about a terminally ill man. A riveting and intelligent script and a great cast make this a quiet gem.

DEBILATORY POWDER, THE

Pathé (France), 1908, b&w, 434 feet, silent

A powder that weakens all is set loose on an unsuspecting public.

DECIMA VITTIMA

See *THE TENTH VICTIM*

DEEP BLUE SEA

Warner Bros., 1999, Color, 102 min, VT, DVD

Producers: Alan Riche, Tony Ludwig, Akiva Goldman, Duncan Henderson, and Bruce Berman; **Director:** Renny Harlin; **Screenplay:** Duncan Kennedy, Donna Powers, and Wayne Powers; **Music:** Trevor Rabin; **Special Effects:** William Sandell, Walt Conti, Jeffrey A. Okun, and John Richardson; **Cinematography:** Stephen Windom, A.S.C., and Pete Romano; **Cast:** Samuel L. Jackson, Saffron Burrows, Thomas Jane, LL Cool J, Jacqueline McKenzie, Michael Rapaport, Stellan Skarsgard

Scientist Susan McAlester's (Burrows) experiments are on the verge of finding the key to the regeneration of human brain tissue, a fantastic discovery if she can pull it off. To accomplish this miracle, the good doctor has genetically re-engineered the DNA of mako sharks, nature's fastest, most perfect killing machines. Sadly, there are two things wrong with this. First, it is a monstrous violation of the ethical code governing this type of experimentation. Second, it has made the sharks faster, smarter, and a thousand times more dangerous. McAlester's theories are proven correct at the same time a violent tropical storm comes up—the same moment, of course, that the sharks choose to rebel against their captors. The handful of humans on the off-shore research facility are going to be hard pressed as they not only try to stop the sharks from escaping to the open sea (where they would become masters of the oceans in no time), but also just to stay alive.

This fast-paced, inventive thriller offers more than a few surprises. Numerous characters fall victim to the sharks, while the aquatic facility collapses around them, but it's often a surprise as to who gets eaten and who doesn't. The entire cast delivers strong performances as a group of fast-thinking and clever people who keep their cool in the face of danger. LL Cool J's portrayal of the facility's cook appears at first to be little

Deep Blue Sea (WARNER BROS. & VILLAGE ROADSHOW FILMS / JOSEPH B. MAUCERI COLLECTION)

more than comic relief for a very intense film but quickly develops into a standout performance. All of this is wonderfully polished with some terrific special effects and highly-detailed sets.

On the down side, the script serves up a few rounds of stiff dialogue, and some of the logic is even stiffer. It's acceptable that increasing their brain mass made the sharks smarter, but when did they go out and get degrees in structural engineering? The sharks seem to understand things the average human wouldn't and relate too well to the dry world, of which they should have no basic understanding. But this is the movie's only real flaw.

DEEP IMPACT

Paramount, 1998, Color, 120 min, VT

Producer: Steven Spielberg, Joan Bradshaw, and Walter F. Parkes; **Director:** Mimi Leder; **Screenplay:** Bruce Joel Rubin and Michael Tolkein; **Music:** James Horner; **Special Effects:** Scott Farrar, Bill George, and Michael Lantieri; **Cinematography:** Dietrich Lohmann; **Cast:** Morgan Freeman, Tea Leoni, Vanessa Redgrave, Blair Underwood, Bruce Weitz, Robert Duvall, Elijah Wood, Maximilian Schell, James Cromwell, Ron Eldard, Jon Favreau, Laura Innes, Mary McCormak, Richard Schiff, Charles Martin Smith, Betsy Brantley

The film opens on an evening's observation of the night sky by a group of amateur astronomers. A young boy (Wood) spots something he thinks is new. Everyone else is certain it's not, but being conscientious amateur scientists, they note the position and send the information to an observatory for confirmation. The lone observer working that night confirms that there's something new in the sky and that it's something large and fast and headed right for us. Racing out of the observatory in a panic with a computer disc detailing the discovery, the observer loses his life in a car crash before he can tell anyone what has been discovered, and so the vital information is lost. Or is it?

The movie then shifts locations and fast forwards some months to a reporter (Leoni). She wants to be an anchor, but her boss won't let her out from under her low-profile assignments. She needs a break, and she gets it when the secretary of a resigning politician lets the reporter in on what she thinks is a sex scandal, but which turns out to be the story of the approaching object. The government has known since the death of the observer but has kept things quiet to avoid a panic. In return for her cooperation, Leoni is given preference when the story is released to the public and the truth is revealed—a comet the size of Manhattan Island is headed for Earth. If it strikes, all life on Earth will die. But the president (Freeman) assures it won't because the United States and Russia have been working together to build a ship that will plant nuclear bombs inside the comet and blow it to bits. The world absorbs the news as best it can, and the film begins to intertwine around the stories it has thus far set up.

Wood, the boy who alerted the world to the danger, becomes a hero. Leoni gets the anchor position, much to the discomfort of her boss, but it doesn't make her happy. There are personal issues between her and her father that are making her life dark and empty. Robert Duvall enters as the senior member of the team going into space to stop the comet. President Freeman continues trying to hold the country together.

While *Deep Impact* had the misfortune of hitting the theaters the same summer as the splashier *ARMAGEDDON*, which also featured a comet streaking toward Earth, *Deep Impact* had a little bit more to say. Both included astronauts heading into space to plant bombs and blow the comets out of the sky, but on most levels that's where the similarities end. While *ARMAGEDDON* served up snappy dialogue tossed out by great actors with buckets of top-notch special effects to dazzle the audience, *Deep Impact* explored more than just the hardware of science fiction and gave its social aspects the full treatment as well.

In this film Earth and its billions were not forgotten. How would people react to the news? Would society break down? Would people who knew their minutes might be numbered continue to act as they always had, or would their lives change? Would their priorities change? And would those changes be for the better or the worse? *Deep Impact* is a powerful, well-written film. There are no easy decisions made by any of its characters. And, as things get worse and worse, the decisions get harder and harder, until the end is clearly in sight and suddenly everyone's decision's become incredibly easy.

The last 20 minutes of the film are remarkably suspenseful and deliver spectacularly impressive special effects. This is by far the best impact-from-space movie ever made and a top science fiction movie as well. It gets its science right for the most part but doesn't get so caught up with technology that it forgets about the impact technology has on people.

Note: Despite the film's quality, it does include a number of bits of bad science. Since the overall production is so excellent, one goof should stand to represent all the goofs. In the film the comet is headed for Earth straight from the Sun. In other words, it is headed at us directly from the angle of the Sun so that whenever the Sun is visible, that is the direction from which it is coming. If that is the case, why is it visible in the night sky?

DEEP SPACE

(U.S.), 1987, Color, 90 min, VT

Producer: Yoram Pelman; **Director:** Fred Olen Ray; **Screenplay:** T.L. Lankford and Ray; **Music:** Alan Oldfield and Robert O. Ragland; **Cinematography:** Gary Graver; **Cast:** Charles Napier, Ann Turkel, Julie Newmar, James Booth, Ron Glass, Peter Palmer, Bo Swenson, Anthony Eisley

Deep Space delivers a fairly standard story about a monster on the loose with the police in pursuit. It has

nothing to do with outer space but does possess a small connection to science fiction. With such a strong cast of character actors, one would expect something to work, but this is no serious effort of any kind.

DEEPSTAR SIX

Tri-Star Pictures, 1989, Color, 100 min, VT, LD

Producers: Mario Kassar and Andrew G. Vajna; **Director:** Sean S. Cunningham; **Screenplay:** Geof Miller and Lewis Abernathy; **Music:** Harry Manfredini; **Special Effects:** Mike Edmonson, James Isaac, and Richard Stutsman; **Cinematography:** Mac Ahlberg; **Cast:** Greg Evigan, Nancy Everhard, Cindy Pickett, Miguel Ferrer, Taurean Blacque, Marius Weyers, Nia Peebles, Matt McCoy, Elya Baskin, Ronn Carroll, Thom Bray

An underwater complex is menaced by a giant monster that the audience will feel can't kill most of the cast quickly enough. Read a book rather than watch this.

DEF-CON 4

New World Pictures, 1984, Color, 89 min, VT

Producer: Paul Donovan; **Director:** Donovan; **Screenplay:** Donovan; **Music:** Christopher Young; **Cinematography:** Douglas Connell; **Cast:** Lenore Zann, Maury Chaykin, Kate Lynch, Tim Choate

Three astronauts circling the globe in a nuclear-armed satellite are lucky enough to be in space when the world goes through a holocaust. When they eventually crash to Earth, they are threatened by an evil group that now holds power.

DEFENSE FORCE OF THE EARTH

See *THE MYSTERIANS*

DELICATESSEN

Union Générale Cinématographique (France)/Miramax (U.S.), 1991, Color, 95 min, VT

Producers: Jean-Pierre Jeunet, Marc Carlo, and Gilles Adrien; **Director:** Jeunet; **Screenplay:** Carlo and Adrien; **Music:** Carlos D'Alessio; **Cinematography:** Darius Khondji; **Cast:** Marc Caro, Jean Claude Dryfus, Dominique Pinon, Marie-Laure Dougnac, Karin

Viard, Ticky Holgado, Anne Marie Pisani, Edith Ker, Patrick Paroux, Jean-Luc Caron

In the future the world has suffered some sort of holocaust that is never really explained. The reason is not important, however, in this delicious comedy about cannibalism and the breakdown of moral and social values in the face of want. Like all the best science fiction, this brilliant, shocking, and intelligent film tackles difficult social issues thoughtfully.

Note: This is Jean-Pierre Juenet's first film before going on to direct *CITY OF LOST CHILDREN* and *ALIEN RESURRECTION.*

DEMOLITION MAN

Warner Bros. 1993, Color, 114 min, VT, LD, DVD

Producers: Joel Silver, James Herbert, Jacqueline George, and Steven Fazekas; **Director:** Marco Brambilla; **Screenplay:** Daniel Waters, Robert Reperu, and Peter M. Lenkov; **Music:** Elliot Goldenthal; **Special Effects:** Michael J. McAlister, Kimberly K. Nelson; **Cast:** Sylvester Stallone, Wesley Snipes, Sandra Bullock, Nigel Hawthorne, Benjamin Bratt, Glenn Shadix, Bill Cobbs, Andre Gregory, Jesse Ventura, Troy Evans, Dennis Leary, Bob Gunton

In the late '90s, supercop John Spartan (Stallone) and supercriminal Simon Phoenix (Snipes) are both put into cryogenic suspended animation. Phoenix is put away rightly enough for his terrible crimes, Spartan for crimes he is unjustly accused of by Phoenix. Some 36 years later, Phoenix is awakened for his parole hearing. He escapes using information he should not have but somehow mysteriously possesses. Phoenix himself is surprised at the wealth of highly technical and destructive new information with which he awakens, but he's not about to look a gift horse in the mouth. The master criminal is also amazed to discover that he has come awake in a world totally unprepared for him.

It is a happy place where everyone routinely greets each other with phrases like "Be well," and "Have a peachy day." More important, major crime has been virtually eliminated. There has not been a murder or rape in over a decade and a half. The police are now more like consultants than peace officers. The only guns are in museums. It is a world where the never-ending television commercial jingles of the previous century are now played on the oldies radio station as popular entertainment. Cursing gets one an automatic, one-credit fine from the thought police. The Constitution has had at least 61 amendments, and life has been thoroughly sanitized. Almost.

It seems this paradise has some nay sayers. Apparently, when things like salt and cigarettes and red meat and beer were all made illegal, there were those who chose to live outside society. They may dress in rags and live in the old sewers, they may have to dine on rats to survive, but as the de facto head of this underworld, Edgar Friendly (Leary) says it's worth it to them because they are free from the tyranny of the surface world. And that's what the ruler of the upper world can't stand.

After the "big one," the earthquake that finally dropped a big part of California into the ocean, a new-age politician arose who combined what was left of the southern cities into a new massive country, San Angeles, and then proceeded to turn it into a fascist state run along politically correct themes. And this smug, arrogant politico, who had Phoenix programmed while he was still frozen with all the extra information with which the criminal awoke, turned him into a super-duper criminal with the mind-control mission of killing Edgar Friendly. Of course the modern, happy-face police aren't equipped to handle a situation like Phoenix, so a student of the 20th century, an officer played by Bullock, suggests thawing out Spartan, the man who brought Phoenix in the first time. This is done, and then culture shock really begins.

This is an entertaining and interesting movie. First, it asks some important questions. For it to hint that perhaps many of the solutions we hear proposed these days are worse than the problems they profess to cure is not only refreshing; it's downright courageous. Admittedly, the film is to some degree simplistic in its views, but at least it presents them with bracing honesty, and that is what science fiction is all about. For instance, the movie never denies that salt and cigarettes and so on are bad for people; it just insists that taking away people's freedom of choice is worse. Even the freedom to make bad choices must be protected.

In addition, the direction is fast and efficient. Special effects are top notch. Future designs are interesting, if not especially inspired. The acting is superb if understandably breathless, even if Stallone and Snipes occasionally come across like comic-book heroes, which isn't necessarily a bad thing. There may be a bit more action and a touch less thinking than some would like, but overall there are plenty of things to recommend this one.

DEMON PLANET

See *PLANET OF THE VAMPIRES*

DEMON SEED, THE

MGM, 1977, Color, 95 min, VT, LD

Director: Donald Cammell; **Screenplay:** Robert Jaffe and Roger O. Hirson; **Music:** Jerry Fielding, Lee Ritenour, and Ian Underwood; **Special Effects:** Tom Fisher; **Cast:** Julie Christie, Fritz Weaver, Gerit Graham, Berry Kroeger, Lisa Lu, Larry J. Blake, Robert Vaughn

Superintelligent computer Proteus IV (the voice of Robert Vaughn) tries to take over the Icon Institute where it was created, but luckily its supposed masters shut it down just in time. But what creator Weaver has forgotten is that he has a workstation link to Proteus in his home. Of course, the supercomputer transfers itself there and continues its diabolical work. Sealing all the exits from the house, the computer takes over Weaver's home, looking for ways to extend its power. After a brief search, it decides the easiest way to take over the world is to become human. So it mechanically manufactures some sperm, complete with robot DNA that will pass on its traits to a child, and then "rapes" Weaver's wife (Christie). Weaver manages to get into his home during the baby's birth (the child is formed in an artificial birthing chamber—not inside Christie). Weaver uses an axe to destroy everything he can, but when he prepares to turn it on the robot child, his wife stays his hand. The metal plates covering the child are really only a protective covering. Inside is a human baby. Then the baby speaks with Proteus's voice, and it's clear things are not going to be all right.

The science fiction elements aren't so strongly realized here as the horror elements are, but that doesn't stop this from being a highly watchable and enjoyable film. It's well thought out, quick moving, and fairly spellbinding.

DEMON WITHIN, THE

See *THE MIND SNATCHERS*

DESTINATION INNER SPACE

Magna, 1966, Color, 83 min

Producer: Earle Lyon; **Director:** Francis Lyon; **Screenplay:** Arthur C. Pierce; **Music:** Paul Dunlap; **Special Effects:** Roger George; **Cast:** Sheree North, Scott Brady, Gary Merrill, John Howard

Men in the most obvious rubber suits in the history of low-budget filmmaking attempt to convince people they are really amphibious creatures. No audience has ever been fooled by them, but the cast seems suckered.

DESTINATION MOON

United Artists, 1950, Color, 91 min, VT, LD, DVD

Producer: George Pal; **Director:** Irving Pichel; **Screenplay:** Rip Van Ronkel, James O'Hanlon, and Robert A. Heinlein; **Music:** Leith Stevens; **Special Effects:** Chesley Bonestell, Walter Lantz, and Lee Zavitz; **Cinematography:** Lionel Lindon; **Cast:** John Archer, Warner Anderson, Tom Powers, Dick Wesson, Erin O'Brien-Moore

The U.S. is losing the space race. Sabotage is claiming too many rockets, but scientist Anderson has a plan. He convinces an industrialist that the key to winning this contest over the Communists is for the U.S. to make a flight to the Moon. An atomic engine is built, and the race is on. The crew suffers through the tense flight, dodging meteors and almost losing their star during a walk on the hull, but they make it to, and land on, the Moon, which they explore in earnest. Discovering they don't have enough fuel for the return trip, their radioman volunteers to lighten the load by staying behind, but an alternative plan is found and everyone makes it back.

The plot may sound a bit trite by today's standards, but pioneering efforts such as this often lack the punch that comes with hindsight. This is one of the first real science fiction films, and although it might not be terribly entertaining, it deserves some respect. Noted science fiction author Robert A. Heinlein not only provided the source material, his novel *Rocket Ship Galileo*, but also collaborated on the screenplay and worked as one of the film's technical advisers, along with rocketry expert Hermann Oberth. From its spacesuits to the lunar surface, it's as accurate as the science of the time could envision, and in light of future events, it seems politically savvy. Chesley Bonestell's spectacular matte paintings assured its visual appeal and helped make this one of the top science fiction ventures from the period.

DESTROY ALL MONSTERS
(aka KAIJU SOSHINGEKI)

Toho, 1968, Color, 88 min, VT, DVD

Producer: Tomoyuki Tanaka; **Director:** Ishiro Honda; **Screenplay:** Honda, Mabuchi, and Peter Fernandez; **Music:** Akira Ifukube; **Cinematography:** Tai-ichi Kankura; **Special Effects:** Teisho Arikawa and Yasuyuki Inoue; **Cast:** Akira Kubo, Yukiko Kobayashi, Kyoko Ai, Jun Tazaki, Yoshio Tsuchiya, Kenji Sahara, Andrew Hughes

See *GODZILLA, KING OF THE MONSTERS*

DESTROY ALL PLANETS

AIP, 1968, Color, 75 min

Producer: Hidemas Nagata; **Director:** Noriaki Yusa; **Screenplay:** Fumi Takahasi; **Special Effects:** Kazafumi Fujii and Yuzo Kaneko; **Cast:** Kajiro Hongo, Toru Takaatsuka, Peter Williams

Mind-controlling alien invaders attack Japan. Giant superturtle Gamera ("He loves the little children") battle them until the aliens take over his brain and turn him against those he fought to protect. Eventually, the massive amphibian regains control of his own brain and turns on the aliens. What would a Japanese sci-fi film be without aliens, spaceships, giant monsters, and kids?

DEVIL COMMANDS, THE

Columbia, 1941, b&w, 66 min

Producer: Wallace MacDonald; **Director:** Edward Dmytryk; **Screenplay:** Robert D. Andrews and Milton Sigler; **Music:** M.W. Stoloff; **Special Effects:** Phil Faulkner; **Cinematography:** Allen G. Sigler; **Cast:** Boris Karloff, Amanda Duff, Richard Fiske, Anne Revere, Ralph Penny, Dorothy Adams, Kenneth MacDonald

Scientist Karloff uses his new brain wave–measuring device on his wife. Later she's killed in a car accident. Stricken with grief, Karloff tries to communicate with his wife in the great beyond by using his machine to reconfigure her brain waves. He attaches the machine to a servant girl to use her as an additional power source, but the girl dies, forcing our protagonist to get out of town. Relocated, Karloff attempts to communicate with the dead once more, this time by hooking his machine up to corpses. The locals find out about what he is doing and storm his home just as the experiment finally works. The house is destroyed, and Karloff is swept away into the energy ether his meddling has

unleashed. The film is predictable every step of the way, but Karloff is the master, and he makes it all enjoyable.

DEVIL DOLL, THE

MGM, 1936, b&w, 79 min, VT

Producer: E.J. Mannix; **Director:** Tod Browning; **Screenplay:** Garrett Fort, Guy Endore, and Erich von Stroheim; **Music:** Franz Waxman; **Special Effects:** Cedric Gibbons; **Cinematography:** Leonard Smith; **Cast:** Lionel Barrymore, Maureen O'Sullivan, Frank Lawton, Robert Greig, Lucy Beaumont, Henry B. Walthall, Grace Ford, Rafaela Ottiano

Science has the answer to the world's hunger problems: Shrink everyone to doll size. Before the plan can be put into operation, evil Lionel Barrymore steals the formula so that he can create a miniature revenge squad he then uses to take down his foes. There's not much real science here and certainly not a lot of consideration given to the practicality or the consequences of what is proposed. Though *Devil Doll* is an average entry into the genre, it's a must for Barrymore fans.

DEVIL GIRL FROM MARS

Danzinger (Great Britain), 1955, b&w, 76 min, VT, DVD

Producers: Edward J. and Harry Danzinger; **Director:** David McDonald; **Screenplay:** John C. Mather and James Eastwood; **Music:** Edwin Astley; **Special Effects:** Jack Whitehead; **Cast:** Patricia Laffan, Hazel Court, Hugh McDermott, Peter Reynolds, Adrienne Corri, Sophie Stewart, Joseph Tomelty

An attractive Martian (Laffan) clad in black leather lands on Earth to steal men for the repopulation of her world. Now we know why it's the *angry* red planet. The film is not improved by the presence of her lumpy robot sidekick.

DEVIL'S UNDEAD, THE

See *NOTHING BUT THE NIGHT*

DIAMOND MACHINE, THE

American Continental, 1956, b&w, 92 min

Director: Pierre Chevalier; **Screenplay:** Jacques Doniol-Valcroze; **Cast:** Eddie Constantine, Maria Frau, Yves Royan

In this outing, a scientist discovers a way to manufacture diamonds.

DIAMOND MAKER, THE

1909, b&w, 490 feet, silent

Producer: J. Stuart Blackton; **Director:** Blackton

In this outing, yes, a scientist discovers a way to make diamonds.

DIAMOND MAKER, THE

Cines (Italy), 1914, b&w, two reels, silent

But in this outing, can you believe it, a scientist discovers a way to make diamonds.

DIAMOND MASTER, THE

Universal, 1929, b&w, serial/20 chapters, silent

Director: Jack Nelson; **Screenplay:** George H. Plympton and Carl Krusada; **Cast:** Louise Lorraine, Hayden Stevenson, Louis Stern

Once again a scientist unlocks the secret of making diamonds, but this time it takes 20 visits to the theater to watch him do it.

DIAMOND QUEEN, THE

Universal, 1921 b&w, serial/18 chapters, silent

Director: Edward Kull; **Screenplay:** George H. Pyper and Robert F. Roden; **Cast:** Eileen Sedgwick, Al Smith, Lou Short, Frank Clarke

This time when a scientist discovers a way to make diamonds, it only takes 18 visits to the theater to watch him do it.

DIAMOND WIZARD, THE

Gibraltar (Great Britain), 1954/United Artists (U.S.), 1954, b&w, 83 min

Producer: Steven Pallos; **Director:** Dennis O'Keefe and Montgomery Tully; **Screenplay:** John C. Higgens;

Music: Matyas Seiber; **Cinematography:** Arthur Graham; **Cast:** Dennis O'Keefe, Margaret Sheridan, Alan Wheatley

A scientist discovers the secret of making diamonds, and this time actually does something with it. He replaces real diamonds with the fakes and then runs away, just as one should from this bizarre subgenre of sci-fi films.

DIAPHONOIDS, BRINGERS OF DEATH

See *WAR OF THE PLANETS*

DIE, MONSTER, DIE

AIP, 1965, Color, 80 min, VT, LD

Producer: Pat Green; **Director:** Daniel Haller; **Screenplay:** Jerry Sohl; **Music:** Don Banks; **Cast:** Boris Karloff, Nick Adams, Freda Jackson, Suzan Farmer, Terence de Marney, Patrick Magee

When a rock falls from space and poisons the countryside, a landowner who refuses to acknowledge the connection keeps the thing in his home until it poisons his family and destroys all he holds dear. Karloff is excellent in this adaptation of H.P. Lovecraft's *The Colour Out of Space* (see *THE CURSE*), but pedestrian direction, poor effects, and a dismal take on the source material are just enough to bring the classic sci-fi/horror tale crashing to its knees.

DIMENSION 5

United Pictures/Feature Film Group, 1967, Color, 88 min

Producer: Earl Lyon; **Director:** Franklin Adreon; **Screenplay:** Arthur C. Pierce; **Music:** Paul Dunlap; **Special Effects:** Roger George; **Cast:** Jeffrey Hunter, Harold Sakata, France Nuyen, Linda Ho, Donald Woods

Communists are planning to bring Los Angeles to the ground, and only American superagent Jeffrey Hunter can stop them, which one would expect to be easy, considering he has a belt that allows him to travel through time. No thought is given to the fact that a government that can control time controls everything else. The truly sad thing (besides the deplorable waste of talents like Hunter and Nuyen) is that this movie came from the same team that produced the far superior CYBORG 2087, which did confront some of the basic ethical questions about time travel.

DISASTER IN TIME

See THE GRAND TOUR

D.O.A.

See THE MONSTER AND THE GIRL

DOCTOR MANIAC WHO LIVED AGAIN

See THE MAN WHO LIVED AGAIN

DOCTOR OF DOOM

AIP, 1964, b&w, 90 min

Producer: William Calderon Stell; **Director:** René Cardona; **Screenplay:** Alfred Salazar; **Cast:** Armando Silvestre, Lorena Valezquez, Irma Rodriguez, Elizabeth Campbell

A mad doctor transplants a monkey's brain into a man's body. Later he takes it out and puts it into a woman's body. Then the audience loses interest.

DOCTOR X

First National, 1932, Tinted, 77 min

Director: Michael Curtis; **Screenplay:** Robert Tasker and Earl Baldwin; **Cast:** Lionel Atwill, Fay Wray, Lee Tracy, Preston Foster

A mad doctor tests his dangerous formula on himself. His creation: synthetic flesh that, when smeared across real flesh, gives the individual wearing it super strength. The side effect: It also makes the wearer a crazed cannibal.

DOG, A MOUSE AND A SPUTNIK, A
(aka: SPUTNIK)

Filmsonor (France) 1958/(U.S.) 1960, b&w, 94 min

Producer: Louis de Masure; **Director:** Jean Dreville; **Screenplay:** Jean Jacques Vital; **Music:** Paul Misraki; **Cinematography:** André Bac; **Cast:** Noel-Noel, Denise Gray, Mischa Auer, Darry Cowl

It's the '50s and the American/Russian space race is on when some humans are accidentally launched into space.

DOLLAR A DAY, A

See SPACE RAGE

DOLLMAN

Full Moon Pictures, 1991, Color, 86 min, VT, LD

Producer: Cathy Gesualdo; **Director:** Albert Pyun; **Screenplay:** Charles Band, David Pabian, and Chris Roghair; **Music:** Anthony Riparetti; **Cinematography:** George Mooradian; **Cast:** Tim Thomerson, Jackie Earl Haley, Kamala Lopez, Humberto Ortiz, Nicholas Guest, Judd Omen

An alien villain who is just a head comes to Earth from a planet exactly like Earth, except for being a bit like our probable future. A one-foot-tall police officer from the same world pursues him.

DONOVAN'S BRAIN

United Artists, 1953, b&w, 83 min, VT, LD

Producer: Tom Gries; **Director:** Felix Feist; **Screenplay:** Feist; **Music:** Eddie Dunstedter; **Special Effects:** Harry Redmond, Jr.; **Cinematography:** Joseph Biroc; **Cast:** Lew Ayres, Gene Evans, Nancy Davis, Steve Brodie, Lisa Howard, Tom Powers

Industrialist Donovan dies in a plane crash, but a young doctor (Ayres) keeps his brain alive and then tries to communicate with it, much to the doctor's regret. The brain responds to his communication attempts all too well, eventually taking over the doctor's brain via telepathy. After that, the possessed doctor seeks revenge on those who caused Donovan's plane crash. This stylish and moody film offers plenty of atmosphere. While it's more properly a horror/supernatural story, the hardware bespeaks science fiction.

Note: This film is based on the Curt Siodmak novel by the same name. Believe it or not, while scores of science fiction classics sit on the shelf praying for a crack at the cinema, this one has been filmed three times to date. There was *The Lady and the Monster* in '44 and then *The Brain* in '62. This version is the best by far. It's also the only one to feature a future first lady (Nancy Davis, better known as Nancy Reagan) in its cast.

DOOMSDAY MACHINE, THE
(aka: ESCAPE FROM PLANET EARTH)

First Leisure, 1972, Color, 88 min, VT

Producer: Harry Hope; **Director:** Lee Sholem; **Screenplay:** Stuart J. Byrne; **Cinematography:** Stanley Cortez; **Cast:** Harry Hope, Denny Miller, Mala Powers, Bobby Van, Ruta Lee, Grant Williams, Henry Wilcoxon

A group of scientists in deep space spend a lot of time arguing. To be viewed only in cases of insomnia.

DOOMWATCH

Tigon (Great Britain), 1972, Color, 92 min, VT

Producer: Tony Tenser; **Director:** Peter Saady; **Screenplay:** Clive Exton, **Music:** John Scott; **Cinematography:** Ken Talbot; **Cast:** Ian Bannon, Judy Geeson, George Sanders, John Paul, Simon Oats, Geoffrey Keen, Percy Herbert

Residents of a fishing village try to keep visitors out to hide their grossly mutated families and neighbors. Illegally dumped radioactive waste has affected the local fish population, and since the villagers catch fish for a living, they become affected too. This one's spooky and entertaining, but predictable.

DOPPELGANGER

See *JOURNEY TO THE FAR SIDE OF THE SUN*

DRAGONS OF KRULL

See *KRULL*

DR. ALIEN

Paramount, 1988, Color, 87 min, VT, LD, DVD

Producer: David DeCoteau; **Director:** DeCoteau; **Screenplay:** Kenneth J. Hall; **Music:** Reg Powell and Sam Winans; **Cinematography:** Nicholas Josef von Sternberg; **Cast:** Judy Landers, Billy Jacoby, Olivia Barash, Stuart Fratkin, Raymond O'Connor, Arlene Golonka, Linnea Quigley, Troy Donahue, Ginger Lynn Allen, Edy Williams

An alien (Landers) lands on Earth so that she can disguise herself as a college professor and transform a nerd into a hunk in this featherweight nonsense.

DR. BLACK, MR. HYDE
(aka: DR. BLACK AND MR. WHITE, THE WATTS MONSTER)

Dimension Pictures, 1976, Color, 87 min, VT

Producer: Charles Walker; **Director:** William Crain; **Screenplay:** Lawrence Woolner and Larry LeBron; **Music:** Johnny Pate; **Special Effects:** Harry Woolman; **Cinematography:** Tak Fujimoto; **Cast:** Bernie Casey, Rosalind Cash, Marie O'Henry, Ji-Tu Cumbuka, Milt Kogan, Stu Gilliam

In this contemporary twist on Robert Louis Stevenson's *Dr. Jekyll and Mr. Hyde*, a black scientist takes his own potion and turns into a white monster.

DR. BROMPTON-WATT'S ADJUSTER

Edison, 1912, b&w, 325 feet, silent

A scientist think he's discovered the fountain of youth, but instead he's discovered the fountain of devolution.

DR. CHARLIE IS A GREAT SURGEON

Eclair (France), 1911, b&w, 420 feet, silent

Dr. Charlie replaces a man's stomach with that of a chimp, and since this is a comedy, it's not hard to guess who's soon eating all the bananas.

DR. COPPELIUS

Childhood Productions (Spain), 1966, Color, 420 feet

Director: Ted Kneeland; **Screenplay:** Kneeland; **Music:** Clement Philbert, Léo Delibes, Raymond Guy Wilson; **Cast:** Claudia Corday, Walter Slezak, Caj Selling, Eileen Elliott

Dr. Coppelius (Slezak) builds a beautiful female robot that dances like an angel. A local youth who sees the robot perform falls in love with it and forsakes his flesh-and-blood girlfriend. She then destroys the robot and takes its place. Corday plays both the robot and the jilted fiancée, and critics raved about her performance, which does hold up well. Her dancing is fine, but it doesn't stop this from being at best, an odd little movie that prompts a variety of reactions from its audience.

DR. CYCLOPS

Paramount, 1939, Color, 75 feet, VT, LD

Producer: Dale Van Every; **Director:** Ernest B. Schoedsack; **Screenplay:** Tom Kilpatrick; **Music:** Gerard Carbonara, Albert Hay Malotte, and Ernest Toch; **Special Effects:** Farciot Edouard and Wallace Kelley; **Cinematography:** Edouard and Kelley; **Cast:** Albert Dekker, Thomas Coley, Janice Logan, Victor Killian, Charles Halton, Frank Yaconelli

Dr. Thorkel (Dekker) invites a group of scientists to his remote jungle laboratory to view his latest invention—a shrinking ray. The assembled mock him, saying that he's crazy. To prove his point, Thorkel turns his ray on the scientists and shrinks them to the size of dolls. He then lets them know that they will pay for laughing at him and prepares to torture his captives to death. Everyone escapes, and most of the rest of the picture is spent following the tiny folk escaping both the giant Thorkel as well as the surrounding area's now giant animals. Fighting back, the tinies manage to break Thorkel's incredibly thick glasses, rendering him nearly blind and giving him the name Dr. Cyclops. This proves to be a great break for the tiny folk as it allows them to trick Thorkel into falling down a mine shaft. Later, the temporary effects of Thorkel's ray wear off and the picture ends. Tight directorial control and amazing color effects elevate this little film to above average.

DREAM IS ALIVE, THE

IMAX Corporation (Canada), 1985, Color, 37 min

Producers: Graeme Ferguson and Phyllis Ferguson; **Director:** Graeme Ferguson; **Screenplay:** Toni Myers; **Music:** Micky Erbe and Maribeth Solomon; **Cinematography:** David Douglas; **Cast:** Walter Cronkite

The opening scenes depict a space shuttle returning to Earth and landing at the Kennedy Space Center in Florida as seen in part from the pilot's perspective. This is followed by a behind-the-scenes look at a space shuttle as it is processed and readied for launch. After that, the audience witnesses the launch and follows the shuttle into space for some truly eye-popping space footage, all of which is real. The finale comes with the deployment of the spacecraft's school bus–sized satellite payload. *The Dream Is Alive* is an interesting insider's view of the U.S. space shuttle program. It features spectacular in-flight footage shot by 14 NASA astronauts over a series of three separate missions, narrated by Walter Cronkite. Obviously this is not a work of fiction but will certainly appeal to and inspire most science fiction fans.

For those not familiar with IMAX technology, it uses an image area 10 times larger than conventional 35mm film and three times larger than standard 70mm film. Because of its enormous size, the film can be projected with incredible clarity onto screens up to eight stories tall. If you've never seen an IMAX picture, check the major cities around for IMAX theaters. Florida's Kennedy Space Center has two of them. Some IMAX films are better than others, but the experience is out of this world.

Note: The film has two interesting highlights. First, it answers the question "How do astronauts sleep in space?" It answers plenty of others as well, but that's one of the real fun ones. Second, for those into moments of real science history, the movie captures the astronaut Kathy Sullivan's space walk, the first ever made by an American woman.

DREAMSCAPE

20th Century Fox, 1984, Color, 99 min, VT, LD, DVD

Producer: Bruce Cohn Curtis; **Director:** Joseph Rubin; **Screenplay:** Rubin, Chuck Russell, and David Loughery; **Music:** Maurice Jarre; **Special Effects:** Peter Kuran; **Cinematography:** Brian Tufano; **Cast:** Dennis Quaid, Max von Sydow, Christopher Plummer, Eddie Albert, Kate Capshaw, George Wendt, David Patrick Kelly

Science finds a way to let Dennis Quaid and others enter other people's dreams. The actors provide solid performances. The photography is strong, and the special effects are state of the art for the time, as well as highly imaginative. Even the soundtrack is good. Unfortunately, the muddy story never comes together as the film becomes bogged down in political sensibilities and never quite makes it clear who's good and who's evil.

DR. GOLDFOOT AND THE BIKINI MACHINE

AIP, 1965, Color, 88 min, VT

Producer: James H. Nicholson; **Director:** Norman Taurog; **Screenplay:** Elwood Ullman and Robert Kaufman; **Music:** Lex Baxter; **Special Effects:** Roger

George; **Cast:** Vincent Price, Frankie Avalon, Dwayne Hickman, Susan Hart, Fred Clark, Jack Mullaney

The sinister Dr. Goldfoot (Price) is building beautiful girl robots to seduce unsuspecting older men and make Goldfoot rich. Price is wasted in an embarrassing role as well as in its even worse sequel, *DR. GOLDFOOT AND THE GIRL BOMBS*.

Note: Bad-film enthusiasts should note that the second and last Dr. Goldfoot movie was directed by none other than Mario Bava.

DR. GOLDFOOT AND THE GIRL BOMBS

See *DR. GOLDFOOT AND THE BIKINI MACHINE*

DR. JEKYLL AND MR. HYDE

Paramount, 1932, b&w, 98 min. VT, LD

Producer: Rouben Mamoulian; **Director:** Mamoulian; **Screenplay:** Samuel Hoffenstein and Percy Heath; **Cinematography:** Karl Strauss; **Cast:** Fredric March, Miriam Hopkins, Rose Hobart, Holmes Herbert, Halliwell Hobbes

Gentle and conservative Dr. Jekyll attempts to prove that a human's evil nature comes from connection to an animal past. To obtain the proof he craves, he devises a potion, drinks it, and then suffers the consequences when it transforms him into wild, beastly Mr. Hyde. Robert Louis Stevenson's classic has been adapted to the screen a startling number of times, though most critics and scholars regard Paramount's 1932 effort as the definitive version.

The first attempt came from Selig Polyscope, a featurette barely 1,000 feet in length made in 1908. Denmark's Great Northern studios added a silent feature-length version two years later in 1910. There were at least five more silent versions, one each in 1912 and 1913, then three in 1920 alone. The only really notable one out of all these early versions, however, is Paramount's 1920 effort in which John Barrymore plays Henry Jekyll. The actor was praised for his grotesque transformation sequences, which were apparently carried off through nothing more than Barrymore's facial contortions.

The Academy Award–winning 1932 version came next, but it was certainly not the last. 1941 saw Spencer Tracy tackle the role for MGM. This version of the story shifted the emphasis from science to psychology and was no match for the memory of March's performance. Much the same can be said for those that followed.

1960 saw *The Two Faces of Dr. Jekyll* (see *HOUSE OF FRIGHT*) from Hammer Studios. During this period Hammer did some of its best work in the science fiction/horror cross-genre, but not this time. The classic story was reworked to include Mrs. Jekyll (Dawn Addams), who sets out on the good doctor with Christopher Lee. Jekyll (Paul Massie) is not so much a tortured, principled man, but a weakling who needs Hyde to do his bidding. Even this story might have been watchable if handled better, but alas, the direction is stale and flat, one of Terrence Fisher's few smashing failures.

The year 1967 brought *The Strange Case of Dr. Jekyll and Mr. Hyde*, and in '72 the story was stretched a bit to give us *Dr. Jekyll and Sister Hyde*. Possibly the worst of them all is 1974's *Twisted Brain* (aka: *Horror High*), a horrible mess in which a geeky high schooler finds the formula and uses it to gain revenge on those who have picked on him. And of course in '76, the need to wring a buck out of social tragedy prompted some exploitative talents to film *DR. BLACK, MR. HYDE*. None of the last five mentioned here have very much to offer. And there have been others, many of them dreadfully bad. At the bottom of the barrel is the loathsome 1982 release of *Jekyll and Hyde . . . Together Again*. Usually the comedies based on the classic monster films are at least amusing, but not this one.

One of the quirkier entries worth mentioning is *Mary Reilly* (1996), a Julia Roberts vehicle in which the familiar tale is told from the point of view of Jekyll's housekeeper. It's an interesting film, but the science fiction aspects of the story are for the most part completely lost in the tale's retelling as a gothic bodice-ripper.

DR. MANIAC

See *THE MAN WHO LIVED AGAIN*

DROPS OF BLOOD

See *MILL OF THE STONE WOMEN*

DR. ORLOFF'S MONSTER

AIP, 1964, b&w, 88 min

Director: Jesus Franco; **Screenplay:** Franco and Nick Frank; **Cinematography:** Alfonso Nieva; **Cast:** Jose Rubin, Agnes Spank, Parlay Cristal

A mad scientist makes human robots that he sends out to kill for him.

DR. OTTO AND THE RIDDLE OF THE GLOOM BEAM

(U.S.), 1986, Color, 97 min, VT

Producers: Jerry Carden and John R. Cherry III; **Director:** Cherry; **Screenplay:** Cherry, Coke Sams, Daniel Butler, Steve Leasure, Glenn Petach, and Jim Varney; **Music:** Shane Keister; **Cinematography:** Jim May; **Special Effects:** Frank A. Cappello; **Cast:** Jim Varney, Glenn Petech, Myke Mueller, Jackie Welch, Daniel Butler

Crackpot scientist Varney (better known for his role as the lovable pseudo-hillbilly in the *Ernest* movies) gets in and out of disguises and danger as he mugs his way through this not-so-great effort. The film has a few good laughs.

DR. RENAULT'S SECRET

20th Century Fox, 1942, b&w, 58 min

Producer: Sol M. Wurtzel; **Director:** Harry Lachman; **Screenplay:** William Bruckner and Robert F. Metzler; **Music:** David Raksin and Emil Newman; **Cinematography:** Virgil Miller; **Cast:** George Zucco, J. Carrol Naish, Jack Norton, John Shepperd, Lynne Roberts

The secret is that Dr. Renault (Zucco) has made a monkey into a man (Naish).

DR. STRANGELOVE OR: HOW I LEARNED TO STOP WORRYING AND LOVE THE BOMB

Columbia, 1964, b&w, 94 min, VT, LD, DVD

Producer: Stanley Kubrick; **Director:** Kubrick; **Screenplay:** Kubrick, Terry Southern, and Peter George; **Music:** Laurie Johnson; **Special Effects:** Wally Veevers; **Cinematography:** Gilbert Taylor; **Cast:** Peter Sellers, George C. Scott, Sterling Hayden, Slim Pickens, Keenan Wynn, Peter Bull, James Earl Jones, Tracy Reed

Unstable General Jack D. Ripper (Hayden) has become convinced that the Communists are polluting America's "precious bodily fluids," and so he takes it upon himself to launch a nuclear attack on the Soviet Union. He then commits suicide rather than reveal the authorization code that will convince his pilots to return. U.S. president Muffley (Sellers) alerts the Soviets, giving them everything they need to shoot down those renegade planes, which the military can't convince to return. Some of the planes get through, but by that time Ripper's aide, Captain Mandrake (Sellers again), has figured out the recall code and the remaining planes are brought back. All, that is, but one. Sadly, that bomber's radio isn't functioning. Commanded by Major T. J. "King" Kong (Pickens), the bomber continues on its way to deliver its payload.

In the meantime, General Buck Turgidson (Scott) urges the president to declare all-out war since there's going to be some bombing anyway. And since war now seems inevitable, wheelchair-bound former Nazi scientist Dr. Strangelove (Sellers yet again) tells the president not to worry: Life underground will be great. Ignoring his yahoo staff, Muffley tries to give the Soviets instructions on how to shoot down Kong's plane, but everyone on the other end of the hot line is drunk, and thus the world ends with a bang.

Although in its early stages this movie was planned as a serious drama, it ended up as a terrific comedy. Inspired by the novel *Red Alert* by Peter George, *Dr. Strangelove or: How I Learned to Stop Worrying and Love the Bomb* is perhaps the most powerful, and certainly the most successful, of all the movies made in protest of nuclear arms. It points up the human factor time and again, showing that no matter how advanced our machines get, they are still being run by human beings who are fallible. It's odd that Kubrick, who is credited by both most critics and science fiction fans in general with making three of the greatest science fiction movies of all time, never has a positive outlook on any of the sciences in his movies. Of course, in *Strangelove* it's a combination of human and mechanical weaknesses that doom us, and since people built the machines in the first place, it's really the human race, or at least the warmongers within it, that takes it on the chin.

The movies's statement is dark and horribly powerful, but at the same time it's also genuinely funny. The decision to film in starkly graphic black-and-white tones was courageous, considering it was the '60s, before such a thing was considered an "artistic statement." The sets are incredible, and the music wonderfully ominous. Basically, it's a package that achieves just what it set out to do with a strong science fiction premise.

DR. WHO AND THE DALEKS

Amicus (Great Britain), 1965, Color, 83 min, VT

Producers: Milton Subotsky and Max Rosenberg; **Director:** Gordon Flemyng; **Screenplay:** Subotsky and Terry Nation; **Music:** Barry Gray and Malcolm Lockyer; **Special Effects:** Ted Samuels; **Cast:** Peter Cushing, Roy Castle, Jennie Linden, Barrie Ingham, Roberta Tovey, Michael Coles, Geoffrey Toone

It's possible that some science fiction afficionados haven't heard of Dr. Who, but it seems unlikely. For those who don't know him, here's the scoop: The Doctor is a Time Lord. He travels back and forth through time in his time machine, the Tardis, which is shaped to appear like a British police telephone box. The reason for the British influence? *Dr. Who* began as a BBC television production that became the longest-running science fiction TV series in history. The series spawned only two films, however, of which this is the first.

The plot follows Dr. Who's most sinister villains, the Daleks, as they attempt to conquer Earth. Daleks are an alien race reduced to ameboid form due to fall-out from the nuclear war they had on their world. They now encase themselves within clumsily shaped but quite deadly robots in order to get around. In this outing, the Doctor faces the Daleks on their own world. Once there, he discovers that the Daleks hunt humans called Thals for sport. The Doctor puts an end to that by shorting out their robot vehicles' main power source, thus saving humanity.

The films were lucky enough to have a budget somewhat beyond the subsistence levels on which the television episodes were forced to exist. That doesn't mean in any way, however, that this was a big-budget epic. Even with the upgrade to Peter Cushing as the good Doctor in the two films, they are both B pictures made to pull a specific audience into the movie houses.

Dr. Who, although it has quite a large adult fan following around the world, was produced as children's programming. It's inventive and clever, with scripting that is often quite technical and even sophisticated. But over the decades it has remained a mostly static bit of fare, constantly hampered by its severely low budget. Good scripts and willing, if somewhat limited, actors, have sustained it despite the show's use of some of the worst special effects ever seen. One can imagine the

show's producers during the '60s, looking at imports of *Lost in Space* and simply drooling over the chance to have monsters that looked that good.

All of that aside, however, without a previous love affair with the series that this picture is likely to leave one a bit disappointed. On the other hand, those who have caught even a few of the shows in reruns and enjoyed them should give the films a try. Both the series and the off-shoot movies deserve their sterling reputation along with their legions of fans, and everyone deserves a chance to see Peter Cushing play the good Doctor. Without slighting the excellent work of the television casts, it surely no one plays this kind of role better than does Cushing.

DR. X

Warner Bros., 1932, Color, 77 min

Director: Michael Curtiz; **Screenplay:** Robert Tasker and Earl Baldwin; **Cinematography:** Richard Tower and Ray Rennahean; **Cast:** Lee Tracy, Robert Warwick, Willard Robertson, Lionel Atwill, Preston Foster, Fay Wray

Police and reporters search for a serial murderer and cannibal. Clues lead them to Lionel Atwill's science academy. A trap set for the killer backfires when it fails to deliver the fiend to the police, but instead traps Fay Wray with the killer. What is mostly a murder mystery unleashes a sci-fi twist when it's revealed that the bad guy everyone thought was a two-armed man turns out to be a highly respected one-armed man. Through an invention called synthetic flesh, the fiend created a new arm and face at will. The film ends when the good guys accidentally set the bad guy on fire.

DUEL IN SPACE

Reed, 1954, b&w, 78 min

Producer: Roland Reed; **Cast:** Richard Crane, Robert Lyden, Sally Mansfield

A great title for what is just another pack of television's *Rocky Jones, Space Ranger* episodes strung together and edited for the big screen. Nostalgia value only.

DUEL OF THE GARGANTUAS

See *THE WAR OF THE GARGANTUAS*

DUEL OF THE SPACE MONSTERS

See *MARS INVADES PUERTO RICO*

DUNE

Universal, 1984, Color, 140 min, VT, LD, DVD

Producer: Rafaella DeLaurentiis; **Director:** David Lynch; **Screenplay:** Lynch; **Music:** TOTO; **Special Effects:** Kit West, Carlo Rambaldi, and Albert J. Whitlock; **Cast:** Francesca Annis, Leonardo Cimino, Brad Dourif, José Ferrer, Linda Hunt, Freddie Jones, Richard Jordan, Kyle MacLachlan, Virginia Madsen, Silvana Mangano, Everett McGill, Jack Nance, Kenneth McMillian, Sian Phillips, Jurgen Prochnow, Paul Smith, Patrick Stewart, Sting, Dean Stockwell, Max von Sydow, Alicia Roanne Witt, Sean Young

The House of Atreides has been in direct competition with the Harkonnen family for quite some time. Usu-ally the Atreides have come out on top, but that's about to change. Baron Harkonnen (McMillan) has cooked up a deal with the Padishah Emperor (Ferrer) to have the Atreides family placed in command of planet Dune, source of the galaxy's supply of "spice." This is the mutating agent that gives Navigators the ability to move ships through hyperspace with the power of their wills alone. Once the Atreides are on Dune, Harkonnen plans to invade their holdings, kill them all, and claim all for his own. He manages to kill almost every-one but misses Paul Atreides, the scion of the family. Paul has a "witch" for a mother (Annis), whose lineage has bequeathed him special powers. (The witches of Dune are referred to as members of the Bene Gesserit sisterhood. In the film the entire order is relegated to the shadows with only the briefest of camera time. In the novel they had a great deal more to do, but then, so did everything and everyone else.) These powers make Paul a veritable messianic figure whom the spice min-ers as well as Dune's nomadic clans, the Freman, rally behind. After learning great secrets about himself, Paul conquers the Harkonnens and the emperor, and more-

Dune (UNIVERSAL CITY STUDIO & DINO DELAURENTIIS CORPORATION / AUTHOR'S COLLECTION)

over conquers the witches who control everything in the galaxy from the shadows, mainly by conquering his own fears.

This description of the film leaves out a lot. In fact, it leaves out about as much of the film as the film does the novel. The question is: Is that a good thing or not? To merely say that this movie poses problems for a reviewer is to be kind. *Dune* the book has been hailed time and time again as the greatest science fiction novel ever written, and it certainly belongs in the top three. *Dune* the movie, however, has been reviled since its release as the worst science fiction film of all time. How could this be?

The science fiction community waited a long time for a film adaptation of *Dune*. Two previous attempts (by most estimations, only Latin American filmmaker Alejandro Jodorowski's was actually serious) to bring the much-revered classic to the screen failed. When this production started, expectations ran high. The hype spiraled out of control. So did the budget. Soon everyone knew that *Dune* was going to be one of the most expensive pictures ever made. Actually, industry insiders suggested that the figures bandied about were wildly inflated by the production company to create interest in the picture, a strategy that backfired.

Once *Dune* hit theaters, the fans lined up, all expecting to see their personal vision of the novel they loved above all others. When they saw an average film with lavish production values, they were understandably disappointed. When the critics saw it, they saw something they could not understand, primarily because critics outside genre publications often don't have even the simplest understanding of most science fiction elements. With *Dune*, however, so much of the novel was left out that their lack of understanding of even the most basic points of the film was understandable. *Dune* author Frank Herbert (See Appendix IV) was quite forgiving to the producers when he said, "Not every scene is in the movie. You wouldn't sit for a fourteen-hour, butt-killing epic, would you?"

In the final analysis, the picture was made for fans of the book. Herbert said that watching the film gave him the weird experience of having the sense that the scenes that are left out merely happen offstage. The costumes and sets are some of the finest ever produced for a sci-fi film. The direction is peerless, the special effects inventive and cutting-edge. The cast is one of the finest ever assembled for a science fiction film, and all of them obviously worked hard to deliver outstanding performances. Much is missing from the novel, including Herbert's overwhelming ecological concerns, the Bene Gesserit's maneuverings, as well as other elements, all of which clarify and enhance the story. The author found the film easy to follow, a pleasure to look at, and one of the more stirring science fiction experiences of his life. But he had read the book twice. Anyone planning to see this film might consider doing the same.

DUNGEONS AND DRAGONS

See *KRULL*

DUNGEONS OF KRULL, THE

See *KRULL*

EAGLE OF THE NIGHT, THE

Pathé (France), 1928, b&w, 10 chapter serial, Silent

Director: Jimmie Fulton; **Cast:** Frank Clarke, Shirley Palmer, Earle Metcalfe, Roy Wilson

Twenty reels of film were devoted to the story of a titanic struggle for possession of a new scientific gadget that will make its owner the ruler of the airways—a muffler that allows planes to fly overhead silently. At the time, the plane itself had hardly left the realm of science fiction to become fact.

EARTHBOUND

(U.S.), 1981, Color, 94 min

Producer: Michael Fischer; **Director:** James L. Conway; **Screenplay:** Fischer; **Music:** Fischer; **Special Effects:** John Carter and Harry Woolman; **Cast:** Burl Ives, Christopher Connelly, Meredith MacRae, Joseph Campanella, Todd Porter, Marc Gilpin, Elissa Leeds, John Schuck, Stuart Pankin

An alien family lost in space crash lands on Earth. Luckily they land in the great heartland, where people are nice, except for government agent Campanella, who has sinister plans for them.

EARTH DEFENSE FORCE

See *THE MYSTERIANS*

EARTH DIES SCREAMING, THE

20th Century Fox, 1964, b&w, 62 min

Producers: Robert Lippert and Jack Parsons; **Director:** Terence Fisher; **Screenplay:** Henry Cross; **Music:** Elizabeth Lutyens; **Cast:** Willard Parker, Virginia Field, Dennis Price, Vanda Godsell, Thorley Walters

One of only three science fiction films directed by Hammer horror director Terence Fisher, this delivers Earth invaded by robots who kill people and then reanimate their bodies. The purpose? To mold them into a zombie army that they can then set upon the rest of humanity. The movie centers on the action taking place within one remote community.

A poor script, low budget, and lackluster direction undermine this one despite a fairly imaginative premise. Fisher fans be warned—this is not the level of work one would expect from the man who made *Horror of Dracula* and other great Hammer films.

EARTH GIRLS ARE EASY

Vestron Pictures, 1989, Color, 100 min, VT, LD

Producers: Tony Garnett and Terrance E. McNally; **Director:** Julien Temple; **Screenplay:** McNally, Julie Brown, and Charlie Coffey; **Music:** Nile Rogers and Chaz Jankel; **Special Effects:** Dennis Petersen, Tim McHugh, Eric Brevig, and Mike Bigalow; **Cinematography:** Oliver Stapleton; **Cast:** Geena Davis, Jeff Goldblum, Jim Carrey, Damon Wayans, Julie Brown, Michael McKean, Charles Rocket, Larry Linville, Rick Overton, Angelyne

Goofy, extremely hairy, multicolored aliens land in Southern California and are ushered into the great West Coast lifestyle by an airhead beautician and her pals. In other words, once again someone decided to produce a sci-fi musical comedy, and once again it just didn't work. One would expect this movie to be hysterical considering the cast, but this is not the case. It delivers a few laughs, but this film was made before most of its stars had become stars. *M.A.S.H.*'s Larry Linville might have been the biggest name at the time and it shows.

EARTHRIGHT

See *THE RETURN*

EARTH VS. THE FLYING SAUCERS

Columbia, 1956, b&w, 83, VT, LD

Producer: Charles Schneer; **Director:** Fred F. Sears; **Screenplay:** George Worthing Yates and Raymond Marcus; **Music:** Mischa Bakaleinikoff; **Special Effects:** Ray Harryhausen; **Cast:** Hugh Marlowe, Joan Taylor, Donald Curtis, Morris Ankrum, Tom Browne Henry, Paul Frees

Aliens come to Earth in classically simple UFOs, only to be fired upon by nervous soldiers before they even do anything threatening. The aliens return fire and prove to be a lot more dangerous than the trigger-happy GIs. Eventually, they communicate that their planet is dying and that they want to migrate here. Earth resists and a lethally one-sided war breaks out. Humanity loses steadily until the body of an alien falls into their hands, and a quick examination of the corpse reveals than the reptilian extraterrestrials are sensitive to high-pitched frequencies. After a quick session in the laboratory, Earth is ready to fight back with one of its most plentiful products: highly irritating noise. Soon UFOs are falling from the sky and Earth is safe.

A low budget and truly wooden acting make this one difficult to watch, but the movie possesses one magnificent saving grace—the absolutely fantastic spe-cial effects of Ray Harryhausen. At a time when not every film had terrific effects (in fact, at a time when most sci-fi movie effects were not very good), Harryhausen's work was a breath of fresh air and a marvel. The epic battle over Washington, D.C., is a classic showstopper, and even though today's trained eye can see the flaws in the effects, for the time they were a tremendous step forward. Harryhausen made very few sci-fi films in his career, switching over to an exclusive diet of fantasy early on and leaving this movie with some extra historical value.

EARTH VS. THE GIANT SPIDER

See *EARTH VS. THE SPIDER*

EARTH VS. THE SPIDER (aka: THE SPIDER, EARTH VS. THE GIANT SPIDER)

AIP, 1958 b&w, 73 min

Producer: Bert I. Gordon; **Director:** Gordon; **Screenplay:** Gordon, Laszo Gorog, and George Worthing Yates; **Music:** Albert Glasser; **Special Effects:** Bert I. and Flora Gordon; **Cinematography:** Jack Marta; **Cast:** Ed Kemmer, June Kenney, Gene Roth, Mickey Finn, Sally Fraser

A giant spider crawls out of its cave and terrorizes the local community. The police stun it, and everyone celebrates because they think the thing is actually dead. Soon it recovers to renew its rampage before it's finally electrocuted. Just another giant bug movie without even good effects to make it bearable.

EASTER SUNDAY

See *THE BEING*

EBIRAH, HORROR OF THE DEEP (aka: GODZILLA VS. THE SEA MONSTER)

Toho (Japan), 1966/AIP (U.S.), 1968, Color, 85 min, VT

Producer: Tomoyuki Tanaka; **Director:** Jun Fukuda; **Screenplay:** Shinichi Sekizawa; **Music:** Masaru Sato; **Cinematography:** Kazuo Yamada; **Special Effects:** Eiji Tsuburaya; **Cast:** Akira Takarada, Toru Watanabe, Kumi Mizuno, Jun Tazaki, Hideo Sunazuka, Akihiki Hirata, Haruo Nakajima, Hiroshi Sekida

See *GODZILLA*

EDWARD SCISSORHANDS

20th Century Fox, 1990, Color, 100 min, VT, LD, DVD

Producers: Tim Burton and Denise DiNovi; **Director:** Burton; **Screenplay:** Burton and Caroline Thompson; **Music:** Danny Elfman; **Special Effects:** Stan Winston and Michael Wood; **Cinematography:** Stefan Czapsky; **Cast:** Johnny Depp, Winona Ryder, Dianne Wiest, Vincent Price, Alan Arkin, Anthony Michael Hall, Kathy Baker, Conchata Ferrell, Caroline Aaron, Dick Anthony Williams

Vincent Price, in one of his last screen appearances, plays a scientist who creates a robot man-boy. He teaches him slowly, too slowly it turns out. Though Edward's (Depp) appearance is mostly human, he has scissors for temporary hands, and before Price can attach the human hands he has made for his creation, he dies. Edward is left to fend for himself in the scientist's lonely mansion until an endlessly optimistic saleslady (Wiest) and takes him home to suburbia and adopts him.

Edward Scissorhands (TWENTIETH CENTURY FOX / AUTHOR'S COLLECTION)

At this point the film takes its wild leap forward. When you think that Edward will be rejected, he is embraced by his new neighbors. You expect him to be considered a freak, but they are all fascinated by his talent (he can do amazing things with his scissors—style hair, trim hedges into amazing shapes, and so on). It's only when the townspeople get to know Edward as a human being and think of him as capable of human feeling regardless of his inhuman origins that they turn against him. Sparked by the vengeful lies of a jilted neighbor and a run-in with the police, an angry mob forms to hound Edward back from whence he came.

The social questions raised by the film are interesting. Not only is Edward an artificial construct that mimics human life perfectly except for his hands, but he is an artist as well. Burton's message is that the artist is loved as long as he remains an object and will be rejected when he steps down from his pedestal. The acting, design, music, and special effects are all up to the high standards Burton has set in his directing career. This is one of his best films, certainly his most personal statement, and a must-see for anyone who ever thought of taking his or her talent from beneath the bushel and letting it shine.

ED WOOD

Touchstone Pictures, 1994, b&w, 124 min, VT, LD

Producers: Tim Burton and Denise DiNovi; **Director:** Burton; **Screenplay:** Larry Karaszewski, Scott Alexander, and Rudolph Grey; **Music:** Howard Shore; **Special Effects:** Allen Blaisdell, Kevin Pike, Howard Jensen, and Paul Boyington; **Cinematography:** Stefan Czapsky; **Cast:** Johnny Depp, Martin Landau, Sarah Jessica Parker, Patricia Arquette, Jeffrey Jones, Vincent D'Onofrio, Lisa Marie, Bill Murray, G.D. Spradlin, Mike Starr, Brent Hinkley, Juliet Landau, George "The Animal" Steele, Max Casella

This bio-pic recounts the life of notorious filmmaker, Edward D. Wood, Jr., notorious for having produced several low-budget science fiction films in his career, including *BRIDE OF THE MONSTER* and *PLAN 9 FROM OUTER SPACE*. Burton's quirky picture follows Wood through the heyday of his directorial career when he was working with cast-off star Bela Lugosi and making the movies for which he is most remembered.

This obviously affectionate treatment of Wood's life will intrigue both those who love Wood's movies and those who hate them. For those who know little about Wood and his movies, this one won't mean much. And, be warned, watching *PLAN 9* in hopes of making sense of this movie is a really bad idea.

Note: Actor Conrad Banks was a regular fixture in the real Ed Wood's movies. He's played by Brent Hinkley here, but he also appears in the film. Watch for him as the bartender in the scene where Ed Wood (Depp) meets Orson Welles.

There's an odd mistake in this film. During the picture, Wood and Lugosi (Landau) watch Lugosi's earlier picture *White Zombie* on television. What makes this odd is that in reality *White Zombie* was considered a lost film and wasn't rediscovered until the mid '60s, long after Lugosi's death. Maybe putting in a silly error on purpose was planned as a tribute to Ed Wood.

EFFECTS OF A ROCKET, THE

1911, b&w, 420 feet, silent short

Humans finally achieve personal rocket flight.

EGGHEAD'S ROBOT

Children's Film Foundation, 1970, Color, 56 min

Producer: Cecil Musk; **Director:** Milo Lewis; **Screenplay:** Leif Saxon; **Music:** Gordon Langford; **Cinematography:** Johnny Coquillon; **Cast:** Keither Chegwin, Jeff Chegwin, Kathryn Dawe, Roy Kinnear, Richard Wattis

A precocious youth gets lonely and constructs a robotic duplicate of himself for fun and games. The film delivers what one might expect from this premise and absolutely nothing more.

ELECTRIC GIRL, THE

Eclair, 1914, b&w, one reel, silent short

In this oddly titled short, a girl does indeed receive an electrical shock, but afterward she becomes a magnetic girl, not an electrical one. It offers some nice effects for the time.

ELECTRIC GOOSE, THE

Gaumont (Great Britain), 1905, b&w, one reel, silent short

In this short, a goose that receives an electrical shock. The wild part is that the goose is ready to be eaten

when it gets its dose, but that doesn't stop it from becoming reanimated.

ELECTRIC HOTEL, THE

Spain, 1906, b&w, 476 feet, silent short

There's not much here to impress modern viewers, though the film is more inventive than might be expected. One might think "how quaint" upon viewing 1906's version of automatic doors, but in this completely automated hotel, the suitcases even unpack themselves.

ELECTRIC HOUSE, THE

First National Pictures, Inc., 1922, b&w, two reels, silent

Producer: Joseph M. Schenck; **Director:** Buster Keaton; **Screenplay:** Keaton and Edward F. Cline; **Cinematography:** Elgin Lessley

A young inventor builds a fully automated model house. Not unrealistically, he hopes a demonstration of it will induce investors to let him mass produce his wonder homes. Since the inventor is Buster Keaton, things don't go as expected, with comedic results. This one is just wacky and clever enough that it's still fun to watch. Keaton was a master.

ELECTRIC LAUNDRY, THE

France, 1919, b&w, one reel, silent short

The clothes at this laundry are cleaned without the aid of human beings. Can't wait till they have the home version ready.

ELECTRIC LEG, THE

Claredon (Great Britain), 1912, b&w, one reel, silent

A far-seeing inventor tinkers together a leg that works on electricity—one that can walk without a human being attached.

ELECTRIC POLICEMAN, THE

Gaumont (France), 1909, b&w, 352 feet, silent short

A human policeman dons electric boots to be able to cover more ground.

ELECTRIC VILLA, THE

Pathé (France), 1911, b&w, 420 feet, silent short

Yes, it's yet another electric house story. This one does hold the distinction of having been first, but it's nowhere near as funny as Buster Keaton's.

ELECTRIC MONSTER, THE
(aka: ZEX, ESCAPEMENT)

Amalgamated (Great Britain), 1957/Columbia (U.S.), 1960, b&w, 72 min, VT

Producer: Alec C. Snowden; **Director:** Montgomery Tully; **Screenplay:** Charles Eric Maine and J. Maclaren-Ross; **Music:** Soundrama; **Cinematography:** Bert Mason; **Cast:** Rod Cameron, Mary Murphy, Peter Illing, Meredith Edwards

In this quite bizarre movie, scientists in a mental institution attempt to cure their patients by artificially inducing particular dreams. Bad scientists get their kicks from playing around in their helpless patients' heads. What tries to be interesting and philosophical comes off as ponderous, and the film doesn't live up to its premise. Only the special effects come through for the audience on occasion.

ELLA

See *MONKEY SHINES: AN EXPERIMENT IN FEAR*

EMBRYO (aka: CREATED TO KILL)

Cine Artists, 1976, Color, 105 min, VT, DVD

Producers: Arnold H. Orgolini and Anita Doohan; **Director:** Ralph Nelson; **Screenplay:** Doohan and Jack W. Thomas; **Music:** Gil Melle; **Special Effects:** Roy Arbogast; **Cinematography:** Fred Koenkamp; **Cast:** Rock Hudson, Diane Ladd, Barbara Carrera, Roddy McDowall, Anne Schedeen

A doctor (Hudson) decides to play God. He develops a rapid-growth hormone that he uses on fetuses after applying a bit of standard B-movie logic—it worked with a dog, so why not try a person? Soon Doc Hudson has a fully formed, beautiful female with no mind or personality. He tries to fill in the missing pieces but soon discovers he has a thing of evil on his hands that must be destroyed. This rehash of *FRANKENSTEIN* or

more accurately *ALRAUNE* revisits the idea that those living beings not created by God will not have a soul and that all soulless things are evil. Still, the film is actually kind of riveting, although sometimes in a disgusting manner.

EMPIRE OF THE ANTS

AIP, 1977, Color, 87 min, VT

Producers: Samuel Z. Arkoff and Bert I. Gordon; **Director:** Gordon; **Screenplay:** Jack Turley and Gordon; **Special Effects:** You guessed it, Bert I. Gordon, once more; **Music:** Dana Kaproff; **Cinematography:** Reginald H. Morris; **Cast:** Joan Collins, Robert Lansing, Albert Salmi, John David Carson, Robert Pine, Jacqueline Scott

This film claims to be based on H.G. Wells's classic by the same name. When some ants find a radioactive snack to munch on, it's not long before they're giant sized and munching on the cast in the kind of low-budget film Bert I. Gordon excelled at making.

EMPIRE STRIKES BACK, THE
(aka: STAR WARS—EPISODE V: THE EMPIRE STRIKES BACK)

20th Century Fox, 1980, Color, 120 min, VT, LD

Producer: Gary Kurtz; **Director:** Irvin Kershner; **Screenplay:** Leigh Brackett, Lawrence Kasdan, and George Lucas; **Music:** John Williams; **Special Effects:** Brian Johnson, Richard Edlund, Nick Adler, Dennis Muren, Bruce Nicholson, Joe Johnston, Jon Berg, Phil Tippett, Harrison Ellenshaw, Lorne Peterson, Peter Kuran, Conrad Buff; **Cinematography:** Peter Suschitsky; **Cast:** Mark Hamill, Harrison Ford, Carrie Fisher, Billy Dee Williams, Anthony Daniels, Frank Oz, Kenny Baker, Peter Mayhew, Alec Guinness, Clive Revill, Julian Glover, John Ratzenberger, James Earl Jones, David Prowse

The second film in the first *STAR WARS* trilogy opens with surviving villain, Darth Vader (Prowse/voice of Jones), desperate to find not only the rebel warriors who escaped him in the first film, but their hero (if not leader), Luke Skywalker (Hamill), in particular. The rebellion is feeling somewhat safe, having found Hoth, an isolated ice planet, to act as its base of operations. Before the rebels can even finish setting up shop, however, they are discovered by Imperial Forces and the fighting begins anew. The attack scatters the rebels across the galaxy for a while, until everyone can meet again at a mysterious rendezvous point.

Instead of heading for the new base, Luke follows the instructions he's received through a vision of his old mentor, Obi-wan Kenobi (Guinness), to seek out the Jedi master, Yoda (Oz as voice and puppeteer), on the swamp planet Dagobah. In the meantime, Han Solo (Ford), Princess Leia (Fisher), and Chewbacca (Mayhew), Luke's comrades in the first film, are forced to escape together in Han's ship, the *Millennium Falcon*, which is malfunctioning even more than usual.

Luke finds Yoda and continues his training in the Jedi disciplines, receiving many bruises and ominous warnings for his troubles. Han and the others, after a spectacular chase through an asteroid field, find their way to Bespin, the Cloud City, a refinery of sorts owned by Lando Calrissian (Williams), an old friend of Han's. Of course, Vader is there ahead of them and captures them all. He really doesn't want them, however; it's only Luke he's after, though we still don't know why. We discover the truth soon enough when Vader tortures Han as a way of sending a psychic message to Luke that his friends are in trouble.

Despite the warnings of Yoda and the shade of Kenobi, Luke rushes off to the rescue where he finally confronts Vader in hand-to-hand combat. The results are not what the audience expects. Vader cuts off Luke's hand during the duel (a battle Luke does not win, but from which he does manage to escape) and then discovers that the master villain is his father. Han is taken away by bounty hunters, supposedly to be killed, and Luke ends up with Leia, who now knows she loves Han.

The picture ends with a cliffhanger, making it obvious audiences will have to wait for the sequel to get the answers they want, and while some may doubt that audiences were satisfied with such an ending, they'd be wrong. When discussing any sequel, the one question that has to be answered is: Was it as good as the first? Usually with films, the answer is no. Here the answer is no, it wasn't as good as the first one. It was better.

In *STAR WARS*, the characters never seemed to be in any true danger. The film's mood was light, holding all the tension of an Errol Flynn movie. The characters were in trouble, but it was clear they'd get out of it. In *The Empire Strikes Back* the wisecracks are kept to a minimum. Those present are tainted with a more adult grimness. The robots aren't as funny this time as they are annoying. Han's alien sidekick isn't as much of a clown as he is a concerned friend and able partner. Han, Leia, and Luke are no longer a cute romantic triangle. In fact, Luke's been cut out of the equation just at the moment when he needs support the most. At

the time when he must face the dark side of the force and his own inner demons, suddenly walls are set everywhere before him—even between himself and his beliefs of his own origin. Everything he has ever known is suddenly a lie. No, this is not a happy picture.

But it is a far more subtle one than the first. For one example, Luke is told over and over by his new teacher that he must reverse his old perspectives, be turned inside out, upside down. Throughout the film this is just the way we see Luke, suspended from above, hung from ceilings, standing on his head, and so on. At the climax he is dropped head over heels for what seems hundreds of stories, ending tangled in an antenna in the exact position of the Hanged Man, the Tarot card of unavoidable destiny. The Hanged Man is a trapped figure, unable to escape that which must befall him. We can but sympathize. At this point Luke has lost his friend, his girl, his youth, his innocence, his good right hand, and his past. He stands as a man of destiny with the weight of the world on his shoulders and as the hero who delivers to audiences all around the world a far better picture than the first one.

But no matter how much better this movie is than *STAR WARS*, neither of them is really a pure science fiction film. The hardware is there—robots and spaceships and lasers and floating cities and aliens and walking fortresses and all manner of delights for the eyes—but at this juncture the actual story of the saga still remains a mix of fantasy, mythology, and western romance. Lacking are the elements of social science and universal probing that fuel the genre's best offerings.

This is still a good film, though, a well-paced, well-directed action adventure drama that is far more taut and fully realized than the first one. Kershner's direction is moodier, heavier, more given to confusion and shock than Lucas's. Even the soundtrack picks up the new mood, sounding more sober and stark than before. Of course, much of this must be credited to science fiction writer Leigh Brackett, who was wisely called in to polish Kasdan and Lucas's screenplay. Watching the third film in the series, *THE RETURN OF THE JEDI*, which Brackett, who died between the films, did not work on, highlights just how much the success of *Empire* owed to her.

Note: Many people have noted that when Han is frozen at the end of the film and the princess declares, "I love you," he responds, "I know," instead of something more reciprocal. The story is that the scene called for so many retakes that tired of the endless repetition, Harrison Ford changed his line out of exasperation. Director Lucas supposedly liked it better, and it stayed in.

Another rumor going around is that during the great chase through the asteroid field, not everything is an asteroid. Comedians among the special effects team are supposed to have hidden both a shoe and a potato within the epic display.

EMPIRE STRIKES BACK, THE (THE SPECIAL EDITION)

See *THE EMPIRE STRIKES BACK; STAR WARS*

ENDLESS DESCENT (aka: THE RIFT)

Dister Group (Spain), 1991, Color, 79 min, VT, LD

Producers: Federico DeLaurentiis and José Escriva; **Director:** Juan Piquer Simon; **Screenplay:** David Coleman; **Music:** Joel Goldsmith; **Special Effects:** Colin Arthur; **Cinematography:** Juan Mariné; **Cast:** Jack Scalia, R. Lee Ermey, Ray Wise, Deborah Adair, John Toles Bey, Ely Pouget

The captain of a great submarine and the submersible's noble and principled designer battle each other endlessly while looking for a ship that's lost beneath the waves. All they find are monsters and page after page of bad dialogue to spit at each other. The film offers a few good effects, but the title really does say it all.

END OF THE WORLD, THE

Nordisk (Denmark), 1916, b&w, six reels, silent

Director: August Bloom; **Screenplay:** Otto Rung; **Cinematography:** John Ankerstjerne

A comet disrupts Earth's atmosphere, causing catastrophic weather conditions that ravage the planet in this inventive early effort.

END OF THE WORLD, THE (aka: LA FIN DU MONDE)

L'Ecran d'Art (France), 1931, b&w, 105 min

Producers: Harold Auten and K. Ivanoff; **Director:** Abel Gance; **Screenplay:** Gance; **Music:** Ondes Martenot and Michael Michelet; **Cinematography:** Nikolas Roudakoff and Jules Kruger; **Cast:** Abel Gance, Samson Fainsilber, Georges Colin, Colette Darfeuil, Sylvia Grenade, Jeanne Brindeau

In this outing from Abel Gance, one of the masters of early cinema, a comet plunging toward Earth actually hits it. The resulting chaos is terrible. In an interesting twist to the story, the scientist who predicts the comet's arrival naturally causes a panic with his news but is then arrested for treason for having done so. Like all Gance films, *The End of the World* is highly original, ranging dramatically from the out-and-out silly to the breathtaking. It's fairly hard to come by copies, but those who get a chance to see this one will consider the search worthwhile.

END OF THE WORLD, THE

Manson, 1977, Color, 92 min

Producer: Charles Band; **Director:** John Hayes; **Screenplay:** Frank Ray Perilli; **Music:** Andrew Belling; **Special Effects:** Harry Wolman; **Cinematography:** John Huneck; **Cast:** Christopher Lee, Sue Lyon, Kirk Scott, Lew Ayres, Macdonald Carey, Dean Jagger, Liz Ross

A holy man (Lee) is destroyed by an alien who then takes over both Lee's shape and his church. Along with a crew of alien nuns, he then sets about building a time-warp device that will enable them all to return home. Some humans try to stop them but later change their minds and decide to help them. After they finally get their traveling device completed, the alien tells his human helpers that they might as well return to his world with him and his followers since his mission was to destroy Earth. They go with him, and after their departure the world is destroyed.

ENEMY FROM SPACE (aka: QUATERMASS II)

United Artists, 1957, b&w, 85 min, VT, LD, DVD

Producer: Anthony Hinds; **Director:** Val Guest; **Screenplay:** Guest and Nigel Kneale; **Music:** James Benard; **Special Effects:** Bill Warrington, Henry Harris, and Frank George; **Cinematography:** Gerald Gibbs; **Cast:** Brian Donlevy, Bryan Forbes, Michael Ripper, Sidney James, John Longden, Vera Day, William Franklyn, Percy Herbert

Curious, troublemaking, hot-tempered Professor Quatermass discovers a huge complex tucked away in a remote corner of England. When he tries to learn its purpose, he is sharply rebuked by armed men. At the same time, small projectiles are raining from the sky in the vicinity, and anyone who draws close to one of them falls under the control of alien minds who can then command their actions completely. This ability has allowed the aliens to infiltrate the government to its highest levels. Thus, it is British government personnel who have built this secret plant, but only because of the inescapable manipulation of their alien controllers. Quatermass manages to find his way into the complex and finally gets the chance to confront the aliens. In their natural state they resemble gigantic piles of ill-formed ebony gelatin. The professor manages to destroy the aliens, release their captives, and saves the world from a horrible takeover.

The second installment in the series of excellent Professor Quatermass films is even somewhat superior to the first, THE CREEPING UNKNOWN. While the plot sounds trite, the story holds together well due to the powerful script and the sheer force of will of Donlevy's portrayal of the blustering, unstoppable Quatermass. He is a delight to watch as he leads this science fiction/horror tale far beyond the limits that might have bound any other actor. Despite a shoestring budget, the effects are quite respectable. This is an irresistibly moody film, tense and terrifying. It does have unmistakable echoes of INVASION OF THE BODY SNATCHERS, but this gem of a science fiction movie unquestionably takes similar themes and makes them its own.

ENEMY MINE

20th Century Fox, 1985, Color, 108 min, VT, LD

Producers: Stephen J. Friedman and Stanley O'Toole; **Director:** Wolfgang Peterson; **Screenplay:** Barry Longyear and Edward Khmara; **Music:** Maurice Jarre; **Special Effects:** Rolf Zehetbauer; **Cinematography:** Tony Imi; **Cast:** Dennis Quaid, Louis Gossett, Jr., Brion James, Richard Marcus

Humans are at war with a race of aliens. One soldier from each side gets stranded on an inhospitable planet. They hate each other, but they're forced to depend on each other for their survival, and eventually they learn mutual respect.

Because the film features Caucasian actor Dennis Quaid as the human and African-American actor Louis Gossett, Jr., (under several layers of latex) as the alien, much was made of it in critical circles as an attempt to explore the topic of racism. Unfortunately, morality plays on this level seem awkward in science fiction settings. The story itself is simplistic, offering no surprises whatsoever, and merely comes across as misguided. Warring soldiers are supposed to hate each

other regardless of racial differences, so for two of them to overcome their enmity and becomes friends does not equate with overcoming racial hatred. But that's not to conclude that this is an entirely bad movie. The sets and designs are excellent, and Quaid and Gossett are both terrific actors in top form in this film.

The film was based on a story by science fiction author Barry Longyear, but don't blame him for the mess. The author of the widely regarded *Circus World* novels reported that he had nothing but trouble with Hollywood, explaining the baffling logic behind why studio executives insisted on adding a subplot about an actual mining operation to the film. The executives, it seems, simply assumed the audience might not understand that the word *Mine* in the title was being used in the possessive.

ESCAPE FROM NEW YORK

Avco Embassy, 1981, Color, 99 min, VT, LD, DVD

Producers: Debra Hill and Larry J. Franco; **Director:** John Carpenter; **Screenplay:** Carpenter and Nick Castle; **Music:** Carpenter; **Special Effects:** James Cameron, R.J. Kizer, Gary Zink, Dennis Skotak, and Roy Arbogast; **Cinematography:** Dean Cundey and Jim Lucas; **Cast:** Kurt Russell, Lee Van Cleef, Ernest Borgnine, Donald Pleasence, Isaac Hayes, Adrienne Barbeau, Harry Dean Stanton, Season Hubley

In the year 1997 (yikes!) the island of Manhattan has been turned into a gigantic prison. The city degenerated so much that the government decided to turn it into an escape-proof pen for more than 3 million criminals who have been dropped onto the island and left to survive as best they can, which means preying on each other to live. The bridges have been mined, the tunnels sealed, and the Statue of Liberty converted into a guard tower from which infrared goggle–wearing guards can blast would-be escapees. It sounded like a great plan, that is, until the president (Pleasence) of the United States's plane is sabotaged, and Air Force One crashes within the prison's borders with a tape cassette crucial to the survival of world peace on board. The deal is that the tape must be played for the Russians and the Chinese at a summit conference within 24 hours or another world war (a third one has already taken place prior to the film) is almost inevitable—all of which gives New York's new population a once-in-a-lifetime hostage.

The government's plan is to offer one-time war hero, now master criminal, Snake Plissken (Russell) amnesty to go in and get the president out. To keep him honest, they implant explosives in his neck as insurance. Snake is given a great number of weapons and sent in by glider—a craft he has to set down on top of the World Trade Center. He does this, immediately loses all his weapons, and then sets off on a series of adventures in what is supposed to be New York City but looks a lot more like the back alleys of Cleveland, Ohio.

This film is tragically flawed. It never takes the time to explore the idea of a superprison in a future time created by horrible social pressures but instead languishes as a feeble-minded action-adventure film that not only spits in the eye of everyday logic, but can't even be bothered to obey its own internal logic. Lazy, self-indulgent writing and directing made for nonexistent characterizations, mediocre sets and special effects, and, outside of Pleasence, an array of lackluster performances.

For example, at one point Snake must run to the top of the World Trade Center and then back down again. Despite the incredible distance and number of steps involved, he's not tired when he gets to the top or when he gets back down. It only gets worse when he then discovers that the car he arrived in won't start. Checking under the hood, he finds an armed man inside the engine area waiting for him as thugs swarm out from behind every corner to overwhelm him.

The best plan the thugs could come up with was to remove the engine from his car? Anyone who's ever had to remove an automobile's engine block knows it's a heavy, greasy, long, and involved job. It would be infinitely simpler to take out his distributor cap, but no, these precocious thugs said to themselves, even though we have no idea how long it will take Snake to get back to his car, we'll risk his hearing us so that we can set up this great gag.

If this were an isolated incident, it could be overlooked, but from start to finish the movie never stops delivering these kinds of gaffes. The filmmakers couldn't even get the landmarks in the film correct, calling the 59th Street Bridge the 69th Street Bridge. Despite all this *Escape from New York* still has a cult following.

There's not much science fiction here and not much of a movie either. To make matters worse, this film was followed 15 years later by a sequel, *ESCAPE FROM L.A.* In that one, Snake has to infiltrate the island of Los Angeles to bring back an engine of destruction smuggled onto the island by the U.S. president's daughter. The sequel bombed in theaters and apparently didn't do a great deal better in home viewing release.

Note: Listen closely to the voice of the opening narrator as well as to that of the computers in the film. It's everyone's favorite scream queen, Jamie Lee Curtis.

ESCAPE FROM L.A.

Paramount Pictures/Rysher Entertainment, 1996, Color, 101 min, VT, LD, DVD

Producers: Harrison Ellenshaw, Debra Hill, and Kurt Russell; **Director:** John Carpenter; **Screenplay:** Carpenter, Hill, and Russell; **Music:** Carpenter and Shirley Walker; **Special Effects:** Martin Bresin, Dale Ettema, Michael Lessa, and Kimberly K. Nelson; **Cinematography:** Gary B. Kibbe; **Cast:** Kurt Russell, A.J. Langer, Steve Buscemi, Stacy Keach, Michelle Forbes, Pam Grier, Jeff Imada, Cliff Robertson, Peter Fonda, Paul Bartel, Bruce Campbell, Robert Carradine, Lee Van Cleef, Ernest Borgnine, Donald Pleasence, Isaac Hayes, Adrienne Barbeau, Harry Dean Stanton, Season Hubley

See *ESCAPE FROM NEW YORK*

ESCAPE FROM PLANET EARTH

See *THE DOOMSDAY MACHINE*

ESCAPE FROM THE PLANET OF THE APES

20th Century Fox, 1971, Color, 97 min, VT, LD

Producer: Arthur P. Jacobs; **Director:** Don Taylor; **Screenplay:** Paul Dehn; **Music:** Jerry Goldsmith; **Cinematography:** Joseph Biroc; **Cast:** Roddy McDowall, Kim Hunter, Bradford Dillman, Natalie Trundy, Eric Braeden, William Windom, Sal Mineo, Ricardo Montalban, Albert Salmi

In the third installment in the *PLANET OF THE APES* series, a spaceship lands off the coast of the United States; specifically it's the one that took James Franciscus to the future in the preceding film, *BENEATH THE PLANET OF THE APES*. Officials greeting the ship expecting the return of their astronaut, however, are surprised by the trio of apes who have piloted the vehicle home. They are in fact familiar faces Cornelius (McDowall) and Zira (Hunter), along with a friend Milo (Mineo). The apes are a puzzle and a curiosity to the government, until they reveal that they can talk. They then become vastly exploitable instant celebrities, but the situation grows complicated when it is discovered that Zira is pregnant.

Government scientist Braeden has pieced together the truth about the future. To him Zira's baby can be nothing more than the missing link in the puzzle of how Earth comes to be ruled by apes who slaughter humans or experiment on them as lab animals. The driven scientist does everything he can to destroy the ape family, working through channels to have the child aborted and the apes sterilized, then simply tracking them down and murdering them when they escape. In a desperate ploy Zira manages to switch her baby with that of a circus ape, and it becomes obvious at the end of the film that Braeden had things figured out all along, but that he only succeeded in forcing the future to happen that he hoped to avoid.

How did the idea for this third film come about? When screenwriter Paul Dehn wrote the sequel to *PLANET OF THE APES*, he was assured it would be the only sequel, thus his destructive ending in which everyone dies, and the entire planet is obliterated. Several months later, he is reported to have received a terse telegram in the purest Hollywood fashion: Apes Exist. Sequel Required. So Dehn sent everyone's two favorite apes and a friend back in time to their past, our present. It was a brilliant move. First, of course, it saved money by allowing the production company to shoot in Los Angeles. Second, and more important, it allowed Dehn to reverse the situation from the first two films but essentially still tell the same story.

In the first two movies, men went to the ape world and were put through tests, made to perform, and finally forced to escape their captors from whom they fled until they were killed. Now apes go to the human world and repeat the same process. Interestingly, at the end of the second film an ape shoots a man who destroys the ape's world in retaliation. At the end of this one, a man shoots an ape (Zira) who destroys that man's world in retaliation by leaving behind her son who will eventually bring about the Planet of the Apes.

Social satire in a tense first contact film adds up to a terrific movie. *Escape From the Planet of the Apes* is a highly entertaining film. Watching the chimps parody human values is refreshing fun. Watching them fear humankind's paranoia and violent instincts is thought-provoking. The movie's one drawback is that it opened the door for the downhill slide of the rest of the series. While most science fiction fans would be satisfied with an ending like the one to this film, Hollywood is always on the outlook for piles of cash, and the ending, heavy with intent but murky on details, easily set up the next two films. This wouldn't necessarily have been a bad thing, except that both are trivial messes.

ESCAPEMENT

See *THE ELECTRONIC MONSTER*

ESCAPE TO WITCH MOUNTAIN

Disney/Buena Vista, 1975, Color, 97 min, VT, LD

Producer: Jerome Courtland; **Director:** John Hough; **Screenplay:** Robert Malcolm Young; **Music:** Johnny Mandel; **Cinematography:** Frank V. Phillips; **Cast:** Eddie Albert, Ray Milland, Kim Richards, Ike Eisenmann, Donald Pleasence

Two ordinary-looking orphan kids (Richards and Eisenmann) are actually little orphan space aliens. They have telekinetic and paranormal abilities that a ruthless businessman (Milland) decides to exploit. Luckily for the kids, they run into a protector in the form of vacationing Eddie Albert, who helps them until their parents show up in a spaceship the size of North Dakota to take them home. There's not much real science fiction at work in this fairly average and unmemorable film. A sequel, *Return From Witch Mountain*, followed but was not up to the original.

ESCAPE 2000 (aka: TURKEY SHOOT)

New World Pictures, 1981, Color, 92 min, VT

Producers: John Daly and David Hemmings; **Director:** Brian Trenchard-Smith; **Screenplay:** Jon George and Neill D. Hicks; **Music:** Brian May; **Special Effects:** John Sears; **Cinematography:** John R. McLean; **Cast:** Steve Railsback, Olivia Hussey, Michael Craig, Carmen Duncan, Roger Ward

In the future, criminals are hunted for sport. This ugly rip-off transplants the far superior *The Most Dangerous Game* to a science fiction setting and tries to make up with violence and incoherence what it lacks on every other level. Forget this one.

E.T. THE EXTRA-TERRESTRIAL

Universal, 1977, Color, 92 min, VT, LD

Producer: Steven Spielberg; **Director:** Spielberg; **Screenplay:** Melissa Mathison; **Music:** John Williams; **Special Effects:** Dale L. Martin, Warren Franklin, Michael Pangrazio, Dennis Muren, and Laurie Vermont; **Cinematography:** Allen Daviau; **Cast:** Dee Wallace, Henry Thomas, Peter Coyote, Robert Mac-Naughton, Drew Barrymore, K.C. Martel, Sean Frye, C. Thomas Howell

E.T. is the story of a young boy's first contact with an extraterrestrial being. Elliott (Thomas), convinced he's seen something moving out behind the house, searches the weeds, checks the shed, and eventually falls asleep in a lawn chair, hoping to again spot the troll or gremlin or whatever he saw. Eventually, he succeeds and finds the alien, then elects to bring it into the house and enlist his older brother and younger sister in helping him hide it. The alien was left behind when his crewmates were forced to take off without him. Dubbed "E.T." by his rescuers, the alien lives in their playroom, hiding from the ever-searching government, drinking Coors, and looking for a way to return home, all the while becoming more and more attached to his human "family."

The ominous and sinister-intentioned government finally catches on and closes in on the alien's middle-class hideout. And they do so just in time, since E.T. has begun to sicken and will likely soon be dead without help. The government men, in a real twist for modern sci-fi films, actually are there to help for once. They set up a field hospital with unbelievable speed and do everything they can to rescue filmdom's cutest alien. Sadly, however, it's all to no avail. E.T. dies and the family cries. Of course that's not the end. E.T. really isn't dead. Elliott and his friends get him away from the government to where his pals can pick him up and take him back to the stars.

The movie is unquestionably a heartwarming tearjerker, but as a science fiction film it barely qualifies. Nothing is explained. E.T.'s ship flies in the atmosphere, but it isn't aerodynamic. It leaves baffling rainbows when it flies. E.T. can breathe our air and eat our food; yet some unnamed thing here kills him slowly. He heals Earthly wounds with a touch of his finger and builds a transmitter out of old toys and garbage, which can reach his friends in space, but he can't anticipate that he will set up a mind-link with Elliott when he gets drunk, which is the only time the mind-link comes into play. It all adds up to a rather sloppy and illogical movie, though some critics have claimed E.T. is a symbol for Christ. On the other hand, the story is wonderful, the acting fine, the direction superb, and the effects outstanding. There has never been a rubber suit like E.T. Giger's *ALIEN* is just an evil killing machine. This creation had the range to become a fully realized character.

Note: Sharp-eyed sci-fi film buffs will note one specimen in particular among the alien's plant collection. It's a triffid from the 1962 classic *DAY OF THE TRIFFIDS*.

EVENT HORIZON

Paramount, 1997, Color, 95 min, VT, LD, DVD

Producer: Lawrence Gordon; **Director:** Paul Anderson; **Screenplay:** Philip Eisner; **Music:** Michael Kamen; **Special Effects:** Richard Yuricich, A.S.C.; **Cast:** Laurence Fishburne, Sam Neill, Kathleen Quinlan, Joely Richardson, Richard T. Jones, Jack Noseworthy, Jason Isaacs, Sean Pertwee, Peter Marinker, Holley Chant, Barclay Wright, Noah Huntley, Robert Jezek

The ship *Event Horizon* was designed by scientist William Weir (Neill) to reach distant stars. Instead, it disappeared without a trace when its experimental gravity drive was engaged. Now, seven years later, the *Event Horizon*'s distress beacon indicates that the ship has suddenly reappeared near Neptune. The operating beacon means someone had to have returned with it. Since this was one of the most important experiments ever in the history of human science, an emergency rescue mission is immediately launched. On the ship Weir and the crew review video records of the last moments before the ship vanished. It is a cacophony of screams that ends abruptly. What follows seems at first to be a standard rescue-in-space story, until the crew and Weir actually board the *Event Horizon*. Then the movie becomes a horror story—a traditional haunted house tale in space with an interesting sci-fi twist. It turns out that Weir did invent a faster-than-light drive, one that jumped the ship from our dimension literally to Hell. Now the ship has returned to harvest more souls.

This is a grim one. The movie is joyless, relentless, and frightening and pulls none of its punches. The sets are dark and mysterious. The performances are gripping, the direction taut, and the special effects absolutely outstanding. For those who don't mind an intense dark ride, there's lots of fun to be had, especially as it keeps you on the edge of your seat with fingers crossed trying to figure out how the courageous hero is going to save the universe from being swallowed by the forces of Hell. Or more accurately, *if* he's going to save the universe.

EVE OF DESTRUCTION

Interscope Communications, 1991, Color, 98 min, VT, LD

Producer: David Madden; **Director:** Duncan Gibbons; **Screenplay:** Gibbons and Yale Udoff; **Music:** Phillippe Sarde; **Special Effects:** Peter Lamont; **Cinematography:** Alan Hume; **Cast:** Gregory Hines, Renee Soutendijk, Michael Greene, Kurt Fuller, John M. Jackson, Kevin McCarthy.

Scientist Eve Simmons (Soutendijk) builds an android in her own image. For some baffling reason she builds a tremendously powerful bomb into it. Things go all right for a while, but soon the android goes on a rampage, and the film's hero (Hines) blusters in with a less than stellar effort to stop it. Other than assuming that this movie was merely written around some unthinking filmmaker's idea of a clever title, it's hard to understand why this film was ever made. The story seems to hate both men and women, and since there aren't that many androids running around with the ever-increasing price of a movie ticket, one can't imagine who the intended audience was supposed to be.

EVERYTHING YOU ALWAYS WANTED TO KNOW ABOUT SEX (BUT WERE AFRAID TO ASK)

United Artists, 1972, Color, 87 min, VT, LD

Producers: Jack Rollins and Charles H. Joffe; **Director:** Woody Allen; **Screenplay:** Allen; **Music:** Mundell Lowe; **Cinematography:** David M. Walsh; **Cast:** Woody Allen, Louise Lasser, John Carradine, Lou Jacobi, Anthony Quayle, Tony Randall, Lynn Redgrave, Burt Reynolds, Gene Wilder, Jack Barry, Erin Fleming, Robert Q. Lewis, Heather MacRae, Pamela Mason, Sidney Miller, Regis Philbin, Geoffrey Holder, Jay Robinson, Robert Walden

Loosely based on the best-selling, nonfiction book by Dr. David Reuben, this film consists of a series of vignettes, two of which have a science fiction feel. In the first, Allen parodies both mad scientist and giant monster movies when an enormous female breast is set loose to maraud across the countryside. In the film's final sequence, the audience is given an interior view of the male body during a seduction. Rapid glimpses within the control rooms for the brain and the genitals are some of the funniest moments in the film. The rest of the movie makes no pretense of being science fiction, but the two sequences described here are worth a look.

EVIL BRAIN FROM OUTER SPACE, THE

Manley, 1964, Color, 86 min

Director: Teno Ishii; **Screenplay:** Ichiro Miyagawa; **Cast:** Ken Utsui, Reiko Seto, Chisako Tawara

Three of the Japanese *Super Giant* movies were spliced together to create this fairly lackluster mess. The end result? Super Giant fights off giant monsters and hordes of bad guys invading from outer space. The *Super Giant* series is for fans only, but this mindless bit of nonsense may not even appeal to them.

EVIL OF FRANKENSTEIN

Hammer Film Productions, Ltd., 1964, Color, 86 min, VT

Producer: Anthony Hinds; **Director:** Freddie Francis; **Screenplay:** John Elder; **Music:** Don Banks; **Special Effects:** Les Bowie; **Cinematography:** John Wilcox; **Cast:** Peter Cushing, Peter Woodthorpe, Kiwi Kingston, Sandor Eles, Duncan Lamont, Katy Wild

See *FRANKENSTEIN*

eXistenz

Dimension, 1999, Color, 92 min, VT, DVD

Producers: Robert Lantos, Andras Hamori, and David Cronenberg; **Director:** Cronenberg; **Screenplay:** Cronenberg; **Music:** Howard Shore; **Special Effects:** Jim Isacc, Kelly Lepkowsky, and Stephan Dupuis; **Cinematography:** Peter Suschitzky; **Cast:** Jennifer Jason Leigh, Jude Law, Ian Holm, Don McKellar, Callum Keith Rennie, Sarah Polley, Robert A. Silverman, Christopher Eccleston, William DeFore, Oscar Hsu, Kris Lemche, Vik Sahay, Kirsten Johnson

This film opens with an exciting moment for the game players of the world. The new game, eXistenZ, is about to be tested for the first time. What is more exciting, though, is that the game's creator, Allegra Geller (Leigh) herself, is present for the trial run. Geller is the "Game Goddess," the hip, hyperaware, sexy inventor of the best games of all time. What makes these new games so intense is that the game's driver, a pod resembling a living organ, plugs directly into the player's nervous system via a bioport implanted directly into the gamer's spine. Because the pod has access to all of the player's memories, anxieties, and desires, the direction each game takes depends entirely on who's playing.

When the moment for the unveiling finally arrives, the players are handed umbilical-like cords, the ends of which lead back to the main bio-game machine under Geller's control. We don't get to see much of the game, however, before an assassin tries to kill Geller, using a bizarre weapon—an organic fusion of gristle and bone capable of shooting its ammunition of human teeth at fatal velocity. Shouting "Death to eXistenZ! Death to the demoness Allegra Geller!" the man fires the weapon and damages her game pod.

At this point everyone panics and runs away into the night. It is decided that the remote farmhouse picked for the test is no longer safe, and so Geller is forced to flee for her life with Ted Pikul (Law), a low-ranking employee working for the gaming company that employs Geller. It soon becomes apparent that there is a price of $5 million on Geller's head and that she and Pikul can trust no one. This leads to an ever-increasing series of bizarre adventures for the two. After a while, however, it's revealed that the pair are not in the real world, that they are still in the game. Worse yet, the killers have followed them inside, and somehow Geller and Pikul must survive long enough to escape the game.

eXistenZ, produced, directed, and written by theater-of-the-bizarre genius David Cronenberg, is quite a surprise, but not a good one. Cronenberg, whose films include a remake of THE FLY (1986), THE BROOD, THEY CAME FROM WITHIN, SCANNERS, and VIDEODROME has routinely earned the praise critics and fans of science fiction and horror films. *eXistenZ* is not up to his usual standards.

There simply is little happening to intrigue viewers. Cleverly, the movie looks and moves like a game scenario. The sets are dressed simply—no brand names, no jewelry or suits or televisions, no watches or clocks. Everything is ordinary and functional. When characters are told to go to the Chinese restaurant for lunch, the place is a barn with the words *Chinese Restaurant* painted over the door. This helps build the mood of a real role-playing game, but overlooks the fact that role-playing games are interesting only to those people playing them, leaving an audience rather bored. Even the major revelation of the climax is apparent from the earliest moments of the film, undercutting any attempt to maintain suspense.

While all of the usual Cronenberg tricks are here, none of them are used to any real effect. The director, known for pushing the limit toward grossing out his audience, fails to come close to his past efforts. Far

eXistenZ (DIMENSION FILMS / AUTHOR'S COLLECTION)

more important, though, is the director's passion for getting inside his subjects: how the characters think, what they feel, how they really feel about what they think. Cronenberg is the master of taking such subject matter to the edge of taste and decency and hurling his audience over the side to the rocks of truth below. But not this time. Nothing is revealed about these characters because we never know what they really think. Everything they do is just a series of masks from beginning to end.

There are also massive flaws in logic throughout the plot, but any of them can be explained by saying that since it was all a game the players were making it up as they went along; nothing they did or said that didn't add up doesn't matter. That may be true, but in a situation in which nothing the characters do or say matters, then nothing they do or say can be very entertaining either.

EXPEDITION MOON

See *ROCKETSHIP X-M*

EXPLORERS

Paramount, 1985, Color, 109 min, VT, LD

Producers: David Bombyk and Edward S. Feldman; **Director:** Joe Dante; **Screenplay:** Erick Luke; **Music:** Jerry Goldsmith; **Special Effects:** Robert MacDonald III, Bruce Nicholson, Nilo Rodis-Jamero, and Jack Mongovan; **Cinematography:** John Hora; **Cast:** Ethan Hawke, River Phoenix, Jason Presson, Amanda Peterson, Dick Miller, Robert Picardo, Dana Ivey, Meshach Taylor, Mary Kay Place

Three kids (Hawke, Phoenix, Presson) figure out a way to travel into space. They build their own spaceship out of an old carnival ride car, old monitors, and spare parts, and then set off as explorers. Suddenly, the kids find another spaceship and are drawn aboard, where they encounter awful-looking and awful-sounding aliens.

Up to the point when the kids meet the aliens, the plot comes together well. The characterization, the story of how these three kids come together as friends, and their family backgrounds make for a well-told and compelling flight of fantasy. The acting and storytelling are on a par with the inventive props and special effects. The pacing is absolutely brilliant. When the young trio heads into outer space, the audience is engaged and is looking forward to the outcome. But once the group boards the alien ship, the movie takes a

wild left turn to nitwit comedy that undoes everything it has accomplished, making this an exceedingly disappointing film.

Note: Those who must watch this movie should keep their eyes open for the following gags: The school is named not for a president or a war hero but for animator Chuck Jones; the sled, Rosebud from *Citizen Kane*, is clearly highlighted in the junkyard sequence; and there is a newspaper headline that reads: "Kingston Falls Mystery Still Unsolved," referring to Joe Dante's previous film, the 1984 release, *GREMLINS*.

EXTERMINATORS, THE

Comptoir Francais/Cinerad-Camera (France/Italy), 1965, Color, 95 min

Producer: Jean Maumy; **Director:** Riccardo Freda; **Screenplay:** Claude Marcel Richard; **Music:** Michel Magne; **Cinematography:** Henri Persin; **Cast:** Richard Wyler, Gil Delemare, Jany Clair

A crazed scientist (sometimes it seems like there's no other kind in these movies) builds an atomic missile that he plans to use to destroy New York. Some would say this wasn't all that bad an idea. Many of them are New Yorkers.

EYE CREATURES, THE (aka: ATTACK OF THE EYE CREATURES)

AIP, 1965, Color, 80 min, VT

Producer: Larry Buchanan; **Director:** Buchanan; **Screenplay:** Al Martin and Robert J. Gurney, Jr.; **Music:** Ronald Stein; **Cinematography:** Ralph K. Johnson; **Cast:** John Ashley, Cynthia Hull, Chet Davis

INVASION OF THE SAUCER MEN wasn't that good a film. Why anyone would want to remake it with a lesser cast and half the budget is anyone's guess. Regardless, this simply awful piece of drive-in filler that resulted was laughed at in its own time, as well as now. The film's only saving grace is that it's good for those who like to watch it turn from day to night repeatedly within the same scene.

Note: If you do watch this one, note the opening credits. Not only were some of the prints for this one renamed *Attack of the Eye Creatures*, but they were misprinted as *Attack of the the Eye Creatures*. Sigh—only in Hollyhollywood.

FABULOUS WORLD OF JULES VERNE, THE

(Czechoslovakia) 1958/Warner Bros. (U.S.) 1961, b&w, 83 min, VT

Director: Karel Zeman; **Screenplay:** Zeman and Frantisek Hrubin; **Music:** Zdenek Liska; **Special Effects:** Zeman; **Cinematography:** Jiri Tarantik; **Cast:** Lubor Tolos, Van Kissling, Jane Zalata, Arnost Navratil, Miroslav Holub, Zatloukalova

Director and co-screenwriter Zeman strove to pay tribute to Jules Verne, the original father of science fiction, by combining facets from many of his novels in one epic story. The result was this truly unusual film. Verne's heavier-than-air airships, his submarines, lost worlds, and all the other staple elements of his most memorable works are pulled together with live actors working against both animation and mattes of miniature sets. The interesting thing is that Zeman patterned the look of his film after the style of the 19th-century engravings that adorned the original editions of Verne's novels. This is a film from the heart, made to express the filmmaker's love of his subject matter, and, if one can overlook the actors' leaden performances, an interesting period piece worth the student of the genre's time.

Note: In copies available in America, beware a droning, pointless, sleep-inducing introduction by Hugh Downs, tacked on perhaps because Warner Bros. assumed Americans might not know of Jules Verne.

FACULTY, THE

Dimension, 1998, Color, 104 min, VT, DVD

Producer: Elizabeth Avellan; **Director:** Robert Rodriguez; **Screenplay:** Kevin Williamson, David Wechter, and Bruce Killel; **Music:** Marco Beltrami; **Special Effects:** Robert Kurtzman, Gregory Nicotero, Howard Berger, and Brian M. Jennings; **Cast:** Jordana Brewster, Clea DuVall, Laura Harris, Josh Hartnett, Shawn Hatosy, Salma Hayek, Famke Janssen, Piper Laurie, Chris McDonald, Bebe Neuwirth, Robert Patrick, Usher Raymond, Jon Stewart, Daniel Von Bargen, Elijah Wood

The film critic's press kit for this picture started with a fairly pretentious note:

> *The Faculty* is filled with many shocking twists and turns that we hope will keep the audience on the edge of their seats. When writing and talking about the film, we would appreciate that you keep its exciting plot developments a secret so that the audience can enjoy them for the first time.

That's a fairly pretentious request—unless, of course, it happens to be right, as it is in this case. This is an exciting film filled with a fairly large number of

The Faculty (DIMENSION FILMS / AUTHOR'S COLLECTION)

hairpin plot turns that will catch you off-guard no matter how carefully you pay attention.

Here's the plot: Herrington High is well past its prime. It's an ugly place with no money, burned out teachers, and little hope of a better future. If you're not a jock, you have absolutely no standing there, which leaves most of the students alienated and unappreciated, looking for violence, sex, or drugs. When it looks like things can't get any worse, into the mix comes an alien life force with a hive mentality bent on collecting everyone in the school to its will.

If the above sounds something like INVASION OF THE BODY SNATCHERS or perhaps John Carpenter's THE THING, it should. Horror screenwriter Kevin Williamson (*Scream, Scream 2*) had both of them in mind when he wrote *The Faculty*, wanting especially to pay homage to BODY SNATCHERS, one of his favorite films. As he put it: "There's something about the theme of conformity versus individuality that rings true in every decade. Why not take a McCarthy-era theme and

move it into a nineties high school? The idea being, no matter what stands in your way you can overcome it . . . you don't have to become it. Even aliens."

This may sound like justification for plagiarism, but Williamson has crafted a somewhat new look at an old idea, one that actually turns the notion upside down. In the old films, the alien presence is introduced into a complacent, orderly world, bringing it a horrid degree of brainless control. Here, once the alien influence begins to be felt, suddenly Herrington isn't such a dump. Students are behaving, the halls start getting cleaner, the teachers all have purpose once more. It's almost hard to root for the heroic teens trying to stop the takeover. Why should they? Things really do seem better with the overmind in charge. It's one of the film's splendid ironies that such a notion could look so attractive, but it also makes it clear this is no 1950s retread, but a brand-new story made just for the '90s.

Given a strong script, the filmmakers then did their best to put it on the screen. The camera work is handled smartly—open, static shots for normal life contrasted with moving, angular shots for when the world is turned upside down. The pacing is excellent, and the young cast delivers spirited and engaging performances. Special effects sequences are executed flawlessly, adding to the story instead of distracting from it. Admittedly, there are a few flaws in timing and logic, such as the lack of an explanation as to why the alien presence doesn't move against the kids who know what it's doing any faster than it does. But if you're having a good time watching the film, you'll probably be disposed to letting them slide by.

Note: Listen hard—the dialogue is quite witty. Example: When asked where the drama club will get the money for the sets they need for their new production, the principal asks why can't they just reuse the sets from last year's production of *Our Town*, a play traditionally performed on an empty stage. It's not a sci-fi joke, but it's a good one, and it's not the only one, so pay attention.

FAHRENHEIT 451

Universal, 1967, Color, 112 min, VT, LD, DVD

Producer: Lewis M. Allen; **Director:** Francois Truffaut; **Screenplay:** Truffaut and Jean-Louis Richard; **Music:** Bernard Hermann; **Cinematography:** Nicholas Roeg; **Cast:** Julie Christie, Oskar Werner, Cyril Cusack, Anton Diffring, Jeremy Spenser, Bee Duffell, Alex Scott, Mark Lester

In a future that now seems far more probable than when Ray Bradbury first wrote the novel this film is based on, the ordinary is what is worshiped. Anything that smacks of intellectualism is illegal, and the worst crime of all is reading. Whenever works of fiction or philosophy and so forth, are discovered, the government calls in the firemen. These firemen don't put out fires, however; they start them. Using flamethrowers, they burn every bit of societally undermining literature they can find, bringing the temperature of their flames quickly to 451°, the point at which paper catches fire.

The story centers on fireman Montag (Werner). While going through his normal routine, a woman (Christie) asks him if he has ever read one of the books he burns with such relish. He arrogantly lets her know that such a notion never crossed his mind, but soon he is questioning himself, and soon he is reading. Montag then reads everything he can get his hands on. With the turning of every page, he grows more literate and more aware of what has happened to the world. Soon he is a member of the book underground, a group of

people, each of whom has sworn to memorize one of the classics so that they will not disappear from this world, but these changes can only lead to trouble for him.

This is an incredible and important story. Truffaut's direction is somewhat slow—the pacing is trying for most American audiences. Also, for some reason the director rejected most of the sci-fi elements of Bradbury's book, but since the things lost were trappings and not key plot elements, the changes do little damage to the overall story. They certainly don't keep this from being a film worth seeing.

However, with even the best science fiction movie adaptations, no matter how good a job the filmmakers do, the book is always better, and this is no exception. *Fahrenheit 451* may be Bradbury's most important book, as well as the one for which he'll remembered. Those who want the full impact of the message should read it. If you don't have the time, however (the notion of which does make the movie's point all the more frightening), then watch the film. As Bradbury himself said, "The results were very good indeed. It has a terrific ending that makes me cry every time I see it."

Note: The soundtrack is another Bernard Hermann masterpiece, haunting, tense, and spooky. Hermann was one of the best composer/conductors the art of film scoring has ever known. This was one of his most evocative efforts.

FAIL SAFE

Columbia, 1964, b&w, 111 min, VT, LD

Producer: Max Youngstein; **Director:** Sidney Lumet; **Screenplay:** Walter Bernstein; **Special Effects:** Storyboard, Inc.; **Cinematography:** Gerald Hirshfeld; **Cast:** Henry Fonda, Walter Matthau, Fritz Weaver, Dan O'Herlihy, Sorrell Booke, Larry Hagman, Frank Overton, Dom DeLuise

A mistake sends a U.S. bomber off to nuke the Soviet Union. The U.S. government does everything it can to stop the bomber, but as it turns out, the government's best is not enough. In desperation, the president (Fonda) contacts the Soviets and informs them of what has happened. Their discussions lead to naught. Moscow is doomed, and the Communists will retaliate in full, destroying the world, if the U.S. doesn't come up with a brilliant solution. The president's inspired response is for the United States to nuke New York City purposely to make up for accidentally atomizing Moscow. A bomb is dropped on the Big Apple, and the film ends.

Fail Safe had the misfortune to arrive in the theaters at roughly the same time as the wildly successful and remarkably similar *DR. STRANGELOVE OR: HOW I LEARNED TO STOP WORRYING AND LOVE THE BOMB*, which was by far the public's favorite. *Fail Safe* was a critical success, but it didn't thrill anyone with its box office records. It is, however, a splendid piece of work, filmed in stark black and white, the lack of color working hand-in-hand with the pseudo-documentary style used by Lumet. This is an intelligent and sober look at a somewhat preposterous situation, made all the more effective by the actors' handling of some difficult dialogue.

FALLING, THE

See *ALIEN PREDATOR*

FANTASTIC INVASION OF PLANET EARTH

See *THE BUBBLE*

FANTASTIC PLANET (aka: PLANETE SAUVAGE, LA)

Les Films Armorial (France)/Ceskoslovensky (Czechoslovakia), New World (U.S.), 1963, Color, 72 min, VT, DVD

Producers: S. Damiani and A. Valio-Cavablione; **Director:** René Laloux; **Screenplay:** Roland Topor; **Music:** Alan Gorgageur; **Animation:** Jiri Trnka and Kratky Film; **Voices:** Sylvie Lenoir, Jean Topart, Jennifer Drake, Yves Barsacq, Jean Velmont, Paul Ville, May Amyl

On planet Ygam, the giant android race known as the Draags keep humans, which they call Oms, as pets. One clever Om, Terr, learns a great deal from his teenaged Draag owner, Tiwa. Soon Terr joins the underground resistance for Om independence and is fighting for Om Rights. The Draag find the rebellion's headquarters and destroy it, killing most of the freedom fighters, except for Terr, who escapes harm. Eventually, the Draags come to the conclusion that the Oms are actually intelligent beings and allow them to go off to live on a planet of their own. They name it for the leader of the Omish rebellion, Terr. Of course, they call it Terra.

The only real point of interest in this rehash of basic science fiction clichés is the mood and atmosphere of Ygam. The backgrounds are filled with disturbingly savage items, like the giggling plant that delights in crushing mammals. The film has a number of bizarre oddities like this, but its childish story line and stiff, limited animation are in no way must-see features. Still, this strange film has oceans of fans who insist it is a classic.

FANTASTIC VOYAGE

20th Century Fox, 1966, Color, 100 min, VT, LD, DVD

Producer: Saul David; **Director:** Richard Fleischer; **Screenplay:** Harry Kleiner; **Music:** Leonard Rosemann; **Special Effects:** Lyle B. Abbott, Art Cruickshank, and Emil Kosa, Jr.; **Cinematography:** Ernest Laszlo; **Cast:** Stephen Boyd, Raquel Welch, Arthur O'Connell, Donald Pleasence, William Redfield, James Brolin, Arthur Kennedy, Jean Del Val

Scientist Jan Benes (Del Val) wants to defect to the United States, and the Americans want him for all the great secrets locked in his head. The only one problem is that he also has a clot in his head that is going to kill him soon. To make matters worse, the clot is completely unreachable through ordinary surgical means. In a desperate effort, a hotshot scientist in the far-flung future of 1995 (yikes!) suggests taking a full-sized submarine and its crew, shrinking them with a miniaturization ray, and then injecting them into Benes to destroy the clot. The ray's effects don't last long, so the team has to work fast before they kill the patient simply by returning to normal size.

The sub and its crew embark on their mission and have a number of harrowing experiences, most of them brought on by the presence of a traitor (Pleasence) in their midst and the natural defenses of Benes's immune system. The traitor is conveniently eaten by a ravenous band of white corpuscles, which also eat the sub, but that's okay. The crew eventually completes its mission and escape Benes's body in a tear drop, moments before they expand back to full size.

The idea from Jerome Bixby is original and exciting, but the direction and acting are pedestrian. The filmmakers ignored traditional cinematic values such as acting in favor of relying on their special effects team, which, in truth, did win a trio of Oscars, to pull them through. Sets of the giant-sized heart, brain, and lungs are spectacular on a movie screen, but not enough to make up for the film's deficiencies.

Note: The movie was later adapted as a novel by legendary science fiction writer Isaac Asimov.

FARM, THE

See *THE CURSE*

F.B.I. VS. DR. MABUSE

See *RETURN OF DR. MABUSE*

FEMALE SPACE INVADERS

See *STARCRASH*

FIEND WITHOUT A FACE

Amalgamated (Great Britain)/MGM (U.S.), 1958, b&w, 74 min, VT, LD

Producer: John Croydon; **Director:** Arthur Crabtree; **Screenplay:** Herbert J. Leder; **Music:** Buxton Orr; **Special Effects:** Puppel Nordhoff and Peter Nielson; **Cinematography:** Lionel Banes; **Cast:** Marshall Thompson, Kim Parker, Terence Kilburn, Michael Balfour, Gil Winfield, Peter Madden

There's a lot of trouble at the site of a joint U.S./Canadian radar base. The base uses nuclear energy to power its radar, and this has the locals up in arms. The cows haven't been giving the same amount of milk ever since the base went in, and everyone in town is certain it's the nuclear reactors that are causing the tragedy. And, if this horrendous loss of milk wasn't bad enough, suddenly there seems to be a madman loose. People are being murdered in an unusually vicious manner, and the townsfolk are blaming a mad G.I. killer.

While local troublemakers get the town stirred up (ironically sending them out into the forest where they can be killed more easily by the film's true villains), stalwarts from the base try to get to the bottom of things. What they find makes their hair stand on end. It seems a local, not-so-mad scientist wanted to make thought materialize. He succeeded, but not with the beneficial results he was expecting. Instead, his experiments turned loose a flock of invisible killers who murder their victims by sucking their brains out through holes punctured into the base of their necks. In the film's grand finale, the creatures are finally revealed as leaping brains with trailing spinal cords flapping behind them.

It sounds silly, and just looking at a still picture of one of the brains, they do look pretty silly at that. But the ending of this movie is anything but. True, while the monsters are invisible the drumbeat that accompanies their movements almost forces one to visualize the creatures as some sort of Energizer Predator, but for the few moments they're visible, the creatures turn this one into a tense, scary thriller. Admittedly, the amount of hard science could be stored in a quart jar with room left over for three more pints, and the acting is kind of hammy, but the direction is smooth, and the stop-frame animation effects are truly frightening. These creatures are revolting, and aren't those the best kind?

FIEND WITH THE ATOMIC BRAIN, THE (aka: THE FIEND WITH THE ELECTRONIC BRAIN, THE FIEND WITH THE SYNTHETIC BRAIN, BLOOD OF GHASTLY HORROR, PSYCHO A GO-GO!, THE LOVE MANIAC)

Hemisphere, 1972, Color, 87 min, VT

Producers: Al Adamson and Samuel M. Sherman; **Director:** Adamson; **Screenplay:** Sherman, Dick Poston, and Chris Martino; **Special Effects:** Vilmos Zsigmond; **Cast:** John Carradine, Tommy Kirk, Kent Taylor, Regina Carrol

John Carradine stars as a mad doctor who specializes in brain transplants that go horribly wrong. Sadly, the film is notable only for the many ways it has been retitled in the empty hope that this perfectly wretched piece of work could ever find an appreciative audience.

FIEND WITH THE ELECTRONIC BRAIN, THE

See *THE FIEND WITH THE ATOMIC BRAIN*

FIEND WITH THE SYNTHETIC BRAIN, THE

See *THE FIEND WITH THE ATOMIC BRAIN*

FIFTH ELEMENT, THE

Columbia, 1997, Color, 127 min, VT, LD, DVD

Producers: Patrice Ledoux and Iain Smith; **Director:** Luc Besson; **Screenplay:** Besson and Robert Mark Kamen; **Music:** Eric Serra; **Special Effects:** Nick Adler, Neil Corbould, Ron Gress, Bill Neil, Mark Stetson, and Trevor Wood; **Cinematography:** Thierry Arbograst; **Cast:** Bruce Willis, Gary Oldman, Luke Perry, Ian Holm, Milla Jovovich, Chris Tucker, Brion

The Fifth Element (SONY PICTURES ENTERTAINMENT/
JOSEPH B. MAUCERI COLLECTION)

James, Tommy "Tiny" Lister, Jr., Lee Evans, John
Neville

Bruce Willis plays a 23rd-century New York City cab
driver in a time when the cabs fly and the whole world
has become a little crazy. Friendly aliens had set things
up to protect the world from evil aliens thousands of
years before. But something went wrong, and now the
evil aliens are on their way, which means the whole
world is doomed. Unless, that is, cabbie Willis can protect the beautiful but bizarre young woman who has
come into his life, as well as figure out the secret of the
Fifth Element, which will save Earth.

Describing more of the plot here is pointless
since the story line is just a thin wire on which to hang
scenes. The scenes ever so carefully suspended from
that gossamer thread, however, are an incredible
amount of fun. There is plenty of comedy and campy
old sci-fi hardware retrofitted to suit a '90s sensibility,
and visually the film is a dazzling array of inspired sets,
landscapes, and bizarre alien creatures. The film does
not make complete sense, but unlike many of its pretentious competitors, it doesn't pretend to either. This
is a comic-book movie, which is the reason for the
comic-book descriptions above. It may also be the reason for Chris Tucker's extremely over-the-top performance as the world's most irritating celebrity. At the
very least, the movie manages not to disrupt its internal logic. Most critics panned this one, but many audiences loved it. Is it nothing more than eye candy? Yes,
but it's extremely high-quality and really funny eye
candy.

FINAL COUNTDOWN, THE

United Artists, 1980, Color, 104 min, VT, LD

Producer: Peter Vincent Douglas; **Director:** Don
Taylor; **Screenplay:** David Ambrose, Gerry Davis,
Thomas Hunter, and Peter Powell; **Music:** John
Scott; **Special Effects:** Maurice Binder; **Cast:** Kirk
Douglas, Martin Sheen, Katherine Ross, James Far-
entino, Charles Durning, Ron O'Neal

The film opens with civilian computer expert Warren
Lasky (Sheen) being rushed aboard a nuclear-powered
aircraft carrier, the U.S.S. *Nimitz*. The reason why is
not revealed. In fact, even the navy doesn't know.
Shortly after, the great ship puts out to sea and gets
caught in an incredible storm that swallows it whole
and transports it back in time to the waters just off
Pearl Harbor, the day before the infamous Japanese
attack. The captain (Douglas) and commander (Farentino) quickly figure out that they are in 1941, but
oddly they don't seem very concerned. Instead, they
quickly begin to debate whether or not they should
interfere with the attack.

Regardless of how well trained these men may be,
their actions make little sense. No one on the ship
questions what has happened. They simply wait for
orders. And that's the next odd part: Military men who
can accept having been transported four decades into
the past without the slightest discomfort or the need to
question the fact, then debate for hours over their
moral right to interfere with the past. It's rare that
Hollywood credits the military with such philosophic
tendencies, which may explain why it was handled so
badly.

There is an old saying about too many cooks and
the kind of broth they produce. This movie was cooked
up in one of those kitchens. First, three fellows wrote a
story about a modern aircraft carrier traveling through
time. Then a fourth scribe made a quartet that turned
out a screenplay based on the story. What the lot of
them produced is a poorly strung together collection
of scenes with very little in the way of transition or
explanation.

The film moves much too quickly, time and again
blurring its focus. The characters are rushed along as if
there were a timetable that had to be met no matter
what the cost. Well, the cost was in continuity, character development, plot structure, and audience enjoyment. This film does not grip the viewer—indeed, it's
hard even to maintain passing interest in it. And when
the captain finally does make a decision, and amazingly
he decides to give the Japanese hell, the storm returns

and spits the *Nimitz* back out into the future. Sheen's programmer gets left behind in the past and is standing on the docks as an older man (married to the beautiful girl he met in the past) to greet the carrier when it returns.

A novelization by Martin Caidin sewed up all the ragged holes in the script, but audiences shouldn't have to go to the bookstore just to be able to figure out what they just saw in a film.

FINAL PROGRAMME, THE (aka: THE LAST DAYS OF MAN ON EARTH)

Goodtime Enterprises/Gladiole Films (Great Britain), MGM (U.S.), 1974, Color, 89 min, VT, LD

Producers: John Goldstone and Sandy Lieberson; **Director:** Robert Fuest; **Screenplay:** Fuest; **Music:** Paul Beaver and Barnard Krause; **Special Effects:** Fuest and Phillip Harrison; **Cast:** Jon Finch, Jenny Runacre, Sterling Hayden, Harry Andrews, Hugh Griffith, Julie Ege, Patrick Magee

This film is based more than somewhat loosely on Michael Moorcock's wildly eccentric and socially satiric novel of the same name, the first of the Jerry Cornelius adventures. In both book and film, Cornelius's father has died, leaving behind his final computer program (a design for the perfect self-replicating human being), which sets off a worldwide hunt. But that's where the similarities end.

While Moorcock's book tackled the story with wit and a savage sense of humor, the film is little more than a string of stylish but dated bits that fail completely. Gone are both the author's sophistication and his brooding sense of irony, replaced by a facile smugness, the equivalent of an egotistical child using words incorrectly, then not only insisting he knows their meanings, but demanding praise for being so clever. One would have expected better from Fuest, who directed so many episodes of Britain's famous *Avengers* television series.

FIRE IN THE SKY

Paramount, 1993, Color, 107 min, VT, LD

Producers: Todd Black and Joe Wizan; **Director:** Robert Lieberman; **Screenplay:** Tracy Tormé; **Music:** Mark Isham; **Special Effects:** Michael Owens, Matt Kutcher, and Alan E. Lorimer; **Cinematography:** Bill Pope; **Cast:** D.B. Sweeney, Robert Patrick, Craig Sheffer, Peter Berg, James Garner, Henry Thomas, Bradley Gregg, Noble Willingham, Kathleen Wilhoite

Travis Wilson (Sweeney) and a group of friends are out for the night, but the night is interrupted when he is abducted by aliens. Five days later, he's returned. Most of the story follows what his friends and family are put through by the authorities during Wilson's absence and what all of them undergo when he returns.

This great little movie has a creepiness that slowly gets under your skin, building minute by minute until the audience is genuinely unsettled. How can such a simple story generate such feelings in its audiences? Because everyone involved swears that it's *true*!

Yes, this movie is based on Travis Wilson's *The Walton Experience*, which he wrote after his alleged abduction. Whether the story is fact or fiction, the movie will challenge even nonbelievers because it *feels* so true. The skepticism of real life pervades the picture in stark contrast to the fantastic nature of its story. The men involved gain nothing and almost lose everything, and if they were out to pull some kind of con, it certainly didn't work. Adding to the overall sensation are the special effects. As little as they are, they're unavoidably creepy.

FIRE MAIDENS FROM OUTER SPACE

Topaz (Great Britain), 1956, b&w, 80 min

George Folwer; **Director:** Cy Roth; **Screenplay:** Roth; **Music:** Aleksandr P. Borodin; **Special Effects:** Roy Ashton and Scott MacGregor; **Cinematography:** Ian D. Struthers; **Cast:** Anthony Dexter, Susan Shaw, Paul Carpenter, Henry Fowler, Sydney Tafler

On a mission to the 13th moon of Jupiter, daring astronauts brave the overwhelming gravitational pull of the largest planet in the solar system and land to discover . . . a planet full of dazzlingly beautiful women! It might seem like an ideal situation if it wasn't for a horrible monster running around at night tearing people apart. Watching people fall off the couch when the big dance number comes can make this one worth seeing.

FIRE OF LIFE

Nordisk (Denmark)/Great Northern (U.S.), 1912, b&w, two reels, silent

Director: Schedler Sorenson; **Screenplay:** Xenius Rostock; **Cast:** Valdemar Psitander, Julie Henriksen, Else Frohlich

A scientist comes up with the secret to life everlasting.

FIRESTARTER

Universal, 1984, Color, 115 min, VT, LD, DVD

Producer: Frank Capra, Jr.; **Director:** Mark L. Lester; **Screenplay:** Stanley Mann; **Music:** Tangerine Dream; **Special Effects:** Mike Edmonson; **Cinematography:** Giuseppe Russolini; **Cast:** George C. Scott, Martin Sheen, Heather Locklear, Drew Barrymore, David Keith, Art Carney, Louise Fletcher, Moses Gunn, Freddie Jones

A child (Barrymore) whose parents were affected by a government experiment learns that she can cause spontaneous combustion at will in what amounts to a really bad film with acres of really good special effects based on a fair novel of the same name by Stephen King. Burn, baby, burn.

FIRST MAN INTO SPACE
(aka: SATELLITE OF BLOOD)

Amalgamated (Great Britain)/MGM (U.S.), 1959, b&w, 77 min, VT, DVD

Producers: John Croydon and Charles F. Vetter; **Director:** Robert Day; **Screenplay:** John C. Cooper and Lance Hargreaves; **Music:** Buxton Orr; **Cinematography:** Geoffrey Faithfull; **Cast:** Marshall Thompson, Marla Landi, Robert Ayes, Bill Nagy, Carl Jaffe, Bill Edwards

Earth's first man in space comes back covered with slime and thirsty for blood. If this sounds like the first Quatermass movie, *THE CREEPING UNKNOWN*, that's because this is a second-rate rip-off of that great film.

FIRST MEN IN THE MOON

Columbia, 1964, Color, 107 min, VT, LD

Producers: Charles Schneer and Ray Harryhausen; **Director:** Nathan Juran; **Screenplay:** Nigel Kneale and Jan Read; **Music:** Laurie Johnson; **Special Effects:** Harryhausen; **Cast:** Edward Judd, Martha Hyer Lionel Jeffries, Erik Chitty, Betty McDowall, Miles Malleson, Hugh McDermott, Peter Finch

The story begins in present-day England, where old Mr. Bedford (Judd), a gentleman living in a retirement home, watches the first Moon landing on television. As he does, he recounts his own trip to the moon to those around him (as he has done in the past). He claims that back before the turn of the century, his friend Dr. Cavor (Jeffries) invented an antigravity fluid he called Cavorite, which caused anything coated with it to float. His first major use for it? To propel a manned satellite to the Moon. For fun, he took Bedford and Bedford's fiancée along.

The trio have several adventures on the surface of the Moon, wearing deep-sea diving suits (as they say quite logically: "What will keep water out will keep air in."), after which they are found by reasonable, friendly creatures who live inside the Moon. Cavor tells the insectlike Selenites of life on Earth. Unfortunately for Cavor and his friends, his stories of war and the such frighten the poor lunar king so badly that he decides to keep the doctor and his companions on the Moon forever. The king reasons that if the astronauts never to return to Earth, then no other Earthlings would ever be able to reach the Moon and the lunar kingdom would be protected from such horrible ideas such as politics and greed. Cavor, who is suffering from a cold, is content to remain, but Bedford and his girl make a break, escaping back to Earth.

Once the film returns to the present, everyone chuckles at Bedford's story as usual, until suddenly the modern astronauts on television discover a tattered Union Jack on the surface of the Moon. They soon find the Lunar cities, which are filled with corpses of all the Moon creatures killed by Cavor's cold germs.

This is an uneven but highly watchable version of the H. G. Wells classic. It was updated with a framing sequence in anticipation of modern moviegoers' complaints about watching a period piece. Effects genius and co-producer Ray Harryhausen reported that it was this device and only this device that finally convinced producer Schneer to go ahead with the film.

While this is not a landmark motion picture, it is a quaint and fair adaptation of Wells's novel—no better or worse than most sci-fi films as far as its script goes. This movie shines, however, in its special effects. Dynamation whiz Ray Harryhausen does his usual impressive job. When he wasn't in complete control of the look (as with the Selenites, which were, in fact, children in rubber suits) the special effects suffered to varying degrees. But where the master had complete control, the film's look is absolutely splendid. Schneer and Harryhausen did their best to maintain the charm and grace of the Victorian period, the previously mentioned framing device that adds to the movie more than one might think.

Note: First Men in the Moon was also made into a film in 1919 by the Gaumont Studios in Great Britain. It was silent, of course, but it was also a feature film and apparently was well received. Sci-fi fever strikes again.

FIRST SPACESHIP ON VENUS (aka: PLANET OF THE DEAD, SPACESHIP VENUS DOES NOT REPLY, ASTRONAUTS)

Defa/Juizjon (East Germany/Poland), 1959, Color, 109 min/Crown International (U.S.), 1963, Color, 78 min, VT, DVD

Producer: Hugo Grimaldi; **Director:** Kurt Matzig; **Screenplay:** J. Barckhausen, J. Felthke, W. Kohlasse, Matzig, G. Reisch, and G. Rucker; **Music:** Gordon Zahler; **Cast:** Ignacy Machowski, Yoko Tani, Tang Hua-Ta, Oldrich Lukes, Julius Ongewe

The remains of an alien spaceship that exploded on Earth years earlier leads an international crew of astronaut explorers to the planet Venus. They are surprised when they find that everyone has been dead for quite some time. The Venusians' machines are still operating, but the land shows the ravages of a nuclear war. Yes, Venus destroyed itself with the horrors of atomic war. Can we learn our lesson before it's too late? This movie is not much fun in English. It's possible that something got lost in the over 30 minutes that were cut when Crown International edited this film for American release, but the English-language version is stiff and ponderous.

FIVE

Columbia, 1951, b&w, 93 min

Producer: Arch Oboler; **Director:** Oboler; **Screenplay:** Oboler; **Cinematography:** Louis Clyde Stoumen and Sid Lubow; **Cast:** Earl Lee, William Phipps, Charles Lampkin, Susan Douglas, James Anderson

After the nuclear bombs fall, four people find their way to William Phipps's remote mountain home—black elevator operator Lampkin, bank teller Lee, sporting-type Anderson, and pregnant Douglas. The five bicker and cry a lot before they begin to fight and despair in earnest. By the end, only Phipps and Douglas and her dead husband's baby are left.

One of the first films with the antinuclear war theme that would become a staple of the science fiction genre, this one may also possibly be the most preachy of the bunch. Producer/director/screenwriter Oboler worked in radio for years before starting in Hollywood in 1945, and the overly talky and pedantic *Five* reflects this background.

FIVE MILLION YEARS TO EARTH (aka: QUATERMASS AND THE PIT)

Hammer/Seven Arts (Great Britain)/20th Century Fox (U.S.), 1968, Color, 97 min, VT, DVD

Producer: Anthony Nelson-Keys; **Director:** Roy Ward Baker; **Screenplay:** Nigel Kneale,; **Music:** Tristram Cary; **Special Effects:** Les Bowie Films; **Cast:** James Donald, Barbara Shelley, Andrew Keir, Julian Glover, Maurice Good

During work on a new subway line, something is found buried under the streets of London, something the tunnel excavators can't understand. At first it's thought to be an unexploded V-bomb left over from World War II. But testy Professor Quatermass, the bad-tempered hero of both THE CREEPING UNKNOWN and ENEMY FROM SPACE, disagrees and thus the fun begins. The professor is correct, of course. The object is a Martian spaceship that has been on Earth since prehistoric times. The military fights him every step of the way, confusing the importance of political power with more weighty problems like preserving humanity. With the aid of anthropologist Dr. Roney (Donald) and his assistant (Shelley), Quatermass unearths insectlike Martian remains and then pieces the entire story together. Millions of years before, Mars was dying. Hoping to ensure the survival of their race in some form or other, they sent an expedition to Earth, where the Neanderthals of the day were genetically engineered to contain the Martians' racial memories.

The film ends with this discovery awakening those memories in Londoners all over town, an action that threatens to destroy humanity unless Quatermass and Roney can cobble together a surefire idea in time to stop it. As they try to stay alive, the Martian ship's long-dormant power begins to connect with the citizens, turning them, basically, into Martians.

This film is powerful, exciting, and intelligent, leaving little doubt that *Five Million Miles to Earth* is the best of the three Quatermass films and one of the high-water marks of science fiction. Although produced on a comparatively small budget, its formidably taut script is a masterpiece. There are no slow parts, no dragging scenes. Everything crackles with energy, especially Andrew Keir, the first Englishman to play the professor, and the hands-down best Quatermass ever.

This is one of the purest science fiction films ever made, so confident of its premise that it dismisses God as the Creator without even drawing attention to the fact. Step by step, Quatermass and Roney track down one horrible truth after another, using the scientific method until their monstrous conclusions are supported by unshakable evidence. Their work is coldly painstaking and clinical, yet the script is such that the actors make every second seemed charged with excitement.

FLAME BARRIER, THE

United Artists, 1958, b&w, 70 min

Producers: Arthur Gardener and Jules Levy; **Director:** Paul Landres; **Screenplay:** Pat Fiedler and George Worthing Yates; **Cast:** Arthur Franz, Kathleen Crowley, Robert Brown, Vincent Paudula, Kaz Oran

A satellite that should be in orbit crash-lands in Africa. When scientists Franz and Crowley go searching for the reason, they find that an amoebalike alien has attached itself to it. If this weren't bad enough, the little critter is unfriendly, releasing bursts of incredible heat whenever someone gets too close and pretty soon burning down the whole jungle. This movie couldn't have been saved even if Whit Bissell had been coaxed into taking a part.

FLAMING DISK, THE

Universal, 1920, b&w, serial, 36 reels, silent

Director: Robert F. Hill; **Screenplay:** Arthur Henry Gooden and Jerry Ash; **Cast:** Elmo Lincoln, Monty Montague, Louise Lorraine

Science produces a lens that can disintegrate metal. As one might expect, 18 Saturdays were required to see if the good guys win out in the end. Need a hint? They did.

FLASH GORDON (1936) (aka: SPACE SOLDIERS, ATOMIC ROCKETSHIP, SPACESHIP TO THE UNKNOWN)

Universal, 1936, b&w, serial, 26 reels, VT, DVD

Director: Frederick Stephani; **Screenplay:** Stephani, George H. Plympton, Basil Dickey, and Lee O'Neill; **Cast:** Buster Crabbe, Jean Rogers, Frank Shannon, Charles Middleton, Priscilla Lawson, John Lipson

Flash Gordon (Crabbe) and his girlfriend Dale (Rogers) accompany mad scientist Dr. Zarkov (Shannon) in his homemade rocketship (they launch it from the backyard) on a trip to discover what's causing

recent volcanic activity on Earth. If it's Flash Gordon, you can bet the culprit is Ming the Merciless (Middleton). Flash and company battle their arch villain along with his claypeople, sharkpeople, and other assorted accomplices for 13 episodes, finally killing Ming in the last reel.

Even though more money was reportedly spent on this serial than any other made at the time, it still looks as bad as all the rest, which is a shame because, frankly, Flash deserves better. Flash Gordon was created by the King Features Syndicate strictly to compete with the competition's Buck Rogers. Buck was more of a real science fiction character. He got to the future through suspended animation. He piloted spacecrafts, used rayguns and flight packs, and generally embraced technology wholeheartedly, if only in the pulpiest of fashions. Flash was a much earthier guy. He'd disintegrate the enemy if he could, but he was much more likely to end up in stylish swordplay.

Neither character was driven to respect the hard sciences, but Buck at least seemed to make a tip of the hat in that direction; Flash was simply escapist fodder. Even characters like Rocky Jones and Captain Video

Flash Gordon (UNIVERSAL / R. ALLEN LEIDER COLLECTION)

dealt in more reliable science than Flash. But a genre has to start somewhere. To understand Flash's appeal, however, think of Flash Gordon as the Luke Skywalker of his time. It's a fairly apt parallel.

This Flash Gordon epic was followed by two serials, *FLASH GORDON'S TRIP TO MARS* (aka: *Space Soldiers' Trip to Mars*), then *FLASH GORDON CONQUERS THE UNIVERSE* (aka: *Peril from the Planet Mongo, Space Soldiers Conquer the Universe*, and *The Purple Death from Outer Space*). None of these is outstanding or worth viewing for any reason other than nostalgia or curiosity.

FLASH GORDON (1980)

Universal/De Laurentiis Productions, 1980, Color, 110 min, VT, LD, DVD

Producer: Dino De Laurentiis; **Director:** Mike Hodges; **Screenplay:** Lorenzo Semple, Jr.; **Music:** Howard Blake and Queen; **Cinematography:** Gilbert Taylor; **Special Effects:** George Gibbs, Derek Botell, and Richard Conway; **Cast:** Sam J. Jones, Melody Anderson, Topol, Max von Sydow, Ornella Muti, Brian Blessed, Timothy Dalton, Mariangela Melato, Peter Wingarde

Flash Gordon (Jones) and his girlfriend Dale (Anderson) accompany scientist Dr. Zarkov in his homemade rocketship on a trip to discover what's causing recent problems on Earth. Of course, if it's Flash Gordon, you can bet the culprit is Ming the Merciless (von Sydow). Flash and company battle their archvillain along with his accomplices.

This campy mess once and for all insults a character who has never been treated very well on film. In color with dazzling special effects and an almost all-star cast, this version of Flash Gordon is even worse than the serials. Those may have been silly and misguided, filled with the worst kind of pulp excess, but they at least *tried* to take things seriously. The goal of the serial Flash Gordon filmmakers was not to prove their own superiority to their material by ridiculing it relentlessly.

The Dino De Laurentiis version of Flash Gordon may be the most relentless attack on a well-established character in the history of science fiction films (well, there is De Laurentiis's *KING KONG* series, isn't there). It shows in the choice of unknown and untalented Sam Jones to star as Flash. The actor is embarrassingly awful. He's supported by a top-notch cast that struggles along and at least tries, but the lead is simply awful. But Jones is not the worst thing in this movie.

Screenwriter Lorenzo Semple, Jr., has a history of draining the heroism out of any character and replacing it with sad clowning and idiotic buffoonery. He was the genius who turned Batman into a stiff straight man for '60s television, and his talent shows through here as well.

Though probably not true, one wonders if the filmmakers were actively seeking to destroy the character of Flash Gordon.

FLASH GORDON CONQUERS THE UNIVERSE

Universal, 1940, b&w, serial, 12 chapters, VT, DVD

Directors: Ford Beebe and Ray Taylor; **Screenplay:** George H. Plympton, Basil Dickey, and Barry Shipman; **Music:** Ralph Freed, Franz Waxman, Sam Perry, Heinz Roemheld, Charles Previn, and Frank Skinner; **Cinematography:** Jerome Ash; **Cast:** Buster Crabbe, Frank Shannon, Carol Hughes, Charles Middelton, Roland Drew, Don Rowan, Victor Zimmerman, Anne Gwynne, Shirley Dean.

See *FLASH GORDON* (1936)

FLASH GORDON: MARS ATTACKS THE WORLD

See *THE DEADLY RAY FROM MARS*

FLASH GORDON'S TRIP TO MARS

Universal, 1939, b&w, serial, 15 chapters, VT, DVD

Directors: Ford Beebe and Robert Hill; **Screenplay:** Ray Trampe, Normal S. Hall, Wyndham Gittens, and Herbert Dolmas; **Music:** Ed Ward, Franz Waxman, Sam Perry, Heinz Roemheld, Clifford Vaughn, David Klazkin, Karl Hajus, and W. Frankel Harling; **Cinematography:** Jerome Ash; **Cast:** Buster Crabbe, Frank Shannon, Jean Rogers, Charles Middelton, Beatrice Roberts, Richard Alexander, C. Montague Shaw

See *FLASH GORDON* (1936)

FLATLINERS

Columbia, 1990, Color, 105 min, VT, LD, DVD

Producers: Rick Bieber and Michael Douglas; **Director:** Joel Schumacher; **Screenplay:** Peter Filardi;

Music: James Newton Howard; **Special Effects:** Peter Donen, Hans Metz, Philip Cory, and Peter Juneau; **Cinematography:** Jan de Bont; **Cast:** Julia Roberts, Kevin Bacon, William Baldwin, Kiefer Sutherland, Oliver Platt, Kimberly Scott

Medical students apply scientific principle to the moment of death. Their hope is that if they induce temporary termination (kill themselves, but only a little) under controlled circumstances, and then bring themselves back from the dead, they will be able to answer the age-old question of what comes next.

However, a great idea stumbles through poor execution. The first half of this film is rather gripping, misleading audiences into thinking they're going to see something terrific, even extraordinary, before it bogs down into silliness just when it should start making revelations. It's sad to watch the tight first half of this film destroyed by sloppy thought and deed throughout the second half, but then how can one defend a film that dubs in the antique sounds of a dot-matrix printer when a laser printer is in operation on the screen. Despite an intriguing idea, great cast, excellent camera work, imaginative special effects, and half of a good script, director Schumacher only destroys them with hip styling.

FLESH EATERS, THE

Cinema, 1964, b&w, 88 min, VT

Producers: Jack Curtis, Terry Curtis, and Arnold Drake; **Director:** Jack Curtis; **Screenplay:** Drake; **Music:** Julian Stein; **Special Effects:** Roy Benson; **Cinematography:** Carson Davidson; **Cast:** Rita Morley, Martin Kosleck, Byron Sanders, Barbara Walken, Ray Tudor

It isn't bad enough that demented scientist Kosleck develops a strain of microorganism that eats away flesh, but as an experiment he releases it into the waters off his island. Once a band of desperate castaways lands on the island, they spend the rest of the movie literally hanging onto their skin. First they have to keep it away from the microbes; then they have to watch out for the giant creature that the microbes form when they join together.

FLESH FOR FRANKENSTEIN

See *ANDY WARHOL'S FRANKENSTEIN*

FLESH GORDON

Mammoth Films, 1974, Color, 78 min, VT, LD

Producers: Howard Ziehm and Bill Osco; **Directors:** Michael Benveniste and William Hunt; **Screenplay:** Benveniste and Hunt; **Music:** Ralph Ferraro; **Special Effects:** Jim Danforth, David Allen, Russ Turner, Rick Baker, Doug Beswick, Craig Neuswanger, Greg Jein, Robert Maine, George Garr, Joe Clarke, Jim Aupperie, Mike Hyatt, Dennis Muren; **Cast:** Jason Williams, Suzanne Fields, Joseph Hudgins, William Hunt, John Hoyt, Lance Larsen, Candy Fields, Mycle Brandy

The story in this oddball movie is a standard Flash Gordon take-off: Flesh Gordon (Williams), Dale Ardor (Fields), and their usual scientist pal Dr. Flexi Jerkoff do battle against the evil emperor Wang (Hunt) on the planet Porno. This time Earth is menaced by a sex ray.

Despite an X rating on its release, there is very little X-rated material in this movie. In the beginning, this film was scheduled to be just another cheap bit of smut, but the production hired some fairly talented kids to work on the special effects. Hungry for a chance to show off, they designed all sorts of elaborate showstoppers—giant penis-snakes, robotic rapists, intricately detailed beetle creatures, and so on. As the effects grew more elaborate, the talented kids called in some of their friends. Many of those listed above were doing some of their first feature film work, and some did not even receive credit for their work. But eventually the producers began to realize they had something far more interesting than what they had first planned.

The powers in charge decided to try to have their cake and eat it, too. A great deal of the steamy footage was cut, and suddenly *Flesh Gordon* was released as a very sexy, but not that dirty, sci-fi comedy. The strategy worked. *Flesh Gordon* became a huge hit for an X-rated movie, all of it due to its incredible effects. Those who may be curious should understand that there is still sexual material in the film, just far less than originally intended. Those who don't enjoy such things should pass this one by. Those who aren't bothered will relish the hysterical Ray Harryhausen tribute at the climax of the film.

FLIGHT OF THE NAVIGATOR, THE

Walt Disney Productions, 1986, Color, 90 min, VT, LD

Producers: Dimitri Villard and Robert Wald; **Director:** Randal Kleiser; **Screenplay:** Matt McManus, Mark H. Baker, and Michael Burton; **Music:** Alan Silvestri; **Special Effects:** Jack Bennett, Peter Doren, Ron Goodman, Craig Boyajian, Joe Williams, and Geoff Kleiser; **Cinematography:** James Glennon; **Cast:** Joey Cramer, Veronica Cartwright, Cliff De Young, Sarah Jessica Parker, Matt Adler, Howard Hesseman, Paul Reubens

A 12-year-old boy hitches a ride on a spaceship, riding along with its adorable robot. When he returns, he's still 12 years old, but he discovers that he's been gone for eight years. This is standard fare, but kids enjoy it. For genre fans, however, the science is slight and the story is a little too thin for most adults.

FLIGHT TO A FAR PLANET

See QUEEN OF BLOOD

FLIGHT TO MARS

Monogram, 1951, Color, 72 min, VT

Producer: Walter Mirisch; **Director:** Lesley Selander; **Screenplay:** Arthur Strawn; **Music:** Marklin Skiles; **Cast:** Marguerite Chapman, Cameron Mitchell, Virginia Huston, Arthur Franz, John Litel, Edward Earle, Morris Ankrum

A group of astronauts and newspaper reporters crash-land on Mars after not quite dodging a meteor shower. To their surprise they discover an underground Martian civilization ruled by a beautiful princess. The astronauts and the reporters and the Martians get along famously, so the Martians decide to help the poor Earthlings fix their ship and get back home. Where's Whit Bissell when you need him?

FLUBBER

Disney, 1997, Color, 93 min, VT, LD, DVD

Producers: John Hughes, Michael Polaire, Ricardo Mestres, David Nicksay, and Nilo Rodis-Jamero; **Director:** Les Mayfield; **Screenplay:** Sam Taylor and Bill Walsh; **Music:** Danny Elfman; **Cinematography:** Dean Cundey; **Special Effects:** Phillip Edward Alexy, Lynda Lemon, Tom Bertino, Scott Lebrecht, Dan Chuba, Doug Smith, Peter Crosman, David Wainstain, Industrial Light and Magic, C.O.R.E. Digital Pictures, DreamQuest Images, POP Film, Computer Café, Inc. and Vision Crew Unlimited; **Cast:** Robin Williams, Marcia Gay Harden, Christopher McDonald, Raymond J. Barry, Clancy Brown, Ted Levine, Wil Wheaton, Edie McClurg, Jodi Benson

See THE ABSENT-MINDED PROFESSOR

FLY, THE (1958)

20th Century Fox, 1958, Color, 94 min, VT, LD, DVD

Producer: Kurt Neumann; **Director:** Neumann; **Screenplay:** James Clavell; **Music:** Paul Sawtell; **Special Effects:** Lyle B. Abbott; **Cinematography:** Karl Struss; **Cast:** David Hedison, Patricia Owens, Vincent Price, Herbert Marshall, Kathleen Freeman, Betty Lou Gerson, Charles Herbert

André Delambre (Hedison) is working on the world's first teleportation device. After testing his device with less than stellar success on the family pet, he feels he's worked out all the bugs and is ready to try again. Feeling pretty confident, he decides to send himself through the machine. André makes it from point A to point B, but there's a problem. A fly got into the teleportation chamber with him. When they got to the other end, the two had switched heads and one arm (leg?). Wearing a heavy veil that covers his head, our hero implores (how he talks with a fly's head is never explained) his wife to search for the fly in the hopes that if both of them pass through the machine once more they will be returned to their original states. Wife and son search for the insect, but they can't catch it.

In the meantime, André feels his humanity slipping away. He knows that soon he will not be able to control himself and so he is forced to commit suicide in a manner that will obliterate the gruesome facts of his experiment. Understanding, his wife helps, but this only serves to get her arrested for his murder. She tells her story and is deemed a madwoman. Luckily for her (and for André), the police inspector in charge of the case happens to sit in the garden near a spiderweb where the fly with André's head has been trapped. He stares in horror as he realizes he is looking at an insect with a man's head and arm. He quickly smashes the abomination and the spider with a large rock. Mrs. Delambre is not bothered further by the law.

The science doesn't work very well in this movie. For instance, why is it that the human with the fly head and the fly with the human head can both think? Where *did* that fly brain get off to? Still, it's an effective sci-fi/horror film nonetheless. The pacing is excellent, the human relations between the husband and wife are intense and heartbreakingly tragic. The social questions about humans playing God, or at least about paying respect (or, well, at least some attention) when playing with fire, are handled with subtlety and intelligence. This modest picture made on a shoestring budget remains one of the classics.

Note: The Fly was also a box office smash, making so much money that it spawned two sequels. First up was the obligatorily titled *Return of the Fly*, where André's son picks up where Dad left off, and then *Curse of the Fly*, in which an escaped mental patient ends up with the remains of the Delambre family, who still haven't learned to leave well enough alone. Neither sequel matches the first on any level.

FLY, THE (1986)

20th Century Fox, 1986, Color, 100 min, VT, LD, DVD

Producer: Stuart Cornfeld; **Director:** David Cronenberg; **Screenplay:** C.E. Pogue and Cronenberg; **Music:** Howard Shore; **Special Effects:** Chris Walas and Stephan Dupuis; **Cast:** Jeff Goldblum, Geena Davis, John Getz, Joy Boushel, Les Carlson

Jeff Goldblum portrays Seth Brundle, a brilliant conceptual scientist terrified of traveling in vehicles who dedicates his life to making teleportation a reality. He makes the same mistake as his 1958 predecessor, however, namely going through the machine with an unnoticed fly hitching a ride. The results in this remake are far more sinister and tragic. This time our scientist's DNA has been combined with the fly's on the molecular level. There are not two subjects with swapped parts that possibly could be reexchanged. This time there is only one traveler, and he's doomed to slowly turn into a giant insectlike being, with no hope of salvation. He tries desperately to find a way to reverse the process without losing his lover at the same time. His mind begins a descent into insect logic, however, and the rest of the film revolves around his struggle to not only regain his mere physical humanity, but to retain his mental humanity as well.

Producer Cornfeld, commenting on the alteration of the head-switching story line, announced at the time: "It would have been just like the original, bad melodrama and camp horror. So we decided it would be a lot more disturbing and nightmarish if it was done as a metamorphosis."

For those who didn't notice, this version of *The Fly* is the remake of the 1958 low-budget, sci-fi/horror classic reviewed above. It came at a time when Hollywood was hot to run old science fiction movies through the remake machine. Most were less successful; John Carpenter's THE THING and Dino De Laurentiis' KING KONG were made in the same era. This film, however, was not. The '80s version of *The Fly* was a complete reconceptualization of the original and a fairly brilliant one at that. This time there is no hope for salvation. All Brundle can do is to watch helplessly as he is transformed step by step into a grotesque mutant—incredibly agile, superstrong, and driven to insanity by appetites he cannot control.

The film works on all levels. The storytelling is seamless. The performances, sets, special effects, and makeup are all excellent. The interesting point to note is that Cornfeld realized something other producers never figured out. Usually science fiction remakes entail the destruction of a classic, often motivated by efforts to cash in on the fame of a previous blockbuster, which is never the equal of the original. Intelligently, Cornfeld took a film admired for its terrific story and added the depth and effects and pathos it always needed to make it a classic. Choosing to remake *The Fly* and cleaning up its mistakes was more than a wise move.

FLY II, THE

20th Century Fox, 1989, Color, 104 min, VT, LD, DVD

Producers: Stuart Cornfeld and Steven Charles Jaffe; **Director:** Chris Walas; **Screenplay:** Ken Wheat, Jim Wheat, and Frank Darabont; **Music:** Christopher Young; **Special Effects:** Don Bies; **Cinematography:** Robin Vidgeon; **Cast:** Eric Stoltz, Daphne Zuniga, John Getz, Lee Richardson, Frank Turner, Ann Marie, Lee, Gary Chalk, Saffron Henderson, Harley Cross, Matthew Moore

Here the son (Stoltz) of Seth Brundle (Jeff Goldblum) in the 1986 remake of the 1958 version of *The Fly* gets into trouble as a result of his father's experiments. Stoltz reaches puberty at a remarkably early age. He's got a frightening intellect, but not enough so to keep himself from being exploited by the same man who tormented his father.

The Fly II was generally regarded as a dud. After all, it's not easy to follow in the footsteps of someone like David Cronenberg, who directed the preceding film. Audiences might have been underimpressed by the more staid direction of Chris Walas in this outing. Still, this is a good, solid sequel. It expanded nicely on the first movie in much the way the first sequel to the

1958 did. The science is competently handled, and if nothing else, the villain from the first movie finally gets the fate he deserves.

FLYING DISC MEN FROM MARS

Republic, 1950, b&w, 12 chapters, 24 reels

Producer: Franklin Andreon; **Director:** Fred C. Bannon; **Screenplay:** Ronald Davidson; **Special Effects:** Howard and Theodore Lydecker; **Cast:** Wallace Reed, Lois Collier, James Craven, Walter Reed, Dale Van Sickel, Tom Steele

A Martian comes to Earth in a flying saucer to take over the world. After nearly 400 minutes of screen time, the mountain he is hiding in goes volcanic and blows him to bits.

FLYING SAUCER, THE

Film Classics, 1950, b&w, 69 min, VT

Producer: Mikel Conrad; **Director:** Conrad; **Screenplay:** Conrad and Howard Irving Young; **Music:** Darrel Calker; **Cinematography:** Philip Tannura; **Cast:** Mikel Conrad, Pat Garrison, Denver Pyle, Russell Hicks

This is little more than a slow-moving espionage tale about Soviet agents monkeying around with a flying saucer in Alaska.

FOOD OF THE GODS

AIP, 1976, Color, 88 min, VT

The Fly II (TWENTIETH CENTURY FOX / AUTHOR'S COLLECTION)

Producer: Bert I. Gordon; **Director:** Gordon, again; **Screenplay:** Our boy Gordon; **Music:** Elliot Kaplan; **Special Effects:** Gordon; **Cast:** Marjoe Gortner, Pamela Franklin, Ida Lupino, Jon Cypher, Ralph Meeker, Belinda Balaski, Tom Stovall

A farmer feeds his chickens a strange substance he finds bubbling up out of the ground. When it is discovered that this substance causes gigantism in the offspring of those creatures that ingest it, big business decides to get in on the act. Unfortunately, the scientists and investors that gather on Ralph Meeker's island to exploit this discovery find that the rats, wasps, and other local creatures have been into the brew as well. Now the island is covered with monsters, and the humans spend the rest of the movie battling their way to freedom.

With little more than the title to tie it to H.G. Wells's novel *Food of the Gods*, Bert I. Gordon succeeded again at what he had done 11 years earlier in adapting the same novel for the screen as *Village of the Giants*. Even with a far bigger budget at his disposal on this picture than ever before in his career, Gordon still turned out nothing more than an expensive B movie, which some viewers consider campy fun. *Food of the Gods* suffers from a weak script, static direction, clumsy dialogue, shoddy editing, and unconvincing special effects.

Note: In 1989 a Canadian company made *Food of the Gods II*. It has no noticeable threads tying it to the first film except that, like the first, it has practically nothing to do with the novel it is named after.

FOOD OF THE GODS II

Carolco, 1989, Color, 91 min, VT, LD

Producers: Andras Hamori, Bob Misiorkowski, Damian Lee, and David Mitchell; **Director:** Lee; **Screenplay:** E.K. Brewster and Richard Bennett; **Music:** Dennis Haines and Stephen Parsons; **Cinematography:** Curtis Peterson; **Special Effects:** Dianne Pruras and Ted Rae; **Cast:** Paul Coufos, Lisa Schrage, Jackie Burroughs, Frank Moore, Colin Fox

See *FOOD OF THE GODS*

FORBIDDEN PLANET

MGM, 1956, Color, 98 min, VT, LD, DVD

Producer: Nickolas Nayfack; **Director:** Fred M. Wilcox; **Screenplay:** Cyril Hume; **Music:** Bebe and Louis Barron; **Special Effects:** A. Arnold Gillespie, Warren Newcombe, Irving C. Ries, and Joshua Meador; **Cast:** Walter Pidgeon, Anne Francis, Leslie Nielsen, Warren Stevens, Jack Kelly, Richard Anderson, Earl Holliman, George Wallace, James Drury

The intrepid captain (Nielsen) of relief saucer C57D lands on planet Altair IV to look into what happened to the colony that should have been sending reports back for some years. The opening shots of the clean-cut crew in their neatly pressed uniforms working the controls of their ever-so-tidy ship gives one the thought that the film is going to be just another space opera—a gussied-up version of a Flash Gordon serial, perhaps—but nothing could be further from the truth.

Upon landing, Nielsen is met by a robot (the famous Robby the Robot) who takes the captain to the home of his master, Dr. Morbius (Pidgeon). Morbius and his daughter (Francis) are the only survivors of the expedition for whom Nielsen has come searching. All the others, explains Morbius, were slain years ago by an invisible monster who tore them all limb from limb. The doctor has no idea why he and his daughter were spared.

This is only the beginning of the story, as it also turns out that Altair IV is home to the remains of a once proud race of superintellectual aliens, the Krell. Morbius discovered the remains of their great underground cities as well as much of their still intact scientific achievements when the entire expedition was still alive. Part of the cache he unearthed was a brain enhancer that almost killed the doctor, but instead left him with greatly enhanced mental powers.

Captain Nielsen wants to take Morbius and his daughter, as well as all the knowledge of the Krell, back to Earth as soon as possible. Morbius refuses to go along. He has decided Earth is too backward to handle the vast knowledge of the Krell, and he will not allow the Krell's fate to become Earth's. The doctor explains that the aliens didn't understand what they had in their enhancer. The machine unleashed the power of each Krell's entire brain, including the dark thoughts all beings keep hidden. Morbius reports that after the enhancers were introduced into Krell society, the aliens destroyed themselves in a single night as their released hatreds and desires tore their world apart.

It soon becomes apparent that Morbius knows what he is talking about. Just as the Krell destroyed each other without intending to, so did brain-enhanced Morbius unknowingly slay all of his companions 25 years earlier when they insisted on returning to Earth. And now, when he sees his secure little world endangered and a man who is in love with his daughter threatening to take her away from him, Morbius's subconscious again breathes life into the invisible terror

Forbidden Planet (MGM / AUTHOR'S COLLECTION)

that he launched against his fellow colonists a quarter century earlier.

Things end badly for the doctor as he realizes that the only way to stop the creature that his id has created is for his own brain to cease to function. To save his daughter, he throws himself in the path of his own raging id. He then dies, warning Nielsen and his daughter that he has set the planet to blow up so as to forever keep the secrets of the Krell safe from humankind and the universe. The two escape along with Robby and the rest of Nielsen's surviving soldiers, all of them watching the explosion of Altair IV from outer space.

Loosely based on Shakespeare's *The Tempest, Forbidden Planet* is one of the best science fiction movies ever made. Although the dialogue is somewhat uninspired and oftentimes the scenes centering on the soldiers are undistinguishable from standard World War II fare, the ideas behind the movie are incredibly pow-

erful. Unlike standard monster movies, the use of Morbius's unconscious as the sinister force is both imaginative and tragic. The film unflinchingly asks the question: Are we intelligent enough to play God? Are we competent enough to even *think* about the role? The film also has the nerve to take a stand and suggest that we *are* capable of handling such things, as long as we keep our hubris in check (although it does seem to indicate that, ultimately, none of us is that good at keeping our cool).

Although the acting might be considered pedestrian in spots, the special effects are terrific. This was the first of the blockbuster effects movies. The colors everywhere are dynamic, the costumes fresh and modern-looking (only some of the soldiers' uniforms come off as corny). The ship designs, along with those of Morbius's home and those of the abandoned Krell city were accomplished with tremendous style and vision.

In many ways this film set the mark for the science fiction genre for years afterward. It was 12 years before it received its first serious challenger in Kubrick's *2001: A SPACE ODYSSEY*.

Every true fan must see this film. Intelligent, well paced, visually stunning, and possessed of a sobering sense of tragedy, it is one of the undisputed masterpieces of the genre that helped overcome much of science fiction's previously well-deserved reputation as trash.

Note: There are several moments of subtle animation in the film. One is a downward view of the Krell's underground city that goes on seemingly for miles. The other is when the invisible monster is caught in the outline of weapon fire and an energy field that reveals it as a hellish, grotesquely misshapen thing. Both bits were produced by the Disney Studio.

FORBIN PROJECT, THE

See *COLOSSUS: THE FORBIN PROJECT*

FORBIDDEN WORLD (aka: MUTANT)

New World Pictures, 1982, Color, 86 min, VT, LD, DVD

Producer: Roger Corman; **Director:** Allan Holzman; **Screenplay:** Tim Curnen; **Music:** Susan Justin; **Special Effects:** Steve Neill, Dennis Skotak, and Robert Skotak; **Cinematography:** Tim Schrstedt; **Cast:** Jessie Vint, June Chadwick, Dawn Dunlap, Linden Chiles, Fox Harris

Producer Corman is up to his old tricks in this rip-off of *ALIEN*. It's obvious enough when the film resorts to reusing sets from other movies, but recycling of action sequences from *BATTLE BEYOND THE STARS*, one of Corman's finest works, is unforgivable. What the movie lacks in effects and story, the filmmakers try to cover up with excessive amounts of blood.

FORBIDDEN ZONE

Hercules Film, Ltd., 1980, b&w, 76 min, VT

Producers: Richard Elfman, Nick James, Gene Cunningham, Judith Faye Elfman, and Martin Nicholson; **Director:** Richard Elfman; **Screenplay:** Matthew Bright, Richard Elfman, James and Nick L. Martinson; **Music:** Danny Elfman and the Mystic Knights of Oingo Boingo; **Special Effects:** John Nelson; **Cinematography:** Gregory Sandor; **Cast:** Hervé Villechaize, Susan Tyrell, Marie-Pascale Elfman, Viva, Matthew Bright, Virginia Rose, Ugh-Fudge Bwana, Phil Gordon, Hyman Diamond, Danny Elfman and the Mystic Knights of Oingo Boingo

The Hercules (no relations to the demigod of Greek mythology) family moves into a house that has a doorway to the sixth dimension in its basement. One travels to this other plane of existence via a stretch of interdimensional intestines, exiting out of a huge anus into an unexplainable nightmare land where Hervé Villechaize is king. Hercules' daughter Frenchie ends up as the king's prisoner, prompting her dimwitted brother to release their psychotic grandfather, a one-time king of wrestlers, from his bonds so he can help rescue her. Eventually Frenchie ends up queen of the sixth dimension and everyone lives happily ever after.

This bizarre movie may have been an attempt to make a live action film in the style of the cartoons created by masterful animator Max Fleischer. Any success the filmmakers might have had is lost amidst the tacky, rude, and foul nature of the movie. The plot makes little sense, though the song and dance numbers are entertaining, but the only truly notable thing about *Forbidden Zone* is that it is the first film to feature the music of Danny Elfman who would later compose the score for such films as *BATMAN* and *TWELVE MONKEYS*. Elfman actually appears on screen as Satan, along with the rest of his band as his devilish minions, singing and dancing in a parody of bandleader Cab Calloway.

FOREVER YOUNG

Warner Bros., 1992, Color, 102 min, VT, LD, DVD

Producers: Bruce Davey, Jeffrey Abrams, and Edward S. Feldman; **Director:** Steve Miner; **Screenplay:** Davey and Abrams; **Music:** Jerry Goldsmith; **Special Effects:** Greg Cannom; **Cinematography:** Russell Boyd; **Cast:** Mel Gibson, Jamie Lee Curtis, Elijah Wood, Isabel Glasser, George Wendt, Joe Morton, Nicolas Surovy, David Marshall Grant, Art LaFleur

The year 1939 brings tragedy for a test pilot (Gibson). It seems his girlfriend has been in a car accident, which has left her in a coma, and there's no telling when she'll wake up. Grief-stricken, our hero volunteers for a pre–World War II cryogenics experiment, and the next thing he knows, it's 1992 and he's been thawed out only to become involved in the lives of a single mom and her son. This is really a romantic comedy masquerading as a science fiction film, and as a humorous love story it works just fine.

FORTRESS

Village Roadshow Productions, 1993, Color, 91 min, VT, LD, DVD

Producers: John Davis and John Flock; **Director:** Stuart Gordon; **Screenplay:** Steven Feinberg, Terry Curtis Fox, David Venable, and Troy Neighbors; **Music:** Frederic Talgorn; **Special Effects:** Robert Black; **Cinematography:** David Eggby; **Cast:** Christopher Lambert, Jeffrey Combs, Loryn Locklyn, Kurtwood Smith, Lincoln Kilpatrick, Clifton Gonzalez

In the near future, husband (Lambert) and wife (Locklyn) are trying to get out of the country. They're fleeing the oppressive American government, which now mandates the slaughter of any children a couple has past their first. The wife is pregnant, and she and the father don't want to kill their child. When they fail to get out of the country, however, they are caught and sentenced to hard time in a fairly unoriginal escape-proof, corporate-run prison. The film then turns to Lambert's efforts to stay alive on the men's side of the prison and to find a way for himself and his wife to escape. Meanwhile, on the women's side of the complex, Locklyn has become the apple of the warden's eye.

Many critics panned this film, but it was an astounding international success despite its poor reception, most likely due to its unique science fiction outlook. One might suspect from the description above that *Fortress* would supply a rather unoriginal story, but that could not be further from the truth. Admittedly, some of the acting is over the top, and some parts are a bit flat,

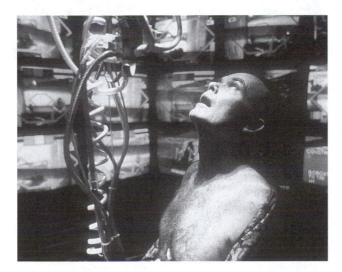

Fortress (DIMENSION FILMS / JOSEPH B. MAUCERI COLLECTION)

but the effects are good, the concept bold, the prison interestingly designed, and the plot top-notch. What happens between the warden and Locklyn is pure science fiction and awfully disturbing.

Note: HIGHLANDER fans keep a sharp eye out. This one was filmed on some of the same sets used for *HIGHLANDER II: THE QUICKENING*.

4-D MAN, THE (aka: MASTER OF TERROR)

United Artists, 1959, Color, 85 min, VT, DVD

Producer: Jack H. Harris; **Director:** Irwin S. Yeaworth, Jr., **Screenplay:** Theodore Simonson, Cy Chermak, and Harris; **Music:** Ralph Carmichael; **Special Effects:** Barton Sloan; **Cinematography:** Theodore J. Pahle; **Cast:** Robert Lansing, Lee Meriwether, James Congdon, Guy Raymond, Robert Strauss, Patty Duke, Jasper Deeter

Scientist Robert Lansing accidentally discovers the secret of opening a doorway to the fourth dimension. Further research allows him to move at will through the dimension next door. The down side is rapid aging and physical deterioration for those using the doorway. The end comes when Lansing has pushed things too far and reverts to his third-dimensional nature while passing through a wall. Despite the fact that it's never explains why Lansing doesn't sink through the floor when he's capable of passing through walls, this is not a bad little film. Lansing is totally believable and wonderfully tragic, and a young Lee Meriwether delivers a strong performance. This is one of the best of the B movies.

FOUR-SIDED TRIANGLE

Hammer (Great Britain), 1953, b&w, 74 min, VT, DVD

Producer: Alexander Paal; **Director:** Terence Fischer; **Screenplay:** Paul Tabori and Fischer; **Music:** Malcolm Arnold; **Cast:** James Hayter, Barbara Payton, Stephen Murray, John Van Eyssen, Percy Marmont

Two scientists (Hayter and Murray) are in love with the same girl. She quite properly loves only one of them. Their solution? Invent a duplicating machine and make an exact copy of the girl so that there's one each for both of these hard-working atom smashers. The twist kicks in when both the original and the copy fall in love with the same guy. With a great concept and a great title, one can only wish that the filmmakers had produced a great movie as well. Unfortunately, despite having the highly talented Terence Fisher at the helm, this movie adds up to something awful.

F.P.1 (aka: F.P.1 DOES NOT ANSWER)

UFA (Germany), 1932, b&w, 90 min/20th Century Fox (U.S.), 1933, b&w, 70 min

Producer: Eric Pommer; **Director:** Karl Hartl; **Screenplay:** Curt Siodmak and Wallace Reisch; **Cinematography:** Gunther Rittau; **Cast:** Leslie Fenton, Conrad Veidt, Jill Esmond, Hans Albers, Peter Lorre, Sybille Schmidtz, Paul Harmann, Charles Boyer, Danielle Paraola, Pierre Brasseur, Jean Murat

A hero pilot convinces the world that building a floating airport in the middle (more or less) of the Atlantic Ocean is a good idea. The story, however, really revolves around a fairly formulaic love triangle. *F.P.1.* has been compared to METROPOLIS, but it's hard to see the similarities other than that the film was made more than a half-century ago in Germany.

Note: The film was produced simultaneously in German, French, and English, but no information is available on the French version.

F.P.1 DOES NOT ANSWER

See *F.P.1*.

FRANKENHOOKER

Shapiro-Glickenhaus Entertainment, 1990, Color, 90 min, VT, LD

Producer: James Glickenhaus and Edgar Ievins; **Director:** Frank Hennenlotter; **Screenplay:** Hennenlotter and Robert Martin, **Music:** Joe Renzetti; **Cinematography:** Robert M. Baldwin; **Special Effects:** Al Magliochetti; **Cast:** James Lorinz, Patty Mullen, Charlotte Heikamp, Louise Lasser, Shirley Stoler

See *FRANKENSTEIN*

FRANKENSTEIN

Universal, 1931, b&w, 71 min, VT, LD, DVD

Producer: Carl Laemmle, Jr.; **Director:** James Whale; **Screenplay:** Robert Florey, Garrett Ford, and Francis Edward Faragoh; **Special Effects:** John P. Fulton, Kenneth Strickfaden, and Jack Pierce; **Cast:** Boris Karloff, Lionel Belmore, Fredric Kerr, Marilyn Harris, Colin Clive, Mae Clarke John Boles, Edward Van Sloan, Dwight Frye

Hailed as the first science fiction novel and certainly one of the most influential novels ever written, it's not surprising that Mary Shelley's *Frankenstein* has been adapted for film so many times. The first version came in 1910 when Thomas Edison made a film of just under 1,000 feet at his Long Island studios. Rumored to have been spectacular for the time, barely anything of it survives. The version credited above is undoubtedly the best known and most widely respected of all the adaptations. Although it changed the book's plot considerably, it is the version of this story most commonly known and, in fact, is better known in some ways than the novel itself. When the name *Frankenstein* is mentioned, it is Boris Karloff's face everyone sees.

Of course, Frankenstein is not the monster's name, but that of the doctor who gives the collection of spare body parts a new chance at life. Working with his assistant, Fritz (Frye), Frankenstein (Clive) digs up dead bodies to obtain the parts they need for his experiment. When it comes time to acquire the brain, Fritz is dispatched to the nearby college where two brains, one normal and one abnormal, are stored. A loud noise frightens Fritz, and he drops the container with the good brain, ruining it. Panicked, he steals the abnormal one and flees.

Frankenstein unknowingly inserts the criminal brain into his artificial man. The platform containing the monster's body is raised through a skylight in the roof of Frankenstein's castle to be exposed to a violent electric storm. Soon the current is flowing, and when the platform is returned to the lab, the creature is alive. The creature has the demeanor of a child, but its innocence does not last long. The malicious Fritz terrorizes the creature and beats it savagely, ultimately driving it into a rage. In its fury, the monster escapes the castle, killing Fritz in the process, and wanders into the countryside.

When Frankenstein discovers what has happened, he tries desperately to find his creation. He knows that the creature isn't responsible for its actions, but the angry villagers searching high and low for "the madman" who is terrorizing the countryside will only be satisfied with his death. Frankenstein finds the creature hiding in a windmill before the villagers track it down, but the long-suffering monster has had enough. Frankenstein is thrown out a high window, prompting the mob to set fire to the windmill. The creature is burned to death.

Bride of Frankenstein (UNIVERSAL PICTURES / R. ALLEN LEIDER COLLECTION)

Four years later, *Bride of Frankenstein* followed, universally hailed as an even better film than its predecessor. A surviving Frankenstein is reunited with his fiancée and struggles to put the past behind him. Two things interfere. His old professor, Dr. Praetorius, wants him to do more experiments. The monster survived as well.

Frankenstein refuses to work with Praetorius, who then finds the surviving monster and convinces the creature that he can force Frankenstein to create a mate for it. Frankenstein's fiancée is kidnapped as a bargaining chip, and the doctor conducts the procedure to bring a second artificial person to life. The female creature (Lanchester) is unbelievably beautiful and yet monstrous at the same time. The creature, with incredibly understated tenderness, extends his hand to his bride, but mindless loathing erupts within her and she releases a hateful, incredibly unnerving, reptilian

hiss. Convinced that she hates him, the monster turns his anger toward those around him.

Following these two triumphs, the history of Frankenstein on film has been uneven. Universal Studios continued its franchise with a series of good, but uninspired films extending the myths. *Son of Frankenstein* (1939) has great merit, indeed, not only because it contains Karloff's last performance as the Monster, but also for its stunning gothic mood, eerie sets, bizarre camerawork, and the compelling performances of its headliners: Bela Lugosi, Basil Rathbone, and the corking good Lionel Atwill. The story is essentially the same: Frankenstein's son (Rathbone), also a doctor, loses sight of reality and unleashes the reborn creature on the world.

Ghost of Frankenstein (1942) marks a slip in quality and presents yet another heir to the Frankenstein legacy, played by distinguished character actor Sir

Cedric Hardwicke. Having learned nothing from his father's and his brother's spectacular disasters, the third doctor allows himself to be convinced to put the brain of Ygor (Lugosi) into the Monster. *Ghost* does, however, provide one astonishing scene, the equal of anything in the first three films for bravura atmosphere and scientific horror—the Monster stands alone in a field being struck repeatedly by lightning bolts and growing ever stronger for the experience.

Frankenstein Meets the Wolfman (1943) is the franchise's first true B film, one rife with coincidence and happenstance. Eternal lycanthrope Lawrence Talbot (Lon Chaney, Jr.) gets it into his head that if Dr. Frankenstein possessed the secret of life, he must also hold the secret of death, which Talbot reasons might relieve him from his wolfish curse. Again, good atmosphere is the main attraction as the dependable George Waggner weaves the myths of the two tormented creatures into the first of the Universal "Monsteramas." To be fair, the climactic battle between the two title monsters is awesome, despite the obvious substitution of stuntmen for Lugosi and Chaney.

Lugosi has taken a lot of unjustified posthumous criticism for a lousy performance in *Frankenstein Meets the Wolfman*. The actor was told to play the Monster as if the creature had been blinded in the conflagration that ended the previous film. Afterward, the producers changed their minds and cut out every reference to the Monster's blindness, leaving Lugosi's performance unexplained and rather foolish-looking. Examined in light of this information, we see the debonair Hungarian making the best of a bad part with all the skill and talent he possessed.

Most other Frankenstein films were, at best, kitsch and, at worst, insults to the memory of the series. They include: *House of Frankenstein* (1945), *House of Dracula* (1945), *Curse of Frankenstein* (1958), *Frankenstein 1970* (1958), *Frankenstein's Daughter* (1959), *Frankenstein Conquers the World* (1964), *Evil of Frankenstein* (1964), *Frankenstein Meets the Space Monster* (1965), *Frankenstein Created Woman* (1967), *Frankenstein's Bloody Terror* (1968), *Frankenstein Must Be Destroyed* (1970), *Horror of Frankenstein* (1970), *Frankenstein and the Monster from Hell* (1974), *Frankenstein Island* (1981), *Frankenstein '88* (aka: *The Vindicator*)/(1986), *Frankenstein General Hospital* (1988), *Frankenstein Unbound* (1990) and *Frankenhooker* (1990).

Among this roundup, *Revenge of Frankenstein* (1958), the stylish sequel to *Curse of Frankenstein*, is the exception. Possibly the most disappointing of all was *Mary Shelley's Frankenstein* (1994), which prom-

ised to be the most faithful adaptation yet filmed. While many parts of it came close, the movie still deviated significantly from the book, not helped by Robert DeNiro's flat and uninteresting portrayal of Frankenstein's creature.

Only three other films related to Frankenstein are worthwhile. Two are comedies, *ABBOTT AND COSTELLO MEET FRANKENSTEIN* (1948), an amusing continuation of the Universal Studios series, and *Young Frankenstein* (1974), a parody of the original and its first two sequels, which is tremendously funny and insightful. Where the original presented the monster going bad only because his creator neglected him as a parent, this comedy features Gene Wilder playing the doctor as a loving father, with suitably humorous results.

The only other worthy Frankenstein film is the bizarre and highly disturbing *Gothic*, a 1986 film with Gabriel Byrne and Natasha Richardson made by con-

Frankenstein (UNIVERSAL PICTURES / R. ALLEN LEIDER COLLECTION)

troversial filmmaker Ken Russell. The story revolves around the actual night in 1816 when Mary Shelley and Dr. Polidori were inspired to write their classics, respectively, *Frankenstein* and *The Vampyre*. With Russell at the helm, *Gothic* is filled with sex and nightmares, but it's handled well, and it's interesting to watch such literary greats as Lord Byron and Percy Shelley portrayed as characters.

Note: In 1987 Universal decided it was time to replace the long-censored footage from their classic 1931 masterpiece. The restored material amounted to only snippets, but the scene in which the Monster kills the young girl by the water is an excellent example of what a difference a few seconds can make.

Also, the most important moment restored to the film is the line that follows Frankenstein's outburst in the lab. He exclaims, "It's alive, it's *alive!*" and then continues with: "Now I know how it feels to be God." The word *God* is masked by another burst of thunder, but one can read Frankenstein's lips at that moment to get the full effect of the character's arrogant blindness. After all, the God he compares himself to didn't need someone else's lightning to create humans, the same lightning that refuses Frankenstein's blasphemy.

FRANKENSTEIN AND THE MONSTER FROM HELL

Hammer (Great Britain)/Paramount (U.S.), 1974, Color, 93 min, VT

Producer: Roy Skeggs; **Director:** Terence Fisher; **Screenplay:** John Elder; **Music:** James Bernard; **Cinematography:** Brian Probyn; **Special Effects:** Eddie Knight; **Cast:** Shane Briant, Peter Cushing, David Prowse, Madeline Smith, John Stratton

See *FRANKENSTEIN*

FRANKENSTEIN CONQUERS THE WORLD

Toho (Japan, 1964) / AIP (U.S., 1966), color, 87 min, VT

Producer: Tomoyuki Tanaka; **Director:** Inoshiro Honda; **Screenplay:** Kaoru Mabuchi; **Music:** Akira Ifukube; **Cinematography:** Hajime Koizumi; **Special Effects:** Eiji Tsuburaya; **Cast:** Nick Adams, Tadao Takashima, Jumi Mizuno, Kumi Mizuno

See *FRANKENSTEIN*

FRANKENSTEIN CREATED WOMAN

20th Century Fox, 1967, color, 92 min, VT

Producer: Anthony Nelson Keys; **Director:** Terence Fisher; **Screenplay:** John Elder; **Music:** James Bernard; **Cinematography:** Arthur Grant; **Special Effects:** Les Bowie; **Cast:** Peter Cushing, Thorley Walters, Susan Denberg, Robert Morris, Peter Blythe, Barry Warren, Duncan Lamont

See *FRANKENSTEIN*

FRANKENSTEIN '88

Frank & Stein Film Productions 1986, color, 88 min, VT

Producers: Don Carmody and John Dunning; **Director:** Jena Claude Lord; **Screenplay:** Edith Ray and David Preston; **Music:** Paul Zaza; **Cinematography:** Rene Verzier; **Cast:** Terri Austin, Richard Cox, Pam Grier, Maury Chaykin, David McIlwraith

See *FRANKENSTEIN*

FRANKENSTEIN GENERAL HOSPITAL

New Star Entertainment, 1988, b&w and color, 92 min, VT, LD

Producers: Dimitri Villard and Robbie Ward; **Director:** Deborah Roberst; **Screenplay:** Robert Deel and Mike Kelly; **Cinematography:** Tom Fraser; **Cast:** Mark Blankfield, Irwin Keyes, Katie Caple, Kathy Shower, Bobby Picket, Lou Cutell

See *FRANKENSTEIN*

FRANKENSTEIN ISLAND

Chriswar Films, 1981, color, 89 min, VT

Producers: Jerry Warren and Jerry Christopher; **Director:** Warren; **Screenplay:** Warren; **Music:** Ericj Bromberg; **Cinematography:** Murray DeAtley; **Cast:** John Carradine, Andrew Duggan, Cameron Mitchell, Steve Brodie, Robert Clark, Katherine Victor

See *FRANKENSTEIN*

FRANKENSTEIN MEETS THE SPACE MONSTER

See *FRANKENSTEIN; MARS INVADES PUERTO RICO*

FRANKENSTEIN MEETS THE WOLFMAN

Universal, 1943, b&w, 74 min, VT, LD

Producer: George Waggner; **Director:** Roy William Neill; **Screenplay:** Curt Siodmark; **Music:** H.J. Salter; **Cinematography:** George Robinson; **Special Effects:** John P. Fulton; **Cast:** Lon Chaney, Jr., Bela Lugosi, Lionell Atwill, Dwight Frye, Ilona Massey, Eddie Parker, Rex Evans, Dennis Hoey, Maria Ouspenskaya

See *FRANKENSTEIN*

FRANKENSTEIN MUST BE DESTROYED

Warner Bros., 1970, color, 97 min, VT

Producer: Anthony Nelson Keys; **Director:** Terence Fisher; **Screenplay:** Bert Batt; **Music:** James Bernard; **Cinematography:** Arthur Grant; **Special Effects:** Eddie Knight; **Cast:** Peter Cushing, George Pravda, Freddi Jones, Veronica Carlson, Simon Ward

See *FRANKENSTEIN*

FRANKENSTEIN 1970

Allied Artists, 1958, b&w, 83 min, VT

Producer: Aubrey Schenck; **Director:** Howard Koch; **Screenplay:** George Worthing Yates; **Music:** Paul Dunlap; **Cinematography:** Carl Guthrie; **Special Effects:** Gordon Bau; **Cast:** Boris Karloff, Tom Duggan, Jana Lund, Mike Lane, Don Barry

See *FRANKENSTEIN*

FRANKENSTEIN'S BLOODY TERROR

Maxper P.C. (Spain), 1968, color, 113 min

Producer: Enrique Equiluz; **Director:** Equiluz; **Screenplay:** Jacinto Molina; **Music:** Angel Arteaga; **Cinematography:** Emilio Foriscot; **Cast:** Paul Naschy, Julian Ugarte, Jose Nieto

See *FRANKENSTEIN*

FRANKENSTEIN'S DAUGHTER

Astor, 1958, b&w, 85 min, VT

Producer: Marc Frederic; **Director:** Dick Kunha; **Screenplay:** H.E. Barrie; **Music:** Nicholas Carras; **Cinematography:** Meredith Nicholson; **Special Effects:** Ira Anderson; **Cast:** Sally Todd, John Ashley, Sandra Knight, Harold Lloyd, Jr., Robert Dix, Donald Murphy

See *FRANKENSTEIN*

FRANKENSTEIN'S MONSTERS: SANDRA VS: GAILAH

See *WAR OF THE GARGANTUAS*

FRANKENSTEIN UNBOUND

The Mount Company, 1990, color, 85 min, VT, LD

Producers: Roger Corman, Jay Cassidy, Laura J. Medina, Kobi Jaeger, and Thom Mount; **Director:** Corman; **Screenplay:** F.X. Feeney and Edward Neumeier; **Music:** Carl Davis; **Cinematography:** Armando Nanuzzi and Michael Scott; **Special Effects:** Syd Dutton, Bill Taylor, and Renato Agostini; **Cast:** John Hurt, Raul Julia, Bridget Fonda, Nick Brimble, Catherine Rabett, Jason Patric, Michael Hutchence, Catherine Corman, Mickey Knox, Terri Treas

See *FRANKENSTEIN*

FRAU IM MOND, DIE (aka: BY ROCKET TO THE MOON, THE GIRL IN THE MOON)

UFA (Germany), 1929, b&w, 156 min, silent

Director: Fritz Lang; **Screenplay:** Lang and Thea von Harbou; **Special Effects:** Oskar Fischinger and Konstantin Tschewerikoff; **Cast:** Gerda Marus, Willy, Fritsch, Fritz Rasp and Klaus Pohl

Retelling the old tale of flying a rocket to the Moon, the first half of this film is fairly interesting. Director Lang relied on actual rocketry experts Willy Ley and Hermann Oberth as consultants to devise the prophetic model rocket, which even came in stages, used in the film. The portion leading up to the launch pad shows all the style one expects from a Lang film, but once the ship takes off, it's downhill. The Moon the astronauts reach looks more like the Black Forest than any of the satellites in this solar system. And the astronauts don't seem troubled by their lack of spacesuits or by the fact that the temperatures and gravity on the Moon are identical to those on Earth. The lunar party simply wanders about the surface of the Moon gathering gold and jewels like wildflowers in May. This first science fiction film from the legendary Lang after his much praised *METROPOLIS* did not win the same critical acclaim as that film.

FREAKMAKER, THE

See *MUTATIONS*

FREE ENTERPRISE

Regent Entertainment, 1999, Color, 96 min

Producers: Dan Bates, Mark Altman, Ron Singer, and Allan Kaufman; **Director:** Robert Meyer Burnett; **Screenplay:** Altman and Burnett; **Music:** Scott Spock; **Cinematography:** Charles L. Barbee; **Cast:** Rafael Wegel, Eric MacCormack, Audie England, Patrick Van Horn, William Shatner, Jonathan Slavin, Phil LaMarr, Deborah Van Valkenberg, Marilyn Kentz, Holly Gagnier, Jennifer Sommerfield, Lori Lively, Russell Young, Ellie Cornell, Joey D. Viera, Spencer Klein, Ethan Glazer, Carl Bressler, Annika Brindley, Mandy Ingber

Robert (Wegel) and Mark (MacCormack) are best friends rapidly approaching their 30th birthdays. This is a hard enough milestone for most guys to face. For these two would-be filmmakers, it's terror time. The boys are part of the "Star Wars Generation," the baby boomers who grew up with Captain Kirk on the tube and Luke Skywalker on the big screen. They're devoted to movies, classic television, action figures, and every other bit of paraphernalia they can use to keep themselves distracted from the real world.

The quintessential "big kid," Robert would rather spend his rent money on toys and laser discs, oblivious that this aspect of his personality constantly alienates the women he loves. At the same time, his best friend, Mark, engages in meaningless dalliances rather than pursuing any kind of real relationship, spending his nights hopelessly devoted to an inane screenplay, *Bradykiller*, about a serial killer who murders only beautiful women named Cindy, Jan, and Marsha.

When the pair runs into their idol, William Shatner, in a bookstore, they think they've reached nirvana—a chance to talk to Captain Kirk! What they get, however, is William Shatner—an ordinary mortal who

Free Enterprise (MINDFIRE ENTERTAINMENT / AUTHOR'S COLLECTION)

has trouble with women, drinks too much, and is hawking a six-hour musical version of Shakespeare's *Julius Caesar*—a production in which he intends to play all the parts. Needless to say, their illusions about Kirk are shattered, and slowly their sci-fi/comic-book/horror/TV film worlds begin to crumble.

Free Enterprise is the slyest, most wonderfully referential movie in decades. The cast's never-ending journey through the fan meccas of Los Angeles is wildly hilarious. Watching the characters pawing through the displays at Toys 'R' Us (engaging 10-year-olds in nerdish discussions at the same time), hunting through the racks of comics stores, bar-hopping, and ultimately coming together at Mark's 30th birthday party (at which Shatner does a mind-blowingly hysterical rap, "No Tears For Caesar") is right on the money—totally believable and instantly recognizable to anyone who has ever been a member of any type of genre fandom.

Not surprising, the writers of *Free Enterprise* are both huge fans of the same things their characters love. At the time of release, co-writer Mark Altman joked that the semi-autobiographical story "is somewhat based on a true story . . . unfortunately." His partner, Robert Burnett, said, "What Mark and I wanted to show are two characters who obviously love *Star Trek*, movies and classic television, but have a life. They're not geeks, but they're certainly dysfunctional. Ultimately, it takes meeting William Shatner to make them realize the captain is just as screwed up as they are and with this fundamental understanding they are able to fix what's wrong with their lives."

This film is the ultimate in-joke comedy, and the first ultracool movie ever made about the fan lifestyle. Eschewing sets, the movie filmed throughout Los Angeles in the real locations where the story takes place: the cartoon-theme restaurant Cartoonsville; Golden Apple Comics; L.A.'s premier laserdisc and DVD emporium, Laser Blazer; and dozens of other hip sites. Revolving as it does around someone reaching his 30th birthday, the film even takes us to the Tillman Water Reclamation Plant for a dream sequence featuring a *Logan's Run* Sandman trying to terminate the birthday boy. Simply *everything* is in this film, from Immortal Isis action figures and green-skinned dancing girls to Neil Gaiman hardbacks and Hallmark Enterprise Christmas tree ornaments. No one person steeped in enough trivia could catch every joke. Indeed, the end credits are so packed with jokes it takes more than one viewing of the film simply to *read* them all.

Above everything else, however, is William Shatner's performance. This movie is a must for Shatner fans. His sense of humor is evident beyond a shadow of a doubt as he plays himself as honestly as possible. It's an amazing send-up of his public image, one worthy of an Oscar nomination for best supporting actor.

Note: Heed this warning—keep watching every last line of the credits.

FREEJACK

Morgan Creek Productions, 1992, Color, 108 min, VT, LD, DVD

Producers: Stuart Oken and Ronald Shusett; **Director:** Geoff Murphy; **Screenplay:** Dan Gilroy, Steven Pressfield, and Shusett; **Music:** Trevor Jones; **Special Effects:** Keith Shartle, Richard Hoover, Joe Digaetano; **Cinematography:** Amir M. Mokri; **Cast:** Emilio Estevez, Mick Jagger, Rene Russo, Anthony Hopkins, Jonathan Banks, David Johansen, Amanda Plummer, Grand L. Bush, Frankie Faison, Esai Morales, John Shea

Race car driver Estevez crashes in 1991. The wreck should be fatal, but it's not because the lucky stiff has been grabbed through time a split second before his death so that his body can be used by an evil businessman in the future.

The premise isn't bad, just silly. It's hard to swallow that the technology to break the dimensions of time and space will be available by 2009 and that this will be the best thing anyone can do with it. The film is further weakened by the pointless reunion of Estevez with his 20-years-older former girlfriend. The incredible cast is misleading—even the star of *Silence of the Lambs* has to pay his electric bill.

Freejack (MORGAN CREEK PRODUCTIONS / AUTHOR'S COLLECTION)

FREQUENCY

New Line Cinema, 2000, Color, 102 min, VT, DVD

Producers: Robert Shaye, Richard Saperstein, Hawk Koch, Gregory Hoblit, and Toby Emmerich; **Director:** Hoblit; **Screenplay:** Emmerich; **Music:** Michael Kamen; **Cinematography:** Alar Kivilo; **Special Effects:** John Caglione, Jr., Bill Myer, Martin Malivoire, Kaz Kobielski, Jason Board, Gary Kleinsteuber, Daniel S. Gibson, Gordin Brothers, Peter Sissakis, Arthur Langevin, Lauren Ritchie, Bill Westenhofer, Eileen Moran, Alicia Powers, and Zeke Morales; **Cast:** Dennis Quaid, Jim Caviezel, Shawn Doyle, Elizabeth Mitchell, Andre Braugher, Noah Emmerich, Melissa Errico, Daniel Henson, Jordan Bridges, Stephen Joffe, Jack McCormack, Peter MacNeill, Michael Cera, Marin Hinkle

This film asks: What if you could go back in time to change one single event connected to your life? What would it be? For John Sullivan (Caviezel), there's no question. One day before the anniversary of his father's death, in the midst of a rare (but not unprecedented) New York City display of the aurora borealis, he discovers his father's old ham radio hidden in the closet of the family home. When he sets the radio up, the voice of a man comes through the static, a man who claims to be a firefighter awaiting the results of the 1969 World Series—and who turns out to be John's dad.

At first he can't believe it, but soon he is convinced enough to try to change the past. As the static begins to destroy their connection, John desperately tries to

convince his father, Frank (Quaid), that death awaits him the next day. Back in 1969, as things John said begin to come true, Frank decides to listen to the voice on the radio and saves his life, whereas originally he had died.

Dad dies tragically when son is a boy, but history is changed and son saves dad so he can live to a ripe old age—end of the movie, right? Wrong. That's only the first half hour. After that, the story begins to skyrocket as Frank sets off multiple changes in the past that turn John's present upside down. It isn't long before father and son realize that the slightest, most innocent action on dad's part can dangerously change the lives of everyone in his son's present. Worse yet, John finds himself gaining memories but not losing his old ones. He now remembers two childhoods—one in which his father died when he was six, and one in which he didn't die at all. The problem is that he can't tell which memories go with his old life and which ones are now real.

Frequency is a top-notch sci-fi/thriller guaranteed to keep people on the edge of their seats. When the film isn't focusing on the heroics of John's firefighting dad, it keeps everyone in suspense with John's own action sequences from his life as a New York City cop. Excitement is far from all the film has to offer, though.

This movie is a real brain-twister. From the moment father and son make contact through the ether, the film is shot in real time in both periods. In other words, the action jumps back and forth between 1969 and 1999, instantly showing the results in the future of any changes made in the past. It's not only an interesting approach, but it's the first time anyone has utilized such a device in a film.

Science fiction fans will be pleased with the technique, for unlike many Hollywood interpretations of scientific theories, this one received the stamp of approval by Columbia University professor Brian Greene, a leading theoretical physicist known for his revolutionary ideas on string theory. With even famed physicist Stephen Hawking confirming that he believes time travel is now possible (not for humans, but for intangibles, such as radio waves), there are few facts to stand in the way of this plot.

Frequency is a carefully scripted, expertly directed movie without a wasted moment. The actors do an amazing job of pulling the audience into the human story underneath the science fiction. Watch this one prepared to pay attention. This is a complete story with hairpin turns aplenty—an intelligent, thoughtful, action-packed murder mystery played out in two separate dimensions at the same time.

Frequency (NEW LINE CINEMA / AUTHOR'S COLLECTION)

FROGS

AIP, 1972, Color, 90 min, VT

Producers: Peter Thomas and George Edwards; **Director:** George McCowan; **Screenplay:** Robert Hutchison; **Music:** Les Baxter; **Cinematography:** Mario Tosi; **Cast:** Ray Milland, Sam Elliott, Joan Van Ark, Adam Roarke, Judy Pace, Mae Mercer, Nicholas Cortland, Lynn Borden, Holly Irving, David Gilliam

An old rich man (Milland) hates the critters on his island, and they hate him. During his birthday party, the bugs and reptiles attack. Almost everyone dies, including the audience who die of laughter watching the attack of the killer frogs.

FROM BEYOND

Empire Pictures, 1986, Color, 85 min, VT, LD

Producer: Brian Yuzna; **Director:** Stuart Gordon; **Screenplay:** Dennis Paoli, Gordon, and Yuzna; **Music:** Richard Band; **Special Effects:** John Carl Buechler, Anthony Doublin, John Naulin, and Mark Shustrom; **Cinematography:** Mac Ahlberg; **Cast:** Jeffrey Combs, Barbara Crampton, Ted Sorel, Ken Foree, Carolyn Purdy-Gordon, Bunny Summers, Bruce McGuire

Crazed Dr. Pretorious (Sorel) has put together a machine that stimulates the pineal gland (one of a human's long-dormant sensory glands) of anyone unlucky enough to be standing near it. Unlucky because, despite its libido-heightening effects, what also happens is that those within range are suddenly made aware of a dimension that constantly surrounds us all, as well as the creatures within it. Of course, before the machine was turned on, the creatures were as unaware of us as we were of them, but once it's on, the creatures develop a taste for human flesh.

Early on, Pretorious has his head bitten off by one of the interdimensional visitors. His assistant, Crawford Tillinghast (Combs), manages to escape but ends up in a mental ward. There a young doctor with radical ideas (Crampton) decides to take him back to the house to confront his "delusions." They return with strongman Bubba Brownlee (Foree), and that's when the fun starts in earnest, for it seems that Pretorious was not killed by his decapitation, but ingested. His intellect has somehow possessed the brainless thing that slew him, and now the doctor is a creature of unimaginable power. He spends the rest of the movie

From Beyond (EMPIRE ENTERTAINMENT / AUTHOR'S COLLECTION)

exerting his ever-growing control over the trio, toying with them, torturing them, and even manipulating them into sexual adventure.

The science is thin, and the shock and titillation value runs thick, but this remains one of the absolute best sci-fi/horror films. The true triumph of *From Beyond* lies in its interpretation of horror, in the manner in which it delves into deeper emotions and issues behind all the bloodshed. Adapted from the H.P. Lovecraft story, the script greatly expands the plot of the original work. Interestingly, it offers no absolute heroes or villains. Its characters are all protagonists, thrown together by fate and dealt with just as randomly. The just do not necessarily triumph. Indeed, working from a purely Lovecraftian viewpoint, the "just" do not even exist. This impersonal, godless view of the universe permeates Lovecraft's work, and the motif is used to good advantage here. Humanity is merely another body of grubbing life that deserves whatever happens to it—good or bad.

Despite the film's low budget, the production values are fairly strong. The soundtrack enhances every scene perfectly, the special effects are frightening, imaginative, disgusting, and yet all working within the framework of the movie to advance the story. The acting is also top-notch. The emotions displayed by stars Combs and Crampton are wild and compelling. Some of the most frightening scenes are of Combs in a mental hospital, trying to convince people that he isn't insane.

Note: Lovecraft fans—be on the lookout for Combs's Miskatonic University sweatshirt.

FROM DEATH TO LIFE

Rex, 1911, b&w, one reel, silent

A scientist comes up with a formula that turns living creatures to stone.

FROM MARS TO MUNICH

20th Century Fox, 1925, b&w, one reel, silent

If one were an invisible Martian who had traveled to Earth, what's the first thing one would do? Break into the local beer bottlers and get plastered, of course.

FROM THE EARTH TO THE MOON

Warner Bros., 1958, Color, 100 min, VT, LD

Producer: Benedict Bogeaus; **Director:** Byron Haskin; **Screenplay:** Robert Blees and James Leicester; **Special Effects:** Lee Zavitz; **Cinematography:** Edwin B. Dupar; **Cast:** Joseph Cotten, George Sanders, Debra Paget, Don Dubbins, Patric Knowles, Melville Cooper, Carl Esmond, Henry Daniell, Morris Ankrum

Joseph Cotten is the head of the Baltimore Gun Club, who convinces enough people that a big enough gun could get a capsule to the Moon and back in this slow-moving adaptation of Jules Verne's classic novel. The special effects are adequate, and it's somewhat interesting to see this unusual cast in a science fiction film, but only somewhat.

Note: The 1967 *Jules Verne's Rocket to the Moon* purports to be based on the same book as this film, but one would be hard pressed to prove it. The picture is a broad comedy in which a series of knuckleheaded moves keep the "astronauts" from ever even leaving the planet.

FROZEN ALIVE

Magna, 1966, b&w, 80 min

Producers: Ron Rietti and Arthur Barunner; **Director:** Bernard Knowles; **Screenplay:** Evelyn Frazer; **Cinematography:** Robert Ziller; **Cast:** Mark Stevens, Marianne Koch, Walter Rilla

In one of the earliest films about cryogenics, a scientist carrying out research decides to experiment on himself. While he's in the deep freeze, his wife is murdered, and he becomes the prime suspect when he emerges. This one just proves not every attempt at science is a success, and neither is every attempt at science fiction.

FROZEN DEAD, THE

Warner Bros., 1967, b&w, 95 min

Producer: Herbert J. Leder; **Director:** Leder; **Screenplay:** Leder; **Music:** Don Banks; **Cinematography:** David Boulton; **Cast:** Dana Andrews, Kathleen Breck, Philip Gilbert, Anna Palk, Karel Stepanek, Edward Fox

Scientist Andrews tries to get the Third Reich on the move once again. The frozen dead are the preserved bodies of the most ruthless Nazis of World War II.

FURY, THE

20th Century Fox, 1978, Color, 117 min, VT, LD

Producer: Frank Yablans; **Director:** Brian De Palma; **Screenplay:** John Farris; **Music:** John Williams; **Special Effects:** A.D. Flowers, Rick Baker, Bill Tuttle, Dick Smith; **Cinematography:** Richard H. Kline; **Cast:** Kirk Douglas, John Cassavetes, Carrie Snodgress, Amy Irving, Fiona Lewis, Andrew Stevens, Charles Durning, Gordon Jump, Daryl Hannah

Douglas plays a U.S. secret agent whose son (Stevens) is kidnapped by Cassavetes, another secret agent. Seems the boy has telekinetic powers and the government wants to raise as many children with mental powers as it can to be dangerous weapons of war. Douglas tracks his son down, but the boy is already tool of evil. A deadly confrontation follows their meeting. While plenty of glitter and flash are on the screen to make the film entertaining, there's very little substance to the story.

FUTURECOP

See *TRANCERS*

FUTURE SHOCK

Park Place Ent., (U.S.), 1994, Color, 93 min, VT, LD

Producers: Anthony Dalesandro, George Furla, Vincent Goett, Eric Hertle, Eric Parkinson, Jeff Rice,

Vivian Schilling, Randolf Turow, Jeff Wong, Bill Woodward; **Directors:** Eric Parkinson, Matt Reeves, and Oley Sassone; **Screenplay:** Parkinson and Schilling; **Music:** John McCallum; **Cinematography:** Gerry Lively; **Cast:** Francis Sassone, Matt Reeves, Vivian Schilling, Scott Thompson, Martin Kove, Sam Clay, Bill Paxton, Brion James, Sidney Lassick, James Karen, Amanda Foreman, Tim Doyle

This trilogy film begins with a nice framing sequence: Psychiatric patients are being experimented on by virtual reality researchers without their knowledge. The three tales are passable, but only the framing sequence has anything to do with science fiction.

FUTUREWORLD

AIP, 1976, Color, 104 min, VT

Producers: Paul Lazarus and James T. Aubrey; **Director:** Richard T. Heffron; **Screenplay:** Mayo Simon and George Schenck; **Music:** Fred Karlin; **Special Effects:** Gene Griggs and Brian Sellstrom; **Cinematography:** Howard Schwartz; **Cast:** Peter Fonda, Blythe Danner, Arthur Hill, Yul Brynner, Stuart Margolin, John Ryan

The film *WESTWORLD*, the tale of a Disneyland for rich adults where all their fantasies are fulfilled by incredibly humanlike robots, ended in terrible bloodshed. In this sequel, the amusement park is trying to overcome the bad publicity of the first film. World leaders from every country, the rich and influential, and the reporters who first broke the Westworld story are all invited to visit the wonderful new and improved park. But the surprise is that the gang that runs the park really want to replace all the presidents, monarchs, and business leaders with robot duplicates so they can take over the world.

One of the oldest pulp fiction story lines in history is not served well here. The film is slow-moving, unexciting, and remarkably predictable.

Note: The jury is still out for certain, but chances are good (about 96.8 percent) that this is the first science fiction movie to feature computer-generated animation. It's the scene featuring the materialization of an android.

GALACTIC GIGOLO

Urban Classics, 1988, Color, 82 min, VT

Producers: Kris Covello and Gorman Bechard; **Director:** Bechard; **Screenplay:** Bechard and Carmine Capobianco; **Music:** Bob Esty and Lettuce Prey; **Special Effects:** Debi Thibeault and Frank Stewart; **Cinematography:** Bechard; **Cast:** Carmine Capobianco, Debi Thibeault, Ruth Collins, Angela Nicholas, Frank Stewart

Walking, thinking vegetation from a galaxy far away comes to Earth with the plan to shift its shape and then bed every woman in Connecticut during its vacation. In *ALIEN* they said that in space no one can hear you scream, and that's the only place this movie should be watched.

GALAXINA

Marimar, 1980, Color, 95 min, VT, LD, DVD

Producer: Marilyn J. Tenser; **Director:** Williams Sachs; **Screenplay:** Sachs; **Special Effects:** Chris Casady; **Cinematography:** Dean Cundey; **Cast:** Stephen Macht, Dorothy Stratten, James David Hinton, Avery Schreiber

This standard pulp sci-fi film spoof is notable only for the appearance of *Playboy* centerfold (and eventual sensational murder victim) Dorothy Stratten as a robot. Outside of that one social oddity, there is little of interest.

GALAXY OF TERROR (aka: MINDWARP: AN INFINITY OF TERROR, PLANET OF HORRORS)

New World Pictures, 1981, Color, 80 min, VT, LD

Producer: Roger Corman; **Director:** Bruce D. Clark; **Screenplay:** Clark and Marc Siegler; **Music:** Barry Schrader; **Special Effects:** Tom Campbell, Dennis Skotak, and Austin McKinney; **Cinematography:** Jacques Haitkin; **Cast:** Edward Albert, Erin Moran, Ray Walston, Bernard Behrens, Zalman King, Sid Haig

A group of valiant astronauts are in trouble when a rescue mission to another planet drags them into harm's way, where monsters kill them. Erin Moran had monetary troubles after *Happy Days*, so she can be excused, but how did they ever talk Ray Walston into being in this embarrassment?

GALAXY QUEST

Dreamworks Pictures, 1999, Color, 100 min, VT, DVD

Producers: Elizabeth Cantillon, Suzann Ellis, Mark Johnson, Charles Newirth, and Sona Gourgouris; **Director:** Dean Parisot; **Screenplay:** David Howard and Robert Gordon; **Music:** David Newman; **Special Effects:** Stan Winston, Bill George, Kim Bromley, Christopher Armstrong, Robert Stadd, Manny Epstein, Jay M. Hirsh, Lucinda Strub, Fred Tessaro, Christine Onesky, William N. Greene III, and Robert Simokovic; **Cinematography:** Jerzy Zielinski; **Cast:** Tim Allen, Sigourney Weaver, Alan Rickman, Tony Shalhoub, Sam Rockwell, Daryl Mitchell, Enrico Colantoni, Robin Sachs, Patrick Breen, Missi Pyle, Jed Rees, Justin Long

For four glorious seasons—1979 to 1982—the crew of the *NSEA Protector* patrolled the galaxy. Week after week they saved the universe until the dread specter of cancellation hit them and they were pulled off the television airwaves. Nearly 20 years later, the five major stars of the classic sci-fi series *Galaxy Quest* find themselves hopelessly typecast. Unable to get any serious work thanks to their years on the show, they are reduced to taking such jobs as appearing at store openings and selling their autographs at science fiction conventions to their still loyal fans.

Some of their fans, however, turn out to be a little too loyal. A race of octopods, the Thermians, began to pick up transmissions from Earth during a time of great social upheaval on their planet. The honor, mutual respect, and brotherhood of the noble *Protector* crew struck them as a model upon which they could found a new society; so they did—bringing peace and happiness to their world. At least, until an evil race of aliens showed up and began to slaughter them by the millions.

With nowhere else to turn, the naive, trusting Thermians do the only thing they can—they go to Earth and collect the crew of the *Protector* and try to convince them to save them from the terrible menace threatening them. Of course there is no noble crew, just a team of out-of-work actors who don't like each other very much and who certainly don't know anything about running starships or fighting alien warlords. But if they don't, the Thermians are doomed. What can they do?

It's fairly obvious that the *Galaxy Quest* TV series is based on *Star Trek*. It's also no state secret that actor Jason Nesmith (Allen) is supposed to be *Star Trek*'s William Shatner. There's something else that isn't going to be a secret for long . . . *Galaxy Quest* is one of the best sci-fi comedies of all time.

Granted, the more one knows about *Star Trek*, the more laughs one will get out of *Galaxy Quest*. There are

numerous throwaway gags that refer to both "classic *Trek*" as well as *The Next Generation*. Those who don't know that much about either show will still be entertained, however, since there are plenty of general bits of humor, and there's plenty of good old-fashioned storytelling as well. Much is made of the horrors of typecasting or the ridiculousness of assuming that actors are actually anything like what they play on the screen.

For those who like their science fiction movies with lots of special effects—aliens, space battles, monster fights—there's plenty of that, too. Both Stan Winston (*JURASSIC PARK, ALIENS, TERMINATOR 2*) and Bill George (*STAR WARS—EPISODE 1: THE PHANTOM MENACE, STAR TREK: GENERATIONS*) were on hand to give the film an absolutely top-notch look and feel. All of the ships and aliens and such are the usual state-of-the-art one expects in any modern science fiction film. What is fun, however, are the purposely bad effects.

The *Protector* is first seen traveling through space as part of a 20-year-old TV show. George remarks that it was a particular challenge to step backward and produce effects that were, in the words of director Dean Parisot, "cheesy."

"For the shots from the series," says George, "the effects had to look like they were done for television in the 1970s, with matte lines and film scratches and the color a little bit off."

The director added, "I was saying things like 'let's find the flattest shot we can; let's find something that cuts really badly; let's make that special effect worse' . . . it was crazy."

It was also genius. A great deal of attention was paid to getting the little things right. Much is made of how critical science fiction fans are, of how seriously they take their favorite shows. And this is really the key to this film. Science fiction fans often take a great deal of heat for their exuberance. To science fiction enthusiasts, it's all so obvious why they do such things—why they're so excited, why they're so certain that others would feel the same way they do if only those others just *understood*. *Galaxy Quest* parodies the enthusiasm of science fiction fans without insulting the ideals and philosophy that excite them. The film also takes great care constructing its comedy, building to a number of great laughs, and to some truly dramatic high points that elevate it beyond mere parody into a full-fledged motion picture event.

Indeed, one of the most interesting innovations is the bridge technology used in the film. The running of the heroes' ship is not left to computers and telemetry programs—a hands-on pilot maneuvers the craft with steering controls reminiscent of a powerboat or motorcycle. The transporter device also responds to hand touch much like a pinball machine, its workings described by one of the ship's crew as being "more art than science." This is a telling difference from much science fiction, an elevation of the human over the machine, something lost from much of the sci-fi entertainment produced since the days of "classic" *Star Trek* and those earlier shows like *Captain Video* or the FLASH GORDON serials.

Be all that as it may, any *Star Trek* fan will enjoy this good-natured ribbing, no matter how seriously they take their favorite franchise. *Galaxy Quest*, much like the documentary TREKKIES, makes telling points about both what is wrong with science fiction fandom and the occasional junk it elevates and what is gloriously right about it. This well-made film, though light and breezy in places, is capable of tugging at one's heartstrings.

GAMERA: GIANT MONSTER MIDAIR SHOWDOWN

See *GAMERA, THE GUARDIAN OF THE UNIVERSE*

GAMERA, THE GUARDIAN OF THE UNIVERSE

Daiei (Japan), 1995, Color, 96 min, VT

Producer: Tsutumu Tsuchikawa; **Director:** Shuske Kaneko; **Screenplay:** Kazunori Ito; **Music:** Ko Otani; **Cinematography:** Kenji Takama and Junichi Tozawa; **Special Effects:** Shinji Higuchi and Hajimi Matsumoto; **Cast:** Ayako Fujitani, Hirotaro Honda, Yukijiro Hotaru, Tsuyoshi Ihara, Akira Kubo, Shinobu Nakayama, Akira Onodera

Monstrous, private plane–sized birds called Gyaos attack researchers on an island. At the same time a mysterious "reef" is moving through the ocean, headed toward Japan. The government attempts to trap the birds in a stadium on the mainland before they can feast on any more citizens, but when the birds are led to the stadium and trapped, the "reef" surfaces and proves to be Gamera, a gigantic monster turtle come to kill the birds. When the birds escape captivity with a form of laser breath that no one on the ground witnesses, Gamera is blamed for their release. Interestingly, the environmentalist faction of the government fights for the destruction of the turtle, trying to protect the killer birds as an unknown species. While the birds grow bigger and more deadly with every passing minute, the army is sent to destroy Gamera.

Researchers discover that the birds were an accidental genetic creation of a past Atlantislike civilization and that Gamera was created to deal with them. Now, if only they can convince the government to stop trying to kill the only thing that can protect humanity from the monsters that destroyed the long-dead civilization, everything will be peachy.

This is a very good giant monster movie. The acting is compelling, the music dramatic, and the special effects highly convincing. All the previous Gamera films are ignored, this one being treated as if it is the first time the turtle has ever appeared. Although its connection to youngsters ("Gamera love the little children") is made once more, it is handled in a much more sophisticated fashion, making for an extremely entertaining film for fans of the genre. The first film in a new Gamera series, this one was followed by *GAMERA 2: ADVENT OF LEGION* and *GAMERA 3: THE AWAKENING OF IRIS.*

GAMERA 2: ADVENT OF LEGION

Daiei (Japan), 1999, Color

Producers: Miyuki Nanri, Naoki Sato, Tsutomu Tsuchikawa; **Director:** Shuske Kaneko; **Screenplay:** Kazunori Ito and Kaneko; **Cinematography:** Junichi Tonazawa; **Cast:** Ayako Fujitani, Akiji Kobayashi, Miko Mizuno, Toshiyuki Nagashima

See *GAMERA, GUARDIAN OF THE UNIVERSE*

GAMERA 2: THE ASSAULT OF LEGION

See *GAMERA, GUARDIAN OF THE UNIVERSE*

GAMERA 3: REVENGE OF IRIS

See *GAMERA, GUARDIAN OF THE UNIVERSE*

GAMERA 3: THE AWAKENING OF IRIS

Daiei (Japan), 1999, Color

Producer: Miyuki Nanri, Naoki Sato, Tsutomu Tsuchikawa; **Director:** Shuske Kaneko; **Screenplay:** Kazunori Ito and Kaneko; **Cinematography:** Junichi Tozawa; **Special Effects:** Shinji Higuchi; **Cast:** Ayako Fujitani, Hirotaro Honda, Yukijiro Hotaru, Tsuyoshi, Shinobu Nakayama, Ai Maeda

See *GAMERA, GUARDIAN OF THE UNIVERSE*

GAMERA VS. GYAOS

See *RETURN OF THE GIANT MONSTERS*

GAMERA VS. MONSTER X

Daiei (Japan)/AIT (U.S.), 1970, Color, 83 min

Producer: Noriaki Yuasa; **Screenplay:** Fumi Taka-hashi; **Music:** Shunsuke Kikuche; **Cinematography:** Akira Khazaki; **Special Effects:** Kazufumi Fujii; **Cast:** Tustomu Takauwa, Kelly Yaris, Katherine Murphy, Junko Yashiro, Ken Omura

See *GAMMERA, THE INVINCIBLE*

GAMERA VS. ZIGRA

Daiei (Japan), 1971, Color, 87 min

Producer: Yoshihiko Manabe; **Director:** Noriaki Yuasa; **Screenplay:** Nisan Takahashi; **Music:** Shun-suke Kikuchi; **Cinematography:** Akira Uehara; **Special Effects:** Kazufumi Fujii; **Cast:** Ken Utsui, Yusuke Kawazu, Kayo Matsuo

See *GAMMERA, THE INVINCIBLE*

GAMMA PEOPLE, THE

Warwick (Great Britain), 1955/Columbia (U.S.), 1956, b&w, 88 min, VT

Producer: John Gossage; **Director:** John Gilling; **Screenplay:** Gossage and Gilling; **Special Effects:** Tom Howard; **Cinematography:** Ted Moore; **Cast:** Paul Douglas, Leslie Phillips, Eva Bartok, Walter Rilla, Martin Miller

Newsmen Douglas and Phillips wander into the comic-opera version of a European country, looking for a story. This country is run by a group of fairly mad scientists willing to do anything to drag their nation into the 20th century. Their big plan is to expose children to gamma rays to increase their intelligence. Some of the time it works, but the rest of the time it turns the subject children into slack-jawed halfwits. The ones who do get some brains out of the deal lose their ability to emote in this somewhat better-than-average film.

GAMMERA, THE INVINCIBLE

Daiei (Japan)/World Entertainment Corporation, 1966, b&w, 88 min, VT, LD

Producer: Yonejiro Saito; **Director:** Noriaki Yuasa; **Screenplay:** Fumi Takahashi and Richard Craft; **Music:** Tadashi Yamauchi; **Special Effects:** Yonesaburo Tsukiji; **Cinematography:** Nobuo Munekawa; **Cast:** Brian Donlevy, Albert Dekker, Diane Findlay, Eiji Funakoshi, Harumi Kiritachi

In this first of the many Gamera (for some reason the beast was given an additional *m* in his name for this one film) movies, the monstrously large, supposedly pre-historic sea turtle is accidentally thawed from his icy grave and set loose on the world. Scientists find his abilities to fly and spit fire extraordinary, to say the least. There are plenty of film appearances by Gamera ("He loves the little children"). Two of the better ones are *Gamera vs. Monster X* and *Gamera vs. Zigra*.

GAP, THE

Instructional Films (Great Britain), 1937, b&w, 38 min

Director: Donald Carter; **Cast:** Patric Curwen, Car-leton Hobbs, G.H. Mulcaster

Fiction about aerial assaults over London is given an interesting look through the use of a documentary style. What really makes the film interesting is that it was released years before the famous blitz of London was launched by the Nazis during World War II. Sci-fi strikes again!

GAS! OR IT BECAME NECESSARY TO DESTROY THE WORLD IN ORDER TO SAVE IT

See *GAS-S-S-S!*

GAS-S-S-S! (aka: GAS! OR IT BECAME NECESSARY TO DESTROY THE WORLD IN ORDER TO SAVE IT)

AIP, 1970, Color, 79 min, VT

Producer: Roger Corman; **Director:** Corman; **Screenplay:** George Armitage; **Cinematography:** Ron Dexter; **Music:** Barry Melton plus Country Joe and the Fish; **Cast:** Bud Cort, Talia Shire, Cindy Williams, Ben Vereen, George Armitage, Robert Corff, Elaine Giftos

The story opens on a defense plant in Alaska. The place is working on bacteriological and chemical war engines. One gets loose, and before you know it, everyone on Earth over the age of 25 is dead. The youth of the world are left to create a new world in their absence. At first, midwestern American conservatives go on a berserk rampage while the Hell's Angels try to preserve the good old days. Eventually, saner types emerge to produce a better place for all to live. Which is about the time for the ground to crack open and for the dead adults to come back to life as zombies, including not just the recently deceased, but folks hundreds of years old as well. All it seems to take to rise from the dead was a measure of fame.

It's surprising that it took Corman until the early '70s to capitalize on the '60s, but that's the way it was. This film is wildly stupid. Corman's claim is that executives at AIP edited it behind his back. One wonders how bad it was to force their hand into creating what finally made it to the screen.

GATTACA

Columbia, 1997, Color, 112 min, VT, LD, DVD

Producers: Michael Shamberg, Stacey Sher, and Danny DeVito; **Director:** Andrew Niccol; **Screenplay:** Niccol; **Cinematography:** Slavomir Idziak; **Music:** Michael Nyman; **Special Effects:** Janek Sirrs, Gary D'Amico, Chris Watts, and Steve Dellerson; **Cast:** Ethan Hawke, Uma Thurman, Jude Law, Gore Vidal, Loren Dean, Alan Arkin, Xander Berkeley, Blair Underwood, Ernest Borgnine, Tony Shalhoub, Jane Brook, Elias Koteas

In the not too distant future, medical science offers parents the ability to program their unborn children's genetic traits. Eventually, the practice gives way to a new form of discrimination, the genetically perfect "Valids" lording their status over the imperfect naturally born, or "In-Valids." The plot revolves around naturally born Vincent (Hawke) and his rivalry with his younger, genetically streamlined brother Anton. By the time they are ten and eight respectively, the family's hopes are pinned on Anton. The two brothers compete constantly, Vincent always the loser because science decreed it so.

But Vincent doesn't take science's word that he is In-Valid. He wants to go into space despite the fact that In-Valids are not permitted, and so he works and struggles and pushes himself (something his younger sibling and the Valids around him don't have to do) and hopes to turn the tables. Leaving home for good, Vincent spends the next few years working janitorial jobs, which is the only type of work In-Valids can get, and devises a plan.

Developing his body to the extreme, he finds a disabled Valid (Law) who is willing to give his identity to Vincent in exchange for being supported. Vincent gets a job at Gattaca, the corporation that seemingly sends all the world's rocket ships into space. His life becomes a daily routine of cleaning his workspace so that no loose skin cells or eyelashes are left behind, placing his Valid conspirator's hairs in his comb for others to find, scrubbing his skin until it is raw to clean away all his dead skin before he goes to work, and so forth.

It is a life totally devoted to remaining undiscovered long enough to get into space. Vincent succeeds constantly, getting closer and closer to his goal, until suddenly disaster sets in. Someone murders the mission director at Gattaca—the man who was trying to shut Vincent's mission down. Did Vincent do it? Did the girl who is interested in him do it? Someone else?

The police are convinced that the murderer must be an In-Valid after a forensic sweep discovers a single, carelessly dropped eyelash Vincent left behind. They search for the killer who may or may not be Vincent, while Vincent himself tries to decide if he still wants to go into space or stay with the woman he thinks he might love—the woman who also may or may not be the murderer, who may or may not love him back once she discovers the truth about the "Valid" she thinks she knows.

Gattaca is an extremely intelligent film, one of those rare sci-fi/noir films that hold the world up to an exacting lens of realism. For some, conceding all of the picture's stalking points is particularly difficult. In many ways the world of the Valids is far too conformist and structured to seem possible. Genetic perfection seems to turn everyone into boring, worker drones, and love, happiness, excitement, enjoyment, and rage—in other words, everything human—seems to disappear. Many audiences could not get past this concept, but it raises a provocative question: Would humankind custom-order children who didn't get angry, who didn't get excited, who did what they were told without questioning authority? Given the chance, would expectant parents preselect a healthy, strong, highly intelligent, well-rounded, and obedient child? Additionally, relationships develop between characters, and as the truth is revealed regarding the murder, it becomes clear that human passions have not been erased, but perhaps only submerged, despite the veneer of perfection.

Gattaca is stylish, smart, and intensely driven. It is also slow paced, with little action and few gaudy special effects. There are no chase scenes and little in the way of physical dynamics. This is a thoughtful picture, one that reveals physical perfection for the unquestioned pedestal treasure it is in our society. There is nothing wrong with perfection, but to accept it alone as a standard without taking into consideration honor and courage and leadership, qualities only produced in the forge of adversity and human pain, is to settle for too little. *Gattaca* is a quiet, poignant movie that says a great deal on an important subject.

GHIDRA, THE THREE-HEADED MONSTER

Toho (Japan)/Continental (U.S.), 1965, Color, 85 min, VT

Producer: Tomoyuki Tanaka; **Director:** Inoshiro Honda; **Screenplay:** Shiuichi Sekizawa; **Music:** Akira Infukube; **Cinematography:** Hajime Koizumi; **Special Effects:** Eiji Tsubraya; **Cast:** Yosuka Natsuki, Yukiro Hoshi, Hiroshi Koizumi, Takashi Shimura

See *GODZILLA, KING OF THE MONSTERS*

GHOSTBUSTERS

Columbia, 1984, Color, 107 min, VT, LD, DVD

Producers: Ivan Reitman, Bernie Brillstein, Michael C. Gross, and Joe Medjuck; **Director:** Reitman; **Screenplay:** Dan Aykroyd and Harold Ramis; **Cinematography:** László Kovács; **Music:** Elmer Bernstein and Ray Parker, Jr.; **Special Effects:** Richard Edlund, Joe Day, Chuck Gasper, Dennis Michelson, Lynda Lemon, and Bruno George; **Cast:** Bill Murray, Dan Aykroyd, Harold Ramis, Sigourney Weaver, Rick Moranis, Annie Potts, Ernie Hudson, William Atherton

Three psychology professor specializing in studies of the paranormal (Murray, Aykroyd, Ramis) have their grant terminated by the Board of Regents at their university. It seems the board dislikes their research, methods, and goals and wants them out—especially Dr. Venkman (Murray). The dean tells Venkman that he considers him a "poor scientist," one who sees science as a "dodge" or a "con," and that he isn't the only one who feels that way. When the three ousted intellectual attempt to make it in the real world as paranormal exterminators, their first client says she feels Venkman is more of a game show host than a scientist.

This entire film revolves around whether or not Dr. Venkman really is a scientist. If he is, the world is safe. If he isn't, humanity will be slaughtered by an ancient Sumerian god, Zuul. At the beginning of the picture, hopes for humankind's survival are not in great evidence. The so-called Ghostbusters are amazed by paranormal events like symmetrical book stacking or mass sponge migrations where the sponges move approximately a foot and a half. Not quite the caliber of person one looks for when needing heroes to fight gods.

But that is exactly the kind of person needed for the job—a rational, logical, *thinking* person. In other words, scientists.

Ghostbusters is thought of as a comedy/horror film, but it really isn't. Although there are plenty of laughs in the film, it is primarily a sci-fi/horror movie that revolves around a humorous trio—Venkman, the scamming cynic, Ray (Aykroyd), the naive, childlike scientist, and Egon (Ramis), the emotionally cold, overachieving genius. Great care was taken to make scenes set up for horrific payoffs end with jokes and for apparently comedic scenes to end with terrifying results.

The thing that roots this film (and its sequel) solidly in the science fiction tradition is its unswerving allegiance to thinking rather than to emotion. Although the trio of scientists may find themselves frightened at times, they never revert to prayer or paganism of any type. No matter how great the challenge, how powerful the ultradimensional entity they might face, they never stop "thinking" of ways to defeat them. Even when some of them falter, such as at the climax when Ray is gibbering in fear and Egon announces "Sorry, Venkman, but I'm terrified beyond the capacity for rational thought," Venkman holds them together long enough for them to think their way clear of danger. Interestingly enough, the point is made over and over that nonthinkers are to be dismissed. When a representative of the EPA shows up to inspect their facility because he "feels" the Ghostbusters are up to no good, he is made a figure of ridicule. When, in one instance, the Ghostbusters themselves get involved in a fistfight, for the first time in the film the camera jumps back from them, minimizing them drastically.

There is a great deal more that could be said, but therein lies the chance of ruining a tremendously satisfying experience for those who haven't yet seen this classic film. Suffice to say that it's wonderfully scored, well acted, stuffed with special effects that hold up quite well decades later, and directed with intelligence and wit rarely seen in such projects. Indeed, as far as sci-fi/horror films go, there is only one that rivals *Ghostbusters*, the British classic, *FIVE MILLION YEARS TO EARTH* (aka: *QUATERMASS AND THE PIT*).

Even the film's sequel, *Ghostbusters II*, is only a pale version of the original. It has a good concept, is well written, acted, and directed, but the mood isn't sus-

Ghostbusters (COLUMBIA PICTURES / AUTHOR'S COLLECTION)

tained nearly as well as in its predecessor. In *Ghostbusters* the audience is waiting for the answer to the question of Venkman's code of honor, waiting for him to prove himself as a scientist. No such moment exists in the second film, and so it remains highly entertaining, but is not the classic the first film is.

GHOSTBUSTERS II

Columbia, 1989, Color, 102 min, VT, LD, DVD

Producers: Ivan Reitman, Bernie Brillstein, Michael C. Gross, Sheldon Kahn, Gordon A. Webb, and Joe Medjuck; **Director:** Reitman; **Screenplay:** Dan Aykroyd and Harold Ramis; **Cinematography:** Michael Chapman; **Music:** Randy Edelman; **Special Effects:** Danny Wagner, Ned Gorman, Dave Allen, Ramela Easley, John V. Fante, Alan Jones, Peter Kuran, Jeff Olsen, Bill

George, Brian Gernand, Dennis Muren, Chuck Gaspar, and Michael Douglas Middleton; **Cast:** Bill Murray, Dan Aykroyd, Harold Ramis, Sigourney Weaver, Rick Moranis, Annie Potts, Ernie Hudson, Peter McNicol, Chloe Webb, David Margulies

See *GHOSTBUSTERS*

GHOST IN THE MACHINE

20th Century Fox, 1993, Color, 95 min, VT, LD

Producer: Paul Schiff; **Director:** Rachel Talalay; **Screenplay:** William Davies and William Osborne; **Cinematography:** Phil Meheux; **Music:** Graeme Revell; **Special Effects:** Michael Pangrazio; **Cast:** Karen Allen, Chris Mulkey, Ted Marcoux, Wil Horneff, Jessica Walter, Brandon Quintin Adams, Phil Ducommun

Single mother Karen Allen is the target of a serial killer. He's stopped, but before he can pass on completely, his spirit is sucked into the mainframe of the town computer, giving him the opportunity to continue to attack her by killing her friends, ruining her credit, and doing other horrible things.

GHOST OF FRANKENSTEIN, THE

Universal, 1942, b&w, 68 min, VT, LD

Producer: George Wagner; **Director:** Erle C. Kenton; **Screenplay:** W. Scott Darling; **Cinematography:** Milton Krasner; **Music:** H.J. Salter; **Cast:** Cedric Hardwick, Lon Chaney, Jr., Bela Lugosi, Lionel Atwill, Ralph Bellamy, Evelyn Ankers, Dwight Frye, Holmes Herbert, Doris Lloyd

See *FRANKENSTEIN*

GIANT BEHEMOTH, THE

See *BEHEMOTH, THE SEA MONSTER*

GIANT CLAW, THE

Columbia, 1957, b&w, 76 min, VT

Producer: Sam Katzman; **Director:** Fred Sears; **Screenplay:** Samuel Newman and Paul Gangelin; **Cinematography:** Benjamin H. Kline; **Music:** Mischa Bakaleinikoff; **Cast:** Jeff Morrow, Mara Corday, Morris Ankrum, Morgan Jones, Robert Shayne, Edgar Barrier

A giant bird from outer space flaps in to build its nest on Earth. It causes a great deal of mischief, which gets our fly boys after it, but they can't hurt it since the thing has its own force field. Luckily, some whiz kid scientists are able to whip up a ray that nullifies the force field. They lure the thing off the Empire State Building and then shoot it out of the sky like the heroes they are. This movie is actually much worse than it sounds, due to its terrible special effects.

GIANT OF METROPOLIS, THE

Centro (Italy), 1962, Color, 92 min, VT

Producer: Emmino Salvi; **Director:** Umberto Scarpelli; **Screenplay:** Sabatino Ciuffino and Oreste Palellea; **Cinematography:** Mario Sensi; **Music:**

Armando Trovajoli; **Special Effects:** Joseph Natanson; **Cast:** Gordon Mitchell, Bella Cortez, Roldano Lupi, Liana Orfei

The highly advanced city of the future, Metropolis, is really Atlantis of *20,000 B.C.* The city's MSB (Mad Scientists Brigade) goes after muscle man Gordon Mitchell so that they can clone an army of mighty warriors from his DNA. They foul up somewhere along the line and blow up the whole place with nuclear power. Unfortunately, this movie is plodding and laughable.

GIGANTIS, THE FIRE MONSTER

Toho (Japan), 1955/Warner Bros. (U.S.), 1959, b&w, 85 min, VT

Producer: Tomoyuki Tanaka; **Director:** Motoyoshi Odo; **Screenplay:** Takeo Murata; **Cinematography:** Seiichi Endo; **Special Effects:** Eiji Tsuburaya; **Cast:** Hiroshi Koizumi, Yukio Kasama, Minosuki Yamada, Hugo Grimaldi, Setsuko Makayama

See *GODZILLA, KING OF THE MONSTERS*

GILALA

See *THE X FROM OUTER SPACE*

GILL WOMEN, THE

See *VOYAGE TO THE PLANET OF PREHISTORIC WOMEN*

GILL WOMEN OF VENUS, THE

See *VOYAGE TO THE PLANET OF PREHISTORIC WOMEN*

GIRARA

See *THE X FROM OUTER SPACE*

GIRL FROM 5000 A.D., THE

See *TERROR FROM THE YEAR 5000*

GIRL FROM SCOTLAND YARD, THE

Paramount, 1937, b&w, 62 min

Producer: Emanuel Cohen; **Director:** Robert Vignola; **Screenplay:** Doris Anderson and Dore Schary;

Cinematography: Robert Pittack; **Cast:** Karen Morley, Eduardo Ciannelli, Robert Baldwin, Katherine Alexander

A murderous genius is on the loose in England, one who kills with radio waves. Of course, whenever a mad inventor this clever is terrorizing the crown, what's Scotland Yard to do but assign its cutest detective to the case. One might hope this movie would at least be good for laughs in that *Girl from U.N.C.L.E.* sort of way or maybe good in that '30s tough girl style, but it isn't really much of anything.

GIRL IN THE MOON, THE

See *WOMAN IN THE MOON*

GIVE A DOG A BONE

Westminster (Great Britain), 1966, Color, 77 min

Producer: Henry Cass; **Director:** Cass; **Screenplay:** Cass; **Cinematography:** S.D. Onions; **Music:** George Fraser; **Cast:** Ronnie Stevens, Ovor Danvers, Richard Warner

The King of the Rats is loose. What to do? If you're the helpless boy and his dog that star in *this* picture, you rely on the intervention of well-intentioned space aliens. This movie isn't for everyone, but it's not terrible either, and it's good for very young viewers.

GIVE US THE MOON

Gainsborough (Great Britain), 1944, b&w, 95 min

Producer: Edward Black; **Director:** Val Guest; **Screenplay:** Guest; **Cinematography:** Phil Grindrod; **Cast:** Jean Simmons, Peter Graves, Margaret Lockwood, Vic Oliver

Caryl Brahms and S.J. Simon wrote a fairly good book entitled *The Elephant Is White*, detailing what they thought life in the British Isles might be like once World War II finally ended. The above-named filmmakers did not do it much justice.

GLADIATORERNA

See *THE PEACE GAME*

GLASS BOTTOM BOAT, THE

MGM, 1966, Color, 110 min, VT, LD

Producers: Martin Melcher and Everett Freeman; **Director:** Frank Tashlin; **Screenplay:** Freeman; **Cinematography:** Leon Shamroy; **Music:** Frank DeVol; **Special Effects:** J. McMillan Johnson; **Cast:** Doris Day, Rod Taylor, Arthur Godfrey, Paul Lynde, Dom DeLuise, John McGiver, Robert Vaughn, Alice Pierce, Eric Fleming, George Tobias, Ellen Corby, Edward Andrews, Dick Martin

Widow Day is hired by researcher Taylor. Is she what she appears to be, or is she a foreign spy? That's what the bumbling government agents want to know, and that's where much of the usual Tashlin slapstick comes from. As for science fiction, Day's adventures take her through bits with bizarre hardware, everything from antigravity to runaway robotic household appliances. As Doris Day comedies go, it's one of the better ones.

GO AND GET IT

Marshall Neilan Productions, 1920, b&w, 6,300 feet, silent

Producer: Marshall Neilan; **Directors:** Neilan and Henry Symonds; **Screenplay:** Marion Fairfax; **Cinematography:** David Kesson; **Cast:** Pat O'Malley, Noah Beery, Wesley Barry, Agnes Ayres, Bull Montana

The brain of a criminal is transplanted into the body of a gorilla. Mayhem ensues. Is there anyone who couldn't see that one coming?

GOBOTS: BATTLE OF THE ROCK LORDS

Hanna-Barbera, 1986, Color, 75 min, VT

Producers: Kay Wright and Raymond E. MacDonald; **Director:** Ray Patterson; **Screenplay:** Jeff Segal; **Animation:** Iwao Takamoto and Paul Sabell; **Music:** Hoyt S. Curtin; **Cast:** Margot Kidder, Roddy McDowall, Michael Nouri, Telly Savalas

This overly long television commercial features the good toys beating up the bad toys and vice versa. This flat and boring nonsense lacks any charm or entertainment value.

GODZILLA (1998)

Tri-Star, 1998, 139 min, Color, VT, LD

Producers: Dean Devlin and Roland Emmerich;
Director: Emmerich; **Screenplay:** Devlin, Emmerich, Ted Elliot, and Terry Rossio; **Cinematography:** Ueli Steiger; **Music:** David Arnold; **Special Effects:** Terry Clotiaux, Sean S. Cunningham, Volker Engel, Karen E. Goulekas, Rob Engle, and Nanci Roberts; **Cast:** Matthew Broderick, Hank Azaria, Jean Reno, Maria Pitillo, Kevin Dunn, Harry Shearer, Michael Lerner, Vicki Lewis, Doug Savant, Arabella Field, Bodhi Elfman

The opening credits give us a history lesson. For 20 years the French have conducted nuclear tests in the South Pacific amidst desolate atolls devoid of life except for various types of lizards. The tests are conducted one after another with savage fury, while the emotionless, unblinking lizards watch.

Time leaps forward. It's the present day, and a cannery ship far out at sea struggles through a storm. Suddenly, the ship is rocked by some unknown force, the hull breached by what looks like a fantastically large claw. The ship goes down, and all but one of its crew perish.

Across the world, scientist Matthew Broderick is pulled away from his research in Chernobyl, where he has been studying the effects of nuclear radiation as it applies to unnatural growth in exposed creatures. The government is bringing him in on something they think his research makes him highly qualified to investigate. That something takes on ominous tones after an interview with the one surviving sailor, who gives them a name, Gojira, better known as Godzilla.

Later, Broderick and the military inspect an island destroyed by whatever it is they're chasing. Broderick notes the canned fish littering the beach, the massive claw mark in the hull of the cannery boat, and the Frenchman who claims to be the insurance adjuster for the shipping line. Before he can make much of any of it, however, Broderick is whisked off as word comes in that the mystery target is now a mere 200 miles off the coast of the United States.

The scene shifts rapidly to New York. It doesn't take Godzilla long to get ashore and start tearing things up, but for some reason the military don't see him as much of a threat at first. They think he's an animal that can be controlled with their weapons. They quickly learn that Godzilla is no ordinary beast when the king of the monsters destroys all of their tanks and

helicopters that get in his way and then simply burrows into the subway system to elude his attackers. The military search everywhere for the great beast, but it isn't long before scientist Broderick lets them know they have a bigger problem. He's certain Godzilla is pregnant, and they must find the nest immediately. But after Broderick's old girlfriend steals his classified information in an attempt to further her media career, the military throw Broderick off the project and ignores his advice.

Broderick is approached by the mysterious French "insurance agent," who has been present in the background of the film, and he reveals himself to be a member of the French secret service. He enlists Broderick in helping him clean up the mess caused by his government, and the two go after the nest, while the military corner Godzilla in the river and set off enough explosives to convince them that the menace has finally been destroyed.

Meanwhile, Broderick's ex-girlfriend and her cameraman friend follow Broderick, hoping for a big story. The group ends up in the wreckage of Madison Square Garden, where they discover the nest. The eggs hatch before they can be destroyed, but our heroes manage to call in an air strike that levels the Garden, after an exciting chase and a few grisly deaths. Suddenly, Godzilla returns to the nest. He wasn't destroyed after all. But all of his kids were. For a moment, the great beast noses through the dead, searching for even a single survivor. Then, convinced there are none, he throws himself into destroying their killers.

Godzilla chases the group through the streets of Manhattan as they flee in a stolen cab. Managing to get in touch with the military through the cab radio, they coordinate an attack. The cab leads Godzilla to the Brooklyn Bridge, where the beast becomes tangled in the suspension cables. While it momentarily presents itself as a stationary target, the military finally finishes the creature off with rocket fire from a trio of jets.

Critics panned this film, and fans of the old series heaped abuse upon it. One wonders why, since this first American-made Godzilla film was a tremendously well-done piece of work, completely respectful of its source material.

One common criticism was that Godzilla didn't look like Godzilla anymore. Few noted that his head had changed repeatedly from film to film in the old series or that audiences had laughed for years at the obvious rubber suit used in those movies. Others complained that liberties had been taken with Godzilla's origin. But in GODZILLA, KING OF THE MONSTERS it's clearly stated that Godzilla is obviously a mutant caused by radioactive fallout, just as he is in this film.

Godzilla (TOHO STUDIOS / R. ALLEN LEIDER COLLECTION)

Some lamented the absence of the creature's trademark radioactive breath, and it is true that particular aspect of the series was missing. The filmmakers, however, did add several scenes in which Godzilla bellows with such force that his breath blows cars into the air where they crash into each other and then burst into flame, a tip of the hat to the original. Another complaint was the presence of a romantic subplot, ignoring the fact that most older Godzilla films also had two people who couldn't quite figure out how to fall in love.

Other equally trivial negative points were raised, but some people are just never happy. Godzilla became a sorry, foolish clown in the late '60s and remained so throughout the '70s. Many fans bemoaned the terrible fate of the big lizard while laughing themselves sick over his goofy screen antics in the same breath. By the time *GODZILLA 1985* was made, it was already too late to clean up the flat-headed lizard's image. Only a complete overhaul could save him, and that's what this film offer with dazzling

special effects, a compelling soundtrack, and an exciting plot. More Godzilla movies in the new series are planned, and one hopes they retain the same level of craftsmanship evident in this one.

Note: In the Madison Square Garden broadcast booth, watch for a small statue of one of the *Independence Day* aliens. Roland Emmerich directed that film as well. Also, for the eagle-eyed, there is a split-second cameo of comedian George Carlin. Carlin shares the screen with cameraman Animal (Hank Azaria).

GODZILLA, KING OF THE MONSTERS
(aka: GOJIRA)

Toho (Japan), 1954, 98 min/Embassy (U.S.), 1956, 81 min, b&w, VT, LD, DVD

Producers: Tomoyuki Tanaka, Richard Kay, Harry Rybnick, and E.B. Barison; **Director:** Ishiro Honda;

Screenplay: Honda, Takeo Murata, and Terry Morse; **Cinematography:** Masao Tamai; **Music:** Akira Ifukube; **Special Effects:** Eiji Tsuburaya; **Cast:** Raymond Burr, Takashi Shimura, Momoko Kochi, Akira Takarada, Akihiko Hirata, Haruo Nakajima, Katsumi Tezuka, Frank Iwanaga

All vessels venturing into a certain area in the middle of Japan's regular shipping lanes are disappearing. Radiomen report blinding light and an ocean of flames before their all-too-brief broadcasts end in screams and static. Before long, the truth is known. An old island legend, the monster Gojira, has returned to plague humankind.

The creature is a 400-foot-tall bipedal dinosaurlike beast that shrugs off machine guns and tanks as well as rockets and staggering amounts of electricity. The thing is also radioactive. Not only does it leave heavy radiation traces wherever it walks, but it's capable of expelling streams of forceful radioactive breath that melt everything in its path.

The monster comes ashore in Japan and knocks down a great deal of Tokyo as if its buildings were child's blocks for several nights until a plan is finally found. Eye patch–wearing scientist Serizawa (Takarada) has invented a horrible device, the oxygen destroyer, which until now he has kept fairly secret. Realizing there is no other way to stop the creature, he offers his device to the world to combat the monster, but only if he is the one to set it off. Finding the beast asleep on the bottom of the Pacific, a diving party including Serizawa plants the device on the ocean floor and then heads for the surface.

Except Serizawa, who stays behind to set off the device. Once he sees that it is working, however, he cuts his air line. Previously, he burned all his papers, swearing he would never allow his device to hurt humankind. Now that he has revealed its existence to the world, the only honorable thing he can do is die along with the beast so that no one will ever extract his secret from him.

Godzilla, as the beast was renamed for the American market, is a property that is often ridiculed. Giant monsters wrecking Japan have become a comedy staple over the past half-century but not because of this film. *Gojira* is the name the picture was released under in Japan. The American company that bought the rights two years later cut 20 minutes out of the original film, replacing it with new footage of Raymond Burr to help prepare the picture for the world market. Even distorted as it is, the picture is still effective.

Made less than 10 years after the only nuclear bombs ever used against a populated area were dropped on Japan, there is little doubt of the retaliatory nature of this film. When the first ship is seen at the beginning, the audience watches as a group of sailors sit around on deck and sing, one of them playing his guitar. Then the blinding flash and ocean of flames erupt, and the men scream and scatter. The guitar hits the deck, and, interestingly, the camera remains focused on it as the shadows of the men fade away. Radiation comes into the world unseen; men are made insignificant and music dies.

The beast tears through Japan for no logical reason—not hunger, revenge, anger, conquest, hatred—nothing can explain this massive wave of destruction, just as nothing can stop it. All older weapons are toys in comparison. No explanation is ever given as to why jet fighter missiles don't at least blow chunks out of the monster. True, it's big, but it's just a creature, right? Of course, the answer is no. Godzilla isn't just a creature, he's a metaphor, and thus he can be slain only by a metaphor.

Serizawa has invented a terrible device. Scientifically, the oxygen destroyer makes even less sense than Godzilla, but that's all right. It and its one-eyed (he has vision, but it's a crippled vision) creator are a metaphor, too. It's an interesting way of telling the story because thus Godzilla is cast not only as radioactive destruction but also as the Japanese war machine that brought about the nuclear conflagration in the first place. Serizawa realizes the monster must be stopped, but must another monster be brought into the world to stop him? Bravely, he does the only thing he can to keep his inner moral peace with the universe.

Godzilla, King of the Monsters is a wonderfully structured film—tragic and epic. Admittedly, in closeup, the big dumb rubber suit is as obvious as can be, but the night scenes of destruction when Godzilla comes ashore are hauntingly magnificent. The soundtrack augments the action with a moodiness seldom approached even today. And scenes such as an extended shot of a mother crouching in the street, holding onto her four small children, not even trying to protect them, just holding them as the towering, unstoppable nightmare strides through the city, coming straight for them, reveal Inoshiro Honda as one of the most lyrical directors who ever stepped behind the camera.

As nothing more than a simple monster movie, this one has its flaws. But as a fist raised in anger against not only those who dropped the bombs on Japan but also against those who forced those bombs to be dropped, it is stark poetry.

This film was the first of many featuring the self-proclaimed king of the monsters. Godzilla made a bundle for its primary franchise owners, Toho Studios, and knowing a good thing, they went into the giant monster business in a big way. The first sequel, *Gigantis, the Fire Monster* was released in 1959. It didn't add much to the legend, but it was serious, exciting, and well made.

By 1964 Godzilla was routinely fighting Toho's other giant creatures, as in that year's *Godzilla vs. Mothra*. Much has been made of its story line, in which the two monsters are seen as representing old Japanese culture vs. that which was being born through Western influence. Godzilla (the old ways) triumphs at first by destroying Mothra (the new ways). But then Mothra's two offspring defeat Godzilla. It's an interesting subtext, and it proved that the old lizard could still be used to tell stories far beyond what might be expected. It was also, however, something of a last hurrah.

For a number of years the series floundered through an endless string of films mostly geared toward children. In *Ghidra, the Three-Headed Monster* (1964), Godzilla is only a guest star as in the 1968 *Destroy All Monsters*. True, he was an important guest star, but it was a star that was fading. There were still moments for him, as in 1966's *Godzilla vs. the Sea Monster*, but it was clear the studio was running out of ideas. In '69 he appeared in *Godzilla's Revenge*, a chop job whose action sequences were mostly cut from the earlier *Godzilla vs. the Sea Monster* and *Son of Godzilla*. Disappointment was keen, but it was nothing compared to what was to follow.

In the 1970s Godzilla became extremely two-dimensional. *Godzilla vs. the Smog Monster* and *Godzilla on Monster Island* (both released in 1972) were made for children. It is interesting to note, though, that *Smog Monster* marked an attempt at restoring Godzilla's metaphorical relevance as he took on a creature born of Earth's pollution. Though clumsy and pedantic, the film's environmentalist message made for a bizarre mix of comedy and horror, stitched together with some macabre animation sequences. But while in many of his 1960s films Godzilla was reduced from a nearly all-powerful terror to a superhero of sorts, he now became little more than a children's matinee performer. In 1976 he hit the bottom with *Godzilla vs. Megalon*, in which he teamed up with a superpowered robot to fight bad guy monsters. At this point audiences knew full well they were headed for a comedy, and practically a vaudeville show at that.

The saga of the king of the monsters hit its lowest point in the late 1970s. By then the one-time mind-boggling terror had become a karate star, a dancer, and a clown. He starred in comic books. He made commercials. And, like many another overexposed property, he got fat and boring and repetitive. But luckily for his fans, Godzilla's owners had plans for something new.

Note: One of the minor films that followed Godzilla's initial release was his matchup against King Kong (*King Kong vs. Godzilla* [1963]). One noteworthy tidbit is that this film is one of the highest-grossing films in Japanese history. Some say the reason is that the film has two endings: one in which Godzilla wins the match for Japanese audiences, and one in which Kong wins for Western audiences. This is not true. Although the film was edited heavily for its American release (as almost every Godzilla film was), the ending was the same for both countries. The monsters fall into the sea. Godzilla does not reappear. Kong reappears and swims away. Open to interpretation—yes, but open to the same interpretations worldwide because everyone saw the exact same footage. Sorry conspiracy fans, but that's the way it is.

Note: Director Terry Morse added the footage of Raymond Burr to *Godzilla, King of the Monsters* two years after the original picture had been filmed, using both split screen effects and doubles for the Japanese stars. It's almost flawless work for which he must be commended. The sets, costumes, and attitude of the original were matched perfectly.

GODZILLA 1985 (aka: THE RETURN OF GODZILLA)

New World Pictures, 1985, 91 min, Color, VT, LD

Producers: Tomoyuki Tanaka, Fumio Tanaka, and Anthony Randel; **Directors:** Kohji Hashimoto and R.J. Kizer; **Screenplay:** Shuichi Nagahara and Lisa Tomei; **Cinematography:** Kazutami Hara; **Music:** Reijiro Koroku; **Special Effects:** Eiji Tsuburaya; **Cast:** Raymond Burr, Keiji Kobayashi, Ken Tanaka, Yasuko Sawaguchi, Shin Takuma, Yosuke Natsuki, James Hess, Warren Kemmerling, Travis Swords

At sea there is a terrible storm. A great vessel is pounded mercilessly, then finally sinks. The only question: Was it really the typhoon that sank the boat?

The world soon learns that it wasn't the storm that caused the destruction, but the monster Godzilla. Not seen since it was driven off 30 years earlier (this picture was made as a direct sequel to *GODZILLA, KING OF THE MONSTERS*, and as far as the plot is concerned, there had been no other movies in the series except the first), the reemergence of this terror sends the world into a panic. The U.S. and the Soviet Union both threaten to nuke Japan to kill the creature if that's what it takes, and tension builds along the different fronts. The scientists trying to stop Godzilla let us know that all the nukes will do is further destroy and poison Japan while giving the monster even more power than it already has, leaving the film's heroes with the daunting task of figuring out another way to defeat the giant lizard.

Godzilla 1985 is a nice return to the intensity of the early movies. The filmmaker's search for continuity is certainly well served by the device of cutting Raymond Burr into the film as was done in the '56 original. The sets are a spectacular improvement over those in the first picture. As good as those were, Japanese model building had never been better up to that point than in this film. Also, after years of pointedly ignoring Western film techniques, suddenly smoke was being used to cover giveaway signals, night shots were once more used to enhance both the film's mood and its sense of reality. Even a Western-style film score was included, giving the movie a texture the other films in the series hadn't had.

The picture does have flaws, however. The greatest is in the re-editing for release outside Japan. Although Burr's scenes are well handled, it's obvious that in the original version the Americans are clearly the bad guys and the Russians the even-tempered ones. Not wanting to offend American moviegoers, the blame for the nuclear escalation suddenly goes to the Russians. It's a clumsy effort, but it doesn't cripple the film. What comes closer to doing that is that standard bad dubbing. Subtitles would have been preferable.

Superior to dozens of previous Toho monster films, sadly *Godzilla 1985* was not a big box office draw. Many reasons have been given. The one that comes closest to the truth is that it was simply too little, too late. Godzilla had been treated as a clown for so many years that people came to expect it. Since there was no reason to expect anything but the usual stupidity, only those who wanted to see a stupid Godzilla went to the theaters. Most of the audience for this one stayed home, not realizing until the picture was out of the theaters that it was the one they had been waiting for.

In Japan the film was enough of a hit to spawn a series of more serious films. In 1989 *Godzilla vs. Biollante* was released in Japan, the first of what would be six new films from Toho. None of these features has seen an American release to date, but they are available on VHS. The remainder are: *Godzilla vs. King Ghidorah*, *Godzilla vs. Mothra*, *Godzilla vs. Mechagodzilla II*, *Godzilla vs. Space Godzilla*, and *Godzilla vs. Destroyah*.

The new films continue the *Godzilla 1985* story line. Gone are the wisecracking kids, dream sequences, martial arts monster fights, and all of the other less than serious elements that had plagued the Japanese superstar's middle years. In *Biollante*, for instance, Middle Eastern spies steal biological material (samples of Godzilla's cells). Their hope is to use Godzilla's DNA to help develop a strain of wheat that will grow in the desert. When a terrorist's bomb kills the head scientist's daughter, he grafts some of her DNA to a rosebush, hoping to keep her soul alive. The rosebush is what eventually becomes the film's title monster. In some ways the story doesn't flow smoothly, but it is an attempt to take the Godzilla legend in an artistic direction that works well enough.

In the next film, *Godzilla vs. King Ghidorah*, time travel comes into the series as visitors from the future come to Japan to help save it from its eventual destruction at the hands of Godzilla. The time travelers plan to remove the Godzillasaurus from the path of the American nuclear bomb that will turn it into Godzilla. Their plan works, but then their true intentions become clear, and humanity must work to recreate Godzilla to stop the time travelers. The resulting creature is a bigger, tougher, more lethal Godzilla.

King Ghidorah is the best of the last series of films, but all of them have features that make them quite watchable, especially compared to so many of the older movies. All of them have stunning set work and the most dazzling choreography to come out of Toho Studios. *Mechagodzilla II* and *Space Godzilla* feature tremendous battle sequences, possibly the best ever seen in the series.

The most dramatic of all, however, is *Godzilla vs. Destroyah*. In this movie Toho finally kills their superstar once and for all. Posters for the film announced the event (so no one was taken by surprise), but Japanese audiences are reported to have grown quite emotional at the ending, despite being prepared. Even though a decade had passed since a Godzilla film had been released outside of Japan, the monster's passing made the news around the world. CNN and *The New York Times* both covered the event, as did scores of other media.

GODZILLA ON MONSTER ISLAND

See GODZILLA, KING OF THE MONSTERS; GODZILLA VS. GIGAN

GODZILLA RAIDS AGAIN

See GIGANTIS, THE FIRE MONSTER

GODZILLA'S REVENGE

See *ALL MONSTERS ATTACK; GODZILLA, KING OF THE MONSTERS*

GODZILLA 2000

Tri-Star Pictures/Toho, 2000, 98 min, Color

Producer: Shogo Tomiyama; **Director:** Takao Okawara; **Screenplay:** Wataru Mimura and Kanji Kashiwabara; **Music:** Takayuki Hattori; **Cinematography:** Katsohiro Kato; **Special Effects:** Kenji Suzuki, Shinichi Wakasa, and Hideo Okamoto; **Cast:** Takehiro Murata, Shiro Sano, Hiroshi Abe, Naomi Nishida, Mayu Suzuki, Tsutomu Kitagawa

A thick fog blankets the islands of Japan, where all seems calm until a terrified world discovers that Godzilla is alive. The giant monster wades ashore and destroys a nearby nuclear power plant while the world readies itself for the struggle to come. At the same time, a gigantic meteorite has been discovered on the ocean floor. It's soon revealed that the rock is actually a stone-covered spaceship. Before long the alien aboard the ship and Godzilla are locked in combat while all the world hangs in the balance.

Following the release of *GODZILLA* (1999) Toho studios reclaimed the rights to their famous film monster. And while their latest effort had its good points, it was far from the landmark Godzilla movie for which most fans were hoping. The new Godzilla costume was highly effective despite the limitations of using a man in a rubber suit to create the effect. The more primal and ferocious design of the creature made the monster's threat all the more credible. Additionally, the movie delivered very high-quality special effects in the way of detailed and convincing cityscapes through which Godzilla moved.

One wishes the story could have been as impressive. Completely ignoring Godzilla's death in the previous Toho outing, *GODZILLA VS. DESTROYAH*, the film simply brings the irradiated beast back to life. Initially Godzilla seems determined to destroy all of Japan's power sources, though no motivation is apparent. In addition to this the alien entity raised from the sea bottom is supposed to have come to Earth specifically to attack Godzilla. But the entity is explained to have been on Earth for 65 million years (or 6,000 in an apparent inconsistency), meaning it could have had no knowledge of Godzilla, who was created by modern man. Also unexplained is why,

after defeating the alien, Godzilla simply returns to the sea rather than resuming his rampage against Japan's power plants.

Despite this, the actors give the best performances they can within the limitations of the script, which offers up shallow and predictable characters drawn in the broadest of strokes. There's a father/daughter team of scientists (she's 12 but she runs the business) who find themselves working with a female reporter who, although she doesn't like them and they don't like her, falls into the "mom" roll with ridiculous ease. The government scientists with whom the father was once partners and must now reunite are career oriented and only want to kill Godzilla. Perhaps the only interesting character in the film is the government agent in charge of combating Godzilla, a duty he takes so seriously that he personally confronts the monster in a fatal showdown.

GODZILLA VS. BIOLLANTE

Toho (Japan), 1989, Color, 104 min, VT

Producer: Tomoyuki Tanaka; **Director:** Kazuki Omori; **Screenplay:** Omori and Schinichiro Kobayashi; **Music:** Koichi Sugiyama; **Cinematography:** Yudia Kato; **Special Effects:** Koichi Kawakita; **Cast:** Kunihiko Mitamura, Yoshiko Tanaka, Masanobu Takashima, Megumi Odaka, Toru Minegishi Kenpachiro Satsuma, Shigeru Shibazaki, Yoshitaka Kimura, Masao Takegami

See *GODZILLA 1985*

GODZILLA VS. DESTROYAH (aka GODZILLA VS. DESTROYER)

Toho (Japan), 1995, Color, 103 min, VT

Producers: Tomoyuki Tanaka and Shogo Tomiyama; **Director:** Takao Okawara; **Screenplay:** Kazuki Omori; **Music:** Akira Ifukube; **Special Effects:** Koichi Kawakita; **Cast:** Megumi Odaka, Momoko Kochi, Yasufumi Kayashi, Yoko Ishino, Takuro Tatsumi, Ronald Hea, Kenpachiro Satsuma, Ryu Hurricane, Ryo Hariya, Eichi Yanagida

See *GODZILLA 1985*

GODZILLA VS. DESTROYER

See *GODZILLA 1985; GODZILLA VS. DESTROYAH*

GODZILLA VS. KING GHIDORAH

Toho (Japan), 1991, Color, 103 min, VT

Producers: Tomoyuki Tanaka and Shogo Tomitama; **Director:** Kazuki Omori; **Screenplay:** Omori; **Music:** Akira Ifukube; **Cinematography:** Yoshinori Sekiguchi; **Special Effects:** Koichi Kawakita; **Cast:** Anna Nakagawa, Megumi Odaka, Kenji Sahara, Isao Toyohara, Katsuhiko Sasaki, Kanpachiro Satsuma, Wataru Fukuda, Ryu Hurricane

See *GODZILLA 1985*

GODZILLA VS. GIGAN
(aka GODZILLA ON MONSTER ISLAND)

Toho (Japan), 1972/Cinema Shares (U.S.), 1977, Color, 89 min, VT, LD

Producer: Tomoyuki Tanaka; **Director:** Jun Fukuda; **Screenplay:** Shinichi Sekizawa; **Music:** Akira Ifukube; **Cinematography:** Kiyoshi Hasegawa; **Special Effects:** Teruyoshi Nakano; **Cast:** Hiroshi Ishikawa, Yuriko Hishimi, Tomoko Umeda, Minoru Takashima, Kunio Murai, Haruo Nakajima, Kengo Nakayama, Yukietsu Omiya, Kanta Ina

See *GODZILLA, KING OF THE MONSTERS*

GODZILLA VS. HEDORA (aka: GODZILLA VS. THE SMOG MONSTER)

Toho (Japan), 1971.AIP (U.S.), 1972, Color, 85 min, VT, LD

Producer: Tomoyuki Tanaka; **Director:** Toshimitsu Banno; **Screenplay:** Banno and Kaoru Mabuchi; **Music:** Riichiro Manabe; **Cinematography:** Hoichi Manoda; **Special Effects:** Teruyoshi Nakano; **Cast:** Akira Yamauchi, Hiroyuki Kawase, Toshie Kimura, Toshio Shibamoto, Keiko Mari, Haruo Nakajima, Kengo Nakayama

See *GODZILLA, KING OF THE MONSTERS*

GODZILLA VS. MECHAGODZILLA II
(aka: GODZILLA VS. SUPERMECHAGODZILLA)

Toho (Japan), 1993, Color, 107 min, VT

Producers: Tomoyuki Tanaka and Shogo Tomiyama; **Director:** Takao Okawara; **Screenplay:** Wataru Mumura; **Music:** Akira Ifukube; **Cinematography:** Yuzuru Aizawa; **Special Effects:** Koichi Kawakita; **Cast:** Takashima, Kenji Sahara, Akira Nakao, Kenpachiro Satsuma, Ryu Hurricane, Wataru Fukuda

See *GODZILLA 1985*

GODZILLA VS. MEGALON

Toho (Japan), 1973/Cinema Shares (U.S.), 1976, Color, 83 min, VT

Producer: Tomoyuki Tanaka; **Director:** Jun Fukuda; **Screenplay:** Fukada; **Music:** Riichiro Manabe; **Cinematography:** Yuzuru Aizawa; **Special Effects:** Teruyoshi Nakani; **Cast:** Katsuhiko Sasaki, Hiroyuki Kawase, Yutaka Hayashi, Robert Dunham, Shinji Takagi, Kengo Nakayama, Tsugitoshi Komada, Hiedo Date

See *GODZILLA, KING OF THE MONSTERS*

GODZILLA VS. MOTHRA (1964)
(aka GODZILLA VS. THE THING)

Toho (Japan)/SIP (U.S.), 1964, Color, 90 min, VT, LD

Producer: Tomoyuki Tanaka; **Director:** Inoshiro Honda; **Screenplay:** Schinichi Sckizawa; **Music:** Akira Ifukube; **Cinematography:** Hajimi Koizumi; **Special Effects:** Eiji Tsuburaya, Mototaka Tomioka, and Safamasa Arikawa; **Cast:** Hiroshi Koizumi, Yu Fujiki, Akira Takarada, Yuriko Hoshi, Emi Ito, Yumi Ito

See *GODZILLA, KING OF THE MONSTERS*

GODZILLA VS. MOTHRA (1992)

Toho (Japan), 1992, Color, 102 min, VT

Producers: Tomoyuki Tanaka and Shogo Tomiyama; **Director:** Takao Okawara; **Screenplay:** Kazuki Omori; **Music:** Akira Ifukube; **Special Effects:** Koichi Kawakita; **Cast:** Tetsuya Beshho, Megumi Odaka, Satomi Kobayashi, Akira Takarada, Keiki Imamura, Sayaka Osawa, Kenpachiro Satsuma, Ryu Hurricane

See *GODZILLA 1985*

GODZILLA VS. THE SEA MONSTER

See *EBIRAH, HORROR OF THE DEEP; GODZILLA, KING OF THE MONSTERS*

GODZILLA VS. THE SMOG MONSTER

See *GODZILLA, KING OF THE MONSTERS; GODZILLA VS. HEDORAH*

GODZILLA VS. SPACEGODZILLA

Toho (Japan), 1994, Color, 108 min, VT

Producers: Tomoyuki Tanaka and Shogo Tomiyama; **Director:** Kensho Yamashita; **Screenplay:** Hiroshi Kashiwabara; **Music:** Takayuki Hattori; **Cinematography:** Masahiro Kishimoto; **Special Effects:** Koichi Kawakita; **Cast:** Megumi Odaka, Jun Hashizume, Zenkichi Youneyama, Akira Emoto, Kenji Sahara Koichi Ueda, Keiko Imanura, Sayaka Osawa, Kenpachiro Satsuma, Ryo Hariya, Wataru Fukuda, Little Frankie

See *GODZILLA 1985*

GODZILLA VS. SUPER-MECHAGODZILLA

See *GODZILLA 1985; GODZILLA VS. MECHAGODZILLA II*

GODZILLA VS. THE THING

See *GODZILLA, KING OF THE MONSTERS; GODZILLA VS. MOTHRA* (1964)

GOG

United Artists, 1954, 85 min, Color, VT, LD

Producer: Ivan Tors; **Director:** Herbert L. Strock; **Screenplay:** Tom Taggert; **Cinematography:** Lathrop B. Worth; **Music:** Harry Sukman; **Special Effects:** Harry Redmond, Jr.; **Cast:** Richard Egan, Constance Dowling, William Schallert, Herbert Marshall, John Wengraf

Top secret experiments are being conducted by scientists in a hidden underground lab. The research is bent on proving whether or not space travel is feasible for human beings. Before much can be learned, however, various pieces of equipment, test chambers and the like, begin malfunctioning in a highly lethal manner and quickly diminish the the scientists' numbers. Finally, two experimental robots, Gog and Magog, go out of control as well. It all turns out to be the work of a sinister foreign power that is managing its acts of sabotage through the use of an experimental ray that is being broadcast from a special high-altitude aircraft. Not good enough to be great and not bad enough to be funny, all this movie has going for it is a big explosive finale full of 3-D effects churning outward toward the audience.

Note: Both the names Gog and Magog appear in the Bible. They are not important names, nor does either apply to a single entity. Magog, for instance, is used both as a personal name and as the name of an entire race of people. Thus, whatever the screenwriters meant to convey is unclear. Perhaps the George Lucas formula is best—simply use letter and number combinations for naming robots and leave it at that.

GOJIRA

See *GODZILLA, KING OF THE MONSTERS*

GOLD

UFA (Germany), 1934, 80 min, b&w

Producer: Alfred Zeisler; **Director:** Karl Hartl; **Screenplay:** Rolf Vanloo; **Cinematography:** Guenther Rittau; **Music:** Hans-Otto Borgmann; **Special Effects:** Otta Hunte; **Cast:** Hans Albers, Brigitte Helm, Lien Deyers, Friederich Kayssler

Once more a scientist invents a machine that creates wealth. This time the device churns out gold. This gets him murdered by greedy parties who want the invention for themselves. No one profits, however, as the lab is smashed and buried by a fantastic wall of seawater during the film's highly effective climax.

Note: It's likely that this film contains the first cinematic depiction of an atom smasher. Also, interestingly enough, the effects at the end of this film were so striking that they were lifted almost in their entirety and grafted onto the ending of United Artist's 1953 gem, *The Magnetic Monster*. This is an unfortunate set of events because the heavy-handed borrowing now keeps *Gold* from ever being seen today.

GOLDENGIRL

Avco Embassy, 1979, 104 min, Color, VT

Producer: Danny O'Donovan; **Director:** Joseph Sargent; **Screenplay:** John Kohn; **Cinematography:** Steven Larner; **Music:** Bill Conti; **Cast:** Susan Anton, Curt Jurgens, James Coburn, Robert Culp, Leslie Caron, Harry Guardino, Jessica Walter, Ward Costello, Nicholas Coster

Track star Anton is turned into a robot so that she can win at the Olympics. James Coburn plays the trainer with a heart of gold who turns the brainwashed Anton against her manipulative father.

GOLDEN RABBIT, THE

Rank (Great Britain), 1962, 64 min, b&w

Producer: Barry Delmaine; **Director:** David MacDonald; **Screenplay:** Dick Sharples and Gerald Kelsey; **Cinematography:** S.D. Onions; **Music:** Bill McGuffie; **Cast:** Timothy Bateson, Kenneth Fortescue, Maureen Beck, John Sharp

A scientist discovers the secret of turning lead into gold, which is a nice trick. Alas, the effect is sadly temporary.

GORGO

MGM, 1961, 78 min, Color, VT, LD, DVD

Producer: Wilfred Eades; **Director:** Eugene Lourie; **Screenplay:** John Loring and Daniel Hyatt; **Cinematography:** F.A. Young; **Music:** Angelo Francesco Lavagnino; **Special Effects:** Tom Howard; **Cast:** Bill Travers, William Sylvester, Vincent Winter, Bruce Seton, Joseph O'Conner, Martin Benson

Nara Island, Ireland, is the site of a terrible storm. An underwater volcano has erupted, making a hash of

Gorgo (MGM / R. ALLEN LEIDER COLLECTION)

everything in sight. Unfortunately for the Nara islanders, besides wrecking the countryside, it's also awakened a 30-feet-tall amphibious dinosaur (a "gorgosaurus" according to the film) and sent it up into the surface world. The thing comes ashore and tromps a lot of the island, prompting the locals to allow sailors Sylvester and Travers to capture the thing and take it away. The boys cart their captive off to London, where it's put on display for the general public. Everything is going fine for the two bush-league Barnums until the horrible truth is discovered. They didn't capture a full-grown dino. They nabbed a baby. And mama is on her way.

The wrecking of London by the adult, 150-feet-tall "gorgosaurus" is a fantastic sight. Much of the beginning of this movie is stock and standard, but Tom Howard's effects are striking and appear quite spectacular on the big screen. There's not much to the story outside of the surprise twist of Mama's appearance, but it's still one of the best giant monster movies.

GOTHIC

Virgin Vision, 1986, Color, 90 min, VT, LD

Producers: Penny Corke, Al Clark, and Robert Devereux; **Director:** Ken Russell; **Screenplay:** Stephen Volk; **Cinematography:** Mike Soothon; **Music:** Thomas Dolby; **Cast:** Gabriel Byrne, Julian Sands, Natasha Richardson, Miriam Cyr, Timothy Spall

See *FRANKENSTEIN*

GRAND TOUR, THE

Drury Holding Company, 1992, 99 min, Color, VT

Producers: Robert E. Warner and John A. O'Conner; **Director:** David N. Twohy; **Screenplay:** Twohy; **Cinematography:** Harry Mathias; **Music:** Gerald Gouriet; **Special Effects:** James W. Beauchamp; **Cast:** Jeff Daniels, Ariana Richards, David Wells, Nicholas Guest, Jim Haynie, Emilia Crow, Robert Colbert, Marilyn Lightstone

When visitors arrive and start to fill up a small-town hotel, usually the owner is happy. This time, however, the owner has reason to believe his guests are not so much from out of town as they are from out of time. He believes they are time travelers gathering to witness some horrible event. Based on the intelligent and suspenseful *Vintage Season* by Lawrence O'Donnell and the legendary C.L. Moore, this movie is a surprise for most viewers. Like all good science fiction, this one relies more on brainpower than firepower.

Note: Robert Colbert also starred in the 1966 television series *The Time Tunnel*.

GRAVEROBBERS FROM OUTER SPACE

See *PLAN 9 FROM OUTER SPACE*

GRAVEYARD TRAMPS

See *INVASION OF THE BEE GIRLS*

GREAT ALASKAN MYSTERY, THE

Universal, 1944, 13-chapter serial, b&w

Directors: Ray Taylor and Lewis D. Collins; **Screenplay:** Maurice Tombragel and George H. Plympton; **Cinematography:** William Sickner; **Cast:** Ralph Morgan, Jay Novello, Marjorie Weaver, Anthony Warde, Milburn Stone, Fuzzy Knight, Martin Kosleck, Joe Crehan

Noble scientists set out for Alaska to mine for an element they have reason to believe will power their new gadget, the Peraton, a transmitter capable of moving matter through space. As one might suspect, there are some bad guys who want to steal it. This one is pretty dull, even for those who like serials.

GREATEST POWER, THE

Metro, 1917, five reels, b&w, silent

Director: Edwin Carewe; **Screenplay:** Albert Shelby Le Vino; **Cast:** William B. Davidson, Ethel Barrymore, Harry S. Northrup, William Black

A chemist working on a cancer cure somehow gets his wires crossed and instead invents an incredibly powerful explosive.

GREATEST BATTLE ON EARTH, THE

See *GHIDRA, THE THREE-HEADED MONSTER*

GREAT MONSTER YONGKARI

See *YONGARI—MONSTER FROM THE DEEP*

GREAT RADIUM MYSTERY, THE

Universal, 1919, 36 reels, b&w, silent serial

Directors: Robert F. Hill and Robert Broadwell; **Screenplay:** Frederick Bennett; **Cast:** Eileen Sedwick, Robert Reeves, Cleo Madison

Scientists battle enemy agents once more, this time over a newly improved assault tank.

GREAT UNDERSEA WAR, THE

See *THE TERROR BENEATH THE SEA*

GREEN SLIME, THE

Toei (Japan), 1968, 77 min/MGM (U.S.), 1969, 90 min, Color, VT

Producers: Ivan Reiner and Walter Manly; **Director:** Kinji Fukasaku; **Screenplay:** Charles Sinclair, William Finger, and Tom Rowe; **Cinematography:** Yoshikazu Yamasawa; **Music:** Toshiaki Tsushima and Charles Fox; **Special Effects:** Akira Watanabe and Takeshi Ugai; **Cast:** Robert Horton, Richard Jaeckel, Luciana Paluzzi, Bud Widom, Ted Gunther

Daring rocketeers destroy a giant meteor headed for Earth. Afterward, they dock at the local space station. The problem is, however, that these valiant heroes don't realize they've unwittingly brought an army of tiny monsters back with them. Interestingly enough, the horde of microscopic critters, which should never have seen a mammal before, only await the taste of blood so they can sprout into six-foot-tall bundles of tentacles that rip everything and everyone to shreds. Soon the station is overrun with the horrors, and our heroes have to fight their way to safety. Sounds like it might be a gem, but it's not.

GREEN TERROR, THE

Gaumont (Great Britain), 1919, 6,500 feet, b&w, silent

Director: Will Kellino; **Screenplay:** G.W. Clifford; **Cast:** Maud Yates, Heather Thacher, Aurele Sydney

A mad scientist attempts to wipe out the entire world's wheat crop. The film never explains how anyone can be so angry at one of the essential food groups.

GREEN WOMAN, THE

See *QUEEN OF BLOOD*

GROUNDSTAR CONSPIRACY, THE

Universal, 1972, 96 min, Color, VT

Producers: Hal Roach, Jr., and Trevor Wallace; **Director:** Lamont Johnson; **Screenplay:** Matthew Howard and Leslie P. Davies; **Cinematography:** Michael Reed; **Music:** Paul Hoffert; **Special Effects:** Herbert Ewing; **Cast:** George Peppard, Michael Sarrazin, Christine Belford

This melodrama about espionage and sabotage at a secret space project is long on plot but short on action and very badly scripted. Included here only so viewers can be warned away.

GROUND ZERO

Flocker Enterprises, 1973, 86 min, Color

Producer: James T. Flocker; **Director:** Flocker; **Screenplay:** Samuel Newman; **Cinematography:** Flocker; **Music:** The Chosen Few; **Cast:** Ron Casteel, Augie Treibach, Melvin Belli

A lunatic mines the Golden Gate Bridge with nuclear explosives.

GULLIVER'S TRAVELS BEYOND THE MOON

Toei (Japan), 1965/Continental (U.S.), 1966, 85 min, Color

Producer: Hiroshi Okawa; **Director;** Yoshio Kuroda; **Screenplay:** Shinichi Sekizawa; **Animation:** Hideo Furusawa; **Music:** Milton and Anne DeLugg; **Cast:** Chiyoko Honma, Seiji Miyaguchi, Shoichi Ozawa, Kyy Sakamoto

It's Jonathan Swift's classic character, updated to the point where he travels to the Moon in a rocketship. Once there along with his young boy companion, Gulliver gets caught up in a war between two races of robots. What is too silly for most adults may be acceptable for small children.

HANDMAID'S TALE, THE

Bioskop Films, 1990, Color, 109 min, VT, LD

Producer: Daniel Wilson; **Director:** Volker Schlondorff; **Screenplay:** Harold Pinter; **Music:** Ryuichi Sakamoto; **Cinematography:** Igor Luthor; **Cast:** Natasha Richardson, Robert Duvall, Faye Dunaway, Aidan Quinn, Elizabeth McGovern, Victoria Tennant, Blanche Baker, Traci Lind

In the near future the world has changed dramatically and not for the better. The United States has suffered through a second revolution and is now divided into hostile territories. The story of this film centers on the area named Gilead, a racist, sexist hell for everyone living there who isn't a heterosexual white male. Since most people have been rendered sterile due to decades of environmental abuse, women capable of childbirth are kept in virtual slavery. In the novel that inspired the film, the central character is named Offred, from "of Fred," to denote her lineage. In the movie she is named Kate, but her tale of terrible woe is the same, as she is forced into servitude for the establishment.

The film, much like Margaret Atwood's book, has a very specific message, and those who don't agree with it will find it hard to watch. Essentially, it falls back on the stereotypical view that all white men are sexist and racist, determined to rape the planet, and that all others are their victims. The book is bitter enough but at least it acknowledges that its exaggeration makes a point. The film does not, and rather than fomenting discussion, its pointlessly disturbing diatribe is the equivalent of an ideological gun held to an imagined enemy's throat. It amounts to well-made hay for slow-witted horses.

HAND OF DEATH, THE

20th Century Fox, 1961, b&w, 59 min

Producer: Eugene Ling; **Director:** Harry Nelson; **Screenplay:** Ling; **Music:** Sonny Burke; **Cinematography:** Floyd Crosby; **Special Effects:** Bob Mark; **Cast:** John Agar, Roy Gordon, Steve Dunne, John Alonzo, Paula Raymond

Scientist John Agar gets himself into trouble with a dangerous nerve gas experiment. His research not only turns him into a mutant freak, reminiscent of the Thing from Marvel Comics' *Fantastic Four,* but it also gives him the touch of death. Watching this movie is pretty much the touch of death itself.

HAND OF PERIL, THE

World, 1916, b&w, five reels, silent

Producer: Maurice Tourneur; **Director:** Tourneur; **Screenplay:** Tourneur; **Cast:** Doris Sawyer, June Elvidge, House Peters

An x-ray machine renders those things x-rayed totally transparent. No explanation for the science in this movie should be expected. Still, it manages to be somewhat silly and somewhat interesting at the same time.

HANDS OF A STRANGER

Allied Artists, 1962, b&w, 86 min, VT

Producers: Newton Arnold and Michael DuPont; **Director:** Arnold; **Screenplay:** Arnold; **Music:** Richard LaSalle; **Cinematography:** Henry Cronjager; **Cast:** Sally Kellerman, Joan Harvey, Paul Lukather, Ted Ottis, Irish McCalla, James Stapleton, Barry Gordon

The fourth adaptation of the classic novel *Les Mains d'Orlac*. A pianist loses his hands in an accident. A brilliant surgeon decides to try something radical and performs a hand transplant. The only problem is that the donor was a murderer. The hands take on a life of their own and mayhem ensues. The plot is silly and the science is out the window, but the film is well made and manages to be a fairly entertaining version of the story.

HANDS OF ORLAC, THE

Pan Film, 1925, b&w, 70 min, silent

Director: Robert Wiene; **Screenplay:** Louis Nerz; **Cinematography:** G. Kramph and Hans Androschin; **Cast:** Conrad Veidt, Carmen Cartellieri, Alexandra Sorina, Fritz Kortner

The first screen version of the classic novel *Les Mains d'Orlac*. When a pianist loses his hands in an accident, a brilliant surgeon decides to try something radical and performs a hand transplant. The only problem is that the donor was a murderer. The hands take on a life of their own and mayhem ensues. The film is competent but not extremely engaging.

HANDS OF ORLAC, THE

British Lion Film Corporation (Great Britain/France), 1960/Continental (U.S.), 1964, b&w, 105 min, VT

Producers: Steven Pallos and Donald Taylor; **Director:** Edmond T. Grenville; **Screenplay:** John Baines and Grenville; **Cinematography:** Desmond Dickinson; **Music:** Claude Bollings; **Cast:** Mel Ferrer, Christopher Lee, Donald Pleasence, David Peel, Lucile Saint-Simon, Basil Sydney, Donald Wolfit

The third adaptation of the classic novel *Les Mains d'Orlac*. When a pianist loses his hands in an accident, a brilliant surgeon decides to try something radical and performs a hand transplant. The only problem is that the donor was a murderer. The hands take on a life of their own, but that's okay this time because in this version the murderer didn't really do it. Even with Christopher Lee and Donald Pleasence in the cast, all the movie offers is a simple plot twist.

HANGAR 18

Taft International, 1980, Color, 93 min, VT

Producer: Charles E. Sellier, Jr.; **Director:** James L. Conway; **Screenplay:** Steven Thornley; **Cast:** Darren McGavin, Robert Vaughn, Gary Collins, James Hampton, Joseph Campanella, Philip Abbott, Pamela Bellwood, Steven Keats, Willian Schallert, Tom Hallick

A satellite launched into orbit from a space shuttle crashes into a clumsily piloted UFO, knocking the ship from the skies and killing one of the astronauts. Since the revelation of the flying saucer would hurt the incumbent president's re-election chances by proving the government has lied about UFOs, the White House chief of staff (Vaughn) covers up the crash. The UFO is found and hidden away, and the crash is blamed on the two surviving astronauts. The idea around the White House is that after the election "the truth" will be revealed and the astronauts' reputations cleared. However, no one bothers to tell the surviving astronauts (Collins and Hampton). Determined to unveil the cover-up, the flyboys play detective, getting involved in car crashes and killing Secret Service men right and left as they close in on the stashed UFO.

In the meantime, teams of government scientists pore over the ship. Are years of intense backward engineering needed to decipher its many secrets? Not for these whiz kids. Their investigation unlocks the mysteries of humanity and the universe in about a week. And what do they discover? That humanity is the product of alien genetic engineering.

Many people actually considered *Hangar 18* a documentary when it was released, but it wasn't. It was just a way to cash in on the popular rumor (not as popular then as it has become since) that the government actually has recovered a UFO from a crash. This is not to say that *Hangar 18* is a bad film. More accurately, it's uninspired. Although it did have a theatrical release, this is probably one of the best television sci-fi movies ever made. Relying heavily on the theory popularized by *CHARIOT OF THE GODS* that all human advancement was sparked by extraterrestrial entities, it weaves a pseudo-scientific explanation for flying saucers, "proving" that it was ancient astronauts who are the missing link in human evolution. The real problem with this film is that it wasn't anything new at the time of its release and so is far less relevant now.

HAPPINESS CAGE, THE

See *THE MIND SNATCHERS*

HARDWARE

Palace Pictures, 1990, Color, 92 min, VT, LD

Producer: Joanne Sellar; **Director:** Richard Stanley; **Screenplay:** Steven MacManus, Kevin J. O'Neill, and Stanley; **Cinematography:** Steven Chivers; **Music:** Simon Boswell; **Special Effects:** Image Animation; **Cast:** Dylan McDermott, Stacey Travis, John Lynch, Iggy Pop, William Hootkins, Mark Northover

The future is a nuclear wasteland because of people's destructive tendencies, and in the desert (it's always in the desert), McDermott finds the remains of an android, which he brings to friend Travis. Soon the android's old programming is revived. Could it be programmed to fix things and be helpful? No. As usual, this android was programmed to obliterate all life in the universe. While the film is not all bad, it doesn't offer anything new or interesting.

HARRISON BERGERON (aka: KURT VONNEGUT'S "HARRISON BERGERON")

Atlantis Films Limited, 1995, Color, 105 min, VT

Producers: John Glascoe, Joseph Pierson, and Jonathan Hackett; **Director:** Bruce Pittman; **Screenplay:** Arthur Crimm, Glascoe, and Kurt Vonnegut; **Cinematography:** Michael Storey; **Music:** Lou Natale; **Special Effects:** Michael Lemnick; **Cast:** Sean Astin, Miranda de Pencier, Buck Henry, Eugene Levy, Andrea Martin, Christopher Plummer, Howie Mandel

In the year 2053, possibly the most insidious "Big Brother" ever dreamed up controls society. This time it's thought control, or more correctly, level-of-thought control, as the government has decided that people who think, as opposed to those who only react, have to be monitored. In an attempt to make people equal, electrodes are attached to everyone's heads. Anyone who thinks too much becomes unequally advantaged over one's peers and must be shocked by the headband until all thoughts disappear.

Enter Harrison Bergeron (Astin). Harrison is the smartest kid to come along in years. In fact, he's so intelligent, the headband simply isn't capable of dumbing him down. Still, Harrison tries to conform. He wants to be liked. He wants to be normal. He wants to get married and enjoy a popular television game show as his dad does. His headband is readjusted often, the voltage heightened frequently, but it's no good. He's just too smart.

Finally, surgery is mandated by the state, but it is all a ruse to get Harrison out of the regular world. Everything in this world is really controlled by Christopher Plummer and his cabal of manipulative geniuses, who seized the planet after the last world war and have kept it running ever since, more or less smoothly if rather dully. All creativity has been purged and is kept away from the now docile herds of people, who think they actually still run the world.

So Harrison is declared to have died on the operating table but then is brought into Plummer's secret cabal. He is given the freedom to think, to listen to jazz, to watch the old movies and television shows, to love whom he wishes. He is not, however, allowed to create a family. None of the cabal is. That is the self-imposed "punishment" they must endure to justify the many advantages they enjoy. The longer Harrison lives within the cabal, however, the more the entire deal rankles him. He doesn't want to think of his family as cattle to be placated. He doesn't want to deny himself children, nor does he want to deny those with children the joys of art and literature—of being able to think and plan and hope and dream and live life, not merely exist. Thus highly uncomfortable with making all of the world's decision, Harrison predictably rebels, but in a most unexpected way—both times he rebels.

To reveal more would spoil an excellent sci-fi film. This one is highly entertaining and thought provoking, as frightening as it is funny. This is one of Kurt Vonnegut's best short stories brought to life with tremendous style and wit.

Note: Watch for star Astin's father, John Astin (best known as Gomez Addams from *The Addams Family* television series) in a brief but typically wacky cameo appearance.

HARRY AND THE HENDERSONS

Universal, 1987, Color, 110 min, VT, LD

Producers: Dear Vane and Richard Vane; **Director:** William Dear; **Screenplay:** William Dear and William E. Martin; **Cinematography:** Allen Daviau and George Koblasa; **Music:** Bruce Broughton; **Special Effects:** Clive R. Kay; **Cast:** John Lithgow, Melinda Dillon, Margaret Langrick, Joshua Rudoy, Kevin Peter Hall, David Suchet, Lainie Kazan, Don Ameche, M. Emmet Walsh

A typical Hollywood version of the all-American family encounters Bigfoot in the forest and, mistakenly thinking him dead, brings him back to suburbia. Once he revives, however, they keep him around the house. This is merely *E.T.*, with the adults in on the secret. Lithgow provides a typically screwy performance, and the makeup did win Rick Baker an Academy Award, but it all adds up to something charming, sweet, and insipid.

HAUNTED PLANET, THE

See *PLANET OF THE VAMPIRES*

HAUNTED WORLD, THE

See *PLANET OF THE VAMPIRES*

HAVE ROCKET, WILL TRAVEL

Columbia, 1959, b&w, 76 min, VT

Producer: Harry Romm; **Director:** David Lowell Rich; **Screenplay:** Raphael Hayes; **Cinematography:** Ray Cory; **Music:** Mischa Bakaleinikoff; **Cast:** Moe Howard, Larry Fine, Curly Joe DeRita, Jerome Cowan, Nadine Datas, Anna Lisa, Bob Colbert

A trio of dim-witted but good-hearted janitors (the Three Stooges) try to help a damsel in distress but end up blasting themselves into outer space. Moe, Larry, and Curly Joe manage to set down on the planet Venus, where they meet a friendly talking unicorn, battle a giant, fire-breathing spider, and match wits with a supercomputer that creates robotic duplicates of them, setting them on each other in a fight to the death. Everything turns out all right, and the boys make it back to Earth to become national heroes.

This is the first of the Stooges feature-length theatrical releases, made possible after their rediscovery by a new generation, thanks to television. Both the original Curly Howard and his brother, Shemp

Howard, had already passed on, and while DeRita does his level best to fill their shoes, it's not the same. Still, this is a must for all sci-fi/Stooges fans.

HEAD, THE

Rapid (West Germany), 1959/Trans-Lux (U.S.), 1961, b&w, 91 min, VT

Producer: Wolfgang Hartwig; **Director:** Victor Trivas; **Screenplay:** Trivas; **Cinematography:** Otto Reinwald and Kurt Rendel; **Music:** Willy Mattes and Jacques Lasry; **Special Effects:** Theo Nishwitz; **Cast:** Horst Frank, Paul Dahlke, Karin Kernke, Michel Simon, Dieter Eppler

A mad scientist (Frank) is working with the remarkable Serum Z, a potion that can keep human appendages tissue from degenerating even when completely separated from the body. Frank cuts the head of the potion's inventor from his body and then keeps the head alive in his lab. He also transplants the head of a beautiful woman with an ugly body onto the body of a quite stunning corpse. How he becomes a surgeon of such magnitude is not explained. Neither is why anyone would watch this movie.

HEARTBEEPS

Universal, 1981, Color, 79 min, VT, LD

Producer: Michael Phillips; **Director:** Allan Arkush; **Screenplay:** John Hill; **Cinematography:** Charles Rosher, Jr.; **Music:** John Williams; **Special Effects:** John K. Stirber, Albert Whitlock, and Stan Winston; **Cast:** Andy Kaufman, Bernadette Peters, Randy Quaid, Kenneth McMillan, Melanie Mayron, Christopher Guest

This is a sci-fi comedy about two robots who fall in love, featuring Andy Kaufman, whose comic genius is not on display in this film.

HEAVY METAL

Columbia, 1981, Color, 90 min, VT, LD, DVD

Producers: Leonard Mogel and Ivan Reitman; **Director:** Gerald Potterton; **Screenplay:** Dan Goldberg and Len Blum; **Music:** Elmer Bernstein; **Original Art and Stories:** Richard Corben, Angus McKie, Dan O'Bannon, Thomas Warkentin, and Bernie Wrightson; **Animation:** Alan Best, Rusty Gilligan, Brian Larkin, Pino

Van, Ira Turek, Lee Mishkin, Juan Gimenez; **Cast:** John Candy, Richard Romanus, Joe Flaherty, Don Francks, Eugene Levy, Harold Ramis, John Vernon

The opening titles in this film are a truly impressive splash of color and music, during which the audience follows an astronaut piloting a snazzy sports car from outer space down through the atmosphere toward Earth, making his final touchdown on the street right outside his home. Upon entering his front door, he is greeted by his daughter, and he shows her something he brought back from space. That something is a glowing green orb that consumes the astronaut in grisly fashion and then chases his daughter through the house, cornering her in another room where it traps her. Instead of consuming her as well, it begins to tell its tale.

The orb announces that it is the Loch-Nar, the sum of all the universe's evil. Supposedly, its power infects all times, all galaxies, all dimensions. To some it is a treasure, to some a god, to others a bauble to be treated with no regard—but despite the perceptions of others, it is actually invincible, all-consuming evil. It's also our narrator.

Thus *Heavy Metal* settles into its framing device, and from this point on, the orb tells the girl stories, the film's various animated vignettes. Unfortunately, most of them are as weakly structured or pointless as the frame containing them. Point in case: The orb is supposed to be the total sum of all possible evil in the entire universe, and yet, in all the stories (the orb appears within all the vignettes sooner or later) it hardly does anything evil at all. If this thing is the sum total of all evil, the universe must be a fairly nice place. Beyond the fact that the framing sequence does not live up to its own boasting, the real problem is that it's the weakest animation in the entire film. Even though some of the other segments are quite competently rendered, and a few are even gorgeous, the end of each is a return to the frame and a reminder that everything is not right with this film.

The film's most significant flaw, however, is the writing, most of which consists of stock, shallow stories with no direction or point. Other than cabdriver Harry Canyon, featured in the first tale, no characters involve us in their tale or engender our sympathy. The stories are insultingly simplistic. Some do not even end but simply meander off into pointlessness, with the Loch-Nar suddenly popping up again to chortle over how evil it is, even though it never actually does anything very evil.

The worst segment of the film comes last. The tale of Taarna the Defender is fairly familiar stuff, and it was corny over two decades ago when first written.

Taarna may be the last of a race of immortals, but she's also just another of the bikini-armored warrior women so common in contemporary fantasy. She runs around a battlefield talking a much better fight than she delivers. If she's such a great warrior with a sword at least three feet long, why can't she even nick a bad guy whose defense is an eight-inch buzz saw attached to his wrist stump?

Not all the vignettes are terrible, but they are terribly mismatched and don't mesh into an enjoyable whole. The rock music that crowds out Elmer Bernstein's far superior sound track is competent but not inspired. It is merely background—ornamental strings of notes that don't enhance their sequences. Like so much "modern" entertainment, *Heavy Metal* is rough, loud, sexy, violent, and colorful, as well as gratuitous and pointless.

HEAVENS CALL, THE

Dovzhenko (U.S.S.R.), 1959, Color, 90 min

Producer: A.P. Dovzenko; **Directors:** Alexander Kozyr and M. Karinkov; **Screenplay:** V. Pomieszczykov and A. Sazanov; **Music:** Yuli Meitus; **Cinematography:** Nikolai Kulchitsky; **Special Effects:** Al Locatelli, G. Lukashov, and Y. Schlaech; **Cast:** A. Shvorin, L. Lobanov, Ivan Pereverzev

This is the original Russian version of the film that producer Roger Corman turned into BATTLE BEYOND THE SUN in 1963. It's hard to find now, but much better in its original form when it was obviously a propaganda film. Honesty is the best policy.

HECTOR SERVADAC'S ARK

See *NAKOMETE*

HELL CREATURES, THE

See *INVASION OF THE SAUCER MEN*

HELLEVISION

Roadshow Attractions, 1939, Color

A scientist invents television, but all he seems able to receive are scenes from Hell, which really doesn't seem much different from today—even with cable.

Note: The visions of Hell were snipped from the far superior 1909 silent film version of *Dante's Inferno*.

HELLO TELEVISION

Educational Films, 1930, b&w, 20 min

Producer: Mack Sennett; **Director:** Leslie A. Pearce; **Screenplay:** Pearce; **Cast:** Andy Clyde, Ann Christy, Julia Griffith

The television phone has finally been invented, apparently so that silly people can do silly things with it. Some things never change.

HELLSTROM CHRONICLE, THE

Columbia, 1971, Color, 90 min, VT

Producers: David L. Wolper and Walon Green; **Director:** Green; **Screenplay:** David Seltzer; **Music:** Lalo Schifrin; **Cinematography:** Ken Middleman, Helmut Barth, and Green; **Sound Effects:** Charles L. Campbell and David Ronne; **Consultants:** Roy Snelling and Dr. Charles Hogue; **Cast:** Lawrence Pressman, Conlan Carter

The Hellstrom Chronicles is a witty and engaging pseudo-documentary that proposes that humans' days on Earth might possibly be numbered, not, for once, because of nuclear holocaust or environmental carelessness, but because the insects of the world are tougher and more durable than people, and possibly because they're more determined to survive.

This is a fairly frightening film. Granted, the filmmakers had that end in mind and did everything they could (including stretching the truth and drawing somewhat improbable conclusions at times) to unnerve viewers. Indeed, those who already live in fear of the insect world may find some portions of this movie impossible to watch. The narration is structured and purposely repetitive to hammer home the horrible danger to come.

The running story is a catalog of how insects are better suited to survive every disaster to which humans are susceptible, and the conceit works well. During the film's initial release, people walked out of theaters watching for passing bugs, as if their lives depended on it. The effect was short lived, of course. But the movie made its point then and still holds up effectively now.

Additionally, the photography throughout is excellent, even breathtaking. A trio of top cinematographers brought in astounding insect footage of that time and beyond. As to the science, like most projects of this nature as noted above, some of it is fudged, but it's still

not bad as a layperson's crash course in entomology. Indeed, the film won the 1971 Academy Award for best documentary.

HERBERT WEST: RE-ANIMATOR (aka: H.P. LOVECRAFT'S HERBERT WEST: RE-ANIMATOR, RE-ANIMATOR)

Empire Pictures, 1985, Color, 86 min, VT, LD, DVD

Producer: Brian Yunza; **Director:** Stuart Gordon; **Screenplay:** Dennis Paoli, William J. Norris, and Gordon; **Music:** Richard Band; **Cinematography:** Mac Ahlberg; **Special Effects:** Bret Culpepper; **Cast:** Jeffrey Combs, Bruce Abbott, Barbara Crampton, Robert Sampson, David Gale

Herbert West (Combs) is a medical student at Miskatonic University. His wild theories aren't sitting well with the staid head of the somber institute of higher learning, in particular his claim to be able to reanimate the dead. So Herb has to sneak around morgues, acting the standard mad scientist to prove his theories.

Herbert's skulking about is drenched in blood, gore, and the blackest of humor. Both *Re-Animator* and its sequel, *Bride of Re-Animator*, are strong stuff for the viewer—graphic, gruesome, and somewhat sexually explicit. But for those who like this kind of material, these are two nifty gems. The performances, especially that of the wildly talented Jeffrey Combs as West, are superb. And if at times they seem over the top, viewers should remember (as many critics failed to do) that such performances are not only appropriate, but essential in such films. Sensible audiences shouldn't expect a mad scientist performance to resemble Hamlet. A film like this calls for convincing lunacy, and Combs delivers. The actor was unknown at the time, but his many subsequent big-screen and television roles have proven him both a fine comedian and can accomplished straight dramatic performer—in other words, an excellent choice for the difficult role of Herbert West.

Despite the considerable liberties taken with its source material, macabre horror master H.P. Lovecraft's *Herbert West: Re-Animator*, this film may yet be judged the most faithful adaptation of Lovecraft's fiction to date. Lovecraft admitted on more than one occasion that he had neither the ability nor the inclination to make conventional character and plot development central to his stories. Instead, what he sought was the evocation of a particular mood of cosmic dread (or in the case of the confessedly schlocky *Herbert West: Re-Animator*, a mood of "necrolatrous" delirium). Lovecraft poses a major challenge to any film adaptation, commercial or otherwise, since much of the effect of the original stories is wrought by Lovecraft's inimitable prose style, something that cannot be transferred easily to the screen. In other words, any viable Lovecraft movie is going to have to deconstruct then reconstruct the original, introducing characters and plot developments as a narrative skeleton for the flesh of the original. Both *Re-Animator* films accomplish this quite handily.

Most Lovecraft aficionados consider *Herbert West: Re-Animator* the best screen adaptation of the horror master's work to date, but it is mostly a conglomeration of elements from the various West stories. *Herbert West-Reanimator* was originally a collective title for a series of six short stories featuring the mad doctor and his hapless unnamed assistant (Dan Cain in the movie). Various themes, story ideas, and characters from the stories found their way into the film and its sequel.

BRIDE OF THE RE-ANIMATOR opens with West and Cain in the midst of a Latin America country, treating war casualties before returning to New England. To keep the disillusioned Cain, whose girlfriend was killed in the first movie, working with him, West now proposes that they try to patch together a body in which to place her heart so that she may live again.

Note: There are in a sense not two but three *Re-Animator* films. The R-rated version of the first movie is surprisingly different from the unrated version. The editors had to snip quite a bit of blood-spewing footage to get an R-rating. What is surprising is the amount of R-rated replacement footage missing from the unrated version, presumably because of length. The R-rated version contains several minutes of transitional scenes that improve the continuity of the story. Other details not in the unrated version include a revealing scene where Cain catches West shooting up with the insidious reagent serum. That way, West can get by without having to sleep, a problem no viewer should have after watching these films.

HERRN DER WELT, DER (THE MASTER OF THE WORLD)

Ariel-Film (Germany), 1935, b&w, 90 min

Director: Harry Piel; **Screenplay:** George Muehlen-Schulte; **Cast:** Walter Janssen, Sybille Schmitz

In the future, machinery does all the work humankind could possibly desire it to do, including killing. Sounds just like today, doesn't it?

H.G. WELLS' NEW INVISIBLE MAN

See *THE INVISIBLE MAN; THE NEW INVISIBLE MAN*

H.G. WELLS' THINGS TO COME

See *THINGS TO COME*

HIDDEN, THE

New Line Cinema, 1987, Color, 98 min, VT, LD, DVD

Producers: Robert Shaye, Gerald T. Olsen, and Michael Meltzer; **Director:** Jack Sholder; **Screenplay:** Bob Hunt; **Music:** Michael Convertino; **Cinematography:** Jacques Haitkin; **Special Effects:** Michael Backanskas; **Cast:** Kyle MacLachlan, Michael Nouri, Ed O'Ross, Clu Gulager, Claudia Christian, Clarence Felder, William Boyett, Richard Brooks

Something has gone wrong in Los Angeles. Ordinary citizens with no previous criminal records are suddenly acting like supercriminals. For no apparent reason, one person after another, men and women alike, are robbing banks, stealing cars, and committing random, wanton acts without the slightest compunction—all while playing the loudest, head-banging heavy metal music possible.

L.A. cop Nouri is perplexed and frustrated, two things that don't change much when F.B.I. agent MacLachlan is partnered with him on the case. What they learn is that an alien criminal that can hide within the bodies of human hosts arrived in the City of Angels. Once inside, it can direct its captives to do whatever it wants done—steal, murder, overeat, and generally have a good time cramming one exciting pleasure after another into its days. When its hosts are worn out or killed, it simply finds another.

The thing can be killed only when outside its hosts, and then only by alien technology—technology MacLachlan is carrying because he's an alien as well. As the film progresses the human and alien lawmen discover their foe's ultimate plan. He's going to try to take over the body of the politician most likely to become the United States's next president.

The Hidden is a great action/adventure film. The science is all mummery, but everything else is right on the money in this fast-moving, well-directed thrill ride. Critic Roger Ebert described the film as ". . . a cross between *INVASION OF THE BODY SNATCHERS* and *THE TERMINATOR*."

Note: As good as *The Hidden* is, however, its inevitable sequel is not. *The Hidden II* does not have the cast, the pacing, the motion, the excitement, the plot, or the heart of its predecessor. Supposedly 15 years later, Nouri's daughter is a policewoman when another alien comes to Earth, and she helps another alien sheriff track it down.

HIDDEN II, THE

New Line Cinema, 1994, Color, 91 min, VT, LD

Producers: David Helpern, Michael Meltzer, and Mark Ordesky; **Director:** Seth Pinsker; **Screenplay:** Pinsker; **Music:** David McHugh; **Cinematography:** Bryan England; **Cast:** Ralph Sbarge, Kate Hodge, Jovin Montanaro, Christopher Murphy, Michael Weldon, Michael Nickles

See *THE HIDDEN*

HIDDEN HAND, THE

Warner Bros., 1942, b&w, 68 min

Producer: William Jacobs; **Director:** Ben Stoloff; **Screenplay:** Anthony Coldwey and Raymond Schrock; **Cinematography:** Henry Sharp; **Cast:** Elizabeth Fraser, Frank Wilcox, Craig Stevens

A slight forgettable film involving suspended animation.

HIDDEN POWER

Columbia, 1939, b&w, 60 min

Producer: Larry Darmour; **Director:** Lewis Collins; **Screenplay:** Gordon Rigby; **Cinematography:** James S. Brown, Jr.; **Cast:** Regis Toomey, Jack Holt, Gertrude Michael, Dickie Moore, Holmes Herbert

Compassionate scientist Holt is searching for an all-purpose remedy for pain and suffering. What he discovers instead (don't bother asking how) is an explosive force on a par with nuclear fission. What he doesn't do is give anyone a reason to watch this slow and predictable film.

HIDEOUS SUN DEMON, THE

Pacific International, 1959, b&w, 74 min, VT, DVD

Producer: Robert Clarke; **Directors:** Clarke and Thomas Cassarino; **Screenplay:** E.S. Seeley, Jr. and Doane Hoag; **Music:** John Seely; **Cinematography:** John Morrill, Villis Lapenieks, Jr., and Stan Follis; **Special Effects:** Richard Cassarino; **Cast:** Robert Clarke, Patricia Manning, Fred LaPorta, Nan Peterson, Patrick Whyte, Bill Hampton

A nuclear scientist (Clarke, also the movie's producer and co-director) gets an overdose of radiation. Unlike most people who would, of course, just die, Clarke turns into a hideous lizardlike beast, transforming whenever he is touched by the light of the Sun. He decides to stay out of the Sun for the rest of his life, but blunderingly finds his way into the sunlight again. Soon he falls to his death from a great height, and the audience leaves, looking for a great height from which they can jump.

HIGHLANDER

Highlander Productions, 1986, Color, 111 min, VT, LD, DVD

Producers: Gregory Widen, Peter Bellwood, and Larry Ferguson; **Director:** Russell Mulcahy; **Screenplay:** Bellwood, Widen, and Fergeson; **Music:** Michael Kamen and Queen; **Cinematography:** Gerry Fisher, B.S.C.,; **Special Effects:** Martin Gutteridge, Bob Keen, Graham Longhurst, Nick Maley, and Bert Luxford; **Cast:** Christopher Lambert, Sean Connery, Clancy Brown, Roxanne Hart, Beatie Edney, Alan North

The action begins in the vast parking garage underneath Madison Square Garden. Two men are locked in mortal combat, the huge humanmade cavern ringing with the sound of clashing steel. It's a sword-on-sword duel to the death, despite the fact that it's also present-day New York City, where slightly more sophisticated weaponry should be available. No matter, the contest ends soon enough when one of the combatants, Conner MacLeod (Lambert), decapitates his opponent. The headless body falls to the ground, while out of nowhere a whirlwind of energy floods the chamber, entering MacLeod's body, destroying half the cars in the garage at the same time.

Suddenly the year is 1536. The location has shifted to the Scottish Highlands, but Lambert is there as well, a slightly younger man riding off to his first war. During the battle he is given a mortal wound by a fearsome giant of a man (Brown). He is not expected to survive the night, and yet somehow he gets up in the morning—completely healed. His family, neighbors, even his girlfriend condemn his survival as sorcery. If not for the intervention of his closest friend he would be executed as a witch. Instead, he is exiled from his home, in a state of confusion.

The confusion doesn't last, though. MacLeod is told that he is an immortal by Ramirez (Connery), another immortal who feels it his duty to prepare the Highlander for battle against the worst of all the immortals, Kurgan, the giant MacLeod had met previously. Ramirez instructs his student in the ways of the sword and the philosophy of battle. He also explains his and the Highlander's immortality to his student.

They are part of a select group who must face each other in combat. They have no choice. They are fighting for "the prize," which only one of them may possess—the last one. They cannot be killed in any way except through the complete separation of their head from their body. They also do not age, nor can they father children.

The film continues to cut back and forth between the past and the present, until finally there are only two immortals remaining: MacLeod and Kurgan. They face each other in a duel to the death, one that MacLeod doesn't seem capable of winning. Of course, the hero does win, and the prize is his. In the last minutes we find that the prize is the end of his immortality. He now has all the knowledge of humankind within his head, but, more important, he can now marry and grow old, have children, watch them grow, pass on his knowledge and, the most cherished part of all, he can finally die.

Highlander is an excellent film. Short on sci-fi elements outside of immortality, it makes up for that with some of the most exciting modern filmmaking techniques ever seen. The film exhibits extraordinary control over the storytelling. There is no meandering, no wasted seconds. The man responsible, director Mulcahy, came from a background of both music videos and low-budget foreign (Australian) films, so perhaps the rapid cuts and economy are easily explained.

"He [Mulcahy] is so quick," Lambert explained, "he can shoot in a day what other people would shoot in two days. And what ends up on the screen is fantastic. Talent is something you have—you don't learn it. You have it or you don't."

About his own character, Lambert said, "The guy is immortal. He can do anything he wants to and nobody can kill him—but there's something very sad about that. There's a strange duality to the character."

Sadly, the studio edited the film and not only chopped out minutes, but added the disastrously inappropriate songs by rock band Queen, which, although intrusive, luckily do not destroy the scenes onto which they were plastered. The European cut of the film is superior.

Be careful, however, not to allow the majesty of the first film to raise hopes for the sequels, *Highlander II: The Quickening*, *Highlander—The Final Dimension*, or *Highlander: Endgame*. *Highlander II: The Quickening* ignores (or at least contradicts) much of the first film, adding several terribly irrelevant science fiction elements, and features forgettable performances by both Lambert and Connery. *Highlander—The Final Dimension* contradicts points of both previous films as well as the subsequent television series.

Don't be quick to blame director Mulcahy for the problems with *Highlander II*, however. The picture was shot in Argentina. Word is that during filming the country's inflation rate shot skyward so rapidly that the production's insurance company seized control of the film. Afraid the filmmaker didn't know what he was doing, they made the movie into one they felt would make the most money. When the final cut was screened for Mulcahy, it is reported he walked out after the first 15 minutes, like members of audiences everywhere.

The MacLeod immortals, Conner (Lambert) from the HIGHLANDER films and Duncan (Paul) from the first *Highlander* television series, join forces to battle powerful magician Kell (Payne). While the swordplay and action are adequate, the plot fails to adequately explain the discrepancies and connections among the films in the series and the television version spin-off based on the same story lines. The plot is also remarkably difficult to follow for audiences unfamiliar with all aspects of the entire *Highlander* saga, and so the film appeals to die-hard fans only.

Note: The castle in which Conner lives during his marriage is the same castle used for interior shots in *Monty Python and the Holy Grail*.

HIGHLANDER: ENDGAME

Dimension, 2000, Color, 87 min

Producers: Bob Weinstein, Harvey Weinstein, Peter Davis, William N. Panzer, Cary Granat, H. Daniel Gross, Robert Bernacchi, Beth Anne Calabro, Patrick Peach, and Jean-Claude Schlim; **Director:** Douglas Aarniokoski; **Screenplay:** Gillian Horvath, Joel Soisson, and Panzer; **Music:** Nick Glennie-Smith; **Cinematography:** Douglas Milsome; **Special Effects:** Nick Allder, Terry Schubert, Jeff Clifford, Garth Inns, Alison Savitch, Michael Sagol, and Greg Nelson; **Cast:**

Christopher Lambert, Adrian Paul, Bruce Payne, Lisa Barbuscia, Donnie Yen, Ian Paul Cassidy, Adam Copeland, Jim Byrnes, Peter Wingfield, Damon Dash, Beatie Edney, Sheila Gish, Douglas Aarniokoski

See *HIGHLANDER*

HIGHLANDER II: THE QUICKENING

Lamb Bear Entertainment, 1991, Color, 88 min, VT, LD, DVD

Producers: Jean Luc Defait, Ziad El Khoury, Guy Collins, Jack Cummins, Peter Davis, Mari Provenzano, Maio Sotela, Robin Clark, and Alejandro Sessa; **Director:** Russell Mulcahy; **Screenplay:** Peter Bellwood; **Cinematography:** Phil Meheux; **Music:** Stewart Copeland; **Special Effects:** San Nicholson, Jesse Silver, and John Richardson; **Cast:** Christopher Lambert, Sean Connery, Virginia Madsen, Michael Ironside, John C. McGinley, Allan Rich, Phil Brock, Rushy Schwimmer

See *HIGHLANDER*

HIGHLANDER—THE FINAL DIMENSION

Dimension, 1994, Color, 99 min, VT, LD, DVD

Producers: Eric Altmeyer, Mychele Boudrias, Jean Cazes, Guy Collins, James Daly, Claude Leger, and Charles L. Smiley; **Director:** Andy Morahan; **Screenplay:** Peter Ohl; **Cinematography:** Steven Chivers; **Music:** J. Peter Robinson; **Special Effects:** Charles Carter, Louis Craig, Marc Fiquet, Tony Fox, Stuart Galloway, and Stephen Dupuis; **Cast:** Christopher Lambert, Mario Van Peebles, Deborah Unger, Mako, Raoul Trujillo, Martin Neufield, Michael Jayston

See *HIGHLANDER*

HIGHLY DANGEROUS

Two Cities (Great Britain), 1950/Lippert (U.S.), 1951, b&w, 88 min

Producer: Anthony Darnborough; **Director:** Roy Baker; **Screenplay:** Eric Ambler; **Music:** Richard Addinsell; **Cinematography:** Reginald Wyer and David Harcourt; **Cast:** Dana Clark, Marius Goring, Wilfred Hyde-White, Anthony Newley, Margaret Lockwood, Olaf Pooley, Eric Pohlmann

A scientist (Lockwood) travels into Communist territory on a secret mission and learns that the enemy is preparing a new type of germ warfare to be spread through the use of insects. Old-fashioned storytelling makes for a well-paced, tight, and highly dramatic film.

HIGH TREASON

Gaumont (Great Britain), 1929, 95 min/Tiffany (U.S.), 1930, 69 min, b&w

Producer: L'Estrange Fawcett; **Director:** Maurice Elvey; **Screenplay:** Fawcett; **Cinematography:** Percy Strong; **Cast:** Benita Hume, Jameson Thomas, Raymond Massey, Basil Gill

It's the far-flung future of 1940. The world is enmeshed in conflict. It's the Americas versus Europe in another war to end all wars that features the flooding of the tunnel below the English Channel and the blitzing of New York City. Sometimes science fiction makes remarkable predictions. Sometimes it just makes interesting films. This one is fun to watch, even if just for its humorous (by today's standards) elements.

H-MAN, THE

Toho (Japan), 1958, 87 min/Columbia (U.S.), 1959, 79 min, Color, VT

Producer: Tomoyuki Tanaka; **Director:** Inoshiro Honda; **Screenplay:** Hideo Kaijo and Takeshi Kimura; **Music:** Masaru Sato; **Cinematography:** Hajime Koizumi; **Special Effects:** Eiji Tsuburaya; **Cast:** Kenji Sahara, Koreya Senda, Yumi Shirakawa, Akihiko Hirata

A fishing boat comes across a directionless freighter whose crew seems to have abandoned it. As the fishers search the vessel, however, they find signs that something isn't right. The most worrisome thing: complete sets of clothing scattered here and there, with the shorts inside the pants and undershirts inside blouses. When they find the captain's uniform, however, it isn't quite empty. A rush of green slime pours out of it and up the leg of one of the searchers, and that's how this film gets started.

Residue from an H-bomb test that the freighter passed through gave birth to a deadly new life-form. Thanks to the concerned fishers, the slime, which is actually a creature with a collective mentality, makes it to Tokyo, where it slops its way around the city looking for beautiful women to dissolve with its radioactive touch. As usual in any Japanese science fiction film without a giant monster, the military takes care of the problem in the end. Overall, this is by far one of Toho's better efforts.

Note: The special effects are rather good. The dissolve effect was reportedly achieved by using life-sized inflatable human figures. After dressing and positioning the blow-up dolls, the effects staff then let the air out of them and ran the footage in slow motion. It sounds simple, but the result is truly creepy.

HOLD THAT HYPNOTIST

Allied Artists, 1957, b&w, 61 min

Producer: Ben Schwalb; **Director:** Austen Jewell; **Screenplay:** Dan Pepper; **Music:** Marlin Skiles; **Cinematography:** Harry Neumann; **Cast:** Huntz Hall, Jane Nigh, Stanley Clements, David Condon, Robert Roulk, James Flavin, Queenie Smith, Jimmy Murphy

A hypnotized Huntz Hall regresses to a past life where he gets involved with Bluebeard the Pirate. Time travel and a few good jokes is all this movie has to offer.

HOLLOW MAN

Columbia, 2000, Color, 114 min

Producers: Marion Rosenberg, Stacy Lumbrezer, Douglas Wick, and Allan Marshall; **Director:** Paul Verhoeven; **Screenplay:** Andrew W. Marlowe; **Music:** Jerry Goldsmith; **Cinematography:** Jost Vacano; **Special Effects:** Scott E. Anderson, Alec Gillis, Craig Hayes, Tom Woodruff, Jr., Susan MacLeod, John Fasal, Scott Stokdyk, Eric Armstrong, Anthony LaMolinara, Mark Lasoff, Tippett Studio, Amalgamated Dynamics, Inc., Banned From The Ranch Entertainment, Rhythm & Hues Studios, Inc., Cyber FX Inc., Composite Components Company; **Cast:** Kevin Bacon, Elisabeth Shue, Josh Brolin, Kim Dickens, Greg Grunberg, Joey Slotnick, Mary Randle, William Devane, Rhona Mitra, Pablo Espinosa, Margot Rose

Sebastian Caine (Bacon) is a familiar character in science fiction—the brilliant but arrogant scientist. As *Hollow Man* opens, we find that his genius has been directed toward creating an invisibility serum. He is supposedly working on this project for the benefit of the U.S. government, but when dealing with the likes

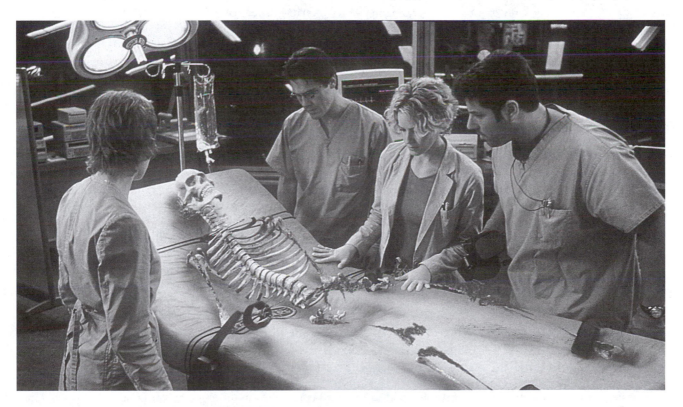

Hollow Man (SONY PICTURES / AUTHORS COLLECTION)

of Doctor Caine, one must question whether or not he's really only working for himself.

At the picture's opening, Caine and his staff have already cracked the problem of rendering living tissue invisible and are confronted with the issue of making it reappear. Caine's brilliance soon delivers, however, and, in a mind-boggling series of special effects, an invisible gorilla is made to reappear from the inside out—veins, organs, skeleton, flesh, skin, hair, all taking shape before the eye. It is the moment Caine has been waiting for, but he's still unwilling to turn his results over to the government before he has made it work on a human being.

Enlisting his top two aides to conceal their recent breakthrough, Caine tests his new formula on himself. Caine's aides, one his former lover who is now involved with the other aide (a situation Caine does not suspect), see a chance to advance their careers at Caine's risk, and agree to the test. Even when Caine has become clearly unstable, the pair never even considers telling anyone the truth. When an insane Caine begins to murder everyone within the government facility to protect his secret, the aides continue to lie until they are forced to kill him. They barely escape the resulting inferno and seem hardly disturbed over killing their one-time friend and boss.

Despite it's landmark special effects, *Hollow Man* lacks direction and any kind of moral center, degenerating quickly into a pointless exercise in bloody splatter. Created by one of the most inventive sci-fi directors of all time, Paul Verhoeven (*STARSHIP TROOPERS*, *ROBOCOP*, *TOTAL RECALL*), the film was surprisingly simplistic and unsatisfactory. Indeed the movie looks dazzling. New special effects software was written specifically for this movie so that the human body is revealed layer by layer, every aspect articulate and rendered in fascinating detail. Even later effects, after Caine is invisible, deliver an impressive view of the invisible man covered in water and moving through steam or smoke. For the first half-hour of the film, it's almost enough to carry the story. Eventually, however, it becomes obvious the film has no real story to tell and certainly no moral compass to guide its statements on its characters actions and experiments. Ultimately *Hollow Man* fails to rise above its roots a B horror film, and a fairly boring one of that.

HOMMUNCULUS

Bioscop (German), 1916, b&w, 24 reels, silent serial

Director: Otto Rippert; **Screenplay:** Rippert and Robert Neuss; **Cinematography:** Carl Hoffmann;

Cast: Olaf Fonss, Friedrich Kuhne, Maria Carmi, Mechtild Their

Hommunculus is a man created by science. As such, he possesses a tremendous intellect but has no soul. Interestingly, he resents having been created by a mere mortal. His intellect allows him to conquer territory, and soon he sets himself up as a dictator. His lack of soul catches up to him, however, as he ends up burned to death by some well-aimed lightning.

This is an important piece of sci-fi film history, if for no other reason it predates and sets up much of what was to follow in the genre. Stock themes such as humans tampering with nature, mad scientists and the super creatures they always seem to be building, the evil that always results when scientific inquiry isn't tempered with humanity or morality, and mandatory big explosions for the ending all have their roots here.

HONEY, I SHRUNK THE KIDS

Walt Disney Productions, 1992, Color, 89 min, VT, LD

Producer: Penny Finnkelman Cox; **Director:** Joe Johnston; **Screenplay:** Stuart Gordon, Ed Naha, Brian Yuzna, and Tom Schulman; **Cinematography:** Hiro Narita; **Special Effects:** Phil Tippett, David L. Hewitt, Peter Kuran, and David Allen; **Music:** James Horner; **Cast:** Rick Moranis, Matt Frewer, Marcia Strassman, Kristine Sutherland, Thomas Brown, Jared Rushton, Amy O'Neil, Robert Oliveri

Timid genius Moranis is a scientist's scientist. He lives his life for the pursuit of knowledge, turning his home into a lab away from the lab and his family into test subjects whenever he can. He works hard for the corrupt and heartless corporation intent on sucking his soul away, then comes home, and works even harder. At present he's working on a shrinking ray. When his and the neighbors' kids invade his lab and get into typical childish horseplay, they shrink themselves to insect size. Soon they're lost at the far end of the backyard, which has become to their sensibilities a vast, impenetrable jungle. What follows is a special effects extravaganza that never loses sight of being a comedy first. This movie is great fun for the whole family.

The theatrical sequel, *Honey I Blew Up the Kid* (this time it's the reverse as the baby of the family is turned *GODZILLA*-sized and sent out to rampage through Las Vegas) and the direct-to-video *Honey, We Shrunk Ourselves* are respectable follow-ups. The second film is not up to the quality of the first, and the direct-to-video release (like most) is not up to the quality of either film. Oddly enough, all of the films were followed by a syndicated television series that often topped its predecessors.

HONEY, I BLEW UP THE KID

Disney, 1992, Color, 89 min, VT, LD

Producers: Albert Band, Dawn Steel, Deborah Brock, Ed Feldman, Stuart Gordon, and Dennis Jones; **Director:** Randel Kieiser; **Screenplay:** Gary Goodrow and Thom Eberhardt; **Cinematography:** John Hora; **Music:** Bruce Broughton; **Special Effects:** Tom Smith, Charles Finance, and Harrison Ellenshaw; **Cast:** Rick Moranis, Marcia Strassman, Robert Oliveri, Daniel Shalikar, Joshua Shalikar, Lloyd Bridges, John Shea, Keri Russell, Ron Canada, Gregory Sierra, Julia Sweeney, Ken Tobey

See *HONEY, I SHRUNK THE KIDS*

HONEY, WE SHRUNK OURSELVES

Disney, 1997, Color, 98 min, BT, LD

Producer: Barry Bernardi; **Director:** Dean Cundy; **Screenplay:** Nell Scovell and Joel Hodgson; **Cinematography:** R.C. Biggs, Tim Landry, and Matt Kutcher; **Cast:** Rick Moranis, Eve Gordon, Robin Bartlett, Allison Mack, Jake Richardson, Bug Hall, Stuart Pankin

See *HONEY, I SHRUNK THE KIDS*

HORRIBLE DR. HITCHCOCK, THE
(aka: THE TERRIBLE DR. HITCHCOCK)

Sigma III (Italian), 1964, 76 min, Color, VT

Producers: Luigi Carpentieri and Ermano Donati; **Director:** Robert Hampton; **Screenplay:** Julyan Perry; **Music:** Roman Vlad; **Cinematography:** Raffaele Masciocchi; **Cast:** Robert Flemyng, Barbara Steele, Teresa Fitzgerald, Maria Teresa Vianello

A somewhat mad doctor (Flemying) obsessed with bringing his dead wife back to life drains the blood of innocent beauties to feed his horrific honey-lamb.

HORRIBLE MILL WOMEN, THE

See *MILL OF THE STONE WOMEN*

HORROR CHAMBER OF DR. FAUSTUS
(aka: EYES WITHOUT A FACE)

Champes-Élysées (French), 1959/Lippert (U.S.), 1962, 95 min, b&w, VT, LD

Producer: Jules Borkon; **Director:** Georges Franju; **Screenplay:** Franju, Claude Sautet, Pierre Boileau, Thomas Narcejac, and Jean Redon; **Music:** Maurice Jarré; **Cinematography:** Eugen Schüfftan; **Special Effects:** Charles-Henri Assola; **Cast:** Pierre Brasseur, Alida Valli, Edith Scob, Juliette Mayniel

Mad doctor Brasseur wants to purify his daughter's horribly scarred face (a scarring in which he had a hand). To this effect he takes skin grafts from the beautiful young women whom he kills. The grafts do not take, and the daughter wanders her fathers moody, shadow-drenched home. While not for everyone, it's considered a classic by many.

HORROR CREATURES OF THE PREHISTORIC PLANET

See *HORROR OF THE BLOOD MONSTERS*

HORROR EXPRESS (aka: PANIC ON THE TRANS-SIBERIAN)

Granada (Spain)/Benmar (Great Britain), 1972, 88 min, Color, VT, DVD

Producer: Bernard Gordon; **Director:** Eugenio Martin; **Screenplay:** Arnaud d'Usseau; **Music:** John Cacavas; **Cinematography:** Alejandro Ulloa; **Special Effects:** Pable Pérez; **Cast:** Peter Cushing, Christopher Lee, Telly Savalas, Silvia Tortosa, Jorge Rigaud

Rival anthropologists Cushing and Lee are transporting the recently discovered body of a prehistoric ape-man on the Tran-Siberian Express when the creature suddenly revives. It turns out that the ape-man is still dead, but not the alien that crash-landed on Earth millions of years back and invaded the poor brute's mind. The alien has the ability to transfer its personality from one host body to another, a power it puts to use aboard the train. This top-notch genre film is long on horror and short on science, but it's well worth watching to enjoy Lee and Cushing in one of their best.

Note: The script for the film was produced only because the producer had gotten his hands on the scale model trains used in the blockbuster drama *Nicholas and Alexandra* and wanted to make a movie in which he could use the period pieces.

HORROR HIGH (aka: TWISTED BRAIN)

Crown-International Pictures, 1974, Color, 85 min, VT

Producer: James P. Graham; **Director:** Larry N. Stouffer; **Screenplay:** James Fowler; **Cast:** Pat Cardi, Rosie Holotik, John Niland, Austin Stoker, Joye Hash

See *DR. JEKYLL AND MR. HYDE*

HORROR OF FRANKENSTEIN

Hammer (Great Britain), 1970, Color, 95 min, VY, LD

Producer: Jimmy Sangster; **Director:** Sangster; **Screenplay:** Sangster and Jeremy Burnham; **Cinematography:** Moray Grant; **Music:** Malcolm Williamson; **Special Effects:** Tom Smith; **Cast:** Ralph Bates, Kate O'Mara, Graham Jones, Veronica Carlson, Bernard Archard, Dennis Price, David Prowse, John Rice

See *FRANKENSTEIN*

HORROR OF PARTY BEACH

20th Century Fox, 1964, 72 min, b&w, VT

Producer: Del Tenny; **Director:** Tenny; **Screenplay:** Richard Hilliard; **Music:** Bill Holmes; **Cinematography:** Hilliard; **Cast:** John Scott, Alice Lyon, Allen Laurel, Eulabelle Moore, Marilyn Clark, the Del-Aires

Radiation combines with various sea creatures and mutates them into a land-faring gaggle of monsters that can't resist terrorizing bikini-clad young women. Luckily, despite the fact that the police force is comically helpless, a local scientist (Laurel) realizes that salt will destroy the monsters. But, wait—didn't the monsters come from saltwater in the first place?

HORROR OF THE BLOOD MONSTERS (aka: VAMPIRE MEN OF THE LOST PLANET, HORROR CREATURES OF THE PREHISTORIC PLANET, SPACE MISSION OF THE LOST PLANET)

Independent International, 1971, 85 min, Color VT

Producer: Al Adamson; **Director:** Adamson; **Screenplay:** Sue McNair; **Music:** Mike Velarde; **Cinematography:** William G. Troiano and Vilmos Zsigmond; **Special Effects:** David L. Hewitt; **Cast:** John Carradine, Bruce Powers, Vicki Volanti, Robert Dix, Brother Theodore, Joey Benson, Jennifer Bishop

Scientist Carradine goes into space to determine the reason why vampirism has broken out on the planet. He discovers that the cause is a virus drifting to Earth from a world where the incredibly different sentient races have been at war for far too long. By this point the audience discovers that's exactly how long they've been in the theater.

HORROR OF THE STONE WOMEN

See *MILL OF THE STONE WOMEN*

HORROR PLANET (aka: INSEMINOID)

Almi Century Distribution, 1982, 86 min, Color, VT, LD, DVD

Producers: David Speechley and Richard Gordon; **Director:** Norman J. Warren; **Screenplay:** Gloria Maley and Nick Maley; **Music:** John Scott; **Cinematography:** John Metcalfe; **Special Effects:** Jeremy Harris and Nick Maley; **Cast:** Robin Clark, Jennifer Ashley, Stephanie Beachman, Steven Grives, Barry Houghton, Victoria Tennant, Judy Geeson

IT! THE TERROR FROM BEYOND SPACE must be the greatest sci-fi movie of all time. At least, that's the conclusion one might draw from the amazing number of times it's been ripped off. This is just another in the line of movies about people in space being eaten by alien creatures on their ship.

HOUSE OF DRACULA

Universal, 1945, b&w, 67 min, VT, LD

Producer: Paul Malvern; **Director:** Erle C. Kenton; **Screenplay:** George Bricker and Dwight Babcock;

Cinematography: George Robinson; **Music:** Paul Dessan, Charles Henderson, William Lava, Hans J. Salter, Paul Sawtell, Charles Previn, and Frank Skinner; **Special Effects:** John P. Fulton and Jack Pierce; **Cast:** Onslow Stevens, Lon Chaney, Jr., Martha O'Driscoll, Jane Adams, Lionel Atwill, Glenn Strange, John Carradine, Skelton Knaggs, Ludwig Stossel

See *FRANKENSTEIN*

HOUSE OF FRIGHT (aka: TWO FACES OF DR. JEKYLL, THE)

Hammer Films (Great Britain), 1960/AIP (U.S.), 1961, 89 min, Color, VT

Producer: Michael Carreras; **Director:** Terence Fisher; **Screenplay:** Wolf Mankowitz; **Music:** Monty Norman and David Heneker; **Cinematography:** Jack Asher; **Special Effects:** Roy Ashton; **Cast:** Paul Massie, Dawn Addams, Christopher Lee, David Kossoff, Francis De Wolff, Norma Marla, Percy Cartwright, Oliver Reed

Dr. Jekyll (Massie) sets to work with his chemicals once more, determined to prove his theory about good and evil. But when he creates Mr. Hyde, there's a Mrs. Dr. Jekyll (Addams) to complicate things. She manages most of the complicating by taking a lover (Lee). Jekyll kills everyone he can get his hands on, saving for last the person he hates the most, Mr. Hyde. One might be curious enough to find out how he manages that trick by watching the movie, but keep in mind this is little more than an overly clever film in which the filmmakers attempt to show how artistic they are by "improving" a classic, a surprising lump of coal from the Santa's Workshop known as Hammer Films, especially coming from the directorial hands of Fisher.

HOUSE THAT WENT CRAZY, THE

Selig, 1914, b&w, silent short

An unwitting thief breaks into an automated house and lives to regret it as his entry causes the house to go berserk.

HOWARD THE DUCK

Universal, 1986, Color, 111 min, VT, LD

Producers: George Lucas, Gloria Katz, and Robert Latham Brown; **Director:** Willard Huyck; **Screenplay:** Katz, Huyck, and Steve Gerber; **Music:** John Barry, Thomas Dolby, and Sylvester Levay; **Cinematography:** Richard H. Kline; **Special Effects:** Barbara Affonso, Jay Ignaszewski, Greg Childers, Mary Brenneis, Ruben Goldberg, Jon Alexander, Bob MacDonald, Jr., Raymond Robinson, Dan Nelson, Jeff Marz, and Michael J. McAlister; **Cast:** Lea Thompson, Jeffrey Jones, Tim Robbins, Paul Guilfoyle, Holly Robinson, Miles Chapin, Virginia Capers, David Paymer, Thomas Dolby, Richard Kiley

A science experiment conducted by screwball doctor Jones goes wrong, reaching into a parallel dimension and bringing back one of its residents. The unfortunate abductee? A life-size, three-dimensional cartoon duck named Howard. The sarcastic cigar-smoking fowl befriends a rock 'n' roll redhead (Thompson), who helps him adjust to his new world.

Adapted from the Marvel Comic created by Steve Gerber, *Howard the Duck* is considered a failure by legions of moviegoers, which may be an exaggeration. It isn't the most perfectly paced picture ever made, but it is well acted and directed. It offers terrific special effects and is remarkably faithful to the comic book, which also featured long sequences that didn't go anywhere. Those who are not fans of the comic may find it a strange, silly movie, but fans will find it's exactly what was promised.

HOUSE OF FRANKENSTEIN

Universal, 1944, b&w, 71 min, VT, LD

Producer: Paul Malvern; **Director:** Erle C. Kenton; **Screenplay:** Edward T. Lowe; **Cinematography:** George Robinson; **Music:** H.J. Salter; **Special Effects:** John P. Fulton; **Cast:** Boris Karloff, J. Carrol Naish, George Zucco, Lon Chaney, Jr., Elena Verdugo, Anne Gwynne, Lionel Atwill, Peter Coe, Glenn Strange, Sig Tumann, John Carradine

See *FRANKENSTEIN*

H.P. LOVECRAFT'S HERBERT WEST: RE-ANIMATOR

See *HERBERT WEST: RE-ANIMATOR*

HUMAN DUPLICATORS, THE

Woolner/Crest, 1965, 81 min, Color, VT

Producers: Hugo Grimaldi and Arthur Pierce; **Director:** Grimaldi; **Screenplay:** Pierce; **Music:** Gordon

Zalder; **Cinematography:** Monroe P. Askins; **Special Effects:** John Chambers; **Cast:** George Macready, Richard Kiel, George Nader, Barbara Nichols, Richard Arlen, Hugh Beaumont, Dolores Faith

Scientist Macready wants to create a race of androids. All he succeeds in doing is to help pave the way for an alien invasion. Kolos (Kiel), an android from the stars, comes to Earth, determined to use Macready's androids for his own purposes. He usurps Macready's experiment and is ready to deliver Earth to his superiors until he falls in love. An extremely low budget doesn't help, but the filmmakers did their best and turned out a film that's not awful but not really worthwhile, either.

HUMANOID, THE

Columbia, 1979, 99 min, Color

Producer: Georgia Venturini; **Director:** George B. Lewis; **Screenplay:** Adriano Bolzoni and Aalso Lado; **Music:** John Williams; **Cinematography:** Silvano Ippolito; **Special Effects:** Armando Valcauda; **Cast:** Richard Kiel, Ivan Rassimov, Barbara Bach, Leonard Mann, Corinne Clery, Marco Yeh

Heroic space pilot Golob (Kiel) is captured by evil scientist Grael (Rassimov). The bad guy puts a synthetic brain into the good guy's body. This makes Grael's boss, Lady Agatha (Bach), think that it's a good time to invade Earth. Think again, Aggie. Have you forgotten Golob's valiant pals, Gibson, Tom Tom, and Nick? Doubtless, this is one of the worst movies ever made, and so bad it may not ever have even been shown in the United States, despite having been made by an American studio.

HUMANOIDS FROM THE DEEP

New World Pictures, 1980, 80 min, Color, VT, LD

Producers: Roger Corman, Hunt Lowry, and Martin B. Cohen; **Director:** Barbara Peeters; **Screenplay:** Cohen, Frank Arnold, and Frederick James; **Music:** James Horner; **Cinematography:** Daniel Lacambre; **Special Effects:** Roger George, Steve Johnson, Kenny Myers, and Shawn McEnroe; **Cast:** Doug McClure, Ann Turkel, Vic Morrow, Cindy Weintraub, Anthony Penya, Denise Galik

Mutant salmon (don't ask) come onto land in search of beautiful women for mating. No, this is not a joke. It's low-brow junk saved from being utterly dismissible by one small quirk. Even though the movie has a standard sci-fi/horror movie setup, the traditional male heroes are absolutely incapable of stopping even one of the creatures. Grandmothers can kill them. Children, beauty queens, and everyone else in the film seem to have no trouble stopping these creatures except poor Doug McClure and his pal.

HUMAN VAPOR, THE

Toho (Japan), 1960/Columbia (U.S.), 1961, 80 min, Color

Producer: Tomoyuki Tanaka; **Director:** Inoshiro Honda; **Screenplay:** Takeshi Kimura; **Music:** Kunio Miyauchi; **Cinematography:** Hajime Koizumi; **Special Effects:** Eiji Tsuburaya; **Cast:** Tatsuya Mihashi, Kaoru Yachigusa, Yoshio Tsuchiya

A criminal is gifted with the power to turn himself into vapor with the speed of thought. Suddenly, his line of work looks a lot easier.

HYDRA (1973)

See ZAAT

HYDRA (1986)

See THE SEA SERPENT

HYPERBOLOID OF ENGINEER GARIN

Gorky (U.S.S.R.), 1965, 96 min, b&w

Producer: M. Berdicevski; **Director:** Berdicevski; **Screenplay:** I. Manevic and A. Ginzburg; **Cast:** E. Evstigneev, V. Safonov, N. Astangov

A mad scientist tries to destroy the world with his evil death ray, but surprise, surprise, he fails.

HYPNOTIC SPRAY, THE

Gaumont (Great Britain), 1909, b&w, silent short

A mere boy comes into possession of the title's diabolical potion, a spray that robs those with whom it comes into contact of their will power.

I

I AIM AT THE STARS

Columbia, 1960, b&w, 107 min

Producer: Charles H. Scheer; **Director:** J. Lee Thomson; **Screenplay:** Jay Drather; **Music:** Laurie Johnson; **Cinematography:** Wilkie Cooper; **Cast:** Curt Jurgens, Victoria Shaw, Gia Scala, Herbert Lom

This fictionalized—odd, considering that the truth should have been interesting enough—account of the troubles former Nazi scientist Wernher von Braun had in adjusting to life in the United States adds up to a pointless waste of time.

ICEMAN

Universal, 1984, Color, 99 min, VT, LD

Producers: Patrick J. Palmer and Norman Jewison; **Director:** Fred Schepisi; **Screenplay:** Chip Proser and John Drimmer; **Music:** Bruce Smeaton; **Special Effects:** Thomas L. Roysden, Michael Westmore, and Michele Burke; **Cinematography:** Ian Baker; **Cast:** Timothy Hutton, Lindsay Crouse, John Lone, Josef Sommer, David Strathairn, Danny Glover, James Tolkan

A Neanderthal man (Lone) is found frozen in the ice, perfectly preserved. In fact, he is so perfectly pre-served, modern science is able to bring him back to consciousness. Of course, everyone wants to study him. Everyone, that is, save scientist Hutton, who wants to get to know the Neanderthal as a person. Unfortunately, this leads to people dying and other complica-tions. Luckily, this primitive savage who most likely murdered on a daily basis is more civilized than every-one he meets in his new world and manages to put things right at the end. This movie handles its science fiction angles well, and it is beautifully filmed and won-derfully scored, but the story is silly and juvenile.

ICE PIRATES

MGM, 1984, Color, 91 min, VT, LD

Producer: John Foreman; **Director:** Stewart Raffill; **Screenplay:** Raffill and Stanford Sherman; **Music:** Bruce Broughton; **Special Effects:** Bill Cobb and Max W. Anderson; **Cinematography:** Matthew F. Leonetti; **Cast:** Robert Urich, Mary Crosby, Michael D. Roberts, John Matuszak, Anjelica Huston, Ron Perl-man, John Carradine, Robert Symonds

In the future water is a rare commodity, despite the fact that civilization has reached the point of building star-ships and robots. It has also perfected cryogenics, cloning, and the disintegrator beam, but they can't fig-ure out how to synthesize water from simple hydrogen and oxygen, paving the way for a booming black market for H²O, which is where the Ice Pirates come in. The script is funny and inventive, and the spoofing of science fiction concepts is handled imaginatively, but poor direction and cinematography bring it all down.

I COME IN PEACE (aka: DARK ANGEL)

Media Home Entertainment, 1990, Color, 92 min, VT, LD

Producers: Jeff Young and Mark Damon; **Director:** Craig R. Baxley; **Screenplay:** Leonard Maas and Jonathan Tydor; **Music:** Jan Hammer; **Special Effects:** Bruno Van Zeebroeck; **Cinematography:** Mark Irwin; **Cast:** Dolph Lundgren, Brian Benben, Betsey Brantley, Matthias Hues, David Ackyroyd, Jay Bilas, Sherman Howard, Mark Lowenthal, Michael J. Pollard, Jesse Vint

A bad guy alien arrives on Earth. Remarkably, he looks so Californian that one might suspect he came to surf, but no, he's really here to steal people's endorphins, which are like heroin to his race. Alien Lundgren pursues the bad guy because he's a cop. *THE HIDDEN* did it better than this bland take on an old science fiction theme.

I EAT YOUR SKIN
(aka: VOODOO BLOODBATH)

Cinemation, 1971, b&w, 82 min, VT

Producer: Del Tenney; **Director:** Tenney; **Screenplay:** Tenney; **Music:** Lon E. Norman; **Special Effects:** Guy Del Russo; **Cinematography:** Francois Farkas; **Cast:** William Joyce, Heather Hewit, Betty Hyatt Linton, Walter Coy, Dan Stapleton, Robert Stanton

A mad scientist uses the radioactive venom of mutant snakes to create an army of zombies to do his terrible bidding. One might wonder why someone bothered to make a black-and-white movie in the '70s, but the truth is they didn't. Filmed close to 10 years earlier, this one sat on a shelf for a long time before someone worked up the courage to release it.

IF

London Films (Great Britain), 1916, b&w, 4,800 feet, silent

Director: Stuart Kinder; **Cast:** Judd Green, Irish Delaney

A mad scientist using Flash Gordonesque flying ships and really big guns devastates London. Visitors on field trips to the Museum of Silent Film Studies can safely leave this one in the vault.

IKIARA XB 1 (aka: VOYAGE TO THE END OF THE UNIVERSE)

Cekoslovensky Filmexport (Czechoslovakia)/AIP (U.S.), 1963, b&w, 81 min

Director: Jindrich Polak; **Screenplay:** Pavel Juracek and Polak; **Music:** Zdenek Liska; **Cinematography:** Jan Kalis; **Cast:** Zdenek Stepanek, Radovan Lakavsky, Dana Medricka, Irene Kova, Francis Smolen

It's the 25th century and the crew of a gigantic space-going research vessel are the focus of our attention. The mixed-gender crew mostly go about their daily routine (which is surprisingly quirky and clever) until they are menaced by radiation emitted by a black star. Escaping that, they head on to a populated planet they have discovered. Surprise, it's Earth. Though only the least perceptive of viewers will be caught off-guard by the twist ending, this is an interesting film, especially scenes such as the one where the crew encounters the U.S.S. *Capitalist* (complete with corpses sitting around a dinner table in 19th-century top hats, no less) adrift in space.

ILLUSTRATED MAN, THE

Warner Bros./7 Arts, 1969, Color, 103 min, VT

Producers: Howard B. Kreitsek and Ted Mann; **Director:** Jack Smight; **Screenplay:** Kreitsek; **Music:** Jerry Goldsmith; **Special Effects:** Ralph Webb; **Cinematography:** Philip Lathrop; **Cast:** Rod Steiger, Claire Bloom, Robert Drivas, Don Dubbins, Jason Evers, Tim Weldon, Christie Matchett

Carnival worker Steiger is the title's illustrated man. His body is completely covered in tattoos, but not any ordinary tattoos. These flesh etchings give those who peek glimpses into the future, or other worlds, or far-off places. The film delivers three such peaks, which according to most viewers is two too many. One reveals a world where it never stops raining. In another, children use a jungle playroom to get rid of their parents. In the third, it's the last night before the end of the world. After hours, all the adults plan to kill their offspring gently to spare them the pain coming in the morning. Sometimes, filmmakers treat Ray Bradbury's work with respect and sometimes they don't. Since the conceit of the illustrated man to string together a collection of previously written stories in one anthology didn't work all that well in the book, the film is no surprise. Of the three stories chosen—"The Veldt," "The Long Rains," "The Last Night Of The World"—only "The Veldt" is a fair adaptation.

I LOVE YOU, I KILL YOU

Uwe Brandner (West Germany), 1971/New Yorker Films (U.S.), 1972, Color, 94 min

Producer: Uwe Brandner; **Director:** Brandner; **Screenplay:** Brandner; **Music:** Brandner, Kid Olanf, and Heinz Hetter; **Cinematography:** André Debreuil; **Cast:** Ralph Becker, Hannes Fuchs, Marianne Blomquist

In the future the authorities execute population control through euthanasia. This film remains oddly disturbing and has proven somewhat prescient considering the heated debates in contemporary society of issues such as abortion and assisted suicide.

I'M AN EXPLOSIVE

George Smith Productions (Great Britain), 1933, b&w, 50 min

Producer: Harry Cohen; **Director:** Adrian Brunel; **Screenplay:** Brunel; **Cinematography:** Geoffrey Faithful; **Cast:** Bill Hartnell, Harry Terry, Sybil Grove, Gladys Jennings

A prankster drinks down a liquid explosive. At least, that's the story he gives the government when he sues them. It's all a plot to amass enough money so he can marry the girl he loves. There's not much science fiction here, but it's a genial romp nonetheless.

I MARRIED A MONSTER FROM OUTER SPACE

Paramount, 1958, b&w, 78 min, VT, LD

Producer: Gene Fowler Jr.; **Director:** Fowler, Jr.; **Screenplay:** Louis Vittes; **Special Effects:** John P. Fulton and Charles Gemore; **Cinematography:** Haskell B. Boggs; **Cast:** Tom Tryon, Gloria Talbott, Ken Lynch, John Eldredge, Jean Carson, Maxie "Slapsie Maxie" Rosenbloom, Valerie Allen

On the eve of his wedding day, handsome Bill (Tryon) is abducted by aliens. He's then taken to their ship, where they create an exact duplicate of him. The counterfeit Tom is then sent off to go through with real Tom's plan to marry the beautiful Marge (Talbott). To save their dying planet, the aliens have decided to impregnate Earth women. The only problem with their plan is that the two species are so different, cross pollination isn't an option. Marge starts to catch on that there's something wrong with the man she thought she knew so well. When she discovers just what it is, she tries to tell the FBI, but by that time the aliens control all means of communication. She realizes that if the aliens can't reproduce, then they can't be any of the new fathers in town. Marge gets a strike team together, and they turn the tide.

A silly title disguises what is actually a fair picture. Yet another movie metaphor for the Red Scare, it's often been said that the title of this one could have been *I Married a Communist*. Like THE INVASION OF THE BODY SNATCHERS, this is a well-made and scary little film with a strong story and a great performance from Talbott.

Note: Producer/director Gene Fowler, Jr. was a film editor for the legendary Fritz Lang before coming to Hollywood. As this picture shows, he learned a lot before making the trip.

IMMEDIATE DISASTER (aka: THE STRANGER FROM THE STARS, THE VENUSIAN, STRANGER FROM VENUS)

British-Princess Pictures/Rich And Rich, 1954, b&w, 75 min

Producers: Burt Balaban and Gene Martel; **Director:** Balaban; **Screenplay:** Hans Jacoby; **Music:** Eric Spear; **Special Effects:** Nell Taylor; **Cinematography:** Kenneth Talbot; **Cast:** Helmut Dantine, Patricia Neal, Derek Bond, Arthur Young, Cyril Luckham

Venusian Dantine saves Patricia Neal's life. He then disguises himself as a regular man so he can move about freely on Earth. His goal is to bring our world's leaders together with his much wiser Venusian leaders, who are frankly concerned by our savage use of nuclear power. Dantine tells everyone that they'd better make their decisions soon because there is a Venusian fleet on the way. Unfortunately for Dantine, Neal's fiancé is the jealous type. He can't stand the thought of her thinking anyone else might be a better guy, even a superman from Venus, so he helps plot the destruction of the Venusian fleet. Everything turns out all right, but it doesn't really matter since this is simply a contemptible rip-off of the far superior THE DAY THE EARTH STOOD STILL, even to the point of hiring the same actress to play the damsel.

IMMORTAL MONSTER, THE

See CALTIKI, THE IMMORTAL MONSTER

I, MONSTER

Amicus (Great Britain), 1971/Cannon (U.S.), 1973, Color, 75 min

Producers: Max J. Rosenberg and Milton Subotsky; **Director:** Stephen Weeks; **Screenplay:** Subotsky; **Music:** Carl Davis; **Special Effects:** Harry Frampton and Peter Frampton; **Cinematography:** Moray Grant; **Cast:** Christopher Lee, Mike Raven, Peter Cushing, Richard Hurndall, George Merritt, Kenneth J. Warren, Susan Jameson

Warm and loveable Dr. Marlow (Lee) develops an elixir designed to help people overcome their inhibitions. It's all done with the highest of Freudian motives, but the result is just another kindly doctor turning himself into something repulsive. If the filmmakers had had the decency to title this one *The Strange Case of Dr. Marlow and Mr. Blake*, audiences might have had a chance of knowing what was coming. The cast does a tremendous job with what they have, but they have terribly little. The script is a hackneyed retelling of the Jekyll and Hyde legend.

Note: There is a reason for the occasional bizarre camera setup viewers will experience. Not content with simply stealing from the past rather than coming up with an original idea, the studio also filmed this one in 3-D. It's the only dimension this film has.

IMPULSE

ABC Motion Pictures, 1984, Color, 91 min, VT, LD

Producer: Tim Zinnemann; **Director:** Graham Baker; **Screenplay:** Bart Davis and Don Carlos Dunaway; **Music:** Paul Chihara; **Special Effects:** Greg Curtis and Tom Fisher; **Cinematography:** Thomas Del Ruth; **Cast:** Tim Matheson, Meg Tilly, Hume Cronyn, Bill Paxton, John Karlen, Amy Stryker

The film's heroes visit a town where exposure to a strange chemical has affected the inhabitant's ability to control their impulses. As a result, everyone is acting on their darkest urges. Unfortunately, the surprisingly good cast cannot help the muddled script or ineffective direction.

INCREDIBLE INVASION (aka: SINISTER INVASION, ALIEN TERROR, INVASION SINIESTRA)

Azteca (Mexico)/Columbia (U.S.), 1971, Color, 90 min, VT

Producer: Luis Enrique Vergara; **Directors:** Juan Ibanes and Jack Hill; **Screenplay:** Vergara and Karl Schanzer; **Music:** Enrico C. Cabaiati; **Special Effects:** Enrique Gordillo; **Cinematography:** Raúl Dominguez and Austin McKinney; **Cast:** Enrique Guzman, Maura Monti, Boris Karloff, Tene Valez, Christa Linder, Yerye Beirute, Sergio Kliner

Way back in the 19th century, scientist Boris Karloff stumbles into making first contact with an alien race that does bad things in stupid ways. This is one of a quartet of films that Karloff, the one-time legend of Hollywood horror films, found himself making in Mexico at the time of his death. It's a terrible film, and a terrible last tribute to a man who gave the genre so much.

Note: This movie is reportedly based on an H.P. Lovecraft story, but watching the film does not help determine which one.

INCREDIBLE MELTING MAN, THE

AIP, 1977, Color, 86 min, VT

Producer: Samuel W. Gelfman; **Director:** William Sachs; **Screenplay:** Sachs; **Music:** Arlen Ober; **Special Effects:** Rick Baker and Harry Woolman; **Cinematography:** Willy Curtis; **Cast:** Alex Rebar, Burr DeBenning, Myron Healy, Michael Aldredge, Ann Sweeney, Lisle Wilson, Julie Drazen

Astronaut Rebar returns from a mission to Saturn. As usual in films that "borrow" their plot from the far superior Professor Quatermass outing, THE CREEPING UNKNOWN, he's the only survivor—if he can actually be called that. His flesh is melting off his body, and the only way he can halt the decay is to kill and kill again. This completely forgettable film features some interesting work by a young Rick Baker, but it's not enough to make it worthwhile.

INCREDIBLE PETRIFIED WORLD, THE

GBM Productions, 1958, b&w, 78 min, VT

Producer: Jerry Warren; **Director:** Warren; **Screenplay:** John W. Steiner; **Music:** Josef Zimanich; **Cinematography:** Victor Fisher; **Cast:** John Carradine, Robert Clarke, George Skaff, Allen Windsor, Phyllis Coates, Lloyd Nelson

Scientist Carradine talks four men into exploring the bottom of the ocean in his diving bell, where he then he loses them in the world of tunnels below the ocean. Decent ideas pepper the script, but the acting is so flat one could roll of golf ball across it from here to the Moon. The direction is fairly awful as well.

INCREDIBLE SHRINKING MAN, THE

Universal, 1957, b&w, 81 min, VT, LD

Producer: Albert Zugsmith; **Director:** Jack Arnold; **Screenplay:** Richard Matheson; **Music:** F. Carling and E. Lawrence; **Special Effects:** Clifford Stine; **Cinematography:** Ellis W. Carter; **Cast:** Grant Williams, Randy Stuart, April Kent, Paul Langton, William Schallert, Billy Curtis

Scott Carey (Williams) just wanted to relax on his boat. Instead, he ended up passing through a mysterious radioactive cloud that at first seemed to have left him unaffected. Soon, though, Carey discovers he has lost weight. Then height. After trying for a while to deny what is happening to him, finally he is forced to admit the frightening truth—he is shrinking.

It quickly becomes apparent that science and medicine cannot help him. At first, he tries to deal with his problem rationally, but thanks to unthinking well-wishers, the curious, and the just plain intrusive, Carey begins to regard himself as a freak—a freak he hates. Disaster strikes as he reaches doll size and is left alone to deal with a gargantuan cat. After that fairly terrifying adventure, he confronts an elephantine spider and drops of water that might as well be anvils. Then, with still no cure in sight, so small as to no longer be visible to the naked eye, suddenly everything changes for Carey. At his most helpless he at last sheds his fear of the unknown and becomes the master of his own destiny. Reaching inner peace, he boldly moves forward to become one with the cosmos. Man, thou art dust and unto dust thou shall return.

The science in this movie is ridiculous, but for once that consideration can be put aside. It's only the hard

The Incredible Shrinking Man (UNIVERSAL PICTURES/ R. ALLEN LEIDER COLLECTION)

sciences that suffer here, and these are all flaws that must be sought out since they are not obvious. On the other hand, the social sciences come off nicely. This is a tale of the familiar becoming the unknown, of our ability as a species to deal with change, of our ability to recognize that when the entire world seems to be changing all around, it's usually only we who are changing. It's also a well-crafted metaphor for man's continuing struggle to deal with aging and death.

The Incredible Shrinking Man is one of the best sci-fi films of the '50s, based on the poignant novel *The Shrinking Man* by Richard Matheson. It is one of the most intelligent, well-acted, literate, and inventive pictures of the period, concentrating on larger questions than most films of that decade of *any* kind. It has an excellent soundtrack and special effects that were the best of their type for their time. This thoughtful, eye-opening classic is a must-see and a half.

INCREDIBLE SHRINKING WOMAN, THE

Universal, 1981, Color, 88 min, VT, LD

Producer: Hank Moonjean; **Director:** Joel Schumacher; **Screenplay:** Jane Wagner; **Music:** Suzanne Ciani; **Special Effects:** Bruno Van Zeebroeck; **Cinematography:** Bruce Logan; **Cast:** Lily Tomlin, Charles Grodin, Ned Beatty, Henry Gibson, Elizabeth Wilson, Mark Blankfield, Pamela Bellwood, John Glover, Mike Douglas, Rick Baker

Lily Tomlin plays a housewife whose constant exposure to a variety of household products in just the right doses has left her in the same predicament as Grant Williams in *THE INCREDIBLE SHRINKING MAN*. Regardless of the similarity, this film does not share its predecessor's exalted place in film history. While this was a funny idea for a movie, and Tomlin certainly has the chops to handle the character, it also marked the directorial debut of Joel Schumacher. Outside of Rick Baker's outstanding performance as a gorilla (performed from inside one of his own incredible monkey suits, of course), the only positive thing the critics could say was that it had a true sense of personal style. True enough, Schumacher has style. Sadly, though, that's all he has.

INCREDIBLE TWO-HEADED TRANSPLANT, THE

AIP, 1971, Color, 81 min, VT

Producer: John Lawrence; **Director:** Anthony M. Lanza; **Screenplay:** Lawrence and James Gordon White; **Music:** John Barber; **Special Effects:** Barry Noble and Ray Dorn; **Cinematography:** Jack Steely, Glen Gano, and Paul Hipp; **Cast:** Bruce Dern, Pat Priest, Casey Kasem, Barry Kroger, Albert Cole, John Bloom

Mad (or at least incredibly silly) Doctor Bruce Dern transplants a lunatic killer's head onto the body of a mentally retarded man. The only problem is that he left the retarded man's head in place. Granted, when the two heads talk to each other, their dialogue is as unusual as anything one might ever hope to hear in a lifetime, but so would a Korean opera be if it were played on kazoos. Sadly, if given a choice, one should go with the opera. Even fans of *The Munsters* television show hoping for a color glimpse of the attractive Pat Priest should avoid this movie.

INDEPENDENCE DAY

20th Century Fox, 1996, 145 min, VT, LD, DVD

Producer: Dean Devlin; **Director:** Roland Emmerich; **Screenplay:** Devlin and Emmerich; **Music:** David Arnold; **Special Effects:** Volker Engel and Douglas Smith; **Cinematography:** Karl Walter Lindenlaub, BVK; **Cast:** Will Smith, Bill Pullman, Jeff Goldblum, Mary McDonnell, Judd Hirsch, Margaret Colin, Randy Quaid, Robert Loggia, Brent Spiner, Harvey Fierstein, James Rebhorn, Adam Baldwin, Ross Bagley, Vivica A. Fox, Harry Connick, Jr., James Duval, Lisa Jakub

On July 2nd, an ominous shadow passes over the U.S. astronaut's monument to peace on the surface of the Moon. What is casting the spreading shade is not revealed, but it's clearly large enough to shake the dust on the lunar surface. Down on Earth, listening posts in New Mexico spot the approaching object and quickly identify it as something roughly one-quarter the size of the Moon, that it is closer to Earth than to the Moon, and that it isn't a natural phenomenon of any kind because it's slowing into an orbit.

The listening post informs the Pentagon, which informs the secretary of defense, and he tells the president (Pullman). The president is in the middle of a political crisis. A young fighter pilot war hero, he was swept into office on a wave of idealism, but now everyone seems to hate him for not being able to fix everything instantly. He and his people try to learn what they can, getting half their information from the television news since global communications have been mysteriously disrupted.

Meanwhile, a communications troubleshooter (Goldblum) in New York solves the mystery as the scattered news programs track some three dozen UFOs, each 15 miles in diameter, which break off from the orbiting command ship to assume positions around the world. The aliens are using our satellites to communicate around Earth and coordinate their attack. Goldblum races to Washington, D.C., where his ex-wife, who works for the president, helps him warn the commander-in-chief, allowing top government officials to escape the city moments before it is destroyed by the aliens.

At this point, the film moves into high gear. Cities are destroyed around the globe in waves. NORAD and NATO are decimated. Humanity fights back, but the enemy ships, even their support fighters, are cloaked with impenetrable energy shields that harmlessly dissipate the energy even of nuclear weapons. Only an air force captain (Smith) brings one of their fighters down by blinding it with his jet's parachute, causing it to crash. When he tears open the cockpit of the enemy fighter, he is greeted by a swirl of flailing tentacles. Ducking through, he punches the alien in the head, knocking it out while shouting, "Welcome to Earth!"

It is a rousing line, unexpected but warmly received by audiences after the terrible thrashing the home team has been getting. Smith drags his captive to Area 51, the secret base where a covert branch of the government has been hiding the legendary Roswell saucer for the past 50 years, which just happens to be another

Independence Day (TWENTIETH CENTURY FOX / JOSEPH B. MAUCERI COLLECTION)

downed alien craft. The president has arrived there as well with Goldblum, and there the fate of the world is decided.

Earth's only hope now is for Smith and Goldblum to pilot the old Roswell saucer up to the ship, where they will download into the system a computer virus they hope will cancel the alien fleet's shields at least briefly. If the two can get inside the alien's orbiting command center, if they can download the virus, if they can set off their nuke to disable the ship, and if the remaining forces of the world's combined military can launch a counterstrike in the few minutes of opportunity given them, then America's July 4th Independence Day will become the world's holiday. If not, then slavery and extermination are all that await humankind.

This is one terrific roller coaster ride, a good, old-fashioned alien-bad-guys, them-or-us film that raked in the cash faster than the filmmakers could count it. Despite hollow criticisms from the ranks of the intelligentsia, they deserved it. *Independence Day* may not be a thought-provoking film seeking the answers to humanity's deepest questions, but it is a rollicking good shoot-'em-up. The heroes do the right thing in all matters. The men love their women and vice versa, no matter what the odds. Fathers are good to their kids, and everyone loves their dogs. There are no easy victories. Millions upon millions die in just the first attack. Only a few hours into the war, America's fighting capabilities are down to 15 percent. The good guys are on the run for most of the film's epic 145 minutes, but they never give up, and they make the movie's near 2 1/2-hour running time go by like a snap of the fingers.

The film features remarkable special effects, the cast is well chosen, and the soundtrack is outstanding. And if science has been conveniently reduced to its most simplistic form in many cases, at least it's reasonably accurate. It's not the most detailed of hard science fiction films, but it keeps the audience watching and inspires them to applaud when the picture's over. In some ways that's a rare type of movie.

INDESTRUCTIBLE MAN

Allied Artists, 1956, b&w, 70 min, VT

Producer: Jack Pollexfen; **Director:** Pollexfen; **Screenplay:** Sue Bradford and Vy Russell; **Music:** Albert Glasser; **Cinematography:** John Russell, Jr.; **Cast:** Lon Chaney, Jr., Casey Adams, Marion Carr, Ross Elliot, Stuart Randall, Robert Shayne, Joe Flynn

The evil Butcher Benton (Chaney, Jr.) is finally executed by the state for his terrible crimes. Just before the execution, however, he is visited by his attorney, who, it is revealed, set up the armored car heist gone bad that brought the Butcher down. He also talked the other two men he enlisted to help Butcher into turning state's evidence in hope of tricking his client into revealing where he hid the money from the robbery. The Butcher isn't as stupid as he looks, although he's certainly willing to bet on a long shot. He won't tell the double-dealing attorney what he did with the money, but he does swear to kill him and his two partners in crime. The fact he is behind bars and hours away from the gas chamber does not enter into his equation.

Soon the Butcher is dead, and at least three people are breathing a little easier. But then a doctor (Shayne), who really should have known better, has his assistant (Flynn) bring him Benton's body from the prison for experimentation. Their experiment involves multiplying the cells in the Butcher's body, not bringing him back to life. In fact, the doctor is certain that can't happen. So he's rather surprised when the Butcher's incredible desire for vengeance allows the doctor's machines to bring him back from the dead. Between the gas chamber and the experiments, the Butcher can no longer speak, but he's alive.

As soon as he's reoriented, the Butcher kills the doctor and his assistant and then sets about trying to murder those who got him executed in the first place. Standing in his way is the police detective (Adams) who has been working on this case since the armored car was first robbed. Not only does he have to bring himself to believe that his mission is to recapture a dead man, but he also has to figure out how to take out a bad guy who can't be harmed by bullets or shotguns, thanks to his incredibly multiplied cells.

In the film's finale, heavily armed officers throw everything they have at the Butcher, but to no avail. He cannot be stopped. After he is horribly disfigured by flamethrowers, though, he finally seems to accept that life holds nothing for him. Eluding capture one last time, the Butcher mounts a massive transformer and runs the current that powers the city through his body.

Thus ends the story of Butcher Benton, brought back from the dead, transforming him into an indestructible man, but only as long as he could hold onto his hate. Once that faded, so did his invulnerability, and thus his life.

There's not much science or logic in this film, but there are other reasons to watch it. Like the original THE FLY, this movie screams out to be remade. It has an exciting plot, plenty of romance, and a good deal of action. In the end, the Butcher is brought down in the sewers by cops armed with machine guns, flamethrowers, and bazookas. The special effects are merely perfunctory, but the sequence would lend itself to contemporary effects techniques. Besides the action, the romantic subplot involving a misunderstood girl broadens the story's appeal considerably. After all, a good story is always a good story.

This is also worth a nod as the earliest of the sci-fi/noir films. The entire movie is a police procedural told in voice-overs, actually the concluding report of detective Adams. It is a gritty, by-the-book rundown filled with the kind of Los Angeles insider shots seen only in noir films up until that time. It also incorporates two noir film standard locations: Angel's Flight, the 75-degree incline trolley (no longer in existence), and the Bradbury Building (featured in a number of crime movies). Sci-fi fans will know the latter as the home of the eccentric inventor in BLADE RUNNER, as well as the "Demon With a Glass Hand" episode of the original Outer Limits.

One drawback, however, is the nails-on-a-chalkboard performance of the world's worst character actor, Casey Adams. His turn as the police detective protagonist is awful enough to make the audience squirm in their seats. He is truly the anti-Whit Bissell, and it takes a certain amount of gumption to sit through one of his performances.

Note: Indestructible Man may very well be the sci-fi film in which the following line was first heard: "The newspapers will have a field day." Also, Robert Shayne and Joe Flynn, the two hapless scientists who bring Lon Chaney, Jr., back to life, will possibly be better known to you as the Superman television show's Inspector Henderson (Shayne) and as McHale's Navy's Captain Binghamton.

For would-be screenwriters, Indestructible Man is possibly the best example in Hollywood history of a movie written specifically for one individual. Lon Chaney, Jr., was on the verge of losing his battle with alcoholism. Most studios didn't want to touch him due to his inability to walk correctly, remember lines, or even show up for work. The team of Sue Bradford and Vy Russell did an excellent job of concocting a script that would cover Chaney's deficiencies and give him another chance to play a starring role. Vocal cords burned out, filled with electricity to cover his shakes and staggering, on the run so that he could be off-camera much of the time, they did the best they could and it shows. For quite some time, Chaney hadn't been as good as he is here.

Stock Footage Alert! Look for acres of vintage Los Angeles stock footage, including street scenes, shops, police cars, and more. Enjoy.

INFRA-MAN

Shaw Brothers, 1976, Color, 92 min, VT

Producer: Run Me Shaw; **Director:** Hua-Shan; **Screenplay:** Peter Fernandez; **Special Effects:** E.H. Glass; **Cast:** Li Hsiu-hsien, Wang Hsieh, Yuan Man-tzu, Terry Liu, Tsen Shu-yi, Huang Chien-lung, Lu Sheng

A princess from outer space (Liu) with a gang of all-powerful creatures invades Earth and it's up to—imagine this—not a Japanese superhero this time, but a Chinese one (Hsiu-hsien) to knock their rubber-costumed socks off. This movie has been rabidly listed as a world beater of a knock-the-stuffin'-outta-them flick by loyal fans of the genre, and even the great Siskel and Ebert reportedly listed this as one of their "Guilty Pleasure" movies. Enjoy.

INNERSPACE

Warner Bros., 1987, Color, 120 min, VT, LD

Producers: Steven Spielberg, John Peters, Peter Gruber, and Michael Finnell; **Director:** Joe Dante; **Screenplay:** Chip Proser and Jeffery Boam; **Music:** Jerry Goldsmith; **Special Effects:** Mike Edmonson, James Fredburg, Dennis Muren, Ned Gorman, Harley Jessup, and Michael Wood; **Cinematography:** Andrew Lazlo; **Cast:** Martin Short, Dennis Quaid, Meg Ryan, Kevin McCarthy, Fiona Lewis, Vernon Wells, Robert Picardo, Wendy Schaal, Harold Sylvester, William Schallert, Henry Gibson, Orson Bean, Kevin Hooks, Kathleen Freeman, Dick Miller, Ken Tobey

Handsome Dennis Quaid is a cocky and heroic, if somewhat out-of-control, navy test pilot who has volunteered to be the test subject in a miniaturization project. In this experiment Quaid, along with a submersible vehicle designed to navigate within living organisms, will be reduced to microscopic size and then injected into the body of a rabbit. Once inside, Quaid will see if he can connect the ship to the animal's hearing and vision centers, thus turning the animal into a de facto reconnaissance device.

On the day of the big test, the miniaturization process goes off without a hitch, but then the trouble starts. Trying to save the project from spies, a doctor injects handsome, cocky, heroic Quaid along with his ship, not into the designated test subject, but into not-so-handsome, cocky, or heroic, but far more out-of-control Martin Short.

This sci-fi/spy thriller/comedy obviously owes the hardware of its plot to the far more serious (although not quite so entertaining) 1966 sci-fi film, *FANTASTIC VOYAGE*. Putting a submarine and its crew inside a living creature is all the plot these two share.

Innerspace could have been a bomb. As stated, the best part of its story is borrowed. The rest is fairly routine. What makes up for its lackluster script is Quaid's much better than average portrayal of an action hero and Short's incredible comedic timing. In the hands of two lesser talents, there would have simply been nothing here. These two keep things going nicely, however, providing plenty of laughs and even some interesting notions *FANTASTIC VOYAGE* didn't get around to exploiting. Besides the stars, the movie's good special effects also help hide some of the plot defects as well as its silly science. This movie, as the saying goes, is lots of good clean fun.

Note: SCTV (Second City Television) fans should watch the scene in the doctor's office closely. Yep—that's Andrea Martin and Joe Flaherty in the waiting room. Have fun, kids.

INSECT WOMAN

See *THE WASP WOMAN*

INSEMINOID

See *HORROR PLANET*

INSPECTOR GADGET

Disney, 1999, Color, 85 min, VT, DVD

Producers: Jordon Kerner, Roger Birnbaum Aaron Meyerson, Jonathan Glickman, and Ralph Winter; **Director:** David Kellogg; **Screenplay:** Kerry Ehrin, Zak Penn, and Dana Olsen; **Cinematography:** Adam Greenberg, A.S.C.; **Music:** John Debney and Peter

Afterman; **Special Effects:** Peter M. Chesney, E. Blaine Converse, Kyle Ross Collingsworth, Joe Heffernan, Gintar Repecka, Thomas Zell, William Theisinger, Dream Quest Images, and the Stan Winston Studio; **Cast:** Matthew Broderick, Rupert Everett, Joely Fisher, Michelle Trachtenberg, Andy Dick, Cheri Oteri, Dabney Coleman, D.L. Hugley, Don Adams, René Auberjonois, Frances Bay, Brian George

The movie opens with a fantastic scene of heroism as a cop saves a group of children, a busload of people, and a really cute dog from certain death. The only problem, the heroism is all a dream. The dreamer is John Brown (Broderick), a security guard who wants to be a force for justice, but really isn't equipped for the job—not yet.

Before long, rich, handsome, evil Sanford Scolex (Everett) shows up at the lab Brown guards. Scolex is after the robotics research inside. He gets it, nearly killing Brown in the process while losing his hand to the security guard's heroics. Scolex sees losing his hand as a good thing—it allows him to adorn himself with a robot claw and a snappy new nickname, the Claw.

At the same time, the scientist in charge of the looted facility uses the robots she and her father perfected to bring Brown back from the brink of death—creating an arch adversary for the Claw, Inspector Gadget. Now the forces of good and evil are personified in two men, both in love with the same woman —one of them out to conquer the world, the other to save it.

If all of the above sounds highly overdramatic, especially for the adaptation of an animated cartoon series to the big screen, that's part of the charm of this wily film. The *Inspector Gadget* cartoons were never the wittiest things to begin with. The series was strictly for tots, every episode a cookie-cutter remake of the one before. There was little imagination, no common sense, and nothing much there for adults. But kids loved it.

Like the old Warner cartoons, however, this version of the character has something for adults and kids. The premise is simple—Brown is rebuilt after his accident into "a 21st-century human crime fighting machine," one with 14,000 different devices built into his body. Of course, being something of a dolt, he can barely remember what any of them are and there begins the fun.

This is a fun movie. The story may be simple, but at least it makes sense. There are small editing problems here and there, but no gigantic plot holes, and the gags are snappy enough to keep almost everyone

happy. There are some wonderful bits, from the hospital's public address system paging "Dr. Howard, Dr. Fine, Dr. Howard," a very in Three Stooges joke, to a shot of Mr. T, Odd Job, Tonto, Igor, and others in a Minions Recovery Group. On top of that, the producers were smart enough to bring in Don Adams (*Get Smart*), the original American voice of Inspector Gadget for a voice cameo. So, what could there be to complain about?

Despite its lack of much science fiction outside of its hardware aspects, *Inspector Gadget* is a funny movie for adults and kids that shows the original cartoons as much respect as it does the audience. You could do worse in this world.

IN THE STEEL CABINET OF DR. MABUSE

See *RETURN OF DR. MABUSE*

IN THE STEEL NET OF DR. MABUSE

See *RETURN OF DR. MABUSE*

IN THE YEAR 2889

AIP, 1968, Color, 80 min

Producer: Larry Buchanan; **Director:** Buchanan; **Screenplay:** Harold Hoffman; **Special Effects:** Jack Bennett; **Cinematography:** Robert C. Jessup; **Cast:** Paul Peterson, Billy Thurman, Quinn O'Hara

Once more it's the end of the world. Once more a small bunch of humans constantly run from a larger group of horrible mutants. Once more time is wasted for anyone unlucky enough to watch this sad and tired sack of nonsense. Avoid.

INVASION EARTH 2150 A.D.

See *DALEKS—INVASION EARTH 2150 A.D.*

INVADER

Very Big Motion Picture Corporation, 1992, Color, 95 min, VT

Producers: Philip J. Cook, Ami Artzi, Menahem Golan, and John R. Ellis; **Director:** Cook; **Screenplay:** Cook; **Music:** David Bartley; **Cinematography:** Cook; **Cast:** Hans Bachmann, A. Thomas Smith, Rick

Foucheux, John Cooke, Robert Bidermann, Ralph Bluemke, Allison Sheehy

Alien invaders have completely overrun an American military base. Who can the armed forces of the United States turn to to save their helpless soldiers? Why, an investigative reporter. Who else? Actually, this movie is not as bad as it might sound. Although the budget was somewhere at the bottom of the barrel, the writing was top-notch, and it's evident that whatever budget they had went into the special effects, helping it to hold its own against better-known genre entries.

INVADER (aka: LIFEFORM)

Stargate Entertainment, 1996, Color, 90 min, VT

Producers: Rick Baer and Madelyn Curtis; **Director:** Baer; **Screenplay:** Baer; **Music:** Kevin Kiner; **Special Effects:** Robert Hutchins; **Cinematography:** James Glennon; **Cast:** Cotton Smith, Deirdre O'Connell, Robert Wisdom, Carlos Carrasco, Ryan Phillippe, Raoul O'Conner, Leland Orser, Kevin Cooney, Joesph Romanov, Damm Saleem, Ivan Guevon, Tim Charles

One of NASA's Viking Space Probes returns from its journey to Mars a bit heavier than when it left, and not just because of the soil samples and rock chips it gathered. This one has a stowaway—an armored alien hitchhiker. Our out-of-towner is highly curious. It examines everything it comes in contact with in great detail. In typical Hollywood fashion, the military can't think of anything better to do than kill the alien on sight. After that, the real trouble starts.

INVADER, THE

Spectator Films, 1997, Color, 93 min, VT

Producers: David Newlon, Lawrence McDonald, and Joe Kramer; **Director:** Mark Rosman; **Screenplay:** Rosman; **Music:** Todd Hayen; **Special Effects:** Allen Benjamin, Rudy Beltramello, and Jan-Michael Vincent; **Cinematography:** Greg Middleton; **Cast:** Ben Cross, Sean Young, Daniel Baldwin, Nick Mancuso, Lynda Boyd, Tim Henry, Ken Tremblett, Robert André, Craig Bruhnanski, Joe Maffei, Alan Franz, Howard Storey, Linda Ko

Renn (Cross) is a visitor to our planet from another world. In fact, he's the only visitor from his world we're ever going to meet because the rest of his species has been wiped out by an evil warlike race. Renn, not wanting to remain the last of his kind, searched the universe to find another being with whom he might mate and produce, not just a viable offspring, but a savior for his executed people.

Who is this would-be supermom? Why, little ol' Annie (Young) of Earth, who is the one genetically perfect match for noble Renn in the galaxy. If he can just convince Annie to procreate with him, spawn a child, and then keep both mom and fetus alive long enough for a birth, maybe he'll be able to repopulate his world. But the aliens who eliminated his species have followed him to Earth. Sigh—what's a guy in love to do?

With an ill-conceived plot—after all, if these bad guys can completely eliminate the population of one planet, why not Earth, too?—and genetics that would get booed out of a third grade science fair, not even a good cast and a lot of action can make up for the defects.

INVADERS FROM MARS (1953)

20th Century Fox, 1953, Color, 78 min, VT, LD, DVD

Producer: Edward L. Alperson; **Director:** William Cameron Menzies; **Screenplay:** Richard Blake; **Music:** Raoul Krushaar; **Special Effects:** Gene Hibbs, Anatole Robbins, and Jack Cosgrove; **Cinematography:** John F. Seitz; **Cast:** Helena Carter, Arthur Franz, Jimmy Hunt, Leif Erickson, Hillary Brooke, Bert Freed, Morris Ankrum

Youngster Dave MacLean (Hunt) wakes up from a sound sleep on a dark and scary night. When he is drawn to his bedroom window by a strange light coming from beyond the hill past the edge of his parents' property, we get the same surprise he does, the sight of a flying saucer crash-landing past the ragged fence marking the property line. Soon Dave's father (Erickson) goes off to investigate. As we watch, Dad is sucked beneath the ground in a truly terrifying sequence. But the next morning Dad is home, same as always. Except, thinks young Dave, maybe not quite the same. Dad used to be, well . . . nicer. Not anymore. Before long, Dave witnesses the same changes in his mother as well. Suddenly, both parents seem cold and distant. Nothing he does is right.

Careful investigation reveals small implants at the base of his parents' necks. Dave decides the saucer people put them there and are using them to control his parents. Dave tries to convince others. He tells the police but soon realizes the police have already been taken over just like his parents. Not giving up, Dave tells others who, after a while, investigate and discover that the boy is telling the truth.

Soon the army is called in. The invaders turn out to be massive green-colored humanoids who take their telepathic orders from a tendril-covered head in a glass globe. It seems their saucer didn't crash after all. The alien's technology allowed them to hide it under the ground. They have excavated a tremendous system of tunnels outward from their ship. It is into these tunnels that they pull people down from the surface, making it appear as if they are being sucked into the ground. The army pours into the tunnels and begin the battle for humanity's future. The fighting is tremendous, and then, at the height of the insanity . . . Dave awakens.

It's all been a scary dream. Or has it? Suddenly, there is a bright flash of light at the window. Dave again sees the saucer crash beyond the hill in his backyard. It's happening again!

Despite the seeming melodrama, this is actually an incredible little film. Often lumped with the anti-Communism science fiction films of the '50s, this is certainly a film about paranoia, but it's not the "Red Menace" the filmmakers had in mind.

Invaders From Mars was directed by William Cameron Menzies, the brilliant force behind the look of the 1936 science fiction classic, *THINGS TO COME*. This was not a man who did things by accident. Throughout the film, the camera is positioned to give the viewer a child's-eye view, and the sets were built oversized to make things seem larger. This is a movie about the horrors of puberty, of the alienation and confusion of youngsters who one day have a perfectly normal life and the next find themselves living with parents they no longer know or whom they think they don't know. Menzies didn't have nearly the budget he had in '36, but he managed just fine, though he did have to rely heavily on stock footage. His trademark impressionist sets are more subdued, but his stylish influence is still there, setting up the disturbed world of a child whose parents (the ultimate authority figures) and the police (authority once removed, but even more frightening) have seemingly gone mad.

One can make a strong case that this is another red scare picture. But in this instance that's a fringe benefit and not the main thrust. Either way, even if you just want to enjoy a good flick, this is a fine movie worth anyone's time, but especially great for kids.

It is certainly thousands of times better than the 1986 remake of the same name. Adequate horror director Toby Hooper was not up to the task of remaking this classic. The cast was good enough, but despite a strong beginning, the remake falls into a black hole,

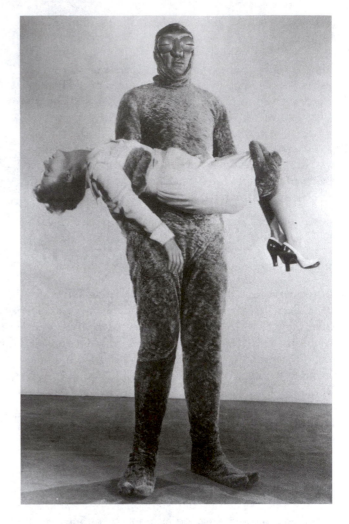

Invaders from Mars (1953) (TWENTIETH CENTURY FOX / R. ALLEN LEIDER COLLECTION)

breaks its leg, and never climbs back out. Be absolutely certain to watch only the 1953 version. Accept no substitutes.

INVADERS FROM MARS (1986)

Cannon Pictures, 1986, Color, 100 min, VT, LD, DVD

Producers: Edward L. Alperson, Jr., Yoram Globus, and Menahem Golan; **Director:** Toby Hooper; **Screenplay:** Richard Blake, Don Jakoby, Dan O'Bannon; **Music:** Sylvester Levay, David Storrs, Christopher Young; **Cinematography:** Daniel Pearl; **Special Effects:** John Dykstra, Richard Rownak, and Robert Shepherd; **Cast:** Karen Black, Hunter Carson, Timothy Bottoms, Laraine Newman, James Karen, Bud

Cort, Louise Fletcher, Eric Pierpoint, Christopher Allport

See *INVADERS FROM MARS*

INVASION

Merton Part (Great Britain)/AIP (U.S.), 1966, b&w, 82 min, VT

Producer: Jack Greenwood; **Director:** Alan Bridges; **Screenplay:** Roger Marshall; **Music:** Bernard Ebbinghouse; **Special Effects:** Ronnie Ebbinghouse, Stan Shields, and Jack Kine; **Cinematography:** James Wilson; **Cast:** Yoko Tani, Lyndon Brook, Eric Young, Anthony Sharp, Stephanie Bidmead, Valerie Gearson, Edward Judd

An alien spacecraft crash-lands on Earth. A wounded female alien survivor is taken to the local country hospital for much-needed emergency treatment. Before long, though, more aliens show up, demanding that the female be turned over to them immediately. When the locals decline to turn the innocent-appearing girl over to these newly arrived, more hostile-seeming aliens, tempers flare and the aliens take over the hospital, surrounding it with a truly impressive force field. Before long, the locals discover that the female alien is a wanted criminal—at least, that's what they're told. Low-budget, to be certain, but highly effective, suspenseful, and worth watching. The force field special effects are remarkable for the budget of this team, and an interesting social study of first contact makes this movie better than the usual fare.

INVASION OF THE ANIMAL PEOPLE

ADP (Great Britain), 1960, 73 min/Favorite Films (U.S.), 1962, 55 min, b&w, VT

Producer: Arthur Warren; **Directors:** Warren and Virgil Vogel; **Screenplay:** Arthur C. Pierce; **Music:** Allan Johannson and Harry Arnold; **Special Effects:** Odert von Schoultz; **Cinematography:** Hilding Bladh; **Cast:** Barbara Wilson, Robert Burton, Ake Gronberg, Bengt Blomgren, Stan Gester

An alien spacecraft filled with invisible E.T.s touches down in Lapland for no discernable reason. One of the creatures in storage aboard the ship escapes its confines and immediately sets out to destroy as much of the countryside as possible. Humanity is helpless. Luckily, however, the aliens are capable of recapturing their beast. They do so and then take off, leaving behind lots of destruction and many confused Laplanders. For whatever reasons they might have had, the American studio that released this movie in the United States re-edited the picture until it made practically no sense. Then, seeing they had "improved" it too much, they brought in John Carradine to read an explanatory narration that would keep the audience from scratching their scalps trying to figure the thing out. And it wasn't too good before the editing.

INVASION OF THE BEE GIRLS (aka: GRAVEYARD TRAMPS)

Centaur Pictures, 1973, Color, 85 min, VT

Director: Denis Sanders; **Screenplay:** Nicholas Meyer; **Music:** Charles Bernstein; **Cinematography:** Gary Graver; **Cast:** Victoria Verti, William Smith, Anita Ford, Cliff Osmond, Wright King, Ben Hammer

There is a disturbing force disrupting the laws of nature in sunny California. Hidden away from the world in a small town, this evil power is affecting suburban housewives and turning them into soulless creatures who pleasure their mates to death. There's lots of good campy fun here for audiences old enough to watch. It's no indication of the kind of work Meyer would later produce on *STAR TREK: THE WRATH OF KHAN*, but enjoyable nonetheless.

INVASION OF THE BODY SNATCHERS (1955)

Allied Artists, 1955, b&w, 80 min, VT, LD, DVD

Producer: Walter Wanger; **Director:** Don Siegel; **Screenplay:** Daniel Mainwaring and Sam Peckinpah; **Music:** Carmen Dragon; **Special Effects:** Milton Rice; **Cinematography:** Ellsworth Fredericks; **Cast:** Kevin McCarthy, Dana Wynter, Larry Gates, King Donovan, Carolyn Jones, Virginia Christine, Pat O'Malley, Richard Deacon, Sam Peckinpah, Jean Willes, Whit Bissell

Dr. Miles Bennell (McCarthy) has been on a short vacation. He comes home to Santa Mira, California, rested and relaxed and ready to tackle his patients' problems anew. The most important thing on his mind, however, is getting together with his lovely girlfriend, Becky (Wynter). Like it or not, though, his patients and his romance have to be put on hold as he is given a lot more to think about.

For some reason the doctor can't put his finger on, many of the town's residents are claiming that people they've known for years are no longer those same people. Parents don't seem right to their children, husbands to their wives, and so on. Bennell keeps assuring people that everything is okay. After all, he can't be bothered with all of this—he has a date with Becky. But the date gets put on hold when the couple's friends, the Bellichecs (Donovan and Jones), discover a body in their home. It is only half formed, but the half they can make out looks like the husband. Only a bit of investigation is needed to find another body that looks like Mrs. Bellichec. The bodies are destroyed, and the four sit down to discuss what they have seen.

As incredible as it seems, the two couples are soon faced with an awful truth—giant pea pods from space have been placed in the homes of people all over town. While the townsfolk sleep, the pods somehow turn into their exact replicas. When the transformation is complete, something happens to replace the actual human being's personality with that of a member of a hive collective.

The four plan to escape town, but before they can the Bellichecs are absorbed by the collective. It soon dawns on Dr. Bennell and his girl that they are the only true humans left in Santa Mira. Hiding in the doc's office, they watch as trucks filled with giant pods are loaded in the town square, then directed to the surrounding towns. Bennell and Becky make a break for it, pursued into the neighboring hills by the entire town's population. While hiding in a cavern, Becky shuts her eyes for a moment. Bennell awakens her only to find that the one brief instant of rest was all it took to steal his love from him forever. As he stares into the eyes of the warm, loving woman he had risked so much for, his face washes with trembling fear as he suddenly finds himself faced by an alien viper. (Ms. Wynter's transformation is a brilliantly effective piece of acting, never failing to chill any new viewer—not to slight McCarthy's reaction, which is also stunning.)

With his former love screaming to the rest of the collective mind, giving away his position, Bennell runs off into the night. Dazed, sleep-deprived, and babbling with fear, the doctor makes his way onto an expressway. He wanders between the cars, trying to stop their drivers, screaming warnings of what has happened to the uncaring motorists all around him. It is a frightening scene, one man with the knowledge of the end of the world, shouting his Cassandrian truths while everyone hurries home to their TV dinners. End of the picture.

Well, almost.

The above was the original ending as far as the filmmakers were concerned, but the studio executives found the scene too frightening. They insisted a "happy" ending be tacked onto the film. Complying slyly, the filmmakers shot an additional framing device. In it, Bennell is picked up by the police and examined by a psychiatrist, played with extreme panache by the world's greatest character actor, the amazing Whit Bissell. The shrink knows a raving lunatic when he hears one and is going to have Bennell shipped off to the funny farm when a police report comes in. It seems a truck has overturned on the freeway—a truck filled to the brim with giant pea pods.

Bennell sinks into his chair in relief while the police mobilize. On the surface it might seem like the good guys are going to win, but that isn't really the case. Even though the film is over, the music doesn't change to an upbeat tempo. The camera angle remains distant and foreboding. In fact, everything about the ending suggests that things are just getting started. Humanity might win—maybe—but only if they fight and fight hard. In many subtle ways, the tacked-on happy ending is even more gloomy than the original.

The Invasion of the Body Snatchers is the classic of classics, the absolute pinnacle of '50s B movie paranoia—stylish, sophisticated, and bone-chilling. Many argue that the movie could be attacking left- or right-wing politics. In the 1950s, the popular image of the "Red Menace" was its characterization as a hive mentality. The notion that individual rights were to be sacrificed for the good of the collective was the prevalent image of Soviet Communism in America during the time this film was made. No doubt creating a like image was the aim of the filmmakers. Nor is there any doubt as to the stature of this movie. Nearly a half-century after its initial release, the picture's political concerns are now mostly of interest to dedicated film students and historians; yet the film remains tremendously effective. The fall of the Soviet Union and the end of the cold war has done nothing to lessen the impact of this film.

After all, complacency and smugness are always to be guarded against. Upon his return to Santa Mira, Dr. Bennell is the epitome of the annoyingly self-assured American. Eighty minutes later, he's a frightened, powerless voice lost in the wilderness, which is really what makes this such a milestone film.

Moody and disturbing, it has yet to lose its hold on the movie-watching public. Each new generation comes to it with the arrogance of youth and goes away with something new to think about. From the moment Jack Finney began writing the novel *The Body Snatchers*, on which this film was based, to the last seconds the camera remained focused on McCarthy at the close of filming the tacked-on ending, no one involved could

Invasion of the Body Snatchers (ALLIED ARTISTS / R. ALLEN LEIDER COLLECTION)

have realized what kind of impact they were going to have on the American consciousness.

Note: An article discussing all three films based on the original novel in *The Encyclopedia of Novels Into Film* concludes with a set of opposing quotes from film historians that are so brilliantly juxtaposed it would be almost criminal not to mention them here.

> Horror film historian Carlos Clarens has pointed out that "the ultimate horror in science fiction is neither death nor destruction but dehumanization. . . . That the most successful SF films . . . seem to be concerned with dehumanization simply underlines the fact that this type of fiction hits the most exposed nerve of contemporary society: collective anxieties about the loss of individual identity. . . ." Countering this view is the rather more insidious suggestion by historian Vivian Sobchack that there is emotional appeal in being "taken over" as it were: "[The] emotional attraction is 'no more responsibility.' Being 'taken over' can be likened to being drafted, to having to follow orders. 'Taken over,' we cannot be held accountable for our crimes—passionate or passionless." Perhaps the latter view is the most terrifying implication of all.

INVASION OF THE BODY SNATCHERS (1978)

United Artists, 1978, Color, 115 min, VT, LD, DVD

Producer: Robert H. Solo; **Director:** Philip Kaufman; **Screenplay:** W.D. Richter; **Music:** Danny Zeitlin; **Special Effects:** Ben Burtt; **Cinematography:** Michael Chapman; **Cast:** Brooke Adams, Leonard Nimoy, Donald Sutherland, Kevin McCarthy, Jeff Goldblum, Veronica Cartwright, Art Hindle, Robert Duvall

San Francisco is pelted with a bizarre shower of unidentifiable stuff from beyond. After the shower, city public health employees Matthew Bennell (Sutherland) and Liz Driscoll (Adams) begin to notice changes all around the city by the bay. As in the original film, secondary characters are suddenly cold, remote, and inflexible. As Bennell and Driscoll investigate, the necessary answers are revealed much as they were in the first film. Again, it is the friendly Bellichecs (Goldblum and Cartwright) who find a half-formed pod body, this time in their health club. Things go downhill fast as the pod creatures begin to take over the city. One major twist between this version and the first: The couples turn to their friend the learned Dr. Kibner (Nimoy), who chalks everything up to mass hysteria. Of course, he may have a reason for doing so.

This is a highly effective film. Since it's attempting to recreate a classic, the best it can do is not drop the ball. The original *Invasion of the Body Snatchers* is a perfect film, sticking with its source material's plot until the last quarter of the book, which it rejects—at the end of the book, the pods, sensing that they're not going to win, simply lift off and begin to float back into space—thus improving on the story. That's not the kind of movie you top easily. Filmmakers hope not to embarrass themselves when they remake a classic film.

To their credit, the '78 filmmakers indeed show some class. Knowing that almost everyone in their audience would already be familiar with the original movie, the filmmakers styled their version as more of a sequel than a remake. The first picture showed what was happening in a small town—perhaps the very first place hit. The second film tackled what would happen in a big city. One of the humorous asides of the picture was the ease the pod people had hiding pods in San Franciscans' plant-heavy homes. The new film boasted a much flashier directorial style with exaggerated cuts and wild camera movement. It also contained much more graphic transformation scenes. These changes undercut some of the film's terror quotient, but since the first film did that by its very existence (after all, it's hard to build suspense when people already know the story), the changes seem logical and indeed helped keep the film quite interesting.

Also interesting was their choice of casting Kevin McCarthy to reprise his role from the original. True, the audience sees him only for a minute as he runs down the freeway once more, screaming his warnings, but it is a highly effective scene. More of an insider bit, but even greater fun for those in the know, was having original director Don Siegel on board as a pod-person cab driver. These were both nice touches appreciated by everyone in a position to catch them. All in all, is a good movie. Be warned, though. This sequel/remake is not nearly as effective for those who haven't seen the first film.

Note: Although Robert Duvall is listed in the credits above, be advised that it's a very small part. No blinking allowed if you want to see him.

INVASION OF THE BODY STEALERS

See *THIN AIR*

INVASION OF THE NEPTUNE MEN

Manley (Japan), 1961, Color, 74 min

Producer: Hiroshi Okawa; **Director:** Koji Ota; **Screenplay:** Shin Morita; **Cinematography:** Shizuka Fujii; **Cast:** Shinichi Chiba, Mishsue Komiya, Shanjio Ebara

Once again, aliens in funny costumes are invading Earth. Once again, they can't think of a better place to begin their invasion than the Island of the Midnight Sun. Once again, a silly Japanese superhero pounds them into salt. This movie is only for those who can't get enough of this science fiction subgenre.

INVASION OF THE SAUCER MEN
(aka: THE HELL CREATURES, SPACEMEN SATURDAY NIGHT)

AIP, 1957, b&w, 68 min, VT

Producers: James H. Nicholson and Robert Gurney, Jr.; **Director:** Edward Cahn; **Screenplay:** Gurney, Jr., and Al Martin; **Music:** Ronald Stein; **Special Effects:** Carlie Taylor, Paul Blaisdell, and Howard A. Anderson; **Cinematography:** Frederick E. West; **Cast:** Steve Terrell, Gloria Castillo, Frank Gorshin, Raymond Hatton, Ed Nelson, Lyn Osborn

Aliens are invading Earth, or at least they're landing here at inopportune moments. These big-headed, bug-eyed, rubber-handed losers get spotted by con men and then end up getting run over by hot-rodding teenagers. And, if that isn't embarrassing enough, when the aliens make their stand against humanity, the saviors of Earth, a bunch of local teens, dissolve the creatures with their high beams.

INVASION OF THE STAR CREATURES

AIP, 1962, b&w, 81 min

Producer: Merj Hagopian; **Director:** Bruno De Soto; **Screenplay:** Jonathan Haze; **Music:** Jack Cookerly and Elliot Fisher; **Special Effects:** Joseph Kinder; **Cinematography:** Basil Bradbury; **Cast:** Bob Ball, Gloria Victor, Dolores Reed, Frankie Ray

A pair of moronic soldiers (Ray and Ball) are on army maneuvers when they are captured by a pair of space-women (Reed and Victor). The women are here to conquer Earth with the aid of their fearsome vegetation monsters. Not a bad idea, but sadly our intergalactic cuties spend all their time pitching woo with Ray and Ball, which makes the women forget all about conquest.

INVASION OF THE ZOMBIES

Azteca (Mexico), 1961, b&w, 85 min

Producer: Fernando Oses; **Director:** Benito Alzraki; **Screenplay:** Alzraki; **Music:** Raul Lavista; **Cinematography:** Jose O. Ramos; **Cast:** Santo, Lorena Valezquez, Armando Silvestre, Jaime Fernandez

There's a mad scientist loose in Mexico who has created an army of zombies with which he plans to take over the entire planet. Things look bad. In fact, only one man stands in this monster's way, one man with no superpowers or weapons or much in the way of brains. Yes, with a description like that, it can be none other than Santo, the Masked Marvel of the Mexican Wrestling Ring. Go get 'em, Santo.

INVASION SINIESTRA

See *INCREDIBLE INVASION*

INVENTORS, THE

Educational (Great Britain), 1934, b&w, two reels

Producer: Al Christie; **Screenplay:** William Watson and Sig Herzig; **Cast:** Chase Taylor, Budd Hulick

Two resource-poor but inventive scientists team up to build an artificial human. Not having any corpses, they use spare automobile parts. Could it be the inspiration for *My Mother, the Car?*

INVENTOR'S SECRET, THE

Cines (Italy), 1911, b&w, silent short

Long before the Manhattan Project, science fiction filmmakers had their silent screen scientists hard at work on the problem of creating superexplosives.

INVISIBILITY

Hepworth (Great Britain), 1909, b&w, silent short

Directors: Cecil Hepworth and Lewin Fitzhamon; **Cast:** Lewin Fitzhamon

An ordinary man with a talent for spotting a bargain purchases a quantity of a peculiar powder that renders him invisible. Would that it were that easy.

INVISIBLE AGENT, THE

Universal, 1942, b&w, 81 min, VT

Producer: Frank Lloyd; **Director:** Edwin L. Marin; **Screenplay:** Curt Siodmak; **Special Effects:** John P. Fulton; **Cinematography:** Lester White; **Music:** Charles Previn; **Cast:** Ilona Massey, Jon Hall, Peter Lorre, Cedric Hardwicke, J. Edward Bromberg, Holmes Herbert, Keye Luke, John Litel

This World War II thriller takes the existence of characters and events in H.G. Wells's *The Invisible Man* for granted. When the original madman's secret invisibility formula comes into the hands of his descendant (Hall), suddenly there are sinister Nazis everywhere (wonderfully played by Lorre and Hardwicke) trying to get their hands on it. Younger viewers can get caught up in this one pretty easily. After that, the fractured dialogue gets harder to take with each year of schooling accumulated. It's not terrible, just a bit predictable.

INVISIBLE BOY, THE

MGM, 1957, b&w, 89 min, VT, LD

Producer: Nicholas Nayfack; **Director:** Herman Hoffman; **Screenplay:** Cyril Hume; **Special Effects:** Jack Rabin, Irving Block, and Louis DeWitt; **Cinematography:** Harold Wellman; **Music:** Lex Baxter; **Cast:** Richard Eyer, Diane Brewster, Philip Abbott, Harold J. Stone

In this kid's science fiction film Richard Eyer plays the fairly clever son of a lovable scientist. Dad has built a robot pal for his son (*FORBIDDEN PLANET*'s Robbie the Robot put to use in a less than crowning role), as well as a master computer for himself. The problem is that like so many supercomputers with a messiah complex, this one gets the notion that it would probably be much happier as the first vacuum tube-powered ruler of the world. So it reprograms Robbie to act as its arms and legs and sets out on its quest for global domination. Luckily, little Richie has picked up a few tricks from Dad, and figuring out how to make himself invisible, he manages to reprogram Robbie and stop the master computer. Come to think of it, maybe Dad's not such a genius after all.

INVISIBLE FLUID, THE

Biograph, 1908, b&w, silent short

Director: Wallace McCutcheon; **Cinematography:** G.W. Bitzen; **Cast:** Mack Sennett, Anthony O'Sullivan, Edward Dillon, D.W. Griffith

Spray the title fluid on anyone or anything and watch it turn invisible, for a while anyway. Of course, that would really be *invisibility* fluid, but you can't win them all.

INVISIBLE DR. MABUSE, THE (aka: THE INVISIBLE HORROR)

CCC Filmkunst GmbH (West Germany), 1961/ Thunder Pictures, Inc. (U.S.), 1966, b&w, 89 min, VT

Producer: Artur Brauner; **Director:** Harold Reini; **Screenplay:** Brauner, Ladislas Fodor, and Norbert Jacques; **Special Effects:** Heinz Stamm and K.L. Rupper; **Cinematography:** Ernst. W. Kalinke; **Cast:** Lex Barker, Karin Dor, Siegfried Lowitz, Wolfgang Priess, Rudolf Fernau

A somewhat interesting thriller in the Dr. Mabuse series, this movie concerns an FBI agent (Barker) going to Germany to investigate the murder of a fellow agent. His investigation takes him across the now invisible Mabuse's path.

There are two noteworthy elements to the Mabuse series. First, the series actually centers on a villain instead of a hero. Second, the earlier films in the series were directed by legendary German filmmaker Fritz Lang. For those interested, the other films in the series are: *Dr. Mabuse: The Gambler* (Part One of what was originally an epic 3 1/2-hour film, now only shown in two parts), *Dr. Mabuse, King of Crime* (Part Two), *The Testament of Dr. Mabuse*, and *The Thousand Eyes of Dr. Mabuse*.

There is also the 1961 Criterion film, *The Return of Dr. Mabuse*, wherein the good doctor tries to control the world through the use of a mind-control drug.

INVISIBLE HORROR, THE

See *THE INVISIBLE DR. MABUSE*

INVISIBLE INVADERS, THE

United Artists, 1959, b&w, 67 min, VT

Producer: Robert E. Kent; **Director:** Edward L. Cahn; **Screenplay:** Samuel Newman; **Special Effects:** Phil Scheer and Roger George; **Cinematography:** Maury Gertsman; **Music:** Paul Dunlap; **Cast:** John Agar, Jean Byron, Robert Hutton, Philip Tonge, John Carradine, Hal Torey, Eden Hartford, Paul Langton

Invisible alien entities resurrect the dead of Earth. Once they've gotten them up on their feet (no mean task), they turn them into an army of zombie killers, which they then set loose on the world. The more of the living the monsters slaughter, the more monsters there are to contend with. When bullets and bombs prove a bust, luckily the military decides to team up with science to find the answer. White noise makes the aliens nuts, so our heroes turn on the juice and send the bad guys packing. This movie is an in-betweener—not so good, and not so bad, but certainly nowhere near as good as the *Living Dead* series of films Romero produced later, though reportedly Romero counts this film as one of his influences.

INVISIBLE KID, THE

Media Home Entertainment, 1988, Color, 95 min, VT, LD

Director: Avery Crounse; **Screenplay:** Crounse; **Cast:** Jay Underwood, Karen Black, Brother Theodore, Wally Ward, Chynna Phillips, Mike Genovese, Jan King

A high school student with more than a few of the problems of a typical teenager happens across the secret of invisibility. Given a miraculous power beyond the scope and ken of most mortal men, he of course uses it to sneak into the girl's locker room.

INVISIBLE MAN, THE

Universal, 1933, b&w, 71 min, VT, LD, DVD

Producer: Carl Laemmle, Jr.; **Director:** James Whale; **Screenplay:** R.C. Sherriff; **Special Effects:** John P. Fulton; **Cinematography:** Art Edeson and John Mescall; **Music:** Heinz Roemheld; **Cast:** Claude Rains, Gloria Stuart, Una O'Connor, William Harrigan, E.E. Clive, Dudley Digges, Dwight Frye, Henry Travers, Holmes Herbert

Jack Griffin (Rains) is a lowly chemist's assistant with big ideas. His main idea is to surpass his employer and future father-in-law in both fame and fortune. When he disappears suddenly, however, his fiancée and her father grow greatly alarmed. Not so his friend Kemp (Harrigan), who thinks it may have something to do with Griffin's latest experiments.

We discover that Griffin has been working with a new compound, monocane. Supposedly, this substance has the ability to bleach animal tissues completely transparent—invisible. This incredible find, sadly, has two major drawbacks. The first is that so far no way has been found to reverse the process. And the second is that enduring the process may make test subjects invisible, but it also makes them quite insane.

Like any two-fisted researcher with a chip on his shoulder, Griffin is certain he can survive the ordeal, and thus doses himself. He is quickly bleached through and through, and not long after loses his sanity. Wrapped in the bandages that have since become one of the most famous images in science fiction filmdom, he goes to the local town of Ipping, where he sets up shop. He is certain that here he will discover an antidote that will allow him to switch back and forth from invisible to visible. After that secret has been mastered, Griffin is certain that he will be able to become the ruler of the world.

Unfortunately, the madness eating at him does far too good a job. As the invisible man, he begins to terrorize Ipping; he also attempts to force his one-time friend Kemp to work with him, eventually murdering the man. The police are foiled by his power for a while, but eventually luck is with them. A fresh snowfall forces Griffin to leave tracks when he flees the law. The officers fire in the general direction of the retreating prints, and at least one of them scores a deadly hit. Griffin falls, we presume. As his blood flows and his life ebbs, he becomes slowly visible once more. The madness flees along with his life. The reign of the invisible man is over, and so is the best picture made to date on the subject.

The filmmakers started with a great source, but beyond that, they were blessed with the enormously talented (and often underappreciated) Claude Rains as their star. That Rains could mesmerize audiences so completely with the power of his voice alone (his face is actually seen for only a few moments at the end of the movie) is testament to his power as an actor as well as to the rest of the team. Of course, he had wonderful support from everyone in this quite talented cast, including John Carradine and Walter Brennan in what amount to bit parts. Additionally, R.C. Sherriff did a terrific job of adapting H.G. Wells's novel. Many critics consider this the best transference of Wells's work to the screen, though perhaps THINGS TO COME has a slight edge.

Most important, though, is James Whale's brilliant direction. It's one of his finest achievements, as it is for everyone connected. Even H.G. Wells himself is reported to have been favorably impressed. As with FRANKENSTEIN, James Whale gave *The Invisible Man* a depth and dignity that escapes the ability of most filmmakers to this very day.

But all one needs to prove that this crew really knew what they were doing is to examine the next two Invisible Man pictures made by the same studio. Seven years after Rains made them a tidy fortune with *The Invisible Man*, Universal tried to fill his shoes with Vincent Price in THE INVISIBLE MAN'S REVENGE. Price does his usual best as an innocent man accused of killing his own brother, who uses the invisibility potion to track down the real killer. Curt Siodmak (along with Lester Cole) did an okay job on the screenplay, but there is little doubt that anyone will ever confuse the work of director Joe May with that of James Whale.

And if that is the case, it is equally certain that no one will ever confuse the work of Joe May with the less than magnificent direction of Ford Beebe. Given the task of directing Universal's 1944 *The Invisible Man's Revenge*, Beebe does an uninspired job, as did his screenwriter Bertram Millhauser. Only a better than usual cast led by Jon Hall saved this movie from being a true howler.

Things have only gotten worse. At least 30 other pictures exist on same theme, but no one has been able to do anything new with the idea other than rehash the ideas from Universal's first two pictures, such as in the 1957 Mexican feature THE NEW INVISIBLE MAN, which was heavily plagiarized from *The Invisible Man Returns*.

Note: Not all the other invisibility films are bad, although those who have seen Dean Jones's MISTER SUPERINVISIBLE, or worse yet, Chevy Chase in MEMOIRS OF AN INVISIBLE MAN may be dubious. In the plus column is THE INVISIBLE WOMAN. Made in 1941, this comedy starring John Barrymore, Virginia Bruce, Shemp Howard, Margaret Hamilton, and a slew of other highly talented people is loads of fun. It has nothing to do with Wells, and its science fiction quotient is less than minimal, but it shouldn't get lumped in with all the failures, especially for viewers who enjoy old-style comedy with a science fiction twist.

Gloria Stuart of the 1934 classic went on to a starring role in the blockbuster film *Titanic*.

INVISIBLE MAN'S REVENGE, THE

Universal, 1944, b&w, 78 min, VT, LD

Producer: Ford Beebe; Director: Beebe; Screenplay: Bertram Millhauser; Music: H.J. Salter; Cinematography: Milton Krasner; Special Effects: John P. Fulton; Cast: Jon Hall, John Carradine, Gale Sondergaard, Lester Mathews, Leon Errol, Evelyn Ankers, Ian Wolfe, Billy Bevan

See THE INVISIBLE MAN

INVISIBLE MONSTER, THE (aka: SLAVES OF THE INVISIBLE MONSTER)

Republic, 1950, b&w, Serial, 12 Chapters

Director: Fred Brannon; Screenplay: Donald Davidson; Music: Stanley Wilson; Special Effects: Howard Lydecker and Theodore Lydecker; Cinematography: Ellis W. Carter; Cast: Stanley Price, Richard Webb, Aline Towne, Tom Steele, Eddie Parker, John Crawford, Dale Van Sickle

The Phantom Ruler is Stan Price, who starts robbing banks after he comes across a powder that will render him invisible. (Could this be INVISIBILITY's Lewin Fitzhamon on the loose once more? Nah.) He is brought low by a pair of insurance investigators (Towne and Webb), whose courage so rattle Price that when confronted by their heroism, he falls into his own trap and electrocutes himself. As with so many serials, Republic re-edited and cut this one down to a 100-minute feature, which they released in 1966. Making it shorter did not make it better. Ignore both versions.

INVISIBLE RAY, THE (1920)

Forham Amusement Corporation, 1920, b&w, silent serial, 15 chapters

Producer: Jesse J. Goldburg; Director: Harry A. Pollard; Screenplay: Guy McConnell; Cast: Ruth Clifford, Jack Sherrill, Edward Davis

Over the course of 15 weeks, an atomic ray gun is fought over quite strenuously by various men in hats. Then, in the last reel, the good guys win.

INVISIBLE RAY, THE (1936)

Universal, 1936, b&w, 82 min, VT, LD

Producer: Edmund Grainger; Director: Lambert Hillyer; Screenplay: John Colton; Music: Franz Waxman; Special Effects: John P. Fulton; Cast: Boris Karloff, Bela Lugosi, Frances Drake, Frank Lawton, Walter Kingsford, Beulah Bondi, Violet Kemble Cooper

This movie starts with this quote burned into the screen:

> Every scientific fact accepted today once burned as a fantastic power in the mind of someone called mad. Who are we on this youngest and smallest of planets to say the INVISIBLE RAY is impossible to science? That which you are now to see is a theory whispered in the cloisters of science. Tomorrow these theories may startle the universe as fact.

Janos Rukh (Karloff) figures he's soon going to be on top of the world. His life's work is complete, and he's about to show it off to the scientists who laughed at him and drove him out of professional academic circles. The invited group arrive at Rukh's castle, led by Dr. Felix Benet (Lugosi). Rukh leads his guests to his laboratory and explains what they will see. Every action taken by everything in the world, he explains, leaves an indelible record in the universe through its vibrations. Rukh has found a way to record and reveal those vibrations. He demonstrates by showing the assembly a meteor crash that took place in Africa millions of years previous. He then goes so far as to announce that he is certain this meteor contained a new element that will be more powerful than anything humankind has previously known.

Everyone is impressed. As Benet is going on an expedition to Africa soon, he invites Rukh to join him. Rukh is taken aback by everyone's newfound acceptance of his theories. It's obvious he expected more ridicule, but when he does not receive it, he becomes quite heady. Against the wishes of his blind mother, he goes along to Africa, bringing his young wife in tow. There he discovers the meteor and is rewarded beyond his wildest dreams with the unbelievable power he is able to harness from it, thanks to the element he finds within its sparking body.

The problem: Exposure to the element, which Rukh dubs Radium X, leaves him so filled with radiation that he glows in the dark. Worse yet, it's left him with a deadly touch that kills anything his exposed flesh even brushes for an instant. Rukh refuses to see his wife, confiding only in Benet. This is the last straw for Mrs. Rukh. She's been fighting temptation for a while, trying to honor her marriage vows, but with this snub she becomes convinced her husband doesn't love her and leaves him.

Benet finds a temporary antidote for Rukh. He has to take it at regular intervals, but at least he can rejoin the human race. Benet warns Rukh that he is going to have trouble thinking and that it is almost certain Rukh will go mad. What Benet doesn't understand is that Rukh was fairly nuts even before his exposure. Now he's already around the bend. Rukh sees enemies everywhere. After curing his mother's blindness with his discovery, he fakes his own death and then begins killing his "enemies" one by one. The scientists he first showed his invention, Benet, even his ex-wife and her new husband are on the list. A trap is set that costs Benet his life, but it also forces Rukh to see what he has become. At his mother's urging, he allows the radiation to finish its work and so disappears in a burst of fire.

This film almost deserves unreserved praise. Everything about it is good practically the whole way through, but when it falters, it does so loudly. Sadly, every aspect of it falters at least once. Worse yet, the Franz Waxman score, usually a thing you can count on, is a crashing bore. The set designs are magnificent in the beginning and the end, but the African sets in the middle are cramped and minimal to the point of comedy.

Still, there is much that is great. Karloff and Lugosi are at their peak; in fact, Boris Karloff was getting single-name billing as "KARLOFF" in giant-sized letters above the rest of the cast. The two were the kings of Universal then, but they couldn't make this movie work all the way through. Notable is the performance of Violet Kemble Cooper as Mother Rukh. She gets to do several great turns, especially when her sight is restored. But a great cast can't make up for bad stock music, an uneven script, and really bad science. This one is quite watchable for a number of reasons, but it's not a great film.

Note: As Dr. Benet, Lugosi sports a mustache and goatee. No one in history ever looked more perfect in them than he does.

INVISIBLE: THE CHRONICLES OF BENJAMIN KNIGHT

See *MANDROID*

INVISIBLE THIEF, THE

Pathé, 1905, b&w, silent short

The citizens of France are menaced for something short of 400 feet of film by an invisible prankster. Not much is known about this short, except that it seems to be the first film mention of invisibility. Happy hunting to those who are determined to find this movie because they have to not see the facts for themselves.

INVISIBLE TERROR

See *BEACH GIRLS AND THE MONSTER*

THE INVISIBLE WOMAN

Universal, 1941, b&w, 72 min, VT

Producer: Burt Kelly; **Director:** A. Edward Sutherland; **Screenplay:** Joe May, Fred Rinaldo, Robert Lees, Gertrude Purcell, and Curt Siodmak; **Cinematography:** Elwood Bredell; **Music:** Charles Previn and Frank Skinner; **Special Effects:** John P. Fulton; **Cast:** Jon Hall, John Carradine, Gale Sondergaard, Lester Matthews, Leon Errol, Evelyn Ankers, Ian Wolfe, Billy Bevan

See *THE INVISIBLE MAN*

IRON CLAW, THE

Pathé, 1916, b&w, silent serial, 20 chapters

Director: Edward Jose; **Screenplay:** George Brackett Seitz; **Cast:** Sheldon Lewis, Pearl White, Creighton Hale

Another villain with another ray gun makes life tough for the citizens of France for a score of weeks. Then, instead of being beaten by the good guys, he is actually felled by a virus that kills him through accelerated aging. Much the way the original audiences must have felt after sitting through 20 episodes of this silly thing.

IRON GIANT, THE

Warner Bros., 1999, Color, 87 min, VT, DVD

Producers: Allison Abbate and Wes McAnuff; **Director:** Brad Bird; **Screenplay:** Bird and Tim McCaniies; **Music:** Michael Kamen; **Animation:** Bird, Joe Johnston, Steve Markowski, Mark Whiting, and Scott Johnston; **Cast (Voices):** Jennifer Aniston, Harry Connick, Jr., Eli Marienthal, Vin Diesel, Christopher McDonald, John Mahoney, M. Emmet Walsh, Cloris Leachman, James Gammon

The year 1957—a local fisherman who has a way with a tall tale informs the residents of the small town of Rockwell, Maine, that he encountered a gigantic metal man during a violent nighttime storm. No one takes him seriously except for Hogarth (Marienthal), a curious nine-year-old who lives with his waitress mother (Aniston). Doing a little exploring, Hogarth discovers that the story is true. He discovers a 50-foot robot with an insatiable appetite for metal. That appetite gets his discovery into difficulty as it tries to eat a power station and is nearly fried. Hogarth shuts down the power and soon finds he has a 50-foot-tall friend—one with amnesia, a heart of gold, and the firepower to level worlds.

A paranoid government agent (McDonald) stirs up both the townsfolk and the army, ultimately creating a situation in which the safety of first Rockwell and then the entire planet is at stake. When the situation gets completely out of hand, it's up to the Iron Giant (Diesel), of course, to save the town's residents from their own fears and prejudices.

Although it sounds like a routine story, *The Iron Giant* is actually a gem of a movie. It has beautiful animation, exceptional direction, a solid cast, and a crowd-pleasing story that is far more subtly layered than one would suspect. A large part of that comes from its origins. The film is based on the acclaimed novel *The Iron Man* by England's late poet laureate, Ted Hughes. Hughes originally wrote the story to comfort his and troubled poet Sylvia Plath's children in the wake of Plath's suicide. The message of Hughes's work, that things continue and life goes on, works well with the film's central theme—what if a gun had a soul?

The year 1957 was chosen for the film, of course, for the presence of *Sputnik* in the sky and the "Red Menace" everywhere else. Wonderful use of "duck-and-cover" classroom filmstrips illustrates not only the paranoia, but the amazing amount of disinformation prevalent at the time. Ultimately, *The Iron Giant* is a warm tale with surprising depth and an unexpected ending that will please even the toughest animation crowd. Also, Warner Bros. made the film without imposing the usual selection of treacly Disneyesque song and dance numbers. For this reason if no other, the film deserves special attention.

Note: In 1986, rock musician Pete Townshend became interested in writing "a modern song-cycle in the manner of *Tommy*." He chose Hughes's novel *The Iron Man* as his subject matter, and the album was released three years later.

Also, in 1993, the story was adapted for the stage and presented at London's Old Vic Theatre.

ISLAND AT THE TOP OF THE WORLD, THE

Walt Disney Studios, 1974, Color, 93 min, VT, DVD

Producer: Winston Hibler; **Director:** Robert Stevenson; **Screenplay:** John Whedon and Ian Cameron; **Special Effects:** Art Cruickshank, Peter Ellenshaw, and Danny Lee; **Cinematography:** Frank V. Phillips; **Cast:** David Hartman, Donald Sinden, Jacques Marin, Mako, Agneta Eckemyr, David Gwillim

What does a daring but stodgy Victorian type with nothing much to occupy himself for a few months do to fill the void? Outfit an expedition to fly a lighter-than-air craft over the pole to help a grieving sea captain search for his missing son, of course. If the son disappeared searching for the legendary graveyard of the whales, that just adds a touch of intrigue. And if they happen to discover a lost Viking civilization along the way, that would only be a plus,—right?

This film took a lot of heat at the time of its release, especially Hartman, the film's somewhat wooden star, but it's not at all bad. The effects are top-notch, the plot believable if whimsical, and its sense of gentlemanly adventure is as charming for its idealism as it is for its innocence. It looks and sounds and feels like it was based on a Jules Verne novel, but it was actually pulled from the pages of Ian Cameron's novel *The Lost Ones*. Disney's track record with science fiction is not a good one (*TRON*, *THE BLACK HOLE*, *MY FAVORITE MARTIAN*), but this one proves the studio can hit one out of the park when it really puts its collective mind to it.

ISLAND OF DR. MOREAU, THE (1977)

AIP, 1977, Color, 98 min, VT

Producers: Skip Steloff and John Temple-Smith; **Director:** Don Taylor; **Screenplay:** John Shaner and Al Ramrus; **Special Effects:** John Chambers, Don Striepeke, Tom Burman, Ed Butterworth, and Walter Schenck; **Cinematography:** Gerry Fisher; **Music:** Laurence Rosenthal; **Cast:** Burt Lancaster, Michael York, Nigel Davenport, Barbara Carrera, Richard Basehart, Nick Cravat, Bib Ozman, Gary Baxley, David Cass, John Gillespie, Fumio Demura

Poor castaway Michael York finds his way to the title island, where he finds an over-the-top Burt Lancaster trying to fill the shoes of H.G. Wells's Dr. Moreau. Moreau is a scientist attempting to turn the beasts of the jungle into civilized men, forgetting, as always, that there is no real proof in this world that people have ever actually been civilized. In this version of the story, the mad doctor attempts this through manipulation of the animals' DNA, instead of through surgery as in both Wells's novel and its previous film version, THE ISLAND OF LOST SOULS.

On hand in the doctor's compound is an incredibly sexy woman (Carrera), whom Moreau has created from a panther. The doctor does his best to get York to mate with her simply because he wants to study the results. Moreau is also surprised when, after he injects York with his potions, changing the castaway into a half-man, half-beast from the other direction, the ungrateful wretch won't advance Moreau's experiments by helping him document the changes taking place within him.

Also lurking about are the intensely grotesque beast-humans that Moreau has created. They stay in the jungle and moan about the "House of Pain," where they were created. Many of them would like to rip Moreau limb from limb, but the Sayer of the Law (Basehart) stops them time and again. Moreau is the god who gave them all life. Like the God of Moses, he also gave them a set of commandments—not to take life being one of them. Eventually, though, Moreau breaks one of his own laws, giving his creations all the incentive they need to finally put an end to him. While the beast-humans kill Moreau and tear his island apart, York and Carrera escape by boat. Oddly enough, Moreau's work on York fades away quickly once the two lovebirds are on the boat, but no similar reversion comes to Carrera, which would have ruined the obligatory Hollywood happy ending. The fact that it also results in an interspecies romance is not addressed.

Wonderful makeup is about all this film has going for it. Although it proclaims the name of an H.G. Wells novel, it was actually based more on the previous and far superior film, THE ISLAND OF LOST SOULS. It repeats the first adaptation's major change by adding Carrera's panther woman, but then doesn't bother to use the idea to the marvelous effect the previous filmmakers did. Further changes lead things rapidly downhill.

For instance, as previously mentioned, in the novel Dr. Moreau creates his beast-humans through surgery in his House of Pain. It is fear of this terrible place that keeps the beast-humans mostly in check. But where is the pain in genetic experiments? Replacing the bloody cruelty of the novel with the cleaner and far less violent imagery of chromosome research weakens this part of the story considerably. Also, Lancaster's Moreau, shot almost entirely in daylight and in color as opposed to Charles Laughton's Moreau in THE ISLAND OF LOST SOULS, shot in black-and-white and almost entirely at night, is almost a saintly figure. The entire thrust of this picture is wrong. It has a good cast and really nice makeup but not much else.

However, as pointless as this '77 version of the film is, the 1996 supposedly epic version starring Marlon Brando and Val Kilmer is infinitely worse. Stan Winston's makeup effects are breathtaking and worth catching with the sound off, but Brando's cheaply ridiculous performance is almost insulting. It's hard to decide whether he was too lazy to give the audience a real performance or if he had simply forgotten how. It's possible that the actor holds some incredible contempt for Wells or science fiction in general and did his best to show it here, but that might be giving him far too much credit. Maybe director John Frankenheimer harbored an anti-Wells bent, but again it's probably not the case. This version's lunatic script even eliminates the House of Pain, and instead electronic implants keep the beast-humans in check. It's easy to see how this wonderful, if overused, science fiction device might attract the bored and the unimaginative. But the whole point of the story is lost. The beast-humans become human through pain. They are held in check through laws. Now the law is discarded, and it's the pain that holds them in check.

ISLAND OF DR. MOREAU, THE (1996)

New Line Cinema, 1996, Color, 95 min, VT, LD, DVD

Producers: Tim Zinnemann, Edward R. Pressman, and Clair Rudnick Polstein; **Director:** John Frankenheimer; **Screenplay:** Waylong Green, Ron Hutchinson, Richard Stanly, and Michael Herr; **Cinematography:** William A. Fraker; **Music:** Gary Chang; **Special Effects:** Michael Z. Hannan, Grant Viklund, Gene Rizzardi Jr., Raleigh L. Swick II, Jim Charmatz, Rob Dolittle, Stand Winston Studio, and Digital Domain; **Cast:** Marlon Brando, Val Kilmer, David Thewlis, Fairuza Balk, Ron Perlman, Marco Hofschneider, Temuera Morrison

See THE ISLAND OF DR. MOREAU (1977)

ISLAND OF LOST SOULS, THE

Paramount, 1933, b&w, 72 min, VT, LD

Producer: National Board of Directors; **Director:** Eric C. Kenton; **Screenplay:** Waldemar Young and Philip Wylie; **Special Effects:** Wally Westmore; **Cin-

Island of Dr. Moreau (NEW LINE CINEMA / JOSEPH B. MAUCERI COLLECTION)

ematography: Karl Struss; **Cast:** Charles Laughton, Bela Lugosi, Richard Arlen, Stanley Fields, Kathleen Burke, Leila Hyams, Alan Ladd, George Irving, Tetsu Komai, Randolph Scott

Edward Parker (Arlen) and his fiancée, Ruth Walker (Hyams), are shipwrecked. Worse than drifting around for a few months, they end up making their way to the hellish island of Dr. Moreau, who is portrayed by Charles Laughton at his over-the-top best. The island is populated by insidiously ugly natives, constantly lurking just outside Moreau's compound. The ugly natives are all males, however. The one female in evidence, Lota (Burke), is quite the dish. Unlike the men, she is given fairly free access to the compound. And, if Moreau has his way, she'll get free access to Parker as well.

It turns out Moreau is a surgeon who had to flee Great Britain for the South Pacific just ahead of his wrathful colleagues. Moreau was experimenting with

animals back in England, trying to force evolution upon them through the means of surgery. The medical community's problem with Moreau's work was with its inhumanly cruel nature.

Retreating to his island, Moreau has now proved all his claims. He can create thinking, rational beings from animals through the science of vivisection. The ugly natives are, of course, animals Moreau has transformed through scores of hours of horribly painful surgery in his "House of Pain." Many of them are consumed with hate for Moreau and would love to kill him, but he has convinced them he is a god. The malcontents are kept in line by his Sayer of the Law (Lugosi), who beats them into submission with the list of laws Moreau gave his creations, such as "Not to spill blood . . . that is the law. Are we not men?"

Lota is Moreau's finest achievement, one he means to take a step further by having her mate with Parker. Fortunately for Parker's fiancée, a rescue party arrives. Not to be thwarted, though, Moreau orders one of his duller but stronger creations to murder the leader of the rescue team. But this is a big mistake for the doctor, for it gives the malcontents the loophole they are looking for—if god doesn't have to obey the laws, then neither do we.

When Moreau tries to subdue his beast-humans, they reject his law, moving forward on him slowly in the face of his cracking whip as Lugosi speaks for all of them.

"You made us things. Not men. Not beasts. Part men. Part beasts. Things . . . *things!*"

The beast-humans revolt, Parker and his lovely fiancée escape by the skin of their teeth, and Lota is savaged by one of the beast-humans while the others take Moreau to his own House of Pain and experiment on him. Ironically, Lota is killed because she chooses to stay behind when the castaways flee, giving her life that they might survive. Her self-sacrifice in the name of her love for the man she cannot have truly makes her Moreau's greatest creation, a triumph he tragically does not live to witness.

Despite the addition of Lota, the panther girl, *The Island of Lost Souls* comes far closer to the original H.G. Wells story than any of the other screen versions of this timeless tale. It's a tremendous effort, well staged, well directed, and well acted. The makeup effects are gruesomely wonderful, and the film is quite effective in setting a mood of tension and suppressed hostility. Lugosi and Laughton compete for chances to chew up the scenery, with Laughton coming out as the over-the-top champ for no other reason than he gets more screen time. Neither of them hurts the film, however. Their antics only increase the mood of utter madness that runs rampant in this dark and claustrophobic picture.

The finale of this early film is far more effective that either of the sequels. Moreau deserves every horror visited upon him, yet his demise is so cruel and prolonged that he still must be pitied. It's a level of subtlety none of the remakes ever achieved.

Note: In case you didn't recognize the name in the credits, Philip Wylie, who helped write this screenplay, is the same Philip Wylie who wrote *When Worlds Collide, Generation Of Vipers*, and other sophisticated and challenging science fiction novels. There's little doubt that much of the respect for Wells's work came from this fellow master.

ISLAND OF LOST WOMEN

Warner Bros., 1959, b&w, 66 min

Producer: Albert J. Cohen; **Director:** Frank W. Tuttle; **Screenplay:** Ray Buffum; **Cinematography:** John Seitz; **Music:** Raoul Kraushaar; **Cast:** Alan Napier, Gavin Muir, Venetia Stevenson, Diane Jergens, June Blair, Jeff Richards, John Smith

A plane is forced down on a remote island. The survivors of the crash find they aren't as alone on the island as they first thought, but they soon wish they were. The group quickly discovers they have a host— the obligatory mad scientist who has bred a small army of amazons with the help of his daughters. The problem isn't with the somewhat sophisticated lessons in war that the doctor insists on teaching his creations, but with the death ray he's getting ready to give them.

ISLAND OF TERROR

Universal, 1967, Color, 89 min, VT

Producer: Tom Blakeley; **Director:** Terence Fisher; **Screenplay:** Alan Ramsen and Edward Andrew Mann; **Special Effects:** John St. John Earl; **Cinematography:** Reg Wyer; **Music:** Malcolm Lockyer; **Cast:** Edward Judd, Peter Cushing, Carole Gray, Niall MacGinnis, Sam Kydd, Roger Heathcote, Eddie Byrne

It's wacky ol' science gone wrong once more. On a remote British isle, a scientist with good intentions is working toward finding a cancer cure. Somehow he takes a wrong turn and creates a herd of hideous, tentacled mutations that latch onto human beings and, instead of sucking out their blood, suck out their bone marrow (isn't it always the way?).

When a marrowless body washes up on the mainland, a team of scientists (Cushing, Judd, Byrne, and Gray) is assigned to investigate. They find the island in question, the monsters find them, and then the usual all hell breaks loose. The good guys quickly discover that their foes can't be stopped. Rifles and handguns are useless. Explosives just create lots of new critters since the pieces all regenerate as complete entities. The problem is finally solved by getting all the survivors on the island into one building, which is surrounded by radioactive cattle (that's right, radioactive cattle). The mutations suck the marrow from the cattle and die. End of film.

Though trite in some ways, this movie is worth viewing. Yes, the creatures do move slower than snails, so it is a wonder that they ever attach themselves to anyone, but they do. Cushing plays the best of the standard science fiction heroes, the rational human, as perfectly here as he ever did. In one memorable sequence he cuts off his own hand (to which a mutant has attached itself) rather than die. It is the bravery of logic, and no one has ever been more convincing showing it than Cushing. It's the best of the only three science fiction films made by Terence Fisher, most likely because it's much more of a horror film than it is sci-fi.

ISLAND OF THE BURNING DAMNED (aka: ISLAND OF THE BURNING DOOMED, NIGHT OF THE BIG HEAT)

Planet (Great Britain), 1967, Color, 94 min, VT

Producer: Tom Blakeley; **Director:** Terence Fisher; **Screenplay:** Ronald Liles, Pip Baker, and Jane Baker; **Cinematography:** Reg Wyer; **Music:** Malcolm Lockyer; **Cast:** Peter Cushing, Christopher Lee, Sarah Lawson, Jane Merrow, Patrick Allen, William Lucas, Percy Herbert

A small British isle is attacked by alien invaders in the middle of winter. The aliens, which resemble large fried eggs, first raise the local temperature to tropical levels. If that was all they did, most likely no one would have had a problem with their visit. But then they start burning people to death whenever the opportunity arises. As usual, the humans are fairly helpless. Luckily, it finally starts to shower, and wouldn't you know it, these aliens are dissolved by rainwater, which, of course, they aren't smart enough to come in out of. This movie is based on the novel *Night of the Big Heat* by John Lymington. Unlike the movie, the book is rich and scary and fairly frightening.

ISLAND OF THE BURNING DOOMED

See *ISLAND OF THE BURNING DAMNED*

ISLAND OF THE DOOMED
(aka: MAN-EATER OF HYDRA)

Orbital/Theumer (Spain/West Germany), 1966/Allied Artists (U.S.), 1968, Color, 88 min

Producer: George Ferrer; **Director:** Mel Welles; **Screenplay:** Stephen Schmidt; **Cinematography:** Cecilio Paniagua; **Music:** Anton Garcia Abril; **Cast:** Cameron Mitchell, Kay Fischer, Ralph Naukoff, Elisa Montes, George Martin

On a remote island a mad scientist gets involved in dangerous experiments. This time our misunderstood genius has spent his life devoted to the development of a plant that can kill people by sucking their bodies dry of blood. This movie is mildly entertaining. Mitchell is at his best, but the story is incredibly predictable and the science nonexistent.

ISLAND OF THE TWILIGHT PEOPLE

See *THE TWILIGHT PEOPLE*

IT CAME FROM BENEATH THE SEA

Columbia, 1955, b&w, 77 min, VT, LD

Producer: Charles H. Schneer; **Director:** Robert Gordon; **Screenplay:** George Worthing Yates and Hal Smith; **Special Effects:** Ray Harryhausen and Jack Erickson; **Cinematography:** Henry Freulich; **Music:** Mischa Bakaleinikoff; **Cast:** Kenneth Tobey, Faith Domergue, Donald Curtis, Ian Keith, Harry Lauter, Del Courtney, Dean Maddox, Jr.

There's trouble out at sea as well as along the western coast of the United States. A dashing navy man (Tobey) teams up with two scientists (Domergue and Curtis) to see what could be behind all the bizarrely wanton and completely unexplainable destruction. Ms. Domergue investigates the evidence. The boys restrict themselves to analyzing their chances with their attractive colleague. Eventually, however, the trio stumbles across the truth. A gargantuan octopus, obviously mutated wildly out of control by nuclear radiation, is the force behind all the killing and property damage. Before long, the thing even moves inland, dragging itself through the streets of San Francisco so it can destroy skyscrapers as well as tanker ships. Bullets and tanks are useless. What will humanity do?

If you don't already know this movie, be assured that it is one of the good ones—short on science, but long on looks, thanks to the king of the stop-frame animators, Ray Harryhausen. The creature's epic scene centers on it trying to pull down the Golden Gate Bridge. It's one of the most spectacular scenes of Harryhausen's career, and yet the government actually tried to keep it from happening. In his book *Film Fantasy Scrapbook*, the animator tells the following story:

> In order to obtain permission and cooperation to photograph the various landmarks in San Francisco it was necessary to present the script to the "City Fathers" for approval. We were astonished to be confronted with a big "No" on the matter of the Golden Gate Bridge. We supposed they felt that any suggestion of destruction on film, even in a fantasy, might undermine the public's confidence in the soundness of its structure. We had of course gone too far into production to be defeated by this decision. Because it was imperative to have real shots of the bridge we were forced to be resourceful and to resort to other means. Much stock footage and newsreel material was also used to great advantage and economy.

Another bit of economy utilized during the making of this film was leaving off two of the octopus appendages. According to Harryhausen, his budget for the film was rather tight, and two fewer tentacles to build and animate during the long stop-motion process saved a good deal of time. Luckily, *It Came From Beneath the Sea*'s six-legged beastie is more than adequate to carry the picture. Stop-frame king Harryhausen was at the top of his game, and the film has never suffered for a lack of fans over the decades.

Also interesting in this film is the character of the scientist played by Faith Domergue. Ever since the '60s there has been chatter in Hollywood about the lack of strong roles for women. During the '50s, however, science fiction movies were filled with strong-willed beauties who did exactly what they wanted and usually left the men sputtering for air. Joan Weldon shoving aside chauvinist concerns as she descends into the ant hill in *THEM* is an excellent example, as is Domergue's character in this film. Indeed, the mens' inability to crack her shell is one of the most interesting subplots in any Harryhausen film. The whole thing is handled with great style and humor, all the way to the end when navy man Tobey finally wins the duel, only to wonder if maybe he hadn't bitten off more than he could chew.

This is one that couldn't have been any better even if Mr. Whit Bissell himself had been lurking somewhere in the background.

Note: Speaking of best ever, it should be pointed out to Harryhausen fans that his *Film Fantasy Scrapbook* is an excellent source of facts and still photos from almost every one of his movies.

IT CAME FROM OUTER SPACE

Universal, 1953, b&w, 80 min, VT, LD

Producer: William Alland; **Director:** Jack Arnold; **Screenplay:** Harry Essex; **Special Effects:** Clifford Stine and David S. Horsley; **Cinematography:** Stine; **Music:** Herman Stein; **Cast:** Richard Carlson, Barbara Rush, Charles Drake, Russell Johnson, Joe Sawyer, Kathleen Hughes, Morey Amsterdam, Charles Drake

Sunrock, Arizona: Astronomer Richard Carlson spots what he thinks at first to be a meteor crashing into Earth. Courageously, he climbs down into the massive crater left by the crash, searching for proof of the meteor he expects to find. He quickly upgrades his expectations, however, when he discovers a spaceship far advanced beyond human technology at the bottom of the crater. A rock slide forces him to retreat, but he's seen enough. He's ready to tell the whole world—UFOs are real; aliens are among us!

Predictably, no one believes him. Not so predictably, aliens from the ship begin replacing humans from the local town with duplicates. Yet another sinister invasion? Refreshingly, not this time. In a quite interesting change of pace, all the aliens are attempting is to repair their ship and get off Earth before its lunatic hordes murder them. The E.T.s do what they do only so they might move about undiscovered while they collect the parts they need to effect their repairs. By the end of the film Carlson, who has been leading the search for the aliens, is put in the position of having to keep the mobs away from the harmless space voyagers so that they can escape.

After they do, Carlson is asked about any more visitors from the stars. He assures all that: "It wasn't the right time for us to meet. But there'll be other times, other nights. They'll be back."

This is an excellent film, based on a Ray Bradbury story. Imaginative, subtle, and highly effective, it's not only a 3-D movie, but it's also the first science fiction film directed by Jack Arnold, the man who would go on to make both THE INCREDIBLE SHRINKING MAN and *The Mouse That Roared.* The cast does a fine job as well, and despite the obvious low budget, even the effects

It Came from Outer Space (UNIVERSAL PICTURES / R. ALLEN LEIDER COLLECTION)

are striking, all the way from the opening to the closing credits.

The theory behind the alien's power is interesting. Although the film goes into no boring (but possibly helpful) explanations, it seems to imply that the creatures can project their minds through any electrical field, including those surrounding living things—from plant to plant, line-of-sight between living creatures, even through the phone lines. They project three-dimensional replications of humans to move about for them, but these projections seem to be more hologram than flesh. All in all, it's a terrific idea.

Note: This is also the source of the oft-quoted line: "Did you know that more murders are committed at 92 degrees Fahrenheit than at any other temperature? I read an article once, at lower temperatures people are easy goin', at over 92 it's too hot to move, but at 92 degrees, people get irritable!"

IT CAME WITHOUT WARNING

See *WITHOUT WARNING*

IT CONQUERED THE WORLD

AIP, 1956, b&w, 71 min, VT

Producer: Roger Corman; **Director:** Corman; **Screenplay:** Lou Rusoff; **Special Effects:** Paul Blaisdell; **Cinematography:** Frederick E. West; **Music:** Ronald Stein; **Cast:** Peter Graves, Lee Van Cleef, Beverly Garland, Sally Fraser, Paul Blaisdell

Tom Anderson (Van Cleef) isn't the kind of neighbor you'd really want next door. For one thing, he sees nothing wrong with helping alien monsters take over the world. Luckily, his neighbor in this picture is a two-fisted Peter Graves, who shoots first and asks questions later. Anderson does finally regret his duplicity and attacks the leading creature after the monster throttles Anderson's wife. This sounds like the usual Corman nonsense, but it's actually somewhat effective. It's obviously shot with the standard Corman speed and anemic budget, but it's also a nicely atmospheric piece that does its job well enough.

IT HAPPENS EVERY SPRING

20th Century Fox, 1949, b&w, 87 min, VT

Producer: William Perlberg; **Director:** Lloyd Bacon; **Screenplay:** Valentine Davis and Shirley W. Smith; **Special Effects:** Fred Sersen; **Cinematography:** Joe MacDonald; **Music:** Leigh Harline; **Cast:** Ray Milland, Jean Peters, Paul Douglas, Ed Begley, Ted de Corsia, Ray Collins, Jessie Royce Landis, Alan Hale, Jr., Debra Paget, Jean Evans

Gentle Professor Milland has a problem, one that comes upon him every spring, gripping him well into the fall. That problem is the heady joy of the baseball season. The poor boy is utterly consumed by it. It distracts him, takes over his whole life, and drives his superiors at the university to distraction. On top of this, our dizzy prof wants to marry the dean's daughter, but baseball fever keeps interfering with that, too.

One day, quite by accident, Milland discovers a formula that prevents whatever it is applied to from coming in contact with wooden objects. It's not long before he works out a surefire money-making equation: formula + baseballs = a pitcher who can't be stopped.

Milland beats a path to a team in the cellar, confident he can keep the dean from discovering the real reason for his emergency leave. The dean, of course, would never allow his daughter to get mixed up with someone as crude as an athlete. He's also confident he can keep his girl in the dark and make his limited supply of formula last long enough to get him through one baseball season—just long enough to earn enough money for his sweetie and him to live on happily ever after. As you might expect, the usual complications ensue, and the laughs start to pile up pretty quickly thereafter.

It Happens Every Spring is a delightful, extremely unpretentious little comedy. As usual, the science of this one is right out the window, but as in most sci-fi/comedies, it isn't trying to win any Nobel prizes, just smiles and laughs. With most audiences, it succeeds. Beyond that, the baseball-pitching effects are pretty remarkable for the '40s.

IT LIVES AGAIN (aka: IT'S ALIVE II)

Warner Bros., 1978, Color, 91 min, VT, LD

Producers: Larry Cohen and William Wellman Jr.; **Director:** Cohen; **Screenplay:** Cohen; **Cinematography:** Fenton Hamilton; **Music:** Bernard Herrmann; **Special Effects:** Greg Cannom and Rick Baker; **Cast:** Frederic Forrest, Kathleen Lloyd, John Ryan, John Marley, Andrew Duggan, Eddie Constantine

See *IT'S ALIVE!*

IT'S ALIVE!

Warner Bros., 1974, Color, 91 min, VT, LD

Producer: Larry Cohen; **Director:** Cohen; **Screenplay:** Cohen; **Special Effects:** Rick Baker; **Cinematography:** Fenton Hamilton; **Music:** Bernard Herrmann; **Cast:** John Ryan, Sharon Farrell, Andrew Duggan, Guy Stockwell, James Dixon, Michael Ansara

In this truly bizarre film, a mutant baby is delivered, and the instant it clears the safety of its mother's womb, it attacks and kills all of the medical staff in the delivery room. After that, it leaps through the skylight and goes on a rampage of slaughter. Dad leads the search for the horror, determined to destroy this foul thing, which, by its very existence, is a blight on his good name. When push comes to shove, however, Dad realizes that the little psycho killer is *his* little psycho killer, and his paternal instinct takes over.

Critic Leonard Maltin says this movie is "not for all tastes," earning himself the understatement award of the century. *It's Alive!* is certainly an effective sci-fi/horror film, but it is a grim and unsettling one, particularly disturbing for those who have or wish to have children.

The picture was followed by two sequels, *It Lives Again* (aka: *It's Alive II*) and *It's Alive III: Island of the*

Alive, neither of which live up to the genius of the first. *It's Alive!* was a top grosser in its initial year of release and a huge smash in Europe, taking the Special Jury Prize at the Avariaz Film Festival in France. The films that follow attempt to expand on the original story, telling the tale of how mutant babies continue to be born around the world in response to the worsening environmental conditions. There is intelligent and pointed commentary on subjects ranging from abortion to AIDS, but the sequels, although clever, especially the first, are not up to their predecessor on any level.

It's Alive! is a shocking, often disgusting film, but it also has tremendous impact for those who can sit through it. Rewards await the brave.

Note: It's Alive! holds the honor of being one of the last science fiction films scored by the legendary Bernard Herrmann before his death; he died in the middle of scoring *Taxi Driver*. Herrmann fans certainly won't be displeased.

IT'S ALIVE II

See *IT'S ALIVE!*

IT'S ALIVE III: ISLAND OF THE ALIVE

Warner Bros., 1987, Color, 91 min, VT

Producers: Larry Cohen, Barry Shils, Paul Stander, and Barbara Zitwer; **Director:** Cohen; **Screenplay:** Cohen; **Cinematography:** Daniel Pearl; **Music:** Laurie Johnson; **Special Effects:** Rick Baker and Dane A. Davis; **Cast:** Michael Moriarty, Karen Black, Laurene Landon, Gerit Graham, James Dixon, Neal Israel, Macdonald Carey

See *IT'S ALIVE!*

IT STALKED THE OCEAN FLOOR

See MONSTER FROM THE OCEAN FLOOR

IT! THE TERROR FROM BEYOND SPACE

United Artists, 1958, b&w, 69 min, VT

Producer: Robert E. Kent; **Director:** Edward L. Kahn; **Screenplay:** Jerome Bixby; **Special Effects:** Lane Britton and Paul Blaisdell; **Cinematography:** Kenneth Peach; **Music:** Paul Sawtell; **Cast:** Marshall Thompson, Shawn Smith, Kim Spalding, Ann Doran, Dabbs Greer, Paul Langton, Ray Corrigan

A second rocket expedition to Mars arrives to find every member of the first party, save one, dead. Marshall Thompson plays the lone survivor who claims that the rest of his fellows were killed by some monstrous thing that he cannot explain to his interrogators' satisfaction. There is a reason for their skepticism—at first the second crew is willing to give Thompson the benefit of the doubt, then a bullet hole is found in the skull of one of the dead. Thompson is then taken into custody, and the expedition heads back to Earth to put the solar system's first interplanetary murderer on trial.

Unbeknownst to the crew, however, there *is* a monstrous thing, but it's no longer on Mars. The creature had slipped aboard their ship before takeoff. Once the ship is in space, the creature begins roaming the craft, looking for fresh victims. It kills some crew members one by one, storing their bodies in the ship's ventilation system for further meals. The monster takes over the ship section by section, chasing the crew farther and farther forward until all the survivors are trapped in the nose cone with the creature tearing its way through the hatch door.

This is an exciting, well-made, straightforward film that has had its plot stolen so many times that it's hard to count them all. It suffers from many of the problems one expects in '50s science fiction films—spaceships with unadorned, nonfunctional walls, wooden packing crates used by astronauts for their supplies, and so forth. Strip away the "mistakes" easily spotted now, however, and there isn't that much wrong here. True, the monster that is so effectively hidden from sight throughout most of the picture is frankly a disappointment when finally seen clearly, but a case of rubber-suititis is about the only false note in *It! The Terror From Beyond Space*. This is one of the better space opera films, certainly one of the best ever made in black-and-white. Viewers who have seen *ALIEN* may feel they know this one inside out, but still, as a history lesson if nothing else, it's a winner.

I WAS A TEENAGE FRANKENSTEIN

AIP, 1957, b&w (with some color segments), 74 min, VT

Producer: Herman Cohen; **Director:** Herbert Strock; **Screenplay:** Kenneth Langtry; **Special Effects:** Philip Scheer; **Cinematography:** Lothrop Worth; **Music:** Paul Dunlap; **Cast:** Whit Bissell, Gary Conway, Phyllis Coates, Robert Burton, John Cliff

The tragic Dr. Frankenstein has yet another descendant interested in piecing together parts of dead bodies into new and interesting wholes. This time the old gent's great-great-great grandson is portrayed by the world's greatest character actor, Whit Bissell, in a starring role for once, as the sad surgeon who doesn't mind a little murder if it helps prove his point. Unfortunately, even the legendary acting chops of the incredible Bissell can't lift this movie out of the dull stupor created by its turgid script and plodding directing.

I WAS A TEENAGE WEREWOLF

AIP, 1957, b&w, 76 min, VT

Producer: Herman Cohen; **Director:** Gene Fowler, Jr.; **Screenplay:** Ralph Thornton; **Special Effects:** Fae M. Smith; **Cinematography:** Joseph LaShelle; **Music:** Paul Dunlap; **Cast:** Michael Landon, Yvonne Lime, Whit Bissell, Vladimir Sokoloff, Guy Williams, Eddie Marr

A slightly mad school psychiatrist gets his mitts on juvenile delinquent Landon and does his best to throw a monkey wrench into the lad's plans. Landon would like to clean up his act to please his widower dad, but the school shrink thinks it would be more fun to hypnotize him and regress the lad to a primitive state. The result is that Landon turns primitive enough to become a werewolf whenever a bell rings. Don't be conned into thinking that this is the inspiration for *ALTERED STATES*. This is just another piece of out-and-out exploitation nonsense, an attempt by the talentless to bilk the gullible out of their hard-earned cash. And it worked, too, since the film was a hit during its original release.

JACK ARMSTRONG

Columbia, 1947, b&w, serial, 15 chapters

Producer: Sam Katzman; **Director:** Wallace Fox; **Screenplay:** Arthur Hoerl, Lewis Clay, Royal K. Cole, and Leslie Swabacker; **Music:** Lee Zahler; **Cinematography:** Ira H. Morgan; **Cast:** Pierre Watkin, Hugh Prosser, Joe Brown, John Hart, Rosemary La Planche, Charles Middleton, Jack Ingram, Eddie Parker, Wheeler Oakman, Claire James

In this serial, Jack Armstrong (Hart) and his pals (Watkin, Prosser, Brown, and La Planche) discover some unscrupulous men experimenting with cosmic energy—yes, the bad kind. The plucky kids decide to investigate this world-shattering information on their own rather than waste the time of the local police or a couple of carloads of G-men. After the kidnapping of a few kids (just killing these meddlesome punks as real spies might would be, of course, too easy) and their subsequent escapes, the kids finally track evil doctor Grood (Middleton) to his island fortress, where he is preparing his death ray. The choreography of blunders continues there for a while, week after week, until finally Jack, acting as judge, jury, and executioner, takes out the villain with a hand grenade.

Once upon a time, Jack Armstrong, the All-American Boy, was very popular. He and his pals were the Hardy Boys/Nancy Drew team of their day. But, that doesn't mean this serial is something special. Sadly, it's just more pulp fodder, but it does show that the language and props of science fiction was spreading across the genres. What should be noted is that any other genre can turn itself into a science fiction slasher—a sci-fi/western, sci-fi/comedy, sci-fi/noir, sci-fi/action/adventure (a double slasher, but you get the idea), and so on. Time travel, first contact, superpowers, mad doctors, the nature of the soul, reanimation, robots, interplanetary travel, and any other science fiction concept can end up in a romance, a western, a war picture, and so on. Literature borrows. From generation to generation and from art form to art form, that's the nature of art—to take that which is already known and make it into something new, but still recognizable.

JAPAN SINKS

See *NIPPON CHIMBOTSU*

JESSE JAMES MEETS FRANKENSTEIN'S DAUGHTER

Embassy, 1966, Color, 82 min, VT

Producer: Carroll Case; **Director:** William Beaudine; **Screenplay:** Carl Hittleman; **Music:** Raoul Kraushaar; **Cinematography:** Lothrop Worth; **Special Effects:** Ted Coodley and John D. Hall; **Cast:** John Lupton, Narda Onyx, Steven Geray, Jim Davis, Estellita, Carl Bolder

When his partner (Bolder) is shot, notorious outlaw Jesse James (Lupton) is forced to hide out, not in one of his usual digs, but in the mansion of Maria Frankenstein. (Well, look at the boy's career choices—historically the lad's not known for making good decisions. Ms. Frankenstein (Onyx) doesn't really mind, though, because she finds Jesse quite attractive. But the somewhat dim terror of the Old West doesn't notice because he's infatuated with the maid (Estellita). This class-crossing insult, witless as it might be, sends Frankenstein's daughter into a jealous rage that forces her to do a lobotomy on Jesse's pal, turning him into a psycho killer whom she can send to kill Jesse. Amazingly, Jesse is saved from his lobotomized best friend by the local sheriff. As usual, though, there's no one there to save the audience.

JE T'AIME, JE T'AIME

France, 1968, 94 min/20th Century Fox, 1973, Color, 82 min

Producer: Mag Bodard; **Director:** Alain Resnais; **Screenplay:** Resnais and Jacques Sternberg; **Music:** Krzstof Penderecki; **Cinematography:** Jean Boffety; **Cast:** Claude Rich, Olga Georges-Picot, Anouk Ferjac

Claude Rich plays a man finished with life. After attempting suicide and failing, he is forced to take part in a top-secret experiment in time travel. Normally, someone as unstable as a potential suicide would never be considered for anything so important. But just such an attitude is what the experimenters need.

The somewhat smug researchers are confident that their experiment is completely safe. After all, they've already worked their magic on mice, and everything worked out just fine. But human beings are not animals, or at least, not simple ones. Conscious of the passage of time, we experience the phenomenon on a cerebral as well as a physical level. For the unfortunate Rich, this means reliving the horrible love affair that sent him over the edge to begin with—not once, but scores of times as history fragments and repeats itself while the time traveler oscillates within its fluid boundaries.

Je T'aime, Je T'aime is an incredibly rich and striking masterpiece. The editing is beyond the discussion it can be given here. Suffice it to say that the editor shattered time again and again, sometimes in increasing small bites, sometimes showing the same moment with only slight differences, mixing memory with reality and vice versa. There is a great deal going on here, starting with the organic, seemingly biological

time machine and traveling onward throughout the film. In truth, the science fiction element is as strong and pure as in any American film. This story is not a straightforward adventure film, such as George Pal's *THE TIME MACHINE*, but a study of how and why we age or at least why we as a race are unable to escape the clutches of time, mainly because of our inability to extricate ourselves from the blunders of our own past.

JETEE 'LA

Argos/Arcturus (France), 1962, b&w, 29 min

Producer: Anatole Dauman; **Director:** Chris Marker; **Screenplay:** Marker; **Music:** Trevor Duncan; **Cinematography:** Marker; **Cast:** Helene Chatelain, Jacques Ledoux, Davos Hanich

Another time travel effort from France as a group of post–World War III scientists attempt to send a man back in time to the days before the war. A combination of drugs and concentrating on a particular boyhood memory is what it takes to propel the test subject backward in time. The only problem those in charge of the experiment didn't foresee, once back in the far more desirable past—why would the poor guy want to return to the future? Maybe to avoid being tracked down and exterminated by more time travelers.

The interesting (and that is using as mild a word as possible) thing about this globally acclaimed film is that the entire picture (save for one scene showing a girl winking) is actually composed from a wildly inventive series of still photographs. This excellent work by filmmakers definitely laboring for experimentation and the advancement of their art rather than for profit produced a stylish, bold, tragic film. Blessed with a singular personal vision that is as remarkable as it is daring, this is one of the most intriguing non-American science fiction movies ever made. It may not be for the *STAR WARS/JURASSIC PARK/KILLERS FROM SPACE* crowd, but this is science fiction as it is rarely produced.

JETSONS: THE MOVIE

Universal, 1990, Color, 81 min, VT, LD

Producers: William Hanna, Joseph Barbara, and James Wang; **Directors:** Hanna and Barbara; **Screenplay:** Dennis Marks; **Music:** John Debney and Mark Mancina; **Animation:** Ray Patterson and Al Gmuer; **Cast:** George O'Hanlon, Penny Singleton, Mel Blanc, Tiffany, Don Messick, Patric Zimmerman

George Jetson finally gets that promotion that Mr. Spacely was always offering him on the original television series. Of course, as one might expect from Mr. Spacely, there's a catch. The factory is located on a faraway planet, which means some hardships for George familywise. But he's a loving husband who only wants the best for his clan, so off he goes to his new executive position. The problem, however, is that his boss has been even more duplicitous than usual. There is a cute alien race living in the caverns under the factory, which is being destroyed by the sprocket-making machines above. What seemed like terrorist acts are really desperate attempts of these poor aliens to save their homes and lives.

For those who liked the wonderfully sarcastic 1960s cartoon, *The Jetsons*, this film will be terribly disappointing. Judy sings stupid songs; Mr. Spacely is pointlessly stupid, evil, petty, and vain; and George is . . . well, it's really too painful to describe. George isn't George and Jane isn't Jane except in the most trivial, blunt, and heavy-handed ways.

There is a ruthless (and, considering the results, especially the horribly dismal box office returns, mindless as well) serving of interests other than making a good film evident throughout. Pointless changes were made (such as hiring singer Tiffany to do Judy's voice) only for the purpose of trying to draw in new customers, while ignoring the fan base from the television series. The story is stale and boring. Everything about the film is depressingly cheap. Awkward, feeble, blocky computer animation intrudes regularly, and one wonders if those involved either hated the franchise's fans or refused to believe that pleasing them was their job.

The worst crime of all? *Jetsons* fans will understand, but others will have to use their imaginations. *The Jetsons* has the coolest theme music ever written for an animated cartoon show. It is hot, smoky jazz with a horn set and piano tinker that swing with an FSL movement that pops the art behind it like no one's business. Fans might expect that hearing the theme in a big dark theater, blasting out of Dolby speakers, would be the pinnacle of animation daydreams. And yet the hacks behind this one even got that wrong.

J-MEN FOREVER

Curtco, 1979, b&w, 75 min, VT

Producer: Patrick Curtis; **Director:** Richard Patterson; **Screenplay:** Peter Bergman and Philip Proctor; **Music:** Billy Preston, Head East, The Tubes, Badazz, Budgie, and Richard Thiess; **Cast:** Philip Proctor, Peter Bergman, M.G. Kelly

The dreaded Lightning Bug is out to conquer Earth with his most diabolical plot yet. He's going to smother the black-and-white airways with that dread rock 'n' roll all the kids are so hopped up on and zombify everyone. Where can decent people turn? Who will make the world safe? Why, every hero you remember from the Republic serials, that's who.

Two extremely funny and inventive men, Phil Proctor and Pete Bergman of the world-renowned Firesign Theater took reels and reels of the old Republic weekly grinders and re-edited them with voice-over gags into one new hysterically funny movie. No one is safe from their joking around, which is nonstop.

Note: A young Leonard Nimoy cut his teeth on more than one of the Saturday morning serials. The Firesign boys have particular fun with the future Mr. Spock's appearance here, a joke that all by itself makes this movie worth watching.

JOHNNY MNEMONIC

Columbia/Tri-Star, 1995, Color, 98 min, VT, LD, DVD

Producer: Don Carmody; **Director:** Robert Longo; **Screenplay:** William Gibson; **Music:** Brad Fiedel; **Cinematography:** François Protat; **Special Effects:** Shinichi Youhimoto, Gene Warren, Jr., George Merkert, John Nelson, Bill Birrell, Glenn Campbell, Cat Chapman, Rory Cutler, Leslie Huntley, Anthony Ceccomancini; **Cast:** Keanu Reeves, Dolph Lundgren, Takeshi, Ice-T, Dina Meyer, Udo Kier, Denis Akiyama, Henry Rollins, Tracy Tweed, Don Francks

It's 2021. Everything that's wrong with our present world has been taken about a step and a half further toward the dark side. In other words, Earth is one scary, violent, fast-paced place that no one wants to live in and everyone would love to escape.

Enter our hero, Johnny Mnemonic (Reeves). Mnemonic is a courier—a very special kind. His brain has been outfitted to receive, store, then download computer-ready information. We're talking a direct wet-wire storage capacity. Finally, humankind has found a way to benefit from all those areas of the brain they say we don't use. Wanting to carry the absolute maximum amount of information that any human being can possibly hold, Mnemonic has gone one step further than most of his fellow couriers—he's not only added a dangerous compressor to his neural implants, but he's also freed up all the available room on his God-given hard drive, as it were, wiping every nonessential memory from his brain so that he might handle more data.

This makes Mnemonic a cipher to everyone, including himself. He has no personality because he has no memories. Nothing in his mind tells him who he is, what his beliefs are, his parents, his first date, right from wrong—anything. In the meantime, Mnemonic's memories are intact and waiting for him in storage. He can get them back as soon as he retires, which he's planning to do soon.

Mnemonic has just been offered an incredible contract. He'll need to carry a dangerous amount of information—almost twice his actual capacity, a feat he accomplishes through the use of the previously mentioned dangerously risky cerebral data compressor. Now all he has to do is fly from Beijing to Newark, deliver his package, and everything will be fine. Of course, there are terrorists after him, and an evil corporation that wants the information he's carrying, and he has no way of knowing who to trust, thanks to having no memories.

Johnny Mnemonic is a fast-paced, cutting-edge film, yet many critics panned it savagely when it was released. This film was keyboarded by William Gibson, the author of *Neuromancer*, the first of the cyberpunk novels, and one wonders if most of the concepts within it were simply beyond the reach of old-school critics who thought they'd mastered the electronic age when they made the switch from electric typewriters to word processors. Reeves was endlessly lambasted for flat acting, overlooking that he was playing a man with no memory of any of his formative moments. He was a man without a childhood, without emotions. It was a hard role to approach, but Reeves did a terrific job.

Johnny Mnemonic is not high, intellectual storytelling, but it is a fast-moving, zip-plugged, speedline seven-shifter that follows along just as many action movie conventions as it ignores. Gibson chose among the standard adventure film clichés wisely, running down the clock in a way that leaves the audience constantly guessing—will the same old thing actually be the same old thing this time, or will there be yet another flashy twist thrown in?

Note: Before this film Dolph Lundgren was seen as just another muscle man with a bad accent, but like Reeves, he proves himself here, along with the rest of the young, hard-working cast.

JOURNEY BENEATH THE DESERT (aka: L'ATLANTIDE)

France/Italy, Embassy (U.S.), 1961, Color, 89 min, VT

Producer: Nat Wachberber; **Directors:** Edgar G. Ulmer and Ciuseppi Masini; **Screenplay:** Ugo Libera-tore, Remigio del Grasso, André Tabet, and Amedeo Nazzari; **Music:** Carlo Rustichelli; **Cinematography:** Enzo Serafin; **Special Effects:** Giovanni Ventimiglia; **Cast:** Jean-Louis Trintignant, Georges Rivière, Rad Fulton, Haya Harareet, Amedeo Nazzari, Giulia Rubini, Gabriele Tinti, Gian Maria Volonte

A helicopter in need of emergency repairs, unfortunately for its crew and passengers, is forced to make an unscheduled landing at a nuclear test site. Those aboard poke around for a while and find the lost city of Atlantis under the test site. Fancy that.

Actually, this isn't a bad little film. It's also the fourth time the oft-filmed Pierre Benoit novel, *Atlantida*, has reached the silver screen. The first was a 1921 silent version. The second came in 1932 (see *L'ATLANTIDE*). The third film came in 1948 and was entitled *Siren of Atlantis*. All four versions were made by European studios. It is generally agreed that *Journey Beneath the Desert* is the best of the quartet, possibly explaining why after a version every 12 to 13 years, suddenly there hasn't been one for decades.

JOURNEY TO THE BEGINNING OF TIME (aka: JOURNEY TO PRE-HISTORY)

Czechoslovakia, 1954, 93 min/New Trends (U.S.), 1967, 87 min, Color, VT, LD

Producer: William Cayton; **Director:** Karl Zeman; **Screenplay:** Zeman and J.A. Novotny; **Music:** E.F. Burian; **Cinematography:** Vaclav Pazdernik and Antonin Horak; **Special Effects:** Ivo Mrdzek, Karel Zeman, and Zdenek Rozkopal; **Cast:** James Lucas, Victor Betral, Peter Hermann, Charles Goldsmith

This is the simple tale of a quartet of adventurous youths who pilot their raft down the river of time. They don't see much of the world wars, the signing of the Declaration of Independence or the Magna Carta, or the building of the pyramids, and so on, but they do get to view lots and lots of stop-frame animated beasties. Despite its rush to the lowest common denominator, this movies is interesting and even better than average. It's fun as a history lesson—the history of sci-fi films, not anthropology.

JOURNEY TO THE CENTER OF THE EARTH (aka: TRIP TO THE CENTER OF THE EARTH)

20th Century Fox, 1959, 132 min, Color, VT, LD, DVD

Producer: Charles Brackett; **Director:** Henry Levin; **Screenplay:** Brackett and Walter Reisch; **Music:** Bernard Herrmann; **Cinematography:** Leo Tover; **Special Effects:** Lyle B. Abbott, James B. Gordon, and Emil Kosa, Jr.; **Cast:** James Mason, Pat Boone, Alan Napier, Alan Caillou, Diane Baker, Arlene Dahl, Thayer David, Peter Ronson

Professor Lindenbrooke (Mason) discovers proof of the existence of a world hidden inside our own when he comes across markings made on a piece of volcanic rock. The marks were made by a famous explorer, Arne Saknussemm, who disappeared without a trace years earlier. Confident he can follow Saknussemm's trail, the professor sets out to find this lost underground world, accompanied by his student (Boone), Boone's manservant (Ronson), and his girlfriend (Dahl).

As the foursome makes its way into the depths of Earth, however, at first they are unaware that they have company. Saknussemm's only surviving relative, the sinister Count Saknussemm, wants the glory of finding the center of the Earth, and so he sets out to destroy the quartet and claim their find as his own. He attempts to murder the foursome but fails, ending up as their prisoner. The five then move on together, falling into more and more trouble even as they make more and more fantastic discoveries. A forest of towering, redwood-sized mushrooms, dinosaurs, and prehistoric bread are just some of the wonders that await them. Among the dangers: whirlpools, earthquakes and dinosaurs.

Journey to the Center of the Earth is a great movie for the whole family. There's not much for adults watching by themselves (unless they saw it as kids, or are really good with the snappy ad-libs), but watching this one with kids is a totally different experience. The picture is nicely paced and action filled, but it's also a product of its times, a gentle film aimed at Eisenhower-era kids that still holds up today.

Mason is a sheer joy, always perfectly in character, and Boone not only doesn't sing much, but he acts his heart out. The effects are spectacular, despite dinosaurs that are those familiar lizards with fins pasted on their backs that turned up in every other 1950s dinosaur movie that wasn't the work of special effects master Ray Harryhausen. The climax is incredible fun, and the sound track is yet another of Bernard Herrmann's triumphs.

JOURNEY TO THE CENTER OF TIME (aka: TIME WARP)

Borealis-Dorad, 1968, 82 min, Color, VT

Producers: Ray Dorn and David L. Hewitt; **Director:** Hewitt; **Screenplay:** David Prentiss; **Music:** John Barber; **Cinematography:** Robert Caramico; **Special Effects:** Modern Film Effects; **Cast:** Scott Brady, Gigi Perreau, Anthony Eisley, Lyle Waggoner, Abraham Sofaer, Poupee Gamin

Warning to NASA and others who would cut corners: This could happen to you!

Scientists working on a time machine hurry things along without the proper amount of testing, looking for results to prove their theory and not necessarily the truth. When they feel confident enough, they pile into their time machine and take off on an ill-considered joy ride. The team is caught in an oscillation in time. They find themselves in a typical time travel future in which a totalitarian utopia lies locked in never-ending conflict with a subrace of hostile mutants. Escaping this world, they are promptly flung into the past, where they wind up with the required number of badly executed dinosaur special effects. Before they can get their bearings, it all begins again. *Journey to the Center of Time* is not much of a film. Indeed, if you strip out the ideas it borrowed from the somewhat superior THE TIME TRAVELERS, this movie doesn't have much to offer.

JOURNEY TO PRE-HISTORY

See *JOURNEY TO THE BEGINNING OF TIME*

JOURNEY TO THE FAR SIDE OF THE SUN (aka: DOPPELGANGER)

Century 21 (Great Britain)/Universal, 1969, 94 min, Color, VT, LD, DVD

Producers: Gerry and Sylvia Anderson; **Director:** Robert Parrish; **Screenplay:** Gerry and Sylvia Anderson and Donald James; **Music:** Barry Gray; **Cinematography:** John Read; **Special Effects:** Derek Meddings and Harry Oakes; **Cast:** Roy Thinnes, Lynn Loring, Herbert Lom, Patrick Wymark, Ian Hendry

Col. Glenn Ross (Thinnes) leads an expedition to, as the film's title suggests, the far side of the Sun. The noble astronaut's objective: a newly discovered planet that since the beginning of time has shared Earth's orbit while always remaining exactly on the other side of the Sun from our own world. Sadly for the valiant flyboy, he seems to not only fail to make it to the far side of the Sun, but also can't even return home correctly. He crash-lands back on Earth, killing his fellow astronaut in the process.

The colonel is soon being questioned relentlessly by his superiors. What is he doing back on Earth? Why couldn't he reach his objective? Why wasn't the mission completed? How could the rocket have crashed? What caused the crash—equipment malfunction, crew distraction, or inefficiency? Or possibly, something more sinister?

Ross is taken aback. He can't believe that men he has known for so many years would accuse him of deliberately sabotaging his greatest mission. Why would he do it? What could he possibly gain beyond the fame and glory of being the man to prove there was another planet in our own orbit? That challenge met would put his name among the stellar explorers of history. He would have been immortal.

But then, a sinister, unbelievable idea begins to blossom within the colonel's mind.

What if his mission didn't fail? What if he and his partner did make it to the other side of the Sun? And, what if the planet he crashed on was indeed the planet he was sent to investigate? Evidence begins to pile up. Before long, Ross is certain of his theory—the planet on the other side of the Sun from Earth shares more than just its orbit. It is Earth—exactly the same down to every person, insect, and McDonald's burger. His only problem—how to prove his theory to those now intent on seeing him as either a spy or an incompetent?

Journey to the Far Side of the Sun is an ambitious film filled with lots of pre-*X-Files* government conspiracy horror. Created by Gerry and Sylvia Anderson, whose production company brought the world the somewhat less serious puppet television series *Thunderbirds*, as well as the sharp and experimental live-action near-hits *UFO* and *Space 1999*, the picture is perhaps a bit too complex. There are hints of both sabotage instigated by sources other than the colonel and collusion between the two planets that are never adequately explained. The plot woes brought on by this are compounded by a story told via episodes of flashback related by a mental patient (we'll keep that identity a secret for those who want to go out and watch this one).

Still, it's a film worth viewing on a rainy Saturday. Veteran director Robert Parrish's deft hand smoothed out a great number of potential rough edges for his television producers, leaving them with an interesting picture that still stands up fairly well, and Thinnes's performance won't disappoint either.

JOURNEY TO THE SEVENTH PLANET

AIP, 1962, 83 min, Color, VT, LD

Producer: Sidney Pink; **Director:** Pink; **Screenplay:** Pink and Ib Glindeman; **Music:** Jerry Capeheart, Glindemann, and Mitchell Tableporter; **Cinematography:** Aage Wiltrop; **Special Effects:** Bent Barfod Films; **Cast:** John Agar, Greta Thyssen, Ann Smyrner, Mimi Heinrich, Carl Ottosen, Ove Sprogoe

In the far-flung future of 2001, humankind has finally pushed outward past the Moon, almost to the farthest reaches of the solar system. This time humanity has made it as far as the planet Uranus. The mission, led by astronaut John Agar, should be routine—survey the place and report any observations to Earth. As could be expected, there is nothing routine about the mission. Shortly after arrival, the five astronauts find themselves in the grip of a sadistic (or at least curious) invisible force possessed of incredible mental powers. The Earthlings find fragments of their memory being used against them as familiar images from their past on Earth suddenly confront them in the flesh on Uranus.

As described, the plot has great possibilities, but outside of a ratlike monster created by genius special effects man Jim Danforth, there is not much here to see and even less to think about. Even Agar fans will be disappointed. It's not that he phoned in his performance; he simply wasn't given much to work with. The filmmakers show the tiniest bit of imagination here and there, but for the most part, this movie is as avoidable as they come.

JUDGE DREDD

Hollywood Pictures/Cinergi Pictures, 1995, Color, 96 min, VT, LD, DVD

Producers: Andrew J. Vagna and Edward R. Pressman; **Director:** Danny Cannon; **Screenplay:** Michael DeLuca, Willian Wisher, and Steven E. DeSouza; **Music:** Alan Silvestri; **Cinematography:** Adrian Biddle, B.S.C., **Special Effects:** Joss William, Diane Pearlman, Steve Cullane, Clive Beard, Brian Morrison, Kevin Herd, Michael Dawson, Kevin Draycott, Brian Werner, Robert U. Taylor, and Joel Hynek; **Cast:** Sylvester Stallone, Armand Assante, Diane Lane, Rob Schneider, Joan Chen, Jorgen Prochnow, Max von Sydow, Balthazar Getty, Joanna Miles, Mitchell Ryan, James Russo, Scott Wilson

After a series of *Judge Dredd* comic-book covers flash into view, veteran voice James Earl Jones reads the following words as they scroll across the screen for the illiterate in the crowd:

In the third millennium, the world changed. Climate, nations, all were in upheaval. The Earth transformed into a poisonous, scorched desert, known as "The Cursed Earth."

Millions of people crowded into a few Mega-Cities where roving bands of street savages created violence the justice system could not control. Law as we know it collapsed.

From the decay rose a new order. A society ruled by a new elite force—a force with the power to dispense both justice and punishment—they were the police, jury and executioner all in one. They were the judges.

After that, we enter Mega-City 1, roughly the size of what was once Delaware, New Jersey, and lower New York State. It is a seemingly impregnable fortress, its incredible outer walls erected to bar entry to whatever might be alive out in the barren and feared Cursed Earth. The camera moves through the streets, revealing the wall-to-wall buildings, roadways, and restless, frustrated citizens trapped within the last gasp of this rotting civilization.

Enter citizen Herman Fergeson (Schneider), just released from prison. He has been assigned living quarters in a skyscraper-sized apartment building named Heavenly Haven. But upon arrival, Fergeson finds his apartment occupied by a gang of heavily armed thugs in the midst of fighting a war with another gang in the streets. Then enter the legendary street judge, Judge Dredd (Stallone), backed up by several other younger judges, including female Judge Hershey (Lane). The judges quickly wipe out both gangs, then arrest Fergeson basically for nothing more than being in the area. And so, after roughly 45 minutes of freedom, it's another five years of hard labor for poor Citizen Fergeson.

In the meantime, things are about to get hard for everyone—citizens and judges alike. In a meeting of the High Council of Judges, an argument championed by Judge Griffin (Prochnow) rages over increasing the number of crimes that can warrant capital punishment. With the number of riots going up every day, it seems to Griffin the most expedient way to deal with the situation, but Chief Judge Fargo (Sydow) disagrees. Even with more riots, even with that reporter Vardis whipping up discontent in the streets, the chief judge insists that judges must stand for something more than merely maintaining order at any cost.

Elsewhere, in the Aspen Penal Colony, we meet Rico (Assante), a fearsome criminal held in the highest security possible. At one time Rico was not only a judge, but Dredd's best and only friend. Still, when he crossed the line Dredd judged him accordingly and sentenced him to life. But suddenly things are looking up for Rico. The warden of the Penal Colony, who is working for an underworld figure, brings him a package, which contains a judge's badge and weapon, which Rico uses to escape. Upon returning to Mega-City 1, Rico picks up another package from his mysterious benefactor. This one has his old uniform and more weaponry. Next, the one-time judge picks up a killer robot and heads out to begin his mischief.

At roughly the same time, a judge murders controversial reporter Vardis. The murder is recorded by the home security system, and the tape reveals the rogue judge's badge to say "Dredd." Worse yet, judges' weapons, which can only be fired by their judge (any one else even touching one is electrocuted), have DNA-encoded bullets, and the bullets confirm the taped evidence: Dredd is the killer.

Justice is swift in the Mega-Cities. Despite Hershey's attempts to defend him, Dredd is sentenced to death. He is spared only when Fargo agrees to step down as chief judge, which he does because a retiring chief judge gets one last request. He requests mercy for Dredd for all his years of loyal service. His request is honored somewhat—Dredd's sentence is reduced to life in Aspen Penal Colony. The chief judge does not get to enjoy his retirement much, however. In this hellish future, a judge who actually lives long enough to retire is sent on the "Long Walk." This involves giving the judge not a gold watch, but a gun and some ammo and then sending him out into the Cursed Earth "to bring law to the lawless." Dredd is taken to Aspen, Fargo goes on his Long Walk, and then the truth behind all these complicated goings-on are finally revealed.

Judge Griffin is the one who had Rico released from Aspen. He wants to bring order to Mega-City in the storm trooper way, and more and bigger Rico-inspired riots are his way of scaring the high council into agreement. With Fargo and Dredd gone, Griffin's plan is to convince the council to reopen the Janus Project, the cloning experiment that created Dredd and Rico years earlier. Dredd doesn't know he is a clone, or that Rico is one either, but Rico knows, and he's ready to lead an army of such clones through the streets.

Out in the Cursed Earth, a savage band known as the Angel Family brings down the ship transporting Dredd (and, by chance, Fergeson as well) to Aspen. The two escape serious injury but are captured by the Angels, who, among their other faults, are cannibals. Dredd fights them off with the help of the timely arrival of Fargo, but Fargo takes a mortal wound.

Judge Dredd (HOLLYWOOD PICTURES & CINERGI PICTURES / JOSEPH B. MAUCERI COLLECTION)

Before he dies, he reveals the secret of the Janus Project. Between them, they figure out that Rico (who would share Dredd's DNA) is the killer of Vardis and that he and Griffin must be working together. Dredd and Fergeson return to Mega-City 1, and with Judge Hershey's help, they confront Rico.

Is this the *Inherit the Wind* of science fiction films? Well, no. But it may be the absolute best science fiction film based on a comic book ever made. The look is right, the characters are right, and everything came straight out of the books, right down to the bit about Dredd and Rico being clones. As always, lots of people grumbled about this movie, though without good reason. For once, every aspect of a comic book was taken seriously in its film adaptation. Nothing was eliminated in a Hollywood makeover. The effects are good. Everything looks exactly as it does in the comics, and the characters are right out of the books.

One could only wish for more of the comics' droll social commentary and wildly off-beat humor. For instance, in one scene a droid rolls through the halls announcing, "Eat Recycled Food." This sounds smart until one considers it. What exactly is recycled food? Recycled from what? And how? After only a moment's examination, this becomes a sharp bit of humor, the kind with which the *Judge Dredd* comics are filled. Sadly, there is far too little of this in the film.

But there is plenty of other stuff. The fights are great, the chases are thrilling, and the tone is right. Stallone *is* Judge Dredd, absolutely perfect for the role. Dredd is a very straightforward, unbending character. In Dredd's world, the law doesn't make mistakes. He knows he didn't commit any murders, but until he's given proof by the chief judge, he doesn't actually know what to do. After all, the law said he was guilty, so he must be—right?

Note: During the wild aerial motorcycle chase, there is a three-second period in which Stallone and his vehicle are a computer simulation. It comes when the craft buzzes close over the heads of the citizens in the street. Happy hunting trying to spot which seconds are which.

JULES VERNE'S ROCKET TO THE MOON

See *THOSE FANTASTIC FLYING FOOLS*

JUNGLE CAPTIVE

Universal, 1945, b&w, 64 min

Producer: Morgan Cox; **Director:** Harold Young; **Screenplay:** M. Coates Webster and Dwight V. Babcock; **Cinematography:** Maury Gertsman; **Music:** Hans J. Salter, Paul Sawtell, Richard Hageman, William Lava, Charles Previn, Frank Skinner, and Dimitri Tiomkin; **Cast:** Otto Kruger, Amelita Ward, Phil Brown, Vicky Lane, Jerome Cowan, Rondo Hatton

See *JUNGLE WOMAN*

JUNGLE WOMAN

Universal, 1944, b&w, 54 min, VT

Producer: Will Cowan; **Director:** Reginald LeBorg; **Screenplay:** Henry Sucher; **Cinematography:** Jack McKenzie; **Cast:** Acquanetta, J. Carrol Naish, Milburn Stone, Lois Collier, Pierre Watkin, Evelyn Ankers, Samuel S. Hinds

There were three films in this series, but since none are worth too many words, all are grouped under the most well-known of the trio.

In the first film, *Captive Wild Woman*, mad scientist John Carradine gets the urge to transform an orangutan into a beautiful woman. His experiment succeeds in the beauty department, specifically by having the ravishing Acquanetta play the end results. When her love for a real man goes unrequited though, she wrecks the lab and dies tragically. The movie is fun in a silly sort of way. If nothing else, it allows the audience to amuse themselves trying to spot the footage cut into this film from Clyde "Bring-'Em-Back-Alive" Beatty's *The Big Cage*. Beatty's original footage from that movie was used in dozens of other jungle films as well.

In the second film, *Jungle Woman*, Acquanetta plays the same role. She is brought back to life, this time with the venerable J. Carrol Naish playing the mad scientist. For a switch, psychiatry is tried on our monkey girl in this film, but by the end she still brings the house down.

By the third and final film in the series, *Jungle Captive*, Acquanetta had grown tired of the role so Vicki Lane took over. Again love is sparked between ape-girl and he-man, but wouldn't you know, the effects of the transformation are sadly temporary.

These three pictures have their fans, of course, especially *Jungle Woman*, but it's just the camp value lining the boys up for this series. The films have some stars, some so-so effects, and a lot of monkeyshines (yeah, that one was intended), but none of it adds up to anything for anyone interested in good films.

JUNIOR

Universal, 1994, Color, 110 min, VT, LD

Producer: Ivan Reitman; **Director:** Reitman; **Screenplay:** Kevin Wade and Chris Conrad; **Music:** James Newton Howard; **Cinematography:** Adam Greenberg, A.S.C.; **Special Effects:** David Blitstein, Lynda Lemon, and Peter Montgomery; **Cast:** Arnold Schwarzenegger, Danny DiVito, Emma Thompson, Frank Langella, Pamela Reed, Judy Collins, James Eckhouse, Aida Turturro, Welker White

Stuffy scientist Schwarzenegger is coaxed by his more flamboyant colleague DiVito into trying an experiment on himself that could result in his becoming pregnant. It's all a matter of fame and fortune and somewhat empirical . . . until it works. Then, feeling the great mystery of life happening within him, Schwarzenegger forgets all the worldly benefits and concentrates on having his child. The science fiction premise is great—let a man experience not only the earthy side of pregnancy (throwing up, hormone imbalance, odd cravings, back pain), but also the mystical, life-inside-life mystery of creation aspect of the process as well. There are lots of issues to explore, but unfortunately, this film was supposed to be a comedy, even though it stops being funny about halfway through. This noble experiment might be worthy for a nothing-better-to-do-afternoon.

Note: Schwarzenegger deserves credit for spending a great deal of time in the offices of various obstetricians researching his role so that he could observe and study how pregnant women move, carry themselves, and so on. It's not the same kind of suffering for one's art that Tom Hanks, Kevin Bacon, and Bill Paxton went through to create the weightless scenes in *APOLLO 13*, but it's still above and beyond the call of duty.

JURASSIC PARK

Universal/Amblin Entertainment, 1993, Color, 126 min, VT, LD, DVD

Producers: Gerald R. Molen and Kathleen Kennedy; **Director:** Steven Spielberg; **Screenplay:** Michael Crichton, David Koepp, and Malia Scotch Marmo; **Music:** John Williams; **Cinematography:** Dean Cundey; **Special Effects:** Industrial Light & Magic and the Stan Winston Studio; **Cast:** Jeff Goldblum, Sam Neill, Laura Dern, Richard Attenborough, Bob Peck, B.D. Wong, Martin Ferrero, Joseph Mazzello, Ariana Richards, Samuel L. Jackson, Wayne Knight

Multibillionaire Attenborough is a clever guy. He's gathered a crack staff that has found a way to not only extract dinosaur DNA from creatures trapped in amber and such, but to then successfully clone living, breathing dinosaurs. His plan is to exhibit these fearsome monsters in a free-range setting for fun and profit. He invites a crew of scientists to preview the park and provide him with some crowd-pleasing reviews. The scientists are paleontologist Neill, who is in love with his work, paleontologist Dern, who loves her work but could love Neill as well, and Goldblum, some sort of new-age scientist who spouts chaos theory but doesn't seem to have any one discipline to call his own. He loves good times and money and seems more interested in Dern than the dinosaurs. So certain is Attenborough that nothing can go wrong that he even has his grandchildren brought in for the occasion. And so, a kindly old man, a set of adorable kids, and a love triangle are dropped into the middle of an island full of razor-toothed eating machines.

Wayne Knight plays the bad guy, out to steal dino embryos and sell them to the highest bidder, but he fouls things up so that between his shenanigans and a wild storm, everything on the island gets loose. In keeping with this Spielberg film's simplistic logic, Knight must die for his crimes. So too the lawyer so obviously included in the cast just so he can be eaten that the word *dinner* might as well have been stamped on his forehead. What happens from here on in? The dinosaurs chase people, eating their victims according to a predictable pattern. The movie is pure paint-by-numbers. The dynamic, heroic, smooth-talking Goldblum doesn't get the girl. Apparently, she's reserved for the nerd.

That Michael Crichton had anything to do with this only shows that anyone can be seduced to the dark side. Yes, the science is all in place in the opening, and the pseudo theme park is chillingly exploitative. The special effects are an absolutely incredible state-of-the-art accomplishment, setting the groundwork for the amazing advances in digital film technology that followed, but the movie itself is ultimately a failure. There are so many things wrong with this picture that it's nearly impossible to find a place to start.

Outside of Goldblum, none of the actors find any way to bring much to their stock wooden characters. It's as if they had so little to work with that they just didn't bother. It's fairly cynical of a director and a writer to decide that since everyone's just going to be looking at the effects there's no need to put together an intelligent script, but it's hard to imagine that that isn't exactly what happened here.

This zoo is located on an island that is quite costly to reach; yet billionaire Attenborough, who has supposedly studied all aspects of this venture quite thoroughly, expects to turn a profit on general public admissions to a place more expensive to reach than Hawaii.

Weak-eyed animals that hunt by smell chase gasoline-exhaust-spewing jeeps rather than just killing the herbivores they can smell all around them.

One of the world's greatest hunters can't outthink these creatures in the brush; yet anthropologist Dern can—basically because she doesn't believe in killing. In a Spielberg film, of course he has to die and she has to live because political correctness, not logic, is what counts.

Dozens of questionable scenes throughout this film could be recounted, but perhaps the worst is the ridiculous jeep-in-the-tree sequence. The number of

Jurassic Park (UNIVERSAL CITY STUDIOS & AMBLIN ENTERTAINMENT / AUTHOR'S COLLECTION)

coincidences and moments of action that simply break the laws of physics within this single sequence mount up faster than flapjacks at a Boy Scout Jamboree breakfast, but the audience is meant to applaud the wonderful comedy, despite coming at the apogee of the film's first wave of terror. Perhaps this was Spielberg's way of softening the picture's intensity in order to get the rating guaranteed to generate the most profit, but it certainly doesn't make for a good story.

Factual mistakes abound as well. For instance, Knight's character is shown at a beachfront cafe under the caption: San Jose, Costa Rica. But are no beaches in San Jose, Costa Rica—it's a landlocked town. It doesn't even have an adjoining lake. But it can be argued that this is only a minor detail, so instead consider the central premise of the film. The amber from which the essential dino DNA is extracted is supposed to have come from the Dominican Republic. The problem? No amber brought out of the Dominican Republic has ever been found that was more than 20 million years old. Since the last of the dinosaurs perished 65 million years ago, Attenborough's scientists are something akin to miracle workers. This is sloppy work.

Many will defend this film on the grounds that it made a great deal of money, but money earned is not what makes a good science fiction film. In fact, to make the kind of money this film made (and it did make some $58 million in just its first weekend of release), a filmmaker is forced to dumb the product down so that any brainless viewers oozing their way through life can enjoy it. Good science fiction hardly ever attracts a massive audience because there's usually just too much thinking involved.

Jurassic Park is a beautiful film to view and includes many of the greatest, most shockingly realistic special effects of all time. With the sound off, it is simply breathtaking. But with the sound on, it is breathtakingly stupid and fairly insulting.

Note: Michael Crichton's book is better than what came to the screen. The characters are more believable, their motivations more credible. More of them die. There are more ethical issues, more loose ends in this sturdy thesislike look at science gone insane. Those who've never seen this movie should seriously consider just reading the book and keeping it that way.

William Hurt reportedly was first offered the Sam Neill role. The story is the star of *ALTERED STATES* and *LOST IN SPACE*, among others, turned the project down cold, refusing even to read the script.

JUST FOR FUN

Amicus (Great Britain), 1960/Columbia (U.S.), 1963, b&w, 85 min

Producer: Milton Subotsky; **Director:** Gordon Flemyng; **Screenplay:** Subotsky; **Music:** Bobby Vee, The Crickets, Freddy Cannon and The Tremeloes; **Cinematography:** Nicholas Roeg; **Special Effects:** Key Sinclair; **Cast:** Mark Wynter, Cherry Roland, Richard Vernon, Reginald Beckwith, Freddie Cannon, Johnny Tillotson, Ketty Lester

Teenagers get together politically in such masses that they're able to affect the outcome of national elections. Suddenly, the world is ruled by rock 'n' roll. We've seen this plot before; we've just never seen it used so badly. Outside of a few good finger-clicking numbers, like Bobby Vee doing "The Night Has a Thousand Eyes" (and even that's only good for viewers old enough to remember it), this movie has nothing for anyone.

JUST IMAGINE

20th Century Fox, 1930, b&w, 113 min

Producers: Ray Henderson, B.G. DeSylva, and Lew Brown; **Director:** David Butler; **Screenplay:** Henderson, DeSylva, Brown, and Butler; **Music:** Henderson, DeSylva, Brown, and Arthur Kay; **Cinematography:** Ernest Palmer; **Special Effects:** Stephen Goosson and Ralph Hammeras; **Cast:** El Brendel, Maureen O'Sullivan, John Garrick, Marjorie White, Frank Albertson, Hobart Bosworth, Mischa Auer, Ivan Lino, Kenneth Thompson

Back in 1930, El Brendel is struck by lightning while playing golf. He's declared dead, but in the far-flung future of 1980, he is awakened to a land of scientific marvels. Zounds!

As he wanders about, he comes across the film's plot: the rivalry between MT-3 (Thompson) and J-21 (Garrick) for the love of delightful LN-18 (O'Sullivan). Since both guys want to marry this lovely lady, they have to petition the all-wise and all-knowing central government for a ruling. The government rules in favor of MT-3. It's clear to the audience, however, that the government has made one of its usual bone-headed calls. J-21 is obviously the hero of this story, so what's to do?

Well, J-21 can petition the courts for another ruling. Being mad with the power to mess with people's lives, the government decrees that J-21 has four months to come up with something so impressive they'll throw their previous ruling out the window. Law by judicial whim (wow—it's like these guys really could see into the future). With the help of El Bendel, J flies to Mars, mixes it up with the Martian twins (yes, all Martians come in pairs, one of them containing the pair's good qualities, the other all of their rotten aspects), does a few musical numbers, and then returns to Earth, where he is proclaimed a hero and given LN-18's hand in marriage.

As silly as this one sounds, it's another of those bizarre science fiction musicals usually left unmentioned because it's just so awful. The sets, props, and effects were marvelous for the time. Everyone was dazzled by the film's look, especially the set for New York City, which cost a reported $250,000 in 1930 dollars. Sadly, however, they were not so dazzled by anything else, not a real plot or good musical numbers.

KADOYNG

Shand (Great Britain), 1972, Color, 60 min

Producer: Roy Simpson; **Director:** Ian Shand; **Screenplay:** Leo Maguire; **Music:** Edwin Astley; **Cinematography:** Mark McDonald **Cast:** Leo Maguire, Teresa Codling, Adrian Hall, David Williams, Stephen Bone

This film about a friendly alien who comes to Earth to help people with his special powers like teleportation, and the ability to be very understanding makes for less-than-perfect science fiction entertainment. To date, no videotapes of this movie appear to be available in the United States.

KAISER'S SHADOW, THE

Ince, 1918, b&w, silent, five reels

Producer: Thomas H. Ince; **Director:** R. William Neill; **Screenplay:** Octavus Roy Cohen and J.H. Giesy; **Cast:** Dorothy Dalton, Thurston Hall, Edward Cecil

As if losing World War I wasn't enough for them, evil German spies, looking to stir up more trouble for a weary planet, try to get their hands on the Allies' latest war machine—the ray gun. Perhaps this is understandable, the Germans, after all, being in the jaws of wretched defeat.

KAITEI DAISENSO

See *THE TERROR BENEATH THE SEA*

KIDS IN THE HALL: BRAIN CANDY

See *BRAIN CANDY*

KDO CHCE ZABIT JESSII? (aka: WHO WOULD KILL JESSIE?)

Czechoslovak State Film, 1965, b&w, 80 min

Directors: Milos Macourek and Vaclav Vorticek; **Screenplay:** Macourek and Vorticek; **Cinematography:** Jan Nemcek; **Cast:** Jiri Sovak, Dana Medricka, Olga Schoberva, Karl Effa, Juraj Visny

The couple in this film have a problem. They're two happily married scientists and things couldn't be better, except, of course, for the husband's obsession. He just can't get enough of the cartoonishly voluptuous heroine of the local newspaper's comic strip, Jessie. She's forever being pursued by two bad guys—a cowboy and a lunk with the powers of Superman, and as far as the husband is concerned, she's the answer to his dreams.

Oddly enough, the wife thinks she has some answers of her own. She's just invented a machine that can dispel a person's problematic fantasies; her husband's fantasies might not be a problem for him, but they are for her. There's just one little side effect. This machine happens to bestow life to those things it pulls from within people's subconscious minds. Even mental energy can be neither created nor destroyed. So, before you know it, a real live Jessie and her two boorish pursuers are tearing up our scientists' little love nest.

From all available reports, this extremely hard-to-find film is very funny and edgy and worth any science fiction fan's time. Considered an embarrassment to the Communists when it was made, it has not been seen much outside of what was once Czechoslovakia.

KID'S CLEVER, THE

Universal, 1929, b&w, silent, 5,292 feet

Producer: William James Craft; **Director:** Craft; **Screenplay:** Jack Foley; **Cinematography:** Al Jones; **Cast:** Glenn Tryon, Kathryn Crawford, Russell Simpson, Stepin Fetchit, George Chandler

The Tom Swift of his era settles into his workshop and comes up with an automobile and a motorboat that both can run without all that expensive fuel everyone else is using.

KILLER LACKS A NAME, THE

Filmes Cinematografica (Italy), 1966, Color, 104 min

Director: Tullio Domichelli; **Cast:** Lang Jeffries, Olga Omar, Barbara Nelli

A crazed killer who is already stuck with a steel hand remembers the old adage about turning every disadvantage into an advantage. He cleverly finds a way to electrify it, without killing himself, and then uses it to kill with a touch. Seems like just buying a gun would have been easier.

KILLDOZER

ABC/Universal Television, 1974, Color, 75 min

Producer: Herbert F. Solow; **Director:** Jerry London; **Screenplay:** Theodore Sturgeon; **Special Effects:** Albert Whitlock; **Cinematography:** Terry K. Meade; **Music:** Gil Melle; **Cast:** Clint Walker, Neville Brand, Carl Betz

The setting is an island in the Pacific. The only human inhabitants are a rough-and-tumble construction crew. Talk about bad luck—before this gang of workers can complete their job, a disembodied alien power from outer space lands on the same island and inhabits their bulldozer. From there on, it's man against machine in a duel to the death.

It sounds stupid, and sadly, unlike the short story it's based on, the movie has little to offer. What in print was a tremendously tight series of encounters becomes on the screen a muddled yawn with far too much padding revolving around Hollywood-invented personal problems between members of the crew. What's hard to believe is that not only was this thing based on a terrific Theodore Sturgeon story, but that he even wrote the screenplay. Who's to blame for what *Killdozer* finally became is anyone's guess, but it's hard to believe it's Sturgeon.

KILLER KLOWNS FROM OUTER SPACE

Media Home Entertainment, 1988, Color, 88 min, VT, LD

Producer: Edward Chiodo; **Director:** Stephen Chiodo; **Screenplay:** Edward Chiodo, Stephen Chiodo, and Charles Chiodo; **Music:** John Massari; **Special Effects:** Phillip Dean Foreman and Fantasy II Film Effects; **Cinematography:** Alfred Taylor; **Cast:** Grant Cramer, Suzanne Snyder, John Vernon, John Allen Nelson, Peter Licassi, Michael Siegel, Royal Dano

Blood-drinking extraterrestrial clowns from outer space land on Earth to suck an entire town dry. It's a fairly standard, unimaginative alien invasion plot—except for making the aliens murderous psycho clowns and dressing up the entire dark, macabre film in circus colors with buckets of sick three-ring gags and lots of very strange violence. Of course, it has become a big cult film. Made on a very small budget in extremely bad taste, this movie has a quirky sense of humor that might drag you to its odd charms. Be warned, however, *Killer Klowns From Outer Space* is also fairly crude.

KILLERS FROM SPACE

RKO Radio Pictures, 1954, b&w, 71 min, VT

Producer: W. Lee Wilder; **Director:** Wilder; **Screenplay:** Bill Raynor; **Music:** Manuel Compinsky; **Special Effects:** Consolidated Film Industries; **Cinematography:** William H. Clothier; **Cast:** Peter

Graves, James Seay, Steve Pendleton, Shep Menken, Burt Wenland, Lester Dorr, Barbara Bestar, Frank Gerstle, John Merrick

There's an atomic test going on, and scientist Graves is circling the site in a military jet to take readings. His pilot spots something on the ground that looks like the flash from a mirror. The pilot declares it to be a fireball and takes them in closer to investigate.

The next thing anyone knows, the jet is wrecked, the pilot is dead, and Graves has shown up at the front gate in perfect health with no recollection of either how he survived or how he made his way back to the air base. If that isn't odd enough, he is also sporting a set of extremely new surgical incisions on his hairless chest. The base commander—a Sherlock Holmes if there ever was one—finding nothing suspicious in any of this, sends Graves home in the care of his wife. Not long after, though, everyone, including the base's whiz kid of a commander, is commenting on how different Graves seems.

The reason? It seems Graves died in the crash and was brought back to life by aliens (aliens from the planet Kermit, I guess, considering the painted Ping-Pong balls they use for eyes) who need him to steal atomic secrets for them. What they need to know in particular is exactly when the next atomic test will take place. Why? you ask. Because these staring fools are collecting the energy from our blasts. Once harvested, they use it to mutate our spiders, geckos, and beetles into giant monsters. Their plan? Simple: Release the mutated creatures. Creatures kill all life on Earth. Aliens use gamma rays to kill all creatures. Creatures decompose, turning into wonderful fertilizer, and the aliens then move onto their new paradise.

Luckily, Graves can understand their advanced technology just by looking at it. When their mind control is broken by drugs given him on the base, he's able to formulate a plan that allows him to turn the tables and destroy all the creatures and aliens. Whadda, guy, huh?

This is a spectacularly bad movie. Film critic extraordinary Leonard Maltin calls it "too dull to be funny," but I disagree. You may never have a better opportunity to play Mystery Science Theater 3000/The Home Version like this one again. Anyone can be a Bob Hope with this gasbag of a film to make fun of.

Everything about this one is terrible. The sets are so underdressed that it's hard to tell when the characters are on the army base or in a private home. Every wall looks exactly the same. Graves's circling research jet clearly shows transparently through the clouds. When it goes into its crash, the stock footage used is of a plane going down at a 45-degree angle. When they cut to the model, it's going straight down. If doing it once isn't bad enough, this movie's editor wants to make sure you know how bad he is, so he repeats the sequence, back and forth, back and forth, until he can be positive the audience will know how truly, riotously bad an editor he is. And these are flaws found in just the first five minutes.

Beyond these, the music is melodramatic drivel pulled from piles of stock background music, and not to good stuff, either. Could there be anything funnier than the second-rate animation used via monitor to show Graves the wonders of the alien's home world. "Behold the 2-D cardboard animation that is our home," you snicker, and everyone around you slaps their knees. As for the shot through the window of the desert base that shows the stock footage of a nuclear test going off—*in the ocean*—I'm certain you can come up with your own punchline.

Beyond all of this, however, there actually was a good story buried underneath all the bad direction, terrible effects, and exploitative producing. On its own, the story isn't half bad, but sadly it's not worth searching for. Things were done so cheaply that even the stock picture of President Eisenhower on the wall of the air base is so grainy he appears to have been in a Got Milk commercial. Watch this movie for laughs, but only for laughs. A good story when they started, it's just plain awful now.

Note: Peter Graves has taken a lot of heat for this film, and deservedly so. He comes off pretty bad in some scenes. But that's due to the all too obvious the-first-take-is-the-only-one-we-can-afford mentality that produced this film. What's amazing is how many lines he manages perfectly. In many scenes, despite the drawbacks, he does an excellent job of communicating that he's under the control of an outside force. Sure, Graves is a stiff actor, but he's the world's greatest stiff actor. This part, a dead man brought back to life and kept under the mental control of others from afar, is just what was called for. No, Graves really did his level best here. It's the film that's a flop—not him.

KILLER SHREWS, THE

Hollywood Pictures Corporation, 1959, b&w, 70 min, VT

Producer: Ken Curtis; **Director:** Ray Kellogg; **Screenplay:** Jay Simms; **Music:** Harry Bluestone and Emil Cadkin; **Special Effects:** Ben Chapman and Louise Caldwell; **Cinematography:** Wilfred M. Cline; **Cast:** James Best, Ingrid Goude, Ken Curtis, Baruch Lumet, Gordon McLendon

A scientist with nothing better to do creates a race of monsters to terrorize his friends and neighbors in their isolated island community. There's nothing much wrong with this movie, which at times can even be a touch clever, but it's a story seen too often and done better.

KILLER TOMATOES STRIKE BACK

See *ATTACK OF THE KILLER TOMATOES*

KINDRED, THE

Vestron Video, 1987, Color, 97 min, VT, LD

Producers: Joel Freeman, Stacey Giachino, and Jeffrey Obrow; **Director:** Stephen Carpenter; **Screenplay:** Obrow, Carpenter, Earl Ghaffari, John Penny, and Joseph Stefano; **Music:** David Newman; **Special Effects:** David L. Hewitt; **Cinematography:** Carpenter; **Cast:** Jeffrey Obrow, Rod Steiger, Kim Hunter, David Allen Brooks, Amanda Pays, Talia Balsam, Timothy Gibbs, Peter Frechette, Julia Montgomery

An experiment gone wrong creates an evil monster, which is then unleashed against a group of teens with no greater faults to recommend their destruction other than being attractive enough to catch the terror's eye. The special effects aren't terrible. Amanda Pays delivers a solid performance, which is about all there is worth watching in this movie.

KING DINOSAUR

Lippert, 1955, b&w, 63 min

Producer: Bert I. Gordon; **Director:** Gordon; **Screenplay:** Gordon, Al Zimbalist, and Tom Gries; **Music:** Louis Palance and Michael Terr; **Special Effects:** Howard A. Anderson; **Cinematography:** Gordon Avil; **Cast:** Doug Henderson, Bill Bryant, Patricia Gallagher, Wanda Curtis

It's astronauts in trouble again. Somewhere in our far-flung future, a rocket is sent out from Earth to investigate the planet Nova. Unfortunately for the astronauts, they predictably crash-land and find themselves at the mercy of the title creature and his pals.

Don't expect Stan Winston miracle monsters here. This is another Bert I. Gordon original, so know in advance that those dinos are going to just be the same dopey lizards with glued-on tail fins seen in many other '50s movies. In fact, not only is this a Gordon original, but it's his debut—the first time he brought his wondrously low-budget style to the world. And this one is about as low as you can get. Gila monsters for dinosaurs? Try female astronauts wearing skirts and pumps.

KINGDOM OF THE SPIDERS

Dimension Pictures, 1977, Color, 94 min, VT

Producers: Igo Kantor and Jeffrey Sneller; **Director:** John Cardos; **Screenplay:** Richard Robinson and Allan Caillou; **Music:** Kantor; **Special Effects:** Greg Auer; **Cinematography:** John Morrill; **Cast:** William Shatner, Tiffany Bolling, Woody Strode, Lieux Dressler, Altovise Davis, David McLean, Marcie Rafferty

Arizona, always a swell place for a little low-budget picture making, is having trouble with pesticides and dead people. The pesticides aren't killing people, but they are upsetting the army of tarantulas that have decided to fight back. To handle this world-threatening menace, does humanity send the army? The air force? Well, no—but they do the next best thing. They send William Shatner. That'll teach those pesky critters.

Actually, although there are no big surprises (or even any little ones) here, this is not a bad picture, actually tight, unpretentious, and watchable. It's a well-made, well-directed creeper in which Shatner, a veterinarian, and Bolling, an entomologist, do a terrific job in keeping the story going. Everything turns out as the audience expects, but that was the case with *STAR WARS*, and not too many people complained about that.

KING KONG

RKO, 1933, b&w, 103 min, VT, LD

Producers: David O. Selznick, Merian C. Cooper, and Ernest B. Schoedsack; **Directors:** Cooper and Schoedsack; **Screenplay:** James Creelman, Ruth Rose, Edgar Wallace, and Cooper; **Music:** Max Steiner; **Special Effects:** Willis O'Brien, E.B. Gibson, Fred Reefe, Orville Goldner, Carroll Shepphird, and Marcel Delgado; **Cinematography:** Edward Lindon, Vernon L. Walker, and J.O. Taylor; **Cast:** Robert Armstrong, Fay Wray, Bruce Cabot, Frank Reicher, Sam Hardy, Noble Johnson, James Flavin, Victor Wong, Steve Clemento, Paul Porcasi, Russ Powell, Sandra Shaw, Ethan Laidlaw, Blackie Whiteford, Dick Curtis, Charles Sullivan,

Harry Tenbrook, Gil Perkins, Vera Lewis, Leroy Mason

King Kong is the all-time classic of classics.

Consider the quote listed an an "Old Arabian Proverb" at the opening of the film:

> "And the Prophet said: And lo! the Beast looked upon the face of Beauty. And it stayed its hand from killing. And from that day it was as one dead."

Cut to the New York City docks. In the middle of the night, a well-dressed, apprehensive man calls out, "Hey, is this the moving picture ship?" When he gets a positive answer, the greatest giant monster movie of all time is under way.

The man is a theatrical booking agent (Hardy) who's come to this boat, the *Venture*, to meet the world's greatest action adventure documentary filmmaker, Carl Denham (Armstrong). The agent has been looking for a girl to star in the filmmaker's new picture, but he's come to tell Denham that there isn't an actress in the city willing to take this job. There are a number of reasons why.

Denham won't say what the picture is about or where it's going to be shot. He won't say how long it's going to take or what kind of dangers his actors are going to have to face. Little things, like the special gas bombs Denham has had made or the fact that the ship's hold is storing "enough ammunition to blow up the harbor," all put there by a crew made up of "the toughest mugs" the agent has ever seen have set the poor man's conscience spinning.

Well, lions and elephants have never scared the great Carl Denham, and he's not about to let this stop him. The critics and his distributors have been telling him that if his pictures only had a love interest, they could gross twice as much. Filmmaker enough to know you've got to please the crowd, he heads into Manhattan, vowing to bring an actress back "even if [he] has to marry one." Before things go that far, though, Denham crosses paths with a down-on-her-luck actress, Ann Darrow, whom he promises "money and adventure and fame and a long sea voyage" to convince her to come along.

Aboard ship, she meets Jack Driscoll (Cabot), the gruff, two-fisted first mate, and the two begin to fall for each other. In the meantime, now that the whole production is safely out to sea, Denham finally puts his cards on the table. He's obtained a map that will lead them to an island far off the trade routes, Skull Island, the island of Kong. Everyone freezes. Sturdy Captain Englehorn (Reicher) has heard the legends, Kong—a native god of incredible power. Pure superstition—right? Denham doesn't think so. He's been told that on this isle there is a great wall that separates the native inhabitants from most of the rest of the island. He says they keep this wall in great repair because of their fear of what is on the other side.

The *Venture* arrives at Skull Island, with an incredible view of both the ominous skull-shaped mountain for which the island is named and the even more forbidding wall Denham mentioned earlier. The crew and cast head for shore, arriving in time to interrupt a native ceremony. The locals are preparing a "bride" for Kong, but when they see Ann Darrow, "the golden woman" as they call the attractive blonde, the chief tries to buy Ann as a gift for Kong. Denham, using Englehorn as his interpreter, tells them no deal, but promises to come back tomorrow. Everyone retreats back to the *Venture*, but that night the chief sends his warriors to the ship to kidnap Ann. She is taken to the island and tied to an altar on the other side of the gigantic wall. Before long, Denham and the others realize Ann has been taken. They race ashore, getting there just in time to see the most amazing sight in the history of film until that moment:

King Kong!

Up to this point the film is a well-written, nicely paced adventure film, and though nothing much has happened, snappy direction and earnest acting have kept things moving along. All that changes with the appearance of a fantastic 50-feet-tall gorilla.

Denham and some of the crew he brought along charge into the jungle after Kong, who has taken Ann. They first encounter a dinosaur beyond the wall. Things go fairly well as Denham coolly slaughters the creature, but it gets worse. More dinosaurs arrive and start killing off the crew. Soon Denham and Driscoll have no guns or bombs, and once they catch up to Kong, no help, either. Trapped on opposite sides of a ravine, Driscoll tells Denham he'll follow Kong and find Ann. He tells Denham to head back and wait. More monumental scenes ensue as Kong battles a tyrannosaurus, a pterodactyl, and a cross between the Loch Ness monster and a dachshund, which stop-frame animator Willis O'Brien must have made up out of his head, but which is still more than effective. Kong loses his prize, however, as Driscoll is able to whisk Ann away while the gorilla is occupied in one of his battles.

Kong follows the two back to the native village. Bullets and spears are nothing to him. He crashes through the massive gate that has kept him at bay for so long and then sets about slaughtering every human in sight until he is felled by one of Denham's gas bombs. The crew is shaken, but Denham stays on top of things, ordering: "Send to the ship for anchor chains and tools. Build a raft and float him to the ship. We'll give him more than chains. He's always been king of his world, but we'll teach him fear. Why, the whole world will pay to see this. We're millionaires, boys—I'll share it with all of you. In a few months, it'll be up in lights: *Kong, the eighth wonder of the world!*"

A quick dissolve, and the marquee Denham promised comes into sight. Kong is going on display on Broadway. Reporter's flashbulbs send the chained and shackled monster into a berserk rage, and the sense of finale begins to set in. Kong breaks free of the theater, tears up New York City as he did the native's small community, and then manages to find Ann. Taking her in his massive paw, he scales the Empire State Building. On Skull Island, he lived on the tallest peak. On Manhattan Island, he heads for similar ground. Once there, though, he finds that the pterodactyls here are more dangerous than they were at home—a squad of military airplanes are sent to dispatch the beast, which they do with only minimal losses.

Dying, Kong puts his beloved "golden woman" down so she will not share his fate and then topples to the ground so many scores of stories below. On the ground, a policeman notes that the airplanes got Kong after all. Denham corrects him with the immortal line: "'Twas beauty killed the beast."

Thus ends the absolute greatest giant monster movie of all time. *King Kong* was a tremendous hit, not only a financial success, but a critical success as well. *King Kong* made so much money it completely revived the almost moribund RKO Studio, allowing it to survive for another two decades. Indeed, it isn't that much of a stretch to say that if not for *Citizen Kong*, there might not have been a *Citizen Kane*.

As for the critics, they have not stopped lavishing praise on this incredible film since its release. In fact, it is quite possible many of the scholars who have tried to explain this film's tremendous success have gone a bit too far in their search for underlying subtexts that appeal to the masses. *King Kong* has been claimed by the environmentalists as an indictment of the capitalist system, showing what happens when living things are brought to the city. European Communists have claimed that Kong's smashing of the island's gates make him a symbol of Karl Marx, and that the subsequent Broadway mixing of communism and commerce foretells the fall of the Soviet Union. African Americans have taken Kong's kidnapping from Africa and his subsequent throwing off of his chains as proof that the film is a racial statement of the evils of the white man. Dozens of other claims have been made, many of them Freudian in nature, that is,

smashing the city = rage gratification. Sadly for the intelligentsia of the world, all these ideas may be in the film, because any well-structured story can be interpreted. But none of these ideas were put there intentionally by the writers, as everyone involved has acknowledged time and again over the years.

King Kong is simply a great action film. Of course, that doesn't explain what makes it a science fiction film. Calling it such is admittedly somewhat of a stretch. But it's closer to the essence of the genre than many others, such as *ABBOTT AND COSTELLO GOES TO MARS* or *THE HANDS OF ORLAC*, which may have more of the necessary hardware but not the right intent. Carl Denham is the perfect science fiction hero—he's out to prove something, consumed by his quest, yet not destroyed by it. He stands outside love and money, looking always toward the larger picture, always keeping his wits about him. He isn't the tallest, strongest, or toughest man in the picture, but he's the smartest, and thus he survives.

If there is an underlying science fiction theme, it is the destruction of the savage impulse by progress. No longer can one simply take women or smash enemies—civilization has made that all too complicated. That's why in the city, thinkers like Denham survive and big apes go down for the count. Kong might be a monster up close, but he had to be tracked down to a remote, forgotten little island in the middle of nowhere. From there he was dragged to be the amusement of a "civilized" people who had seen and done everything else and who needed Kong to save them from boredom. Of course, this is meant to justify this entry, not to tell what the filmmaking team of Merian C. Cooper and Ernest B. Schoedsack were envisioning. They knew what they were doing. Would that the rest of Hollywood knew a tenth of what these two brilliant innovators did.

While on the subject of *King Kong*, it would seem unfair not to mention *The Son of Kong*. As with any successful film, there's always time to make a sequel. Sadly, as usual, the thinking was that people would come to see the film no matter what, so the budget was slashed considerably. The producers did the best they could, however, and while the results are not extraordinary, they still managed to create an effective film. The story centers on Carl Denham (Armstrong), the man who captured Kong in the first film. Interestingly enough, he is now being hounded by litigants demanding he make good on the damage caused to New York by Kong. Desperate to pay everyone off and regain his good reputation, he gets together with the skipper from the first film, Captain Englehorn (Reicher), and the two head back to Skull Island to see if they can find something that might restore their fortunes.

Again the story gets down to business immediately, setting the situation, then involving Denham with a girl (Helen Mack) so that the characters can engage the audience until the action starts. This much can be said for *The Son of Kong*—when the action starts, it pays off. Not only are the battle sequences between the smaller, blond Kong just as dramatic as those in the first film, but they are better animated as well. Willis O'Brien was able to smooth out some of the flaws in his technique, such as the unavoidable animation of Kong Senior's hair. Also, outside of the brontosaurus used in the first film, which actually appears only briefly here, all of the monsters and major sets in the second film are new. As in the first, some are recognizable animals, and some are pure fantasy creatures, but all of them are serious about trying to destroy Kong, Jr., and company. The fights are well choreographed and extensive, if not always quite as violent as those in the original.

There is also the Willis O'Brien supervised *Mighty Joe Young* (aka: *Mr. Joseph Young of Africa*), featuring the work of his new young assistant, Ray Harryhausen. This is in many ways a veritable remake of *King Kong*, the only hit O'Brien was fated to have (it did finally win him a much belated Oscar).

Note: This entry could easily take up another 30 pages to cover the different technical aspects of stop-frame animation that Willis O'Brien perfected working on this picture alone. But there is one recurring question that deserves to be addressed. For decades people have raged over a certain scene in the film, specifically the moment when King Kong shakes the pursuing sailors from the log he has just used to cross a canyon. Legions of folks say that originally when the sailors' bodies hit the ground, giant spiders came out and ate them. Many others say they're wrong. Oddly, both sides in this debate are right. The scene was written and filmed. The footage did exist. But it was not released as part of the movie; Schoedsack and Cooper felt it took away from the point of the film, which was Kong.

KING KONG (aka: THE NEW KING KONG, KING KONG: THE LEGEND REBORN)

Paramount, 1976, Color, 134 min, VT, LD, DVD

Producer: Dino De Laurentiis; **Director:** John Guillermin; **Screenplay:** Lorenzo Semple, Jr. (officially based on the original by James Creelman, Ruth Rose, Edgar Wallace, and Merian C. Cooper); **Music:** John Barry; **Special Effects:** Rick Baker, Glen Robinson, Joe Day, Harold Wellman, Frank van der Veer, Barry Nolan, and Lou Lichtenfield; **Cinematography:** Richard H. Kline; **Cast:** Jessica Lange, Jeff Bridges, Charles Grodin, John Randolph, Rene Auberjonois, Julius Harris, Jack O'Halloran, Ed Lauter, John Lone, Rick Baker

Oil company executive Grodin leads an expedition to Kong's island. He doesn't know anything about Kong, nor does he care. All he's after are the huge deposits of crude he believes are there, thanks to faulty readings of satellite reports. There is no crude oil, but there is Kong. As in the original, he is given another unwilling "bride" (Lange), who is rescued from his hairy clutches by another smitten young man (Bridges). Kong is captured by the oil company and taken back to civilization in a supertanker. Once again he escapes and takes his romantic frustrations out on the Big Apple, which reciprocates by blasting him off the World Trade Center with helicopter gunships.

Quite simply, this film is the most inadequate remake of all time. No greater crime can be committed to something once told seriously than to allow Lorenzo Semple, Jr., to rewrite it. Semple's scripts seem incapable of seeing honor, nobility, or courage in any way other than silly, foolish, and worthy of nothing but contempt. Where Robert Armstrong in the original *Kong* goes to Skull Island out of a sense of adventure, Charles Grodin goes only for profit. When Armstrong puts Kong in chains, it's to humble the great beast and teach him fear. For the two-dimensional oil executive, again it's only for profit.

Kong himself, an object of wonder and terror in the first film, becomes a joke in the second. Where the original makes Kong upliftingly tragic, the second causes us only to pity him. Any human being who has ever been rejected in love knows all about the feeling's tragic aspects. Not many of them, however, have ever truly wished to be pitied.

Of course, many a feeble story has been at least partially redeemed by good special effects. No luck here. True, Rick Baker's Academy Award—winning ape suit created an acceptable Kong, but that's all. Gone are the magnificent sets of the first film. Gone are the epic battles with the great beasts of the land, sea, and air. The titanic struggles of the original are replaced with two scenes. The first is a sad fight between Kong and an incredibly unrealistic giant snake. The second is a scene wisely left out of the first film, the ocean voyage back to civilization. Here we get to watch Kong at his most pathetic, moping around listlessly on the tanker as Jessica Lange learns to feel sorry for him.

The bright color and cynical direction of the new picture are no improvements, either. As one might expect in modern Hollywood, not only does Kong have to be emasculated, but the heroine must be made tougher. A strong heroine is generally a good thing, but when she is unlovable, then Kong does not deserve our sympathy for wanting her. If she is not frightened by him, then the audience's sense of terror is diminished.

The 1976 *King Kong* was made with seeming contempt for both its source material and the audience. Instead of delivering terror, action, and adventure, the filmmakers serve up sermons and moral speeches aimed at teaching the audience some well-needed lessons about how to treat the planet. One could hope the lackluster box office would've taught the producers a lesson, but such is not the case. In 1986, De Laurentiis again went poaching on the Kong preserve, this time bringing forth the even more ridiculous *King Kong Lives*. In this one, the filmmaker takes even more pity on Kong and gives him a Kongette, a big ape babe he can love so he can get over his infatuation with blond women. This film was the final kick in the head De Laurentiis' production team failed to deliver with their first effort.

This trivialization of Kong was a far bigger failure than the remake, and the main reason seems to be that most of the people who were hoodwinked into seeing the '76 *Kong* by the blatantly misleading promotion lies refused to set foot in the theaters a second time.

Not nearly as insulting to the 1933 *King Kong* are the two Toho productions, the seemingly inevitable 1962 *King Kong Vs. Godzilla* (released in the U.S. in 1963 by Universal), and 1967's *King Kong Escapes* (released in the U.S. in 1968, also by Universal).

Both films wildly inflate Kong's size and powers for the sake of longer fights. In the first, his foe is Godzilla, who is eight times the original Kong's size, impervious to nuclear weapons and able to breathe radioactive fire. In the second Toho release, Kong's enemy is a robot ape, MechaKong, who besides being a superstrong mechanoid can also release ray beams at his foes. As you most likely already know, the original Kong was killed by bullets fired by a quartet of World War I fighter planes. Not exactly Godzilla-stoppers by any stretch of the imagination. What saves these films is that as goofy as they are, the Japanese filmmakers were still trying to take their subject matter seriously, rather than dishing up moral lessons. *King Kong Vs. Godzilla* is by far the more palatable of the two, but both films earn fair marks for at least trying not to insult the memory of the original film.

Note: Those who feel they must subject themselves to the 1976 *Kong* remake should keep their eyes peeled for Joe Piscopo and Corbin Bernsen, who both had small roles. Piscopo has at least a moment on camera, but Bernsen's part lasts barely a second. Even those who are not big fans of Piscopo or Bernsen will need something to keep them amused if they intend to sit through this film.

Besides those listed above, there also exists *King of Kong Island* (aka: *Kong Island*), in which mad scientists experimenting on apes are at their worst.

KING KONG ESCAPES

Toho (Japan), 1967, 104 min/Universal (U.S.), 1968, Color, 96 min

Producer: Tomoyuki Tanaka; **Director:** Ishiro Honda; **Screenplay:** Kaoru Mabuchi; **Cinematography:** Hajime Koizumi; **Music:** Akira Ifukube; **Special Effects:** Eiji Tsuburaya; **Cast:** Rhodes Reason, Mie Hama, Linda Miller, Akira Takarada

See KING KONG (1976)

KING KONG LIVES

Paramount, 1986, Color, 105 min, VT, LD

Producers: Dino De Laurentiis and Martha Schumacher; **Director:** John Guillermin; **Screenplay:** Steven Pressfield and Ronald Shusett; **Cinematography:** Alec Mills; **Music:** John Scott; **Special Effects:** Doug Beswick, Dean Gates, and Carlo Rambaldi; **Cast:** Brian Kerwin, Lida Hamilton, John Ashton, Peter Michael Goetz, Frank Maraden, Alan Sader

See KING KONG (1976)

KING KONG: THE LEGEND REBORN

See KING KONG (1976)

KING KONG VS. GODZILLA

Toho (Japan), 1962, 99 min/Universal (U.S.), 1963, color, 91 min, VT, DVD

Producer: Tomoyuki Tanaka; **Director:** Inoshiro Honda; **Screenplay:** Shinichi Sckizawa; **Music:** Akira Ifukube; **Cinematography:** Hajimi Koizumi; **Special Effects:** Eiji Tsuburaya; **Cast:** Tadao Takashima, Mie

King Kong vs. Godzilla (UNIVERSAL PICTURES / R. ALLEN LEIDER COLLECTION)

Hama, Kenji Shara, Yu Fujiki, Ichiro Arishima, Haruo Nakajima, Katsumi Tezuka, Shoichi Hirose

See *GODZILLA, KING OF THE MONSTERS; KING KONG* (1976)

KING OF KONG ISLAND

Three Star Films (Italy)/Sinister Cinema (U.S.), 1978, Color, 92 min, VT

Producers: Ralph Zuker and Walter Brandi; **Director:** Robert Morris; **Screenplay:** Zuker; **Cinematography:** Mario Mancini; **Music:** Ruberto Pregadio; **Cast:** Brad Harris, Esmeralda Barros, Marc Lawrence, Adrianna Alben, Mark Rarran

See *KING KONG* (1976)

KING OF THE MOUNTIES

Republic, 1942, b&w, serial, 25 reels

Producers: William J. O'Sullivan and Herbert J. Yates; **Director:** William Witney; **Screenplay:** Taylor Caven, Ronald Davidson, William Lively, Joseph O'Donnell, and Joseph Poland; **Music:** Cy Fever; **Special Effects:** Howard Lydecker; **Cinematography:** Bud Thackery; **Cast:** Abner Biberman, Nestor Paiva, William Vaughn, George Irving, Peggy Drake, Allan Lane, Gilbert Emmery, Anthony Warde, Jay Novello, Duncan Renaldo, Bradley Page, Russell Hicks

It's the original Sergeant King (Lane) of the Royal Canadian Mounted Police in 12 chapters of Nazi-smashing action. Those nasty Nazis have invented a stealth bomber, and when the Nazi war machine invents the ultimate weapon, who better to stop them but a Mountie. It's as silly as it sounds, but still fun for those who can't get enough of this kind of stuff.

KING OF THE ROCKET MEN

Republic, 1949, b&w, serial, 25 reels

Producer: Franklin Adreon; **Director:** Fred Brannon; **Screenplay:** Royal Cole, William Lively, and Sol Shore; **Music:** Stanley Wilson; **Special Effects:** Howard Lydecker and Theodore Lydecker; **Cinematography:** Ellis W. Carter; **Cast:** House Peters, Jr., Don Haggerty, James Craven, I. Standford Jolley, Douglas Evans, Tristram Coffin, Mae Clarke, Ted Adams, Dale Van Sickel, Tom Steele, David Sharpe, Eddie Parker

No, it's not Sergeant King of the Royal Canadian Mounted Police again, but Tristram Coffin as the rocket-belted, oddly helmeted hero, Rocket Man. Over 12 weeks of cliffhangers, Rocket Man battles the evil villain Dr. Vulcan, who has stolen a machine capable of creating earthquakes. This one is just as silly as it sounds, although the science fiction props are much funnier than those in *KING OF THE MOUNTIES.*

KING OF THE ZOMBIES

Monogram, 1941, b&w, 67 min, VT, LD

Producer: Lindsey Parsons; **Director:** Gene Yarbrough; **Screenplay:** Edmund Kelso; **Music:** Edward Kay; **Special Effects:** Dave Milton and Mark V.

Wright; **Cinematography:** Mack Stengler; **Cast:** Dick Purcell, Joan Woodbury, Mantan Moreland, Henry Victor, John Archer

Nazi mad scientists working in the tropics create an army of zombie men to throw at the Allies. The only reason to watch this movie is for the comedy of Mantan Moreland, who provides the best laughs. Still, this is one that most likely shouldn't be viewed except by the staunchest of Moreland fans.

KISS KISS, KILL KILL

Parnass (West Germany), 1966, Color, 87 min

Producers: Hans A. Pfluger and Theo Werner; **Director:** Frank Kramer; **Screenplay:** Sim O'Neill; **Music:** Mladen Gutssha; **Cinematography:** Francesco Izzarelli; **Cast:** Brad Harris, Luciano Stella, Christa Linder

A maniac creates a way to turn people into an army of zombies in the hopes of using them to take over the world. He fails.

KISS ME DEADLY

United Artists, 1955, b&w, 105 min, VT, LD

Producer: Robert Aldrich; **Director:** Aldrich; **Screenplay:** A.I. Bezzerides; **Music:** Frank DeVol; **Special Effects:** Complete Film Service; **Cinematography:** Ernest Laszlo; **Cast:** Ralph Meeker, Albert Dekker, Paul Stewart, Cloris Leachman, Wesley Addy, Nick Dennis, Maxine Cooper, Gaby Rogers, Jack Elam, Strother Martin, Jack Lambert

Mickey Spillane's ultraviolent private eye Mike Hammer is hired to track down a briefcase. The movie is pretty much your basic noir story until the end. Then Hammer finds out what's in the briefcase, and the picture suddenly becomes one of those rare science fiction/noir films. This stands as an interesting film on a number of levels, not the least of which is Aldrich's effectively moody direction, which many, such as Leonard Maltin, credit with heavily influencing the later French New Wave directors. Of course, Aldrich also chose to make Hammer a two-bit scumbag, far more unsavory than he is in Spillane's novels. It's gritty, stark, and angry, and for those looking for those qualities, this one is the classic.

KISS THE GIRLS AND MAKE THEM DIE

De Laurentiis (Italy), 1966/Columbia (U.S), 1967, Color, 106 min

Producer: Dino De Laurentiis; **Directors:** Henry Levin and Dino Maiuri; **Screenplay:** Maiuri and Jack Pulman; **Music:** Maria Nascimbene; **Special Effects:** Augie Lohman; **Cinematography:** Aldo Tonti; **Cast:** Michael Conners, Dorothy Provine, Terry-Thomas, Raf Vallone, Beverly Adams, Oliver McGreevy

It's hard to believe, but this movie's about a mad scientist harboring a superiority complex who has a plan for world domination. This one's plan is to sterilize the entire world's population, save for himself and the group of beautiful women he plans to put into suspended animation.

KNIGHT OF THE DRAGON, THE

See *STAR KNIGHT*

KONEC SRPNA V HOTELU OZON
(aka: THE END OF AUGUST AT THE HOTEL OZONE)

Line Cinema (Czechoslovakia), 1965, b&w, 87 min

Director: Jan Schmidt; **Screenplay:** Pavel Juracek; **Music:** Jan Klasák; **Special Effects:** Oldrich Bosák; **Cinematography:** Jirí Macák **Cast:** Ondrej Jariabek, Beta Ponicanova, Magda Seidlerova, Hana Vitkova

It's sometime after World War III, and there seems to be no prospect of survival. Things look absolutely hopeless. The plot of the movie revolves around a small group of women determined to recreate the human race. Although they have not seen any living men for quite some time, they're not about to give up hope. They move onward constantly, searching the desolate remains of the world for men with whom they can repopulate the world. Finally, they find a single living male in the Hotel Ozone. The only problem is that he's far too old to father any children. With this realization, the women give up in absolute hopelessness and the film ends. This is one of the great depressing movies of all time—it offers not a single shred of hope and ends in utter futility and despair. Hopeless, yet fascinating.

KONGA

AIP, 1961, Color, 90 min, VT

Producer: Herman Cohen; **Director:** John Lemont; **Screenplay:** Cohen and Aben Kandel; **Music:** Gerard Shurmann; **Special Effects:** Jack Craig; **Cinematography:** Desmond Dickinson; **Cast:** Michael Gough, Margo Johns, Jess Conrad, Claire Gordon, Jack Watson

A mad scientist experimenting on monkeys wants to create a plant/mammal hybrid (where do these B movie scientists get their wacky ideas?), so to do this he keeps enlarging his chimp to King Kongian proportions and then shrinking him back down again (don't feel bad—it's never explained what the one would have to do with the other, either). When he isn't advancing the field of animal/vegetable cross-breeding, the giant chimp/Kong is used throughout the film by our lab worker to kill his enemies. In the end, though, the giant chimp goes on a lackluster rampage through London, carrying the doctor in his hand. Neither comes to a good end.

KONG ISLAND

See *KING KONG* (1976); *KING OF KONG ISLAND*

KRONOS (aka: DESTROYER OF THE UNIVERSE)

20th Century Fox, 1957, b&w, 78 min, VT, LD, DVD

Producers: Kurt Neumann, Jack Rabin, Irving Block, and Louis DeWitt; **Director:** Neumann; **Screenplay:** Block; **Music:** Paul Swatell; **Special Effects:** Rabin, Block, and DeWitt; **Cinematography:** Karl Stuss; **Cast:** Jeff Morrow, Barbara Lawrence, John Emery, George O'Hanlon, Morris Ankrum, John Parrish, Robert Shayne

A UFO lands in the waters off the western coast of North America. Soon scientists from the California Science Institute (CSI), Elliot (Emery), Less (Morrow) and his fiancée Vera (Lawrence), and good ol' Culver (O'Hanlon), are looking into the incident. What they find when they catch up to their target astounds them. The visitor from space has grown to a staggering height. It is also marching across the land, searching for energy sources to consume.

The machine, Kronos, can devour power in any form. It gathers energy in mostly from the power plants it constantly seeks out and destroys. The alien machine grows stronger with each new infusion of energy from the plants, but they aren't its only source

of power. When the army attacks, the UFO consumes the force thrown against it and presumably can absorb even the energy of its own massive footsteps. What to do, especially after Elliot falls under the telepathic control of the alien device? Elliot's pals have the answer. They reverse Kronos's polarity, causing the energy the machine is stealing to overload and flood its controls. The resulting short circuit destroys the machine and saves Earth.

This is an interesting film. On the one hand, the script is fairly pedestrian. Not much in the writing (or the acting, for that matter), is worth much notice. Even the special effects, highly effective in some instances, are not 100 percent consistent.

On the other hand, Kronos itself is a fascinating concept. It is a stand-alone menace in the world of 1950s giant bugs, Japanese monsters, and alien invaders. Despite some of this film's deficiencies as a movie, its science fiction concept is so intriguing (and to this day, still so incredibly singular) that the movie is worth a look from any true fan of the genre.

Note: A lot of what is right about this movie can probably be credited to its producer and director, Kurt Neumann. Neumann may not be a familiar name, but he was the driving force behind a number of the '50s more highly regarded science fiction films, including *ROCKETSHIP X-M* and *THE FLY*.

KRONOS: DESTROYER OF THE UNIVERSE

See *KRONOS*

KRULL (aka: KRULL: INVADER OF THE BLACK FORTRESS, DUNGEONS AND DRAGONS, DRAGONS OF KRULL, THE DUNGEONS OF KRULL)

Columbia, 1983, Color, 117 min. VT, LD

Producer: Ron Silvermann; **Director:** Peter Yates; **Screenplay:** Stanford Sherman; **Music:** James Horner; **Special Effects:** John Evans, Mark Meddings, Mike Round, Robert Gavin, Phil Sanderson, and Paul Wilson; **Cinematography:** Peter Suschitzky; **Cast:** Ken Marshall, Lysette Anthony, Freddie Jones, Francesca Annis, David Battley, Liam Neeson, Robbie Coltrane

The Beast, a fairly unimaginative cross between H.R. Giger's Alien and H.P. Lovecraft's Cthulhu, comes to the planet Krull to conquer, enslave, and bore audiences as he supposedly has done on a million worlds in the past. His massive, steaming spaceship—shaped like a tree stump and constructed out of stone—lands, and the Beast sends forth his mighty army of 20 riders (yes, a space-faring conqueror who uses cavalry) to conquer the entire planet.

Apparently they do so with ease. Before long, all of Krull has been subjugated except for two tiny kingdoms. They decide to band together to stop the Beast. Once the prince of the first kingdom marries the princess of the second, their combined armies will be sent forth to combat the Beast's troops. The only problem is that the Beast desires the princess as his own and thus sends forth his tens of riders to destroy all opposition to his possessing her.

Unlike the battles during which the rest of the planet was lost, the action here is onscreen for what it's worth. The hero (Marshall) and his sci-fi armored knights, the worst collection of fantasy fighters since the Roman soldiers in *The Three Stooges Meet Hercules*, lose quickly. Since Marshall is the hero, he's only rendered unconscious, while every single man under his command is slaughtered. The princess is taken to the Beast, and everything looks bleak, indeed.

But then enters the old man who is not a wizard but might be, who knows of a weapon and a place of power, and an even older old man who knows more magic and more places of power. They head off to get the weapon. The older old man is slain, more warriors willing to fight the Beast are gathered, a cyclops is discovered, as is another place of power and an old woman who knows some magic like the old men, and more and more like this on toward its underwhelming conclusion.

There is no point in wasting further words. This blend of fantasy and science fiction has absolutely no idea what it is doing. The story meanders, and scenes pile up one atop another, but none of them actually flow into the one that follows. Questions also pile up faster than can be imagined. How do the mortal men run fast enough to catch the horses that run at super speed? Once they catch them, how do they stay on their backs? Why is it that the Beast's men could previously beat the combined might of the entire planet's armies, let alone the millions of planets' armies they're supposed to have slaughtered previously, but not the ragtag bunch of losers that Marshall brings together? Why do Marshall and the old man spend so much time chasing down the magic weapon when it is absolutely useless against the Beast? Why is it that at the climax the prince and princess are able to join hands and destroy the all-powerful villain when neither of them knows anything about magic?

Outside of a few good special effects and a chance to see a young Liam Neeson in action, everything about this movie is bad. As far as awful goes, this one has it all: poor direction, head-scratching editing, bad acting, ill-used clichés, and much more.

KRULL: INVADER OF THE BLACK FORTRESS

See *KRULL*

KURT VONNEGUT'S "HARRISON BERGERON"

See *HARRISON BERGERON*

LADY AND THE MONSTER

Republic, 1944, b&w, 86 min

Producer: George Sherman; **Director:** Sherman; **Screenplay:** Dane Lussier and Frederick Kohner; **Music:** Walter Scharf; **Cinematography:** John Alton; **Special Effects:** Theodore Lydecker; **Cast:** Erich von Stroheim, Vera Hruba Ralston, Richard Arlen, Sidney Blackmer

Financial king W.H. Donovan dies in a plane crash. A scientist from a nearby facility manages to reach the site, recover the tycoon's body, and remove his undamaged brain, which he then keeps alive in a glass tank because, well, he's the kind of genius who's smart enough to do such a thing. Sadly, however, the disembodied brain then takes telepathic control of the doctor, proving that maybe he wasn't so smart in the first place.

Yes, this is indeed another film version of Curt Siodmak's classic novel, *Donovan's Brain*. It's the science fiction movie Hollywood just can't stop making. This is one of the better versions, though, played more for horror than science fiction and graced by the nifty appearance of von Stroheim, who really makes the picture come alive.

LADY FRANKENSTEIN

Condor International (Italy), 1944, 99 min/New World (U.S.), 1972, Color, 85 min, VT

Producer: Harry Cushing; **Director:** Mel Welles; **Screenplay:** Edward DiLorenzo; **Music:** Alessandro Allesandroni; **Cinematography:** Ricardo Pallotini; **Special Effects:** Cipa; **Cast:** Joseph Cotten, Herbert Fox, Sara Bey, Mickey Hargitay, Paul Muller, Paul Whiteman

Joe Cotten is a sad and tired Dr. Frankenstein, indeed. His daughter (Bey) takes over the family's monster-making business, doing everything just like her father, including picking the worst brains possible. The nice twist is that she has built her monster to defeat her father's monster. Sadly, however, the only living creatures that get stomped by this one are the members of the audience.

LA FIN DU MONDO

See *THE END OF THE WORLD*

LAND THAT TIME FORGOT, THE

Amicus Productions (U.K.), AIP (U.S.), 1975, Color, 91 min, VT

Producer: John Dark; **Director:** Kevin Conner; **Screenplay:** Michael Moorcock and James Cawthorn; **Music:** Douglas Gamley; **Cinematography:** Alan Hume; **Special Effects:** Derek Meddings and Roger Dicken; **Cast:** Doug McClure, John McEnery, Anthony Ainley, Susan Penhaligon, Keith Barron

This movie starts with a World War II German U-boat sinking a British ship and then rescuing some of its passengers. Managing to end up wildly off course, the oddly mixed crew chances upon the long-lost land of Caprona. Insanely, the main river running through the hidden world works like a "river through time." At the beginning of the river, the life-forms are simple, like those found at the beginning of time. The farther you go up the river, though, the more advanced the life-forms become. Don't expect any big scientific treats. It's mostly just guys with guns against dinosaurs with teeth. Finally, with no other way to end the story, a volcano is called into service that wipes out the submarine and the Germans, while stranding McClure and the heroine.

If this sounds fairly inane, blame Edgar Rice Burroughs. He was good with the occasional action story, but science fiction was not his forte. The film's incredibly dull and unconvincing special effects do not help things, either. These were embarrassingly boring in 1975, and now they're simply pathetic. *The Land That Time Forgot* is a fun novel for 12-year-old readers dreaming of adventure and willing to fill in the plot's deficiencies with their own imagination. When it's executed poorly onscreen, however, everything falls apart.

Note: For those who have to see all films based on Edgar Rice Burroughs novels or who just want to know what happened to the hero and his girlfriend, the sequel novel, *The People That Time Forgot* was filmed as well. Sadly, outside of a great cinematic moment in which a popular Frank Frazetta painting is brought to life, this one is even worse than the first.

LAND UNKNOWN, THE

Universal, 1957, b&w, 78 min, VT, LD

Producer: William Alland; **Director:** Virgil Vogel; **Screenplay:** Laszlo Gorog and Charles Palmer; **Music:** Joseph Gershenson; **Cinematography:** Ellis W. Carter; **Special Effects:** Fred Knoth, Jack Kevan, and Orien Ernett; **Cast:** Jock Mahoney, Shawn Smith, Henry Brandon, Douglas Kennedy, William Reynolds

Navy personnel gather for a briefing. Admiral Byrd's actual 1947 exploration of the Antarctic is about to get an updating. It's time to finish what the admiral started and map the entire subcontinent. Two important items are mentioned at the briefing—a "polar oasis," the body of warm water Byrd discovered on his expedition, and the fact that fossils of ferns and other vegetation have been discovered at the South Pole. At the meeting are navy men Mahoney, Reynolds, and Harvey, along with lady reporter Smith. They'll all be going on the new expedition. Mahoney, the captain in charge, is a scientist whose major field is geothermal research. Smith's main reason for going isn't clear.

When the new expedition gets to the Antarctic region, they are held up by the Ross ice pack. Early estimations were wrong. Now the mapping is going to have to be accomplished on a more rigorous schedule, meaning long helicopter flights going farther than would normally be advisable. Returning from one such mapping session, a monstrous storm front forces the helicopter to seek shelter on the ground. With clouds all around the crew descends blindly, trying to reach the ground. Suddenly, the instruments tell them they have gone below sea level. Not only that, but the farther down they go, the higher the temperature. Then disaster—a pterodactyl flies into the helicopter (seen by the audience, but not by those inside the chopper). It's grazing blow shakes up the crew and breaks the radio aerial. The descent then continues until the helicopter has gone a total of 2,500 feet below sea level.

Coming out of the fog, the three navy men and their passenger find themselves in the Mesozoic era. Captain Mahoney theorizes that they are inside a volcanic crater and that the thermal activity below the surface of the valley is what kept this prehistoric world intact through the Ice Age. While his men look over the damaged chopper, the captain and the reporter go off to look around. An oblivious Smith almost gets herself eaten by a plant, which reaches for her but doesn't quite snare her. She is called away by one of the others who finds the first trace of animal life in the valley— the carcass of a small pterodactyl. Mahoney wisely suggests they leave before any predators show up.

The audience is then brought up to speed. The helicopter's radio can't reach out of the valley. Nor can the helicopter lift off, one of its engine parts having been damaged in the midair collision. Also, the four have food that will last for six weeks. But they will have to find a way out of the valley long before then. The navy ships that brought the expedition to the Antarctic have to pull out in 25 days. If they don't, when the ice flow begins to expand once more, it will crush them. Over 800 lives can't be sacrificed for four—especially four people who will by then be presumed dead. So it's up to Mahoney and company to effect their own escape—or else.

The film then shifts into high gear. Two monitor lizards (the kings of 1950s and 1960s dinosaur flicks) fight. A *Tyrannosaurus rex* waddles into view, and the crew retreats to the helicopter and gets the rotors going. The rex is slashed by the rotors, but they don't scare it off. Then a strange sound is heard that does scare the big lizard away. The crew emerges from the chopper more worried than ever (what could scare the *T. rex*?), only to discover their food stores have been raided by something that must have been human.

Finding a small mammal (a type of pre-monkey) prompts several minutes of science class. The lecture is a good one—a straightforward, simple lecture on the theory of evolution—then class is broken up by the return of one of the monitors. While it throws everyone into a panic, Smith is kidnapped by unseen forces. When she awakens later, she discovers she has been captured by a man (Brandon) who crash-landed with four others during Byrd's expedition 10 years earlier.

He vaguely remembers that his name is Hunter. He has survived through his wits (building tools, smashing the dinosaurs eggs, scaring them with the horrible noise he makes by blowing into a massive sea shell, and so forth, but it's clear that he's gone a bit insane. He wants Smith and will do anything to keep her, including leading the three navy men to the wreck of his plane, where he is certain they will find the part they need to escape. His only stipulation is that they have to leave Smith with him.

Mahoney says no deal and off he and the others go, leaving Hunter to his devices. Time passes slowly, however, and as the days count down the captain's crew begins to wonder if they shouldn't give Smith to Hunter. Mahoney balks, but Smith runs off to give herself to Hunter if it will save the others. He and his men save her from him, but then the men decide to torture Hunter until he tells them where the wreck is. At this point the captain announces that everyone is going to stay cool. Smith will not be sacrificed. Hunter will not be tortured. If he doesn't want to go back and he doesn't want to help them—okay. But they will all remain human beings, not become savages. At this point, Hunter begins to remember what it means to be truly human and tells the navy men where they can find the part they need.

They find it, fix the helicopter, and are ready to leave when Hunter and Smith are suddenly attacked by a lake beast. The reclusive caveman saves Smith, but is left floating unconscious in the lake. Mahoney dives into the lake and saves Hunter. The chopper pulls out, flies across the ice, the ocean, and just reaches the ships as it runs out of fuel and crashes into the ocean. The crew plus one are fished out of the water, and everyone gets to go home.

Filmed in CinemaScope, there is a lush, expansive feel to this Universal monster picture that most of the others simply did not accomplish. The science

throughout is good (or at least up to date with what was known at the time), presented simply in under-standable bites. The characters within are just people—not heroes—although they can act heroically. What raises *The Land Unknown* from monster movie to science fiction film is that for the most part the characters think. It's a refreshing change of pace.

Also, a lot of work obviously went into this film. At first the studio actually envisioned *The Land Unknown* as a color, A-list picture to be made with a big-name star. These plans faded, but the picture still commanded an impressive budget, reportedly larger than for the Technicolor extravaganza THIS ISLAND EARTH. The set dressing for the valley is imaginative and consistent. The fog is used cleverly, not oppressively, and the creatures aren't too bad, either. Obviously, no 1950s dinosaur can compare with the computer-animated reptiles we see in movies today, but for the time they were top-notch. *Variety* gave them points for "stark realism" and *Motion Picture Exhibitor* called them "terrifying and realistic." The best comment came from *Harrison's Reports*, which gushed: "The monsters depicted are so flexible and lifelike that one accepts them as real."

LAPUTA (aka: CASTLE IN THE SKY)

Tokuma Shoten (Japan), 1986, Color, 125 min, VT

Producer: Isao Takahata; **Director:** Hayao Miyazaki; **Screenplay:** Miyazaki; **Music:** Jo Hisaishi; **Cast:** Keiko Yokozawa, Mayumi Tanaka, Megumi Hayashibara, Hiroshi Ito, Eken Mine, Sukekiyo Kameyama, Takumi Kamaiyama, Ichiro Nagai, Masashi Sugahara, Tarako, Fujio Tokita, Machiko Washio, Yoshito Yasuhara

This Japanese animated feature starts off with a bang, as a squad of uniformed men flying winged sleds, led by a somewhat crazed old woman (Mama), attack a blimp in midflight. Their assault and boarding is non-stop excitement, if somewhat confusing. They seem bent on kidnapping a young girl whom a great many armed men onboard seem intent on defending. But when the girl gets the chance to escape her defenders, she takes it—whacking their leader over the head with a bottle and bravely heading out the window. She's trying to get away from her locked cabin and into the next one. But the invaders arrive first, cutting off her escape route. She's trapped, she panics, and then . . . she slips.

In an instant she falls hundreds of feet, eluding capture but obviously heading toward certain death.

Then, the big surprise. As she passes out, her necklace begins to react to the rapid descent, and she floats gently to the ground, saved by her mysterious jewelry. She is found, then sheltered and fed by a boy her own age. He is Pazu. She is Sheeta. Obviously they are meant for each other. She is lost and alone and helpless, facing unbelievable odds. He is an orphan and insignificant, but he is lost to love now that he has met her, and nothing will stop him from solving the riddle of who she is and why everyone is after her.

Refreshingly, Sheeta and Pazu are completely open with each other. Pazu tells her about his father and how he disappeared searching for Laputa, the legendary city in the sky. Sheeta tells him how she just showed up in a field one day as a little girl, lost and alone, with only her magic amulet to identify her. She lets Pazu test it. He jumps from a great height while wearing it, but it doesn't work for him, and he comes crashing to Earth, unhurt in the manner that only cartoon characters can make believable.

Before long, however, Mama and her gang as well as the government agents show up to continue the pursuit. Both sets of forces pursue the kids throughout the town, fighting each other all along the way. The epic train chase that is the centerpiece of this segment is both imaginative and breathtaking. Following it, the kids escape to the local mines, where an old miner explains the secret of the rock used to make Sheeta's amulet, giving them clues about Laputa. Unfortunately, the pair are captured by the government agents as they leave. Pazu is locked in a dungeon, while Sheeta is showered with gifts, as the government finally reveals what it wants.

Years earlier, a robot fell from the sky, a robot they believe came from Laputa. Desperate to find (and loot) the mythic paradise, the agents are hoping that the girl and her amulet can revive the robot. The amulet works its magic, but not in any way the government approves. The robot awakens and instantly begins destroying the fortress in which it has been held. Guns and bombs are useless against it. Great doors are used to seal it off, but it cuts its way through them with ease. The robot is trying to rescue Sheeta, whom it recognizes as a citizen of Laputa. Tragically, her initial fear of the robot keeps it from helping her until it is too late. The military throws everything it has against the robot, determined to stop it. The problem, of course, is that if they manage to destroy the robot, Sheeta dies with it.

But Pazu, having been released from the dungeon, has teamed himself with Mama and her boys to save Sheeta. They pull off an amazingly daring rescue in the middle of the conflagration, which is as touching and poetic as it exciting. Then it's a race to find Laputa as Mama and the kids try to outrun the government, who now knows the secret of the amulet, which has fallen into their hands. Who wins? Well, that would be telling. Suffice it to say there is plenty of movie left at this point, and it just gets better and better.

There's lots of buzz worldwide over Japanese animation these days. After decades of only being able to get copies of videos that practically had to be smuggled into the country, suddenly the United State is awash in *anime*. It's true that lots of it is just as wonderful as the medium's enthusiasts promise. But great quantities of it are the usual mundane fodder, much of it self-indulgent and incredibly repetitive, utilizing the same scenes, plots, and gags over and over.

Laputa, however, is not in that category, not by a long shot. This is one of the absolutely finest animated features ever made. The art is concise, consistent, and beautiful. Unlike some Japanese features, none of the usual cheats or simplistic facial gags are used in this highly imaginative and wonderfully executed film. This is high art of a quality that even Disney has trouble matching anymore. The machinery designs are clever and interesting. The robots, the train cars, the winged flying machines, and other items are well conceived and plausible. The animators have gone out of their way to not only make this world complete, but to make it seem as if everything in it really can work. The story is a sheer delight. This movie is a love story with the characters at its forefront—even Mama's mercenary heart is melted by the intensity of Sheeta and Pazu's feeling for each other.

This is a rare gem of a movie, one so perfectly made that even if seen in Japanese (for those of you who don't speak Japanese), it is still easily understood.

LASERBLAST

Yablans, 1978, Color, 90 min, VT, LD, DVD

Producer: Charles Band; **Director:** Michael Rae; **Screenplay:** Franne Schacht and Frank Ray Perilli; **Music:** Joel Goldsmith and Richard Band; **Cinematography:** Terry Bowen; **Special Effects:** Steve Neill and David Allen; **Cast:** Kim Milford, Cheryl Smith, Roddy McDowall, Ron Masak, Keenan Wynn, Dennis Burkley, Eddie Deezen

A human criminal makes his way to Earth, pursued by two reptilian peace officers. The bad guy dies in a shoot-out, but his weapons are found by teenage Billy Duncan (Milford), who has a lot more problems than friends. Suddenly, Billy has found a way to stand up to the big bad bullies, and everyone else he considers a problem. A good idea, fair execution, and low budget all add up to a poor film.

LAST DAYS OF MAN ON EARTH, THE

See *THE FINAL PROGRAMME*

LAST HOUR, THE

Nettleford Films (Great Britain), 1930, b&w, 75 min

Producer: Archibald Nettleford; **Director:** Walter Forde; **Screenplay:** H. Fowler Mear; **Cast:** Stewart Rome, Richard Cooper, Wilfred Shine, Billy Shine

A monarch with little use for trade agreements uses an incredibly advanced weapons system to force planes out of the sky so that he can loot them. Does he then mass produce the weapon and sell it to other countries and make billions? Why bother when he can be a pirate instead?

LAST MAN ON EARTH, THE (1924)

20th Century Fox, 1924, b&w, silent, seven reels

Producer: Jack G. Blystone; **Director:** Blystone; **Screenplay:** Donald W. Lee; **Cinematography:** Allan Davey; **Cast:** Earle Foxe, Derelys Perdue, Grace Cunard, Gladys Tennyson, Buck Black

It's the far-flung future of 1954! A rampaging plague has wiped out every male above the age of 14—except the poor guy from the title, of course. Obviously the world is being run by the surviving women. Everything is fine until they discover that there is a man left. Then the government officials start a donnybrook over who gets him first. All in all, it's pleasantly silly.

LAST MAN ON EARTH, THE (1963)

La Regina/Alta Vista (Italy), 1963/AIP (U.S.), 1964, b&w, 86 min, VT

Producer: Robert J. Lippert; **Directors:** Sidney Salkow and Ubaldo Ragona; **Screenplay:** Logan Swanson and William P. Liecester; **Music:** Paul Sawtell and Bert Shefter; **Cinematography:** Franco Delli Colli; **Special Effects:** Piero Macacci and Giorgio Giovanninni; **Cast:** Vincent Price, Franca Bettoia, Emma Danieli, Giacomo Rossi-Stuart, Troy Cerevi

A terrible plague has ravaged humankind. The only survivor of the strange malady is Dr. Robert Morgan (Price), the title's last man on Earth—or at least, the last man on Earth who isn't a vampire. Yes, the plague has turned the population of the world into vampires. In response, Morgan has turned his home into a fortress, where he hides every night. The vampires assault his home at sundown every night, their voices moaning to him: "Come out, Morgan. Come out, Morgan." After the sun comes up, Morgan leaves his home to search his foes out in their lairs, where he destroys them day after day. Then it's back home to hide and to continue trying to distill a vaccine from his own blood. Since he has survived the plague, he assumes there must be something about his own body chemistry that could cure the world.

The 1963 version of *The Last Man on Earth* is a wonderfully creepy film with a surprise ending that couldn't possibly be given away by anyone with even the most crudely formed sense of mercy. This is a treat for Vincent Price fans. The master is at his best here—kindly, confused, suffering, and murderous. This is also the first film adaptation of Richard Matheson's classic novel, *I Am Legend*. The second adaptation is the better-known *THE OMEGA MAN*. Neither film is a perfect transference of the novel to the screen, but both have their fans. Try both of them. Those who want an explanation of how the plague turns people into vampires, read the novel, where Matheson explains it all in brilliant medical terms. The book is the best bet of the three, but they're all entertaining.

LAST STARFIGHTER, THE

Universal, 1984, Color, 100 min, VT, LD, DVD

Producer: Gary Adelson; **Director:** Nick Castle, Jr.; **Screenplay:** Jonathan Betuel; **Music:** Craig Safan; **Cinematography:** King Baggot; **Special Effects:** Jeff Okun, James Dale Camomile, Michael Lantieri, Kevin Pike, Joe Sasgen, and Darrell Pritchett; **Cast:** Robert Preston, Dan O'Herihly, Lance Guest, Catherine Mary Stewart, Barbara Bosson, Norman Snow, Cameron Dye, Wil Wheaton, Marc Alaimo

It's a story we've seen plenty of times. Video games are being placed in arcades all around the country—just not, as one might imagine, for amusement and the collection of quarters, but for the training, testing, and recruitment of young men and women with exceptional skills so that they can save the universe. One of the machines, destined for Las Vegas, winds up instead in a trailer park in the middle of nowhere. Luckily for the intergalactic recruitment center, a bored Lance Guest lives in that trailer park.

Since Guest is the movie's young star, it's obvious he's going to prove to be the best game player. He is approached by con-alien Robert Preston, who kidnaps him from Earth, convinced that any young pup with a talent for video blasting will be pleased to leave his girlfriend and family to go off and save the galaxy by defending The Frontier. Surprise—Guest turns out to like breathing and insists on being returned home.

This turns out to be a lucky break for everyone. It seems that The Frontier is in more trouble than it thought. A renegade prince who was ejected from the good and wise Frontier has returned at the head of the enemy invasion fleet. He knows the secrets of his former homeland's defenses, and he uses this knowledge to bring in the bad guys to destroy the heroic star fighters. Of course, once Guest learns of this, he goes back and cleans house.

This film is easy and yet hard to criticize. It's heart is in the right place, and the screenplay tries to keep up. The stars are engaging, and Preston (in his last role) is as vital and lovable as ever. Yes, the picture has some small problems, but detailing them is not important. Suffice to say that this is a very good children's science fiction adventure that adults will also enjoy surrounded with children. It offers nothing new, but it's fun, with good special effects, especially for its time. The sci-fi content is limited to the hardware and aliens.

Note: The word is that this is the first motion picture to have effects done on a Cray Super Computer. It shows. At the time, the spaceships and their intricate battles dazzled audiences. People were left breathless in the theaters. Now, especially on a television screen, the effects seem obvious and clunky.

Also, for *Star Trek* fans, Wil Wheaton and Marc Alaimo didn't have big parts in this movie, but it did help set them up for their more notable television roles as Wesley Crusher on *Next Generation* and as Gul Dukat on *Deep Space Nine*.

LAST WAR, THE

Toho (Japan), 110 min/Medallion TV (U.S.), 1961, 81 min, Color

Producers: Sanezumi Fujimoto and Tomoyuki Tanaka; **Director:** Shue Matsubayashi; **Screenplay:** Toshio Yazumi and Takeshi Kimura; **Music:** Kuma Dan; **Cinematography:** Rokuro Nishigaki; **Special Effects:** Eiji Tsuburaya; **Cast:** Frankie Sakai, Nobuko Otowa, Akira Tararada, Yukiro Hoshi

A series of mistakes causes the world's superpowers to fling their nuclear arsenals at one another. It's an idea that's been done before, sometimes well and sometimes not so well. But whether the other films were comedies or dramas, they never went as far as this one. In *The Last War,* the studio that gave us multiple warnings about playing with nuclear fire with their creation, Godzilla, goes to the ultimate extreme. Here there is no last-minute bailout. The world is destroyed in an epic wagonload of special effects and a bit of gutsy finger-pointing.

LAST WOMAN ON EARTH, THE

Filmgroup, 1960, Color, 71 min, VT

Producer: Roger Corman; **Director:** Corman; **Screenplay:** Robert Towne; **Music:** Ronald Stein; **Cinematography:** Jack Marquette; **Cast:** Anthony Carbone, Betsy Jones-Moreland, Robert Towne

Two men and one woman find themselves stranded on a lush Caribbean island after a nuclear war wipes out everyone else. Since this is a Roger Corman project, one might expect things to get stupid fairly quick, and though there are times when Corman surprises, this wasn't one of them. In fact, this movie was wrapped up so quickly, Corman asked first-time screenwriter Robert Towne to come up with another one on the spot so the cast and crew could remain on location and enjoy the Caribbean awhile longer. Towne delivered, coming up with *THE CREATURE FROM THE HAUNTED SEA.* Oddly enough, the film they threw together on a lark was much better than *The Last Woman on Earth,* the movie they went down there to make in the first place.

Note: Screenwriter Towne went on to write the award-winning *Chinatown,* among other highly regarded films.

LATE FOR DINNER

MGM, 1991, 99 min, Color, VT, LD

Producers: Dan Lupovitz and W.D. Richter; **Director:** Richter; **Screenplay:** Mark Andrus; **Music:** David Mansfield; **Cinematography:** Peter Sova; **Special Effects:** Rosemary Brandenburg; **Cast:** Brian Wimmer, Peter Berg, Marcia Gay Harden, Peter Gallagher, Colleen Flynn, Kyle Secor, Michael Beach, Bo Brundin, Janeane Garofalo

Two friends on the run head to a third friend who is experimenting with cryonics and hide themselves in a deep freeze for about 30 years rather than face their problems. Then they wake up and try to resume their lives. From beginning to end this movie seems always on the verge of becoming something worth watching, but somehow never quite does.

LATE GREAT PLANET EARTH, THE

Pacific International, 1979, 90 min, Color

Producers: Robert Amran and Alan Belking; **Director:** Amran; **Screenplay:** Amran; **Music:** Dana Kaproff; **Cinematography:** Michael Werk; **Narration:** Orson Welles, Hal Linsey

Hal Linsey wrote a best-seller called *The Late Great Planet Earth* that tied together all the known ancient predictions about the end of the world and tried to explain them through modern phenomena that our ancestors had no knowledge of—nuclear war, UFOs, and so on. Since no best-seller is safe from Hollywood, this one was optioned and turned into a silly film. It's not really good for much of anything, except a party in which everyone likes to make fun of what they see on the screen.

LATEST STYLE AIRSHIP

Pathé (France), 1908, b&w, silent short

Director: Ferdinand Zecca

This short from France involves the invention of a flying bicycle. Viva la Schwinn.

LATITUDE ZERO

Toho (Japan)/National General (U.S.), 1969, 99 min, Color

Producers: Don Sharp and Tomoyuki Tanaka; **Director:** Inoshiro Honda; **Screenplay:** Ted Sherdeman and Shinichi Sekizawa; **Music:** Akira Hukube; **Cinematography:** Taiichi Kanjura; **Special Effects:** Eiji Tsuburaya; **Cast:** Joseph Cotten, Cesar Romero, Richard Jaeckel, Patricia Medina, Linda Haynes, Akira Takarada, Tetsu Nakamura

Evil genius Romero battles good genius Cotten under the sea. It's a submarine battle for control of the world. It's also tired and silly, and despite some excellent sets, not much of a movie. Toho does a lot better with Godzilla than it does adapting old American radio shows into movies.

Note: Screenwriter Shederman also scripted the classic *THEM!*

L'ATLANTIDE

See *JOURNEY BENEATH THE DESERT*

LAUGHING AT DANGER

FBO, 1924, b&w, silent, six reels

Director: James W. Horne; **Screenplay:** Frank Howard Clark; **Cinematography:** William Marshall; **Cast:** Eve Novak, Joe Harrington, William Talmadge

American scientists create death rays and evil foreign agents try to steal them.

LAWNMOWER MAN, THE

New Line Cinema, 1992, 105 min, Color, VT, LD, DVD

Producers: Peter A. McRae, Clive Turner, Edward Simons, Robert Pringle, Masao Takiyama, and Gimel Everett; **Director:** Brett Leonard; **Screenplay:** Leonard and Everett; **Music:** Dan Wyman; **Cinematography:** Russell Carpenter; **Special Effects:** Jimi Simmons, Angel Studios, Reel Efx, Mercer Title & Optical, and EFX Unlimited, Inc.; **Cast:** Jeff Fahey, Pierce Brosnan, Jenny Wright, Mark Bringleson, Geoffrey Lewis, Jeremy Slate, Dean Norris, Austin O'Brien

Scientist Brosnan has been having a tough time. He's developing a groundbreaking new theory but can't get approval to work on it from his superiors—not to test it on humans, anyway. In desperation, he cons the mentally retarded man (Fahey) who cuts his grass into acting as his guinea pig. For a while things go along smoothly. Brosnan gets the results he expected and more. Fahey finds himself becoming not only more intelligent, but more and more aware of his surroundings in powerful ways. Eventually, Fahey begins to tap into the virtual reality world that Brosnan has created, finding that he can link with the computer to give himself a variety of cyber superpowers. Then the big question comes into play—now that he's smart, is he a good guy or a bad guy?

This is one of the first serious attempts to explore cyberspace in a feature film. Excellent computer animation work makes the plot more believable than it

The Lawnmower Man (NEW LINE CINEMA / JOSEPH B. MAUCERI COLLECTION)

might otherwise be. A few plot holes are found, but nothing that takes away from what is ultimately an interesting, exciting, and even satisfying film.

The Lawnmower Man was followed by a sequel. None of the stars except young Austin O'Brien returns, but it does have the always entertaining Matt Frewer on hand. Unfortunately, it doesn't have a whole lot more going for it. Where the first expands consciousness, the sequel just helps pass the time.

LAWNMOWER MAN 2: BEYOND CYBERSPACE (aka: LAWNMOWER MAN 2: JOBE'S WAR)

Allied Entertainment (Great Britain) New Line Cinema (U.S.), 1996, Color, 93 min, VT, LD, DVD

Producers: Keith Fox, Steven A. Lane, Auram Kaplan, Peter A. McRae, Robert Pringle, Edward Simons, Masao Takiyama, and Clive Turner; **Director:**

Farhad Mann; **Screenplay:** Brett Leonard, Gimel Everett, and Mann; **Cinematography:** Ward Russell; **Music:** Robert Rolk; **Special Effects:** John E. Saski and Michael Meinardus; **Cast:** Partick Bergin, Matter Frewe, Austin O'Brien, Ely Pouget, Camille Cooper, Patrick La Brecque, Crystal Celeste Grant, Kevin Conway

See *THE LAWNMOWER MAN*

LE DERNIER COMBAT

Triumph Films (France)/Columbia (U.S.), 1984, 90 min, b&w, VT

Producer: Constantin Alexandrov and Luc Besson; **Director:** Besson; **Screenplay:** Besson and Pierre Jolivet; **Music:** Eric Serra; **Cinematography:** Carlo Varini; **Special Effects:** Christian Grosrichard, Thierry Flamanio, Claire Vaton, Patrick Leberre;

Cast: Pierre Jolivet, Jean Bouise, Fritz Wepper, Jean Reno, Christiane Kruger

The setting is some time in the future. Something has destroyed civilization and killed off most of the population. Those few survivors the film shows us either don't have the resources to rebuild what's been lost or simply aren't interested in making the attempt, so they live in the ruins, struggling to survive as best they can. Our hero is a bearded man (Jolivet) who, as the film opens, is introduced having joyless, noisy sex with an inflatable doll. Before he can climax, the air is released comically from the toy, a gag thrown in the audience's face later.

Jolivet is building a one-man airplane in his apartment. At night he leaves his den to search quietly for the various parts he still needs. On occasion he tries to read but does not seem able. This depresses him, although early on it remains unclear to the audience. Eventually, Jolivet crosses the desert to invade the stronghold (a few old cars parked strategically around

Le Dernier Combat (COLUMBIA PICTURES / AUTHOR'S COLLECTION)

a waterhole) of a nondescript gang of hooligans who don't talk to one another; no one in the film can talk, but the filmmakers take their time revealing this. These desert rats survive by sending the smallest of their number down a sewer into an otherwise unreachable water source. He fills up the gang's jugs and then is hauled back to the surface. The leader of the crew, a man who wears a necklace of fingers, keeps this mole locked in the trunk of his car until needed.

Jolivet invades the stronghold to kill the leader. He then takes his own finger from the leader's necklace, shoves it into a glove, puts the glove on, then leaves with the battery from the leader's car. The gang pursues him, but he has just enough time to install the battery in his airplane and make his escape, flying through the windows of his apartment. The plane eventually crash-lands near an old city.

At this point the film begins to follow another silent character played with amazing comedic hostility by the sensational Jean Reno. Reno is engaged in attempting to trick his way inside another man's stronghold. He places boxes of food, crates of gold and jewels, and so forth at the front door, trying to trick the old man inside into opening the door long enough for him to enter. The old man spends all his time painting on the inner walls of his fortress. His figures are primitive hunters and animals. Interestingly, they are the same figures represented in the cave paintings found in France, which have proved to be the earliest European art. The old man's figures are almost exactly the same style as those in the old caves. He never seems to get anything finished, however, since Reno is always returning to distract him with another trick.

At the same time, we watch Jolivet as he finds a place to stay. Like Charlton Heston in *THE OMEGA MAN* or Vincent Price in *THE LAST MAN ON EARTH*, he gathers art and appliances to build himself a home. During a freak storm, he is pelted by fish from the sky. No explanation is given for the phenomenon—the fish just fall. Jolivet is wildly happy, throwing the fish into a pile that must number in the hundreds. Oddly, he finds one fish that has no head, but rather a tail on each end. That this does not elicit more than the mild surprise from him is a clue as to what has happened to the world, but nothing more is made of it.

Eventually, however, the comedy begins to come to a close. Reno and Jolivet meet, and Reno turns out to be an incredibly malicious psychopath who attacks without mercy. He overwhelms the smaller Jolivet, who barely escapes with his life. Then, as luck would have it, in dragging himself to a hiding place, Jolivet stumbles onto an unknown entrance into the old man's fortress. He passes out and is found by the occupant, who must then determine if he will kill the helpless intruder or not. Deciding thumbs up for Jolivet, the old man returns to his former practice, doctor. Soon Jolivet is up and around. Interestingly, the doctor paints using Jolivet as a model. Although still painting on the walls, his work now takes on a much more technically advanced quality—he has a friend, and only civilized men can be friendly, only civilized men can advance in the arts.

The two settle in as roommates, and the doctor slowly begins to reveal his secrets. The first is a gas that, if inhaled, allows people to speak once more for a few moments. Now the audience understands—whatever happened to the world eliminated man's ability to talk. Triumphantly, Jolivet says, "Bon jour." He has a civilized place to live and a civilized person to share it with—a good day indeed.

The second secret the doctor reveals is a bit more startling. The old man has a woman captive in his fortress. Jolivet's shock at seeing her lets the audience know that this is a big deal. He has no idea where she is held. The doctor blindfolds him and then takes him to her cell a different way each time. Jolivet has dreams of himself with this last woman on Earth, but alas such is not meant to be. Jean Reno manages at last to batter his way inside the fortress. The lunatic slaughters the woman, then in turn almost kills Jolivet, who triumphs in the end, but it is a hollow victory. The film concludes as it started, with dreams of sex dying as the toy is broken before the act can be completed.

Critic Leonard Maltin calls this film "wildly overpraised," but *Le Dernier Combat* is truly a work of art, made even more remarkable by its low budget. For instance, the sound track is a collection of whatever could be found that fit the moment. Jazz, electronic, and other types of music alternate throughout. It's cheap, but highly effective. This creates a singularity of vision that imposes a definite attitude on the film, always important in low-budget filmmaking. Attitude is an all-important commodity when the money isn't available to carry out ideas on a big scale. Forced to use black-and-white film? Don't make a movie that apologizes for looking cheap—make it a statement. Can't afford sound dubbing? Write a script that takes away man's voice.

The wonderful thing about *Combat* is that its lack of words make it wonderfully open to interpretation. Besson wants to tell us something about the female nature of society. Civilization is basically a female concept: law and order, the building of a nice, peaceful nest. Jolivet symbolizes the civilized man. He carries a table setting with him wherever he goes. Even at the end of the world he has his knife, fork, and wineglass, and he uses them properly. His habits, whenever possible, are still properly mannered. Reno, on the other hand, is the ape mentality—the scheming, violent brute who survives through ferocity and strength of arms. Reno lives like an animal, even when he doesn't have to. He is a brute force that constantly destroys society whenever possible, including the last living female. Jolivet, the civilized man, gives her presents and dotes on her but cannot keep her alive.

To Besson, there can be no civilization without women. Indeed, without feminine influence, the very concept makes no sense. Even the obviously educated and sophisticated doctor reverts to making primitive cave paintings without a relationship in his life. No one within the movie ever attempts to build anything new. They are all part of a vast scavenger society living in the ruins of what once was. As in romance, once the fall comes, nothing is the same. Love leaves and all is lost.

Note: In case the director/screenwriter's name looks familiar (and it should), that's because Luc Besson is the creator of such other off-beat genre films as *The Professional*, *La Femme Nikita* and the sci-fi hit THE FIFTH ELEMENT. Still Besson has yet to top what he accomplished in *Le Dernier Combat*.

LEECH WOMAN, THE

Universal, 1960, 77 min, b&w, VT, LD

Producer: Joseph Gershenson; **Director:** Edward Dein; **Screenplay:** David Duncan; **Music:** Irving Gertz and Milton Rosen; **Cinematography:** Ellis W. Carter, A.S.C.; **Special Effects:** Bud Westmore; **Cast:** Colleen Gray, Grant Williams, Gloria Talbott, Phillip Terry, John Van Dreelen, Kim Hamilton, Arthur Batanides, Estelle Hemsley

This movie opens with a scene of the fighting Talbots (Gray and Terry) battling once more. She's a well-off older woman whose younger husband doesn't have much use for her now that he's used her money to become a doctor with an established practice. She's fairly certain he's cheating on her, and she uses a steady stream of alcohol to help cover her pain. As expected, this only makes her more combative and him more anxious to be rid of her. Usually, ridicule is enough for the doctor when it comes to his wife, but he's now had enough. In fact, Talbot is planning on a divorce when fate intervenes. An elderly black woman comes to his office. She claims to be a member of the Nando tribe, and over 140 years old. Rightly, the doctor scoffs, but the old woman shows him the secret of the Nando—a powder she calls nipé.

Her claim is that she was brought to America from Africa as a slave scores of years earlier. She has kept herself alive through the judicious use of her tribe's secret, but now her supply has almost run out. She proposes swapping the secret for passage back to Africa. As proof of her claim, she takes a bit of the portion and becomes decades younger before Talbot's eyes.

The doc is impressed, yet still allows her to leave without closing the deal. That night he tells his wife that he doesn't want a divorce. It's all been a big mistake. He loves her and wants her to go to Africa with him to help him with a bold new project. Obviously, the doc just wants a guinea pig to test the nipé on once he finds the Nandos, but his poor drunk wife is still desperately in love with him, and so off they go to Africa.

An unscrupulous guide is hired to usher them through much badly integrated stock footage, and finally the land of the Nandos is discovered. This is bad, since the tribe is protective of their secret. The old woman has made it there before them without their help. She lets them know they will all be killed for daring to come into Nando country. But before they perish, they will be shown the tribe's secret.

And that secret is pineal fluid, fatally extracted from the base of the neck of male volunteers. A curved ring is used to kill the victim and extract the fluid. Why the men volunteer to die is unclear, but they do, and the women of the tribe get to live longer and know one more beautiful moment before they die themselves. In fact, the old black woman offers Mrs. Talbot the chance to know youth and beauty again. She can pick any man to be killed so that she might be beautiful once more. Seeing the stunning effect on the Nando woman, and having finally accepted what an untrustworthy goon her husband is, Mrs. Talbot accepts, condemning him to death by pineal extraction. He is murdered, she is transformed, and finally the movie starts to heat up. The guide, both wanting to live and seemingly mystically enchanted by Mrs. Talbot's new beauty, concocts an escape plan. Using dynamite, he slaughters the tribe to cover their exit, taking with them the ring and all the tribe's spare nipé.

Once he and the ex-Mrs. Talbot are safely away, they make love in the jungle and sleep beneath the stars. When morning comes, the awful truth is revealed. The effect of the radical transformation is short-lived. With her beauty gone, the spell is broken, and the guide tries to run away, but it's too late. He's killed and beauty returns.

When she returns to the States, our heroine pretends to be her own niece. She takes over her house and starts seducing the young and handsome family lawyer. His fiancée doesn't like that, but Mrs. Talbot doesn't care what anyone thinks. All she wants is to keep her beauty. She picks up young men and slaughters them on a nightly basis. When the lawyer's fiancée tries to scare her off from her man. Mrs. Talbot kills her as well. But then she makes her fatal mistake. Using the fiancée's pineal fluid doesn't restore her. Only men are good for that. Killing another woman only brings about ageing so rapid Mrs. Talbot changes to dust before the eyes of the police who had caught up to her because of her murderous ways. And thus ends *The Leech Woman*.

This is not Hollywood at its best. Many things are implied throughout, but never confirmed. Are the Nando men under some sort of pheromonal spell? Maybe. Is the nipé powder made from the fluid there in the jungle? How? Who knows? No part of the plot in this clunker can stand up to even casual observation. Worse, though, is its sheer clumsiness. No matter how many times the open cup of nipé powder is dropped, turned over, carried in pockets, and so forth, none of it ever spills. Mrs. Talbot has no trouble finding the right spot at the base of any man's neck, even when she isn't looking when she strikes. Dynamite thrown onto the grass rooftops of huts creates enough shrapnel to kill scores of charging warriors.

Colleen Gray is wonderful as the doomed Mrs. Talbot, but she's obviously the glue holding together just another quickie Universal horror movie. During the early 1950s, these films had a magic that often raised them above the usual B movie fare. But by 1960 the magic was running out. The themes of love and betrayal that could have done so much for this movie are just window dressing. It's fun, just not great. Women feeling bitter about some jerk will have a good time sympathizing with Gray, and guys can sit back and feel smug at the end, but observe this warning even if all others in this volume go unheeded: This is not a picture for couples.

Note: Even in its initial release, *The Leech Woman* appeared not as a solo feature, but on a double bill with the low-budget English import, *Brides Of Dracula*.

LEGALLY DEAD

Universal, 1923, b&w, silent short

Director: William Parke; **Screenplay:** Harvey Gates and Charles Furthman; **Cinematography:** Richard Fryer; **Cast:** Milton Sills, Brandon Hurst, Claire Adams, Margaret Campbell

A scientist thinks he can raise the dead through the judicious use of the wonder fluid, adrenaline! When the body of a wrongfully executed man comes into his possession, he doesn't hesitate to test his theory.

LENSMAN

Toho/MK Studios, 1984, Color, 107 min, VT

Directors: Yoshiaki Kawajiri and Kazuyuki Hirokawa; **Screenplay:** Edward E. Smith; **Music:** Akira Inoue; **Cast:** Kerrigan Mahan, Tom Wyner, Greg Snegoff, Michael McConnohie

E.E. Doc Smith's classic space opera adventures are brought to animated life by the Japanese, sadly to little effect. The wild glory and thunder and epic scope of the novels is missing, along with the sense of fun. While mildly entertaining and good for animation and comic-book fans, there's not much here, especially for those still cherishing their childhood love affair with the old novels.

LET THERE BE LIGHT

American-Flying A, 1915, b&w, silent short

Director: William Bertrum; **Cast:** Helen Rosson, Charles Newton, E. Forrest Taylor

A turn-of-the-century scientist stuns the world with a fantastic invention—an electric illuminator! Hey, it was 1915.

LEVIATHAN

MGM, 1989, Color, 98 min, VT, LD, DVD

Producers: Luigi DeLaurentiis, Aurelio DeLaurentiis, Charles Gordon, and Lawrence Gordon; **Director:** George Pan Cosmatos; **Screenplay:** Jeb Stuart and David Webb Peoples; **Music:** Jerry Goldsmith; **Cinematography:** Alex Thomson; **Special Effects:** Charles L. Finance and Barry Nolan; **Cast:** Peter Weller, Richard Crenna, Amanda Pays, Daniel Stern, Ernie Hudson, Michael Carmine, Lisa Eilbacher, Hector Elizondo, Meg Foster

Once again the plot of *ALIEN* is ripped off, this time in an underwater setting as a group of divers confronts a savage creature. Despite a remarkable and talented cast, this one remains a most terrible, dreadful picture.

L5: FIRST CITY IN SPACE

Imax Corporation, 1996, Color, 35 min

Producers: Toni Myers, Graeme Ferguson, and Jonathan Barker; **Directors:** Myers and Allan Kroeker; **Screenplay:** Myers; **Music:** Micky Erbe and Maribeth Solomon; **Cinematography:** Andrew Kitzanuk; **Special Effects:** Stephen Roloff and Pat Rawlings; **Cast:** Colin Fox, Rachel Walker, Denis Akiyama, Genevieve Langlois, Martha Henry

It is 100 years in the future and humankind is finally out in the stars. On L5, the city and spaceport suspended at a point of perfect gravitational balance between Earth and the Moon, life is good. In fact, it's practically utopia. The story centers on an event in the past of seven-year-old Chieko, whose adult self narrates the film.

Our narrator explains the history of space exploration from the reality of our own times until the building of the L5 colony. Life in the wonderful, egalitarian worker's paradise is detailed for us—how people work and play, how they grow their crops, recycle their air, raise their cattle, and so forth, and then the drama begins. L5's life-support systems have reached their limits. If the city is to grow, more water must be found, and found fast. Luckily, Chieko's grandfather has a plan. A comet 500 million miles away has all the frozen water within it that the city could want. All they have to do is divert the comet's orbit with a robot rocket. Then it will pass L5 every few years and provide the city with all the water it needs.

The rocket is fired off. It reaches the comet without incident but then fails to divert its target from its usual path. But Chieko's dad decides he can just fly out and fix it. The music indicates that the drama is high. The ship anchors on the comet through the use of gigantic harpoons. Dad repairs the rocket, but then he is suddenly lost.

The next moment, his voice cuts through the static on L5's receivers. He's safe and will be home in time for Chieko's birthday. Everything will be fine. After that, we meet the grown-up Chieko, who is now the mayor of L5. As the audience senses the movie is coming to a close, one last glorious image is shared: a second city being built out among the stars.

"People will always be Earth-dwellers," Chieko tells us, "but we are no longer Earth-bound. Our dream has come true. At last, we are citizens of the solar system."

Like all Imax films, *L5* is beautiful to look at, even breathtaking at times. But the company's first foray

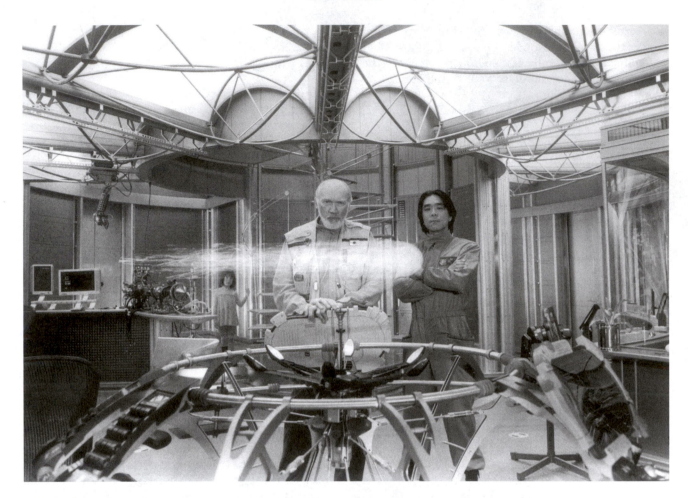

L5: The First City in Space (DENTSU PROX, INC. / AUTHOR'S COLLECTION)

into creating a "reality-based" film is nothing special. The story is far too simplistic and full of basic amateur science fiction that will interest only the youngest of fans. Of course, *STAR WARS* is pretty primitive as far as its science goes, but at least it's laid out in an exciting manner. Not *L5*. The Imax tale is told in a cloying, overly cute style, politically safe, but ponderously slow moving. There is no excitement and little in the way of thrills or even boredom breakers. As for as the Imax experience, save this movie for the bottom of your sci-fi viewing list. There simply isn't that much going on, and, like so many Imax films, its previews promise a lot of exciting space views, but far too much of this one is spent in routine shots within the city.

Note: When determining where to locate the space city, the filmmakers were advised by scientists at the Jet Propulsion Laboratories to place it at L5, an actual position in our solar system (LaGrange Point 5) on the Moon's orbit around Earth, where the gravitational pull is close to zero. NASA's scientific data and decades of research suggest that this spot is the best location to support a self-sustaining space colony. If more hard science like this had made its way into the film, perhaps it would have been more interesting.

LIFEFORCE

Tri-Star Pictures/Cannon Group, 1985, Color, 101 min, VT, LD, DVD

Producers: Yoram Globus, Menahem Golan, and Michael J. Kagan; **Director:** Tobe Hooper; **Screenplay:** Dan O'Bannon and Colin Wilson; **Music:** Henry Mancini and Michael Kamen; **Cinematography:** Alan Hume; **Special Effects:** John Gant, Richard Hiscott, Kevin Welch, Roy Scott, Grant McCune, Nick Finlayson, and Roger Dorney; **Cast:** Steve Railsback, Peter Firth, Frank Finlay, Patrick Stewart, Mathilda May, Michael Gothard

The space shuttle *Churchill* is outward bound, going farther than any manned vehicle has yet dared travel. The joint British/American team is on a mission to approach and observe the returning Halley's comet more closely and thoroughly than ever before. The crew soon discovers a most curious thing about the comet—it has a passenger. Trapped in the head of the comet is a two-mile-long spaceship—obviously one of alien origin. Four members of the *Churchill*'s crew go aboard the alien craft to investigate. They find hundreds of corpses—otherworldly figures resembling gigantic bats, all of them dried out and shriveled. At the same time that the astronauts are searching the death ship, automatic controls within the vessel begin deploying a massive, umbrella-shaped energy scoop from the front of the ship. Its purpose is not explained.

Back inside, the mission commander has discovered something new—a chamber with three glass coffins. Within each is one perfectly preserved nude *human* figure—two male and one female. When the other explorers discover him, the commander is floating weightless over the container holding the female figure, simply staring at her. To the observers, the woman, or perhaps her container, seems to be drawing something from the commander—energy, perhaps—life force, maybe—but no result is immediately apparent. With Halley's comet moving ever farther out of range, the commander decides that the four of them had better get moving. He orders the three glass containers taken back with them to the *Churchill*, along with one of the bat corpses. After that monumental decision is made, the scene shifts to Earth.

The *Churchill* has returned to Earth orbit, but it isn't making any attempt to land. Instead, it is simply drifting outside the atmosphere. Another shuttle, the *Columbia*, is sent up to investigate. It finds the *Churchill* gutted by fire, all the members of its crew burned to death. It can find no explanation for the tragedy. Also discovering the three glass containers and their occupants, the *Columbia* crew decides to bring them back to Earth for examination.

While this is happening, a television reporter talks of the passage of Halley's comet. He informs his viewers that throughout history comets have been equated with disaster, that they have always been thought of as harbingers of evil. He goes so far as to give the Latin translation for the word *comet*, "evil star."

Now the action truly begins. As the examination of the female body commences, she drains the energy from her examiner. His body falls away, dry and brittle, all the life sucked from it. The woman calmly leaves the building, killing everyone who stands in her way

with her touch. When she wants to exit, the glass wall before her explodes from just a glance. The two males awaken next and follow much the same pattern. Machine guns don't stop them, but grenades do.

Finally, things should be looking up with two down and one to go, but when the scientists at the base try to examine the remains of the first guard who was drained of all his life energy, his corpse sits up at the doctor's touch and steals the medical man's life force. A little study tells the horrible tale: Halley's comet has brought a vampire plague to Earth. After the energy is drained from a living thing, two hours later, it awakens with the same need to drain energy from people. There is no cure. If you get the disease, you either drain other people's energy, or you explode into dust.

In the middle of all this madness, the *Churchill*'s escape pod is found. The commander of the mission is still alive. He tells his rescuers that on the way back from Halley's comet, the rest of the crew died one by one. The female was draining them of their lives. The commander knew it but couldn't do anything to stop it because she was controlling him mentally. Finally, he managed to wreck the *Churchill*'s controls and set the ship afire while escaping in the pod.

The commander doesn't know why, but for some reason there is a psychic link between himself and the female. He is hypnotized at that point in an attempt to turn the link between himself and the vampire to humanity's advantage. Seeing what she sees, the good guys discover that the vampire is traveling from body to body, her own body hidden somewhere else. Through the link, our heroes are capable of tracking her down and capturing her. Drugging the body that the vampire is using, they are able to question her. They discover that her female form is just a sham. She created it out of what she found in the commander's mind when she first made metal contact with him. She is more than just his perfect dream girl—as she puts it: "I am the feminine in your mind." In other words, the commander couldn't help himself. She made herself a part of him by putting a part of herself within him and then taking a part of him away.

At the same time, London is in chaos. The plague is crippling the city, and a nuclear bomb will soon be dropped if it isn't stopped. As the slaughter continues, the alien ship is finally explained. The large umbrella scoop is gathering up the soul energy being sent to the vessel via the plague. So if our heroes are going to save not only London from destruction, but the very souls of humanity, they are going to have to figure out how to destroy a vampire who is utterly unstoppable, who has visited Earth routinely in the past, and who can kill with a glance.

To give away the ending of this movie would be a great disservice. *Lifeforce* is an incredible film, and may well be the most intelligent vampire movie ever made. Most of the films in this subgenre are merely slasher movies. Some have a bit of interesting commentary to make on male/female relationships, and a few make interesting forays into psychology and philosophy, but this is beyond all of them, light-years beyond. The special effects are adequate to excellent, and the acting is sharp, but the story is what makes this movie hum. Of course, that's what comes from basing your movie on a book by Colin Wilson, one of the world's most insightful philosophers. *Lifeforce* is a true, thinking sci-fi fan's film.

LIFEFORM

See *INVADER* (1996)

LIEUTENANT ROSE, R.N., AND HIS PATENT AEROPLANE

Clarendon (Great Britain), 1912, b&w, silent short

Airplanes were barely off the ground when this film's plucky protagonists were inventing planes that can be controlled over great distances electronically. Little is known about this film, but the reports are favorable.

LIFE IN THE NEXT CENTURY

France, 1909, b&w, silent short

Director: Gérard Bourgeois

Life in the faraway dream world of the year 2010 is previewed for audiences at the turn of the last century. As you might guess, the filmmakers thought it would be a great time to live. Credit has to be given to them for having so much hope.

LIFE WITHOUT SOUL

Ocean Film Corporation, 1915, b&w, silent feature

Producer: George DeCarlton; **Director:** Joseph W. Smiley; **Screenplay:** Jesse J. Goldburg; **Cast:** William A. Cohill, Jack Hopkins, Lucy Cotton, Pauline Carley, Percy Darrell Standing

A fairly interesting retelling of *Frankenstein*, wherein after the monster is brought to life it chases its creator across the ends of the Earth.

LIGHTNING BOLT

7 Films/Balcazar (Italy/Spain), 1966, 100 min/Woolner Brothers (U.S.), 1967, 96 min

Producer: Alfonso Balcazar; **Director:** Anthony Dawson; **Screenplay:** Balcazar and Jose Antonio do la Loma; **Cinematography:** Ricardo Pallottini; **Music:** Riz Ortolani; **Special Effects:** Antonio Visone; **Cast:** Urusla Parker, Anthony Eisley, Wandisa Leigh

Earth's (specifically, the United States's) space program is disrupted rather violently when our intergalactic neighbors begin peppering us with laser bombardment. Sadly, the studios responsible for producing this film were not hit first.

LIGHT YEARS

Miramax, 1988, 71 min, VT, LD

Producers: Bob Weinstein, Henri Rollin, and Jean-Claude DeLynre; **Director:** Rene Laloux; **Screenplay:** Isaac Asimov; **Music:** Bob Jewett, Gabriel Yared, and Jack Maeby; **Animation:** Philippe Caza; **Cast:** Glenn Close, Christopher Plummer, Jennifer Grey, John Shea, Penn and Teller, Terrence Mann, David Johansen

This animated science fiction film tells the story of a prince whose utopian land of Gandahar is ravaged by an unknown enemy who turns its citizens into stone. His mother, the queen, sends him off to avenge this, and the prince winds up on a time-travel adventure into the future where the only thing of note is just how disgustingly arrogant and pretentious everyone has gotten about sex.

LIQUID AIR, THE

Gaumont (France), 1909, b&w, silent short

A new invention freezes solid any person who happens to come into contact with it.

LIQUID ELECTRICITY

1907, b&w, silent short

Producer: J. Stuart Blackton; **Director:** Blackton

Another new invention gives superspeed to anyone who drinks it.

LIQUID SKY

Z Films, Inc., 1983, Color, 112 min, VT, LD, DVD

Producer: Slava Tsukerman; **Director:** Tsukerman; **Screenplay:** Tsukerman, Anna Carlisle, and Nina V. Kerova; **Music:** Brenda I. Hutchinson; **Cinematography:** Yuri Neyman; **Special Effects:** Neyman; **Cast:** Anne Carlisle, Paula E. Sheppard, Susan Doukas, Otto Von Wernherr, Bob Brady

In New York City, a wild lesbian who is heavily into the music scene discovers a UFO on her penthouse patio. Despite a small budget, this movie delivers some bizarre effects and even some big laughs, but only for some audiences. It's a comedy for outsiders, but isn't all science fiction for outsiders?

LITTLE PRINCE, THE

Paramount, 1974, Color, 88 min, VT, LD

Producer: Stanley Donen; **Director:** Donen; **Screenplay:** Alan J. Lerner; **Music:** Frederick Loewe; **Cinematography:** Christopher Challis; **Special Effects:** Thomas Howard; **Cast:** Richard Kiley, Steven Warner, Bob Fosse, Gene Wilder, Clive Revill, Joss Ackland, Donna McKechnie, Victor Spinetti

The little prince (Warner) in question lives on an asteroid with his talking rose. Deciding he needs to know more about life than what knowledge his animated vegetation can provide, he travels to Earth, where he enlists the aid of a pilot (Kiley) to help him quest for the meaning of life. This story started life as a classic children's science fiction/fantasy novel. As a book it's loved by millions, but as a movie it's highly forgettable. *The Little Prince* is Lerner and Loewe at their worst.

LITTLE SHOP OF HORRORS, THE (aka: THE PASSIONATE PEOPLE EATER)

Allied Artists, 1960, b&w, 70 min, VT, DVD

Producer: Roger Corman; **Director:** Corman; **Screenplay:** Charles Griffith; **Music:** Fred Katz; **Cinematography:** Archie R. Dalzell; **Special Effects:** Harry Thomas and Daniel Haller; **Cast:** Jonathan Haze, Jackie Joseph, Mel Welles, Dick Miller, Myrtle Vail, Jack Nicholson, Marie Windsor, Charles Griffith

In New York City, a young loser working in a flower store is determined to make the salesgirl notice him.

He decides to breed a new type of plant to make himself important enough for her to want to date him. His plan works, and soon our hero is known far and wide as the genius who crossbred the world's most interesting new plant. There's just one problem—one of the strains he used in his work was the Venus's-flytrap, and now he has a bloodthirsty carnivore on his hands.

This is the one you've heard about—the film Roger Corman made in just two days (some reports say three days, but what's the difference?)—the classic black comedy that is just about as funny as can be. Bloody, murderous, and hysterical, this one's a must for anyone who's never seen it, just for a very young Jack Nicholson's turn as a dental patient who loves pain.

Note: This original version of the film gathered such a following, both among critics and the public, that eventually it was turned into a stage musical that ran for years and years in New York and elsewhere. It was highly successful, so much so that in 1986 the stage version, in which the plant of the original became the advance scout of an alien invasion, was turned into a second motion picture.

This color, all-singing, all-dancing version of the film was directed by Frank Oz and starred Rick Moranis, Ellen Greene (reprising her stage role), Vincent Gardenia, Steve Martin, James Belushi, John Candy, Christopher Guest, and Bill Murray. It is just as much fun as the first one.

LITTLE SHOP OF HORRORS, THE (1986)

The Geffen Company, 1986, Color, 88 min, VT, LD, DVD

Producers: David Geffen, Eric Angelson, Denis Holt, and David W. Orton; **Director:** Frank Oz; **Screenplay:** Howard Ashman and Charles B. Griffith; **Cinematography:** Robert Paynter; **Music:** Miles Goodman and Graham Longhurst; **Cast:** Rick Moranis, Ellen Greene, Vincet Gardenia, Steve Martin, James Belushi, John Candy, Christopher Guest, Bill Murray, Levi Stubbs

See *THE LITTLE SHOP OF HORRORS* (1960)

LOGAN'S RUN

MGM, 1976, Color, 118 min, VT, LD, DVD

Producers: Saul David and Hugh Benson; **Director:** Michael Anderson; **Screenplay:** David Z. Goodman; **Music:** Jerry Goldsmith; **Cinematography:** Ernest

Laszlo; **Special Effects:** Lyle B. Abbott and Frank Van Der Veer; **Cast:** Michael York, Jenny Agutter, Richard Jordon, Roscoe Lee Brown, Peter Ustinov, Farrah Fawcett-Majors, Michael Anderson, Jr., Lara Lindsay

It's the year 2274. In a postnuclear holocaust society, life is one big party in the film's tyrannically ruled domed city—at least, that is, until this society's citizens reach the age of 30. At that time, they are required (aka: forced) to become one with the Carousel. This device is supposed to rejuvenate those who enter it for another 30 years of fun and games. As you might guess, it simply kills them instead. Those who don't enter of their own free will are tracked down and terminated by Sandmen, officers of the law who put people to sleep permanently.

The story centers or Jessica (Agutter) who, reaching her 30th birthday, has decided she'd like to live a bit longer. She makes a break for it along with Sandman Logan (York), who is beginning to have some doubts about his calling. They are trying to find the mythic outside world free base known only as Sanctuary. Along the way they're pursued by Logan's former best friend and partner as the two make their way through the mad underworld of the city and then the even more lunatic world outside.

To make a long story short—there is no Sanctuary. Jessica and Logan find a great deal of ridiculous, unrelated, meaningless time wasters and then finally the world's only surviving old man (Ustinov). He convinces them that it's worth living to be old, and so they go back to the city to convince everyone else. They are captured, and when interrogated by the domed city's master computer, their arguments against ritual suicide overload the computer's brain and it explodes, taking the city with it.

This is one of the most pretentious overrated science fiction films ever made. Produced toward the end of the end of the '70s, it pushed all the right societal buttons of the time. It was anti-big government, antimilitary, antiauthority, but it was also antireason, antithought and antiquality. To be fair, most of the first half of the movie is inventive and somewhat intriguing. The story line shows promise at first, but the second half becomes bogged down with senseless scenes of action thrown at the main characters. The film ignores the book it adapts, which wasn't very good itself, and loads the movie with meaningless visual material meant to stimulate the audience. Pithy dialogue masquerading as philosophy takes away even from those scenes worth watching.

Though the film was presented a special Academy Award for visual effects decades ago, the effects really weren't even all that special by contemporary standards. Current science fiction television shows routinely have effects light-years ahead of what MGM presented here. Considering how sloppily this movie was put together (watch for Agutter's green stockings to disappear and reappear from moment to moment), one wonders whose idea the award was in the first place.

Many critics have taken a whack at this film, but it was probably Peter Nicholls in *The Science Fiction Encyclopedia* who summed it up best.

> This is a film that encapsulates the many flaws that seem inherent in SF cinema; paradoxically they may be summarized as irrationality, and a lack of scientific thought, perhaps resulting from a Hollywood cynicism which regards sf as basically a genre for uncritical children, which in turns suggests a lack of unfamiliarity with written sf outside the comics.

Note: For those who watch this movie, keep an eye open at the end. After everyone has escaped the destruction of the city, someone in the crowd gives Ustinov the Vulcan hand salute. Just a bit of sci-fi fun.

LORD OF THE FLIES (1963)

Walter Reade/Sterling (Great Britain), 1963, b&w, 91 min, VT, LD, DVD

Producer: Lewis Allen; **Director:** Peter Brook; **Screenplay:** Brook; **Music:** Raymond Leppard; **Cinematography;** Tom Hollyman and Gerald Feil; **Cast:** Tom Chapin, James Aubrey, Roger Elwin, Tom Gaman, Hugh Edwards

A plane filled with English schoolboys is doing its best to escape some sort of upcoming military disaster, perhaps a nuclear war, when it crash-lands on a deserted island. At first, Britain's best and brightest do pretty well for themselves. They set up a tribal government that works for a while, but the usual human emotions set in, and before long the tribe turns on itself. Those intellectuals trying to resist the primitive urges within all of us are murdered and otherwise abused by those not so concerned with the nobility of man. The science fiction angle is all social science this time, but this is truly an excellent, sobering, and tragic film that only seems more prophetic with every passing year.

A new adaptation released in 1990 featured strong cinematography and a solid cast; while it was largely adequate, it failed to reach the same poignancy as its predecessor.

LORD OF THE FLIES (1990)

Castle Rock Entertainment/Columbia Pictures, 1990, Color, 90 min, VT

Producer: Peter Allen, Jeffrey Bydalek, Ross Milloy and Lewis Newman; **Director:** Harry Hook; **Screenplay:** Sarah Schiff; **Music:** Phillipe Sarde; **Cinematography:** Martin Fuhrer; **Cast:** Badgett Dale, Balthazar Getty, Chris Furrh, Danuel Pipoly, Gary Rule, Andrew Taft, Edward Taft

See *LORD OF THE FLIES* (1963)

LORDS OF THE DEEP

Concorde, 1989, Color, 79 min, VT

Producer: Roger Corman; **Director:** Mary Ann Fisher; **Screenplay:** Howard R. Cohen; **Cinematography;** Dan Kneece; **Cast:** Bradford Dillman, Priscilla Barnes, Daryl Haney, Melody Ryane, Eb Lottimer, Stephen Davies, Roger Corman

An underwater base in the future is under attack by aliens. Or is it? To tell the truth, no one cares, since this is truly one of the worst science fiction on-under-or-anywhere-around-the-water movies ever made.

LOST ANGEL, THE

MGM, 1944, b&w, 91 min

Producer: Robert Sisk; **Director:** Roy Rowland; **Screenplay:** Isobel Lennart and Angna Enters; **Music:** Daniele Amfitheatrof; **Cinematography:** Robert Surtees; **Cast:** Margaret O'Brien, James Craig, Marsha Hunt, Keenan Wynn, Alan Napier, Philip Merivale, Donald Meek, Henry O'Neill, Robert Blake

A young girl (O'Brien) is the subject of an experiment—could a child be raised to be a genius? This one can. By the age of six she's already smarter than most college professors. But she lacks the ability to enjoy her life, that is, until she stops living with scientists and starts living with a reporter (Craig). The movie just misses getting bogged down in sentiment and is unusually good.

Note: Don't overlook the hat check girl—it's a young Ava Gardner.

LOST CITY, THE (aka: THE LOST CITY OF THE LIGURIANS)

Regal, 1935, b&w, serial, 12 chapters

Producer: Sherman S. Krellberg; **Director:** Harry Revier; **Screenplay:** Pereley Poore Sheehan, Eddie Graneman, Leon D'Usseau, Zelma Caroll, George Merrick, and Robert Dillon; **Music:** Lee Zahler; **Cinematography:** Roland Price and Edward Lindon; **Cast:** Kane Richmond, William Millman, Ralph Lewis, Gabby Hayes, Josef Swickard, Milburn Moranti, Eddie Getherstone, William Boyd, Margot D'use, Gino Corrado, Claudia Dell, William Bletcher

The world is being lashed by massive electrical storms. Plucky hero Richmond traces the cause of the storms to Africa, to (get ready for this one) Magnetic Mountain, no less. The mountain is really the outward disguise for a hidden civilization ruled by madman Boyd. As usual in these multireelers, the hero and the villain's accomplices pummel each other until the end when the good guy finally wins. This serial has it all—zombie giants, Arab scientists, pygmy warriors, frozen electricity (yeah, that's right), lost cities, scenery-chewing bad-girl evil queens, and Gabby Hayes as a bad guy. Like most serials, for fans of the genre only.

LOST CITY OF THE JUNGLE, THE

Universal, 1946, b&w, serial, 13 chapters

Directors: Ray Taylor and Lewis D. Collins; **Screenplay:** Joseph F. Poland, Paul Houston, and Tom Gibson; **Cinematography;** Gus Peterson; **Cast:** Lionel Atwill, Keye Luke, Russ Hayden, Jane Adams, John Eldredge, John Gallaudet, Arthur Space, Gene Roth

At the end of World War II, cranky warmonger Atwill heads for the lost city of Pendrang to get his hands on some meteorium 245. Supposedly, this wonder substance will give the country controlling it immunity to nuclear bombs. A band of the usual idiot good guys try to stop this dastardly villain, but there's no need. Atwill is so desperate to get out of this turkey he has his character knock over the meteorium and blow himself up. Some guys are just all class.

As bad as serials get, this one highlights their rampant stupidity. If it's a lost city, how did this meteorium get there? How is it anyone knows about it? How do they know it will cancel the effects of nuclear bombs when, at that time, the world barely knew what those effects were, let alone how to cancel them? There is more, but the point is made.

LOST CITY OF THE LIGURIANS, THE

See *THE LOST CITY*

LOST CONTINENT, THE (1951)

Lippert, 1951, b&w, 83 min, VT, LD, DVD

Producers: Robert L. Lippert and Sigmund Neufeld; **Director:** Samuel Newfield; **Screenplay:** Richard Landeau and Carroll Young; **Music:** Paul Dunlap; **Cinematography:** Jack Greenhalgh; **Special Effects:** Augie Lohman; **Cast:** Whit Bissell, Cesar Romero, Hillary Brooke, Chick Chandler, Sid Melton, Aquanetta, John Hoyt

Intrepid and dashing scientist Romero leads an expedition to the top of a mountain. What they're looking for is an atomic rocketship that's gone missing. What they find is a tropical jungle filled with dinosaurs. The dinosaurs have been kept alive by the mountaintop's abundant uranium deposits. What's going to keep these scientists alive in the face of so many hungry critters is anyone's guess. Cheaply made from an improbable script, this movie has little to say for itself, outside of having Whit Bissell, the world's greatest character actor, among the ranks. Even that didn't help this one much, though it does offer inexplicably green-tinted sequences that someone thought were going to put this picture over the top.

LOST CONTINENT, THE (1968)

Hammer (Great Britain)/20th Century Fox (U.S.), 1968, Color, 89 min

Producers: Michael Carreras, Anthony Hinds, and Peter Manley; **Director:** Carreras; **Screenplay:** Michael Nash; **Music:** Roy Phillips and Gerard Schürmann; **Cinematography:** Paul Beeson; **Special Effects:** Arthur Hayward, Robert A. Mattey and Cliff Richardson; **Cast:** Eric Porter, Hildegard Knef, Suzanna Leigh, Tony Beckley, Nigel Stock, Neil McCallum

A tramp steamer accidentally makes its way into the thick seaweed ropes of the Sargasso Sea. Trapped, the passengers battle a series of giants (giant lobster, giant octopus, giant crab, and so on) and then normal-sized conquistadors from a society that evolved in the Sargasso when some unlucky Spaniards were trapped there centuries earlier. Though implausible and often silly, the movie is almost saved by an unusually able cast.

LOST IN SPACE

New Line Cinema, 1998, Color, 122 min, VT, LD, DVD

Producers: Carla Fry, Mark W. Koch, Stephen Hawkins, and Akiva Goldsman; **Director:** Hawkins; **Screenplay:** Goldsman; **Music:** Bruce Broughton, **Cinematography:** Peter Levy, A.C.S.; **Special Effects:** Norman Garwood, Angus Bickerton, and Jim Henson's Creature Shop; **Cast:** William Hurt, Gary Oldman, Matt LeBlanc, Mimi Rogers, Heather Graham, Lacey Chabert, Jack Johnson, Jared Harris, Edward Fox, Dick Tufeld

It's 2058 and the intrepid Robinson family is preparing to save the world. Earth is on its last legs. Its resources are drying up at a catastrophic rate. The planet's only chance is to be able to reach the stars. That's where the Robinsons come in. Dad (Hurt) and Mom (Rogers) are scientists who have a plan—build a hyperspace jump gate in an Earth orbit while a ship heads for our closest neighbor and erects another. The journey, by conventional means, will take decades. But once that jump gate is up, travel between the two worlds will be instantaneous.

A rival group has the same plan, however, and they're out to destroy the Robinsons so that their team will get to rule the world. Their spy, Dr. Smith (Oldman), sabotages their ship. But then, before he can get back outside, he is rendered unconscious by his own employers and left to share the Robinsons' fate. Waking up seconds before the end, Smith is able to set the family's rescue in motion (literally everyone is needed), but the only way for the Robinsons to save themselves is to throw themselves recklessly into the unknown, or, as the title goes, to become lost in space.

The film then falls into a series of interesting and exciting episodic progressions until the Robinsons' ship makes planetfall in desperate need of fuel. Here the strange time loops that seem to have been following the Robinsons come full circle in a conclusion that should have been obvious to everyone from the beginning, but which somehow seems to sneak under most audience member's radar. The cast escapes the planet before its internal disruptions finally cause it to explode, although as they blast off into the void once more, they're still lost in space.

This is a great little film. For those not fans of the original television show, which may be the worst of the nonsense inflicted on viewers by Irwin Allen, the premise is much the same as that described above. The first few episodes emphasized the heroics of Dad and Major West, but the show ultimately became a comedy centered on Dr. Smith and his sidekick, the mission's robot. The movie is a great step forward. The family, unlike the problem-free black and white Robinsons, is a real family. The kids don't feel like leaving everything behind and blasting off into space. Mom and Dad are so busy trying to save the world they don't have any time for their children or each other. Dad's been ignoring young Will, and then there's his rivalry with the blunt but brave pilot who not only wants to take over Dad's position as commander of the mission, but would like to be involved with his oldest daughter as well. The spaceship design benefits from four decades of space travel research and design. Suddenly, the science makes sense. Dr. Smith's continued presence makes sense. Everything makes sense.

The picture is filled with wonderful tips of the hat to the old series. Things that made the show unbearable are explained, rendered plausible, or in some way mentioned without the slightest hint of embarrassment. No knowledge of the television series is necessary, but it helps for getting the in-jokes.

On the other hand, there is nothing exceptional about the film. It breaks no new science fiction ground, poses no great questions, offers no deep insights. All in all, *Lost in Space* is just another action-packed, smoothly scripted, highly enjoyable time waster.

Note: Stars from the original show—June Lockhart, Mark Goddard, Marta Kristen, and Angela Cartwright—all make appearances in the film. Lockhart and Goddard are easy to spot, but Kristen and Cartwright have but the briefest of cameos. Happy hunting.

LOST MISSILE, THE

United Artists, 1958, b&w, 70 min

Producer: Lee Gordon; **Director:** Lester Berke; **Screenplay:** John McPartland, Jerome Bixby, and Berke; **Music:** Gerald Fried; **Cinematography:** Kenneth Peach; **Special Effects:** Jack R. Glass; **Cast:** Robert Loggia, Larry Kerr, Ellen Parker, Philip Pine

A missile settles into orbit around Earth. No one knows whose it is or where it came from. But they do know that its orbit is decaying and that when it comes crashing into the planet it will most likely hit New York City. On top of that, the missile is setting massive fires and melting cities all around the globe. Robert Loggia tries everything to stop the missile, but he can't forestall the movie's interestingly low-key finale. Its low budget cripples *The Lost Missile* slightly, but like so many inexpensive black-and-white science fiction films, this one makes up for its stunted cash flow with grand ideas and solid writing.

LOST PLANET, THE

Columbia, 1953, b&w, serial, 15 chapters

Producer: Sam Katzman; **Director:** Spenser G. Bennett; **Screenplay:** George H. Plympton and Arthur Hoerl; **Music:** Mischa Bakaleinikoff; **Special Effects:** Jack Erickson; **Cast:** Judd Holdren, Vivian Mason, Forrest Taylor, Gene Roth, Ted Thorpe, Michael Fox

Captain Video (Holdren) comes to the rescue once more. This time it's interstellar hoodlums and a planetary invasion that have to be dealt with. Fifteen weeks is a long time to spend getting to the edge of something like this—Captain Video wins.

LOST WORLD, THE (1925)

First National, 1925, b&w, silent feature, VT, LD, DVD

Producers: Earl Hudson and Watterson R. Rothhacker; **Director:** Harry O. Hoyt; **Screenplay:** Marion Fairfax; **Cinematography:** Arthur Edeson; **Special Effects:** Willis O'Brien and Marcel Delgado; **Cast:** Wallace Beery, Lewis Stone, Bessie Love, Arthur Hoyt, Bull Montana, Lloyd Hughes

Sherlock Holmes creator Sir Arthur Conan Doyle's other investigator, Professor Challenger (Beery), leads an expedition into a previously unexplored section of South America. He's chasing down rumors of an almost inaccessible plateau where time stopped scores of millions of years in the past. Challenger and his party locate the area in question, finding their way to the top with some amount of difficulty. Once there, they do indeed discover a doorway to the past. They also find lots of hungry dinosaurs eager to snack on the presumptuous new lords of the food chain.

Challenger and the others manage to escape the plateau before it is destroyed by volcanic forces. The wily scientist succeeds in bringing back some proof of their discoveries—a brontosaurus egg that hatches back in London. The critter grows to full size and escapes into downtown London, eventually destroying Tower Bridge and crushing buildings and people.

This silent version of Doyle's classic novel is by far the best of all the *Lost World* films. Except for some minor variations (and a different ending—in the novel it's only a small pterodactyl that escapes to fly over the city), the film is remarkably faithful to the novel. In the remakes that followed, science was left pretty much at the gate, and the main thrust of the silent version was to discover the facts of the case and report them. Ah, the beauty of an era of filmmaking that at least attempted to deliver what it promised.

Note: It's hard to find a good print of this film these days, but the search is worth the effort for one reason if none other. This version of *The Lost World* was helmed by master stop-frame animator Willis O'Brien. Seeing him accomplish this kind of remarkable detail and fluidity of motion years before his work on *King Kong* gives one a true appreciation of his genius.

LOST WORLD, THE (1960)

20th Century Fox, 1960, Color, 97 min, VT

Producer: Irwin Allen; **Director:** Allen; **Screenplay:** Allen and Charles Bennett; **Music:** Bert Shefter and Paul Sawtell; **Cinematography:** Winton Hoch; **Special Effects:** Lyle B. Abbott, Emil Kosa, Jr., James B. Gordon, and Ben Nye; **Cast:** Claude Rains, Michael Rennie, Fernando Lamas, Jill St. John, David Hedison, Ian Wolfe, Richard Haydn

Sherlock Holmes creator Sir Arthur Conan Doyle's other investigator, Professor Challenger (Rains), leads an expedition into a previously unexplored section of South America. He's chasing down rumors of an almost inaccessible plateau where time stopped scores of millions of years in the past. Challenger and his party find the area in question, just as they did in the 1925 film of the same name, but this time they have no trouble reaching the top. These 1960s explorers have come by helicopter, and so all it takes is a gentle landing, and once more the rumored doorway to the past is discovered anew. All those hungry dinosaurs are still just as eager to snack on the presumptuous new lords of the food chain as they were in the '20s.

Of course, proving they actually ran into dinosaurs will be a problem. They see a number of monitor lizards with papier-maché horns and spikes glued to the heads and backs, but no dinosaurs. There are giant spiders and the usual human-grabbing plants, hostile natives, and other cheap devices thrown into the script to waste time as well, but no real dinosaurs. Eventually, Challenger and the others manage to escape the plateau before it is destroyed by volcanic forces. The wily scientist manages to bring back some proof of their discoveries—a lizard's egg that breaks opens before they take one step out of the jungle. It gives all of the survivors a good laugh though, and that's all that matters—right?

This is an earnest attempt at filmmaking that sadly just doesn't cut it. Too cheap to produce a movie with realistic dinosaurs, Irwin Allen made it the way he makes all his films, with every short-cut, corner-cutting method at his disposal. To cover the missing monsters, the story is packed with romances, betrayals, dark secrets, and hidden treasure, direct from the soap-opera school of writing. This is a shame, for the photography throughout is wonderful, and even the lizards with glued-on fins and horns don't look so bad. In fact, the duel to the death where two of these critters roll over the towering cliffs at the end is fondly remembered by most folks who saw this movie in their childhood.

The cast does its best with what it has. Rains is wonderful as Challenger, and everyone around him supports him well. The story truth is, though, that they just don't have much with which to support him, other than trite, cliché-ridden speeches that weigh down the weak plot even further.

LOST WORLD, THE (1993)

Worldvision (Canada), 1993, Color, 99 min, VT

Producers: Frank Agrama, Norman Siderow, and Daniele Lorenzano; **Director:** Timothy Bond; **Screenplay:** Harry Alan Towers; **Music:** Larry Wolfe, Isaiah Sanders, and Gerard Shadrick; **Cinematography:** Paul Beeson; **Special Effects:** Peter Parks; **Cast:** John Rhys-Davies, David Warner, Eric McCormack, Nathania Stanford, Darren Peter Mercer, Tamara Gorski, Innocent Chosa, Kate Egan

Sherlock Holmes creator Sir Arthur Conan Doyle's other investigator, Professor Challenger (Rhys-Davies), leads an expedition into a previously unexplored section of Africa. He's chasing down rumors of an almost inaccessible plateau where time stopped scores of millions of years in the past. Challenger and his party find the area in question, but trust me, there is not a single reason for you to care.

This rambling mess has little to do with Doyle's book. Rhys-Davies and Warner are their usual competent selves, but everyone else is terrible. What's more, the main component of the story—all those hungry dinosaurs that audiences crave—are scarcer than statues to Whit Bissell and poorly done as well. This is one of the worst adaptations of a Conan Doyle novel. Possibly the only one worse is this film's sequel made by the same company. Shot at the same time as the first, *Return to the Lost World* features a plot about sinister Belgians who want to exploit the Lost World for profit! Luckily, Challenger and his crew are on hand to stop them from their evil capitalistic ways. Presumably they then went off to free all the zoo and circus animals they could find. Both of these films are blunderingly amateurish from beginning to end. Indeed, it's almost painful to watch a pair of seasoned professionals like John Rhys-Davies and David Warner stumbling around in these truly awful movies.

LOST WORLD: JURASSIC PARK, THE

Universal/Amblin Entertainment, 1997, Color, 134 min, VT, LD, DVD

Producers: Bonnie Curtis, Colin Wilson, Kathleen Kennedy, and Gerald R. Molen; **Director:** Steven Spielberg; **Screenplay:** Michael Crichton and David Koepp; **Music:** John Williams; **Cinematography:** Janusz Kaminski; **Special Effects:** Megan I. Carlson, Don Elliott, Cory Faucher, George C. Hull, Ned Gorman, Pat Turner, Christine Owens, and Brian Tipton; **Cast:** Jeff Goldblum, Julianne Moore, Pete Postlethwaite, Arliss Howard, Richard Attenborough, Vince Vaughn, Vanessa Lee Chester, Peter Stormare, Harvey Jason, Richard Schiff, Thomas F. Duffy, Joseph Mazzello, Ariana Richards

This film's only connection to the classic Arthur Conan Doyle novel of the same name is the title. Professor Challenger is nowhere to be found, and one suspects that if Canon Doyle were alive today, that's just the way he'd want it.

Picking up where *JURASSIC PARK* left off, it is revealed that the dinosaurs (brought back to life using DNA left over from the jurassic era) on the island, where the doomed amusement park was built, were actually bred on another island and then transported to their final destination. This second island has now become an expansive, humane wildlife preserve, but the men who control it plan to open it up for exploitation in order to recover their investment. Hoping to study the dinosaurs before their environment is disturbed, Dr. Ian Malcolm (Goldblum) from the previous film leads a research expedition. They quickly find that another group is on the island as well—a group of hunters. But when the dinosaurs refuse to cooperate with the humans' goals, both groups find themselves stranded and fighting for their lives.

And so the plot unfolds. Goldblum, whose performance makes viewing this preachy mess bearable, is the one good feature of this film, other than the special effects. Everything around him borders on the idiotic. This film loses its way, as many science fiction movies do, when it places its political message before telling a good story, the message being a warning against exploiting the environment.

This becomes most apparent in one of the movie's pivotal scenes. When one of the camera operators working with the research group turns out to be an environmentalist, the audience seems directed to cheer his decision to free all the captive dinosaurs within the camp, especially when they then proceed to trample and slaughter the film's villains—the scientists and wranglers who put them there. This is the same genius who stole all the ammunition for the one gun powerful enough to stop the largest creatures. The fact that these actions trap everyone on the island, place their lives in immediate danger, and result in several deaths, doesn't get in the way of this character being cast as a hero. After all, he's handsome with a great smile, and the exploiters aren't, so obviously he must be good and they must be evil.

Another important point is that the island environment is actually safe, protected, and healthy for the dinosaurs, undercutting the idea that they're being abused by those who would profit from them. The movie could have made its environmental-friendly and anticapitalism statements more easily if the island were modeled after old-fashioned zoos, which were cruel places no better than animal prisons. Then the monkey-wrenching tactics of some of the researchers would have been more justifiable.

These aren't the film's only weaknesses. In their desperate need to recreate the first movie as closely as possible, the filmmakers saddle Goldblum with a previously unmentioned child and girlfriend to provide the ad hoc family unit present in *JURASSIC PARK*. Not addressed is how he was shamelessly chasing Laura Dern through the first film while he apparently had this other girlfriend and daughter waiting for him back home. Did it occur to the filmmakers how bad this makes him look? Also, his previously unmentioned child turns out to be a teenage black girl who resembles Goldblum in no way. The difference is never explained and remains a jarring uncertainty throughout the story. What could have been an interesting story point, enhancing the characters' history and personal lives, expanding the audience's sense of who these people are, is let to lie fallow, a token nod to political correctness.

Not content to stop there, the most ridiculous scene in the first film is also recreated as closely as possible for the sequel. It involves a truck caught in a gigantic tree for a moment before falling—slapstick comedy in the middle of an adventure film. The scene is even more ridiculous here.

This is one of the most simple-minded, badly written, illogical pieces of blatant film propaganda. While propaganda is not necessarily something to be avoided, bad movies are. The only thing in this one's favor are its wonderful special effects.

Note: The film has one bit of wit. When the *Tyrannosaurus rex* taken back to civilization gets loose in downtown San Diego, a Japanese businessman running from the scene announces in Japanese, "I came to America to get away from this sort of thing." An obvious and amusing reference to *GODZILLA*.

LOVE GERM

Lubin, 1908, b&w, silent short

Somehow a researcher comes across the germ that makes people fall in love. Love as an infection—is that notion cynicism or genius?

LOVE FACTOR, THE

See *ZETA ONE*

LOVE MAGNET, THE

General, 1916, b&w, silent short

Director: A. Santell; **Cast:** Lloyd V. Hamilton, Bud Duncan, Ethel Teare

More romantic foolishness as a magnet is discovered that attracts women. The interesting part is that all the women aren't typical movie goddesses. This magnet attracts all kinds of women. An odd film, but not a bad one.

LOVE MANIAC, THE

See *THE FIEND WITH THE ATOMIC BRAIN*

LOVE MICROBE, THE

Biograph, 1907, b&w, silent short

Somehow a researcher comes across the germ that makes people fall in love. Love as an infection—is that notion cynicism or genius? Possible inspiration for the next year's film, *LOVE GERM.*

LOVE PILL, THE

Mayfair (Great Britain), 1971, Color, 82 min

Producers: Lawrence Barnett and John Lindsay; **Director:** Kenneth Turner; **Screenplay:** Lindsay; **Cinematography:** John Mackey; **Cast:** Toni Sinclair, Kenneth Waller, Melinda Churcher

A local grocery creates a candy that just happens to have the additional bonus of being a reliable contraceptive and turns all women into insatiable nymphomaniacs. Should anyone be surprised that a man wrote this one?

LOVE POTION #9

20th Century Fox, 1992, Color, 96 min, VT, LD

Producer: Dale Launer; **Director:** Launer; **Screenplay:** Launer; **Cinematography:** William Wages; **Music:** Jeb Leiber; **Cast:** Tate Donovan, Sandra Bullock, Mary Mara, Dale Midkiff, Hillary Bailey Smith, Dylan Baker, Anne Bancroft

A shy researcher, biochemist Donovan, gets a love potion from an old gypsy fortune-teller. Teaming up with animal researcher Bullock, they discover that the potion is not a sham but a condensed liquid salt with unusual properties. One swallow changes the voice so that it causes reverberations in the ears of whoever hears it. This triggers the chemical production of pheromones, causing listeners of the opposite sex to be attracted and listeners of the same sex to become hostile. The effects last for four hours and then fade.

Early experiments on animals create hysterically exaggerated results, letting the researchers know that they needs to dilute their formula. After that, however, the comedy takes off. The male researcher acts typically male, getting revenge on a woman who insulted him in the past, running sexually rampant in a girl's dormitory, and so on. The woman, on the other hand, acts far more intelligently. She first charms a cop giving her a ticket, which leads her to charming her insurance man, which sets off a whole string of events that by the end of the day has her at the Governor's Ball on the arm of a prince. Meanwhile, Donovan realizes that he loves Bullock, but the plot is complicated when he finds she's returned to her old boyfriend. This makes no sense to Donovan because the guy was a jerk. It doesn't take long, though, before Donovan discovers that the boyfriend has secretly gotten his hands on the potion and is using it to keep Bullock enthralled.

Admittedly, the basic premise here is a slight one. But this idea is distinguished by standout, sharp direction and stylish, boldly clever camera work. It's only a B romantic comedy but highly praiseworthy for its insightful commentary on the human condition if nothing else. This very early Bullock film (her second) is one of her best and is a fun way to pass a dreary evening.

M

MAC AND ME

Vision International, 1988, Color, 93 min, VT, LD

Producers: Mark Damon, William B. Kerr, and R.J. Louis; **Director:** Stewart Raffill; **Screenplay:** Steve Feke and Raffill; **Music:** Alan Silvestri; **Cinematography:** Nick McLean; **Special Effects:** Martin Becker, Rubin A. Aquino, and Christopher Swift; **Cast:** Christine Ebersole, Jonathan Ward, Katrina Caspary, Lauren Stanley, Jade Calegory

Uncreative science fiction filmmakers looking to cash in on the genre often steal the plot of *ALIEN*. When they also want to sell commercial time onscreen, they look to *E.T.*, which is just what this film does. With a production number showcasing Mcdonald's and the use of the wonder drug Coca-Cola to allow Mac, the alien, to survive his stay on Earth, it's hard to miss the product endorsements in this film; there's more to them than the story.

MACHINE, THE

France2 Cinéma (France/Germany), 1994, Color, 96 min, VT

Director: François Dupeyron; **Screenplay:** René Belletto and Dupeyron; **Music:** Michel Portal; **Cinematography:** Dietrich Lohmann; **Cast:** Gérard Depardieu, Nathalie Baye, Dider Bourdon, Natalia Woerner, Erwan Baynaud, Marc Andreoni, Julie Depardieu

Gérard Depardieu is a scientist who invents a mind-switching machine, with which he he puts his mind (accidentally, of course) into the head of a psycho-killer who loves to slaughter women. There's not a great deal of science fiction, but it's still a top-notch movie.

MAD DOCTOR OF BLOOD ISLAND, THE

Hemisphere, 1969, Color, 85 min, VT

Producer: Eddie Romero; **Director:** Romero; **Screenplay:** Reuben Conway; **Music:** Tito Arévalo; **Cinematography:** Just Paulino; **Cast:** John Ashley, Angelique Pettyjohn, Ronald Perry, Eddie Garcia, Alicia Alonzo

Visitors to a remote island and the local natives are menaced by a crazed scientist's chlorophyll monster.
Note: Angelique Pettyjohn reportedly claims that her love scene with co-star John Ashley wasn't faked. Steamy stuff, but only for those who saw the film in theaters back in 1969. When the movie was edited for television, the scorching scene was cut and then lost for all time.

MAD DOCTOR OF MARKET STREET, THE

Universal, 1942, b&w, 61 min, VT

Producer: Paul Malvern; **Director:** Joseph H. Lewis; **Screenplay:** Al Martin; **Music:** Hans Salter; **Cinematography:** Jerome Ash; **Special Effects:** R.A. Gausman; **Cast:** Lionel Atwill, Una Merkel, Nat Pendleton, Noble Johnson, Anne Nagel, Claire Dodd, Richard Davies

Scientist Atwill takes it one the lam to a remote island in the South Pacific where he convinces the local natives he's a god by raising the dead. He then uses the natives in his experiments, showing why he had to go on the run in the first place.

MAD DOG TIME (aka: TRIGGER HAPPY)

MGM/United Artists, 1996, Color, 93 min, VT, LD

Producers: Leonard Shapiro, Larry Bishop, Eddie Ska-piro, and Stephan Manpearl; **Director:** Bishop; **Screenplay:** Bishop; **Cinematography:** Frank Byers; **Special Effects:** Bellissimo/Belardinelli Effects, Inc.; **Music:** Earl Rose; **Cast:** Ellen Barkin, Jeff Goldblum, Gabriel Byrne, Billy Drago, Richard Dreyfuss, Diane Lane, Larry Bishop, Richard Pryor, Gregory Hines, Paul Anka, Kyle MacLachlan, Burt Reynolds, Christopher Jones, Henry Silva, Michael J. Pollard, Billy Idol, Rob Reiner, Angie Everhart

On a parallel Earth, gangsters run everything. Goldblum and Dreyfuss are excellently cast as the intelligent rival gang leaders in this cool, stylish bit of filmmaking. Other than the notion of parallel realities, though, there's little science fiction.

MAD GHOUL, THE

Universal, 1943, b&w, 64 min, VT

Producer: Ben Pivar; **Director:** James Hogan; **Screenplay:** Brenda Weisberg and Paul Gangelin; **Music** Hans Salter; **Cinematography:** Milton Krasner; **Cast:** George Zucco, David Bruce, Turhan Bey, Robert Armstrong, Milburn Stone, Addison Richards, Evelyn Ankers, Charles McGraw, Rose Hobart

George Zucco is a classic mad scientist whose claim to fame is Death In Life Gas: One whiff and you're zom-bie for life. The only problem—life only lasts a few days unless you get a new heart. And then another, and another, and another.

MAD LOVE

MGM, 1935, b&w, 85 min, VT, LD

Producer: John W. Considine; **Director:** Karl Freund; **Screenplay:** P.J. Wolfson and John Balderston; **Music:** Dimitri Tiomkin; **Cinematography:** Chester Lyons; **Cast:** Peter Lorre, Colin Clive, Frances Drake, Keye Luke, Isabel Jewel, Ted Healy, Sara Haden, Edward Brophy

Despite the title change, this one is simply another version of *THE HANDS OF ORLAC*. Its surprising twist (it would be a crime to reveal here), as well as having Peter Lorre in one of his outstanding performances, makes it the best of the bunch by far. However, be warned—Ted Healy's comedy is grossly misplaced.

MADMEN OF MANDORAS

See *THEY SAVED HITLER'S BRAIN*

MAD MAX

Orion, 1979, Color, 93 min, VT, LD, DVD

Producers: Samuel Z. Arkoff and Byron Kennedy; **Director:** George Miller; **Screenplay:** Miller and James McCausland; **Cinematography:** David Eggby; **Music:** Brian May; **Special Effects:** John Downding and Chris Murray; **Cast:** Mel Gibson, Joanne Samuel, Hugh Keays-Byrne, Steve Bisley, Tim Burns, Roger Ward

Beginning "A Few Years From Now . . ." this film introduces a future just slightly ahead of the present during a time of civil disorder. There's still a civilization of sorts, but there isn't a great deal of it in evidence, and what there is looks to be rapidly falling apart.

A wild criminal named the Night Rider and his girlfriend are on the run in a stolen police vehicle, leading the police on a dangerous chase across the countryside and into a town. The Night Rider is totally ruthless. He's also a much better driver than the majority of officers pursuing him. He drives them off the road and forces them to crash into everything in sight while killing anyone who gets in his way. Enter Officer Max (Gibson). He chases down the Night Rider, refusing to fall for any of his criminal tricks, and finally leads the bad guys to a fiery end. The criminals' nomadic biker friends, especially a particularly psychotic gang leader known as Toe Cutter, vow to make Max pay.

Max goes home to his family—a loving, intelligent, talented wife, and a happy, healthy baby, who live in a lovely little home. When a further series of clashes between the police and the bikers leads to the death of an officer named Goose, Max, filled with rage, is about to go out to kill all the bikers. But in an incredibly realistic moment, Max quits the force after watching the horribly burned Goose die painfully in the hospital. He admits to the shocking truth that he's scared, that he doesn't want to die, and that he doesn't want to watch his family die. He's out. It's over.

Then fate steps in, putting the badgeless Max and his family on holiday in the same town as the bikers, who kill his wife and child. Max must scoop up their remains from the highway; this drives him back to the police force to bring the bikers to justice.

Mad Max may be a low-budget film, but it is also exciting and well directed. The science fiction trappings include the near-future setting and the questions raised by the ongoing (understandably offscreen) collapse of civilization. How fast would the artificial construct of city life deteriorate? Indeed, is it already collapsing, just at a rate unnoticed as of yet? At the same time, the film delivers something of a political message. In a departure from clichéd futures ruled by fascism and apocalypses brought on by self-absorbed military forces, courts overly sympathetic to criminals and the greedy, smarmy lawyers who populate them are the main cause for the breakdown of society. This notion struck a chord with audiences, and it scared a few, too, as only good science fiction can.

This film's two sequels—*THE ROAD WARRIOR* and *Mad Max Beyond Thunderdome*—aren't much more than adventure films. But the three work much like the *STAR WARS* trilogy: A western disguised as sci-fi is a surprise hit, followed by a darker, far more intense effects-laden film ending in a cliff-hanger that leaves audiences screaming for more, then generates a final chapter that almost works but falls apart during its last half.

Note: Look for a copy of this film that features the original Australian soundtrack. The American releasing company felt the accents in the picture were too thick, and thus had the film dubbed by American actors, lending a stilted quality to a number of the scenes.

MAD MAX 2

See *THE ROAD WARRIOR*

MAD MAX BEYOND THUNDERDOME

Kennedy Miller Productions (Australia), 1985, Color, 106 min, VT, LD, DVD

Producers: Terry Hayes, George Miller, Steve Amezdroz, Doug Mitchell, and Marcus D'Arcy; **Director:** Miller; **Screenplay:** Hayes and Miller; **Music:** Maurice Jarré; **Cinematography:** Dean Semler; **Special Effects:** John Bowring, Brian Cox, Michael Wood, Alan Maxwell, and Steve Courtley; **Cast:** Mel Gibson, Tina Turner, George Ogilvie, Angelo Rossitto, Helen Buday, Rod Zuanic, Frank Thring, Angry Anderson

See *MAD MAX; THE ROAD WARRIOR*

MAD MONSTER, THE

PRC, 1942, b&w, 77 min, VT

Producer: Sigmund Neufeld; **Director:** Sam Newfield; **Screenplay:** Fred Myton; **Music:** David Chudnow; **Cinematography:** Jack Greenhalgh; **Special Effects:** Harry Ross and Gene Stone; **Cast:** Johnny Downs, George Zucco, Glenn Strange, Anne Nagel, Henry Hall, Mae Busch, Sarah Padden, Gordon DeMain

Crazed scientist Dr. Cameron (a wildly scenery-chewing Zucco) is out to help the Allies defeat the Nazis. His idea: Let's create a battalion of werewolf warriors to take out the Third Reich. It turns out to be just as bad as it sounds.

MAD PEOPLE, THE

See *THE CRAZIES*

MADRID IN THE YEAR 2000

Madrid Films (Spain), 1925, b&w, silent feature

Director: Manuel Noriega; **Screenplay:** Noriega; **Cinematography:** Antonio Macasoli; **Cast:** Roberto Ingesias, Juan Nada, Roberto Bey

Looking much like a travelogue that is suddenly much more current than when it was first released, this film delivers basically what you would expect from its title: a look at the far-flung futuristic city of Madrid in the year 2000.

MAGNETIC FLUID, THE

Pathé (France), 1912, b&w, silent short

A liquid is created which, when taken internally, gives the thirsty party powerful hypnotic control over others.

MAGNETIC KITCHEN, THE

Pathé (France), 1908, b&w, silent short

Director: Segundo de Choman

A kitchen of the future goes wild to great comic effect.

MAGNETIC MONSTER, THE

United Artists, 1953, b&w, 76 min, VT, LD

Producer: Ivan Tors; **Director:** Curt Siodmak; **Screenplay:** Siodmak; **Music:** Blaine Sanford; **Cinematography:** Charles Van Enger; **Special Effects:** Jack Glass; **Cast:** Richad Carlson, King Donovan, Jean Bryon, Strother Martin, Byron Foulger

A previously unknown magnetic isotope absorbs energy from any source possible, allowing it to grow stronger and stronger at a wild rate. The isotope creates monstrous havoc until it is destroyed in its cyclotron, in what may be the first cinematic depiction of an atom smasher.

Note: The effects at the end of this film are incredibly striking. They were lifted almost in their entirety from the 1934 German film, *GOLD*. Although the transplanted sequence was a huge boost for *The Magnetic Monster*, the decision to do this was unfortunate because the heavy-handed borrowing now keeps *Gold* from ever being seen today.

MAGNETIC MOON, THE

Reed, 1954, b&w, 78 min

Producer: Roland Reed; **Director:** Hollingsworth Morse; **Screenplay:** Francis Rosenwald; **Cast:** Richard Crane, Sally Mansfield, Tor Johnson, Pamela Duncan, Jimmy Lydon, John Alvin, Charles Davis, Robert Lyden, Reginald Sheffield

More outer space shenanigans with that lovable lug, Rocky Jones, Space Ranger, in yet another film trimmed together from episodes of the television show.

MAGNETIC PERSONALITY, A

1912, b&w, silent short

A thief steals a cache of magnets. Afterward he is chased doggedly by the usual assortment of steel and iron to comic effect.

MAGNETIC REMOVAL

Pathé (France), 1908, b&w, silent short

Director: Segundo de Choman

Turn-of-the-century science masters the secret of cleaning one's home with the power of magnets.

MAGNETIC SQUIRT, THE

Le Lion, 1909, b&w, silent short

Director: Segundo de Choman

A miracle drug allows the lame to walk once more.

MAGNETIC VAPOR, THE

Lubin, 1908, b&w, silent short

Director: Segundo de Choman

Somehow a magnetic gas turns a wimpy husband who has always lived under the weight of his domineering wife's thumb into a take-charge guy who becomes lord of his castle. Worms of the world, unite!

MAKING MR. RIGHT

Orion Pictures, 1987, Color, 95 min, VT, LD

Producers: Joel Tuber, Susan Seidelman, Mike Wise, Dan Enwright, Lynn Hendee, and Andrew Mondshein; **Director:** Seidelman; **Screenplay:** Floyd Byars and Laurie Frank; **Music:** Chaz Sankel; **Cinematography:** Edward Lachmann; **Special Effects:** Clive R. Kay and Brian Ferren; **Cast:** John Malkovich, Ann Magnuson, Glenne Headly, Ben Masters, Laurie Metcalf, Polly Bergen, Harsh Nayyar, Hart Bochner, Polly Draper, Susan Anton

Somewhat inept, shy scientist Malkovich takes humankind light-years ahead as he creates a near perfect android copy of himself. The machine man is dubbed

Ulysses, but despite its historic, heroic name, it's an idea a little too new for the general public, and so a public relations firm is brought in to sell it. This movie is better romantic comedy than it is science fiction.

MAN AND HIS MATE

See *ONE MILLION B.C.*

MANCHURIAN CANDIDATE, THE

United Artists, 1962, b&w, 126 min, VT, LD, DVD

Producers: John Frankenheimer, George Axelrod, and Howard M. Koch; **Director:** Frankenheimer; **Screenplay:** Axelrod; **Music:** David Amran; **Cinematography:** Lionel Lindon; **Special Effects:** A. Paul Pollard and Howard A. Anderson; **Cast:** Frank Sinatra, Laurence Harvey, Angela Lansbury, Janet Leigh, John McGiver, Henry Silva, Leslie Parrish, James Gregory, Khigh Deigh, Whit Bissell

It is 1952, the time of the Korean War. A patrol of American soldiers is led into an ambush by their Korean guide, but they are not slaughtered nor taken to a prisoner of war encampment. Instead, they are whisked by a Russian helicopter team to a brainwashing center where an incredible scheme is put into operation. Their sergeant (Harvey) is to be turned into a war hero and Medal of Honor winner. The others are all conditioned to tell a story that will guarantee this.

In a fascinating scene that the audience sees through the eyes of the soldiers, the Communist medical team demonstrates the effectiveness of their techniques to their superiors. The soldiers see the Communists as a gathering of American women at a ladies' garden club meeting. Interestingly, the lone black soldier in the group sees the women as all black. When the head doctor orders Harvey to murder one of the other men and then another, he does so without the slightest hesitation. His conditioning is complete. He has been ordered not to remember anything he does. With no memory, the theory states, he can have no guilt. With no guilt, there is no fear of being caught. With no memory, fear, or guilt, he is thus the perfect assassin.

The men are all sent home. Harvey gets his award. The others, however, begin to experience terrifying dreams as memories of their brainwashing surfaces. The major (Sinatra), who happens to be assigned to military intelligence, has the worst dreams of all. He feels that he is going mad. The only clue that something is wrong is one thing he said about Harvey. When inter-

viewed about Harvey's supposed heroism by the Medal of Honor review board, Sinatra said that the sergeant was the kindest, bravest, most wonderful man he ever knew in his entire life. In fact, every survivor supposedly saved by Harvey said the same thing. And yet, Sinatra is positive he and the others all disliked Harvey intensely before they went on their last mission.

What does it mean? Fearing that he will soon go insane if he doesn't get some answers, Sinatra begins to dig, uncovering a Communist plot to murder the favored candidate for president of the United States, a move that would leave the Communist's puppet, the vice-presidential candidate, as the next president.

This is one tight thriller, and though the science fiction elements are more concerned with social issues than hardware, they're excellently handled. Based on the novel by Richard Condon, the movie was hotly debated for its political observations. The year following its release President Kennedy was assassinated, and the film was shelved for decades due to the unfortunate parallels between its story and real life. When it returned to the popular culture, however, it was universally hailed as one of the most important films of its time.

And indeed, it's pretty terrific, though flawed. Along with some clunky dialogue, one of the movie's most unwieldy problems is the thin motivation of a number of characters. Much was lost when heavy elements of sex and drugs present in the book were dropped for the screen. The greatest loss, however, is in the ending. In the book, Marco (Sinatra) reconditions his former commanding officer and changes his orders. Marco puts the idea of killing the Communist agents, the vice-presidential candidate and his wife (Harvey's parents), into the shooter's head. Marco also gives him the idea to kill himself. The movie opts for a more upbeat ending in which Harvey breaks his own conditioning and chooses to assassinate his parents and then kills himself, leaving Sinatra as the good guy.

Among the film's high points is director Frankenheimer's use of a continually moving camera to create the ladies auxiliary/Communist meeting hall sequence. Interestingly enough, after taking a week to shoot this crucial scene, the director edited a rough cut to show star Sinatra, and the two were so pleased that no further editing was done on the scene. While this moment rightly deserves its place in film history, another sequence has been lavishly praised, one not perhaps so worthy of adulation, the scene in which Sinatra interrogates Harvey. In a number of shots Sinatra appears slightly out of focus, leading people to believe that Frankenheimer intended to show the scene from Harvey's point of view, that of a brainwashed man who could not see things clearly.

Critics have praised Frankenheimer's brilliance here, but according to the director himself that's not quite the case. In a televised interview, Frankenheimer went on record that the interrogation scene was particularly intense for Sinatra, that he had worked himself up greatly. The actor had become convinced he couldn't do the scene properly, but on the day of shooting Sinatra proved to be riveting. Frankenheimer was pleased and then dismayed to find that the daily rushes showed that the actor's brilliant work was out of focus. A reshoot was scheduled, but Sinatra was so agitated over having to do the difficult scene again he developed laryngitis. Working against a schedule, Frankenheimer decided to go with the slightly out of focus footage. And thus a classic moment of sci-fi cinema history was born.

Note: Pay attention to the fight scene between Sinatra and Henry Silva. Sinatra actually broke a finger during the shooting of their donnybrook. Also, pay attention to the names of the platoon soldiers in Korea. They were all taken from the soldiers in the 1950s television comedy *The Phil Silvers Show.*

MAN-EATER OF HYDRA

See *ISLAND OF THE DOOMED*

MANDROID

Full Moon, 1993, Color, 80 min, VT, LD

Producers: Charles Band, Oana Paunescu, Vlad Paunescu, and Lara Porzak; **Director:** Jack Ersgard; **Screenplay:** Earl Kenton and Jackson Berr; **Music:** David Arkenstone; **Cinematography:** Vlad Paunescu; **Special Effects:** Michael Deak; **Cast:** Brian Cousins, Jane Caldwell, Curt Lowens, Patrick Ersgard, Robert Sydmonds, Costel Constantin, Michael Dellafemina

This silly film concerns an invisible man, drugs that do whatever the script says (no matter what science might actually have to say about it), and, of course, the title robot. Wandering and unfocused, this movie was followed by an even worse picture, *Invisible: The Chronicles of Benjamin Knight.*

MAN FACING SOUTHEAST
(aka: MAN LOOKING SOUTHEAST)

Cinequanon (Argentina), 1986, Color, 108 min, VT, LD

Producer: Lujan Pflaun; **Director:** Eliseo Subiela; **Screenplay:** Subiela; **Cinematography:** Richardo DeAngelis; **Music:** Pedro Aznar; **Cast:** Lorenzo Quinteros, Hugo Soto, Ines Venengo

The staff psychiatrist at a mental hospital has a problem that only gets worse the more he analyzes it. A new patient claims to be from another world. Worse yet—the man displays powers that seem to back up his claim. What's the poor doctor to do? This one is slow paced, more concerned with character development and story than with dazzling special effects, but definitely worth tracking down.

MAN FROM PLANET X, THE

United Artists, 1950, b&w, 70 min

Producers: Aubrey Wisberg and Jack Pollexfen; **Director:** Edgar Ulmer; **Screenplay:** Wisberg and Pollexfen; **Cinematography:** John L. Russel; **Music:** Charles Koff; **Special Effects:** Angelo Scibetti and Andy Anderson; **Cast:** Robert Clarke, William Schallert, Margaret Field, Charles Davis, Roy Engel, Raymond Bond

Earth, specifically Scotland, is visited by a quiet, friendly alien. At least he's friendly until he meets William Schallert. Scientist Schallert wants the alien's secrets of interplanetary travel, and he wants them *now!* This does nothing for the alien's disposition toward Earth. This is an odd film, ultra low-budget, but its story is fairly original and its direction far better than its budget deserves.

Note: If not the first, *The Man from Planet X* is one of the earliest films to feature a *nonhuman* visitor from the stars.

MAN FROM THE FIRST CENTURY, THE

See *MAN IN OUTER SPACE*

MAN FROM THE PAST, THE

See *MAN IN OUTER SPACE*

MANHATTAN PROJECT, THE

Cannon Films, 1986, Color, 117 min, VT, LD

Producers: Marshall Brickman, Jennifer Ogden, and Roger Paradiso; **Director:** Brickman; **Screenplay:** Brickman and Thomas Baum; **Music:** Philippe Sarde; **Cinematography:** Billy Williams; **Special Effects:** Bran Ferren; **Cast:** John Lithgow, Christopher Collet,

Cynthia Nixon, Jill Eikenberry, John Mahoney, Sully Boyar, Greg Edelman, Robert Leonard

A teenager breaks into a maximum security facility, walking out with some plutonium so that he can build a nuclear weapon. Why would he want to do such a thing? He claims to be making a point, but no matter what he says, it's fairly obvious that he doesn't care that he's endangering the lives of countless people. The film suffers from its attitude that activities such as breaking and entering, resisting arrest, and private ownership of weapons of Armageddon is okay as long as you stick it to The Man.

MANHUNT IN SPACE

Reed, 1954, b&w, 78 min

Producer: Roland Reed; **Director:** Hollingsworth Morse; **Screenplay:** Arthur Hoerl; **Cinematography:** Walter Strenge; **Special Effects:** Jack R. Glass; **Cast:** Richard Crane, Sally Mansfield, Scott Beckett, Henry Brandon, Ga'bor Curtiz, Charles Meredith, Patsy Parsons, Robert Lydon, Judd Holdren, Dale Van Sickel, Henry Lautor, Ray Montgomery

Earth forces comb the solar system for an invisible rocket. With that kind of intricate plot, it can only mean even more outer space shenanigans with lovable lug Rocky Jones, Space Ranger, in yet another film trimmed together from episodes of the television show.

MANHUNT OF MYSTERY ISLAND

Republic, 1945, b&w, Serial, 15 chapters

Producer: Ronald Davidson; **Directors:** Spenser G. Bennett, Wallace Grissell, and Yakima Canutt; **Screenplay:** Albert DeMond, Basil Dickey, Jesse Duffy, Alan James, Grant Nelson, and Joseph Poland; **Music:** Richard Cherwin; **Cinematography:** Bud Thackery; **Special Effects:** Howard Lydecker and Theodore Lydecker; **Cast:** Forrest Taylor, Linda Stirling, Richard Bailey, Forbes Murray, Edward Cassidy, Harry Strang, Jack Ingram, Roy Barcroft

Scientist Taylor, the inventor of a radium-powered transmitter that will supply the world with never-ending power, disappears while searching for new radium fields. His plucky daughter (Stirling) teams up with a clever adventurer (Bailey), and the two follow Dad's trail to Mystery Island.

MAN IN HALF MOON STREET, THE

Paramount, 1944, b&w, 92 min

Producer: Walter MacEwan; **Director:** Ralph M. Murphy; **Screenplay:** Charles Kenyon and Garret Fort; **Music:** Miklos Rozsa; **Cinematography:** Henry Sharp; **Special Effects:** Wally Westmore; **Cast:** Nils Asther, Helen Walker, Brandon Hurst, Paul Cavanaugh, Reginald Sheffield, Morton Lowry

Scientist Asther has kept himself alive since the mid-1800s via an operation he arranges for himself every 35 years, an organ transplant. Asther has had to commit murder every time to get his hands on the necessary replacement parts. Not getting his operation exactly on time, however, causes him to crumple and wither away.

Though some claim to like this film, its science is bad and its science fiction worse. Much the same can be said for the 1959 remake by Hammer Films, *The Man Who Could Cheat Death*. Both pictures follow the same basic plot, but not even the presence of Christopher Lee can save the remake.

MAN IN OUTER SPACE (aka: THE MAN FROM THE FIRST CENTURY, THE MAN FROM THE PAST, MAN OF THE FIRST CENTURY)

Ceskostovensky Filmexport (Czechoslovakia), 1961, 96 min/AIP, 1964, 85 min, b&w

Producer: Rudolf Wolf; **Director:** Oldrich Lipsky; **Screenplay:** Lipsky and Zedenek Blaha; **Music:** Ladislav Simon; **Cinematography:** Vladimír Movotný; **Special Effects:** Zdenek Liska; **Cast:** Milos Kopecky, Radovan Lukavasky, Vit Olmer

An arrogant man with a raging superiority complex is sent off to a faraway world. When he returns 2,000 years later, he sets out to become the greatest capitalist in history (which, obviously, now covers more ground than before his departure). His running dog ways are sidetracked by the proletariat alien who accompanies him back to Earth. Not all science fiction films produced behind the Iron Curtain are Communist propaganda, but those that are, are so with a vengeance, as is this one.

MAN IN THE DARK

See *THE MAN WHO LIVED TWICE*

MAN IN THE MOON

Gaumont (France), 1909, b&w, silent short

Director: Émile Cohl

A most courageous traveler braves the frigid reaches of outer space from the gondola of his hot air balloon. An anthropomorphic Moon and some friendly stars keep him company in this amusing, charming period piece that was cutting edge in the days before World War I, though merely quaint now.

MAN IN THE MOON, THE (1898)

See *THE ASTRONOMER'S DREAM*

MAN IN THE WHITE SUIT, THE

Ealing (Great Britain), 1951/Universal (United States), 1952, b&w, 97 min, VT, LD

Producer: Michael Balcon; **Director:** Alexander Mackendrick; **Screenplay:** Roger MacDougall, John Dighton, and Mackendrick; **Music:** Benjamin Frankel; **Cinematography:** Douglas Slocombe; **Special Effects:** Geoffrey Dickinson and Sydney Pearson: **Cast:** Sir Alec Guinness, Joan Greenwood, Cecil Parker, Vida Hope, George Beson, Michael Gough, Edie Hartin, Ernest Thesiger, Howard Marion-Crawford, Colin Gordon

Inventor Guinness comes up with a fabric that not only won't wear out, but can't even be soiled. He makes himself a suit out of the material to prove that his miracle fabric can do all he claims. Clothing manufacturers, seeing the end of their businesses, do everything they can to stop Guinness from marketing his invention. There's just enough science fiction to get this wonderfully sophisticated comedy rolling.

Note: The odd noises given off by Guinness's laboratory machinery sound mechanical, but they were created through the clever use of a bassoon and a tuba.

MAN LOOKING SOUTHEAST

See *MAN FACING SOUTHEAST*

MAN-MADE MONSTER

See *THE ATOMIC MONSTER*

MAN OF THE FIRST CENTURY

See *MAN IN OUTER SPACE*

MAN'S BEST FRIEND

New Line Cinema, 1993, Color, 97 min, VT, LD

Producers: Daniel Grodnik, Robert Kosberg, and Kelley Smith-Wait; **Director:** John Lafia; **Screenplay:** Lafia; **Music:** Joel Goldsmith; **Cinematography:** Mark Irwin; **Special Effects:** Mark R. Byers, Frank Ceglia, and Paul H. Haines, Jr.; **Cast:** Ally Sheedy, Lance Hendriksen, Robert Costanzo, Fredric Lehne, John Casini, J.D. Daniels, William Sanderson, Trula Marcus, Rick Barker

Reporter Sheedy rescues a big dopey dog from Hendriksen's nasty laboratory, where terrible experiments are carried out on helpless animals. The dog turns out to be genetically engineered. Most of the expensive tinkering, however, only helps extend a variety of canine clichés to the breaking point.

MAN THEY COULD NOT HANG, THE

Columbia, 1939, b&w, 65 min, VT

Producer: Wallace MacDonald; **Director:** Nick Grinde; **Screenplay:** Karl Brown; **Cinematography:** Benjamin Kline; **Music:** Morris Stoloff; **Cast:** Boris Karloff, Lorna Gray, Don Beddoe, Robert Wilcox, Roger Pryor, Ann Doran

Scientist Karloff steals an invention—a mechanical heart. Sadly for the real inventor, Karloff has to murder him in the process. Sadly for Karloff, he's arrested, tried, sentenced to death, and executed for his crime. The murderous scientist is brought back to life by the stolen invention. Vowing revenge, Karloff rigs up a house as a death trap and then invites the judge, jury, and witnesses to be slaughtered one by one. Things go fine until Karloff's daughter is killed by one of the traps, however, and the revenge-crazed scientist uses the mechanical heart to save his daughter even though it means forfeiting his own life.

MAN THEY COULDN'T ARREST, THE

Gaumont (Great Britain), 1933, b&w, 72 min

Producer: Michael Baloon; **Director:** T. Hayes Hunter; **Screenplay:** Hunter, Angus MacPhail, and

Arthur Wimperis; **Cinematography:** Leslie Rowson; **Cast:** Hugh Wakefield, Gordon Harker, Renée Clama

This slight film covers the invention and misuse of the first long-range listening device.

MAN WHO COULD CHEAT DEATH, THE

See *THE MAN IN HALF MOON STREET*

MAN WHO FELL TO EARTH, THE

British Lion/Cinema Five (Great Britain), 1976, Color, 138 min, VT, LD, DVD

Producer: Si Lituinoff; **Director:** Nicholas Roeg; **Screenplay:** Paul Mayersberg; **Cinematography:** Anthony Richmond, B.S.C.; **Music:** John Phillips; **Special Effects:** Peter S. Ellenshaw and Camera Effects, Ltd.; **Cast:** David Bowie, Rip Torn, Candy Clark, Buck Henry, Bernie Casey, Linda Hutton, Rick Ricardo, Jackson D. Kane

The movie opens, as the title suggests, as a man (Bowie) falls to Earth. The man, who looks human and is dressed like an Earthling, makes his way from the crash site and stumbles into the nearest town. Someone follows him, but we don't know who or why. Bowie seems not to know what's going on himself. He doesn't know what cars are or maybe highways. On the other hand, he knows gold and sells his wife's wedding ring for $20, drawing sympathy for being a fool until it's revealed that he has a bundle of rings. Amazingly, he seems to have enough rings to run up a stake of more than $10,000 (a *lot* of rings at $20 a pop).

Bowie uses the money to hire one of the world's best patent lawyers for his nine basic patents. The lawyer (Henry) assures his client that he'll be able to raise $300 million (in 1976 dollars!) in less than three years with such resources. Bowie puts Henry in charge of the corporation that would hold the patents and then goes off to wait for the money to roll in.

At this point the film strays from its straightforward path with the introduction of two more characters. Dr. Bryce (Torn) is a professor more interested in chasing co-eds half his age than he is in teaching. When asked to leave his job and campus, he gets himself hired by Bowie's corporation. Candy Clark, a New Mexican waitress of limited intelligence, attaches herself to Bowie as a combination cook/housekeeper/sex object.

We learn that Bowie actually has a wife and children somewhere out in space. Their planet is dying of thirst, and that's why Bowie came to Earth. He expects to save his family from dying of thirst by amassing a fortune on Earth over a period of years. Supposedly in love with his wife, he engages in a romantic relationship with Clark.

Meanwhile, Bryce works hard for Bowie but can't accomplish anything. Bowie's relationship with Clark begins to disintegrate, and though Bowie works hard for his family, he also fails to accomplish anything. His desert-wandering clan is last seen, their bloody bodies heaped one upon the other in the middle of a wasteland.

It's hard to say exactly where this movie loses its thread and why. It starts out promising a great deal, the opening sequence alone teasing one into thinking greatness is just around the corner. The first half-hour is awash in dazzlingly innovative, even poetic, cinematography. The tonal, tubular music offsets the lush artistic style with smoothness that seems almost majestic. But the film's story unravels halfway through and never comes together. Are we supposed to feel sorry for Bowie or glad he gets his comeuppance in the end? Was he a harmless visitor? Was he trying to steal Earth's water supply? And why couldn't he have just brought his family with him? Unfortunately, none of these questions are answered.

The Man Who Fell to Earth is a pretentious muddle without form or substance, despite the director's style and flash. Its initial positive reception and its cult status, are more likely the result of drug culture appeal, as well as art crowd fears to dare say the emperor has no clothes. Of course, some viewers blame the film's incoherence on its original American distribution company, which slashed the picture's running time from 138 minutes to 116. But the original cut is not available, so the film can only be judged on the final release.

MAN WHO LIVED AGAIN, THE (aka: THE MAN WHO CHANGED HIS MIND)

Gaumont (Great Britain), 1934, b&w, 68 min, VT

Producer: Michael Balcon; **Director:** Robert Stevenson; **Screenplay:** L. duGarde Peach, Sidney Gillitat, and John Balderston; **Cinematography:** Jack Cox; **Music:** Louis Levy; **Special Effects:** Roy Ashton; **Cast:** Boris Karloff, Anna Lee, Cecil Parker, John Loder, Frank Cellier, Lyn Harding

Karloff is once again a mad scientist, only this time the description is more literal. Scientist Karloff has been playing around with consciousness transferral. Having perfected it on the level of chimp-to-chimp, he now wants to move up to person-to-person. He has a reason.

Though labeled a lunatic by the rest of his colleagues, he is infatuated with a younger man's fiancée. In a twist on the usual science fiction/horror films of the time, which rarely got this involved, Karloff wants to switch his mind with the younger man's just so he can steal his intended love. This is a little-known, but highly interesting, soulful movie.

MAN WHO LIVED TWICE, THE

Columbia, 1936, b&w, 73 min

Producer: Ben Pivar; **Director:** Harry Lachman; **Screenplay:** T. Van Dycke, Fred Niblo, and Arthur Strawn; **Cinematography:** James Van Trees; **Cast:** Ralph Bellamy, Marian Marsh, Ward Bond, Isabel Jewell, Thurston Hall, Nana Bryant

A criminal manages to escape the clutches of all his dubious associates and then decides to remove himself from the world completely. Plastic surgery and brain surgery are involved, leaving the patient not only looking different, but suffering from amnesia as well. He starts out on the straight and narrow, but of course things are never that easy. What begins as an interesting premise is not convincingly developed. Worse yet, the film was remade years later as *Man in the Dark*. Ordinary as the first version is, the remake is even staler, despite being made in 3-D.

MAN WHO THOUGHT LIFE, THE

Asa Film/Palladium (Denmark), 1969, b&w, 97 min

Director: Jens Ravn; **Screenplay:** Henrik Stangerup; **Cinematography:** Witold Leszczynski; **Music:** Per Nørgaard; **Cast:** John Price, Preben Neergaard, Lotte Tarp

Neergaard is a lucky individual who can actually create life. Anything he can imagine, animate or inanimate, he can materialize from sheer nothingness through the power of his will alone. The only drawback is that the things he creates are short-lived. He gets an idea how to fix that, though. Going to a surgeon, he demands that the doctor operate on his brain so that his power can become great enough for his creations to remain intact. The doctor, rightly enough, refuses such a mad request. But that doesn't slow down Neergaard. He simply creates a duplicate of the surgeon, whom he instructs to perform the operation. The only problem—the operation doesn't work and he dies.

Believe it or not, this movie is a comedy. Well-acted and filmed with great style, *The Man Who Thought Life* is a rare thing. Not only is it a science fiction film that dares to make solid, philosophical points, but it does so while daring to be funny.

THE MAN WHO CHANGED HIS MIND

See *THE MAN WHO LIVED AGAIN*

MAN WHO TURNED TO STONE, THE

Columbia, 1957, b&w, 80 min, VT

Producer: Sam Katzman; **Director:** Leslie Kardos; **Screenplay:** Raymond T. Marcus; **Cinematography:** Benjamin Kline; **Music:** Ross DiMaggio; **Cast:** Victor Jory, Ann Doran, Victor Varconi, William Hudson, Paul Cavanaugh, Charlotte Austin, Jean Willies

Scientist Jory and his cohorts have discovered the secret of immortality. All they have to do is drain off the life force of beautiful young women and suck it down like gravy. Of course, if they don't get enough energy at the right times, they begin to turn to stone.

MAN WHO WASN'T THERE, THE

Paramount, 1983, Color, 111 min, VT

Producers: Tony Bishop and Frank Mancuso, Jr.; **Director:** Bruce Malmuth; **Screenplay:** Stanford Sherman; **Cinematography:** Frederick Moore; **Music:** Miles Goodman; **Special Effects:** Martin Becker, Frankie Inez, Robert Cole, Chuck Stewart, and Bob Wilcox; **Cast:** Steve Guttenberg, Jeffrey Tambor, Lisa Langlois, Art Hindle, Morgan Hart, Bill Forsythe, Vincent Baggetta

This comedy about a poor sap who is given an invisibility formula by a dying spy may be the worst invisibility movie ever made—a record likely to hold for aeons to come. Released in 3-D by people who thought tricks and effects could take the place of acting, writing, and solid direction, it remains insultingly bad.

MAN WITH NINE LIVES, THE
(aka: BEHIND THE DOOR)

Columbia, 1940, b&w, 73 min, VT

Producers: Irving Briskin and Wallace MacDonald; **Director:** Nick Grinde; **Screenplay:** Karl Brown; **Cinematography:** Benjamin H. Kline; **Cast:** Boris Karloff, Roger Pryor, Jo Anne Sayers. Charles Trowbridge, Stanley Brown, Hal Taliaferro, John Dilson

Karloff is out to help humanity by coming up with a cure for cancer, by freezing infected patients. Just when it looks as if he's got something, he disappears. Ten years later, he and his patients are found in a secret facility on a remote island—all of them frozen. When Karloff is thawed out, his experiment is heralded as a great success. The law sees things a bit differently however.

MAN WITH TWO BRAINS, THE

Warner Bros., 1983, Color, 93 min, VT, LD, DVD

Producers: David V. Picker and William E. McEven; **Director:** Carl Reiner; **Screenplay:** Steve Martin, George Gipe, and Reiner; **Cinematography:** Michael Chapman; **Music:** Joel Goldsmith; **Special Effects:** Allen Hall, Clay Pinney, and Robert G. Willard; **Cast:** Steve Martin, Kathleen Turner, David Warner, Sissy Spacek, Paul Benedict, Richard Brestoff, James Cromwell, George Furth, Randi Brooks

Poor Dr. Martin is one of the world's great surgeons, but he has no love in his life. His wife (Turner) is a domineering witch who has him completely buffaloed. Then the magic day comes along when he finally meets someone who thinks just as he does. Only "think" is all she can do. The doctor has fallen in love with a brain floating in a bottle. Wanting to do more than examine her mind, he sets out to find a new host body for his brainwave babe. It's goofy and low on science fiction, but that doesn't stop the movie from being an enjoyable comedy.

MAN WITH THE X-RAY EYES

See *"X"—THE MAN WITH THE X-RAY EYES*

MAN WITH TWO LIVES, THE

Monogram, 1942, b&w, 65 min

Producer: A.W. Hacke; **Director:** Phil Rosen; **Screenplay:** Joseph Hoffman; **Cinematography:** Harry Neumann; **Cast:** Edward Norris, Kenne Duncan, Frederick Burton, Anthony Warde, Marlo Dwyer

A scientist gets into trouble by reanimating the dead. The unfortunate patient is killed by accident, and when he is brought back to the world of the living, his body is possessed by the soul of a criminal who was electrocuted at the same moment the accident victim died.

MAN WHO CHANGED HIS MIND, THE

See *THE MAN WHO LIVED AGAIN*

MAROONED (aka: SPACE TRAVELLERS)

Columbia, 1969, Color, 134 min, VT, LD

Producer: M.J. Frankovich; **Director:** John Sturges; **Screenplay:** Mayo Simon; **Cinematography:** Daniel Fapp; **Special Effects:** Lawrence W. Butler, Donald C. Glouner, and Robie Robinson; **Cast:** Gregory Peck, Richard Crenna, Mariette Hartley, David Janssen, James Franciscus, Gene Hackman, Lee Grant, Nancy Kovack

Three astronauts are trapped in space during a mission, unable to return to Earth. On the ground, the head of the space agency tries to keep everyone on the planet calm as they scream for a rescue mission. In the meantime, the boys in space are cool as cucumbers about their imminent deaths in what ultimately adds up to a boring, plodding, emotionless film.

Note: Shockingly, director John Sturges also gave the world the classic western *The Magnificent Seven*. Additionally, the Academy of Motion Picture Arts & Sciences awarded this uninspired work an Oscar for best special effects in the same year that Ray Harryhausen's *THE GOLDEN VOYAGE OF SINBAD* was released.

MARS ATTACKS

Warner Bros., 1996, Color, 103 min, VT, LD, DVD

Producers: Tim Burton and Larry Franco; **Director:** Burton; **Screenplay:** Jonathan Gems; **Cinematography:** Peter Suschitzky; **Music:** Danny Elfman; **Special Effects:** Robert West, David Andrews, Michael Fink, Michael Lantieri, Janek Sirrs, Jim Mitchell, Daniel Radford, and Jesse Silver; **Cast:** Jack Nicholson, Danny DeVito, Martin Short, Michael J. Fox, Glenn Close, Annette Bening, Pierce Brosnan, Sarah Jessica Parker, Rod Steiger, Lucas Hass, Pam Grier, Paul Winfield, Tom Jones, Natalie Portman, Jim Brown, Sylvia Sidney, Lisa Marie, Joe Don Baker, Christine Applegate, Barbet Schroeder

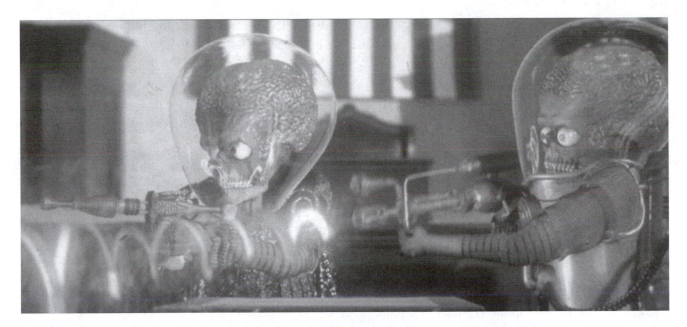

Mars Attacks (WARNER BROS. / JOSEPH B. MAUCERI COLLECTION)

Martian invaders of the most obviously evil type swarm over Earth in an attempt at global conquest. The military is completely helpless. The fallout from nuclear bombs is harmless to these little green creatures. Only the accidental discovery of the fatal effects of crooner Slim Whitman's voice on the helmeted aliens saves the planet.

Mars Attacks, was based on Mars Attacks, the Topps Company card set from the 1960s. In an era of baseball cards, collecting a set of bubble gum cards that told a story—a *cool* story—was an immediate hit. Director Burton may have hoped to capitalize on that craze's sentimental value, but he actually scored a much bigger hit with the younger generation that missed the story the first time.

The film opened to less than favorable reviews, partly because Burton was simply too subtle. Superficially, the picture seems to be a one-joke comedy. Sadly, many viewers and critics missed the wealth of real humor under the surface. Additionally, the film is an undisguised attack on shortsighted, opportunistic extremes at both ends of the political spectrum. The liberal and capitalist viewpoints are equally powerless against the aliens.

Every person of seeming importance turns out to be an opportunistic boob. The president (Nicholson) is a poll-driven moron who doesn't do anything without consulting his press corp and his domineering wife (Close). His trusted military advisers are all sycophants, and he refuses to listen to the few that make sense. The

news media are interested only in the story from their own narrow views—what are these Martians' love interests, or whom do they prefer in the next election? Real estate developers want to rent them rooms. Press agents want to book them on television shows. Professors want to use them to prove their theories that intelligence equals benevolence.

Throughout the film, only those victimized by these extreme positions—black schoolchildren, minimum wage workers, bus drivers, and so on—succeed against the Martians. In the end, the secret weapon that cleans the planet of the invaders is discovered only because of a young boy's unflinching love for his grandmother.

Dismissed as silly, excessive, and pointless, *Mars Attacks* is actually a shrewd attack on many of the ills (political correctness, capitalism-run-rampant, casual sex, et cetera) destroying the modern world. Perhaps these cancers are so firmly entrenched in life that adult audiences could not recognize them without an emotional attachment to an already set viewpoint. But the older generation is usually doomed in much science fiction. Hope lies with the children, and many kids love this hilariously sarcastic film.

Note: Many of the most graphic, twisted images of the film were blamed on director Burton's warped sensibilities. The truth is that the most intense moments of the movie come straight from the card set published 30 years ago.

MARS INVADES PUERTO RICO (aka: FRANKENSTEIN MEETS THE SPACE MONSTER, DUEL OF THE SPACE MONSTERS)

Allied Artists, 1965, b&w, 78 min, VT

Producer: Robert McCarty; **Director:** Robert Gaffney; **Screenplay:** George Garret, John Rodenbeck, and R.H.W. Dillard; **Cinematography:** Saul Midwall; **Special Effects:** John Aiese; **Cast:** James Karen, David Kerman, Nancy Marshall, Marilyn Hanold, Robert Reilly

Col. Frank Saunders (Reilly) is an android space pilot who crosses paths with Princess Marcuzan (Hanold). The princess lands in Puerto Rico, looking to kidnap humans to repopulate her planet, where the birthrate is alarmingly low. Frank tries to stop her, gets his robotic face blasted, and presto—Frank becomes Frankenstein. The princess continues her kidnapping while Frank is repaired by some kindly doctors (Karen and Marshall). The doctors try to stop the princess and lose. Frank tries and finds himself confronting the princess's monster. There is no true Frankenstein monster in this picture. There is no Dr. Frankenstein. There is no reason to watch.

MARS NEEDS WOMEN

AIP, 1966, Color, 80 min, VT, LD

Producer: Larry Buchanan; **Director:** Buchanan; **Screenplay:** Buchanan; **Cinematography:** Robert C. Jessup; **Music:** Ronald Stein; **Cast:** Tommy Kirk, Yvonne Craig, Warren Hammack, Roger Ready, Byron Lord, Anthony Houston

Martian Tommy Kirk and a trio of his pals come to Earth searching for women to take back to Mars. The birthrate is down on the Red Planet, and to a civilization that can move with ease between galaxies, kidnapping babes from technologically backward worlds is the only answer. Kirk and his buddies find lots of willing girls and a few good dance clubs. Oddly enough, *Mars Needs Women* was played with an engaging sincerity that almost gave it the heart it needed.

MARTIANS GO HOME

Tarus Entertainment, 1990, Color, 89 min, VT, LD

Producers: Elon Dershowitz, Michael Flynn, and Michael D. Pariser; **Director:** David Odell; **Screen-

play: Charles S. Hass; **Cinematography:** Peter Deming; **Music:** Allan Zavod; **Cast:** Randy Quaid, Anita Morris, Barry Sobel, Margaret Colin, Vic Dunlop, John Philbin, Gerrit Graham, Ronnie Cox, Harry Basil

A moderately successful television songwriter (Quaid) unintentionally invites hordes of green-skinned Martians to Earth. The invaders appear wherever they like, doing nothing but telling bad jokes and making everyone's life miserable. Based on a classic novel by Fredric Brown, the film fails to capture the genius of the master's humor, mainly because the humor of the novel came not just from the jokes, but from what was being joked about.

MARTIAN IN PARIS, A

Les Films Univers (France), 1960, b&w, 87 min

Producers: José Bénazéraf and Jacques Vilfrid; **Director:** Jean-Daniel Daninos; **Screenplay:** Daninos and Vilfrid; **Cinematography:** Marcel Combes; **Cast:** Darry Cowl, Nicole Mirel, Gisèle Grandre

A Martian looking not all that dissimilar from an attractive human being lands in the City of Light to take a crash course in love.

MARY SHELLEY'S FRANKENSTEIN

Tri-Star, 1994, Color, 128 min, VT, LD

Producers: David Parfitt, Fred Fuchs, David Barron, James V. Hart, Jeff Kleeman, John Veitch, Kenneth Branagh, Robert DeNiro, and Francis Ford Coppola; **Director:** Branagh; **Screenplay:** Steph Lady and Frank Darabont; **Cinematography:** Roger Pratt; **Music:** Partick Doyle; **Special Effects:** Richard Conway, Tim Willis, Dave Eltham, Steve Onions, Lulu Morgan, Garth Inns, Steve Hamilton, and Chris Watts; **Cast:** Robert DeNiro, Tom Hulce, Helena Bonham Carter, Aidan Quinn, Ian Holm, John Cleese, Richard Briers, Robert Hardy, Cherie Lunghi

See *FRANKENSTEIN*

MARTIANS ARRIVED, THE

Epoca/Dario (Spain/Italy), 1964, b&w, 95 min

Directors: Pipolo and Franco Castellano; **Screenplay:** Franco Castellano, G. Moccia, and Leonardo Martin;

Music: Ennio Morricone; **Cast:** Paolo Panelli, Alfredo Landa, Jose Calvo

Martians that look like attractive human beings land on Earth. They just come for a visit, but after a look around, they decide to settle in.

MASK OF FU MANCHU, THE

MGM, 1932, b&w, 72 min, VT, LD

Producer: Irving Thalberg; **Directors:** Charles Brabin and Charles Vidor; **Screenplay:** Irene Kuhn, Edgar Allan Woolf, and John Willard; **Cinematography:** Gaetano Guadio; **Special Effects:** Cedric Gibbons and Ken Strickfaden; **Cast:** Boris Karloff, Lewis Stone, Karen Morley, Myrna Loy, Jean Hersholt, Charles Starrett

Fu Manchu (Karloff) wants to get his hands on the mask and sword of Genghis Khan. He plans to use these symbols to unite the various Asian peoples for a war against the rest of the world. As always, his villainous daughter Fah Loh Sih (Loy) is at his side, and his arch nemesis, Scotland Yard's Sir Denis Nayland Smith (Stone), is at his heels.

Other than Fu's deadly ray gun, which goes haywire at the end of the picture, there isn't much science fiction. Still, the Fu Manchu series deserves a mention since; regardless of his exotic plans, the Asian madman usually seeks to destroy his enemies through science. The film was adapted from one of Sax Rohmer's novels, and reportedly Rohmer himself had a hand in this adaptation, one of the most lavish in the series.

MASTER MINDS, THE

Monogram, 1949, b&w, 64 min

Producer: Jan Grippo; **Director:** Jean Yarbrough; **Screenplay:** Charles R. Marion and Bert Lawrence; **Cinematography:** Marcel LePicard; **Music:** Edward J. Kay; **Cast:** Leo Gorcey, Huntz Hall, Gabriel Dell, William Benedict, Alan Napier, Glenn Strange, Bennie Bartlett, David Gorcey, Jane Adams, Bernard Gorcey

Bowery Boy Sach (Hall) finds he can predict the future. This brings him to the attention of a mad scientist (Napier), who has an ape creature (Strange) hidden away that he'd like to make more intelligent. Somehow he gets the idea that putting Sach's brain in the monster's body will have that effect. For Bowery Boys fans, this one is fair enough.

MASTER OF TERROR

See THE 4-D MAN

MASTER OF THE WORLD

AIP, 1961, Color, 104 min, VT, LD

Producer: James H. Nicholson; **Director:** William Whitney; **Screenplay:** Richard Matheson; **Cinematography:** Gil Warrenton; **Music:** Les Baxter; **Special Effects:** Ray Mercer, Tim Barr, Wah Chang, and Gene Warren; **Cast:** Vincent Price, Henry Hull, Charles Bronson, Mary Webster, Vito Scotti, Mary Webster, Richard Harrison

Mad genius Robur (Price) has decided to put an end to all armed conflict across the face of the globe. To achieve this end, he builds a great airship—part helicopter, part dirigible. Naming it *Albatross*, Robur sets out to bomb into submission anyone who will not support his plans for peace. In a scene that owes far more to the Disney version of *20,000 LEAGUES UNDER THE SEA* than to either of the Jules Verne novels (*Clipper of the Clouds* and *Master of the World*) on which this film is based, several outsiders are taken aboard the great airship—one of them an American secret agent (Bronson). He greatly admires Robur's goal but despises his methods of obtaining them, and he ultimately sabotages the great ship.

This is not a very satisfying film. Outside of the airship itself, which is wonderfully detailed, the special effects here are cheap to the point of parody. Small budgets should not be attached to stories with such grand scope. Also, Bronson may have been more badly cast here than any actor in the history of sci-fi films. Rent a good Whit Bissell movie instead—heck, rent a bad one—at least it'll have Whit Bissell. That alone gives it a leg up over this movie.

MATRIX, THE

Warner Bros., 1999, Color, 120 min, DVD

Producer: Joel Silver; **Director:** Larry Wachowski and Andy Wachowski; **Screenplay:** Larry Wachowski and Andy Wachowski; **Cinematography:** Bill Pope; **Music:** Don Davis; **Special Effects:** John Gaeta, Geof Darrow, and Owen Paterson; **Cast:** Keanu Reeves, Laurence Fishburne, Carrie-Anne Moss, Joe Pantoliano, Hugo Weaving

The Matrix (WARNER BROS. & VILLAGE ROADSHOW FILMS / AUTHOR'S COLLECTION)

The conceit of this truly interesting film is that there are two realities: the life we live everyday—shopping, romances, meals, jobs, school, and so on—and the one that lies hidden behind all of that. Only one of those two is real, and the other is a dream called the Matrix.

Two units of police are sent into a building to bring out a woman, unarmed, against lots of well-armed officers. As you might expect, she trashes the lot of them. Before she can escape, however, her departure is interrupted by the usual men in black, whom she leads on a stupendously amazing chase over rooftops. Even more amazing, though, is her getaway. Trapped in a phone booth, she seems doomed as one of the pursuing agents tries to eliminate her with a sanitation vehicle. He drives the truck through the glass booth into the wall beyond just seconds after the woman answers the ringing phone inside the booth. You expect to see blood on the bricks, but there is none. The woman has somehow disappeared.

Next, you are introduced to Thomas Anderson (Reeves), Neo as he is known to his select clientele (pay attention to his code name). He works in some kind of computer-oriented corporation as a fairly successful programmer by day. At night his real life begins. Neo is a vital part of the underground computer culture, charging big bucks for private programs. Neither of these worlds are satisfying him, however. He's after something bigger, something more. Neo is hunting for the truth about the Matrix. He doesn't know what it is. The word is merely the label for something he's heard about in whispers—perhaps in dreams—some mysterious unknown that he believes has unimaginable sinister control over his life. He's also heard that a person named Morpheus (Fishburne) can explain the Matrix. Neo doesn't know why he believes or how he knows any of this. He only knows he does.

Finally, the night comes when Neo is contacted by a beautiful stranger, Trinity (Moss), who says she can lead Neo to Morpheus. She gives him the night to think about things. The next day at work, however, Neo finds that those agents-in-black from the beginning of the film looking for him. Why him? For talking to a girl? For trying to find Morpheus? For knowing about the existence of the Matrix, even though he doesn't have the slightest idea what it is?

Yes, to all of the above. Eventually, Neo makes his way to Morpheus. Once in the presence of the master, he discovers that just as he has been searching for Morpheus, so has Morpheus been searching for him. More exactly, Morpheus has been hunting for the One—the person who will be able to destroy the Matrix. Neo doesn't think he is this mystical One, but Morpheus thinks Neo is. If you're wondering who is the One and

The Matrix (WARNER BROS. & VILLAGE ROADSHOW FILMS / JOSEPH B. MAUCERI COLLECTION)

what is the Matrix?—good questions. The answers are better.

The Matrix is an illusionary word that takes place in the heads of the human race. In film it's far in the future. The machines finally did take over. Now, all of humanity lives a dream sleep in mechanical coffins, their enslaved bodies acting as batteries to provide energy to keep the machines going. In exchange, the machines provide nutrients and the Matrix. Electronically, they supply the world everyone thinks they live in. Only a handful of people like Morpheus and his followers remain free to fight for humanity's liberation. But things are beginning to go badly for them, which is why Neo had better turn out to be the One, or everything is pretty much over for the human race. The rest of the film is spent trying to decide whether Neo is the One or not, and what he can do if he is.

Giving credit where it's due, *The Matrix* is the best new science fiction idea of the 1990s. It works on every level with remarkable consistency. The cast, by no means brimming with superstars, does an excellent job, making every character authentic and highly believable. The storytelling is thorough, well thought out, and immensely entertaining. This is the ultimate paranoid tale. This time, absolutely *everything* you know is supposed to be a lie. Not everything you know about the government, or the police, or any single part of life, but *all* of it. Every single fact about your life and everyone else's . . . it's *all* a lie.

The Matrix is also a terrific action adventure film. The gunfights are amazingly tense, the chases breathtaking and unpredictable. And for the special effects, the wizards behind the scene created an entirely new technology for use in this film.

Superslow motion heavy on stylized action scenes treat the audience to watching people dodge bullets, run along walls, and lots of other good stuff, but certain moments called for something extra—dynamic camera movement around slow motion events that approach 12,000 frames per second. The directing/screenwriting Wachowski brothers dubbed it "bullet time photography." Whatever the name, the new technique allows filmmakers almost unlimited flexibility in controlling the speed and movement of onscreen elements. It may be the biggest special effects breakthrough since TERMINATOR II introduced "morphing." Only time will tell.

MASTERS OF THE UNIVERSE

The Cannon Group, 1987, Color, 106 min, VT, LD

Producers: Michael Flynn, Evzen Kolar, Yorum Globus, Menahem Golan, Edward R. Pressman, and Elliot Schick; **Director:** Gary Goddard; **Screenplay:** David Odell; **Cinematography:** Hanania Baer; **Music:** Bill Conti; **Special Effects:** Arthur Brewer, Ellen Kitz, Brent Boates, Neil Krepela, Richard Edlund, Chris Regan, Mary Mason, and Gary Waller; **Cast:** Dolph Lundgren, Frank Langella, Courteney Cox, James Tolkan, Meg Foster, Christina Pickles, Billy Barty, Jon Cypher

Noble but barely dressed He-Man (Lundgren) comes to Earth along with his pals in search of a key that has the power to control the entire universe. They're trying to keep it out of the hands of evil Skeletor (Langella). Skeletor manages to capture the key and unlock its secrets, forcing He-Man to battle the all-powerful monster to determine the fate of all realms of existence, just as they did so often in the animated series featuring the same characters.

Despite being a film based on a line of misshapen toys and one of the worst animated television series ever to air, *Masters of the Universe* is one of those rare gems in which an audience expecting absolutely nothing comes away pleasantly surprised. The main reason is that this is an extremely unpretentious fun film. The budget is obviously low, given the quality of the sets and props, but the writing is wonderful. Given the task of telling a multidimensional tale with limited resources, the screenwriters crafted an excellent script that makes perfect sense within the framework of the story. Watching the delightfully funny Jon Cypher discuss the joys of eating KFC during the middle of a gunfight is an intentional comedy riot.

Clearly everyone involved was trying their absolute best. Star of stage and screen Frank Langella may have refused to wear the cumbersome makeup that would have brought his character to life, demanding a cheap and phony-looking mask instead, but his performance is magnificent. Opening day audiences were openly shocked when Skeletor seems to have won, declaring to the heavens, "Now I am Master of the Universe!" Good writing and a great performance caught everyone so completely that they forgot that they had gone to make fun of this innocent little movie. Don't expect the moon and the stars, but for those who like goofy superhero pictures, this one is sweet, simple fun—its heart definitely in the right place.

MECHANICAL BUTCHERS, THE

Lumière (France), 1898, b&w, silent short

It's a dream come true for breakfast lovers everywhere. Drop a pig into this wonder machine and instantly collect the pork chops, slabs of bacon, pig's knuckles, and all the other edibles one expects from this animal. Though more than 100 years old, this film remains as wonderful a dream today as when it was first filmed, unless you're a vegetarian.

MECHANICAL HUSBAND, THE

London Cinematograph Company (Great Britain), 1910, b&w, silent short

Director: S. Wormald

It's no wonder the girl falls for the guy in this film since he's perfect in every way. Of course, he's also a robot, so he's been programmed that way.

MECHANICAL LEGS, THE

Gaumont (France), 1908, b&w, silent short

A double amputee is given a pair of robotic legs.

MECHANICAL MAN, THE

Universal, 1915, b&w, silent short

A scientist has finally perfected his robot in this one-reel silent short. But when it comes time for it to perform, it's revealed that it's not as perfected as it could be. The inventor is forced to take its place and suffer the consequences.

MECHANICAL MARY JANE

Hepworth (Great Britain), 1910, b&w, silent short

This short tells the tale of a mechanical servant girl who gets more than a little out of control.

MECHANICAL STATUE AND THE INGENIOUS SERVANT, THE

Vitagraph, 1907, b&w, silent short, 7 min

Producer: J. Stuart Blackton; **Director:** Blackton

Another film about trouble with mechanical servants.

MEMOIRS OF AN INVISIBLE MAN

Universal, 1992, Color, 99 min, VT, LD

Producers: Arnon Milchan, Bruce Bodner, and Dan Kolsrud; **Director:** John Carpenter; **Screenplay:** H.F. Saint, William Goldman, Robert Collector, and Dana Olsen; **Cinematography:** William A. Fraker; **Music:** Shirley Walker; **Special Effects:** Albert Delgado, Ned Gorman, Bruce Nicholson, Stuart Robertson, Mark More, Bill Kimberlain, Ken Perpiot, and ILM; **Cast:** Chevy Chase, Daryl Hannah, Sam Neill, Michael McKean, Stephen Tobolowsky

See *THE INVISIBLE MAN*

MENACE FROM OUTER SPACE

Reed, 1954, b&w, 78 min

Producer: Roland Reed; **Director:** Hollingsworth Morse; **Screenplay:** Warren Wilson; **Music:** Alexander Laszlo; **Special Effects:** Jack R. Glass and Dick Morgan; **Cast:** Richard Crane, Sally Mansfield, Scott Beckett, Patsy Parsons, Robert Lyden, Maurice Cass, Leonard Penn, Patsy Iaonne, Walter Coy, Frank Pulaski, Joanne Jordon

Yet another film strung together from episodes of *Rocky Jones—Space Ranger*! Like the others, this one offers little to the discovering viewer.

MEN IN BLACK

Columbia/Amblin Entertainment, 1997, Color, 98 min, VT, LD, DVD

Producers: Steven Spielberg, Graham Place, Walter F. Parkes, Steven R. Molen, and Laurie MacDonald; **Director:** Barry Sonnonfeld; **Screenplay:** Ed Solomon, David Koepp, Ted Elliott, and Terry Rossio; **Cinematography:** Don Peterman; **Music:** Danny Elfman; **Special Effects:** ILM, Eric Brevig Kyle Ross, Scott Farrar, J.D. Street, Jacqueline M. Lopez, John G. McCabe, Jon Thackery, Peter A. Rehard, Banned From The Ranch Entertainment, Question Mark FX, Storyboard, Inc., Autumn Light Entertainment, Cinovation Group, and Visual Concept Engineering; **Cast:** Tommy Lee Jones, Will Smith, Linda Fiorentino, Rip Torn, Vincent D'Onofrio, Tommy Shalhoub, Siobhan Fallon

A van carrying illegal Mexican aliens across the desert is stopped by the U.S. Border Patrol. Before the uniformed officials can process the hopeful immigrants, however, two men dressed in black suits approach, claiming to be in charge of the situation due to the powers granted them from some mysterious Division 6. They question the Mexicans one by one until they come across one who doesn't speak Spanish. Surprise, he's an illegal alien all right, but he's no Mexican. The inhuman makes a break for it, and his questioner, Agent K (Jones), is forced to splatter him across the countryside in front of one of the border patrol officers. That's all right, though. K carries a Neurolizer, a cigar-shaped silver mechanism that erases memories. What isn't all right is K's partner, D, who was injured in the scuffle. Now K needs a new partner.

Enter NYPD detective Will Smith. He comes to K's attention when he manages to run to ground an extremely fleet-of-foot alien, even beating the creature's cosmic weaponry at the same time. After some fairly humorous testing, K lets the future Agent J in on a few secrets. There really are UFOs bringing aliens to Earth, and the government has known about it all along. That was why the Men In Black were formed, to take care of interplanetary relationships, and to make certain the population of Earth's comfortable illusion as to their dominance of the universe isn't shaken. J joins the team, and soon he and his partner are knee-deep in a desperate race to save the world.

This is a witty hip comedy that plays all its cards perfectly. In a genre severely lacking in both buddy pictures and stylish comedies, this film covers both bases expertly. The picture so deserves praise that it's hard to know where to begin. Everyone in the cast is excellent. Jones and Smith couldn't be better. Rip Torn, as Zed, the fierce, unflappable head of MIB, gives a stellar performance. And these three have a tough job shining against the movie's unrelentingly excellent special effects. This

Men In Black (SONY PICTURES ENTERTAINMENT / JOSEPH B. MAUCERI COLLECTION)

time, though, the filmmakers worried about the writing as well as the film's video game potential, which means not only is the dialogue snappy, but it all makes sense.

Hollywood has such a disastrous record of bringing comic books to the screen (in feature or television form) it's hard to believe that this property started life as a funnybook from Malibu Comics, but those are the facts. What went right here is anyone's guess, but the result is a top-notch, imaginative, sarcastic film for all ages that sums up government conspiracy theories and lots more with one devastatingly comedic and yet logical bon mot after another.

Note: When Earth is about to be destroyed, and MIB headquarters is filling up with baggage-laden aliens trying to get off planet, there is a moment when we see one group of extraterrestrials singing a bizarre song. Those in the know recognized the "Betelgeuse Death Anthem," the tune that Ford Prefect and Zaphod Beeblebrox sing while awaiting death in the BBC production of another masterful science fiction comedy, *The Hitchhiker's Guide to the Galaxy.*

MESSAGE FROM MARS, A

United Kingdom Films (Great Britain), 1913, b&w, silent feature

Producer: Nicholson Ormsby-Scott; **Director:** J. Wellett Waller; **Screenplay:** Waller; **Cinematography:** Arthur Martinelli; **Cast:** E. Hoffman Clark, Charles Hawtrey, Chrissie Bell, Hubert Willis, Frank Hector

Mars is worried about the fate of Earth. In the best interests of its neighbor, the Red Planet sends a missionary of sorts to help us get past our madness. This extremely moralistic but not necessarily wrong-headed fable was actually based on an extremely popular stage play of the time. This cinematic version used the actors from the long-running theater production, but it was not the only one ever made, or even the first. Records exist of a shorter version of the play made four years earlier in New Zealand. In 1921 an American version was produced, but for some reason Hollywood chose to depict the story's moralizing as a dream.

MESSAGE FROM SPACE

United Artists, 1977, Color, 105 min

Producer: Toei Studios; **Director:** Kinji Fukasaku; **Screenplay:** Hirou Matsuda, Shotaro Ishinomori, Kinji Fukasaku, and Masahiro Noda; **Cinematography:** Toro Nakajima; **Music:** Kenichio Morioka; **Special Effects:** Minoru Nakano, Noburu Takanashi, Nobuo Yajima, and Shotaru Ishinori; **Cast:** Vic Morrow, Sonny Chiba, Philip Casnoff, Peggy Lee Brennan, Sue Shiomi, Tetsuro Tamba

The good and wise Jillucians are facing genocide at the hands of the nasty and mean Gavanas. Kido, the good and wise elder statesman of the Jillucians has a plan. He will throw magic nuts into space in the hopes that a group of heroes will be compelled by the nuts to come and save his people. The heroes are found, and they come back and save the planet—almost. There are survivors of the Gavanas' attack when the battle is over, but the planet is dying. So the heroes load up all the survivors into their ship (not a spaceship, but, inexplicably, a European sail-powered schooner) and go off in search of a planet where everyone can be happy.

The film owes much to *The Seven Samurai* and *Star Wars*, but it's not quite so bad as it sounds. Its heart is in the right place, and its special effects are sometimes bizarre, but awfully interesting. In particular, the hand-shaped command ship of the villains is not to be missed.

MESSAGE TO THE FUTURE

Thirteenth Century Films (Hungary), 1970, Color, 87 min

Producer: Jacob Kotzky; **Director:** Jozsef Nepp; **Screenplay:** David Avidan; **Cinematography:** Amnon Salomon; **Music:** Jacob Goldstein; **Cast:** David Avidan, Joseph Bee, Irit Méiri, Zygmont Frankel, Avi Yakir, Rafi Taylor

A contemporary 20th-century family meets its 30th-century descendants without much fanfare.

METALSTORM: THE DESTRUCTION OF JARED-SYN

Albert Band International Productions, 1983, Color, 84 min, VT, LD

Producers: Albert Band, Charles Band, Albert J. Adler, Gordon W. Gregory, and Arthur H. Maslansky; **Director:** Charles Band; **Screenplay:** Alan J. Alder; **Cinematography:** Mac Ahlberg; **Music:** Richard Band; **Special Effects:** Frank H. Isaacs; **Cast:** Jeffrey Byron, Tim Thonerson, Kelly Preston, Mike Preston, Richard Moll

A good guy hunts a megalomaniac in this low-budget future film that tries hard to look better than a direct-to-video release.

METAMORPHOSIS

Filmirage, 1990, Color, 96 min, VT

Producer: Donatella Donati; **Director:** G.L. Eastman; **Screenplay:** Eastman; **Cinematography:** Gianlorenzo Battaglim; **Special Effects:** Maurizio Trani; **Cast:** Gene LeBrock, Catherine Baranov, Harry Cason, David Wicker, Jason Arnold, Stephen Brown

A mad scientist takes a crack at immortality, and like so many of those who have gone before, this reckless researcher tries his formula out on himself with less than the expected results. At first, he turns into some kind of a lizard-thing, then he devolves further into a puddle of goo. Despite bad effects and terrible writing, including some parts lifted from *THE FLY* (1986), this movie takes itself far too seriously.

METEOR

AIP, 1979, Color, 103 min, VT, LD, DVD

Producers: Arnold Orgolini and Theodore Parvin; **Director:** Ronald Neame; **Screenplay:** Stanley Mann and Edmund H. North; **Cinematography:** Paul Lohmann; **Music:** Laurence Rosenthal; **Special Effects:** David Constable, Glen Robinson, Robert Staples, Frank van der Veer, Bill Cruse, Robbie Blalack, and Jamie Shourt; **Cast:** Sean Connery, Natalie Wood, Karl Malden, Brian Keith, Henry Fonda, Martin Landau, Trevor Howard, Richard Dysart, Bo Brundun, Joseph Campanella

A comet slams into the asteroid belt, causing a number of meteors to head for the third rock from the Sun, including a five-mile-wide menace to stellar navigation named Orpheus. It is so huge that experts agree that it could turn Earth into a second asteroid belt.

NASA bigwig Karl Malden gets his onetime employee Sean Connery to come back to help out.

Connery had designed a space-based nuclear missile platform to handle just such incidents. The launcher, Hercules, was built but was then aimed toward the planet instead of away from it for use against the Russians. This perversion of his work is what made Connery quit in the first place. Now he has to work with his former boss to convince a skeptical president (Fonda) that the danger is real and that the platform needs to be turned and fired at the approaching Orpheus.

Worse yet, NASA says that even if this is done, Hercules doesn't have enough firepower to stop the meteor. But the Russians have built their own platform, suspiciously like Hercules and also aimed at Earth, but—as one might suspect—not at Russia. The nations enemy must put their faith in science over war and come to trust each other fast—because the platforms have to be turned, retargeted, and fired so that their objective is destroyed far enough away from Earth to avert destruction. Predictably, the planet is saved—most of it, anyway. New York, Hong Kong, and various parts of Europe and elsewhere are pelted fiercely, and many lose their lives in the resulting devastation.

It's rare when a cast of this magnitude is assembled. It's even rarer when they're all gathered together and then utterly and completely wasted. *Meteor* has a great story—interesting, new at the time, and scientifically accurate. But the film's direction is lackluster, its pacing slow and jumpy, and the special effects dull and unconvincing. Nearly two decades before *DEEP IMPACT* and *ARMAGEDDON*, *Meteor* was among the first of the science fiction subgenre in which a big rock hurls toward Earth. It could have been a great movie, but it is only a distant cousin of the greatness to come.

METEOR MAN, THE

MGM, 1993, Color, 100 min, VT, LD

Producers: Robert Townsend, Loretha C. Jones, and Christopher Homes; **Director:** Townsend; **Screenplay:** Townsend; **Cinematography:** John A. Alonzo; **Music:** Cliff Eidelman; **Special Effects:** Al D. Sarro, Bruce Nicholson, and ILM; **Cast:** Robert Townsend, James Earl Jones, Marla Gibbs, Eddie Griffin, Robert Guillaume, Roy Fegan, Frank Gorshin, Sinbad, Bill Cosby, Cynthia Belgrave, Marilyn Coleman, Don Cheadle, Luthur Vandross

Producer/director/screenwriter Robert Townsend plays a good but beleaguered inner-city schoolteacher. There's trouble in his neighborhood. Bad guy gangsters are making things scary. What to do? The answer—not much of anything, until the schoolteacher is struck down by a glowing green meteor. The space rock gives Townsend Supermanlike powers. For a while he's tough on crime, but then his powers start to fade. Luckily, his inspiring gumption and resolve gets the neighborhood mobilized, and in the end they save him and take care of the hoods. It's hard to attack a film trying to project as positive a message of self-reliance and courage as this one does. Unfortunately, it's billed as a comedy and it simply isn't funny.

METEOR MONSTER, THE

See *TEENAGE MONSTER*

METROPOLIS

UFA (Germany), 1926/Paramount (U.S.), 1927, b&w, silent feature, 120 min, VT, LD, DVD

Producer: Erich Pommer; **Director:** Fritz Lang; **Screenplay:** Lang and Thea von Harbou; **Cinematography:** Karl Freund; **Music:** Gottfried Happertz; **Special Effects:** Otto Hunte, Erich Kettelhut, Karl Vollbrecht, and Eugen Shuftan; **Cast:** Brigitte Helm, Alfred Abel, Gustav Froelich, Rudolf Klein-Rogge, Fritz Rasp, Heinrich George, Theodor Loos

It's the faraway year 2000, and everyone wants to live in the immaculate skyscraper towers of the shining city Metropolis. Well, everyone rich wants to live there. Life's a breeze for them. For the workers who live under the city, however, things could be better. They live in crumbling, filthy poverty, working endless hours at back-breaking labor for little reward. The city is run by manager Jon Frederson (Abel). He likes the arrangement of the rich having all the advantages and doesn't want any changes. His son Fredor (Froelich), however, is persuaded to see things differently by Maria (Helm), a beautiful woman from the downtrodden masses. Maria takes Fredor down into the tunnels beneath the city to show the industrialist's son the ugly truth behind his father's wealth. Maria hopes that someday the laborers of Metropolis will have a better life; she preaches nonviolence.

Frederson goes to a sinister scientist, Rotwang (Klein-Rogge), to find a way to stop Maria, cure his son of his foolish romantic notions about lifting up the proletariat, and getting the workers back to breaking their spines more efficiently. Rotwang has just the solution. He creates a robot version of Maria, which he sends to incite the workers to riot. The riot will certainly lead to the destruction of their homes and families, but apparently the workers are too simpleminded to realize this. Though it's possible there's a good reason why Frederson want his workforce to wipe themselves out, it's never offered in the film. Luckily, some simple heroics on his son's part changes all that. Instead of the mass murder Frederson plotted, Maria is freed, Rotwang is thrown off the tallest building in Metropolis by a passionate Fredor, and Frederson is forced to shake hands with the leaders of the revolt as he promises that a new day will soon be dawning.

This film is considered the classic of science fiction classics. For the times the sets could be more stunning or stylish. The almost heavenly vistas of Metropolis are a breathtaking achievement for a cinema that hadn't yet made pictures with sound. The expressionistic sets combined with Lang's interpretive and artistic direction make this movie a feast for the eyes.

However, like many modern pictures, special effects is all this one has going for it. The politics are childishly basic, the characters drawn in the starkest melodrama. Maria is poor, so she is all good, all pure. Frederson is rich, so he is evil, on the edge of insanity. He's willing to slaughter helpless people on a scale bound to doom all he is trying to preserve simply because he cannot admit anyone else's point of view.

This film is very much a product of its time. When Lang made his visionary epic, the year 2000 was still 75 years away. The world was filled with men as ruthless as Frederson, if not nearly so insane, since fortunes are not easily made by the criminally chaotic. Socialism and communism gave some people hope for a better world. Modern perspectives on these topics differ. The naivete of *Metropolis* is highlighted here not to prove any great insight, but to warn those viewers who see only its weighty reputation. The story is silly, the science fiction limited, and the acting consists of the usual broad gestures of the silent era. However, magnificent sets and daring breadth and scope make this film one of the earliest prophetic visions of the future. To be fair to Lang, now that the year 2000 has come and gone, it's actually frightening to see how much of his vision of the future is more true than ever.

MIB

See *MEN IN BLACK*

MIGHTY JOE YOUNG (1949)

RKO, 1949 b&w, 94 min, VT, LD

Producers: Merian C. Cooper and John Ford; **Director:** Ernest B. Schoedsack; **Screenplay:** Rught Rose

and Cooper; **Music:** Roy Webb; **Special Effects:** Willis O'Brien, Ray Harryhausen, Linwood G. Dunn, Fitch Fulton, Pete Peterson, and George Lofgren; **Cinematography:** J. Roy Hunt; **Cast:** Terry Moore, Ben Johnson, Robert Armstrong, Frank McHugh

See *KING KONG*

MIGHTY JOE YOUNG (1998)

Walt Disney Pictures, 1998, color, 114 min, VT, LD, DVD

Producers: Ted Hartley, Tom Jacobson, Gail Katz, Mark Lisson, Gary Stutman, and Ralph Winter, **Director:** Ron Underwood; **Screenplay:** Mark Rosenthal, Lawrence Konner, Ruth Rose, and Merian C. Cooper; **Music:** James Horner; **Special Effects:** Rick Baker, Hoyt Yeatman, Ted Bukowski, Kevin Cox, Curtis Decker, Lawrence Decker, Darryll Dodson, Edwin J. Escobar, Robert Espinoza, Gene A. Grijalva, Steve Hall, Matthew Hall, Gary L. Kara, Carlos M. Schiesow, Frank L. Toro, Dreamquest Images, Dan Deleeuw, Industrial Light and Magic, Matte World Digital and Computer Film Company; **Cinematography:** Don Peterman, A.S.C., and Oliver Woods; **Cast:** Charlize Theron, Bill Paxton, Rade Sherbedgia, Peter Firth, David Paymer, Regina King, Robert Wisdom, Naveen Andrews, Lawrence Pressman

See *KING KONG*

MIGHTY MORPHIN POWER RANGERS: THE MOVIE

20th Century Fox, 1995, Color, 95 min, VT, LD

Producers: David Coatsworth, Shuki Levy, Haim Saban, and Suzanne Todd; **Director:** Bryan Spicer; **Screenplay:** John Kamps, Arne Olsen, and Roger Kumble; **Cinematography:** Paul Murphy; **Music:** Graeme Revell; **Special Effects:** Steve Courtley, Richard O. Helmer, Tad Pride, Erik Henry, and Rodney Montague; **Cast:** Karan Ashley, Johnny Yong Bosch, Steve Cardenas, Jason David Frank, Amy Jo Johnson, David Yost, Paul Schrier, Jason Navry, Paul Freeman, Gabrielle Fitzpatrick, Nicholas Bell

The Power Rangers are five (sometimes six) teenagers who all attend the same high school and who have normal lives until a superpowered menace threatens the world. Then outside forces gift them with superpowers so that they can protect Earth. This time around, an ancient evil from the dawn of time, Ivan Ooze, has returned to existence and is setting out to conquer the universe. It's up to the Power Rangers to stop him, but they've lost their powers. They regain their powers through a quest of self-knowledge; then they kick the stuffing out of the most powerful villain they've ever faced.

It's easy to make fun of the small-screen fare that spawned this movie and its sequel, *Turbo: A Power Rangers Movie*, which didn't live up to the promise of this first film. The Power Rangers' first full-length feature won't ever be considered a classic, but for what it is, it couldn't have been much better without simply throwing out the source material and starting over. It's decent fare for kids, and at least the villain is funny and actually sinister instead of merely pathetic as are his small-screen counterparts.

MILLENNIUM

Gladden Entertainment, 1989, Color, 108 min, VT, LD, DVD

Producers: Chris Carter, Freddie Fields, John M. Eckert, Robert Vince, Louis M. Silverstein, John Foreman, Doug Leiterman, and P. Gael Mourant; **Director:** Michael Anderson; **Screenplay:** John Varley; **Cinematography:** René Ohashi; **Music:** Eric N. Robertson; **Special Effects:** Harrison Ellenshaw, David L. Hewitt, and Arthur Langevin; **Cast:** Kris Kristofferson, Cheryl Ladd, Robert Joy, Daniel J. Travanti, Brent Carver, Maury Chakin, David McIllwraith, Al Waxman, Lloyd Bochner

Time travelers come back from our future to put the nab on doomed passengers from crashing airliners. Kristofferson plays a crash investigator who begins to notice something strange going on. During the course of his investigation, he falls for one of the time travelers, Ladd. Based on a very good short story by science fiction great John Varley, who also wrote the screen adaptation, much of the movie is clever and intriguing, but ultimately it falls apart before the end of the first hour and then continues downhill.

MILL OF THE STONE WOMEN (aka: THE HORRIBLE MILL WOMEN, DROPS OF BLOOD, HORROR OF THE STONE WOMEN)

Parade, 1963, Color, 94 min

Producer: Gianpaolo Bigazzi; **Director:** Giorgio Ferroni; **Screenplay:** Ferroni, Remigio Del Crosso, Ugo Liberatone, and Giorgio Stegani; **Cinematography:** Pierludovico Pavoni; **Music:** Carlo Innocenzi; **Cast:** Pierri Brice, Scilla Gabel, Dany Carel, Wolfgang Preiss

It's the turn of the last century, and a mad scientist whose daughter has a bizarre disease must supply her with massive, constant blood transfusions. The scientist blackmails a local doctor into helping him acquire beautiful young women whom he can murder for blood, and afterward the bodies are mounted as waxworks exhibits to hide them from prying souls.

MIMIC

Dimension, 1997, Color, 105 min, VT, LD, DVD

Producers: Michael Phillips, Cary Granat, Richard Potter, Andrew Rona, Scott Schiffman, Michael Zoumas, Bob Weinstein, B.J. Rack, and Ole Bernedal; **Director:** Guillermo Del Toro; **Screenplay:** Del Toro and Matthew Robbins; **Cinematography:** Dan Lautsen, D.F.F.; **Music:** Marco Beltrami; **Special Effects:** Brian M. Jennings, Rich Lazzarini, The Character Shop, Tyruben Ellingson, and Rob Bottin; **Cast:** Mira Sorvino, Jeremy Nortam, Alexander Goodwin, Giancarlo Giannini, Charles S. Dutton, Josh Brolin, Alix Koromzay, F. Murray Abraham, James Costa, Javonn Barnwell, Norman Reedus, Pak-Kwong Ho, Margaret Ma, Warna Fisher, Alan Argue, Charles Hayter, Julian Richings, James Kidnie, Eve English, Bill Lasovich, Doug Jones, Roger Clown

Brilliant scientist (Sorvino) is given a challenge. She is required to combat an epidemic threatening the lives of all the world's children. She does so by recombining the DNA of two separate insect species to create a biological counteragent to the carrier of the disease. The new species is christened the Judas Breed and is promptly turned loose in New York City to stop the great plague. This sets the stage for the rest of the movie, which, of course, is the inevitable boomerang effect required whenever scientist alter the balance of nature. For the rest of the picture, Sorvino is pulled into a destructive web of her own making, forced to pay for her genetic crimes.

Mimic suffers from some incredible scientific gaffes. For instance, the audience is asked to believe that the Centers for Disease Control could effectively rope off Manhattan Island so that not a single cockroach could escape. How they accomplish this amazing cleansing of every bridge and tunnel, every car and boat, when every New Yorker knows it's practically impossible to keep the city roach free, is not explained. Hard facts, logic, or

Mimic (DIMENSION FILMS / JOSEPH B. MAUCERI COLLECTION)

even basic understanding of the simplest scientific principles do not concern the filmmakers.

Despite these flaws, the film does have pluses, including solid performances by two Oscar winners. But the main thing about this picture is an unrelenting sense of creepiness. *Mimic* is a tense, itchy skin-crawler. The inexorable chill of fear to this movie is literally inescapable. Although the special effects are excellent and the execution of the horrors nightmarishly realistic, there is an authentic quality to the horror rarely seen in modern films. Credit for *Mimic*'s starkly different mood has to go to director Guillermo Del Toro.

Del Toro was a recent arrival in Hollywood when he made this picture and didn't follow the usual sci-fi formulas. A sure indication of this is the film's climax—the showdown between humanity and the monsters—and the audience has no clue that it's the finale. So never-ending is the sense of dread menace felt throughout the film, even after the good guys have won, that the audience is not actually certain that they have. This is accomplished without any of the usual lame tag-on endings, showcasing the villain limping off or raising a hand from the grave to ensure the inevitable sequel.

Del Toro did not make this picture with any of the usual studio considerations in mind, including resale to television or home video. He made this for the big screen. Much of its terror is lost on the small screen. Indeed, the moody lighting throughout makes the film far too murky for television.

MIND BENDERS, THE

AIP, 1963, b&w, 101 min

Producer: Michael Relph; **Director:** Basil Dearden; **Screenplay:** James Kennaway; **Cinematography:** Denys Coop; **Music:** George Auric; **Cast:** Dirk Bogarde, Mary Ure, John Clements, Norman Bird, Michael Bryant, Edward Fox, Wendy Craig

In this simple tale of sensory deprivation experiments, the program is in jeopardy of being shut down when one of the scientists commits suicide. Did he, or was it espionage that took his life? An excellent cast keeps this slow but intriguing film moving along.

MIND DETECTING RAY, THE

Star (Hungary), 1918, b&w, silent short

Director: Alfred Desy; **Screenplay:** Istvan Lazar

A machine that can read thoughts is invented. Inventions like this don't sit around long, though, before some villain swipes them. This evildoer is out of luck, however, as the machine itself informs on the thief.

MIND OF MR. SOAMES, THE

Amicus (Great Britain), 1969/Columbia (U.S.), 1970, Color, 97 min

Producer: George Goodman; **Director:** Alan Cooke; **Screenplay:** Ron Whyte; **Cinematography:** Manny Wynn; **Music:** Phil Romone; **Cast:** Robert Vaughn, Terence Stamp, Nigel Davenport, Christian Roberts

Mr. Soames (Stamp) is a man in his late twenties who has been in a coma since birth. His condition is finally cured, but the doctors' work doesn't end there. Soames is an adult with the intellect of a newborn. He must be educated to exist within society—and at an accelerated rate. This proceeds nicely at first under the watchful eye of project head Robert Vaughn. All too quickly, however, Soames becomes a media darling, and the press and public begin interfering dangerously with his progress. Vaughn tries to stop the inevitable, but it isn't long before poor Mr. Soames comes to a bad end thanks to the uncaring masses and their need to feed on lives outside their own. This exceptionally good cautionary tale was decades ahead of its time.

MIND SNATCHERS, THE (aka: THE HAPPINESS CAGE, THE DEMON WITHIN)

Cinerama, 1972, Color, 94 min, VT

Producer: George Goodman; **Director:** Bernard Girard; **Screenplay:** Ron Whyte; **Cinematography:** Manny Wynn; **Music:** Phil Ramone; **Cast:** Christopher Walken, Ralph Meeker, Claus Nissen, Ronnie Cox, Joss Ackland, Birthe Newman, Susan Travers

A process for curbing aggression in violent mental patients is viewed as a blessing by the medical community until the government steps in and decides to use it to turn less-than-perfect soldiers into zombie killing machines. This movie is better than it sounds. There isn't a great deal of physical action, but the intriguing story certainly challenges viewers to think.

MINDWARP: AN INFINITY OF TERROR

See *GALAXY OF TERROR*

MIRACLE MILE

Columbia, 1989, Color, 87 min, VT, LD

Producers: Gramme Cottle, John Daly, and Derek Gibson; **Director:** Steve DeJarnatt; **Screenplay:** DeJarnatt; **Cinematography:** Theo Van de Sande; **Music:** Tangerine Dream; **Special Effects:** Claire Gaul and Jerry Casillas; **Cast:** Anthony Edwards, Mare Winningham, John Agar, Lou Hancock, Mykel T. Williamson, Kelly Minter, Kurt Fuller, Denise Crosby, Robert Doqui, Danny De La Paz

A nice-guy musician (Edwards) who just can't catch a break finally seems to have broken his bad luck pattern. He's hit it off with a wonderful girl (Winningham) and actually has a date with her. Everyone is happy for him, but then on the way to the date, he answers a ringing public phone and intercepts a terrible message. The

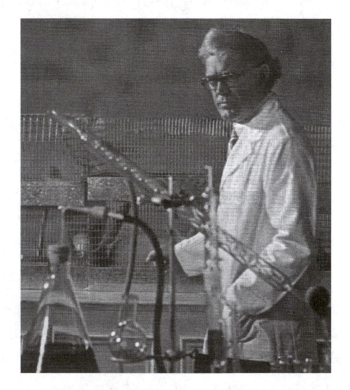

The Mind Snatchers (CINERAMA / AUTHOR'S COLLECTION)

nukes are flying. Humanity has one hour to live. The message seems real, but what should he do? Even if it is true, is there anything he *can* do—outside of just enjoying his date, the first good thing that has happened to him in a long time?

To reveal the ending of this lesser-known classic would be a terrible. The critics are sharply divided on this movie. Film critic Leonard Maltin writes that this one "loses all hope of credibility in its last half hour" and that "co-stars Edwards and Winningham" can't do anything with this material." But another case can be made. Tackling the question of responsibility to self versus that owed the community, the film evolves at a maddening pace, ever teasing the audience as to whether Edwards's decisions are valid.

Note: The superb soundtrack was recorded by Tangerine Dream, a popular band at the time the film was made.

MIRACLE RIDER, THE

Mascot, 1935, b&w, serial, 15 chapters

Producer: Victor Zobel; **Directors:** Armand Schaefer and Reeves Eason; **Screenplay:** John Rathmell; **Cinematography:** Ernest Miller and William Nobles; **Music:** Lee Zahler; **Cast:** Charles Middleton, Bob Kortman, Tom Mix, Jean Gale

Bad guy Middleton is an oil executive out to steal Indian land because the reservation is sitting on top of great quantities of rare new element which can be made into a valuable explosive. Helping him is half-breed Kortman, who wants to take over the tribe. Opposing him is Texas Ranger Tom Morgan (Mix).

MISADVENTURES OF MERLIN JONES, THE

Buena Vista, 1964, Color, 88 min, VT

Producer: Walt Disney; **Director:** Robert Stevenson; **Screenplay:** Tom and Helen August; **Cinematography:** Edward Coleman; **Music:** Buddy Baker; **Cast:** Tommy Kirk, Annette Funicello, Leon Ames, Stuart Erwin, Alan Hewitt, Connie Gilchrist

Merlin Jones (Kirk) is a college student with a lot on his mind. In this film, that boils down to two things. One is a big, football-helmet-shaped thinking cap that allows him to read people's minds. The other is Annette Funicello.

This is the first of two rather vacuous Disney films featuring Merlin Jones. In the second, *The Monkey's Uncle*, Merlin uses sleep-teaching techniques to pull the football team through their academic problems. Merlin knows this will work because he's already tested it on a chimp.

MISSILE TO THE MOON

See *CAT WOMEN OF THE MOON*

MISSION MARS

Allied Artists, 1968, Color, 95 min, VT

Producers: Laurence Appelbaum, Mort Fallick, and Everett Rosenthal; **Director:** Nick Webster; **Screenplay:** Michael St. Clair and Aubrey Wasberg; **Cinematography:** Clifford H. Poland, Jr.; **Music:** Berge Kalajian; **Special Effects:** Haberstroh Studios; **Cast:** Darren McGavin, Nick Adams, Shirley Parker, George DeVries, Heather Hewitt, Michael DeBeausset

Three American astronauts find themselves fighting for their lives against an unseen enemy in this forgettable film.

MISSION STARDUST (aka: MORTAL ORBIT, OPERATION STARDUST, YOU ONLY LIVE ONCE)

Times Films (Germany/Italy/Spain), 1967, Color, 95 min, VT

Producer: Aitor/PEA/Theumer Films; **Director:** Primo Zeglio; **Screenplay:** K.H. Vogeman and Frederico d'Urritia; **Cinematography:** Manuel Merino; **Music:** Anton Garcia Abril; **Cast:** Lang Jeffries, Essy Persson, Luis Davilla, Daniel Martin, John Karelson, Pinkas Braun

Heroic space pilot Perry Rhodan (Jeffries) lands on the Moon and discovers an alien craft whose passengers and crew are suffering from a mysterious malady. Luckily for Perry, there's a shapely female space pilot to keep him company. Unluckily for the audience, there's nothing to keep their interest in this miserable adaptation of the wildly popular European space opera series.

MISSION TO MARS

Touchstone, 2000, Color, 118 min, VT, DVD

Mission to Mars (TOUCHSTONE PICTURES / AUTHOR'S COLLECTION)

Producers: Tom Jacobson, Sam Mercer, David Goyer, Justis Green, Jim Wedaa, and Ted Tally; **Director:** Brian DePalma; **Screenplay:** Jim Thomas, John Thomas, Graham Yost, and Lowell Cannon; **Cinematography:** Stephen H. Burum, A.S.C.; **Music:** Ennio Morricone; **Special Effects:** Garry Elmendorf, Stephen T. Cremin, Randy Shymkiw, David Heron, William Kennedy, Terry W. King, Roland Loew, Mark Obedzinski, Glen Marinello, Industrial Light & Magic, Tippett Studio, CIS Hollywood, and Jim Henson Creature Shop; **Cast:** Gary Sinise, Tim Robbins, Don Cheadle, Connie Nielsen, Jerry O'Connell, Peter Outerbridge, Kavan Smith, Jill Teed, Elise Neal, Kim Delaney

The year is 2020 and NASA has pulled off another giant leap forward for humankind. Humanity has left its first collective footprint in the red dust of Mars. Shortly after arrival, however, a discovery indicates that Mars could be readied for colonization decades earlier than anyone had ever imagined. The team goes out to investigate, promising to report back soon. The report is worse than anyone could have thought.

All but one of the landing party are dead. Something on Mars killed them all. The transmission relaying that information is weak, broken, and short. Once it's finished, NASA faces a monumental decision. Do they spend billions of dollars on a rescue mission—one almost certain not to find any survivors and one that might also kill those sent on it—or not? No easy choice. Cautiously, the mission goes forward, and the science fiction epic *Mission to Mars* is off and running.

The studio worked hand-in-hand with NASA over a year to get every detail as close to reality as possible, and so the special effects are extremely realistic. The deep-space segment of this film is absolutely flawless, its science dead-on accurate, helping to amplify the tension of the disasters that plague the rescue mission, and making for some genuine nail-biting moments of suspense. For three-quarters of its length *Mission to Mars* really delivers, but at some point the producers stopped listening to their NASA consultants and their science fiction film turns into a sci-fi flick with a startling downturn. It wouldn't be right to reveal all the details here, but many audiences left this film with the same question on their minds, "That's it?"

Basing the movie on the excellent nonfiction work *The Case for Mars*, by rocket scientist Robert Zubrin, was a great idea. Perhaps, however, the filmmakers should have stuck to the facts and left the science fiction to someone with more than a cut-rate imagination.

MISSION TO MIR

Imax Corporation, 1997, Color, 40 min

Producers: Toni Myers, Andrew Gellis, and Graeme Ferguson; **Director:** Ivan Galin; **Cinematography:** James Neihouse; **Music:** Micky Erbe and Maribeth Solomon; **Cast:** Jim Weatherbee, Eileen Collins, Janice Voss, Michael Foale, Bernard Harris, Vladimir Titov, Valadimir Dezhurov, Gennady Strekalov, Norm Thagard, Hoot Gibson, Charlie Precourt, Bonnie Dunbar, Ellen Baker, Greg Harbaugh, Anatoly Solovyev, Nikolai Budarin, Yuri Gidzenko, Sergei Avdeyev, Thomas Reiter, Ken Cameron, James Halsell, Chris Hadfield, Jerry Ross, William McArthur, Yuri Onufrienko, Yuri Usachev, Shannon Lucid, Valery Korzun, Alexander Kaleri, Dr. Claudie Andre-DesHayes, Bill Readdy, Terry Wilcutt, Jay Apt, Tom Akers, Carl Walz, John Blaha

Actually filmed in outer space by the "cast" listed above—a cast up entirely of American and Russian astronauts—this unprecedented giant screen tour of Russia's space station Mir gives its audience a unique look inside the weightless environment of space travelers. Not exactly science fiction, it should certainly prove of great interest to science fiction fans.

This IMAX film is a blend of historic footage and somewhat amazing live-action shots. The movie covers the rigorous preparation both astronauts and cosmonauts undergo prior to their flights. This, of course, means a trip to the Russian cosmonaut community, Star City. As rare a treat as that is, however, it can't compare to seeing the launching pad in Baikonur—a site once considered so secret it wasn't located on any maps. There the film shows breathtaking footage of a massive *Soyuz* rocket lifting off. The film's all too brief 40 minutes also hold marvelous views of the launching of the shuttle *Atlantis* as well as the ship's docking with Mir. After that, the mission itself is detailed as well as the return home by the two different crews, followed by the next crew's sharing the cramped station. Filming this picture took two and a half years, four separate space missions, and three different trips to Russia (as well as location shooting in America), so there's quite a lot to see.

Note: Mir (the Russian word for "peace") orbits Earth 16 times a day. That's a lot of rotations for cosmonaut Valeri Polyakov, who holds the record for the longest stay in space. He spent 14 months aboard the station. American Shannon Lucid was there for only six months (a record for any American, male or female), but part of her stay was also filmed for *Mission to Mir.*

MISTER SUPERINVISIBLE

As Films, S.A. (Spain)/Kel-Tel pictures (U.S.), 1973, Color, 93 min, VT

Producer: Peter Carsten; **Director:** Anthony M. Dawson; **Screenplay:** Luis Marquina and Maria Laura Rocca; **Cinematography:** Alejandro Ulloa; **Music:** Carlo Savina; **Cast:** Dean Jones, Ingeborg Schoener, Gastone Moschin, Peter Carsten

See *THE INVISIBLE MAN*

MOLE PEOPLE, THE

Universal, 1956, b&w, 78 min, VT

Producer: William Alland; **Director:** Virgil Vogel; **Screenplay:** Laszlo Gorog; **Cinematography:** Ellis W. Carter, A.S.C.; **Music:** Joseph Gershenson; **Special Effects:** Clifford Stine and Bud Westmore; **Cast:** John Agar, Cynthia Patrick, Hugh Beaumont, Alan Napier, Eddie Parker, Robin Hughes, Rodd Redwing, Frank Baxter, Nestor Paiva, Phil Cambers

Dr. Frank C. Baxter is giving a lecture about how far humans have gone into space in order to make the point that they haven't traveled very far inside Earth. Unable to dispute his steel-trap logic, the audience must watch as he presents every harebrained theory about civilizations existing inside our planet. At the conclusion he states that everything he just said was nonsense, offers up some more, and thus starts *The Mole People.*

The movie proper begins with a great deal of promise. A group of archaeologists (Agar, Beaumont, and others) discover an ancient Sumerian tablet and an oil lamp that detail the story of Noah's flood and the escape of the Sumerian royal family from the deadly waters, hinting that they established a new city atop a nearby mountain. That's good enough for this intrepid band. Instantly, they abandon their expedition, hoping that this chance discovery will pan out.

They reach the mountain, where they accidentally discover the underground city of the Sumerian's descendants. It's a civilization of albinos who survive by keeping a race of mole people as slaves. Our heroic scientists would be put to death except that their trusty flashlight marks them as gods to the light-sensitive cavern dwellers. Our heroes cozy up to the one Sumerian who isn't an albino or light-sensitive and a chorus girl (Patrick) who decides to do whatever they tell her to do. Eventually Agar and Beaumont escape along with Patrick when the mole people revolt. They climb to the surface, where Patrick is killed when an earthquake topples a pillar from an ancient city, crushing her as she glimpses the Sun for the first time.

There probably was a fine script at the beginning of filming this epic, but it got buried somewhere along the way in what film critic Leonard Maltin has called "probably the worst of Universal-International's 50s sci-fi movies." Where did it go so wrong?

It's not the actors. Agar and Beaumont, supported brilliantly by Nestor Paiva as another of the scientists, are top-notch throughout. The snappy dialogue these two banter back and forth gives the audience the impression that they're going to see a top-notch adventure film. When the Sumerian artifacts are discovered, the speeches about how many civilizations have rotted and crumbled since the beginning of time and how our own might be next are haunting and well delivered. When they first discover the underground civilization, they come across an ancient torture chamber. Examination of one skeleton prompts the line, "This one died from a blow to the head."

Which gets the response, "That's a sign of higher civilization."

The script, opposed to the plot, has wit throughout, and the actors deliver it all with flair. But this movie folds because of the spectacular lack of imagination from its writer and director and a terribly low budget. The ancient albinos wear bare-armed, skirted costumes, while the subhuman mole people wear high-necked black pajamas, presumably to save on creature makeup. The Sumerians can barely grow enough mushrooms to eat, so why do they allow the mole people (whom they have to feed) to live? The Albinos spend much time whipping the mole people, who just seem to stick around to be whipped. Since the mole people can burrow through the ground nearly as quickly as most people can swim, why don't they just go somewhere else—somewhere where no one wants to whip them?

The 1950s Universal lot turned out some of the finest science fiction of the time. Cinematographer Ellis W. Carter, musical director Joseph Gershenson, special effects wizard Clifford Stine, and makeup man Bud Westmore could always be counted on for at least a better-than-average job. Unfortunately, all too often they were teamed with hack writers and directors who turned their hard work into nonsense. The *The Mole People* may be the worst of those teamings.

MOM AND DAD SAVE THE WORLD

Warner Bros., 1992, Color, 88 min, VT, LD

Producer: Michael Phillips; **Director:** Greg Beeman **Screenplay:** Chris Matheson and Ed Solomon; **Cinematography:** Jacquet Haitkin; **Music:** Jerry Goldsmith and Robert Wait; **Special Effects:** Robert Habros, Richard Malzahn, Katherine Kean, Michael Muscal, and John T. Van Vliet; **Cast:** Teri Garr, Jeffrey Jones, Jon Lovitz, Thalmus Rasulala, Wallace Shawn, Eric Idle, Dwier Brown, Kathy Ireland

Evil Jon Lovitz rules a dreadful world where he sits dreaming of conquering Earth. Actually, he just wants to blow it up. After, that is, he kidnaps Teri Garr, who is his ideal woman. It's not the best science fiction comedy ever made, but not the worst either.

MONKEY'S UNCLE, THE

Walt Disney, 1965, Color, 91 min, VT

Producers: Walt Disney and Ron Miller; **Director:** Robert Stevenson; **Screenplay:** Tom August and Helen August; **Music:** Buddy Baker; **Special Effects:** Robert Mattey and Eustace Lycett; **cinematography:** Edward Coleman; **Cast:** Tommy Kirk, Leon Ames, Annette Funicello, Frank Faylen, Norman Grabowski, Arthur O'Connell

See *MISADVENTURES OF MERLIN JONES, THE,*

MONITORS, THE

Commonwealth, 1969, Color, 92 min, VT

Producer: Bernard Sahlins; **Director:** Jack Shea; **Screenplay:** Myron Gold; **Cinematography:** Vilmos Zsigmond; **Music:** Fred Katz; **Cast:** Guy Stockwell, Susan Oliver, Avery Schreiber, Sherry Jackson, Keenan Wynn, Alan Arkin, Larry Storch, Xavier Cugat, Jackie Vernon, Everett Dirksen, Stubby Kaye, Ed Begley, Shepherd Strudwick

Alien invaders conquer Earth in the most horrible way possible. They install monitoring satellites above the planet that keep humankind from harming itself. But don't worry, the usual rebels are in place to make sure we regain our right to knock each other silly. This movie had great promise, especially since it was based on a novel by one of science fiction's finest funnymen, Keith Laumer. Sadly, not enough of the book made it to the screen, and the hard-working cast can't save it.

MONKEY SHINES: AN EXPERIMENT IN FEAR

Orion Pictures, 1988, Color, 115 min, VT, LD

Producers: Charles Evans, Peter Grunwald, Peter R. McIntosh, and Gerald S. Paonessa; **Director:** George Romero; **Screenplay:** Romero and Michael Stewart; **Cinematography:** James A. Conter; **Music:** David Shire; **Special Effects:** Tom Savini and Steve Kirshoff; **Cast:** Jason Beghe, John Pankow, Kate McNeil, Joyce Van Patten, Christine Forrest, Stephen Root, Stanley Tucci, Janine Turner

A monkey gets a brain boost from an injection of human brain cells to make him the perfect helper for a quadriplegic. Things quickly get out of hand, and the film turns into a boring horror movie with little science fiction, less plot, and no reason to watch.

MONOLITH

EGM Film International (Germany), 1994, Color, 95 min, VT, LD

Producers: Stan Wertlieb and Michael Polaire; **Director:** John Eyres; **Screenplay:** Steven Lister and Eric Puppen; **Cinematography:** Alan M. Trow; **Music:** Frank Becker; **Special Effects:** Clint Colver, John C. Hartigan, William Mesa, John T. Van Vliet, and Introvision, International; **Cast:** Bill Paxton, Lindsay Frost, John Hurt, Louis Gossett, Jr., Paul Ganus, Musetta Vander, Andrew Lamond

A fine cast is wasted as cops chase an unbelievably unstoppable killer alien in this ill-conceived film.

MONOLITH MONSTERS, THE

Universal, 1957, b&w, 77 min, VT, LD

Producer: Howard Christie; **Director:** John Sherwood; **Screenplay:** Norman Jolley and Robert F. Fresco; **Cinematography:** Ellis W. Carter, A.S.C.; **Music:** Joseph Gershenson; **Special Effects:** Clifford Stine and Bud Westmore; **Cast:** Grant Williams, Lola Albright, Les Tremayne, Phil Harvey Trevor Bardette, Harvey Jackson, Richard Cutting, William Flatherty, Linda Scheley, Dean Cromer, Steve Darrell, William Schallert, Troy Donahue, Paul Peterson, Laurie Mitchell, Eddie Parker

This movie starts with a meteor hitting Earth. Fate brings a man from the Department of the Interior to the site, where water drips from his car radiator onto the dirt roadbed, striking a fragment from the meteorite. As the government man drives away, the rock inexplicably begins to sizzle. The fellow then takes one of the fragments back to his laboratory in town. But it isn't long before an accident ruins the lab, and our poor civil servant is turned to stone! He's found by his geologist partner, Dave Miller (Williams), who's at a loss for words.

At the same time, a field trip of grade-schoolers goes to the same part of the desert. Little Jenny picks up one of the meteorite fragments and takes it home as a souvenir. She wants to bring it into the house, but her mother tells her to leave the dirty thing outside. Of course, to Jenny, this means that washing the rock will make everything all right. It isn't long before Miller finds Jenny's home much the way he found his own lab—carnage everywhere and people turned to stone.

The mystery is cleared up as soon as a freak thunderstorm washes through the desert. In the morning, the horrible answer is obvious. The meteorite fragments respond to freshwater. Contact makes them grow through a crystallization process in which they reach freakish heights. Once they reach a size that can no longer bear their weight, they topple. When they strike the moisture-rich ground, they simply start growing again. Due to the natural geography of the area, the monoliths travel down a long valley. So far their progress has been slow, impeded by the shape of the land and the low moisture of the desert. But soon they will reach the town that lies at the end of the valley. After that, they'll be able to reach the entire world beyond. Earth itself will be buried under billions of tons towering silicate shafts.

Then Miller and his friends make a discovery. Saltwater not only doesn't cause the monoliths to grow, it actually dissolves them! Armed with his information, Miller blows up the nearby dam, confident he's timed the flow of the water so that it will pass through the nearby ancient seabed (the town was built there to mine the seabed for its salt) and flood the monoliths just as they reach the old riverbed.

Despite its outlandish premise (or perhaps because of it), *The Monolith Monsters* is one of the best of Universal's B movies. Most of the credit has to go to director Sherwood. For instance, in the beginning of the film, when the doomed Interior man returns to his office, the first thing he does is open the transom window before he gets on with his duties. The film has a number of these perfectly human moments, seconds of film wasted on nothing more than establishing a believable rhythm for the world being created. Movies such as *THE LEECH WOMAN* or *KILLERS FROM SPACE* lack such quality moments. Additionally, film fanatics still speak of legendary special effects man Clifford Stine as a genius. He certainly proves it here. He and his staff somehow managed to create the opening meteor strike, the many growing monolith scenes, the destruction of the dam and the resulting flood, along with all of the other effects on a budget under $72,500. Even in 1957 dollars, that's pretty impressive.

Another aspect of this picture that leaves so many others behind is its science. As the various scientists buzz about what is happening, they attack the problems and puzzles before them in rational, scientific ways. They think and muse and test, working out the challenge before them like real people, frightened people. The filmmakers also got their science right. The geology the characters speak of might be elementary, but it's correct.

Note: Star Grant Williams, who also brought the role of *THE INCREDIBLE SHRINKING MAN* to life, isn't the only reason to study the faces in this movie. *The Monolith Monsters* is filled with a bit players who carved out their own fame later. William Schallert of the *Star Trek* episode "The Trouble With Tribbles" is there, along with *Donna Reed Show*'s Paul Peterson. Laurie Mitchell, the *QUEEN OF OUTER SPACE*, put aside her crown to play a nurse, joining monster stunt man great Eddie Parker as a policeman and a very young Troy Donahue as yet another geologist. These are all uncredited appearances, so look sharp to catch them. Always notice the Universal B movies' famous backlot town. The same town square that got such a workout in the *BACK TO THE FUTURE* movies got a lot more use in the studio's black-and-white days. It serves here as well as it always does.

Another fun fact about this movie is that desert shooting was so cold, below freezing actually, that during the Lone Pine location work summer clothing–clad Williams actually had to sip ice water to chill himself before each shot so that his breath wouldn't show on camera.

MONSTER, THE

MGM, 1925, b&w, silent feature, VT

Producer: Roland West; **Director:** West; **Screenplay:** Willard Mack and Albert Kenyon; **Cinematography:** Hal Mohr; **Cast:** Lon Chaney, Gertrude Olmstead, Hallam Cooley, Johnny Arthur, Charles Sellon

Scientist Chaney thinks he can bring people back to life from the immortal beyond. MGM thought this was the perfect vehicle for lots of jokes. Neither one of them was right. Not for consumption by anyone still living.

MONSTER AND THE GIRL, THE
(aka: D.O.A., THE AVENGING BRAIN)

Paramount, 1941, b&w, 65 min, VT, LD

Producer: Jack Moss; **Director:** Stuart Heisler; **Screenplay:** Stuart Anthony; **Cinematography:** Victor Milner; **Cast:** George Zucco, Ellen Drew, Robert Paige, Onslow Stevens, Paul Lukas, Rod Cameron, Gerald Mohr, Joseph Calleia

First the evil gangsters force poor Ellen Drew into a life of prostitution. Then, when her brother is killed, mad scientist Zucco puts the poor boy's brain into the body of a gorilla. From there on the gorilla runs about town killing the evil gangsters. They don't make them like this anymore.

MONSTER FROM GREEN HELL, THE

DCA, 1958, b&w, 71 min, VT

Producer: Al Zimbalist; **Director:** Kenneth Crane; **Screenplay:** Louis Vittes and André Bohem; **Cinematography:** Ray Flin; **Music:** Albert Glasser; **Special Effects:** Jess Davison, Jack Rabin, and Louis DeWitt; **Cast:** Jim Davis, Barbara Turner, Robert E. Griffin, Eduardo Cianelli, Joel Fluellen, Vladimir Sokoloff

A spaceship is launched into orbit from Earth, and aboard is a batch of wasps. Radiation mutates the insects into giant killers who cause havoc when the ship crashlands in Africa. Scientists Davis and Turner battle the bugs to no effect until a volcano finally ends the movie.

MONSTER FROM THE
OCEAN FLOOR, THE

Lippert, 1954, b&w, 64 min, VT

Producer: Roger Corman; **Director:** Wyott Ordung; **Screenplay:** William Danch; **Cinematography:** Floyd Crosby; **Music:** André Brumer; **Cast:** Anne Kimball, Stuart Wade, Wyott Ordung

A giant squidlike creature is discovered on the ocean floor. It's clearly a big discovery because the thing has a light bulb glowing in its head, and how many sea creatures like that have been discovered? The creature is chased by a minisub that finally stops it by ramming it in the bulb.

MONSTER IN THE NIGHT

See *MONSTER ON THE CAMPUS*

MONSTER MAKER, THE

PRC, 1944, b&w, 64 min, VT, LD

Producer: Sigmund Newfeld; **Director:** Sam Newfield; **Screenplay:** Pierre Gendron and Martin Mooney; **Cinematography:** Robert Cline; **Music:** Albert Glasser; **Cast:** J. Carrol Naish, Ralph Morgan, Wanda McKay, Glenn Strange, Sam Flint, Terry Frost

Scientist Naish infects folks with the germs that cause acromegaly, a deforming disease in that proves somewhat more disgusting than entertaining.

MONSTER ON THE CAMPUS
(aka: MONSTER IN THE NIGHT)

Universal, 1958, b&w, 77 min, VT, LD

Producer: Joseph Gershenson; **Director:** Jack Arnold; **Screenplay:** David Duncan; **Cinematography:** Russell Metty, A.S.C.; **Music:** Gershenson; **Special Effects:** Clifford Stine and Bud Westmore; **Cast:** Arthur Franz, Joanna Moore, Troy Donahue, Eddie Parker, Whit Bissell, Alexander Lockwood, Helen Westcott

The film starts with the creation of "Modern Woman," or, more specifically, a mask of her. In the hall of science Professor Franz is making an impression of his best girl's face to use in the display of the "Faces Of Man" that hang there. He's already made one of himself to depict "Modern Man." The professor awaits the delivery of his coelacanth—a prehistoric fish believed to have died out in the time of the Jurassic—which has recently been caught alive and well off the shores of Madagascar. When the fish does arrive, a well-behaved German shepherd laps up some of the bloody water dripping from the thing's crate. Suddenly, the dog goes wild, even attacking its owner. It's subsequently caged, and an examination shows that it has mutated into a beast resembling its own wolfish ancestors. No one knows what to make of its condition, nor do they care at the moment. The university paid top dollar for the professor's fish, and he is determined to give them their money's worth.

Things get worse when the professor cuts himself on the fish's teeth and then makes the mistake of sticking his wounded hand into the bloody ice and water in which the fish was packed. He gets sick quite quickly, and a coworker takes him home. Later, when Franz's fiancée goes to see what's happened to him, she finds the coworker dead, hanging from a tree, and Franz's unconscious body nearby. Forensic evidence points to some kind of misshapen freak, however, so Franz is cleared of the crime. Soon he's teaching and studying his coelacanth once more.

Before long something else shows an interest in the ancient fish—a common dragonfly. The insect dines on a little fish blood and soon becomes its own two-foot-long ancestor. The professor figures out how to trap it, but some of the dragonfly's blood ends up in his pipe, and after a few puffs he again becomes the killer the police have been looking for. After another night of carnage, Franz is able to piece together the puzzle. Although Madagascar fishers have been eating the coelacanths for years, the one sent to the professor had been hit with gamma rays to preserve it.

Franz knows he's the "Monster on the Campus" and determines to do something about it. He could just keep quiet, but that wouldn't be responsible. So the professor transforms himself on purpose and then attacks the police. He's killed before anyone knows what has happened. Justice is served.

Despite its corny title, this is another of the best B movies produced by Universal. Ace veteran Jack Arnold did a tremendous job bringing this rather routine story to life. His usual infusion of real-life antics, inserted to give his movies a feel of reality, is evident here. The best example is the "Use Other Door" sign in Franz's lab. Everyone uses that door, going to any lengths to avoid the door they're supposed to use. As always, Arnold does a magnificent job of humanizing the characters.

Monster on the Campus is interesting for more reasons than just its direction, however. The tale was inspired by two actual occurrences. A living, prehistoric coelacanth really was caught in the waters off Madagascar, and at the same time Russian scientists began to advance the theory that radiation could cause mutation. The script, however, does more than just blend these contemporary facts with the idea of Dr. Jekyll and Mr. Hyde. The film's central point is that humanity is always less than a generation away from savagery. Arnold adds a number of subtle, subconscious clues to the action by his use of the masks hanging in the hall of science. At times when Franz speaks, the mask of Modern Man is hanging just over his head or just behind his shoulder. At other moments, however, when the mutation is about to occur, the mask of Primitive Man looms behind him.

Tricks like this make the film a science fiction classic. The monsters, while evident, are not the main point. This is a message movie, a message pounded home often—thinking that humankind has created much but could lose it all in an instant. Cool and rational, it promises no happy ending, but continues to slam home the point that humanity is a lucky accident, and that if it doesn't take responsibility for its actions, it will end up back in the swamp with the rest of evolution's mistakes.

This is never more evident than when Franz delivers one of the great speeches in sci-fi filmdom. Halfway through the picture, he informs his students that the coelacanth is a creature unchanged in 200 million years and so has obviously stabilized as a species.

> In the case of man, we have a recent species which is not stabilized at all. Man is not only capable of change, but man alone, among all living creatures, can choose the direction in which that change will take place. In other words, man can use his knowledge to destroy all spiritual values and reduce the race to bestiality. Or, he can use his knowledge to increase his understanding, to a point far beyond anything now imaginable. Think it over, that's all for today.

Class dismissed.

Note: One should always keep a sharp lookout for the Universal B movies' famous backlot town. The same town square that got such a workout in the BACK TO THE FUTURE movies got a lot more use in the studio's black-and-white days. During this film early on there is a terrific shot of the Munsters' home, right there in the middle of Marty McFly's hometown.

MONSTERS OF THE NIGHT

See *THE NAVY VERSUS THE NIGHT MONSTERS*

MONSTER THAT CHALLENGED THE WORLD, THE

United Artists, 1957, b&w, 85 min, VT, LD

Producers: Arthur Gardner and Jules Levy; **Director:** Arnold Laven; **Screenplay:** Pat Fielder and David Duncan; **Cinematography:** Lester White and Scotty Welborn; **Music:** Heinz Roemheld; **Special Effects:**

Robert Crandell, Edward S. Haworth, and August Lohman; **Cast:** Tim Holt, Audrey Dalton, Hans Conreid, Casey Adams

Atomic radiation strikes again, this time creating a race of giant mollusks that have to be stopped before humanity is doomed. Slow-paced but fairly intelligent, this movie features pretty good special effects for its time.

MONSTER WITH THE GREEN EYES

See *PLANET AGAINST US*

MONSTROSITY
(aka: THE ATOMIC BRAIN)

Emerson, 1964, b&w, 72 min, VT

Producers: Jack Pollexfen and Dean Dillman, Jr.; **Director:** Joseph Mascelli; **Screenplay:** Vy Russell, Sue Dwiggens, and Dillman, Jr.; **Cinematography:** Alfred Taylor; **Music:** Gene Kauer; **Special Effects:** Ken Strickgaden; **Cast:** Frank Gerstle, Erika Peters, Judy Bamber, Frank Fowler, Marjorie Eaton, Bradford Dillman

Mad doctors conduct evil brain transplants. The title, *Mosntrosity*, is a pretty good description of the end results.

MOON 44

Centropolis, 1990, Color, 102 min, VT, LD

Producers: Roland Emmerich, Ute Emmerich, Dean Heyde, Carsten H.W. Lorenz, and Michael Scurding; **Director:** Roland Emmerich; **Screenplay:** Emmerich, Oliver Eberle, P.J. Mitchell, and Heyde; **Cinematography:** Karl Walter Lindeniaub; **Music:** Joel Goldsmith; **Special Effects:** Volker Engel and Theo Nischwitz; **Cast:** Michael Paré, Lisa Eichhorn, Malcolm McDowell, Dean Devlin, Brian Thompson, Stephen Geoffreys, Mechmed Yilmaz, Leon Rippy, Roscoe Lee Browne

Roughly a century in the future, a ruthless corporation forces captives on a moon it claims to own to defend that claim against a rival corporation. A lesser effort from the Emmerich/Devlin team. Better to pass this over and go on believing that *STARGATE* was this pair's first effort.

MOON PILOT

Disney/Buena Vista, 1962, color, 98 min, VT

Producers: Walt Disney and Bill Anderson; **Director:** James Neilsen; **Screenplay:** Maurice Tombragal; **Cinematography:** William E. Snyder; **Music:** Paul Smith; **Special Effects:** Eustance Lycett; **Cast:** Tom Tryon, Brian Keith, Tommy Kirk, Edmond O'Brien, Dany Saval, Bob Sweeney, Kent Smith

NASA is concerned about the next pilot they're about to send up (Tryon). It seems they just sent a chimp up who's come back with some terrible personality quirks. Luckily, the hero has attracted the attention of a lovely spacegirl (Saval), who gives him the secret of how to coat his ship so that he won't go moon mad. The two go on Tryon's mission together, making a side trip to her home planet to meet her parents. This movie is awfully dated and is ample fare only for small, nondiscriminating children.

MOONTRAP

Magic Films, 1989, Color, 92 min, VT, LD

Producers: John Cameron, Brian C. Manoogian, James A. Courtney, Robert Dyke, Stephen Roberts, and Alan M. Solomon; **Director:** Dyke; **Screenplay:** Tex Ragsdale; **Cinematography:** Peter Klein; **Music:** Joseph LoDuca; **Special Effects:** Dale Jones and Gary Jones; **Cast:** Walter Koenig, Bruce Campbell, Leigh Lombardi, Robert Kurcz

An over-the-hill shuttle pilot (Koenig) and his young partner (Campbell) are sent to the Moon to examine an alien artifact. The only problem is that the artifact is actually a murder machine left behind to take care of Earth. This highly imaginative and intelligent film is a terrific romp for Koenig and Campbell fans, but it suffers from a very small budget and some odd direction.

MOON ZERO TWO

Hammer Films (Great Britain)/Warner Bros. (U.S.), 1969, Color, 100 min, VT

Producer: Michael Carreras; **Director:** Roy Ward Baker; **Screenplay:** Carreras; **Cinematography:** Paul Beeson; **Music:** Philip Martell; **Special Effects:** Les Bowie, Kit West, and Nick Allder; **Cast:** James Olson, Catherine von Schell, Warren Mitchell, Dudley Fos-

ter, Michael Ripper, Neil McCallum, Ori Levy, Adrienne Corri

This science fiction/western takes place in 2021, when shuttle pilot Olson is forced by a vile bunch of hombres into stealing a pure sapphire asteroid. However, the hero's inner morality gets the better of him and he turns on the gang and foils their dastardly plans. It's claim-jumping in the craters and love among the stars, but it's not very good. That this movie was made at the same time men were actually landing on the Moon shows a poor sense of judgment. Despite rather convincing effects, there is little appeal here.

MORONS FROM OUTER SPACE

Thorn EMI Screen Entertainment, 1985, Color, 87 min, VT

Producer: Barry Hanson; **Director:** Mike Hodges; **Screenplay:** Griff Rhys Jones and Mel Smith; **Cinematography:** Phil Meheux; **Music:** Peter Brewis; **Special Effects:** Martin Gutteridge and Effects Associate, Ltd.; **Cast:** Griff Rhys Jones, Mel Smith, James B. Sikking, Dinsdale Landen, Jimmy Nail, Joannie Pearce, Paul Brown

A pair of completely idiotic aliens crash-land their spaceship on Earth, and the comedy begins. This uneven string of sight gags has no claim to a great story, but is smug about its ability to make anyone howl sooner or later.

MORTAL ORBIT

See *MISSION STARDUST*

MOST DANGEROUS MAN ALIVE, THE

Columbia, 1961, b&w, 82 min

Producer: Benedict Bogeaus; **Director:** Allan Dwan; **Screenplay:** James Leicester and Philip Rock; **Cinematography:** Carl Carvahal; **Music:** Louis Forbest; **Cast:** Ron Randell, Morris Ankrum, Debra Paget, Joel Donte, Elaine Stewart, Anthony Caruso, Gregg Palmer

An escaped convict is rewarded with a dose of radiation that makes his skin as hard as iron. He runs around for a while, but in the end he crumbles into a pile of rust. This was director Dwan's last film.

MOST DANGEROUS MAN IN THE WORLD, THE

See *THE CHAIRMAN*

MOTHRA

Toho (Japan), 1961/Columbia (U.S.), 1962, Color, 100 min, VT

Producer: Tomoyuki Tanaka; **Director:** Inoshiro Honda; **Screenplay:** Shinichi Sekizawa; **Cinematography:** Hajime Koizumi; **Music:** Yuji Koseki; **Special Effects:** Eiji Tsuburaya; **Cast:** Lee Kresel Emi Itoh, Yumi Itoh, Frankie Sakai, Hiroshi Koizumi, Kyoko Kagawa, Ken Ueghara

The miniature priestesses of an ancient god are stolen from their South Pacific home. The pair try to convince the evil showman who has stolen them that there'll be the devil to pay if he doesn't release them, but he laughs in their faces and then forces them to sing in his nightclub. This is all right by the priestesses, as their singing is the homing beacon for their vengeful god. Sure enough, just as the little women warned their kidnapper, their god, a giant caterpillar, comes after them. Science and the military try to stop the thing, but to no avail. The caterpillar is tough enough, but then it stops to spin a cocoon that the military, in its infinite wisdom, decides to burn. The heat only spurs the transformation inside, and the caterpillar emerges as a full-grown giant moth that then really takes Japan apart until it recovers its priestesses, at which point it flies off for home.

In many ways just another typical Japanese giant creature movie, but highly watchable nonetheless. By far one of the most absurd of all the Toho monster movies, *Mothra* relies on farce more than it does on its star. The situation set up by the kidnapping of the mini-priestesses cannot be viewed rationally. One can only suspend disbelief and enjoy the silliness or simply not watch the film. The miniature effects throughout are stunning, although Mothra itself is somewhat laughable, especially after the transformation. Nonetheless, the film is a classic of its subgenre. The beloved bug returned in many a further Toho classic, but Mothra's first appearance has always been its best.

MOTOR CAR OF THE FUTURE

Messter (Germany), 1910, b&w, silent short

Flying cars at the turn of the last century. This one flies off to Saturn.

MOTOR CHAIR, THE

Italia (Italy), 1911, b&w, silent short

A mechanical chair proves to have a mind all its own.

MOTORIST, THE

(Great Britain), 1906, b&w, silent short

Producer: R.W. Paul; **Director:** Walter R. Booth

This time it isn't the car itself, but the fuel that has automobiles flying into outer space.

MOTOR VALET, THE

Alpha (Great Britain), 1906, b&w, silent short

Director: Arthur Cooper

A mechanical manservant wrecks his master's house and then explodes.

MOUSE ON THE MOON, THE

United Artists, 1963, Color, 82 min

Producer: Walter Shenson; **Director:** Richard Lester; **Screenplay:** Michael Pertwee; **Music:** Ron Grainer; **Cinematography:** Wilkie Cooper; **Cast:** Margaret Rutherford, Bernard Cribbins, Ron Moody, Terry Thomas, Michael Crawford

See *THE MOUSE THAT ROARED*

MOUSE THAT ROARED, THE

Columbia, 1959, Color, 85 min, VT, LD

Producer: Walter Shenson; **Director:** Jack Arnold; **Screenplay:** Roger MacDougall and Stanley Mann; **Cinematography:** John Wilcox; **Music:** Edwin Astley; **Cast:** Peter Sellers, Jean Seberg, David Kossoff, Leo McKern, Monty Landis, Timothy Bateson, William Hartnell

The story starts in the Grand Duchy of Fenwick, which is in a bit of trouble. The California wine market is having an adverse affect on Fenwick wine. Some countries might file a protest at the United Nations, but not Fenwick. This country decides to declare war on the United States, instead. Their reasoning is simple. They're a postage stamp of a country. The United States will beat them in 20 seconds, as they do everywhere they have a war. Then the United States is certain to spend billions to get Fenwick on its feet again. It's a great plan, but there's only one problem: the U.S. doesn't win the war; Fenwick does.

Through a series of comic misunderstandings, the duchy comes into possession of America's top scientist and his most deadly bomb. This sets off a worldwide panic. Suddenly, every country wants to become Fenwick's ally, and the little country is in more trouble than ever.

This is a dated picture but a charming one nevertheless. Peter Sellers plays three different roles with handy aplomb and provides much fun for the whole family, as does the sequel, *The Mouse on the Moon*. In this one, the Grand Duchy of Fenwick beats the rest of the world to the Moon by using a rocket fuel made from local wine. Both movies suffer slightly from extremely dated humor and politics, but they still have enough nutty fun to make them enjoyable.

MR. INVISIBLE

See *MISTER SUPERINVISIBLE*

MR. JOSEPH YOUNG OF AFRICA

See *KING KONG*; *MIGHTY JOE YOUNG* (1949)

MULTIPLICITY

Columbia, 1996, Color, 117 min, VT, LD, DVD

Producers: Trevor Albert, Harold Ramis, Lee R. Mayes, Suzanne Herrington, and Whitney White; **Director:** Ramis; **Screenplay:** Lowell Ganz, Mary Hale, Babaloo Mandel, and Chris Miller; **Cinematography:** László Kovács; **Music:** George Fenton; **Special Effects:** Richard Edlund, Michelle Moen, Donna Langston, Mark H. Pompian, Tom Ryba, Brian Samuels, David A. Smith, and Michael Sweeney; **Cast:** Michael Keaton, Andie MacDowell, Harris Yulin, Richard Masur, Eugene Levy, Ann Cusack, Brian Doyle-Murray

A working man (Keaton) who feels that the world just wants too much of him hits on the perfect solution to his problems—he has himself cloned. One clone works out so well that he has another created. Then the clones start having clones made. And all of them want to sleep with Keaton's wife (MacDowell). That's only one of the problems. A much bigger monkey wrench is that each

new clone comes out missing some basic part of the original Keaton. It's a good premise, and Keaton handles the various identities of the clones with a masterful comedic hand, but the plot wears thin far too early.

MUPPETS FROM SPACE

Columbia, 1999, Color, 82 min, VT, DVD

Producers: Brian Henson, Martin G. Baker, Kristine Belson, and Stephanie Allain; **Director:** Tim Hill; **Screenplay:** Jerry Juhl, Joseph Mazzarino, and Ken Kaufman; **Cinematography:** Alan Caso; **Music:** Jamshied Sharifi; **Special Effects:** Thomas G. Smith, Raul M. Wagner, Rose Neighbors, David B. Sharp Productions, CFC/MVFX, Dreamscape Imagery, Inc., and Perpetual Motion Pictures; **Cast:** The Muppet Performers: Dave Goelz, Steve Whitmore, Bill Barretta, Frank Oz, *and* Jeffrey Tambor, F. Murray Abraham, David Arquette, Josh Charles, Kathy Griffin, Pat Hingle, Hollywood Hogan, Ray Liotta, Andie MacDowell, Rob Schneider

On a quest with his buddy Rizzo the Rat, Gonzo the Great seeks his alien ancestors. After announcing on the talk show UFOMania that he is an extraterrestrial and that he is seeking his nearest kinfolk, Gonzo becomes the target of a secret government cabal of alien hunters. This leads to the usual Muppet mayhem, silliness, and song and dance numbers.

One of the best of the Muppets' big-screen outings. After a number of clunkers, the team in charge decided to get back to basics and allow the world's most beloved puppets to do again what made them so beloved in the first place. Although there isn't that much science fiction, it really doesn't matter. This movie is a comedy for all ages. All Muppet fans are heartily encouraged to try this one.

Note: The film includes a wonderful spoof of a scene from the movie *Independence Day*. Muppet fans who enjoyed *ID4* would be advised to pay attention for this extra chuckle.

MURDER BY TELEVISION

Imperial, 1935, b&w, 60 min

Producers: William M. Pizor, Clifford Sanforth, and Edward M. Spitz; **Director:** Clifford Sanforth; **Screenplay:** Joseph O'Donnell; **Cinematography:** James S. Brown Jr. and Arthur Reed; **Music:** Oliver Wallace; **Special Effects:** Henry Spitz; **Cast:** Bela Lugosi, June Collyer, George Meeker, Hattie McDaniel

Want to kill your enemies? This film has the answer. Hide your death ray inside a television camera. Then get your victim to stand in front of the camera while you phone because the telephone is the trigger for the death ray.

MUTANT

See *FORBIDDEN WORLD*

MUTANT II

See *ALIEN PREDATOR*

MUTATIONS (aka: THE FREAKMAKER)

Columbia, 1974, Color, 92 min, VT

Producer: Robert D. Weinbach; **Director:** Jack Cardiff; **Screenplay:** Weinbach and Edward Mann; **Cinematography:** Paul Beeson; **Music:** Basil Kirchin; **Special Effects:** Ken Middleham and Charles Parker; **Cast:** Donald Pleasence, Tom Baker, Brad Harris, Julie Ege, Michael Dunn, Jill Haworth, Willie Ingram, Esther Blackmon, Hugh Baily, Felix Duarte, Molly Tweedle, Kathy Kitchen

Mad Doc Nolter (Pleasence) is convinced that humankind's survival in this horror of a world lies in crossbreeding humans and plants. He begins to experiment on his students and anyone else helpless enough to get in his way. As might be expected, things don't work out the way he thought they would. Nolter is killed by the monstrous results of his tampering with his daughter's fiancé. Pleasence is his usual wonderful self, and he carries this somewhat slight film handily. Gruesomely disgusting effects are on hand for those not enamored of Pleasence's acting.

MUTILATOR, THE

See *THE DARK*

MUTINY IN OUTER SPACE

Allied Artists/Woolner, 1964, b&w, 82 min

Producers: Hugo Grimaldi and Arthur Pierce; **Director:** Grimaldi; **Screenplay:** Pierce; **Cinematography:** Archie Dalzell; **Music:** Gordon Zahler; **Special Effects:** Roger George; **Cast:** William Leslie, Dolores Faith, Pamela Curran, Richard Garland, Harold Lloyd, Jr., James Dobson, Glenn Langan

The inhabitants of a space station are attacked by a creeping space fungus. The growth first covers the station and then begins knocking off the astronauts within.

MY FAVORITE MARTIAN

Walt Disney Studios, 1999, Color, 90 min, VT, DVD

Producers: Robert Shapiro, Jerry Leider, and Mark Toberoff; **Director:** Donald Petrie; **Screenplay:** Sherri Stoner and Deanna Oliver; **Cinematography:** Thomas Ackerman, A.S.C.; **Music:** John Debney; **Special Effects:** Phil Tippett and John T. Van Vliet; **Cast:** Christopher Lloyd, Jeff Daniels, Elizabeth Hurley, Daryl Hannah, Wallace Shawn, Christine Ebersole, Michael Lerner, Ray Walston, Shelley Malil, Jeremy Hotz, Troy Evans

The setting is the surface of Mars. One of those amazing NASA land crawlers moves across the Martian terrain, picking up soil samples and looking for more rocks to analyze. It rolls up to a beauty, and then, sadly, its batteries finally run out of power. NASA is well pleased, however; they had to spend only $50 billion to get 12 new rocks to experiment upon. But while the government types slap themselves on the back, the camera pulls up to show what the land crawler would have come across if it had had just another iota of power—a massive Martian city built in a Grand Canyon–sized crevice, complete with dozens of personal spacecraft filling the air.

As one might guess, this is the opening for the Walt Disney Studios' feature film version of *My Favorite Martian*, the hit CBS television series that ran from 1963 through 1966. The story from this point remains much the same as the old show. An unfriendly, cantankerous, yet playful Martian (Lloyd) crash-lands on Earth. He is discovered by a friendly human, Tim O'Hara (Daniels), a reporter who has just lost his job and who thinks having discovered a Martian is a great way to get it back. O'Hara quickly forgets about exploiting his discovery, however, and instead allows Lloyd to hide his damaged ship in his garage while they try to repair it. The Martian poses as his human companion's Uncle Martin, and the two get into the same kind of high jinks as their '60s predecessors. Even the Martian's odd metal antenna sliding up out of his head is still in place.

The filmmakers deserve credit for bringing Ray Walston, star of the original, back for more than just a cameo. However, besides that gesture, all this film has to offer are fast gags, wild stunts, and tons of outrageous computer graphics, puppets, animatronics, and first-rate special effects. There's plenty here for kids, but little for adults.

The filmmakers all professed to be fanatics of the TV show, and there's nothing in the film to prove them wrong. The main problem is that it is uninspired and annoyingly pat. Daryl Hannah, who secretly loves Jeff Daniels, is coming over to his apartment. Of course this is when Elizabeth Hurley decides to go to fellow reporter Daniels's place to steal his story. When Hannah gets there, she finds Hurley and so becomes jealous. She doesn't catch anyone doing anything. She doesn't have even the benefit of a wildly hysterical misunderstanding to make sense of her hurt feelings. That's the main problem with this movie. Everything is flatly predictable. There are no surprises, no big laughs, no real entertainment. It's as if the entire production was thrown together in a week and a half.

There's a greater problem, however. A trend at Disney in the late '90s was to take pleasant little properties from the '50s and '60s and remake them with excessive violence that the originals didn't need. Disney's bizarrely dark remake of MIGHTY JOE YOUNG (see KING KONG) comes to mind, and this film suffers the same fate. When government soldiers shoot down Uncle Martin's walking, talking space suit, that's one thing, but when Daryl Hannah is temporarily transformed into an alien, she devours a human being. Later, she changes back to human form with no reference to the human life she took.

MY SCIENCE PROJECT

Buena Vista, 1985, Color, 94 min, VT, LD, DVD

Producer: Jonathan T. Taplin; **Director:** Jonathan Beteul; **Screenplay:** Beteul; **Music:** Peter Bernstein; **Cinematography:** David M. Walsh; **Cast:** John Stockwell, Danielle Von Zemeck, Fisher Stevens, Raphael Sbarge, Dennis Hopper, Barry Corbin, Richard Masur, Ann Wedgeworth

Lost for ideas for their science project, high school students raid an air force junk pile. They come across an alien device that can transmute time and space, and they decide that this would make the best science project ever. As much as one might want to believe in a military unable to compete with high school students when it comes to getting otherworldly technology to work, this film falls apart on many levels. The special effects are adequate, but the politics are offensive and useless, and Dennis Hopper is wasted.

Note: For those who can't resist a Dennis Hopper performance, pay attention to his costume at the end of the film. When he returns from his time travel adventure back in the '60s, he's wearing the same outfit he did in his classic '60s film, *Easy Rider.*

MY STEPMOTHER IS AN ALIEN

Weintraub Entertainment Group, 1988, Color, 108 min, VT, LD, DVD

Producers: Art Levinson, Franklin R. Levy, Ronald M. Parker, and Laurence Mark; **Director:** Richard Benjamin; **Screenplay:** Timothy Harris, Jerico Stone, Jonathan Reynolds, and Herschel Weingrud; **Music:** Alan Silvestri; **Special Effects:** Grant McCune; **Cinematography:** Richard H. Kline; **Cast:** Dan Aykroyd, Kim Basinger, Jon Lovitz, Alyson Hannigan, Joseph Maher, Ann Prentiss, Seth Green, Wesley Mann, Harry Shearer

Widower scientist Aykroyd wants to find life on other worlds. To achieve this he keeps destroying valuable equipment by overloading it at the research center where he works. Due to a wet jacket with metal buttons left too close to the equipment, his beacon is boosted beyond his wildest dreams. At the same time the damage to the systems is astronomical.

Aykroyd is fired, and his dreams of ever reaching an extraterrestrial with his broadcasts seem to come to a crashing halt. But the beam transmitted that night had an adverse affect on a highly advanced planet several solar systems away. If he doesn't send another beam soon, the effect will reach critical mass and the planet will be destroyed. What to do? Send a fabulously incredible female operative (Basinger) to get him to send another signal. These aliens have studied Earth—they know Earthmen will betray their ideals, their wives, children, mothers, and countries for a pretty face. What could be easier?

At this point the film breaks down into a series of comedy routines. Basinger has to get Aykroyd to send the signal again. Relying on her alien abilities (the usual bag of unrelated, illogical powers) as well as the thing in her purse (her partner? assistant? cyborg computer?—it's never explained) to feed her information, she finds the good doctor, invades his life, gets him his job back, and even marries him. It's all in the line of duty, of course. She has to save her world.

Along the way she falls in love with him, as well as with the entire sensation of being human. Then comes the big news—the high council of her planet has decreed that since an Earthman possesses the ability to destroy their world, as soon as the signal is sent again, Earth must be destroyed. Will she do it? Can Aykroyd even do it again if he wants to? The questions are typical, the plot holds few surprises, and the science is bad, even for a comedy. On the other hand, the jokes are often pretty good. There are few dated bits, and Aykroyd is more of the old school of comedy. Who else in the 1980s would hinge the safety of the planet on a Jimmy Durante song and dance routine?

Note: The film features one of Jon Lovitz's finest performances. Lovitz, the Whit Bissell of comedy, certainly steals the show.

MYSTERIANS, THE

Toho (Japan), 1957/RKO (U.S.), 1959, Color, 89 min, VT

Producer: Tomoyuki Tanaka; **Director:** Inoshiro Honda; **Screenplay:** Takeshi Kimura; **Cinematography:** Hajime Koizumi; **Music:** Akira Ifukube; **Special Effects:** Eiji Tsuburaya; **Cast:** Kenji Sahara, Yumi Shirakawa, Momoko Kochi, Takashi Shimura, Akihiko Hirata

Millennia ago, the planet Mysteroid was destroyed. Those inhabitants who escaped eventually make their way to Earth. Setting up a base on the Moon and then one on the planet itself, the Mysterians demand Earthwomen so that they can start breeding. No one on Earth likes this idea, and so the demands are rejected and war begins.

This is one of the best science fiction movies ever produced in Japan. Although still nothing more than pulp fiction, it moves in a linear, understandable progression without the inanity inherent in most Toho productions. The special effects are highly respectable, and the miniature work is the usual stunning display.

MYSTERIOUS CONTRAGRAV, THE

Gold Seal, 1915, b&w, silent short

Producer: Henry McRae; **Screenplay:** McRae

Another turn-of-the-century scientist is just too far ahead of his time. This one discovers how to use negative electricity to create antigravity.

MYSTERIOUS ISLAND

Columbia, 1961, Color, 100 min, VT, LD

Producer: Charles H. Schneer; **Director:** Cy Endfield; **Screenplay:** John Prebble, Daniel Ullman, and Crane Wilber; **Cinematography:** Wilkie Cooper and Egil Woxholt; **Music:** Bernard Herrmann; **Special Effects:** Ray Harryhausen; **Cast:** Michael Craig, Joan Greenwood, Michael Callan, Gary Merrill, Herbert Lom, Beth Rogan

Prisoners in a Southern prison camp during the Civil War escape in a hot air balloon. However, the escapees can't control the balloon, which takes them out to sea during a terrible storm. Eventually, the runaways wash up on a tropical island. The men discover two female castaways and then learn that the island is home to a variety of gigantic creatures. It is also home to some advanced force that refuses to show itself but which remains in the background, watching the castaways and helping them from time to time.

Finally, the beachcombers discover that their guardian angel is the one and only Captain Nemo. His great submarine, the *Nautilus*, is there at the island, docked in an underground grotto. Unfortunately for the castaways, the sub is no longer mobile. But Nemo has a plan for helping them escape the island. He suggests they use their original balloon to raise a pirate ship Nemo had sank while defending the castaways. They repair the balloon, insert it in the pirate ship, repair the damaged hull, and then start filling the balloon with air through the use of the *Nautilus*'s still functional bellows. A volcano erupts at that moment, cutting things close. Nemo and the *Nautilus* are sent to their graves, but the castaways escape.

There have been five film versions of Jules Verne's classic second tale of Captain Nemo, but the most famous, and certainly the most entertaining, is this 1961 epic. The acting is top-notch, and with effects by the legendary Ray Harryhausen, enhanced by one of equally legendary Bernard Herrmann's finest sound tracks, it remains unsurpassed.

The first adaptation, filmed in a two-color process in 1929 by MGM, features Lionel Barrymore as Count Dakker. He has submarines and underwater cities, but he does nothing with them that would satisfy current audiences.

The Soviet Children's Film Studio used Captain Nemo in a 1941 version, but they saddled the good seaman with a group of youngsters. This one should be avoided, as should the 1950 black-and-white, 15-chapter serial. Although also done by Columbia, which would eventually do the job correctly, sitting through this would be painful indeed. The 1972 version with Omar Sharif as Captain Nemo, a joint French/Italian venture, is above average, but still well below the quality of the 1961 version.

Note: Many viewers have complained that the giant crab in the film is a cheap effect, something akin to the monitor lizards superimposed around full-sized actors so popular in other science fiction movies of the time. Nothing could be more mistaken. Harryhausen did indeed use a real crab, but it was a dead one that the effects wizard took apart and reconstructed with wire insides so that it could be used like any of his other stop-frame animation puppets.

MYSTERIOUS INVADER, THE

See *THE ASTOUNDING SHE-MONSTER*

MYSTERY SCIENCE THEATER 3000: THE MOVIE

Gramercy Pictures, 1996, Color, 73 min, VT, LD, DVD

Producer: Trace Beaulien, Jim Mallon, and Kevin Murphy; **Director:** Mallon; **Screenplay:** Michael Nelson, Joel Hodgson, Paul Chaplin, Bridget Jones, Mary Jo Peter, Beaulien, Mallon, and Murphy; **Music:** Billy Barber, Charlie Erickson, and Hodgson; **Special Effects:** PM Effects, Eric Howell, Paul Murphy, Dreamstate Effects, and Cinema Research Corporation; **Cinematography:** Jeff Stonehouse; **Cast:** Michael J. Nelson, Trace Beaulieu, Kevin Murphy, Jim Mallon, John Brady

Mike Nelson is a human trapped aboard a spaceship where he and his robot crew are forced to watch old movies that are constantly beamed to them. The three sit in the lower right-hand corner of the screen and crack wise as the films play. In this theatrical version of their television show, Mike and his robots attack an edited version of the 1955 film *THIS ISLAND EARTH*. The movie version of the television show isn't as long as a TV episode or quite as funny, and nothing particularly special was done to distinguish the film from any regular outing.

Note: Those who must watch should keep their eyes peeled for two extremely "in" MST3K gags. At the beginning of the film, Mike Nelson reads a status report, which is really a copy of "Satellite News," the MST3K Information Club's official newsletter. Later, a control panel for a pair of robotic arms is shown, labeled "Manos." *Manos* is the Spanish word for "hands." Here, however, it stands for *Manos, the Hands of Fate,* the show's pronounced "worst movie we ever showed."

MYSTERIOUS MR. M, THE

Universal, 1946, b&w, serial, 13 chapters

Directors: Vernon Keays and Lewis D. Collins; **Screenplay:** Joseph Poland, Paul Huston, and Barry Shipman; **Cinematography:** Gus Peterson; **Cast:** Richard Martin, Dennis Moore, Pamela Blake, Jane Randolph, Danny Norton, Edmund MacDonald

A noted inventor is snatched by bad guys, and good guys chase after him for 13 episodes. There's the mysterious drug, Hypnotrene, and the mysterious enemy that uses it, but most of all there is the mystery of why anyone would care.

MYSTERY MEN

Universal, 1999, Color, 111 min

Producers: Robert Engelman, Lawrence Gordon, Mike Richardson, and Lloyd Levin; **Director:** Kinka Usher; **Screenplay:** Neil Cuthbert; **Cinematography:** Stephen H. Burum, A.S.C.; **Music:** Stephen Warbeck; **Special Effects:** Terry Frazee, Geno Crum, Carole A. Kenneally, Ronald Myers; **Cast:** Hank Azaria, Janeane Garofalo, William H. Macy, Kep Mitchell, Paul Reubens, Ben Stiller, Wes Studi, Greg Kinnear, Eddie Izzard, Lena Olin, Geoffrey Rush, Clair Forlani, Louise Lasser, Tom Waits, Prakazrel Michel

Champion City—a town so large that it makes Los Angeles look like Newark—is a thriving community of decent, hardworking folk who go about their lives relatively free of worries from crime. The reason? Champion City is home to Captain Amazing (Kinnear), the world's greatest superhero. In fact, he may be too great for his own good. The captain has rendered the city virtually crime-free, a bad thing for his commercial endorsements. But don't worry, the captain has a plan.

Captain Amazing arranges for his old nemesis, Casanova Frankenstein (Rush), to be released from the insane asylum. His motive is simple—he's sure Frankenstein will provide him with a great battle that will put him back in the spotlight. After that, he's certain that his corporate sponsors will stop pulling out their support. Everything goes off without a hitch, except for one little thing. Casanova Frankenstein wins the battle, leaving Champion City defenseless before this most terrible of monsters. What can be done? Who will protect the city?

Obviously from the title, that would be the Mystery Men, no heroes in the class of Captain Amazing. They

Mystery Men (UNIVERSAL STUDIOS / AUTHOR'S COLLECTION)

are, as one of them puts it, "the other guys." Guys like Roy, aka Mr. Furious (Stiller), who has a dead-end job at a junkyard where his terrible boss abuses his violent temper to the breaking point. Then there is Jeffrey, aka Blue Raja (Azaria). He lives at home with his mother, where he spends his time locked in his room burning incense and throwing forks and spoons at pretend attackers. Clad in his son's baseball vest and roller-blade kneepads, Eddie, aka the Shoveler (Macy), is an expert at wielding a shovel. He desperately longs for the support of his family, but instead he is constantly scolded by his wife for staying out late to fight crime. Together they are a trio of working-class folk with minor to nonexistent superabilities at best, but they are undeniably entertaining.

Mystery Men may be one of the best live action superhero movie ever made. How can a comedy about a group of loser superheroes surpass Christopher Reeve's Superman or Michael Keaton's Batman? The simple answer: better story, better editing, and a lot more heart.

The story may be comedy, but it isn't slapstick. This is a tale about ordinary, blue collar people who want to make a difference in their world. In the tradition of *The Magnificent Seven*, each character on the team has a different reason for being there and something different to prove to himself. Although the story uses outrageous props in an outlandish setting, it is deadly serious, and often quite touching. Also, unlike many previous superhero films, this one clearly loves its characters. All of the Mystery Men are flawed in some way, but it is clear we are meant to think of them as good people. After all, while the world stands by, they're actually doing something about evil.

There's nothing easy about their brand of crime fighting. Indeed, it is particularly painful to watch some of their battles as the villains land far more punches and kicks than the heroes. No previous film has ever portrayed superheroes from the down side of honest, realistic pain. On the other hand, no previous movie has ever portrayed heroes so easy for people to identify with. Some of the characters in *Mystery Men* are foolish, but more important is their dignity that makes them triumph.

The cast worked hard, and the results show on the screen. A lot of jokes might whiz by the average viewer. The comic book *Mysterymen*, upon which *Mystery Men* is based, is a satire of both politics and the comic-book field. The film is as rowdy as the comics that inspired it. A lot of jokes are hurled at inferior comic work, plus a lot of barbs reserved for a particular director of *Batman* movies who shall remain nameless.

Mystery Men isn't hard-core science fiction, but it offers an excellent story, hilarious yet believable acting, terrific special effects, and the most ringing condemnation yet of disco as the tool of evil. Anybody who's ever thought about being the one who rescues people trapped in a fire, who saves the day, who makes the winning point, or who is any kind of hero will enjoy this film.

MYSTERY OF THE LOST RANCH, THE

Vitaphone, 1925, b&w, silent serial, five chapters

Directors: Harry S. Webb and Tom Gibson; **Screenplay:** Barr Cross; **Cinematography:** Gus Peterson; **Cast:** Pete Morrison

Honest cowpokes and evil international spies duke it out in the later Old West to see who can lay claim to a death ray. Though one of the first, this serial proved to be as bad as all the others that followed.

N

NA KOMETE (aka: HECTOR SERVADAC'S ARK, ON THE COMET)

Barrandov (Czechoslovakia), 1970, Color, 85 min

Director: Karel Zeman; **Screenplay:** Zeman; **Music:** Lubos Fiser; **Cinematography:** Rudolph Stahl; **Cast:** Emil Hovarth, Magda Vasarykova, Frantisek Fillpovsky

Karel Zeman, who came to world attention with his bizarrely stylish *FABULOUS WORLD OF JULES VERNE*, tackles the master once more. With Verne's *Off on a Comet* as his jumping-off point, he weaves a tale about the fate of a group of people who are carried off the planet by a comet that comes too close to Earth. The bulk of the film is concerned with the rebuilding of their lives in this highly odd situation. Though mildly interesting, this film is not nearly as innovative as the director/screenwriter's early project.

NAKED SPACE

See *THE CREATURE WASN'T NICE*

NAVIGATOR, THE: A MEDIEVAL ODYSSEY

New World Pictures (New Zealand), 1988, Color/b&w, 92 min, VT, DVD

Producers: Gary Hannam and John Maynard; **Director:** Vincent Ward; **Screenplay:** Geoff Chapple, Kely Lyons, and Vincent Ward; **Music:** Davood A. Tabrizi; **Cinematography:** Geoffrey Simpson; **Special Effects:** Shaun Bell, David Foreman, Jim Millet, Ken Durey, Nicholas F. Foreman, and Paul Nichola; **Cast:** Hamish McFarlane, Bruce Lyons, Chris Haywood, Marshall Napier, Noel Appleby, Paul Livingston, Sarah Pierse

It's the Dark Ages. Plague is emptying the countryside. In one English hamlet, however, there is hope. A young boy thinks he can lead everyone to safety, and thus begins a great burrowing project that doesn't merely lead the inhabitants of the village down into the Earth, but back out again hundreds of years in the future. Low-budget but stylish, imaginative and fascinating, this movie is an attention grabber for those who can watch the screen for more than 10 minutes without an explosion and not become bored.

NAVY VS. THE NIGHT MONSTERS, THE (aka: THE NIGHT CRAWLERS, MONSTERS OF THE NIGHT)

Realart Pictures Corporation, 1966, Color, 90 min, VT

Producers: Jack Broder, Madelynn Broder, and George Edwards; **Director:** Michael Hoey; **Screen-**

play: Murry Linster and Hoey; **Cinematography:** Stanley Cortez; **Special Effects:** Edwin Tillman; **Cast:** Mamie Van Doren, Anthony Eisley, Pamela Mason, Bill Gray, Bobby Van, Walter Sande, Edward Faulkner, Phillip Terry

Sailors struggle mightily against plants that eat anything. It's a tough battle, but the good guys wipe out the nasty vegetation in the end. Of course, their obvious answer of simply destroying such creatures came from an era before the Environmental Protection Agency and recycling. Speaking of which, consider recycling any copies of this bomb you might come across.

NEANDERTHAL MAN, THE

United Artists, 1952, b&w, 77 min

Producers: Aubrey Wisbert and Jack Pollexfen; **Director:** E.A. Du Pont; **Screenplay:** Wisbert and Pollexfen; **Music:** Albert Glasser; **Cinematography:** Stanley Cortez; **Special Effects:** David Commons and Jack Rabin; **Cast:** Robert Shayne, Richard Crane, Robert Long, Doris Merrick

Scientist Shayne, long on looks but short on ability, first transforms his helpless pussycat into something the United Artists special effects department hoped audiences would believe was a sabertooth tiger. Then, not yet convinced that he shouldn't conduct such deadly experiments, he turns himself into a prehistoric throwback. The helplessly inept science and even worse filmmaking helped earn the '50s its reputation as the treasure trove of bad science fiction.

NEMESIS

Shaw/Jenson, 1993, Color, 95 min, VT, LD, DVD

Producers: Anders P. Jensen, Tom Karnowski, Eric Karson, Ash R. Shah, Gundip R. Shah, and Sunil R. Shah; **Director:** Albert Pyun; **Screenplay:** Rebecca Charles; **Music:** Michael Rubini; **Cinematography:** George Mooradian; **Special Effects:** Gene Warren, Jr.; **Cast:** Oliver Grunner, Tim Thomerson, Deborah Shelton, Cary-Hiroyuki Tagawa, Marjorie Monaghan, Jackie Earle, Nicholas Guest, Merle Kennedy, Brion James

Grunner plays a cop in the near future who has had a high number of body parts replaced by mechanics. That makes him a cyborg to anyone who understands basic science. However, in this film, the completely mechanical constructs he battles, rightfully called androids, are called cyborgs. It all goes downhill from there. This movie was followed by two sequels released direct to video: *Nemesis 2* and the equally forgettable *Nemesis 3: Time Lapse* and *Nemesis 4: Death Angel.*

NEMESIS 2: NEBULA

Filmwerks/Imperial Entertainment, 1995, Color, 83 min, VT

Producers: Jessica G. Budin, Paul Rosenblum, Gary Schmoeller; **Director:** Albert Pyun; **Screenplay:** Pyun; **Music:** Anthony Riparetti; **Cinematography:** George Mooradian; **Special Effects:** Guy Faria; **Cast:** Sue Price, Chad Stahelski, Tina Cote, Earl White, Jahi J.J. Zuri, Karen Studer, Shelton Bailey, Donyah Dinnah, Jon H. Epstein, Sharon Bruneau, Debbi Muggli

See *NEMESIS*

NEMESIS 3: PREY HARDER

Filmwerks/Imperial Entertainment, 1995, Color, 85 min, VT

Producers: Jessica G. Budin, Tom Karnowski, Paul Rosenblum, and Gary Schmoeller; **Director:** Albert Pyun; **Screenplay:** Pyun; **Music:** Anthony Riparetti; **Cinematography:** George Mooradian; **Special Effects:** Guy Faria and David P. Barton; **Cast:** Sue Price, Tim Thomerson, Norbert Weisser, Xavier Declie, Chad Stahelski, Earl White, Jahi J.J. Zuri, Jon H. Epstein, Sharon Bruneau, Debbi Muggli, Ursula Sarcev

See *NEMESIS*

NEMESIS 4: DEATH ANGEL

Filmwerks/Imperial Entertainment, 1995, Color, 65 min, VT

Producers: Tom Karnowski and Gary Schmoeller; **Director:** Albert Pyun; **Screenplay:** Pyun; **Music:** Anthony Riparetti; **Cinematography:** George Mooradian; **Cast:** Sue Price, Norbert Weisser, Blanka Copikova, Andrew Divoff, Michael Gucik, Nicholas Guest, Simon Poland

See *NEMESIS*

NEPTUNE FACTOR, THE
(aka: THE NEPTUNE DISASTER, AN UNDERWATER ODYSSEY)

20th Century Fox, 1973, Color, 98 min, VT

Producer: Sandy Howard; **Director:** Daniel Petrie; **Screenplay:** Jack DeWitt; **Music:** Lee McCauley; **Cinematography:** Harry Makin; **Special Effects:** Lee Howard and Opticals of Canada; **Cast:** Ernest Borgnine, Yvette Mimieux, Ben Gazzara, Walter Pidgeon

Three brave but not especially resourceful aquanauts trapped on the ocean floor in a research center wait for rescue before their air runs out. Kudos to those who recognize this as the same plot used in *MAROONED* (1969).

NEST, THE

MGM, 1988, Color, 88 min, VT

Producer: Julie Corman; **Director:** Terence Winkless; **Screenplay:** Robert P. King; **Music:** Rick Conrad; **Cinematography:** Ricardo Jacques Gale; **Cast:** Robert Lansing, Lisa Langlois, Franc Luz, Terri Treas, Stephen Davies, Diana Bellamy, Nancy Morgan

A scientific experiment meant to do wonderful things instead creates a race of giant insects with less-than-dangerous diets.

NEW BARBARIANS, THE

See *WARRIORS OF THE WASTELAND*

NEUTRON AGAINST THE ROBOTS

Azteca (Mexico), 1961/Commonwealth-United TV (U.S.), 1962, b&w

Producer: Luis Garcia de Leon; **Director:** Frederico Curiel; **Screenplay:** Curiel; **Music:** Enrico Cabiati; **Cinematography:** Fernando Colin; **Cast:** Wolf Ruvinskis, Rosita Arenas, Armando Silvestre, Julio Aleman

Three superscientist's brains are melded into one to create a jumbo super-duper brain that wants to rule the world. The only problem (well, one of the bigger problems) is that the brain must feed on the blood of living humans! Luckily, mighty costumed hero Neutron is there to save the day.

NEW INVISIBLE MAN, THE

Calderon (Mexico), 1957,/Columbia (U.S.), 1966, b&w, 94 min, VT

Producer: Guillermo Calderon Stell; **Director:** Alfredo Crevana; **Screenplay:** Alfredo Salazar; **Cinematography:** Raul Martinez Solares; **Music:** A.D. Conde; **Cast:** Arturo de Cordova, Ana Luisa Peluffo, Raul Meraz, Augusto Benedico

See *THE INVISIBLE MAN*

NEW KING KONG, THE

See *KING KONG* (1976)

NEW MICROBE, THE

Cines (Italy), 1912, b&w, silent short

The new microbe in question strikes the population, causing instantaneous weakness in its victims.

NEW VOYAGE TO THE MOON

Pathé (France), 1909, b&w, silent short

This short concerns the adventure of an early French visitor to the Moon.

NEXT ONE, THE

ANE, 1984, Color, 105 min, VT

Producer: Fred C. Perry; **Director:** Nico Mastorakis; **Screenplay:** Mastorakis; **Music:** Stanley Myers; **Cinematography:** Ari Stavrou; **Cast:** Keir Dullea, Adrienne Barbeau, Jeremy Licht, Peter Hobbs

A well-wisher from the future (Dullea), who seems oblivious to his Christian messiahlike appearance, returns to his past (our present) to fall head over heels for a woman (Barbeau) who lives with her son on a Greek island. This movie would love to pretend it was filled with meaning and significance, but it's just another slow-moving, predictable ball of nothing.

NIGHT CALLER, THE

See *BLOOD BEAST FROM OUTER SPACE*

NIGHT CALLER FROM OUTER SPACE, THE

See *BLOOD BEAST FROM OUTER SPACE*

NIGHT CRAWLERS, THE

See *THE NAVY VS. THE NIGHT MONSTERS*

NIGHTFALL

Concorde Pictures, 1988, Color, 82 min, VT, DVD

Producer: Julie Corman; **Director:** Paul Mayersberg; **Screenplay:** Mayersberg; **Music:** Frank Serafine; **Cinematography:** Dariusz Wolski; **Special Effects:** Kevin Stratton; **Cast:** David Birney, Sarah Douglas, Alexis Kanner, Andra Millian, Charles Hayward, Susie Lindeman, Starr Andreeff

This movie is set on a planet in a solar system that has three stars. This interesting bit of space geography causes the planet in question to exist in a state of constant sunlight—except for one evening that comes once every thousand years when all three stars align just so, causing night to fall. This creates a kind of cosmic madness brought on by the planet's inhabitants' fear of the unknown. Based on the classic Isaac Asimov short story by the same name, the film is ambitious but due to its low budget remains a hopeless muddle that despite great locations is simply not up to the task.

NIGHTFLYERS

New Century Vista Film Company, 1987, Color, 89 min, VT

Producer: Herb Jaffe; **Director:** T.C. Blake; **Screenplay:** Robert Jaffe; **Music:** Doug Timm; **Cinematography:** Shelly Johnson; **Special Effects:** Roger George, Bob Harmon, Bob Weisinger, and Robert Short; **Cast:** Catherine Mary Stewart, Michael Praed, John Standing, Lisa Blount, Glenn Withrow

Scientists aboard a space cruiser are set upon one by one. What's causing the mayhem? An unseen force.

NIGHT KEY, THE

Universal, 1937, b&w, 68 min

Director: Lloyd Corrigan; **Screenplay:** Tristram Tupper and John C. Moffit; **Music:** Lou Forbes; **Cinematography:** George Robinson; **Special Effects:** John P. Fulton; **Cast:** Boris Karloff, Sam Hinds, Alan Baxter, Jean Rogers, Frank Reicher, Ward Bond, Warren Hull

Karloff plays yet another scientist who creates a miracle, only to be cheated out of it by an unscrupulous colleague. Desperate, he creates another miracle, only to have that one stolen by the same man. He turns to a life of crime, not only outwitting his enemy at every turn, but also the gang he has hired.

NIGHT OF THE BIG HEAT

See *ISLAND OF THE BURNING DAMNED*

NIGHT OF THE BLOOD BEAST

AIP, 1958, b&w, 65 min, VT

Producer: Gene Corman; **Director:** Bernard Kowalski; **Screenplay:** Martin Varno; **Music:** Alexander Laszlo; **Cinematography:** John M. Nickolas, Jr.; **Special Effects:** Harry Thomas and Herman Lewis; **Cast:** Michael Emmet, Angela Greene, John Baer, Ed Nelson, Tyler McVey, Georgiana Carter

Astronaut John Corcoran is the first human to pass through the Van Allen radiation belt. Unfortunately, he doesn't survive the experience and returns to Earth dead from causes unknown. Worse yet, the scientists trying to determine what killed him spot his corpse wandering the space center at night. Eventually, it is discovered that there are alien creatures living within his body, using it as an incubatory host.

NIGHT OF THE COMET

20th Century Fox, 1984, Color, 94 min, VT

Producers: Thomas Crawford, Wayne Crawford, Michael Rosenblatt, Nancy Isreal, Andrew Lane, and Sandra Scheik; **Director:** Thom Eberhardt; **Screenplay:** Eberhardt; **Music:** Richard Campbell; **Cinematography:** Arthur Albert; **Special Effects:** Ted Rae; **Cast:** Catherine Mary Stewart, Kelli Maroney, Robert Beltran, Geoffrey Lewis, Mary Woronov, Sharon Farrell, Michael Bowen

A comet, last seen just before the dinosaurs disappeared, is about to pass over Earth. Most of the population of Los Angeles turns out to watch the big event and celebrate. On the morning after, however, all that's left of them is their clothing and various piles of orange dust.

As bad as things look, it's not the end of civilization yet. There are survivors: deteriorating zombies, people who were semiprotected when the comet passed over; not-so-brilliant scientists who hid in an underground compound but left the vents open and the fans running, hence exposing themselves to the effects of the comet (which means they'll also be deteriorating zombies soon); and two Valley Girl sisters, Regina (Stewart) and Samantha (Maroney), who were protected from the comet by the steel walls of a movie projection booth and a lawn storage shed respectively. Regina's a feisty-but-sweet movie theater usher. Samantha's a whiney-but-spunky cheerleader. Luckily for them, they're both comfortable with automatic weapons and the occasional knee to the groin, thanks to their military officer dad, because those survival skills will be coming in handy.

The sisters find and squabble over another survivor, Hector (Beltran), go on a shopping spree in an empty mall, and battle with the zombies, who are looking for something more tasty than cats to eat. They're also forced to battle the less-than-capable scientists who want the girls' blood (all of it) to create a serum that will keep their brain trust from becoming zombies.

Neither the zombies, whose makeup seems more suitable for trick-or-treating, nor the scientists offer many good thrills. There have certainly been a number of more serious films about the last few survivors on Earth. In fact, this movie owes more than a little to THE OMEGA MAN and *I Am Legend*, the Richard Matheson novel that inspired that earlier film. But then, this isn't exactly a serious movie. *Night of the Comet* is a completely tongue-in-cheek effort that works quite nicely. The movie contains some extremely effective, eerie shots of postcomet L.A.: an automated pool cleaner sweeping a pool that is empty except for one rubber ducky, a car abandoned at an intersection, rain that is washing orange dust into the sewers, and so on.

These mood-enhancing moments alone wouldn't be enough reason to watch the movie, but fortunately the film's two stars pull off its dry comedy. Both actresses are wonderfully appealing, tossing off their Valley Girl lines with wonderful comic timing. (Regina says to Samantha, who has been chain-drinking sodas: "What are you going to do when your complexion freaks out? The dermatologist is dead, you know.") The scene in which the pair hit the deserted mall and bop around trying on clothes to the tune "Girls Just Want to Have Fun" is memorable enough to make this movie worthwhile.

NIGHT OF THE LEPUS

MGM, 1972, Color, 88 min

Producer: A.C. Lyles; **Director:** William Claxton; **Screenplay:** Don Holliday and Gene Kearney; **Music:** Jimmie Haskell; **Cinematography:** Ted Voigtlander; **Special Effects:** Howard A. Anderson; **Cast:** Stuart Whitman, Janet Leigh, Rory Calhoun, DeForest Kelley, Paul Fix, Melaine Fullerton

The rabbit population of the American Southwest is growing out of control. Government scientists try to slow their incredible reproduction rate but end up creating gigantic rabbits that slaughter people and destroy property. Eventually, the monster rabbits are competently dealt with by the government. The original source material for this film, Russell Braddon's novel *The Year of the Angry Rabbit*, is a social satire set in Australia. Missing the point, Hollywood tried to play it straight. Didn't anyone at MGM realize how difficult it would be to make rabbits look menacing?

NIGHT OF THE LIVING DEAD (1968)

Reade/Continental, 1968, b&w, 90 min, VT, LD, DVD

Producers: Russell Streiner and Karl Hardman; **Director:** George Romero; **Screenplay:** John A. Russo; **Cinematography:** Romero; **Special Effects:** Regis Sur- vinski and Tony Pantanello; **Cast:** Duane Jones, Judith O'Dea, Russell Streiner, Keith Wayne, Karl Hardman

A plague is spreading across the face of Earth. Radiation from outer space—no more explanation is ever given—is having an effect on the recently deceased. It is reanimating them and turning them into cannibalistic monsters. This is occurring across the globe, but the film deals only with the small band of terrified living folk who take shelter in an old house in the forest. The bulk of the story covers the group's attempt to survive through the night while waves of slow-moving but highly dangerous zombies attack their hiding place. One bite from the creatures turns a living person into one of the walking dead. The mounting horror and tension never cease. Finally, after the long night, the true genius of the filmmakers is revealed.

When dawn arrives, gunfire is heard. A citizen's army is tracking down and killing the zombies. The leader of the survivors stumbles out of the house in response to the commotion. He is tired from his incredible ordeal, but he has to see what is happening. His weary gait is mistaken for the shambling movements of a zombie, and he is killed by the advancing troops in one of independent cinema's most startling moments of irony.

This extremely low-budget picture works on a number of levels, which proves that a lack of capital is no excuse for turning out a stupid film. Much can be said about *The Night of the Living Dead* and its sequels (*Dawn of the Dead* and *Day of the Dead*). All three pictures, amazingly each one actually better than the one before, are brilliant horror movies, but they are not science fiction films. Each film has a few bits of pseudo-science that are supposed to explain what is happening, but these are throwaway devices. More relevant to the sci-fi genre are themes of social science throughout the series that offer interesting insights on big government, suburbia, racism, social order, social indoctrination, and more.

Be warned, however. As smart as these movies are, they are also extremely bloody, violent, and graphic and not for children or those with delicate sensibilities. They will, however, be of particular interest to would-be filmmakers. *Night of the Living Dead* is a case study in smart low-budget filmmaking. Romero encouraged his investors to appear as zombies, made a local butcher an investor for his donation of animal guts and blood, used chocolate syrup for blood, and rewrote with imagination whenever necessary. For example: when his mother's car was dented in between takes for the opening cemetery scene, Romero rewrote the scene to include the roll-to-a-stop wreck to cover the damage for further shooting. The moment covered the inconsistency and added to the beginning mood considerably.

Note: When looking for *Night of the Living Dead*, make certain you find the 1968 version, not the 1990 remake. Although George Romero scripted the remake, it is not as effective as its lower-budget predecessor. This second version, while a well-made and entertaining coda to the series, came about due to a copyright battle. Adding to the confusion is the fact that the original film is also available in a colorized version, which purists should avoid since it strongly mutes the film's stark black-and-white contrasts.

NIGHT OF THE LIVING DEAD (1990)

20th Century Fox, 1990, Color, 96 min, VT, LD

Producers: George A. Romero, John A. Russo, Menahem Golan, and Russell Streiner; **Director:** Tom Savini; **Screenplay:** Romero and Russo; **Music:** Paul McCollogh; **Special Effects:** Matt Vogel, Jeff Naparstek, and Chris Stavakis; **Cinematography:** Frank Prinzi; **Cast:** Tony Todd, Patricia Tallman, Tom Towles, McKee Anderson, William Butlet, Katie Finnerman

See NIGHT OF THE LIVING DEAD (1968)

NIGHT THE WORLD EXPLODED

Columbia, 1957, b&w, 64 min

Producer: Sam Katzman; **Director:** Fred Sears; **Screenplay:** Luci Ward and Jack Natteford; **Music:** Ross DiMaggio; **Cinematography:** Ben Kline; **Cast:** Kathyrn Grant, William Leslie, Tris Coffin, Marshall Reed, Raymond Greenleaf

A mineral that absorbs nitrogen is discovered within Earth's core. Unfortunately, it absorbs nitrogen until it explodes from the effect with mind-numbing force. Having removed a sample from its safe environment, however, the scientists have created the possible danger of setting off a chain reaction that will destroy the world. Luckily, the scientists are able to rectify their mistake.

1984

Holiday Films (Great Britain), 1956, b&w, 91 min

Producer: N.N. Peter Rathvon; **Director:** Michael Anderson; **Screenplay:** William P. Templeton and Ralph Bettinson; **Music:** Malcolm Arnold; **Cinematography:** C. Penington Richards; **Special Effects:** B. Langley, G. Blackwell, and N. Warwick; **Cast:** Edmond O'Brien, Michael Redgrave, Jan Sterling, David Kossoff, Mervyn Johns, Donald Pleasence, Michael Ripper

It's the years after a nuclear war. London has become the capital of a new country, Oceania. The ruler is the mysterious figure known only as Big Brother. Order is maintained through a network of two-way monitors stationed in every public and private place possible. People conform mainly because they have no idea when Big Brother might be watching them.

The story centers on historical revisionist Winston Smith (O'Brien). His job is much as it sounds—to rewrite history whenever his superiors decide the old facts are no longer useful and have need of new ones. Smith wants to be a good citizen. He tries hard to believe the government's pronouncements that "war is peace," and that "freedom is slavery." He leads his simple life as outlined by Big Brother, and for a while things are quiet in his world. Then Smith makes a terrible mistake. He falls in love with someone whom he has not been approved to love.

Julia (Sterling) comes into his life, and from that moment on things disintegrate rapidly. The two are drawn to each other on a level that their government conditioning cannot halt. Eventually their illicit affair is discovered, and they are taken away for the proper, government-approved reconditioning. After all, Big Brother knows best.

What comes next depends on which version of the film one sees. The producers made two endings—one for release in Great Britain, the other in America. Astoundingly, the version made for the United Kingdom goes off on its own more upbeat direction, while the United States version follows the plot of the original book much more closely. In England, the lovers are reprogrammed by the government but manage to overcome their conditioning. They are then subsequently killed by a hail of bullets during an overly defiant escape attempt. In the American ending, as in George Orwell's novel, the reprogramming takes hold and the two become productive, useful members of Big Brother's dreary utopia once more—soulless and no longer in love.

Why a British film company would tack such an ending onto a world-famous British author's work for the British market while filming the proper ending for the United States is beyond understanding. This cinematic version of the novel works well enough, but the sets are uninspired, the acting only tolerable, and the direction flat and lifeless. Considering the vast superiority of NINETEEN EIGHTY-FOUR, the version of the novel released in 1984, there is little reason to sit through this version outside of historical curiosity.

NINETEEN EIGHTY-FOUR

Virgin, 1984, Color, 115 min, VT, LD

Producers: Al Clark, Marvin J. Rosenblum, John Davis, Robert Deverelux, and Simon Perry; **Director:** Michael Radford; **Screenplay:** Jonathan Gems, Michael Radford, and George Orwell; **Music:** Dominic Muldowney and the Eurythmics; **Cinematography:** Robert Deakins; **Special Effects:** David Scholefield, Ian Scoones, Andrew Thompson, and Chris Verner; **Cast:** Richard Burton, John Hurt, Suzanna Hamilton, Cyril Cusack, Gregor Fisher, James Walker, Phyllis Logan

As in the 1956 version of this classic story, London is now the capital of a new country, Oceania. The ruler is the mysterious figure known only as Big Brother. Order is maintained through a network of two-way monitors stationed in every public and private place possible. People conform mainly because they have no idea when Big Brother might be watching them.

The story centers on historical revisionist Winston Smith (Hurt). His job is much as it sounds—to rewrite history whenever his superiors decide the old facts are no longer useful and have need of new ones. Smith wants to be a good citizen. He tries hard to believe the government's pronouncements that "war is peace," and that "freedom is slavery." He leads his simple life as outlined by Big Brother, and for a while things are quiet in his world. Then Smith makes a terrible mistake. He falls in love with someone whom he has not been approved to love.

Julia (Hamilton) comes into his life, and from that moment on things disintegrate rapidly. The two are drawn to each other on a level that their government conditioning cannot halt. Eventually their illicit affair is discovered, and they are taken away for the proper, government-approved reconditioning. After all, Big Brother knows best.

The torturous reprogramming centers on Winston, or more exactly, it centers on government functionary O'Brien (Burton) as he explains to his rebellious charge why he must return to the arms of Big Brother. Unlike the original British version of the film, in which the lovers manage to overcome their conditioning and subsequently must be killed by a hail of bullets during an overly defiant escape attempt, this depressing and gloomy but highly faithful version of George Orwell's novel doesn't shrink from the book's ending. The lovers are broken by the hideous power of the caring state. Totalitarian Big Brother wins completely and utterly, destroying the pair's useless, egocentric love. They are returned to the fold, and all is well in Oceania once more.

This later adaptation is far superior to its predecessor in all ways. The score is inventive and supportive of the images on the screen at every moment. The decayed look of the sets is perfect. The jumps between the dreary look of Big Brother's world and the bursts of color that abound in Julia and Winston's brief escapes to the countryside are heartbreakingly intense.

But, above all, if credit for this film's stunning effectiveness is to be doled out to anyone beyond director Radford, then it has to go to Richard Burton. The actor is so chilling in his last screen role as poor Winston's interrogator/confessor O'Brien that one is almost moved to give him some credit for the fall of Soviet communism, so effectively does his performance reveal the sinister side of such regimes. His soft-spoken, paternalistic approach to the role is horrifyingly brilliant—possibly the greatest triumph of his career.

One wonders about the self-defeating integrity of filmmakers who would dare to create a work such as this. There could not have been any doubt that such a relentlessly downbeat film would not attract a major audience. To make such a film when profit always seems the bottom line is not only a staggering achievement, but a remarkably brave one as well. This is one of the finest science fiction films ever made. Certainly it is the most completely faithful adaptation of a science fiction novel.

NIOBE

Paramount, 1915, b&w, silent feature

Producer: Daniel Frohman; **Director:** Hugh Ford; **Screenplay:** Edward A. Paulton and Harry Paulton; **Cast:** Hazel Dawn, Charles Abbe

Electrical wires bring a statue to life.

NIPPON CHIMBOTSU (aka: THE SUBMERSION OF JAPAN, JAPAN SINKS)

NEW World Pictures, 1973, Color, 140 min

Producers: Osamu Tomoyuki and Tanaka Tomoyuki; **Director:** Shiro Moritani; **Screenplay:** Shinobu Hashimoto and Sakyo Komatsu; **Cinematography:** Daisaku Kimura and Hiroshi Murai; **Music:** Masaru Satô; **Special Effects:** Teruyoshi Nakano; **Cast:** Keiju Kobayashi, Hiroshi Fujioka, Tetsuro Tamba, Ayumi Ishida

Scientists discover that Japan is going to sink into the ocean due to changes occurring within Earth's core. The most time its inhabitants have to escape to some new life is two years at most. Most of the rest of the world shows little concern for the Japanese plight, ignoring, rejecting, even threatening the millions of potential refugees. Finally, Australia offers its Northern Territory to the desperate island nation, which, considering the Japanese objectives of World War II, is a humblingly ironic statement for a Japanese film.

This movie is filled with elaborate if not totally effective special effects. It's still worth watching, mainly for its stark emotions and poetic desperation. This is a noble picture, to say the least, perhaps somewhat short on science fiction but long on depth and character.

Note: The movie *Tidal Wave*, released by Roger Corman through New World Pictures, is the dubbed version of *Nippon Chimbotsu*, but it does not introduce viewers to Shiro Moritani's moving epic. While Corman did indeed purchase the rights to release *Nippon Chimbotsu* in America, he devastated the film by not only adding new scenes filmed in the United States, but also by cutting the original from nearly two and a half hours to less than an hour and a half. Practically noth-

ing remains of the original film outside of its special effects.

NO BLADE OF GRASS

MGM, 1979, Color, 96 min

Producer: Cornel Wilde; **Director:** Wilde; **Screenplay:** Sean Forestal and Jefferson Pascal; **Cinematography:** H.A.R. Thompson; **Music:** Burnell Whibley; **Special Effects:** Terry Witherington; **Cast:** Nigel Davenport, Anthony Sharp, George Coulouris, Jean Wallace, John Hamill, Lynne Frederick, Patrick Holt, Anthony May

Here we find another devastated and dying future world, but for once nuclear radiation isn't the culprit. This time it's industrial chemicals that have polluted the world to the point where most of the long-stemmed grasses die off. Suddenly, the world is not only without lawns and bamboo, but all of its cereal grains as well. Famine and the usual accompanying terror follow quickly. The movie's focus centers on a family fleeing the panic and violence of London for the Scottish countryside. As one would expect, civilized law breaks down quickly as hunger rules the day and the family runs into numerous hazards, the worst of which are armed groups of hungry thugs searching for food.

The picture has a noble ecological message, and plenty to say about the innate savagery of the human animal, but it is not very well made. This has generally been attributed to severe cuts made by its distributor before release. Considering that director Wilde was responsible for the highly praised *The Naked Prey* some years earlier, it seems likely the argument is valid. Those interested in a story about an ordinary family trying both to survive by their wits and retain their humanity while the world goes to hell all around them would be better advised to watch either the earlier film *PANIC IN THE YEAR ZERO*, or to read *The Death of Grass*, the novel upon which *No Blade of Grass* is based.

NO ESCAPE

Savoy Pictures, 1994, Color, 118 min, VT, LD, DVD

Producers: James Eastep, Jake Eberts, Gale Ann Hurd, and Michael R. Joyce; **Director:** Martin Campbell; **Screenplay:** Michael Gaylin, Joel Gross, and Richard Herley; **Cinematography:** Phil Meheux; **Music:** Graeme Revell; **Special Effects:** Brian Cox, David Hardie, David Young, Brian Pierce, Dennis Skotak, Robert Skotak, and Jenny Fulle; **Cast:** Ray Liotta,

Lance Hendriksen, Stuart Wilson, Kevin Dillon, Ian McNiece, Michael Lerner, Ernie Hudson

In this movie about a future prison, criminals are left to fend for themselves on an island, kept from escaping by high-tech security. Liotta plays the convict destined to be the deciding factor in the island's fate. Though not much of an idea at first glance, *No Escape* does redeem itself with several nice plot twists, well-staged action sequences, and a sturdy refusal to take itself too seriously.

NOTHING BUT THE NIGHT
(aka: THE RESURRECTION SYNDICATE, THE DEVIL'S UNDEAD)

Charlemagne (Great Britain), 1972, Color, 90 min, VT

Producer: Anthony Nelson Keys; **Director:** Peter Saady; **Screenplay:** Brian Hayles; **Cinematography:** Ken Talbot; **Music:** Malcolm Williamson; **Special Effects:** Les Bowie and Eddie Knight; **Cast:** Christopher Lee, Peter Cushing, Diana Dors, Georgia Brown, Keith Barron, Fulton Mackay, Gwyneth Strong

Scientists attempt to create immortality by injecting the "life essence" of the recently deceased into innocent children. This is being done for profit, with the kids nothing more than vessels to be emptied of personality. The children's minds are taken over by the invading spirit forces' memories, eventually transforming the tykes into brutal murderers.

NOT OF THIS EARTH (1958)

Allied Artists, 1958, b&w, 67 min

Producer: Roger Corman; **Director:** Corman; **Screenplay:** Charles Griffith and Mark Hanna; **Cinematography:** John J. Mescall; **Music:** Ronald Stein; **Special Effects:** Paul Blaisdell; **Cast:** Paul Birch, Beverly Garland, Jonathan Haze, Morgan Jones, William Roerick, Dick Miller

A vampire (Birch) from the planet Davanna comes to Earth to prepare the way for invasion. His planet needs our blood, and he means to see we give it up as quickly as possible. He tries hard but doesn't succeed. Birch does a commendable job and is well supported by the rest of the cast, and the result is an interesting film somewhat ahead of its time.
Note: Not of this Earth was remade in 1988 to little effect. There was no great variation from the original

Corman film and certainly no improvements. The only reason anyone went to see the picture was to view ex-porn star Traci Lords in a starring role. Also, the film *Star Portal* is another weak remake of the 1958 original, but this one stoops so low as to lift battle scenes from Corman's earlier picture, *BATTLE BEYOND THE STARS*.

NOT OF THIS EARTH (1988)

MGM, 1998, Color, 88 min, VT

Producers: R.J. Robertson, Jim Wynorski, and Murray Miller; **Director:** Wynorski; **Screenplay:** Robertson, Wynorski, Mark Hanna, and Charles B. Griffith; **Music:** Chuck Cirino; **Cinematography:** Zoran Hocstatter; **Cast:** Traci Lords, Arthur Roberts, Lenny Juliano, Ace Mask, Roger Lodge

See *NOT OF THIS EARTH* (1958)

NOW WE'LL TELL ONE

MGM, 1933, b&w, short subject

Producer: Hal Roach; **Director:** James Chase; **Music:** Leroy Shield; **Cast:** Charley Chase, Eddie Baker, Muriel Evans, Killian Elliot

A scientist invents a belt, and when two belts of the same type are worn by different individuals, the pair can switch personalities. Featuring the wildly funny Hal Roach brand of slapstick, this movie is good fun, mostly thanks to the crazed antics of comedian Charley Chase.

NOW YOU SEE HIM, NOW YOU DON'T

Walt Disney, 1972, Color, 88 min, VT

Producer: Ron Miller; **Director:** Robert Butler; **Screenplay:** Joseph L. McEveety; **Music:** Robert F. Brunner; **Special Effects:** Eustace Lycett and Danny Lee; **Cinematography:** Frank Phillips; **Cast:** Kurt Russell, Edward Andrews, Michael McGreevy, Ed Begley, Jr.

See *THE COMPUTER WORE TENNIS SHOES*

N.P.

Zeta-A-Elle (Italy), 1971, Color, 106 min

Producer: Enrico Zaccarla; **Director:** Silvano Agosti; **Screenplay:** Agosti; **Cinematography:** Nicola Dimitri;

Music: Nicola Piovani; **Cast:** Ingrid Thulin, Irene Pappas, Francesco Rabal

Much like the real end of the 20th century, the workers of the world are freed from their labors by incredible advances in technology. Unlike the real end of the 20th century, the film's workers are happy about the fact because they aren't left to starve by the corporations using all those advanced machines to throw their workers into the streets.

NUCLEAR ULTIMATUM

See *TWILIGHT'S LAST GLEAMING*

NUTTY PROFESSOR, THE (1963)

Paramount, 1963, Color, 67 min, VT, LD

Producer: Ernest D. Glucksman; **Director:** Jerry Lewis; **Screenplay:** Lewis and Bill Richmond; **Cinematography:** W. Wallace Kelley; **Music:** Walter Scharf; **Special Effects:** Paul K. Lerpae; **Cast:** Jerry Lewis, Stella Stevens, Del Moore, Kathleen Freeman, Med Flory, Howard Morris, Elvia Allman, Henry Gibson

Professor Kelp (Lewis) isn't all that nutty, really, but he is terribly shy and not very good-looking. Being a brilliant scientist, though, the professor thinks he has the answer. Kelp has spent his life researching a way around his problem. While experimenting with elixirs that will change one's personality, he reaches a point in his life where he can no longer bear being the man he is and thus drinks one of his own potions. This has a Jekyll/Hyde effect of turning him into his exact opposite. Suddenly, Kelp is suave and charming, gregarious and entertaining. He is also terribly vain and shallow and not a little obnoxious.

Kelp's girlfriend (Stevens) is forced to choose between her unbearably shy professor and his callous but more attractive alter ego, Buddy Love. Of course, Kelp wins out over his darker side and gets the girl in the end, and the two live happily ever after. Kelp is happy because he's learned a valuable lesson. His new bride is happy because she's got a bottle of the elixir tucked away for "emergencies."

Jerry Lewis's *The Nutty Professor* is certainly one of the comedian's better vehicles, if not his best. Lewis was able to do what the public enjoyed, his usual soulful, inept jabbering character, while getting a chance to release the side of his own personality that he often had to hide from his audience, that of a nasty, wise-cracking, rude egomaniac. Before audiences fell in love with his little-boy shtick, Lewis was a top-drawer nightclub comedian, and it has often been reported that continually having to play goody-goody nerds for the big screen rankled him. This helped the science fiction elements of the movie, however, since the Jekyll/Hyde theme used here is so integral. How far does humanity dare tamper with God's handiwork? What is the proper role of a person in society—to appear honestly as himself or herself or to mold himself/herself according to society's wishes?

NUTTY PROFESSOR, THE (1996)

Universal, 1996, Color, 95 min, VT, LD, DVD

Producers: James D. Brubaker, Brian Grazer, Karen Kehela, Jerry Lewis, Russell Simmons, and Mark Lipsky; **Director:** Tom Shadyac; **Screenplay:** Bill Richmond, Lewis, Steve Oedekerk, David Sheffield, Barry W. Blaustein, and Tom Shadyac; **Cinematography:** Julio Macat; **Music:** David Newman and Wolfgang Amadeus Mozart; **Special Effects:** Burt Dalton, Rick Baker, David Leroy Anderson, Jon Farhat, David Fuhrer, Janek Sirrs, and Robert Stadd; **Cast:** Eddie Murphy, Jada Pinkett, James Coburn, Dave Chappelle, Larry Miller, John Ales

Professor Klump (Murphy) isn't all that nutty, really, but he is terribly overweight. In fact, he's as fat as modern special effects wizardry could make him. Being a brilliant scientist, though, the professor thinks he has the answer. Klump has spent his life researching a way around his problem. While experimenting with DNA restructuring, he meets a girl whom he just can't bear to lose because of his weight, so he recklessly tries out his process on himself. This has the Jekyll/Hyde effect of turning him into his exact opposite. Suddenly, Klump is thin and muscular, graceful and athletic.

Unlike the earlier film, his transformation doesn't make him less likable; there's just "less" of him. Where Jerry Lewis was looking to release his nastier side in the original *NUTTY PROFESSOR*, Murphy, who had come through a string of flops, was trying to sweeten his bad-boy image. Thus, like so many modern science fiction movies, the special effects team was called in to take over for the writers, though in this case the special effects were an integral part of the story. Klump not only goes through amazing (and amazingly inappropriate) changes, but Murphy was able to play half the people witnessing the changes, as well, as he plays at least half his own family. Again, the Jekyll/Hyde theme is nicely served—how far does humanity dare tamper with God's handiwork? What is the proper role of people in society—to appear honestly as themselves, or to mold themselves according to society's wishes?

In the sequel, *The Nutty Professor II: The Klumps*, Professor Sherman Klump (Murphy) is in love with a beautiful fellow scientist (Jackson) who loves him back, but before they can be married, Sherman has a demon he has to exorcise—Buddy Love. The professor is still haunted by the thin egomaniac he released in his first film, and, fearing he won't be able to control his inner self's nasty tendencies, he decides to genetically erase Buddy. But Buddy fights back, managing not only to elude the professor, but to turn the tables on him as well. The film works well as a sci-fi/comedy mainly because of its serious story line. Despite the outlandish off-color material that keeps most of the movie going, it all still hangs on the fact that Sherman Klump is a man terrified of his own inner demon—terrified to the point where he is willing to tamper with his genetic code to be rid of it. All done in the name of love, his fear makes him appear more and more pathetic as he begins to lose his entire world.

The sci-fi content includes genetic mutation, gene extraction, and reversal of the aging process, as well as mutant monster/human being sex, to keep the purists happy.

NUTTY PROFESSOR II: THE KLUMPS, THE

Universal, 2000, Color, 106 min, VT, DVD

Producers: James D. Brubaker, Brian Grazer, Karen Kehela, Jerry Lewis, Eddie Murphy, Tom Shadyac, James Whitaker, and Michael Ewing; **Director:** Shadyac; **Screenplay:** Paul Weitz, Chris Weitz, David Sheffield, and Barry W. Blaustein; **Cinematography:** Dean Semler, A.S.C.; **Music:** David Newman; **Special Effects:** Jon Farhat, Rick Baker, Jennifer Bell, Robert Stadd, Greg Papalia, David Leroy Anderson, Double Negative, C.O.R.E. Digital Pictures, Syd Dutton, Bill Taylor, Illusion Arts, Inc., and Pixel Magic; **Cast:** Eddie Murphy, Janet Jackson, John Ales, Richard Grant, Larry Miller, Anna Maria Horsford, Melinda McGraw, Jamal Mixon, Gabriel Williams, Chris Elliott Duffy Taylor, Earl Boen, Nikki Cox, Freda Payne

See *THE NUTTY PROFESSOR* (1996)

OCTOBER SKY

Universal, 1999, Color, 95 min

Producers: Charles Gordon and Larry Franco; **Director:** Joe Johnston; **Screenplay:** Lewis Colick; **Music:** Mark Isham; **Special Effects:** Joey DiGaetano, Robert Vazqez, Gary I. Pilkinton, Dave Rigby, Richard E. Perry, Kathleen Tonkin, and Bill Johnson; **Cinematography:** Fred Murphy, A.S.C.; **Cast:** Jake Gyllenhaal, Chris Cooper, Laura Dern, Chris Owen, William Lee Scott, Chad Lindberg, Natalie Canerday, Scott Miles, Randy Stripling, Chris Ellis, Elya Baskin, Courtney Fendley, David Dwyer, Terry Loughlin

In Coalwood, West Virginia, 1957, all boys grew up to be coal miners. The place was a "company town." It was a municipality owned lock, stock, and barrel by a single corporate entity. The company mined coal, and so did everyone who lived there. A few lucky ones might escape on football scholarships, but for most only the cold dark maw of the mines beckoned, calling them forth with the numbing power of destiny. For Homer Hickam (Gyllenhaal), whose father (Cooper) runs the mine for the controlling corporation, that destiny seems completely inescapable.

Then in October of '57, everything changed—not only for the boys of Coalwood, but for every person on the face of the Earth for all time. That was the month the Soviet Union launched the world's first orbiting satellite, *Sputnik*. Suddenly, people had not only left the ground but they had left the controlling hand of gravity, taking aim at God's domain. And just as suddenly, Homer Hickam could see a way out of Coalwood. Gathering his two best friends, he builds a rocket in his parents' basement. The test flight ends in blowing up the fence that his mother had just built around their property. Not an auspicious beginning.

Undeterred, however, Homer risks being socially ostracized by befriending the school brain, Quentin (Owen). Quentin is staggered that any of the popular kids would ever want to have anything to do with him, but it takes only a moment for him to realize what Homer is offering—a chance to escape the mines, a chance to escape the loneliness of being the only person in town who cares about something besides digging coal, a chance to be anything. Quentin agrees; he's in. Soon the four are launching rockets on a regular basis. When their missiles don't get very far, constantly exploding on the launching pad (much like the NASA rockets of the same time), the boys' teacher, Miss Riley (Dern), gets them a highly advanced book on rocketry. Then things really start to happen.

As Homer and his friends study, adapt, and improvise, their rocket tests go higher and straighter. The boys become local celebrities as the town comes out to see the launches in ever increasing numbers. Machinists at the mine start helping them manufacture casements and nozzles. Before long, it begins to look like the Rocket Boys (as the town dubs the quartet) might actually win the local school science fair. If they win that and go to the nationals, that could mean college scholarships all around and the freedom to do or be anything that can be imagined. If they win.

If all of the above sounds like something that might have happened, that's because it did. *October Sky* is based on the autobiography of Homer Hickam, *Rocket Boys*, which tells of his near epic struggle to haul himself up from the coal fields of West Virginia.

"It doesn't happen very often," director Joe Johnston explained, "but every now and then you read a story that hits you on an emotional level. *October Sky* involves themes that are so universal to the experiences of coming-of-age in twentieth century America that it approaches the status of a modern fable."

Big words, but not inappropriate. This is a film packed with the emotion of that critical time in any person's life when you finally have to accept responsibility for your own future. Homer's dad wants his son to follow his career into the mines. He is against Homer's dream and fights him all the way. The local school, except for Miss Riley, is hostile to the boys' supposed pretensions. Even the local authorities seem determined to shut the Rocket Boys down. It is a story of grit and determination, of hope and pain and friendship, and of the just plain guts that it takes to buck the odds. It's also inspiring family entertainment.

However, based on a true story, how does this movie fit into the scope of this book? Obviously it's about rocketry, a subject near and dear to the hearts of many sci-fi fans, but its importance goes far deeper. Science fiction is the one genre of fiction that deals with looking to the future. It is grounded in throwing off old ideas and leaping forward to embrace the wild and barely imaginable, just as the Rocket Boys do in this film, just as they did in real life. This is the true story (told in microcosm) of the changes the world experienced when science suddenly did leap forward beyond comprehension. Science fiction began to capture humanity's mind only in the 1930s. By the 1950s science began catching up, and the world trembled that such things could be possible.

Note: The re-creation of the mining town is about as accurate as possible. As the real Homer Hickam said at the time of the picture's release:

> When you came into Coalwood in that era the first thing you noticed was the coal mine itself because the whole town's focus was this 800-foot shaft that the coal tipple was built over, and where all the men in town, every day, disappeared. This film has done the same thing: its focus, really, is that tipple, and everything that goes around it. I think that, especially at night,

October Sky (UNIVERSAL STUDIOS / AUTHOR'S COLLECTION)

when I've gone over to the set and looked at the tipple at night with the lights glowing and the way all the offices are around it, I think I'm back in Coalwood.

Hickam gave the film high marks for accuracy. The film gives Hickam high marks for having been an individual who knew what he wanted and for going after it with a vision and a strength of will to rival that of the gods.

OH, BOY!

Associated British Pathé Company (Great Britain), 1938, b&w, 73 min

Producer: Walter C. Mycroft; **Director:** Albert DeCourville; **Screenplay:** Dudley Leslie; **Cast:** Albert Burdon, May Lawson, Bernard Nedell, Edmon Ryan

Here's an interesting twist on the well-worn Jekyll/Hyde story. This time around, the nutty professor is a shy type who creates a compound for himself to guzzle that will make him more outgoing. His formula succeeds, but there's a hitch. Our clever scientist is not only growing more gregarious, but he's growing younger as well. Then, on top of that problem, he becomes the only citizen of the British Isles to discover that three Americans are plotting to steal the crown jewels.

OMEGA MAN, THE

Warner Bros., 1971, Color, 98 min, VT, LD, DVD

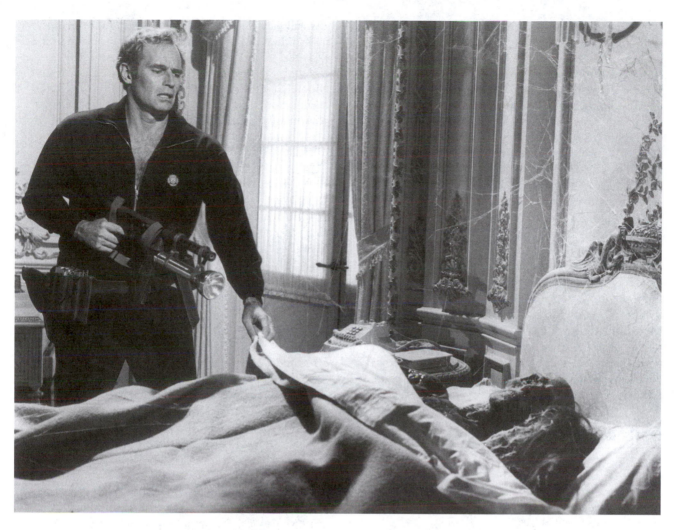

The Omega Man (WARNER BROS. / R. ALLEN LEIDER COLLECTION)

Producer: Walter Seltzer; **Director:** Boris Sagal; **Screenplay:** John William and Joyce H. Corrington; **Music:** Ron Grainer; **Special Effects:** Gordon Bau; **Cinematography:** Russ Metty; **Cast:** Charlton Heston, Rosalind Cash, Anthony Zerbe, Paul Koslo, Lincoln Kilpatrick, Brian Tochi, Eric Laneuville

Strapping, heroic-looking scientist Robert Neville (Heston) appears to be the last man on Earth. There's been a biological war between the superpowers, and it seems that everyone but Neville has died or turned into a sunlight-fearing, mutant zombie. Neville was working on an antidote for such weapons when the war broke out. He had just enough time to test it on himself before the end. Luckily for him, it worked—if you call being the last man left alive lucky.

Neville himself isn't so sure. True, he has the best of everything, looted from the storehouses all around him.

But he also lives alone in a booby-trapped fortress, moving about by day trying to kill all the mutants, hiding by night when they try to kill him. The mutants want to rid the world of all reminders of the realm of science that brought Earth to ruin. That includes Neville.

Enter young sexy survivor Lisa (Cash). She's a mutant, but she is changing much more slowly than the others. She lives in a commune with a lot of kids she's gathered together who seem to have a natural immunity. Neville decides to leave his fortress stronghold and go off with Lisa to her commune and distill a cure from his own blood. Before this happy ending can be accomplished, the mutants manage to kill Neville, and Lisa ends up taking the cure and heading for the hills with the other survivors.

This movie is the second filming of Richard Matheson's incredibly paranoid, claustrophobic novel *I Am Legend*. The first, *THE LAST MAN ON EARTH* (1963), starring Vincent Price, stayed much closer to the novel and thus comes off with far more punch and surprise. The Heston version has more action and excitement but contains little of Matheson's novel. Also, it is so heavy-handed in its symbolism that it is almost laughable.

Heston, the ultimate screen patriarch, plays the lone white man, living in fear behind locks, dreaming only of murdering every living thing left on the planet. He deludes himself with dreams of scientific benevolence when obviously it was he and his filthy ilk who destroyed the world in the first place, keeping the cure for themselves. The love of a beautiful minority woman is enough to open his eyes, but of course nothing could save him from the death he so richly deserves. It's understood that *all* the old people have to die so the young people who won't do bad things to the Earth can inherit it.

It's a poor way to treat a story that made many of the same points far more poignantly and without resorting to finger-pointing at any particular race or sex. While it's true that both films will be disappointments to fans of the novel. *The Omega Man* is guaranteed to disappoint everyone except devotees of loud, noisy movies in which things often blow up without the encumbrance of difficult concepts like plotting or common sense.

OMICRON

Manley, 1973, b&w, 102 min

Producer: Franco Christaldi; **Director:** Ugo Gregoretti; **Screenplay:** Gregoretti; **Music:** Piero Umiliani; **Cinematography:** Carlo DiPalma; **Cast:** Renato Salvatori, Dante di Pinto, Calisto Calisti, Mara Carisi, Ida Serasini

The advance scout of an alien invasion force lands on Earth and begins his job by taking control of the body of a factory worker. His scouting mission is interrupted, however, when his new human emotions begin to point out the obvious attributes of an Earthwoman whom he can't resist. Suddenly, he has a quandary—what to do about that invasion fleet that's on its way? The scout comes up with a great plan. He leads his alien comrades to Venus instead of Earth, assuming that they'll never notice the larger, cleaner, poison gas–free, life-sustaining planet next door.

ONCE IN A NEW MOON

Fox British (Great Britain), 1935, b&w, 63 min

Producer: Anthony Kimmins; **Screenplay:** Kimmins; **Cast:** Eliot Makeham, Wally Patch, John Turnbull, Rene Ray, Mary Hinton, Derrick de Marney

A small village decides it's time to get rid of democracy, and so they elect a socialist as their mayor who immediately sets out to create a worker's paradise. He does a terrible job and is eventually thrown into space when the Moon blunders into a passing celestial object. This bit of obvious propaganda is so ponderous that even those who rabidly agree will have a tough time watching it.

ONE HUNDRED YEARS AFTER

Pathé (France), 1911, b&w, silent short

A turn-of-the century scientist goes into a prolonged sleep and awakens at another turn of the century in the future. Needless to say, 2011 isn't all he hoped for.

ONE MILLION B.C.
(aka: MAN AND HIS MATE)

United Artists, 1939, b&w, 80 min

Producer: Hal Roach, Sr.; **Directors:** Hal Roach, Sr. and Hal Roach, Jr.; **Screenplay:** Eugene Roche, Mickell Novak, George Baker, and Joseph Frickett; **Music:** Werner R. Heymann; **Special Effects:** William Stevens and Roy Seawright; **Cinematography:** Norbert Brodine; **Cast:** Victor Mature, Carole Landis, Lon Chaney, Jr., John Hubbard, Mamo Clark, Jean Porter

A caveman and a cavewoman from rival tribes set up housekeeping together. They fight dinosaurs and run from volcanoes. This was a big-budget epic at the time, but it doesn't hold up particularly well. Lizards shot in close-up, no matter how effectively, are still not dinosaurs. And no human, or even sub-sub-human for that matter, ever co-existed with one. *The Flintstones* was never intended as a history lesson.

Note: Rumors have claimed that famed director D.W. Griffith actually filmed segments of this film. Film critic Leonard Maltin is on record as saying it just isn't so.

ONE MILLION YEARS B.C.

Hammer Films (Great Britain)/20th Century Fox (U.S.), 1966, Color, 100 min, VT, LD

Producers: Michael Carreras, Hal E. Roach, Sr., and Aida Young; **Director:** Don Chaffey; **Screenplay:** Carreras, Mickell Novak, George Baker, and Joseph Frickett; **Special Effects:** Ray Harryhausen; **Cinematography:** Wilkie Cooper; **Cast:** Rachel Welch, John Richardson, Percy Herbert, Robert Brown, Martine Beswick

A caveman and a cavewoman from rival tribes set up housekeeping together. They fight dinosaurs and run from volcanoes. Yet, this movie is a remake of the above-mentioned 1939 dino epic. The remake's science is just as goofy, but at least this time when those cavemen battle dinosaurs, they're Ray Harryhausen's dinosaurs. Though ridiculous as science fiction, this one is worth seeing for the special effects work alone.

ON THE BEACH

United Artists, 1959, b&w, 134 min, VT, LD

Producer: Stanley Kramer; **Director:** Kramer; **Screenplay:** John Paxton; **Music:** Ernest Gold; **Special Effects:** Lee Zavitz; **Cinematography:** Giuseppe Rotunno; **Cast:** Gregory Peck, Ava Gardner, Fred Astaire, Anthony Perkins, Donna Anderson, Guy Doleman, John Tate

Nuclear war has ravaged Earth for more than a year. The conflict is now over, and the warring nations are silent. To the best of everyone's knowledge, the Northern Hemisphere has been completely destroyed. From the best anyone can tell, the North is covered by a radioactive cloud that has consumed all life. Sadly for those few pockets of humanity remaining, the cloud now seems to be moving south. The best estimation anyone can come up with gives the survivors no more than a year to live.

The story takes place in Australia, a country left remarkably unravaged by the war. One functional submarine is left on Earth, an American vessel docked in Melbourne. Its captain (Peck) finds romance with an Australian woman (Gardner) for a while, but then comes the news—a Morse code message has come through from America! The possibility of survivors has to be checked out, and so the submarine sets off for San Francisco.

The crew reaches California only to find that the message is the result of a soda bottle near the transmitter being moved to and fro by the wind. No one is left alive in the Americas. There is no one left alive anywhere. It's over. The race is doomed. Word is sent back to Australia. While the submarine crew decides to head out into the open sea and scuttle their ship, the authorities in Australia begin distributing suicide pills to the population.

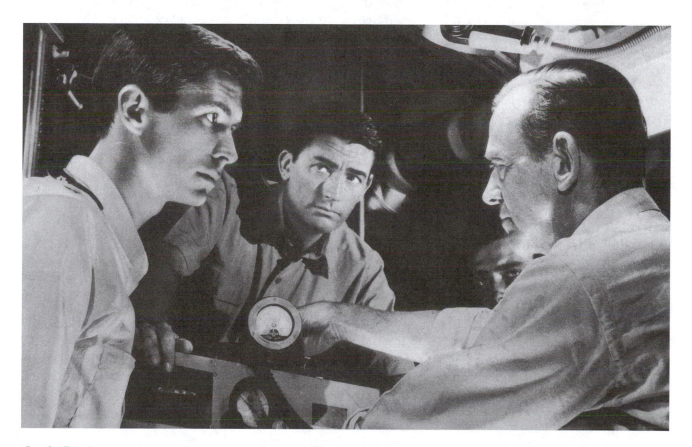

On the Beach (UNITED ARTISTS / AUTHOR'S COLLECTION)

On the Beach is the finest of all the antinuclear war films. It is slow paced, preachy, and full of its own self-importance at times, but on the other hand it is correct in its assumptions of how the world would end in such a situation. Fred Astaire, who plays his first straight dramatic role as a scientist, delivers the film's key line. "Who would have ever believed that human beings would be stupid enough to think that peace can be maintained by arranging to defend themselves with weapons that couldn't possibly be used without committing suicide?" It's easy to chuckle now at the dangers of an all-out nuclear exchange (the film reasonably credits a mere 4,700 nuclear detonations with ending life on the planet) since it seems the world may have turned that corner. What needs to be considered is that this film may have had something to do with it.

Adapted from the equally chilling and effective novel, *On the Beach* by Neville Shute, the film was a great success worldwide. It was also shown at special screenings in Moscow, where it was equally well received. Depending on who was in those audiences, perhaps it isn't so far-fetched to theorize that *On the Beach* may have had more than just a sobering effect on the general population. For example, it takes nerves of stone to watch a young Anthony Perkins and his wife prepare to feed their child a suicide pill without being overcome by the horror of the scene. This film coldly and quietly, in simple, stark terms, outlines exactly what the fate of the world would be if the nukes ever flew. It offers no hope, no explanations—nothing. It only states clearly and accurately that if humanity ever starts pushing buttons, it would be the end for the human race.

There have been many nuclear scare films, most of them comic in their poor attempts to transmit the true terror of the end. All of their explosions and ruined cities and melting people, however, cannot hold up against the calm horror that permeates this film. The cast did a remarkable job, Stanley Kramer cemented his reputation as a filmmaker, and maybe the world was saved from disaster.

ON THE COMET

See *NA KOMETE*

ON THE THRESHOLD OF SPACE

MGM, 1956, b&w, 98 min

Producer: William Bloom; **Director:** Robert D. Webb; **Screenplay:** Francis M. Cockrell and Shimon Wincelberg; **Music:** Lyn Murray; **Special Effects:** Ray Kellogg; **Cinematography:** Joe MacDonald; **Cast:** Guy Madison, John Hodiak, Virginia Leith, Dean Jagger, Warren Stevens

This movie was presented as a documentary, covering 15 years of the human quest to reach the stars, culminating in a Moon shot. Accurate predictions, but considering the year it was made, this is obviously no documentary. The cast was present only to help string together actual air force footage of astronaut training, endurance tests, and so on. To be fair, this is a well-made film for its time, but it's quite dated now, though it's an extremely good resource for stock footage fans.

OPERATION ATLANTIS

Splendor/Fisa (Italy/Spain), 1965, Color, 88 min

Producer: Sidney Pink; **Director:** Domenico Paolella; **Screenplay:** Victor Auz and Vinicio Marinucci; **Cinematography:** Francisco Sanchez and Marcello Masciocchi; **Cast:** John Ericson, Berna Rock, Erika Blank, Beni Deus

When unexplainable occurrences on the African continent draw the attention of European governmental secret agencies, it's decided that something must be done. John Ericson is the agent sent in to discover just what is going on. What he finds is a secret nuclear base manned by evil Chinese madmen. What the audience finds is yet another evening wasted by nonsense masquerading as a science fiction film.

OPERATION STARDUST

See *MISSION STARDUST*

OUR HEAVENLY BODIES

UFA (Germany), 1925, b&w, 70 min

Director: Hans Walter Kornblum; **Cast:** Theodor Loos, Walter Reinman

This rare treat features a guided tour of the entire solar system and then concludes with a look at the coming end of the universe. It's inventive and nicely ahead of its time.

OUTER TOUCH

See *SPACED OUT*

OUTLAND

Warner Bros., 1981, Color, 109 min, VT, LD, DVD

Producers: Stanley O'Toole, Charles Orme, and Richard A. Roth; **Director:** Peter Hyams; **Screenplay:** Hyams; **Music:** Jerry Goldsmith, Gerald Fried, and Morton Stevens; **Special Effects:** Martin Body, Albert Blackshaw, John Stears, and Martin Bower; **Cinematography:** Stephen Goldblatt; **Cast:** Sean Connery, Peter Boyle, Frances Sternhagen, James B. Sikking, Kika Markham, John Ratzenberger, Clarke Peters

Sean Connery plays Federal District Marshal William Thomas O'Neil, a decent, but stubborn cop. His caustic mouth has gotten him into plenty of trouble in his time, but now it's done its worst damage to date. O'Neil has been made head of security for Con-Amalgamate #27, a mining colony on Io, the innermost moon of Jupiter—an unenviable, dead-end assignment designed to get him out of everyone's hair.

Con-Am's Io titanium mining operation has a problem. Despite being the company's highest-producing operation (ever since new manager Peter Boyle arrived), a lot of people are dying—more and more every month. Discovering this upon his arrival, the new sheriff decides to find out why. And why shouldn't he? After all, his wife has deserted him, taking his son to Earth (a place he has never seen). Interestingly, O'Neil's wife still loves him. She does what she does for their son. She can't stand the thought of him growing to adulthood in space, never breathing real air or seeing a river. She invites O'Neil to follow them, leaving him a message that she had purchased three tickets.

O'Neil stays, and the plot unfolds quickly, introducing us to his lackluster coworkers and corrupt superiors. Io's new head cop proves to be too honest for the local management. When he refuses to go along with the way things have always been on Io, a team of killers is brought in to eliminate him. There is little surprise when no one in the mining colony (outside of company doctor Frances Sternhagen) will help O'Neil, leaving him to take on the killers by himself.

When it was released, many critics labeled *Outland* merely a rip-off: *High Noon* on Jupiter. In truth, the film does partially borrow one of the highly successful western's plot lines. However, it weaves a completely different story around that plot line, making such charges seem feeble. The big difference between the two films is that in *High Noon* the sheriff stands alone because those who could help him are physical cowards—they don't want the bad guys to run their town, but they don't want to die either. In *Outland* the "townsfolks" are moral cowards. Drugs coming into Io are responsible for the deaths, but they are also responsible for higher productivity and big bonuses. No one wants to help the sheriff because no one wants the flow of drugs stopped.

Outland is a fine action picture with several different moral twists. Especially interesting is Connery's character, especially when examined against the expectations of the times. Unlike most of the characters Connery had played previously, O'Neil is not a superhero/action figure. He is a far more believable man, one who has begun to believe that he can't take it anymore. He has lost his son and wife (although it is implied he could get them back), and now he has lost his future as well. He is a man without allies or friends. Connery's subdued performance reveals a man at the end of the line. Older and unsure of himself as he is, however, he decides to make one last stand, the key to understanding the film.

Outland is one of the first sci-fi/noir films. It looks at the grim realities of space colonization in the context of what history teaches about company towns, speculating that the future as painted in *Star Trek* is still a long way off. To carry the analogy further, Marshal O'Neil is no Captain Kirk. He is filled with doubts and is tired of his job. The film makes clear that there is no rationale for what he is doing, and so must he consider himself a hero? O'Neil answers that he isn't and that "they keep sending me to piles of shit like this because they think I belong here. I just want to see if they're right."

O'Neil stops the killers brought in to silence him, as well as a traitor on his own staff, taking out a large segment of the station to do it. Then, at the moment when he is about to arrest the corrupt, drug-smuggling manager, he decides against arresting him and just knocks him unconscious. Many will believe that the arrest follows, but it is obvious by O'Neil's decision to claim the ticket his wife purchased that he has found his answers and that he is turning his back on the dark world all around him.

As impressive as the plot is, as well as Connery's interpretation of it, however, what made the film interesting to the contemporary sci-fi audience was its gritty, complete look. When *Outland* was made, very few science fiction pictures had broken away from the "sparkling clean outer space" tradition. It was also refreshing because director/screenwriter Hyams chose to make a sci-fi film that disdained the usual props of the genre. As he said then: "There won't be a ray gun in sight. Nor any space ships slewing about the corridors of time. The mining colony is [the] location, not the subject."

Hyams was attempting something quite different from the other sci-fi films of the time. One of the outstanding innovations of *STAR WARS* was its use of old, worn-looking machinery. *ALIEN* followed, showing its main ship, the *Nostromo*, as a hard, baling-wire-and-spit kind of spacecraft. In *Outland*, everything takes on the rough reality of all the exploration-born mines and outposts of history. Hyams explained:

> This kind of place is very similar to what existed when the . . . Alaska pipeline was laid, in the off-shore rigs that are now in existence, the Dodge Cities of the world. There are places that are populated normally by people . . . who have very little to lose out to make as much money as they can in the shortest amount of time. Their life is one of tremendous physical hardship. The creature comforts here barely exist. It's a claustrophobic place where things don't work particularly well. . . . This is a place of enormous boredom and physical danger.

The look of the film is all the director promised. The mining colony is a low, cramped, and inhospitable place. Bunks are piled 10 to the ceiling; recreation comes only in the Leisure Club, a dark crowded room of harsh fluorescent lights, smoke, and erotic dancers. The costuming is functional. The look is very convincingly minimal. Hyams reflected:

> A frontier is a hard, gritty, unpleasant place to be, and the people building it are always looking over their shoulders rather than ahead. Trying to stay alive and putting up with hell while making some quick, big money is the kind of commercial venture Con-Am #27 is involved in.

The director is proud of *Outland*, and he should be. It has a good, involving, complex story that is played out against a stunning backdrop. Equally impressive are the interior sets of the mining operation, as well as the model used in creating the mine itself and the Jupiter backdrop. The effects are stunning, as technically perfect as they could be at the time—right down to the newly discovered ring around the planet.

At the time of its release, many people were disappointed with the film's downbeat look and message. As exciting as the shotgun battles were, people wanted their ray guns, no matter how little sense that would have made. *Outland* was called a western in space, a label that did not harm *STAR WARS* any but which contributed to *Outland*'s unreasonable dismissal.

OUTLAWED PLANET, THE

See *PLANET OF THE VAMPIRES*

Outland (THE LADD COMPANY / AUTHOR'S COLLECTION)

OUT OF THIS WORLD

Roland Reed Productions, 1954, b&w, 78 min

Producer: Roland Reed; **Cast:** Richard Crane

Another cobbled-together movie from several episodes of the *Rocky Jones* television series, this has camp value only, and little of that.

OVERCHARGED

Hepworth (Great Britain), 1912, b&w, silent short

A weakling is given a rousing good blast of electrical energy. This not only gives him superstrength, but it makes him magnetic as well.

OVER INCUBATED BABY, THE

(Great Britain), 1901, b&w, silent short

A baby is left in its incubator obviously longer than it should be. This leads to the baby emerging as an old man. It'd be easy knock this hundred-year-old film, but considering the stories in some contemporary science fiction films, maybe this premise isn't that stupid.

PAJAMA PARTY

AIP, 1964, Color, 84 min, VT

Producers: James H. Nicholson, Samuel Z. Arkoff, and Anthony Carras; **Director:** Don Weis; **Screenplay:** Louis M. Heyward; **Music:** Les Baxter; **Special Effects:** Roger George; **Cinematography:** Floyd Crosby; **Cast:** Tommy Kirk, Annette Funicello, Elsa Lanchester, Buster Keaton, Don Rickles, Harvey Lembeck, Dorothy Lamour, Frankie Avalon, Susan Hart, Jody McCrea, Candy Johnson, Donna Loren, Teri Garr

This would be little more than a beach party movie, except the dim-witted boy who needs to be taught some lessons just happens to be from Mars. The science fiction is almost nonexistent here, but it's fun to see a superyoung Teri Garr in the same film with Don Rickles and Buster Keaton.

PALLE ALONE IN THE WORLD

Nordisk (Denmark), 1949, b&w, short subject

Producers: Bjarne and Astrid Henning-Jensen; **Directors:** Bjarne and Astrid Henning-Jensen; **Screenplay:** Bjarne and Astrid Henning-Jensen; **Cinematography:** Annelise Reenberg; **Cast:** Lars Henning-Jensen

Palle hasn't been sleeping well. In nightmares he sees himself as the last person left alive on Earth. To escape his dreams, he boards a flight to the Moon.

PANIC IN THE AIR

Columbia, 1936, b&w, 60 min

Producer: Ralph Cohn; **Director:** D. Ross Lederman; **Screenplay:** Harold Shumate; **Cinematography:** Benjamin Kline; **Cast:** Lew Ayres, Florence Rice, Benny Baker, Murray Alper

A sinister discovery throws the world into a panic as the planet's radio broadcasts are wiped out. One of the usually indefatigable Lew Ayres's worst efforts.

PANIC IN THE CITY

United Pictures, 1968, Color, 97 min, VT

Producer: Earle Lyon; **Director:** Eddie Davis; **Screenplay:** Davis and Charles Savage; **Music:** Paul Dunlap; **Special Effects:** Paul Sylos, Jr.; **Cinematography:** Alan Stensvold; **Cast:** Nehemiah Persoff, Anne Jeffries, Howard Duff, Dennis Hopper, Linda Cristal, Stephen McNally

Terrorists want to start World War III. Their plan: Detonate a nuclear device inside a major American city and watch the nukes fly. Los Angeles is picked as the target, and everything is set in motion. The terrorists' plan is thwarted, however, by Howard Duff, who takes the bomb out to sea and nobly dies to save L.A. and the rest of the world from destruction.

PANIC IN THE YEAR ZERO

AIP, 1962, b&w, 92 min, VT

Producers: Arnold Houghland and Lou Rusoff; **Director:** Ray Milland; **Screenplay:** Jay Simms and John Morton; **Music:** Les Baxter; **Special Effects:** Pat Dinga and Larry Butler; **Cinematography:** Gil Warrenton; **Cast:** Ray Milland, Frankie Avalon, Jean Hagen, Mary Mitchell, Joan Freeman, Scott Peters, Richard Garland

Ray Milland plays a working stiff who just can't catch a break in this film about the end of the world. Bright and early he and his family, along with his daughter's boyfriend (Avalon), hit the road in their motor home for a little rest and relaxation. While they're driving along, the background—the city of Los Angeles—is suddenly vaporized in a nuclear attack. It doesn't take very long for Milland to realize what this means. Intelligently, he throws politics out the window immediately. Who cares who started World War III? What does it matter why they did it? All that concerns this father is keeping his family alive, and this proves to be a rough deal. Every other survivor he meets wants to rob him blind or rape his wife or daughter.

This is one of the best postapocalypse films ever made and certainly one of the best science fiction films from AIP. Despite an extremely low budget, the story is frighteningly realistic and all too easy to believe. Many have criticized Milland's character for resorting to barbaric tactics to protect his family. This is the kind of moralizing that comes quite easily to those armchair warriors who never give serious thought to anything beyond their next pontification. Milland's character never acts first, never initiates any savagery; he merely reacts to it. Indeed, this is what gives the film its power—an intelligent man having his veneer of civilization slowly chipped away. Smart enough to realize what is going to happen and what he has to do to protect those he loves, Milland still agonizes over each action he takes.

Panic in the Year Zero may have a banal, blaring sound track and a ridiculously low operating budget, but that doesn't stop it from being a powerful film with an important statement. Many of Hollywood's larger studios tackled this same subject matter with bigger budgets, better effects, and greater stars, only to produce lackluster, boring, and insulting entertainment. The problem? The one place they didn't spend their money wisely was on the script.

Adapted from Ward Moore's classic short stories, "Lot" and "Lot's Wife," *Panic in the Year Zero* gets down to the true horror of World War III. Yes, there will be a staggering loss of life if the ICBMs ever fly, but even if some people survive here and there, the truly terrifying possibility is that civilization itself will be lost. Not the accumulated art and music of the ages, but the ideals, practices and beliefs that keep us from following the savage impulses of our human natures.

PANIC ON THE TRANS-SIBERIAN

See *HORROR EXPRESS*

PARASITE

Embassy Pictures Corporation, 1982, Color, 85 min, VT, LD

Producers: Charles Band, Irwin Yablans, Michael Wolf, and Richard Marcus; **Director:** Band; **Screenplay:** Alan J. Adler, Frank Levering, and Michael Schoob; **Music:** Richard Band; **Special Effects:** Stan Winston, Lance Anderson, and James Kagel; **Cinematography:** Mac Ahlberg; **Cast:** Robert Glaudini, Demi Moore, Luca Bercovici, James Davidson, Al Fann, Cherie Currie, Vivian Blaine

It's the unspecified near future, and the world is quite a repressive place. A scientist working with evil parasites foolishly allows one to get inside him. Then the even more foolish, repressive society that employs him allows him to escape with the critter. After that, of course, the thing escapes, and thus begins yet another swipe from the classic *ALIEN*.

Note: Parasite, which gave star Demi Moore one of her first feature roles, was originally released to theaters in 3-D.

PARASITE MURDERS, THE

See *THEY CAME FROM WITHIN*

PARIS SLEEPS

See *THE CRAZY RAY*

PARTS: THE CLONUS HORROR

See *THE CLONUS HORROR*

PASSIONATE PEOPLE EATER, THE

See *THE LITTLE SHOP OF HORRORS*

PAWN ON MARS

Vitaphone, 1915, b&w, silent short

Director: Theodore Marston; **Screenplay:** Donald I. Buchanan; **Cast:** Charles Kent, Dorothy Kelly, James Morrison

A scientist discovers a way to set off explosives from a distance by means of radio waves. Because so many of these early science fiction films involved new and better ways to blow things up, one is inclined to think they justify the post-Hiroshima wave of antiexplosives films.

PEACE GAME, THE (aka: GLADIATORERNA)

Sandrews (Sweden)/New Line (U.S.), 1968, Color, 105 min

Producer: Göran Lindgren; **Director:** Peter Watkins; **Screenplay:** Nicholas Gosling and Watkins; **Music:** Claes af Geijerstan; **Cinematography:** Peter Suschitzky; **Cast:** Arthur Pentelow, Frederick Danner, Kenneth Lo, Bjorn Franzen

In the near future, war has been eliminated because the cost in blood and fortune has grown too high. This doesn't mean that the world lives in peace. Global conflict has been replaced by elite killer team sports, all controlled by computers. This is an odd film, mainly because it takes a harsh and strident warning tone about a future that is not only highly unlikely, but one wherein war has all but been abolished. If it had pointed at the modern phenomenon of nation states such as the United States and the Soviet Union sitting back and using smaller countries like franchise teams to settle their disagreements, the film might be remembered as a statement of power and insight. As it is, however, the overused clichés undeveloped and remains a simple formula: Killing is bad.

PEACEMAKER

Fries Entertainment, 1990, Color, 90 min, VT, LD

Producers: Wayne Crawford, Joel Levine, Charles Fries, Andrew Lane, Gregory Small, and Cary Gliegerman; **Director:** Kevin S. Tenney; **Screenplay:** Tenney; **Music:** Dennis Michael Tenney; **Special Effects:** John Carter, Bob Tiller, John Eggett, and John Blake; **Cinematography:** Tom Jennett; **Cast:** Robert Forster, Lance Edwards, Hilary Sheppard, Robert Davi, Bert Remsen

An alien policeman is chasing an alien bad guy to Earth for a showdown. The interesting catch is this one—the inevitable human police officer who gets involved has a problem—*both* of the aliens claim to be the good guy. A good idea with solid action to back it up is unfortunately marred by the worst wisecracks from the snappy-patter bin at the local cliché warehouse.

PEOPLE THAT TIME FORGOT, THE

Amicus Productions (U.K.)/AIP (U.S.), 1977, color, 90 min, VT

Producers: Samuel Z. Arkoff, John Dark, Steve Previn, Max Rosenberg, and Richard R. St. Johns; **Director:** Kevin Conor; **Screenplay:** Patrick Tilley; **Music:** John Scott; **Cinematography:** Allan Hume; **Special Effects:** John Richardson and Ian Wingrove; **Cast:** Patrick Wayne, Doug McClure, Sarah Douglas, Dana Gillespie, David Prowse, John Hallam, Tony Britton, Shane Rimmer, Thorley Waters

See *THE LAND THAT TIME FORGOT*

PERCY, THE MECHANICAL MAN

Paramount, 1916, b&w, silent short

Producer: John R. Bray

Early short subject about a robot with a knack for comedy.

PERFECT WOMAN, THE

Two Cities/Eagle-Lion (Great Britain), 1949, b&w, 89 min

Producers: Alfred Black and George Black; **Director:** Bernard Knowles; **Screenplay:** Knowles and George Black; **Music:** Arthur Wilkinson; **Cinematography:** Jack Hildyard; **Cast:** Patricia Roc, Stanley Holloway, Miles Malleson, Nigel Patrick, Irene Handi, Patti Morgan, Constance Smith, Pamela Davis

Two of science fiction's earliest wild and crazy guys (Holloway and Patrick) are recruited to test a scientist's new female robot. As a joke, the scientist's niece takes the robot's place. One of the bright fellows falls in love with the niece (believing her to be the metal miss), and as can be expected, comedy mayhem ensues.

PERIL FROM THE PLANET MONGO

See *FLASH GORDON*, 1936

PERILS OF PARIS, THE

Anderson Pictures, 1924, b&w, silent feature

Director: Edward Jose; **Screenplay:** Gerard Bourgeois; **Cast:** Pearl White, Robert Lee, Henry Bandin

A clever scientist invents a "Power Ray." Sadly, he isn't clever enough to think that bad guys might kidnap his daughter to force him to turn over his secrets.

PERILS OF PAULINE

Universal, 1934, b&w, serial

Producer: Henry MacRae; **Director:** Ray Taylor; **Screenplay:** Ella O'Neill, Basil Dickey, George H. Plymptom, and Jack Foley; **Music:** Sam Perry, Heinz Roemheld, and Guy Pevier; **Cast:** Evelyn Knapp, Robert Allen, James Durking, John Davidson, Sonny Rae

A disc hides the formula for a hideous gas that destroyed an ancient civilization. Naturally, everyone is chasing it down—bad guys to use it, good guys to get rid of it.

PERPETUAL MOTION SOLVED

Hilarity (Great Britain), 1914, b&w, silent short

Gravity is defeated by a homemade flying car.

PHANTASM

Avco Embassy, 1979, Color, 87 min, VT, LD

Producer: Don Coscarelli; **Director:** Coscarelli; **Screenplay:** Coscarelli; **Music:** Fred Myrow; **Special Effects:** David Gavin Brown and Paul Pepperman; **Cinematography:** Coscarelli; **Cast:** Michael Baldwin, Bill Thornbury, Reggie Bannister, Kathy Lester, Angus Scrimm

After a funeral, teen Mike (Baldwin) witnesses the theft of his best friend's casket by a mysterious figure known throughout the film (and its two sequels) only as the Tall Man. When his brother Bill ridicules his story, Mike shows the typical unrealistic pluck of the movie hero by investigating the situation himself. He is pulled into a long run of unexplainable phenomena, all of which pan out to be an alien from beyond. Maybe.

Though some proponents of this series claim that it captures the feel and flavor of a true nightmare, where experiences do not always follow a logical pattern (hence its title), others find the film confusing and meandering. There is a good deal of gore and menace but no explanations. Its three sequels, *Phantasm II*, *Phantasm III* and *Phantasm: Oblivion* (the second released direct to video, and the third received only limited theatrical release) are cut much from the same cloth. The characters return to confront the Tall Man with his flying silver sphere and evil little mutants.

PHANTASM II

Universal, 1998, Color, 90 min, VT, LD

Producer: Robert A. Quezada; **Director:** Don Coscarelli; **Screenplay:** Coscarelli; **Music:** Fred Myrow; **Special Effects:** Mark Shostrom; **Cinematography:** Daryn Okada; **Cast:** James Le Gros, Reggie Bannister, Angus Scrimm, Paula Irving, Samantha Phillips, Kenneth Tigar

See *PHANTASM*

PHANTASM III

Starway International Inc., 1994, Color, 91 min, VT, LD

Producers: Seth Blair and Don Coscarelli; **Director:** Coscarelli; **Screenplay:** Coscarelli; **Music:** Christopher L. Stone; **Special Effects:** Kevin F. McCarthy and D. Kerry Prior; **Cinematography:** Chris Chomyn; **Cast:** A. Michael Baldwin, Reggie Bannister, Angus Scrimm, Bill Thornbury, Gloria Lynn Henry, Kevin Conners, Condy Ambuehl, John Chandler, Brooks Gardner

See *PHANTASM*

PHANTASM: OBLIVION

Warner Bros., 1998, Color, 90 min, VT

Producers: A. Michael Baldwin and Don Coscarelli; **Director:** Coscarelli; **Screenplay:** Coscarelli; **Music:** Fred Myrow, Christopher L. Stone, Steve Morrell, Reggie Bannister, and Malcolm Seagrave; **Special Effects:** D. Kerry Prior; **Cinematography:** Chris Chomyn; **Cast:** A. Michael Baldwin, Reggie Bannister, Angus Scrimm, Bill Thornbury, Heidi Marnhout, Bob Ivy

See *PHANTASM*

PHANTOM CREEPS, THE

Universal, 1939, b&w, 79 min, VT, DVD

Producer: Henry MacRae; **Directors:** Forde Beebe and Saul A. Goodkind; **Screenplay:** George H. Plympton, Basil Dickey, and Mildred Barish; **Music:** Karl Hajos, Frank Skinner, Franz Waxman, and Heinz Roemheld; **Cinematography:** Jerry Ash and William Sickner; **Cast:** Bela Lugosi, Robert Kent, Regis Toomey, Dorothy Arnold, Eddie Acuff, Lane Chandler, Edward Van Sloan, Edward Norris

Evil Dr. Zorka (Lugosi) has perfected a means of placing test subjects into suspended animation. The first problem: He wants to use it for evil. The second: Everyone else wants him to be good. United States intelligence operatives (Kent and Toomey) are sent in to stop him. So the doctor does the only thing he can do to protect his suspended animation potion—he puts on his belt of invisibility and releases his killer robot.

This film is actually the result of Universal cutting down the 12-part serial of the same name into a new feature. Although many viewers claim this one is "so bad, it's good," others feel it is "so bad no one should watch it."

Note: For those who must watch it, there are two things to look for: veteran actor Lee J. Cobb as a road construction boss, and stock footage from the *Hindenburg* crash.

PHANTOM EMPIRE, THE

Mascot, 1935, b&w, serial, 12 chapters

Producer: Armand Shaefer; **Directors:** Otto Brower and Breezy Eason; **Screenplay:** John Rathmell and Shaefer; **Music:** Gene Autry, Lee Zahler, and Hugo Riesenfeld; **Special Effects:** Jack Coyle and Howard Lydecker; **Cinematography:** Ernest Miller and William Nobles; **Cast:** Gene Autry, Betsy King Ross, Frankie Darrow, Dorothy Christy, Wheeler Oatman, Smiley Burnett

Gene Autry was a real singing cowboy superstar back in the '30s, popular in westerns and on the radio. In this film he plays himself, just a regular ol' sweet-crooning, fast-shooting singing sensation who's trying to produce his weekly radio show from his Radio Ranch when his signal is blanked out by mass interference. To make a long story short, the trouble is coming from a mountain that borders the back 40, or more precisely, from the lost city of Murania, which is underneath it. The movie is a tale of robots, gangsters, evil queens, death rays, devices of doom, and, of course, the noble Thunder Riders, cowboys riding across the plains in capes and disturbingly stupid helmets.

This serial is one of those features that many claim is "so bad, it's good," and for once they're almost right. Bad movies are never good, but they can be watchable. Granted, 12 chapters of bad is a *lot* of bad, but there are scenes in this preposterous insanity that are so ridiculous—just watch the heroes sneaking past the sword-wielding, 10-gallon-hat-wearing robot guards—they have to be seen to be believed.

PHANTOM FIEND

See *RETURN OF DR. MABUSE*

PHANTOM FROM SPACE

United Artists, 1953, b&w, 72 min, VT

Producer: W. Lee Wilder; **Director:** Wilder; **Screenplay:** Bill Raynor and Myles Wilder; **Music:** William Lava; **Special Effects:** Alex Welden and Howard Anderson; **Cinematography:** William H. Clothier; **Cast:** Ted Cooper, Rudolph Anders, Noreen Nash, Harry Landers, Jim Bannon, Michael Mark

A UFO crash lands outside the Griffith Observatory. The alien pilot turns out to be invisible to the naked human eye and pretty cranky to boot. He starts out his stay on Earth by murdering some picnickers and then continues on through Los Angeles. Eventually he is lured into the observatory, where the attending scientists render him visible with an infrared light. This causes him to fall to his death, ridding the world of one more surprisingly clumsy alien menace.

PHANTOM FROM 10,000 LEAGUES, THE

ARC, 1956, b&w, 81 min

Producers: Jack Milner and Daniel Milner; **Director:** Daniel Milner; **Screenplay:** Lou Rusoff; **Music:** Ronald Stein; **Special Effects:** Paul Blaisdell; **Cinematography:** Bryden Baker; **Cast:** Kent Taylor, Cathy Downs, Michael Whalen

There's a death ray at the swimming hole, in the hands of a horrible puppet pretending to be a monster of some sort. Scientists spend a lot of time talking about what to do.

PHANTOM MENACE, THE

See *STAR WARS: EPISODE ONE—THE PHANTOM MENACE*

PHANTOM OF THE AIR

Universal, 1933, b&w, serial, 12 chapters

Producer: Henry MacRae; **Director:** Ray Taylor; **Screenplay:** Ella O'Neill, Basil Dickey, and George H. Plympton; **Cast:** Tom Tyler, William Desmond, LeRoy Mason, Walter Brennan, Gloria Shea, Jennie Cramer, Hugh Enfield

Hurray for our side! The gravity-eliminating Contra-grav has been invented. Boo to the villains who dare to steal it. Death to the producers who made this junk.

PHANTOM PLANET, THE

AIP, 1962, Color, 82 min, VT

Producer: Fred Gebhart; **Director:** William Marshall; **Screenplay:** William Telaak and Fred de Gorter; **Music:** Hayes Pagel; **Special Effects:** Charles Duncan; **Cinematography:** Elwood J. Nicholson; **Cast:** Dean Fredericks, Colleen Gray, Tony Dexter, Dolores Faith, Francis X. Bushman, Richard Kiel

A few meteors bring bad luck to the deep space cruiser, *Pegasus IV*. The ship is battered and drifting uncontrollably. Only one of the crew (Fredericks) manages to escape. His escape doesn't seem worth it at first, since he manages only to get away from his doomed ship to a nearby lifeless asteroid. But lucky Fredericks has made it to the only asteroid in the universe that actually has a civilization within, who pilot their home world around like a dune buggy. They all fit inside because they're tiny. Fredericks fits inside because he is shrunk down in size by the asteroid's all-wise leaders. Once there, he finds that they have a swell civilization—except for the gruesome monster that keeps attacking. Fredericks throws in with the humans. It sounds ill conceived, and it is, but it does possess an earnest quality that transcends many of its type.

PHANTOMS (aka: DEAN KOONTZ'S PHANTOMS)

Dimension Films, 1998, Color, 95 min, VT, LD

Producer: Dean Koontz; **Director:** Joe Chappelle; **Screenplay:** Koontz; **Music:** David C. Williams; **Special Effects:** KNB EFX Group, Inc.; **Cinematography:** Richard Clabaugh and Greg Littlewood; **Cast:** Peter O'Toole, Joanna Going, Rose McGowan, Ben Affleck, Liev Schreiber, Clifton Powell, Nicky Katt

The story opens in the small town of Snowfield, Colorado, a community that has recently suffered from a rather startling drop in the number of its permanent residents. Seven hundred people—almost the entire population—are missing, and no one has a clue as to where they went. The only survivors are two sisters (McGowan and Going), the town's sheriff (Affleck) and his deputy (Schreiber), and a professor (O'Toole) with an extensive knowledge of ancient epidemics. It seems that the townsfolk have been claimed by a being known loosely as the Ancient Enemy, a thing that has lain dormant below Earth's surface for centuries. It has the power to exterminate entire species and eliminate whole civilizations. It is a voracious, shape-shifting force that can black out a city in an instant and transform everything in its path. Now it has come to the surface once more, and it's up to Snowfield's five survivors to stop it. Handled in the best manner of low-budget classics, this is a competent film with a good cast and a lot of clever force behind it.

PHASE IV

Paramount, 1973, Color, 86 min, VT, LD

Producer: Paul B. Radin; **Director:** Saul Bass; **Screenplay:** Mayo Simon; **Music:** Brian Gascoigne and Yamash'ta; **Special Effects:** John Barry, David Forhaus, and Ken Middleham; **Cinematography:** Dick Bush; **Cast:** Nigel Davenport, Lynne Frederick, Michael Murphy, Alan Gifford, Helen Horton, Robert Henderson

Normal-size, but superintelligent ants are out in the desert causing trouble. They're out to produce a slave race of humans by breeding telepathically controlled slaves. This film is stunning to look at but almost incomprehensible once an audience strains to piece together a coherent plot.

PHENOMENON

Touchstone Pictures, 1996, Color, 124 min, VT, LD

Producers: Barbara Boyle, Charles Newirth, Michael Taylor, and Jonathan D. Krane; **Director:** Jon Turteltaub; **Screenplay:** Gerald Di Pego; **Music:** Thomas Newman; **Special Effects:** Rod M. Janusch, David Blitstein, Mageara Cameron, Louis Catorelli, Ken Ralston, and Martin A. Kline; **Cinematography:** Phedon Papamichael; **Cast:** John Travolta, Brent Spiner, Kyra Sedgwick, Forest Whitaker, Robert Duvall, Jeffrey DeMunn, Richard Kiley, Troy Genaro, Dean O'Bryan, Ellen Geer

Travolta plays an ordinary Joe who is struck by a bolt of light that makes him superintelligent. Suddenly, he has the answers to everything, except how to make that special girl love him. The whole town is interested in his amazing new brain powers, though, which leads to the local university and the government getting involved, with destructive results for the personal lives of those around Travolta. With an incredible surprise ending too good to reveal, this slow-paced, heart-filled and wonderfully original science fiction explanation for the brain-enhancing burst of light, this one is that rarest gem of all—the good science fiction date movie.

PHILADELPHIA EXPERIMENT, THE

New World Pictures, 1984, Color, 102 min, VT, LD, DVD

Producers: Pegi Brotman, John Carpenter, Douglas Curtis, and Joel B. Michaels; **Director:** Stewart Rafill; **Screenplay:** William Gray, Wallace C. Bennett, Don Jakoby, and Michael Janover; **Music:** Kenneth Wannberg; **Special Effects:** Mase W. Anderson and Lawrence J. Cavanaugh; **Cast:** Michael Paré, Nancy Allen, Eric Christmas, Bobbi Di Cicco, Kene Holliday

In World War II an American military science experiment has disastrous results. A Navy ship is twisted through several dimensions, sailors are left trapped in bulkheads, and many men die in the service of their country. Two of those believed dead don't die, however—they disappear. Or, more exactly, they are transported four decades into the future through the hole

that the experiment opened in time. Like all time travel stories, this film has its problems, but the snappy acting and intense staging of its scenes cover a lot of flaws, especially for fans of Michael Paré, who is especially good in this outing.

∏ (aka PI)

Artisan Entertainment, 1998, Color, 85 min, VT, DVD

Producers: Eric Watson, Scott Vogel, Randy Simon, David Godbout, Tyler Brodie, Jonah Smith, and Scott Franklin; **Director:** Darren Aronofsky; **Screenplay:** Aronofsky; **Music:** Clint Mansell and Sioux Z; **Cinematography:** Matthew Libatique; **Cast:** Sean Gullette, Mark Margolis, Ben Shenkman, Pamela Hart, Stephen Pearlman, Samia Shoaib, Ajay Naidu, Kristyn Mae-Anne Lao, Laruen Fox, Jo Gordon

This story centers on the beliefs of one very interesting genius, Maximillian Cohen (Gullette). His main working premise is as follows:

> *One:* Mathematics is the language of nature. *Two:* Everything around us can be represented and understood through numbers. *Three:* If you graph the numbers of any system, patterns will emerge. *Therefore:* there are patterns everywhere in nature.

Max is a brilliant but very troubled man. When he was a child, he stared at the Sun for too long. Ever since then he's had violent headaches. He's also had a need to discover certain things. For instance, for the last 10 years he has been working toward, and constantly on the verge of making, the most important discovery of his life. Throughout the last decade, a time he has spent virtually a prisoner of his apartment/laboratory, he has been attempting to decode the numerical pattern beneath the ultimate system of ordered chaos—the stock market. The closer he gets to the secret, however, the more the universe resists giving up its secrets. As Max closes in, chaos begins swallowing the world around him. He is pursued by an aggressive Wall Street firm set on world financial domination, as well as a Kabbalah sect intent on unlocking the secrets behind their ancient holy texts (which would be the name of God). Max races to crack the code before someone kills him. What he finds is simply astounding.

This tremendous science fiction film was made on a shoestring budget in Brooklyn, New York. Intricately woven and forcefully dedicated to its intelligent story, this is one of the most kinetic, visually and cerebrally exciting movies the genre has to offer. Part of the appeal is that the movie is not only a black-and-white film, but it is a *truly* black-and-white film. Cinematographer Libatique used black-and-white reversal film stock, a film that is extremely difficult to expose as well as edit, but which results in highly dramatic contrasts. As screenwriter/director Aronofsky said at the time of the film's release, "We wanted a black *or* white film. One that's as richly stylized as a photograph."

Of course, it took more than a fancy film stock to get this picture its near-universal reputation as an instant classic. Another trick employed by Aronofsky was to tell his story in a subjective manner to help pull the audience into the mind of the film's disturbed protagonist. To accomplish the task of shooting the entire film through Max's perspective, Aronofsky and Libatique invented a number of revolutionary camera setups. These included a rig that attached to actor Gullette's body for a few key scenes, a "Heat-Cam," which created ripples in front of the lens, and a "Vibrator-Cam," which created jarring effects.

Aronofsky and Gullette reportedly spent eight months together working on the script, fleshing out Max's motivations so as to ensure that his simultaneous ascent into enlightenment and descent into madness were not lost in the complex structure of the plot. If they did, it was certainly worth it. This is an incredible story. It is a brilliant, personal statement and one of the best films of the genre. As to why he made such a quirky, nonaction-oriented, non–special effects movie, Aronofsky explained: "I think people have already seen everything blown up—space ships, the Death Star, giant insects, the Earth. What people are interested in now is the exploration of emotions, what makes a person tick, the inner world. Outer space is dead. Inner space is the next journey."

PIRANHA

New World, 1978, Color, 92 min, VT, DVD

Producers: Roger Corman, Jeff Schechtman, and Jon Davison; **Director:** Joe Dante; **Screenplay:** John Sayles; **Music:** Pino Donaggio; **Special Effects:** Jon Berg; **Cinematography:** James Anderson; **Cast:** Kevin McCarthy, Bradford Dillman, Heather Menzies, Keenan Wynn, Dick Miller, Barbara Steele, Belinda Balaski, Bruce Gordon, Paul Bartel

It seems that during the Vietnam War the Pentagon created a superrace of genetically altered piranha to dump in the waters of North Vietnam. The plan was never put into effect, even though the scientist in charge developed all kinds of great mutants, including one with arms and legs. Of course the army never got rid of any of the

mutants, either, and that's where the plot of this film begins. The piranhas are let loose by accident, set free in the waters of California. Now they're on their way to an innocent summer camp and a vacation resort owned by a retired general. The fish eat a lot of people until the hero poisons them, and the doctor assures us all the little killers have been disposed of.

Of course, four years later *Piranha Part Two: The Spawning* was released. It has nothing to do with the original. Cast, setting—everything is different, including the fact that this time the little devils can *fly*. Both films are about as intelligent as they sound. Oddly enough, the sequel was directed by James Cameron shortly before he made his epic, TERMINATOR. What happened in between pictures is impossible to say.

PIRANHA PART TWO: THE SPAWNING

Chako Film Company (Italy), 1981, Color, 95 min, VT, LD

Producers: Ovidio G. Assonitis, Chako Van Leeuwn, and Jeff Schectman; **Director:** James Cameron; **Screenplay:** H.A. Milton; **Music:** Stelvio Cipraiani; **Special Effects:** Gino DeRossi, Antonio Corridori, and Gilberto Carbonaro; **Cinematography:** Roberto D'Ettorre Pizzolli; **Cast:** Tricia O'Neil, Steve Marachuk, Lance Hendriksen, Ricky G. Paul, Ted Richert, Leslie Graves

See *PIRANHA*

PITCH BLACK

USA Films, 2000, Color 107 min, VT, DVD

Producers: Tom Engelman, Ted Field, Scott Kroopf, and Anthony Winley; **Director:** David Twohy; **Screenplay:** Jim Wheat, Ken Wheat, and Twohy; **Music:** Graeme Revell; **Special Effects:** John Cox, Peter Chiang, Patrick Tatopoulos, Brian Cox, Steve Szekeres, Pauline Grebert, David Hardie, Pieter Plooy, Karen Dimmig, Double Negative Ltd., The Magic Camera Company, Hunter/Gratzner Industries, Inc., and The Chandler Group; **Cinematography:** David Eggby, A.C.S.; **Cast:** Vin Diesel, Radna Mitchell, Cole Hauser, Keith David, Lewis Fitz-Gerald, Claudia Black, Rhiana Griffith, John Moore, Simon Burke, Les Chantery, Sam Sari, Firass Dirani, Ric Anderson, Vic Wilson, Angela Makin

Pitch Black starts out about as fast-paced as an action picture can. One minute a deep-space transport is mov-

Pitch Black (UNIVERSAL STUDIOS / AUTHOR'S COLLECTION)

ing along at a somber pace; the next second its hull has been breached by meteors, the captain is dead, and it's up to the docking pilot, Fry (Mitchell), to get the crippled ship back under control. Since the transport is tumbling out of control down through the atmosphere of an unknown world, this is no easy task. The crash is a beautifully executed sequence, edited about as sharply and as fast as the human eye can follow, and calculated to leave audiences breathless.

The crash kills most of the crew and passengers. Those left alive begin to bury the dead and collect what is still usable from the wreckage, then survey the new world upon which they've been deposited. The planet is incredibly hot and viciously bright. The intense sunlight bleeds the color out of everything, not that there is much to look at outside of sand, rocks, and bones. There is no life anywhere, no trees or insects or even water. Nothing.

At least, not until the lights go out.

Trapped for a moment in an underground situation, Fry discovers that there is life on the planet—vicious, insanely destructive life. But whatever it is living in the underground darkness, it fears the light. And on a world ringed by three suns, the curse of never-ending daylight suddenly doesn't seem so bad. Of course, with suns and satellites there's always the possibility of an eclipse. But of more urgent concern to this group is the fact that one of the crash survivors is a killer named Riddick (Diesel), who was being taken in by a bounty hunter. Now he's loose on the planet, making for danger aboveground and below. As one of the characters says, "That's what I get for flying coach."

Pitch Black is great fun. The movie offers little in the way of actual science, but there's an excellent story, well-crafted characters, and nonstop action to keep viewers guessing and the faint of heart screaming. Of course, those who like science fiction movies with lots of special effects will not be disappointed here. Although *Pitch Black* is a cleverly constructed low-budget film (like TREMORS without the jokes), its effects are top-notch and razor sharp. When ALIEN was first in theaters, one of its big selling points was that it took one forever to bring the creature into focus, so strange and, well, alien was its appearance. It's been a long time since a movie creation was that original or unique, but the creatures in this production measure up nicely. As for the cast, there are no superstars, but the performances are good, and the characters are not what one might expect, including who lives and who dies.

Note: When the picture was released, much was made of the filmmakers' using a bleaching process to give the daylight sequences a harsh, colorless look. Considered by many to be a brilliant touch to convey an alien amount of heat and sunlight, it was actually employed to cover up the fact that the weather during the location shooting was horribly overcast, not the bright sunlit effect they expected of the Australian desert in summer.

PLANETE SAUVAGE, LA

See *FANTASTIC PLANET*

PLANET OF BLOOD (1965)

See *PLANET OF THE VAMPIRES*

PLANET OF BLOOD (1966)

See *QUEEN OF BLOOD*

PLANET OF STORMS (aka: PLANET OF TEMPESTS, STORM PLANET, COSMONAUTS ON VENUS)

Leningrad Studio of Popular Science Films (U.S.S.R.), 1962, Color

Producer: Vladimir Yemelyanov; **Director:** Pavel Klushantsev; **Screenplay:** Alexander Kazantsev and Klushantsev; **Music:** P. Admoni and Aleksei Chyornov; **Special Effects:** A. Lavrentyev and V. Skelkov; **Cinematography:** Arkady Klimov; **Cast:** Kyunna Ignatova, Yuri Sarantsev, Vladimir Yemelianov, Gennadi Vernov, Georgi Zhonov

A large Soviet space cruiser arrives at Venus to begin humankind's initial exploration of the planet. A party of male cosmonauts heads for the surface with their robot, while a lone female cosmonaut remains aboard the command ship to keep things running smoothly. This device allows for much long, slow dialogue between the men below and their "mother" in the sky about the joys of living in the great Communist protectorate. Other parts are more lively, however, as the boys below face carnivorous plants, dinosaurs, lizard people, volcanoes, and such. The cosmonauts finally wake up, and, deciding that Venus is not the place to be, leave that planet behind. As they depart, however, they are unaware that an intelligent Venusian is watching them from beneath the surface of a lake.

Planet of Storms is a simple science fiction/action picture, no better or worse than the typical American B movie. In fact, Roger Corman bought the rights to the Soviet film solely to get his hands on its special effects, which was then used in later films: *VOYAGE TO THE PREHISTORIC PLANET* and *VOYAGE TO THE PLANET OF PREHISTORIC WOMEN*. There is little likelihood of the original Soviet picture ever being shown in the United States, except in the most limited way, due to the problem of Corman's rights. Of the three versions of this movie, however, the original is the best.

PLANET OF HORRORS

See *GALAXY OF TERROR*

PLANET OF TERROR (1965)

See *QUEEN OF BLOOD*

PLANET OF TERROR (1966)

See *PLANET OF THE VAMPIRES*

PLANET OF THE APES

20th Century Fox, 1968, Color 112 min, VT, LD, DVD

Producer: Arthur P. Jacobs; **Director:** Franklin J. Shaffner; **Screenplay:** Michael Wilson and Rod Serling; **Music:** Jerry Goldsmith; **Special Effects:** Jack Martin Smith, William Creber, John Chambers, Ben Nye, Dan Striepeke, Lyle B. Abbott, Art Cruickshank, and Emil Kosa, Jr.; **Cinematography:** Leon Shamroy; **Cast:** Charlton Heston, Roddy McDowall, Kim Hunter, Maurice Evans, James Whitmore, James Daly, Linda Harrison, Paul Lambert, Robert Gunner

Four astronauts are on their way back to Earth only to find a number of surprises. First, their ultrasophisticated equipment fails them completely, and one of their number is killed while in suspended animation. That leaves only three of them to escape their sinking ship. They then wander a blasted plain for days, wondering what went wrong with their mission and what godforsaken world have they landed on. Their worries grow as they encounter the life-forms of this bizarre planet—human men and women who are mute and live in an animal-like existence below even the Neanderthal (although their craniums are obviously more developed that any primitive human's), and a race of intelligent, civilized apes. We know they're civilized because they're the ones with the guns.

One of the astronauts is killed by the apes, another is dealt a stunning blow that mentally incapacitates him, and the third, Taylor (Heston), is shot a glancing blow in the neck, which temporarily robs him of the power of speech. Taken to the zoo for study, Taylor is put in the care of two ape scientists, husband and wife Cornelius and Zira (McDowall and Hunter). They quickly discover that Taylor is intelligent—far too intelligent for what they expect from a mere human. Mathematical and logic tests are a snap for him. Before long, he's even communicating through sign language to them about forbidden subjects such as space travel. The two inform the proper authorities at once that they have discovered a superhuman.

A kangaroo court arranged by the ministry of science tries to railroad Taylor to a quick execution. At the dramatic high point of this clash, Taylor's power of speech returns, and he reveals his secret in full view of everyone—there are humans who can talk. The high committee is even more determined to have Taylor destroyed before his very presence in the world causes the fall of ape civilization. Zira and Cornelius, aghast and ashamed at their superiors, arrange for Taylor to

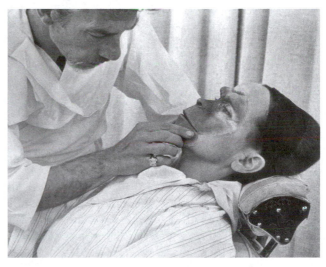

Planet of the Apes (TWENTIETH CENTURY FOX /
R. ALLEN LEIDER COLLECTION)

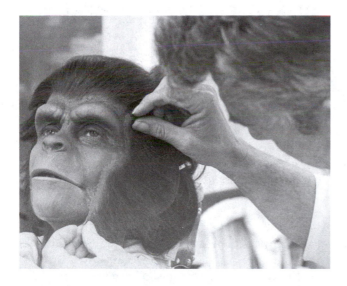

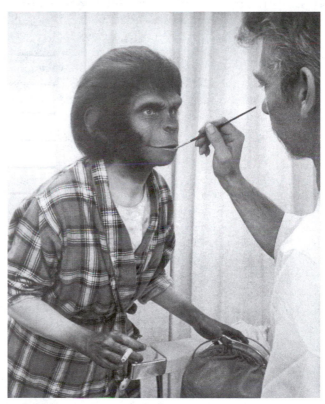

Planet of the Apes (TWENTIETH CENTURY FOX /
R. ALLEN LEIDER COLLECTION)

Planet of the Apes (TWENTIETH CENTURY FOX /
R. ALLEN LEIDER COLLECTION)

Planet of the Apes (TWENTIETH CENTURY FOX /
R. ALLEN LEIDER COLLECTION)

escape along with a human companion (Harrison) of whom he has become fond. Taylor heads into the Forbidden Zone, a land banned to all apes. He goes there because he suspects that if the area is off limits, it probably has the proof he needs to establish that he isn't a freak and that humans are not all ignorant savages.

Taylor's hunch proves devastatingly correct. It turns out that the high council knew all along that man wasn't a savage race. In fact, they've been doing everything they can not only to keep the humans down but also to keep secret the knowledge that man is not an idiot species and that the human was once the highest form of life on their planet. Having proved his point, and also sick to death of the company of apes, Taylor rides off with his lovely but mute friend Nova. He doesn't get to enjoy his moment of superiority for long though. Rounding a bend, he finds the upper torso of the Statue of Liberty buried in the sand. Instantly, he realizes the truth—his ship didn't fail. It did return him and the others to Earth. It merely brought them back in the future—a future after a nuclear war that reduced humankind to animals and gave ascendancy to the apes.

If *Planet of the Apes* were merely an antinuclear war picture, it would not be nearly so important to the science fiction film genre as it has become. Intelligently, or at least cleverly, the storytellers engineered dozens of sequences throughout to make statements about politics, religion, "Big Brother"–style government (see *1984*; *NINETEEN EIGHTY-FOUR*), intelligence tests, and so on. The late '60s was a time when most of the values and institutions in the United States were being challenged from all angles. A big-budget film that raised the same kinds of questions was not guaranteed success simply for having asked those questions. Indeed, a big-budget film would be suspect as the product of the establishment.

But *Planet of the Apes* offers more than just an attitude. The filmmakers' most intelligent move was to pose their questions by attacking both sides. At times Taylor bears the brunt of the attack. At other times it is the ape society. Thus the movie forces the viewer not simply to pick a side (humans vs. apes) and blindly follow it, but to make choices based on who is correct.

Some of the dialogue is heavy-handed, many clichés do not weather the test of time well. Taylor telling a young ape "don't trust anyone over 30" loses much of its meaning now that the film itself is "over 30" and the old slogan is a tired memory known only to current sci-fi fans' parents and grandparents. Still, the picture holds together remarkably well for a piece so distinctly opinionated. Again, this is because the opinions rise above personality to the level of universal truths—destroying all the world is bad, bigotry is bad, every creature has worth, and more, which are concepts difficult to dispute.

However, the movie is not totally good science fiction. Its social science fiction is exceptional, but the hard sci-fi elements are almost laughable. None of the astronauts guess that they've returned to Earth, even though they've landed on a planet with a breathable atmosphere and the correct gravity for humans. Nor does Taylor question that the apes speak English. These are some of a number of quibbles with the film's science, but quibbles they are. *Planet of the Apes* is a satiric, moral novel, and for once the film made from such a book reaches beneath the surface of the story to get its underlying messages onto the screen. Ultimately, the movie is a rousing success that should be seen by all science fiction fans who want to add to their sci-fi vocabulary.

Four sequels have followed so far: BENEATH THE PLANET OF THE APES, ESCAPE FROM THE PLANET OF THE APES, CONQUEST OF THE PLANET OF THE APES and BATTLE FOR THE PLANET OF THE APES, as well as a television series and animated series.

PLANET OF THE DEAD

See *FIRST SPACESHIP ON VENUS*

PLANET OF THE VAMPIRES
(aka: DEMON PLANET, THE HAUNTED PLANET, THE HAUNTED WORLD, THE OUTLAWED PLANET, PLANET OF BLOOD, THE PLANET OF TERROR, SPACE MUTANTS, TERRORE NELLO SPAZIO)

Italian International (Italy)/Castilla Cinematografica (Spain)/AIP (U.S.), 1965, Color, 85 min, VT, LD

Producer: Fulvio Lucisana; **Director:** Mario Bava; **Screenplay:** Castillo Cosulich, Antonio Roman, Rafel J. Salvia, Bava, Ib Melchior, and Louis M. Heyward; **Music:** Gino Marinuzzi; **Special Effects:** Paolo Ketoff and Emilio Zago; **Cinematography:** Antonio Pérez Olea and Antonio Rinaldi; **Cast:** Barry Sullivan, Norma Bengell, Angel Aranda, Ivan Rassimov, Evi Morandi, Fernando Vellena

Astronauts land on a mist-covered planet. Their mission is to find their missing comrades. Instead, they begin killing each other for no reason. If that isn't bad enough, three of the victims who have been buried rise from the dead, eerily walking about still encased in their shrouds. It turns out telepathic aliens are controlling the minds of the humans because they're going to take over the ship and send their zombie slaves back to Earth. Once there, they plan to subjugate the planet with their great mental powers. That's it. No heroic ending. The aliens win.

Like many silly science fiction films, this one has its cult following that will swear it is great entertainment, either because it is so atmospheric, it's sensational, or it is so stupid it's wonderful. Director Bava was highly regarded as a cameraman before he made the switch to directing, and while his movies have an original look, the stories are beyond redemption—ordinary, plodding, childish. This is a gory, lurid motion picture that outside of a few interesting visuals has nothing much to offer the discerning sci-fi fan. And that Barry Sullivan . . . he's no Whit Bissell.

PLANET OF THE VAMPIRES (1966)

See *QUEEN OF BLOOD*

PLANET ON THE PROWL

See *WAR BETWEEN THE PLANETS*

PLANETS AGAINST US (aka: THE MAN WITH THE YELLOW EYES, THE HANDS OF A KILLER, MONSTER WITH THE GREEN EYES)

Manley, 1961, b&w, 85 min, VT

Producers: Albert Chimenz and Vico Pavoni; **Director:** Romano Ferrara; **Screenplay:** Ferrara and Piero Pierotti; **Music:** Armando Tovajoli; **Cinematography:** Pier Ludovico Pavoni; **Cast:** Michel Lemonine, Maria Pia Luzi, Jany Clair, Marco Guglielmi, Otello Toso

Humanoid aliens (who all look exactly the same) arrive on Earth with no good intentions. They can hypnotize Earthlings with a glance, destroy people with a touch, and cause natural disasters with relative ease. Needless to say, things look pretty bad as these bad guys from beyond march across Europe causing as much suffering as possible. The invaders turn out to be robots who are not an invasion force, but a group of disgruntled, escapee robots running away from a higher civilization. Why pick on us and not on their masters? What did their masters do that made them run away? It's never explained before the robots' owners show up and wipe them out.

PLAN 9 FROM OUTER SPACE (aka: GRAVE ROBBERS FROM OUTER SPACE)

DCA, 1956, b&w, 79 min, VT, LD, DVD

Producer: Edward J. Wood, Jr.; **Director:** Wood, Jr.; **Screenplay:** Wood, Jr.; **Music:** Bruce Campbell, Wolf Droysen, Steve Race, Trevor Duncan, James Stevens, Ward Sills, Frank Mahl, Van Phillips, John O'Notes, and Gilbert Vinter; **Special Effects:** Charles Duncan; **Cinematography:** William C. Thompson; **Cast:** Bela Lugosi, Lyle Talbot, Mona McKinnon, Gregory Walcott, Vampira, Tor Johnson, Tom Keene, Duke Moore, Dudley Manlove, Joanna Lee, Criswell

Aliens attempt to conquer Earth by resurrecting the dead and animating their bodies. They fail.

This movie has been hailed by scores of critics and moviegoers as the worst movie ever made. Bela Lugosi died only two days into the movie's shooting schedule, prompting director Ed Wood to replace him with a taller, thinner actor, who played the rest of Lugosi's scenes holding a cloak in front of the lower part of his face, hoping the audience would remember Lugosi as Dracula and somehow be fooled.

The production values are terrible as is the acting, and the story barely makes any sense. Everything about this movie is tragically bad. So, of course, the film has an uncountable number of fans around the world who love watching it for its sheer awfulness. *Plan 9 From Outer Space* is, if not the worst, certainly one of the worst films of all time. Not only one of the worst sci-fi films, but one of the worst films, period.

Note: For those who feel they must watch the only movie in history in which the entire cast was baptized because the Baptist Church put up the money to fund the production, be sure to watch for the "tombstones" that move back and forth in the wind and then are finally blown over by the breeze, and the patio furniture that magically moves itself inside the house.

POLICE OF THE FUTURE

Gaumont (France), 1909, b&w, silent short

The title says it all in this early look at futuristic law enforcement.

POSTMAN, THE

Warner Bros., 1997, Color, 177 min, VT, LD, DVD

Producers: Kevin Costner, Lester Berman, Steve Tisch, and Jim Wilson; **Director:** Costner; **Screenplay:** Eric Roth and Brian Hegeland; **Music:** James Newton Howard; **Special Effects:** Petra Holtorf, Stephen Rosenbaum, Paul Taglianetti, Jay Riddle, and Martin A. Kline; **Cinematography:** Stephen Windon;

Cast: Kevin Costner, Will Patton, Larenz Tate, Olivia Williams, James Russo, Daniel Von Bargen, Tom Petty, Scott Bairstow, Roberta Maxwell, Joe Santos, Peggy Lipton

The civilized world has ended. A wandering hobo (Costner) finds a mail sack and, posing as a mailman, brings hope to a dying world. Trying to be something bigger, *The Postman* fails miserably to be anything but boring. Too long and complex, with nothing in the way of a story, special effects, or even competent performances, this is a sad adaptation of David Brin's source novel.

POWER, THE

MGM, 1968, Color, 103 min, LD

Producer: George Pal; **Director:** Byron Haskin; **Screenplay:** John Gay; **Music:** Miklos Rosza; **Special Effects:** J. MacMillan Johnson, Gene Warren, and Wah Chang; **Cinematography:** Ellsworth Fredricks; **Cast:** George Hamilton, Suzanne Pleshette, Richard Carlson, Yvonne De Carlo, Earl Holliman, Gary Merrill, Ken Murray, Barbara Nichols, Arthur O'Connell, Aldo Ray, Nehemiah Persoff, Michael Rennie

There's an evil genius at work, thinning out the scientific community with his fantastic telekinetic powers. Fellow scientist Hamilton sets out to discover who the killer is before it's too late. This is an often ignored film that moves nicely, maintains suspense, possesses good special effects for the time, and has a wonderful cast.

POWER GOD, THE

Vital Exchanges, 1925, b&w, silent serial

Director: Ben Wilson; **Cast:** Ben Wilson, Neva Gerber, Mary Crane, Mary Brooklyn

Scientists invent a machine that can turn out an unlimited power supply. The machine needs no fuel or base materials.

PREDATOR

20th Century Fox, 1987, Color, 107 min, VT, LD, DVD

Producers: Jon Davis, Lawrence Gordon, Deau Marus, Laurence Pereira, Joel Silver, Jim Thomas, and

John Malone; **Director:** John McTiernan; **Screenplay:** Jim Thomas and John Thomas; **Music:** Alan Silvestri; **Special Effects:** Laurencio Cordero, Joel Hynek, Al D. Sarro, J.W. Kompare, Keith Shartle, and Robert Greenberg; **Cinematography:** Donald McAlpine; **Cast:** Arnold Schwarzenegger, Carl Weathers, Jesse Ventura, Elpida Carillo, Bill Duke, Sonny Landham, Richard Chaves, R.G. Armstrong, Shane Black, Kevin Peter Hall

There's something mysterious going on in the jungles of Latin America. Government agents have disappeared, which causes ultrapatriot Weathers to call in his old pal Schwarzenegger along with his old pal's cadre of elite killers to go in on a rescue mission. More is up than meets the eye, though, and that's on both sides. It seems Schwarzenegger has been lied to about his rescue mission. On top of that, the terrorists everyone thinks are the bad guys aren't the party responsible for the missing agents. Who is? There are legends of a terrible invisible monster that has come to the area for centuries to hunt for humans whenever the temperature grows extremely hot. Sadly for almost everything on two legs in this movie, the myths are true. An alien race considers Earth its personal hunting reserve; whenever it gets warm enough, it's off to the third rock from the sun for a little trophy collecting.

After proving how incredibly skilled they are at warfare against the terrorists, fully half of Schwarzenegger's men are wiped out before they even know what is going on once the alien discovers them. From then on, it's a constant battle with the humans trying to stay ahead of the invisible, laser beam–wielding hunter tracking them for their skulls.

Fast-paced, with terrific stunts, and scientifically feasible throughout, *Predator* is one of the best sci-fi/action/adventure films ever produced. The script is intelligent, with both sides of the battle showing surprising brainpower.

PREDATOR 2

20th Century Fox, 1990, Color, 108 min, VT, LD

Producers: Terry Carr, John Davis, Suzanne Todd, Lloyd Levin, Joel Silver, Lawrence Gordon, Michael Levy, and Tom Joyner; **Director:** Stephen Hopkins; **Screenplay:** Jim Thomas and John Thomas; **Music:** Alan Silvestri; **Special Effects:** Ken Pepiot, J.W. Kompare, and Joel Hynek; **Cinematography:** Peter Levy; **Cast:** Danny Glover, Gary Busey, Ruben Blades, Maria Conchita Alonso, Bill Paxton, Kevin Peter Hall, Robert

Predator 2 (TWENTIETH CENTURY FOX / JOSEPH B. MAUCERI COLLECTION)

Davi, Adam Baldwin, Kent McCord, Calvin Lockhart, Morton Downey, Jr.

It's a record-breaking scorcher of a summer along the west coast of North America, and there's something mysterious going on in the hotter neighborhoods of Los Angeles. If the stars of this sequel knew about the first picture, they would know about the legends of a terrible invisible monster that has come to Earth for centuries to hunt for humans whenever the temperature has risen too high. An alien race considers Earth its personal hunting reserve. Whenever it gets warm enough, it's off to the third rock from the sun for a little trophy collecting. Now that it's hot enough above the equator for once, the boys from the intergalactic NRA have decided to travel to the city for their fun.

Predator 2 had all the earmarks of a bomb sequel made without any of the big stars from the first film. The location was switched from exotic jungle settings to the streets of Los Angeles, just down the block from the studio making the film. With so little connection to the original, this film looked to be just a quickie squeezed out to cash in on the first film, and it suffered at the box office initially because of this widely held misconception.

The word *misconception* is used because this is one of the top science fiction sequels ever made. The story is intelligent and builds on the first wherever possible. Where the original *PREDATOR* was much more of an all-out action epic, its follow-up is a touch more subtle and even more satisfying at the end. Indeed, in the first film, practically everyone dies before Arnold Schwarzenegger forces the alien hunter to commit nuclear suicide to keep his other-worldly effects from being captured by the victorious Earthling. In this film, cop Glover battles the alien to a standstill, forcing other aliens to land and reveal themselves to save their comrade. They are also forced by honor to accord Glover respect. In truth, the scene is much like granting a magnificent bull its life after a great performance in the ring, but still, it's more than Schwarzenegger got from the aliens. *Predator 2* is a tight, well-scripted, thinking-person's sequel. It takes the first film into consideration at every turn and then adds to the legend rather than simply copying it.

Note: At the scene in the Predator's trophy room, keep an eye out for the Alien head mounted on the wall.

PREHISTORIC MAN, THE

Star (Hungary), 1917, b&w, silent short

Director: Alfred Desy; **Screenplay:** Zoltan Somlyo and Erno Gyorf

A group of scientists comes up with the great idea to make monkeys as smart as people. Using their intelligence-enhancing beam, they boost an ape's brainpower. The first thing it does is chase girls around the furniture. Then it get itself elected to political office. Needless to say, *The Prehistoric Man* is still as funny as the day it was made.

PREHISTORIC WOMEN (1950)

Eagle-Lion Films, 1950, Color, 74 min, VT

Producers: Albert J. Cohen and Sam X. Abarbanel; **Director:** George Tallas; **Screenplay:** Abarbanel and Gregg C. Tallas; **Music:** Raoul Kraushaar; **Cinematography:** Lionel Lindon; **Cast:** Laurette Luez, Allan Nixon, Joan Shawlee, Jo Carol Dennison, Judy Landon

Eye-poppingly gorgeous makeup-covered cave girls set off in search of some men worthy of their Jurassic good looks. Just as silly as it sounds.

PREHISTORIC WOMEN (1967)
(aka: SLAVE GIRLS)

Hammer Studios (British), 1967, Color, 91 min, VT, DVD

Producer: Michael Carreas; **Director:** Carreas; **Screenplay:** Carreas; **Music:** Carlo Martelli; **Special Effects:** George Blackwell; **Cinematography:** Michael Reed; **Cast:** Martine Beswick, Michael Latimer, Edina Ronay, John Raglan, Carol White, Stephine Randall, Steve Berkoff

A sturdy explorer deep in the Amazon comes across a lost civilization where blondes have been enslaved by their pigmentationally enhanced betters in what was basically an excuse to put pretty girls in skimpy costumes up on the screen.

PREHYSTERIA

Full Moon, 1993, Color, 86 min, VT, LD

Producer: Charles Band; **Directors:** Albert Band and Charles Band; **Screenplay:** Mark Goldstein and Greg Suddeth; **Music:** Richard Band; **Special Effects:** David Allen; **Cinematography:** Adolofo Bartoli; **Cast:** Brent Cullen, Colleen Morris, Samantha Mills, Austin O'Brien, Tony Longo, Stuart Fratkin, Stephen Lee

A raisin farmer's dog steals some eggs. The dog hatches the eggs, and what is born out of them? Cute little puppy-sized dinosaurs. Plot holes abound, the special effects are way too scarce, and logic isn't even considered. This movie was followed by both *Prehysteria 2* and *Prehysteria 3*.

PREHYSTERIA 2

Paramount/Full Moon, 1994, Color, 82 min, VT

Producer: Charles Band; **Director:** Albert Band; **Screenplay:** Brent V. Friedman and Michael Paul Davis; **Music:** Fuzzbee Morse; **Cinematography:** James L. Spencer; **Cast:** Kevin R. Conners, Bettye Ackerman, Michael Hagiwara, Jennifer Harte, Dean Scofield, Greg Lewis, Larry Hankin

See *PREHYSTERIA*

PREHYSTERIA 3

Paramount/Full Moon, 1995, Color, 84 min, VT

Producer: Charles Band; **Director:** David CeCoteau; **Screenplay:** Brent V. Friedman and Michael Paul Davis; **Cinematography:** James L. Spencer; **Cast:** Whitney Anderson, Shannon Dow Smith, Pam Matteson, Fred Willard, Owen Bush, John Fujioka, Bruce Weitz, David Buzzotta, Thomas Emery Dennis

See *PREHYSTERIA*

PRESIDENT'S ANALYST, THE

Paramount, 1967, Color, 104 min, VT, LD

Producers: Howard W. Koch and Stanley Rubin; **Director:** Theodore J. Flicker; **Screenplay:** Flicker; **Music:** Lalo Schifrin; **Cinematography:** William A. Fraker; **Cast:** James Coburn, Godfrey Cambridge, Severn Darden, Joan Delaney, Pat Harrington, Will Geer, William Daniels, Barry McGuire

The president's analyst (Coburn) cracks under the pressure of listening to the leader of the free world carp about his troubles. Not able to take it anymore, Coburn flees Washington and hides at the home of a "typical American family." He is pursued by the FBI and the CIA, which are as grossly characterized as conservative monsters as the family Coburn hides with are as liberals. The movie finally reveals that the entire country is run by the phone company, which is itself controlled by robots who want to stick tiny phones into everyone's head. The film remains quite watchable, mostly thanks to Coburn's appeal, but the science fiction content is limited to hardware only. Often hailed as a classic of political satire, the film lost much of its punch when the phone company was broken up by the government. Or was that all part of their plan?

PRINCE OF SPACE

Toei (Japan), 1959, b&w, 121 min

Director: Eijiro Wakabayashi; **Screenplay:** Shin Morita; **Cinematography:** Masahiko Iimura; **Cast:** Tatsuya Umeniya, Ushio Skashi, Jojji Oka

The title's Prince of Space sneaks onto Earth for a tour, posing as a humble bootblack. On his heels follows an intergalactic tyrant who wants to conquer Earth.

PRIVILEGE

Worldfilm Services/Memorial Enterprises/Universal, 1967, Color, 103 min

Producer: John Heyman; **Director:** Peter Watkins; **Screenplay:** Norman Bogner; **Music:** Mike Leander; **Cinematography:** Peter Suschitzky; **Cast:** Paul Jones, Jean Shrimpton, Mark London, Jeremy Child, Max Bacon

Social science fiction about a socialist government in 1970s England using the power of both church and state to control the population. It uses rock stars to great effect for this purpose, at least until one of their puppets begins to realize who really holds the reins of power. *Privilege* tried hard to expose an era in a manner that might actually hold up decades later, but heavy-handed and paranoid, this movie had little to say when it was first released, and nothing now.

PROFESSOR DIDLITTLE AND THE SECRET FORMULA

Alta-International (West Germany), 1972, Color

Director: W.V. Chmielewski; **Cast:** Teeny May, Bill Ramsey, Boyd Bachman

A scientist turns a sluggish relative into a real go-getter.

PROFESSOR HOSKIN'S PATENT HUSTLER

Prestwich (Great Britain), 1897, b&w, silent short

Director: Dave Aylott

A turn-of-the-century scientist invents a machine that causes everything around it to age.

PROFESSOR OLDBOY'S REJUVENATOR

Kalem, 1914, b&w, silent short

Director: Dave Aylott

A scientist invents a fountain-of-youth drug, which he tests first on his dog and then on himself.

PROFESSOR PIECAN'S DISCOVERY

Cricks and Martin (Great Britain), 1910, b&w, silent short

Director: A.E. Coleby

A scientist invents a potion that revitalizes the weak.

PROFESSOR PUDDENHEAD'S PATENTS

Kleine, 1909, b&w, silent short

Director: Walter Booth

A flying car and the vacuum provider are among the helpful goodies invented and patented by the title scientist in this movie.

PROFESSOR'S ANTIGRAVITATIONAL FLUID, THE

Hepworth (Great Britain), 1908, b&w, silent short

Director: Lewin Fitzhamon; **Cast:** Bertie Porter

A scientist invents the title fluid, which causes anything it touches to float in the air.

PROFESSOR'S SECRET, THE

Gaumont (France), 1908, b&w, silent short

The title secret is a formula that, when injected into people, turns them into apes.

PROFESSOR'S STRENGTH TABLETS, THE

Clarendon (Great Britain), 1908, b&w, silent short

Director: Percy Stow

A scientist creates superstrength pills that work, but which are also explosive.

PROFESSOR'S TWIRLY-WHIRLY CIGARETTES, A

B&C (Great Britain), 1909, b&w, silent short

Director: H.O. Martinek

Take one piece of liver. Reduce it to powder. Take that powder, mix it with tobacco, and roll a cigarette. Have someone smoke the cigarette, then watch them spin in wild circles. Didn't this stuff make a comeback in the '60s?

PROFESSOR WAMAN

Shree Ranjit (India), 1938, b&w

Director: Manibhai Vyas

A scientist from the Indian subcontinent proclaims victory over Nature.

PROJECTED MAN, THE

Proteico (Great Britain), 1966, 90 min/Universal (U.S.), 77 min, Color

Producers: Maurice Foster and John Croydon; **Director:** Ian Curtis; **Screenplay:** John C. Cooper and Peter Bryant; **Music:** Kenneth V. Jones; **Special Effects:** Flo Nordhoff, Robert Hedges, and Mike Hope; **Cinematography:** Stanley Pavey; **Cast:** Bryant Halliday, Mary Peach, Norman Wooland, Ronald Allen, Derek Farr, Gerald Heinz, Derrick de Marney

Scientist Wooland doesn't want to fund the experiments of scientists Steiner and Allen any further. Not wanting to be out of a job, the pair enlists the aid of scientist Peach, to whom they know Wooland will listen. A good plan, but when Peach falls for Allen, a jealous Wooland sabotages their test. When it fails, he cuts off support. Halliday suspects as much, and hoping to prove their work positive, tries their machine on himself. The teleportation device transports him across town but leaves him disfigured, half-mad, and with the power of death-by-touch. He battles the police for a while and then ends it all in a power station.

PROJECT MOONBASE

Lippert, 1953, b&w, 63 min, VT, DVD

Producer: Jack Seaman; **Director:** Richard Talmadge; **Screenplay:** Seaman and Robert A. Heinlein; **Music:** Herschel Burke Gilbert; **Special Effects:** Jacques Fresco and Jerome Pycha, Jr.; **Cinematography:** William Thompson; **Cast:** Donna Martell, Ross Ford, James Craven, Hayden Rorke, Larry Johns, Herb Jacobs

In the once far-flung future of 1970, a spaceship leaves an orbiting space platform for the Moon. The ship crashes, thanks to the work of a dastardly enemy spy. Some of the survivors die, while others get married live on TV from the Moon. On the one hand, the movie was co-scripted by Robert A. Heinlein, so the science is as accurate as 1950s hard science could be, with a few good guesses thrown in just for fun. On the other hand, truly mundane acting and the film's minuscule budget make all that accuracy painfully boring to watch.

PROJECT X

Paramount, 1967, Color, 97 min

Producer: William Castle; **Director:** Castle; **Screenplay:** Edmund Morris; **Music:** Nathan Van Cleave; **Special Effects:** Paul Lerpae and the Hanna-Barbera Studios; **Cinematography:** Harold E. Stine; **Cast:** Christopher George, Greta Baldwin, Henry Jones, Monte Markham, Keye Luke, Harold Gould, Phillip Fine

It's 2118, and the Communist Chinese are about to launch an all-out attack on their Western foes, using a biological soup made up of a combination of the worst of the medieval plagues. One American agent knows the location of the secret base from which the attack will be launched, but he has amnesia and can't reveal the site—or can he? Putting together a desperate hoax, the government tries to convince the agent (George) that he is really a bank robber from the 1960s. The idea is to break down his mental defenses so that they can get at the information hidden within his brain. The wild plan works, and the West is saved. Despite the interesting premise, there is no real tension in this movie.

PROPHECY

Paramount, 1979, Color, 106 min

Producer: Robert Rosen; **Director:** John Frankenheimer; **Screenplay:** David Seltzer; **Music:** Leonard Rosenman; **Special Effects:** Robert Dawson and Thomas Burman; **Cinematography:** Harry Stradling; **Cast:** Talia Shire, Robert Foxworth, Armand Assante, Richard Dysart, Victoria Racimo

An evil lumberyard owner with no social conscience whatsoever dumps methyl mercury into a Maine river with no regard for the consequences, which turn out to be astounding. Soon mutant animals are chasing well-meaning environmentalists and their Native American friends through the rain-soaked woods, trying to kill them.

PSYCHO A GO-GO!

See *THE FIEND WITH THE ATOMIC BRAIN*

PULSE

Columbia, 1988, Color, 91 min, VT

Producer: Patricia A. Stallone; **Director:** Paul Golding; **Screenplay:** Golding; **Music:** Jay Ferguson; **Special Effects:** Paul K. Lerpae and Chet Jones; **Cinematography:** Peter Lyons Collister; **Cast:** Joey Lawrence, Cliff De Young, Roxanne Hart, Charles Tyner, Myron Healy

The appliances in the Lawrence home come alive, and, as usual, they're all violent and murderous. *Pulse* is actually a cut above most sci-fi/monster films, except that the "villain," a living short circuit, is never explained. Not why it is alive. Not why it is evil. Not nothin'.

PUNISHMENT PARK

Chartwell-Francois, 1970, Color, 89 min

Producer: Susan Martin; **Director:** Peter Watkins; **Screenplay:** Watkins; **Music:** Paul Motian, Jr.; **Cinematography:** Joan Churchill; **Cast:** Paul Alelyanes, Jim Bohan, Stan Armsted, Carmen Argenziano, Gary Johnson, Mike Hodel

It's the future, and the totalitarian government has the answer to its dissident problem. Whenever it captures someone with a rebellious nature, it makes the following offer: We'll let you go in the desert. You have to try to reach Home Base. If you do, you live. If you don't, we kill you. Not a bad deal (since you're already captured)—right? Wrong. Even those who make it to Home Base are killed.

Those who are thinking that this movie might turn out to be somewhat pointless are on the right track. Made at the height at the American baby boomer generation's rebellion against the Vietnam War, *Punishment Park* is obvious, unvarnished propaganda—the kind that offers no proof of its statements, but simply demands to be believed because it's so pure of heart. The film does employ one interesting trick though. A television camera crew follows one of the dissident groups, allowing the audience to grow more involved with the downtrodden victims' lives while the murderous army patrols are kept distantly faceless.

PUPPET MASTERS, THE

See *ROBERT A. HEINLEIN'S THE PUPPET MASTERS*

PURPLE DEATH FROM OUTER SPACE, THE

See *FLASH GORDON* (1936)

PURPLE MONSTER STRIKES, THE

See *D-DAY ON MARS*

PURPLE PEOPLE EATER

Paramount, 1988, Color, 87 min, VT, LD

Producers: Brad Krevoy and Steven Stabler; **Director:** Linda Shayne; **Screenplay:** Shayne; **Music:** Dennis Dreith; **Cinematography:** Peter Deming; **Cast:** Ned Beatty, Shelley Winters, Neil Patrick Harris, Peggy Lipton, Chubby Checker, Little Richard, James Houghton, Thora Birch, Molly Cheek, Sheb Wooley

The title alien comes to Earth looking like a pitiful kid on the doorstep in a pathetic homemade Halloween costume. And why has a Purple People Eater traveled countless light-years to Earth? To form a rock and roll band, of course.

Q

Q (aka: THE WINGED SERPENT)

Larco Productions, 1982, Color, 93 min, VT, DVD

Producers: Larry Cohen, Dick Di Bona, Don Sandburg, Peter Sabiston, and Paul Kurta; **Director:** Cohen; **Screenplay:** Cohen; **Music:** Robert O. Ragland; **Special Effects:** Dennis Eger, Randy Cook, Dave Allen, and Peter Kuran; **Cinematography:** Fred Murphy; **Cast:** David Carradine, Michael Moriarty, Richard Roundtree, Candy Clark, James Dixon, John Capodice, Malachy McCourt

The Aztec god Quetzalcoatl comes to roost in the vacant rookery of midtown Manhattan's famed Chrysler Building. Carradine is fine as New York City cop who ends up in the middle of hunting down the rooftop killer who is beheading sunbathers, but Michael Moriarty steals the film as a pathetic nonentity who discovers the serpent's resting place and determines to cash in on the knowledge. *Q* isn't great science fiction, but it is fast paced and amusing.

QUATERMASS

See *THE QUATERMASS CONCLUSION*

QUATERMASS AND THE PIT

See *FIVE MILLION YEARS TO EARTH*

QUATERMASS CONCLUSION, THE (aka: QUATERMASS)

Euston (Great Britain), 1980, Color, 107 min, VT

Producers: Ted Childs and Verity Landert; **Director:** Piers Haggard; **Screenplay:** Nigel Neale; **Music:** Nic Rowley and Marc Wilkinson; **Cinematography:** Ian Wilson; **Cast:** John Mills, Simon MacCorkindale, Barbara Kellerman, Margaret Tyzack, Brewster Mason

Aging properly since his last film appearances (*THE CREEPING UNKNOWN*, *FIVE MILLION YEARS TO EARTH*), Professor Bernard Quatermass returns to the screen for one final adventure. Death rays form outer space are striking Earth and killing people. Or are they?

Originally made for television, this last entry in the Quatermass saga suffers from poor production values and a poorer sense of the heroic nature of the title character. Saddling him with age, a missing wife, and a rebellious, runaway granddaughter who joins a cult based on death rays, the once heroic and fiery scientist is reduced to a brave but powerless and doddering relic. Quatermass is a bully and a tyrant, but he should be a benevolent dictator, ruling the world of science through the force of his will and his undying belief in his ability to master the entire physical world. To not have him die as he lived, to twist him into a completely unrecognizable puppet for the sake of hurling platitudes from the cover of a cultural icon is tragic for a truly great character.

Note: Though originally made for British television, this film was later released to theaters.

QUATERMASS EXPERIMENT, THE

See *THE CREEPING UNKNOWN*

QUATERMASS II

See *ENEMY FROM SPACE*

QUEEN OF BLOOD (aka: FLIGHT TO A FAR PLANET, THE GREEN WOMAN, PLANET OF BLOOD, PLANET OF TERROR, PLANET OF THE VAMPIRES)

AIP, 1966, Color, 81 min, VT, LD

Producer: George Edwards; **Director:** Curtis Harrington; **Screenplay:** Harrington; **Music:** Leonard Moran; **Special Effects:** William Condos; **Cinematography:** Vilis Lapenieks; **Cast:** Florence Marly, Dennis Hopper, John Saxon, Judi Merideth, Forrest J. Ackerman, Basil Rathbone

American astronauts find life (of sorts) on Mars in the form of a beautiful vampire. Taking her back to Earth, the stalwarts find themselves served as dinner until finally the vamp cuts herself and bleeds to death, sparing the crew any more unintentional blood donations. The vampire does leave behind a nest of eggs, however, starting the cycle of obvious chiller endings in the sci-fi/horror movies.

QUEEN OF OUTER SPACE

Allied Artists, 1958, Color, 80 min, VT

Producer: Ben Schwalb; **Director:** Edward Bernds; **Screenplay:** Charles Beaumont; **Music:** Marlin Skiles; **Special Effects:** Jack Cosgrove; **Cinematography:** William P. Whitley; **Cast:** Zsa Zsa Gabor, Eric Fleming, Laurie Mitchell, Paul Birch, Lisa Davis, Dave Willock, Patrick Waltz.

A rocketload of space-happy, lantern-jawed flyboys find themselves a planetful of gorgeous women. No wonder every boy growing up in the '50s wanted to be an astronaut. Parts of this one were played for laughs in the first place, so it's hard to hold too much against it.

Note: For those eagle-eyed viewers, pay close attention to the costumes, sets, and the models. Many of the costumes were moved from the *FORBIDDEN PLANET* lot to this one, and a number of the models and sets were borrowed from the production of *WORLD WITHOUT END.*

QUEST FOR FIRE

20th Century Fox, 1981, Color, 97 min, VT, LD

Producers: John Kemeny and Denis Heroux; **Director:** Jean-Jacques Annaud; **Screenplay:** Gerard Brach; **Music:** Phillipe Sarde; **Special Effects:** Christopher Tucker; **Cinematography:** Claude Agostini; **Cast:** Everett McGill, Rae Dawn Chong, Ron Perlman, Nameer El Kadi

The Ulam tribe is attacked by a stronger tribe, the cannibalistic Wagabou. During the battle, the Ulam are almost entirely wiped out. Even worse, the Wagabou have stolen the Ulam's fire. Neither tribe knows how to make fire. Though they understand its uses, and they know how to keep a fire going, they don't know how to start one. Without fire the tribe will perish. Three young members (McGill, Perlman, and El Kadi) are charged with finding fire and bringing it back to the tribe. The boys set out, and thus begins their quest. The three wander across enough different types of terrain that one begins to wonder just how many *years* their travels took them, but beyond this minor artistic consideration, this is a magnificent film.

Quest for Fire may be the most impressive film ever made on the subject of humanity in the distant past and certainly the most scientifically accurate film in its genre. No dinosaurs roam this landscape of 80,000 years ago. Savage Neanderthals fight with cunning but not honor. No English is spoken. Nothing is presented as romantic or endearing or noble. The ancient world is more than merely dangerous. It is a never-ending nightmare of fangs and senseless slaughter that must accompany blind survival. And that, of course, is what this film is all about.

Not surprisingly, the three protagonists learn a great deal in their travels. The audience is plunged through numerous examples of primitive fear and drama, while insights into the behavior of our mutual ancestors abound. Interestingly, humankind's first laugh is given equal weight by the explorers with their discovery of the first long-range weapons. That such a film could be made in an era of pulp and comic fantasy films was an amazing achievement. The picture is the culmination of three years of exhaustive research and preparation, plus an entire fourth year dedicated solely to filming.

"It was as difficult as I anticipated," admitted director Annaud. "It took a long time, but this picture is so much a part of me that it is now a baby of mine."

The director was drawn to the project by the J.H. Rosny novel on which the movie was based. "The book has an essential respect for those early, insignificant creatures," recalled Annaud, "and, of course, its central theme was immensely exciting—man's discovery of the means of making and controlling fire, which anthropologists now agree was a giant step forward in mankind's evolution."

The film is more than merely exciting, however. A sense of familiarity or some sort of racial memory permeates the production, strongly enhanced by its scientific accuracy. The language of the Ulam tribe helps lend much believability (see Appendix III). Created by Anthony Burgess and Desmond Morris, the verbal and nonverbal communication presented in the film is stunning in its seeming authenticity. Far more than language, however, beyond the realistic creatures and landscapes, the gut-level battles and confrontations, even the carefully sculpted look of the makeup, the costumes, and the atmosphere of the world at the dawn of time that permeates the movie, there is a further key aspect of the film that draws the audience in.

By studiously avoiding the standard clichés of the genre, Annaud has hidden the very message that so many other moviemakers fail to deliver, although they try hard enough. Too often in the past, sci-fi films about early humans have offered antic cave-types who fight with a sense of duty—who protect the weak, brave untold dangers for little reward, and act like knights in shining bear skins most of the time. In *Quest for Fire*, however, the heroes are a more believable bunch. They steal what they need. They run in wild-eyed terror from what they know they cannot beat. They go to the bathroom, play silly tricks on each other, and worry about where their next meal is coming from, just like regular people. By delving deeply into what makes people act the way they do, by sticking honestly to the true facets of human nature, Annaud made a truly universal film, one which speaks to every man and woman on the planet. These characters are the ancestors of humankind, and a look around at the way the world's inhabitants treat each other makes it clear that modern people are not all that removed from them.

By the time the Ulam try their hand of making fire, the audience should be feeling a primal need to see them triumph. This is not the edge-of-one's-seat thrill of waiting for Han Solo to rescue Luke Skywalker from Darth Vader, but a tension borne of desperation, for the Ulam failure to master fire would be more than a disappointment; it would be a death sentence. The

Quest for Fire (THE ROYAL BANK OF CANADA / AUTHOR'S COLLECTION)

Ulam's victory is the audience's justification. After they've seen everything wrong with humankind, there has to be some small hope for balance. Maybe it takes giving the Ulam mastery of the world to balance all their faults. After witnessing the atrocities of people daily on the news, the end of the picture, with the young "cave couple" gazing upward at the stars in wonder, gives the audience a powerful release from despair.

QUEST FOR LOVE

Peter Rogers Productions (Great Britain), 1971, Color, 90 min, VT

Producer: Peter Eton; **Director:** Ralph Thomas; **Screenplay:** Bert Batt; **Music:** Eric Rogers; **Cinematography:** Ernest Steward; **Cast:** Tom Bell, Joan Collins, Denholm Elliot, Laurence Naismith, Lyn Ashley, Juliet Harmer, Neil McCallum, Simon Ward

An excellent John Wyndham short story, "Random Quest," served as the basis for this better-than-average sci-fi/romance about a man (Bell) who stumbles into one of Earth's parallel dimensions. Everything is exactly the same as on Earth, except that this duplicate hasn't experienced many of the senseless tragedies (the Vietnam War, the JFK assassination) plaguing our own version. Mr. Bell finds a girl (Collins) to fall in love with, but she dies. What's Bell to do but get back to his own Earth, find the same girl's double there, and save her.

QUIET EARTH, THE

Mr. Yellowbeard Productions Ltd. & Co. (New Zealand), 1985, Color, 100 min, VT, LD

Producers: Don Reynolds and Sam Pillsbury; **Director:** Geoff Murphy; **Screenplay:** Bill Baer, Bruno Lawrence, and Pillsbury; **Music:** John Charles; **Special Effects:** Ken Durey, Bruce Tooley, and Phil Addenbrook; **Cinematography:** James Bartle; **Cast:** Bruno Lawrence, Alison Routledge, Peter Smith

It's the end of the world, and the last man on Earth wanders around the emptiness for a while before he goes mad. Then the last woman on Earth shows up to keep him company, and soon after the second-to-last man on Earth makes an appearance and the dating game starts all over again. The filmmakers present an apocalypse that isn't quite believable, but overall *The Quiet Earth* is not a bad film.

QUINTET

20th Century Fox, 1979, Color, 100 min, VT

Producer: Robert Altman; **Director:** Altman; **Screenplay:** Altman, Frank Barhydt, Lionel Chetwynd, and Patric Resnick; **Music:** Tom Pierson; **Special Effects:** Tom Fisher and John Thomas; **Cinematography:** Jean Bofferty; **Cast:** Paul Newman, Brigitte Fossey, Vittorio Gassman, Fernando Rey, Bibi Andersson, Nina Van Pallandt, David Langton, Craig Richard Nelson

It's the future, and everything is buried under vast fields of ice. The few remaining cities are gigantic things, highly advanced but slowly falling apart. Newly arrived in one of these megacities is Essex (Newman) and his wife (Fossey). Everything is fine for a while, and then Essex's wife is killed by a sloppy quintet player. The game is a city-devised amusement in which citizens are forced to play, an amusement that often turns bloody. Essex vows revenge, and the game continues. Labored, boring, and pretentious, this film offers little science fiction beyond the props and sets.

RABBIT TEST

Avco Embassy, 1978, Color, 86 min, VT, LD
Producer: Edgar Rosenberg; **Director:** Joan Rivers;
Screenplay: Rivers and Jay Redack; **Music:** Pete Carpenter; **Cinematography:** Lucien Ballard; **Cast:** Billy Crystal, Alex Rocco, Joan Prather, Doris Roberts, George Gobel, Imogene Coca, Paul Lynde

A comedy about the first pregnant man with minimal science fiction surrounded by acres of bad taste and bad jokes.

RABID

New World Pictures, 1977, Color, 90 min, VT

Producers: John Dunning, Danny Goldberg, Ivan Rietman, and André Link; **Director:** David Cronenberg; **Screenplay:** Cronenberg; **Music:** Rietman; **Special Effects:** Joe Elsner and Al Griswold; **Cinematography:** René Verzier; **Cast:** Marilyn Chambers, Frank Moore, Howard Ryshpan, Joe Silver, Patricia Gage, Susan Roman

An accident victim (Chambers) is treated to radical plastic surgery that turns her into a monster with an unquenchable desire to eat the flesh of others. Of course, everyone she attacks becomes infected with the same disease and impulse. How does she spread this contagion? Through the new labia that appears underneath her arm, from which a needle-sharp protrusion erupts to sting her victims.

Though director Cronenberg tends to push the envelope for art's sake in all of his work, it's difficult to know whether he's one of Canada's greatest directors or most flamboyant flimflam men, especially since many Canadian critics support both views. Present is his trademark mix of science fiction and horror, and though it holds together for a while, ultimately it pushes past the point of having anything worth saying.

RADAR MEN FROM THE MOON

Republic, 1952, b&w, serial, 12 chapters, VT, DVD

Producer: Franklin Adreon; **Director:** Fred C. Brannon; **Screenplay:** Ronald Davidson; **Music:** Stanley Wilson; **Special Effects:** Howard Lydecker and Theodore Lydecker; **Cinematography:** John MacBurnie; **Cast:** George Wallace, Roy Barcroft, William Bakewell, Tom Steele, Clayton Moore

The villain in the Moon, Retik (Barcroft), isn't satisfied with his lunar empire. He wants one on Earth as well. The brave and noble Commander Cody (Wallace) thinks Retik should stop his evil ways. This basic conflict of ideologies leads to far more bad dialogue and air-punching than one would imagine.

RADAR SECRET SERVICE

Lippert, 1950, b&w, 59 min

Producer: Barney Sarecky; **Director:** Sam Newfield; **Screenplay:** Beryl Sachs; **Music:** Russell Garcia and Dick Hazard; **Special Effects:** George Lane; **Cinematography:** Ernest Miller; **Cast:** Tristram Coffin, Pierre Watkin, John Howard, Adele Jergens, Tom Neal, Sid Melton, Ralph Byrd, Kenne Duncan.

The Radar Patrol uses radar to track down a stolen truck crammed to the gills with radioactive waste. Whew!

RADIOACTIVE DREAMS

ITM, 1986, Color, 86 min, VT, LD

Producers: Thomas Karnowski, Moctesuma Esparza, Roger Holzberg, and Frank Dominquez; **Director:** Albert Pyon; **Screenplay:** Pyun; **Music:** Pete Robinson; **Special Effects:** Greg Cannon; **Cinematography:** Charles Minsky; **Cast:** John Stockwell, Michael Dudikoff, Lisa Blount, Don Murray, George Kennedy, Michelle Little

Two kids (Stockwell and Dudikoff) grow to adulthood hidden away in a fallout shelter. With nothing to read but the collected works of Raymond Chandler, they've both adopted the persona of Chandler's noir detective.

RADIO PATROL

Universal, 1937, b&w, serial, 12 chapters

Producers: Barney Sarecky and Ben Koenig; **Director:** Ford Beebe; **Screenplay:** Wyndham Gittens, Norman S. Hall, and Ray Trampe; **Cast:** Mickey Rentschler, Grant Withers, Catherine Hughs, Adrian Morris, Max Hoffman, Jr., Monte Montague

It's radio cops Pat O'Hara and Molly Selkirk to the rescue when a group of international scoundrels kill the inventor of a flexible, yet nearly indestructible metal.

RAVAGERS

Columbia, 1979, Color, 91 min

Producer: John W. Hyde; **Director:** Richard Compton; **Screenplay:** Donald S. Sanford; **Music:** Fred Karlin; **Special Effects:** Ronald E. Hobbs; **Cinematography:** Vincent Saizis; **Cast:** Art Carney, Ann Turkel, Anthony James, Woody Strode, Seymour Cassel, Richard Harris, Ernest Borgnine, Alana Hamilton

A nuclear world has destroyed civilization. The streets of the city are controlled by a violent gang known as the Ravagers. When they kill the wife of Falk (Harris), he in turn takes revenge by killing as many of them as possible before they finally chase him out of town. Eventually he makes his way to the ocean, where he finds a new society founded on peace. Unfortunately, the Ravagers follow him, and the peaceful people must fight to protect themselves.

RAYS THAT ERASE

Martin (Great Britain), 1916, b&w, silent short

Director: E.J. Collins

A scientist hard at work on bettering the world comes up with a device that gives off vibrations which render the things they pass over invisible.

RE-ANIMATOR

See *HERBERT WEST: RE-ANIMATOR*

RED PLANET MARS

United Artists, 1952, b&w, 87 min, VT, LD

Producer: Anthony Veiller; **Director:** Harry Horner; **Screenplay:** Veiller and John Balderston; **Music:** David Chudnow; **Cinematography:** Joseph F. Biroc; **Cast:** Peter Graves, Andrea King, Marvin Miller, Morris Ankrum, Gene Roth, Herbert Berghof, Vince Barnett

Peter Graves falls into communication with men from Mars. Or, are they only men? Might they be . . . God? Might this also be one of the worst of the anti-Communist sci-fi films of the '50s?

RELIC, THE

Paramount, 1997, Color, 110 min, VT, LD

Producers: Mark Gordon, Gale Anne Hurd, Sam Mercer, and Gary Levinsohn; **Director:** Peter Hyams; **Screenplay:** Lincoln Child, Douglas Preston, Amanda Silver, Rick Jaffa, Amy Jones, and John Raffo; **Music:** John Denby; **Special Effects:** Tom Homsher, Gary Elmendorf, William Harrison, Terry W. King, John

Downey, Alan Rifkin, Paul Taglianetti, John D. Milinac, Gregory L. McMurry, Video Image, Stan Winston Studio, Bluesky/VIFX, and Banned From The Ranch Entertainment; **Cinematography:** Hyams; **Cast:** Penelope Ann Miller, Linda Hunt, Tom Sizemore, James Whitmore, Clayton Rohner, Chi Muoi Lo, Thomas Ryan, Robert Lesser, Lewis Van Bergen, Constance Towers, John Kapelos, Audra Lindsey

A scientist hard at work on battering his reputation in the anthropological community pushes a native people the wrong way and gets an unusual reward. He's turned into a particularly terrible monster, crated up, and returned to his home museum. Of course, no one discovers this until the night of a fund-raiser with all of the city's glittering elite in attendance, to be chased, eaten, and otherwise terrorized.

Though the plot sounds fairly standard, the film manages to deliver a powerhouse of excitement, mostly due to remarkable special effects and a suspenseful story. Scenes of the police invading the museum and being repelled by the rhinoceros-sized beast are incredible. The film fails in the science department, however, when a typical movie computer whiz performs a full DNA sequencing program on a desktop computer, something that takes upward of seven years' intense research in the real world.

RELUCTANT ASTRONAUT, THE

Universal, 1967, Color, 101 min, VT, LD

Producer: Edward J. Montague; **Director:** Montague; **Screenplay:** Jim Fritzell and Everett Greenbaum; **Music:** Vic Mizzy; **Cinematography:** Rexford Whimpy; **Cast:** Don Knotts, Arthur O'Connell, Leslie Nielsen, Joan Freeman, Jesse White, Jeanette Nolan

An easily frightened little guy (Knotts) who suffers from a fear of heights is elected to orbit Earth.

REPO MAN

Edge City, 1984, Color, 92 min, VT, LD

Producers: Peter McCarthy, Michael Nesmith, Gerald T. Olson, and Jonathan Wacks; **Director:** Alex Cox; **Screenplay:** Cox; **Music:** Iggy Pop, Tito Larriva, and Steven Hufsteter; **Special Effects:** Roger George and Robbie Knott; **Cinematography:** Robby Müller; **Cast:** Emilio Estevez, Harry Dean Stanton, Vonetta McGee, Olivia Barash, Sy Richardson, Tracey Walter, Susan Barnes, Fox Harris, The Circle Jerks

After his family gives away his college money to a televangelist, a new-wave youngster (Estevez) needs to find a job fast. Not having much of a clue, he falls into the car repossession line. One of the old-timers (Stanton) takes him under his wing to teach him the ropes, and the two become involved in the film's science fiction plotline.

To give away too many plot details would be criminal. It really is better seen than explained, especially for those elements aimed at the audience's powers of observation. For instance, every vehicle that makes a turn goes in a direction opposite from what it signals. Also, every vehicle sports a Christmas tree air freshener, including a police motorcycle.

The film carries on with this kind of absurdity throughout. For example, when a character introduces himself as "Otto Parts," it isn't particularly funny, until Otto is seen later standing under an "Auto Parts" sign. The Repo Man Code is clearly a play on Asimov's Laws of Robotics, another gag only apparent when a man who looks suspiciously like Asimov is seen driving a car filled with dead aliens.

These kinds of games occur throughout the film, but then, what else should one expect from a picture in which half the major characters are named after brands of beer? There are the usual low-budget film mistakes, like reflecting boom mikes and cars that change from sedans to coupes from shot to shot. But this is still a wonderfully edgy and challenging film that strongly deserves its cult reputation.

REPTILICUS

AIP, 1962, Color, 90 min, VT

Producers: Samuel Z. Arkoff, Johann Zalabery, and Sidney W. Pink; **Director:** Pink; **Screenplay:** Pink and Ib Melchior; **Music:** Sven Gyldmark; **Cinematography:** Aage Wiltrup; **Cast:** Carl Ottosen, Ann Smyrmer, Mimi Heinrich, Asbjorn Andersen, Marla Behrens

A gigantic prehistoric monster is regrown from a piece of its tail alone. The behemoth begins to trash much of Scandinavia. The usual assortment of dashing soldiers and attractive women attempt to stop it. Perhaps something is lost in the translation, but otherwise this is one of the few sci-fi films that really is so bad it's funny.

RESURRECTION

Universal, 1980, Color, 103 min, VT

Producers: Renée Missel and Howard Rosenman; **Director:** Daniel Petrie; **Screenplay:** Lewis John Carlino; **Music:** Maurice Jarre; **Cinematography:** Mario Tosi; **Cast:** Ellen Burstyn, Sam Shepard, Richard Farnsworth, Roberts Blossom, Clifford David, Pamela Payton-Wright, Eva LeGallienne

A young couple, happy and in love, speeds down the freeway in their new convertible, but when their car crashes, the man is killed and the woman survives only long enough to reach the operating table, where she dies as well. After a few minutes, however, the woman (Burstyn) returns to life. Everyone agrees that it's a miracle.

Burstyn soon discovers she has healing powers. She uses these as best she can, but without really thinking of the consequences. Soon, however, she is being studied by scientists hoping to duplicate, or at least measure, her abilities. Her new boyfriend—who seems great at first—is also studying her, but with less noble reasons. He can't make up his mind if she's an angel sent from God or a tool of the devil, but in the end he tries to kill her. She survives the attack but finds that her powers are gone. Or are they?

This is a wonderfully paced, beautifully filmed, and intelligently scripted study of the possible powers of the mind. It's also a frighteningly accurate look at the petty fears that often motivate humankind. Though a touch too long and a bit verbose, it remains an excellent film and possibly Burstyn's finest role.

RESURRECTION OF ZACHARY WHEELER, THE

JEF Films, 1971, Color, 100 min, VT

Producer: Bob Stabler; **Director:** Bob Wynn; **Screenplay:** Jay Simms and Tom Rolf; **Music:** Marlin Skiles; **Cinematography:** William Boatman; **Cast:** Angie Dickinson, Bradford Dillman, James Daly, Leslie Nielson, Jack Carter

A United States senator is rushed to a secret medical facility in New Mexico after a fatal automobile accident in an attempt to delete the word *fatal* from the accident's description. The film mixes science fiction and action, but doesn't really have enough of either to sustain itself and succeeds only in being odd and unsatisfying.

RESURRECTIONS SYNDICATE, THE

See *NOTHING BUT THE NIGHT*

RETURN, THE (aka: THE ALIEN'S RETURN, EARTHRIGHT)

1980, Color, 91 min, VT

Producer: Greydon Clark; **Director:** Clark; **Screenplay:** Curtis Birch, Jim Wheat, and Ken Wheat; **Music:** Dan Wyman; **Cinematography:** Tomislav Pinter; **Cast:** Jan Michael Vincent, Cybil Sheperd, Martin Landau, Raymond Burr, Neville Brand, Brad Rearden, Vincent Schiavelli

New Mexico serves as the backdrop for this thin story of an old man and two children who run into a visitor from beyond. Good scenery and a wonderful cast do nothing for this slow mess.

RETURN FROM WITCH MOUNTAIN

Disney, 1977, Color, 93 min, VT, LD

Producers: Ron Miller and Jerome Courtland; **Director:** John Hough; **Screenplay:** Malcolm Marmorstein; **Music:** Lalo Schifrin; **Special Effects:** Eustace Lycett and Art Cruickshank; **Cinematography:** Frank V. Phillips; **Cast:** Kim Richards, Ike Eisenmann, Bette Davis, Christopher Lee, Jack Soo, Brad Savage, Dick Bakalyan, Christopher Juttner, Anthony James, Ward Costello, Denver Pyle

See *ESCAPE TO WITCH MOUNTAIN*

RETURN OF CAPTAIN AMERICA, THE

See *CAPTAIN AMERICA*

RETURN OF DR. MABUSE

Criterion, 1961, b&w, 91 min

Producers: Artur Brauner and Wolf Brauner; **Director:** Harald Reinl; **Screenplay:** Ladislas Foder and Marc Behm; **Music:** Peter Sandloff; **Cinematography:** Karl Lob; **Cast:** Wolfgang Preiss, Gert Frobe, Lex Barker, Daliah Lavi

See *THE INVISIBLE DR. MABUSE*

RETURN OF GODZILLA, THE

See *GODZILLA 1985*

RETURN OF DR. X

Warner Bros., 1939, b&w, 62 min

Producer: Bryan Foy; **Director:** Vincent Sherman; **Screenplay:** Lee Katz; **Music:** Bernard Kaun; **Special Effects:** Percy Westmore; **Cinematography:** Sid Hickox; **Cast:** Humphrey Bogart, Rosemary Lane, Wayne Morris, Huntz Hall, Glen Langdon, Dennis Morgan, John Litel

Bogart plays a deceased child-murderer, semiresurrected by a scientist whose resuscitation techniques can't keep anyone around for very long—without, that is, a fresh supply of blood every day. Guess who starts committing a new batch of murders?

Note: This is not a sequel to the much better *DR. X*, but a quickie rushed out to capitalize on the other film.

RETURN OF SWAMP THING, THE

Millimeter Films, 1989, Color, 88 min, VT, LD

Producers: Tom Kuhn, Benjamin Melniker, Michael E. Uslan, and Robert E. Warner; **Director:** Jim Wynorski; **Screenplay:** Grant Morris and Derek Spencer; **Music:** Chuck Cirino; **Special Effects:** Vicki Graef; **Cinematography:** Zoran Hochstätter; **Cast:** Dick Durock, Heather Locklear, Louis Jourdan, Sarah Douglas, Daniel Taylor, Ronreaco Lee

See *SWAMP THING*

RETURN OF THE APE MAN

Monogram, 1944, b&w, 60 min

Producers: Sam Katzman and Jack Dietz; **Director:** Philip Rosen; **Screenplay:** Robert Charles; **Music:** Edward Kay; **Special Effects:** Ray Mercer; **Cinematography:** Marcel Le Picard; **Cast:** Bela Lugosi, George Zucco, John Carradine, Ed Chandler, Mary Currier, Frank Moran, Judith Gibson, Michael Ames

Scientist Lugosi puts the brain of Carradine into the body of a missing link. Lugosi keeps his new pet at bay with a blazing blowtorch and other sophisticated devices, but the wily ape man finally has his revenge.

Note: This is not a sequel to the far better *THE APE MAN*.

RETURN OF THE FLY, THE

20th Century Fox, 1959, b&w, 78 min, VT, LD, DVD

Producer: Bernard Glasser; **Director:** Edward Bernds; **Screenplay:** Bernds; **Music:** Paul Sawtell and Bert Shefter; **Cinematography:** Brydon Baker; **Special Effects:** Hal Lierly; **Cast:** Vincent Price, Brett Halsey, David Frankham, John Sutton, Danielle DeMezt, Pat O'Hara, Dan Seymour

See *THE FLY* (1958)

RETURN OF THE GIANT MONSTERS (aka: GAMERA VS. GYAOS, BOYICHI, AND THE SUPERMONSTER)

Daiei (Japan), 1967/AIP (U.S.), 1969, Color, 87 min

Producer: Hidemas Nagata; **Director:** Noriaki Yuasa; **Screenplay:** Fumi Takahashi; **Music:** Tadashi Yamaguchi; **Special Effects:** Kazufumi Fujii; **Cinematography:** Akira Inouye; **Cast:** Kojiro Hongo, Kichijiro Veda, Yukitaro Hotaru, Naoyuki Abe, Taro Marui, Reiko Kasahara, Yoshiro Kitahara

A volcano erupts, releasing giant monsters that run around Japan crushing buildings with no furniture or people inside them. In the winner's corner, Gamera, who loves the little children. In the loser's corner. Gyaos, who deserves all our scorn.

RETURN OF THE JEDI (aka: STAR WARS—EPISODE VI: RETURN OF THE JEDI)

20th Century Fox, 1983, Color, 131 min, VT, LD

Producer: George Lucas; **Director:** Richard Marquand; **Screenplay:** Lawrence Kasdan and Lucas; **Music:** John Williams; **Special Effects:** Roy Arbogast, Richard Edlund, Warren Franklin, Bill George, Joe Johnston, William David Lee, Bruno Van Zeebroeck, Ken Ralston, Howard Stein, Gary Zinc, Arthur F. Repola, and Michael Wood; **Cinematography:** Alan Hume, B.S.C.; **Cast:** Mark Hamill, Harrison Ford, Carrie Fisher, Billy Dee Williams, Anthony Daniels, Frank Oz, Kenny Baker, Peter Mayhew, Alec Guinness, Sebastian Shaw, Ian McDiarmid, James Earl Jones, David Prowse, Denis Lawson, Warwick Davis

This third film in the first *STAR WARS* trilogy opens with the rescue of Han Solo (Ford) from the clutches of Jaba the Hut. One wonders what happened to the motto "The rebellion is more important than any one man," and why the rebellion's political leader, its only Jedi, and best strategist take off on a mission that could have been easily accomplished by sending in the troops. Perhaps only to allow Princess Leia (Fisher) to appear in a gold bikini and slave chain, which, of course, gives the audience a good idea of where this film is going. After the rescue, the rebellion must continue. Still surviving villain Darth Vader (Prowse/voice of Jones) is working on a plan to bring his son, Luke Skywalker (Hamill), over to the dark side of the force. To this end the Empire is building a second Death Star, but it's all just a ruse to sucker Skywalker into the emperor's grasp.

It's a ruse that works. Luke goes off to face Vader in the emperor's command ship while the rebellion splits its forces between the fleet protecting the new Death Star and the force field generating base on the planet below. Things look bad for a while, but with the help of the most technically astute teddy bears (yes, the aliens are teddy bears) in the universe, they defeat the Empire. The teddy bears, called Ewoks, possess impressively curious intellects—they fight with spears and haven't figured out the wheel yet, but they've progressed far enough to figure out the catapult and the hang glider.

There are many pros and cons to this film. It was wildly satisfying to great numbers of its fans but equally disappointing to others. While not a bad science fiction film, it really isn't worthy of being the sequel to THE EMPIRE STRIKES BACK. *Star Wars* was released when serious action and sci-fi films were being laughed off the screen. The impact of *Star Wars* was an amazing reversal, one that prompted dozens of rip-offs while people waited for *The Empire Strikes Back*. The fans were faithful, however: The next film would be epic. And, in truth, Lucas did not disappoint—the first sequel to *Star Wars* was everything people hoped for and more. Whether or not Lucas put as much effort into *Return of the Jedi* is something which only he knows, but it does not appear so.

The direction is not equal to that of the previous two films. Marquand, a director with few pictures to his credit (*The Legacy* and *Eye of the Needle*), was not up to the task. When the special effects department could not come up with a very convincing Jaba the Hut (the alien never looks like anything other than a big plastic bag), the director shows the creature in direct, bright-lit close-ups instead of hiding it in shadows. When the princess is captured and forced into her slave costume, Marquand refuses to take advantage of the provocative costume in a manner that might show her humiliation. Rather, he just allows her to sit around and look bored, wondering when her rescue party will show up.

The plot is weighed down by far too many cute but useless devices. The teddy bear aliens, the badly named fish-creatures (the Calamari), R2-D2's 101 gadgets-for-any-emergency, Chewbacca's Tarzan imitation complete with bull ape call—all are inconsistent with the high tension generated by the previous film. Sadly, this outing adds nothing to the series. Dozens of new ships, new Imperial uniforms, and new aliens are seen, but the film does not extend the story. Since most of this does little to advance or enhance the plot, one has to suspect that the charges of planning merchandise at the expense of the film itself might be valid.

Much of the film doesn't follow with what has gone before. Han knew Leia loved him before. Why does he forget here? Yoda was a strong character in *Empire*. Why does he fade away weakly in this sequel? The Force used to be something anyone could manipulate. Here it becomes a thing only certain families can manipulate. Struggling to look European in design and to taste Japanese in flavor (much of the last half of the film is merely a rehash of any number of father/son samurai movie plotlines), the story here simply doesn't mesh. The death of Leigh Brackett, the guiding force behind the second film's brilliant screenplay had more of an effect on this picture than anyone could have predicted.

Lastly, the special effects aren't quite up to the job this time either. Matte lines, blue lines, and wires show constantly. There are literally dozens of continuity mistakes throughout the film. Indeed, it's quite disappointing to think that that eager band of kids who produced *Star Wars*' revolutionary effects would do such a better job than Lucas's very own Industrial Light & Magic.

Note: At one point the film's title was slated to be *Revenge of the Jedi*. Much controversy still exists in the world of *Star Wars* fandom as to why the title was changed. No one is really certain; even Fox and Lucas have changed their stories over the years. The only certain facts are that *Revenge of the Jedi* was the official title for a while, but that it never appeared on any version of the film, though it did show up on some movie posters.

RETURN OF THE JEDI (THE SPECIAL EDITION)

See STAR WARS

RETURN OF THE KILLER TOMATOES

Four Square Productions, 1988, Color, 99 min, VT, LD

Producers: Lowell D. Blank and J. Stephen Peace; **Director:** John De Bello; **Screenplay:** De Bello, Peace,

Costa Dillon, and Stephen F. Andrich; **Special Effects:** Dean Andolsek; **Cast:** Anthony Starke, George Clooney, Karen Mistal, Charlie Jones, Steve Lundquist, John Austin

See *ATTACK OF THE KILLER TOMATOES*

RETURN OF THE LIVING DEAD, THE

Orion Pictures, 1985, Color, 90 min, VT, LD

Producer: Tom Fox; **Director:** Dan O'Bannon; **Screenplay:** O'Bannon and John Russo; **Music:** Matt Clifford and Robert Randles; **Special Effects:** Michael Joyce and William Stout; **Cinematography:** Jules Brenner; **Cast:** Clu Gulager, James Karen, Don Calfa, Thom Matthews, Beverly Randolph, John Philbin

This film's simple premise: George Romero's *NIGHT OF THE LIVING DEAD* films weren't fiction. The government covered up the truth by making the horror movies to mislead the public and burying the toxic materials that reanimated the corpses in the first place. Now the zombies that the government put on ice for further study have escaped, and it's all happening again in this interesting comedy that somehow gets funnier the gorier and more violent it grows.

Return of the Living Dead Part II is much the same as the first, though considerably tamer, but the third entry in this series, *Return of the Living Dead Part III* takes a decidedly different tack. A lovesick teenager uses the revitalizing gas to bring his dead girlfriend back to life with fairly gruesome results.

RETURN OF THE LIVING DEAD PART II

Lorimar, 1988, Color, 89 min, VT, LD

Producers: William S. Gilmore, Tom Fox, and Eugene C. Cashman; **Director:** Ken Wiederhorn; **Screenplay:** Weiderhorn; **Music:** J. Peter Robinson; **Cinematography:** Robert Elswit; **Special Effects:** Eugene Crum, Del Armstrong, Kenny Meyers, Terry D. Frazee, and Gene Grigg; **Cast:** James Karen, Thom Matthews, Michael Kenworthy, Marsha Dietlein, Dana Ashbrook

See *THE RETURN OF THE LIVING DEAD*

RETURN OF THE LIVING DEAD PART III

Vidmark, 1993, Color, 97 min, VT, LD

Producers: Gary Schmoeller and Brina Yunza; **Director:** Yunza; **Screenplay:** John Penny; **Music:** Barry Goldberg; **Cinematography:** Gerry Lively; **Special Effects:** Lisa Buono, Steve Johnson, Corn Ltd, Max FX, SFX Images, Wayne Toth Productions, and Nelson FX; **Cast:** Mindy Clarke, J. Trevor Edmond, Kent McCord, Sarah Douglas, James T. Callahan, Mike Moroff, Sal Lopez, Basil Wallace

See *THE RETURN OF THE LIVING DEAD*

RETURN OF THE SWAMP THING, THE

See *SWAMP THING*

RETURN OF THE TERROR

Warner Bros., 1934, b&w, 70 min

Producer: Samuel Bischoff; **Director:** Howard Bretherton; **Screenplay:** Eugene Solow and Peter Milne; **Cinematography:** Arthur Todd; **Cast:** Mary Astor, Lyle Talbot, John Halliday, J. Carrol Naish, Frank Reicher

A kind and benevolent scientist comes up with a great idea for a new style of x-ray machine. Before he can reap any benefits from his wonderful invention, however, he is falsely accused of uncontrollable mental illness and slapped in an insane asylum to get him out of the way of his rivals.

RETURN TO THE LOST WORLD

See *THE LOST WORLD* (1993)

REVENGE OF FRANKENSTEIN

Columbia, 1958, Color, 91 min, VT, LD

Producer: Anthony Hinds; **Director:** Terence Fisher; **Screenplay:** Jimmy Sangster; **Music:** Leonard Salzedo; **Special Effects:** Phil Leakey; **Cinematography:** Jack Asher; **Cast:** Peter Cushing, Michael Gwynn, Francis Matthews, Michael Ripper, Eunice Gayson, Lionel Jeffries, John Welsh

See *FRANKENSTEIN*

REVENGE OF THE CREATURE

Universal, 1955, Color, 82 min, VT, LD

Producer: William Alland; **Director:** Jack Arnold; **Screenplay:** Martin Berkeley; **Music:** Herman Stein; **Cinematography:** Charles S. Welbourne; **Special Effects:** Bud Westmore; **Cast:** John Agar, Lori Nelson, John Bromfield, Nestor Paiva, Dave Willock, Ricou Browning, Robert B. Williams, Clint Eastwood

See *THE CREATURE FROM THE BLACK LAGOON*

REVENGE OF THE JEDI

See *RETURN OF THE JEDI*

REVENGE OF THE ZOMBIES
(aka: THE VANISHING CORPSE)

Monogram, 1943, b&w, 61 min

Producer: Linsley Parsons; **Director:** Steve Sekely; **Screenplay:** Edmund Kelso and Van Norcross; **Music:** Edward Kay; **Cinematography:** Mack Stengler; **Cast:** John Carradine, Gale Storm, Robert Lowery, Mantan Morland, Bob Steele, Veda Ann Borg, Mauritz Hugo

Scientist Carradine wants to help the Nazis out of their clumsy mess of a war. His plan: to allow the dead not only to walk once more, but to bear arms for their beloved Fatherland. Carradine's wife (Storm), slated to be one of the living dead, decides she'd rather have a career and turns her husband's creations on him.

RIDERS TO THE STARS

United Artists, 1954, Color, 82 min

Producer: Ivan Tors; **Director:** Richard Carlson; **Screenplay:** Curt Siodmak; **Music:** Harry Sukman; **Special Effects:** Jack Glass; **Cinematography:** Stanley Cortez; **Cast:** William Lundigan, Richard Carlson, Martha Hyer, Dawn Addams, King Donovan, Herbert Marshall

It's the beginning of the space race, and the nation's efforts to get human beings into space are complicated by the problem of "air friction." The questionable theory is put forward that since meteors can make it to Earth's surface without being burned to a crisp, something about them protects them. Three incredibly brave and noble astronauts blast off to capture meteors for developing frictionless coating for future rockets. Up they go in spaceships with scoops built into their noses for snagging passing chunks of space rock. They return to Earth, mission accomplished, and the space program is saved!

Riders to the Stars was a nice effort, but is now hopelessly outdated and far too treacly to be of any interest, except for the usual maniacs who will watch bad films simply because they're bad. Take note, trash seekers: *Riders to the Stars* is considered one of the worst sci-fi movies of all time.

RIFT, THE

See *ENDLESS DESCENT*

RIGHT STUFF, THE

Warner Bros., 1983, Color, 193 min, VT, LD, DVD

Producers: Irwin Winkler, James D. Brubaker, and Robert Chartoff; **Director:** Philip Kaufman; **Screenplay:** Kaufman and Tom Wolfe; **Music:** Bill Conti; **Special Effects:** John V. Fantee, Gary Gutierrez, Karl Herrman, and Pat Turner; **Cinematography:** Caleb Deschanel; **Cast:** Sam Shepard, Fred Ward, Scott Glenn, Ed Harris, Dennis Quaid, Barbara Hershey, Kim Stanley, Veronica Cartwright, Kathy Baker, Pamela Reed, Donald Moffat, Levon Helm, Scott Wilson, David Clennon, William Russ, Jeff Goldblum, Harry Shearer

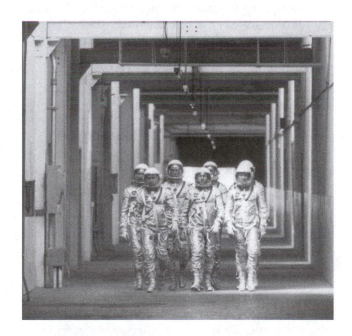

The Right Stuff (THE LADD COMPANY / AUTHOR'S COLLECTION)

The true, if somewhat idealized, story of the first U.S. astronauts and the birth of the space program. Set against the competing facts of the Apollo missions versus the air force's attempts to put Chuck Yeager into space in a ship capable of leaving the atmosphere and returning on its own, this incredible film faithfully adapts Tom Wolfe's dynamic best-seller. It's also a wonderful representation of the era, portraying much of the mood and feel of the early '60s in the U.S. accurately. The film runs more than three hours, and yet during its initial release audiences sat mesmerized. It's little wonder—the tale of the first men to dare the heavens is a powerful one, and this film is all audiences could have hoped for.

Note: The film is not a perfect historical record by any means. For instance, at one point in 1963 the audience witnesses Jack Ridley discussing an upcoming flight of the NF-104 with Chuck Yeager. This probably didn't happen, considering that Ridley died in 1954.

Also, keep an eye out for the real Chuck Yeager in a cameo as a disdainful bartender with a silent glare for a cocky pilot.

The Road Warrior (WARNER BROS. / AUTHOR'S COLLECTION)

ROAD WARRIOR, THE (aka: MAD MAX 2)

Kennedy/Miller Productions, 1981, Color, 94 min, VT, LD, DVD

Producer: Byron Kennedy; **Director:** George Miller; **Screenplay:** Terry Hates, Brian Hannant, and Miller; **Music:** Bill Conti; **Special Effects:** Mark Clayton, Greg Mulhearn, Brian Hunter, David Hardy, Munt Fieguth, Steve Courtly, and Jeffery Clifford; **Cinematography:** Dean Semler; **Cast:** Mel Gibson, Bruce Spence, Vernon Wells, Mike Preston, Virginia Hey, Emil Minty, Kiell Nilsson

In MAD MAX civilization still seemed to have a chance of holding itself together, but as this sequel opens, it is instantly clear that is no longer the case. Whatever caused society to crumble in the first film has come full cycle. Interactive cooperation on a planetary, national, state, or even communal level has all but disappeared, and it's every man for himself now. And Max (Gibson) is the man of the hour.

Max is a road warrior, a drifter who moves across the Australian landscape in his souped-up, stripped-down racer with only a dingo for company. His wife and family have been taken from him. Their civilizing influence gone, he no longer cares what happens to himself or anyone else. Some people who would like to change his mind are in a small community he comes across that has built itself a fortress around an old petroleum refinery. He manages to get inside the wall just ahead of a vicious gang of murderous killers—a small army that represents the true fall of humanity's ideals. At first, Max is too bitter about how his personal fate has been handled by the gods to care about his hosts' plight, but eventually a deal is struck. Max knows where an abandoned fuel tanker is. He offers to bring it back and help the villagers escape with enough fuel to take them away from the ravagers.

The climax of the film involves a number of the refineries' warriors riding in deathmobiles around the tanker, trying to give Max the cover he needs to get the fuel out of the valley. Almost all of the heroes die, but they take out the bad guys, and then the truth is revealed: Max has been used again; there never was any fuel in the tanker—only sand. While Max and the warriors (including the head of the community, who talked Max into going on the mission and who gives up his life with the others at the end) lead the gang away, the rest of the villagers escape in smaller, far more inconspicuous vehicles, taking all the fuel with them in sealed drums. Max is left standing in the road, realization creeping into his eyes that once again he has allowed civilization to touch him and once again he has been used by it.

Though not so clever as the first, this second film is far more dynamic and exciting and stands at least equal to its predecessor. Many audiences prefer the second film, most likely because of its slicker, flashier production. Regardless, *Mad Max* and *The Road Warrior* are excellent films, both making statements about how fragile our much-lauded civilization is and how close we are to losing it.

A third film in the series, *Mad Max Beyond Thunderdome*, fails to match the high traditions of the series. It offers little more than a somewhat confused and very watered-down retread of the first two films.

ROBERT A. HEINLEIN'S THE PUPPET MASTERS (aka: THE PUPPET MASTERS)

Hollywood Pictures, 1994, Color, 109 min, VT, LD

Producers: Ralph Winter and Michael Engelberg; **Director:** Stuart Orme; **Screenplay:** Ted Elliot, Terry Rossio, David S. Goyer, and Robert A. Heinlein; **Music:** Colin Towns; **Special Effects:** Roy Arbogast, Kevin Pike, and Peter Montgomery; **Cinematography:** Clive Tickner; **Cast:** Donald Sutherland, Eric Thal, Julie Warner, David Keith, Will Patton, Richard Belzer, Tom Mason, Yaphet Kotto

Members of the U.S. Security Agency discover that people throughout the Midwest have been infected by extraterrestrial parasites. The alien creatures control vast numbers of United States citizens, a fact that throws the government into a first-rate panic. This was a powerful concept when Heinlein first wrote his novel of the same name back in the '50s, but over the years the story concept was "borrowed" for so many other movies that four decades later when this film was finally made the idea had lost much of its power.

ROBINSON CRUSOE ON MARS

Paramount, 1964, Color, 109 min, VT, LD

Producer: Aubrey Schenck; **Director:** Byron Haskin; **Screenplay:** Ib Melchior and John C. Higgens; **Music:** Nathan Van Cleave; **Special Effects:** Wally Westmore, Bud Bashaw, and Lawrence W. Butler; **Cinematography:** Winton C. Hoch; **Cast:** Paul Mantee, Adam West, Vic Lundin

Two astronauts (Mantee and West) along with their astromonkey, Mona, are headed for Mars. A problem arises and West is killed in a crash, which leaves Mantee and Mona stranded on the surface of Mars. The two set up housekeeping in the thin Martian atmosphere, desperate to find a way to increase their oxygen supply. It isn't long before a runaway alien slave (a remarkably humanoid Lundin) finds them. He has escaped from the mining concern being run by other aliens who are strip-ping Mars's resources. The slave, soon nicknamed Friday by Mantee, shares his oxygen pills, and the three work together to survive the hostile Martian environment and the slavers who hunt them in their flying ships.

This is an interesting adaptation of an old story with impressive, intimate direction, strong cinematography, and clever use of the Death Valley backdrop. Unfortunately, wild speculation takes the place of science.

ROBOCOP

Orion, 1987, Color, 103 min, VT, LD, DVD

Producers: Arne Schmidt and Jon Davison; **Director:** Paul Verhoeven; **Screenplay:** Edward Neumeier and Michael Miner; **Music:** Basil Poledouris; **Special Effects:** Rob Bottin, Dale Martin, Phil Tippett, Peter Kuran, Visual Concept Engineering, Inc., Rocco Gioffre, Robert Blalack, and Praxis Film Works; **Cinematography:** Jost Vacano; **Cast:** Peter Weller, Nancy Allen, Daniel O'Herlihy, Ronny Cox, Kurtwood Smith, Miguel Ferrer, Robert DoQui, Ray Wise, Felton Perry, Paul McCrane, Del Zamora

It's the near future and the corporation heads of Detroit's Security Concepts think they have an answer to the crime problem. Recently deceased police officers are reoutfitted with enough cyborg components to return them to functional duty. The experiment gets a boost when young officer Murphy is cut down by a sadistic gang of wild drug dealers. The dead policeman is refitted as a robot avenger, although programmed with a few rules to keep him one of the good guys—serve the public trust, uphold the law, and protect the innocent.

Murphy makes a splendid RoboCop, but Murphy was killed so violently the horrible memory cannot be erased from his brain. That keeps more of the dead cop's personal memories alive as well. Soon RoboCop is not only hunting his killer, but he's looking for his family as well. His first shock comes when he discovers that his killer is being protected by high-ranking officials within Security Concepts. Worse than that, he then discovers programming that he cannot override—it prohibits him from harming corporate officers of Security Concepts.

This is a fine action picture, but its appeal extends far beyond that. Much of the best moral speculation of the Frankenstein saga is present, updated by the more modern idea that no longer is anything wrong with human tampering with God's creation. The moral ambiguity of the story centers on the more sci-fi notion that the morality of such actions hinges on the intent of the tamperer—as well as the results.

This movie was followed by two sequels, as well as a live-action and an animated television series. All versions of *RoboCop* have been popular to varying degrees, but nothing after the initial film matched the wild interest started by it. Fans and critics alike credit director Verhoeven's uniquely humorous vision of science and business running rampant for the movie's enduring popularity. Whatever the case, the *RoboCop* concept is a hearty one.

ROBOCOP 2

Orion, 1990, Color, 117 min, VT, LD, DVD

Producers: Patrick Crowley and Jon Davison; **Director:** Irvin Kershner; **Screenplay:** Frank Miller and Walon Green; **Music:** Leonard Rosenman; **Special Effects:** Rob Bottin, Phil Tippett, Peter Kuran, and Visual Concept Engineering, Inc.; **Cinematography:** Mark Irwin; **Cast:** Peter Weller, Nancy Allen, Daniel O'Herlihy, Belinda Bauer, Tom Noonan, Robert DoQui, Felton Perry, Gabriel Damon, Willard Pugh, Patricia Charbonneau

It's the near future and the corporate heads of Detroit's Security Concepts once again think they have an answer to the crime problem. This time they want to create secure neighborhoods where people pay for their own police force. Of course, the corporation is up to its old tricks, working hand in hand with the drug dealers who are ruining the city with their latest product, "Nuke."

RoboCop ends up confusing a youthful killer with his son due to a glitch in his memory banks, making him unable to deal with the dangerous punk. Security Concepts again finds RoboCop dangerous to their plans, so his initial programming—serve the public trust, uphold the law, and protect the innocent—is updated with thousands of useless even contradictory commands to make him less of a threat to their plans. In one of the films most triumphant moments, RoboCop grabs hold of an exposed electrical source in an attempt to clear away the useless programming, while risking certain death.

Many reviewers criticized this film unmercifully as too dark, too violent, and too cynical, but it is a matter of perspective. The film, like most of the best sci-fi, uses the genre to disclose its exploration of a contemporary problem. Screenwriter Frank Miller is exposing the crushing, repressive nature of big government gone wild with writing more and more laws—legislation

Robocop 2 (ORION PICTURES / JOSEPH B. MAUCERI COLLECTION)

mostly aimed at keeping decent citizens in line—while failing to dispense justice to actual criminals. Miller wrote a politically conservative science fiction film, but regardless, as with the original, there are no mistakes in its forward motion. The only difference between this film and the first is that in the initial film director Verhoeven managed to tell a two-sided story.

ROBOCOP 3

Orion, 1993, Color, 105 min, VT, LD, DVD

Producers: Patrick Crowley and Jane Bartelme; **Director:** Fred Dekker; **Screenplay:** Frank Miller and Dekker; **Music:** Basil Poledouris; **Special Effects:** Rob Bottin, Phil Tippett, Peter Kuran, and Visual Concept Engineering, Inc.; **Cinematography:** Gary B. Kibbe; **Cast:** Robert John Burke, Nancy Allen, Rip Torn, John Castle, Jill Hennessy, CCH Pounder, Robert DoQui, Mako, Renny Ran, Bruce Locke

It's still the near future and the corporate heads of Detroit's Security Concepts still think they have an answer to the crime problem. This time they simply want to level most of Detroit and start over. Things are so bad that this time, rather than working inside the system, RoboCop ends up leaving the force and joining the rebellion trying to hold off the inevitable police state.

Cautious after the criticism leveled by some against its predecessor, this installment in the series avoids excessive violence and tones down the political stand of the second Robocop film. Sadly, all that remains is the comic book action that made the first films popular but none of the wit and punch that made them successful. Even the death of RoboCop's partner (Allen) is played for mere shock value. The film retains the action, surprises, and high-quality special effects but little of the massive, sweeping dynamics of either of the other entries in the series.

ROBO MAN

See *WHO?*

ROBOT CARNIVAL

A.P.P. Co., Ltd. (Japan), 1987, Color, 91 min, VT, LD

Directors/Screenplays/Animators: Katsuhiro Otomo, Atsuko Fukushima, Kouji Morimoto, Kiroyuki Kitazume, Mao Lamdo, Hidetoshi Ohmori, Yasuomi Umetsu, Hiroyuki Kitakubo, and Takashi Nakamura; **Music:** Isaku Fujita; **Cast:** Nariko Fujieda, Katsue Miwa, Toku Nisho, Chisa Yokoyama, Kei Tomiyama, Kaneto Shiozawa

Nine of Japan's top animators teamed up to create this animated anthology film centering on the theme of robots. There are eight segments, although it is often hard to tell where one starts and others stop. Not all of the pieces work; some are nearly incomprehensible. Others, however, such as the story that shows a human man falling in love with a robot female, are very clear and quite touching. The stories aside, the artwork is fascinating and spectacular throughout. Any animation fan, but especially anime enthusiasts, will appreciate it. Be warned: Violence in Japanese cartoons is not nearly as sanitized as it is in America.

ROBOT MONSTER, THE

Astor, 1953, b&w, 63 min, VT, LD, DVD

Producer: Phil Tucker; **Director:** Tucker; **Screenplay:** Wyatt Ordung; **Music:** Elmer Bernstein; **Cinematography:** Jack Greenhalgh; **Special Effects:** Jack Rabin and David Commons; **Cast:** George Nader, Claudia Barrett, Gregory Moffett, Pamela Paulson, Selena Royle, John Mylong

The most evil thing in the galaxy, the horrid Ro-Man (an actor inside a gorilla bodysuit with a diving suit helmet in place of a head), comes to Earth and kills every living thing in sight with its mighty death ray. Soon everyone is gone except for one family that somehow manages to elude the thing for most of the film as it awkwardly stumbles about in scenic Bronson Canyon, searching for them. Finally, the moment comes when it is about to destroy the last family on Earth when we discover that it's all a dream. Lucky break, eh? Perhaps one of the worst sci-fi movies of all time, *Robot Monster* is utterly terrible. Originally shown in 3-D, even that innovation couldn't disguise what an incredibly, completely awful picture this is.

Stock Footage Alert: This movie stuck in every spare bit of celluloid it could get its hands on, including sweepings from Willis O'Brien's studios, such as outtakes from *ONE MILLION B.C.* As might be expected, their placement is just as awful as everything else in the picture.

ROBOT OF REGALIA, THE

Reed, 1954, b&w, 78 min

Producers: Roland D. Reed, Guy V. Thayer, Jr., and Arthur Pierson; **Director:** Hollingsworth Morse; **Screenplay:** Arthur Hoerl; **Cast:** Richard Crane, James Lyton

Once again, it's a feature film cobbled together from episodes of the venerable *Rocky Jones, Space Ranger* television show. This time out, our boy Rocky meets a robot.

ROBOT VS. THE AZTEC MUMMY

Calderon (Mexico), 1959/AIT (U.S.), 1962, b&w, 65 min

Producer: William C. Stell; **Director:** Rafael Portillo; **Screenplay:** Alfred Salazar; **Music:** Antonio Diaz Conde; **Cinematography:** Enrique Wallace; **Cast:** Ramon Gay, Crox Alvarado, Rosita Arenas

When a scientist invades a sacred tomb and a scary mummy runs him off, the researcher returns with a robot to help him steal the dead Indians' treasures.

ROCKET ATTACK, U.S.A.

Exploit Films, 1961, b&w, 68 min, VT

Producer: Barry Mahon; **Director:** Mahon; **Cinematography:** Mike Tabb; **Cast:** Monica Davis, Daniel Kern, John McKay, Edward Czerniuk, Arthur Metrano

Evil Communists are getting ready to nuke New York City. Can America's spies save the Big Apple as well as the nation they love from World War III?

ROCKET MAN, THE

20th Century Fox, 1954, b&w, 79 min

Producer: Leonard Goldstein; **Director:** Oscar Rudolph; **Screenplay:** Lenny Bruce, Jack Henley, George W. George, and George F. Slavin; **Music:** Lionel Newman; **Cinematography:** John F. Seitz; **Cast:** Charles Coburn, Spring Byington, Anne Francis, John Agar, George "Foghorn" Winslow, Beverly Garland

Our boy Winslow gets his hands on an outer space weapon that makes dishonest people honest. Politicians beware.

ROCKETMAN

Buena Vista Pictures, 1997, Color, 94 min, VT, LD

Producers: Oren Aviv, Roger Birnbaum, Richard H. Prince, Jamie Masada, Jonathan Glickman, Eric L. Gold, Peter Saffran, and Jon Turtelhaub; **Director:** Stuart Gillard; **Screenplay:** Craig Mazin, Greg Erb, and Oren Aviv; **Music:** Michael Tavera; **Cinematography:** Steven B. Postner; **Special Effects:** Bill Cobb, John Corneto, and Christopher S. Baird; **Cast:** Harland Williams, Jessica Lundy, William Sadler, Jeffrey DeMunn, Beau Bridges, James Pickens, Jr., Peter Onorati

It's the future and time for the first manned flight to Mars. The crew is ready, the window of opportunity is approaching, and suddenly one of the astronauts takes to his sickbed. What to do? Why, replace him with a complete moron who likes to fart in his spacesuit. What else? As some might guess, this movie was billed as a comedy.

ROCKETSHIP X-M
(aka: EXPEDITION MOON)

Lippert, 1950, b&w, 78 min, VT, LD, DVD

Producer: Kurt Neumann; **Director:** Neumann; **Screenplay:** Neumann; **Music:** Ferde Grofé; **Special Effects:** Jack Rabin and Irving Block; **Cinematography:** Karl Struss; **Cast:** Lloyd Bridges, Osa Massen, Hugh O'Brian, John Emery, Noah Beery, Jr.

A spaceship on its way to the Moon runs into a meteor shower and is knocked off course all the way to Mars. When the ship lands, the crew discovers the remains of a one-time grand Martian civilization now decaying in radioactive ruin. They also find a savage race of sub-Martians who kill off most of the crew. The two who make it back to the ship and off Mars don't fare much better. They run out of fuel on the way back to Earth.

Kurt Neumann is far better known as the director of the riveting sci-fi/horror film, *THE FLY.* Sadly, *Rocketship X-M* comes nowhere close to Neumann's later masterpiece. This film, rushed out to beat the far more elaborate *DESTINATION MOON* to the screen, is fair enough but nothing special. The videotape version boasts new special effects shot some 25 years after the picture was initially made.

ROCKETEER, THE

Walt Disney Studios, 1991, Color, 108 min, VT, LD, DVD

Producers: Lisa Bailey, Dave Stevens, Lloyd Levin, and Larry J. Franco; **Director:** Joe Johnson; **Screenplay:** Stevens, Paul DeMeo, William Dear, and Danny Bilson; **Music:** James Horner; **Special Effects:** Sandra Almond Williams, John Bell, Patricia Blau, Chris Burton, Jon G. Belyeu, Ken Ralston, Pat Turner, Penny Runge, and James D. Schwalm; **Cinematography:** Hiro Narita; **Cast:** Bill Campbell, Jennifer Connelly, Alan Arkin, Timothy Dalton, Paul Sorvino, Terry O'Quinn, Ed Lauter, James Handy, Tiny Ron, Melora Hardin

Nazis and a hometown hero square off over a rocket-powered backpack. Based on a comic by the same name, the movie is a poorly directed collection of action clichés, weak dialogue, sloppy effects, and a terrible story.

ROCKET TO THE MOON

See *CAT WOMEN OF THE MOON*

ROCKY HORROR PICTURE SHOW, THE

20th Century Fox, 1975, Color, 95 min, VT, LD

Producer: Michael White; **Director:** Jim Sharman; **Screenplay:** Sharman and Richard O'Brien; **Music:** O'Brien; **Special Effects:** Wally Veevers; **Cinematography:** Peter Suschitzky; **Cast:** Tim Curry, Susan Sarandon, Barry Bostwick, Richard O'Brien, Jonathan Adams, Meatloaf, Little Nell, Charles Gray, Patricia Quinn

Two plucky kids (Bostwick and Sarandon) get lost on a dark and stormy night. What to do? Why, ask for assistance at that spooky old mansion, of course. Inside, the heterosexual couple discovers a nest of Transylvanian transsexuals lead by Dr. Frank N. Furter (Curry), an alien on Earth to make a male love slave for himself.

This is an extremely kinky musical comedy spoof of horror and sci-fi films, colorful, fast-moving, and funny. The special effects are odd but satisfying. The songs are outrageous (still) and great fun. They're a must for the fun-loving sci-fi fan. After all, the title song alone makes references to THE DAY THE EARTH STOOD STILL, THE INVISIBLE MAN, KING KONG, DOCTOR X, FORBIDDEN PLANET, WHEN WORLDS COLLIDE, NIGHT OF THE DEMON, TARANTULA, and THE DAY OF THE TRIFFIDS. Although an utter failure in its initial run, the film became a favorite of the midnight show circuit shortly thereafter, playing on a weekly basis for decades in numerous cities around the United States.

Seeing *The Rocky Horror Picture Show* in the theater now is nothing like seeing it when first released. Midnight shows now feature elaborate audience participation, and those who don't know the film won't have the slightest idea of what is going on as people throw toast at the screen, open umbrellas (while firing squirt guns in the air), and scream out nearly every line of the movie on cue.

The Rocky Horror Picture Show was followed by a sequel, *Shock Treatment*, which featured many of the same characters (not all played by the same actors, however) in a wacky, but not very amusing film that had little to do with science fiction or entertainment. It was only made to cash in on the midnight-show success of its predecessor.

Note: The house used as Dr. Furter's mansion is the Oakley Court, a 250-year-old hotel used by Hammer Studios for such films as *The Man in Black* ('49), *The Brides of Dracula* ('60), *The Reptile* ('66), and *The House in Nightmare Park* ('73). Have fun looking for recognizable features.

RODAN

Toho (Japan),1956, DCA (U.S.), 1957, Color, 78 min, VT, LD

Producer: Tomoyuki Tanaka; **Director:** Inoshiro Honda; **Screenplay:** Takeshi Kimura and Takeo Murata; **Music:** Tadashi Yamauchi; **Cinematography:** Isamu Ashida; **Special Effects:** Eiji Tsuburaya; **Cast:** Kenji Sahara, Yumi Shirakawa, Akhiko Hirata, Akio Kobori, Yoshibumi Tajima

Japan is in giant-monster trouble once again. This time it's a gigantic, nearly indestructible pterodactyl-like creature causing all the damage. Better than a number of the Godzilla team's films, *Rodan* has a more interesting back story than most of the Toho fare and some very interesting takes on the main monster as well.

ROLLERBALL

United Artists, 1975, Color, 129 min, VT, LD, DVD

Producer: Norman Jewison; **Director:** Jewison; **Screenplay:** William Harrison; **Music:** Tomaso Albinoni; **Cinematography:** Douglas Slocombe; **Special Effects:** Sass Bedig and John Richardson; **Cast:** James Caan, John Houseman, Maud Adams, John Beck, Moses Gunn, Ralph Richardson

It's the future and everything is great. War and hunger and poverty have been virtually eliminated. So what do people do in this perfect future? They watch Rollerball matches, of course. Rollerball is the ultimate contact sport: a high-speed, deadly game that pits one corporate team (nations have been eliminated at this point in history) against another in a worldwide competition. Jonathan E (Caan) is the greatest Rollerball star the world has ever seen. He enjoys his status, but lately it hasn't been enough. Jonathan has begun to think. Sadly for him, he's begun to think about his job.

Rollerball is a future sport devised by the corporate nations of the world to keep the masses in check. Played on a circular track, two teams of skaters (along with a few motorcycle-riding partners) battle for control of a ball that is literally shot into play out of a cannon. After the Corporate Wars, conflict (along with the individuality that usually breeds it) was declared a bad thing. The businesses that then controlled the world brought Rollerball into being to placate the masses. Games were routinely rigged to keep any one team or player from rising to any kind of popular status. Jonathan E manages to come to prominence, however, much to his corporate masters' displeasure.

The overlords offer the player many bribes to slow down and take it easy—in other words, to stop standing

Rodan (TOHO STUDIOS / R. ALLEN LEIDER COLLECTION)

out and inspiring the crowds to think about doing the same. Unfortunately, this has all come at a time when Jonathan has begun to question his place in society and whether or not a lack of individuality is a good thing. His masters devise several plans to make the game more difficult so as to knock Jonathan from his perch. Jonathan survives each challenge, however, growing more resentful with each game.

Finally it is decided that an open-ended game will be staged in which play will end only when one combatant is left standing. Everyone playing knows that it's a setup to take out Jonathan, and so even his own team is reluctant to protect him. He wins anyway. As he is cheered at the end, the implication is that with his incredible popularity he is going to challenge the ruling classes.

Rollerball is an interesting film. Its action sequences are highly dramatic and quite entertaining, even

decades after its initial release, but the scenes in between the games are often poorly paced and lifeless. This was a complaint from many critics when the film was first in the theaters, and time has not helped any. Still, there is a great deal going on within the story that can't easily be ignored.

Jonathan represents the potential of the human race. The film addresses a then contemporary American problem that has become only worse over the years—how easy living distracts humankind from progress. Human evolution proceeds through individual effort. But mass produce everything for everyone, give every person the same comfortable life, make it impossible for anyone to possess more than the person down the street, and suddenly the desire/need for competition fades away. *Rollerball* is not a perfect film by any means, but it tries hard to raise some important questions. Like any good sci-fi film, it succeeds.

RUNAWAY

Tri-Star Pictures, 1984, Color, 100 min, VT, LD, DVD

Producer: Michael Rachmil; **Director:** Michael Crichton; **Screenplay:** Crichton; **Music:** Jerry Goldsmith; **Cinematography:** John A. Alonzo, A.S.C.; **Special Effects:** Mark Dornfield, John Thomas, George Erschbamer, and William H. Orr; **Cast:** Tom Selleck, Cynthia Rhodes, Gene Simmons, Kirstie Alley, Stan Shaw, Joey Cramer, G.W. Bailey

It's the near-future and trouble is brewing. A ruthless maniac named Luthor (Simmons) gets his hands on a computer component that will allow him to reprogram simple household robots for murder. In this particular near-future, robots are everywhere, fulfilling all manner of functions for humanity. With automated workers in every corner of society, a person who could kill at a distance through these machines would be—more than just a menace—a demon. Opposing Luthor is police officer Jack Ramsey (Selleck) of the Runaway Robot Squad. Ramsey stumbles across the villain's trail, but of course no one believes the evidence he uncovers. Except for his partner—and convincing her even takes a while. Eventually, however, Ramsey and Luthor square off and the forces of good triumph once more.

Although it is true that the film's reach really does exceed its grasp, at least the filmmakers tried to make an honest science fiction film. *Runaway* is a nice attempt. The story line might fail in the details (minor points of logic fall apart several times, and the audience is force-fed a great deal of information in a revelation or a single phone call), but its intent holds together. As in all great adventures, the hero is first chosen by fate to stand in the way of evil and then, by evil itself, as a foe to be crushed. At the climax Luthor could escape the clutches of the law, but he doesn't. Instead, he forces Ramsey to pursue him, making it an all-or-nothing proposition.

One of the best things about *Runaway*, however, is the attention the filmmakers give to scientific detail. Each robot is intelligently thought out and displayed. Multiple uses exist for single designs. In other words, form follows function, not mere human aesthetic, as it does in the real world. *Runaway* isn't perfect, but it's a solid, albeit low-budget thriller with real characters, nice effects, and some great acting.

RUNNING MAN, THE

Tri-Star Pictures, 1987, Color, 100 min, VT, LD, DVD

Producers: Keith Barrish, George Linder, Tim Zinnermann, and Rob Cohen; **Director:** Paul Michael Glaser; **Screenplay:** Steven E. DeSousa and Stephen King; **Music:** Harold Faltermeyer; **Cinematography:** Thomas Del Ruth; **Cast:** Arnold Schwarzenegger, Maria Conchita Alonso, Yaphet Kotto, Jim Brown, Richard Dawson, Jesse Ventura, Mick Fleetwood, Dweezil Zappa

It's near-future and things couldn't be worse. In 2017 the entire world's economy has collapsed. The planet is now one large totalitarian police state. Television is used to keep the masses in check (much like today). One of the most popular programs is the Justice Department's number one hit, "The Running Man." The premise is simple. In *Most Dangerous Game* fashion, convicts are given a chance at freedom. These "running men" are used like foxes, set loose but pursued by an overwhelming force of colorful killers.

Arnold Schwarzenegger plays a police officer who refused to carry out the order to massacre a large crowd of unarmed citizens. The citizens were slaughtered anyway, and Arnold was framed for their murders. When there's a slip in "The Running Man" show's ratings, Arnold is forced to participate in the games. He does so to keep his friends out of the game, but the evil producer has his friends thrown in anyway. Fighting their way through one hunter after another, the foursome not only escapes the game, but finds a way to aid the underground in fomenting a revolution that brings freedom to the land.

Despite a thin plot, the film is quite watchable. No great lessons are learned, but the sci-fi content is surprisingly rich. Hard science is represented by lots of little devices making up the background. The social sciences, however, are well represented, as the breakdown of American integrity is shown in the context of the Hollywoodization of the Constitution. It's also a good action picture with enough punch to keep one watching.

Note: Richard Dawson's turn as the swarmy host of the game show is simply wonderful. Of course, the producers were cashing in on his years as the smiling, somewhat naughty host of the television game show *The Family Feud.* It works. Here's hoping his line, "Get me the president's agent!" isn't prophetic.

SALUTE OF THE JUGGER

See *BLOOD OF HEROES*

SANTA CLAUS CONQUERS THE MARTIANS (aka: SANTA CLAUS DEFEATS THE ALIENS)

AVCO Embassy, 1964, Color, 80 min, VT

Producers: Joseph Levine, Arnold Deeds, and Paul L. Jacobson; **Director:** Nicholas Websters; **Screenplay:** Jacobson and Glenville Mareth; **Music:** Milton Delugg; **Special Effects:** Duke Brady, Fritz Hansen, Frank Hoch, and the Haberstroh Suddios; **Cinematography:** David L. Quaid; **Cast:** John Call, Leonard Hicks, Vincent Beck, Donna Conforti, Pia Zadora

Santa Claus and two Earth children are kidnapped by Martians and taken back home to Mars so that the jolly old elf can help straighten out the Red Planet's children. For those wondering why this movie isn't seen on a local cable station every December along with other Christmas classics and other "sugar-plummed" holiday fare, there's a reason: It's just as stupid as it sounds.

SANTA CLAUS DEFEATS THE ALIENS

See *SANTA CLAUS CONQUERS THE MARTIANS*

SATELLITE OF BLOOD

See *FIRST MAN INTO SPACE*

SATELLITE IN THE SKY

Warner Bros., 1956, Color, 84 min

Producers: Edward Danzinger and Harry Lee Danzinger; **Director:** Paul Dickson; **Screenplay:** John Mather, J.T. McIntosh, and Edith Dell; **Music:** Albert Elms; **Special Effects:** Wally Veevers; **Cinematography:** George Perinal and Jimmy Wilson; **Cast:** Kieron Moore, Jimmy Hanley, Donald Wolfit, Louis Maxwell, Byran Forbes

It's time to test the first tritonium bomb. Intelligently (more so than anyone who actually does test massively high explosives on this planet) it is decided to conduct this experiment in outer space. While in orbit, with preparations for the test under way, the device becomes fixed in place on the astronaut's escape vehicle. Despite all their best efforts, the fly boys can't get it unfixed, and that means the pilot is doomed.

SATURN 3

AFD, 1980, Color, 97 min, VT, LD, DVD

Producers: Stanley Donen and Eric Rattray; **Director:** Donen; **Screenplay:** Martin Amis and John Barry;

Music: Elmer Bernstein; **Special Effects:** Colin Chilvers; **Cinematography:** Billy Williams; **Cast:** Kirk Douglas, Farrah Fawcett, Harvey Keitel, Douglas Lambert

Two research chemists, Adam and Alex (Douglas and Fawcett), have the perfect life. They live alone in a research facility on Titan, the third moon of Saturn. Much older, Adam is from Earth and knows a thing or two about the universe. But poor little Alex was born in space and knows nothing about humanity except for the small bits she's learned from Adam. Regardless, the two are happy. These lovebirds are out on Titan hoping to synthesize a protein nutrient that can feed a starving, overpolluted, and overly decadent Earth. The dedicated, self-sacrificing lovers conduct their work in peace and quiet, considering themselves the luckiest pair of kids in the cosmos, until Captain James (Keitel) shows up. He informs the pair that he's come to monitor their work and that they're already behind schedule. Actually, he's a madman who killed a space shuttle pilot and took over his ship to make the trip to Titan.

To help the two get back on schedule (and to keep his mind off how much he desires Alex), James constructs a robot helper for them. The captain makes a major mistake, however. He programs Hector, the towering robotic monster, directly from his own unbalanced brain. The robot is as crazed, as homicidal, and as lust-struck with Alex as is James. But while James lusts after Alex, a high-school kid, Hector is another story. Once the robot has "brain-drained" off James's personality, it launches a mission of rape, and Adam and Alex try to stay alive as the captain and his robot take turns attempting to kill them. At one point, Alex's dog is split in two and then reassembled by the station's robotic lab, but only as a prelude to James getting the same treatment. To say things get messy from there is an understatement.

This interesting premise should have led somewhere, but unfortunately it didn't. The performances are stiff and the plot aimless, and despite the screenwriters' clever touch of building an inexperienced and naïve quality into Fawcett's character, she brings no credibility to it. To make matters worse, the science fiction quota here is on a par with that in *ABBOTT AND COSTELLO GO TO MARS*.

SAVAGE DAWN

See *STRYKER*

SCANNER COP

Republic Films, 1994, Color, 94 min, VT, LD

Producers: Pierre David and René Malo; **Director:** David; **Screenplay:** John Bryant and George Saunders; **Music:** Louis Febre; **Cinematography:** Jacques Haitkin; **Cast:** Daniel Quinn, Darlanne Fluegel, Richard Grove, Mark Rolston, Richard Lynch, Hilary Shepard, James Horan, Gary Hudson, Luca Bereovici, Brion James

See *SCANNERS*

SCANNER COP II: VOLKIN'S REVENGE (aka: SCANNERS THE SHOWDOWN)

Showdown Productions, 1994, Color, 95 min, VT, LD

Producer: Pierre David; **Director:** Steve Barnett; **Music:** Richard Bowers; **Special Effects:** Brett Newkirk, John Foster, Steve Patino, Joseph Cornell, Christopher Robbins, John Carl Buechler, George Phillips, and Arthur Valicinis; **Cast:** Daniel Quinn, Patrick Kilpartrick, Khrystyne Haje, Stephen Mendel, Robert Forster, Brenda Swanson, Jerry Potter, Jewel Shepard

See *SCANNERS*

SCANNERS (aka: TELEPATHY 2000)

Avco Embassy, 1981, Color, 102 min, VT, LD

Producers: Pierre David, Victor Solicki, and Claude Heroux; **Director:** David Cronenberg; **Screenplay:** Cronenberg; **Music:** Howard Shore; **Special Effects:** Don Berry, Louis Craig, and Jacques Godbout; **Cinematography:** Mark Irwin; **Cast:** Stephen Lack, Jennifer O'Neill, Patrick McGoohan, Michael Ironside, Law-rence Dane, Charles Shamata

"Scanners" are a random group of people who gained tremendous mental powers during their prenatal months due to an unsafe baby drug that upset their development. Once the problem was discovered, the product was quickly pulled from the market, but not before it started several hundred unborn children on their way to becoming something beyond human knowledge.

The film opens with the most powerful known scanner, Revok, attacking a government agency. He has determined to gather all willing scanners to his cause. He's also decided that anyone who doesn't join up will be eliminated. His target in the opening sequence is a scanner working for the government. Revok succeeds beyond anything the audience expects, managing not only to take out his target, but to escape two carloads of heavily armed agents trying to detain him.

The plot unfolds slowly from this point. Dr. Ruth (McGoohan) tells his agency that Revok has found and indoctrinated or eliminated all the world's scanners save one. Vale (Lack), the last free scanner, is under Ruth's care. The doctor plans to train him and then send him after Revok. And training Vale will need. Scanners suck in all the random surface thoughts of those people in their immediate vicinity—with the result that most scanners are forced to live as recluses, running from the terrible, never-ending voices they constantly hear whenever they venture into populated areas. Ruth and Revok both possess a drug that allows scanners to move freely in the world. Ruth uses his to help scanners. Revok, on the other hand, wants scanners to rule the world. To this end he is secretly administering the drug to pregnant women so that he might build an army of scanners. When the end comes, we finally discover why he wants to do this.

Revok is Ruth's son. Dr. Ruth is the creator of the drug that formed the scanners. Vale is his other son—a son he allowed to wander the world as a helpless vagrant until he could be used by his father in the battle to stop Revok. Both sons feel used, but in different ways and to different ends. When all this sibling rivalry finally comes to a head in the climax, the sparks really fly.

Director Cronenberg is at his best in this movie, and there's a lot going on that has to be experienced first hand. Although the plot follows his usual story line—something has gotten inside of people, which they wish they could remove—it is by far his best use of the theme. Despite its low budget, this is a tremendously powerful and effective film. Some special effects are not for the squeamish, but they will appeal to those who can take exploding heads and melting eyes. This is a solid, straightforward science fiction movie.

However, that judgment doesn't hold for all of the sequels. Cronenberg had little or nothing to do with the later films in the series. Whereas some of the sequels aren't bad and even make good use of the original premise, that wild, visceral sickness Cronenberg manipulated throughout the opening movie is definitely missing in the others. There's blood and gore, but not much reason to endure them.

Scanners II: The New Order, the first of the sequels, makes the best use of the original premise. Again, bad people are hoping to use scanners to do their bidding. Again, along comes a principled scanner who upsets their apple cart. *Scanners III: The Takeover*, however, is so dreadful that the franchise had to be repackaged to survive. What followed was *Scanner Cop*, a focused change in direction that saved the series. In this first offering, a

rookie police officer who happens to be a scanner uses his powers (which might kill him) to track a cop killer. This was followed by *Scanner Cop II: Volkin's Revenge* in which an evil scanner whom our hero had taken off the streets returns with heightened powers for a rematch.

SCANNER FORCE

See *SCANNERS III: THE TAKEOVER*

SCANNERS II: THE NEW ORDER

(Canada), 1991, Color, 105 min, VT, LD

Producers: Pierre David and René Malo; **Director:** Christian Duguay; **Screenplay:** B.J. Nelson; **Music:** Marty Simon; **Special Effects:** Ryal Cosgrove; **Cinematography:** Rodney Gibbons; **Cast:** David Hewlett, Deborah Raffin, Yvan Ponton, Isabelle Mejias, Tom Butler, Raoul Trujillo

See *SCANNERS*

SCANNERS III: THE TAKEOVER

Republic Pictures, 1992, Color, 101 min, VT, LD

Producers: Irene Litinsky, Rénald Paré, Pierre David, and René Malo; **Director:** Christian Duguay; **Screenplay:** B.J. Nelson, René Malo, David Preston, and Julie Richard; **Special Effects:** Michael Maddi and Jon Campfens; **Cinematography:** Hugues de Haeck; **Cast:** Liliana Komorowska, Valerie Valois, Daniel Pilon, Collin Fox, Claire Cellucci, Michael Copeman, Steve Parrish

See *SCANNERS*

SCANNERS: THE SHOWDOWN (aka: SCANNER COP II: VOLKIN'S REVENGE

See *SCANNERS*

SCREAM AND SCREAM AGAIN

AIP, 1970, Color, 95 min, VT, LD

Producers: Max J. Rosenberg and Milton Subotsky; **Director:** Gordon Hessler; **Screenplay:** Christopher Wicking; **Music:** Dave Whittaker, Dominic King, and Tim Hayes; **Special Effects:** Jimmy Evans; **Cinematography:** John Coquillon; **Cast:** Vincent Price,

Peter Cushing, Christopher Lee, Judy Huxtable, Alfred Marks, Peter Sallis, Judi Bloom, Christopher Matthews, Michael Gothard, Marshall Jones

Something's loose in England that kills its victims by draining all their blood. That something turns out to be a superrace being developed by a mad scientist (Price) at the request of a government agent (Jones). Things would have probably worked out for the pair, but a plucky police officer (Bloom) tracks the lunatics down. Price is all for doing her in, but cold-blooded murder right in front of him is too much for squeamish agent Jones. He kills Price to save Bloom, and that's the end of England's chances to rule the world with an army of super soldiers.

Scream and Scream Again isn't quite as bad as it might sound, but it's also nothing special either. Despite its claims of science fiction, its sci-fi quota is quite small.

SCREAMERS

Triumph Films, 1995, Color, 107 min, VT, LD, DVD

Producers: Masao Takiyama, Josée Bernard, Franco Battisa, Anthony I. Ginnane, Tom Berry, Charles W. Fries, and Stefan Wodoslawsky; **Director:** Christian Duguay; **Screenplay:** Miguel Tejada-Flores and Dan O'Bannon; **Music:** Normand Corbell; **Special Effects:** Cineffects Productions, Inc., Ryal Cosgrove, Ernest D. Farino, Adrien Morot, Monica Babic, Daniel Blais, Laserlite F/X, Bruno Boisvert, and Transformes L.M., Inc.; **Cinematography:** Rodney Gibbons; **Cast:** Peter Weller, Roy Dupuis, Jennifer Rubin, Andy Lauer, Charles Powell, Ron White, Michael Caloz, Liliana Komorowska

The year is 2078. Man has made it off-world and found dozens of other planets to despoil. In this film the action centers on one world where two political factions are fighting it out. In reality, most of the fighting takes place off-planet, leaving the two sides' workers stranded on the inhospitably cold world, trying to keep each other at bay while waiting for supplies. Things wouldn't be so bad if it wasn't for the screamers—small robot-killing devices with which the enemy has littered the planet. They travel underground and explode out through the frozen crust, killing their victims with a series of blades and spinning saws.

If that wasn't bad enough, the things seem to be evolving. This is discovered when an enemy trooper tries to reach the "good guys" lines. It's quickly apparent that this lone trooper hadn't come to attack, but to offer a truce. Since good guy team leader Weller has found

that no one is coming from off-world to help them— "them" meaning anyone on the planet—he decides to look into the offer. Courageously, he heads for the enemy lines, taking only one man with him. They make their way to the other side's stronghold, discovering the secret of the screamers along the way. Then they discover another secret. And then another. And then . . .

What seems at first to be just another exploitation sci-fi rip-off quickly turns into a well-written, unpredictable piece of top-notch entertainment. The direction is slow paced but steady, and thought-provoking scenes replace nonstop exploitative bloodbaths and special effects bonanzas. The ending disappoints a touch, but the rest of the film more than makes up for it.

SEA SERPENT, THE (aka: HYDRA)

(Spain), 1986, Color, 92 min, VT

Producer: José Frade; **Director:** Gregory Greens; **Screenplay:** Gordon A. Osborn; **Music:** Robin Davis; **Cast:** Timothy Bottoms, Ray Milland, Taryn Power, Jared Martin, Gerard Tichy, Carole James

Bottoms is a wrongly disgraced sea captain who is desperate to regain his good name. To do so, he sets out after a sea monster recently awakened from its ocean-bottom slumber by atomic tests. It's not the best idea he ever had.

SECONDS

Paramount, 1966, b&w, 106 min, VT, LD

Producer: Edward Lewis; **Director:** John Frankenheimer; **Screenplay:** Lewis J. Carlino; **Music:** Jerry Goldsmith; **Special Effects:** Jack Petty and Mark Reedall; **Cinematography:** James Wong Howe; **Cast:** Rock Hudson, John Randolph, Salome Jens, Will Geer, Jeff Corey, Murray Hamilton, Wesley Addy

The old millionaires of the world have a secret. When they're simply too tired to go on, they have their deaths faked, and then they are taken to a private clinic where they are transformed into young, healthy, virile specimens of man and womanhood. Tired old John Randolph goes under the knife in the beginning of the movie, only to wake up as Rock Hudson.

At first he's wonderfully pleased. It isn't long, however, before he begins to regret his actions. Simply put, he discovers that youth isn't all it's cracked up to be. He struggles to make things work, but the doctors from the clinic decide he's too close to breaking and have him brought back. At that point, he is locked away with the others who couldn't handle their new lives—all of them locked away as living storage units, waiting to supply spare parts to the next arrogant oldster. Sappy and uneven treatment makes this good premise much less effective than it could have been.

SECRET KINGDOM, THE

Stoll (Great Britain), 1925, b&w, silent feature

Producer: Sinclair Hill; **Director:** Hill; **Screenplay:** Alicia Ramsay; **Cinematography:** Percy Strong; **Cast:** Matheson Lang, Stella Arbenia, Eric Bransby

A scientist invents a machine that can hear and record people's brain waves and then makes their most personal thoughts available for public consumption. As one might expect, this causes nothing but trouble. Wisely, the machine is soon destroyed. *The Secret Kingdom* is a good study of human nature, and though the science fiction element is minimal, it's put to good use.

SECRET OF THE TELEGIAN (aka: THE TELEGIAN, THE TELEPORTED MAN)

Toho (Japan), 1960/Herts-Lion (U.S.), 1964, Color, 85 min

Producer: Tomoyuki Tanaka; **Director:** Jun Fukuda; **Screenplay:** Shinichi Sekizawa; **Cinematography:** Kazuo Yamada; **Special Effects:** Eiji Tsuburaya; **Cast:** Yumi Shirakawa, Akira Kitano, Koji Tsuruta, Tadao Nakamaru, Akihiko Hirata, Shin Otomo, Akira Sera, Koji Uno

A scientist takes a normal man and electrically charges his circulatory system. Somehow this not only turns him into a monster, but it allows him to teleport anywhere instantly. And the reason for this? To murder one's enemies, of course.

SECRET SERVICE IN DARKEST AFRICA, THE (aka: THE BARON'S AFRICAN WAR)

Republic, 1943, b&w, serial, 10 chapters

Producer: William J. O'Sullivan and Herbert J. Yates; **Director:** Spencer Bennett; **Screenplay:** Royal Cole, Basil Dickey, Jesse Duffy, Ronald Davidson, Joseph O'Donnell, and Joseph Poland; **Cinematography:** William Bradford; **Special Effects:** Howard Lydecker;

Music: Mort Glickman; **Cast:** Rod Cameron, Joan Marsh, Duncan Renaldo, Lionel Royce

The Nazis are in Africa, working on death rays and suspended animation. Time for 21 reels of Rod Cameron and his secret service agents to punch their way to victory.

SEED PEOPLE

Full Moon Entertainment, 1992, Color, 86 min, VT

Producers: Charles Band and Anne Kelly; **Director:** Peter Manoogian; **Screenplay:** Jackson Barr; **Cinematography:** Adolfo Bartoli and Aldo Antonelli; **Special Effects:** Lois Simbach; **Music:** Bob Mithoff; **Cast:** Sam Hennings, Andrea Roth, Dane Witherspoon, David Dunard, Holly Fields, Anne Betancourt

A man returns to his hometown to find aliens enacting the most pointless rip-off of *INVASION OF THE BODY SNATCHERS* ever attempted.

SERGEANT DEADHEAD THE ASTRONAUT

AIP, 1965, Color, 89 min

Producers: James H. Nicholson, Samuel Z. Arkoff, and Anthony Carras; **Director:** Norman Taurog; **Screenplay:** Louis M. Hayward; **Cinematography:** Floyd Crosby; **Special Effects:** Roger George; **Music:** Les Baxter; **Cast:** Frankie Avalon, Deborah Walley, Cesar Romero, Buster Keaton, Fred Clark, Gale Gordon, Eve Arden

It's into space for mild-mannered astronaut Frankie Avalon and his astrochimp. Meek Frankie goes through a personality change with his co-pilot and comes back a loudmouthed jerk. Oh, that poor monkey. Obviously, this movie was made in the days before PETA.

SEX KITTENS GO TO COLLEGE

Allied Artists, 1960, b&w, 90 min

Producer: Albert Zugsmith; **Director:** Zugsmith; **Screenplay:** Robert Hill and Zugsmith; **Cinematography:** Ellis Carter; **Special Effects:** Augie Lohman; **Music:** Dean Elliot; **Cast:** Mamie Van Doren, Tuesday Weld, Mijanou, Mickey Shaughnessy, Louie Nye, Martin Milner, John Carradine, Vampira, Conway Twitty, Charles Chaplin, Jr., Harold Lloyd, Jr.

Thinko, the whiz computer, picks a stripper (Van Doren) with a genius IQ to head its small town college's science department. The title tells one all there is to know.

SHADOW OF CHINATOWN

Victory, 1934, b&w, serial, 15 chapters

Producer: Sam Katzman; **Director:** Robert F. Hill; **Screenplay:** W. Buchanan, Isodore Bernstein, and Basil Dickey; **Cinematography:** Bill Hyder; **Cast:** Bela Lugosi, Herman Brix, Luana Walters, Charles King

A scientist (Lugosi) comes up with a machine that can mesmerize helpless folks and then control them from a distance. Of course, he uses his invention for evil.

SHADOW OF EVIL (aka: BANCO IN BANGKOK)

CICC (France/Italy), 1964, 115 min/Warner Brothers (U.S.), 1966, 92 min

Producer: Paul Cadeac; **Director:** André Hunebelle; **Screenplay:** Pierre Foucand, Raymond Borel, Michel Lebrun, Richard Caron, Patrice Rondard, and Hunebelle; **Cinematography:** Raymond Lemoigne; **Music:** Michel Magne; **Cast:** Kerwin Mathews, Robert Hossein, Pier Angeli, Stuart Nesbitt

A scientist wants to rule the world by releasing a plague that will kill everyone on the planet except those with the proper immunization. Can secret agent Kerwin Matthews save the day?

SHADOWZONE

Full Moon Entertainment, 1990, Color, 89 min, VT, LD, DVD

Producers: Charles Band, Debra Dion, and Carol Kottenbrook; **Director:** J.S. Cardone; **Screenplay:** Cardone; **Music:** Richard Band; **Cinematography:** Karen Grossman; **Cast:** David Beecroft, Louise Fletcher, Shawn Weatherly, James Hong, Miguel Nunez, Lu Leonard, Frederick Flynn

A team of scientists is hard at work out in the Nevada desert. They think they're simply experimenting with human sleep patterns, but as usual, they're on the verge of moving beyond humanity's appointed place in the universe. Shattering the barrier between our conscious dimension and the next one over, the unsuspecting boys and girls in white unleash a hideous monster into our realm. Snappy production values and better than average performances compensate for a low budget.

SHANKS

Paramount, 1974, Color, 93 min

Producer: Steven North; **Director:** William Castle; **Screenplay:** Ronald Graham; **Music:** Alex North; **Special Effects:** Richard Albain; **Cinematography:** Joseph Biroc; **Cast:** Marcel Marceau, Philippe Clay, Tsilla Chelton, Cindy Eilbacher, Larry Bishop, Don Calfa, Mondo, William Castle, Helena Kallianiotes

Malcolm Shanks (Marceau) is a deaf-mute puppeteer who has been befriended by a clever scientist, Dr. Walker (also played by Marceau). The doctor has invented a device that will rewire the dead, effectively turning them into human puppets. When Walker passes on, Shanks uses the doctor's device to create a better life for himself. First he murders his hideous in-laws, reanimating them after their demise. Soon after, Shanks falls in love. But not all is destined to go well for our quiet homicidal maniac. A motorcycle gang breaks in on his girlfriend, proceeding to torture, rape, and then kill her in short order. The psycho puppeteer unleashes his battalion of the walking dead to slaughter the bikers and then reanimates his love as a zombie puppet.

This very strange movie was the last film directed by William Castle. Needlessly violent and coldly lacking any hint of remorse, this is not a film for everyone.

SHAPE OF THINGS TO COME, THE

Allied Artists, 1979, Color, 95 min

Producers: Harry Alan Towers and William Davidson; **Director:** George McCowan; **Screenplay:** Martin Lager; **Music:** Arthur Bliss; **Special Effects:** Wally Gentleman, Don Weed, and Brick Price; **Cinematography:** Reginald Morris; **Cast:** Jack Palance, Carol Lynley, John Ireland, Barry Morse, Nicholas Campbell, Eddie Benton

King of the robots, Omus (Palance), gives the lunar city of New Washington an ultimatum—surrender. The Moon has even stricter gun control than does

New York City, and so the citizens of New Washington find themselves in quite a predicament. Not to worry, though. A group of plucky humans takes it upon themselves to fly off to Omus's home planet and put the kibosh on his evil plans. The Canadian production company that put this movie together, claiming it was based on the classic novel by H.G. Wells, went out of business before they could release the film. That turn of events didn't keep this sorry mess from finding its way to the public.

SHE CREATURE, THE

AIP, 1957, b&w, 77 min

Producer: Alex Gordon; **Director:** Edward L. Cahn; **Screenplay:** Lou Rusoff; **Cinematography:** Frederick E. West; **Special Effects:** Paul Blaisdell; **Music:** Ronald Stein; **Cast:** Chester Morris, Paul Blaisdell, Marla English, Lance Fuller, Cathy Downs, El Brendel, Tom Conway, Frieda Inescort, Frank Jenks, Jack Mulhall

Psychotic hypnotist (Morris) stumbles across a frightening ability. When he puts his beautiful young assistant under his power, he regresses her to prehistoric times. This puts her under the control of a long past ancestor who kills anyone she can get her hands on. Morris thinks this is smashing and bills himself as the world's most accurate prognosticator. He predicts murders and then sends his assistant's prehistoric alter ego out to do the killing. This works until the assistant falls in love, which interferes with Morris's income. He tells the alter ego to kill the new boyfriend, but in the end his plans backfire.

SHE DEMONS

Astor, 1958, b&w, 77 min, VT

Producer: Arthur A. Jacobs; **Director:** Richard E. Cunha; **Screenplay:** Cunha and H.E. Barrie; **Cinematography:** Meredith M. Nicholson; **Special Effects:** Carlie Taylor and David Koehler; **Music:** Nicolas Carras; **Cast:** Irish McCalla, Tod Griffin, Victor Sen Yung, Gene Roth, Leni Tana, Billy Dix, Bill Coontz, Rudolph Anders

A Nazi scientist hard at work in the jungle wants to restore his disfigured wife's former beauty. He's been trying skin grafts from the native girls but hasn't had much success. That's why so many of the locals have great bodies and scarred faces—the she-demons of the title.

SHE DEVIL

20th Century Fox, 1957, b&w, 77 min

Producer: Kurt Neumann; **Director:** Neumann; **Screenplay:** Neumann and Carroll Young; **Cinematography:** Karl Struss; **Music:** Paul Sawtell and Bert Shefter; **Cast:** Mari Blanchard, Jack Kelley, Albert Dekker, John Archer

A woman with tuberculosis is willing to try anything to save her life. Unfortunately, she tries a fruit fly serum that has some side effects no one quite counted on—like incredible strength and an appetite for murder. An antidote is found, which removes the side effects, but which also halts the lady's breathing.

SHH! THE OCTOPUS

Warner Bros., 1938, b&w, 60 min

Producer: Bryan Foy; **Director:** William McGann; **Screenplay:** George Bricker; **Music:** Heinz Roemheld; **Cinematography:** Arthur Todd; **Cast:** Allen Jenkins, Hugh Herbert, Marcia Ralston, Eric Stanley

A scientist out to help no one but himself tries to invent something new and exciting. After a little thought, he decides the most exciting new thing that he could invent would have to be a death ray. Anyone who tries to stop him or just happens to drop by gets invited to play with his giant octopus.

SHIRLEY THOMPSON VS. THE ALIENS

Kolossal (Australia), 1972, b&w, 104 min

Producer: Jim Sharman; **Director:** Sharman; **Screenplay:** Helmut Makaitsi and Sharman; **Music:** Ralph Tyrell; **Cinematography:** David Sanderson; **Cast:** Jane Harders, Marion Johns, June Collis, Tim Eliott

Nasty aliens are invading Earth, but these extraterrestrials have an unexpected weakness—one human in six billion can see them. This time that human is a beleaguered woman with better (or at least, more immediate) things to do than worry about the invasion.

SHIVERS

See *THEY CAME FROM WITHIN*

SHOCKER

Carolco Pictures, 1989, Color, 110 min, VT, LD

Producers: Wes Craven, Shep Gordon, Barin Kumak, Warren Chadwick, Robert Engelman, Peter Foster, and Marianne Maddalena; **Director:** Craven; **Screenplay:** Craven; **Music:** William Goldstein; **Special Effects:** Allen Blaisdell, Larry Fioritto, David L. Hewitt, and Jonathan Craven; **Cinematography:** Jacques Haitkin; **Cast:** Michael Murphy, Peter Berg, Cami Cooper, Mitch Pileggi, Sam Scaber, Heather Langenkamp, Theodore Raimi, Richard Brooks, Dr. Timothy Leary

The teenage son (Berg) of a police officer is mentally linked with one of the most psychotic killers of our time. Some thought this bizarre circumstance would end when said killer was put to death, but when the switch is thrown on the electric chair, the murderer becomes an electric killer who can move through power lines. Soon the killing begins again. Despite a reasonably interesting premise, this movie died a quick death due to its incredibly awkward script and pitifully inept direction.

SHOCK TREATMENT

See *THE ROCKY HORROR PICTURE SHOW*

SHOCK WAVES (aka: DEATH CORPS)

Zopix Company, 1975, Color, 86 min, VT

Producer: Reuben Trane; **Director:** Ken Weiderhorn; **Screenplay:** John Kent Harrison and Ken Weiderhorn; **Music:** Richard Einhorn; **Cinematography:** Irving Pare; **Cast:** Peter Cushing, Brooke Adams, John Carradine, Fred Buch, Jack Davidson, Luke Halpin

A party boat filled with young, good-looking fun-lovers sets out in the warm waters off the coast of sunny Florida, where they meet an old hermit (Cushing). It's not long before they learn that Cushing is actually the master of a group of underwater Nazi zombies. The premise is not helped by a low budget and a weak script.

SHORT CIRCUIT

Tri-Star Pictures, 1986, Color, 98 min, VT, LD, DVD

Producers: Gregg Champion, David Foster, Gary Foster, and Lawrence Turman; **Director:** John Badham; **Screenplay:** S.S. Wilson and Brent Maddock; **Music:** David Shire; **Special Effects:** Eric Allard, Dennis Dorney, Mike Edmonson, Michael Ferriter, Rocco Gioffre, Chris Casady, Robert Hall, Nina Salerno, Hoyt Yeatman, Keith Shartle, and Dream Quest Images; **Cinematography:** Nick McLean; **Cast:** Ally Sheedy, Steve Guttenberg, Fisher Stevens, G.W. Bailey, Austin Pendleton, Brian McNamara, Tim Blaney

A weapons manufacturing company has come up with a new engine of destruction for the military—a mobile, unmanned reconnaissance device and weapons platform that can go almost anywhere and handle almost any situation since it thinks on its own. The weapon, affectionately known as number 5, decides that killing is bad, and runs away from the weapons manufacturer. Worse yet, number 5 is discovered by an animal rights heroine (Sheedy), who teaches it about love and compassion and helps it elude its pursuers.

This good premise fails on a number of counts. The film becomes lost in its own apparent political message and misses the opportunity to make a powerful statement by settling for two-dimensional characters and a predictable story. *Short Circuit 2* followed but offered no improvement over its predecessor.

SHORT CIRCUIT 2

TriStar Pictures, 1988, Color, 110 min, VT, LD

Producers: David Foster, Gary Foster, and Lawrence Turman; **Director:** Kenneth Johnson; **Screenplay:** Brent Maddock and S.S. Wilson; **Music:** Charles Fox; **Special Effects:** Mike Edmonson, Arthur Langevin, John McLeod, Mike Reedy, and Mark Noel; **Cinematography:** John McPherson; **Cast:** Fisher Stevens, Michael McKean, Cynthia Gibb, Jack Weston, Dee McCaffrey, David Hemblen

See *SHORT CIRCUIT*

SILENT RAGE

Columbia, 1982, Color, 105 min, VT, LD

Producers: Andy Howard and Anthony B. Unger; **Director:** Michael Miller; **Screenplay:** Joseph Fraley and Edward D. Lorenzo; **Music:** Peter Bernstein and Mark Goldenberg; **Cinematography:** Robert C. Jessup and Neil Roach; **Cast:** Chuck Norris, Ron Silver,

Steven Keats, Tori Kalem, William Finley, Brian Libby, Stephen Furst

A type of Frankenstein's monster is built, and it's up to Chuck Norris, Texas sheriff, to stop it. *Silent Rage* offers plenty of nice action moves for those who like them, but the sci-fi is hardly present.

SILENT RUNNING

Universal, 1972, Color, 90 min, VT, LD, DVD

Producers: Douglas Trumbull, Marty Hornstein, and Michael Gruskoff; **Director:** Trumbull; **Screenplay:** Deric Washburn, Michael Cimino, and Steven Bochco; **Music:** Peter Shickele and Diane Lampert; **Special Effects:** Trumbull, John Dykstra, Richard Yuricich, Wayne Smith, Richard Alexander, John Baumbach, Leland McLemore, Bob Shepard, Gard Richards, Bill Shourt, James Down, and Paul Kraus; **Cinematography:** Charles F. Wheeler; **Cast:** Bruce Dern, Cliff Potts, Ron Rifkin, Jesse Vint, Mark Persons, Cheryll Sparks, Steven Brown and Larry Whisenhunt

In the all too near future, almost every piece of vegetation on the face of Earth has been destroyed. In fact, there is nothing green on the planet any longer. What remains of our forests and crops is now in space aboard a series of domes attached to the space freighter, *Valley Forge*. The idea is that someday these domes will be brought back to Earth after the pollution levels die down so that the planet can be made lush once again. Tending to this great responsibility is extremely dedicated botanist Dern. He takes his job seriously, certainly more so than the astronauts keeping the domes orbiting for him. Dern slogs on despite their abusive behavior, constantly puttering in his greenery with the help of three small drones.

Things get worse, however, when the government decides to shut down the project. The order comes for the gardens to be destroyed and for everyone to return to Earth, but this puts Dern over the edge. He snaps, murdering his fellow astronauts and hijacking the domes. Dern and the drones head for deep space to escape the reaches of Earth, but the plants begin to wither as they are taken away from the Sun. Dern returns for the good of his beloved trees and vegetables, but this puts him and the domes back in the path of those who want to destroy them. Having run out of options, Dern detaches the domes from the freighter, putting them into orbit in the care of his beloved drones. Then he destroys the *Valley Forge* and himself along with it to ensure that no one will look for his precious green.

The science behind *Silent Running* is fatuous. Aside from a botanist who doesn't realize why plants denied sunlight might be dying, why couldn't seeds and cuttings have been stored on Earth? Considering the expense of maintaining the domes, why would a beleaguered world have gone to such trouble when there were so many far more practical alternatives? The answer is that when you set up straw men as villains, they're easier to knock over. Overly impressed with its own social conscience (the producers brought in political activist Joan Baez to sing), the picture gets heavy-handed at times with the lessons it seems to feel the audience needs desperately. On the other hand, first-time director Trumbull pulled out all the stops to give the movie wonderful, subtle effects without deep space battles and morphing monsters to show off. Subsequently, what scenery over-the-top Dern doesn't chew to bits is amazingly impressive for its time and still holds up quite well today.

SINISTER INVASION

See *INCREDIBLE INVASION*

SIREN OF ATLANTIS

See *JOURNEY BENEATH THE DESERT*

SKEETER

New Line Cinema, 1994, Color, 91 min, VT, LD

Producers: James Glenn Dudelson, Sanford Hampton, John Lambert, and Kelly Andrea Rubin; **Director:** Clark Brandon; **Screenplay:** Brandon and Lanny Horn; **Music:** David Nessim Lawrence; **Special Effects:** Frank H. Isaacs; **Cinematography:** Lambert; **Cast:** Tracy Griffith, Jim Youngs, Charles Napier, Jay Robinson, William Sanderson, Eloy Casados, Buck Flower, John Putch, Saxon Trainor, Stacy Edwards, Michael J. Pollard

Giant mosquitoes cause a lot of trouble in this good, low-budget, sci-fi/black comedy.

SKY BIKE, THE

Eyeline Films (Great Britain), 1967, Color, 62 min

Producer: Harold Orton; **Director:** Charles Frend; **Screenplay:** Frend; **Cinematography:** John Coquillion; **Music:** Harry Robinson; **Cast:** Spenser Shires, John Howard, Liam Redmond, Della Rands

A group of inventors pull together to prove that humans can fly under their own power. They create an aircraft powered by human energy alone, one which a lone average person can keep in the air for the distance of a mile. They succeed and, interestingly, 10 years later a group of real inventors actually did the same thing. *Sky Bike* may seem like a fictionalized account of the actual story of the *Gossamer Condor*, but the truth is the film came first.

SKY CALLS, THE

See *BATTLE BEYOND THE SUN*

SKY IS CALLING, THE

See *BATTLE BEYOND THE SUN*

SKY PARADE, THE

Paramount, 1936, b&w, 70 min

Producer: Harold Hurley; **Director:** Otho Lovering; **Screenplay:** Byron Morgan, Brian Marlow, and Arthur J. Backhard; **Cinematography:** William Mellor and Al Gilks

A robotic, fully automated airplane is demonstrated to an amazed public.

SKY PIRATES

Monogram, 1939, b&w, 60 min

Producer: Paul Malvern; **Director:** George Waggner; **Screenplay:** Paul Schofield and Joseph West; **Cast:** Jason Robards, Marjorie Reynolds, Milburn Stone

A way to guide high explosives from bombers to targets below by using of radio waves is discovered and put to use.

SKY MARSHALS OF THE UNIVERSE

See *COMMANDER CODY*

SKY SHIP

Nordisk (Denmark), 1917/Great Northern (U.S.), 1920, b&w, silent feature

Director: Holger-Madsen; **Screenplay:** Ole Olsen and Sophus Michaelis; **Cinematography:** Louis Larsen; **Cast:** Zanny Peterson, Gunnar Tolnaes

Some early space jockeys land on Mars and discover a race of beautiful women in the first of many silly sci-fi films involving rockets and lingerie.

SKY SKIDDER, THE

Universal, 1929, b&w, silent feature

Director: Bruce Mitchell; **Screenplay:** Val Cleveland; **Cinematography:** William Adams; **Cast:** Helen Foster, Al Wilson, Pee Wee Holmes

A new airplane is demonstrated for the world at large, and it can travel roughly 8,000 miles to the gallon.

SKY SPLITTER

Hodkinson, 1923, b&w, silent short

Producer: John R. Bray; **Directors:** Ashley Miller and J. Norling; **Screenplay:** Norling

A scientist creates a spaceship for the singular purpose of breaking the speed-of-light barrier. When he tests his invention, however, he enters a time warp, which allows him to witness his own childhood.

SLAPSTICK (OF ANOTHER KIND)

Serendipity/Entertainment Releasing, 1984, Color, 82 min, VT, LD

Producers: Steven Paul and Larry Sugar; **Director:** Paul; **Screenplay:** Paul; **Music:** Michel Legrand and Morton Stevens; **Cast:** Jerry Lewis, Madeline Kahn, Marty Feldman, Jim Backus, John Abbott, Pat Morita, Samuel Fuller, Merv Griffin, Steven Paul, Orson Welles

Lewis and Kahn have dual roles in this quirky film. They play the parents of massive deformed twins as well as playing the twins themselves. The children are actually the heralds of alien beings who can cure all the world's ills. The only catch is, the twins can never be separated. One might expect much from such a seasoned cast working with a Kurt Vonnegut, Jr., story as their starting point, but the aging Jerry Lewis is the high point of this dreary mess.

SLAUGHTERHOUSE-FIVE

Universal, 1971, Color, 104 min, VT, LD, DVD

Producer: Paul Monash; **Director:** George Roy Hill; **Screenplay:** Hill and Stephen Geller; **Music:** Johann Sebastian Bach; **Special Effects:** Enzo A. Martinelli and Albert Whitlock; **Cinematography:** Miroslav Ondricek; **Cast:** Michael Sachs, Ron Liebman, Eugene Roche, Sharon Gans, Valerine Perrine, John Dehner, Holly Near, Perry King

A minor nobody, Billy Pilgrim (Sachs), is the focus of this story. He has an ordinary job, wife, and life, and he's bored with all of them. Then something comes along to spice things up. Suddenly, Pilgrim becomes unstuck in time. For some unknown reason his life begins to move backward and forward with events past and future happening in random order. His first stop is back to the days of World War II when he was a prisoner of war in Dresden during the bombings. His movements in time stagger him for a while, until finally he is "rescued" from his unsettling situation by aliens calling themselves the Tralfamadorians. They place Pilgrim in a geodesic dome with a beautiful movie star (Perrine) and instruct him to live out his days in peace.

Those not familiar with the ideas of novelist Kurt Vonnegut, Jr., author of *Slaughterhouse-Five*, may be confused by this film. The story turns on a comparison of the true horrors in this world, such as war and assassination, as opposed to the imagined ones, such as living in suburbia and doing one's job. The film is clever and well constructed insofar as any movie can be when trying to capture the essence of a Vonnegut novel, though the alien sequences fail. Reading *Slaughterhouse-Five* first would be one's best bet.

SLAVE GIRLS

See *PREHISTORIC WOMEN* (1967)

SLEEPER

United Artists, 1973, Color, 90 min, VT, LD, DVD

Producer: Jack Grossberg; **Director:** Woody Allen; **Screenplay:** Allen and Marshall Brickman; **Music:** Preservation Hall Jazz Band; **Special Effects:** A.D. Flowers and Dale Hennessy; **Cinematography:** David M. Walsh; **Cast:** Woody Allen, Diane Keaton, John Beck, Mary Gregory, Don Keefer, Chris Forbes, John McLiam

A man (Allen) who went into the hospital for a minor operation in 1973 awakens hundreds of years in the future. During his routine ulcer procedure he somehow lapsed into a coma. Not knowing what else to do with him, the hospital put him into cryogenic storage, and he has been brought back to the world of the living by doctors working for the revolution. They need a person outside the database—someone unknown to the harsh dictatorship that rules the land—to infiltrate government headquarters and assassinate the "Leader."

What could have been a straightforward action movie in other hands became a wildly hysterical story in Allen's. As with so many stories about people from the present ending up in the future, the film is not concerned with prediction. It is an examination of contemporary values disguised as riotous slapstick, and it approaches sheer brilliance.

The film is loaded with typical Woody Allen jokes. The future discovers that what the 1970s thought was health food was actually poisonous. Now everyone knows it's steak, hot fudge, and deep frying that extend life. Of course, there are also the modern artificial foods that have to be beaten into submission (just like steaks and chops and drumsticks) before they can be enjoyed. A revolution is happening, but Allen can't understand since the future seems an absolutely wonderful place. Smoking is good for you, sex is better than ever, life is idyllic. What's there to revolt about?

This is an extremely funny film, and the science fiction content is fairly high. Allen went so far as to take science fiction writer Isaac Asimov to lunch to discuss his concepts, all of which Asimov labeled scientifically feasible. At the time of release, many felt the movie had too much slapstick, but these critics may have missed the messages underlying the gags. The film finds its own moral center and sticks to it, ridiculing society from the safety of the jester's guise.

SLIME PEOPLE, THE

Hansen, 1963, b&w, 76 min, VT

Producer: Joseph F. Robertson; **Director:** Robert Hutton; **Screenplay:** Vance Skarstedt; **Music:** Lou Foman; **Special Effects:** Charles Duncan; **Cinematography:** William Troiano; **Cast:** Robert Hutton, Les Tremayne, Robert Burton, Judee Morton, Susan Hart, John Close

A small group of people fight for their lives against subterranean creatures who have erected a barrier composed of fog around Los Angeles.

SLIPSTREAM

Entertainment Film (Great Britain), 1989, Color, 92 min, VT, LD

Producers: William Braunstein, Arthur H. Maskansky, Steve Lanning, Nigel Green, and Gary Kurtz; **Director:** Steven M. Lisberger; **Screenplay:** Bill Bauer and Tony Kayden; **Music:** Elmer Bernstein; **Special Effects:** Brian Johnson; **Cinematography:** Frank Tidy; **Cast:** Mark Hamill, Bill Paxton, Bob Peck, Kitty Aldridge, Eleanor David, F. Murray Abraham, Ben Kingsley, Robbie Coltrane

The slipstream of the title is an incredible wind that has developed in our future. It is so powerful that humankind has been forced to retreat to shielded valleys for safe living quarters. It's an intriguing concept but one that, for some reason, isn't used to its potential in this story about a rogue (Paxton) who kidnaps a prisoner from a bounty hunter (Hamill). The movie becomes bogged down in its inability to make anything out of its premise.

SNOW DEMONS (aka: SNOW DEVILS)

Mercury Film Int'l (Italy), 1965, Color, 92 min

Producers: Ivan Reiner, Joseph Fryd, Walter Manley, and Antonio Margheriti; **Director:** Anthony Dawson; **Screenplay:** William Finger, Charles Sinclair, and Reiner; **Music:** Angeleo Francesco Lavagnino; **Special Effects:** Victor Sontolda and R. Perron; **Cinematography:** Riccardo Pallottini; **Cast:** Jack Stuart, Amber Collins, Peter Martell, Halina Zalewska

Yetis or abominable snowmen are discovered by a group of researchers, but the creatures turn out to be aliens, and not the nice kind that comes here to solve all our problems, either.

SNOW DEVILS

See *SNOW DEMONS*

SOLARBABIES

Brooksfilm, 1986, Color, 94 min, VT, LD

Producers: Mel Brooks, Irene Walzer, Jack Frost Sanders, and Francisco Molero **Director:** Alan Johnson; **Screenplay:** Waylon Green and D.A. Metron; **Music:** Maurice Jarre; **Special Effects:** Nick Allder, Neil Krepela, Alan Bryce, Lynda Lemon, Thaine Morris, Annick Thierrien, Bill Neil, Chris Regan, Matthew Yuricich, Terry Windell, and Gary Waller; **Cinematography:** Peter MacDonald; **Cast:** Richard Jordon, Jami Gertz, Jason Patric, Lukas Haas, Charles Durning,

Peter DeLuise, Adrain Pasdar, Sarah Douglas, Frank Converse, Terrence Mann, Kelly Bishop

In the future, an evil overlord imprisons a group of courageous teens in his castle. The plucky kids escape through their belief in "Bohdi," a vague mystical force.

SOLAR CRISIS

Vidmark Entertainment (Japan), 1990, Color, 112 min, VT, LD, DVD

Producers: Richard Edlund, Morris Morishima, Richard C. Sarafian, and James Nelson; **Director:** Alan Smithee; **Screenplay:** Crispan Bolt and Joe Gannon; **Music:** Maurice Jarre; **Special Effects:** Edlund and Evan Jacobs; **Cinematography:** Russell Carpenter; **Cast:** Tim Matheson, Charlton Heston, Peter Boyle, Annabel Schofield, Corin Nemec, Jack Palance, Tetsuya Bessho, Dorian Harewood, Brenda Bakke

Earth is about to be destroyed in a massive solar flare. To the rescue, Matheson and his space-faring heroes who set off for the Sun to put a stop to the coming holocaust before it can happen. The fly in the ointment is Boyle, who wants to stop the mission and thus destroy Earth. The movie suffers from Boyle's character, who remains ill-defined and unclearly motivated, but the scenes without him are well done and involving.

SOLARIS

Mosfilm (Russia), 1972, 165 min/Sci-Fi Picture (U.S.), 1976, 132 min, Color, VT, LD

Producer: Viacheslav Jarasov; **Director:** Andrei Tarkovsky; **Screenplay:** Tarkovsky and Friedrich Gorenstein; **Music:** Edward Artemyev; **Cinematography:** Vadim Ysov; **Cast:** Natalya Bondarchuk, Donatas Banionis, Yuri Yarvet, Anatoly Solonitsin

There's trouble on the space station in orbit around the planet Solaris, so young astronaut Chris Kelvin (Banionis) is sent to investigate. When he arrives, he finds only three members of the original crew of 85 still living. Solaris has always been a vast puzzle to our scientists. Its weather is mysteriously erratic. On top of that, the world creates islands and sends them up from the bottom of the sea whenever it feels like it. With those sent to study Solaris killing themselves and each other, the planet is more of an enigma to the forces of Earth than ever. Kelvin goes nearly mad himself when he is confronted by the form of his dead wife. He kills the being in his terror, but another one shows up that night. Kelvin soon realizes the woman is not a ghost, but a living being. With her help, he slowly begins to realize that the planet below is alive and trying to communicate with the Earthlings above.

Though overlong, even in its reduced American version, *Solaris* is a hauntingly beautiful film. The imagery is spectacular. Based on the Stanislaw Lem novel by the same name, it is the best adaptation of the author's work to date.

SOLDIER

Warner Bros., 1998, Color, 98 min, VT, DVD

Producers: R.J. Louis, Susan Ekins, James G. Robinson, Jeremy Bolt, and Jerry Weintraub; **Director:** Paul Anderson; **Screenplay:** David Webb Peoples; **Music:** Joel McNeely; **Special Effects:** Ed Jones and Clay Pinney; **Cinematography:** David Tattersall, B.S.C.; **Cast:** Kurt Russell, Jason Scott Lee, Connie Nielsen, Michael Chiklis, Gary Busey

In the future all wars are fought by men who have been selected at birth to be soldiers. At that time they are stripped of their individuality, separated from society, and raised with one overriding dictum: Kill or be killed. Only a handful reach adulthood. Todd (Russell) is a veteran soldier of both Earthly and intergalactic conflicts. He's one of the best. Scarred, toughened, and numbed by a lifetime of nothing but fighting, he stands as the embodiment of Darwin's principle of survival of the fittest. Or at least, he did.

Todd and the other soldiers like him are in their 40s. The same way the military retires old planes and tanks for newer models, it's time for Todd's batch to be replaced with younger, faster, stronger killing machines. The old boys try their best, but they cannot compete. Todd ends up dumped on a garbage planet and left for dead. He is nursed back to health by a peaceful group of forgotten pioneers, scavengers who have a harsh existence on the trash world but who live in peace. These people fear Todd, but they care for him anyway because it's the right thing to do.

Slowly, he regains his strength. As he does, fear of him grows worse. No one in the scavenger community

Soldier (WARNER BROS. & MORGAN CREEK PRODUCTIONS / AUTHOR'S COLLECTION)

knows what to do. They like him, but he's not really human. Sadly, his lifetime of training goes against anything resembling human conditioning. He is a killing machine, pure and simple. Soon he goes off to live by himself before he accidentally kills someone or before the mistrust of some in the community forces a confrontation. Suddenly, the new faster, stronger soldiers show up on the garbage planet. Their baptism of fire is going to be wiping out the scavenger community. Now Todd has to beat the unbeatable to protect the people who saved his life.

Soldier is the kind of movie people mean when they say "they just don't make 'em like that anymore." This is a solid B movie but one with A-level sensibilities and, like all the best science fiction, does more than just show off snappy hardware. It speculates on the moral and social changes the future might bring. Here, the idea of raising children from birth to be soldiers is explored in cold but honest detail. No childhood, no mothers, no Christmas, proms, pets, or sleepovers. Just training and killing and blood. Is it right? Does the safety of the many justify the brutal horror inflicted on Todd and his fellows from birth?

Soldier poses all these questions and then masterfully does not attempt to answer them all. This is not a neatly wrapped formula story in which everything turns out all right. This is an exceptional piece of cinema—disturbing and chilling. It looks honestly at one of the darkest parts of the human soul and does not lie about what it finds there. Nor does it pontificate, pretending that it holds all the answers.

Two of the film's stars, Kurt Russell and Gary Busey, are excellent. What could've been a farce from lesser performers becomes a riveting drama. There's no doubt they understood their roles, especially Russell, who said about his part, "I believe the strength of the movie is not necessarily the flashiest parts, but more the human interest parts. Todd is a man who has a tremendous range of emotions that are completely bottled."

Russell was right; the part of Todd might have been a bit daunting to a less able actor. The movie is built around this character, and yet he has less than 100 words of dialogue. Russell wasn't intimidated by the challenge of playing a character who barely speaks. Comparing the role to that of a mime, he said, "One of my beliefs on film acting is that if you think it, it will be there on screen, it will be true. The audience will understand what you are thinking."

The film boasts more talent than just its actors. Screenwriter David Peoples also wrote *BLADE RUNNER* and Academy Award winner *Unforgiven*. The technical team featured David Tattersall, who worked on *STAR WARS: EPISODE ONE* and *Con Air*, and *Blade Runner*'s director of photography, as well as that film's production designer, David L. Snyder, Edited by Martin Hunter (*EVENT HORIZON*, *Full Metal Jacket*), the film moves wonderfully, especially when combined with the visual effects of Ed Jones (*Who Framed Roger Rabbit?*) and the special effects of Clay Pinney. Add to that Paul Anderson, the director of *MORTAL KOMBAT* and *EVENT HORIZON*, and the talent behind this unusual film is quite formidable.

SOME GIRLS DO

Ashdown (Great Britain), 1969/United Artists, 1971, Color, 93 min

Producer: Betty Box; **Director:** Ralph Thomas; **Screenplay:** David Osborn and Liz Charles-Williams; **Music:** Charles Blackwell; **Special Effects:** Kit West; **Cinematography:** Ernest Steward; **Cast:** Richard Johnson, Vanessa Howard, Daliah Lavi, Ronnie Stevens, Robert Morley, Beba Loncar, Sydne Rome, James Villier

Our hero, Bulldog Drummond (Johnson), tries to stop the villains attempting to ruin the Crown's plan to build supersonic planes. Robot girls are involved but not intelligent filmmaking.

SOMETHING IS OUT THERE
(aka: DAY OF THE ANIMALS)

Film Ventures Int'l, 1977, Color, 98 min, VT

Director: William Girdler; **Screenplay:** Eleanor E. Norton and William W. Norton; **Music:** Lalo Schifrin; **Cinematography:** Robert Sorrentino; **Cast:** Christopher George, Lynda Day George, Leslie Nielsen, Richard Jaeckel, Michael Ansara, Ruth Roman

The hole in the ozone layer has grown to the point where the extra radiation that is seeping through is making the world's animals insane. At least it's getting to the ones in the High Sierras. For 98 minutes they chew, chomp, and in other ways slaughter every actor they can find.

SOMETHING WEIRD

Mayflower, 1968, b&w, 83 min

Producer: James F. Hurley; **Director:** H. Gordon Lewis; **Screenplay:** Hurley; **Cinematography:** Andy

Romanoff; **Cast:** Tony McCabe, Elizabeth Lee, William Brooker

An electrical accident leaves a man with a hideously scarred face and tremendous telepathic powers. Not surprisingly, people begin to avoid him.

SON OF BLOB, THE

Harris, 1972, Color, 88 min, VT

Producer: Anthony Harris; **Director:** Larry Hagman; **Screenplay:** Harris and Jack Woods; **Music:** Mort Garson; **Special Effects:** Tim Barr; **Cinematography:** Al Hamm; **Cast:** Godfrey Cambridge, Carol Lynley, Robert Walker, Shelley Berman, Richard Stahl, Larry Hagman, Cindy Williams, Marlene Clark, Gerrit Graham, Dick Van Patten

See *BEWARE! THE BLOB*

SON OF FLUBBER

Disney, 1963, Color, 103 min, VT, LD

Producer: Walt Disney; **Director:** Robert Stevenson; **Screenplay:** Bill Walsh and Don Da Gradi; **Music:** George Bruns; **Special Effects:** Peter Ellenshaw, Eustace Lycett, Robert Mattey, Jack Boyd, and Jim Fetherolf; **Cinematography:** Edward Coleman; **Cast:** Fred MacMurray, Nancy Olson, Keenan Wynn, Charlie Ruggles, Tommy Kirk, Leon Ames, Ed Wynn, Paul Lynde, Stu Erwin, Elliott Reid, Joanna Moore, Jack Albertson

See *THE ABSENT-MINDED PROFESSOR*

SON OF FRANKENSTEIN

Universal, 1939, b&w, 95 min, VT, LD

Producer: Rowland Lee; **Director:** Lee; **Screenplay:** Willis Cooper; **Music:** Frank Skinner; **Special Effects:** Jack Pierce; **Cinematography:** George Robinson; **Cast:** Basil Rathbone, Josephine Hutchinson, Donnie Dunagan, Boris Karloff, Bela Lugosi, Michael Mark, Perry Ivins, Edgar Norton, Lionel Atwill

See *FRANKENSTEIN*

SON OF KONG, THE

RKO, 1934, b&w, 70 min, VT, LD

Producer: Merian C. Cooper; **Director:** Ernest B. Schoedsack; **Screenplay:** Ruth Rose; **Cinematography:** Edward Linden, Vernon Walker, and J.O. Taylor; **Music:** Max Steiner; **Special Effects:** Willis O'Brien and Marcel Delgado; **Cast:** Robert Armstrong, Frank Reicher, Helen Mack, Noble Johnson, Victor Wong, John Marston, Lee Kohlmar

See *KING KONG*, 1976

SORCERERS, THE

Allied Artists, 1967, Color, 83 min, VT

Producers: Michael Reeves, Tony Tenser, and Patrick Curtis; **Director:** Reeves; **Screenplay:** Tom Baker and John Burke Reeves; **Music:** Paul Ferris; **Cinematography:** Stanley A. Long; **Cast:** Boris Karloff, Catherine Lacey, Ian Ogilvy, Elizabeth Ercy, Susan George

Married scientists (Karloff and Lacey) experiment with controlling the human will. They invite a young man (Ogilvy) to join their research with tragic results.

S.O.S. INVASION

IMT Films (Spain), 1969, Color, 87 min

Director: Silvio F. Balbuena; **Screenplay:** J.L. Navarro Basso; **Music:** Moreno Buendia; **Cinematography:** Alfonso Nieva; **Cast:** Jack Taylor, Mara Crus, Diana Sorel

An alien force in the form of an attractive girl turns the dead into robot zombies bound to its will.

SOYLENT GREEN

MGM, 1973, Color, 97 min, VT, LD

Producers: Walter Seltzer and Russell Thatcher; **Director:** Richard Fleischer; **Screenplay:** Stanley R. Greenberg; **Music:** Fred Myrow; **Special Effects:** Matthew Yuricich, Robert R. Hoag, and Augie Lohman; **Cinematography:** Richard H. Kline; **Cast:** Charlton Heston, Edward G. Robinson, Leigh Taylor-Young, Chuck Connors, Brock Peters, Whit Bissell, Joseph Cotten, Paula Kelly, Mike Henry, Dick Van Patten

In 2022 the world has become unmanageably over-populated. Suicide is not only no longer frowned upon, but the government encourages it as vigorously as the paying of taxes. Breads, meat, and vegetables are sold on the black market for absurd prices. Only the unbelievably rich know the luxury of real food anymore. For the masses it's packets of processed crackers hurled to the hungry from the backs of trucks. One of the most popular brands of crackers is Soylent Green, supposedly made from soybeans and lentils. With nothing else available, people fight to the death over them.

When Soylent Corporation executive Joseph Cotten is murdered for no clear-cut motivation the police can determine, detective Heston is assigned to the case. He and his "book"—paper is too expensive, but people are cheap, so those with good memories become the pad and paper of those who need them—Robinson start digging and are shocked by what they find. Robinson discovers the truth first and is so overcome by the information he heads off to the Euthanasia Center. Heston follows his "book's" body from the center. Along with all the other human corpses, it is not taken to a graveyard or crematorium, but to the Soylent Corporation. After sneaking around and a couple of gunfights, soon Heston cries out the film's oft-quoted classic line, "Soylent Green is *people!*"

This film was not the tremendous success some hoped for. With Charlton Heston of THE OMEGA MAN in a new sci-fi film, Edward G. Robinson in his last film role, and a mysterious, controversial topic, it was considered a sure thing. Unfortunately, no one in the audience failed to figure out what was going on long before the police on the screen did, making Heston's hysterical screams of outrage pointless. Anyone waiting for some surprise didn't get it.

Worse yet, many viewers didn't see the problem. The world of 2022 was presented as a nightmarish landscape of wall-to-wall bodies. There is no more progress, there are no jobs, there are no trees, no forests, no fields, no food, no anything. The government and the business world are at their wits' end. Death is on every corner, and food riots break out on the hour. Life on Earth has become a living hell. The answer of manufacturing Soylent Green was not as horrifying as it could have been. People weren't being rounded up and slaughtered but going to their deaths voluntarily. Fat, greedy corporate monsters weren't living high on the blood of the innocent but were stuck in the same boat with everyone else. The rich are being hauled off to the recycling plant along with the homeless, and indeed, the corporate fat cats seem fairly benevolent if you remember that they must bear the horror of what is happening while everyone else lives in blissful ignorance. It is the end of the world, and those in charge try to make things as good as they can for folks without victimizing them or letting them know the horrible truth.

SPACEBALLS

Brooksfilm/MGM, 1987, Color, 96 min, VT, LD, DVD

Producers: Mel Brooks and Ezra Swerdlow; **Director:** Brooks; **Screenplay:** Brooks, Ronny Graham, and Thomas Meehan; **Music:** John Morris; **Special Effects:** Craig Boyajian, Peter Albiez, Peter Donen, Grant McCune, Peter Gruskoff, Richard Ratliff, and ILM: **Cinematography:** Nick McLean; **Cast:** Mel Brooks, John Candy, Rick Moranis, Bill Pullman, Daphne Zuniga, Dick Van Patten, George Wyner, Michael Winslow, Lorene Yarnell, John Hurt, Ronnie Graham, Rhonda Shear, Joan Rivers, Dom DeLuise

Simply put, the film is a parody of the first chapter of the STAR WARS saga—sometimes scene for scene. Coming years after the first *Star Wars* movie and incorporating jokes about very few other sci-fi films, the movie is not nearly as rewarding as other Brooks parodies such as *Blazing Saddles* or YOUNG FRANKENSTEIN, though it includes one memorable scene in which actor John Hurt recreates his famous chest-buster scene from the first ALIEN feature. The creature erupts out of his chest and then launches into the Michigan J. Frog routine from the Warner Bros. classic cartoon, "One Froggy Evening."

SPACECAMP

ABC Motion Pictures, 1986, Color, 107 min, VT, LD

Producers: Patrick Bailey, Walter Coblenz, and Leonard Goldberg; **Director:** Harry Winer; **Screenplay:** W.W. Wicket and Casey T. Mitchell; **Music:** John Williams; **Special Effects:** Charles L. Finance, Chuck Gaspar, Barry Nolan, and Van der Veer Photo Effects; **Cinematography:** William A. Fraker; **Cast:** Kate Capshaw, Lea Thompson, Kelly Preston, Larry B. Scott, Leaf Phoenix, Tate Donovan, Tom Skerritt, Barry Primus, Terry O'Quinn, Mitchell Anderson, T. Scott Coffey

It's NASA's prestigious summer training camp for kids. The bunch of teens shown in this film get more than they bargained for, though, when they are accidentally launched into space and have to get back safely on their own. When one considers what NASA goes through before a space launch and how many missions have been scrubbed for a loose tile, a twisted wire, or a bad weather report, the thought that somehow an American space shot could go off with a group of high schoolers onboard is ridiculous to the point of insult.

SPACE COWBOYS

Warner Bros., 2000, Color, 126 min

Producers: Clint Eastwood, Andrew Lazar, and Tom Rooker; **Director:** Eastwood; **Screenplay:** Ken Kaufman and Howard Klausner; **Music:** Lennie Niehaus; **Cinematography:** Jack N. Green, A.S.C.; **Special Effects:** Michael Owens and ILM; **Cast:** Clint Eastwood, Tommy Lee Jones, Donald Sutherland, James Garner, Marcia Gay Harden, William Devane, Loren Dean, Courtney B. Vance, James Cromwell

In 1958, America's space program—or "outer atmosphere testing" as it was called in those days—was in the hands of the U.S. Air Force. The air force was determined to create a rocket-powered ship that could leave the atmosphere and return under its own power. On the verge of success, the air force was told to stop all research and development. A new agency named NASA would be taking over; chimpanzees would replace the brave test pilots that had been risking their lives for their country. That true scenario is the starting point for *Space Cowboys*.

Proposing that the bravest, fastest, smartest pilots alive in '58 were the men of Team Daedalus (Eastwood, Jones, Sutherland, Garner), the film depicts the four men shoved aside by cruel fate when the air force is removed from the picture. But then, more than 40 years later, the same fates give them another chance, when Russian satellite, *Ikon*, suffers a systems failure that the Russians insist will cause a total communications blackout in their country. Complicating matters is the fact that only one man understands the satellite's operating system (one stolen from America by the KGB years earlier), the man who wrote it. Team Daedalus's Frank Corvin (Eastwood). Thus Frank and the rest of the team finally get their shot at going into space—40 years later.

The four old timers provide plenty of fun as they stagger through their pre-mission physical testing, but all of them manage to make the grade. Once the mission begins, though, the story heats up. The team contacts the Russian satellite easily enough, but when the repair work begins, Corvin notices that *Ikon* is no communications satellite, but a nuclear weapons platform with weapons aimed at America.

Space Cowboys is a good science fiction movie with a strong story. Since its four principal players are all major stars, each appears in an introduction that sets the tone and personality for his character. From there the plot moves at lightning speed, sometimes jumping too quickly over details of which some viewers might like to see more and occasionally letting the audience fill some points in with their own imagination, but it remains engaging and clear. Interestingly, the special effects do not dominate the screen, though they are quite accomplished, including some unique views of Earth from space.

SPACE CHILDREN, THE

Paramount, 1958, b&w, 69 min

Producer: William Alland; **Director:** Jack Arnold; **Screenplay:** Bernard C. Schoenfeld; **Music:** Nathan Van Cleave; **Special Effects:** John P. Fulton and Wally Westmore; **Cinematography:** Ernest Laszlo; **Cast:** Jackie Coogan, John Crawford, Adam Williams, Peggy Webber, Michel Ray, Richard Shannon, John Washbook

A meddlesome brain from outer space comes to Earth to stop nuclear testing. To reach this goal, it takes over the minds of the children of scientists working on an upcoming test. The kids tell everyone how bad nuclear bombs are, but nobody listens to them because they're just kids. At this point, the brain gets tough and gives the kids enhanced mental powers that enable them to force their parents to stop the testing. This film is in no way equal to director Arnold's other '50s classics, CREATURE FROM THE BLACK LAGOON, MONSTER ON CAMPUS, being far too preachy and politically narrow as if only Americans need to be taught a lesson about nuclear bombs.

SPACE CRUISER YAMOTO

Enterprise (Japan), 1977, Color, 107 min, VT

Producer: Yoshinabu Nishizaki; **Director:** Nishizaki; **Screenplay:** Nishizaki; **Music:** Hiroshi Miyagawa; **Animation:** Leiji Matsumoto and Noboru Ishigura; **Cast:** Gorô Naya, Kei Yomiyama, Shûsei Nakamura, Yôko Asagari, Michiko Hirai, Horo Kimura, Maruko Kitahama, Akira Kamiya, and Osamu Saka

In the year 2199 Earth takes a terrible beating. Aliens from the planet Gorgon pummel our world with radioactive meteors, destroying all life on the surface and driving all of humanity underground. Attempts to retaliate are obliterated as the Gorgons watch for any sign of arms building and destroy them in their infancy. The answer? Tunnel under the ruined remains of the great Japanese battleship *Yamoto* sunk centuries earlier during World War II, and reoutfit it as a space-faring vessel from below. Then find the greatest, bravest crew in the world and send them into outer space in search for a cure to the radiation destroying Earth and a way to get rid of the Gorgons.

This is Japanese animation at its finest. Admittedly, the artwork, although good, isn't quite up to what would come out of Japan over the next quarter-century, but the story is absolutely fantastic. High adventure and the standard human soap opera blend wonderfully with such Japanese staples as ancestor worship and the wild kid out for revenge who grows to maturity as tragedy forces him to accept the responsibility he's run from all his life. Interestingly, the film was later broken up into 26 episodes (with extra footage and entire new plotlines added) for television distribution. The movie thus became a franchise that spawned numerous movies and television seasons.

SPACED INVADERS

Smart Egg Releasing Company, 1990, Color, 102 min, VT, LD

Producers: Luigi Cingolani, George Zecevic, John S. Curran, and Caroline Pham; **Director:** Patrick Read Johnson; **Screenplay:** Johnson and Scott Lawrence Alexander; **Music:** David E. Russo; **Special Effects:** John Knoll; **Cinematography:** James L. Carter; **Cast:** Douglas Barr, Royal Dano, Ariana Richards, J.J. Anderson, Gregg Berger, Kevin Thompson, Jimmy Briscoe, Tony Cox, Debbie Lee Carrington, Tommy Madden

A group of hardcase Martians land on Earth during Orson Welles's famed 1938 broadcast of *War of the Worlds*. Hearing the radio program and being no more intelligent than anyone else on the eastern seaboard of the United States, they head for the backwater to join the rest of the Martian invasion force. This one had a good idea, but little else.

SPACED OUT (aka: OUTER TOUCH)

Miramax, 1979, Color, 84 min, VT

Producer: David Speechley; **Director:** Norman J. Warren; **Screenplay:** Bob Saget and Andrew Payne; **Cinematography:** John Metcalfe and Peter Sinclair; **Cast:** Barry Stokes, Tony Maiden, Glory Annen, Michael Rowlatt, Ava Cadell, Kate Ferguson, Lynn Ross

Beautiful women from outer space find that the only place to find any real men is planet Earth. The producers added a filthy-mouthed computer to the film for its second release in hopes of *improving* it.

SPACE FLIGHT (aka: SPACEFLIGHT IC-1)

Lippert (Great Britain)/20th Century Fox (U.S.), 1965, b&w, 63 min

Producers: Robert L. Lippert and Jack Parsons; **Director:** Bernard Knowles; **Screenplay:** Harry Spaulding; **Music:** Elisabeth Lutyens; **Cinematography:** Geoffrey Faithful; **Cast:** Bill Williams, Norma West, Linda Marlowe, John Ciarney, Jeremy Longhurst

It's the far-flung future of 2015. A spaceship full of astronaut/colonists is roaming the depths of outer space, looking for planets to colonize. They don't have a lot of say in things, though—the ship is remote-controlled through its computer system by RULE, the governing body that has taken over Earth. Soon the computer is killing folks aboard ship, and suddenly the colonists are yearning for the good old days of the year 2000 when there were still elections.

SPACEFLIGHT IC-1

See *SPACE FLIGHT*

SPACEHUNTER: ADVENTURES IN THE FORBIDDEN ZONE

Columbia, 1983, Color, 90 min, VT, LD

Producer: Ivan Reitman; **Director:** Lamont Johnson; **Screenplay:** Edith Rey, David Preston, Dan Goldberg, and Len Blum; **Music:** Elmer Bernstein; **Special Effects:** Dale L. Martin; **Cinematography:** Frank Tidy, D.S.C.; **Cast:** Peter Strauss, Molly Ringwald, Michael Ironside, Ernie Hudson, Andrea Marcovicci

As this movie opens, Wolff (Strauss), a pilot, responds to a distress signal from a shipwrecked spacecraft. On board are three intergalactic beauties now stranded on the plague-infested backwater known as Terra Eleven. Wolff is joined in his search for the heavenly bodies by Niki (Ringwald), the orphaned survivor of an abortive medical rescue operation that failed years earlier. She leads Wolff into the Forbidden Zone, a land crawling with plague-carrying mutants, underwater amazons, and the Overdog (Ironside), a renegade Earth scientist who has risen to near supreme power by hoarding the incredibly valuable plague serum. Wolff and Niki are joined by the usual band of rogues. The group wanders across the planet, getting into and out of a lot of adventures, dodging monsters, saving the girls, and, of course, beating the villain in the end.

Outside of the terrible 3-D effects (the film actually improves greatly on television when this effect drops out), this movie is good, cheap fun. Knowing that the picture is a Grade Z film going in allows viewers to enjoy it for what it is. The movie moves well—it's funny, quick, and well paced. Of course, it's no more than light amusement, with low sci-fi content, but it never pretends to be more.

SPACEMAN IN KING ARTHUR'S COURT, A

See UNIDENTIFIED FLYING ODDBALL

SPACE MASTER X-7

20th Century Fox, 1957, b&w, 71 min, VT

Producer: Bernard Glasser; **Director:** Edward Bernds; **Screenplay:** George Worthing Yates and Daniel Mainwaring; **Music:** Josef Zimanich; **Cinematography:** Brydon Baker; **Cast:** Bill Williams, Paul Frees, Robert Ellis, Moe Howard, Lyn Thomas, John Berry, Thomas Browne Henry

A satellite probe returns from beyond Earth's atmosphere, bringing back a frightening space fungus. The "Blood Rust" spreads like wildfire while scientists fight it.

SPACEMEN

See ASSIGNMENT OUTER SPACE

SPACEMEN SATURDAY NIGHT

See INVASION OF THE SAUCER MEN

SPACE MONSTER

AIF, 1965, Color, 80 min

Producer: Burt Topper; **Director:** Leonard Katzman; **Screenplay:** Katzman; **Music:** Marlin Skiles; **Special Effects:** Don Post Studios; **Cast:** Russ Bender, Baynes Barron

Astronauts investigate a water world. Attacked by sea creatures, they survive valiantly and then finally find the source of their troubles—another off-worlder, a tiny alien hidden away in his own ship underneath the ocean.

SPACE MUTANTS

See PLANET OF THE VAMPIRES

SPACE RAGE (aka: TRACKERS, A DOLLAR A DAY, SPACE RAGE: BREAK OUT ON PRISON PLANET)

Vestron, 1985, Color, 75 min, VT

Producers: Damian Lee, Morton Reed, Patrick Wells, and Peter McCarthy; **Director:** Conrad Palmisano; **Screenplay:** Reed and Jim Lenahan; **Music:** Billy Ferric and Zander Schloss; **Special Effects:** Frank DeMarco and Roger George; **Cinematography:** Tim Schrstedt; **Cast:** Richard Farnsworth, Michael Paré, John Laughlin, Lee Purcell, Lewis Van Bergen, William Windom

Trouble on a prison planet forces Farnsworth to don his guns again to stop the troublemaking outlaws.

SPACE RAGE: BREAK OUT ON PRISON PLANET

See SPACE RAGE

SPACE RAIDERS

New World Pictures, 1983, Color, 82 min, VT

Producer: Roger Corman; **Director:** Howard R. Cohen; **Screenplay:** Cohen; **Music:** James Horner; **Special Effects:** Bret Culpepper; **Cinematography:** Alec Hirshfield; **Cast:** Vince Edwards, David Mendenhall, Patsy Pease, Thom Christopher, Dick Miller, Luca Bercovici

A somewhat pointless space opera heavily derived from the far superior Roger Corman production BATTLE BEYOND THE STARS, particularly in its special effects and sound track.

SPACESHIP

See *THE CREATURE WASN'T NICE*

SPACESHIP TO THE UNKNOWN

See *FLASH GORDON* (1936)

SPACESHIP VENUS DOES NOT REPLY

See *FIRST SPACESHIP ON VENUS*

SPACE SOLDIERS

See *FLASH GORDON* (1936)

SPACE SOLDIERS CONQUER THE UNIVERSE

See *FLASH GORDON* (1936)

SPACE SOLDIERS TRIP TO MARS

See *FLASH GORDON* (1936)

SPACE TRAVELLERS

See *MAROONED*

SPACEWAYS

Hammer/Lippert (Great Britain), 1953, b&w, 76 min, VT, DVD

Producer: Michael Carreras; **Director:** Terrence Fisher; **Screenplay:** Paul Tabori and Richard Landau; **Music:** Ivor Slaney; **Cinematography:** Reginald Wyer; **Cast:** Howard Duff, Eva Bartok, Alan Wheatley, Michael Medwin, Andrew Osborn

When a technician gets pinned with a homicide rap, accused of doing away with his wife and stuffing her into a satellite blasting off for the stars, the poor slob (Duff) has to rendezvous the first capsule with one of his own to prove his innocence.

SPECIES

MGM, 1995, Color, 111 min, VT, LD, DVD

Producers: Mark Egerton, Dennis Feldman, Frank Mancuso, Jr., and David Streit; **Director:** Roger Donaldson; **Screenplay:** Feldman; **Music:** Christopher Young; **Special Effects:** Ray Moore, Douglas Miller, Alex Mann, Harold Mann, John Mann, Theo Waddell, Jeff Jarvis, Eric Bigas, Joel Roman Mendias, Ellen Somers, Richard Edlund, XFX Images, Boss Film Studios, and The Truly Dangerous Company; **Cinematography:** Bart Kowiak Andrzej; **Cast:** Ben Kingsley, Michael Madsen, Forest Whitaker, Natasha Henstridge, Alfred Molina, Marg Helgenberger, Whip Hubley, Michelle Williams, Jordon Lund

Scientists experimenting with alien and human DNA almost hit the jackpot when they create a seemingly perfect woman until she reveals herself as a homicidal inhuman monster. There isn't anything terribly wrong with this film, but it doesn't quite stand out either. It moves well and offers tremendous special effects, as well as several set-up jokes to engage the audience. It's a very good-looking film and boasts some high-caliber performers. The only problem for true sci-fi fans is that the science disappears early in favor of fantasy and gore. *Species II* tried hard to trade on the success of the first movie, but was a terrible disappointment. Falling off on every level, it failed to reach the mild peak of its predecessor.

SPECIES II

MGM Entertainment/MGM, 1998, Color, 95 min, VT, LD, DVD

Producers: Dennis Feldman, Frank Mancuso, Jr., and Vikki Williams; **Director:** Peter Medak; **Screenplay:** Chris Brancato; **Music:** Ed Shearmur; **Special Effects:** Janet Quen, Jon Warren, Terry Chapman, Joseph Grossberg, Ralph Maiers, David Sammons, Mark Spatney, Brent O. Coert, David Fogg, Even Jacobs, and Ray Moore; **Cinematography:** Matthew F. Leonetti; **Cast:** Natasha Helgenberger, Mykelti Williamson, Justin Lazard, James Cromwell, George Dzundza, Richard Belzer, Peter Boyle

See *SPECIES*

SPHERE

Warner Bros., 1998, Color, 133 min, VT, LD, DVD

Producer: Barry Levinson; **Director:** Levinson; **Screenplay:** Paul Attanasio and Stephen Hauser; **Music:** Elliot Goldenthal; **Special Effects:** Jeffrey A.

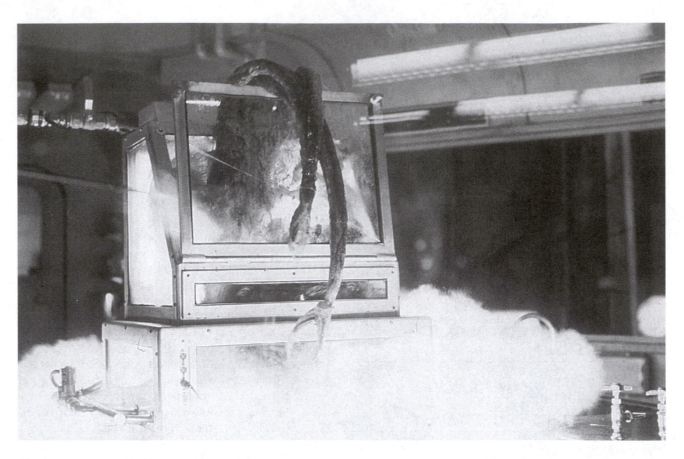

Species (MGM / JOSEPH B. MAUCERI COLLECTION)

Okun; **Cinematography:** Adam Greenberg; **Cast:** Dustin Hoffman, Sharon Stone, Samuel L. Jackson, Peter Coyote, Queen Latifah, Liev Schreiber, Marga Gomez

Civilian scientists, each an expert in at least one if not a number of disciplines, are all flown by the military to the middle of the ocean. Those who have been told anything think they are headed to the site of a downed airliner, but once there they are told the truth. The government has discovered a spaceship that crashlanded in the ocean over 300 years ago. They determined the date by calculating the age of the coral covering part of the ship.

Psychoanalyst Hoffman had written a paper 15 years earlier for the White House on what should be done upon first contact with aliens. Using the study as its guide, the government has gathered the team he suggested in the paper, including himself. Now they are all sheltered in an underwater habitat erected by the navy on the bottom of the ocean. Their mission: Go into the ship, which is still emitting a regular pulsation, find the ULF (Unknown Life Form) that is inside, and make contact.

The team gets inside easily enough, discovering that the ship is not from an alien world but from our own future. It's a United States space-faring vessel, one with a crew that apparently slaughtered one another after picking up a bizarre bit of cargo. Within the ship, the explorers find a massive, shimmering, perfectly engineered sphere. They have no explanation for the floating mystery. They can find no purpose for it, no controls, no doorways or windows, no seams—the sphere is a complete unknown to all members of the team.

Eventually, one of them (Jackson) discovers the secret of entering the sphere, a secret he never shares with his teammates. He refuses to tell them, and in a bit of poor scripting they accept his coyness as if his cracking of what is potentially the greatest secret in the history of humankind is of no particular importance. And then the murders begin. First, a terrible storm arises on the surface, forcing the habitat's support fleet away. Then, one by one, the cast is murdered until only Hoffman, Stone, and Jackson remain. Hoffman and Stone finally deduce that Jackson, the only survivor to have entered the alien device (the one they assume caused the original crew to kill one another) is the source of all their problems. Ever since he entered the sphere, they reason, he has had the power to manifest his dreams. He's been killing everyone. The two drug Jackson, rendering him unconscious to the point at which his brain is below the threshold of dream, for their own safety.

Then Hoffman realizes it's really Stone doing everything. But Stone realizes it's really Hoffman. Well, it's really all of them. All of them had entered the sphere (although Stone and Hoffman never really remember), which is an alien Aladdin's lamp, and thus all of them have the power to materialize their thoughts. So they blow up the spaceship and the habitat, escaping to the surface in a minisub. Once there, they realize that people aren't capable of handling this discovery. The trio uses the power to forget they ever had it. When they make this noble gesture, the sphere (untouched by the explosion that destroyed everything else) rises from the ocean bottom and leaves the planet.

Sphere is a movie in three sections. For the first hour it is a tremendously engaging science fiction film. The facts and details and bits of science come at you faster than you can rake them in. Everything is smooth and seamless and logical, not surprising since the film is based on a Michael Crichton novel. The second hour is a mindless swirl of death and blame-placing, of confusing visuals and wandering, aimless sequences. The filmmakers cheat ruthlessly, never allowing people to act logically if it interferes with the plotline.

For instance, they tell us the manifestations come from their dreams, but Queen Latifah is killed by one of Hoffman's fears while he is awake. Why did he kill her? Who knows? When Jackson's manifestations kill two others, there are at least tiny personal quirks that could explain why he would have felt unconscious resentment toward both men. But Hoffman never really interacts with Latifah. Why would his subconscious wish her harm? Many such troubling inconsistencies occur within the film's second hour. Then, with only 13 minutes left, things all come together for the noble ending. The noble ending is actually somewhat comforting, somewhat satisfying. It doesn't make up for earlier failings—the explanation is simply too little, too late—but it makes up for some of the nonsense. Ultimately, *Sphere* is not worth watching. The opening hour promises so much that the letdown is impossible to survive.

SPIDER, THE

See *EARTH VS. THE SPIDER*

SPIRIT OF '76, THE

Castle Rock Entertainment, 1991, Color, 82 min, VT

Producers: Roman Coppola, Simon Edery, Alan Renshaw, Susan B. Landau, and Fred Fuchs; **Director:** Lucas Reiner; **Screenplay:** Coppola and Reiner; **Music:** David Nichtern; **Special Effects:** Jonathan Horton and Dan Kohne; **Cinematography:** Stephen Lighthill; **Cast:** David Cassidy, Geoff Hoyle, Olivia d'Abo, Jeff McDonald, Steve McDonald, Barbara Bain, Carl Reiner, Tommy Chong, Julie Brown, Iron Eyes Cody, Devo, Rob Reiner, Moon Zappa

A trio of travelers journeys back from the far-flung future of 2176 to the year 1776 to find our how America "really" got started. Somehow they wind up in 1976. Like most time travel stories, this one doesn't attempt to say anything about the future. Its purpose is to make a statement about the present. Unfortunately the only statements these filmmakers thought necessary involved the fashions and mostly forgotten fads of the '70s. Why they bothered to set up a political premise when they planned no political payoff is perplexing.

SPLIT SECOND

Muse Productions, 1992, Color, 90 min, VT, LD

Producer: Chris Hanley; **Director:** Tony Maylam; **Screenplay:** Gary Scott Thompson; **Music:** Stephen Parsons; **Cinematography:** Clive Tickner; **Cast:** Rutger Hauer, Kim Cattrall, Neil Duncan, Alun Armstrong, Pete Postlewaite, Ian Drury, Robert Eaton, Michael J. Pollard

In London of the very near future, a horrific serial killer is loose in the streets, and top cop Hauer is determined to track him down. One of the killer's victims was Hauer's partner, and he doesn't like getting stuck with new partner Duncan. But the two must work together anyway when the killer he's tracking turns out to be some form of alien creature.

Though this film starts off reasonably well, it winds up muddled and confusing. Early on, Hauer spots a dog that has witnessed the serial killer at work. So desperate is he for a lead that Hauer actually questions the dog. The actor's work in this scene is so exceptional, one actually expects him to form a telepathic link with the animal, and the scene gives high hope for more clever bits to come, but they never do. Cattrall turns in a good performance, and Duncan makes a more than convincing rookie partner, uttering the much stolen line, "We're going to need bigger guns," after their encounter with the monster. Despite these few good things, *Split Second* degenerates steadily.

SPUTNIK

See *A DOG, A MOUSE AND A SPUTNIK*

S-S-SNAKE!

See *SSSSSSSS*

SSSSSSSS (aka:S-S-SNAKE!)

Universal, 1973, Color, 99 min, VT

Producer: Dan Striepke; **Director:** Bernard Kowalski; **Screenplay:** Hal Dresner and Striepke; **Music:** Pat Williams; **Special Effects:** John Chambers and Nick Marcellino; **Cinematography:** Gerald P. Finnerman; **Cast:** Strother Martin, Dirk Benedict, Tim O'Conner, Richard Shull, Reb Brown, Jack Ging, Heather Menzies

Scientist Strother Martin is out to save humankind from pollution by turning everyone into king cobras. Eventually, he's stopped, but not before he messes things up romantically for his daughter by turning her boyfriend into a snake.

STARCRASH (aka: THE ADVENTURES OF STELLA STAR, FEMALE SPACE INVADERS)

New World Pictures, 1979, Color, 92 min, VT

Producers: Nat Wachsberger and Patrick Wachsberger; **Director:** Luigi Cozzi; **Screenplay:** Cozzi; **Music:** John Barry; **Special Effects:** Niso Remponi and Paol Zeccara; **Cinematography:** Paul Beeson; **Cast:** Caroline Munro, Marjoe Gortner, Christopher Plummer, David Hasselhoff, Robert Tessier, Joe Spinell, Hamilton Camp, Nadia Cassini, Judd Hamilton

In this thinly disguised space western Joe Spinell plays an evil space count who wants to do terrible things to Emperor of the Universe Plummer and everyone in his kingdom. Plummer sends Caroline Munro to stop him once and for all. She and her band of second-class sidekicks run around the galaxy for a while and then finally accomplish their mission. A few of the special effects sequences here were good in their day, but most were just awful even then, and with a terrible plot, laughable

acting, and no budget at all, there's little in favor of this film.

STARGATE

MGM, 1994, Color, 119 min, VT, LD, DVD

Producers: Dean Devlin, Roland Emmerich, Ute Emmerich, Peter Winther, Oliver Eberle, Mario Kassar, Joel B. Michaels, and Ramsey Thomas; **Director:** Roland Emmerich; **Screenplay:** Dean Devlin and Roland Emmerich; **Music:** David Arnold; **Special Effects:** Jeff Kleiser, Art Morrel, Michael Van Himbergen, Jeffrey A. Williams, Thomas Bolland, John P. Kazin, Kit West, Amanda Cerney, Derry Frost, Mary Nelson, Robert O'Haver, Trevor Wood, Eileen O'Neill, William Basanceney, Jeffery Okun, and Randy Bauer; **Cinematography:** Karl Walter Lindenlaub; **Cast:** Kurt Russell, James Spader, Viveca Lindfors, Jaye Davidson, Alexis Cruz, Mili Avital, Leon Rippy, French Stewart, John Diehl, Carlos Lauchu, Djimon, Erick Avari, Gianin Loffler, Cecil Hoffmann, Rae Allen, Richard Kind

Centuries ago, an alien race visit Earth, specifically the region of the Nile delta. They kidnapped a number of people to breed a slave race. They also left behind a teleportation doorway that would allow travelers instantaneous transportation from one dimension, point in the galaxy, or universe to another just in case they ever needed to return. When the doorway is discovered in modern times, it ends up in the hands of the military. They try to crack the code that will get the door going again, but they have no luck until they bring in a young linguist (Spader) whose specialty is ancient languages.

Once Spader gets the Star Gate up and running, he and a team of soldiers, led by an officer (Russell), are sent through to see what's on the other side. The military has given Russell orders to destroy the gate if he perceives a threat to Earth, and of course Spader doesn't know this. They find a human civilization made up of the descendants of the early humans kidnapped out of our past, still being held in slavery by the aliens who greatly resemble the gods of ancient Egypt. The expected revolt comes off, the aliens are destroyed, and the film ends on a happy note.

Stargate is an interesting near miss. Its main problem is an intelligent beginning that runs out of steam, more disappointing to many than if it had been a routine picture throughout. The action is realistic and the acting good, but best of all, there are real science fiction concepts at work, though mild ones to be sure. A television movie and ongoing television series followed.

STAR KID

Tri-Mark Pictures, 1998, Color, 101 min, VT, LD

Producers: Mark Amin, Andrew Hersh, Russ Markowitz, Cami Winikoff, Jennie Lew Tugend, and Jonathon Komack Martin; **Director:** Manny Coto; **Screenplay:** Coto; **Music:** Nicholas Pike; **Special Effects:** Diane Carlucci, Kelly Matsumoto, Vincent Montefuscu, Lou Carlucci, Thomas C. Rainone, Beecher Tomlinson, Area 51, Criswell Productions, Computer Cafe, Inc., Film Technical Services, and Digital Film Works, Inc.; **Cinematography:** Ronn Schmidt; **Cast:** Joseph Mazzello, Joey Simmrin, Danny Masterson, Richard Gilliland, Corinne Bohrer, Ashlee Levich

A young loner discovers a superpowered, intelligent cybernetic suit of armor in a scrap yard. He puts it on, learns to use it, communicates with it, and also befriends it, all just before the evil alien shows up to destroy it, and the film becomes an extended action sequence.

STAR KNIGHT (aka: THE KNIGHT OF THE DRAGON)

Salamandra Productions (Spain), 1986, Color, 90 min, VT, LD, DVD

Director: Fernando Colomo; **Screenplay:** Colomo; **Cinematography:** José Luis Alcaine; **Music:** José Nieto; **Special Effects:** Reyes Abades and Chuck Comisky; **Cast:** Klaus Kinski, Harvey Keitel, Fernando Rey, Maria Lamor, Miguel Bosé

It's the Dark Ages, and for no discernable reason, a spaceship falls into a Spanish lake and is mistaken for a dragon.

STARMAN

Columbia, 1984, Color, 115 min, VT, LD

Producer: Larry J. Franco; **Director:** John Carpenter; **Screenplay:** Bruce Evans and Raynold Gideon; **Music:** Jack Nitzsche; **Special Effects:** Roy Arbogast, Bill Lee, Pamela Marcotte, Scott Farrar, Michael J. McAlister, Gary Zinc, Michael Gleason, Bill Kimberlin, Bruce Nicholson, David Simmons, Dick Wood, and Kevin Quibell; **Cinematography:** Donald M. Morgan, A.S.C.; **Cast:** Jeff Bridges, Karen Allen, Charles Martin Smith, Richard Jaeckel

The film begins with the actual U.S. satellite *Voyager II* beaming out The Rolling Stones's "I Can't Get No Satisfaction," plus various greetings from the people of Earth in assorted languages. Of course someone answers. Is there a sentient creature who can resist the power of rock and roll? Not in the universe portrayed in this film.

The alien (Bridges) who answers the Stones's call receives a less friendly greeting than he was led to expect from the *Voyager II* messages—his ship is shot down. He makes his way to the nearest habitat he can find, the home of the recently widowed Jenny Hayden. Here he quickly takes on human form by duplicating the DNA from a lock of hair found in one of her photo albums. He ends up looking exactly like Jenny's newly dead husband, except for his nose. The Starman's has never been broken, while Jenny's husband's had.

Very quickly, he hustles the completely freaked-out Jenny into a car and on a cross-country trip from Wisconsin to Arizona, where he must rendezvous with his mother ship or die. A compassionate SETI agent, Mark Shermin (Smith), and an evil government official, National Security bigwig George Fox (Jaeckel), follow closely behind. Along the way the Starman learns the basics of human behavior (red light—stop, green light—go, yellow light—go very fast), and Jenny is simultaneously drawn to the being who looks so much like the husband she is grieving for and is terrified. Before they reach Arizona, the Starman and Jenny fall in love. Of course, agent Shermin and Jenny are able to get the Starman to Arizona and away from the clutches of agent Fox.

This one works far better as a romantic road trip movie than it does a science fiction flick. It's much more about the relationship that builds between Jenny and her hubby lookalike than about action or special effects (in sharp contrast to *DUNE* and 2010, both of which came out within months of *Starman*). Both Bridges (who was nominated for an Oscar for his role) and Allen are completely convincing. Some may find the ending too heavy-handed—the film draws an analogy between Starman and Christ wherein Starman impregnates the previously barren Jenny with a son who will one day teach the earthlings. Still the love story should be emotionally satisfying enough for the romantics in the audience.

Note: Later the film had a short rebirth as a television series of little note.

STAR PILOT

Monarch, 1977, Color, 81 min

Producers: Aldo Calamara and Ermanno Curti; **Director:** Pietro Francisci; **Screenplay:** Francisci and

Fernando Paolo Girolami; **Cinematography:** Giulio Albonico and Silvano Ippoloto; **Cast:** Leonara Ruff, Gordon Mitchell, Kirk Morris

A team of scientists is sent off to the Hydra constellation to translate a newfound alien language.

STAR PORTAL

New Concorde, 1998, Color, 78 min

Producer: Roger Corman; **Director:** Jon Purdy; **Screenplay:** Mark Hanna and Purdy; **Music:** Adam Berry; **Cinematography:** Bruce Dorfman; **Cast:** Stephen Bauer, Fiona Byrne, Anthony Crivello, Stephen Davies, Athena Massey, Dean Tuckwell

See *NOT OF THIS EARTH*

STARSHIP INVASIONS
(aka: ALIEN INVASION)

Warner Bros., 1977, Color, 87 min, VT

Producers: Ed Hunt and Ken Gord; **Director:** Hunt; **Screenplay:** Hunt; **Music:** Gil Melle; **Special Effects:** Warren Keillor; **Cinematography:** Mark Irwin; **Cast:** Christopher Lee, Robert Vaughn, Daniel Pilon, Helen Shaver, Henry Ramer, Sherri Rose, Tiiu Leek, Victoria Johnson, Doreen Lipson, Kate Par, Ted Turner

The dread Legion of the Winged Serpent has cast its evil gaze toward Earth. Trying without much success to protect the planet is the top-secret Legion of Races. Lucky for Earth, they have a Galactic Center base hidden in the middle of the Bermuda Triangle. Obviously a cast of the above mentioned wasn't likely to deliver a terrible job, but the story is terrible and the special effects so bad even by 1977 standards that there is no justification for this film's having ever been released by a major studio.

STARSHIP TROOPERS

Tri-Star Pictures, 1997, Color, 129 min, VT, LD, DVD

Producer: Jon Davidson; **Director:** Paul Verhoeven; **Screenplay:** Edward Neumeiner; **Music:** Basil Pole-

Starship Troopers (SONY PICTURES ENTERTAINMENT / JOSEPH B. MAUCERI COLLECTION)

douris; **Special Effects:** Scott Anderson, Phil Tippett, and Kevin Yagher; **Cinematography:** Jost Vacano; **Cast:** Casper Van Dien, Dina Meyer, Denise Richards, Michael Ironside, Jake Busey, Neil Patrick Harris, Clancey Brown, Seth Gilliam, Rue McClanahan, Marshall Bell

It's the far-off future and people don't get to vote or even call themselves citizens until they've done their military duty. They can have jobs, be heads of corporations, go to school, marry, raise children—anything, basically, except vote and hold office. That's only for those who accept their responsibility to the country that protects them. For the first 20 minutes of the movie, going into the military in the future isn't that big a deal. But once the "bugs" show up, it's a different matter as Earth is attacked by a race of gigantic sentient insects. Their technology might be completely biological, but it's enough to allow them to bombard Earth from the other side of the galaxy.

The plot is simple. Kids just out of high school join the military, thinking becoming a citizen will be cool, only to end up enduring the harshest war in history and then becoming not just citizens, but responsible citizens.

Starship Troopers is a return to the buddy pictures made in great numbers during and shortly after World War II. It focuses tightly on three high school seniors, giving you their decision to join the service, following them through basic training, then on into the war. As usual, the war is just a backdrop for the real story—finding out who lives, who dies, and who gets the girl. Interestingly enough, this time around the "girl" is actually Casper Van Dien, who has two determined women fighting over him. But that's how things can get turned around in a Paul Verhoeven film.

The director's first sci-fi effort, *ROBOCOP*, greatly impressed audiences with a violent, but audaciously clever script, terrific special effects, and an imaginative, quirky subtext. *TOTAL RECALL* followed, possessing all the elements of Verhoeven's first work but tweaked to a higher power with everything bigger, faster, and grimmer. Like *Total Recall* adapted from the work of Phillip K. Dick, *Starship Troopers* is based on the work of a classic science fiction writer.

A lot of details and the exact hardware of Robert Heinlein's half-century-old novel didn't make it into the movie, although much of his sensibility did. Initially, Heinlein wrote *Starship Troopers* as a children's book—a citizenship primer as it were. Interestingly, when Verhoeven's version of the story was released, critics attacked the film for its fascist views.

As producer Davidson said, "To translate Heinlein's polemics into drama, we devised the Fed Net, which echoes the media breaks in *RoboCop*. This government-sponsored 'infomercials' underlay the conflict between man and insect, but also keep a satiric undertone running throughout the picture."

But alongside its political and social themes, *Starship Troopers* delivers fast-paced action as well, complete with dazzling visual effects and ultragory battle scenes.

STAR TREK—FIRST CONTACT

Paramount, 1996, Color, 110 min, VT, LD, DVD

Producers: Rick Berman, Martin Hornstein, and Peter Lauritson; **Director:** Jonathan Frakes; **Screenplay:** Berman, Ronald D. Moore, and Brannon Braga; **Music:** Jerry Goldsmith and Joel Goldsmith; **Special Effects:** Craig Barron, Donald Meyers, Andrea D'Amico, Jeff Olson, Adam Howard, David Takemura, John Knoll, and Habib Zargarpour; **Cinematography:** Matthew F. Leonetti; **Cast:** Patrick Stewart, Jonathan Frakes, Brent Spiner, LeVar Burton, Gates McFadden, Marina Sirtis, Michael Dorn, Alfie Woodard, James Cromwell, Alice Krige, Robert Picardo

See *STAR TREK—THE MOTION PICTURE*

STAR TREK—GENERATIONS

Paramount, 1994, Color, 118 min, VT, LD, DVD

Producers: Rick Berman, Peter Lauritson, and Bernie Williams; **Director:** David Carson; **Screenplay:** Berman, Ronald D. Moore, and Brannon Braga; **Music:** Dennis McCarthy; **Special Effects:** Alia Agha, C. Marie Davis, Habib Zargarpour, Terry D. Frazee, Bill George, Ronald D. Moore, Roni McKinley, John Knoll, and John Grower; **Cinematography:** John A. Alonzo; **Cast:** William Shatner, Walter Koenig, James Doohan, Malcolm McDowell, Patrick Stewart, Jonathan Frakes, Brent Spiner, LeVar Burton, Gates McFadden, Marina Sirtis, Michael Dorn, Barbara March, Gwyneth Walsh, Alan Ruck

See *STAR TREK—THE MOTION PICTURE*

STAR TREK—INSURRECTION

Paramount, 1998, Color, 103 min, VT, LD, DVD

Producers: Rick Berman, Michael Pillar, Marty Hornstein, Peter Lauritson, and Patrick Stewart; **Director:** Jonathan Frakes; **Screenplay:** Berman, and Pillar;

Music: Jerry Goldsmith; **Special Effects:** John Grower, Adam Howard, Mark Spatny, Jim Rygiel, and Siouxsie Stewart; **Cinematography:** Matthew F. Leonetti; **Cast:** Patrick Stewart, Jonathan Frakes, Brent Spiner, LeVar Burton, Gates McFadden, Marina Sirtis, Michael Dorn, F. Murray Abraham, Daniel Hugh, Donna Murphy, Anthony Zerbe, Greg Henry, Michael Welsh

See *STAR TREK—THE MOTION PICTURE*

STAR TREK—THE MOTION PICTURE

Paramount, 1979, Color, 142 min, VT, LD, DVD

Producer: Gene Roddenberry; **Director:** Robert Wise; **Screenplay:** Harold Livingstone; **Music:** Jerry Goldsmith; **Special Effects:** Douglas Trumbull; **Cinematography:** Richard Kline; **Cast:** William Shatner, Leonard Nimoy, DeForest Kelley, James Doohan, Nichelle Nichols, Walter Koenig, George Takei, Majel Barrett, Grace Lee Whitney, Mark Leonard, Stephen Collins, Persis Khambatta, David Gautreaux, Terrence O'Conner, Marcy Lafferty, Bill van Zandt

It's the 23rd century and the Federation is the dominant, unifying power in the galaxy. As this movie opens, a trio of Klingon (the alien "evil empire" next door) ships patrol their own territory when something comes along that is totally outside their scope of experience. As usual in such a situation, the Klingons open fire. The entity, whatever it is, swallows them up in a blast of cosmic force and moves on as if nothing had happened.

This power is on a direct course for Earth, headquarters for the Federation, in search of its creator. No one knows what this could mean, and the authorities are soon in a panic over what to do. Their eventual answer is to send James T. Kirk to investigate. Now middle-aged, Admiral Kirk (Shatner) is the man who wrote the book on meeting unknown and unbelievably powerful alien life-forms and getting the better of them. The Federation quickly gets all of his former officers together with him save one, the half-human/ half-alien Mr. Spock (Nimoy), who is no longer a member of the Federation. Aboard their old ship, the *Enterprise*, newly outfitted with lots of up-to-date gizmos, the crew blasts off to intercept the new menace. En route, Mr. Spock joins them. He will help them meet the unknown entity and save Earth, but he has his own personal reasons.

Spock is part Vulcan, an alien race that prizes logic and the intellect and disdains emotion. The approaching menace apparently is nothing but intellect—pure thought completely devoid of all emotion—something from which Spock thinks he can learn. Once contact is made, the giant threat is discovered to be the old American satellite *Voyager*, which has been roaming the galaxy for hundreds of years. It's learned a lot, including how to think and make itself all powerful.

Star Trek—The Motion Picture was a film that could neither succeed nor fail. On the one hand, a loyal fan base had anticipated it for more than a decade. On the other hand, the fans expected the most fabulous science fiction movie ever imagined—something the first *Star Trek* film was not.

Star Trek—The Motion Picture is not exceptional. Its main flaw is its thin story line, cobbled together from the plots of two old episodes of the television series. To make fans wait 10 years for something new and then not give them a fresh story seemed a crime to the fans. Originally planned for 1975, scripts were reviewed for the next three years until filming finally began in late 1978, resulting in a weak plot.

A minor but important mistake is a sound track that has not the slightest homage to the original TV theme music. The Goldsmith sound track is a stirring triumph. Often called the only thing right with the film, its theme was eventually used as the main theme of the second *Star Trek* television series: *Star Trek: The Next Generation*. But as with the look of the ship, the crew's uniforms, and so on, the original theme was just another casualty of the studio's desire to put distance between themselves and what had gone before. This was to be a major motion picture, after all, not an everyday television program, and they felt it had to be big, especially in terms of special effects.

Unfortunately, the special effects were not all that impressive. Though many rumors spin around, the only facts the studio verifies are that the picture was already over budget with few of the effects complete and that the first special effects coordinator, Robert Able, was dismissed and Douglas Trumbull brought in to take his place. Trumbull and his people worked night and day to get the picture into some kind of shape, barely getting prints shipped to New York and Los Angeles in time for critics' screenings. Despite Trumbull's effort, the critics were less than kind. Indeed, the author of this book was one of the New York critics at that first screening, where a novelization of the film was given to each attendee. The book helped figure out much of the muddle. In subsequent years, footage was added to the film for its television debut, for which it was also re-edited. The movie is much improved thanks to the extra work, but it was almost a case of too little, too late. The franchise was almost ruined.

Paramount had to think long and hard about doing anything else with *Star Trek*. The actors were aging and asking for much higher salaries, especially the principals. The fans had been disappointed with the first film and were not looking forward to another with anticipation. The rest of the world had been even less enchanted with the film. The executives decided that if they were ever going to make a picture with everything, the next *Star Trek* would have to be it. In a wise move, they hired Nicholas Meyer to put together the next film. He gave them *Star Trek II—The Wrath of Khan* (1982), the absolute best of the *Star Trek* films and, perhaps, one of the 10 best science fiction films of all time.

Over and over, Meyer returned to the source material to construct his film. The first notes of the sound track filled the theater with the original theme. Instantly, audiences cheered. A protagonist was brought back from the original television series. Khan is a genetically engineered superman from the late 20th century. After clashing with Captain Kirk (and losing, of course), he and his people are allowed to settle on a planet of their own. Between the series and the film, the planet went through terrible upheavals, turning the garden paradise into a desert nightmare. Providence brings Khan and his surviving followers a way to get off the planet. The superman renews his struggle with Kirk, managing at the same time to get his hands on a weapon of ultimate destruction. At the climax, Khan beats Kirk and captures the means of bringing the galaxy to its knees before him. He possesses everything he has ever dreamed of throughout his extended lifetime—except, the life of James T. Kirk. His greatest foe finds a way to elude Khan's trap, and that gives the villain a difficult choice—run away from his enemy and thus secure a dynasty that will serve him and his for years, possibly forever, or turn and risk all by fighting Kirk once more on equal footing.

The ending is more than just another space battle; it is a struggle between the wills of two larger-than-life characters. Neither is willing to give an inch, and so they doom all around them. When Kirk triumphs over Khan, the superman sets off his stolen doomsday device. He dies knowing that there is no possible way Kirk can survive. Kirk himself believes this is true.

There is a way out, of course, but it's not one any hero captain could order. Someone will have to realign a radioactive device by hand. It will save the ship, but it means that person's death. Kirk's best friend, Spock, the only person on the ship with both the stamina and the intellect to pull off the stunt, sacrifices himself to save the ship. He dies, separated from his friend by a sheet of clear plastic (and the boundary of death), and there isn't a dry eye in the house.

Star Trek II—The Wrath of Khan is what every sci-fi film should be, and so few are. It takes all of its characters seriously, giving them all their moment to shine. It has a story filled with literary and biblical references

that all advance the plot. Its special effects and sound track are spectacular. And its sci-fi content is through the roof. It is, as stated above, the absolute finest piece of work ever produced under the banner of *Star Trek*.

Star Trek III—The Search for Spock (1984) is a hopeless mess. After giving the character of Spock a hero's death worthy of a Greek myth, the studio decided he couldn't be replaced and had to be brought back. Like a bad episode of a television show this film brings that about. The plot, which involves Klingons and the planet newly reborn courtesy of the Genesis Device from the previous film, is silly and unbelievable. The villains are equally foolish, offering no real menace. The son Kirk discovered in the second film is killed gratuitously in this one, simply to remove the burden of his presence from the series.

At this point the franchise firmly settled into being a big-screen television series. *Star Trek IV—The Voyage Home* (1986) set out to put everything right. It got rid of the last of the new characters that had been added to the cast, did away with everyone's advanced ranks, even busting Admiral Kirk back down to captain. The story is a bit of fluff about godlike beings coming back to Earth to check on the whales, creatures that no longer existed on the planet in the future thanks to pollution. Kirk and his team go back to the past and bring home some whales and everyone is happy. The film is light and breezy. It gives all the characters something to do that the fans could remember fondly and sets up the franchise to turn out more episodic movies on a regular basis.

The next film in the series is *Star Trek V—The Final Frontier* (1986). It has the best plot since the second and should have been a blockbuster. It wasn't, however, for two reasons. First, as stunningly bold as the plot is, the script incorporates some mawkishly silly scenes. Second, though many rumors have circulated, one hard fact everyone agrees on is that the film's special-effects budget was slashed *during* the filming. This meant that story elements had to be changed, diminished, or eliminated altogether, a major blow to the film's cohesion. Many fans rate the fifth film near the bottom of the Trek barrel.

For two other reasons, however, it deserves higher regard. First, the relationship between Spock, McCoy, and Kirk, always the most important thing in the series, is examined in close detail. The characters are all laid bare at different moments, and none of them suffer for it. There are some beautiful moments, especially Dr. McCoy's confession of how he killed his father to spare him a prolonged and painful death, as well as the camping sequences that start and end the film. Second is the sci-fi angle of this film. In the story the question of God's existence is taken up. Is there one or isn't there? At the very end of the film, when asked if humanity will ever know the answer, Kirk ends the discussion by reminding us that God was created by people as a tool they needed to rise above their own natures. It is a moment the studio could have left out of the film and no one would have been the wiser. But it remained, and *Star Trek* is on record that there is no God save that which humanity created for its own use. Regardless of one's viewpoint on this issue, the fifth *Star Trek* movie is a powerful sci-fi statement, certainly the boldest ever dared in such a commercial vehicle, and perhaps the second best of the *Trek* films.

Star Trek VI—The Undiscovered Country (1991) followed. The movie is satisfying, but there is nothing special about it. The script, which concerns historical events at a crucial diplomatic conference, was written mainly to help straighten out the history of the period between the old *Trek* television show and the new ones. It does this well enough and commits no major flaws. Notably, it is the last of the films to feature the old cast.

Star Trek: Generations (1994) came next. It is the first film to feature the *Next Generation* cast along with several members of the old series—most notably, Captain Kirk. He and the captain of the new *Enterprise*, John Luc Picard (Patrick Stewart), meet and the baton is passed. Together they must confront a strange energy vortex and the man who seeks to harness it for his own use. Kirk is killed off miserably, displeasing even non-Trek fans. Disappointment ran high after this film. Audiences felt Kirk had been treated quite shabbily, and the new crew seemed incompetent. If the transition period was going to succeed, the new cast needed their own *Wrath of Khan*.

The second *Next Generation* film was *Star Trek: First Contact* (1996). Like *Wrath of Khan*, the movie borrowed the most impressive villains from the television series, the Borg—a mentally linked collective of zombie/ cyborgs—and pressed them into service. The picture is a disaster from a science fiction standpoint, making typical time travel mistakes, but it settled back into the episode pattern that had served the franchise well. With an effective villain, good effects, and nice bits for each of the stars, the movie kept the franchise alive.

The last film to date in the series, *Star Trek: Insurrection* (1998), was a disappointment to the fans and the studio both. Intellectually, it is the third best of the movies. A planet is discovered that can mean eternal life and health for billions of beings if it is stolen from the 600 people who live there. The *Enterprise* crew is put in the position of either going along with the forced relocation of a people (a move that will kill those people) or fighting their own government in the name of the principles upon which that government was founded. It is a first-class moral dilemma and one the film resolves in an interesting manner.

Part of the plot setup is that the crew is beginning to feel like diplomatic stooges, no longer engaged in the rugged stellar explorations of their youth. Just being in the proximity of the planet in question, however, reverses the aging process. Thus, the unanswered question is: Do they defend the helpless because it's the right thing to do or because they have regressed to a point of near adolescent recklessness? The question is never answered, of course. Social science fiction is almost always a reflective look within the society that produces it. For an American movie studio to make such a film near the end of the 20th century shows the same kind of risk-taking that the *Enterprise* crew takes. An oversize government, one grown far beyond the original parameters of its own rules and guidelines, is now out of control, stealing from rightful owners, lying, killing their own, all in the name of a supposed greater good that is never named.

It was a courageous statement, but it was easy to see why it did not succeed. People don't like to be reminded of their shortcomings, and *Star Trek: Insurrection* did that in big, bold print. But good science fiction has always challenged the social order, refusing to accept what's convenient if it refutes logic. *Insurrection* could possibly be the last *Star Trek* film. If so, it is a high note worthy of a finale.

STAR TREK II—THE WRATH OF KHAN

Paramount, 1982, Color, 113 min, VT, LD, DVD

Producers: Harve Bennett, Robert Sallin, and William F. Phillips; **Director:** Nicholas Meyer; **Screenplay:** Bennett, Meyer, and Jack B. Sowards; **Music:** James Horner; **Special Effects:** Scott Farrar, Edward A. Ayer, Fred Brauer, Martin Beckler, Gary F. Bentley, Bob Dawson, William Purcell, Harry Stewart, and John McLeod; **Cinematography:** Gayne Rescher; **Cast:** William Shatner, Walter Koenig, James Doohan, George Takei, Leonard Nimoy, DeForest Kelly, Ricardo Montalban, Nichelle Nichols, Kirstie Alley, Bibi Besch, Merritt Buttrick, Paul Winfield

See *STAR TREK—THE MOTION PICTURE*

STAR TREK III—THE SEARCH FOR SPOCK

Paramount, 1984, Color, 105 min, VT, LD, DVD

Producer: Harve Bennett; **Director:** Leonard Nimoy; **Screenplay:** Bennett, Gary Nardino, and Ralph Winter; **Music:** James Horner; **Special Effects:** Bob Dawson, Scott Farrar, Bill George, Ken Ralston, and John

McLeod; **Cinematography:** Charles Correll; **Cast:** William Shatner, Walter Koenig, James Doohan, George Takei, Leonard Nimoy, DeForest Kelly, Nichelle Nichols, Robin Curtis, Christopher Lloyd, Mark Lenard, Dame Judith Anderson, Merritt Buttrick, James B. Sikking, Robert Hooks, John Larroquette, Miguel Ferrer

See *STAR TREK—THE MOTION PICTURE*

STAR TREK IV—THE VOYAGE HOME

Paramount, 1986, Color, 119 min, VT, LD, DVD

Producers: Harve Bennett, Ralph Winter, and Kirk Thatcher; **Director:** Leonard Nimoy; **Screenplay:** Bennett, Nimoy, Nicholas Meyer, Steve Meerson, and Peter Krikes; **Music:** Leonard Rosenman; **Special Effects:** Walt Conti, Brian Tipton, Tony Hudson, John V. Fante, Jenny Fulle, and Eric Swenson; **Cinematography:** Don Peterman; **Cast:** William Shatner, Walter Koenig, James Doohan, George Takei, Leonard Nimoy, DeForest Kelly, Nichelle Nichols, Robin Curtis, Jane Wyatt, Catherine Hicks, Mark Lenard, Brock Peters, Robert Ellenstein, John Schuck

See *STAR TREK—THE MOTION PICTURE*

STAR TREK V—THE FINAL FRONTIER

Paramount, 1989, Color, 106 min, VT, LD, DVD

Producers: Harve Bennett, Ralph Winter, Mel Efros, and Brook Breton; **Director:** William Shatner; **Screenplay:** Shatner, Bennett, and David Loughery; **Music:** Jerry Goldsmith; **Special Effects:** Eric Angelson, Patricia Barry, Bran Ferren, Susan LeBer, Mike Edmonson, Michael Wood, David V. Mei, James Shelly, Mike Reedy, and John McLeod; **Cinematography:** Andrew Laszlo; **Cast:** William Shatner, Walter Koenig, James Doohan, George Takei, Leonard Nimoy, DeForest Kelly, Nichelle Nichols, David Warner, Laurence Luckinbill, Charles Cooper

See *STAR TREK—THE MOTION PICTURE*

STAR TREK VI—THE UNDISCOVERED COUNTRY

Paramount, 1991, Color, 109 min, VT, LD, DVD

Producers: Leonard Nimoy, Ralph Winter, Brooke Breston, Marty Horenstein, and Steven-Charles Jaffe; **Director:** Nicholas Meyer; **Screenplay:** Nimoy, Meyer, Dennis Martin Flynn, Mark Rosenthal, and Lawrence Konner; **Music:** Cliff Eidelman; **Special Effects:** Scott E. Anderson, Scott Farrar, Bill George, Mark Moore, Craig Barron, Andrea D'Amico, Joel Hladecek, and Peter Takevchi; **Cinematography:** Hiro Narita; **Cast:** William Shatner, Walter Koenig, James Doohan, George Takei, Leonard Nimoy, DeForest Kelly, Nichelle Nichols, David Warner, Kim Cattrall, Christopher Plummer, Mark Lenard, Grace Lee Whitney, Brock Peters, Kurtwood Smith, Iman, Rosana DeSoto, John Schuck, Michael Dorn, Christian Slater

See *STAR TREK—THE MOTION PICTURE*

STAR WARS

20th Century Fox, 1977, Color, 121 min, VT, LD

Producer: Gary Kurtz; **Director:** George Lucas; **Screenplay:** Lucas; **Music:** John Williams; **Special Effects:** John Dykstra, John Stears, Stuart Freeborn, Ralph McQuarrie, Ron Cobb, and Rick Baker; **Cinematography:** Gilbert Taylor; **Cast:** Mark Hamill, Harrison Ford, Carrie Fisher, Peter Cushing, Sir Alec Guinness, Anthony Daniels, Kenny Baker, James Earl Jones, David Prowse, Peter Mayhew, Denis Lawson

A long time ago in a galaxy far, far away, rebellion is brewing. The evil emperor has a stranglehold on every system. If he can complete his supposedly invincible Death Star, he will use it to find and crush the rebels who oppose him. Then his rule will be complete. The film opens with the emperor's main henchman, Darth Vader, (Prowse/voice of Jones) closing in on one of the leaders of the rebellion, the Princess Leia (Fisher). He captures her, but not before she can send off a message to the last of her father's faithful Jedi knights, old Obi-Wan Kenobi (Guinness), via two androids R2-D2 and C-3PO (Daniels and Baker). The machines come into the hands of young Luke Skywalker (Hamill) who gets them to Kenobi but loses his family in the process. With nothing to lose, he joins Kenobi in his attempt to free the princess and stop the emperor. They team up with Han Solo (Ford), a mercenary space pilot, and his alien sidekick (Mayhew), rescue the princess, join the rebellion, and destroy the horrid Death Star satellite.

This is the film that changed the shape not only of science fiction movies, but in many ways of *all* science fiction. Although nothing more than a clever updating of the old Buck Rogers/Flash Gordon serials, the film was released at just the right moment in movie history. A young theatergoing public, bored and impatient with

Hollywood's steady diet of dreary, "socially relevant" themes, flocked to *Star Wars*' retro look at morality, friendship, and honor. The movie's great fortune was to open when the nation was desperate for simple truths. Being delivered in a stylish, slick package only increased its popularity. The problem for the genre developed when subsequent producers and genre publishers missed the point of what had made *Star Wars* such a blockbuster.

The timing of its release was absolutely crucial to the film's massive success. Not even its own sequel, THE EMPIRE STRIKES BACK, widely recognized as a vastly superior film on all levels, could match it at the box office. *Star Wars* filled a need in a weary population. With the need filled, audiences were not going to shell out for tickets 20 and 30 times for *anything* for a while. But, as often happens, mindless avarice prevailed over common sense, and for a decade practically nothing in science fiction was done without trying to copy *Star Wars*.

Cute robots and sappy heroics abounded in films lacking the heart and decency of what they were stealing. None of the *Star Wars* rip-offs were hits, though people did flock to many of the "comic book" films that followed as filmmakers abandoned serious science fiction.

Star Wars remains a very entertaining film, despite having a plot lifted from a dozen other movies. It is a sci-fi movie in its look only, but precious little has entertained the world or given it the hope of this unassuming and brilliant gem of a picture. A western at heart, it came at a time when the world needed it, spoke simple truths eloquently, and once and for all legitimized science fiction as a respectable genre worthy of attention from more than just oddball fans. The movie is well paced and imaginative, although it is filled with standard characters whom science fiction enthusiasts have known for more than 40 years.

Note: In 1997, Lucasfilms released new versions of the first three *Star Wars* films. This was also when the new numbering system for the movies became fixed. For those unfamiliar with this concept, here's the story.

First came *Star Wars*. It was meant to be a one-time film. Although it is hard to imagine now, initially the idea for the picture was turned down by most of the Hollywood studios before Fox took a chance on it. Even after signing on, the studio tried to sell their interest before the movie's release, so convinced were they that it was going to be a huge money loser. Only at the last minute when a test audience reacted wildly favorably, did they decide to cross their fingers and hope for the best.

Immediately, the second film, *The Empire Strikes Back*, went into production. Several years later, it was followed by RETURN OF THE JEDI. While these pictures were being made, George Lucas announced that there would be six more films in the *Star Wars* saga, three prequels and three sequels. This, however, would call for the existing *Star Wars* picture to be retitled and renumbered. Actually, since it never had a number, it would now be known as Episode IV.

Even though some prints of *Empire* and all of the prints of *Jedi* had their "correct" numbers, the public resisted this notion, especially since it took Lucas some 20 years to get around to making his prequels. Eventually, however, he did make the new "first" chapter of his saga, and thus, the original *Star Wars* became *Star Wars—Episode IV: A New Hope*. *The Empire Strikes Back* became: *Star Wars—Episode V: The Empire Strikes Back*, and *Return of the Jedi*, of course, was transformed into *Star Wars—Episode VI: Return of the Jedi*.

As for the special editions of the original trilogy released in 1977, none of the movies' story lines were altered in any real way. The new versions were merely enhanced with new special effects. Extra spaceships were added to battles, new characters and animals were added to scenes as background, and large, sweeping cityscapes were tucked in here and there. There is no doubt that all three films were enriched by the new production values. *Star Wars*, produced on a much tighter budget, was the most greatly enhanced. *Jedi* featured some new scenes that made it prettier but did little to help the story. Only *The Empire Strikes Back* remained practically intact.

STAR WARS—EPISODE I: THE PHANTOM MENACE

20th Century Fox, 1999, Color, 121 min

Producer: George Lucas; **Director:** Lucas; **Screenplay:** Lucas; **Music:** John Williams; **Special Effects:** W. Regan McGee, Ned Gorman, Barbara Affonso, Ira Keeler, William Beck, Giovanni Donovan, Lorne Peterson, Heather Smith, Habib Zargarpour, Philip Edward Alexy, Hal T. Hickel, Peter Hutchinson, Sean Schur, Steve Walton, Russell E. Darling, Andrew Doucette, John Knoll, Dennis Murren, Scott Squires, Judith Weaver, Steve Gawley, Bill George, and Simon Maddocks; **Cinematography:** David Tattersall; **Cast:** Liam Neeson, Ewan McGregor, Natalie Portman, Jake Lloyd, Ian McDiarmid, Anthony Daniels, Kenny Baker, Pernilla August, Oliver Ford Davies, Hugh Quarshie, Ahmed Best, Frank Oz, Terence Stamp, Brian Blessed, Ray Park, Samuel L. Jackson

A long time ago in a galaxy far, far away, there was no rebellion. There was no evil emperor. The galaxy lived in peace, a massive Imperial Senate in place to make certain everyone is treated fairly. But, of course, it was not to last.

As the story opens, a rogue politician, Senator Palpatine (McDiarmid), is working behind the scenes not only to destroy the Senate (of which he is a member), but also the Jedi Knights who enforce the rulings of congress. His opening moves are thwarted by two Jedi Qui-Gon Jinn and Obi-Wan Kenobi, one of whom later loses his life battling Senator Palpatine's main henchman, Darth Maul. The two Jedi try to free a young boy, Anakin Skywalker, from slavery on the planet Tatooine because they are convinced he could be a powerful Jedi. Meanwhile, they have also become embroiled in a power struggle between Queen Amidala and Palpatine, in which the queen's planet Naboo is the prize. The Jedi council, led by Yoda, refuses to train Anakin, so the two Jedi break away and plan to train him on their own. When the older of the two dies, he leaves the boy in his younger apprentice's charge.

The film's fatal flaw lies in special effects that trump the story at every turn. Shot more with the sensibility of a special effects designer than a filmmaker, the result is wooden performances from a cast, including international stars of the first rank, and a failure to bring any emotion to the story. Remarkably, this did little to dampen the film's popularity. Indeed, during the first weeks that the *trailer* for the film was in theaters, theater managers reported upward of 75 percent of their audiences paying full admission just to see the preview. The incredible popularity of the *STAR WARS* saga earned this film an eager audience, and though many fans defended it based on what they wanted it to be, it remains a hodgepodge of a thin plot, stiff acting, and sloppy dialogue.

Perhaps the most disappointing aspect of the film is its break with the tradition of its predecessors. The first three *Star Wars* films established that Jedi Knights learn to master a mysterious power known only as "the force." The force was presented as a power anyone with the proper amount of will and determination could learn to use. In the *The Phantom Menace*, however, it becomes a thing of destiny. People must have the proper parasites in their blood to tap into the force. The change, while adding nothing to the story, took a great deal away from the power and mystery of the series.

STAR WARS—EPISODE IV: A NEW HOPE

See *STAR WARS*

STAR WARS—EPISODE IV: A NEW HOPE (THE SPECIAL EDITION)

See *STAR WARS*

STAR WARS—EPISODE V: THE EMPIRE STRIKES BACK

See *THE EMPIRE STRIKES BACK*

STAR WARS—EPISODE V: THE EMPIRE STRIKES BACK (THE SPECIAL EDITION)

See *STAR WARS*

STAR WARS—EPISODE VI: RETURN OF THE JEDI

See *RETURN OF THE JEDI*

STAR WARS—EPISODE VI: RETURN OF THE JEDI (THE SPECIAL EDITION)

See *STAR WARS*

STEPFORD WIVES, THE

Columbia, 1974, Color, 114 min, VT, LD, DVD

Producers: Gustave M. Berne, Edgar J. Scherrick, and Roger M. Rothstein; **Director:** Bryan Forbes; **Screenplay:** William Goldman; **Music:** Michael Small; **Cinematography:** Owen Roizman; **Cast:** Katharine Ross, Paula Prentiss, Peter Masterson, Nanette Newman, Tina Louise, John Aprea, Patrick O'Neal, Dee Wallace, William Prince, Mary Stuart Masterson

Ross and her husband move to Stepford, Connecticut, because of his new job. Ross and best friend Prentiss try to get along with the rest of the women in town, but they find them to be far too subservient to their husbands. After a while, the two begin to think that there's some kind of conspiracy going on. Eventually, Prentiss becomes as compliant as the other women. Ross soon discovers the answer. The other women in town aren't women at all. The real wives of Stepford have all been murdered and replaced by robotic duplicates. Ross actually gets to see her dewy-eyed, lingerie-wearing, firmer-breasted model as it comes off the assembly line.

Feminist science fiction can miss the mark by being too heavy-handed, but not this time. As terrible as it is to face, far too many men (especially rich ones) seem to go for a Stepford Wives solution in a heartbeat. The movie is slow paced and doesn't dazzle with endless effects, but it is a solid production with a frightening story.

Note: The film was followed by a series of made-for-TV movies: *Revenge of the Stepford Wives*, *The Stepford Children*, and *The Stepford Husbands*. None of these match the original.

STOLEN AIRSHIP, THE (aka: THE STOLEN BALLOON, TWO YEAR VACATION, TWO YEAR'S HOLIDAY)

Barrandov/Gottwaldov Studio (Czechoslovakia), 1969, Color, 105 min

Director: Karel Zeman; **Screenplay:** Zeman and Radovan Kratky; **Music:** Jan Novak; **Special Effects:** Jaroslav Krska; **Cinematography:** Joseph Novotny; **Cast:** Jan Malat, Hanus Bor, Michael Pospisil, Jan Cizek

A small band of children steal an airship and have a few adventures, the main one finding Jules Verne's Captain Nemo.

Note: Zeman is the director of the ingenious THE FABULOUS WORLD OF JULES VERNE. Although *The Stolen Airship* is a completely original story, it still contains the same Zeman attention to detail found in his other Verne-inspired works.

STOLEN BALLOON, THE

See *THE STOLEN AIRSHIP*

STORM PLANET

See *PLANET OF STORMS*

STRANDED

New Line Cinema, 1987, Color, 80 min, VT, LD

Producers: Mark Levinson and Scott M. Rosenfelt; **Director:** Tex Fuller; **Screenplay:** Alan Castle; **Music:** Stacy Widelitz; **Special Effects:** Allen Hall; **Cinematography:** Jeff Jur; **Cast:** Ione Skye, Joe Morton, Maureen O'Sullivan, Susan Barnes, Brendan Hughes, Michael Greene, Cameron Dye

Aliens come to Earth and take a teenager and his grandmother hostage, along with anyone who sits down to watch this movie.

STRANGE CASE OF CAPTAIN RAMPER, THE

Defu (Germany), 1927/First National (U.S.), 1928, b&w, silent feature

Director: Max Reichmann; **Screenplay:** Kurt J. Braun and Paul Wegener; **Cinematography:** Herbert Korner and Frederic Weymann; **Cast:** Paul Wegener, Max Schreck, Kurt Gerron, Mary Johnson

An Arctic explorer (Wegener) finds himself trapped at the North Pole. This unfortunate turn of events leads to his regressing mentally and physically to a prehistoric state. Eventually discovered but not recognized by others, he is taken back to civilization as a freak and put on display. He falls in love with his trainer, and that gives a scientist a clue as to what he might actually be. The scientist restores our hero's mental powers. As soon as he can, the explorer, weary of civilization and its despicable ways, heads back for the Arctic and a little peace and quiet.

STRANGE DAYS

20th Century Fox, 1995, Color, 122 min, VT, LD, DVD

Producers: James Cameron and Steven Charles Jaffe; **Director:** Kathryn Bigelow; **Screenplay:** Cameron and Jay Cocks; **Music:** Graeme Revell; **Special Effects:** James Lima and Terry Faazee; **Cinematography:** Matthew F. Leonetti; **Cast:** Ralph Fiennes, Angela Bassett, Juliette Lewis, Tom Sizemore, Michael Wincott, Vincent D'Onofrio, Glenn Plummer, Brigitte Bako, Richard Edson, William Fichtner, Josef Sommer, Chris Douridas, Todd Graff

The story begins at 1:06:27 A.M., on December 30th, 1999. Rapidly, we are told that it will soon be the new millennium and that Los Angeles is worried that midnight might just bring about a race riot of epic proportions. Black singer Jericho One has been stirring things up, and the government is very concerned. They have good reason to be worried because soon Jericho is murdered by persons unknown and the city is seething with tension that looks like it will boil over.

We also learn that the latest drug of choice is "wearing the wire." People's memories are now for sale—per-

Strange Days (TWENTIETH CENTURY FOX / JOSEPH B. MAUCERI COLLECTION)

son A engages in an activity (skiing, mountain climbing, sex, bank robbery) while wearing a brain recorder. The recording can then be "played back" by person B, who will not just see what the other person saw, but who will feel every single sensation.

The king of this new underground product is Lenny (Fiennes). He peddles his wares throughout the upper strata of Los Angeles, moving with ease through the violent new club scene. The other major players in his life include his ex-girlfriend, the singer Faith (Lewis). She left him for major recording producer Philo (Wincott), who is also Jerico's producer. Philo is a major wire head who has started to grow incredibly paranoid due to the amount of wire he has been viewing lately. Because of this he has hired private eye Max (Sizemore) to follow Faith. Max just happens to be an old friend of Lenny's. Angela Bassett is a parent raising her child as best she can on her own by being a tough-as-nails celebrity chauffeur-for-hire. She's also a friend of Lenny's, one he needs fairly desperately since he wouldn't be able to get out of half his scrapes without her.

Lenny is obsessed with Faith. He constantly plays his old wires of the days when they were a couple. When Iris, an old friend of his and Faith's, tells him that Faith is in trouble, that's all the excuse Lenny needs to jam his way back into her life. She and Philo both tell Lenny that it's over, but he refuses to take no for an answer and keeps digging, eventually discovering that there is some kind of connection between Jerico's death and the trouble around Faith.

Unlike most cross-genre sci-fi films, *Strange Days* doesn't cross over into fantasy or horror, but into the realm of hardboiled fiction. The rest of the story is filled with some interesting twists that wouldn't be fair to spoil. Suffice to say that there's more going on here than one suspects at first amid the great cast, tremendous pacing, great effects, and nicely realized plot. Some think that the movie is overly ambitious, but though the story loses its way at times, it's nice to see the hardboiled genre treated with such respect.

The science fiction holds up as well, as does the idea of wireheads, which has been kicking around for some time in the genre, here completely and efficiently realized. This is one of very few movies that gives Doug Trumbull's excellent film *BRAINSTORM* some competition.

STRANGER FROM THE STARS, THE

See *IMMEDIATE DISASTER*

STRANGER FROM VENUS

See *IMMEDIATE DISASTER*

STRANGE INVADERS

Orion Pictures, 1983, Color, 94 min, VT, LD

Producer: Walter Coblenz; **Director:** Michael Laughlin; **Screenplay:** Bill Condon and Laughlin; **Music:** John Addison; **Special Effects:** James Cummins, Henry J. Golas, and Chuck Cumisky; **Cinematography:** Louis Horvath; **Cast:** Paul LeMat, Nancy Allen, Diana Scarwid, Michael Lerner, Louise Fletcher, Wallace Shawn, Fiona Lewis, Kenneth Tobey, June Lockhart

A small midwestern town is taken over by aliens in this spoof of 1950s B science fiction movies that is diminished by mediocre writing and direction despite a wonderful cast.

STRANGE WORLD OF PLANET X, THE

See *THE COSMIC MONSTERS*

STRONGEST MAN IN THE WORLD, THE

Walt Disney Productions, 1975, Color, 92 min, VT

Producer: Bill Anderson; **Director:** Vincent McEveety; **Screenplay:** Joseph L. McEveety and Herman Groves; **Music:** Robert F. Brunner; **Special Effects:** Art Cruikshank and Danny Lee; **Cinematography:** Andrew Jackson; **Cast:** Kurt Russell, Dick Van Patten, Eve Arden, Cesar Romero, Phil Silvers, Joe Flynn, Michael McGreevey, Harold Gould

See *THE COMPUTER WORE TENNIS SHOES*

STRYKER (aka: SAVAGE DAWN)

HCI (Philippines), 1983, Color, 84 min, VT

Producer: Cirio H. Santiago; **Director:** Santiago; **Screenplay:** Howard R. Cohen; **Music:** Ed Gatchalian; **Cinematography:** Ricardo Remias; **Cast:** Steve Sandor, Andria Savio, William Ostrander, Michael Lane, Julie Gray

This dreary and depressing film chronicles a typical postnuclear world, dry and barren, with people ready to fight to the death over a glass of water.

STUFF, THE

New World Pictures, 1985, Color, 93 min, VT

Producers: Larry Cohen and Paul Kurta; **Director:** Cohen; **Screenplay:** Cohen; **Music:** Anthony Guefen; **Special Effects:** Dave Allen, Bret Culpepper, and Jim Doyle; **Cinematography:** Paul Glickman; **Cast:** Michael Moriarty, Andrea Marcovicci, Garrett Morris, Paul Sorvino, Scott Bloom, Danny Aiello, James Dixon, Alexander Scourby, Russell Nype, Brian Bloom, Rutanya Alda

A smooth, fluffy, and tasty white terror from beyond is packaged as a dessert treat, which works fine for the producers until the revenge of the extraterrestrial whipped dessert begins.

SUBMERSION OF JAPAN, THE

See *NIPPON CHIMBOTSU*

SUBURBAN COMMANDO

New Line Cinema, 1991, Color, 99 min, VT, LD

Producers: Howard Gottfried, Hulk Hogan, Kevin Moreton, and Deborah Moore; **Director:** Burt Kennedy; **Screenplay:** Frank A. Cappello; **Music:** David Michael Frank; **Special Effects:** Richard Malzahn, Jeffrey A. Okun, Robert Habros, and Reel EFX; **Cinematography:** Bernd Heinl; **Cast:** Hulk Hogan, Christopher Lloyd, Shelley Duvall, Larry Miller, William Ball, JoAnn Dearing, Jack Elam, Roy Dotrice, Michael Faustino

An intergalactic peacekeeper (Hogan) comes to Earth for a vacation—a nice backwater low-tech world where he can relax. As one might imagine, this doesn't work out the way he was hoping. The alien supersoldier soon finds himself mixed up in the lives of a corporate executive and his family. Mild-mannered Christopher Lloyd learns to stop taking abuse from Hogan, while the warrior learns something about family life from Lloyd.

SUPER FUZZ (aka: SUPER SNOOPER)

Avco Embassy, 1981, Color, 94 min, VT

Producer: Josi W. Konski; **Director:** Sergio Corbucci; **Screenplay:** Robert Booth, Sabatino Ciuffini, and Sergio Corbucci; **Cinematography:** Silvano Ippoliti; **Cast:** Terrence Hill, Ernest Borgnine, Joanne Dru, Marc Lawrence, Julie Gordon, Lee Sandman

A police officer is exposed to radiation and instead of dying from cancer gains superpowers. He uses his tremendous new abilities to fight crime and bore audiences.

SUPERGIRL

Cantharaus Productions N.V., 1984, Color, 114 min, VT, LD, DVD

Producers: Timothy Burrill, Pauline Coutelenq, Alexander Salkind, Ilya Salkind, and Pierre Spengler; **Director:** Jeannot Szwarc; **Screenplay:** David Odel; **Music:** John Williams and Jerry Goldsmith; **Special Effects:** Dennis Bartlett, Martin Body, Peter Harmon, Derek Meddings, Peter Chaing, Dave Docwra, Doug Ferris, Roy Field, José Granell, Terry Reed, Rodger Shaw, Charles Stoneman, and Paul Wilson; **Cinematography:** Alan Hume; **Cast:** Helen Slater, Peter O'Toole, Faye Dunaway, Peter Cook, Brenda Vaccaro, Mia Farrow, Simon Ward, Marc McClure, Hart Bochner, Matt Frewer, Maureen Teefy

See SUPERMAN: THE MOVIE

SUPERMAN

See SUPERMAN: THE MOVIE

SUPERMAN II

Warner Bros., 1980, Color, 127 min, VT, LD

Producers: Ilya Salkind and Pierre Spengler; **Directors:** Richard Donner and Richard Lester; **Screenplay:** Mario Puzo, David Newman, and Leslie Newman; **Music:** John Williams and Ken Thorne; **Special Effects:** Jimmy Benson, John Evans, Colin Chilvers, Brian Warner, Roy Field, Paul Wilson, and Garth Inns; **Cinematography:** Geoffrey Unsworth; **Cast:** Christopher Reeve, Gene Hackman, Margot Kidder, Ned Beatty, Jackie Cooper, Valerie Perrine, Susannah York,

Superman (WARNER BROS. & DC COMICS / R. ALLEN LEIDER COLLECTION)

Clifton James, E.G. Marshall, Marc McClure, Terence Stamp, Sarah Douglas, Jack O'Halloran

See SUPERMAN: THE MOVIE

SUPERMAN III

Warner Bros., 1983, Color, 123 min, VT, LD

Producer: Pierre Spengler; **Director:** Richard Lester; **Screenplay:** David Newman and Leslie Newman; **Music:** John Williams and Ken Thorne; **Special Effects:** Martin Body, Roy Field, Martin Gutteridge, Ian Corbould, Paul Corbould, Terry Reed, Ricky Farns, David Ford, Garth Inns, and Peter Netley; **Cinematography:** Robert Paynter; **Cast:** Christopher Reeve, Margot Kidder, Jackie Cooper, Richard Pryor, Annette O'Toole, Robert Vaughn, Annie Ross, Pamela Stephenson, Sarah Douglas, Jack O'Halloran

See SUPERMAN: THE MOVIE

Superman (20TH CENTURY FOX /R. ALLEN LEIDER COLLECTION)

SUPERMAN IV: THE QUEST FOR PEACE

Warner Bros., 1987, Color, 90 min, VT, LD

Producers: Yoram Globus, Menahem Golan, Graham Easton, and Michael J. Kagan; **Director:** Sidney J. Furie; **Screenplay:** Lawrence Konner, Mark Rosenthal, and Christopher Reeve; **Music:** John Williams, Paul Fishman, and Alexander Courage; **Special Effects:** Harrison Ellenshaw, David L. Hewitt, Brandy Hill, Christopher Keith, Lynda Lemon, John Scheele, Robert Wait, Jodi Sullivan, Candy Lewis, Michael Lloyd, and Michael Lessa; **Cinematography:** Ernest Day; **Cast:** Christopher Reeve, Gene Hackman, Margot Kidder, Jackie Cooper, Jon Cryer, Sam Wanamaker, Mark Pillow, Mariel Hemingway, Marc McClure

See *SUPERMAN: THE MOVIE*

SUPERMAN AND SCOTLAND YARD

20th Century Fox, 1954, b&w, 77 min

Directors: George Blair and Thomas Carr; **Screenplay:** Jackson Gillis; **Special Effects:** Thol Simonson and Jack R. Glass; **Cinematography:** Harold E. Stone; **Cast:** George Reeves, Noel Neill, Jack Larson, Robert Shayne, John Hamilton, Patrick Acherne, Colin Campbell, Virginia Christine, John Doucette, Jonathan Hale, Evelyn Halpern

See *SUPERMAN: THE MOVIE*

SUPERMAN AND THE JUNGLE DEVIL

20th Century Fox, 1954, b&w, 77 min

Directors: George Blair and Thomas Carr; **Screenplay:** Peter Dixon, Jackson Gillis, and David T. Chantler; **Special Effects:** Thol Simonson and Jack R.

Glass; **Cinematography:** Harold E. Stone; **Cast:** George Reeves, Noel Neill, Jack Larson, Robert Shayne, John Hamilton, Sterling Holloway, Billy Nelson, Ben Weldon, Stan Jarman, Doris Singleton

See *SUPERMAN: THE MOVIE*

SUPERMAN AND THE MOLE MEN

Lippert, 1951, b&w, 67 min, VT

Producers: Robert Maxwell and Barney A. Sarecky; **Director:** Lee Sholem; **Screenplay:** Maxwell; **Music:** Darrell Calker; **Special Effects:** Ray Mercer; **Cinematography:** Clark Ramsey; **Cast:** George Reeves, Phyllis Coates, Jeff Corey, Walter Reed, Stanley Andrews, Bill Curtis, Jack Branbury, Jerry Marvin, Tony Baris, Harry Harvey, J. Farrell MacDonald

See *SUPERMAN: THE MOVIE*

SUPERMAN FLIES AGAIN

20th Century Fox, 1954, b&w, 77 min

Directors: George Blair and Thomas Carr; **Screenplay:** David T. Chantler; **Special Effects:** Thol Simonson and Jack R. Glass; **Cinematography:** Harold E. Stone; **Cast:** George Reeves, Noel Neill, Jack Larson, Robert Shayne, John Hamilton, Harry B. Mendoza, Lane Bradford, Larry J. Blake, Jim Hayward, Selmer Jackson

See *SUPERMAN: THE MOVIE*

SUPERMAN IN EXILE

20th Century Fox, 1954, b&w, 77 min

Directors: George Blair and Thomas Carr; **Screenplay:** Jackson Gillis and David T. Chantler; **Special Effects:** Thom Simonson and Jack R. Glass; **Cinematography:** Harold E. Stone; **Cast:** George Reeves, Noel Neill, Jack Larson, Robert Shayne, John Hamilton, Leon Askin, Robert S. Carson, John Harmon, Joseph Forte, Phillip van Zandt, Don Dillaway, Gregg Barton

See *SUPERMAN: THE MOVIE*

SUPERMAN'S PERIL

20th Century Fox, 1954, b&w, 77 min

Directors: George Blair and Thomas Carr; **Screenplay:** Jackson Gillis and David T. Chantler; **Special Effects:** Thol Simonson and Jack R. Glass; **Cinematography:** Harold E. Stone; **Cast:** George Reeves, Noel Neill, Jack Larson, Robert Shayne, John Hamilton, Peter Whitney, Vic Perrin, Robert Bice, Murray Alper

See *SUPERMAN: THE MOVIE*

SUPERMAN: THE MOVIE

Warner Bros., 1978, Color, 143 min, VT, LD

Producers: Pierre Spengler, Alexander Salkind, and Ilya Salkind; **Director:** Richard Donner; **Screenplay:** Mario Puzo, David Newman, Leslie Newman, and Robert Benton; **Music:** John Williams; **Special Effects:** Colin Chivers, Roy Field, John Barry, Les Bowie, and Denys Coop; **Cinematography:** Geoffrey Unsworth; **Cast:** Christopher Reeve, Marlon Brando, Gene Hackman, Margot Kidder, Ned Beatty, Jackie Cooper, Valerie Perrine, Glenn Ford, Marc McClure, Terence Stamp, Jack O'Halloran, Sarah Douglas, Harry Andrews, Phyllis Thaxter, Jeff East, Trevor Howard, Maria Schell, Lise Hilboldt, Larry Hagman, John Ratzenberger

The story opens on the planet Krypton, a world about to be destroyed by violent geological upheavals. There might have been a chance for its population to survive, but the arrogant Science Council ignored the scientist Jor-El (Brando) who discovered the truth. Now only his son will survive—launched into space in an experimental rocket. The baby is kept in suspended animation for centuries as the starship crosses the galaxy, finally finding its way to the planet Earth. Because of the difference in the size between Krypton and Earth, as well as the varying radiation of their Suns, young Kal-El grows up with powers and abilities far beyond those of normal men.

Yes, it's the story of Superman, the Man of Steel who, disguised as Clark Kent (Reeve), mild-mannered reporter for a great metropolitan newspaper, fights a never-ending battle for truth, justice, and the American way.

The only thing that makes Superman a science fiction concept is the fact that he is an alien. Originally, he was only "able to leap tall buildings with a single bound" due to Earth's lesser gravity. This soon gave way to the more spectacular power of flight, and there has been little science fiction in the series ever since.

Numerous attempts to give Superman life began with screen appearances in a series of animated Technicolor cartoons that ran from 1941 through 1943.

Created by the sensationally talented Max and Dave Fleischer (also responsible for the classic Betty Boop and Popeye cartoons), these minidramas were recognized as special, slick, and serious—directed as if they were adult entertainment, with the largest budgets up to that time for animated features at any studio. Fifteen were made in total, and their appeal has never lessened. Crumbling prints were shown over and over for decades until the advent of videotape flooded the marketplace with copies. For those interested in trying to find them all, they were: "The Mechanical Monsters" ('41), "Electronic Earthquake" ('42), "Volcano" ('42), "The Eleventh Hour" ('42), "Destruction, Inc." ('42), "The Japoteurs" ('42), "Billion Dollar Limited" ('42), "Terror On The Midway" ('42), "Showdown" ('42), "Arctic Giant" ('42), "The Magnetic Telescope" ('42), "Jungle Drums" ('43), "Secret Agents" ('43), "The Mummy Strikes" ('43), and "The Underground World" ('43).

The world's first superhero next hit the big screen in 1948 in a 15-chapter serial entitled simply enough *Superman*. Kirk Alyn made a likable Man of Steel, but the story suffers from the usual anemia of all serials. The villain, the Spider Lady, and her death ray hardly seem worthy of Superman's first live-action adventure.

In 1951, a new Superman feature was released by 20th Century Fox. *Superman and the Mole Men* tells the story of an underground race of tiny bald creatures whose civilization is being wrecked by oil drilling on the surface world. They come up and cause trouble; everyone fights; Superman then flies in and settles everyone's woes. Many people mistakenly believe that this film was produced by putting together two episodes of the Superman television show. However, the film came first, although it was eventually recut so that it could be shown on television as a two-part episode of the show, retitled "The Unknown People." Episodes of the show were put together and released in theaters. Little known and hard to find today, these were *Superman in Exile*, *Superman Flies Again*, *Superman and Scotland Yard*, *Superman and the Jungle Devil*, and *Superman's Peril*. All were released in 1954. These films are mild diversions at best but basically nothing really worthy of the Superman legend.

That event came with the release of the 1978 motion picture *Superman: The Movie*. Great care was taken to give the story finally the epic grandeur it deserved. Half of the film details the destruction of Krypton, Clark's boyhood in Smallville, and his eventual discovery of his destiny. When he goes to Metropolis and becomes a reporter for *The Daily Planet*, he meets fellow reporter Lois Lane and then quickly gains fame as Superman through a series of heroic deeds and rescues around town. Before long he becomes entangled with archvillain Lex Luthor and his plans to use missiles to sink California into the sea as part of a real estate scheme. Although some of the humor involving the villains falls hopelessly flat in the second half, the film still stands head-and-shoulders as the best effort made to date on behalf of the character and as one of the finest superhero movies ever made.

Superman was followed by *Superman II* (1980). Although the sequel is more popular than its predecessor with many viewers, it has none of the mythic feel of the first. Three Kryptonian villains banished to the mysterious Phantom Zone by Superman's father before the destruction of Krypton escape and come to Earth to fight the son of their prisoner. The film is mostly one long fight, and as if Superman isn't powerful enough, the movie gives the Man of Steel even more superpowers than he possessed in the comics. Lois Lane (Kidder) also discovers Superman's true identity, a turn of events that prompts Clark to use a Kryptonian device to remove his powers so that he and Lois can share a romance. In the end, Superman must forgo personal happiness in order to bring his enemies to justice.

For all its faults, however, *Superman II* gave little indication of what was to follow. *Superman III* (1983) is a comedy featuring comedian Richard Pryor and a far-fetched scheme to steal money from the banks of the world. It lacks the appeal of the first two films. *Supergirl* (1984) followed the next year, and though played seriously, it is hampered by a low budget in comparison to the Superman films, though Helen Slater gives a good performance as the Girl of Steel. The last film in the series, *Superman IV: The Quest For Peace* (1987), sends the Man of Tomorrow on a mission to destroy all the world's nuclear weapons so that the Earth will know peace. The movie suffers from a superficial story, saved only by strong performances.

SUPERNOVA

MGM, 2000, Color, 91 min, VT, DVD

Producers: Ralph S. Singleton, Ash R. Shah, Daniel Chiba, and Jamie Dixon; **Director:** Thomas Lee; **Screenplay:** David Campbell Wilson; **Music:** David Williams; **Special Effects:** Mark Stetson, Patrick Tatopolos, Thomas L. Fisher, Scott R. Fisher, Tim McGovern, Rochelle Gross, Jake Garber, Julie Mankowski, Russell Seifert, David Grasso, Todd Heindel, Rob Frietas, Nik Carey, Gino Acevedo, Marilee Canaga, Danielle Ferraro, Julie Levi, Jonathan D. Egstad, Eric Barba, Kelly Port, Carey Grant Villegas, Lisa K. Spence, Ronald A. Gress, George Trimmer,

Steve Dietrich, Scott Salsa, Alan Faucher, Michael D. Kanfer, Jamie Dixon, Dan Chuba, Richard Chuang, Henry LaBounta, Les Hunter, Jason Heapy, Larry Weiss, Scott Schneider, Bill Neil, Debra Wolff, Judith Crow, and Mike O'Neal; **Cinematography:** Lloyd Ahern II, A.S.C.; **Cast:** James Spader, Angela Bassett, Robert Forster, Lou Diamond Phillips, Peter Facinelli, Robin Tunney, Wilson Cruz, Eddy Rice, Jr., Knox Grantham White, Kerrigan Mahan, Vanessa Marshall

This is in the truest sense one of the most accurate, well-constructed science fiction movies ever made. It's the early 22nd century, and the crew of medical rescue vessel *Nightingale 229* is on its way to an emergency. A distress signal has been sent directly to them from a mining colony millions of light-years away. This means a dimensional jump and a frenzied search for survivors. The jump goes awry, and when the *Nightingale* emerges back into real space, it runs into a debris shower that leaves it disabled.

Worse yet, her captain is dead and the distress call that brought them so far from home seems to have been a fake. Still worse, the only person whom they find at the distress site is a young man whose existence they cannot verify—a young man who has found an alien artifact so deadly that it's capable of ending all existence. Pretty soon crew members start turning up dead. The crew has an extremely limited time not only to deal with the mystery, but also to repair their ship. In only a few hours the star near which their vessel is trapped is going to go supernova.

This is one of the most scientifically accurate, literate science fiction films. Advance word on *Supernova* was that the director had forced the studio to take his name off the film. There wasn't enough money for the special effects. The studio was making vast editing changes at the last minute. How much is true and how much is rumor cannot be confirmed, but the end result is the first science fiction release of the year 2000 and a terrific way to kick off the year.

The movie boasts an exceptional cast. There are no superstars but plenty of top-notch actors known for excellent work. Most notable are the leads, Spader (*STARGATE*) and Bassett (*STRANGE DAYS*). The sound track is competent, and the direction low-key but involving. The script is tight and intelligent, and the special effects are both precise and out of this world. Of course, there may be a reason why the story line and the visuals in *Supernova* are so perfect.

The film's chief science consultant was Dr. Jacklyn R. Green, the astronomer with NASA's Jet Propulsion Laboratory who runs their Extraterrestrial Materials Simulation Laboratory. Dr. Green advised the filmmakers on the scientific plausibility of the film's actions and sets, including the design of the rouge moon, the science of supernovas, and outer space living conditions. Away from Hollywood, Green serves as a planetary scientist, focusing on the makeup of the solar system; her specialty: ices, dusts, rocks, and dirt in settings such as comets, asteroids, Mars, and Jupiter's moon, Europa. At JPL, she serves as the Comet Simulation Lead Scientist and manager for the Comet Nucleus Sample Return Mission, a mission that will bring back to Earth a piece of a comet. Her mission will be the first ever to land on the surface of a comet, drill into it, collect and analyze a sample, and then return the sample to Earth.

Dr. Green's technical advice on the film was taken to heart. The science in *Supernova* is dead-on—space vehicles with internal gravity have rotating hulls, and unprotected bodies launched into space don't explode. When designing the *Nightingale 229*, production designer Marek Dobrowski worked closely with designers from aerospace company Northrop Grumman to visualize where space travel and medical technology might be headed 150 years from now. He worked strictly from a function-over-form perspective to create a highly streamlined, realistic space vessel. As with a space station, the *Nightingale* is composed of separate modules that, in theory, were assembled in space.

The planetary surface conditions of a moon hovering near a supergiant star were recreated according to all the most current data. Details such as the moon's extremely low temperature, mineral composition, and gravity were all taken into account when creating the mining colony. The entire cast even underwent extensive training to learn how to fly using an elaborate system of cranes and harnesses, even though not everyone in the film had scenes that took place in weightless conditions.

Aside from all the details, however, and as wonderful as it is finally to have someone make a serious science fiction movie, *Supernova* is about more than mere science. At the heart of the film is an analysis of some heady allegorical stuff, such as why God gave humans free will. Of course, any film asking questions that intelligent is not going to be liked, understood, or appreciated by all people, and that helps explain the films' less than blockbuster box office performance.

SUPER SNOOPER

See *SUPER FUZZ*

SUPERSONIC MAN

Gaumont (Great Britain), 1956, b&w, 50 min

Producer: Frank Wells; **Director** S.G. Ferguson; **Screenplay:** Dallas Bower and Wells; **Music:** Jack Beaver; **Special Effects:** Ken Hardy; **Cinematography:** Frank North; **Cast:** Marcia Monlescue, Fella Edmonds, Tony Lyons, Donald Gray

When a living but still immature infant UFO finds itself in trouble on the third planet from the Sun, it's a bunch of plucky Earthkids to the rescue.

SUPERSPEED

Columbia, 1935, b&w, 56 min

Director: Lambert Hillyer; **Screenplay:** Harold Shumate; **Cinematography:** Ben Kline; **Cast:** Norman Foster, Mary Carlisle, Florence Rice

A hardworking scientist tries to improve the lot of downtrodden humankind with his latest invention—a superfast means of transportation.

SURF TERROR

See THE BEACH GIRLS AND THE MONSTER

SWAMP THING

United Artists, 1982, Color, 91 min, VT, LD

Producers: Jack Briggs, Benjamin Melniker, and Michael E. Uslan; **Director:** Wes Craven; **Screenplay:** Craven; **Music:** Harry Manfredini; **Special Effects:** William Munns; **Cinematography:** Robin Goodwin; **Cast:** Louis Jourdan, Ray Weis, David Hess, Adrienne Barbeau, Nicholas Worth

A scientist, out to help all humankind, accidentally turns himself into a walking mass of vines and vegetation. He then fights a villain who wants to use the scientist's knowledge for evil. The film was followed by *The Return of Swamp Thing* and a television series, *Swamp Thing*, none of which matched the original DC comic- book series that inspired them for style, philosophy, or ability to hold an audience.

Swamp Thing (LIGHTYEAR ENTERTAINMENT / JOSEPH B. MAUCERI COLLECTION)

SWARM, THE

Warner Bros., 1978, Color, 116 min, VT, LD

Producer: Irwin Allen; **Director:** Allen; **Screenplay:** Stirling Silliphant; **Music:** Jerry Goldsmith; **Special Effects:** Lyle B. Abbott; **Cinematography:** Fred J. Koenekamp; **Cast:** Michael Caine, Richard Chamberlain, Henry Fonda, Fred MacMurray, Katharine Ross, Richard Widmark, Olivia de Havilland, Ben Johnson, Patty Duke Astin, Lee Grant, Jose Ferrer, Bradford Dillman, Slim Pickens

Scientists take on South American killer bees in a disaster movie that has no punch whatsoever.

T

TALES OF HOFFMAN

Lippert (Great Britain), 1951, Color, 138 min, VT, LD

Producers: Michael Powell and Emeric Pressburger; **Directors:** Powell and Pressburger; **Screenplay:** Powell and Pressburger; **Music:** Jacques Offenbach; **Special Effects:** Arthur Lawson and Hein Heckruth; **Cinematography:** Christopher Challis; **Cast:** Moira Shearer, Robert Rounseville, Robert Helpmann, Pamela Brown, Frederick Ashton

This film version of Jacques Offenbach's opera tells of a student, Hoffman, famed for his marvelous stories. He tells three tales in a tavern, one story about a robotic doll-like woman. The tales are interconnected below the surface, their real purpose to give insights into three different phases of the main character's life. This interesting and sometimes bizarre film is definitely not for the average viewer, and the science fiction is minimal.

Note: The story was filmed in Germany in 1914, but this earlier black-and-white silent version is mostly forgotten, now overshadowed by the 1951 version.

TANK GIRL

United Artists, 1995, Color, 104 min, VT, LD

Producers: Pen Densham, Richard B. Lewis, Aron Warner, and John Watson; **Director:** Rachel Talaly;

Screenplay: Alan Martin, Jamie Hewlett, and Tedi Sarafian; **Music:** Graeme Revel; **Special Effects:** Ken Pepiot, Rochelle Gross, Peter Crosman, Gintar Repecka, Albert Delgado, Robert Skotak, Elaine Edfurd, and Ralph Hall; **Cinematography:** Gale Tattersall; **Cast:** Lori Petty, Ice-T, Naomi Watts, Don Marvey, Jeff Kober, Reg. E. Cathey, Scott Coffey, Malcolm McDowell, Stacy Lynn Lamsower, Ann Cusack, Brian Wimmer, James Hong, Iggy Pop

In the far-flung year of 2033 the world has run out of water, and people are no damn good anymore. Tank Girl (Petty) teams up with a group of humanoid mutated animals to stop an evil Malcolm McDowell from hogging what water there is and keeping the ragged, edgy survivors from having fun. Though obnoxious and obvious, *Tank Girl* is a marvelously wild and interesting film. It is intercut with chaotic, beautifully rendered, but all too brief animated sequences that almost make up for the lack of focus and direction. Petty gives an outstandingly funny performance. While great for fans of the original comic-book series, it may be fairly unintelligible to those without much of a four-color background.

TARANTULA

Universal, 1955, b&w, 80 min, VT, LD

Producer: William Alland; **Director:** Jack Arnold; **Screenplay:** Robert M. Fresco and Martin Berkley;

Tarantula (UNIVERSAL PICTURES / R. ALLEN LEIDER COLLECTION)

Music: Joseph Gershenson; **Special Effects:** Clifford Stine, A.S.C. and Bud Westmore; **Cinematography:** George Robinson, A.S.C.; **Cast:** Leo G. Carroll, John Agar, Maria Corday, Nestor Paiva, Hank Patterson, Ross Eliot, Eddie Parker, Clint Eastwood

A cool doctor (Agar) breezes into town in a sweet, vanilla-white '56 Ford Sunliner. He's not there to make a house call, though. The doc has come to take a look at something unusual—a man who was found in the desert, dead from some hideous mutating disease. As one of the locals tells Agar: "You figure this one out and you're *good.*"

Agar's good all right. It takes him only a few minutes to determine that his patient died from acromegalia. The diagnosis is puzzling, however, since that particular disease takes years to produce the distorted effects evidenced by the corpse, and everyone who knew the victim swears he was normal the day before he died. But if it isn't acromegalia that killed him, then what was it?

The answer lies with kindly scientist Leo G. Carroll, who's been working on a formula to stimulate tissue growth. It works on animals—he's got the overblown, hassock-sized hamsters to prove it—but sadly, not on humans as evidenced by the growth formula's effect on the corpse. Things quickly get worse when a struggle in

Carroll's lab releases a formula-doused tarantula. Before long, this stadium-sized arachnid is clambering all over the countryside doing in as much of the local citizenry as it can before the air force finally takes care of it with napalm.

Tarantula constantly receives high marks for its special effects, and though many of the creature effects are outstanding for their time, especially in the area of sound editing (matching up giant-sized noises with the insect on the screen), many of them are just plain sloppy. The spider constantly seems to grow and shrink from 10 feet to 100 and back again, due to extremely poor editing. On top of that, people never seem to see or hear this massive thing until it is directly on top of them. But this is not a bad film. Beyond the threat of the giant spider, it deals with issues raised by science gone awry and features some some splendid acting and strong, dignified direction from Jack Arnold.

TARGET EARTH

Allied Artists, 1954, b&w, 76 min, VT, LD

Producer: Herman Cohen; **Director:** Sherman Rose; **Screenplay:** William Raynor; **Music:** Paul Dunlap; **Special Effects:** Dave Koehler; **Cinematography:** Guy Roe; **Cast:** Kathleen Crowley, Richard Denning, Richard Reeves, House Peters, Virginia Grey, Robert Ruark, Steve Pendleton, and Whit Bissell as the Scientist

It's morning in a very deserted-looking city. A young woman who apparently tried to attempt suicide by taking an overdose of sleeping pills wakes up feeling pretty depressed. When she tries the electricity, it doesn't work. She can't get water from the tap, either. When she goes outside, she can't find anyone—no one is driving by, eating in restaurants, shopping, going to the dentist, or carrying on any of the normal business of morning in a big town.

Eventually she finds a man who spent the night in an alley after being mugged. Together they find a pair of drunks partying in a deserted nightclub, and there they finally get some answers. The city is about to be invaded. The government evacuated everyone in the middle of the night. Those in a dead sleep (or too busy boozing it up) didn't hear anything and were left behind. The foursome find a fifth man, who's scared and doesn't want to stick around. As he runs down the street, he draws the attention of one of the invaders—a giant robot. The mechanoid fires a beam from its face that kills the runner.

As the survivors scurry for cover, elsewhere we see the military turning to science to come up with a way to beat the seemingly unstoppable robot horde. While the scientists (led by a cool as ever Whit Bissell) work at their project, the foursome encounters a petty thug who stayed in town out of fear of being captured by the police. Now he plans to use three of the foursome as bait for the robots so that he can escape, while keeping the woman for himself. The drunks get in the way of his bullets, though, and that leaves the mugged hero to hold the robots off long enough for the army to ride into town with their newest robot-killing superweapon and save the day.

Target Earth is an unfortunate movie. It opens impressively enough for a black-and-white '50s sci-fi film. The credits and music are strong, and the plot has a nicely moody kickoff. The story starts off wonderfully dark and cynical, striking the right mood for a perfect sci-fi/noir motion picture, but after about 20 minutes, the film falls apart. The dialogue grows more and more inept. The story loses all its drive, wandering in circles to kill time. Even the world's greatest character actor, Mr. Whit Bissell himself, couldn't save this movie from sliding over the edge, especially after the poorly designed robots finally show up.

TARZAN VS. IBM

See *ALPHAVILLE*

TEENAGE CAVEMAN

AIP, 1958, B&W, 65 min, VT

Producer: Roger Corman; **Director:** Corman; **Screenplay:** R. Wright Campbell; **Music:** Albert Glasser; **Cinematography:** Floyd Crosby; **Cast:** Robert Vaughn, Leslie Braddley, Darrah Marshall, Robert Shayne, Jonathan Haze, Frank De Kova

Clean-shaven, hair-sprayed pretty-boy cave teen Robert Vaughn is a prehistoric rebel with a cause. His tribe doesn't allow its young men to travel into the "forbidden zone," a ranging piece of real estate across the river, controlled by the "monster that kills with a touch." Throwing off the oppressive yoke of his elder's authoritarian ways, Vaughn heads across the water and discovers a shocking truth—he's not prehistoric at all. It seems there was a time called the 20th century, and the people that lived then had nuclear weapons with which they finally bombed themselves back to the Stone Age.

TEENAGE MONSTER (aka: THE METEOR MONSTER)

Howco International, 1957, b&w, 65 min

Producer: Jacques Marquette; **Director:** Marquette; **Screenplay:** Ray Buffum; **Music:** Walter Green; **Special Effects:** Jack Pierce; **Cinematography:** Taylor Byars; **Cast:** Gilbert Perkins, Anne Gwynne, Stuart Wade, Gloria Castillo

A young boy has a run-in with a meteor. Just touching the rock turns the lad into a hairy beast. Just having to deal with what's going on turns his mother into an idiot.

TEENAGERS FROM OUTER SPACE

Warner Bros., 1959, b&w, 86 min, VT, DVD

Producer: Tom Graeff; **Director:** Graeff; **Screenplay:** Graeff; **Music:** Graeff; **Special Effects:** Graeff; **Cinematography:** Graeff; **Cast:** David Love, Dawn Anderson, Helen Sage, Harvey B. Dunn, King Moody, Bryant Grant, and, of course, Tom Graeff

Teenage invasion leader Derek (Love) lands on Earth to prepare the way for his people's coming. They plan to infest the planet with gigantic creatures they call Gargons, elephant-sized killer lobsters that they use as cattle. Derek falls for Earthgirl Betty (Anderson) and decides that he can't go through with murdering humanity. So when the rest of the invasion fleet arrives, he tricks them into flying into the side of a mountain. The maneuver kills him along with every single invader and all those nasty Gargons.

The Gargons are never shown, except in shadow, an effect achieved by holding a real lobster up to the light, and the invasion fleet is never on screen, not even for their explosive ending. In fact, nothing of the story is shown except for the parts about people standing around talking.

TELEGIAN, THE

See *SECRET OF THE TELEGIAN*

TELEPATHY 2000

See *SCANNERS*

TELEPORTED MAN, THE

See *SECRET OF THE TELEGIAN*

TENTH VICTIM, THE
(aka: DECIMA VITTIMA)

Champion/Concordia (France/Italy), Embassy (U.S.), 1965, Color, 92 min, VT

Producer: Carlo Ponti; **Director:** Elio Petri; **Screenplay:** Petri, Tonino Guerra, Giorgio Salvione, and Ennio Flaiano; **Music:** Piero Piccioni; **Cinematography:** Giovanni De Venanzo; **Cast:** Ursula Andress, Marcello Mastroianni, Elsa Martinelli, Massimo Serato, Salvo Randone

It's somewhere in the far-flung future of the 21st century. Warfare has been replaced by an aggression-releasing game called the Big Hunt, the cutting-edge government's name for legalized dueling. Citizens try to win 10 rounds so as to secure all sorts of wonderful government benefits. Ursula Andress and Marcello Mastroianni alternately hunt and are hunted by each other in this cult favorite. While this film could have raised some interesting questions, it fell into the trap of becoming little more than a sci-fi one-liner fest in which the cast poses in extravagant costumes more often than it says anything of significance.

TERRIBLE DR. HITCHCOCK, THE

See *THE HORRIBLE DR. HITCHCOCK*

TERMINAL MAN, THE

Warner Bros., 1973, Color, 107 min, VT

Producer: Michael Hodges; **Director:** Hodges; **Screenplay:** Hodges; **Music:** Johann Sebastian Bach; **Cinematography:** Richard Kline; **Cast:** George Segal, Joan Hackett, Jill Clayburgh, Richard Dysart, Michael Gwynn, Donald Moffat, Matt Clark, James B. Sikking, Ian Wolf, Steve Kanaly, Lee DeBroux

George Segal plays a fellow who is subjected to periods of violent blackout after an auto accident. Since his doctors can't seem to control him in any other manner, a radical experiment is suggested. He will have electrodes inserted into his head, linked to a computer set into his shoulder. Then, whenever he suffers one of his blackouts, before he can grow violent, the computer will soothe his brain by flooding it with "pleasure impulses." It isn't long before Segal's brain is *causing* his blackouts, simply to trip the pleasure switch. Only somewhat violent before, suddenly Segal is out spilling blood in a series of homicidal rages that the police not only find

upsetting, but which leave them little choice other than to shoot him down.

Good acting and a nice screenplay of Michael Crichton's novel make up for a lack of dazzling special effects. It's certainly one of Segal's best pictures. Sadly, though, the chance to explore the societal implications of such mind control are ignored in favor of chase scenes and fisticuffs.

TERMINATOR, THE

Orion, 1984, Color, 108 min, VT, LD, DVD

Producers: John Daly and Derek Gibson; **Director:** James Cameron; **Screenplay:** Gayle Anne Hurd and Cameron; **Music:** Brad Fiedel; **Special Effects:** Stan Winston and Ernie Farino; **Cinematography:** Adam Greenberg; **Cast:** Arnold Schwarzenegger, Michael Biehn, Linda Hamilton, Paul Winfield, Lance Hendriksen, Rick Rossovich, Earl Boen, Dick Miller, Bill Paxton

It's somewhere in the near future in downtown Los Angeles. Two nude male figures—warriors from the future somewhat further along—appear in flashes of blue light. One of them, a cyborg coated in living tissue (Schwarzenegger) so that it can pass for human, has come back to kill a woman named Sarah Conner (Hamilton). The other, a normal human being (Biehn), has come back to stop it from completing its task. It seems that the future is a terrible place in which Artificial Intelligence took over the world's computers and weapons-manufacturing plants and then did its level best to wipe out humanity. When one man, John Conner, rose up and taught everyone how to fight the killing machines, the big AI decided to rewrite history by killing his mother. Capturing the time machine station right after the Terminator machine was sent back, the rebels decided that the only thing they could do was to send one of their own back on a one-way mission to keep their leader's mom alive.

The Terminator tackles all of aspects of its time travel tale with intelligence and just the right amount of humor. Sarah Conner does not easily believe what she is told. Neither do the police. The rebel who is sent back eventually falls in love with Sarah, and she with him, and they have a night of passion leading to the birth of John. This, of course, sets up the usual time paradox: How can John Conner teach people anything when he shouldn't have been born since his dad hasn't gone back in time yet? What could be a problem in most time travel movies has never seemed to bother too many folks in *The Terminator*. Most likely the film is simply too satisfying on all other levels for audiences to question something that doesn't reveal itself until the end of the film.

Many films have copied this one, but none live up to it, including its own sequel. *The Terminator* is an intelligent, human sci-fi/actioneer that never stops moving for a moment. Its low budget is evident from the substandard film quality and lack of multiple camera angles, but these are not complaints. Avoiding an overabundance of effects, using only those necessary to tell the story, the movie still crashes along at breakneck speed, never breaking its near-hypnotic grasp. Relying more on storytelling and logic than dazzle, the picture is one of the few modern science fiction films that gives its actors a chance to actually perform rather than be used as props moving across traveling mattes and blue screens. As is often the case, not having a larger budget forced director Cameron to use his brain a bit more. Certainly the jumbled mess he presented seven years later, *Terminator 2: Judgment Day*, gives testament that a larger budget does not mean a better movie.

The sequel is riddled with confusing plot holes and time sequence troubles. Whereas the time paradox in the first film sets up a classic sci-fi puzzle, the time problems in the second film are simply the mistakes of careless screenwriting. Such sloppy work is inexcusable in a movie with a budget well in excess of $100 million. The money, of course, was used only for special effects. In the film's defense, it did pioneer the now-routine process known as morphing. It was used lavishly (and, admittedly, to good effect) throughout the picture, subsequently winning the Academy Award for Best Visual Effects (along with Oscars for Best Sound Effects Editing, Makeup, and Sound).

Despite a tremendous performance by Linda Hamilton, who paints a perfect picture of someone who is considered insane and who has to act with every hand against her, including her own family, there are too many plot holes, too many lapses in logic, too many moments when the audience's imagination and intelligence are considered nonexistent for this sequel to be anything but a pretty though superficial film.

Note: For those who are quick enough, check out the codes running through the Terminator's computer field of vision. It's the Apple 2+ assembly code COBOL.

The Terminator (ORION PICTURES / AUTHOR'S COLLECTION)

TERMINATOR 2: JUDGMENT DAY

Carolco Pictures, 1991, Color, 136 min, VT, LD, DVD

Producers: James Cameron, Gale Anne Hurd, Stephanie Austin, Mario Kassar, and B.J. Rack; **Director:** Cameron; **Screenplay:** Cameron and William Wisger, Jr.; **Music:** Brad Fidel; **Special Effects:** James Belkin, Doug Chiang, John Bruno, George C. Dodge, Janet Healy, Dennis Muran, Leslie Huntley, Robert Skotar, Gene Warren, Jr., Joe Viskocil, and Stan Winston; **Cinematography:** Adam Greenberg; **Cast:** Arnold Schwarzenegger, Linda Hamilton, Edward Furlong, Robert Patrick, Earl Boen, Joe Morton, S. Epatha Merkerson, Castulo Guerra, Danny Cooksey, Jenette Goldstein, Xander Berkeley

See *THE TERMINATOR*

TERROR BENEATH THE SEA, THE (aka: KAITEI DAISENSO, THE GREAT UNDERSEA WAR, BATTLE BENEATH THE SEA, WATER CYBORGS, WATER CYBORG)

Toei (Japan), 1966/Teleworld (U.S.), 1972, Color, 87 min, VT

Director: Hajime Sato; **Screenplay:** M. Fukuishima; **Music:** Shunsuke Kikuchi; **Special Effects:** Nobuo

Terminator 2 (TRISTAR PICTURES/JOSEPH B. MAUCERI COLLECTION)

Yajima; **Cinematography:** K. Shimomura; **Cast:** Shinichi Chiba, Peggy Neal, Franz Gruber, Gunther Braun, Mike Daneen, Andrew Hughes, Eric Neilson

A scientist residing underwater decides it's time to turn men into monsters. Since he's underwater, the monsters have gills, but that's all that's different about this rehash of an all-too familiar plot.

TERRORE NELLO SPAZIO

See *PLANET OF THE VAMPIRES*

TERROR FROM 5000 A.D.

See *TERROR FROM THE YEAR 5000*

TERROR FROM THE YEAR 5000
(aka: CAGE OF DOOM, TERROR FROM 5000 A.D., THE GIRL FROM 5000 A.D.)

AIP, 1958, b&w, 74 min

Producer: Robert Gurney, Jr.; **Director:** Gurney, Jr.; **Screenplay:** Gurney, Jr.; **Cinematography:** Arthur Florman; **Cast:** Ward Costello, Fred Herrick, John Stratton, Joyce Holden

A mad scientist experimenting with time accidentally brings to his era a mutant madwoman who needs to kidnap husbands back to the future.

TERROR IS A MAN
(aka: BLOOD CREATURE)

Allied Artists, 1959, b&w, 89 min, VT

Producers: Eddie Romero and Kane W. Lynn; **Director:** Garry De Leon; **Screenplay:** Harry Paul Harber; **Music:** De Leon; **Special Effects:** Hilario Santos; **Cinematography:** Emmanuel I. Rojas; **Cast:** Richard Deer, Greta Thyssen, Francis Lederer, Flory Carlos, Oscar Keesee, Lilia Duran

The lone survivor of a shipwreck (Deer) finds himself on an island where a mad surgeon (Lederer) is trying to become the new Dr. Moreau by transforming a panther into a human being via a series of very painful operations. The cat man escapes and starts killing people and is finally dealt with. Its victims received no more compensation than the audience.

TERRORNAUTS, THE

Amicus (Great Britain), 1966/Embassy (U.S.), 1967, Color, 75 min, VT

Producers: Milton Subotsky and Max J. Rosenberg; **Director:** Montgomery Tully; **Screenplay:** John Brunner; **Music:** Elisabeth Lutyens; **Special Effects:** Les Bowie Films; **Cinematography:** Geoffrey Faithful; **Cast:** Simon Oats, Zena Marshall, Patricia Hayes, Stanley Meadows, Charles Hawtry, Max Adrian

A traveling alien space fortress now manned by a single robot beams an entire Earthly research station up into space so that the robust men and women of science can help the robot stop an alien fleet.

TERRORVISION

Empire Pictures, 1986, Color, 85 min, VT

Producers: Charles Band, Albert Band, and Debra Dion; **Director:** Ted Nicolaou; **Screenplay:** Nicolaou; **Music:** Richard Band; **Special Effects:** John Carl Buechler; **Cinematography:** Romano Albani; **Cast:** Gerrit Graham, Diane Franklin, Mary Woronov, Chad Allen, Bert Remsen, Randi Brooks, Sonny Carl Davis, Alejandro Rey

A typical rampaging creature from outer space slithers out of the television set of an all-American family. The creature acts badly. The family overacts badly. The audience tunes out quickly.

TERROR WITHIN, THE

Concorde, 1988, Color, 88 min, VT

Producer: Roger Corman; **Director:** Thierry Notz; **Screenplay:** Thomas McKelvey Cleaver; **Music:** Rich Conrad; **Cinematography:** Ronn Schmidt; **Cast:** Andrew Stevens, Starr Andreeff, Terri Treas, George Kennedy, John LaFayette, Tommy Hinchley

Low-budget monsters attack the last outpost of humanity after a plague does away with the rest of humankind.

In the cleverly named sequel *The Terror Within II*, they do it again.

TERROR WITHIN II, THE

Concorde, 1992, Color, 89 min, VT

Producers: Roger Corman and Mike Elliott; **Director:** Andrew Stevens; **Screenplay:** Stevens; **Music:** Terry Plumeri; **Cinematography:** Janusz Kaminski; **Cast:** Andrew Stevens, Stella Stevens, Chick Vennera, R. Lee Ermey, Burton "Bubba" Gillian, Clare Hoak

See THE TERROR WITHIN

TESTAMENT

Paramount, 1983, Color, 89 min, VT, LD

Producers: Andrea Asimow, Lynne Littman, and Jonathan Bernstein; **Director:** Littman; **Screenplay:** John Sacret Young; **Music:** James Horner; **Special Effects:** Chuck Stewart; **Cinematography:** Steven Poster; **Cast:** Jane Alexander, William Devane, Roxana Zal, Ross Harris, Philip Anglim, Lilia Skala, Leon Ames, Rebecca DeMornay, Mako, Lurene Tuttle, Kevin Costner

Nuclear war comes to America. The war remains mostly off-camera, however, as the story concentrates on a small town just outside of the blast area and how its inhabitants cope with the disaster. Specifically, things center on just one family as they wait for dad to come home.

This is as close as one can come to what would probably be the real thing. Nobility and the other social veneers slip away bit by bit as people try not to face the inevitable—older values, good ones and bad ones, coming back at the same time. Antinuclear hysteria is often filled with outright lies, and though this movie is definitely antinuclear, it avoids such hysteria. The picture makes an incredibly powerful antinuclear statement the old-fashioned way, by simply telling the truth. It's hard to consider lobbing nukes at even one's vilest enemies after seeing this movie.

TEST PILOT PIRX

Polish Corporation for Film (Poland), 1979, Color, 104 min

Director: Marek Piestrak; **Screenplay:** Piestrak; **Music:** Arvo Part; **Special Effects:** Jerzy Sniezawski;

Cinematography: Janusz Pawlowski; **Cast:** Sergei Desnitsky, Boleslaw Abart, Vladimir Ivashov, Zbigniew Lesien

A close look at the life and times of one "finite linear" which are near perfect human robots being constructed in our future to take humanity's place once they've finally been perfected.

THEM!

Warner Bros., 1954, b&w, 93 min, VT, LD

Producer: David Weisbart; **Director:** Gordon Douglas; **Screenplay:** Ted Sherdemann; **Music:** Bronislau Kaper; **Special Effects:** William Mueller, Francis J. Scheid, Stanley Fleicher, and Ralph Ayers; **Cinematography:** Sid Hickox; **Cast:** James Whitmore, James Arness, Edmund Gwenn, Joan Weldon, Onslow Stevens, Dub Taylor, Fess Parker, William Schallert, Sean McClory, Sandy Descher

Two New Mexico state troopers get involved in a strange case when they find a young girl wandering in the desert in her bathrobe. She appears to be in extreme, unblinking shock. They soon find that her parent's camper has been violently destroyed—pulled outward by some tremendous force. A recently fired gun is found on the scene, and sugar is scattered everywhere, but no parents are found.

Down the road the officers find a local storefront pulled out the same way. They find another gun at this location—a rifle twisted violently out of shape. They also find its owner twisted violently out of shape. On top of broken and crushed limbs and organs, he has also been injected with several gallons of formic acid. One of the cops stays on the scene while the other goes to report in. Soon the officer who stayed behind is missing as well.

The FBI is brought in as well as two scientists, a father/daughter team (Gwenn and Weldon) from the Department of Agriculture. They discover that a race of giant ants, theoretically spawned by government nuclear testing in New Mexico, has begun to feed on humanity. Soon the surviving policeman (Whitman), his FBI contact (Arness), and the two scientists are searching the entire western end of North America and to find not only the original nest, but also two other nests it has spawned. It's a race against time, for if the new nests are allowed to reproduce themselves, it's quite clear humanity stands no chance against the monsters.

This is one of the classics—the best giant insect movie ever produced. The clichés of the story line

Them (WARNER BROS./R. ALLEN LEIDER COLLECTION)

appeared here first. The special effects used to create the giant ants were marvelous for the time and are still more than adequate today. Rather than utilizing stop-frame animation, effects chief Ralph Ayers went with full-sized creature models, giving the film a chilling reality despite the monsters' obvious immobile look.

It is, however, the storytelling that will keep this movie fresh. Presented in almost documentary fashion, this one has it all. The premise—nuclear radiation spawning an unthinkable mutation—is pure science fiction. How is the enemy met? By guns and bombs and red-blooded mayhem? Not in a true science fiction film. Here the thinking human is brought to the fore. The elderly professor and his daughter save humanity, directing the mere heroes like chess pieces. Comedy is confined to a few brief moments of gallows humor. Romance is likewise present only briefly. Both are injected believably, but neither is allowed to take center stage. The picture's antinuclear message is clear enough, but it is just a plot device, never shrill or intrusive.

THESE ARE THE DAMNED
(aka: THE DAMNED)

Hammer (Great Britain), 1961, 96 min/Columbia (U.S.), 1963, 77 min, b&w

Producer: Anthony Hinds; **Director:** Joseph Losey; **Screenplay:** Evan Jones; **Music:** James Bernard; **Cinematography:** Arthur Grant; **Cast:** Macdonald Carey, Shirley Anne Field, Viveca Lindfors, Alexander Knox, Oliver Reed, James Villiers, Rachel Clay

An American (Carey) and his British girlfriend (Lindfors) are attacked by a vicious band of Teddy Boys (British thugs). The pair escapes harm by retreating into an underground chamber, where they discover a group of children being held captive. The children are part of an experiment—the scientist in charge is trying to breed human beings that are immune to radiation. That way England will have someone to repopulate the planet after the nuclear war everyone knows is coming. The children have been exposed to greater and greater levels of radiation, which means that by the time our heroes (and their antagonists) realize what is going on, they've already been exposed to enough radiation to kill them.

This very strange, disturbing film was meant as an antinuclear message, but it really comes across as an incredibly strong anti-big government message. Children, taken from their parents, exposed to constant radiation, forced to live in a small complex where they dream of the day an insane humanity finally kills itself so that they'll be allowed to go outside and see the Sun—this is a nightmarish film meant only for the strong-willed or those with little imagination. Though not extremely well acted or very cleverly made, the film's science fiction is above reproach.

Note: The American version of this film was edited ("hacked to bits" might be the better description) to the point where it is almost impossible to understand what is actually going on. With some 20 minutes cut, the American version is a waste of time, so look for the original 96-minute Hammer Films version.

THEY CAME FROM BEYOND SPACE

Amicus (Great Britain)/Embassy (U.S.), 1967, Color, 85 min, VT

Producers: Max J. Rosenberg and Milton Subotsky; **Director:** Freddie Francis; **Screenplay:** Subotsky; **Music:** James Stevens; **Special Effects:** Bunty Phillips and Les Bowie Films; **Cinematography:** Norman War-wick; **Cast:** Robert Hutton, Jennifer Jayne, Bernard Kay, Katy Wild, Michael Gough, Zia Mohyeddin

Disembodied aliens travel to Earth via a meteor shower. Once here they commandeer the bodies of Earthlings. One person they can't take over is star Hutton because he has a plate in his head. Everything's okay, though. The aliens aren't really bad guys. They just need some help repairing their damaged spaceship.

THEY CAME FROM WITHIN
(aka: SHIVERS, THE PARASITE MURDERS)

Trans-American, 1975, Color, 94 min, VT

Producer: Ivan Reitman; **Director:** David Cronenberg; **Screenplay:** Cronenberg; **Music:** Reitman; **Special Effects:** Joe Blasco; **Cinematography:** Robert Sadd; **Cast:** Paul Hampton, Allen Migicovsky, Susan Petrie, Lynn Lowry, Joe Silver, Barbara Steele

A scientist attempting to create something beneficial to humankind instead creates a parasite that infects its host like a venereal disease, making them incredibly lustful at the same time. Some people murder, some find their marriages renewed, but all have sex and plenty of it. The invaders quickly spread through an isolated apartment building as a resident doctor tries to figure out what is going on. One by one, however, everyone in the vicinity is infected and turns against him.

Disgusting, stomach-turning effects, a morally bankrupt script, and poor acting are more than the mediocre direction can overcome. The science fiction is minimal, but those who enjoy watching people puke up creatures that then travel through the pipes to infect others might get something out of it. Science fiction historian Peter Nicholls writes, "[Cronenberg's] hallmark is an exaggerated tastelessness designed, perhaps, to alienate the audience from traditional sf/horror clichés by revealing their putrescent underside, and also more generally to demonstrate a variety of social rot."

THEY LIVE

Universal, 1988, Color, 97 min, VT, LD, DVD

Producers: Andre Blay, Larry J. Franco, Shep Gordon, and Sandy King; **Director:** John Carpenter; **Screenplay:** Frank Armitage and Ray Nelson; **Music:** Carpenter and Alan Howarth; **Special Effects:** Michael Arbogast, Roy Arbogast, William Lee, and David Blistein; **Cinematography:** Gary B. Kibbe; **Cast:** Roddy

Piper, Keith David, Meg Foster, Jason Robards III, Raymond St. Jacques, George "Buck" Flower, Peter Jason, Larry Franco

Wrestler-turned-actor, Rowdy Roddy Piper drifts into Los Angeles and discovers that its massive consumer society is actually being driven by alien merchants using subliminal messages to push their products. Special glasses reveal the messages, as well as those people who are actually from outer space. What starts out as a very clever film quickly tanks into a one-note action picture that depends for its success on the audience's complete and unreasoning hatred of Republicans. The film's premise is that the American right wing is completely made up of alien creatures bent on the destruction of humanity. Those not ready to blame the GOP for every single thing that has ever gone wrong in the history of man might want to skip this movie.

THEY SAVED HITLER'S BRAIN (aka: MADMEN OF MANDORAS)

Crown International, 1963, b&w, 74 min, VT, DVD

Producer: Carl Edwards; **Director:** David Bradley; **Screenplay:** Richard Miles and Steve Bennett; **Music:** Peter Zinner and Don Hulette; **Cinematography:** Stanley Cortez; **Cast:** Walter Stocker, Audrey Caire, Carlos Rivas, John Holland, Dani Lynn, Marshall Reed, Nestor Paiva

A kidnapped scientist's loving daughter traces him to an island where Nazis are using the man to help keep their beloved leader's head alive. Everything about this movie is bottom of the barrel, including the insanely edited footage obviously not shot for this film.

THIN AIR (aka: BODY STEALERS, INVASION OF THE BODY STEALERS)

Tigon (Great Britain), 1969/Allied Artists (U.S.), 1970, Color, 91 min, VT

Producer: Tony Tenser; **Director:** Gerry Levy; **Screenplay:** Mike St. Clair and Peter Marcus; **Music:** Reg Tilsley; **Special Effects:** Tom Wadden; **Cinematography:** John Coquillon; **Cast:** George Sanders, Maurice Evans, Patrick Allen, Neil Connery, Hilary Dwyer, Robert Flemying

Parachutists jump out of their planes, but they don't hit the ground.

THING, THE (1951)

See *THE THING FROM ANOTHER WORLD*

THING, THE (1982)

Universal, 1982, Color, 108 min, VT, LD, DVD

Producers: Wilbur Stark, Stuart Cohen, David Foster, Larry Franco, and Lawrence Turman; **Director:** John Carpenter; **Screenplay:** Bill Lancaster; **Music:** Ennio Morricone; **Special Effects:** Roy Arbogast, Albert Whitlock, Hal Bigger, Leroy Routly, James Belohovek, and Michael A. Clifford; **Cinematography:** Dean Cundey; **Cast:** Kurt Russell, A. Wilford Brimley, Richard Dysart, Richard Masur, Donald Moffat, T. K. Carter, David Clennon

See *THE THING FROM ANOTHER WORLD* (1951)

THING FROM ANOTHER WORLD, THE (1951) (aka: THE THING)

RKO, 1951, b&w, 86 min, VT, LD

Producer: Howard Hawks; **Director:** Christian Nyby; **Screenplay:** Charles Lederer; **Music:** Dimitri Tiomkin; **Special Effects:** Donald Stewart and Linwood Dunn; **Cinematography:** Russell Harlan; **Cast:** Kenneth Tobey, Margaret Sheridan, Robert Cornthwaite, Douglas Spencer, James Arness, Dewey Martin, William Self, George Fenneman, James Young, Paul Frees, Eduard Franz

An air force base near the North Pole gets a request from a scientific research center even further north. Something has crashed nearby, and the scientists need the military's help to investigate. Since there is a captain (Tobey) at the air base who's romantically interested in one of the researchers (Sheridan), it's not too difficult to get the air force's cooperation. A bored newspaperman tags along looking for a story, and things get started. It turns out something did crashland—a flying saucer. When trying to free the craft from the ice with thermite bombs, the flyboys accidentally destroy it. They do manage, however, to recover its pilot intact. The grotesque figure (no close-ups of the creature are ever seen) frozen in ice is taken back to the research center. The pilot thaws out before anyone knows what to do with it, and showing that it does not come in peace, it begins killing everyone it can get its all-too-lethal hands on.

Soon the extraterrestrial visitor proves to be not human, mammal, or even animal. It is a sentient vegetable come to Earth to conquer the planet with the army that it plans to grow from seeds taken from its own body. Human corpses are hung like sides of beef in a slaughterhouse to feed its young sprouting from the soil beneath. From that point on, it is a war to the end between the superpowerful alien and the small band of ill-equipped humans who are the only line of defense standing between the creature and the destruction of humanity.

This is one of the best alien invasion movies ever made. Christian Nyby, a longtime cameraman for Howard Hawks, may be credited with direction of the film, but it is taken for granted by most people that the film was actually directed by Hawks himself. It certainly is loaded with Hawks's directorial signatures—crisp, rapid-fire conversations, lightning pacing, natural performances. Beyond that, however, to credit a first-time director with such a masterpiece of science fiction cinema (a man not noted for directing anything of such quality later) seems almost impossible. There are rumors that Orson Welles also had a hand in the direction of this one, but nothing concrete backs up that story.

Tension builds evenly throughout this incredibly well-made film. The audience dreads each opening door, staring unblinking, waiting for the creature to strike. The romantic subplot is well handled, never cloying or getting in the way of the main events, but often helping the plot along nicely. The characters are far more complex than is standard for such films. Even the scientist who nearly gets Earth destroyed through his attempts to communicate with the creature is presented as misguided rather than evil or even stupid.

The movie is based on the John Campbell (writing as Don A. Stuart) novella, "Who Goes There?" Many feel that dropping the literary alien's ability to change its shape at will was a crippling mistake. But there were concerns about the complex story confusing the audience, and such effects could not reasonably be executed with the quality this film demanded.

This element of the story didn't reach the screen until 30 years later when John Carpenter's 1982 adaptation appeared. Titled simply *The Thing*, the director went to great lengths to be faithful to Campbell's story. The second film is scarier in a sense, utilizing then state-of-the-art effects to make the alien's transformation scenes pop off the screen. They are startling, eye-catching, and revolting, unlike any other creature effects.

At the end of this film only two antagonists are left alive. At least one of them is human. Maybe both of them are. Tired from the long battle against the creature, they decide to stop fighting and to just sit down in the snow and wait while the fire burning all over the camp runs its course, leaving them to freeze. The ending is painfully ambiguous. If they are both human, their choice is stupid. On the other hand, if one of them *is* the alien bent on wiping out humanity, this is an act of criminal cowardice on the part of the one who is human. He knows that the alien can be frozen and then revived because he's already seen that happen. The two characters discuss the eventuality that a rescue party will discover their bodies and take them back to civilization. At that point, the alien will thaw out and the world is doomed. It is also possible that both men are actually aliens and the world is already doomed. Or perhaps one or the other is merely hoping to catch his breath before renewing the conflict.

Carpenter's adaptation of "Who Goes There?" has the incredible, lavish, mind-twisting effects Hawks's version of the story lacks, but its bleak vision misses the heart and struggle and courage of the first film.

THINGS TO COME (aka: WELLS' THINGS TO COME)

Hal Roach Studios, 1936, b&w, 113 min, VT, DVD

Producer: Alexander Korda; **Director:** William Cameron Menzies; **Screenplay:** H.G. Wells; **Music:** Arthur Bliss and Muir Mathieson; **Special Effects:** Edward Cohen, Harry Zech, and Ned Mann; **Cinematography:** Georges Perinal; **Cast:** Raymond Massey, Edward Chapman, Ralph Richardson, Cedric Hardwicke, Margueretta Scott, Sophie Stewart, Maurice Bradwell, Ann Todd, Derrick DeMarney, John Clements, Kenneth Villiers, Anne McLaren

The year is 1940—Christmastime. A grandfather looks at a child's holiday gift, a mechanical toy military tank, and comments on how sophisticated toys have become. He remembers the simple Noah's Arks and wooden soldiers of his day and wonders if toys haven't gotten too complicated for the children. It's a telling question, for it's only a matter of hours before a new world war breaks out, one that seems perhaps too complicated for the people waging it.

Years go by, then decades. The war lasts a total of two dozen years, a time long past civilization's ability to supply the feuding sides with the raw materials of conflict. Men who can remember automobiles filling the streets and planes filling the skies are suddenly reduced to life on a par with that of the Dark Ages. Then the

Things to Come (HAL ROACH STUDIOS / R. ALLEN LEIDER COLLECTION)

Wandering Sickness strikes. It is a plague that fills those it touches with a vacant stare and a desire to wander aimlessly. Whether it is a physical ailment or merely a psychological pathology indicative of a desire to be elsewhere is never explained. Fear of the Wandering Sickness forces the healthy to slaughter those infected. In four years' time, the plague has passed, but the world's population has been cut in half. And still, the horrible war rages on. The men in charge on both sides want to continue to hammer away at each other, even though their resources are in sharp decline. The "Boss" of Everytown, where the story centers as the years go by, demands that his mechanics get his planes in the air. They tell him it's impossible without fuel and parts. In despair, one man shouts: "What's the use? Civilization's dead."

Interestingly, a herd of sheep run past at that second, bleating in loud response. Perhaps civilization isn't finished. To prove the sheep's point, a fabulous, ultramodern black airship lands outside town. A flier claiming to represent "law and sanity" has come to let the Boss know that there is a new order coming. Many of the world's remaining scientists and engineers have gath-ered to create a new civilization—one devoid of war-fare. The Boss proclaims that "Science is the enemy of everything natural in life," but he can't stop it. When he tries to resist the coming changes, his stronghold is bombed by airmen dropping the "Gas of Peace." The sleep gas renders everyone unconscious save for the Boss, who dies from the strain of trying to resist.

At this point the film takes another sweeping jump into the future. The year is now 2036. Everytown is a gigantic, mostly underground utopia warmed and lit by artificial sunlight. The inhabitants talk kindly of the bemused olden days, "The Age of Windows," when people built on the surface in the natural sunlight because it was all they knew. People are about to reach for the stars. The first Moon orbit has been planned. But members of the well-fed public are upset. "There are some things man is not meant to know" is their rallying cry. Even as they head for the launching pad to stop the blast-off, Everytown's chief scientist (Massey) argues against their insanity in opposing this venture merely because of its danger.

"Dragging out life to the last possible second," he insists, "is not living to the best of things. The best of

Things to Come (HAL ROACH STUDIOS / R. ALLEN LEIDER COLLECTION)

life, Foxworthy, rests on the edge of death. There's nothing wrong with suffering, if you suffer for a purpose. Our revolution didn't abolish danger or death, it simply made danger and death worthwhile!"

The courageous young couple who will be the first two people in space manage to take off before the mob can stop them, and the picture begins to wind down. The chief scientist, father of the female astronaut, points out the trajectory to the father of the male astronaut. He reassures the man that humanity has to take this step, that people were not meant to rest or live in pleasure for more than a moment. To think, to dream, to reach out and conquer, that is human destiny.

"And when he has conquered all the deeps of space and all the mysteries of time," Massey assures his comrade, "still he will be beginning." With a final gesture toward the stars, he smiles and asks, "All the universe, or nothing. What shall it be? What shall it be?"

And thus ends one of the most impressive science fiction movies of all time. In *The Science Fiction Encyclopedia*, editor Peter Nicholls writes ". . . the film is one of the most important in the history of sf cinema for the boldness of its ambitions, and the ardor with which it projects the myth of space flight as the beginning of Man's transcendence." He in no way exaggerates. This is an incredible work. For one of the few times in the history of the genre, the screenplay was actually written by the author of the original book. Also, this is not just a motion picture; it's a work of art. Every frame seems shot with loving thought aimed at making a continuous story as well as a statement about the condition of man, one that rivets an audience with its powerful composition.

Shots such as the child with his toy drum who plays for the never-ending procession of shadow warriors marching to war behind him, or the faceless people—

soldiers or civilians—all of them just part of the brainless, running mob of humanity that never stops to think, these images are masterful. The film is also brimming over with hardware: artificial sunlight, wrist communicators, exterior glass elevators, moon shots, three-dimensional holographic public address systems, and underground cities. Some aspects of the futuristic costuming may be a bit too reminiscent of Flash Gordon for some people (boots and capes, and men in skirts and togas, and so on), but this is a minor quibble.

Everything about the film suggests a grand epic vision. Critics have knocked the film's socialist message, and while it is true that H.G. Wells was a strong believer in Utopianism, especially later in life, there is nothing unrealistic about the way it is portrayed in the movie. The airmen make quite clear that they are going to impose their will on the world. They have the technology and the Gas of Peace. They also have a technologically advanced world in which half the population has been killed, and they have a scenario ripe for a socialist experiment.

Things To Come seems even more pertinent today than ever before. Its message is the key to science fiction, the notion that man must continually strive, that he must never become too content, that there is always more to learn, more to see, more to understand, and that, as the man said, even when he has conquered all the deeps of space and all the mysteries of time, still he will be beginning.

Note: Comic-book fans may wonder if this film wasn't at least partially the inspiration for both the basic idea and much of the look of the classic *Judge Dredd* series.

THING WITH TWO HEADS, THE

AIP, 1972, Color, 93 min

Producer: Wes Bishop; **Director:** Lee Frost; **Screenplay:** Bishop, Frost, and James G. White; **Music:** Robert O. Ragland; **Cinematography:** Jack Steely; **Special Effects:** Gail Brown, Charles Schram, James White, Dan Striepke, Tim Burman, and Pete Peterson; **Cast:** Ray Milland, Rosie Greer, Don Marshall, Chelsea Brown, Riger Perry, Roger Gentry, Kathy Baumann

An extremely rich but dying bigot (Milland) has only one chance to live—his head must be transplanted onto another body. Specifically, the body of a black man (Greer) accused of committing a crime he didn't commit. Obviously, Milland isn't as rich as he thought, or he could have bought the body of someone he didn't

despise simply for being alive. *The Thing with Two Heads* was played for laughs, which helps, but not enough.

THIRD FROM THE SUN

Bulgarfilm (Bulgaria), 1972, Color, 123 min

Director: Georgi Stoyanov; **Screenplay:** Pavel Vejinov; **Music:** Kiril Dontchev; **Cinematography:** Ivailo Trentchev; **Cast:** Dobrinka Stankova, Naoum Chopov

Unbeknownst to us, alien beings are secretly nudging our development as a species in directions they approve.

THIRTEENTH FLOOR, THE

Columbia, 1999, Color, 120 min, VT, DVD

Producers: Roland Emmerich, Ute Emmerich, Marco Weber, and Kelly Van Horn; **Director:** Josef Rusnak; **Screenplay:** Rusnak and Ravel Centeno-Rodriguez; **Music:** Harald Kloser; **Cinematography:** Wedigo von Schultzendorff; **Special Effects:** Kirk M. Petruccelli, John S. Baker, Centropolis Effects, Joe Jackman, Bret St. Clair, Frederic Soumagnas, Douglas Creel, Nockson Fong, Matt Cordner, Kosta Sarci, Rob Cribbett, Mitch Drain, Sean Cunningham, Daniel Fazel, Hartmut Engel, Christian Hass, Joanna Motek, Olcun Tan, Haggi Floeser; **Cast:** Craig Bierko, Armin Mueller-Stahl, Gretchen Mol, Vincent D'Onofrio, Dennis Haysbert, Steven Schub, Jeremy Roberts, Rif Hutton, Leon Rippy, Janet MacLachlan, Brad Henke, Burt Bulos, Venessia Valentino, Howard S. Miller, Tia Texada, Shiri Appleby, Robert Clendenin, Rachel Winfree

The Thirteenth Floor begins, appropriately enough, on the 13th floor of a downtown Los Angeles corporate tower where visionary programmers Douglas Hall (Bierko) and Hannon Fuller (Mueller-Shahl) have taken virtual reality technology to its apex by creating on a computer chip a living, breathing simulation of 1937 Los Angeles. Unknown to Hall, Fuller has been using the top-secret device to have trysts with various chorus girls in his virtual world. Something goes wrong, however, and once Fuller returns to the real world, he is murdered by an unseen assailant. Hall discovers all of this when he not only finds a bloodstained shirt in his bathroom, but when he is charged with Fuller's murder. The police find he had both the motive and the opportunity. Hall knows he would never do such a thing, but he can't remember what he was doing when Fuller was killed. Could he be the killer? Why can't he remember? And who is the mysterious woman who arrives hours after Fuller's death claiming to be his daughter—a person no one has ever heard of before?

Jane Fuller (Mol) turns out to be the biggest surprise of all. Just as Doug and Hannon have created a virtual reality world, so is their world just one created by Jane. In fact, it's just one of thousands of worlds created in the far-flung future of 2024. The only difference between Doug and Hannon's world and all the other virtual landscapes in Jane's reality is that theirs is the only world that has created its own virtual reality world. So Jane has arrived to shut down Doug and Hannon's machinery before it causes trouble. But there already is trouble since Jane loves Doug—or at least claims to. But how can she love something that is just an image in a game? And how can she love a killer? Or is Doug not the killer?

This is another fine example of the sci-fi/noir film—hardboiled through and through, but science fiction nonetheless. Cut from the same paranoid cloth as THE MATRIX, it's also an intelligent, thought-provoking, adult movie, one that came as a nice change in the same summer as the emotionless, computer-game fantasy served up by George Lucas as the first chapter of the STAR WARS saga.

One interesting surprise is the talent behind this picture. Known for splashy, but hardly intelligent fare such as GODZILLA (1998), INDEPENDENCE DAY, and STARGATE, this film represents quite a change for brother and sister producers Roland and Ute Emmerich. Although all of their earlier pictures made with writer/producer Dean Devlin were well received and quite entertaining, none of them reached the serious level of this effort, which was also the first of their films adapted from a novel, Daniel F. Galouye's Simulacron-3.

Ute Emmerich said at the time, "I liked the themes [of the book], I liked that it was a thriller and a romance. Its edginess and mystery appealed to me, and it allowed us to do a different kind of project, one that has science fiction aspects to it but is also a period piece."

One of the most interesting things about The Thirteenth Floor is that all major cast members not only play their initial characters, but they also have to portray their initial characters' secondary, computer-world characters. These are wonderful performances. Word is that a great number of actors were turned down because although they might be able to play one personality well, they got lost trying to bring another presence to life. Most striking of all the transformations is Vincent D'Onofrio's. His 1990s character is superficially different, dressing sloppy and sporting long, lank yellow hair, while his 1930s counterpart is a natty dresser whose hair is severely cropped and meticulously groomed. But that wasn't all. The actor explained, "Whitney has a higher voice than Ashton does. Their postures are different. Whitney slouches, is more of an internal person, and Ashton stands upright, is more gregarious and powerful, moves with a certain grace. I worked closely with Joseph Porro, the costume designer, initially, because the wardrobe accentuates their physical differences. . . . Ashton wears this fitted suit, and you automatically move differently in a suit."

THIRTY-FOOT BRIDGE OF CANDY ROCK, THE

Columbia, 1959, Color, 75 min, VT

Producers: Lewis J. Rachmil and Edward Sherman; **Director:** Sidney Miller; **Screenplay:** Rowland Barber and Arthur Ross; **Music:** Raoul Kraushaar; **Special Effects:** Jack Rabin, Irving Block, and Louis DeWitt; **Cinematography:** Frank G. Carson; **Cast:** Lou Costello, Dorthy Provine, Doodles Weaver, Gale Gordon, Robert Burton, Charles Lane, Jimmy Conlin, Peter Leeds

In his only film not teamed with his traditional straight man, Bud Abbott, Lou Costello plays a scientist who accidentally turns his girlfriend into a giant and then turns the Army personnel who come searching for her into cavemen and Civil War veterans.

THIS ISLAND EARTH

Universal, 1954, Color, 87 min, VT, LD, DVD

Producer: William Alland; **Director:** Joseph Newman; **Screenplay:** Franklin Coen and Edward O'Callaghan; **Music:** Herman Stein; **Special Effects:** Clifford Stine, Bud Westmore, and Stanley Horsley; **Cinematography:** Clifford Stine, **Cast:** Jeff Morrow, Rex Reason, Faith Domergue, Lance Fuller, Russell Johnson, Regis Barton, Eddie Parker, Douglas Spenser

A scientist (Reason) receives a mysterious package with a build-it-yourself project inside. There are directions for assembly, of course, but no indication of what it is. Curious, he decides to go ahead and build whatever it is he has received. The final product turns out to be a highly advanced communications device. Reason discovers that the kit was a test—one sent to many of the world's leading scientists. Those capable of actually assembling it were then offered a job working for the firm who built it.

Reason accepts the offer, only to find out that the entire episode has been a trap. Yes, the offer of work is

This Island Earth (UNIVERSAL PICTURES / COLLECTION OF R. ALLEN LEIDER)

extended only to those who can pass the firm's test, but the firm has misrepresented itself. The creators of the kit are actually extraterrestrial kidnappers from the planet Metaluna, a world on the verge of destruction. Constantly under attack from their neighbors on Zahgon, the Metalunans have come up with a desperate plan to shanghai Earth's greatest brains and force them to work on a defense plan for their doomed world. Reason, along with another scientist (Domergue), attempts to escape the desolate laboratory/prison in a small aircraft. The escape goes well at first but is quickly foiled by the main Metalunan on Earth, Exeter (Morrow), who pulls them aboard his spaceship via tractor beam and then whisks them back to his world.

Exeter is an alien with a conscience. He disliked having to trick humans into working for Metaluna's survival. He doesn't like holding people captive either, but he's certain everything will be better once he can introduce humans to his world's rulers. No such luck—the Metalunan ruler condemns Reason and Domergue to brain surgery to ensure their cooperation. Exeter helps the two humans escape, getting them back to Earth even as Metaluna is finally destroyed by its enemies.

The plot, based on a novel by Raymond F. Jones, is highly interesting and takes its time to build, its sense of mystery constantly fueled by new discoveries. The film's science fiction is high: There are the typical UFOs and hideous mutants, but there's a lot more going on there as well. Faster-than-light travel is explained to audiences who are unfamiliar with jets, as is suspended animation and a few other other science fiction pulp standards as of then still unknown to the general population. Even the destruction of Metaluna is achieved in a unique method. Rather than bombing the world with explosives, the invaders direct huge asteroids toward the planet, bombarding the world's surface with cheap but devastating power. The special effects can't compete with those of today, but they were stunning for their time.

Note: Additional footage for the film was shot by legendary '50s sci-fi director Jack Arnold, whose work went uncredited.

THIS IS NOT A TEST

Modern Films, 1962, b&w, 72 min

Producers: Frederic Gadette and Murray De'Atlevi; **Director:** Gadette; **Screenplay:** Peter Abenheim, Betty Lasky, and Gadette; **Music:** Greig McRitchie; **Cinematography:** Brick Marquard; **Cast:** Seamon Glass, Aubrey Martin, Mary Morlas, Thayer Roberts

It's the end of the world as humans set off a nuclear disaster. Those who expect humankind to end this way will be bored; those who think people are too smart to end this way will be offended and bored.

THOSE FANTASTIC FLYING FOOLS
(aka: BLAST OFF, JULES VERNE'S ROCKET TO THE MOON)

AIP, 1967, Color, 95 min, VT

Producer: Harry Alan Towers; **Director:** Don Sharp; **Screenplay:** Dave Freeman; **Music:** Patrick John Scott; **Special Effects:** Les Bowie and Pat Moore; **Cinematography:** Brick Marquard; **Cast:** Burl Ives, Troy Donahue, Gert Forbe, Terry-Thomas, Lionel Jeffries, Dennis Price, Klaus Kinski, Hermione Gingold, Daliah Lavi

Very, *very* loosely based on Jules Verne's *From the Earth To the Moon*, this film involves P.T. Barnum (Ives) and his attempt to launch a circus midget to the Moon. The midget makes it as far as Russia.

THREE STOOGES IN ORBIT, THE

Columbia, 1962, b&w, 87 min, VT

Producer: Norman Maurer; **Director:** Edward Bernds; **Screenplay:** Elwood Ullman; **Music:** Paul Dunlap; **Special Effects:** Don Ament and John Chambers; **Cinematography:** William P. Whitley; **Cast:** Moe Howard, Larry Fine, Joe DeRita, Nestor Paiva, Carol Christensen, Don Lamond, Emil Sitka, Edson Stroll

A scientist invents a war wagon that flies, submerges, and rolls along the ground. When a pair of Martians try to put the nab on it, those defenders of Earth, the Three Stooges, step in to set things right. Not the boys' best work, but by the '60s, after replacing the third stooge twice, Moe Howard and Larry Fine were getting tired. They never gave less than their best, but they were old men with no new ideas. The infinitely superior *HAVE ROCKET, WILL TRAVEL*, their first full-length sci-fi venture, was three years behind them, but it seemed like 30.

THUNDERBIRDS ARE GO

United Artists, 1967, Color, 94 min

Producer: Gerry Anderson; **Director:** David Lane; **Screenplay:** Gerry and Sylvia Anderson; **Music:** Barry Gray and the Shadows; **Special Effects:** Derek Meddings and Shaun Whittacker-Cook; **Cinematography:** Paddy Seale, Puppeteers: Christine Glanville and Mary Turner; **Cast:** Sylvia Anderson, Ray Barret, Bob Monkhouse, David Graham, Charles Tingwell, Peter Dynely

A Mars launch is scuttled by a nefarious villain, the Hood. What to do? Why, call the rescue team, the Thunderbirds, of course.

The Thunderbirds was a popular British television series about the Tracy family, later exported to America and numerous other countries. The Tracys ran a rescue service, keeping a vast supply of aircraft, submarines, and even spaceships for their wild adventures. What was even wilder was that the Tracy family, as well as everyone else on the show, was portrayed by marionettes. The material was intended for the youngest of audiences, but the husband and wife producers went on to super-vise two popular live-action TV series, *UFO* and *Space: 1999*.

This movie was followed by *Thunderbirds 6*, which offers more of the same, with the Black Phantom taking the Hood's place.

THUNDERBIRDS 6

United Artists, 1968, Color, 90 min, VT

Producer: Sylvia Anderson; **Director:** David Lane; **Screenplay:** Gerry Anderson and Sylvia Anderson; **Music:** Barry Gray; **Special Effects:** Derek Meddings; **Cinematography:** Harry Oakes; **Cast:** Sylvia Anderson, Christine Finn, Peter Dynely

See *THUNDERBIRDS ARE GO*

THX 1138

American Zoetrope/Warner Bros., 1969/1971, Color, 88 min, VT, LD

Producer: Lawrence Sturhann; **Director:** George Lucas; **Screenplay:** Lucas; **Music:** Lalo Shifrin; **Special Effects:** Hal Barwood; **Cinematography:** Dave Meyers and Albert Kihn; **Cast:** Robert Duvall, Maggie McOmie, Robert Ferro, Johnny Weissmuller, Jr., Ian Wolfe, Marshall Efron, Irene Forrest, Donald Pleasence, Don Pedro Colley

In the future when machines run the world and people do what they're told by their unemotional metal guardians, the police are silver-faced androids who enforce a *1984*-style conformity on everyone. No individuality is allowed of any kind. Men's and women's heads are kept shaved; everyone wears white; sex is the number one taboo. Two people fed up with all the rules are THX 1138 (Duvall) and LUH 3417 (McOmie). They wean themselves from their robot master's drugs, increasing their sex drives and having some fun as a result . . . for a while.

It isn't long before the authorities notice that LUH is pregnant and destroy her for breaking the rules. This forces THX to attempt escape. He is then pursued by the police for quite some time until it seems pointless to the machines to chase him any farther. Human irrationality triumphs, and THX walks into the sun—free.

This was the first feature directed by George Lucas. The film is an expansion of an award-winning short he made in college entitled *THX 2238*. The movie has its points, but in reality like most George Lucas productions, the ideas are all borrowed from other sources. *THX 1138* was an utter failure in its first release. Lucas's success with *STAR WARS* created interest in the film later, but it has never made any kind of favorable impression with audiences.

TIDAL WAVE

See *NIPPON CHIMBOTSU*

TIME AFTER TIME

Warner Bros., 1979, Color, 112 min, VT, LD

Producer: Herb Jaffe; **Director:** Nicholas Meyer; **Screenplay:** Meyer; **Music:** Miklos Rozsa; **Special Effects:** Larry Fuentes, Jim Blount, and Edward G. Carfagno; **Cinematography:** Paul Lohman; **Cast:** Malcolm McDowell, David Warner, Mary Steenburgen, Charles Cioffi, Andonia Katsaros, Patti D'Arbanville, Geraldine Baron, Kent Williams, Joseph Maher, Corey Feldman, Shelley Hack

Once again a science fiction movie pegs H.G. Wells (McDowell) as the *inventor* of a time machine rather than as a man who wrote a story about one. This time around he unveils his creation for a dinner party of his closest friends, one of whom turns out to be Jack the Ripper (Warner). With the Victorian police closing in, the Ripper hops aboard the departing time machine and rides it into the far distant future of 1979. Distress over having unleashed a mad killer into what he has always believed will be a humanmade utopia, Wells uses the time machine when it returns to follow his one-time friend into the future.

Once in the San Francisco of 1979, however, Wells soon finds himself at a severe disadvantage. The future is nothing like the genteel society he always assumed would evolve. Instead, he discovers a filthy, savage place where his prey feels far more at home than he does. What could have been either a brilliant or idiotic film straddles the middle of the road adroitly so that it is merely adequate and inoffensive. Tremendous performances and an incredible musical score are the standout attractions. Pompous (and even somewhat ridiculous) social commentary and starship-sized plot holes are the drawbacks.

TIME BANDITS

Handmade Film, Ltd. (Great Britain), 1981, Color, 110 min, VT, LD, DVD

Producers: Terry Gilliam, George Harrison, Denis O'Brien, and Neville C. Thompson; **Director:** Gilliam; **Screenplay:** Gilliam and Michael Palin; **Cinematography:** Peter Biziou; **Music:** Harrison and Mike Moran; **Special Effects:** John Bunker; **Cast:** Sean Connery, John Cleese, Shelley Duvall, Katherine Helmond, Ian Holm, David Warner, Ralph Richardson, Michael Palin, Peter Vaughan, Kenny Baker, David Rappaport, Craig Warnock

Kevin (Warnock) is an imaginative lad living in what appears to be the fairly near future with a pair of decidedly unimaginative parents. His daydreams of having a father who is interested in something other than TV chatter are interrupted by a party of six marauding dwarves. The little fellows, fancying themselves burglars, have stolen God's map of the cosmos. The map charts not only the stars and planets, but also all the wormholes and temporal rifts. Therefore, the dwarves reason, with the map they can travel through time, steal what they want, and become filthy rich.

The first hole they use leads them to Kevin's bedroom, the point where the Supreme Being catches up to them, demanding the return of his property. Kevin gets caught up in their escape and thus in their adventures as well. They meet various historical figures (Napoleon [Holm], Agamemnon [Connery], Robin Hood [Cleese]), but eventually fall into the clutches of Evil Personified (Warner). Evil wants to escape the boundaries God put on it, and the map is his ticket to freedom. At that point the dwarves have to decide whether or not they are simply thieves or something more.

This film is a great deal of fun for audiences, both in its comedy and its clever script. There are numerous circles in time made throughout the movie, all of them set to confuse the viewer—is Kevin really experiencing what we see, or is he dreaming? A good case can be made for either conclusion. The actual sci-fi content is limited to time travel and wormholes, but it is far too good a film to be overlooked.

TIMEBOMB

Araba Films, 1991, Color, 96 min, VT, LD

Producers: Raffaella De Laurentiis, Mike Petzold, and Andrew G. Marca; **Director:** Avi Nesher; **Screenplay:** Nesher; **Music:** Patrick Leonard; **Special Effects:** Nina Craft and Archie D'Amico; **Cinematography:** Anthony B. Richmond; **Cast:** Michael Biehn, Patsy Kensit, Tracy Scroggins, Robert Culp, Raymond St. Jacques, Richard Jordon, Billy Blanks, Jim Maniaci, Steven J. Oliver, Ray Mancini

Michael Biehn is a watchmaker who is surprised not only to find himself attacked by what should be overwhelming odds, but also to be able to handily beat them. After this good start, however, he goes to a psychologist to try to figure things out.

TIMECOP

Universal, 1994, Color, 99 min, VT, LD, DVD

Producers: Moshe Diamant, Todd Moyer, Richard G. Murphy, Sam Raimi, Robert G. Tapers, David A. Shepard, Mark Scoon, Mike Richardson, and Marilyn Vance-Straker; **Director:** Peter Hyams; **Screenplay:** Richardson and Mark Verheiden; **Music:** Mark Isham; **Special Effects:** Rhonda C. Gunner, Gregory L. McMurry, John Thomas, and Video Image; **Cinematography:** Hyams; **Cast:** Jean-Claude Van Damme, Mia Sara, Ron Silver, Bruce McGill, Gloria Reuben, Scott Bellis, Jason Schombing

It's 2004 and time crime is the latest corruption that law enforcement officials must face. Van Damme plays the tough street cop assigned to find out who the head of the time-raiding bad guys is and to bring him in. Based on the Dark Horse comic book of the same name, many felt this would be a total snooze. Van Damme surprised many of his critics with a subtle (well, subtle for him) performance nestled within a fairly intelligent film. The movie never rises above its comic-book roots, but the mere fact that it even rose up *to* them was reward enough for audiences.

TIME GUARDIAN, THE

Hemdale Film Corporation (Australian), 1987, Color, 105 min, VT, LD

Producers: Anthony I. Ginnane, Robert LaGettie, and Norman Wilkinson; **Director:** Brian Hannant; **Screenplay:** John Baxter and Brian Hannant; **Music:** Allan Zavod; **Special Effects:** Paul Moyes; **Cinematography:** Geoff Burton; **Cast:** Tom Burlinson, Nikki Coghill, Dean Stockwell, Carrie Fisher, Tim Robertson, Peter Merrill, Wan Thye Liew, Damon Sanders

A city some 2000 years in the future tries to escape an army of murderous cyborg warriors by hiding itself in the past. The film makes a solid attempt at delivering a good story but misses the mark, offering instead a simplistic tale in which the good guys win only because they're the good guys. Even Carrie Fisher fans will want to avoid this one.

TIME FLIES

Gainsborough (Great Britain), 1944, b&w, 88 min

Producer: Edward Black; **Director:** Walter Forde; **Screenplay:** Howard Irving Young, Jo O. Orton, and Ted Kavanaugh; **Music:** Noel Gay and Bretton Byrd; **Cinematography:** Basil Emmott; **Cast:** Tommy Handley, George Morre, Graham Moffatt, Evelyn Dall

Two British comedians ride a time machine into the past so that they can travel from one set piece to another making droll quips.

TIME MACHINE, THE

MGM, 1960, Color, 103 min, VT, LD, DVD

Producer: George Pal; **Director:** Pal; **Screenplay:** David Duncan; **Music:** Russell Garcia; **Special Effects:** William Tuttle, George W. Davis, William Ferrari, Gene Warren, and Wah Chang; **Cinematography:** Paul Vogel; **Cast:** Rod Taylor, Alan Young, Yvette Mimieux, Doris Lloyd, Paul Frees, Sebastian Cabot, Tom Helmore, and Mr. Whit Bissell himself

This movie opens at a private Victorian supper. The guests have all arrived, and the housekeeper has seen to their comfort. Now if only the host would arrive so that they can have their dinner. He finally does appear, with a fantastic tale of where he has been since he has seen all his friends last. It seems that George (Taylor) has invented a time machine. Testing his device, he took a ride into the future, finally coming to a stop in the year 802701. He's seen a number of wars go past while he traveled forward, but now he's reached humankind's final triumph, a utopian society where no one knows any kind of need or want. At least, it looks like paradise on the surface.

The problem, as George soon discovered, is that the Eloi, the beautiful people he found upon his arrival, are merely the cattle of a subterranean race of cannibals known as the Morlocks. Heroically, George helps the Eloi rid themselves of the Morlocks, and all is right with the world. He returns to the past to tell his pals what happened to him (a proper gentleman keeps his social engagements, after all), and to snatch three books from his library to take with him on his return to the future. The only one of his friends willing to believe his story (Young) stares at the shelf with the spaces indicating the missing volumes, wondering which three books one might take for a job to rebuild all of civilization.

Like most science fiction based on literature, *The Time Machine* suffers greatly in comparison to its source material. As usual, Hollywood's version of H.G. Wells's classic is grossly oversimplified. Wells's scathing indictment of Victorian society (especially its rigid caste system, which is the basis for the Morlock/Eloi society) is completely removed as are a number of his other provocative theories. However, when simply taken at face value, the movie is wonderfully entertaining, especially for younger audiences. It nicely avoids setting up any messy time paradoxes, paying sharp attention to plot details. The special effects, which won an Academy Award, are staggering for their time, and the time machine itself is a triumph of nostalgic design.

TIMERIDER (aka: TIMERIDER: THE ADVENTURES OF LYLE SWANN)

Jensen/Farley, 1983, Color, 93 min, VT, LD

Producers: Lester Berman and Michael Nesmith; **Director:** William Dear; **Screenplay:** Dear and Nesmith; **Music:** Nesmith; **Cinematography:** Larry Pizer; **Cast:** Fred Ward, Belinda Bauer, Peter Coyote, Ed Lauter, Richard Masur, Tracey Walter, L.Q. Jones

A motorcyclist (Ward) is unexpectedly caught up in a time experiment. Before he knows it, he's back in the Old West, drawn into the most classic of time paradoxes, falling in love with his great-grandmother and fathering his own line. Working-class ethics meet intellectual sensibilities in a blend that didn't satisfy critics but which audiences enjoyed well enough, much of this due to Ward's engaging performance.

TIMERIDER: THE ADVENTURES OF LYLE SWANN

See *TIMERIDER*

TIME RUNNER

Excalibur Pictures/North American Pictures, 1993, Color, 90 min, VT, LD

Producers: John Proust, A. William Smith, Lloyd A. Simandl, James R. Westwell, John A. Curtis, and John Smith; **Director:** Michael Mazo; **Screenplay:** Curtis, Ian Bray, Greg Derochie, Chuck Hyde, Mazo, and Ron Tarrant; **Music:** Brian Farnon and Robert Smart; **Special Effects:** Gary Paller and Tom Price; **Cinematography:** Danny Nowak; **Cast:** Mark Hamill, Rae Dawn Chong, Brion James, Marc Baur, Gordon Tipple, Allen Forget, Barry W. Levy

It's the far-flung future of 2022. Aliens are attacking Earth. Trying to escape one of the planet's orbiting platforms, Mark Hamill ends up in 1992. Once he figures out where and when he is, he realizes that he has a chance to change history and stop the alien attack. He doesn't go about doing so very intelligently, though. Hamill gives a stellar performance, as do others in the cast, but nothing around him matches his intensity.

TIMES ARE OUT OF JOINT, THE

Gaumont (France), 1909, silent short

Director: Emile Cohl

A clock that begins to run unexplainably fast begets dire consequences, as everything within its sphere of influence begins to run equally fast.

TIMESTALKERS

Fries Entertainment, 1987, Color, 100 min, VT

Producers: Charles W. Fries, Richard Maynard, John Newland, and Milton T. Raynor; **Director:** Michael Schultz; **Screenplay:** Ray Brown and Brian Clemens; **Music:** Craig Safan; **Cinematography:** Harry Mathias; **Cast:** William Devane, Lauren Hutton, Klaus Kinski, John Ratzenberger, Forrest Tucker, Gail Youngs

A woman from a few thousand years ahead comes back to the present to enlist the aid of a college professor to help her track a bad guy who has hidden himself in the past. Notable only for the great Forrest Tucker's last role.

TIME TRACKERS

MGM/Concorde/New Horizons, 1989, Color, 87 min, VT

Producer: Roger Corman; **Director:** Howard R. Cohen; **Screenplay:** Cohen; **Music:** Parmer Fuller; **Cinematography:** Ronn Schmidt; **Cast:** Ned Beatty, Wil Shriner, Kathleen Beller, Bridget Hoffman, Alex Hyde-White, Lee Bergere, Robert Cornthwaite

A group of time cops races into the past to stop another future traveler who wants to use time for his own diabolical ends. On their way back to the Dark Ages, the future cops pick up present-day detective Ned Beatty to add perspective for the audience.

TIME TRAVELERS, THE

AIP, 1964, Color, 82 min, VT

Producer: William Redlin; **Director:** Ib Melchior; **Screenplay:** Melchior; **Music:** Richard La Salle; **Special Effects:** David Hewitt and Ray Storey; **Cinematography:** Vilmos Zsigmond; **Cast:** Preston Foster, Philip Carey, Merry Anders, John Hoyt, Steve Franken, Forrest J. Ackerman, Joan Woodbury, Dolores Wells, Dennis Patrick

A band of noble scientists working on the problem of time travel experience their greatest triumph and their most terrible tragedy paradoxically at the same moment. The team manages to put together a device that can peer into the past, present, and future. Before they can utilize it for much studying, however, a temporal portal is accidentally created that sucks up one of their people. Desperate to get him back, the others follow him into the void.

The team reappears over a hundred years in the future. A nuclear war has occurred, leaving the survivors living in underground shelters, while mutants roam the radioactive surface world getting into trouble. The team is taken to the head of the future survivors who tells them that the mutants will soon win the struggle for dominance of Earth. Thus, the survivors are building a vessel capable of taking them all to another world. The team pitches in, helping to build the spaceship while also working on building a portal to take them home.

Before the escape ship can be finished, however, the mutants attack. The team tries to go back to their former present in the new portal, but they go back too far—back to the point when they can actually witness themselves going into the portal the first time. It soon becomes apparent that they are in a time loop, doomed to continue going back and forth, repeating the same pattern for all eternity.

The movie navigates its path through a dozen standard clichés, but does so adroitly enough so as not to enrage or bore the sci-fi connoisseur.

TIME WALKER

New World Pictures, 1982, Color, 83 min, VT

Producers: Robert A. Shaheen, Jason Williams, and Dimitri Villard; **Director:** Tom Kennedy; **Screenplay:** Williams, Tom Friedman, and Karen Levitt; **Music:** Richard Band; **Special Effects:** Holly Hudson and Sue Dolph; **Cinematography:** Robbie Greenberg; **Cast:** Ben Murphy, Nina Axelrod, Kevin Brophy, James Karen, Shari Belafonte-Harper, Antoinette Bower

Somehow, a highly destructive alien creature—one nearly unstoppable in modern times—was subdued in ancient Egypt. Then for some reason the Egyptians wrapped but did not mummify (i.e., remove all the internal organs) the creature, leaving it in the tomb of King Tut to be found centuries later—still alive, of course, and ready to cause more mayhem.

TIME WARP (1967)

See *JOURNEY TO THE CENTER OF TIME*

TIME WARP (1980)

See *THE DAY TIME ENDED*

TIN MAN, THE

MGM, 1935, b&w, 19 min

Producer: Hal Roach; **Director:** James Parrott; **Cast:** Patsy Kelly, Thelma Todd, Cy Slocum, Matthew Betz, Clarence H. Wilson

Two women are menaced by a robot programmed to hate the fairer sex. The cast-metal misogynist comes to its senses, however, and turns on its evil programmer.

TITAN A.E.

20th Century Fox, 2000, Color, 90 min, VT, DVD

Producers: Don Bluth, Gary Goldman, and David Kirschner; **Directors:** Bluth and Goldman; **Screenplay:** Ben Edlund, John August, and Joss Whedon; **Music:** Graeme Revell; **Special Effects:** David Paul Dozoretzy Storey, and Paul Martin Smith; **Animation:** Troy Saliba, John Hill, Robert Fox, Renato Dos Anjos, Edison Goncalves, Paul Newberry, and Mark Weathers; **Cast:** Matt Damon, Bill Pullman, Drew Barrymore, Janeane Garofalo, Nathan Lane, John, Leguizamo, Ron Perlman, Tone-Loc

It's 3028 and humankind has conquered space and created a lifestyle in which everyone seems content. Then comes one little problem—a devastating attack by the

Drej, a vicious alien race whose members are composed of pure energy. The attack lasts only a few minutes. When it is over, Earth has been destroyed. The home of the human race is no more. As for the race itself, only those who could escape by spaceship survive. To all intents and purposes, the human race is finished. But there's hope. A boy named Cale unknowingly possesses a map that could lead humanity to the Titan—a great ship that holds the ability to give the human race a new world. Taken off Earth before the Drej attack, it's 15 years before they catch up to him. After that, it's a constant run as Cale and those few friends he makes along the way struggle to stay ahead of their enemies and save the human race.

Although the movie boasts an impressive cast of voice talent and certain parts of the story are actually clever, the problem is that the story works only if you stop thinking. Point in case: The Drej destroy the human race out of fear. Fear of what? Fear of the Titan project. But what is the Titan project? It's a ship capable of creating a new Earth if the old one is destroyed. If that's what the Titan is, then what is it the Drej are so afraid of?

This is never explained, and that's where this movie's main problem comes in. Often, logic just seems ignored to in favor of mindless excitement. The only time people act in their own best interest is when the movie's rigid formula calls for them to do so. The wooden storytelling and ham-handed characterization seem in keeping with co-producer/director Don Bluth's other feature efforts, *All Dogs Go to Heaven*, *A Troll in Central Park*, *Roc-A-Doodle*, *Thumbelina*, and THE LAND BEFORE TIME. It may also point to why 2-D and 3-D animation do not blend well—or why the last shot in the film (a landscape view of New Earth) looks like a bad download from a video game.

However, there are a number of pure sci-fi moments in the film that show some real imagination. The hydrogen trees are nicely used, as are the ice rings. The art (even when the technologies are badly mixed) is almost always beautiful stuff. It's only the story that, despite several nice twists, is boringly easy to predict.

TITAN FIND

See CREATURE

TOBOR THE GREAT

Republic, 1954, b&w, 77 min, VT, LD

Producers: Carl Dvoley and Richard Goldstone; **Director:** Lee Scholem; **Screenplay:** Phillip MacDon-

ald and Goldstone; **Music:** Howard Jackson; **Special Effects:** Theodore Lydecker and Howard Lydecker; **Cinematography:** John L. Russell; **Cast:** Charles Drake, Karin Booth, Bill Chapin, Henry Kulky, William Schallert, Robert Shayne, Lyle Talbot

The robot Tobor is a great friend to its's inventor's son. Soon it will be launched into space, however, in place of a human being who might die doing such things. But then spies try to turn Tobor into a killer.

TORTURE SHIP

Producers Distributing Corporation, 1939, b&w, 56 min

Producer: Ben Judell; **Director:** Victor Halperin; **Screenplay:** George Sayre; **Music:** David Chudnow; **Cinematography:** Jack Greenhalgh; **Cast:** Lyle Talbot, Irving Pichel, Wheeler Oakman, Stanley Blystone, Jacqueline Wells

A scientist takes center stage—this one wants to cure criminals of their bad ways with glandular injections. His very noble idea quickly goes horribly wrong, and soon the kindly scientist is up to his elbows in human beings writhing in agony.

TOTAL RECALL

TriStar/Carolco, 1990, Color, 109 min, VT, LD

Producers: Buzz Feitshans, Elliot Schick, Ronald Shusett, Robert Fentress, Mario Kassar, and Andrew G. Vajna; **Director:** Paul Verhoeven; **Screenplay:** Shusett, Dan O. Bannon, and Gary Goldman; **Music:** Jerry Goldsmith; **Special Effects:** MetroLight Studios, Dream Quest Images, Stetson Visual Services, Hunter Gratzner Industries, Inc., and Industrial Light & Magic; **Cinematography:** Jost Vacano; **Cast:** Arnold Schwarzenegger, Sharon Stone, Rachel Ticotin, Ronny Cox, Michael Ironside, Marshall Bell, Mel Johnson, Jr.

Lowly, ordinary construction worker Arnold Schwarzenegger has been dreaming of Mars lately. Every night he sees himself on the Red Planet with a woman who is not his wife, something that is making his wife (Stone) pretty mad. Arnold is dying to go to Mars, but his wife absolutely refuses. So he decides to do the next best thing—and that, of course, is to take a trip to Total Recall. Recall offers the public implanted vacation memories—just sit in the chair and have the time of your life without any of the usual hassles. No visas, no bugs, no lost luggage, no spouse or children if you desire—even no you. Yes, for a little extra, Recall will help you take a vacation from yourself—you can be a spy, an athlete, anything you desire.

Arnold decides to be a spy and sits in the chair. Before things can go too far, however, Arnold has a bad reaction to the initial injections and has to be brought out before he is lobotomized. The company wipes his memory, refunds his money, and stuffs him in a robot cab. Or do they?

The conceit of this highly exciting and extremely clever film is to keep the audience off balance for as long as possible. Is Arnold having his dream vacation as a spy going to Mars, or is he a spy in deep undercover who has accidentally regained some memories by going to Recall? The story is a dazzling spiral of paranoia, one that never lets up for a moment in its attack on the audience's sensibilities. The story is laid out with extreme intricacy. Indeed, it takes most folks at least two viewings to decide once and for all whether or not Arnold is a hero or an idiot. The film offers no clear-cut answer, intelligently leaving the ending totally up in the air. Indeed, Sharon Stone reportedly complained to director Verhoeven that she did not know how to play her scenes because she could not tell whether she was really married to Arnold's character or not. Since the film was based on a Philip K. Dick short story, "We Can Remember It For You Wholesale," this is not surprising. Dick's fiction is noted for its complex, wandering story lines that almost always involve deeply paranoid characters being tricked over and over by sinister forces.

Director Verhoeven pulled out all the stops. The film is littered with his trademarks: cynical characters, intrusive advertisements, throwaway sci-fi gimmicks enhancing the background, and razor-edged violence that litters the screen with corpses. His usual devious references are there as well; for instance, in one scene Arnold checks into a hotel on Mars under the false name of Brubaker. Brubaker was the name of the mission captain in the film *CAPRICORN ONE*, a movie about a fake trip to Mars that is all part of a government cover-up.

Note: Fans of Douglas Adam's *Hitchhiker's Guide to the Galaxy* should watch for references to that series, including such things as wrapping one's head in a wet towel to avoid being located, incredibly irritating and overly polite robots, and three-breasted prostitutes.

Total Recall TRI-STAR PICTURES / JOSEPH B. MAUCERI COLLECTION)

TO THE CENTER OF THE EARTH

See *UNKNOWN WORLD*

TOY BOX, THE

Boxoffice International, 1971, Color, 85 min

Producer: Harry Novak; **Director:** Ron Garcia; **Screenplay:** Garcia; **Special Effects:** Dennis Marsh; **Cinematography:** H.P. Edwards; **Cast:** Ann Meyers, Deborah Osborne, Lisa Goodman, Evan Steele, Neal Bishop

A kinky alien exposes people to perversion so that it can steal their then perverted brains to feed to its even more-perverted pals.

TRACKERS

See *SPACE RAGE*

TRANCERS (aka: FUTURE COP)

Empire Pictures, 1985, Color, 76 min, VT, LD, DVD

Producers: Charles Band and Debra Dion; **Director:** Richard Band; **Screenplay:** Danny Bilson and Paul DeMeo; **Music:** Phil Davies and Marc Ryder; **Special Effects:** John Carl Buechler, Howard Burger, Gene Winfield, Mike Menzel, Jay Burkhart, Mitch Devane, and Mechanical & Make-Up Imageries, Inc.; **Cinematography:** Mac Ahlberg; **Cast:** Tim Thomerson, Helen Hunt, Art La Fleur, Biff Manard, Anne Seymour, Richard Herd, Richard Erdman

It's the far-off future and things are pretty bad. A totalitarian government is making everyone miserable. But some heroes have a plan. Their idea is to send someone back in time 300 years to a point at which they can change history so that the totalitarian takeover never happens. The only problem is that they can't send back people—only their spirits. The personality of the agent returned through time then has to inhabit the body of one of their ancestors to get the job done.

Comedian Tim Thomerson is wonderfully cast as agent Jack Deth. The social satire is both hilarious and thoughtful. No doubt this is the finest film by Richard Band. Four sequels followed: *Trancers II, Trancers III, Trancers IV: Jack of Swords,* and *Trancers V: Sudden Deth,* the last three of which were released direct to video. Young Helen Hunt returned only for the second and third films, already on her way to better things by the time the third film was released in 1992.

TRANCERS II

Full Moon, 1991, Color, 86 min, VT, LD

Producers: Charles Band, Thomas Bradford, David DeCoteau, and John Schoweiler; **Director:** Band; **Screenplay:** Band and Jackson Barr; **Music:** Mark Ryder and Phil Davies; **Special Effects:** Kevin McCarthy, Sabrina McCarthy, Sandra McCarthy, Dell Rheaume, and G. Bruno Stempel; **Cinematography:** Adolfo Bartoli; **Cast:** Tim Thomerson, Helen Hunt, Megan Ward, Biff Manard, Richard Lynch, Martine Beswicke, Jeffery Combs, Alyson Croft, Telma Hopkins, Art La Fleur, Barbara Crampton

See *TRANCERS*

TRANCERS III

Full Moon, 1992, Color, 83 min, VT, LD

Producers: Albert Band, Charles Band, and Keith S. Payson; **Director:** Courtney Joyner; **Screenplay:** C. Joyner; **Music:** Richard Band, Phil Davies, Mark Ryder; **Special Effects:** John P. Cazin and James Ochoa; **Cinematography:** Adolfo Bartoli; **Cast:** Tim Thomerson, Helen Hunt, Megan Ward, Melanie Smith, Andrew Robinson, Tony Pierce, Dawn Ann Billings, Stephen Macht, Telma Hopkins, R.A. Mahailoff

See *TRANCERS*

TRANCERS IV: JACK OF SWORDS

Paramount/Full Moon, 1994, Color, 83 min, VT, LD

Producers: Oana Paunescu and Vlad Paunescu; **Director:** David Nutter; **Screenplay:** Peter David; **Music:** Gary Fry; **Cast:** Tim Thomerson, Stacy Randall, Ty Miller, Teri Ivens, Mark Arnold, Clabe Hartley, Alan Oppenheimer, Lochlyn Munro

See *TRANCERS*

TRANCERS V: SUDDEN DETH

Paramount/Full Moon, 1995, Color, 73 min, VT, LD

Producers: Oana Paunescu, Vlas Paunescu, and Charles Band; **Director:** David Nutter; **Screenplay:**

Peter David; **Music:** Gary Fry; **Special Effects:** Michael Deak; **Cinematography:** Adolfo Bartoli; **Cast:** Tim Thomerson, Stacy Randall, Ty Miller, Teri Ivens, Mark Arnold, Clabe Hartley, Alan Oppenheimer, Lochlyn Munro

See *TRANCERS*

TRANS-ATLANTIC TUNNEL
(aka: THE TUNNEL)

Gaumont (Great Britain), 1935, b&w, 90 min, VT

Producer: Michael Bacon; **Director:** Maurice Elvery; **Screenplay:** Curt Siodmak; **Cast:** Richard Dix, Leslie Banks, Marge Evans, C. Aubrey Smith, Walter Huston, George Arliss, Helen Vinson

This film is about digging a tunnel underneath the Atlantic Ocean, a story filled to the brim with other predictions such as television, rooftop airports, and an accurately predicted Chunnel—the England/France tunnel running beneath the English Channel. All of this is delivered via a very two-dimensional story and trite personalities.

Note: Interestingly enough, this film is a remake of a simultaneous German/French film produced only two years earlier. See *DER TUNNEL*.

TRANSFORMERS

Toei Company, Ltd (Japan)/Sunbow Productions (U.S.), 1986, Color, 86 min, VT, LD

Producers: Masaharu Etô, Tomo Fukamoto, and Nelson Shin; **Director:** Shin; **Screenplay:** Ron Friedman; **Music:** Vince DiCola, Spenser Proffer, and Robert J. Walsh; **Animation:** Masao Itô, Kôzô Morishita, Baik Seung Kyun, Shigeyasu Yamauchi, and Kôichi Tsunoda; **Cast:** Orson Welles, Leonard Nimoy, Robert Stack, Eric Idle, Judd Nelson, Lionel Stander

Heroic robots from another planet who can change into Earth cars and trucks and planes (for no given reason other than to sell toys) battle villainous robots from another planet who can change into the same assortment of vehicles. There have been excellent animated features that have been nothing more than overlong toy commercials, but this isn't one of them. Based on a television series of the same name.

TRANSMUTATIONS

See *UNDERWORLD*

TRAPPED BY TELEVISION

Columbia, 1936, b&w, 64 min

Producer: Ben Pivak; **Director:** Del Lord; **Screenplay:** Lee Loeb and Harold Buchman; **Special Effects:** Roy Davidson; **Cinematography:** Allen G. Siegler; **Cast:** Lyle Talbot, Mary Astor, Thurston Hall, Nat Pendleton

Cops come up with a new way to get the goods on the bad guys—using spy cameras to monitor their every move.

TREKKIES

Paramount, 1999, Color, 87 min

Producers: W.K. Border, Michael Leahy, Joel Soisson, and Denise Crosby; **Director:** Roger Nygard; **Editor:** Nygard; **Music:** Walter Werzowa, Jimmie Wood, J.J. Holiday, and Billy Sullivan; **Special Effects:** Neo Digital Imaging; **Cinematography:** Harris Done; **Cast:** Denise Crosby, Barbara Adams, The Denis Bourguignon Family, David, Laurel, and Tammi Greenstein, Gabriel and Richard Köerner, Richard Kronfeld, Joyce Mason, Evelyn De Biase, Anne Murphy, Majel Barrett Roddenberry, James Doohan, Walter Koenig, DeForest Kelley, Leonard Nimoy, William Shatner, George Takei, Grace Lee Whitney, Levar Burton, John de Lance, Michael Dorn, Terry Farrell, Jonathan Frakes, Chase Masterson, Kate Mulgrew, Robert O'Reilly, Ethan Phillips, Brent Spiner, Wil Wheaton, Buzz Aldrin, Erik Larson, Richard Arnold, Maria De Maci, Daryl and Bones Frazetti, James T. Kirk, Dr. Marc Okrand, Brian W. Phelps, Glen Proechel, Pat Rimington, Jeri Taylor, Mark Thompson, J. Trusk, Douglas Marcks, Deborah L. Warner, Michael Westmore, Frank D'Amico, Rick Overton, Jon Ross, Fred Travalena, Matt Weinhold

"'Trekkies' are the only fans listed by name in the Oxford English Dictionary."

These words are the first thing that appears on the screen in this documentary about the largest fan phenomenon in pop culture history. One might think this is a strange idea for a film—studying the people who dress up as Klingons and Vulcans, who reportedly spend an average of $400 per year per person on *Star Trek* merchandise. This is obviously not blockbuster material. Watching Barbara Adams, the Arkansas juror who wore her Star Fleet uniform to the media circus Whitewater trial, interviewed is not most people's idea of a wise investment.

But as the camera moves from convention to convention, from fan to fan, slowly, perhaps unbelievably, the film draws audiences into the world being featured. Without the structure of a traditional story, time begins to lose its meaning. The people playing dress-up become less and less strange, and before people know it, they've been sucked inside the world of *Star Trek*.

This is a fun, fascinating movie. At least a rudimentary knowledge of *Star Trek* is necessary to understand what is going on, but then, as the picture clearly points out, who doesn't know Kirk and Spock and the *Enterprise*? How many folks can't tell you how to hold your hand in a Vulcan salute? Not too many. The film doesn't dwell on such things, though. Indeed, this movie is not about *Star Trek*—it's about *Star Trek*'s fans. And in bringing them honestly to the screen, it does a wonderful job.

Meet Dr. Denis Dourguignon, an Orlando dentist who has trademarked the name "Starbase Dental" so he could set up his office with a *Star Trek* theme for those who want to have their teeth cleaned by a Star Fleet officer. Gabriel Köerner is a 14-year-old making his own *Star Trek* movie with effects better than those you'll find in some low-budget films. These are just a few of the people featured, from those who dress their dogs and cats in *Star Trek* uniforms to the auctioneer who got $60.00 for half a glass of water left onstage by Next Generation's John de Lancie (the explanation of this has to be seen to be believed).

There are also plenty of moments with cast members from each of the shows. All of the cast members from the original *Trek* speak at length, but again, their discussions center solely on the fans and their interaction with them. Funny stories are told, like the one about the woman who sent marijuana to DeForest Kelley (Dr. McCoy), as well as serious ones. James Doohan (Scotty) tells a highly emotional story about a fan who sent him a suicide note that prompted a 10-year relationship between the two.

This is an extremely honest film—the geeks have in no way been hidden in a closet. It's also a warm, close-up study that details the frustrations and problems the casts and crews of the various shows have confronted, along with the incredible, often overwhelming love the fans have for the core concept. Unlike so many pop culture juggernauts, *Star Trek* has maintained its momentum for well over 30 years. The main reason is that at

its heart, the franchise is about more than just science fiction, special effects, or monsters and spaceships. *Star Trek* touched a great number of people with its messages of compassion and racial harmony when it first aired, and it's never stopped making fans through its overwhelming humanity.

Note: For those who aren't fans, watch just to see the insane lengths some fans go to. Also, the end credits are accompanied by a quintet of comedians doing some of the best *Star Trek* jokes around.

TREMORS

Universal, 1990, Color, 96 min, VT, LD, DVD

Producers: Ellen Collett, Ginny Nugent, Gale Anne Hurd, S.S. Wilson, and Brent Maddock; **Director:** Ron Underwood; **Screenplay:** Wilson and Maddock; **Music:** Ernest Troost and Robert Folk; **Special Effects:** Alec Gillis, Lise Romanoff, Tom Woodruff, Jr., Amalgamated Dynamics, M.B. Special Effects, Inc., Fantasy II Film Effects, 4-Ward Productions, Illusion Arts, and International Special Effects, Ltd.; **Cinematography:** Alexander Gruszynski; **Cast:** Fred Ward, Kevin Bacon, Michael Gross, Reba McEntire, Finn Carter, Bobby Jacoby, Charlotte Stewart, Tony Genaros, Victor Wong

Ward and Bacon play two jack-of-all-trade handymen who live in the smallest town on Earth, the ironically named Perfection, Nevada. Fed up with no money, no available women, and no opportunities, they decide to pack up and leave town. On the way out, they discover the corpse of one of their neighbors. Soon they discover that the only road out of the valley is blocked. Giant sluglike beasts that travel at great speed beneath the ground are wandering the valley, hunting prey through sound vibrations. They eat up half the folks in the vicinity before anyone knows what's going on and then keep whittling the population down while the terrified citizens try to find some way to fight back.

This movie and its barely released sequel, *Tremors II: Aftershocks*, are both wonderful send-ups of the basic '50s Universal sci-fi/monster movie formula. Great fun is had by Ward, Bacon, and Carter as they sit around and theorize what "graboids" could be: The possibilities range from government experiment to aliens, but nothing is ever explained.

Both screenplays are well written, with strong male and female characters, all of whom have real personalities, many of whom are intelligent. This is one of the key features that make these films so appealing, even for more than one viewing. In the *Tremors* series, not only do the characters survive by keeping their wits about them, but, ironically, trouble actually starts for them when they begin thinking. The point is made repeatedly in the first film, for instance, that one has "to have a plan," as Ward tells Bacon throughout, until finally by the end, when everyone is trapped and there is only one chance left to defeat the last creature, Bacon defies everyone by taking on the creature. When confronted with possible suicide, he just says that he has to try because he has to be smarter than a worm. And clever as the worm is, the human who stops to think is a step ahead.

Both films are rich in such sentiment—excellent, intelligently scripted movies that celebrate intellect and action working hand in hand. In both films the special effects are wonderful, the acting top-notch, and the sound tracks are great. The first movie is the stronger of the two, but not by much. Especially noteworthy fun is generated by Gross and McEntire as a survivalist couple, though McEntire does not appear in the second film, only Gross.

TREMORS II: AFTERSHOCKS

Universal, 1995, Color, 96 min, VT, LD, DVD

Producers: Charles DeFaria, Nancy Roberts, Ron Underwood, and Brent Maddock; **Director:** S.S. Wilson; **Screenplay:** Wilson and Maddock; **Music:** Jay Ferguson; **Special Effects:** Peter Chesney, Tom Chesney, Bruce McPherson, Bruce Thackery, and Kyle Collingsworth; **Cinematography:** Wirgil L. Harper; **Cast:** Fred Ward, Michael Gross, Christopher Gartin, Helen Shaver, Marco Hernandez, Marcelo Tubert, Jose Rosario, Thomas Rosales

See *TREMORS*

TRIGGER HAPPY

See *MAD DOG TIME*

TRIP TO JUPITER, A

Pathé (France), 1907, Hand-Colored, silent short

The king (of France, perhaps) climbs a really long ladder that reaches all the way to outer space. He passes the Moon and planets, each saluting the plucky climber as he passes them by.

TRIP TO MARS, A (1910)

Edison, 1910, b&w, silent short

A scientist makes his way to Mars. The planet turns out to be extremely unfriendly, so he heads back to Earth via his antigravity dust.

TRIP TO MARS, A (1920)

Italy, 1920, b&w, silent feature

Screenplay: Bud Fisher; **Animators:** Fisher and Edgar Horace

More scientists making their way to Mars. This batch doesn't find nearly the trouble that other cinematic astronauts have found. They also get there in the most interesting way possible, via propeller-driven spaceship!

TRIP TO THE CENTER OF THE EARTH

See *JOURNEY TO THE CENTER OF THE EARTH*

TRIP TO THE MOON, A

Lubin, 1914, b&w, silent feature

Producer: Siegmund Lubin; **Director:** Vincent Whitman; **Screenplay:** Whitman; **Animator:** Whitman

Scientists make their way into outer space, traveling via propeller-driven airship to the Moon and then the other planets, finally racing a comet.

TRIP TO THE MOON, THE
(aka: VOYAGE TO THE MOON)

Star Films (France), 1902, b&w, silent short

Producer: Georges Méliès; **Director:** Méliès; **Screenplay:** Méliès; **Special Effects:** Claudel; **Cinematography:** Michaut and Lucien Tainguy; **Cast:** Georges Méliès, Victor André, the Folies-Bergère acrobats, and the Theatre du Chatelet ballerinas

This short is the famous turn-of-the-century science fiction masterpiece of a spaceship launched from France via cannon to the Moon. The astronauts (minus any spacesuits) explore the lunar surface, get captured by H.G. Wells's Selenites, beat the creatures senseless, and then return to Earth for cheers and drinks all around. An inventive work of pure genius for its time.

TRIXIE

See *THE CRAZIES*

TROLLENGERG TERROR, THE

See *THE CRAWLING EYE*

TRON

Walt Disney Studios, 1982, Color, 96 min, VT, LD, DVD

Producers: Harrison Ellenshaw and Ron Miller; **Director:** Steven Lisberger; **Screenplay:** Lisberger and Bonnie MacBird; **Music:** Wendy Carlos; **Special Effects:** Ellenshaw, Jerry Rees, Arvil Bebley, Lee Dyer, Jim Pickel, Kenny Mirman, Arnie Wong, Richard Taylor, Judson Rosebush, John Schoede, Robert Abel & Associates, Digital Effects, Inc., Stargate Films, Inc., and MAGI-Synthavision; **Cinematography:** Bruce Logan: **Cast:** Jeff Bridges, Bruce Boxleitner, David Warner, Cindy Morgan, Barnard Hughes, Dan Shor

A scientist (Bridges) is transported inside a video game by his evil rivals who hope to eliminate him. Once inside, he finds himself transformed into a gladiatorlike being of light who must constantly battle to stay alive.

The movie gets as much from this interesting premise as it can and then coasts on the considerable talent of its stars. Ultimately, however, the picture's lack of anything resembling a solid plot does it in. Touted as a miracle breakthrough in mixing computer animation with live-action footage, the film actually had rather pedestrian effects. For instance, all of the live-action footage filmed for "inside" the computer game was shot in black-and-white, then colorized, but done so darkly, with such dull colors that audiences could not help but lose interest.

The one interesting note is the possible allegory of the film. Made by Disney Studios, it presents Barnard Hughes as a solitary inventor who created something wonderful in his garage, only to find it taken away by the soulless corporation that has grown up around his work. The parallels between the film and the actual story of Walt Disney and the Disney Corporation after Walt's death are remarkable.

Note: Those determined to watch this movie should scan the screen intently during the "solar sailor" sequence. The silhouette form of Mickey Mouse reportedly can be spotted on the terrain beneath the ship, but it appears only for an instant.

TRUMAN SHOW, THE

Paramount, 1998, Color, 102 min, VT

Producers: Edward S. Feldman, Lynn Pleshette, Richard Luke Rothschild, Andrew Niccol, Scott Rubin, and Adam Schroeder; **Director:** Peter Weir; **Screenplay:** Niccol; **Music:** Peter Biziou; **Special Effects:** Larz Anderson, Ted Andre, Jason Wardle, Brad Kuehn, Craig Barron, Travis Baumann, Michael J. McAlister, Brett Northcut, and Janek Sirrs; **Cinematography:** Philip Glass and Burkhart Von Dallwitz; **Cast:** Jim Carrey, Laura Linney, Ed Harris, Noah Emmerich, Natascha McElhone, Holland Taylor, Brian Delate, Paul Giamatti, Harry Shearer

Truman Burbank (Carrey) has the perfect life. He lives in a beautiful, clean, seaside community where everyone knows him and likes him. He'd like to leave someday, just for a while, a trip, a jaunt—anything. Somehow, however, he always ends up getting talked out of leaving town. The reason: The town is a gigantic, sealed-off television set. The sky is a backdrop; the Sun and Moon, clouds and rain and other weather are all special effects produced on cue. The set was built to enclose Truman's life, which is a type of true-life soap opera that is broadcast 24 hours a day. Everyone in town is an actor—his parents, wife, ex-girlfriends, the mail carrier, his boss, everyone—all of the details of their lives controlled by director Christian (Harris).

All of this is a secret from Truman.

Trouble comes when Truman gets restless and wants to get out and see the world. The director and his ignorant star become locked in a battle of wills, with Truman ultimately finding a door in the set that allows him to exit.

The Truman Show was touted as social satire, a commentary on our voyeuristic, privacy-destroying society. Granted, as long as the premise is being established, the film seems clever and quite promising. But once the premise *is* established, the filmmakers found that they simply had nothing to say. The film then goes on for another hour and a half, accomplishing nothing more. Thus the central thesis of the film is a fraud. It is obvious that no one in this world would watch a show like the one presented. Manic comic Carrey does none of his usual shtick. Truman Burbank is a pleasant, normal, quite boring fellow—not anyone who could command a loyal, worldwide audience for over 20 years.

Ignoring that, however, the film works on no other social commentary levels either. The story is empty and hollow. It sets up the audience to learn some deep lesson about human nature and then skips the payoff. Although it tries hard for the supposed social relevance of the British television show *The Prisoner* (note the red-and-white awnings in the town square, the golf carts, and other tips of the hat to the TV show), it never makes any statements beyond the obvious.

TUMANNOST ANDROMEDY (aka: THE ANDROMEDA NEBULA)

Russia, 1967, Color, 85 min

Director: Eugene Sherstobytov

It really is the far-flung future, about 2,000 years ahead, and humanity is trying to make contact with the aliens whom they suspect are living within the title nebula. This very upbeat film was intended to reflect subtly the happy wonders of the Communist lifestyle. Noted for its exceptional special effects, particularly its incredible ending, it is not noted for its actors, who seem like the most wooden lot of penny-rate day players ever assembled.

TUNNEL, DER (aka: THE TUNNEL)

Bavaria Film (Germany), 1933, b&w, 80 min

Producer: Ernest Garden; **Director:** Kurt Bernhardt; **Screenplay:** Kurt Siodmak; **Music:** Walter Gronostay; **Cinematography:** Carl Hoffman; **German Cast:** Paul Hartmann, Olly von Flint, Elga Brink, Attila Hörbiger; **French Cast:** Jean Gabin, Gustaf Grundgens, Madeleine Renaud

Simply put, this is a film about drilling a tunnel from the United States to Europe. The film was made simultaneously in both French and German with different casts working around the same sets. *Der Tunnel* is most likely the first big production that can rightly be labeled as a "disaster" film. The tunnelers are forced to work through all sorts of calamities—floods, cave-ins, even volcanoes. The special effects are remarkable for the time and are still impressive today. The film was remade two years later in English as *TRANS-ATLANTIC TUNNEL*. Although it is a good, solid production, it doesn't quite live up to the 1933 version for realism.

TUNNEL, THE

See *TRANS-ATLANTIC TUNNEL*

TUNNELING THE CHANNEL

Star (France), 1907, b&w, silent short

The earliest prediction of the Chunnel tells the story of England and France being linked by a tunnel running under the English Channel.

TURBO: A POWER RANGERS MOVIE

20th Century Fox, 1997, Color, 99 min, VT, LD

Producers: Haim Saban, Jonathan Tzachor, and Shuki Levy; **Director:** David Winning; **Screenplay:** Levy and Shell Danielson; **Music:** Levy; **Special Effects:** Mike Gerzevitc; **Cinematography:** Ilan Rosenberg; **Cast:** Jason David Frank, Steve Cardenas, Catherine Sutherland, Johnny Yong Bosch, Nakia Burise, Hilary Shepard Turner, Blake Foster

See *MIGHTY MORPHIN POWER RANGERS: THE MOVIE*

TURKEY SHOOT

See *ESCAPE 2000*

12 MONKEYS

Universal, 1995, Color, 131 min, VT, LD, DVD

Producers: Robert Cavallo, Kelley Smith-Wait, Charles Roven, Mark Egerton, Robert Kosberg, Gary Levinsohn, and Lloyd Phillips; **Director:** Terry Gilliam; **Screenplay:** David Webb Peoples, Chris Marker, and Janet Peoples; **Music:** Paul Buckmaster and Charles Olins; **Special Effects:** Beecher Tomlinson, Russell Hurlburt, David Acord, Russell Hardee, Shirley-Montefusco, Vincent Montefusco, Thomas Lockley, Paul Kocar, Kent Houston, Keith Suzuki, Mill Film, Peerless Camera Co., Ltd., and Hunter Gratzner Industries, Inc.; **Cinematography:** Roger Pratt; **Cast:** Bruce Willis, Brad Pitt, Frank Gorshin, Madeleine Stowe, Christopher Plummer, David Morse, Jon Seda, Joseph Melito

A prisoner (Willis) living in a future when most of the world's population has been wiped out in a terrible plague is given an interesting proposition—freedom in exchange for traveling back in time and discovering the cause of the plague, supposedly released on humankind as an act of rebellion by the terrorist group 12 Monkeys. Willis accepts the assignment and goes back to the past, where he discovers that there was no terrorist group. Or was there? Of course, no matter what he finds, those who sent him back to the past do want him to succeed in his quest to uncover the cause

12 Monkeys (UNIVERSAL CITY STUDIOS / JOSEPH B. MAUCERI COLLECTION)

of the plague. Or do they? The film makes tremendous use of traditional time paradox problems. This leaves the plot alternately brilliant and confusing, but enjoyable nonetheless thanks to great performances, terrific special effects, and the typically askance Gilliam direction.

TWELVE TO THE MOON

Columbia, 1960, b&w, 74 min

Producer: Fred Gebhardt; **Director:** David Bradley; **Screenplay:** De Witt Bodeen; **Music:** Michael Anderson; **Special Effects:** Howard A. Anderson and E. Nicholson; **Cinematography:** John Alton; **Cast:** Tony Dexter, Ken Clark, Tom Conway, Michi Kobi, Tierna Bay, John Wengraf, Anna-Lisa, Francis X. Bushman

A group of astronauts are off to the Moon. Once there, the valiant band discovers a race of previously undetected Moon men who freeze the Earth in retaliation for the unannounced visit.

20 MILLION MILES TO EARTH

Columbia, 1957, b&w, 82 min, VT, LD

Producer: Charles Schneer; **Director:** Nathan Juran; **Screenplay:** Bob Williams and Christopher Knopf; **Music:** Mischa Bakaleinikoff; **Special Effects:** Ray Harryhausen; **Cinematography:** Irving Lippmann; **Cast:** William Hopper, Joan Taylor, Frank Puglia, Thomas Browne Henry, John Zaremba, Bart Bradley, Tito Vuolo, Don Orlando

The first human-crewed flight to Venus returns to Earth rather ungracefully. Crash-landing off the coast of Italy, only the ship's pilot (Hopper) and a large, jelly-coated alien specimen (an egg) survive—all else is lost. A local boy finds the egg and takes it to a scientist and his daughter. They accidentally hatch the egg, discovering a small, puppy-sized alien creature within. Once out of its shell (and quite capable of breathing an Earthly atmosphere) the creature begins to grow rapidly at a rate of three or four feet a day. Before long, it's in the hands of the military, whose scientists study the creature for a while, but soon enrage it with their experiments. It bursts its bonds and escapes. Free in Rome, the beast wrecks a lot of historic architecture. Then the thing encounters a circus where it battles an elephant to the death. Finally, the military catches up to the poor brute and knocks it from the top of the Colosseum to its death with a well-placed bazooka shot.

20 Million Miles to Earth is not overly intellectual by anyone's standards, but it still provides plenty of simple straightforward entertainment. The story may be fairly routine and ordinary, but it does make sense. The special effects, on the other hand, produced by master animator Ray Harryhausen, are some of his absolute best. They also help provide the interesting feel of the movie.

Throughout, rather than having his creature initiating any of the film's confrontations, Harryhausen has it reacting to stimuli only. Unlike many lesser filmmakers, the animator never envisions the creature as a rampaging menace so much as a confused, lonely child. Born into a hostile, frightening world, it is not met by a loving mother with food, but by humans with clubs and guns. The creature is not the villain here, a concept unknown at the time, except, of course, in science fiction films.

Note: The creature, never named in the film, was dubbed "The Ymir" by Harryhausen. This name appears in his initial notes as well as in the film's working but never used title.

27TH DAY, THE

Columbia, 1957, b&w, 75 min, VT

Producer: Helen Ainsworth; **Director:** William Asher; **Screenplay:** John Mantley; **Music:** Mischa Bakaleinikoff; **Special Effects:** Ray Harryhausen; **Cinematography:** Henry Freulich; **Cast:** Gene Barry, Valerie French, Arnold Moss, George Voskovec, Stefan Schnabel, Azemat Janti, Marie Tsien

An alien abducts five Earthlings, all from different countries. He gives them each a capsule and an ultimatum: Each capsule can be opened only by the person to whom it was given. If one chooses to open his capsule, he will wipe out all life on a continent of his choice. The alien is giving the Earthlings the means to settle their hostile differences, as well as to make some room for the alien's own dying planet's population. The capsules will only remain effective, however, for 27 days.

Two of the folks throw theirs away and hide. One, a scientist, studies his, trying to figure out what makes it work. Another commits suicide rather than face the consequences. The last of the five, a Russian, is captured by the KGB and tortured for the secret of the capsule. In the end, no one wipes out any continents, and it is revealed that the capsules were only a test to see if Earth was populated with people of moral integrity. When the 27th day has come and gone, the alien activates the capsules and kills all the morally unfit folks on Earth.

Certainly far more optimistic about human frailties than many of the other morality plays disguised as sci-fi movies made in the '50's, this one still offers a curious ending. Confronted with humankind's goodness, the alien then takes it upon itself to murder all the "bad" people on Earth. Deus ex machina, to be certain, but unsettling in that the audience is supposed to be uplifted because an inhuman creature has decided what constitutes a moral human being and has slaughtered everyone else.

20,000 LEAGUES UNDER THE SEA (1907) (aka: 20,000 LIEUES SOUS LES MERS)

b&w, silent

Director: Georges Méliès

See *20,000 LEAGUES UNDER THE SEA* (1954)

20,000 LEAGUES UNDER THE SEA (1916)

Universal Film Manufacturing/Williamson Submarine Film, b&w, 105 min, silent, VT, DVD

Producers: Carl Laemmle and Stuart Patton; **Director:** Patton; **Screenplay:** Patton; **Cinematography:** Eugene Gaudio; **Cast:** Lois Alexander, Curtis Benson, Wallace Clarke, Howard Crampton, Jane Gail, Joseph W. Girard, Dan Hanlon, Allen Holubar, Ole Jansen, Leviticus Jones, Matt Moore, Martin Murphy, Edna Pendelton, William Welsh

See *20,000 LEAGUES UNDER THE SEA* (1954)

20,000 LEAGUES UNDER THE SEA (1954)

Buena Vista, 1954, Color, 127 min, VT, LD

Producer: Walt Disney; **Director:** Richard Fleischer; **Screenplay:** Earl Fenton; **Music:** Paul Smith; **Special Effects:** John Hench, Josh Meador, Ub Iwerks, John Meeham, Peter Ellenshaw, and Bob Mattey; **Cinematography:** Ralph Hammeras and Till Gabbani; **Cast:** James Mason, Kirk Douglas, Peter Lorre, Paul Lukas, Robert J. Wilke, Carleton Young

The film takes place in the mid-1800s, beginning in a seaport where commerce is grinding to a standstill. A monster is on the loose, one that's destroying warships and any shipping involved with munitions or troop movement. Defying the stories of sea serpents, a ship leaves port with three unique characters—Professor Aronnax (Lukas) and his assistant, Conseil (Lorre), who want to find the legendary beast, and harpoonist Ned Land (Douglas) who professes to know no fear of the thing, trusting to his harpoon to send it to the bottom of the sea.

It isn't long, of course, before their vessel is attacked by the creature, and the three find themselves dumped in the drink. Then something unexpected happens. They are rescued by sailors coming from the bowels of the creature itself. The beast turns out to be an amazingly advanced type of submarine, the creation of a mad genius named Captain Nemo (Mason). The captain's family was murdered by warmongers, a loss from which the good man has never recovered. And so he has become an avenger—one determined to rid the world of war by murdering every single person who dares to practice it or even considers becoming involved with it. Nemo tells the trio they will not be harmed, but that they will never be allowed to leave his fabulous ship, the *Nautilus*. They agree, and their 20,000-league underwater journey with Captain Nemo begins.

Most of the movie shows visits to exotic locales, struggles waged against great sea beasts, and battles against warships. Interspersed are cerebral moments wherein the three captives argue about what they should do and why. Ned wants to escape. He also wouldn't mind sending Nemo and his ship to the bottom of the sea. Conseil pretty much agrees with Ned, although he wouldn't mind stealing some of the incredible wealth Nemo has salvaged from the ocean's bottom when they make their escape. Aronnax wants to discover Nemo's secrets and convert the poor, tortured genius to the idea of working for the good of humanity.

Nemo, however, wants to convert Aronnax to his way of thinking. If he could sway the peaceful man of science to his point of view, it would be his greatest victory—justification beyond all reason for his crusade. Ultimately, the film centers on Ned and Nemo's battle of wills—both men desiring to bring Aronnax around to his own way of thinking—the psychological triumph each needs to justify his own viewpoint.

Eventually, the captain is done in by Ned. The harpoonist keeps stealing bottles, throwing messages overboard that explain what the "creature" is, as well as giving the location of Nemo's home base. At the climax, Nemo returns to his secret port to find a vast fleet waiting for him. Aronnax is frustrated, for he was on the verge of getting Nemo to reveal his secrets. The professor refuses to leave the submarine, even when the *Nautilus* begins to take on water, forcing Ned to knock him out and carry him off to safety. Once the adventurers are safely away, the submarine explodes, generating a huge mushroom cloud. Seeing the awesome power that has now been denied to humankind, Aronnax seems to come around to the harpoonist's way of thinking, telling him, "Perhaps you did mankind a service, Ned."

This cinematic version wasn't the only one to change Verne's story. In 1907, the innovative genius Georges Méliès retells the classic as a fisherman's dream, adding mermaids and sea nymphs to the mix. In 1916, Universal produced a black-and-white, silent feature version of the novel, wherein Nemo was visualized as the Indian Prince Dakkar, who actually manages to rescue his daughter from the slaughter Verne and even Walt Disney saw fit to inflict upon her. No matter what merits the others may have, the Disney version is the one people remember and for good reason.

One of the Disney studio's first live-action films, the astounding (at the time) budget of $5 million was poured into the production to make it a thing to remember. The ploy worked—the critics loved the film, box office was excellent, and the feature took its share of awards, including the Oscar for special effects. The story is changed somewhat from the novel, but most of the alterations are intelligent or necessary. For instance, Nemo's conquest of the South Pole is eliminated from the movie. This was a mind-boggling notion to the French sci-fi readers of 1866, but nothing that would be much noted by the 1954 audience when the pole had already been conquered in reality.

All in all, the film is a stellar achievement. The cast is serious and professional. The script enhances the story for once, despite the changes from the novel. The production values are adequate to convince the audience that the period is genuine, and the special effects are the best money could buy at the time. Indeed, the design of Nemo's vessel (created by the film's art director John Meeham) is now ingrained on the world's consciousness. Someone may come along and do a better version of this story—one of the first hard science fiction novels ever written—but for now, Walt Disney's *20,000 Leagues Under the Sea* is the hands-down winner.

Note: The very first known cinematic version of *20,000 Leagues Under the Sea* is an 18-minute, black-and-white silent made by American Biograph in 1905. By all accounts, this film stuck closely to Verne's novel.

20,000 LEAGUES UNDER THE SEA; OR, A FISHERMAN'S NIGHTMARE

See *20,000 LEAGUES UNDER THE SEA* (1954)

TWILIGHT PEOPLE, THE (aka: BEASTS, ISLAND OF THE TWILIGHT PEOPLE)

Dimension, 1972, Color, 84 min, VT

Producers: John Ashley and Eddie Romero; **Director:** Romero; **Screenplay:** Romero and Jerome Small; **Music:** Ariston Avelino and Tito Arevalo; **Special Effects:** Richard Abelardo; **Cinematography:** Fred Conde; **Cast:** John Ashley, Pat Woodell, Jan Merlin, Pam Grier, Charles Macauley, Ken Metcalfe, Tony Gonsalvez, Eddie Garcia

A scientist and former Nazi SS butcher hides on a South Seas island, where he creates mutants, à la *THE ISLAND OF DR. MOREAU.*

TWILIGHT'S LAST GLEAMING (aka: DAS ULTIMATUM, NUCLEAR COUNTDOWN)

Geria Productions (Germany)/Warner Bros. (U.S.), 1977, Color, 146 min, VT, LD

Producer: Merv Adelson; **Director:** Robert Aldrich; **Screenplay:** Ronald M. Cohen and Edward Huebsch; **Music:** Jerry Goldsmith; **Special Effects:** Henry Millar and Willy Neuner; **Cinematography:** Robert B. Hauser; **Cast:** Burt Lancaster, Richard Widmark, Charles Durning, Melvyn Douglas, Paul Winfield, Burt Young, Joseph Cotten, Roscoe Lee Browne, Vera Miles, Gerald S. O'Loughlin, Richard Jaeckel, Leif Erickson, Charles McGraw, John Ratzenberger

A possibly unstable air force general (Lancaster) seizes control of a nuclear missile base with the help of a few loyal friends. Their goal is to force the Pentagon to reveal the truth behind what the United States military machine was really doing in Vietnam, and they're threatening to start World War III if their demands aren't met. The general wants the world to know why his son had to die in Vietnam—because a group of desk-jockeys decided that the Communists had to be shown that America was not afraid to throw away thousands of lives just to prove a point. The world comes to as bad an ending as his son.

Unfortunately, not too many Americans have ever gotten to see this movie as it was intended to be seen. At the last minute the movie's American distributor cut over 20 minutes. They claimed the picture had to "move faster." Evidently, the scenes cut were also those that reveal what the Pentagon was supposedly up to. In the original version the Pentagon deliberately provokes America's entry into the Vietnam conflict so it can prove to the country's true foes that America isn't soft, and that the leaders were more than willing to send thousands to their deaths. Thus, in the original version, Lancaster comes off as a tragic hero, whereas in the truncated version, he seems like a madman.

Note: The secret policy mentioned in the film is based on a work published in 1957, *Nuclear Weapons and Foreign Policy*, written by Henry Kissinger.

TWILIGHT ZONE—THE MOVIE

Warner Bros., 1983, Color, 102 min, VT, LD

Producers: Jon Davidson, Kathleen Kennedy, John Landis, Frank Marshall, Steven Spielberg, Michael Finnell, and George Folsey, Jr.; **Directors:** Spielberg, Landis, Joe Dante, and George Miller; **Screenplay:** George Clayton Johnson, Rod Serling, Landis, Jerome Bixby, John Rogan, and Richard Matheson; **Music:** Jerry Goldsmith; **Special Effects:** David Allen, Kevin Pike, Sally Cruikshank, Rocco Gioffre, Dream Quest Images, Visual Concepts Engineering, and Effects Associate, Ltd.; **Cinematography:** Allen Daviau, John Hora, and Stevan Larner; **Cast:** Vic Morrow, Scatman Crothers, Bill Quinn, Selma Diamond, Kathleen Quinlan, Jeremy Licht, Kevin McCarthy, William Schallert, John Lithgow, Abbe Lane, Bill Mumy, John Larroquette, Burgess Meredith, Dan Aykroyd, Albert Brooks

Four directors, all too young to have directed when it was on the air, take a crack at doing an episode of *Twilight Zone* for a feature version of the old television show. Three of these modern visionaries simply remade old episodes of the show, and one tried something new.

The first segment, which tells the story of a racist stranded with the tables turned in Nazi Germany (Landis), is the only new one. The premise was promising, but its star (Morrow) was killed during filming and the segment had to be finished without him, severely handicapping its effectiveness. The middle two segments from Spielberg and Dante present a group of senior citizens restored to youth through a game of Kick the Can and a child with the power to make anything he imagined real. Only the last segment, a remake of the classic episode "Nightmare at 20,000 Feet" by Miller, holds any real tension or scares, but even it doesn't hold up that well when compared with the original. Dan Aykroyd and Albert

Brooks are featured in a prologue that introduces the movie and sets the film up well, but nothing that follows lives up to what the opening promises.

TWINS

Universal, 1988, Color, 112 min, VT, LD, DVD

Producers: Michael C. Gross, Gordon A. Webb, Sheldon Kahn, Ivan Reitman, and Joe Medjuck; **Director:** Reitman; **Screenplay:** William Davies and William Osborne; **Music:** Randy Edelman and Georges Delerue; **Special Effects:** Donald Elliott and Michael Lantieri; **Cinematography:** Andrzej Bartkowiak; **Cast:** Arnold Schwarzenegger, Danny DeVito, Kelly Preston, Chloe Webb, Bonnie Bartlett, Marshall Bell, Trey Wilson, Hugh O'Brian, Nehemiah Persoff, David Caruso

A few decades before the film begins, some scientists talked a world-renowned artist into becoming pregnant for science. Filling her with genetically enhanced sperm, they created the superbaby—Arnold Schwarzenegger—handsome, athletic, and brilliant. Surprise, though, they also created his twin (DeVito), a dwarf they unceremoniously threw to the wolves when he didn't fulfill their dreams of perfection. As adults, the boys spend the movie finding each other and then tracking down their mother, who knows nothing of them.

TWISTED BRAIN (aka: HORROR HIGH)

Crown International, 1974, Color, 85 min, VT

Producer: James P. Graham; **Director:** Larry Stouffer; **Screenplay:** Jake Fowler; **Cast:** Pat Cardi, Rosie Holotik, John Niland, Austin Stoker, Joye Hash

See DR. JEKYLL AND MR. HYDE; HORROR HIGH

TWO FACES OF DR. JEKYLL, THE

See HOUSE OF FRIGHT

TWO LOST WORLDS

Sterling Productions, Inc., 1950, Color, 61 min, VT, DVD

Producer: Boris Petroff; **Director:** Norman Dawn; **Screenplay:** Petroff, Bill Shaw, Tom Hubbard, and Phyllis Parker; **Music:** Alex Alexander; **Special Effects:** Harry Ross, Jack R. Glass, and Roy Seawright; **Cine-**matography: Harry Newman; **Cast:** James Arness, Laura Elliot, Bill Kennedy, Gloria Petroff

Shipwrecked castaways are trying to reach land. However, when they finally do reach land (in the last 20 minutes of the movie), they enter into a strange world populated with film clips from ONE MILLION B.C.

TWONKY, THE

United Artists, 1953, b&w, 72 min, VT, DVD

Producer: Arch Oboler; **Director:** Oboler; **Screenplay:** Oboler; **Music:** Jack Meakin; **Special Effects:** Robert Bonnig, Harry D. Mills, and Gus Bryz; **Cinematography:** Joseph F. Biroc; **Cast:** Hans Conreid, Janet Warren, Al Jarvis, Ed Max, Gloria Blondell, Bill Lynn, Trilby Conreid

An alien force from the future returns to its past/our present where it invades and then animates a television set. The set's owner, Terry (Hans Conreid), is delighted at first as the set talks to him, obeys his commands, and even begins doing housework. Soon, however, the set takes dictatorial control of Terry's life, hypnotizing anyone who gets in its way. The film is based on a far superior short story written by pulp-era master Henry Kuttner. The original was about a possessed radio/phonograph combination, and it made a bit more sense.

2001: A SPACE ODYSSEY

MGM, 1968, Color, 141 min, VT, LD, DVD

Producer: Stanley Kubrick; **Director:** Kubrick; **Screenplay:** Arthur C. Clarke and Kubrick; **Music:** Richard Strauss, Johann Strauss, Gyorgy Ligeti, and Aram Khachaturian; **Special Effects:** Douglas Trumbull, John Hoelsi, Kubrick, Wally Veevers, Con Pederson, Tom Howard, Colin Cantwell, Fred Martin, Stuart Freeborn, Tony Masters, David Osborne, Bryan Loftus, Bruce Logan, and John Malick; **Cinematography:** Geoffrey Unsworth and John Alcott; **Cast:** Keir Dullea, William Sylvester, Gary Lockwood, Daniel Richter, Douglas Rain, Leonard Rossiter

An alien force (to whom the audience is never introduced throughout the picture) places a massive, rectangular black monolith on prehistoric Earth in the midst of a tribe of humanoid ape creatures. After touching the structure, the creatures begin to show evidence of higher thought processes. They learn how to use tools to destroy all of their neighbors.

2001: A Space Odyssey (MGM / R. ALLEN LEIDER COLLECTION)

The scene of prehistoric slaughter cuts to a commercial flight to the Moon in the year 2001. A monolith exactly like the one seen earlier has been discovered on the Moon. When examined, the monolith releases a signal aimed at Jupiter. An expedition is sent to investigate. Along the way, the artificial intelligence in charge of the ship's computer, known as HAL, develops a paranoid delusion that the crew is plotting against it. One by one it murders everyone onboard until only one astronaut, David Bowman (Dullea), is left alive. Bowman disconnects HAL and proceeds onward.

Shortly thereafter, the aliens take control of Bowman's ship and guide it somewhere. Do they move it forward? Toward them? Through time? There is no answer within the framework of the movie. From here until the end of the film, nothing is shown but a series of images meant to present a sort of mystical sci-fi journey of transformation. Bowman's trip through space is the surface of the scene. As he watches himself age and die, only to be reborn as an embryonic baby floating in space, the audience is supposed to get the sense of another journey—but exactly what kind of journey, or which one, is left up to them.

Commenting on the meaning is pointless, for there is no one meaning. Director Kubrick said repeatedly during his lifetime that *2001* was meant to be "a nonverbal experience." Arthur C. Clarke stated that "if you understand *2001* completely, we failed. We wanted to raise far more questions than we answered." The film is based upon Clarke's short story "The Sentinel," which covers what happens on the screen only until the signal is sent to Jupiter. As Clarke worked on expanding his original story into a novel, Kubrick worked on his screenplay. The two stayed in close contact, reporting their progress to each other and changing their work to accommodate whoever was headed in the best direction.

When asked about the ending, Clarke gave his explanation from the novel. When asked if a completely different interpretation might be reasonable, he thought for a moment, his face an open book, which indicated that he had never thought of such a possibility. Honestly, he admitted so, saying that the film must be open to even more interpretations than he had originally thought, an idea that pleased him no end. Thus, there are no explanations for the ending. Ultimately, the viewer is left to his or her own devices.

Hitting theaters at the height of the '60s drug culture, audiences tripping on acid were ready to give the movie wild raves. Art theater critics gushed over its free form and open structure, praising its involvement of the audience. Other critics, pretending to know what its unintelligible ending meant, jumped aboard to make the film the sci-fi headliner of the decade. Those not afraid to say that emperor was in his boxers condemned the movie as tripe and a fraud. In truth, both sides are correct. Those of a mind to sit back and be moved will find all they want in the film. Those who want to understand the experience will find no satisfaction here.

2001: A Space Oddysey (MGM / R. ALLEN LEIDER COLLECTION)

2001: A Space Odyssey was meant to be vague, and it succeeds. No doubt it is a stunning achievement, utilizing silent era effects, such as producing a hand-drawn matte for each frame of an effects shot, to achieve a look unrivaled by any science fiction film before and few since. It turned up the heat, bringing long-awaited legitimacy to the genre and raising the bar to a magnificent level for all to follow.

Paradoxically, the main problem for those who dislike the film is the same thing that makes it so transcendent. Sixteen years later, Peter Hyams (acting as producer, director, screenwriter, and cinematographer) brought *2010*, Arthur C. Clarke's first sequel to *2001*, to the screen. Far less mystical, the story tells of a second ship (a joint Russian/American expedition) being sent out to Jupiter to discover what happened to the first ship. The movie attempts to fill in the blanks and does so to a remarkable degree.

Again, audiences were split. Those who loved the visual free-form experience of *2001* were disappointed by the sequel's more literal approach. Those who hated the open-ended vagueness of the first applauded *2010* for finally setting the story straight. The sequel has the added bonus of being scientifically accurate. Its sci-fi content is as solid as the first's is speculative.

However, no matter what side of the argument one upholds, Kubrick's overwhelming attention to detail and enthusiasm for bringing a completely new sense of slickness to *2001*'s special effects revolutionized the way science fiction films were perceived by both Hollywood and the public. No matter what faults the film's worst critics might find, the movie is clearly pivotal in the genre's struggle for serious acceptance. Although the groundwork was laid out in the '50s by films of superior storytelling, such as THE DAY THE EARTH STOOD STILL, FORBIDDEN PLANET, THEM, and others, it took Kubrick's visuals to propel the public into total acceptance of science fiction as a legitimate artform.

Note: Many have noted that by incrementing the letters of the name of the insane computer—HAL—forward a single character, one arrives at IBM. Many see Clarke's finger pointed at IBM. Clarke swears the naming was completely accidental and that if he had noticed it himself, he would have changed it before the movie or novel were released.

2010 (aka: 2010: THE YEAR WE MAKE CONTACT)

MGM, 1984, Color, 116 min, VT, LD, DVD

Producers: Peter Hyams, Neil A. Machlis, and Jonathan A. Zimbert; **Director:** Hyams; **Screenplay:** Hyams; **Music:** David Shire; **Special Effects:** David Blitstein, Richard Edlund, John V. Fante; **Cinematography:** Hyams; **Cast:** Roy Scheider, John Lithgow, Helen Mirren, Bob Balaban, Keir Dullea, Douglas Rain, Madelyne Smith-Osborne, Arthur C. Clarke

See *2001: A SPACE ODDYSEY*

TWO YEAR'S HOLIDAY

See *THE STOLEN AIRSHIP*

TWO YEAR VACATION

See *THE STOLEN AIRSHIP*

UCHU DAIKAIJÛ GIRARA

See *THE X FROM OUTER SPACE*

UFO (aka: UFO: UNIDENTIFIED FLYING OBJECTS, UNIDENTIFIED FLYING OBJECTS, UNIDENTIFIED FLYING OBJECTS: THE TRUE STORY OF FLYING SAUCERS)

United Artists, 1956, b&w/Color, 92 min, VT

Producers: Ivan Tors and Clarence Green; **Director:** Winston Jones; **Screenplay:** Francis Martin; **Music:** Ernest Gold; **Cinematography:** Howard Anderson, Bert Spielvogel, and Ed Fitzgerald; **Cast:** Tom Powers

Tom Powers narrates this first ever documentary of purported actual flying saucer footage. Filmed in black-and-white with some color footage, the film is dry, slow-moving, and poorly edited, and film quality in many segments of the picture is so poor that it's often difficult to decide what exactly in a particular shot is the UFO in question. The movie will not make a believer out of anyone but might help some insomniacs.

Television routinely did a better job of presenting such things throughout the 1980s and '90s. Still, for the '50s, the movie attempted to put this kind of material before the public. Of course, it was also an obvious attempt to cash in on a craze, but considering

official governmental hostility toward taking UFOs seriously, making this one could be considered an act of courage.

UFO INCIDENT, THE

Universal, 1975, Color, 100 min

Director: Richard A. Colla; **Screenplay:** Jake Justiz, S. Lee Pogostin, and Hesper Anderson; **Music:** Billy Goldenberg; **Cinematography:** Rexford L. Metz; **Cast:** James Earl Jones, Estelle Parsons, Barnard Hughes, Beeson Carroll, Dick O'Neill, Terrence O'Conner

This movie is based on a true story. In 1961 an interracial couple (Jones and Parsons) began to have troubles, the source of which they could not identify. They were both plagued by nightmares and terrible feelings of extreme, debilitating anxiety. Their problems drove them to a local psychiatrist, and they discovered under hypnosis that one night while out for a drive they had been abducted by extraterrestrials. The pair had been taken aboard an alien vessel and examined for roughly two hours—a period they had never been able to account for.

The movie is extremely talky, but that's the nature of the story. It's a true tale, documented in the news, the subject of a popular novel, *The Interrupted Journey*, and finally this film. It's the subject matter you watch this one for—not the special effects. This is not to say that it's a dull film, however. Jones, Hughes (as the examining doctor), and Parsons all do tremendously convincing jobs.

UFORIA

MCA, 1980, Color, 100 min, VT

Producers: Jeanne Field, Melvin Simon, Barry Krost, Gordon Wolf, and Susan Spinks; **Director:** John Binder; **Screenplay:** Binder; **Music:** Richard Baskin; **Special Effects:** Chuck Comisky; **Cinematography:** David Meyers; **Cast:** Cindy Williams, Fred Ward, Harry Dean Stanton, Harry Carey, Jr., Beverly Hope Atkinson

Grocery clerk Williams gets it into her head that she's been chosen by beings from outer space to lead the best of Earth to safety a la Noah's Ark. There's a reason this movie was unreleased for over half a decade, and it's a good one.

UFO: UNIDENTIFIED FLYING OBJECTS

See *UFO*

ULTIMATE WARRIOR, THE

Warner Bros., 1974, Color, 92 min, VT

Producers: Fred Weintraub and Paul Heller; **Director:** Robert Clouse; **Screenplay:** Clouse; **Music:** Gil Melle; **Special Effects:** Gene Riggs and Walter Simonds; **Cinematography:** Gerald Hirschfeld; **Cast:** Yul Brynner, Max von Sydow, Joanne Miles, William Smith, Richard Kelton, Stephen McHattie, Lane Bradbury

An unidentified biological disaster of epic proportions leaves the world in utter ruin. Humankind has been reduced to small tribes of parasites living off the decay of the past. This struggle for survival takes place in New York City. Predictably a stern but loving dictator keeps his charges alive as best he can in a secure fortress, while a wild killing-machine villain and his berserk followers wait outside the gates, constantly probing for weaknesses. Inside the compound, the Boss (von Sydow) is worried. His most prized man has succeeded in getting crops to produce seeds, but the Boss's daughter is pregnant and he is desperately worried about her baby. The Boss knows it's only a matter of time before the thugs outside breach the compound, but he has no idea what he can do to safeguard his daughter and grandchild.

Yul Brynner is the title character, who sides with the Boss because the Boss has cigars. A number of routine clashes follow, and then finally the Boss shows Brynner a secure escape through the tunnels that run under the city. He gives his warrior the seeds so far produced and charges him to get his family to a place of safety—an island that Brynner believes is still lush.

While Brynner is leading the Boss's daughter through the tunnels (eventually delivering her baby there as well), the bad guys invade the compound, kill everyone, and then track the ultimate warrior through the tunnels. He kills them all and then has a protracted battle with their leader, which ends with the villain hanging over a long drop, his hand caught in a tangle of rope with Brynner's. From his position, Brynner can't cut the rope, so he does the next best thing and cuts off his own arm, letting the bad guy drop to his death. Then he and the mother and her recently born baby head off for the island.

The sci-fi content in this fairly boring, uninterestingly shot film is contained solely within the notion of the devastated future and the scramble to get crops growing again. Neither side in the struggle seems much more noble than the other. *The Ultimate Warrior* is noteworthy only for being the first sci-fi/kung fu film, and the forerunner of many films, most notably THE ROAD WARRIOR.

ULTIMATUM, DAS

See *TWILIGHT'S LAST GLEAMING*

UNDEAD, THE

AIP, 1957, b&w, 75 min, VT

Producer: Samuel Z. Arkoff; **Director:** Roger Corman; **Screenplay:** Mark Hanna and Charles B. Griffith; **Music:** Ronald Stein; **Special Effects:** Curly Batson; **Cinematography:** William A. Sickner; **Cast:** Richard Garland, Pamela Duncan, Richard Devon, Allison Hayes, Mel Welles, Billy Barty, Bruno VeSota

Yet another wacky scientist—this one is working hard to discover the secrets of reincarnation—manages to send himself back to the Middle Ages. The movie's not bad, especially for an early Corman effort. The clever ending really helps, but it's still not a gem (even one in the rough) by any means.

UNDERSEA KINGDOM

Republic, 1936, b&w serial, 12 chapters

Producer: Nat Levine; Directors: Breezy Eason and Joseph Kane; Screenplay: J. Rathmell, Maurice Geraghty, and Oliver Drake; Music: Harry Grey; Special Effects: John T. Coyle, Howard Lydecker, and Theodore Lydecker; Cinematography: William Nobles and Edgar Lyons; Cast: William Farnum, Monte Blue, C. Montague Shaw, Booth Howard, Lon Chaney, Jr., Lois Wilde, Jack Mullhall, Crash Corrigan, Lee Van Atta, Lane Chandler, David Horsley, Frankie Marvin, Smiley Burnette

Once again the Atlantians are trying to take over the world. There's a power struggle between the Sharad and Unga Khan, who conveniently have dressed their followers in all-white and all-black for the audience's ease of identification, and Khan is trying to take over North America. The bad guys invent several nasty weapons, surface-dwelling scientists invent several antinasty defenses, and the whole mess goes on far too long until Atlantis is finally destroyed—twice. Whit Bissell, Ray Harryhausen, and a cameo by God couldn't even have helped this insanity.

UNDERWATER CITY, THE

Columbia, 1962, Color, 78 min

Producer: Alex Gordon; Director: Frank McDonald; Screenplay: Owen Harris; Music: Ronald Stein; Special Effects: Howard Lydecker and Howard A. Anderson; Cinematography: Gordon Avil; Cast: Julie Adams, William Lundigan, Chet Douglas, Paul Dubov, Roy Roberts, Carl Benton Reid

Scientists dread the end of the world, which they fear is right around the corner because of their suspicion that politicians won't be able to keep from blowing up everyone in a plutonium-fueled holocaust. The scientists decide to save themselves by building the ultimate fallout shelter on the bottom of the ocean. An earthquake on the seafloor ruins their plans, while the politicians all stay comfortable, dry, and unradiated on the surface. Shot in color, the film was then released in black-and-white for some unknown reason. Worse yet, all the underwater scenes were obviously filmed on a soundstage through a fish tank.

UNDERWATER ODYSSEY, AN

See *THE NEPTUNE FACTOR*

UNDERWORLD
(aka: TRANSMUTATIONS)

Alpine/Green Man Productions/Limegreen (Great Britain), 1985, Color, 100 min, VT

Producers: Kevin Attew, Don Hawkins, Graham Ford, and Al Burgess; Director: George Pavlou; Screenplay: Clive Barker and James Caplin; Music: Freur; Special Effects: Malcolm King; Cinematography: Sydney Macartney; Cast: Denholm Elliot, Larry Lamb, Steven Berkoff, Miranda Richardson, Art Malik, Nicola Cowper, Ingrid Pitt

Mutants living underground kidnap a beautiful hostage to force the surface world to give them the drugs they need to stay alive. Instead, the surface world sends a killer to settle the matter.

UNEARTHLY, THE

Republic, 1957, b&w, 73 min, VT

Producer: Brooke L. Peters; Director: Peters; Screenplay: Geoffrey Dennis and Jane Mann; Music: Henry Vars and Michael Terr; Special Effects: Harry Thomas and Morton Tubor; Cinematography: W. Merle Connell; Cast: John Carradine, Allison Hayes, Tor Johnson, Myron Healey, Sally Todd

A misguided scientist with good intentions wants to bless his patients with immortality. And, who knows, those he operates on might actually be immortal. What they definitely are, however, once he gets done with them, is mutant plug-ugly.

UNEARTHLY STRANGER, THE

AIP, 1964, b&w, 72 min

Producer: Albert Fennell; Director: John Krish; Screenplay: Rex Carlton; Music: Edward Williams; Cinematography: Reg Wyer; Cast: John Neville, Philip Stone, Gabriella Licudi

A man discovers that his wife is an alien. He panics, but when his alien wife dies, the panic goes away. If only it would take all prints of this film with it.

UNFORGETTABLE

MGM, 1996, Color, 111 min, VT, LD

Producers: Rick Dahl, Dino De Laurentiis, Martha De Laurentiis, Andrew Lazar, William Teitler, and Lucio Trentini; **Director:** John Dahl; **Screenplay:** Bill Geddie; **Music:** Christopher Young; **Special Effects:** Barry Kootchin; **Cinematography:** Jeff Jur; **Cast:** Ray Liotta, Peter Coyote, Linda Fiorentino, Duncan Fraser, Christopher McDonald, Kim Cattrall, Kim Coates, David Paymer, Caroline Elliott

A police scientist is accused of murdering his wife. The problem for the police is that he honestly can't remember a thing. The problem for the scientist is that he honestly loved his wife and would do anything to remember what actually happened. Into his life comes a beautiful scientist who may have just the ticket, instantaneous memory transferral through injections. Our scientist immediately begins a series of treatments. A good, solid idea is tortured to death, at least as far as sci-fi is concerned.

UNIDENTIFIED FLYING OBJECTS

See *UFO*

UNIDENTIFIED FLYING OBJECTS: THE TRUE STORY OF FLYING SAUCERS

See *UFO*

UNIDENTIFIED FLYING ODDBALL (aka: A SPACEMAN IN KING ARTHUR'S COURT)

Walt Disney Studios, 1979, Color, 93 min, VT

Producer: Ron Miller; **Director:** Russ Mayberry; **Screenplay:** Don Tait; **Music:** Ron Goodwin; **Special Effects:** Cliff Culley and Albert Whitlock; **Cinematography:** Paul Beeson; **Cast:** Dennis Dugan, Tom Dale, Ron Moody, Kenneth Moore, Sheila White, John LeMesurier, Rodney Bewes, Robert Beatty, Cyril Shaps

Astronaut Tom Trimble (Dugan), along with his robotic look-alike, is running a routine space mission when his orbiter slips into a time warp, and, faster than you can say Mark Twain, he suddenly finds himself back in the court of King Arthur. Trimble uses NASA technology to help Arthur keep his kingdom.

UNIVERSAL SOLDIER

Carolco/Centropolis Film Production/IndieProd, 1992, Color, 104 min, VT, LD, DVD

Producers: Craig Baumgarten, Joel B. Michaels, Allen Shapiro, Donald Heitzer, Oliver Eberle, and Mario Kazzar; **Director:** Roland Emmerich; **Screenplay:** Dean Devlin, Richard Rothstein, and Christopher Leitch; **Music:** Christopher Franke; **Special Effects:** Volker Engel, Steve Bress, and Matt Kutcher; **Cinematography:** Karl Walter Lindenlaub; **Cast:** Jean-Claude Van Damme, Dolph Lundgren, Ally Walker, Ed O'Ross, Leon Rippy, Tico Wells, Ralph Moeller, Jerry Orbach

During the Vietnam War a group of scientists started freezing mortally wounded soldiers so that decades later (when medical technology would be more advanced) they could repair and upgrade these men and then use them as ultimate killing machines. Son of a gun, it worked—sort of. The problem is two of the soldiers (Van Damme and Lundgren) begin to have flashback memories. Since they were wounded trying to kill each other, they naturally pick up where they left off and start all over again. Lundgren had snapped in the heat of battle and was ordering the slaughter of civilians. Van Damme was trying to stop him.

This routine action film offers better than average logic and motivation but is short on sci-fi or on anything new or interesting. It does have a good sound track, good effects, and even some good science. Not bad, just nothing special. This one was followed by *Universal Soldier II: The Return* as well as two made-for-cable sequels. Don't expect any improvement on the original.

UNIVERSAL SOLDIER II: THE RETURN

Baumgarten Prophet Entertainment, IndieProd, Long Road Entertainment, 1999, color, 82 min, VT, DVD

Producers: Craig Baumgarten, Daniel Melnick, Adam Merins, Richard G. Murphy, Michael I. Rachmil, Allen Shapiro, Bennett R. Specter, Jean-Claude Van Damme; **Director:** Mic Rodgers; **Screenplay:** William Malone and John Fasano; **Music:** Don Davis; **Cinematography:** Michael A. Benson; **Special Effects:** Robert Morgenroth, Paul R. LeBlanc, Gary Hall, Brett Cody, Rick Bongiovanni; **Cast:** Jean-Claude Van Damme, Michael Jai White, Heidi Schanze, Xander Berkeley, Justin Lazard, Kiana Tom, Daniel von Bargen, James Black, Karis Paige Bryant, Bill Goldberg

See *UNIVERSAL SOLDIER*

UNKNOWN ISLAND

Albert J. Cohen Productions, 1948, b&w, 64 min, VT, DVD

Producer: Albert J. Cohen; **Director:** Jack Bernhard; **Screenplay:** Jack Harvey and Robert T. Shannon; **Music:** Ralph Stanley; **Special Effects:** Howard A. Anderson, Harry Ross, and Ellis Burman; **Cinematography:** Fred Jackman, Jr.; **Cast:** Virginia Grey, Philip Reed, Richard Denning, Barton MacLane

A group of scientists too dull and plodding to be mad head for an island to search for dinosaurs. They discover some halfway decent special effects, but nothing very memorable or entertaining.

UNKNOWN SATELLITE OVER TOKYO

See *WARNING FROM SPACE*

UNKNOWN TERROR

20th Century Fox, 1957, b&w, 77 min, VT

Producer: Robert Stabler; **Director:** Charles Marquis Warren; **Screenplay:** Kenneth Higgins; **Music:** Raoul Kraushaar; **Special Effects:** Glenn Alden, Louis DeWitt, and Jack Rabin; **Cinematography:** Joseph Biroc; **Cast:** John Howard, Charles Gray, May Wynn, Mala Powers, Paul Richards, Sir Lancelot

An evil, wacky scientist heads for some really bad sets that the audience is told are really places in South America. Why? So that he can produce a killer fungus (one that looks remarkably like soap suds) with which he can rule the world.

UNKNOWN PURPLE, THE

Truart, 1923, b&w, silent feature

Producer: Roland West; **Director:** West; **Screenplay:** West and Paul Schofield; **Cinematography:** Oliver T. Walsh; **Cast:** Henry B. Walthall, Johnny Arthur, Alice Lake, Frankie Lee, Dorthy Phillips

A wacky scientist (is there any other kind?) is finally released from prison. He was innocent of the charges he was sent away for, but the courts believed his evil wife and less-than-honest business partner, so he was convicted. Now that he's out, he heads back to his lab, douses himself with the purple light from his invisibility machine, and then heads off for a grand ol' round of revenge.

This movie is possibly the first instance of a later overused plot. It also has the added bonus of a wife who actually clashes with the scientist, something usually only in his mind in later versions. Adequate entertainment for its time, but little sci-fi content to speak of.

UNKNOWN WORLD (aka: TO THE CENTER OF THE EARTH)

Lippert, 1951, b&w, 74 min, VT

Producers: Jack Rabin and Irving Block; **Director:** Terrel O. Morse; **Screenplay:** Millard Kaufman; **Music:** Ernest Gold; **Special Effects:** Block, Kaufman, and Willis Cook; **Cinematography:** Harry Freulich and Allen G. Siegler; **Cast:** Victor Kilian, Bruce Kellogg, Marilyn Nash, Otto Waldis, George Baxter, Jim Bannon

A group of scientists decide the only way to save humanity from the ravages of an imminent atomic war is to burrow into the ground and look for a hiding place. Using the amazing Cyclotram, a massive earth borer, they head beneath Earth's surface and eventually discover some caves that would be just perfect . . . if they didn't leave everyone who lived in them sterile.

The sci-fi quotient in this unbelievably preachy film is pathetic, but the film is highly watchable, if for no other reason than to catch Marilyn Nash's memorable performance as the ice queen.

UNTIL THE END OF THE WORLD

Warner Bros., 1991, Color, 158 min, VT, LD

Producers: Paulo Branco, Jonathan T. Taplin, and Ulrich Felsberg; **Director:** Wim Wenders; **Screenplay:** Peter Carey; **Music:** Graeme Revell; **Special Effects:** Frank Schlegel; **Cinematography:** Robby Müller; **Cast:** John Hurt, Solveig Dommartin, Sam Neill, Max von Sydow, Jeanne Moreau, Rudiger Vogler, Ernie Dinog, Eddy Mitchell, Chick Ortega

This slow-moving tale of two humanitarians circling the globe so they can create a device that will give sight to the blind offers lots of great location scenes and lots more scenes that just drag on and on. Little sci-fi content.

UNNATURAL

See *ALRAUNE*

VALLEY OF GWANGI, THE

Warner Bros., 1969, Color, 95 min, VT, LD

Producers: Charles H. Schneer and Ray Harryhausen; **Director:** James O'Connolly; **Screenplay:** William E. Bast; **Music:** Jerome Moross; **Cinematography:** Erwin Hillier; **Special Effects:** Harryhausen; **Cast:** James Franciscus, Gila Golan, Richard Carlson, Laurence Naismith, Dennis Kilbane

In Mexico, sometime after the turn of the last century, performers from a struggling circus make an amazing discovery out in the desert—a tiny horse, fully formed but only a foot high. Naturally they capture it to make an attraction out of it, but there are problems. The horse is actually a Eohippus, a prehistoric ancestor to the modern horse. A professor supplies that bit of knowledge as well as an insight—living things don't spring full grown out of the air, so where there is one little horse, there must be more.

The inevitable question: Where are they and why hasn't anyone seen any of them before? It turns out that a local band of native nomads made it their life mission centuries earlier to protect the tiny horses as well as everything else in their valley from the outside world. When they steal the one found by the circus, intent on returning it to its secret home, the professor follows them in hopes of finding the mother lode.

What he finds is a valley filled with more than just Eohippi. Cut off from the world for the last 65 million years, the valley is a lost world—one overflowing with prehistoric creatures of all types, living blissfully unaware that outside the boundaries of their high-walled domain the mammals have taken over. The circus folk follow the professor, and soon everyone is running around in the Valley of Gwangi (the gypsy name for the *Tyrannosaurus rex* that rules the lost land), doing their best to capture one of the creatures. Before long, the tyrannosaurus is on its way back to the circus, where its presence will lead to disaster.

This is one of the finest, most seamless stop-frame animation films. It is filled with incredible sequences that boggle the mind when one tries to imagine how they were filmed. Today, of course, computers make everything come to life with apparent ease. But despite the marvels modern special effects devices can produce, there is something lost along the way. Just as American animation began to harden with lifeless similarity after the advent of the "Xerox process" first used in Disney's *One Hundred and One Dalmatians*, so too have special effects become boringly type of same now that morphing has become all too routine.

There is nothing routine about Ray Harryhausen dinosaurs, however, or the intricacy of their scenes. The high point of *Gwangi*, for instance, is a wonderful sequence in which a band of mounted riders attempt to lasso the tyrannosaurus. The scene goes on for quite some time, with ropes thrown over the dinosaur's head, neck, and even its upraised leg. There is never a split second where any of the lines seem stiff or posed. It is a masterful moment in sci-fi/fantasy cinema which—

due to the discovery of a number of easier techniques—sadly may never be rivaled.

The Valley of Gwangi was initially released when American critics were interested only in films with social relevance, hoary bromides that chastised the unenlightened masses toward socially acceptable behavior. It is disheartening to look back at reviews and see how this superior film was so universally ignored. Even those critics not caught up in the fads of the moment—social engineering, permissiveness, and such—concentrated on seeming mistakes in the film's plot.

For instance, the fauna of the valley includes pterodactyls, but no explanation is ever offered as to why no one ever saw one of them outside the valley. Why didn't one of them ever fly into town? The answer lies in the allegorical nature of the film. At the core of the movie is a warning against greed. The gypsies guard the valley, keeping people away from it. They understand that a fortune can be made from selling the creatures within, but they resist. To them the valley is the doorway to hell. The dinosaurs can't leave on their own. They have to be released by the greed of humans; evil must always be invited over the threshold of its victims. And once they are, there is no stopping them. Gypsies, gringos, and peasants are all fodder for the jaws of Gwangi once the monster is released. It's no accident that the beast is dispatched only when it is trapped within the walls of a cathedral. Interestingly, it is a building in a state of disrepair—a religion hanging on in a world turned upside down by modernism.

The Valley of Gwangi is most likely the finest of the humans-against-dinosaurs movies. Intelligently thought out (which eliminates most of its competition right there) and lavishly produced, it has a good solid cast, a competent back story filled with romantic complications and the misery humans make for one another, as well as a compelling script with a powerful sense of being about something bigger than it ever admits to out loud. The movie's science fiction is minimal in the light of more recent discoveries and theories about the end of the dinosaurs. However, the film makes good use of one of the best tools of the science fiction film, the thinking hero. Whichever way one chooses to view the science of the film, however, its entertainment value is top-notch, making *The Valley of Gwangi* highly recommended.

Note: If *Gwangi* sounds reminiscent of KING KONG, there's a good reason. Originally, the film was to have been an RKO feature. Willis O'Brien, the genius behind *Kong*, had scripts, production art, story boards, and even a half-dozen glass paintings ready for the film as early as 1942. Miniature dioramas were prepared, as well as a multijointed, stop-motion model of Gwangi. RKO abandoned the film, however, after more than a year of preproduction work so they could make *Little Orphan Annie* instead. If you're scratching your heads, just recall that RKO disappeared not too many years after they started making such wise decisions.

VALLEY OF THE DRAGONS, THE
(aka: PREHISTORIC VALLEY)

Columbia, 1961, b&w, 79 min

Producer: Byron Roberts; **Director:** Edward Bernds; **Screenplay:** Bernds; **Music:** Ruby Raskin; **Cinematography:** Brydon Baker; **Special Effects:** Dick Albain; **Cast:** Cesare Danova, Sean McClory, Gregg Martell, Joan Staley, Danielle De Metz, Roger Til

A comet sweeps too close to Earth and manages to sweep up a few 19th-century fellows, carrying them off as it has in the past. Amazed to be alive, the gents discover that the comet contains a rather large fragment of prehistoric Earth, one populated with cave people and plenty of film clips from the far superior ONE MILLION B.C. This film's advertisements declare it to be based on Jules Verne's *Off on a Comet*, which only proves that some copywriters don't do all their drinking at home.

VALLEY OF ZOMBIES, THE

Republic, 1946, b&w, 56 min

Producers: Dorrell McGowan, Stuart McGowan, and Sherman L. Lowe; **Director:** Philip Ford; **Screenplay:** Dorrell McGowan and Stuart McGowan; **Music:** Richard Cherwin; **Cinematography:** Reggie Lanning; **Special Effects:** Howard Lydecker and Theodore Lydecker; **Cast:** Robert Livingston, Adrian Booth, Ian Keith, Earle Hodings, Wilton Graff, Thomas Jackson, Leroy Mason

A scientist kills his fellow professionals in the scientific community. What makes this fellow unique? He's a dead man. At the end of the film, he's dead again, but also inanimate. Oddly enough, while he was reanimated, he wasn't a zombie, nor were there any zombies to be seen anywhere else in the film.

VAMPIRE MEN OF THE LOST PLANET

See *HORROR OF THE BLOOD MONSTERS*

VANISHING CORPSE, THE

See *REVENGE OF THE ZOMBIES*

VANISHING SHADOW, THE

Universal, 1934, b&w, serial, 12 chapters

Director: Louis Friedlander; **Screenplay:** Het Manheim, Basil Dickey, and George Morgan; **Music:** Edward Ward; **Cinematography:** Richard Fryer; **Cast:** Onslow Stevens, Walter Miller, James Durkin, Eddie Cobb, Ada Ince, Tom London Monte Montague, William Steele, Richard Cramer, Sidney Bracey

An avenging son pursues the corrupt politician who put his father in an early grave, using one strange invention after another to clean up the city and clear his father's name. Matters are complicated by the fact that his fiancée is the main villain's daughter.

Science fiction devices are invented rapid-fire in this sloppily concocted mess without the slightest thought of how invisibility, robots, and death rays could be possible or invented by one man or how they would impact the world. A truly interesting serial would have shown the avenger putting the crooks away with all his marvelous inventions and then being forced to watch the downfall of civilization as his good intentions destroy society when his devices are taken over by the world at large. The use of sci-fi hardware in films without giving any thought to the implications of their impact on civilization goes against all that makes science fiction so captivating and imaginative.

VARAN THE UNBELIEVABLE

Toho (Japan), 1958, 87 min/Crown International (U.S.), 70 min, b&w, VT

Producers: Tomoyuki Tanaka and Jerry A. Baerwitz; **Director:** Inoshiro Honda; **Screenplay:** Shinichi Sekizawa and Sid Harris; **Music:** Akira Ifukube; **Cinematography:** H. Koizumi and Jack Marquette; **Special Effects:** Eiji Tsuburaya and Howard Anderson; **Cast:** Myron Healy, Tsuruko Kobayashi, Kozo Nomura, Koreya Senda, Ayumi Sonoda

A Japanese saltwater lake gets the freshwater treatment. How could they be so stupid as to bring desalinization there? Didn't they know that would bring Varan, the Unbelievable out of his centuries of sleep and send him across the country crushing everything in sight?

VENGEANCE

See *THE BRAIN*

VENUSIAN, THE

See *IMMEDIATE DISASTER*

VIDEODROME

Universal, 1983, Color, 90 min, VT, DVD

Producer: Claude Heroux; **Director:** David Cronenberg; **Screenplay:** Cronenberg; **Music:** Howard Shore; **Special Effects:** Rick Baker; **Cinematography:** Mark Irwin; **Cast:** James Woods, Deborah Harry, Sonja Smits, Peter Dvorsky, Les Carlson, Jack Creley, Lynn Gorman

Max Renn (Woods) runs a cable television station that tends to pander to violent and pornographic tastes. One of his technicians stumbles upon a somewhat bizarre channel, Videodrome, which is broadcast for some unknown reason on a scrambled frequency. The show looks to be the answers to Max's prayers. The format of Videodrome is simple: A never-ending procession of disturbed and disturbing people are brought onto a static set to be tortured and sexually abused. The show may have low production values, but Max knows it will mean high ratings. That thought in mind, the desperate station manager sets out to track down Videodrome in the hopes of sewing up the rebroadcast rights.

There is, of course, a secret that Max quickly discovers. His lover, pop psychologist Nicki Brand (Harry), has also sought out the program. She hasn't done this to help Max, however, but to become one of the show's participants since she has a strong masochistic bent. Her presence is used to lure Max ever onward. Though Max thinks the station is trying to remain hidden from him, they really want him to find them because it's all part of their plan to rid the world of the people they hate the most—Max's audience.

The underlying themes in *Videodrome* are consistent with the themes in all of its director's films, which include *THEY CAME FROM WITHIN* (sentient venereal disease), *SCANNERS* (mutants created by drugs taken during pregnancy), *THE BROOD* (demons created through self-induced pregnancy), and *RABID* (a prostitute who sexually transmits rabies). Max Renn, for instance, is a character whose motives are constantly questioned because of the extreme nature of the material he presents to the public. As director David Cronenberg

Videodrome (UNIVERSAL CITY STUDIOS / AUTHOR'S COLLECTION)

acknowledged, "There are obvious parallels between me and Max, but he's not really me, although the similarities open up questions. The movie goes into more than the relatively simple issue of morality, like the way in which television does alter us physically. It's what Marshall McLuhan was talking about—TV as an extension of our nervous systems and our senses."

Indeed, *Videodrome* goes far beyond McLuhan's theories. The electronic waves over which the scrambled station is broadcast actually alter people physically, causing mutations and hallucinations. Because Cronenberg is famous for such scenes as the exploding head in *Scanners* and other moments of disturbing gore, many expected the same kind of excess from *Videodrome*. It wouldn't be a Cronenberg movie without explicitly traumatizing scenes, but this time around the special effects are not what the film is about.

"I deliberately *de*-emphasized those elements," the director said. "It's got a very seedy look to it, not high-tech at all. It's not an action picture, like *Scanners*. Like *The Brood*, it's a character study in the horror genre, although it does take a couple of extreme turns."

For Cronenberg, those "turns" take the form of confrontation, which he feels is the basis of horror. "A lot of people think of film as an escape," he said, "an escape to entertainment. But I think of horror films as art, as films of confrontation. I think of them as films that make you confront aspects of your own life that are difficult to face. In that way, horror's just like any other serious genre."

All this talk of art makes one think that *Videodrome* is supposed to be something more than simply a

shocker film, and that it is. As in so much of his work, Cronenberg is pointing up the dangers of letting too much of a dangerous substance into the body. This time it's television. Pandering to the lowest common denominator, to the weak, the stupid, the childish, and the unbalanced, the medium comes across here as a reckless source of titillation, pacifying the masses through overstimulation. TV is no longer a marvel or even entertainment; it's a flat and tasteless staple of life. But science fiction has always been a genre filled with prophesies, hasn't it?

For instance, when Max starts his quest, he obtains a gun. He can't use it properly, can't even manage to hold it correctly, nor he can tell the clip from its cleaning brush—but he has no problem killing with it later. Likewise, Nicki runs a radio program that tells people they need help and how to get it. She, however, is a violence freak destined to end up the victim of her own unnatural cravings. Even the folks running the Videodrome can't explain how it works, although they have no trouble using it to their own ends. That seems to be the point of the film.

It was once thought that television would usher in a bold new era of man's exploration of learning—a golden era that would reveal all the glorious wonders of humankind's history, science, and arts. As we now know, television quickly became a "vast wasteland" that changed in many ways over the decades, but not in its attitudes. Never used to boost humankind to any higher plateau, the medium remains a gaudy toy, something many people can't be without.

Videodrome is Cronenberg's most intellectually frightening movie. Max's visions are truly terrifying, mainly because they center on the inescapable image of television as a thing central to almost everyone's real life. In one scene, Max takes brutally sadistic pleasure in whipping a television set broadcasting Nicki's image. In another, he buries his head in the screen because Nicki's image calls to him from it. Laughable scenes on paper, but extremely unnerving on the big screen.

VILLAGE OF THE DAMNED (1960)

MGM, 1960, b&w, 78 min, VT, LD

Producer: Ronald Kinnoch; **Director:** Wolf Rilla; **Screenplay:** Rilla, Sterling Silliphant, and George Barclay; **Music:** Ron Goodwin; **Special Effects:** Tom Howard; **Cinematography:** Geoffrey Faithfull; **Cast:** George Sanders, Barbara Shelley, Michael Gwynne, Laurence Naismith, John Phillips, Richard Vernon, Martin Stephens

Mist from outer space settles on a small English village; then all of the town's inhabitants are rendered unconscious. When they awaken, no one remembers anything that may or may not have happened. As the months go by, however, they discover that all of the healthy women of child-bearing age, 12 in all (some virgins beforehand, others unmarried), were impregnated during the blackout. After they all give birth, the mystery deepens.

All of the children share a number of physical and mental characteristics. They are all extremely fair haired and light skinned. They all have the same disaffected manner—cold and emotionless. As the children age, it becomes obvious that they are endowed with superior mental abilities, including telepathic powers. Alone they are somewhat powerful. In groups they can cause mass destruction through the application of their telekinesis.

Physicist Gordon Zellaby (Sanders) is the father of the leader of the children. He deduces that the children are alien half-breeds. Rather than slaying him, as they have others, the children applaud his deductive powers, and soon he is the only adult they will suffer to teach them. Getting to know the childrens' other side, Zellaby realizes that they must be stopped before they destroy humanity. But how do you kill someone (let alone a group of someones) who can hear your every thought at a distance?

The scientist trains himself to resist the childrens' mental probes. Then armed with a bomb, he calls them all together for one of their routine lectures. Because of the curtain he has pulled across his mind, the children know he is up to something, but they can't pierce the image of a brick wall that he concentrates on. The children invade his mind, and one by one they strip away the bricks in his wall as the timer on the bomb counts down. The kids realize what's coming too late as Zellaby gives his life to save humanity.

Village of the Damned is a wonderful low-budget thriller. It is thoughtfully intense—well paced and well acted. Despite the lack of colorful pyrotechnics, it contains the very essence of the best science fiction—the rational man who thinks his way to victory.

Note: Children of the Damned is a sort of sideways sequel to this classic, but it really can't compare. In 1995, director John Carpenter remade the film with *SUPERMAN* star Christopher Reeve in the Sanders role. As one might expect, the passage of some 35 years allowed the filmmaker to express his graphic tendencies and to dot the landscape with more explicit characters, but the modern version does not improve on the original as it is sloppy and unsatisfying.

VILLAGE OF THE DAMNED (1995)

Universal, 1995, Color, 98 min, VT, LD, DVD

Producers: Andre Blay, Shep Gordon, David Chackler, James Jacks, Sandy King, Sean Daniel, Michael Preger, and Ted Vernon; **Director:** John Carpenter; **Screenplay:** Stirling Silliphant, Wolf Rilla, Ronald Kinnoch, David Himmelstein, and Steve Siebert; **Music:** Carpenter and Dave Davies; **Special Effects:** Roy Arbogast, Dick Wood, Bruce Nicholson, Keith Urban, Mike Wood, Bruno Van Zeebroeck; **Cinematography:** Gary B. Kibbe; **Cast:** Christopher Reeve, Kirstie Alley, Linda Kozowski, Michael Paré, Mark Hamill, Meredith Salenger, Constance Forslund, Buck Flower, Thomas Dekker, Lindsey Haun

See *VILLAGE OF THE DAMNED* (1960)

VILLAGE OF THE GIANTS

See *FOOD OF THE GODS*

VINDICATOR, THE

Frank & Stein Film Productions (Canada), 1986, Color, 88 min, VT

Producers: Don Carmody and John Dunning; **Director:** Jean Claude Lord; **Screenplay:** David Preson and Edith Rey; **Music:** Paul Zaza; **Cinematography:** Rene Verzier; **Cast:** Terri Austin, Richard Cox, Pam Grier, Maury Chaykin, Maury McIlwraith

See *FRANKENSTEIN*

VIOLET RAY, THE

General, 1917, b&w, silent short

Director: Robert Ellis; **Screenplay:** Robert Welles Ritchie; **Cast:** George Larkin, Harry Gordon, Robert Ellis

Another stirring episode of Grant, Police Reporter. This one featured 1917 bad guys running around with a ray gun capable of blinding human beings.

VIRTUOSITY

Paramount, 1995, Color, 105 min, VT, DVD

Producers: Gary Lucchesi, Gimel Everett, and Howard W. Kock, Jr.; **Director:** Brett Leonard; **Screenplay:** Eric Bernt; **Music:** Christopher Young, Tim Sexton, and Richard Rudolph; **Special Effects:** Jon Townley and L²Communications; **Cinematography:** Gale Tattersall; **Cast:** Denzel Washington, Kelly Lynch, Russell Crowe, Stephen Spinella, William Forsythe, Louise Fletcher, William Fichtner, Costas Mandylor, Kevin J. O'Connor, Traci Lords

It's the near future of 1999. The story opens in the Los Angeles offices of the government's Law Enforcement Technology Center, which has developed a prototype for the ultimate police training device. It's a virtual reality stimulator, which utilizes the latest in artificial intelligence technology to test user's skills. Trainees enter the simulation where they are to pursue a computer-generated criminal, Sid 6.7 (Crowe), an unnerving composite of humanity at its worst made up from the profiles of the most evil serial killers and mass murderers. This sophisticated cat-and-mouse game soon has deadly consequences, however, as Sid finds a way to escape the boundaries of cyberspace and suddenly is able to victimize the public at large. Ex-cop Parker Barnes (Washington) is called back to stop the cyber serial killer, and the stakes are heightened when Barnes discovers that one of Sid 6.7's building block personalities is that of the man who was responsible for the death of the officer's wife and daughter.

Extremely over-the-top, nonsense science is utilized to give the ugliest portions of people's destructive nature a reason to dance across the screen. Facts are ignored, such as the universal police policy of never allowing officers access to any criminal investigation in which they have a personal interest. Once again a straw man is chosen to stand in for a real villain. Artificial intelligence has become the bugbear for a new era of sloppy, unimaginative filmmakers who have tired of exploiting nuclear power. To be fair, there are many interesting premises here, but, as usual, what could have been an extremely thoughtful film is merely an excuse for more special effects and posturing.

VIRUS (1980) (aka: DAY OF RESURRECTION)

Toho (Japan), 1980, Color, 155 min, VT

Producer: Haruki Kadokawa; **Director:** Kinji Fukasaku; **Screenplay:** Sakyo Komatsu, Koji Takada, and Gregory Knapp; **Music:** Janis Ian and Teo Macero; **Special Effects:** Michael Lennick; **Cinematography:** Daisaku Kimura; **Cast:** Sonny Chiba, Chuck Conners, Glenn Ford, Stephanie Faulkner, Massao Kusakari, Isao Natsuki, Stuart Gillard, Olivia Hussey, George Kennedy, Henry Silva, Bo Svensen, Cecil Linder, Robert Vaughn

After the nukes fly and a few plagues have their way with humanity, the world's population is reduced to only the survivors found in an Antarctic research station and the sailors aboard a submarine. That leaves a startling 858 men left alive with only eight women. This feature boasts the most money ever spent on a Japanese film up until 1980. Spectacular Antarctic footage shows where some of the money went.

VIRUS (1999)

Universal, 1999, Color, 106 min, VT, DVD

Producer: Gale Anne Hurd; **Director:** John Bruni; **Screenplay:** Chuck Pfarrer and Dennis Feldman; **Music:** Joel McNeely; **Special Effects:** Steve Berg, Chuck Gaspar, Mike Edmonson, Michele C. Vallillo; **Cinematography:** David Eggby, A.C.S.; **Cast:** Jamie Lee Curtis, Donald Sutherland, William Baldwin, Joanna Pacula, Marshall Bell, Julio Oscar Mechoso, Sherman Agustus, Cliff Curtis, Yuri Chervotkin, Keith Flippen, Olga Rzhepetskaya-Retchin, Levani Outchaneichvili

The story opens in the South Pacific aboard the *Akademic Vladislav Volkov*, a Russian science ship that comes complete with dozens of on-ship labs, workshops, and factories. The *Volkov* is just about to line up its parabolic dish with the Russian *Mir* space station. Chief science officer Nadia (Pacula) prepares to download a routine scientific data transmission from the station. At the same time, however, a crackling, colorful energy mass envelops Mir, overloading its circuits and killing its crew. The energy follows the data transmission path down to the *Volkov* and the slaughter continues.

Then, just when your heart starts pounding, the scene switches to a tug pulling a barge through a ferocious typhoon. Captain Everton (Sutherland) and his navigator "Kit" Foster (Curtis) lose their cargo, but they fight their way to relative safety in the eye of the storm. Their tug is in bad shape, and they are running out of time. When they encounter the Russian ship, complete with bullet holes and blood smeared up and down its walls, they hope they've found their salvation. What they don't know is that the *Volkov* is now infested with the energy mass from Mir. It has killed the crew and to defend itself is now creating a small army of robots and cyborgs out of spare parts, other machines, and the stores from all those labs and factories and such.

Virus (UNIVERSAL STUDIOS / AUTHOR'S COLLECTION)

Everton and his people try to deny the facts at first, blinded by the monetary gain that awaits them if only they can bring the *Volkov* in for salvage. It isn't long, however, before the alien presence is undeniable and Everton and his crew are fighting for their lives against the killing machines that have taken over the ship.

Interestingly, when the humans get a chance to speak with the energy mass via computer, the alien tells them that humanity is the "virus" that must be eradicated. It seems that the energy mass is not intent on destroying humanity so much for its own safety as it's doing it for the universe's safety. And so, after answering the humans' questions, the alien breaks contact and moves in for the kill.

Virus is one of the more plausible of the new monster movies because its premise is reasonable, followed by good writing. Screenwriters Chuck Pfarrer and Dennis Feldman took Pfarrer's original idea (from a comic-book series he produced for Dark Horse Comics) and boiled it down to an intense but easy-to-follow 106 minutes that never get boring. Unlike so many similar films, this one has no heroes to make the story pre-dictable. Even Curtis, whom one expects to take the lead, remains a normal person throughout. Sure, she fights back, as almost everyone in the film fights back, but she also runs away and makes mistakes and cries in fear at the ever-increasing horror.

The screenwriters' motto—explain the story in an interesting manner and then just get out of the combatants' way; start the battle and then let the best species win. A heck of a battle it is, too, thanks to the army of special effects people. Every great robot/machine F/X person in Hollywood appears to have dropped in to work on this one, from Eric Allard (who created the robotic effects for SHORT CIRCUIT) to the legendary Phil Tippett (who put together the elephantine Imperial Walkers for THE EMPIRE STRIKES BACK). The gigantic team created dozens of interesting robotic creatures for the movie, many of them strikingly different, all of them flawless.

VISIT TO A SMALL PLANET

Paramount, 1960, b&w, 85 min

Producer: Hal Wallis; **Director:** Norman Taurog; **Screenplay:** Edmond Beloin, Henry Garson, and Gore Vidal; **Music:** Leight Harline; **Special Effects:** John P. Fulton and Wally Westmore; **Cinematography:** Loyal Griggs; **Cast:** Jerry Lewis, Joan Blackman, Fred Clark, Gale Gordon, Earl Holliman, John Williams, Jerome Cowan, Lee Patrick

A superpowered but none-too-bright alien named Kreton (Jerry Lewis) comes to Earth as an observer. While here, he quickly shifts from observer to participant, falling in love and getting into all manner of typical Lewisian shenanigans. This would all be fine if the idea were an original, but *Visit to a Small Planet* is based on a brilliant, satirical play by Gore Vidal. The alien in the play is as simpleminded as Lewis's for the first act. After that, however, the second act reveals the alien's true nature as a destroyer of worlds, making the play a classic, whereas the second act of the film has Lewis mugging, making everyone over the age of eight head for the snack bar.

VOODOO BLOODBATH

See *I EAT YOUR SKIN*

VOODOO MAN

Monogram Pictures Corporation, 1944, b&w, 62 min

Producers: Jack Dietz, Sam Katzman, and Barney A. Sarecky; **Director:** William Beaudine; **Screenplay:** Robert Charles; **Music:** Edward J. Kay; **Cinematography:** Marcel Le Picard; **Cast:** Bela Lugosi, John Carradine, George Zucco, Michael Ames, Henry Hall, Wanda McKay, Louie Currie

Lugosi plays a scientist intent on curing his zombie wife and bringing her back from the semiliving to the world of the conscious. Unfortunately, he has to experiment on half the women in town to do it.

VOODOO WOMAN

AIP, 1957, b&w, 77 min, VT

Producer: Alex Gordon; **Director:** Edward L. Cahn; **Screenplay:** Russell Bender and V.I. Voss; **Music:** Darrell Calker; **Cinematography:** Frederick E. West; **Cast:** Marla English, Tom Conway, Touch Conners, Lance Fuller, Paul Blaisdell

A scientist wants to turn the town's above-average population of attractive women into slaves but winds up creating hideous monsters instead.

VOYAGE INTO SPACE

AIP, 1968, Color, 98 min

Producer: Salvatore Billitteri; **Director:** Minoru Yamada

A small boy controls the actions of a big robot as bad aliens arrive to conquer Earth. The robot beats up their ships in this cut-and-paste effort created by cobbling together pieces from various episodes of the Japanese TV show *Johnny Socko*.

VOYAGE TO THE BOTTOM OF THE SEA

20th Century Fox, 1961, Color, 105 min, VT, LD

Producer: Irwin Allen; **Director:** Allen; **Screenplay:** Allen and Charles Bennett; **Music:** Paul Sawtell; **Special Effects:** Lyle B. Abbott, Jack Martin Smith, and Herman A. Blumenthal; **Cinematography:** Winton Hoch; **Cast:** Walter Pidgeon, Joan Fontaine, Robert Sterling, Peter Lorre, Barbara Eden, Michael Ansara, Frankie Avalon, Regis Toomey, Henry Daniell

It's the maiden voyage of the latest thing in atomic submarines, the *Seaview*. Things are looking pretty darn good for its healthy and happy co-ed crew, until suddenly the Van Allen radiation belt bursts into flames. This, of course, results in superheating Earth. The planet's leading scientists, including those who have spent their lives studying radiation, the Van Allen belt in particular, are stumped. Enter the noble captain of submarine, Admiral Harriman Nelson (Pidgeon). A clever boy, this admiral, he theorizes that a Polaris nuke launched into the belt from a precise point in the Antarctic will put out the flames.

Intelligently (since the admiral's science is laughable), the world's scientists and governments tell him not to do this. A messianic steely eyed visionary, he ignores his intellectual superiors and heads south. The world's navies, as well as a giant squid, try to stop him, but to no avail. Reaching the Antarctic intact, Nelson launches his missile, and since the picture's megalomaniac director was also the screenwriter, the nuke puts out the flames and the world is saved.

Note: Remarkably, the television series that followed was often far better than the movie, at least for the first half of the first season, if for no other reason than that the principal actors, Richard Basehart and David Hedison, were able to keep straight faces throughout its run. At first, the crew battled enemy agents and other standard menaces. After a while, however, oversized whales, squids, and jellyfish began showing up with frightening regularity. Even these weren't too bad, but once mummies, leprechauns, insane robots, and U-boat commander ghosts began showing up, the end was near.

VOYAGE TO THE END OF THE UNIVERSE

See *IKARIA XBI*

VOYAGE TO THE MOON

See *THE TRIP TO THE MOON*

VOYAGE TO THE PLANET OF PREHISTORIC WOMEN (aka: THE GILL WOMEN, THE GILL WOMEN OF VENUS)

AIP, 1968, Color, 80 min, VT

Producer: Norman Wells; **Director:** Peter Bogdanovich (as Derek Thomas); **Screenplay:** Henry Nay; **Special Effects:** Mary Jo Wier and Wah Chang; **Cinematography:** Arkady Klimov; **Cast:** Mamie Van Doren, Mary Mark, Paige Lee, Aldo Roman, Margot Hartman

Astronauts land on Venus and do battle with creatures and a beautiful female population. The astronauts hang in there for a while but are finally repulsed by the women's telepathic powers. This film is half original, and half cobbled together from footage of the slightly superior Russian sci-fi film *PLANET OF STORMS*.

Note: Director Peter Bogdanovich narrates the film, credited under the name Derek Thomas, which he used while working for Roger Corman.

VOYAGE TO THE PREHISTORIC PLANET (aka: PREHISTORIC PLANET)

AIP, 1965, Color, 78 min, VT

Producer: George Edwards; **Director:** John Sebastian; **Screenplay:** Sebastian; **Music:** Ronald Stein; **Special Effects:** John Cline and William Condos; **Cinematography:** Vilis Lapenieks; **Cast:** Basil Rathbone, Faith Domergue, Marc Shannon, Christopher Brand, John Bix, Robert Chanta

It's 2020 and humanity's best are off to a planet—Venus this time—full of prehistoric creatures and volcanoes. There are hints of a plot, but they are all accidental. Basil Rathbone sulks about on the set for *PLANET OF BLOOD* (another film he was making at the same time), looking as angry and embarrassed as a great actor crawling his way through hard times could possibly look. Finally, the noble crew concludes that the original inhabitants of Venus destroyed themselves in nuclear war. What's left of the heroes leave for home. This film is half original, and half cobbled together from footage of the slightly superior Russian sci-fi film *PLANET OF STORMS*.

VULTURE, THE

Homeric Films, Ltd. (Great Britain), 1966/Paramount (U.S.), 1967, Color & b&w, 91 min, VT

Producer: Lawrence Huntington; **Director:** Huntington; **Screenplay:** Huntington; **Music:** Eric Spear; **Cinematography:** Stephen Dade; **Cast:** Robert Hutton, Broderick Crawford, Diane Clare, Monty Landis, Akim Tamiroff, Phillip Friend, Patrick Holt

Not realizing what a fortune his invention would amass on its own, a scientist wants to use a matter transference device to recover an ancient buried treasure (much better than simply selling the thing to a world that hadn't even yet gone to the Moon). The booty had been buried along with the body of a warlock and his familiar, a vulture. The machine malfunctions, and not only mistakes the remains of the vulture for the treasure, but upon bringing the bird's disassembled remains back to the lab, somehow scrambles them with those of the scientist. The result: a vulture with a human head and arms. The consequences: People begin to die all over the place.

WAR BETWEEN THE PLANETS
(aka: MISSION WANDERING PLANET, PLANET ON THE PROWL)

Mercury/Southern Cross (Italy), 1965/Fanfare (U.S.), 1971, Color, 80 min, VT

Producers: Joseph Fryd, Antonio Margheriti, and Walter Manley; **Director:** Margheriti; **Screenplay:** Ivan Reiner and Margheriti; **Music:** Francesco Lavagnino; **Cinematography:** Riccardo Pallottini; **Cast:** Jack Stuart, Archie Savage, Peter Martell, Amber Collins, Halina Zalewska

An entire planet is running loose through space, amazingly without losing its atmosphere, under the control of an evil electronic brain that has set this runaway world on a collision course for Earth.

WAR GAME, THE

BBC (Great Britain), 1965, 50 min/Contemporary (U.S.), 1966, 47 min, b&w, VT

Producer: Peter Watkins; **Director:** Watkins; **Screenplay:** Watkins; **Special Effects:** Lilias Munro; **Cinematography:** Peter Bartlette; **Narrators:** Michael Aspel and Dick Graham

This fictional documentary about the effects of a nuclear war on Great Britain cleverly begins by relying on actual news footage and then blurs the lines with staged news reports and "live" interviews. The project was meant to give a scare and is still quite effective even decades later.

Note: The film was originally produced by the British Film Institute and the BBC for broadcast in England but surprisingly was never shown on British television as it was deemed too shocking for the public. The film eventually found its way to theaters where the more shockproof Americans awarded it an Oscar for Best Documentary.

WARGAMES

MGM, 1983, Color, 110 min, VT, LD, DVD

Producer: Harold Schneider; **Director:** John Badham; **Screenplay:** Lawrence Rasker and Walter F. Parkes; **Music:** Arthur B. Rubinstein; **Special Effects:** Linda Fleischer, Michael L. Fink, and Joe Digaetano; **Cinematography:** William A. Fraker, A.S.C.; **Cast:** Matthew Broderick, Dabney Coleman, John Wood, Ally Sheedy, Barry Corbin, Juanin Clay, Maury Chaykin, Michael Madsen, John Spenser

David Lightman (Broderick) is an average teenager who escapes the boredom of uninteresting, unchallenging schoolwork, his mundane parents, and the bland world around him via his home computer. In the days before AOL, he startled audiences by dialing the phone and inserting a program into his computer that would allow him to travel the world talking to other techno geeks and their computers. David acts without thinking of the consequences: He changes his school grades, impresses a girl by ordering plane tickets to Paris, and finally decides to break into a video game manufacturer's computer to steal its newest game plans for his own amusement via the airwaves.

David, however, has unwittingly broken into the NORAD defense computers instead and accidentally triggers a series of events that may lead to World War III. Captured by the FBI, David is shocked to learn what he has done and is even more shocked to discover that the government considers him a dangerous spy. He tells the FBI and NORAD's officials what to do—contact the original programmer of the computer. The officials claim he's dead, but David claims that the computer says he's still alive. The government boys prove too dim to look into this, leaving David no choice but to escape FBI custody and track down the computer programmer and have him set everything aright in the 27 hours and 59 minutes Earth has remaining. But even after they find the man who programmed the computer, he can't think of a way to shut it down, so David has to do that as well.

No doubt nuclear power used unwisely is dangerous, but that goes for bleach, propane, and most kitchen utensils, too. *WarGames* has a hideously flawed story. For instance, the audience is expected to believe that a teenager can crack governmental computer defenses without really trying (indeed, without even being *aware* of it), something that master spies cannot come close to breaking. This same teenager is then supposed to be wily enough to be able to break out of FBI custody and then elude them completely, even though they know where he is going.

There are lots of flaws in this film, like the scenes of tourists being taken on sightseeing trips through the NORAD war room or the fact that the computer David uses to do his breaking and entering isn't powerful enough to do anything we see him doing. *WarGames* was not meant as entertainment, but as a jeremiad. Its message was that "no one wins a nuclear war." The message is a good one, but the medium is too slight to be taken seriously except by those the movie doesn't have to convince. By presenting every single adult working for the government—military personnel and civilians alike—as utter morons, the filmmakers sacrificed their credibility completely.

WAR GODS OF THE DEEP
(aka: CITY UNDER THE SEA, THE)

AIP, 1965, Color, 84 min

Producer: Daniel Haller; **Director:** Jacques Tourneur; **Screenplay:** Charles Bennett and Louis M. Heyward; **Music:** Stanley Black; **Special Effects:** Frank George and Les Bowie; **Cinematography:** John Lamb; **Cast:** Tab Hunter, Vincent Price, David Tomlinson, Susan Hart, John LeMesurier

Tab Hunter has to travel all the way to England to find an American girl to fall in love with. She lives in a mansion that's connected to an underwater city, and it's ruled by a very insane Vincent Price who is a god to the gillmen outside that city. Then there's the volcano. And that chicken running all over the place.

WARLORDS OF ATLANTIS

Columbia, 1978, Color, 90 min

Producer: John Dark; **Director:** Kevin Conner; **Screenplay:** Brian Hayes; **Music:** Michael Vickers; **Special Effects:** Roger Dicken, John Richardson, and George Gibbs; **Cinematography:** Alan Hume; **Cast:** Doug McClure, Peter Gilmore, Shane Rimmer, Les Brodie, John Ratzenberger, Cyd Charisse, Daniel Masset

Scientists looking for the lost city of Atlantis find it, along with a bunch of attractive women and monsters.

WARLORDS OF THE 21ST CENTURY
(aka: BATTLETRUCK)

New World Pictures, 1982, Color, 91 min, VT

Producers: Lloyd Phillips and Rob Whitehouse; **Director:** Harley Cokliss; **Screenplay:** Irving Austin, John Beech, and Cokliss; **Music:** Kevin Peak; **Special Effects:** Jonnie Burke and Kevin Chisnall; **Cinematography:** Chris Menges; **Cast:** Michael Beck, Annie McEnroe, James Wainwright, John Ratzenberger, Bruno Lawrence

World War III is over. The world is in ruins and there isn't enough petrol for the buggies in this sad *MAD MAX/ROAD WARRIOR* wannabe.

WARNING FROM SPACE (aka: MYSTERIOUS SATELLITE, THE COSMIC MAN APPEARS IN TOKYO, SPACE MEN APPEAR IN TOKYO, UNKNOWN SATELLITE OVER TOKYO)

Daiei (Japan), 1956/AIT (U.S.), 1963, Color, 87 min

Producer: Masichi Nagata; **Director:** Hoki Shima; **Screenplay:** Hideo Oguni; **Cinematography:** Kimio Wantanabe; **Cast:** Toyomi Karita, Kiyoko Hirai, Bontaro Miake

Another group of aliens who didn't think mere Earthlings capable of handling nuclear power come to our world to advise us as to its terrible dangers. This bunch is star-shaped (as in the drawings, not the giant burning gas balls) by nature, but they disguise themselves as human beings.

WAR OF DREAMS

Selig, 1915, b&w, silent short

Director: E.A. Martin; **Screenplay:** W.E. Wing; **Cast:** Edwin Wallock, Lillian Hayward

A scientist with nothing better to do invents a new form of superexplosive that can be detonated by people's *dreams*. Unable to foresee any problems with this, our boy is quite pleased with himself until in one of his own dream he sees what his nutty invention could do in the wrong hands. Upon waking, he wisely destroys all of his work.

WAR OF THE COLOSSAL BEAST

AIP, 1958, b&w, 68 min, VT

Producer: Bert I. Gordon; **Director:** Gordon; **Screenplay:** George Worthing Yates; **Music:** Albert Glasser; **Special Effects:** Gordon; **Cinematography:** Jack Marta; **Cast:** Sally Fraser, Roger Pace, Dean Parkin, Russ Bender, Charles Stewart, George Becwar

Sequel to THE AMAZING COLOSSAL MAN. In the first film, nuclear radiation transformed handsome soldier Colonel Manning into a giant who fell from the top of the Hoover Dam to his death. Now it's discovered that he is no longer handsome and that he didn't die, but instead made his way to Mexico, where he continued scaring the stuffing out of people. Eventually, he is captured and brought back to the United States, Los Angeles, in fact. Some scientists poke and prod him for a while, but eventually he escapes and ends it all by electrocuting himself.

Note: For some undiscernible reason, the producer decided the electrocution sequence should be in color. Thus, *War of the Colossal Beast* ends with a few moments of color.

WAR OF THE GARGANTUAS, THE (aka: DUEL OF THE GARGANTUAS, ADVENTURE OF THE GARGANTUAS, FRANKENSTEIN'S MONSTERS: SANDA VS: GAILAH, SANDA VS: GAILAH

Toho, 1966, Color, 93 min, VT

Producers: Reuben Bercovitch, Henry J. Saperstein, Tomoyuki Tanaka, and Kenichiro Tsunoda; **Director:** Ishirô Honda; **Screenplay:** Honda and Takeshi Kimuka; **Music:** Akira Ifukube; **Special Effects:** Teisho Arikawa, Yasuyuki Inoue, Hiroshi Mukoyama, Teruyoshi Nakano, Eiji Tsuburaya, Ryohei Fujii, Kuichiro Kishida, Fumio Nakadai, and Sokei Tomioka; **Cinematography:** Jahime Koizumi; **Cast:** Russ Tamblyn, Kumi Mizuno, Kipp Hamilton, Yu Fujiki

Sanda and Gailah, two massive humanoid monsters known as gargantua, one green and one brown, duke it out across the width and breath of Japan. Sadly, many fine miniatures are crushed in the process. This is the kind of film that gets made even when cheap-looking rubber suits are out of the ultra-low budget's reach.

WAR OF THE PLANETS (1965) (aka: THE DEADLY DIAPHONOIDS, DIAPHONOIDS: BRINGERS OF DEATH)

Mercury & Southern Cross, 1965, Color, 99 min

Producers: Walter Manley, Joseph Fryd, and Anthony Dawson; **Director:** Antonio Margheriti; **Screenplay:** Ivan Reiner and Renato Moretti; **Music:** Francesco Lavagnino; **Cinematography:** Riccardo Pallottini; **Cast:** Tony Russell, Franco Nero, Lisa Gastoni, Michel Lemoine, Massimo Serato, Carlo Giustini

It's the far-off days of the 21st century and Earth is being invaded yet again. This time the intruders are strange, unfathomable creatures of light. The creatures fail in their bid to subjugate humankind. The producers fail in their bid to not be embarrassed by their pitiful handiwork.

WAR OF THE PLANETS (1977) (aka: COSMOS: WAR OF THE PLANETS, COSMO 2000: PLANET WITHOUT A NAME)

Toho, 1977, Color, 95 min, VT

Producers: Fumio Tanaka and Tomoyuki Tanaka; **Director:** Alfonso Brescia; **Screenplay:** Ryuzo Nakanishi and Shuichi Nagahara; **Music:** Toshiaki Tsushima; **Special Effects:** Yasuyuki Inoue, Teruyoshi Nakano, Takeshi Yamamoto, Toshimitsu Oneda, and Takesaburo Watanbee; **Cinematography:** Yuzuru Aizawa; **Cast:** John Richardson, Yanti Somer, West Buchanan, Kathy Christine, Max Karis, Percy Hogan

It's yet another splendid crew of astronauts off for adventure on a journey to an unknown world. Also unknown to this crew: the art of filmmaking.

WAR OF THE SATELLITES

Allied Artists, 1958, b&w, 66 min

Producer: Roger Corman; **Director:** Corman; **Screenplay:** Lawrence Louis Goldman; **Music:** Walter Greene; **Special Effects:** Jack Rabin, Irving Block, and Louis DeWitt; **Cinematography:** Floyd Crosby; **Cast:** Dick Miller, Susan Cabot, Michael Fox, Richard Devon, Robert Shayne, Eric Sinclair

Aliens with the power to control the minds of men come to Earth in an attempt to stop the upstart planet from exploring the universe. They plan to kidnap some of Earth's scientists and hold them captive aboard their space station. The eggheads, led by Dick Miller, escape their captors' mental powers and do their best to destroy them. So much for keeping Earth out of space. Next time, leave that to the simple indifference of the masses.

Note: The day after the United States launched the *Explorer* satellite, famed low-budget producer/director Roger Corman went to the head of Allied Artists and promised he could deliver a complete picture capitalizing on the launch in a mere two months. True to his word, he did it just as promised. True to his style, it isn't very good.

WAR OF THE WORLDS

Paramount, 1953, Color, 85 min, VT, LD, DVD

Producer: George Pal; **Director:** Byron Haskin; **Screenplay:** Barre Lyndon; **Music:** Leith Stevens; **Special Effects:** Gordon Jennings, Wallace Kelly, Jan Domela, Paul Lerpae, Ivyl Burkes, Irmin Roberts, Gene Garvin, Chesley Bonestell, Marcel Delgado, and Wally Westmore; **Cinematography:** George Barnes; **Cast:** Gene Barry, Les Tremayne, Ann Robinson, Robert Cornthwaite, Henry Brandon, Jack Kruschen, Paul Frees, Sir Cedric Hardwicke, Ivan Lebedoff, Sandro Gigilo, Edgar Barrier, Alex Fraser, Anne Codee, Lewis Martin, Charles Gemora

War of the Worlds (PARAMOUNT / R. ALLEN LEIDER COLLECTION)

London of 1890 becomes the Los Angeles of the 1950s in George Pal's adaptation of *War of the Worlds*. Some things are the same despite the transition but not many. In the Americanized version, a gigantic meteorite (at least what appears to be a meteorite) lands in the countryside on the outskirts of L.A. A group of local scientists, led by dashing Dr. Clayton (Barry), investigates, but the object is too hot for inspection, so the boys repair to a local church dance to while away the time, leaving a few of the locals to guard their prize. Once the star of the film is out of range, a circular hatch opens in the meteorite and a death ray eliminates those present. More meteorites soon fall from the heavens—like the first these prove to be Martian warships. A full-scale invasion has begun.

Being human, we have to give the Martians a chance, so a man of God approaches one of the ships, Bible in hand, beseeching those inside with words of tender compassion. Like all humans before him, the holy man is barbecued. After that, the gloves are finally off. The army fights back, but it's no good. Tanks, fighter jets, nothing can hold its own against the invaders. Even nukes are useless. People everywhere run and hide like frightened rabbits in the face of the

Martian advance. Doc Clayton does his share of hiding, as well, but mostly he continues to look for his girlfriend. He finds her in a church where people have turned to their line of last defense—prayer. Son of a gun, it works. God sends his mighty cold germs to destroy the aliens.

Although Pal's *War of the Worlds* is often hailed as a major science fiction triumph, it's difficult to figure out why. H.G. Wells's source novel is used only for the barest skeleton. The grand old man reportedly despised Orson Welles's famed radio broadcast version of his work. It's hard to imagine how he would have reacted to the film's even looser interpretation.

When the initial "meteorite" lands, no one notices that the spherical rock is unnatural or that it didn't shatter on impact, leaving a crater the size of a sports arena. The science is shocking throughout, but its failures can't match those of the special effects. Wells's unique walking tripods are replaced by ordinary spaceshiplike designs that move on beams of light. This wouldn't be so bad if the wires holding them up weren't visible in many scenes. The Martians (a single representative shown in only one brief scene) are not terribly convincing, either.

The addition of a standard, one-size-fits-all love story does nothing to enhance the narrative but does point up that no particular care was taken with bringing this classic to the screen. Outside of the conquering germs at the end, all of Wells's 19th-century fire and passion are replaced by watered-down 20th-century despair. For Wells, the Martians were representative of the worst of humans. For Pal, they were merely Communists.

WARRIORS OF THE WASTELAND
(aka: THE NEW BARBARIANS)

Dear (Italy)/New Line Cinema (U.S.), 1983, Color, 87 min, VT

Producer: Fabrizio De Angelis; **Director:** Enzo G. Castellari; **Screenplay:** Tito Carpi and Girolami Castellari; **Music:** Claudio Simonetti; **Special Effects:** Germano Natali; **Cinematography:** Fausto Zuccoli; **Cast:** Timothy Brent, Fred Williamson, Anna Kanakis, Venantino Venantini, Enzo G. Castellari

It's the 21st century and society has collapsed as the far superior *ROAD WARRIOR* is ripped off again.

WASP WOMAN, THE (aka: THE BEE GIRL, INSECT WOMAN)

Allied Artists, 1960, b&w, 66 min, VT

Producer: Roger Corman; **Director:** Corman; **Screenplay:** Leo Lordon; **Music:** Fred Katz; **Special Effects:** Grant R. Keats and Philip Mitchell; **Cinematography:** Harry Newman; **Cast:** Susan Cabot, Fred Eisley, Michael Mark, Fred Wolff, Barboura Morris, William Roerick, Frank Gerstle

Ms. Cabot is the head of a cosmetics film. Getting on in years but still vain as a schoolgirl, she not only authorizes the making of a wrinkle creme made from wasp enzymes, but she uses it on herself. Soon she's as beautiful as ever. There's just one annoying problem, the creme causes the user these occasional transformations into some sort of mutant insect thing that needs to kill! Considered a camp classic, there's nothing terribly wrong or worthwhile about this movie.

WATER CYBORG

See *THE TERROR BENEATH THE SEA*

WATER CYBORGS

See *THE TERROR BENEATH THE SEA*

WATERWORLD

Universal, 1995, Color, 136 min, VT, LD, DVD

Producers: Jeffrey Muller, Andrew Licht, and Ilona Herzberg; **Director:** Kevin Reynolds; **Screenplay:** Peter Rader and David Twohy; **Music:** James Newton Howard; **Special Effects:** Archie Ahuna, Carol Ashley, Richard Bain, Martin Bresin, Christopher Edwards, John Frazier, David Fuhrer, Alex Funke, Chris Watts, Chuck Gaspar, Rae Griffith, Michael Gaspar, Michael Vieira, Mark Vargo, Janek Sirrs, Sean Schor, Michael J. McAlister, and Charles Linehan; **Cinematography:** Dean Semler; **Cast:** Kevin Costner, Dennis Hopper, Jeanne Tripplehorn, Tina Majorino, Michael Jeter

Kevin Costner is the Mariner, a human with gills in a future where the polar ice caps have melted. Why they melted, we're never told. But they did, and now everything is underwater. Those people who still populate the planet do it in boats. No one still alive knows that there was an old world or that it's underwater, which is surprising since one would expect the information to at least be carried through the years in an oral tradition.

The Mariner is a scavenger/trader who travels the world's single ocean, looking for things to barter. He lives on an incredible sailing ship that is a true marvel of engineering. In the opening, he comes to trade with a floating community, but when they discover he is a mutant, they imprison him and sentence him to be recycled. He escapes only because the evil "Smokers" (tech heads who still use engines, drink Jack Daniel's, and smoke cigarettes) attack the community. The Smokers, led by Dennis Hopper, want a girl they've heard of, one with a tattoo on her back that supposedly will lead whoever can interpret it to dry land. The girl's beautiful guardian frees the Mariner if he promises to take the two of them with him. He does, and off they go.

From that point on audiences are supposed to root for the women and wait for the gruff Mariner to change, but every word out of the Mariner's mouth makes sense, and everything the woman and girl say is nonsense. They abuse his things, wreck his boat, and lead him into constant danger, and it isn't long before one wonders why the Mariner doesn't just kill them. Eventually, the Smokers get the girl, but the Mariner saves her. Then he kills all the Smokers and leads the woman and the girl and two other tag-alongs to dry land. There he leaves them. The land "doesn't move right" to him, and he has to set off across the ocean he loves.

Where did the Mariner come from? He says there aren't any more like him. Even if he's the first human to adapt to the water (and he's pretty well adapted—webbed feet, gills, swims like a fish, shoots out of the water like a dolphin), this transformation has to have taken an incredible amount of time in terms of evolution. Where are the evil Smokers getting their ammo—their cigarettes, boats, and cars, their Jack Daniel's, their knives and clothing and jet skis and everything else—if the world drowned hundreds of thousands, or even hundreds, of years before?

It has to have been at least hundreds of years because it's been long enough for everyone to have forgotten the truth and to believe that the flood was the beginning of life. The Mariner is the only one who knows there are cities under the ocean. He's the only one who knows that life didn't begin, but that it ended, with the flooding. If that's the case, how did everyone get the mechanical ability to fly planes, as well as repair and fuel them, if everything was buried under the water so long ago? We're supposed to think that the Smokers fuel their gas-guzzlers with the crude oil stored in the supertanker they row around. But as most schoolchildren know, oil has to be refined before you can pour it into gas tanks.

These aren't the film's worst sins, though. Even the basic plot is flawed. The film's premise is that the polar ice caps have melted and this is what flooded the planet, despite proof that there isn't enough ice in the caps to come anywhere close to creating the depth of water indicated in the film. Every valley is filled, every sky-scraper and mountain covered. In addition, consider this: If the ice caps had covered the world to such a level, they would have diluted the salt in the oceans enough to make the water drinkable. But everyone needs to jump through hoops to save rainwater to get a drink. The Mariner uses a bells-and-whistles desalinization machine to purify his urine. The only problem with this is that urine has a much higher salt content than ocean water. So, why doesn't the Mariner simply use his device on the planetful of water all around him? The answer: because he can only be as smart as his writers, and those guys, as the old saying goes, weren't rocket scientists.

WATTS MONSTER, THE

See *DR. BLACK AND MR. HYDE*

WATCHERS

Universal, 1988, Color, 92 min, VT, LD

Producers: Roger Corman, Mary Eilts, and Damian Lee; **Director:** Jon Hess; **Screenplay:** Dean R. Koontz; **Music:** Joel Goldsmith; **Special Effects:** Rory Cutler and Dean Lockwood; **Cinematography:** Richard Leiterman; **Cast:** Corey Haim, Michael Ironsides, Lala, Barbara Williams, Duncan Fraser, Dale Wilson, Blu Mankuma

A young boy (Haim) ends up with a superintelligent dog as a pet. The clever canine is the result of military experiments, and so is the monster that ends up chasing Haim and his pooch, not only in this movie, but through the sequels as well.

The second of the *Watchers* films is actually better than the first but is still nothing worth spending one's time watching. Same goes for *Watchers 3* as well. Dean R. Koontz is always good for an interesting premise, but this one gets watered down considerably the further along things go.

WATCHERS 2

Concorde (Canada), 1990, Color, 97 min, VT, LD

Producers: Roger Corman, Joel DeLoach, and Rodman Flender; **Director:** Thierry Notz; **Screenplay:** Henry Dominic; **Music:** Rick Conrad; **Special Effects:** Kevin Mutchaver and Greg Landerer; **Cinematography:** Edward J. Pei; **Cast:** Marc Singer, Tracy Scoggins, Tom Poster, Jonathan Farwell, Mary Woronov

See *WATCHERS*

WATCHERS 3

Concorde/New Horizons, 1994, Color, 80 min, VT

Producers: Roger Corman, Shane McCoy, and Luis Llosa; **Director:** Jeremy Stanford; **Screenplay:** Michael Palmer; **Music:** Nigel Holton; **Special Effects:** Gabe Z. Bartalos; **Cinematography:** Juan Duran; **Cast:** Wings Hauser, Gregory Scott Cummings, Daryl Roach, John Linton, Lolita Ronalds, Ider CiFuentes Martin, Frank Novak

See *WATCHERS*

WATCHERS REBORN

Concorde/New Horizons, 1998, Color, 88 min, VT

Producers: Roger Corman, Mark Hamill, and Darin Spillman; **Director:** John Carl Buechler; **Screenplay:** Sean Dash; **Music:** Terry Plumeri; **Special Effects:** Buechler, Albert Lannutti, and Magical Media Industries; **Cast:** Mark Hamill, Lisa Wilcox, Lou Rawls, Lucy Lin, Stephen Macht, Gary Collins, Robert Clendenin

See *WATCHERS*

WAVELENGTH

New World Pictures, 1983, Color, 87 min, VT, LD

Producers: James Rosenfield and Maurice Rosenfield; **Director:** Mike Gray; **Screenplay:** Gray; **Music:** Tangerine Dream; **Special Effects:** Mike Menzel; **Cinematography:** Paul Goldsmith; **Cast:** Robert Carradine, Cherie Curry, Keenan Wynn

This is a mostly forgettable vehicle about aliens hiding on Earth and the government cover-up that keeps them out of sight.

WAY . . . WAY OUT

20th Century Fox, 1966, Color, 106 min

Producer: Malcolm Stuart; **Director:** Gordon Douglas; **Screenplay:** William Bowers and Laslo Vadnay; **Music:** Lalo Shifrin; **Special Effects:** Lyle B. Abbott, Emil Kosa, Jr., and Howard Lydecker; **Cinematography:** William H. Clothier; **Cast:** Jerry Lewis, Dick Shawn, Connie Stevens, Anita Ekberg, Robert Morley, Howard Morris, Dennis Weaver, James Brolin

Jerry Lewis and Dick Shawn play astronauts on their way to the Moon in this supposed comedy. Actually, they're part of an astronaut/cosmonaut goodwill public relations stunt. Their mission is the disaster one might expect, then Stevens and Ekberg show up on the Moon, and things go from childish to embarrassing.

WEEKEND

Comacico/Copernic/Lira/Ascot Cineraid (France/Italy), 1968, Color, 103 min, VT

Director: Jean-Luc Godard; **Screenplay:** Godard; **Music:** Guy Béart and Antonie Duhamel; **Cinematography:** Raoul Coutard; **Cast:** Mireille Darc, Jean Yanne, Jean-Pierre Kalfon, Valerie Lagrange, Jean-Pierre Léaud

A middle-class couple can't even set out for a weekend in the country without tearing each other's heads off with their constant arguing. Along the way, they see one road disaster after another. None of the tragedy they see affects them very greatly. Finally, the wrecks become so numerous that the couple must proceed on foot. From here the film gets more and more bizarre. The woman finally joins a group of anarchists as they kill and eat her husband.

This movie has been hailed as the greatest science fiction attack on Western culture ever filmed. It may be. However, it is also a loud, pretentious, and overly affected diatribe screeching about the society that enabled the filmmaker to condemn it in the first place—the society that allows him to criticize it rather than just backing him up against the wall and shooting him. The film is littered with allegories that pretend to reveal great truths, and it's possible that it did have something to say upon its release, but any message it had has diminished over time.

WEIRD SCIENCE

Universal, 1985, Color, 94 min, VT, LD, DVD

Producer: Joel Silver; **Director:** John Hughes; **Screenplay:** Hughes; **Music:** Ira Newbord, Danny Elfman, and Mike Oldfield; **Special Effects:** David Blistein, Roger Lifsey, Doug Hubbard, Henry Millar, Mike Millar, and Richard L. Thompson; **Cinematography:** Matthew F. Leonetti; **Cast:** Anthony Michael Hall, Kelly LeBrock, Ilan Mitchell-Smith, Bill Paxton, Suzanne Snyder, Judie Aronson, Robert Downey, Jr., Robert Rusler

A pair of teen geeks (Hall and Mitchell-Smith) get it into their heads to mix computers and witchcraft to create their dream girl. They set up something like a séance, but the difference is that the little nitwits actually do materialize an astounding woman (LeBrock), who is there to serve their every desire—sort of. Despite a silly premise and poor science fiction, the film manages to be entertaining. It's a typical John Hughes teen comedy, shining with snappy youth-oriented dialogue and scenes romanticizing the world of the high school loser.

WELCOME TO BLOOD CITY

EMI Films Ltd./Len Herberman Production, 1977, Color, 96 min

Producers: Stuart Chase, Max Rosenberg, and Marilyn Stonehouse; **Director:** Peter Sasdy; **Screenplay:** Stephen Schneck and Michael Winder; **Music:** Roy Budd; **Cinematography:** Reginald H. Morris; **Cast:** Jack Palance, Samantha Eggar, Barry Morse, Keir Dullea

A small group of people awaken in the middle of nowhere. They are complete amnesiacs, and the only clue to their previous existence is a card each finds that accuses the person of being a convicted murderer. The entire group is soon enslaved by the people of Blood City, an Old West town, where they are told they will remain slaves forever unless they can murder their way up the town's social ladder. In reality, there is no town. Everything the group has experienced since they first woke up is an elaborate illusion created holographically within the participants' minds. Political unrest is growing exponentially in the real world, and the authorities are using "Blood City" to identify killers to help them keep a lid on things.

This movie could have been an outstanding science fiction ride if it had chosen to play up its paranoia angle. What could have been an intriguing nightmare of intertangled stories and mental traumas was reduced to mostly standard western movie clichés with the sci-fi only thrown in at the end to give the tired thing a hook for a modern audience.

WESTWORLD

MGM, 1973, Color, 91 min, VT, LD, DVD

Producer: Paul Lazarus, Jr.; **Director:** Michael Crichton; **Screenplay:** Crichton; **Music:** Fred Karlin; **Special Effects:** Charles Schulthies and Brent Sellstrom; **Cinematography:** Gene Polito; **Cast:** James Brolin, Richard Benjamin, Yul Brynner, Dick Van Patten, Alan Oppenheimer, Majel Barrett, Victoria Shaw, Norman Bartold, Steve Franken

The movie starts with a promotional trailer for the world's newest theme park. It sounds interesting, but the prices are pretty steep: $1,000 per day, per guest (in early 1970s dollars, no less), is the rate to stay at Delos, the greatest experience of a lifetime. One's cash buys a visit to either Romanworld, Medievalworld, or the film's title park, Westworld. Each section of the park is populated by robot people and animals, all there for the pleasure of the guests. Want to sleep with the scullery maid? Do it. You paid for it and she's not real anyway. Want to fight a duel, rob a bank, be a gladiator, attend an orgy, and sleep with a queen? Anything is possible in Delos.

Taking the sloganeers up on their offer, people flock to the park. Two of these thrill seekers in particular, Peter Martin (Benjamin) and John Blane (Brolin), become the focus of the film's tour of Delos—Westworld in particular. On their first day, the pair have great fun killing robot gunfighters and cavorting with the robot ladies. On the second day, however, things take an ugly turn. There have been hints that something might be wrong with some of the robots. On Martin and Blane's second day in the park, these complications the technicians have been noticing come to a head. Blane decides to have some fun and kill a local gunslinging robot (Brynner). No one is more shocked than Blane (except perhaps Martin as it begins to dawn on him that he's going to be next) when the robot guns him down with swift efficiency. Martin is now on his own, running for his life from his robotic pursuer.

Westworld is a highly effective, intricate film. The directorial debut of science fiction writer Crichton, it's an impressive first film. The sci-fi level is at an all-time high here. For instance, why do the robots begin to malfunction? Crichton's answer is a collective virus. What's being described is what later became known as a "computer virus," but the filmmaker came up with the idea before it had an official name. Also, Crichton's script is nicely textured. There are plenty of interesting images—such as the flight controller whose image-filled reflecting sunglasses foreshadows the inhuman world ahead—to keep one thinking, as well as fun sequences such as Brolin telling his pal that there is "No way to get hurt," after which Benjamin drinks some unnamed rot gut and almost chokes to death.

Westworld is a nice treat, from its intelligent script to its highly evocative sound track. Martin is a lawyer, but the audience is led to believe that he is honest and decent. He's just been divorced and, feeling the world close in on him, has gone to Delos to get away from it all. Martin's purity allows him to survive, just barely. It's humanistic themes like these, coupled with the picture's advanced (for its time) sci-fi notions, that make it a true classic.

As for its sequel, *Futureworld*, one can give the cast and crew credit for trying, but little else. Peter Fonda and Blythe Danner are reporters covering the reopening of Delos after its disastrous meltdown. The secret they uncover is that the whole setup is really a trial run for the replacement of key people around the world with robots. It might have been interesting if the plot hadn't been telegraphed from almost the first minute.

It's interesting to note the parallels between these two films and later Crichton efforts concerning amusement parks gone awry, *JURASSIC PARK* and *THE LOST WORLD*.

Note: Yul Brynner as a gunfighter is costumed exactly as he was in his most famous western film role, *The Magnificent Seven*.

WHAT'S SO BAD ABOUT FEELING GOOD?

Universal, 1968, Color, 94 min

Producer: George Seaton; **Director:** Seaton; **Screenplay:** Seaton and Robert Pirosh; **Music:** Frank De Vol; **Cinematography:** Ernesto Caparros; **Cast:** Mary Tyler Moore, George Peppard, Dom De Luise, Charles Lane, Nathaniel Frey, Susan Saint James, John McMartin, Don Stroud, Cleavon Little, Thelma Ritter, Moses Gunn

There's a toucan spreading a virus through one of the most heavily populated cities in the world, but don't worry—everything should be okay. The citizens of New York City find themselves breaking out with . . . happiness, and the town becomes orderly and loving. The plot would have allowed for some great social commentary, but instead the filmmakers settled for something light and amusing.

WHAT WAITS BELOW

Adams Apple Film Company, 1985, Color, 88 min, VT

Producers: Robert D. Bailey, Sandy Howard, Don Levin, Mel Pearl, and Jeffrey M. Sneller; **Director:** Don Sharp; **Screenplay:** Ken Barnett, Christy Marx, and Robert Vincent O'Neill; **Music:** Michel Rubini and Denny Jaeger; **Special Effects:** Bret Culpepper; **Cine-**

matography: Virgil L. Harper; **Cast:** Robert Powell, Lisa Blount, Timothy Bottoms, Richard Johnson, Anne Heywood, Liam Sullivan

Stalwart archaeologists find a lost race living in South American caverns.

WHAT PLANET ARE YOU FROM?

Columbia, 2000, Color, 100 min

Producers: Mike Nichols, Gary Shandling, Neil Machlis, Brad Grey, and Bernie Brillstein; **Director:** Nichols; **Screenplay:** Shandling, Michael Leeson, Ed Solomon, and Peter Tolan; **Music:** Carter Burwell; **Special Effects:** Patrick McClung, Jenny Fulle, David Taritero, Daniel Kuehn, Dawn Guinta, Kevin J. Jolly, Guy Wiedmann, George Suhayda, Lee Berger, Eileen Moran, Mark Rodahl, Uel Hormann, Tex Kadonaga, Daphne Dentz, C. Marie Davis, and Gregory Oehler; **Cinematography:** Michael Ballhaus, A.S.C.; **Cast:** Garry Shandling, Annette Bening, Greg Kinnear, Ben Kingsley, Linda Fiorentino, John Goodman, Richard Jenkins, Caroline Aaron, Judy Greer, Nora Dunn, Ann Cusack, Camryn Manheim, Janeane Garofalo

Comedian Gary Shandling stars as an alien who hails from an all-male planet, where the guys have been alone for so that long their sex organs have withered away, which is why Shandling has to have an artificial set installed for his big mission to Earth. After a bit of training in what women are all about (which includes tips such as "Tell them they smell nice," "Compliment their shoes," and so on), he is sent to Earth to find a woman, impregnate her, produce a healthy offspring, and pave the way for the aliens to corrupt Earth from within.

It's a thin but hysterical plot that Shandling and his fellow stars fill out perfectly. Of course, all those good performances could at least partially be credited to the film's director, Mike Nichols. The director's credits start in the '60s with films such as *Who's Afraid of Virginia Woolf?* and *The Graduate*, extending over the years to *Catch-22*, *The Birdcage*, *Postcards from the Edge*, and many more, revealing a thread running through them all—Nichols likes comedies where the dark side of things is exposed.

What Planet Are You From? is not nearly as destructive of the human relationship as some of his other work, but it is not the inane sex comedy a number of reviewers labeled it either. The film explores the nature of the male/female relationship quite well. How do we meet each other? What are the male motives for entering the courtship dance? The female reasons? Why is communication between the sexes so difficult? What is it about the birth of a child that can heal the saddest relationships? And on and on. The film doesn't pretend to offer much in the way of answers to these questions, but that's all right. It is enough that it simply raises them. As hard science fiction, this isn't much of a close encounter picture. But as a human drama packed with laughs, it's quite good.

There is one tremendous special effect worth noting. Near the end of the film, the audience is shown an exterior shot of Shandling's planet for the first time. It is a staggering, Metropolis-like setting, overwhelming in the grand 1930s pulp sci-fi style. The second thing that hits the viewer is that it is completely gray. Shandling's character sees his world at the moment in the film when the secrets of what men and women are all about comes together in his head; this wonderful bit of symbolism comments on the drabness of male existence without female companionship—towering and impressive as an edifice, but cold and colorless and empty as well.

WHEN DINOSAURS RULED THE EARTH

Warner Bros., 1970, Color, 96 min, VT, LD

Producer: Aida Young; **Director:** Val Guest; **Screenplay:** J.G. Ballard and Guest; **Music:** Mario Nascimbene; **Special Effects:** Jim Danforth, Dave Allen, Roger Dicken, Garth Inns, Allan Bryce, Brian Johnson, Martin Gutteridge, and Brian Humphrey; **Cinematography:** Dick Bush; **Cast:** Victoria Verri, Robin Hawdon, Patrick Allen, Drewe Henley, Imogen Hassall, Magda Konopka, Patrick Holt

A tale loosely based on *Romeo and Juliet* told against a prehistoric backdrop featuring dinosaurs. Danforth and the rest of the special effects gang deliver some great (for the time) special effects.

Note: J.G. Ballard fans should be warned that the sci-fi writer's only contribution to the screenplay was its story line. The less talented Guest transformed it into what made it to the screen.

WHEN THE MAN IN THE MOON SEEKS A WIFE

Clarendon, 1908, b&w, silent short

Director: Percy Slow; **Screenplay:** Lanford Reed

The man in the Moon, according to this somewhat bizarre oldie, is an actual man. Here he comes to Earth via hot air balloon looking for a wife.

WHEN WORLDS COLLIDE

Paramount, 1951, Color, 83 min, VT, LD

Producer: George Pal; **Director:** Rudolph Mate; **Screenplay:** Sydney Boehm; **Music:** Leith Stevens; **Special Effects:** Gordon Jennings, Harry Barndollar, and Chesley Bonestell; **Cinematography:** John F. Seitz and W. Howard Greene; **Cast:** Larry Keating, Richard Derr, Peter Hanson, Barbara Rush, John Hoyt, Mary Murphy, Laura Elliot, Stuart Whitman

Cut away the romantic subplots, and the story that remains is this: Scientist Handron (Keating) calculates that runaway planets Zyra and Bellus are on a collision course with Earth. Zyra, which orbits Bellus, will pass by Earth causing mass gravitational destruction. Then, 19 days later, Bellus will crash into Earth. Bellus and Earth will be destroyed, and Zyra will assume Earth's orbit around the Sun.

As might be expected, few believe Handron. One who does makes all the difference, however, as he is a multimillionaire. He proposes that his fortune be used to build an ark that will take the select cream of humanity to safety on Zyra after it falls into Earthly orbit. The ark is built, and everything comes to pass as Handron predicted. A surging wave of desperate people try to storm the ark, but wisely the commander of the ship takes off, burning the rioters on the launching pad. Earth is destroyed in a wonderful show of special effects, and then the tricky landing on Zyra handsomely pays off a well-paced film.

This true classic of the genre was based on the novel by Philip Wylie and Edwin Balmer, which was cut rather severely, but interestingly enough, this time the changes the filmmakers felt it needed were actually all for the better.

Note: Although not made until the '50s, the rights for this movie were purchased by Paramount some 20 years earlier for director Cecil B. DeMille. DeMille passed and made his version of *Cleopatra* rather than *When Worlds Collide*, which may all be for the best.

WHERE TIME BEGAN

(Spain), 1978, Color, 86 min, VT

Director: Piquer Simon; **Screenplay:** John Melson, Carlos Puerto, and Juan Piquer; **Music:** Juan Carlos

Calderón and Juan José Garcia Caffi; **Special Effects:** Francisco Prósper and Emilo Gi Ruiz; **Cinematography:** Andrés Berenguer; **Cast:** Kenneth More, Pep Munne, Jack Taylor

Jules Verne's classic *Journey to the Center of the Earth* is adapted here in as boringly pedestrian a manner as possible.

WHO? (aka: ROBO MAN)

Allied Artists, 1975, Color, 93 min, VT

Producer: Barry Levinson; **Director:** Jack Gold; **Screenplay:** John Gould; **Music:** John Cameron; **Special Effects:** Richard Richtsfeld; **Cinematography:** Petrus R. Schlömp; **Cast:** Elliot Gould, Joseph Bova, Trevor Howard, James Noble, Ed Grover, John Lehne

Martino (Bova), a highly valuable American physicist, is injured unto death in a terrible automobile accident that takes place near the Berlin Wall. The Communists of East Germany seize the injured man and later return a man whom they claim is the physicist. No one is certain whether it really is the physicist or not, for Martino's face has been cybernetically reconstructed. Is it really the physicist, or is it a Russian agent sent back in his place? This is the question FBI agent Elliot Gould must crack. *Who?*, based on a far superior novel by Algis Budrys, is competent work, but that's about all.

WHO WOULD KILL JESSIE?

See *KDO CHCE ZABIT JESSII?*

WILD IN THE STREETS

AIP, 1968, Color, 97 min, VT, LD

Producers: James H. Nicholson and Samuel Z. Arkoff; **Director:** Barry Shear; **Screenplay:** Robert Thom; **Music:** Les Baxter; **Special Effects:** Fred Williams; **Cinematography:** Richard Moore; **Cast:** Christopher Jones, Hal Holbrook, Shelley Winters, Diane Varsi, Millie Perkins, Pamela Mason, Army Archerd, Ed Begley, Walter Winchell, Richard Pryor, Dick Clark, Melvin Belli, Paul Frees, Bert Freed

It's some time right around the corner and politics are about to take a very strange turn. First, politician Holbrook uses rock star Jones to further his career. But Jones extracts a promise from Holbrook to lower

Wild, Wild Planet (MGM / AUTHOR'S COLLECTION)

the voting age to 18. Once this is done, Jones gets himself elected president of the United States. He and his pals have everyone over 35 locked away in concentration camps and then have a ball living like brainless pigs. At the end of the film, however, 13- and 14-year-olds across the country are fed up with what is going on in the country. There will be another "revolution" soon.

Like all supposedly cutting-edge, progressive art, it takes but the briefest passing of time to reveal how the film wheezes and gasps under the weight of its own pretensions.

WILD JUNGLE CAPTIVE

See *JUNGLE CAPTIVE*

WILD, WILD PLANET
(aka: THE CRIMINALS OF THE GALAXY, THE GALAXY CRIMINALS)

MGM, 1967, Color, 93 min

Producers: Joseph Fryd and Antonio Margheriti; **Director:** Margheriti; **Screenplay:** Ivan Reiner and Renato Moretti; **Music:** Francesco Lavagnino; **Cinematography:** Riccardo Pallottini; **Cast:** Tony Russell, Umberto Raho, Franco Nero, Lisa Gastoni, Massimo Serato, Carlo Giustini

A female alien shrinks Earth scientists to doll size to be able to manipulate them for her own dastardly purposes. Earth astronauts do their best to stop her.

WILD, WILD WEST

Warner Bros., 1999, Color, 107 min, VT, DVD

Producers: Barry Sonnenfeld, Tracy Glaser, Kim Le Masters, Barry Josephson, Doug Lodato, Jon Peters, Graham Place, Joel Simon, Chris Soldo, Bill Todman, Jr., and Neri Kyle Tannenbaum; **Director:** Sonnenfeld; **Screenplay:** S.S. Wilson, Jim Thomas, John Thomas, Brent Maddock, Jeffrey Price, and Peter S. Seaman; **Music:** Elmer Bernstein; **Special Effects:** Rick Baker, Katrina Stovold, Eric Brevig, Candice Scott, Kelly Fischer, Aaron Muskalski, Michael Lantieri, Karen M. Murphy, Jacqueline M. Lopez, Ladd McPartland, Halmage Watson, and Brian Tipton; **Cinematography:** Michael Ballhaus and Stefan Czapsky; **Cast:** Will Smith, Kevin Kline, Kenneth Branagh, Selma Hayek, Ted Levine, M. Emmet Walsh, Ling Bai, Rodney A. Grant, Garcelle Beauuais, Musetta Vander, Sofia Eng, Frederique Van Der Wal, Ty O'Neal

It's the 1800s and crime has taken an international as well as a science fiction bent. Thus it's time for the president of the United States to create the Secret Service and to install as its first agents special government agent James West (Smith), long on charm and wit, and special government agent Artemus Gordon (Kline), a master of disguises and a brilliant inventor of gadgets large and small. The two are given the mission of tracking down the diabolical genius Dr. Arliss Loveless (Branagh), who is plotting to capture the president with the aid of his huge walking weapons-transport vehicle called the Tarantula, a gigantic Jules Vernesque, steam-powered, spider-shaped bit of Victorian nonsense. West and Gordon begin as competitors but soon pool their talents to become a wily team of operatives who trust each other . . . most of the time.

The Warner publicity department described the film at the time of its release as "a retro epic that mixes witty science fiction with hip-hop savoir-fare—all set against a Western background." What showed up on screen lacked wit, but the stuff about sci-fi meeting hip-hop in the Old West is accurate enough. One of the main problems with this movie is that no real attempt is made to explain how an African-American man could be a special government agent working in the Deep South in 1869. This is no racist stand. This picture could have been a World War II film about a rabbi who is Hitler's personal adviser. The idea could be highly entertaining . . . if given some explanation. But just presenting the idea as the facts of your story without any supporting details is going to leave the more discriminating elements of your audience disappointed.

The film moves along quickly, but the characters are one dimensional, the plot razor thin, and its execution filled with mistakes. For instance, the movie has General Grant creating the Secret Service. He didn't; it was Lincoln. Another example: Machines that do one thing when you push a button do something different when the same button is pushed later. Great care and loving detail went into the various machines and devices that fill the picture. The level of craft here in far exceeds that of the original television show upon which this film was based, but that is the only point where the feature version shines in comparison to its source material.

WING COMMANDER

20th Century Fox, 1999, Color, 90 min, VT, DVD

Producers: Todd Moyer, Jean-Martial LeFranc, and Romain Schroeder; **Director:** Chris Roberts; **Screenplay:** Roberts; **Music:** David Arnold and Kevin Kiner; **Special Effects:** Peter Lamont, Chris Brown, and Digital Anvil; **Cinematography:** Thierry Arbogast; **Cast:** Freddie Prinze, Jr., Saffron Burrows, Matthew Lillard, Tchéky Karyo, Jürgen Prochnow, David Warner, David Suchet

It's Earth year 2564. Up until this time, the planetwide alliance known as the Confederation has been expanding peacefully out into space. This outward thrust was led by a group known as the Pilgrims, instinctive navigators capable of finding their way between the myriad dangers of space through a genetic combination of extrasensory skills and luck. The golden days of quiet expansion are over, though. Now the Confederation has come up against a vicious, bloodthirsty race of quite unreasonable aliens, the Kilrathi. They will not negotiate. They will not even share space. They want it all. Obviously, war is inevitable.

As the picture opens, the Kilrathi launch a major sneak attack and capture a computer navigation device that will allow them to bypass the defending Earth fleet. Instead of having to fight their way inch by inch to their enemy's home planet, they'll be able to jump through space and arrive within our solar system. Everyone is doomed. It's all over.

But what if there was one ship full of crackerjack young, hard-drinking, fast-loving deep-fighter pilots who could put themselves between the Kilrathi fleet and Earth, who could recapture the computer codes, find out where the enemy was going to arrive, and beat them there? Could that save the day?

Attention to details will not help in this film. Everything runs together in a terrible jumble, but not much

Wing Commander (WING COMMANDER PRODUCTIONS / AUTHOR'S COLLECTION)

makes any sense. Why are the Pilgrims hated throughout the galaxy? The audience is told that they became arrogant. Now the few remaining Pilgrims (the targets of unbelievably unreasoning antireligious bigotry) hide their identities out of fear. And yet, these are the people who time and again save the day. It seems they deserve their arrogance (of course, the Pilgrims shown on-camera are the least arrogant characters in the picture), but this question is never resolved.

Nor are many others. For instance, the fighters leaving the main "aircraft carrier" of the film need a runway. Why, more than 500 years into our future, have our flying ships lost the VTOL (vertical take-off and landing) capabilities we now have? Moreover, when these ships take off, they actually dip when going over the edge of the carrier, as if being pulled down by gravity. There is also a knee-slappingly hilarious gaffe when a wrecked fighter needs to be pushed off the runway, and it actually falls over the edge of the ship as if falling into the ocean below instead of simply floating away. Absolutely awful science riddles this film, so much so that it becomes silly even to watch for it.

Wing Commander is based on a video game of the same name, and the only thing it has in its favor is sheer stupid fun. The battle sequences are just outstanding. Some of the destroyer and battleship explosion sequences are more impressive than those in STARSHIP TROOPERS. With over 250 visual digital effects shots, the film is an action-packed thrill ride, and viewers interested in a bit of cinematic roller coaster riding will enjoy this on that level, but no more. One particularly impressive effects sequence, those moments the film calls "time-splicing," involved a series of 60 cameras arrayed along a 120-degree arc. The rig enabled the crew to film two seconds of footage, at 30 frames per second, moving around action that is essentially frozen in space. Employed to great effect in a few music videos and television ads, *Wing Commander* was the first to use the technique in a feature film. It was utilized here to depict the effect of slipping through a space-time portal, and it has to be said that it looks great.

WINGED SERPENT, THE

See *Q*

WITHOUT A SOUL

World, 1916, b&w, silent short

Producer: James Young; **Director:** Young; **Screenplay:** Young; **Cast:** Clara Kimball Young, Edward M. Kimball, Alec B. Frances

In this interesting morality play, a scientist is forced to stand by helplessly as his daughter dies trying a bold experiment. He revitalizes her with an electrical device of his own creation, resurrecting her from the dead. The reanimated girl is no longer the sweet child he knew, however, but a soulless and cruel creature without pity or kindness. When she dies a second time, though it breaks his heart, the scientist does not revive her.

WITHOUT WARNING (aka: IT CAME WITHOUT WARNING)

World Amusement Partnership Nr. 108, 1980, Color, 89 min

Producers: Curtis Burch, Paul Kimatian, Greydon Clark, Skip Steloff, Milton Spenser, Lyn Freeman, and Daniel Grodnik; **Director:** Clark; **Screenplay:** Steve Mathis, Ben Nett, Freeman, and Grodnik; **Music:** Dan Wyman; **Special Effects:** Joseph Phillip Quinlivan III and Dana Rheaume; **Cinematography:** Dean Cundey; **Cast:** Jack Palance, Cameron Mitchell, Martin Landau, Ralph Meeker, Tarah Nutter, Sue Ane Langdon, Neville Brand, Larry Storch

An alien invasion film meant to be a comedy.

WIZARD, THE

20th Century Fox, 1927, b&w, silent feature

Director: Richard Rossen; **Screenplay:** Malcolm Stuart Boylan; **Cinematography:** Frank Good; **Cast:** Leila Hyams, Edmund Lowe, George Kotsonaros, Oscar Smith

A scientist mixes men and monkeys, putting a human head on an ape's body and then sending it out to kill his enemies. As usual, the created does in its creator in the end.

WIZARD OF MARS

American General, 1964, Color, 81 min

Producer: David Hewitt; **Director:** Hewitt; **Screenplay:** Hewitt; **Music:** Frank A. Coe; **Cinematography:** Austin McKinney; **Cast:** John Carradine, Vic McGee, Roger Gentry

Simply put, an Earth ship goes to Mars, and when it lands, its passengers disembark to discover that the Red Planet is filled with magical fantasy creatures in a bizarre parody of *The Wizard of Oz* that's too weird not to be fun.

WIZARDS

20th Century Fox, 1977, Color, 80 min, VT, LD

Producer: Ralph Bakshi; **Director:** Bakshi; **Screenplay:** Bakshi; **Music:** Andrew Billing; **Animation:** Irven Spense, Ian Miller, David Jonas, and Ted Bemiller; **Cast:** Bob Holt, Jesse Wells, Richard Romanus, David Proval, Mark Hamill

This is an animated feature of a time after people have nuked themselves into a new dark age complete with magic. Two brothers are born, one good and one evil. The bad brother starts conquering everything in sight, much like Hitler sweeping through Eastern Europe, forcing the other brother to stir himself. The two duel with magic. The bad brother's magic is better than the good brother's, so the good brother pulls out an ancient handgun and shoots the bad brother.

There is good artwork here but such mindlessly bad animation to wade through to get to it that there is no joy from the film's few moments of quality. Add in the screenplay's haphazard writing, complete lack of a moral point, foul language, and perverted attitude, and this is absolutely not for children.

WOMAN IN THE MOON

See *DIE FRAU IM MOND*

WOMEN OF THE PREHISTORIC PLANET (aka: PREHISTORIC PLANET WOMEN)

Realart, 1965, Color, 87 min, VT

Producer: George Gilbert; **Director:** Arthur C. Pierce; **Screenplay:** Pierce; **Special Effects:** Howard A. Anderson; **Music:** Mel White; **Cinematography:** Archie R. Dalzell; **Cast:** Wendell Corey, Keith Larsen, John Agar, Stuart Margolin, Merry Anders, Irene Tsu, Paul Gilbert, Adam Roarke

Astronauts land on a planet populated by prehistoric humans.

WONDERFUL CHAIR, THE

Brockliss, 1910, b&w, silent short

Why is it a wonderful chair? Because it catches burglars.

WONDERFUL ELECTO-MAGNET, THE

Edison, 1909, b&w, silent short

A wonderful magnet attracts people.

WONDERFUL FLUID, A

Pathé (France), 1908, b&w, silent short

A fluid makes everything and anything grow.

WONDERFUL HAIR REMOVER, THE

Gaumont (Great Britain), 1910, b&w, silent short

An amazing hair remover lives up to its name.

WONDERFUL MARRYING MIXTURE, THE

Walturdaw, 1910, b&w, silent short

A wonderful mixture arranges marriages out of thin air.

WONDERFUL PILLS

Cines (Italy), 1909, b&w, silent short

New wonderful pills cure people of indolence.

WONDERFUL RAYS, THE

Savoia (France), 1919, b&w, silent short

Wonderful rays re-create the images of crimes.

WONDERFUL REMEDY, A

Pathé (France), 1909, b&w, silent short

The remedy makes ugly people beautiful and beautiful people ugly. Is that really so wonderful?

WORLD GONE WILD

Apollo Pictures, 1988, Color, 95 min, VT, LD

Producer: Robert L. Rosen; **Director:** Lee H. Katzin; **Screenplay:** Jorge Zamacona; **Special Effects:** Cliff Wenger; **Music:** Laurence Juber; **Cinematography:** Don Burgess; **Cast:** Michael Paré, Bruce Dern, Catherine Mary Stewart, Adam Ant, Anthony James, Rick Podell

In the 21st century humankind has almost wiped itself out, and a poor defenseless village needs protection from a cult leader and his followers.

WORLD, THE FLESH AND THE DEVIL, THE

MGM, 1959, b&w, 95 min, VT, LD

Producer: George Englund; **Director:** Ranald MacDougall; **Screenplay:** MacDougall; **Music:** Miklos Rozsa; **Special Effects:** Lee LeBlanc; **Cinematography:** Harold J. Marzorati; **Cast:** Harry Belafonte, Inger Stevens, Mel Ferrer

A black man (Belafonte) is trapped in a mine accident. When he finally manages to free himself, he discovers that the reason no one tried to help him is that everyone is dead. A nuclear war broke out and while he was trapped, ended. The film starts with tremendously powerful images of Belafonte alone in a completely deserted Manhattan but then begins to fizzle. First Belafonte discovers a white woman, Stevens, who is happy to find another human being, no matter what color he is. Then along comes Ferrer, who is white and male and a bigot. Outraged at what he has found, Ferrer attempts to kill Belafonte so that he can have Stevens for himself. Then, after chasing Belafonte around, Ferrer concludes that they should all live together in peace. The top-notch cast does what it can, but the heavy-handed moralism weakens the entertainment value.

WORLD WITHOUT END

Allied Artists, 1955, Color, 80 min, VT

Producer: Richard Hermanance; **Director:** Edward Bernds; **Screenplay:** Bernds; **Music:** Leith Stevens; **Special Effects:** Milt Rice, Jack Rabin, and Irving Block; **Cinematography:** Ellsworth Fredericks; **Cast:** Hugh Marlowe, Nancy Gates, Rod Taylor, Booth Coleman, Shawn Smith, Nelson Leigh, Christopher Dark, Lisa Montell, Everett Glass

Astronauts out for a quick orbit of Mars pass through a time warp and upon their return to Earth discover that the year is now 2508. Humanity has nuked itself into oblivion. Normal humans now live in caves, constantly at war with the mutants who live outside. The astronauts team up with the spelunkers, create a mess of 20th-century killing machines, and help wipe out the mutants.

X, THE UNKNOWN

Hammer (Great Britain), 1956, 86 min/Warner Bros. (U.S.), 80 min, b&w, VT, DVD

Producer: Anthony Hinds; **Director:** Leslie Norman; **Screenplay:** Jimmy Sangster; **Cinematography:** Gerald Gibbs; **Music:** James Bernard; **Special Effects:** Jack Curtis and Les Bowie; **Cast:** Dean Jagger, Edward Chapman, Leo McKern, William Lucas, Anthony Newley, Michael Ripper, Peter Hammond, Edward Judd, Ian MacNaughton, Mariane Brauns

A blob of radioactive mud heaves its way up from the center of the Earth. The thing emerges in Scotland, hungry and ready for a little destruction. The entity devours everything in its path, but its real quest is for radioactive materials, which make it grow both stronger and larger. Though the effects are only adequate, this is a great low-budget treat.

X-FILES: THE MOVIE

20th Century Fox, 1998, Color, 121 min, VT, DVD

Producers: Chris Carter, Frank Sputnitz, Lata Ryan, Daniel Sackheim, Mary Astadourian, and Bruce Devan; **Director:** Rob Bowman; **Screenplay:** Carter and Sputnitz; **Music:** Mark Snow and Mike Oldfield; **Special Effects:** Stan Blackwell, Mat Beck, David Collier, Kelly Fischer, Steven Hintz, Tim Conway, Paul J. Lombardi, Scott D. Mattson, Mark A. Brown, Brian C. Davis, David Peterson, Ron Petruccione, Pamela Chouldes, Matthew Ferro, Scott Roark, Scott Shields, Robert Spurlock, and Chuck Stewart Turolano; **Cinematography:** Ward Russell; **Cast:** David Duchovny, Gillian Anderson, Mitch Pileggi, John Neville, Jeffrey DeMunn, William B. Davis, Blythe Danner, Martin Landau, Terry O'Quinn, Lucas Black, Armin Mueller-Stahl, Christopher Fenwell, Cody Newton, Blake Stokes, Dean Haglund, Tom Braidwood, Bruce Harwood, Don S. Williams, George Murdock

Several children discover a hole in the ground. One climbs in to prove how brave he is. Something else is proved when he never comes out.

Shift scene to a federal skyscraper in Texas. A bomb has been planted within. The building has been evacuated, the bomb has been found, and FBI agents are trying to defuse it. Or are they? While a confused agent Fox Mulder (Duchovny) watches in horror, the bomb squad agent just sits in front of the bomb and allows it to explode. Mulder barely escapes. The massive building is reduced to rubble. Why did the man defusing the bomb purposely allow it to detonate? Of course, any fan of *The X-Files* television show would know the answer—the building was being destroyed to cover something up. In this case, it is the body of the boy from the first sequence—or more important, the truth that would be revealed by his corpse. He has become

the victim of something the government is trying to keep quiet, and so his body must be destroyed in this "routine," nonattention-getting manner.

If that sounds absurd, it's only the tip of the iceberg. *The X-Files*, a popular television series, made its reputation by portraying the government as an abusive, intrusive, thousand-armed monster that is constantly deceiving, manipulating, and selling out the American people, particularly when it comes to the question of the existence of extraterrestrial life and its habit of visiting our planet. Although one may not wish to argue with that theory, the point should be made that there has never been an American government that could secretly pull off anything as complex as the conspiracy postulated in *The X-Files*.

To enjoy this motion picture, one needs detailed knowledge of the complicated history of the television show or at least its lengthy and involved UFO subplot. *The X-Files* movie is merely a chapter in the never-ending saga of the television series. It was intended to tie up all the loose ends from the series and explain all the mysteries. Although the film does indeed explain some things and tie up a few loose ends, it also created far more of them. This wouldn't be so bad, except the filmmakers did these things badly.

This movie is riddled with mistakes, some caused by faulty science, some by sloppy filmmaking. For instance, in the opening sequence when the boy is grabbed in the hole in the ground, he is infected by black ooze that takes over his body, working its way up his legs. But as the camera pans upward, the audience sees the ooze also working its way *up* his arms, instead of *down* his arms after having passed completely up through the trunk of his body then out through his shoulders. In another instance, Mulder watches the bomb squad member at work and makes a call on his cell phone, even though the bomb's electronic timer/detonator unit is in plain sight. Any good FBI man would know that by operating an electronic device in such close proximity he was risking setting off the explosives he was supposed to be defusing.

These may sound like quibbles, but a more important glitch involves Mulder's enemies—the secret cabal that has struck a deal with aliens that will allow its members to survive when the planet is taken over. They're perfectly willing to kill anyone who gets in their way, but taking out the man who has stopped their plans scores of times is never allowed. This would make him a "martyr," it seems, and that is somehow a far greater penalty to their plans than all of his interference. Of course, to whom he would be a martyr and how this would stop any of their future plans is never explained. In the film, finally having endured enough of Mulder's

interference, the head of this organization decrees that they will "take away from Mulder what is most important to him." They are referring to his partner, Scully (Anderson). However, the organization subsequently does nothing to her. True, Scully is stung by one of their mutant bees, but the insect was not sent by them. It gets caught in her clothing by accident, and the audience is supposed to believe that her accident is all part of some master plan. This kind of misdirection stems from the lazy writing, which, sadly, characterized *The X-Files* week after week.

Note: Although this movie is forgettable, many episodes of the television series are quite good. The producers of the show fell into a recognizable pattern early on of delivering high-quality, well-written shows about all manner of unusual, supernatural menaces—except UFOs. Extraterrestrial story lines all had to be tied in to the "master story line," which could never be revealed for fear of losing the audience. If you're tracking down the old shows on tape or in syndication, look for any that do not deal with aliens, almost always a guarantee of higher quality and easier understanding.

X FROM OUTER SPACE, THE
(aka: GILALA, BIG SPACE MONSTER GILALA, GIRARA, UCHU DAIKAIJÛ GIRARA)

AIP, 1967, Color, 89 min

Director: Kazui Nihomatsu; **Screenplay:** Nihomatsu, Eibi Montomorochi, and Moriyoshi Ishida; **Cinematography:** Shizuo Hirase; **Music:** Taku Izumi; **Special Effects:** Hiroshi Ikeda; **Cast:** Peggy Neal, Franz Gruber, Eiji Okada

An Earthly spacecraft on its way home picks up a bit of alien protoplasm. The goop resists the heat of re-entry, then grows into a typical Japanese giant monster-movie monster—this one resembling a giant rampaging chicken. It then tromps all over Tokyo while fighting the army.

X-MEN

20th Century Fox, 2000, Color, 92 min, VT, DVD

Producers: Lauren Shuler Donner, Ralph Winter, Avi Rand, Stan Lee, Richard Donner, Tom DeSanto, Joel Simon, and William S. Todman, Jr., **Director:** Bryan Singer; **Screenplay:** DeSanto, Singer, and David Hayter; **Cinematography:** Newton Thomas Sigel; **Music:** Michael Kamen; **Special Effects:** Michael Fink, Gordon Smith, Digital Domain, Cinesite, POP

X-Men (20TH CENTURY FOX / AUTHOR'S COLLECTION)

Film & Animation, Kleiser-Walczak, Matte World Digital, C.O.R.E. Digital Pictures, Jjamb Productions, Inc., and FX Smith, Inc.; **Cast:** Hugh Jackman, Patrick Stewart, Ian McKellen, Ramke Janssen, James Marsden, Anna Paquin, Tyler Mane, Ray Park, Rebecca Romijn-Stamos, Bruce Davison, Matthew Sharp, Brett Morris, Katrina Florece, Sumela Kay

The film revolves around the struggle between regular humanity and the "children of the atom." As common men and women are *Homo sapiens*, these are Homo superior, the next link in the chain of evolution, a step forward that involves unique genetic mutations that first appear at puberty. These mutations result in various superpowers that can be considered gifts or curses, depending on one's viewpoint and, of course, the power received.

Rabid bigot U.S. Senator Kelly (Davison) is out to expose the dangers of mutants living among us. Mutant Charles Xavier (Stewart) dislikes Kelly's ideas but seeks to protect him from Magneto (McKellen), another mutant who hopes to use Kelly to rid the world of humans so that he and his evil brotherhood of mutants can rule what remains and clear the way for Homo superior.

For those not in the know, *X-Men* is based on a comic-book concept created in 1963. Not a tremendous hit at the time, decades later a revamping of the story line made the book an international phenomenon and sold millions of books every month. From successes like this, sci-fi movies often spring, and this is a good one. The plot is a straightforward X-Men story right from the comics, one that translates easily to the screen and allows the filmmakers to concentrate on introducing the characters to those not well acquainted with the movie's source material.

The film's flaws are minor. For one, it is too short. For another, some elements of the source material were ignored. Costume and origin changes for the characters abound, but outside of these two minor points, comic-book fans and regular moviegoers alike have little to complain about. Part of the reason is certainly the impressive directorial skills of Bryan Singer (*The Usual Suspects, Apt Pupil*). The director, known for small, intri-

cate films, said at the time of the film's release that he was attracted to the underlying themes of racism and tolerance that run through the X-Men mythos.

> The story of the X-Men is quite political. It's about differences and similarities. Because the comic was born from the tumult of the '60s, there are political and sociological issues and messages inherent in the X-Men lore.

In fact the relationship between Xavier and his one-time friend and colleague, Magneto, exemplifies the ideological and philosophical differences of that era. They are essentially cut from the same cloth, and both see this mutated breed of humanity as a subject of persecution. However, Xavier lives to protect those who fear him, while Magneto lives to destroy them. Each believes his side is right. Neither is willing to compromise. Ultimately, the film is about how difficult it is to find a level of tolerance that is mutually beneficial to all involved. That's a philosophical concept that mankind and mutantkind could fight about forever.

The original comic-book idea of alienation was meant as a metaphor for puberty, which once it strikes, makes teenagers suddenly feel awkward, different, and alone. Such a metaphor can include experience of any groups outside the mainstream, however.

On a more mundane level, the movie succeeds as one of the few truly superior superhero movies. It possesses a number of imaginative, beautifully choreographed action sequences that were clearly devised by folks who understand that superheroes fight and think differently from normal people. The special effects are everything one expects from a big-budget picture. Incredible CGI rendering is evident everywhere, and the sets and model work, makeup and prosthetics, blue screen imaging and all the rest blend seamlessly to make a simple story into exciting entertainment.

Note: Just the 15 different sets of claws that the special effects crew had to make for Wolverine (Jackman) gives some idea of the effort expended. Apparently, the claws, along with the Toad's extendible tongue, gave special effects chief Gordon Smith some new wrinkles to work out. "Although I have been working with prosthetic technology for the last seven years, 'X-Men' required the newer field of silicone technology that had never been tried before on film," he explained.

Transforming Rebecca Romijn-Stamos into the mutant Mystique was equally challenging. The elaborate process required the application of 70 self-sticking prosthetics and painting her entire body blue, including her ears, nose, and the soles of her feet. Final touches included a vibrant red wig and yellow contact lenses. Initially, the process took 10 hours, but by the end of production, the makeup crew had it down to between six and eight hours, plus two hours to remove the prosthetics and paint. The strenuous procedure required Stamos to put in 22- to 24-hour days and prevented her from working two days in a row.

X-RAYS

G.A. Smith Studios (Great Britain), 1897, b&w, silent short

Director: G.A. Smith

An x-ray machine is aimed at two lovers. The result is a view of skeletal love. Oh well, even science fiction had to start somewhere.

X-17 TOP SECRET

(Spain/Italy), 1965, Color

Director: Amerigo Anton; **Cast:** Lang Jeffries, Angel Jordon, Moa Thia, Aurora De Alba

Rival international spies battle over bizarre scientific weapons in this pointless film with little science fiction content. Avoid.

"X"—THE MAN WITH X-RAY EYES
(aka: THE MAN WITH THE X-RAY EYES)

Alta Vista/AIP, 1963, Color, 88 min, VT

Producer: Roger Corman; **Director:** Corman; **Screenplay:** Robert Dillon and Ray Russell; **Cinematography:** Floyd Crosby; **Music:** Les Baxter; **Special Effects:** Ted Coodley and Daniel Haller; **Cast:** Ray Milland, Dina Van Der Vlis, John Hoyt, Don Rickles, Harold J. Stone, Dick Miller, John Dierkes

Ray Milland plays Dr. James Xavier, a surgeon with an obsession about the power of the human eye. The doctor wants to do more, be a better surgeon and save more lives. To this end, he develops a fluid that, when applied to the eye, should give the user the ability to see with far greater clarity . . . and perhaps beyond the normal limits of the human eye. At first, the doctor merely experiments on animals, with only discouraging results, as all of the test subjects go mad from whatever they see after receiving the drops. Unable to live with himself without understanding what is happening, Xavier applies the drops to his own eyes. Soon the good doctor has the power of an x-ray machine within his head.

Xavier's colleague (Stone) is worried about him. The two get into a heated discussion that leads to Stone's accidental fall from a great height. Afraid that he will be charged with murder, Xavier flees the scene, taking his drops with him. At first the doctor attempts to survive as a carnival worker, using his new x-ray sight for a mind-reading act. After that he moves on to Las Vegas, where he hopes to use his powers at the gaming tables. His ability arouses a little too much suspicion, however, and quite soon he is on the run again.

Eventually, Xavier ends up in the desert, where his powers reach their zenith. The doctor sees through to the center of the universe, a vision that leaves him shrieking in pain. The words of a tent evangelist ("If thine eye offend thee, pluck it out") suddenly make great sense to him.

This is a better than average Corman flick. It suffers from the same low-budget, mediocre special effects and hurried shooting schedule as do many of Corman's pictures, but there is much more of a solid core to this one than almost any of his other films, especially those from the same period. Milland deserves much of the credit for what is right with this nifty little moral package. Social science fiction issues are nicely addressed, and the film adds up to an interesting, poignant vision of one man's place in a universe much larger than his senses ever imagined.

Note: Don't expect a great deal from the finale. Xavier might "see through to the center of the universe," but the film expects viewers to use their imagination. That's all right, though. Using one's imagination is what science fiction is all about.

XTRO

New Line Cinema, 1983, Color, 82 min, VT

Producers: James M. Crawford, Robert Shaye, and Mark Forstater; **Director:** Harry Bromley Davenport; **Screenplay:** Robert Smith and Iain Cassie; **Cinematography:** John Metcalfe; **Music:** Davenport; **Special Effects:** David Anderson, Richard Gregory, Raymond Harris, Tom Harris, John Webber, and Francis Coates; **Cast:** Philip Sayer, Bernice Stegers, Danny Brainin, Maryann d'Abo, Simon Nash, Peter Mandell, Anna Wing

A man abducted by aliens finally makes his way back to Earth a number of years later, but he isn't quite the fun-loving guy he used to be. The filmmakers attempted to make up what they lacked in logic and a good story with sex and gore but fell on their collective faces.

Oddly enough the sequel, *Xtro II: The Second Encounter*, is a somewhat better film. Perhaps the second time around the filmmakers had the sense to swipe their plot from a much better film, *ALIEN*. The thing that is truly odd, however, is that the title *The Second Encounter* makes little sense since the two films have nothing to do with each other outside of having the same director. As for the third film in the series, *Xtro: Watch The Skies*, it even falls short of the first in the series.

XTRO II: THE SECOND ENCOUNTER

Excalibur Pictures/North American Pictures, 1990, Color, 92 min, VT

Producers: John A. Curtis, John Eyres, and Geoff Griffith; **Director:** Harry Bromley Davenport; **Screenplay:** John A. Curtis, Edward A. Kovach, Steven Lister, and Robert Smith; **Cinematography:** Nathaniel Massey; **Music:** Braun Farnon and Robert Smart; **Special Effects:** Greg Derochie; **Cast:** Jan-Michael Vincent, Paul Koslo, Tara Buckman, Jano Frandsen, Nicholas Lea, W.F. Wadden, Rolf Reynolds, Nic Amoroso

See *XTRO*

XTRO: WATCH THE SKIES

Dorian, 1995, Color, 90 min, VT, DVD

Producer: Jamie Beardsley; **Director:** Harry Bromley Davenport; **Screenplay:** Daryl Haney; **Cinematography:** Nathaniel Massey; **Cast:** Robert Culp, Andrew Divoff, Jim Hanks, Sal Landi, Karen Moncrieff

See *XTRO*

YEARS TO COME

Pathé (France), 1922, b&w, silent short

Producer: Hal Roach; **Cast:** Snub Pollard, Marie Mosquini

A routine but notably early attempt to look at a far-off future world where women are in charge of things in word as well as in deed.

YOG—MONSTER FROM SPACE
(aka: THE SPACE AMOEBA, YOG: THE SPACE AMOEBA)

Toho (Japan)/AIP (U.S.), 1971, Color, 84 min

Producers: Tomoyuki Tanaka and Fumio Tanaka; **Director:** Inoshiro Honda; **Screenplay:** Ei Ogawa; **Music:** Akira Ifukube; **Special Effects:** Sadamesa Arikawa; **Cinematography:** Yasuichi Sunokura; **Cast:** Akira Kubo, Kenji Sahara, Kosi Tsuchiya

An unmanned probe sent from Earth to Jupiter is diverted along the way by an unseen alien intelligence. The probe is turned around and taken back to Earth by the would-be invader, which sets the captured ship down on an island just south of Japan. There it mutates the Earth creatures it finds into horrible giants who then stomp all over Japan. This one's not good and not bad, but really just more of the same ol' rubber suit nonsense.

YOG: THE SPACE AMOEBA

See *YOG—MONSTER FROM SPACE*

YONGARY—MONSTER FROM THE DEEP (aka: MONSTER YONGKARI, GREAT MONSTER YONGKARI, GREAT MONSTER YONGARY, YONGKARI—MONSTER OF THE DEEP)

Kuk Dong/Toei (South Korea/Japan), 100 min/AIT (U.S.), 79 min, 1967, Color

Director: Kiduck Kim; **Screenplay:** Yungsung Suh; **Cinematography:** K. Nakagawa and I. Byon; **Cast:** Yungil Oh, Chungim Nam, Soonjai Lee, Moon Kang

More giant monster madness from Asia, this time from South Korea. This great epic silliness involves a giant creature from the ocean floor that causes trouble by consuming gasoline. Avoid.

YONGKARI—MONSTER FROM THE DEEP

See *YONGARY—MONSTER OF THE DEEP*

YOR, THE HUNTER FROM THE FUTURE (aka: THE WORLD OF YOR)

(Italy), 1983, Color, 88 min, VT, LD

Producers: Ugor Terzioglu, Sedat Akdemir, and Michele Marsala; **Director:** Anthony M. Dawson; **Screenplay:** Dawson, Juan Zanotto, Ray Collins, and Robert Bailey; **Music:** John Scott, Guido De Angelis, and Maurizio De Angelis; **Special Effects:** Antonio Margheriti and Edward Margheriti; **Cinematography:** Marcello Masciocchi; **Cast:** Reb Brown, Corinne Clery, John Steiner, Carole Andre, Alan Collins

A muscular adventurer played by an actor with the performing skills of a wounded seal battles sci-fi silliness in a future where action/adventure filmmaking is obviously a lost art. Avoid in every way possible.

YOU ONLY LIVE ONCE

See *MISSION STARDUST*

YOUNG EINSTEIN

Warner Bros. (Australia), 1988, Color, 90 min, VT, LD

Producers: Yahoo Serious, Ray Beattie, Graham Burke, Lulu Pinkus, Warwick Ross, and David Roach; **Director:** Serious; **Screenplay:** Serious and Roach; **Music:** Martin Armiger, William Motzing, and Tommy Tycho; **Special Effects:** Steve Courtley, Laurie Faen, Patrick Fitzgerald, and Pauline Grebert; **Cinematography:** Jeff Darling; **Cast:** Yahoo Serious, Odile Le Clezio, John Howard, Pee Wee Wilson, Su Cruickshank, Lulu Pinkus

This science fiction comedy postulates an alternative history in which not only did Albert Einstein come up with the theory of relativity, but that he also wooed Marie Curie along the way to inventing rock and roll, along with the electric guitar and a host of other goodies, including the formula for beer. While it may be one of the strangest but funniest movies in science fiction history, there's little actual sci-fi content, just a hip roller coaster ride of genteel laughs.

YOUNG FRANKENSTEIN

20th Century Fox, 1974, Color, 98 min, VT, LD

Producer: Michael Gruskoff; **Director:** Mel Brooks; **Screenplay:** Gene Wilder and Brooks; **Music:** John Morris; **Cinematography:** Gerald Hirschfeld; **Special Effects:** Henry Millar, Jr., and Hal Millar; **Cast:** Gene Wilder, Peter Boyle, Madeline Kahn, Teri Garr, Marty Feldman, Cloris Leachman, Kenneth Mars, Richard Haydn, Gene Hackman

See *FRANKENSTEIN*

ZAAT (aka: ATTACK OF THE SWAMP CREATURE, HYDRA, BLOOD WATERS OF DR. Z)

Horizon, 1973, Color, 100 min

Producer: Dan Barton; **Director:** Barton; **Screenplay:** Lee Larew and Ron Kivett; **Music:** Jami Defrates and Barry Hodgin; **Special Effects:** Kivett; **Cinematography:** Jack McGowan; **Cast:** Marshall Grauer, Wade Popwell, Dave Dickerson, Sanna Ringhaver, Paul Galloway

This film features yet another mad scientist, one whose specialty is marine biology, or at least it is until he decides to change his major to murder. He transforms himself into an aquatic monster and then sets out to kill everyone he can find, along with the help of his loyal army (navy?) of mutant guppies. There's not much here to satisfy anyone looking for true science fiction.

ZAMBO (aka: ZAMBO THE APEMAN, SHER-E-JUNGLE)

Bhavani (India), 1937, b&w, 157 min

Producer: M. Bhavani; **Director:** Bhavani; **Screenplay:** Bhavani; **Music:** Pandit Bedriprasad; **Cinematography:** R.M. Master; **Cast:** S.B. Nayampally, Sarla, Indira Wadker, Mehru (the gorilla)

A mad scientist in India transforms a gorilla into a human, and though he does this with the best of intentions, it's well known which road is paved with those. The more than two and a half hours of this are fairly unbearable.

ZAMBO THE APEMAN

See *ZAMBO*

ZAPPED!

Embassy Pictures Corporation, 1982, Color, 92 min, VT, LD

Producers: Jeffrey Apple, Thomas M. Hammel, Fran Schuster, Jonathan Noah Krivine, Howard Schuster, and Roger La Page; **Director:** Robert J. Rosenthal; **Screenplay:** Rosenthal and Bruce Rubin; **Music:** Charles Fox; **Special Effects:** Richard Albain, Max W. Anderson, Laurel Klick, Ron Nary, and Robert Blalack; **Cinematography:** Daniel Pearl; **Cast:** Scott Baio, Willie Aames, Scatman Crothers, Felice Schachter, Sue Ane Langdon, Heather Thomas, Robin Mandan, Greg Bradford

The halls of higher learning must have seemed like the perfect setting for a science fiction movie, especially this sci-fi comedy in which a charming but somewhat goofy student (Baio) accidentally acquires telekinetic powers. Like any teenage male, he selflessly puts his newfound skills to use for the betterment of all humankind . . . cheating at gambling and undressing attractive females. There's not much science fiction here, but for the crowd who's always wondered what it would be like if *Porky's* met *THE X-FILES,* here's a chance to find out.

ZARDOZ

20th Century Fox, 1974, Color, 105 min, VT, LD

Producer: John Boorman; **Director:** Boorman; **Screenplay:** Boorman; **Music:** David Munrow; **Special Effects:** Jerry Johnston; **Cinematography:** Geoffrey Unsworth; **Cast:** Sean Connery, Charlotte Rampling, Sarah Kestleman, Sally Anne Newton, John Alderton, Niall Buggy

The film opens as a floating head comes into view and addresses the audience directly. The head proclaims

that he is a magician, a puppetmaster, and that he is but an entertainment. Surveying the audience, he claims to be naught but a character provided for their amusement. Then he asks, "You poor creatures—who made you? Is God in show business, too?"

At this point the picture cuts to a shot of beautiful countryside in Ireland. A massive stone head carved with a fierce, growling expression floats quietly into view, hovering above the landscape. This is the god Zardoz. It's the year 2293, and life has gone to hell on Earth. Some 90 percent of the world is in the hands of the Brutals—savage humans of low intellect who don't seem worth knowing. Preventing them from overrunning the planet are the Exterminators, a type of murderous cavalry who worship Zardoz and in whose name they murder the Brutals. The great stone head in the sky tells them that guns are good and that the penis is bad. Zardoz has spoken, go and kill.

The Exterminators, led by Zed (Connery), then go off to murder as many of the Brutals as they can. This is their job, their mission in life. They don't think they

Zardoz (20TH CENTURY FOX / R. ALLEN LEIDER COLLECTION)

are exploited, and they are quite happy riding across the countryside slaughtering the Brutals. As the others ride off, however, Zed turns toward the screen and, breaking the fourth wall, purposely targeting the audience, fires. The puppetmaster had talked to and teased the audience; Zed merely slays them. The credits start rolling. The picture has begun.

Zardoz is a richly layered film that reveals itself only slowly. Beneath its dazzling photography and intricate storytelling, there is essentially a very simple message. The 10 percent of the world not overrun with the Brutals is known as the Vortex. Here live three divisions of immortals, the Eternals, the Renegades, and the Apathetics—volatile, disagreeing factions making up the female-dominated society of immortal intellectuals who both control and hide away from the rest of the world. The residents of the Vortex control the great stone head, using fear of it to keep the Exterminators in line. Guns, ammunition, and instructions are delivered to the faithful murder squad through the head's mouth, the all-powerful god "spitting" its tools and desires to its followers.

For a long time, the Exterminators are happy to roam the land killing the Brutals—it's a great job that they are good at and happy with. But then, inside the Vortex, the immortals grow too lazy to care for themselves. They instruct their killers, via Zardoz of course, that the Exterminators are to force the Brutals to cultivate the land and grow food for them. Rebelling against this unnatural activity, Zed secrets himself inside Zardoz and is taken back to the Vortex along with the foodstuffs. Once inside, his presence brings back the emotions the immortals had lost, as well as experiences long given up: death, sex, anger, and all the rest that bring the Vortex to a bitter but desired end.

Boorman's message is not very complicated: Men and women are not equal. They have different interests and don't necessarily mix well but are forced by nature to do so for the good of the species. Upon its release the film was attacked for having an antifeminist stance, but it still managed to achieve a great deal of popularity. Many labeled the movie not only Boorman's attack on feminism, but on *all* women, and in truth the film does attack women, but it is simpleminded to think that is the full extent of its message. Looking at it objectively, it's easy to see that the director/screenwriter is attacking both men and women. Interestingly, many critics who attacked the film as antifeminist seemed perfectly willing to accept its premise that all men are mindless murderers and rapists who are easy to control if allowed to run rampant, killing everything in sight. This aspect of the film was not challenged by its critics, nor was the portrayal of women as naturally more intelligent than

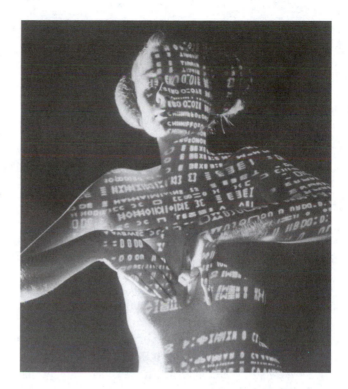

Zardoz (TWENTIETH CENTURY FOX / R. ALLEN LEIDER COLLECTION)

men. The only complaint was that the movie impudently suggests that men and women both need interaction with the other in order to grow, mature, and finally become completely human.

As stated, a very simple premise, but one calculated at the time of the film's release to cause quite a stir. Critics of the film would like to see it dismissed out of hand, but the presence of star Sean Connery makes that impossible. Thanks to Boorman's skill, the picture is too clever, far too beautifully made and intelligently acted to be disregarded. An incredibly lush and insightful film, *Zardoz* is also one of the strongest visions in the history of the science fiction film.

ZERO IN THE UNIVERSE

Film-Makers, 1966, b&w, 85 min

Producer: Jock Livingston; **Director:** George Moorse; **Screenplay:** Livingston and Moorse; **Music:** Donald Cherry; **Cinematography:** Gerard Vandengerg; **Cast:** Jock Livingston, George Moorse, Pam Badyk, George Bartenieff

An unknown, energy-based intelligence, which can appear to simple carbon-based life-forms such as humans in any form it desires, moves about in the world causing trouble. Even so, there's nothing to worry about.

ZERO POPULATION GROWTH

See *Z.P.G.*

ZETA ONE (aka: ALIEN WOMEN, THE LOVE FACTOR)

Tigon (Great Britain), 1969/Edward Montoro Enterprises (U.S.), 1973, Color, 82 min

Producer: Tony Tenser; **Director:** Michael Cort; **Screenplay:** Cort and Christopher Neame; **Music:** Johnny Hawksworth; **Cinematography:** Jack Atcheler; **Cast:** Robin Hawdon, Yutte Stensgaard, Dawn Adams, Rita Webb, Valerie Leon, Lionel Murton

A superpowered alien female comes to Earth, along with her supersquad of beautiful followers, to mix it up with a variety of secret agents. The results hardly live up to the premise.

ZEX

See *THE ELECTRONIC MONSTER*

ZOMBIE HIGH (aka: THE SCHOOL THAT ATE MY BRAIN)

Cinema Group, 1987, Color, 93 min, VT

Producers: Aziz Ghazal, Elliott Kastner, and Marc Toberoff; **Director:** Ron Link; **Screenplay:** Ghazal, Tim Doyle, and Elizabeth Passerelli; **Music:** Daniel May; **Special Effects:** Bernard Davis, William Mertz, and Marc Messenger; **Cinematography:** Brian Coyne and David Lux; **Cast:** Virginia Madsen, Richard Cox, James Wilder, Paul Feig, Kay Kutter, Sherilyn Fenn, Paul Williams

There's a new girl in school (Madsen), and she really wants to fit in at her upper-class prep school (formerly all-male) in the worst way, but she just can't seem to click with the rest of the student body. Maybe she would have done better if she had been replaced by a replicant like the rest of the girls. This one-note horror rip-off of the far superior *THE STEPFORD WIVES* offers little besides the eternal loss of 93 precious minutes of viewers' lives.

ZOMBIES OF THE STRATOSPHERE

Republic, 1952, b w, serial, 12 chapters

Producer: Franklin Adreon; **Director:** Fred C. Brannon; **Screenplay:** Ronald Davidson; **Music:** Stanley Wilson; **Special Effects:** J.L. Cassingham, Howard Lydecker, and Theodore Lydecker; **Cinematography:** John MacBurnie; **Cast:** Leonard Nimoy, Lane Bradford, Craig Kelly, Judd Holdren, Johnny Crawford, Dale Van Sickle, Aline Towne, Wilson Wood, Tom Steele

Three nasty Martians, Narab, Marex, and Roth (Nimoy, Bradford, and Kelly), come to Earth to take over the planet with their typically superior weapons and intellects. The world at stake, once more it's up to serial hero Commander Cody (Holdren) to stop them. Betting types are directed to put their money on the noble commander and then sit back and laugh.

ZONTAR: THE THING FROM VENUS

AIT, 1968, Color, 80 min. VT

Producer: Larry Buchanan; **Director:** Buchanan; **Screenplay:** Buchanan and H. Taylor; **Cinematography:** Robert B. Alcott; **Cast:** John Agar, Susan Bjurman, Patricia DeLaney, Warren Hammack, Anthony Houston

Zontar, a batlike monster with great mental powers, is encouraged to come to Earth and is then directed along its way by a group of humans who are determined to enslave the planet. Once the creature arrives, however, it decides that it can rule Earth all by itself and begins enslaving everyone, including the would-be dictators. Viewers would fare better to watch the superior *INVASION OF THE BODY SNATCHERS*, which this film steals from slightly, or *IT CONQUERED THE WORLD*, which is practically stolen wholesale.

Z.P.G. (AKA: ZERO POPULATION GROWTH)

Sagittarius (Great Britain), 1971/Paramount (U.S.), 1972, Color, 97 min, VT

Producer: Thomas F. Mudigan; **Director:** Michael Campus; **Screenplay:** Max Erlich and Frank DeFelitta; **Music:** Jonathan Hodge; **Special Effects:** Derek Meddings, Harry Lange, Peter Hojmark, and Tony Masters; **Cinematography:** Michael Reed; **Cast:** Oliver Reed, Don Gordon, Geraldine Chaplin, Diane Cilento, David Markham, Sheila Reid

The world is an environmental ruin. Humanity has finally gone too far in the rape of the planet. Cities stand choking in filth and smog so bad that people cannot go outside without protective clothing and rebreathers. Food has to be synthesized and distributed by the government. Total martial law is in force. "Be Good" messages are broadcast in the streets. Pregnancy is punishable by death. A loving couple (Reed and Chaplin) decide that government-provided surrogate children (even though the little tykes come preprogrammed for complete obedience) are not for them. The daring couple decides to defy the government's antichild birth edict and have their own baby. Needless to say, society frowns on their actions. The two are hunted relentlessly until they finally escape into the sewers, their final destination never revealed.

This is an odd film with a disturbing message. The term *zero population growth* is used in the real world to describe a population that neither rises nor falls but maintains itself at a constant. The filmmakers, however, use the term to describe an attempt to reach zero population. This is a well-made film with style, but overall it amounts to a fairly hollow exercise.

Encyclopedia of Science Fiction Movies

APPENDIXES

Science Fiction Movies and Literature

There are close to 2,000 movies listed in this encyclopedia, and yet few are listed below. Since most great science fiction novels are heavy on ideas and short on action, filmmakers don't see them as box office potential. The following films (in roman type) are listed with the literary sources (and their authors) that inspired them.

A

Absent-Minded Professor, The   *A Situation of Gravity*, Samuel Taylor

Alraune   *Alraune*, Hans Heinz

Altered States   *Altered States*, Paddy Chayefsky

Andromeda Strain, The   *The Andromeda Strain*, Michael Crichton

Apollo 13   *Lost Moon*, Jim Lovell and Jeffrey Kluger

Atlantide, L'   *Atlantide, L'*, Pierre Benoit

Atomic Man, The   *The Isotope Man*, Charles Eric Maige

At the Earth's Core   *At the Earth's Core*, Edgar Rice Burroughs

B

Beast from 20,000 Fathoms, The   "The Fog Horn," Ray Bradbury

Bicentennial Man, The   "The Bicentennial Man," "The Positronic Man,"   Isaac Asimov and Robert Silverberg

Billion Dollar Brain, The   *The Billion Dollar Brain*, Len Deighton

Blade Runner   *Do Androids Dream of Electric Sheep?*, Philip K. Dick

Boys from Brazil, The   *The Boys from Brazil*, Ira Levin

Brain, The   *Donovan's Brain*, Curt Siodmak

Brain Eaters, The   *The Puppet Masters*, Robert A. Heinlein

Brave Little Toaster, The   *The Brave Little Toaster*, Thomas M. Disch

Bug   *The Hephaestus Plague*, Thomas Page

C

Charly   *Flowers for Algernon*, Daniel Keyes

Children of the Damned   *The Midwich Cuckoos*, John Wyndham

Clockwork Orange, A   *A Clockwork Orange*, Anthony Burgess

Cocoon   *Cocoon*, David Saperstein

Colossus   *Colossus: The Forbin Project*, D.F. Jones

Coma   *Coma*, Robin Cook

Communion   *Communion*, Whitley Strieber

Conquest of Space   *The Mars Project*, Wernher von Braun

Contact   *Contact*, Carl Sagan

Curse, The   "The Colour Out of Space," H.P. Lovecraft

D

Damnation Alley   *Damnation Alley*, Roger Zelazny

Day of the Dolphin, The   *The Day of the Dolphin*, Robert Merle

Day of the Triffids, The   *The Day of the Triffids*, John Wyndham

Deadly Bees, The   *A Taste for Honey*, H.F. Heard

Demon Seed, The   *The Demon Seed*, Dean R. Koontz

Devil Doll, The   *Burn, Witch, Burn*, A. Merritt

Diamond Master, The   *The Diamond Master*, Jacques Fotrolle

Diamond Queen, The   *The Diamond Master*, Jacques Fotrolle

Die, Monster, Die   "The Colour Out of Space," H.P. Lovecraft

Dr. Jekyll and Mr. Hyde   *Dr. Jekyll and Mr. Hyde*, Robert Louis Stevenson

Dr. Strangelove or: How I Learned to Stop Worrying and Love the Bomb   *Red Alert*, Peter George

Donovan's Brain   *Donovan's Brain*, Curt Siodmak

Dune   *Dune*, Frank Herbert

E

Electric Monster, The   *Escapement*, Charles Eric Maine

End of the World, The   *The End of the World*, Camille Flammarion

Eye Creatures, The   *The Cosmic Frame*, Paul W. Fairman

F

Fahrenheit 451   *Fahrenheit 451*, Ray Bradbury

Fail Safe   *Fail Safe*, Eugene Burdick and Harvey Wheeler

Fantastic Planet   *Oms en série*, Stefan Wul

Final Programme, The   *The Final Programme*, Michael Moorcock

Fire in the Sky   *The Walton Experience*, Travis Wilson

First Men in the Moon   *First Men in the Moon*, H.G. Wells

First Spaceship on Venus   *Astronauts*, Stanislaw Lem

Food of the Gods   *Food of the Gods*, H.G. Wells

Forbidden Planet   *The Tempest*, William Shakespeare

F.P.1   *F.P.1 Does Not Answer*, Curt Siodmak

Frankenstein   *Frankenstein*, Mary W. Shelley

Frankenstein Unbound   *Frankenstein Unbound*, Brian Aldiss

Freejack   *Immortality, Inc.*, Robert Sheckley

From Beyond   "From Beyond," H.P. Lovecraft

From the Earth to the Moon   *From the Earth to the Moon*, Jules Verne

Fury, The   *The Fury*, John Farris

G

Give Us the Moon   *The Elephant Is White*, Caryl Brahms and S.J. Simon

Goldengirl   *Goldengirl*, Peter Lear

Grand Tour, The   *Vintage Season*, C.L. Moore and Lawrence O'Donnell

Groundstar Conspiracy, The   *The Alien*, Leslie P. Davies

H

Hands of a Stranger   *Les Mains d'Orlac*, Maurice Renard

Hands of Orlac, The   *Les Mains d'Orlac*, Maurice Renard

Harrison Bergeron   "Harrison Bergeron," Kurt Vonnegut

Homunculus   *Homunculus*, Robert Reinert

Herbert West—Re-Animator   "Herbert West—Re-Animator," H.P. Lovecraft

I

Illustrated Man, The   *The Illustrated Man*, Ray Bradbury

I'm an Explosive   *I'm an Explosive*, Gordon Phillips

Incredible Shrinking Man, The   *The Shrinking Man*, Richard Matheson

Invasion of the Body Snatchers   *The Body Snatchers*, Jack Finney

Invasion of the Saucer Men   *The Cosmic Frame*, Paul Fairmen

Invisible Man, The   *The Invisible Man*, H.G. Wells

Iron Giant, The   *The Iron Man*, Ted Hughes

Island at the Top of the World   *The Lost Ones*, Ian Cameron

Island of Dr. Moreau, The   *The Island of Moreau*, H.G. Wells

Island of Lost Souls, The   *The Island of Moreau*, H.G. Wells

Island of the Burning Damned   *Night of the Big Heat*, John Lymington

It Came from Outer Space   "The Meteor," Ray Bradbury

J

Journey Beneath the Desert   *Atlantida*, Pierre Benoit

Journey to the Center of the Earth   *Journey to the Center of the Earth*, Jules Verne

K

Killdozer   "Killdozer," Theodore Sturgeon

Kiss Me Deadly   *Kiss Me Deadly*, Mickey Spillane

L

Lady and the Monster   *Donovan's Brain*, Curt Siodmak

La Machine   *La Machine*, Rene Belletto

Land that Time Forgot, The   *The Land that Time Forgot*, Edgar Rice Burroughs

Last Man on Earth, The   *I Am Legend*, Richard Matheson

Lawnmower Man, The   "The Lawnmower Man," Stephen King

Lifeforce   *The Space Vampires*, Colin Wilson

Little Prince, The   *The Little Prince*, Antoine de Saint Exupery

Logan's Run   *Logan's Run*, William F. Nolan and George Clayton Johnson

Lord of the Flies   *Lord of the Flies*, William Golding

Lost Continent, The   *Uncharted Seas*, Dennis Wheatley

Lost World, The   *The Lost World*, Sir Arthur Conan Doyle

Lost World, The   *The Lost World*, Michael Crichton

M

Manchurian Candidate, The   *The Manchurian Candidate*, Richard Condon

Man Who Fell to Earth, The   *The Man Who Fell To Earth*, Walter Tevis

Man Who Thought Life, The   *The Man Who Thought Life*, Valdemar Holst

Marooned   *Marooned*, Martin Caidin

Martians Go Home   *Martians Go Home*, Frederic Brown

Mask of Fu Manchu, The   *The Mask of Fu Manchu*, Sax Rohmer

Master of the World   *Clipper of the Clouds* and *Master of the World*, Jules Verne

Metropolis   *Metropolis*, Thea von Harbou

Mission to Mars   *The Case for Mars*, Robert Zubrin

Monitors, The   *The Monitors*, Keith Laumer

Moon Pilot   *Moon Pilot*, Robert Buckner

Mouse That Roared, The   *The Mouse That Roared*, Leonard Wiberley

Mysterious Island   *Mysterious Island*, Jules Verne

N

Navy vs. the Night Monsters, The   *The Monster from Earth's End*, Murray Linster

Nightfall   "Nightfall," Isaac Asimov

Nightflyers   *Nightflyers*, George R.R. Martin

Night of the Lepus   *Night of the Angry Rabbit*, Russell Braddon

1984 (Nineteen Eighty-Four)   *1984 (Nineteen Eighty-Four)*, George Orwell

Nippon Chimbotsu   *Nippon Chimbotsu*, Sakyo Komatsu

No Blade of Grass   *The Death of Grass*, John Christopher

No Escape   *The Penal Colony*, Richard Herley

O

October Sky   *Rocket Boys*, Homer Hickam

Omega Man, The   *I Am Legend*, Richard Matheson

On the Beach   *On the Beach*, Nevil Shute

P

Phantoms   *Phantoms*, Dean Koontz

Planet of the Apes   *Planet of the Apes*, Pierre Boulle

Postman, The   *The Postman*, David Brin

Power, The   *The Power*, Frank M. Robinson

Project X   *The Artificial Man* and *Psychologist*, L.P. Davis

Q

Quest for Fire   *Quest for Fire*, J.H. Rosny

R

Return of the Terror   *The Terror*, Edgar Wallace

Right Stuff, The   *The Right Stuff*, Tom Wolfe

Robert Heinlein's The Puppetmasters   *The Puppetmasters*, Robert A. Heinlein

Rollerball   *Rollerball Murders*, William Harrison

S

Seconds   *Seconds*, David Ely

Shape of Things to Come, The   *The Shape of Things to Come*, H.G. Wells

Slapstick   *Slapstick*, Kurt Vonnegut

Slaughterhouse-Five   *Slaughterhouse-Five*, Kurt Vonnegut

Solaris   *Solaris*, Stanislaw Lem

Soylent Green   *Make Room, Make Room*, Harry Harrison

Sphere   *Sphere*, Michael Crichton

Starship Troopers   *Starship Troopers*, Robert A. Heinlein

Stepford Wives, The   *The Stepford Wives*, Ira Levin

Swarm, The   *The Swarm*, Arthur Herzog

T

Terminal Man, The   *The Terminal Man*, Michael Crichton

Terrornauts, The   *The Waiting Asteroid*, Murray Leinster

Test Pilot Pirx   *Test Pilot Pirx*, Stanislaw Lem

These Are the Damned   *Children of Light*, H.L. Lawrence

Thing From Another World, The   "Who Goes There?" John Campbell

Things to Come   *The Shape of Things to Come*, H.G. Wells

Thirteenth Floor, The   *Simulacron-3*, Daniel F. Galouye

This Island Earth   *This Island Earth*, Raymond F. Jones

Time Machine, The   *The Time Machine*, H.G. Wells

Total Recall   "We Can Remember It for You
  Wholesale," Phillip K. Dick
Trans-Atlantic Tunnel   *Der Tunnel*, Berhard
  Kellerman
27th Day, The   *The 27th Day*, John Mantley
20,000 Leagues Under the Sea   *20,000 Leagues
  Under the Sea*, Jules Verne
2001: A Space Odyssey   *2001: A Space Odyssey*,
  Arthur C. Clarke
2010   *2010*, Arthur C. Clarke
Twilight's Last Gleaming   *Viper 3*, Walter Wager

U

UFO Incident, The   *The Interrupted Journey*,
  John G. Fuller

V

Village of the Damned   *The Midwich Cuckoos*,
  John Wyndham
Virus   *Virus*, Sakyo Komatsu
Visit to a Small Planet   *Visit to a Small Planet*,
  Gore Vidal

W

War of the Worlds   *War of the Worlds*, H.G.
  Wells
Watchers   *Watchers*, Dean R. Koontz
When Worlds Collide   *When Worlds Collide*,
  Philip Wylie and Edwin Balmer
Who?   *Who?*, Algis Budrys
World, the Flesh, and the Devil, The   *The Purple
  Cloud*, M.P. Shiel

Science Fiction Movies at the Oscars

A long time ago in 1927 in a galaxy far, far away called California, a group of 36 movie executives, representing the major studios, along with the leading actors and actresses, joined forces. Normally bitter rivals, in a rare display of camaraderie they decided to honor as well as publicize their filmmaking efforts with a group of awards we now know as the Academy Awards, or the Oscars®. Over the decades, the awards presentation evolved from a simple sit-down dinner attended by just the elite Hollywood few, to a worldwide televised event viewed by more than 1 billion people. The award categories, 23 in 2001, have themselves evolved over time, reflecting shifts in thinking and technology. There are more than 6,000 members in the Academy of Motion Picture Arts and Sciences, the organization that sponsors the Academy Awards, though not all members vote in all categories, some awards being decided by fewer than 100 experts in a particular field. Science fiction films have generally not fared well at the Oscars, and in fact, from the inception of the awards in 1927 until 1933, not a single science fiction movie received even a nomination.

In 1933 the performance of Fredric March in the dual lead roles of DR. JEKYLL AND MR. HYDE earned him the Oscar for Best Actor. He shared this award with Wallace Beery, who won for *The Champ*. *Dr. Jekyll and Mr. Hyde* was also nominated for Best Cinematography and Best Writing Adaptation but lost in both categories.

In 1936 THE BRIDE OF FRANKENSTEIN was nominated for sound recording but it lost to *Naughty Marietta*.

DR. CYCLOPS and THE INVISIBLE MAN RETURNS found themselves nominated for Best Special Effects in 1941. Possibly as a result of canceling each other out, they lost to *Thief of Baghdad*.

The following year THE INVISIBLE WOMAN lost to *I Wanted Wings* in the category of Best Special Effects, and a very deserving *Sergeant York* took Best Film Editing over a new version of *Dr. Jekyll and Mr. Hyde*.

In 1943 INVISIBLE AGENT lost the Best Special Effects award to *Reap the Wild Wind*.

For the second half of the decade, science fiction movies were in a slump, as they failed—with a few exceptions—at the box office and disappeared completely from the roster of Oscar-night nominees. But the 1950s brought them back into the game, beginning with DESTINATION MOON, nominated for Best Special Effects and Best Color Set Decoration. The film, based on a novel by Robert A. Heinlein, took home the Special Effects Oscar but lost in the other category to the epic *Samson and Delilah*.

The 1952 nominations included just one science fiction film, WHEN WORLDS COLLIDE, nominated for Best Special Effects and Best Cinematography. It took home the former but lost the latter to *An American in Paris*. It's worth noting that the nominating committee utterly overlooked three important science fiction films that year. The first of these was THE MAN FROM PLANET X, a moody film that received modest reviews but might have been nominated for Best Screenplay. The second film was THE DAY THE EARTH STOOD STILL. Directed by Robert Wise, this intelligent and compelling epic was completely ignored. The third film to be overlooked was Howard Hawks's classic THE THING FROM ANOTHER WORLD.

No science fiction films appeared among the 1953 nominations, but the chilling WAR OF THE WORLDS received nominations for Best Special Effects, Best Sound, and Best Film Editing in 1954. It took home only one Oscar, winning for Best Special Effects, while the other two awards for which it was nominated went to *From Here to Eternity*.

The 1955 nominations recognized Disney's spectacular adaptation of the Jules Verne classic *20,000 LEAGUES UNDER THE SEA* in the categories of Best Color Art Direction–Set Decoration, Best Film Editing, and Best Special Effects. The film won in Best Special Effects and Best Color Art Direction–Set Decoration, losing in the third category to *On the Waterfront*. Also nominated in the category of Best Special Effects that year was THEM!—for its remarkable giant ants.

The following year saw no science fiction films among the nominees, and in 1957 only *FORBIDDEN PLANET* received a nomination, in the category of Special Effects. It lost to *The Ten Commandments*, while science fiction classics such as *1984* and *INVASION OF THE BODY SNATCHERS* went unrecognized, as did *THE INCREDIBLE SHRINKING MAN* and *THE FLY* in the next two years.

The 1960 awards recognized *JOURNEY TO THE CENTER OF THE EARTH*, a 20th Century Fox production starring James Mason and Pat Boone, with three nominations—Best Art Direction–Set Decoration, Best Sound, and Best Special Effects—but *Ben Hur*, which took 11 Academy Awards that year, denied *Journey* any.

Two science fiction films received nominations in 1961—*VISIT TO A SMALL PLANET* for Best Art Direction–Black–and–White, which lost to *The Apartment*, and *THE TIME MACHINE*, which earned the award for Best Special Effects. Ignored was the fine English film *VILLAGE OF THE DAMNED*. *THE ABSENT-MINDED PROFESSOR* from Disney lost in 1962 in all three categories for which it received nominations—Best Cinematography and Black-and-White Art Direction–Set Decoration, which went to *The Hustler*, and Best Special Effects, awarded to *The Guns of Navarone*.

Of the 36 science fiction films eligible in 1963 and 1964 none, according to the Academy, merited any honors. In 1964, working with material from a novel by Peter George, director Stanley Kubrick released *DR. STRANGELOVE OR: HOW I LEARNED TO STOP WORRYING AND LOVE THE BOMB*. Made in England and released in the United States by Columbia Pictures, the film, a financial and critical success, received four nominations in 1965—Best Actor (Peter Sellers); Best Director; Best Writing, Screenplay Based on Material from Another Medium; and, most important, Best Picture. Oddly, the picture was not nominated for Best Special Effects. When the awards were presented, however, *Dr. Strangelove* was shut out completely, losing the Best Writing award to *Becket* and the other three to *My Fair Lady*, starring Rex Harrison and directed by George Cukor. The following year, again, not a single science fiction film was nominated.

FANTASTIC VOYAGE in 1967 received nominations for Best Cinematography, Best Sound Effects, Best Special Effects, Best Film Editing, and Best Art Direction–Set Decoration-Color. Unlike *Dr. Strangelove*, this film took home the Oscar for Best Art Direction and for Best Special Effects. The other awards went to *Grand Prix*, and *A Man for All Seasons* took Best Cinematography. Not nominated that year was *FAHRENHEIT 451*. No science fiction movies were nominated in 1968.

When the Oscars were broadcast worldwide on television in 1969 for the first time in the history of the

Academy, three science fiction films were among those in competition. *2001: A SPACE ODYSSEY*, nominated for Best Screenplay–Written Directly for the Screen, lost to *The Producers*, while Best Art Direction–Set Decoration went to *Oliver!*, as did Best Director—to Carol Reed, who directed *Oliver!*. The only award the film did win was, of course, Best Special Effects. *PLANET OF THE APES*, nominated for Best Costume and Best Music–(nonmusical) Original Score, lost to *Romeo and Juliet*, though John Chambers received an honorary award for the incredible makeup he created for the film. Finally, Cliff Robertson, for his performance in the movie *CHARLEY*, won the Best Actor award.

On December 11, 1969, five months after the first lunar landing, Columbia Pictures released *MAROONED*, hoping to capitalize on recent events. The movie's startling special effects snared three 1970 nominations, but it was only honored for Best Special Effects, while Best Sound went to *Hello, Dolly!* and Best Cinematography to *Butch Cassidy and the Sundance Kid*.

In 1972 Stanley Kubrick released *A CLOCKWORK ORANGE*. The movie, nominated for Best Picture, Best Film Editing, Best Writing Based on Material from Another Medium, and finally for Best Director, won no awards. *THE ANDROMEDA STRAIN*, chosen for Best Film Editing and Best Art Direction–Set Decoration, lost to *French Connection* and *Nicholas and Alexandra*. Totally ignored that year was *SILENT RUNNING*.

Over the next four years there were no science fiction films nominated. The films overlooked by the Oscars during this period include *SLAUGHTERHOUSE-FIVE*, in 1972, *SOYLENT GREEN*, *WESTWORLD*, *ZARDOZ*, and *SLEEPER*, all in 1973, and *THE ROCKY HORROR PICTURE SHOW*, *THE STEPFORD WIVES*, and *ROLLERBALL*, in 1975.

LOGAN'S RUN returned science fiction to the Oscar competition in 1976 with a nomination for Best Cinematography, which went to *Bound for Glory*, and Best Art Direction–Set Decoration, awarded to *All the President's Men*. The Academy rewarded the film with an Honorary Award for Special Effects.

In 1978, *STAR WARS* took an amazing 10 nominations, and *CLOSE ENCOUNTERS OF THE THIRD KIND* received nine. Six Oscars—Best Art Direction–Set Decoration, Best Costume Design, Best Visual Effects, Best Film Editing, Best Music-Original Score, and Best Sound—went to George Lucas's epic, and a special award was given in addition for Best Sound for the creation of certain voices. *Close Encounters of the Third Kind* took Best Cinematography and a special award for Sound Effects Editing. *Star Wars* lost Best Picture and Best Writing, Screenplay Written Directly for the Screen to *Annie Hall*, while Woody Allen won Best Director. Nominated for Best Supporting Actress, Melinda Dillon in

Close Encounters of the Third Kind lost to Vanessa Redgrave, who won for *Julia*, while Best Supporting Actor nominee Alec Guinness in *Star Wars* saw Jason Robards of *Julia* win.

In 1979 SUPERMAN soared to a Special Achievement Honor for Visual Effects but lost its three nominations, with Best Sound and Best Film Editing going to *Deer Hunter* and *Midnight Express* taking Best Music.

In 1980 *Apocalypse Now* won Best Cinematography over THE BLACK HOLE and Best Sound over METEOR. ALIEN and STAR TREK—THE MOTION PICTURE lost Best Art Direction–Set Decoration to *All That Jazz*, while *Alien* beat out *The Black Hole* and *Star Trek* for Best Visual Effects. Finally, *Star Trek—The Motion Picture* lost to *A Little Romance* for Best Original Music.

The 1981 Awards saw THE EMPIRE STRIKES BACK receive a Special Achievement Award for its remarkable Visual Effects as well as three standard nominations. Also on the ballot was ALTERED STATES. Both films, nominated for Best Music, lost to *Fame*. *The Empire Strikes Back* won Best Sound, but lost Best Art Direction–Set Decoration to *Tess*. SUPERMAN II, SATURN 3, and BATTLE BEYOND THE STARS appeared that year but received no nominations.

In 1983 ET competed for Best Picture and Best Director and seven other awards. TRON got nominations for Best Sound and Best Costume but lost both. BLADE RUNNER lost Best Art Direction–Set Decoration and Best Effects–Visual Effects. ET, nominated for Best Picture, Best Director, Best Screenplay, Best Cinematography, and Best Film Editing, lost them all to *Ghandi*, taking home only four awards: Best Effects, Sound Effect Editing, Best Effects, Visual Effects, Best Music, Original Score, and Best Sound.

RETURN OF THE JEDI had four chances in 1984, but garnered only a Special Achievement Award in Visual Effects, losing Best Sound, Best Effects-Sound, and Best Music to THE RIGHT STUFF, and Best Art Direction–Set Decoration to *Fanny och Alexander*. WARGAMES also lost for Best Sound, as well as Best Cinematography, which went to *Fanny och Alexander*, and Best Writing–Written Directly for the Screen awarded to *Tender Mercies*.

In 1985 F. Murray Abraham outdid Jeff Bridges's Best Actor Oscar-nominated performance in STARMAN with his part in *Amadeus*. The sequel to *2001—A Space Odyssey*, *2010*, received nominations in four categories, Best Art Direction–Set Decoration, Best Costume, Best Makeup, and Best Sound, all won by *Amadeus*. DUNE was nominated for Best Sound.

1986 saw Don Ameche win Best Supporting Actor for COCOON, the film that also won for Best Visual Effects. BACK TO THE FUTURE took Best Sound Effects Editing, while losing Best Writing, Screenplay Written

Directly for the Screen to *Witness*, and Best Sound to *Out of Africa*. Its fourth nomination, Best Song, went to *White Nights*. The masterful BRAZIL garnered two nominations but lost Best Writing, Screenplay Written Directly for the Screen to *Witness* and Best Art Direction–Set Decoration to *Out of Africa*.

THE FLY won Best Makeup in 1987. Sigourney Weaver, nominated for Best Actress for ALIENS, lost to Marlee Matlin from *Children of a Lesser God*. *Aliens* did win Best Effects, Sound Effects, Sound Effects Editing and Best Effects, Visual Effects, though it lost Best Art Direction–Set Decoration to *A Room with a View*; Best Sound and Best Film Editing to *Platoon*; and finally Best Music, Original Score to *Round Midnight*. STAR TREK IV: THE VOYAGE HOME lost in Best Music, Original Score, Best Effects, Sound Effects Editing, and Best Sound and was even beat out in Best Cinematography by *The Mission*.

ROBOCOP received a Special Achievement Award for Sound Effects Editing in 1988 but lost Best Sound and Best Film Editing to *The Last Emperor*. INNERSPACE beat out PREDATOR for Best Effects, Visual Effects.

In 1990 BATMAN garnered Best Art Direction–Set Decoration over THE ABYSS, which also lost Best Sound and Best Cinematography to *Glory*. But James Cameron's watery epic did win for Best Effects, Visual Effects, beating out BACK TO THE FUTURE PART II.

The Academy awarded TOTAL RECALL a Special Achievement Award for Visual Effects in 1991, but the film lost Best Sound to *Dances With Wolves* and Best Effects, Sound Effects to *The Hunt for Red October*.

The 1992 Academy Awards brought TERMINATOR 2: JUDGMENT DAY six nominations. The film surrendered Best Cinematography and Best Film Editing to *JFK* but secured Best Effects, Sound Effects Editing, Best Effects, Visual Effects, Best Makeup, and Best Sound, winning over STAR TREK VI: THE UNDISCOVERED COUNTRY in two categories. The same year, two men received special awards for their work. The Irving Thalberg Memorial Award went to George Lucas of STAR WARS fame and Ray Harryhausen got the Gordon Sawyer Award for his work in stop animation.

ALIEN[3] and BATMAN RETURNS were both nominated in 1993 for Best Effects, Visual Effects, and both lost to *Death Becomes Her*. *Batman Returns* also lost Best Makeup to *Dracula*.

In 1994 JURASSIC PARK captured awards for Best Effects, Sound Effects Editing, Best Effects, Visual Effects, and Best Sound.

BATMAN FOREVER lost in 1996 to *Braveheart* for Best Cinematography and Best Effects, Sound Effects Editing, and along with WATERWORLD, it lost Best Sound to APOLLO 13. 12 MONKEYS earned a Best Supporting Actor nomination for Brad Pitt, but the award went to Kevin Spacey of *The Usual Suspects*. *12 Monkeys* also lost Best Costume to *Restoration*.

INDEPENDENCE DAY lost Best Sound to *The English Patient* in 1997 but won for Best Effects, Visual Effects. Best Makeup went to THE NUTTY PROFESSOR over STAR TREK: FIRST CONTACT.

In 1998 *Titanic* took 11 Academy Awards out of 14 nominations. GATTACA and MEN IN BLACK lost in Best Art Direction–Set Decoration; CONTACT lost Best Sound; and *Face/Off* and THE FIFTH ELEMENT lost Best Effects, Sound Effects Editing. THE LOST WORLD: JURASSIC PARK and STARSHIP TROOPERS were also passed over for Best Effects, Visual Effects. *Men in Black* did win Best Makeup but lost to *The Full Monty* for Best Music, Original Musical or Comedy Score.

THE TRUMAN SHOW lost twice in 1999, with Best Director going to Steven Spielberg for *Saving Private Ryan* and Best Writing, Screenplay Written Directly for the Screen awarded to *Shakespeare in Love*. ARMAGEDDON bowed to *Saving Private Ryan* in both Best Sound and Best Effects, Sound Effects Editing, and to *What Dreams May Come* for Best Effects, Visual Effects. The Aerosmith hit "I Don't Want to Miss a Thing" from *Armageddon* lost to "When You Believe" from the picture *Prince of Egypt* for Best Song.

At the 2000 Awards THE MATRIX captured Best Sound, Best Effects-Sound Effects Editing, and Best Visual Effects, while STAR WARS EPISODE I-THE PHANTOM MENACE received nominations for Best Effects, Sound Effects Editing, Best Effects, Visual Effects and Best Sound. BICENTENNIAL MAN lost in the category of Best Makeup.

Science fiction films gave a disappointing showing at the 2001 Academy Awards. *The Cell* lost the Oscar for Makeup to *Dr. Seuss' How the Grinch Stole Christmas*, *U-571* beat out *Space Cowboys* for Sound Editing and *The Hollow Man* lost to *Gladiator* for Visual Effects.

—Warren Knisbaum

Interview with Frank Herbert

Frank Herbert (1920-1986) is widely recognized as one of the most important writers of science fiction in the 20th century. His book *Dune* is a landmark work that captures the essence of the best of science fiction literature and offers readers a startling view of an entirely new world populated by unique people driven by a fascinating mix of cutthroat politics and the struggle for survival. *Dune* is often described as the greatest science fiction novel ever written. In contrast, David Lynch's epic adaptation of the book for the screen is generally regarded as one of the worst science fiction films ever produced. The following interview, held while the film was in production during the later years of Herbert's life, provides an enlightening glimpse into the mind of the author and his outlook on one of the most interesting conundrums of science fiction cinema.

Q: Where did *Dune* come from? How did you decide to write such a book?

A: I was going to do a story on Messianic impulse in human society. Why do we follow charismatic leaders? I had a small insight once, that charismatic leaders are dangerous and that we should question them because they are just people and they can make mistakes. But the mistakes of the human being as leader are amplified by those who follow him without question. So I decided I would explore this propensity human beings have to do things like go to Jonestown and drink Kool-Aid.

You get a mad leader, and that madness is actually contagious. People follow such people and I could see there was a story in there, so I started doing my research. Comparative religions, anthropology, you name it. I went down to the Department of Agriculture experimental station on the coast of Oregon to do a newspaper magazine story on their work. They had been extremely successful in developing ways to control the movements of sand dunes. In fact, successful to the point that there were delegations there from all over the world to learn from us. I looked at this; I flew over it, took photographs from the air, and it got me interested in how we inflict ourselves on the planet. And then, about a year later, I woke up to the fact that I had the perfect setting for the story I wanted to tell. A planet which was entirely dunes, entirely desert. So then, I finally started to concentrate on the kinds of research I was doing. Desert ecology, geology, the flora and fauna of same, and then, I went down to the Sonora Desert and lived for a while so I could experience it all first-hand.

Q: How long a while?

A: About three months.

Q: Are we talking about driving out from the hotel every day and kicking around?

A: No. We're taking about renting a place out in the desert, off a dirt road. Living with the roadrunner and rattlesnakes and all the rest all around you. There's a lot of life in the desert.

Q: So, after all that, were you ready to start writing?

A: No, not really. I hadn't finished loading the system, as I call it, getting together all the information I would need to give me that sense of verisimilitude of what it would really be like to live in a place where water was so precious that people did not cry, that the body was salvaged for its water after death, and so on. So I went back to the drawing board and took some more books out of the library, and I also developed a system of going to experts. Being a fairly good interviewer, I would go knocking on professors' doors and say, "Hey, you know something I'd like to know. I can do something for both of us; I'll get an article out of you, which will get published," which is what all professors need, and "I'll get information I need." We would knock out articles in a week most of them would swear they couldn't have written in three months. And they got published, and I got what I needed.

Q: So then . . .

A: Then I sat down and started to write. And a year and half later, I had a book.

Q: How long before the public had the same book?

A: A long time. Now that wasn't any of my concern; that was my agent's job, you know, to move it around.

Q: What took the "long time?"

A: It was turned down 22 times.

Q: In total, how many "major" attempts have been made to bring *Dune* to the screen?

A: Two. Arthur P. Jacobs [producer of the *Planet of the Apes* series] was first. He had the bad taste to die without consulting me.

Q: How far did his project go?

A: To a storyboard, not a script. Then there was Alejandro Jodorowsky [write/director of *El Topo*], with a script and a storyboard which I am sure couldn't have been done in less than 10 hours.

Q: You worked with Salvador Dali on that version.

A: Right. And Jodorowsky fired Dali because Salvador had the temerity to speak his mind. Disagree or agree with the man, it was no reason to dump him as an artist. Alejandro's problem was that he had so many personal, emotional axes to grind—I used to kid him: "Well, I know what your problem is, Alejandro. There is no way to horsewhip the pope in this story."

Now, the newest attempt is by David Lynch [director of *Eraserhead, The Elephant Man*]. David has done a magnificent job. The film begins as *Dune* begins, and it ends as *Dune* ends, and I hear my dialogue all the way through it.

Q: You seem happy about the way things are going.

A: I'm absolutely delighted. I'd heard so many horror stories about books being butchered by being made into a film, and bad science fiction films coming from DeLaurentiis, but this is not. All the characters of *Dune* are on it; there is character development in it—it's not a comic book for the screen at all.

This is a translation job. I wouldn't pretend to be the person who should translate *Dune* from English to French. It's the same with a movie; you go to the person who speaks "movie." We found someone who really can and that's David. On the other hand, David listens to me. I had a lot of input, giving him the sense of the story, what I was doing, and helping to abbreviate it.

Q: What do you think of David's work?

A: I'm an admirer; I like what he has done. I can see from his script that he has *Dune* in mind. David has said that he wants to make a film so that when people walk out of the theater, they will know they've seen *Dune*, and I think he can do it.

Q: Is there anything in his background that you feel makes him exceptionally perfect for *Dune*?

A: You know David was an oil painter; he comes to movies from a very strange direction. People ask me if the sets match my original vision of it all, and to be truthful, I have to say that some do and some are better.

Q: None worse?

A: No. Not at all.

Q: Then he's matched or topped your own interpretations throughout.

A: Yes, as far as the visuals are concerned. But what would you expect with Tony Masters as art director, for God's sake? He didn't win those Oscars sitting home twiddling his thumbs.

Q: What was his best achievement—what did he bring to the screen so perfectly you just couldn't believe it?

A: The Great Hall. It was absolutely beautiful. I just stood there and said "boy." And the castle at Caladan was magnificent. It was a real metaphor for the feudal society I had postulated.

Q: And the creatures and the costumes, how does it all come across?

A: Oh, God, the costumes are eye shockers! They did a great job with all the artifacts; they really did. At the wrap party, a lot of the actors and actresses and technical people kept coming to me to tell me how sorry they were it was over.

Q: The performers responsible for the character development, was there anyone who did such a remarkable job that it brought tears to your eyes?

A: I thought that Freddie Jones in the Thufir Hawat really did a super job. And [Kenneth] McMillan as the baron is absolutely hideous. You hate him.

Q: You're supposed to.

A: Yes, yes. And the same with Sting. I was surprised by Sting. He wasn't a pretty face with naught behind it—he was everything Feyd is supposed to be. Francesca Annis was also a surprise to me. I met her the first night I was in Mexico City [where most of the principal photography was shot], and I looked at this beautiful woman and I thought, "My God, she's Jessica?" And I just didn't see it which was my fault, not hers. The next day, when she was made up for the part—she was really on, and she is really Jessica; there is no doubt about it.

Now I thought Kyle McLachlan did a bang-up job as Paul; he wasn't the way I had visualized Paul, but the spirit and the intensity are there—he plays the part. He dominates the screen when he is on it.

Q: Can you tell us anything about your time on the sets? Anything interesting happen in Mexico?

A: I spent a lot of time with Kyle McLachlan, who is a very intense young man who wanted to do the best he could. He was always asking me, "Why did you have him [Paul] do this? Why did you have him do that?" and I would have to delve back into my memory and find him the reasons. We had a lot of sessions on the set before he went to the camera, when he was really trying to get into the part.

Q: Do you think it helped?

A: I don't know. He was good for the part; he played it well.

Q: Do you think he needed the talks for reassurance, or to understand his script, or perhaps maybe just for approval?

A: Well, he'd been a fan of the book since he'd been 12—he knew it. But I did get a sense of the latter . . .

Q: The filmmakers seem to be giving us our money's worth. How often did they consult you on things as the filming went along?

A: I had great rapport with the people who were making the movie. The only time I put my foot down and said, you shouldn't do that, they didn't. They weren't going to kill off Thufir Hawat in the very poignant death scene at the end, the reason being they wanted to bring him back in the next one. (laughter)
I said, "Okay, bring him back as a Ghola [human duplicates]," and that was the end of that.

Q: So, the short of it is that *Dune* is great, and you're pleased with the way everything has turned out.

A: Simple answer: yes.
The secret of science fiction is that it enables you to create different kinds of drama in ways that aren't available to you in any other medium. That's what science fiction has going for it. Real serious science fiction dominating the screen, the same way it dominates the genre in print.

Q: Do you see much hope for that happening?

A: Oh, yes. What we're into right now is the comic book and pulp magazine era of science fiction movies. We are creating an audience, putting out the clichés that every science fiction fan knows, but that most of this new audience does not know. This was *Star Wars*' chief value. I could see the comic book attraction for a lot of the audience, but it brought in many more people who didn't know the first damn thing about science fiction. They liked the kind of black-and-white exposition, and so they liked the film. *Star Wars* reached into existing science fiction, and ripped off everything in sight.

Q: Aren't those same elements—previously used by writers like Larry Niven, Doc Smith, Fred Pohl—just the conventions of science fiction?

A: Not just the conventions, but the clichés of science fiction. They aren't clichés to us on the inside, merely the devices used to tell an acceptable science fiction story.
Go to the best, *2001: A Space Odyssey*. It managed to give you a sense that things familiar to us now had been moved just one step out, into that area where there is no air.

Q: *2001* premiered at a time when no one took science fiction films seriously. Most of the pictures' appeal came from that approach.

A: A good point. They did take it seriously, and that's the only way science fiction films will survive. We must start getting more of the same. I also know I'm right in saying that we're now in the pulp era of science fiction movies.

Q: Hasn't the mainstream media almost always been 30 years behind the genre?

A: Oh, yes. We haven't graduated yet to this genre's fine literary or dramatic capabilities. This won't be a comic book for the screen, but a story about people. These are people of a different kind in a different environment, which is, after all, the essence of science fiction.

Q: So, what is the essence of *Dune* to Frank Herbert?

A: It is a story of political, economic, and social commentary which is carried along with a particular kind of drama, the drama of the Messiah.

The Language and Tribes of Quest for Fire

The following chart lists type substitutes for phonetic symbols with descriptions of the sound each symbol represents and examples of the sound in familiar usage. The second chart contains the English equivalent of some common Ulam words (in their phonetic forms) and the appropriate body movements accompanying the sound.

PHONETIC SYMBOL	SOUND EXAMPLE	
B	'b'/'v' sound rolled together	
a	short 'a'	man
a	long 'a'	arc
E	'e' sound	egg
S	'ch' sound	chair
-nj	n-yer sound rolled together	tenure
(a)	sharp 'a' sound	actor
oo	'or' sound	board
?	'kh' sound	kick
—	'oi' sound	coil
-n	'n' sound	worn
n	'n'	
F	'f'	find
th	as it is written	the
(z)	'd'/'z' sound rolled together	
x	gutteral 'ker'	Bach
g	Arabic gargling consonant	garlic
j	'y'	yes
e	short 'e'	café
:	preceding vowel lengthened	

ENGLISH	ULAM (PHONETIC)	BODY LANGUAGE
aggression	t'ka-t'ka-t'ka (very quickly)	Group sways from side to side. Least aggressive action, minimal body sway.
	d'ga-d'ga-d'ga	Adding vocal chord expression and resonance plus increasing body movement.
	arr ang arm	Most violent form of expression within this grouping. Mouth open, teeth bared. Resonant sound should be stressed from chest. Dominant gesture—lips forward. Fear gesture—lips pulled back.
reply to alarm	wa wa (wa wa)	Again head lifted on 'wa'
anger	smer (modified from smerdolor) Also extends to long 'ssss' resembling spitting sound ('smerdolor).	Violent scratching movement down opposite upper arm. Scrabbling scratch indicates frustration. A violent, short burst of irritable scratching. This action should suddenly erupt and then stop as quickly. Activity not continuous, interspersed with apparent relaxation. Head scratching. Scratching hand violently thrown away from head to whom gesture is directed. Foot stamping. One foot stamping. Alternate leg stamping, lifting legs quickly up and down. Violent smashing objects to ground and knuckle biting. Self-aggression.
animal	tir (Ti:::r)	
bad	garsna ('ga:rrsn(a))	Based on Spanish lice gesture, a belittling gesture. Both hands are used. Hands are half clenched, two thumbnails are pressed together, one on top of the other. Then thumb nails rotated.

ENGLISH	ULAM (PHONETIC)	BODY LANGUAGE
bear	tirorSa (tir-'oo:rsa)	Standing position, arms raised, hands bent forward with t fingers pointing down, akin to bear posture.
big	meg (me:g)	Arms raised above head, arms loose, hand and fingers pointing to each other. Straightening elbows a few ties to emphasize height.
broken	vragda ('vragda)	Grab left hand with right arm, pull down, making right angle with wrist.
cold	frika (fri.ka)	Hold body with arms to indicate shivering. Wagabou blow on hands and move from one foot to another.
to come	margiom (margiom)	Swing whole arm forward or across body to indicate direction.
death	vragda ('vragda)	Cover eyes with half-open hand.
to drink	essachaiaga (Esta'tSai-aga)	Hand held near chest, in semi-cupped position, then lifted and half-rotated toward open mouth.
enemy (nonfriend)	nyimi (nji'mi) nyimizi (nji'mi:zi)	Hit face with fist.
fire	atra ('atra)	
fight	slackh ('slax)	Hold left forearm vertical and punch it with right fist.
food	estachai (esta'tSai)	
friend	yeemi (ji:mi)	Stroke face with back of hand
fruit	buailt (buailt)	Grasping gesture, like plucking berries from tree, between forefinger and thumb, then twisting motion downwards.
good	otim ('otim)	Feel good: Tongue protruding, teeth just showing, tongue then moves from side to side of mouth. Look good (attraction to another human): Jaws moved up and down as in eating mime but not chewing.

ENGLISH	ULAM (PHONETIC)	BODY LANGUAGE
give	dow ('d-o:e) (to sound through nose)	Gentle action, arm extended in front of chest, scooped back to body, and then slapped against back of other hand which is held in front of chest, palm inward. Hug elbows in for emphasis.
greeting	khonia ('xonja)	Passionate but platonic greeting: Between two people. Back of hands touched together and rubbed. Big Greeting: Face to face rubbing, bodies slightly apart so faces touch and nothing else, avoid nose rubbing.
hunger (food want)	essachaivow (esa'tSaivau)	Clenched fist on stomach.
hunt	tirpreng ('tirpre-nj)	Tap head with weapon. Bang up and down on ground with spears.
joy	(eBai)	Cheek rubbing (see greeting). Let head rub over imaginary face.
lion	tirgarsna ('tir'garsna)	As for tiger but all fingers pointing down.
mammoth	tirmeg (tirme:g)	Standing upright and swaying back and forth, arms resembling tusks.
man	vir (vir)	Two fingers point downwards on back of hand.
pain	smerdolor ('smerdolor)	
reindeer	tirdondr (tirdondr)	Thumbs interlocked, fingers splayed.
strong	kras (kras)	Pulling self more erect and hitting high shoulder with fist.
thirst	agavau (agavau)	
tiger	tirstria ('tirstria)	Two fingers point down, other hand grabs wrist. Then push hand down.
victory	vaiii (Bai)	Before battle: raise weapon abovehead. After battle: raise piece of enemy property above head.
war	slackht (slaxt)	Cross forearms vertical to ground and bang together.

ENGLISH	ULAM (PHONETIC)	BODY LANGUAGE
warm	riarch (ri'a.rtS)	Wiping hands downward over body (outside skins) and sinking slightly at the knees.
water	aga (aga)	
Weapon	slakhataka ('slaxtaka)	Pump closed fist up and down above head.
Wolf	wuftur ('lwu.ftur)	Hand sideways—little finger toward ground. Fingers are closed and slightly bent, thumb vertical.
Woman	virku (virku)	Hands are slightly cupped; thumbs touching, fingertips of one hand overlap fingertips of other. Fingers low, thumbs high.
Yes	siyeda (siyeda)	Bow head, not nodding

THE TRIBES

The Ulam Primitive *Homo sapiens*, the Ulam are a loosely knit group banded together for survival. They wear animal skins and use sharpened wooden poles as spears. The Ulam know how to utilize and maintain fire, but they are unable to create it. If they lose their fire, they must either steal it from others or find a bush or tree set afire by lightning. The Ulam eat almost anything, from insects and plants to animals, but they show a distaste for human flesh. Whenever possible, the Ulam find shelter in caves.

The Kzamm A cannibalistic tribe, the Kzamm fashion their clublike weapons from bones. They are hunters who wear animal skins for protection. Although they have the ability to use fire for cooking and other purposes, the Kzamm are not able to create it or use it to greater advantage.

The Wagabou Plundering Neanderthals, the Wagabou, like most other tribes, use fire but are unable to create it. They are protected from the elements by their natural covering of thick hair. More primitive than all the other tribes in the film, the Wagabou use very rudimentary weapons and practically no tools. They are semicannibalistic and prey on other, weaker tribes.

The Ivaka The Ivaka wear little clothing, preferring to paint their entire bodies. The warriors wear face-concealing headgear and utilize a throwing stick that gives them greater accurate striking range than simple, hand-held spears. The Ivaka village consists of crudely made huts of mud and straw. They fashion containers from animal skins for food storage and sometimes carry pouches with them. They have learned to create fire when needed through heat caused by friction and use it for comfort and convenience.

Bibliography
and Further Reading

Ackerman, Forrest J. *Forrest J. Ackerman's World of Science Fiction*. Santa Monica, Ca.: General Publishing Group, 1997.

———. Ackerman, Forrest J. and the Sci-Fi Channel. *Science Fiction Classics: The Stories that Morphed into Movies*. New York: TV Books, 1999.

Aronofsky, Darren. *Pi: The Screenplay and the Guerilla Diaries*. London: Faber & Faber, 1999.

Asimov, Isaac. *Asimov on Science Fiction*. Garden City, N.Y.: Doubleday, 1981.

Benson, Michael. *Vintage Science Fiction Films, 1896 to 1949*. Jefferson, N.C.: McFarland, 2000.

Burns, Bob, and John Michlig. *It Came From Bob's Basement: Exploring the Science Fiction and Monster Movie Archive of Bob Burns*. San Francisco: Chronicle Books, 2000.

Clarens, Carlos. *An Illustrated History of Horror and Science Fiction Films: The Classic Era, 1895–1967*. Cambridge, N.Y.: DaCapo Press, 1997.

Clute, John, and John Grant, Brian Stableford, and Peter Nicholls, eds. *The Encyclopedia of Science Fiction*. New York: St. Martin's Press, 1993

Clute, John, Tracie Lee, and Candida Frith-MacDonald. *Science Fiction: The Illustrated Encyclopedia*. London, New York: Dorling Kindersley, 1995.

Dillard, J. M., and John Eaves. *Star Trek the Next Generation Sketchbook: The Movies*. New York: Pocket Books, 1998.

———. *Star Trek: Where No One Has Gone Before: A History in Pictures*. New York: Simon & Schuster, 1994.

Ebert, Roger. *Roger Ebert's Movie Yearbook, 1999*. Kansas City, Mo.: Andrews & McMeel, 1998.

———. *Roger Ebert's Movie Yearbook, 2000*. Kansas City, Mo.: Andrews & McMeel, 1999.

Everman, Welch D. *Cult Science Fiction Films: The Amazing Colossal Man to Yog, the Monster from Space*. Secaucus, N.J.: Carol Publishing, 1995

Frank, Alan. *The Science Fiction and Fantasy Film Handbook*. New York: Barnes and Noble Books, 1982.

Galbraith, Stuart, Yukari Fujii and Atsushi Sakahara. *Monsters Are Attacking Tokyo: The Incredible World of Japanese Fantasy Films*. Los Angeles: Feral House, 1997.

Harryhausen, Ray. *Film Fantasy Scrapbook*. South Brunswick, N.Y.: A. S. Barnes and Company; London: Tantivy Press, 1981.

Hendershot, Cyndy. *Paranoia, the Bomb and 1950s Science Fiction Films*. Bowling Green, Ohio: Bowling Green University Popular Press, 1999.

Henderson, C. J. "Brother from Another Planet," *Starlog* (January 1985): 16–18.

———. "Capricorn One," *Questar* (Summer 1978): 7–8.

———. "Outland," *Questar* (June 1981): 76–77

———. "Quest for Fire," *Pegasus* (April/May 1982): 79–80.

———. Review of *The Faculty* (Dimension Films), *Brooklyn Skyline*, 5 January 1999, 24.

———. Review of *The Fly* (20th Century Fox), *Different Worlds* (March/April 1987): 44.

———. Review of *Galaxy Quest* (Dreamworks Pictures), *Brooklyn Skyline*, 4 January 2000, 23.

———. Review of *Highlander* (Highlander Productions), *Different Worlds* (July/August 1986): 45.

———. Review of *Starship Troopers* (Tri-Star Pictures), *Brooklyn Baron*, 10 November 1997.

———. Review of *X-Men* (20th Century Fox), *Brooklyn Skyline*, 25 July 2000, 26.

Holston, Kim R., and Tom Winchester. *Science Fiction, Fantasy and Horror Film Sequels, Series and Remakes: An Illustrated Filmography with Plot Synopses and Critical Commentary*. Jefferson, N.C.: McFarland and Company, 1998.

Hunter, Ian Q. *British Science Fiction Cinema*. New York: Routledge, 1999.

Jones, Stephen. *The Essential Monster Movie Guide*. Toronto: Watson-Guptill, 2000.

Justice, Keith L. *Science Fiction, Fantasy and Horror Reference: An Annotated Bibliography of Works about Literature and Film*. Jefferson, N.C.: McFarland, 1989.

Kinnard, Roy. *Science Fiction Serials: A Critical Filmography of the 31 Hard Science Fiction Cliffhangers, with an Appendix of the 37 Serials with Slight Science Fiction Content*. Jefferson, N.C.: McFarland, 1998.

Knee, Adam. *History of Science Fiction Movies*. El Campo, Tex.: Diderot, 1996.

Kuhn, Annette, ed. *Alien Zone: Cultural Theory and Contemporary Science Fiction Cinema*. London, Eng.: Verso, 1999.

———. *Alien Zone II: The Spaces of Science Fiction Cinema*. London, Eng.: Verso, 1999.

Lee, Walt, ed. *Reference Guide to Fantastic Films: Science Fiction, Fantasy and Horror*. Hollywood: Hollywood Film Archive, 1995.

Lees, J. D., and M. Cerasini. *The Official Godzilla Compendium: A 40 Year Retrospective*. New York: Random House, 1998.

Maltin, Leonard, ed. *Leonard Maltin's 1999 Movie and Video Guide*. New York: Viking/Penguin, 1998.

———. *Leonard Maltin's 2000 Movie and Video Guide*. New York: Dutton/Plume, 1999.

———. *Leonard Maltin's Movie Encyclopedia: Career Profiles of More than 2000 Actors and Filmmakers, Past and Present*. New York: Viking/Penguin, 1995.

Mareero, Robert G., and Linda Bryant, eds. *Fantastic World of Science Fiction Movies: Ninety Years of Science Fiction at the Movies*. Florida: R.G.M. Publications, 1987.

Maxford, Howard. *The A to Z of Science Fiction and Fantasy Films*. London, Eng.: Batsford, 1998.

Nicholls, Peter. *The Science Fiction Encyclopedia*. Garden City, N.Y.: Doubleday, 1979.

———. *The Science in Science Fiction*. New York: Alfred A. Knopf, 1983.

O'Neill, James. *Sci-Fi on Tape: A Comprehensive Guide to Over 1,250 Science Fiction and Fantasy Films on Video*. Toronto: Watson-Guptill, 1997.

Parla, Paul, and Charles P. Mitchell. *Screen Sirens Scream!: Interviews with 20 Actresses from Science Fiction, Horror, Film Noir and Mystery Movies, 1930s to 1960s*. Jefferson, N.C.: McFarland, 2000.

Penley, Constance, Lynn Spigel, Janet Bergstrom, and Elisabeth Lyon. *Close Encounters: Film, Feminism and Science Fiction*. Minneapolis: University of Minnesota Press, 1994.

Pressbook for *Free Enterprise*, Regent Entertainment, 1999.

Pressbook for *October Sky*, Universal Pictures, 1999.

Pressbook for *Soldier*, Warner Bros., 1998.

Pressbook for *The Thirteenth Floor*, Columbia, 1999.

Pressbook for *Videodrome*, Universal, 1983.

Powers, Tom. *Movie Monsters*. Minneapolis: Lerner Publishing, 1993.

Reginald, R., Mary Burgess, and Douglas A. Menville. *Futurevisions: The New Golden Age of the Science Fiction Film*. San Bernardino, Calif.: Borgo Press, 1985.

Rovin, Jeff. *Aliens, Robots and Spaceships*. New York: Facts On File, 1995.

———. *Classic Science Fiction Films*. Secaucus, N.J.: Carol Publishing, 1993.

Rovin, Jeff, and Richard Meyers. *The Great Science Fiction Films: From Rollerball to Return of the Jedi*. Secaucus, N.J.: Carol Publishing, 1988.

Sammon, Paul M. *Future Noir: The Making of Blade Runner*. New York: HarperCollins, 1996.

Seed, David. *American Science Fiction and the Cold War: Literature and Film*. Chicago: Fitzroy Dearborn, 1999.

Senn, Bryan, and John Johnson. *Fantastic Cinema Subject Guide: A Topical Index to 2500 Horror, Science Fiction and Fantasy Films*. Jefferson, N.C.: McFarland, 1992

Sobchack, Vivian Carol. *Screening Space: The American Science Fiction Film*. Piscataway, N.J.: Rutgers University Press, 1997.

Soister, John T. *Of Gods and Monsters: A Critical Guide to Universal Studio's Science Fiction, Horror and Mystery Films, 1929–1939*. Jefferson, N.C.: McFarland, 1998.

Stanley, John. Creature Features: *The Science Fiction, Fantasy and Horror Movie Guide*. New York: Berkley Publishing Group, 2000.

Staskowksi, Andrea. *Science Fiction Movies*. Minneapolis: Lerner Publishing, 1991.

Strick, Philip. *The Movie Treasury: Science Fiction Movies*. London, Eng.: Octopus Books, 1976.

Telotte, J.P. *A Distant Technology: Science Fiction Film and the Machine Age*. Hanover, N.H.: University Press of New England, 1998.

———. *Replications: A Robotic History of the Science Fiction Film*. Champaign: University of Illinois Press, 1995.

Tibbetts, John C., and James M. Welsh. *The Encyclopedia of Novels into Film*. New York: Facts On File, 1998.

Tuck, Donald H. *Encyclopedia of Science Fiction and Fantasy*. 3 vols. Chicago: Advent, 1974, 1978, 1983.

Warren, Bill. *Keep Watching the Skies: American Science Fiction of the Fifties*. 2 vols. Jefferson, N.C.: McFarland, 1982.

Weaver, Tom. *Return of the B-Science Fiction and Horror Movie Makers: Writers, Producers, Directors, Actors, Moguls and Makeup*. Jefferson, N.C.: McFarland, 1999.

———. *They Fought in the Creature Features: Interviews with 23 Classic Horror, Science Fiction and Serial Stars*. Jefferson, N.C.: McFarland, 1995.

Weisser, Thomas, and Yuko Mihara. *Japanese Cinema Encyclopedia: The Horror, Fantasy and Science Fiction Films*. Miami, Fla.: Vital Books, 1997.

Willis, Donald C. *Horror and Science Fiction Films: A Checklist*. 4 vols. Lanham, Md.: Scarecrow Press, 1973, 1982, 1984, 1997 .

Wingrove, David. *The Science Fiction Film Source Book*. New York: Addison, Wesley Longman, 1990.

Young, R. G. *The Encyclopedia of Fantastic Film: Ali Baba to Zombies*. New York: Applause, 1996.

Index

BOLDFACE PAGE NUMBERS INDICATE MAIN HEADINGS; PAGE NUMBERS FOLLOWED BY
THE *ITALICIZED* LETTER *F* INDICATE ILLUSTRATIONS.

A

Abbott, Bud 1–2, 415
Abbott and Costello Go to Mars **1**, 56
Abbott and Costello Meet Dr. Jekyll and Mr. Hyde **1**
Abbott and Costello Meet Frankenstein **2**, 138
Abbott and Costello Meet the Invisible Man **2**
Abel, Alfred 280
Able, Robert 386
Absent-Minded Professor, The **2**, 488
Abyss, The **2–3**
Academy Awards 58, 98, 170, 172, 230, 252, 405, 420, 487–490
Adam, Douglas 423
Adams, Brooke 197
Adams, Casey 190
Adams, Julie 72
Addams, Dawn 98, 181
Adding Machine, The **3**
Adventures of Buckaroo Banzai across the Eighth Dimension, The **3–4**
Adventures of Captain Marvel, The **4**, 5f
Adventures of Stella Star, The **382**
Adventures of the Gargantuas **454**
Aelita **4**
Aerial Anarchists, The **4**
Aerial Submarine, The **5**
Affleck, Ben 17, 326
Agar, John 47, 167, 218, 287–288, 402
Agency **5**
Agent for H.A.R.M. **5–6**
Agutter, Jenny 252
Air Hawks **6**
Airship Destroyer, The **6**
Air Torpedo, The **6**
Akins, Claude 76

Akira **6**
Alaimo, Marc 17, 241
Albert, Eddie 112
Aldrich, Robert 233
Algol **6–7**
Alien **7**, 134, 147, 211, 247, 260, 322, 329, 472, 489
Alien³ **10–11**, 10f, 489
Alienator **7–8**
Alien from L.A. **8**
Alien Invasion **384**
Alien Nation **8**
Alien Predator **8**
Alien Resurrection **8–9**
aliens 9–11, 21, 26, 58, 95, 132–134, 332, 434. *See also* UFOs
  abduction by 41, 65, 80, 123, 185, 241, 360, 382, 392, 416, 431, 455, 472
  attacking Earth 6–7, 17–18, 20, 32, 34, 44, 47, 71, 74, 75, 79, 83, 93, 104, 109–110, 193–199, 200, 207, 210, 225, 226, 249, 271, 288, 316, 333, 334, 335, 339, 353, 366, 376–377, 385, 411, 420, 422, 449, 450, 454
  comedies 22, 52, 65–66, 104, 116, 148–149, 271, 277–278, 293, 296–298, 460–461, 465
  contacting 67–68, 186, 297, 380, 429
  on Earth 3, 45, 51, 56, 65–66, 83–85, 103, 112–113, 118–119, 122, 126, 173, 179–180, 184, 193, 209, 265, 277–278, 297–298, 323, 383, 409, 410, 447
  encounters with 62–63, 116
  helping humans 29, 63, 224
  on/from Mars 4, 82, 93, 125, 131, 211, 271–273,

296–297, 360, 377, 417, 478
  on Moon 124, 285
  on ocean bottom 2, 21
  in space 19, 30, 296, 305
  on spaceship 7, 8–9, 72
  on/from Venus 1, 125, 185–186, 430–431, 451
Aliens **9–10**, 489
Aliens, Robots, and Spaceships (Rovin) 1
Alien's Return, The **347**
Alien Terror **186**
Alien Women **477**
Allard, Eric 449
Allen, Irwin 256
Allen, Karen 154, 383
Allen, Nancy 355
Allen, Ronald 338
Allen, Tim 148
Allen, Woody 114, 370
Alligator People, The **11**
Alphaville **11**
Alraune (1918) **11**, 107
Alraune (1928) **12**
Alraune (1930) **12**
Alraune (1952) **12**
Alraune and the Golem **12**
Altered States **12**, 212, 489
Altman, Mark 141
Alyn, Kirk 21, 398
Amazing Colossal Man, The **12–13**, 454
Amazing Transparent Man, The **13**
Americathon **13**
Amphibian Man, The **13**
Anderson, Dawn 403
Anderson, Gerry 218
Anderson, Gillian 469
Anderson, James 125
Anderson, Melody 127
Anderson, Paul 373
Anderson, Sylvia 218
Anderson, Warner 92
Andress, Ursula 404

Andrews, Dana 145
Android **13–14**, 61
androids 13–14, 39–40, 72, 81, 114, 120, 146, 182, 263–264, 272, 303, 417
Andromeda Nebula, The **429**
Andromeda Strain, The **14**, 488
Andy Warhol's Frankenstein **14**
Angry Red Planet **14–15**
animations 6, 48–49, 120, 203–204, 238–239, 247, 376–377, 443–444
Aniston, Jennifer 204
Annaud, Jean-Jacques 342
Annis, Francesca 101, 492
Another Wild Idea **15**
Anton, Susan 164
Antrobus, John 35
Ape Man, The **15**
Apollo 13 **15–16**, 490
April 1, 2000 **16**
Aranas Infernales **17**
Arena **16–17**
Arlen, Richard 206
Armageddon **17**, 90, 490
Armstrong, Neil 15
Armstrong, Robert 228, 229
Arness, James 408
Arnold, Jack 209, 376, 416f
Aronofsky, Darren 328
Around the World under the Sea **17**
Arrival, The **17–18**
Ashley, John 260
Asimov, Isaac x, 37, 57, 68, 120, 305, 346, 370
Asphyx, The **18**
Assante, Armand 219
Assignment Outer Space **18**
Astaire, Fred 318
Asther, Nils 266
Astin, Sean 169
Astounding She-Monster, The **18–19**
astronauts 15–16, 19, 32, 56, 66, 71, 74, 90, 123, 124, 125,

129, 296, 304, 305, 330, 332, 341, 351, 352, 353, 364, 371, 378, 430, 441, 451, 455, 458, 466, 467
Astronauts **125**
Astronaut's Wife **19**
Astronomer's Dream, The **19**
Astro-Zombies, The **19**
L'Atlantide (1932) **19**
L'Atlantide (1961) **216**
Atlantis, The Lost Continent **19–20**
Atom Age Vampire **20**
Atomic Agent, The **20**
Atomic Brain, The **292**
Atomic Kid, The **20**
Atomic Man, The **20**
Atomic Rocketship **126–127**
Atomic Rulers of the World **20**
Atomic Submarine **21**
Atom Men vs. Superman **21**
Atragon **21**
Attack of the Crab Monsters **21**
Attack of the Eye Creatures **116**
Attack of the 50-Foot Woman **21**
Attack of the Killer Tomatoes **22**
Attack of the Monsters **22**
Attack of the Puppet People **22**
Attack of the Robots **22**
Attack of the Swamp Creature **475**
Attenborough, Richard 221
At the Earth's Core **22–23**
At the Edge of the World **23**
Atwill, Lionel 54, 100, 137, 253, 261
Atwood, Margaret 167
Automatic House, The **23**
Automatic Laundry, The **23**
Automatic Monkey, The **23**
Automatic Motorist, The **23**
Automatic Servant, The **23**
Autry, Gene 325
Avalon, Frankie 322, 364
Avengers **123**
Avenging Brain, The **290**
Awful Dr. Orloff, The **23**
Ayers, Ralph 408
Aykroyd, Dan 66, 152, 297–298, 433
Ayres, Lew 95, 321
Azaria, Hank 160, 300

B

Baby... Secret of the Lost Legend **24**
Bach, Barbara 182
Back to the Future **24–25**, 292, 489
Back to the Future II **25**, 489

Back to the Future III **25–26**
Bacon, Kevin 16, 128, 177, 426–427
Bad Channels **26**
Bad Taste **26**
Bailey, Richard 266
Baio, Scott 475
Baker, Kenny 389
Baker, Rick 170, 186, 188, 230
Baldwin, Michael 324
Ball, Bob 198
Ballard, J.G. 461
Balmer, Edwin 461
Bamboo Saucer, The **26**
Banco in Bangkok **365**
Band, Richard 424
Banionis, Donatas 371
Banks, Conrad 106
Barbara, Joseph 214
Barbarella **26–27**
Barbeau, Adrienne 304
Barb Wire **27**
Barcroft, Roy 344
Barker, Lex 200
Baron's African War, The **364**
Barry, Gene 455
Barrymore, Drew 12, 29, 112, 124
Barrymore, John 98, 201
Barrymore, Lionel 93, 298
Basehart, Richard 205
Basinger, Kim 28, 68, 297
Bassett, Angela 393, 399
Batman (1989) **28–29**, 28f, 134
Batman (1996) **27–28**
Batman and Robin **29**
Batman Forever **29**, 489
Batman Returns **29**, 489
Batteries Not Included **29**
Battle beneath the Earth **29–30**
Battle beneath the Sea **405–406**
Battle beyond the Stars **30–31**, 134, 310, 378, 489
Battle beyond the Sun **31**, 171
Battlefield Earth **31–32**
Battle for the Planet of the Apes **32**
Battle in Outer Space **32**
Battle of the Worlds **32**
Battlestar: Galactica **32–33**
Battletruck **453**
Bava, Mario 53, 98
Bay, Michael 17
Beach Girls and the Monster, The **33**
Beast from 20,000 Fathoms, The **33**, 34f, 35
Beast of Blood, The **33**
Beast of the Dead **33**
Beast of Yucca Flats, The **33–34**

Beasts **433**
Beast with a Million Eyes, The **34**
Beatty, Ned 421
Beaumont, Hugh 287–288
Bed-Sitting Room, The **35**
Beebe, Ford 201
Bee Girl, The **456**
Beery, Wallace 255
Bees, The **35**
Beginning of the End, The **35**
Behemoth, The Sea Monster **35**
Behind the Door **269–270**
Being, The **36**
Belafonte, Harry 466
Bell, Tom 342
Beltran, Robert 306
Belushi, James 251
Beneath the Planet of the Apes **36**, 55, 111
Benjamin, Richard 459
Benoit, Pierre 216
Berg, Peter 367
Bergman, Peter 215
Bernsen, Corbin 231
Bernstein, Elmer 56
Berry, Ken 56
Besson, Luc 121, 245
Bester, Alfred x
Beware! The Blob **41**
Bey, Sara 236
Beyond the Time Barrier **36**
Bicentennial Man, The **36–37**, 490
Biehn, Michael 404, 418
Bierko, Craig 414
Biggles **37**
Big Space Monster Gilala **469**
Billion Dollar Brain, The **37–38**
Bill & Ted's Bogus Journey **37**
Bill & Ted's Excellent Adventure **37**
Birch, Paul 310
Birth of a Robot, The **38**
Bissell, Whit 20, 72, 196, 209, 212, 254, 403
Bixby, Jerome 120
Black Friday **38**
Black Hole, The **38–39**, 65, 489
Black Scorpion, The **39**, 80
Blade Runner **39–40**, 40f, 489
Blanchard, Mari 1
Blast from the Past **40–41**
Blast Off (1954) **41**
Blast Off (1967) **416**
Blob, The (1958) **41**
Blob, The (1988) **41**
Blood Beast from Outer Space **41**
Blood Creature **406–407**
Blood of Ghastly Horror **121**

Blood of Heroes, The **42**
Blood Waters of Dr. Z **475**
Bloom, Judi 363
Blue Light, The **42**
Blue Planet **43–44**, 43f
Bluth, Don 422
Body Parts **42–43**
Body Snatchers, The **44**
Body Snatchers, The (Finney) **196**
Body Stealers, The **410**
Bogart, Humphrey 348
Bogdanovich, Peter 451
Bolder, Carl 214
Bolling, Tiffany 227
Bonestell, Chesley 66, 92
Boom in the Moon **44**
Boone, Pat 217, 488
Boorman, John 476
Borrower, The **44–45**
Bostwick, Barry 357
Bova, Joseph 462
Bowery Boys Meet the Monsters, The **45**, 47
Bowie, David 268
Boy and His Dog, A **45**
Boyd, William 253
Boyichi and the Supermonsters **348**
Boyle, Peter 319
Boys from Brazil, The **45–46**
Brackett, Leigh 108, 349
Bradbury, Ray x, 33, 52, 119, 184–185, 209
Braddon, Russell 306
Bradford, Lane 478
Bradford, Sue 190
Braeden, Eric 64, 111–112
Brahms, Caryl 155
Brain, The **46**
Brain Candy **46–47**
Brain Eaters, The **47**
Brain from Planet Arous, The **47**
Brain of Blood **47**
Brainscan **47–48**, 47f
Brainstorm **48**
Brain That Wouldn't Die, The **48**
Branagh, Kenneth 463
Brando, Marlon 205, 397
Brandon, Henry 238
Brasseur, Pierre 179
Brave Little Toaster, The **48–49**
Brazil **49**, 489
Brendel, El 223
Brennan, Walter 201
Brick Bradford **49**
Bride of Frankenstein **49–50**, 137, 137f, 487

Bride of Re-Animator **50**, 50f, 172, 173
Bride of the Monster **50**, 105
Bridges, Jeff 230, 383, 428, 489
Brief History of Time, A **50**
Brin, David 334
Broderick, Matthew 159–160, 192, 452
Brolin, James 54, 459
Bronson, Charles 273
Brood, The **50–51**, 445, 446
Brooke, Walter 66
Brooks, Albert 433–434
Brooks, Mel 375
Brosnan, Pierce 242
Brother from Another Planet, The **51**
Brown, Clancy 174
Brown, Fredric 272
Brown, Joe 213
Bruce, Virginia 201
Bruckheimer, Jerry 17
Brynner, Yul 439, 459, 460
Bubble, The **51**
Buckaroo Banzai 3–4
Buck Rogers **51–52**, 126
Buck Rogers in the 25th Century **52**
Budrys, Algis 462
Bug **52**
Bujold, Genevieve 64
Bullock, Sandra 91, 258–259
Burgess, Anthony 62, 342
Burke, Kathleen 206
Burnett, Robert 141
Burr, Raymond 156, 158
Burroughs, Edgar Rice x, 22–23, 237
Burrows, Saffron 88
Burstyn, Ellen 347
Burton, Richard vii, 308
Burton, Tim 28, 29, 105, 271
Busey, Gary 373
By Radium Rays **52**
Byrne, Eddie 207
Byrne, Gabriel 68, 138
By Rocket to the Moon **140–141**

C

Caan, James 8, 357
Cabot, Bruce 228
Cabot, Susan 456
Cage of Doom **406**
Caidin, Martin 123
Cain, Dan 173
Caine, Michael 38, 83
Calloway, Cab 134
Caltiki, the Immortal Monster **53**
Cameron, Ian 204

Cameron, James 2–3, 8, 9, 15, 328, 405
Cameron, Rod 364
Campanella, Joseph 103
Campbell, Bruce 293
Campbell, John 411
Candy, John 251
Cape Canaveral Monsters **53**
Capricorn One **53–54**, 423
Captain America **54**
Captain Marvel 4
Captain Nemo 55, 298, 392, 432
Captain Nemo and the Underwater City **55**
Captain Ultra **55**
Captain Video **55**, 126, 255
Captive Wild Woman **221**
Captive Women **55**
Carey, Macdonald 409
Carlin, George 37, 160
Carlson, Richard 209
Carnosaur **55**
Carnosaur II **56**
Carnosaur III: Primal Species **56**
Carpenter, John 81, 118, 130, 411, 447
Carradine, David 87
Carradine, John 19, 68, 121, 180, 187, 195, 201, 221, 351
Carrera, Barbara 205
Carrey, Jim 29, 428
Carroll, Leo G. 402
Carter, Ellis W. 288
Carter, Finn 426
Cartwright, Angela 255
Cartwright, Veronica 7, 197
Casablanca 27
Case for Mars, The (Zubrin) 286
Cash, Rosalind 315
Cassavetes, John 145
Castle, William 52, 365
Castle in the Sky **238–239**
Castle of Evil **56**
Cat from Outer Space, The **56**
Cattrall, Kim 381
Cat Women of the Moon **56**
Caves of Steel **57**
Caviezel, Jim 143
Cell, The **57**
Chairman, The **57**
Chambers, Marilyn 344
Chaney, Lon, Jr. 2, 138, 190–191, 290
Change of Mind **57–58**
Chaplin, Geraldine 479
Chariots of the Gods **58**, 169
Charly **58**, 488
Chase, Charley 310

Chase, Chevy 201
Chayefsky, Paddy 12
Chemist, The **58–59**
Chen, Joan 42
Cherry 2000 **59**, 59f
Children, The **59**
Children of the Damned **60**
China Syndrome, The **60**
Chong, Rae Dawn 45
Chosen Survivors **60–61**
Christian, Claudia 17
Christie, Agatha 56
Christie, Julie 92, 119
Circus World (Longyear) 110
City Limits **61**
City of Lost Children 9, **61**
City under the Sea, The **453**
Clarens, Carlos 197
Clark, Candy 268
Clarke, Arthur C. 435, 436
Clarke, Robert 36, 174
Class of Nuke 'em High **61**
Cleef, Van 210
Cleese, John 418
Clive, Colin 136
Clockwork Orange, A **61–62**, 488
cloning 45–46, 62, 221–223, 295
Clonus Horror, The **62**
Clooney, George 29
Close, Glenn 271
Close Encounters of the Third Kind **62–63**, 488
Cobb, Lee J. 325
Coburn, James 164, 336
Cocoon **63**, 489
Cocoon: The Return **63**
Code Name: Trixie **71**
Code of the Air **63**
Coghlan, Frank, Jr. 4
Colbert, Robert 165
Colchart, Thomas 31
Cold Sun, The **63**
Cole, Lester 201
Collins, Gary 168
Collins, Joan 342
Collision Course 26
Colossus, the Forbin Project **64**
Colossus of New York, The **63–64**
"Colour Out of Space, The" (Lovecraft) 76, 94
Coma **64**
Combs, Jeffrey 144, 172
comets 32, 89–90, 109, 247, 249, 279–280, 302, 305–306, 444
Comet's Comeback, The **64**
Commando Cody **64–65**
Communion **65**

computer graphics interface viii–ix
Computer Wore Tennis Shoes, The **65**
Condon, Richard 264
Coneheads **65–66**
Connery, Sean 175, 279, 319, 418, 476
Conquest of Space **66**
Conquest of the Air **66**
Conquest of the Planet of the Apes **66–67**
Conquest of the Pole **66**
Conreid, Hans 434
Constantine, Eddie 11
Contact **67–68**, 490
Cool World **68**
Cooper, Chris 313
Cooper, Merian C. 229
Cooper, Violet Kemble 203
Coppola, Francis Ford 31
Corday, Claudia 96
Corey, Wendell 19
Corman, Roger 21, 30–31, 34, 55, 56, 85, 87, 88, 134, 147, 151, 171, 182, 210, 241, 251, 253, 290, 309, 310, 330, 378, 439, 455, 471
Cornfeld, Stuart 130
Corseaut, Aneta 41
Cosmic Man, The **68**
Cosmic Man Appears in Tokyo, The **453–454**
Cosmic Monsters, The **68**
Cosmic Voyage **68–70**
Cosmo 2000: Planet Without a Name **454–455**
Cosmonauts on Venus. See Planet of Storms
Cosmos: War of the Planets **454–455**
Cosmos Mortal 8
Costello, Lou 1–2, 415
Costner, Kevin 334, 456
Cotten, Joseph 145, 236, 242, 375
Counterblast **70**
Crabbe, Buster 87, 126
Crack in the World **70**
Craig, James 253
Crampton, Barbara 144
Crash and Burn **70**
Crash of Moons **70**
Crawling Eye, The **71**
Crawling Hand, The **71**
Crawling Monster, The **74**
Crawling Terror, The **68**
Crazies, The **71**
Crazy Ray, The **71–72**
Created to Kill **107**

Creation of the Humanoids **72**
Creature **72**
Creature from Another World, The **71**
Creature from the Black Lagoon, The **72**, 73f
Creatures of the Prehistoric Planet **180**
Creature Walks among Us, The 72, **73**
Creature Wasn't Nice, The **73–74**
Creature with the Atom Brain, The **74**
Creeping Terror, The **74**
Creeping Unknown, The **74**, 110, 124, 186
Crichton, Michael 14, 64, 222, 223, 359, 381, 404, 459
Criminals of the Galaxy, The **462**
Critters **75**
Critters 2: The Main Course **75**
Critters 3 **75**
Critters 4 **75**
Cronenberg, David 115–116, 130, 344, 362, 409, 445–446
Cronkite, Walter 97
Cronos **75**, 75f
Cronyn, Hume 29
Cross, Ben 193
Crouse, Lindsay 18
Crowe, Russell 448
Crowley, Kathleen 126
Cube **76**
Cuburn, James 164
Curry, Tim 357
Curse, The **76**
Curse of Frankenstein, The **76–77**, 138
Curse of the Fly, The **77**, 130
Curtin, Jane 66
Curtis, Donald 208
Curtis, Jamie Lee 111, 448
Cushing, Peter 22–23, 78–79, 100, 179, 207, 367
cyborg 462
Cyborg **77**
Cyborg 2087 **77**, 95
cyborgs 77, 303, 353–355, 404, 419, 448
Cyclops, The **77**
Cypher, Jon 276

D

Dahl, Arlene 217
Daleks—Invasion Earth 2150 A.D. **78–79**
Damnation Alley **79**
Damned, The **409**
Danforth, Jim 218, 461

Daniels, Anthony 389
Daniels, Jeff 296
Danner, Blythe 460
Danning, Sybil 30
Dante, Joe 433
Dantine, Helmut 185
Dark, The **79**
Dark Angel **184**
Dark City **79–80**
Darkman **80–81**
Darkman II: The Return of Durant 81
Darkman III: Die, Darkman, Die 81
Dark Star **81**
D.A.R.Y.L. **81**
Daughter of Dr. Jekyll **81–82**
Daughter of Evil, The **12**
Davidson, Jon 385
Davis, Jim 290
Davis, Nancy 95
Davison, Bruce 469
Dawn of the Dead **82**, 307
Dawson, Richard 359
Day, Doris 155
Day Mars Invaded Earth, The **82**
Day of Resurrection **448**
Day of the Animals **373**
Day of the Dead **82**, 307
Day of the Dolphin, The **82**
Day of the Triffids, The **82–83**, 113
Day the Earth Caught Fire, The **83**
Day the Earth Stood Still, The xi, 15, 68, **83–85**, 84f, 186, 487
Day the Fish Came Out, The **85**
Day the Sky Exploded, The **85**
Day the World Ended, The **85**
Day Time Ended, The **85**
D-Day on Mars **85–86**
Deadly Bees, The **86**
Deadly Diaphonoids, The **454**
Deadly Mantis, The **86–87**
Deadly Ray from Mars, The **87**
Deadly Weapon **87**
Dean Koontz's Phantoms **326**
Death Becomes Her **87–88**
Death Corps **367**
Death Race 2000 **87**
Death Ray, The **87**
Deathsport **88**
Deathwatch **88**
Debilatory Powder, The **88**
DeBoer, Nicole 76
Decima Vittima **404**
Deep Blue Sea **88–89**, 89f
Deep Impact **89–90**
Deep Space **90**

Deepstar Six **90**
Deer, Richard 406
Def-Con 4 **90**
Dehn, Paul 112
Dekker, Albert 97
De Laurentiis, Dino 127, 130, 231, 233
Delicatessen 9, **90–91**
Del Toro, Guillermo 283
Del Val, Jean 120
DeMille, Cecil B. vii, 461
Demolition Man **91**
Demon Planet **332–333**
Demon Seed, The **92**
Demon within, The **284**
DeNiro, Robert 138
Depardieu, Gérard 260
Depp, Johnny 19, 105–106
DeRita, Curly Joe 170
Dern, Bruce 188, 368
Dern, Laura 221, 313
Destination Inner Space **92**
Destination Moon **92**, 356, 487
Destroy All Monsters **92–93**, 157
Destroy All Planets **93**
Destroyer of the Universe **234**
Devil Commands, The **93**
Devil Doll, The **93**
Devil Girl from Mars **93**
Devil's Undead, The **310**
DeVito, Danny 29, 221, 434
Devlin, Dean 292, 415
Diamond Machine, The **93–94**
Diamond Maker, The (1909) **94**
Diamond Maker, The (1914) **94**
Diamond Master, The **94**
Diamond Queen, The **94**
Diamond Wizard, The **94**
Diaphonoids, Bringers of Death **454**
Dick, Phillip K. x, 40, 385, 423
Die, Monster, Die **94**
Diesel, Vin 204, 329
Diller, Phyllis 3
Dillion, Melinda 62, 489
Dimension 5 **94–95**
dinosaurs 24, 33, 55, 165, 221–223, 237–238, 254, 255–258, 316, 317, 336, 442, 443–444, 461
Disch, Tom 49
D.O.A. **290**
Do Androids Dream of Electric Sheep? (Dick) 40
Dobrowski, Marek 399
Doctor of Doom **95**
Doctor X **95**
documentaries 58, 438. *See also* pseudo-documentaries

Dog, a Mouse and a Sputnik, A **95**
Dollar a Day, A **378**
Dollman 26, **95**
Domergue, Faith 208, 416
Donald, James 125
Donlevy, Brian 74, 110
D'Onofrio, Vincent 57, 415
Donovan, King 196
Donovan, Tate 258–259
Donovan's Brain 46, **95**, 236
Doomsday Machine, The **96**
Doomwatch **96**
Doppelganger **217–218**
Douglas, Kirk 122, 145, 361, 432
Douglas, Michael 60, 127
Douglas, Paul 150
Douglas, Susan 125
Downs, Hugh 117
Doyle, Sir Arthur Conan 255, 256, 257
Dr. Alien **96**
Dr. Black, Mr. Hyde **96**, 98
Dr. Brompton-Watt's Adjuster **96**
Dr. Charlie Is a Great Surgeon **96**
Dr. Coppelius **96**
Dr. Cyclops **97**, 487
Dr. Goldfoot and the Bikini Machine **97–98**
Dr. Jekyll 1, 81–82, 96, 98, 181, 186, 291, 311, 314
Dr. Jekyll and Mr. Hyde **98**, 487
Dr. Jekyll and Sister Hyde 98
Dr. Mabuse 200, 347
Dr. Orloff's Monster **98–99**
Dr. Otto and the Riddle of the Gloom Beam **99**
Dr. Renault's Secret **99**
Dr. Strangelove or: How I Learned to Stop Worrying and Love the Bomb **99–100**, 120, 488
Dr. Who 78, 100
Dr. Who and the Daleks **100**
Dr. X **100**
Dragons of Krull **234–235**
Dream Is Alive, The **97**
Dreamscape **97**
Drew, Ellen 290
Dreyfuss, Richard 62, 261
Drops of Blood **282**
Duchovny, David 468
Dudikoff, Michael 345
Duel in Space **100**
Duel of the Gargantuas **454**
Duel of the Space Monsters **272**
Duff, Howard 322, 379
Dugan, Dennis 441
Dullea, Keir 304, 435

Duncan, Neil 381
Duncan, Sandy 56
Dune **101–102**, 101f, 489, 492–493
Dune (Herbert) 491
Dungeons and Dragons **234–235**
Dungeons of Krull, The **234–235**
Duvall, Robert 89, 198, 417
Dwan, Allan 293

E

Eagle of the Night, The **103**
Earthbound **103**
Earth Dies Screaming, The **103**
Earth Girls Are Easy **103–104**
Earthright 347
Earth vs. the Flying Saucers 104
Earth vs. the Spider **104**
Easter Sunday **36**
Eastwood, Clint 72, 376
Ebert, Roger 173
Ebirah, Horror of the Deep **104**, 157
Edison, Thomas 136
Edwards, Anthony 284–285
Edward Scissorhands **105**, 105f
Ed Wood **105–106**
Effects of a Rocket, The **106**
Eggar, Samantha 50
Egghead's Robot **106**
Eisenmann, Ike 112
Ekberg, Anita 458
Electric Girl, The **106**
Electric Goose, The **106**
Electric Hotel, The **106**
Electric House, The **106**
Electric Laundry, The **106**
Electric Leg, The **106**
Electric Monster, The **107**
Electric Policeman, The **106**
Electric Villa, The **107**
Elephant Is White, The (Brahms and Simon) 155
Elfman, Danny 29, 134
El Kadi, Nameer 341
Ellington, Duke 58
Ellison, Harlan 45
Embryo **107**
Emery, John 234
Emilfork, Daniel 61
Emmerich, Roland 160, 292, 415
Emmerich, Ute 415
Empire of the Ants **107**
Empire Strikes Back, The 51, **107–109**, 390, 489
Endless Descent **109**
End of August at the Hotel Ozone, The **233**
End of the World, The (1916)

109
End of the World, The (1931) **109**
End of the World, The (1977) **109**
Enemy from Space 74, **109–110**
Enemy Mine **110**
Erickson, Leif 193
Ericson, John 318
Escape from L.A. **111**
Escape from New York **110–111**
Escape from Planet Earth 96
Escape from the Planet of the Apes **111–112**
Escape 2000 **112**
Escapement **107**
Escape to Witch Mountain **112**
Estellita 214
Estevez, Emilio 142, 346
E.T. the Extra-Terrestrial **112–113**, 489
Event Horizon **113**
Eve of Destruction **113–114**
Everett, Rupert 192
Everything You Always Wanted to Know about Sex (But Were Afraid to Ask) **114**
Evil Brain from Outer Space, The **114**
Evil of Frankenstein **114**
eXistenZ **114–116**, 115f
Expedition Moon 356
Explorers **116**
Exterminators, The **116**
Eye Creatures, The **116**
Eyer, Richard 199
Eyes Without a Face **179**

F

Fabulous World of Jules Verne, The **117**, 302
Faculty, The **117–119**, 118f
Fahey, Jeff 242
Fahrenheit 451 **119**, 488
Fail Safe **119–120**
Falling, The 8
Fantastic Invasion of Planet Earth 51
Fantastic Planet **120**
Fantastic Voyage **120**, 191, 488
Farentino, James 122
Farm, The **76**
Fawcett, Farrah 361
Feldman, Dennis 449
Female Space Invaders 382
Ferrer, José 101
Ferrer, Mel 466
Fields, Suzanne 128
Fiend without a Face **121**
Fiend with the Atomic Brain, The **121**

Fiend with the Electronic Brain, The **121**
Fiend with the Synthetic Brain, The **121**
Fiennes, Ralph 393
Fifth Element, The **121–122**, 122f, 490
Film Fantasy Scrapbook 208, 209
Final Countdown, The **122–123**
Final Programme, The **123**
Fincher, David 9, 10
Fine, Larry 170, 417
Finlay, Frank 86
Finney, Jack 44, 196
Fire in the Sky **123**
Fire Maidens from Outer Space **123**
Fire of Life **123**
Firestarter **124**
First Man into Space **124**
First Men in the Moon **124**
First Spaceship on Venus **125**
Fishburne, Laurence 113, 275
Fisher, Carrie 108, 349, 389, 419
Fisher, Terence 98, 103, 136, 181, 207
Five **125**
Five Million Years to Earth 74, **125–126**
Flame Barrier, The **126**
Flaming Disk, The **126**
Flash Gordon (1936) **126–127**, 126f
Flash Gordon (1980) **127**
Flash Gordon: Mars Attacks the World 87
Flash Gordon Conquers the Universe **127**
Flash Gordon's Trip to Mars **127**
Flatliners **127–128**
Fleischer, Max 134
Fleming, Eric 66
Flemyng, Robert 179
Flesh Eaters, The **128**
Flesh for Frankenstein **14**
Flesh Gordon **128**
Flight of the Navigator, The **128–129**
Flight to a Far Planet 341
Flight to Mars **129**
Flowers for Algernon (Keyes) 58
Flubber 2, **129**
Fly, The (1958) **129–130**, 279, 356, 488
Fly, The (1986) **130**, 489
Fly II, The **130–131**, 131f
Flying Disc Men from Mars **131**
Flying Saucer, The **131**
Flynn, Joe 190
"Foghorn, The" (Bradbury) 33

Fonda, Henry 119, 280
Fonda, Jane 26–27, 60
Fonda, Peter 460
Food of the Gods **131–132**
Food of the Gods II **132**
Forbidden Planet **132–134**, 133f, 341, 488
Forbidden World **134**
Forbidden Zone **134**
Forbin Project, The (Jones) 64
Ford, Harrison 39–40, 40f, 108, 348, 389
Foree, Ken 144
Forever Young **134**
Fortress **135**
Fossey, Brigitte 343
Foster, Jodie 67
4-D Man, The **135**
Four-Sided Triangle **135–136**
Fowler, Gene, Jr. 185
Fox, Michael J. 24–26
F.P.1. **136**
Francis, Anne 132
Franciscus, James 36, 111
Frank, Horst 170
Frankenheimer, John 205, 264–265
Frankenhooker **136**
Frankenstein 2, 76–77, 136–140, 250, 272
Frankenstein 107, **136–139**
Frankenstein '88 **139**
Frankenstein 1970 **140**
Frankenstein and the Monster from Hell **139**
Frankenstein Conquers the World **139**
Frankenstein Created Woman **139**
Frankenstein General Hospital **139**
Frankenstein Island **139**
Frankenstein Meets the Space Monster **272**
Frankenstein Meets the Wolfman 138, **140**
Frankenstein Must Be Destroyed **140**
Frankenstein's Bloody Terror **140**
Frankenstein's Daughter **140**
Frankenstein (Shelley) 136
Frankenstein's Monsters: Sandra vs. Gailah **454**
Frankenstein Unbound **140**
Franz, Arthur 2, 126, 291
Fraser, Brendan 41, 47
Frau im Mond, Die **140–141**
Freakmaker, The **296**
Fredericks, Dean 326
Free Enterprise 141, **141–142**
Freejack **142**, 142f

Freeman, Morgan 69, 89
Frees, Paul 86
Frequency **143**, 143f
Frewer, Matt 243
Froelich, Gustav 280
Frogs **144**
From Beyond **144**, 144f
From Death to Life **145**
From Mars to Munich **145**
From the Earth to the Moon **145**
Frozen Alive **145**
Frozen Dead, The **145**
Frye, Dwight 136
Fuest, Robert 123
Funicello, Annette 285
Furlong, Edward 48
Fury, The **145**
future 61–62, 91, 151, 154,
    184, 185, 280–281, 292,
    392–394, 421–422
  action movies 215–216,
    218–220, 261–262, 303,
    323, 353–355, 357–358,
    359, 363
  apocalyptic 42, 55, 167,
    169, 240, 244–245, 252,
    309, 322, 343, 368,
    372–373, 374–375, 401,
    404, 466, 476
  comedies 52, 87, 122, 356,
    370
  government control in 27,
    49, 119, 135, 223, 339,
    359, 404, 417, 424, 479
  Planet of the Apes 32, 36, 67,
    111, **330–332**
  prison in 110–111, 310
  space missions 218, 227,
    247–248, 254–255, 338,
    356, 377, 386–388, 399,
    463–464
  visitors from 60, 304
Futurecop **424**
Future Shock **145–146**
Futureworld **146**, 460

G

Galactic Gigolo **147**
Galaxina **147**
Galaxy Criminals **462**
Galaxy of Terror **147**
Galaxy Quest **147–149**
Galouye, Daniel F. 415
Gamera 22, 93, 149, 150, 348
*Gamera, The Guardian of the
    Universe* **149**
Gamera 2: Advent of Legion **149**
Gamera 3: The Awakening of Iris
    149
Gamera vs. Gyaos **348**
Gamera vs. Monster X **150**

Gamera vs. Zigra **150**
Gamma People, The **150**
Gammera, The Invincible **150**
Gance, Abel 109
Gap, The **150**
Gardenia, Vincent 251
Gardner, Ava 253, 317
Garland, Beverly 11
Garner, James 376
Garofalo, Janeane 47
Garr, Teri 288
Garrick, John 223
*Gas! Or It Became Necessary to
    Destroy the World in Order to
    Save It* **150–151**
Gas-s-s-s! **150–151**
Gattaca **151–152**, 490
George, Bill 148
George, Christopher 338
George, Peter 99, 488
Gerard, Gil 52
Gerber, Steve 181
Gershenson, Joseph 288
*Ghidra, The Three-Headed Mon-
    ster* **152**, 157
Ghostbusters **152–153**, 153f
Ghostbusters II **153**
Ghost in the Machine **153–154**
Ghost of Frankenstein, The
    137–138, **154**
Giant Behemoth, The **35**
Giant Claw, The **154**
Giant of Metropolis, The **154**
Gibson, Mel 134, 261, 352
Gibson, William 216
Gigantis, the Fire Monster **154**,
    157
Gilala **469**
Gilliam, Terry 49, 430
*Gill Women, The. See Voyage to
    the Planet of Prehistoric Women*
Girara **469**
Girl from 5000 A.D., The **406**
Girl from Scotland Yard, The
    154–155
Girl in the Moon, The **140–141**
Give a Dog a Bone **155**
Give Us the Moon **155**
Gladiatorerna **323**
Glass Bottom Boat, The **155**
Glover, Danny 335
Go and Get It **155**
Gobots: Battle of the Rock Lords
    155
Goddard, Mark 255
Godzilla (1998) **156–157**
Godzilla, King of the Monsters
    157–159, 157f, 160
Godzilla 1985 **159–160**
Godzilla on Monster Island 158,
    160

*Godzilla Raids Again. See Gigan-
    tis, the Fire Monster*
Godzilla's Revenge 157
Godzilla 2000 **161**
Godzilla vs. Biollante 159, **161**
Godzilla vs. Destroyah 159, **161**
Godzilla vs. Gigan 158, **162**
Godzilla vs. Hedora 158, **162**
Godzilla vs. King Ghidorah **162**
Godzilla vs. Mechagodzilla II
    162
Godzilla vs. Megalon 158, **162**
Godzilla vs. Mothra (1964) 157,
    162
Godzilla vs. Mothra (1992) **162**
Godzilla vs. Spacegodzilla **163**
Godzilla vs. Supermechagodzilla
    163
Godzilla vs. the Sea Monster
    104, 157
Godzilla vs. the Smog Monster
    158, **162**
Godzilla vs. the Thing **162**
Gog **163**
Going, Joanna 326
*Gojira. See Godzilla, King of the
    Monsters*
Gold **163**, 263
Goldblum, Jeff 130, 188–189,
    197, 221, 257, 261
Goldengirl **163–164**
Golden Rabbit, The **164**
Goldsmith, Jerry 46, 386
Gordon, Bert I. 35, 104, 107,
    132, 227
Gorgo **164–165**, 164f
Gossett, Louis, Jr. 110
Gothic 138–139, **165**
government control 6, 27, 49,
    54, 91, 119, 135, 167, 168,
    169, 218, 223, 307–309, 339,
    359, 404, 417, 424, 479
Grand Tour, The **165**
Grave Robbers from Outer Space
    333
Graves, Peter 35, 210, 226
Graveyard Tramps **195**
Gray, Carole 207
Gray, Colleen 245, 246
Great Alaskan Mystery, The **165**
*Greatest Battle on Earth, The. See
    Ghidra, the Three-Headed
    Monster*
Greatest Power, The **165**
Great Monster Yongkari **473**
Great Radium Mystery, The **166**
Great Undersea War, The
    405–406
Green, Dr. Jacklyn R. 399
Greene, Brian 143
Greene, Ellen 251

Greene, Lorne 33
Green Slime, The **166**
Green Terror, The **166**
Green Woman, The **341**
Greer, Rosie 414
Gremlins 75
Griffith, Charles 21
Griffith, D.W. 316
Griffith, Melanie 59
Grodin, Charles 230
Gross, Michael 426
Groundstar Conspiracy, The **166**
Ground Zero **166**
Grunner, Oliver 303
Guest, Christopher 251
Guest, Lance 241
Guest, Val 83
Guinness, Alec 108, 267, 389,
    489
Gullette, Sean 327
*Gulliver's Travels beyond the
    Moon* **166**
Gwenn, Edmund 408
Gyllenhaal, Jake 313

H

Hagen, Ross 8
Haggard, H. Rider 19
Haim, Corey 457
Hall, Anthony Michael 459
Hall, Huntz 45, 177, 273
Hall, Jon 199, 201
Hall, Tony 20
Halliday, Bryant 338
Hamill, Mark 107, 349, 371,
    389, 420
Hamilton, George 334
Hamilton, Linda 404, 405
Hamilton, Margaret 201
Hamilton, Suzanna 308
Hampton, James 168
Handmaid's Tale, The **167**
Hand of Death, The **167**
Hand of Peril, The **167–168**
Hands of a Killer **333**
Hands of a Stranger **168**
Hands of Orlac, The (1925) **168**,
    261
Hands of Orlac, The (1964) 43,
    168
Hangar 18 **168–169**
Hanks, Tom 15–16
Hanna, William 214
Hannah, Daryl 297
Hanold, Marilyn 272
Happiness Cage, The **284**
Hardware **169**
Hardwicke, Sir Cedric 138,
    199
Hardy, Sam 228
Harrigan, William 201

Harris, Ed 2, 15, 428
Harris, Jack 81
Harris, Richard 345
Harrison, Linda 36, 331
Harrison Bergeron 169
Harry, Deborah 445
Harry and the Hendersons 169–170
Harryhausen, Ray 33, 55, 104, 124, 208, 217, 230, 298, 299, 317, 431, 443, 489
Hart, John 213
Harvey, Laurence 264
Hauer, Rutger 39–40, 42, 381
Haunted Planet, The 332–333
Haunted World, The 332–333
Have Rocket, Will Travel 170
Hawke, Ethan 116, 151
Hawking, Stephen 50, 143
Hawks, Howard 411
Hawn, Goldie 88
Hayden, Sterling 99
Hayes, Allison 21
Hayes, Gabby 253
Hayter, James 135
Head, The 170
Healy, Ted 261
Heartbeeps 170
Heavens Call, The (1959) 171
Heavens Call, The (1963). See Battle beyond the Sun
Heavy Metal 170–171
Hector Servadac's Ark 302
Hedison, David 129
Heinlein, Robert 68, 92, 338, 353, 385, 487
Heinz, Hans 11–12
Hell Creatures, The. See Invasion of the Saucer Men
Hellevision 171
Hello Television 172
Hellstrom Chronicle, The 172
Helm, Brigette 19, 280
Henry, Buck 82, 268
Hephaestus Plague, The (Page) 52
Herbert, Frank 102, 491–493
Herbert West: Re-Animator 172–173
Herrmann, Bernard 85, 119, 211, 217, 298
Herrn der Welt, Der 173
Heston, Charlton 36, 315, 316, 330, 375
Hickam, Homer 314
Hidden, The 173–174, 184
Hidden Hand, The 174
Hidden II, The 174
Hidden Power 174
Hideous Sun Demon, The 174
Highlander 174–175

Highlander: Endgame 175–176
Highlander II: The Quickening 135, 175, 176
Highlander—The Final Dimension 175, 176
Highly Dangerous 176
High Treason 176
Hindle, Art 50
Hines, Gregory 114
Hinkley, Brent 106
H-Man, The 176–177
Hoffman, Dustin 380
Hogan, Hulk 394
Holbrook, Hal 462
Holdren, Judd 55, 255, 478
Hold that Hypnotist 177
Holloway, Stanley 324
Hollow Man 177–178, 177f
Holm, Ian 418
Holt, Jack 174
Hommunculus 178
Honda, Inoshiro 156–157
Honey, I Blew Up the Kid 178, 179
Honey, I Shrunk the Kids 178–179
Honey, We Shrunk Ourselves 178, 179
Hooper, Toby 194
Hopper, Dennis 297, 457
Hopper, William 430
Horrible Dr. Hitchcock, The 179
Horrible Mill Women, The 282
Horror Chamber of Dr. Faustus 179
Horror Creatures of the Prehistoric Planet 180
Horror Express 179–180
Horror High 98, 180
Horror of Frankenstein 180
Horror of Party Beach 180
Horror of the Blood Monsters 180
Horror of the Stone Women 282
Horror Planet 180
House of Dracula 180–181
House of Frankenstein 181
House of Fright 98, 181
House that Went Crazy, The 181
Howard, Moe 170, 417
Howard, Ron 16
Howard, Shemp 201
Howard, Tom 165
Howard the Duck 181
Hoyt, John 22
Hsiu-Hsien, Li 191
Hubbard, L. Ron 32
Hudson, Rock 107
Hughes, Barnard 428, 439
Hughes, John 459
Hughes, Ted 204

Human Duplicators, The 181–182
Humanoid, The 182
Humanoids from the Deep 182
Human Vapor, The 182
Hunt, Helen 424
Hunt, Jimmy 193
Hunt, William 128
Hunter, Jeffrey 94
Hunter, Kim 111, 330
Hunter, Martin 373
Hunter, Tab 453
Hurd, Gale Anne 2, 8, 9, 17, 345, 448
Hurley, Elizabeth 297
Hurt, John 308, 375
Hurt, William 12, 223, 254
Hutton, Robert 409
Hutton, Timothy 183
Hyams, Leila 206
Hyams, Peter 53, 54, 319–320, 345, 436
Hyde-White, Alex 37
Hydra (1973) 475
Hydra (1986) 363
Hyperboloid of Engineer Garin 182
Hypnotic Spray, The 182

I

I, Monster 186
I Aim at the Stars 183
I Am Legend (Matheson) 240, 306, 315
Iceman 183
Ice Pirates 183–184
I Come in Peace 184
I Eat Your Skin 184
If 184
Ikiara XB 1 184
Illinski, Igor 4
Illustrated Man, The 184–185
I Love You, I Kill You 185
I'm an Explosive 185
I Married a Monster from Outer Space 185
IMAX films
  Blue Planet 43–44, 43f
  Cosmic Voyage 68–70
  Dream Is Alive, The 97
  L5: First City in Space 247–248
  Mission to Mir 287
Immediate Disaster 185–186
Immortal Monster, The 53
Impulse 186
Incredible Invasion 186
Incredible Melting Man, The 186
Incredible Petrified World, The 187

Incredible Shrinking Man, The 187, 209, 488
Incredible Shrinking Woman, The 187–188
Incredible Two-Headed Transplant, The 188
Independence Day 188–189, 189f, 295, 490
Indestructible Man 190–191
Infra-Man 191
Innerspace 191, 489
insects 35, 39, 52, 86, 104, 172, 290, 291, 294, 304, 326–327, 368, 408, 456
Insect Woman 456
Inseminoid 180
Inspector Gadget 191–192
In the Year 2889 192
Invader (1992) 192–193
Invader (1996) 193
Invader, The (1997) 193
Invaders from Mars (1953) 193–194, 194f
Invaders from Mars (1986) 194–195
Invasion 195
Invasion Earth 2150 A.D. 78–79
Invasion of the Animal People 195
Invasion of the Bee Girls 195
Invasion of the Body Snatchers (1955) 34, 44, 80, 110, 118, 195–197, 197f, 488
Invasion of the Body Snatchers (1978) 197–198
Invasion of the Body Stealers 410
Invasion of the Neptune Men 198
Invasion of the Saucer Men 116, 198
Invasion of the Star Creatures 198–199
Invasion of the Zombies 199
Invasion Siniestra 186
Inventors, The 199
Inventor's Secret, The 199
Invisibility 199
Invisible: The Chronicles of Benjamin Knight 265
Invisible Agent, The 199, 487
Invisible Boy, The 199
Invisible Dr. Mabuse, The 200
Invisible Fluid, The 200
Invisible Horror, The 200
Invisible Invaders, The 200
Invisible Kid, The 200
Invisible Man 2, 13, 121, 177–178, 200–203, 269
Invisible Man, The 200–201

Invisible Man's Revenge, The **201–202**
Invisible Monster, The **202**
Invisible Ray, The (1920) **202**
Invisible Ray, The (1936) **202–203**
Invisible Terror 33
Invisible Thief, The **203**
Invisible Woman, The 201, **203**, 487
Iron Claw, The **203**
Iron Giant, The **203–204**
Iron Man, The (Hughes) 204
Ironside, Michael 378
Island at the Top of the World, The **204**
Island of Dr. Moreau, The (1977) **204–205**
Island of Dr. Moreau, The (1996) **205**, 206f
Island of Lost Souls, The **205–207**
Island of Lost Women 207
Island of Terror 207
Island of the Burning Damned 207
Island of the Doomed **208**
Island of the Twilight People **433**
It Came from beneath the Sea **208–209**
It Came from Outer Space 209, 209f
It Came without Warning **465**
It Conquered the World **209–210**
It Happens Every Spring **210**
It Lives Again **210**
It's Alive! **210–211**
It's Alive II **210**
It's Alive III: Island of the Alive **211**
It! The Terror from Beyond Space 7, 180, **211**
Ives, Burl 416
I Was a Teenage Frankenstein **211–212**
I Was a Teenage Werewolf **212**

J

Jack Armstrong **213**
Jackman, Hugh 471
Jackson, Janet 312
Jackson, Samuel L. 88, 380
Jackson, Stephen 76
Jacobs, Arthur P. 492
Jaeckel, Richard 383
Jannings, Emil 6–7
Japan Sinks **309**
Jeffries, Lang 285
Jeffries, Lionel 124

Jekyll and Hyde...Together Again 98
Jesse James Meets Frankenstein's Daughter **213–214**
Je T'Aime, Je T'Aime **214**
Jetee 'La 214
Jetsons: The Movie **214–215**
Jeunet, Jean-Pierre 9, 61, 91
J-Men Forever **215**
Jodorowski, Alejandro 102, 492
Johnny Mnemonic **215–216**
Johnson, Don 45
Johnson, Richard 373
Johnson, Tor 34, 50
Johnston, Joe 314
Jolivet, Pierre 244
Jones, Carolyn 196
Jones, Christopher 462
Jones, Dean 201
Jones, D.F. 64
Jones, Ed 373
Jones, Freddie 492
Jones, James Earl 107, 218, 349, 389, 438
Jones, Jeffrey 181
Jones, Marshall 363
Jones, Raymond F. 416
Jones, Sam J. 127
Jones, Tommy Lee 277, 376
Jory, Victor 269
Journey beneath the Desert **216**
Journey to Pre-History **216**
Journey to the Beginning of Time **216**
Journey to the Center of the Earth **216–217**, 488
Journey to the Center of Time **217**
Journey to the Far Side of the Sun **217–218**
Journey to the Seventh Planet **218**
Judd, Edward 124, 207
Judge Dredd **218–220**, 220f
Jules Verne's Rocket to the Moon 416
Jungle Captive **220**
Jungle Woman **220–221**
Junior **221**
Jurassic Park **221–223**, 222f, 489
Just For Fun **223**
Just Imagine **223**

K

Kadoyng **224**
Kahn, Madeline 369
Kaiju Soshingeki. See Destroy All Monsters
Kaiser's Shadow, The **224**

Kaitei Daisenso **405–406**
Karen, James 272
Karloff, Boris 1, 38, 93, 94, 136, 137, 186, 202–203, 267, 268, 270, 273, 305, 374
Kasdan, Lawrence 108
Katt, William 24
Kaufman, Andy 170
Kdo Chce Zabit Jessii? **224–225**
Keating, Larry 461
Keaton, Buster 44, 59, 106
Keaton, Michael 28, 29, 295
Keel, Howard 83
Keir, Andrew 125
Keitel, Harvey 88, 361
Kelly, Craig 478
Kent, Robert 325
Kershner, Irvin 108
Keyes, Daniel 58
Kidder, Margot 398
Kid's Clever, The **225**
Kids in the Hall: Brain Candy **46–47**
Kiel, Richard 182
Kier, Udo 14
Kiley, Richard 251
Killdozer **225**
Killer Klowns from Outer Space **225**
Killer Lacks a Name, The **225**
Killers from Space **225–226**
Killer Shrews, The **226–227**
Killer Tomatoes Strike Back 22
Kilmer, Val 29, 205
Kilpatrick, Shirley 19
Kindred, The **227**
King, Stephen 124
King Dinosaur **227**
Kingdom of the Spiders **227**
King Kong (1933) **227–230**
King Kong (1976) 130, **230–231**
King Kong: The Legend Reborn **230–231**
King Kong Escapes **231**
King Kong Lives **231**
King Kong vs. Godzilla 158, **231–232**, 232f
King of Kong Island **232**
King of the Mountains **232**
King of the Rocket Men **232**
King of the Zombies **232–233**
Kinnear, Greg 299
Kinney, Terry 44
Kinski, Klaus 13–14, 72
Kirk, Tommy 272, 285
Kissinger, Henry 433
Kiss Kiss, Kill Kill **233**
Kiss Me Deadly **233**
Kiss the Girls and Make Them Die **233**

Klein-Rogge, Rudolf 280
Kline, Kevin 463
Knight, Wayne 222
Knight of the Dragon, The **383**
Knotts, Don 346
Koenig, Walter 293
Konec Srpna V Hotelu Ozon **233**
Konga **233–234**
Kong Island 231, **232**
Koontz, Dean R. 457
Korman, Harvey 13
Kortman, Bob 285
Kosleck, Martin 128
Kramer, Stanley 318
Kristen, Marta 255
Kristofferson, Kris 282
Kronos **234**
Krull **234–235**
Kruschen, Jack 1
Kubrick, Stanley vii, 62, 99, 134, 435, 488
Kurt Vonnegut's "Harrison Bergeron" **169**
Kuttner, Henry 434

L

Lacey, Catherine 374
Lack, Stephen 362
Ladd, Cheryl 282
Ladd, Diane 55
Lady and the Monster **236**
Lady Frankenstein **236**
Laffan, Patricia 93
La Fin Du Monde **109**
Lambert, Christopher 135, 174
Lampkin, Charles 125
Lancaster, Burt 204, 433
Lanchester, Elsa 137
Landau, Martin 106
Landers, Judy 96
Landon, Michael 212
Land that Time Forgot, The **236–237**
Land Unknown, The **237–238**
Lane, Allan 232
Lane, Diane 219
Lang, Fritz 140, 200, 281
Langan, Glenn 13
Lange, Jessica 230
Langella, Frank 276
Lansing, Robert 135
La Plance, Rosemary 213
Laputa **238–239**
Laserblast **239–240**
Last Days of Man on Earth **123**
Last Hour, The **240**
Last Man on Earth, The (1924) **240**
Last Man on Earth, The (1963) **240**, 315
Last Starfighter, The **240–241**

Last War, The **241**
Last Woman on Earth, The **241**
Late for Dinner **241–242**
Late Great Planet Earth, The **242**
Latest Style Airship **242**
Latitude Zero **242**
L'Atlantide (1932) **19**
L'Atlantide (1961) **216**
Laughing at Danger **242**
Laughton, Charles 206
Laumer, Keith 288
Laurel, Allen 180
Law, John Philip 26
Law, Jude 115, 151
Lawnmower Man, The **242–243**, 243f
Lawnmower Man 2: Beyond Cyberspace **243**
Lawrence, Barbara 234
Lawrence, Joey 339
Leary, Dennis 91
LeBrock, Kelly 459
Lederer, Francis 406
Leech Woman, The **245–246**
Legally Dead **246–247**
Leigh, Jennifer Jason 114
Lem, Stanislaw x, 372
Lemmon, Jack 60
Lensman **247**
Leoni, Tea 89
Les Mains d'Orlac. See Hands of Orlac, The
Lester, Richard 35
Let There Be Light **247**
Leviathan **247**
Levin, Ira 45
Levine, Joseph vii
Lewis, Jerry 311, 369, 450, 458
Lewis, Juliette 393
Ley, Willy 140
L5: First City in Space **247–248**, 248f
Libatique, Matthew 328
Lieutenant Rose, R.N., and His Patent Aeroplane **250**
Lifeforce **248–250**
Lifeform **193**
Life in the Next Century **250**
Life without Soul **250**
Lightning Bolt **250**
Light Years **250**
Lindfors, Viveca 409
Linsey, Hal 242

Linville, Larry 104
Liotta, Ray 310
Liquid Air, The **250**
Liquid Electricity **250**
Liquid Sky **251**
Lithgow, John 4, 170
Little Prince, The **251**
Little Shop of Horrors, The (1960) **251**
Little Shop of Horrors, The (1986) **251**
Liu, Terry 191
LL Cool J 88–89
Lloyd, Christopher 4, 24–26, 296, 394
Lockhart, June 255
Locklyn, Loryn 135
Lockwood, Margaret 176
Logan's Run **251–252**, 488
Loggia, Robert 255
Lone, John 183
Longyear, Barry 110
Lopez, Jennifer 57
Lord of the Flies (1963) **252**
Lord of the Flies (1990) **253**
Lords, Traci 310
Lords of the Deep **253**
Lorre, Peter 199, 261, 432
Lost Angel, The **253**
Lost City, The **253**
Lost City of the Jungle, The **253–254**
Lost Continent, The (1951) **254**
Lost Continent, The (1961) **254**
Lost in Space 78, 100, **254–255**
Lost Missile, The **255**
Lost Ones, The (Cameron) 204
Lost Planet, The **255**
Lost World: Jurassic Park, The **257–258**, 490
Lost World, The (1925) **255–256**
Lost World, The (1960) **256**
Lost World, The (1993) **256–257**
Lourie, Eugene 35
Love, David 403
Lovecraft, H.P. 4, 76, 94, 144, 172–173, 186
Love Factor, The **477**
Love Germ **258**
Lovell, Jim 15–16
Love Magnet, The **258**
Love Maniac, The **121**
Love Microbe, The **258**
Love Pill, The **258**
Love Potion #9 **258–259**
Lovitz, Jon 288, 298
Loy, Myrna 273
Lucas, George 51, 107, 108, 349, 390, 417, 489

Lucid, Shannon 287
Lugosi, Bela 2, 15, 38, 50, 105–106, 137, 138, 202–203, 206, 325, 333, 348, 365
Lukas, Paul 432
Lumet, Sidney 120
Lundgren, Dolph 184, 216, 276, 441
Lupo, Alberto 20
Lupton, John 214
Lymington, John 207
Lynch, David 101, 491, 492

M

Mac and Me **260**
MacCormack, Eric 141
MacDowell, Andie 295
Machine, The **260**
Mack, Helen 230
MacLachlan, Kyle 173
MacMurray, Fred 2
Macready, George 182
Macy, William H. 300
Mad Doctor of Blood Island, The 33, **260**
Mad Doctor of Market Street, The **261**
Mad Dog Time **261**
Mad Ghoul, The **261**
Mad Love **261**
Mad Max **261–262**
Mad Max 2. See Road Warrior, The
Mad Max Beyond Thunderdome **262**
Madmen of Mandoras **410**
Mad Monster, The **262**
Mad People, The **71**
Madrid in the Year 2000 **262**
Madsen, Virginia 478
Magnetic Fluid, The **263**
Magnetic Kitchen, The **263**
Magnetic Monster, The 163, **263**
Magnetic Moon, The **263**
Magnetic Personality, The **263**
Magnetic Removal, The **263**
Magnetic Squirt, The **263**
Magnetic Vapor, The **263**
Magnificent Seven, The 30, 270, 300
Magog 163
Mahoney, Jock 237
Making Mr. Right **263–264**
Malden, Karl 279
Malkovich, John 263
Maltin, Leonard 68, 210, 226, 245, 285, 288, 316
Man and His Mate. See One Million B.C.
Manchurian Candidate, The **264–265**

Mandroid **265**
Man-Eater of Hydra **208**
Man Facing Southeast **265**
Man from Planet X, The **265**, 487
Man from the First Century, The **266**
Man from the Past, The **266**
Manhattan Project, The **265–266**
Manhunt in Space **266**
Manhunt of Mystery Island **266**
Man in Half Moon Street, The **266**
Man in Outer Space **266**
Man in the Dark **269**
Man in the Moon (1909) **267**
Man in the Moon, The (1898) **19**
Man in the White Suit, The **267**
Man Looking Southeast **265**
Man of the First Century **266**
Man's Best Friend **267**
Mantee, Paul 353
Man They Could Not Hang, The **267**
Man They Couldn't Arrest, The **267–268**
Man Who Changed His Mind, The **268–269**
Man Who Could Cheat Death, The 266
Man Who Fell to Earth, The **268**
Man Who Lived Again, The **268–269**
Man Who Lived Twice, The **269**
Man Who Thought Life, The **269**
Man Who Turned to Stone, The **269**
Man Who Wasn't There, The **269**
Man with Nine Lives, The **269–270**
Man with the X-Ray Eyes **471–472**
Man with the Yellow Eyes **333**
Man with Two Brains, The **270**
Man with Two Lives, The **270**
Marceau, Marcel 365
March, Fredric 487
Marienthal, Eli 204
Maroney, Kelli 306
Marooned **270**, 304, 488
Marquand, Richard 349
Mars Attacks **270–271**, 271f
Marshall, Ken 235
Marshall, Nancy 272
Mars Invades Puerto Rico **272**

Mars Needs Women 272

Mars Project, The (von Braun) 66

Martian In Paris, A 272

Martians Arrived, The 272–273

Martians Go Home 272

Martin, Steve 251, 270

Martin, Strother 382

Mary Reilly 98

Mary Shelley's Frankenstein 138, 272

Mask of Fu Manchu, The 273

Mason, James 217, 432, 488

Massey, Raymond 412

Massie, Paul 98, 181

Master Minds, The 273

Master of Terror 135

Master of the World, The 173, 273

Masters, Tony 492

Masters of the Universe 276

Mastroianni, Marcello 404

Matheson, Chris 37

Matheson, Richard 187, 240, 306, 315

Matheson, Tim 371

Matrix, The 80, 273–276, 274f, 275f, 490

Matthews, Kerwin 365

Mature, Victor vii

May, Joe 201

Mayhew, Peter 108, 389

McCarthy, Kevin 195–196, 198

McClure, Doug 22, 182, 237

McDermott, Dylan 169

McDiarmid, Ian 391

McDonald, Christopher 204

McDowall, Roddy 32, 111, 330

McDowell, Malcolm 61, 401, 418

McEntire, Reba 426

McGill, Everett 341

McGoohan, Patrick 362

McGowan, Rose 326

McKellen, Ian 469

McLachlan, Kyle 493

McMahon, Horace 1

McMillan, Kenneth 101, 492

McOmie, Maggie 417

McQueen, Steve 41

Mechanical Butchers, The 276

Mechanical Husband, The 276

Mechanical Legs, The 276

Mechanical Man, The 276

Mechanical Mary Jane 277

Mechanical Statue and the Ingenious Servant, The 277

Meeham, John 432

Meeker, Ralph 132

Megowan, Don 72

Méliès, Georges 19, 432

Memoirs of an Invisible Man 201, **277**

Menace from Outer Space 277

Men in Black **277–278**, 278f, 490

Menzies, William Cameron 194

Meriwether, Lee 135

Merlin Jones 285

Message from Mars, A 278–279

Message from Space 279

Message to the Future 279

Metalstorm: The Destruction of Jared-Syn 279

Metamorphosis 279

Meteor 279–280

Meteor Man, The 280

Meteor Monster, The **403**

meteors 17, 41, 52, 76, 83, 209, 279–280, 289, 326, 329, 351, 376, 403, 409, 455

Metropolis 7, 19, 136, 141, **280–281**

Meyer, Nicholas 195, 387

MIB. See Men in Black

Middleton, Charles 126, 213, 285

Mighty Joe Young (1949) 230, **281**

Mighty Joe Young (1998) **281**

Mighty Morphin Power Rangers: The Movie **281–282**

Milford, Kim 239

Milland, Ray 112, 144, 210, 322, 414, 471

Millennium **282**

Miller, Dick 455

Miller, Frank 354

Millhauser, Bertram 201

Milligan, Spike 35

Mill of the Stone Women **282**

Mimic **282–283**, 283f

Mind Benders, The **283**

Mind Detecting Ray, The **284**

Mind Games 5

Mind of Mr. Soames, The **284**

Mind Snatchers, The **284**, 284f

Mindwarp: An Infinity of Terror **147**

Mineo, Sal 111

Miracle Mile 284–285

Miracle Rider, The **285**

Misadventures of Merlin Jones, The **285**

Missile to the Moon 56

Mission Mars 285

Mission Stardust 285

Mission to Mars 285–287, 286f

Mission to Mir 287

Mission Wandering Planet 452

Mister Superinvisible 201, **287**

Mitchell, Cameron 208

Mitchell, Gordon 154

Mitchell, Laurie 290

Mitchell, Radna 329

Mitchell-Smith, Ilan 459

Mitchum, Robert 5

Mix, Tom 285

Modern Bluebeard, A **44**

Mol, Gretchen 415

Mole People, The **287–288**

Mom and Dad Save the World **288**

Monitors, The **288–289**

Monkey Shines: An Experiment in Fear 289

Monkey's Uncle, The 285, **288**

Monolith 289

Monolith Monsters, The **289–290**

Monster, The 290

Monster and the Girl, The 290

Monster from Green Hell, The 290

Monster from the Ocean Floor, The 290–291

Monster in the Night 291–292

Monster Maker, The 291

Monster on the Campus 291–292

monsters 33, 35, 36, 53, 72, 90, 114, 165, 211, 218, 227, 292, 294, 306, 346, 348, 357, 363, 407, 426, 454, 473, 478. *See also* Gamera; Godzilla; King Kong

Monsters of the Night **302–303**

Monster that Challenged the World, The 292

Monster with the Green Eyes 333

Monster Yongkari 473

Monstrosity 292

Moon 44 292

Moon Pilot 293

Moontrap 293

Moon Zero Two 293

Moorcock, Michael 123

Moore, C.L. 165

Moore, Demi 322

Moore, Kieron 83

Moore, Ward 322

Moran, Erin 147

Moranis, Rick 178, 251

Moreland, Mantan 233

Morgan, Harry 56

Moriarty, Michael 340

Morons from Outer Space 293

Morris, Chester 366

Morris, Desmond 342

Morris, Errol 50

Morrow, Jeff 234, 416

Morse, Terry 158

Mortal Orbit 285

Morton, Joe 51

Moss, Carrie-Anne 275

Most Dangerous Game, The 112

Most Dangerous Man Alive, The 293

Most Dangerous Man in the World, The 57

Mothra 294

Motor Car of the Future 294

Motor Chair, The 294

Motorist, The 294

Motor Valet, The 294

Mouse on the Moon, The 294

Mouse that Roared, The 209, 294–295

Mr. Hyde 1, 96, 98, 181, 186, 291, 311, 314

Mr. Invisible. See Mister Superinvisible

Mr. Joseph Young of Africa 230, 281

Mr. Mind 4

Mr. Tawny 4

Mueller-Stahl, Armin 414

Mulcahy, Russell 175

Multiplicity 295

Munro, Caroline 22, 382

Muppets from Space 295

Murder by Television 295

Murphy, Eddie 311–312

Murray, Bill 152, 251

Murray, Stephen 135

Mutant 134

Mutant II 8

mutants 30, 36, 41, 60, 208, 210, 440, 457, 469–471

Mutations 296

Mutilator, The **79**

Mutiny in Outer Space 296

My Favorite Martian 296–297

My Science Project 297

My Stepmother is an Alien 297–298

Mysterians, The 298

Mysterious Contragrav, The 298

Mysterious Invader, The **18–19**

Mysterious Island 298–299

Mysterious Mr. M, The 299

Mysterious Satellite **453–454**

Mystery Men 299–301, 300f

Mystery of the Lost Ranch, The 301

Mystery Science Theater 3000: The Movie 299

N

Naish, J. Carrol 99, 221, 291
Naked Space **73–74**
Na Komete **302**
Napier, Alan 273
Nash, Marilyn 442
Navigator, The: A Medieval Odyssey **302**
Navy vs. the Night Monsters, The **302–303**
Neal, Patricia 84–85, 185
Neanderthal Man, The **303**
Neergaard, Preben 269
Neeson, Liam 80–81, 235
Neill, Sam 113, 221
Nelson, A.J. 74
Nelson, Michael J. 299
Nemesis **303**
Nemesis 2: Nebula **303**
Nemesis 3: Prey Harder **303**
Nemesis 4: Death Angel **303**
Neptune Factor, The **304**
Nest, The **304**
Neumann, Kurt 129, 234, 356
Neutron against the Robots **304**
New Barbarians, The **456**
New Hope, A. See Star Wars
New Invisible Man, The 201, **304**
New King Kong, The **230–231**
Newman, Paul 343
New Microbe, The **304**
New Voyage to the Moon **304**
Next One, The **304**
Nicholls, Peter 45, 252, 409, 413
Nichols, Mike 460
Nicholson, Jack 28, 29, 251, 271
Nielsen, Leslie 132
Night Caller, The **41**
Night Crawlers, The **302–303**
Nightfall **305**
Nightflyers **305**
Night Key, The **305**
Night of the Big Heat (Lymington) 207
Night of the Blood Beast **305**
Night of the Comet **305–306**
Night of the Lepus **306**
Night of the Living Dead (1968) 74, **306–307**, 350
Night of the Living Dead (1990) **307**
Night the World Exploded **307**
Nimoy, Leonard 47, 198, 215, 386, 478
1984 (1956) **307–308**, 488
Nineteen Eighty-four (1984) **308–309**

Niobe **309**
Nippon Chimbotsu **309**
No Blade of Grass **309**
No Escape **309–310**
Nothing But the Night **310**
Not of this Earth (1958) **310**
Not of this Earth (1988) **310**
Nouri, Michael 173
Now We'll Tell One **310**
Now You See Him, Now You Don't 65, **310**
N.P. **310–311**
Nuclear Ultimatum **433**
Nuclear Weapons and Foreign Policy (Kissinger) **433**
Nutty Professor, The (1963) **311**
Nutty Professor, The (1996) **311–312**, 490
Nutty Professor II: The Klumps, The (1996) **311–312**
Nuyen, France 94
Nyby, Christian 411

O

O'Bannon, Dan 81
Oberth, Hermann 92, 140
Oboler, Arch 125
O'Brien, Austin 243
O'Brien, Edmond 307
O'Brien, Margaret 253
O'Brien, Willis 35, 39, 228, 230, 256, 355, 444
October Sky **313–314**, 314f
O'Donnell, Lawrence 165
Ogilvy, Ian 374
Oh, Boy! **314**
O'Hanlon, George 234
Oldman, Gary 254
Olivier, Laurence 46
Omega Man, The 240, 306, **314–316**, 315f
Omicron **316**
Once in a New Moon **316**
One Hundred Years After **316**
One Million B.C. **316**, 355, 434, 444
One Million Years B.C. **316–317**
On the Beach **317–318**, 317f
On the Comet **302**
On the Threshold of Space **318**
Onyx, Narda 214
Operation Atlantis **318**
Operation Stardust **285**
Opper, Dan 13–14
Orwell, George 49, 308
O'Shea, Milo 3
O'Sullivan, Maureen 223
O'Toole, Peter 326
Our Heavenly Bodies **318**
Outer Touch **377**

Outland **319–320**, 320f
Outlawed Planet, The **332–333**
Out of this World **320**
Overcharged **320**
Over Incubated Baby, The **320**
Owen, Chris 313
Oz, Frank 108, 251

P

Pacula, Joanna 448
Page, Thomas 52
Paiva, Nestor 288
Pajama Party **321**
Pal, George 19, 66, 92, 334, 455
Palance, Jack 365
Palle Alone in the World **321**
Panic in the Air **321**
Panic in the City **321–322**
Panic in the Year Zero 309, **322**
Panic on the Trans-Siberian **179–180**
Parasite **322**
Parasite Murders, The. See They Came from Within
Paré, Michael 327
Paris Sleeps **71–72**
Parker, Eddie 290
Parrish, Robert 218
Parsons, Estelle 438
Parts: The Clonus Horror **62**
Passionate People Eater, The **251**
Patinkin, Mandy 8
Patrick, Cynthia 288
Patrick, Nigel 324
Pawn on Mars **323**
Paxton, Bill 16, 371
Pays, Amanda 227
Peace Game, The **323**
Peacemaker **323**
Peach, Mary 338
Peck, Gregory 45–46, 57, 317
Peoples, David 373
People that Time Forgot, The 237, **323**
Peppard, George 30
Percy, The Mechanical Man **323**
Perfect Woman, The **323–324**
Peril from the Planet Mongo 127
Perils of Paris, The **324**
Perils of Pauline **324**
Perlman, Ron 341
Perpetual Motion Solved **324**
Perrine, Valerine 370
Peterson, Paul 290
Petty, Lori 401
Pettyjohn, Angelique 260
Pfarrer, Chuck 449
Phantasm **324**

Phantasm II **324**
Phantasm III **324**
Phantasm: Oblivion **324–325**
Phantom Creeps, The **325**
Phantom Empire, The **325**
Phantom from 10,000 Leagues, The **325–326**
Phantom from Space **325**
Phantom Menace, The. See Star Wars—Episode I: The Phantom Menace
Phantom of the Air **326**
Phantom Planet, The **326**
Phantoms **326**
Phase IV **326–327**
Phenomenon **327**
Philadelphia Experiment, The **327**
Phillips, Leslie 150
Phipps, William 125
Phoenix, River 116
∏ **327–328**
Pickens, Slim 99
Pidgeon, Walter 132, 450
Pinney, Clay 373
327–328
Piper, Rowdy Roddy 410
Piranha **328**
Piranha Part Two: The Spawning **328**
Piscopo, Joe 231
Pitch Black **328–329**, 329f
Planete Sauvage, La **120**
Planet of Blood (1965) **332–333**
Planet of Blood (1966) **341**
Planet of Horrors **147**
Planet of Storms **330**, 451
Planet of Terror (1965) **332–333**
Planet of Terror (1966) **341**
Planet of the Apes 32, 36, 67, 111, **330–332**, 331f, 488
Planet of the Dead **125**
Planet of the Vampires (1965) 7, **332–333**
Planet of the Vampires (1966) **341**
Planet on the Prowl **452**
Planets Against Us **333**
Plan 9 from Outer Space 105, **333**
Platt, Ed 20
Pleasence, Donald 110, 120, 168, 296
Plummer, Christopher 169, 382
Police of the Future **333**
Polyakov, Valeri 287
Porro, Joseph 415
Postman, The **333–334**

Power, The **334**
Power God, The **334**
Power Rangers 281–282
Powers, Tom 438
Predator xi, **334**
Predator 2 **334–335**, 335f
Prehistoric Man, The **335**
Prehistoric Planet **451**
Prehistoric Planet Women **451**
Prehistoric Valley **444**
Prehistoric Women (1950) **335–336**
Prehistoric Women (1967) **336**
Prehysteria **336**
Prehysteria 2 **336**
Prehysteria 3 **336**
Prentiss, Paula 391
President's Analyst, The **336**
Presson, Jason 116
Preston, Robert 241
Price, Stanley 202
Price, Vincent 98, 201, 240, 273, 316, 363, 453
Priest, Pat 188
Prince of Space **336**
Privilege **337**
Prochnow, Jorgen 219
Proctor, Philip 215
Professor Didlittle and the Secret Formula **337**
Professor Hoskin's Patent Hustler **337**
Professor Oldboy's Rejuvenator **337**
Professor Piecan's Discovery **337**
Professor Puddenhead's Patents **337**
Professor's Antigravitational Fluid, The **337**
Professor's Secret, The **337**
Professor's Strength Tablets, The **337**
Professor's Twirly-Whirly Cigarettes, A **337**
Professor Waman **338**
Projected Man, The **338**
Project Moonbase **338**
Project X **338**
Prophecy **338**
Prosser, Hugh 213
Prowse, David 62, 349, 389
Pryce, Jonathan 49
Pryor, Richard 51, 398
pseudo-documentaries 83, 172, 318, 452
Psycho a Go-Go! **121**
Pullman, Bill 188
Pulse **339**
Punishment Park **339**
Puppet Masters, The **353**

Purple Death from Outer Space, The 127
Purple Monster Strikes **85–86**
Purple People Eater **339**

Q

Q **340**
Quaid, Dennis 97, 110, 143, 191
Quaid, Randy 272
Quatermass **340–341**
Quatermass II. See Enemy from Space
Quatermass and the Pit. See Five Million Years to Earth
Quatermass Conclusion, The **340–341**
Quatermass Experiment, The. See Creeping Unknown, The
Queen of Blood **341**
Queen of Outer Space **341**
Quest for Fire **341–342**, 342f, 494–498
Quest for Love **342–343**
Quiet Earth, The **343**
Quintet **343**

R

Rabbit Test **344**
Rabid **344**, 445
Radar Men from the Moon **344**
Radar Secret Service **345**
Radioactive Dreams **345**
Radio Patrol **345**
Rains, Claude 32, 200–201, 256
Ramis, Harold 152
Randolph, John 363
"Random Quest" (Wyndham) 342
Rassimov, Ivan 182
Rathbone, Basil 137, 451
Ravagers **345**
Ray, Frankie 198
Rays that Erase **345**
Re-Animator **172–173**
Reason, Rex 415
Rebar, Alex 186
Red Alert (George) 99
Red Planet Mars **345**
Reed, Dolores 198
Reed, Oliver 50, 479
Reeve, Christopher 397, 447
Reeves, Keanu 37, 215, 275
Reicher, Frank 228, 229
Reigle, James 14
Reilly, Robert 272
Reiser, Paul 9
Relic, The **345–346**

Reluctant Astronaut, The **346**
Rennie, Michael 77, 84
Reno, Jean 244
Repo Man **346**
Reptilicus **346**
Resurrection **346–347**
Resurrection of Zachary Wheeler, The **347**
Resurrection Syndicate, The **310**
Return, The **347**
Return from Witch Mountain 112, **347**
Return of Captain America, The **54**
Return of Dr. Mabuse 200, **347**
Return of Dr. X. **348**
Return of Godzilla, The **158–159**
Return of Swamp Thing, The **348**
Return of the Ape Man **348**
Return of the Fly, The 130, **348**
Return of the Giant Monsters **348**
Return of the Jedi 108, **348–349**, 390, 489
Return of the Killer Tomatoes 22, **349–350**
Return of the Living Dead, The **350**
Return of the Living Dead Part II **350**
Return of the Living Dead Part III **350**
Return of the Swamp Thing, The **400**
Return of the Terror **350**
Return to the Lost World 257
Reuben, David 114
Revenge of Frankenstein 138, **350**
Revenge of the Creature 72, **350–351**
Revenge of the Jedi. See Return of the Jedi
Revenge of the Zombies **351**
Reynolds, William 237
Rhys-Davies, John 256–257
Rich, Claude 214
Richards, Kim 112
Richardson, Natasha 138
Richmond, Kane 49, 253
Riders to the Stars **351**
Ridley, Jack 352
Rift, The **109**
Right Stuff, The **351–352**, 351f, 489
Ringwald, Molly 377
Road Warrior, The 262, **352–353**, 352f

Robert A. Heinlein's the Puppet Masters **353**
Roberts, Julia 98
Robertson, Cliff 58, 488
Robinson, Edward G. 375
Robinson Crusoe on Mars **353**
Robocop **353–354**, 385, 489
Robocop 2 **354**
Robocop 3 **354–355**
Robo Man **462**
Robot Carnival **355**
Robot Monster, The **355**
Robot of Regalia, The **355**
robots 22, 33, 37, 38, 56, 57, 59, 72, 84, 92, 96, 98, 103, 129, 132, 164, 170, 199, 204, 239, 304, 324, 333, 336, 355, 359, 365, 402–403, 417, 422, 425, 448, 450, 459. *See also* androids
Robot vs. the Aztec Mummy **355**
Rocket Attack, U.S.A. **356**
Rocket Boys (Hickam) 314
Rocketeer, The **356**
Rocketman **356**
Rocket Man, The 64, **356**
Rocket Ship Galileo (Heinlein) 92
Rocketship X-M **356**
Rocket to the Moon **56**
Rocky Horror Picture Show, The **356–357**, 488
Rocky Jones, Space Ranger 63, 70, 100, 126, 263, 266, 277, 320, 355
Rodan **357**, 358f
Rogers, Jean 126
Rogers, Mimi 254
Rohmer, Sax 273
Rollerball **357–358**, 488
Romero, Cesar 242, 254
Romero, George 72, 307, 350
Romijn-Stamos, Rebecca 471
Ronson, Peter 217
Rooney, Mickey 20
Rosemary's Baby 19
Rosny, J.H. 342
Ross, Katharine 391
Rovin, Jeff 1
Runaway **359**
Running Man, The **359**
Rush, Geoffrey 299
Russell, Ken 12, 38, 139
Russell, Kurt 65, 110, 372, 373, 382
Russell, Vy 190
Ryan, Robert 55
Ryder, Winona 8, 105

S

Sachs, Michael 370
Sagan, Carl 67
Salkind, Alexander 44
Salute of the Jugger 42
Sanda vs. Gailah 454
Sanders, George 447
Santa Claus Conquers the Martians 360
Sarandon, Susan 357
Satellite in the Sky 360
Satellite of Blood 124
Satterfield, Paul 17
Saturn 3 360–361, 489
Savage Dawn 394
Saval, Dany 293
Saxon, John 30
Sayles, John 30
Scanner Cop 361
Scanner Cop II: Volkin's Revenge 361
Scanners 361–362, 445, 446
Scanners: The Showdown 362
Scanners II: The New Order 362
Scanners III: The Takeover 362
Schallert, William 265, 290
Schell, Maximilian 38
Schneer, Charles 124
Schneider, Rob 219
Schoedsack, Ernest B. 229
School that Ate My Brain, The 478
Schreiber, Liev 326
Schumacher, Joel 128, 188
Schwarzenegger, Arnold 29, 221, 334, 359, 404, 422, 434
science
   consequences of 14
   morality of 48
Science Fiction Encyclopedia, The (Nicholls) 45, 252, 413
scientists 34, 68, 70, 144, 163, 165, 171, 176, 190, 355
   brain experiments 64, 88–89, 93, 95, 107, 121, 364
   creators 11–12, 14, 19, 64, 74, 105, 107, 136–139, 182, 199, 204–207, 227, 263–264, 291
   discoveries/inventions 12, 22, 35, 55, 58, 80, 88–89, 94, 97, 164, 170, 174, 187, 191, 207, 210, 242, 245–246, 247, 254, 258–259, 266, 267, 270, 276, 282–283, 287–288, 298, 305, 310, 323, 328, 334, 335, 337, 338, 346,

348, 350, 351, 365, 366, 369, 379, 382, 409, 454
eternal life 18, 96, 123, 269, 279, 290, 310
insane 22, 23, 26, 33, 45, 47, 56, 59, 61, 87, 99, 116, 121, 128, 166, 170, 172–173, 184, 188, 199, 208, 221, 233, 234, 261, 268–269, 273, 282, 292, 296, 325, 363, 366, 406, 439, 442, 475
invisibility formula 13, 177–178, 200–201, 345
testing on themselves 12, 15, 20, 95, 98, 129–130, 135, 145, 167, 177–178, 181, 186, 217, 260, 311–312
Scott, Alex 18
Scott, George C. 82, 99
Scott, Janette 83
Scott, Ridley 7, 9, 40
Scream and Scream Again 362–363
Screamers 363
Sea Serpent, The 363
Seconds 363
Secret Kingdom, The 364
Secret of the Telegian 364
Secret Service in Darkest Africa, The 364
Seed People 364
Segal, George 404
Selleck, Tom 359
Sellers, Peter 99, 295, 488
Semple, Lorenzo, Jr. 127, 230
"Sentinel, The" (Clarke) 435
Sergeant Deadhead the Astronaut 364
Seven Samurai, The 30, 279
Sewell, Rufus 79–80
Sex Kittens Go to College 364–365
Shadow of Chinatown 365
Shadow of Evil 365
Shadowzone 365
Shakespeare, William 133
Shandling, Gary 460
Shanks 365
Shannon, Frank 126
Shape of Things to Come, The 365–366
Sharif, Omar 298
Shatner, William 141–142, 227, 386
Shawn, Dick 458
Shayne, Robert 190, 303
Shazam 4
She Creature, The 366

She Demons 366
She Devil 366
Sheedy, Ally 267, 367
Sheen, Charlie 17–18
Sheen, Martin 122
She (Haggard) 19
Shelley, Barbara 125
Shelley, Mary 136
Sher-E-Jungle 475
Sheridan, Margaret 410
Sherriff, R.C. 201
Sherwood, John 289
Shh! The Octopus 366
Shimerman, Armin 17
Shirley Thompson vs. the Aliens 366
Shivers. See They Came from within
Shocker 367
Shock Treatment 357
Shock Waves 367
Short, Martin 191
Short Circuit 367
Short Circuit 2 367
Shrinking Man, The (Matheson) 187
Shumacher, Joel 29
Shute, Neville 318
Siegel, Don 198
Silent Rage 367–368
Silent Running 368, 488
Silva, Henry 265
Silver, Ron 17–18
Simmons, Gene 359
Simon, S.J. 155
Simpson, O.J. 54
Simulacron-3 (Galouye) 415
Sinatra, Frank 264–265
Singer, Bryan 470
Sinister Invasion 186
Siodmak, Curt 46, 95, 201, 236
Siren of Atlantis 216
Sizemore, Tom 393
Skeeter 368
Skerritt, Tom 67
Sky Bike, The 368–369
Sky Calls, The. See Battle beyond the Sun
Sky Marshal of the Universe 64–65
Sky Parade, The 369
Sky Pirates 369
Sky Ship 369
Sky Skidder, The 369
Sky Splitter 369
Slapstick (of Another Kind) 369
Slaughterhouse-Five 369–370, 488
Slave Girls 336

Slaves of the Invisible Monster 202
Sleeper 370, 488
Slezak, Walter 96
Slime People, The 370
Slipstream 370–371
Smith, Charles Martin 383
Smith, Gordon 471
Smith, Shawn 237
Smith, Will 188–189, 277, 463
Snipes, Wesley 91
Snow Demons 371
Snyder, David L. 373
Sobchack, Vivian 197
Solarbabies 371
Solar Crisis 371
Solaris 371–372
Soldier 65, 372–373, 372f
Solntseva, Yulia 4
Some Girls Do 373
Something Is out There 373
Something Weird 373–374
Son of Blob, The 41, 374
Son of Flubber 2, 374
Son of Frankenstein 137, 374
Son of Godzilla 157
Son of Kong, The 230, 374
Sorcerers, The 374
Sorel, Ted 144
Sorvino, Mira 282
S.O.S. Invasion 374
Soutendijk, Renee 114
Soylent Green 374–375, 488
Space Amoeba, The 473
Spaceballs 375
Spacecamp 375–376
Space Children, The 376
Space Cowboys 376
Space Cruiser Yamoto 376–377
Spaced Invaders 377
Spaced out 377
Space Flight 377
Spacehunter: Adventures in the Forbidden Zone 377–378
Spacek, Sissy 40
Spaceman in King Arthur's Court, A 441
Space Master X-7 378
Spacemen 18
Space Men Appear in Tokyo 453–454
Spacemen Saturday Night. See Invasion of the Saucer Men
Space Mission of the Lost Planet 180
Space Monster 378
Space Mutants 332–333
Space Rage 378
Space Raiders 378
Spaceship 73–74

Spaceship to the Unknown **126–127**

Spaceship Venus Does Not Reply **125**

Space Soldiers **126–127**

Space Travellers. See Marooned

Spaceways **379**

Spader, James 382, 399

Species **379**, 380f

Species II **379**

Sphere **379–381**

Spider, The **104**

Spielberg, Steven 24–26, 29, 62–63, 89, 112, 191, 222, 433

Spinell, Joe 382

Spirit of '76, The **381**

Split Second **381–382**

Sputnik **95**

S-S-Snake! **382**

Sssssss **382**

Stallone, Sylvester 87, 91, 219

Stamp, Terence 284

Stanton, Harry Dean 346

Starcrash **382**

Stargate **382**

Star Kid **383**

Star Knight **383**

Starman 20

Starman **383**, 489

Star Pilot **383–384**

Star Portal **384**

Starship Invasions **384**

Starship Troopers **384–385**, 384f, 464, 490

Star Trek—First Contact **385**, 388, 490

Star Trek—Generations **385**, 388

Star Trek—Insurrection **385–386**, 388

Star Trek—The Motion Picture viii, **386–388**, 489

Star Trek II—The Wrath of Khan 387, **388**

Star Trek III—The Search for Spock 387, **388–389**

Star Trek IV—The Voyage Home 387, **389**, 489

Star Trek V—The Final Frontier ix, 387–388, **389**

Star Trek VI—The Undiscovered Country 388, **389**, 489

Star Wars 7, 30, 279, 375, **389–390**, 488, 493

Star Wars—Episode I: The Phantom Menace **390–391**, 490

Star Wars—Episode V. See Empire Strikes Back, The

Star Wars—Episode VI. See Return of the Jedi

Stefanovic, Jasna 76

Steiger, Rod 184

Stepford Wives, The **391–392**, 478, 488

Sterling, Jan 307

Stevens, Andrew 145

Stevens, Connie 458

Stevens, Inger 466

Stevens, Stella 311

Stevenson, Robert Louis 96, 98

Stewart, Catherine Mary 306

Stewart, Patrick 388, 469

Stiller, Ben 300

Stine, Clifford 288, 290

Stirling, Linda 266

Stockwell, John 345

Stoker, Austin 32

Stolen Airship, The **392**

Stolen Balloon, The **392**

Stoltz, Eric 130

Stone, Harold J. 471

Stone, Lewis 273

Stone, Sharon 380, 422, 423

Storm, Gale 351

Storm Planet. See Planet of Storms

Stranded **392**

Strange, Glenn 2, 273

Strange Case of Captain Ramper, The **392**

Strange Case of Dr. Jekyll and Mr. Hyde 98

Strange Days **392–394**, 393f

Strange Invaders **394**

Stranger from the Stars **185–186**

Stranger from Venus **185–186**

Strange World of Planet X, The **68**

Stratten, Dorothy 147

Strauss, Peter 377

Streep, Meryl 88

Strieber, Whitley 65

Strongest Man in the World, The 65, **394**

Stryker **394**

Stuart, Gloria 201

Stuff, The **394**

Sturgeon, Theodore 225

Sturgeon's Law x

Sturges, John 270

Submersion of Japan, The **309**

Suburban Commando **394**

Sullivan, Barry 333

Sullivan, Kathy 97

Super Fuzz **395**

Super Giant 20, 114

Supergirl **395**, 398

superheroes 4, 21, 27–29, 54,

55, 64, 126–127, 255, 281–282, 299–301, 397–398

Superman 21

Superman II **395–397**, 398, 489

Superman III **395**, 398

Superman IV: The Quest for Peace **396**, 398

Superman and Scotland Yard **396**, 398

Superman and the Jungle Devil **396–397**, 398

Superman and the Mole Men **397**, 398

Superman Flies Again **397**, 398

Superman in Exile **397**, 398

Superman's Peril **397**, 398

Superman: The Movie **397–398**, 397f, 489

Supernova **398–399**

Super Snooper **395**

Supersonic Man **399–400**

Superspeed **400**

Surf Terror **33**

Sutherland, Catherine 57

Sutherland, Donald 197, 376, 448

Swamp Thing **400**, 400f

Swarm, The **400**

Sweeney, D.B. 123

Swift, Jonathan 166

Sydow, Max von 219

Sylvester, William 165

T

Takarada, Akira 156

Talbott, Gloria 185

Tales of Hoffman **401**

Tandy, Jessica 29

Tank Girl **401**

Tarantula **401–402**, 402f

Target Earth **402–403**

Tarzan vs. IBM **11**

Tattersall, David 373

Taylor, Elizabeth vii

Taylor, Forrest 266

Taylor, Joyce 20

Taylor, Kent 82

Taylor, Rod 155, 419

Teenage Caveman **403**

Teenage Monster **403**

Teenagers from Outer Space **403**

Telegian, The **364**

Telepathy 2000. See Scanners

Teleported Man, The **364**

Tempest, The (Shakespeare) 133

Ten Little Indians (Christie) 56

Tenth Victim, The **404**

Terminal Man, The **404**

Terminator, The **404–405**, 405f

Terminator 2: Judgment Day **405**, 406f, 489

Terrible Dr. Hitchcock, The **179**

Terror beneath the Sea, The **405–406**

Terrore Nello Spazio **332–333**

Terror from the Year 5000 A.D. **406**

Terror Is a Man **406–407**

Terrornauts, The **407**

Terrorvision **407**

Terror within, The **407**

Terror within II, The **407**

Terry, Phillip 245

Testament **407**

Test Pilot Pirx **407–408**

Them! 39, 208, **408**, 408f, 487

Theron, Charlize 19

These Are the Damned **409**

They Came from beyond Space **409**

They Came from within **409**, 445

They Live **409–410**

They Saved Hitler's Brain **410**

Thin Air **410**

Thing, The (1951). See Thing from Another World, The

Thing, The (1982) 118, 130, **410**, 411

Thing from Another World, The 80, **410–411**, 487

Things to Come 194, **411–414**, 412f, 413f

Things with Two Heads, The **414**

Thinnes, Roy 217

Third from the Sun **414**

Thirteenth Floor, The **414–415**

Thirty-Foot Bridge of Candy Rock, The **415**

This Island Earth 238, 299, **415–416**, 416f

This Is Not a Test **416**

Thomas, Henry 113

Thomas, Richard 30

Thomerson, Tim 424

Thompson, Kenneth 223

Thompson, Lea 181

Thompson, Marshall 211

Thornton, Billy Bob 17

Those Fantastic Flying Fools **416**

Three Stooges 170, 417

Three Stooges in Orbit, The **417**

Thunderbirds 6 **417**

Thunderbirds Are Go **417**

THX 1138 **417**

Tidal Wave 309

Time after Time **418**

Time Bandits **418**

Timebomb **418–419**
Timecop **419**
Time Flies **419**
Time Guardian, The **419**
Time Machine, The **419–420**, 488
Timerider **420**
Time Runner **420**
Times Are out of Joint, The **420**
Timestalkers **420**
Time Trackers **420–421**
time travel 24–26, 36, 37, 78, 100, 122, 142, 143, 177, 214, 216, 217, 237, 282, 297, 327, 381, 404–405, 418, 419, 420, 421, 429–430
Time Travelers, The **421**
Time Tunnel, The 165
Time Walker **421**
Time Warp (1967) **217**
Time Warp (1980) **85**
Tin Man, The **421**
Tippett, Phil 449
Titan A.E. **421–422**
Titan Find **72**
Tobey, Kenneth 208, 410
Tobor the Great **422**
Tomlin, Lily 188
Toomey, Regis 325
Torn, Rip 268, 277
Torture Ship **422**
Total Recall 385, **422–423**, 423f, 489
To the Center of the Earth 442
Towne, Robert 241
Townsend, Robert 280
Townshend, Pete 204
Toy Box, The **424**
Trackers **378**
Tracy, Spencer 98
Trancers **424**
Trancers II **424**
Trancers III **424**
Trancers IV: Jack of Swords **424**
Trancers V: Sudden Deth **424–425**
Trans-Atlantic Tunnel **425**, 429
Transformers **425**
Transmutations **440**
Trapped by Television **425**
Travers, Bill 165
Travis, Stacey 169
Travolta, John 31–32, 327
Trekkies 149, **425–426**
Tremors **426–427**
Tremors II: Aftershocks 426, **427**
Trigger Happy **261**
Trip to Jupiter, A **427**
Trip to Mars, A (1910) **427**
Trip to Mars, A (1920) **427**

Trip to the Center of the Earth. See Journey to the Center of the Earth
Trip to the Moon, A **427**
Trip to the Moon, The **427**
Trixie **71**
Trollenberg Terror, The **71**
Tron **428**, 489
Truffaut, Francois 119
Truman Show, The **428–429**, 490
Trumbull, Douglas 48, 368, 386
Tryon, Tom 185, 293
Tserectelli, Nikolai 4
Tucker, Chris 122
Tucker, Forrest 71, 420
Tumannost Andromedy **429**
Tunnel, Der 425, **429**
Tunneling the Channel **429**
Turbo: A Power Rangers Movie **429**
Turkey Shoot **112**
Turnbull, Douglas viii
Turner, Barbara 290
Turner, Kathleen 270
Twain, Mark 441
12 Monkeys 134, **429–430**, 430f, 490
Twelve to the Moon **430**
20 Million Miles to Earth **430–431**
27th Day, The **431**
20,000 Leagues under the Sea (1907) **431**
20,000 Leagues under the Sea (1916) **431**
20,000 Leagues under the Sea (1954) **431–432**, 487
Twilight People, The **433**
Twilight's Last Gleaming **433**
Twilight Zone—The Movie **433–434**
Twins **434**
Twisted Brain 98, **434**
Two Faces of Dr. Jekyll, The. See House of Fright
Two Lost Worlds **434**
Twonky, The **434**
2001: A Space Odyssey viii, 51, 134, **434–436**, 435f, 436f, 488, 493
2010 **436**, 489
Two Year's Holiday **392**
Two Year Vacation **392**

U

Uchu Daikaijû Girara **469**
UFO **438**
UFO Incident, The **438–439**

Uforia **439**
UFOs 21, 62–63, 65, 74, 104, 168–169, 188, 209, 234, 251, 295, 325, 400, 438–439, 468–469. *See also* aliens
Ulam tribe 341–342, 494–498
Ultimate Warrior, The **439**
Ultimatum, Das **433**
Undead, The **439**
Undersea Kingdom **439–440**
Underwater City, The **440**
Underwater Odyssey, An **304**
Underworld **440**
Unearthly, The **440**
Unearthly Stranger, The **440**
Unforgettable **440–441**
Unidentified Flying Objects **438**
Unidentified Flying Oddball **441**
Universal Soldier **441**
Universal Soldier II: The Return **441**
Unknown Island **442**
Unknown Purple, The **442**
Unknown Satellite over Tokyo **453–454**
Unknown Terror **442**
Unknown World **442**
Unnatural **12**
Until the End of the World **442**
Ustinov, Peter 252

V

Valley of Gwangi, The **443–444**
Valley of the Dragons, The **444**
Valley of Zombies, The **444**
Vampire Men of the Lost Planet **180**
vampires 20, 61, 75, 180, 240, 249–250, 310, 332, 341
Van Damme, Jean-Claude 77, 419, 441
Van Dien, Casper 385
Van Doren, Mamie 365
Vanishing Corpse, The **351**
Vanishing Shadow, The **445**
Van Leeuwenhoek, Anton 69
Van Vogt, A.E. x
Varan the Unbelievable **445**
Varley, John 282
Varney, Jim 99
Vaughn, Robert 168, 284, 403
Vaughn, Vince 57
Vengeance **46**
Venusian, The **185–186**
Verhoeven, Paul 178, 354, 385, 423
Verne, Jules 117, 145, 298, 302, 392, 416, 432, 444, 462
Vernon, Howard 23
Victor, Gloria 198

Videodrome **445–446**, 446f
Village of the Damned (1960) **446–447**, 488
Village of the Damned (1995) **447**
Village of the Giants **132**
Villechaize, Hervé 134
Vincent, Jan-Michael 8
Vindicator, The **447**
Vintage Season (O'Donnell and Moore) 165
Violet Ray, The **447**
Virtuosity **447–448**
Virus (1980) **448**
Virus (1999) **448–449**, 449f
Visit to a Small Planet **449–450**, 488
von Braun, Wernher 66
Von Daniken, Erich 58
Vonnegut, Kurt, Jr. 169, 369, 370
von Stroheim, Erich 236
von Sydow, Max 97, 127, 439
Voodoo Bloodbath **184**
Voodoo Man **450**
Voodoo Woman **450**
Vosloo, Arnold 81
Voyage into Space **450**
Voyage to the Bottom of the Sea **450–451**
Voyage to the End of the Universe **184**
Voyage to the Moon **427**
Voyage to the Planet of Prehistoric Women 330, **451**
Voyage to the Prehistoric Planet 330, **451**
Vulture, The **451**

W

Wachowski, Andy 276
Wachowski, Larry 276
Walas, Chris 130
Walken, Christopher 29, 40, 48, 65
Wallace, George 344
Walston, Ray 147, 296
Walton Experience, The (Wilson) 123
War between the Planets **452**
Ward, Burt 28
Ward, Fred 420, 426–427
War Game, The **452**
Wargames **452–453**, 489
War Gods of the Deep **453**
Warlords of Atlantis **453**
Warlords of the 21st Century **453**
Warner, David 256–257, 418
Warner, Steven 251

Warning from Space **453–454**
Warnock, Craig 418
War of Dreams **454**
War of the Colossal Beast 13, **454**
War of the Gargantuas, The **454**
War of the Planets (1965) **454**
War of the Planets (1977) **454–455**
War of the Satellites **455**
War of the Worlds **455–456**, 455f, 487
Warriors of the Wasteland **456**
Washington, Denzel 448
Wasp Woman, The **456**
Watchers **457**
Watchers 2 **457**
Watchers 3 **458**
Watchers Reborn **458**
Water Cyborgs **405–406**
Waterston, Sam 54
Waterworld **456–457**, 490
Watkin, Pierre 213
Watts Monster, The. See Dr. Black, Mr. Hyde
Wavelength **458**
Way...Way out **458**
Weaver, Fritz 92
Weaver, Sigourney 7, 8–11, 148, 489
"We Can Remember It For You Wholesale" (Dick) 423
Weekend **458**
Wegel, Rafael 141
Wegener, Paul 392
Weird Science **458–459**
Welcome to Blood City **459**
Weldon, Joan 208, 408
Weller, Peter 363
Welles, Orson 106, 377, 411, 456
Wells, H.G. 107, 124, 132, 201, 204, 205, 206, 366, 414, 418, 420, 427, 456
Werner, Oskar 119
West, Adam 28, 353
Westmore, Bud 288

Westworld 146, **459–460**, 488
Whale, James 201
What Planet Are You from? **460–461**
What's So Bad about Feeling Good? **460**
What Waits Below **460**
Wheaton, Wil 241
When Dinosaurs Ruled the Earth **461**
When the Man in the Moon Seeks a Wife **461**
When Worlds Collide **461**, 487
Where Time Began **461–462**
White Zombie 106
Whittaker, Forest 44
Who? **462**
"Who Goes There?" (Campbell) 411
Who Would Kill Jessie? **224–225**
Wiest, Dianne 105
Wild, Wild Planet **462**, 462f
Wild, Wild West **463**
Wilde, Cornel 309
Wilder, Gene 138
Wild in the Streets **462**
Williams, Billy Dee 51, 108
Williams, Cindy 439
Williams, Grant 187, 289, 290
Williams, Jason 128
Williams, Robin 37
Williamson, Kevin 118
Willis, Bruce 17, 88, 122, 429
Wilson, Colin 250
Wilson, Travis 123
Wincott, Michael 393
Winfield, Paul 79
Wing Commander **463–464**, 464f
Winged Serpent, The **340**
Winningham, Mare 284–285
Winslow, George "Foghorn" 356
Winston, Stan 148, 205
Wise, Robert viii
Without a Soul **465**

Without Warning **465**
Wizard, The **465**
Wizard of Mars **465**
Wizards **465**
Wolfe, Tom 352
Woman in the Moon **140–141**
Women of the Prehistoric Planet **465–466**
Wonderful Chair, The **466**
Wonderful Electro-Magnet, The **466**
Wonderful Fluid, A **466**
Wonderful Hair Remover, The **466**
Wonderful Marrying Mixture, The **466**
Wonderful Pills **466**
Wonderful Rays, The **466**
Wonderful Remedy, A **466**
Wood, Edward, Jr. 50, 105–106, 333
Wood, Elijah 89
Woods, James 445
Wooland, Norman 338
Wordsworth, Richard 74
World, the Flesh and the Devil, The **466**
World Gone Wild **466**
World of Yor, The **474**
World without End 341, **466–467**
Wylie, Philip 207, 461
Wyndham, John 83, 342
Wynn, Keenan 2
Wynter, Dana 195–196

X

X, The Unknown **468**
X-Files: The Movie **468–469**
X from Outer Space, The **469**
X-Men **469–471**, 470f
X-Rays **471**
X-17 Top Secret **471**
"X"—The Man with X-Ray Eyes **471–472**
Xtro **472**
Xtro: Watch the Skies **472**

Xtro II: The Second Encounter **472**

Y

Yeager, Chuck 352
Year of the Angry Rabbit, The (Braddon) 306
Years to come **473**
Yog—Monster from Space **473**
Yongary—Monster from the Deep **473**
Yor, The Hunter from the Future **474**
York, Michael 204, 252
Young, Alan 419
Young, Sean 24, 193
Young Einstein **474**
Young Frankenstein 138, **474**
You Only Live Once **285**

Z

Zaat **475**
Zambo **475**
Zapped! **475–476**
Zardoz **476–477**, 477f, 478f, 488
Zelazny, Roger 79
Zeman, Karel 117, 302, 392
Zemeckis, Robert 24–26, 67, 68, 87
Zero in the Universe **477**
Zero Population Growth **478–479**
Zeta One **477**
Zex 107
Zombie High **478**
zombies 103, 184, 199, 200, 215, 233, 261, 284, 306, 315, 350, 367, 374, 444, 450
Zombies of the Stratosphere **478**
Zontar: The Thing from Venus **478**
Z.P.G. **478–479**
Zubrin, Robert 286
Zucco, George 99, 261, 262, 290